M A C M I L L A N

INFORMATION NOW ENCYCLOPEDIA

The Confederacy

The Encyclopedia of the Confederacy

RICHARD N. CURRENT, EDITOR IN CHIEF
Emeritus, University of North Carolina, Greensboro

EDITORIAL BOARD

PAUL D. ESCOTT
Wake Forest University

LAWRENCE N. POWELL
Tulane University

JAMES L. ROBERTSON, JR.
Virginia Polytechnic Institute and State University

EMORY M. THOMAS
University of Georgia

MACMILLAN
INFORMATION NOW ENCYCLOPEDIA

The Confederacy

SELECTIONS FROM THE
FOUR-VOLUME
Simon & Schuster *Encyclopedia of the Confederacy*

MACMILLAN REFERENCE USA
Simon & Schuster Macmillan
New York

Prentice Hall International
London Mexico City New Delhi Singapore Sydney Toronto

Designed by Kevin Hanek. Composition by G&H Soho, Inc.

Cartography by Donald S. Frazier, Abilene, TX USA

Macmillan Reference USA
Simon & Schuster Macmillan
1633 Broadway
New York, NY 10019

Manufactured in the United States of America.

printing number
1 2 3 4 5 6 7 8 9 10

ISBN: 0-02-864916-8
LC #:   97–23462

Library of Congress Cataloging-in-Publication Data

The Library of Congress has catalogued another edition of this work as follows:

The Confederacy
        p.   cm.—(Macmillan compendium)
Includes index.
1. Confederate States of America—History—Dictionaries. 2. United States—History—Civil War, 1861–1865—Dictionaries. I. Series.
E487.C723   1997
973.7′13—dc21   97–23462
                                                                              CIP

This paper meets the requirements of ANSI/NISO Z39.48–1992 (Permanence of Paper).

Table of Contents

Cover Image: This photo of the Confederate Memorial in Stone Mountain, Georgia shows three giants of the Confederacy, (from left to right) Jefferson Davis, Robert E. Lee, and Stonewall Jackson.

DAVE HOUSER/CORBIS

M

N

O

P

Q

R

Preface

ORIGINS

The Confederacy looms large in American history. A recent explosion of interest in this topic has accompanied the increasing fascination with the Civil War. Brief and tenuous though their government was, the Confederates left an impressive record of heroism and self-sacrifice in their devotion to the Lost Cause. The history of the Confederacy is a record that continues to appeal to many in the North as well as in the South; Confederate general Robert E. Lee is an American hero as well as a Southern hero.

Those curious about the Confederacy have learned to rely on the distinguished four-volume *Encyclopedia of the Confederacy* published by Simon and Schuster. Since its publication in 1994, general readers, historians, and students have expressed an interest in a condensed version of this prestigious work. The *Information Now Encyclopedia of the Confederacy* is designed to meet that need.

CRITERIA FOR SELECTION AND ORGANIZATION

Broad in scope, *The Information Now Encyclopedia of the Confederacy* is organized in an A-to-Z format. This extraordinary volume presents the Confederate States of America in all its complexity—its structure and internal conflicts as well as its violent history. In preparing this one-volume version of the *Encyclopedia of the Confederacy*, it was agreed that articles would be excerpted in their entirety in order to retain historical accuracy. Our goal was to present a coherent overview of the subject. Relying on advice from a team of scholars, articles were chosen to represent the most significant battles, events, concepts, and terms of the Confederacy. Also included are biographies of the military officers, statesmen, and thinkers who were central to the development of this would-be nation. Entries have been titled and organized in a manner we hope readers will be most likely to consult first. A comprehensive index appears at the end of the volume to provide additional aid for the reader.

FEATURES

To add visual appeal and enhance the usefulness of the volume, the page format was designed to include the following helpful features.

- **Cross-Reference Quotations:** These quotations, extracted from related articles in the volume, will lead to further exploration of the subject. Page numbers are provided for easy reference.

- **Notable Quotations:** Found throughout the text in the margin, these thought-provoking quotations will complement the topic under discussion.

- **Definitions and Glossary:** Brief definitions of important terms in the main text can also be found the margin and in the glossary at the end of the book.

- **Sidebars:** Appearing in a gray box, these provocative asides relate to the text and amplify topics.

- **Index:** A thorough index provides thousands of additional points of entry into the work.

ACKNOWLEDGMENTS

The *Information Now Encyclopedia of the Confederacy* contains over two hundred illustrations from *The Encyclopedia of the Confederacy*. Acknowledgments of sources for illustrations can be found in captions. Because most of the photographs used are over one hundred years old, their quality will vary. Every effort has been made to improve the clarity of these reproductions.

In addition to the articles, photographs, etchings, and maps that appear in the encyclopedia, we have included in the appendix the complete texts of several key documents of Confederate history, ranging from South Carolina's ordinance of secession to the various surrender treaties signed by Confederate commanders.

We are grateful to our colleagues who publish the *Merriam Webster's Collegiate® Dictionary*. Definitions used in the margins and most of the glossary terms come from the distinguished *Webster's Collegiate® Dictionary*, Tenth Edition, 1996.

The articles herein were written for the *Encyclopedia of the Confederacy* (the parent set of this volume) by leading authorities at work in various fields of study. Richard N. Current was General Editor of the original set. Dr. Current is Distinguished Professor, Emeritus, at the University of North Carolina at Greensboro and past president of the Southern Historical Association. The four historians selected for the editorial board are associated with universities in North Carolina, Virginia, Georgia, and Louisiana, thus representing a wide geographical range from the upper to the lower South. Each of these historians is the author of numerous relevant studies reflecting the broad spectrum of approaches to understanding the Confederate era. Paul D. Escott, of Wake Forest University, has been the Reynolds Professor of History since 1990. Lawrence N. Powell, of Tulane University, is associate professor of history. James I. Robertson, Jr. of Virginia Polytechnic Institute and State University, has been the Alumni Distinguished Professor since 1992. Emory M. Thomas, of the University of Georgia, has been Regents Professor of History since 1987.

This book would not have been possible without the hard work and creativity of our staff. We offer our deepest thanks to all who helped create this marvelous work.

Macmillan Reference USA

Foreword

Some historians maintain that the Confederate States of America was a determined effort by the Old South to cling to the past. Other writers see the attempt at nationhood as the actions of a New South in which eleven individual and bustling states banded together to forge a future based on prosperity from land and slaves. Although only a small percentage of Southerners had direct involvement with the institution of slavery, the majority considered their way of life inviolate enough to defend it by force of arms. Safeguarding birthright, home, and family are natural stimuli, and allegiance to state was an ingrown Southern tradition.

Initially the North dismissed secession as little more than a small conspiracy by a handful of hotheads. The Confederacy was an oxymoron: it wanted to pursue freedom for a society economically predicated on slavery. Many observers likened the Southern government to a head full of ideas attached to a body too weak to do much more than stumble unsteadily.

It is true that from the beginning the Confederate experiment stood on shaky legs. That did not deter its political leaders. Looking to the past, they assured the Southern people that courage and dedication would be ample substitutes for limited resources, a shallow manpower pool, and lack of foreign aid.

That worked for a time; yet as all but the most patriotic of Southerners came to realize, time was the Confederacy's worst enemy. Its smaller armies could not stand still and continually swap punches with far more powerful Union hosts. A Richmond newspaper boasted early in the war that "the idea of waiting for blows instead of inflicting them is altogether unsuited to the genius of our people." However, President Jefferson Davis would confess years later: "The simple fact was, the people had gone to war without counting the cost."

Nor was the Southern Confederacy established enough, and stable enough, to sustain a people—and the war being waged against them—for an indefinite period. The Confederacy began as an association of independent and equal states. It never left that mold to acquire the all-for-one concentration that offered a realistic hope for victory.

What made the Civil War so bloody and so fundamental to America was an intensity that neither side anticipated. The South's goal of independence was as absolute as the North's aim of union. Hence, the objectives of the opposing governments could be neither compromised nor harmonized. The Civil War would have to be a fight to the finish.

Americans have never been a military people by nature, but the struggle of the 1860s forced them to become so. The all-American conflict was unlike any war the world had ever seen. It was a total war for total ends, with no aspect of the opponent left immune. The enemy's armies remained the basic targets, but the social and economic foundations on which those armies rested had to be destroyed, if the armies were to collapse. In short, tearing up a railroad was as vital as blowing up breastworks.

The Confederate struggle for freedom captured the imagination—and in some quarters the respect—of the world. For four years, against incredible odds, the South defended and fought, persevered and suffered. It accepted honorable defeat in 1865, wrapped itself in nostalgia, and became again a vital part of the now-United States. The South's postwar vision of "The Lost Cause"—good men fighting for a good cause and surrendering with honor—became a soothing balm for the sores of war.

James I. Robertson Jr.
Alumni Distinguished Professor in History at Virginia Polytechnic Institute and State University.

Abbreviations and Symbols

A.D.	*anno Domini,* in the year of the (our) Lord	**f.**	and following (pl., ff.)
Adj. Gen.	adjutant general	**1st Lt.**	first lieutenant
Adm.	admiral	**fl.**	*floruit,* flourished
Ala.	Alabama	**Fla.**	Florida
A.M.	*ante meridiem,* before noon	**frag.**	fragment
Ariz.	Arizona	**ft.**	feet
Ark.	Arkansas	**Ga.**	Georgia
b.	born; beam (interior measurement of width of a ship)	**Gen.**	general
B.C.	before Christ	**Gov.**	governor
brig.	brigade	**HMS**	Her Majesty's ship
Brig. Gen.	brigadier general	**ibid.**	*ibidem,* in the same place (as the one immediately preceding)
c.	*circa,* about, approximately	**i.e.**	*id est,* that is
Calif.	California	**Ill.**	Illinois
Capt.	captain	**Ind.**	Indiana
cf.	*confer,* compare	**Kans.**	Kansas
chap.	chapter (pl., chaps.)	**km**	kilometers
cm	centimeters	**Ky.**	Kentucky
Col.	colonel	**l.**	length
Colo.	Colorado	**La.**	Louisiana
Comdr.	commander	**lb.**	pound (pl., lbs.)
Como.	commodore	**Lt.**	lieutenant
Conn.	Connecticut	**Lt. Col.**	lieutenant colonel
Cpl.	corporal	**Lt. Comdr.**	lieutenant commander
C.S.	Confederate States	**Lt. Gen.**	lieutenant general
C.S.A.	Confederate States of America, Confederate States Army	**m**	meters
CSS	Confederate States ship	**M.A.**	Master of Arts
cwt.	hundredweight (equals 772 lbs.)	**Maj.**	Major
d.	died	**Maj. Gen.**	major general
D.C.	District of Columbia	**Mass.**	Massachusetts
Del.	Delaware	**mi.**	miles
diss.	dissertation	**Mich.**	Michigan
div.	division	**Minn.**	Minnesota
dph.	depth of hold	**Miss.**	Mississippi
ed.	editor (pl., eds.); edition; edited by	**Mo.**	Missouri
e.g.	*exempli gratia,* for example	**Mont.**	Montana
Eng.	England	**n.**	note
enl.	enlarged	**N.C.**	North Carolina
Ens.	ensign	**n.d.**	no date
esp.	especially	**N.Dak.**	North Dakota
et al.	*et alii,* and others	**Neb.**	Nebraska
etc.	*et cetera,* and so forth	**Nev.**	Nevada
exp.	expanded	**N.H.**	New Hampshire
		N.J.	New Jersey
		N.Mex.	New Mexico
		no.	number (pl., nos.)
		n.p.	no place
		n.s.	new series
		N.Y.	New York

Okla.	Oklahoma
Oreg.	Oregon
p.	page (pl., pp.)
Pa.	Pennsylvania
pdr.	pounder (weight of projectile in pounds; pl., pdrs.)
pl.	plural, plate (pl., pls.)
P.M.	*post meridiem,* after noon
Pres.	president
pt.	part (pl., pts.)
Pvt.	private
r.	reigned; ruled; river
Rear Adm.	rear admiral
regt.	regiment
Rep.	representative
rev.	revised
R.I.	Rhode Island
S.C.	South Carolina
S.Dak.	South Dakota
sec.	section (pl., secs.)
2d Lt.	second lieutenant
Sen.	senator
ser.	series
Sgt.	sergeant
sing.	singular
sq.	square
supp.	supplement; supplementary
Tenn.	Tennessee
Tex.	Texas
trans.	translator, translators; translated by; translation
U.S.	United States
USS	United States ship
Va.	Virginia
var.	variant; variation
vol.	volume (pl., vols.)
Vt.	Vermont
Wash.	Washington
Wis.	Wisconsin
W.Va.	West Virginia
Wyo.	Wyoming
°	degrees
′	feet; minutes
″	inches; seconds
£	pounds
?	uncertain; possibly; perhaps

Key to Map Symbols

Troops, Confederate

Troops, Union

Cavalry, Confederate

Cavalry, Union

Tactical Movement, Confederate

Tactical Movement, Union

Strategic Movement, Confedederate

Strategic Movement, Union

Retreat

Engagement

Artillery

Encampment

Headquarters

Fortifications

Entrenchments

Casemate Ironclad

Gunboat

Monitor

Warship

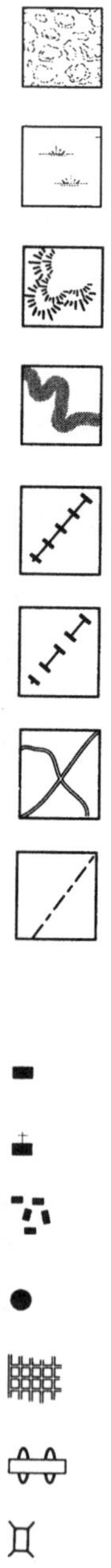

Trees

Marshes

Elevation

River

Railroad

Unfinished Railroad

Road

State Boundary

Building

Church

Village

Town, Strategic

Town, Tactical

Pontoon Bridge

Bridge

The Confederacy

AFRICAN AMERICANS IN THE CONFEDERACY

More than a third of the population of the Confederate States of America was African American. The 9.1 million people living in the eleven future Confederate states as of 1860 consisted of 5.5 million whites and 3.6 million blacks. Of the latter, approximately 3.5 million were slaves. During the Civil War, these blacks played an important role in keeping the Confederate war machine functioning. The Confederacy was dealt a heavy blow, therefore, when President Abraham Lincoln's Emancipation Proclamation impelled at least half a million and perhaps as many as a million of the Confederate blacks to flee their posts in order to follow or serve with the Union forces.

Following the firing on Fort Sumter and Lincoln's call to arms in April 1861, some Southern free blacks rallied to the cause of their region. Historian Emory Thomas has written that "during 1861 several groups of free black Southerners offered themselves as soldiers to the Confederate War Department, and although the War Office rejected each of these applications, some blacks did serve in the Southern armies." In Louisiana, some well-to-do African Americans from New Orleans were allowed to form regiments of free blacks who served as home guards. Their function was to protect their state against invaders. In the light of subsequent developments—emancipation and the antislavery crusade into which the war turned—it seems strange that some Southern blacks volunteered to aid the bastion of slavery. Most were caught up, however, in the general Southern view of Northerners as aggressively bent on imposing their materialistic way of life on the South. Moreover, the president, the U.S. Congress, and the Republican party declared vigorously at the beginning of the war that the North's sole aim was to preserve the Union and that there was no intention to disrupt slavery where it existed.

Although the Union had twice as many states and people as the South and far more naval, financial, and industrial resources, the Confederacy had better generals at the outset and was fighting a defensive war on home ground with soldiers accustomed to hunting, riding, and outdoor life. Alongside these strong points of the Confederacy should be placed the value of its

black population, only 3 percent of which was free. (In contrast, in the five border slave states on the Union side—Delaware, Maryland, Kentucky, Missouri, and later West Virginia—the 150,000 free blacks constituted 25 percent of the black population of 591,000. Baltimore alone had nearly 26,000 free blacks, more than any other city North or South.) In the North, all 238,000 blacks listed in the 1860 census were free persons, since slavery had ceased north of the Mason-Dixon line and the Ohio River. Often overlooked is the importance to the Confederacy of having 3.4 million persons who could be forcibly mobilized for the war effort. They were used in two ways: first, as military laborers, freeing white males to fight, and second, as workers on the home front.

African-Americans conscripted as soldiers by the Confederate forces

Free African-Americans enlisted by the Confederacy

African-American slaves not actively participating in the war

African-American slaves working as laborers for the Confederate forces

BLACKS AS MILITARY LABORERS. The Confederate armies were greatly aided by the use of blacks, especially slaves, as military laborers. The historian Bell I. Wiley has written that

> much of the hard work entailed by military activities of the Confederacy was performed by Negroes. The aversion of the white soldier to menial tasks was one reason for this, but it was not the only one. Conservation of white man-power for fighting purposes was an appreciable factor. Every [black] wielding a shovel released a [white] for the ranks.

Southern blacks loaded, transported, and unloaded supplies. They dug trenches, built roads, erected barricades, constructed fortifications, repaired and built railroads, bridges, trestles, and tunnels, and cooked and

Enslavement of African Americans in what became the U.S. formally began during the 1630s and 1640s.

PAGE 552

AFRICAN AMERICANS INVOLVED IN THE CONFEDERATE WAR EFFORT

Figures taken from records of the period 1860–64

U.S. CENSUS BUREAU

served food. Some troops raised money to hire black cooks, and in 1862 the Confederate Congress enacted a law authorizing four black cooks per company, to be paid fifteen dollars a month if free and used with their master's permission if slave. Blacks washed uniforms, shined boots, mended clothes and tents, moved ordnance, and generally did much of the drudgery for the armed forces. Wiley points to the use of blacks "as teamsters, many of whom were expert from prior plantation experience," and adds that "slaves and free Negroes were employed as hospital attendants, ambulance drivers, and stretcher bearers." In contrast, far more Union army soldiers were tied down in such tasks, since the Union did not have a large pool of free black labor to take over these noncombat duties.

BLACKS' WORK ON THE HOME FRONT. African Americans in the Confederacy were also essential as workers throughout the economy. Plantations continued to function under the supervision of the mistress of the house when masters, sons, overseers, and neighbors enlisted. Even though overseers supervising twenty or more slaves were exempted from the draft in 1862, many plantations and smaller farms functioned without the presence of any white males to supervise the slaves' labor.

Blacks manned the factories of the Confederacy, too, such as the Tredegar Iron Works in Richmond, the South's leading manufacturer and a crucial cog in turning out Confederate war goods. Historian James H. Brewer says that this firm "at the peak of its productivity . . . employed over 1,200 Negroes, free and slave, and 1,200 whites. Negro manpower enabled this plant to fulfill vital contracts with the various bureaus of the War Department." As the war continued, the plant became increasingly dependent on blacks, who were "engaged in highly skilled tasks previously performed almost exclusively by white technicians."

SLAVE-MASTER RELATIONS. These wartime experiences affected the relationships of slaves and

BLACKS AS SOLDIERS
Flee your Masters and Serve the Union Army

As in the Confederacy, free blacks in the Union volunteered to serve at the start of the war, hoping to strike a blow at slavery. But since the Lincoln administration had five border slave states on the Union's side (Virginia's western counties seceded from that state in 1861 and became West Virginia in 1863), it could not initially make the conflict an antislavery war, nor did it especially want to. Hence, free blacks were turned away. But pressures by abolitionists, Congress, and generals, coupled with Union losses in the East, caused Lincoln to conclude, as he later recalled, that "things had gone on from bad to worse, until I felt that we must change our tactics, or lose the game. I now determined upon the emancipation policy." In a preliminary proclamation on September 22, 1862, and the final proclamation in 1863, he declared slaves in areas still in rebellion on January 1, 1863, to be free. He also urged slaves to flee their masters and serve in the Union armies.

The first unit of free Southern blacks accepted by the Union was the First Louisiana Native Guards, which entered the army on September 27, 1862, five days after the preliminary proclamation.

Confederate defenders had fled when Union forces seized New Orleans on April 26, 1862, but the home guard regiments that had been formed by free blacks remained. Union Gen. Benjamin Butler was puzzled as to why they were fighting for the Confederacy, and their leaders explained that they volunteered so they could serve on their own terms in a dignified role rather than being impressed as military laborers and that they hoped to improve the standing of blacks and increase their chances for equality by serving alongside whites. With Federal forces occupying the city, they were willing to switch to the side more likely to end slavery.

As soon as he received word of Lincoln's proclamation, Butler enrolled this unit officially. Two other regiments entered in October and November 1862 as the Second and Third Louisiana Native Guards. These men were the first of what would become a torrent of Southern blacks, mostly former slaves, joining the Union army. Nearly 200,000 soldiers and sailors of African descent served in all, about 140,000 of them former slaves and the rest free blacks, mostly from the North. The first regiment of former slaves

to enlist was the First South Carolina Volunteers. This regiment had been organized in April 1862 by Union Gen. David Hunter. He had done so contrary to the policy at that time of the Lincoln administration. Hunter commanded the Port Royal and Sea Islands area of the South Carolina and Georgia coast, which had been taken by Union forces in November 1861. Lacking authority and funds to pay or provision this regiment, Hunter had had to disband it in August, keeping together only Company A (about one hundred men) as a nucleus around which to rebuild the regiment when policy changed and authorization was forthcoming. During November 1862, Company A participated in a coastal raid in which they freed 155 slaves and killed or captured a dozen Confederate defenders. With Company A as a nucleus, the First South Carolina Volunteer Regiment was rebuilt and taken into the Union army in January 1863. Also joining that month was the First Kansas Colored Volunteers, a regiment made up primarily of runaway slaves congregated in Kansas.

—EDGAR A. TOPPIN

masters. When large numbers of slaves were pulled from plantations and urban households to work as military laborers or in arms production, subtle changes developed in how they viewed themselves. Their sense of self-esteem and relative freedom inevitably increased as they fulfilled important duties under new circumstances. Their newfound attitude of self-confidence did not escape the notice of whites, who worried about the consequences. According to historian Joseph Reidy, slavemasters objected to slaves being employed in ways other than as field hands and house servants. To have them taken over by governmental and military authorities for other uses in the war effort tended, they thought, to undermine the institution of slavery.

Objections were made to the use of slaves as mechanics in work outside of the plantation. The trouble, according to one observer, was that slaves were brought "into habitual contact with white men, beyond those to whom they owe obedience. It is at the hazard of themselves and of society when this occurs." Others nevertheless saw the need to utilize slaves in any fashion necessary to save the Confederacy, since President Lincoln seemed increasingly determined to free them and use them against the South.

The dislocations caused by the war also had an impact on slave-master relations. For example, the flight of coastal plantation owners inland with their entire plantations temporarily saved them from the invading Union armies, but the uprooting of the plantation made it almost impossible physically and psychologically to retain the traditional patterns. As historian Clarence Mohr has written, "the entire refugee process served to undermine the traditional authority structure of previously autonomous and self-contained plantation units."

EMANCIPATION POLICY. President Lincoln became increasingly convinced that emancipation was the key to victory. In August 1864, he noted that emancipation was "inducing the colored people to come bodily over from the rebel side to ours." Answering a suggestion that the emancipation policy should be abandoned as soon as the Union was victorious, Lincoln replied that blacks would desert the Union ranks and return to the Confederate side in the face of such betrayal. He pointed out: "Drive back to the support of the rebellion the physical force which the colored people now give and promise us, and neither the present nor any coming administration can save the Union. Take from us and give to the enemy the hundred and thirty, forty, or fifty thousand colored persons now serving us as soldiers, seamen, and laborers, and we can not longer maintain the contest." He told Judge Joseph Mills of Wisconsin that "no human power can subdue this rebellion without using the Emancipation lever as I have done. Freedom has given us the control of 200,000 able

bodied men, born and raised on southern soil. It will give us more yet. Just so much has it subtracted from the strength of our enemies." And in September 1864 he wrote in a letter of the physical force represented by the African American soldiers: "Keep it and you can save the Union. Throw it away and the Union goes with it."

Lincoln's enthusiasm was not shared universally in the North. Some Union commanders were very pleased with the African American troops, but others had less regard for them. Early in the war, before the Emancipation Proclamation was issued, some Union generals—such as William S. Harney in Missouri, Don Carlos Buell in Tennessee, and George B. McClellan in Virginia—had enforced the Fugitive Slave Law and restored to their owners those slaves who escaped and made their way to the Union lines.

A different stance was taken by Gen. Benjamin Butler. When three runaway slaves came to Fort Monroe, along Virginia's southeastern coast at Hampton, on May 23, 1861, Butler questioned them closely and learned that they were field hands who were being employed along with other slaves to build fortifications for the Confederates. When a Southern major came on behalf of Col. Charles Mallory to reclaim the three runaways, Butler labeled them "contrabands of war," saying they were being used by the Confederate States as part of the war effort. Hence, he confiscated them and claimed them as property of the United States.

In August 1861 the U.S. Congress, seeing the value of drawing black labor from the Confederates, passed a law confiscating any property, including slaves, used in the Confederate war effort. In July 1862 Congress enacted another law freeing the slaves of masters who were "disloyal or treasonous" or bore arms against the United States. Lincoln's Emancipation Proclamation, issued by the commander in chief, struck yet another blow at slavery. Finally, the Thirteenth Amendment ending slavery was proposed by Congress early in 1865 and ratified by the states in December.

TREATMENT OF BLACK SOLDIERS. Confederate reaction initially caused much hardship for black soldiers in the Union army. Authorities announced two somewhat contradictory policies concerning Union soldiers of African descent: first, that none would be allowed to surrender, meaning they would be killed on the field of combat; and second, that any free blacks captured would be sold into slavery in the Deep South. Both policies were abandoned before long, however, because of the consequences. Black soldiers, with no chance to surrender, fought to the death, even in hopeless situations, adding to Confederate casualties. And the Lincoln administration pledged to impose "hard labor" on one Confederate prisoner of war for every Union soldier sold into slavery.

Newspapers in the Confederacy denounced the Emancipation Proclamation as a call upon the slaves to revolt.

PAGES 188–89

The Confederacy was seriously weakened by the long-term effects of Lincoln's emancipation policy.

PAGE 189

The Richmond Examiner *in 1863 called the Emancipation Proclamation "the most startling political crime in American history."*

PAGE 189

DESERTION
Small's Escape

In the famous encounter between USS *Monitor* and CSS *Virginia* in March 1862, about one-third of the *Monitor*'s crew was black. African Americans, usually slaves, served on Confederate ships, too, both merchant and naval. Robert Smalls and his fellow slave crewmates on the Confederate vessel *Planter* took that steamship out of Charleston Harbor early one morning in May 1862 when its three white officers were ashore. In a well-planned escape, the crew members were joined by seven women and children, including two wives, one sister, and four youngsters. They steamed past the Confederate guns with Smalls wearing the captain's hat and waving as if he were the captain. Then they hastily ran up a flag of truce to keep the Union blockading ships from firing on them. *Planter,* which was an armed steamer used for dispatch and transportation purposes, was taken over by the U.S. Navy, along with its six guns.

— EDGAR A. TOPPIN

Black soldiers in the Union army suffered other discrimination, also. They were paid less than their white counterparts until Congress equalized their pay in 1864, and they did not receive the bonuses, pensions, and support for dependents other troops did. Moreover, black soldiers served in segregated units under white officers; only one hundred African Americans were officers, mostly in the Louisiana Native Guard regiments or as chaplains or physicians. Nonetheless, they fought valiantly. Some 37,000 died in combat, a mortality rate 40 percent higher than for white Union soldiers.

DESERTIONS BY SOUTHERN BLACKS. Naval forces, Union and Confederate, had integrated crews (not until World War I did the U.S. Navy become segregated).

Smalls's escape was spectacular, but many other slaves abandoned their masters in less dramatic ways. Most were inspired by the Emancipation Proclamation, but some fled to the Union lines before the proclamation was issued. Partly they were driven by Confederate actions, state and national, to force slaves and free blacks to contribute to the South's war effort. In Virginia, for example, the state legislature passed laws, such as those in October 1862 and February 1863, that required slave owners to furnish their bondmen for military labor with compensation to the owners and also required free blacks to pay, along with whites, a poll tax to support the

war. The tax on free blacks was set at sixty cents in February 1863 and then was increased to two dollars two months later, with slave owners required to pay ninety cents for every slave twelve years of age and older. Many free blacks resented having to pay a tax to support a war intended to keep their people in slavery.

Fears of slave uprisings and conspiracies permeated the South's white population, although later, it became a staple of Southern belief that the slaves had been loyal. True, most remained at their stations and worked as before, and there were only a few isolated cases of slaves attacking their masters. But about a million deserted to the Union side at the first opportune moment, usually when Northern troops reached their vicinity. This steady erosion, which began before the Emancipation Proclamation and swelled thereafter, played a large role in weakening the Confederate side. The twin impact of drawing African Americans away from the Confederate side and of adding nearly 180,000 fresh troops to the war-weary Union ranks during the last two and a half years of the war helped tip the scales. At one point there were more black soldiers on the Union side than the total number of men able to engage actively in combat on the Confederate side. In addition, the emancipation policy persuaded England, France, and other European nations not to come to the aid of the Confederacy. This turn of events caused the Confederates to consider enlisting black soldiers and inaugurating a diplomatic approach based on ending slavery.

ARMING SLAVES AS SOLDIERS IN THE SOUTH. As early as the summer of 1863, a council of Confederate officers had considered the question of arming slaves and enlisting them in the military but rejected the idea. During 1864, more talk of developing black soldiers to fight in the Confederate ranks was heard. President Jefferson Davis opposed the plan in November 1864, but by March of the next year, he was converted to the proposal. While still believing that slavery was the best way for the two races to coexist in the South, Gen. Robert E. Lee said in January that if military necessity made it imperative to use black soldiers he would do so, though on the basis that any such troops would be set free and that slavery in time would have to be abandoned. Writing on February 18, Lee indicated his support of a bill in the Confederate House to arm and free 200,000 slaves: "I think the measure not only expedient but necessary. The enemy will certainly use them against us if he can get possession of them. . . I think those who are employed should be freed. It would be neither just nor wise, in my opinion, to require them to serve as slaves."

Opposition to enlisting the slaves was strong. Gen. Howell Cobb, an ardent secessionist from Georgia, said that the proposal *to make soldiers of our slaves is the most pernicious idea that has been suggested since the war began. . . . Use all the Negroes you can get for all purposes for which you need them but don't arm them. The day you make soldiers of them is the beginning of the end of the revolution. If slaves make good soldiers, our whole theory of slavery is wrong.*

The Confederate Congress, after considerable debate, enacted a modified law on March 13, 1865, permitting the arming of 300,000 slaves as soldiers. The measure came too late. Lee surrendered to Ulysses S. Grant less than a month later at Appomattox on April 9. Meanwhile, a number of black units were formed and began drilling, but the war ended before they could be mustered in.

The decision to arm slaves virtually sounded the Southern death knell for slavery. The Confederate States had been founded on the idea that the institution was to be preserved forever, as Vice President Alexander H. Stephens had asserted at his inauguration. Now the Confederacy in 1865 was moving to abandon the practice. Confederate envoys James Mason and John Slidell made approaches to the British and French governments, respectively, in early 1865 indicating the South's readiness to abandon slavery in exchange for help. The Confederacy's last desperate moves—arming the bondmen and offering to end slavery—are indicative of the importance of blacks in the Southern nation.

[*See also*; Contraband; Emancipation Proclamation; Miscegenation; Navy, *article on* African Americans in the Confederate Navy; Slavery.]

— EDGAR A. TOPPIN

ALABAMA

In June 1861, Comdr. James Dunwoody Bulloch of the Confederate navy arrived in England to purchase ships, guns, and ammunition for the Navy Department. The following month Bulloch contracted with Laird's Shipyard in Birkenhead, across the Mersey from Liverpool, for a wooden barkentine. According to the contract for vessel number *290*, the ship was to be:

- 220 feet in length
- 32 feet in beam
- 15 foot draft
- rigged for sail
- 300 horse power
- steam engine powered by patented screw propeller system

The organization of the Confederate navy was patterned after that of the U.S. Navy.

PAGE 387

FIVE GENERATIONS

A slave family on a plantation near Beaufort, South Carolina, sits for a portrait by Timothy O'Sullivan, 1862.

LIBRARY OF CONGRESS

On the Alabama,
Rear Admiral
Raphael Semmes
sank USS
Hatteras, *a new*
U.S. Navy ironclad
side-wheeler.

PAGE 529

In spite of protests by Charles Francis Adams, American minister to London, British authorities determined that the *290* did not violate Queen Victoria's May 1861 proclamation of neutrality, which prevented the sale of warships to either the United States or the Confederacy. After the *290* had been launched and christened *Enrica*, Bulloch took the ship down the Mersey on a trial and never returned. Later in the Azores *Enrica* rendezvoused with the bark *Agrippina* and transferred ordnance, ammunition, provisions, and coal that Bulloch had previously purchased in England. Four days later the vessel had been fitted out for war and, under the command of Raphael Semmes, *Enrica* was rechristened CSS *Alabama*. Captain Semmes assembled the crew and informed them of his orders from President Jefferson Davis to use the ship against the U.S. Merchant Marine.

Semmes initiated an unparalleled campaign with an attack on U.S. whaling ships in the vicinity of the Azores and merchant vessels off Newfoundland. After moving operations into the Gulf of Mexico *Alabama* encountered and sank in only thirteen minutes USS *Hatteras* off Galveston, Texas. After putting the rescued crew of *Hatteras* ashore at Port Royal, Jamaica, Semmes took the Confederate warship south to the coast of Brazil. With supplies from more than a dozen captured vessels, Semmes headed *Alabama* across the South Atlantic. En route to the Cape of Good Hope, Semmes captured the bark *Conrad*. Instead of destroying it, Semmes armed the vessel, put a small crew aboard, rechristened it CSS *Tuscaloosa*, and sent that vessel commerce raiding as well. Following a visit to Cape Town and a moderately successful cruise across the Indian Ocean, *Alabama* returned to Cape Town

before recrossing the South Atlantic. It was apparent to Semmes that the ship was badly in need of repairs after nineteen months at sea, and he headed the raider for Cherbourg, France.

At Cherbourg USS *Kearsarge*, one of more than a dozen U.S. warships in pursuit of the Confederate raider, finally caught up with Captain Semmes. He considered his vessel a close match for *Kearsarge* and informed its captain, John A. Winslow, of his intention to fight. On June 19, 1864, *Alabama* steamed out of the French port and opened fire on *Kearsarge* at 10:57 A.M. Although one of *Alabama*'s initial shots lodged in the sternpost of *Kearsarge*, the shell failed to explode. As the engagement intensified, shots from *Kearsarge* began to take effect, while those of *Alabama* hit the Union warship only twenty-eight times. In seventy minutes *Alabama* began sinking, and Semmes struck his colors to avoid continued loss of life. The U.S. Navy had destroyed *Alabama*, but Semmes and forty members of the crew escaped capture when the British yacht *Deerhound* came to their rescue.

In 1984 the wreck of the Confederate ship was discovered by a French navy mine hunter. Expeditions to the site carried out by divers and archaeologists of the CSS *Alabama* Association have documented the wreck and uncovered a unique collection of artifacts that illuminate life aboard the commerce raider.

During *Alabama*'s cruise Semmes had captured and burned fifty-five Union merchant vessels valued at more than $4.5 million. Ten other vessels were bonded at $562,000 and released. The impact of commerce raiding by *Alabama* and other Confederate warships was disastrous for the U.S. Merchant Marine. In what has been described as an unparalleled "flight from the flag," hundreds of U.S. vessels were sold or shifted to

CSS ALABAMA

The Alabama *menaced the*
U.S. Merchant Marine until
it was sunk in a battle with
the USS Kearsarge *near*
Cherbourg, France, in 1864.

NAVAL HISTORICAL CENTER,
WASHINGTON, D.C.

foreign registration in an effort to avoid capture and destruction. That impact on the Merchant Marine was felt until the end of the century.

— GORDON WATTS

ALABAMA CLAIMS

During the Civil War commerce raiders fitted out by the Confederate navy carried out a series of successful campaigns against the U.S. Merchant Marine. Vessels like *Alabama, Georgia, Florida,* and *Shenandoah* cruised the routes of Union commerce and captured, destroyed, or released on bond millions of dollars worth of ships and cargoes. *Alabama* alone was credited with losses totaling $5 million. The success of Confederate commerce raiders caused a "flight from the flag" that forced 750 U.S. merchant ship owners to sell or shift their vessels to foreign registration in an effort to avoid capture or destruction. Whereas 65 percent of New York's maritime commerce was carried in American bottoms in 1860, U.S. ships carried only 25 percent three years later. Although the decline of U.S. maritime commerce was not entirely the result of Confederate attacks, they were a major factor.

Because many of the Confederacy's most effective commerce raiders were built in Great Britain, the United States maintained that Britain should be held responsible for their destructive activities. The U.S. government asserted that Great Britain had violated its May 1861 neutrality proclamation by permitting Confederate agents to obtain vessels for purposes of war with virtual impunity. When the Confederacy collapsed in 1865, the United States moved to press its claims against Great Britain. Both countries prepared arguments to support their position, and Charles F. Adams, U.S. minister to Great Britain, relayed that "nothing remains but arbitration." But in spite of Adams's optimism, the issue of reparations was far from arbitration or resolution.

Neither Great Britain nor the United States was willing to make significant concessions. The United States expected Britain to recognize the validity of U.S. claims before any negotiations could begin. Britain, to the contrary, refused to admit culpability for the commerce raiders' actions and adamantly refused to have a third power involved in deciding if it had been right or wrong in the matter. Negotiations reached an impasse and were suspended. When Lord Russell's government collapsed in June 1866, William H. Seward ordered Adams to reopen the issue. Though the attitude of both nations was more conciliatory and each informally offered to make concessions, both Seward and Lord Stanley, Lord Russell's

successor, refused to compromise on the issue of British violation of the neutrality proclamation. Again the negotiations collapsed.

In 1868 the status of the negotiations was complicated by Adams's resignation and the need to resolve other issues that arose, but in November, President Andrew Johnson redirected attention to the *Alabama* claims. By January 1869 he and British Foreign Secretary George W. F. Clarendon had developed an agreement that both parties signed concerning the method of resolving the dispute.

A commission of two Britons and two Americans would hear the claims and decide on resolution. Wherever they could not come to an agreement, an arbitrator would be mutually approved and those matters submitted to his consideration. In the event that the commission could not agree on an arbitrator, two would be selected and lots cast to determine which would rule on the matter at hand. Heads of state could be selected as arbitrators by any two members of the commission. The agreement was anything but satisfactory, and the U.S. Senate voted against it in April 1869.

After the vote Senator Charles Sumner of Massachusetts voiced such vehement opposition to the agreement that it created a wave of renewed public resentment against Great Britain. In his speech Sumner reiterated U.S. grievances and condemned the Johnson-Clarendon agreement because there was no admission of British responsibility, no provisions for future policy on the matter, and no reparations for the United States. Sumner also claimed that Great Britain's violation of Queen Victoria's neutrality proclamation had prolonged the war by several years and resulted in over $100 million in damages to the American Merchant Marine. His accusations not only increased public antagonism against Britain but raised expectations for reparations to unrealistic levels. In Congress Michigan Senator Zachariah Chandler demanded that Canada be ceded to the United States to compensate for fully half of the expense of the Civil War.

The atmosphere made resolution of the issue seem unlikely, but when President Ulysses S. Grant came into office in 1869, his secretary of state, Hamilton Fish, moved to reopen negotiations. Although Great Britain and the United States appeared as polarized as ever, Grant was receptive to compromise within the bounds of political expediency, and the British appeared to be similarly disposed. After a year of delicate negotiations that were complicated by peripheral issues of British dominion in Canada, Canadian-American fishing and trading agreements, and the San Juan Island water boundary, both countries agreed on the formation of a joint high commission to resolve all issues between the United States, Great Britain, and Canada. The commission met in Washington, D.C., in March, and

Alabama's crew, an international mix, required a firm discipline tempered with mercy.

PAGE 531

after considerable deliberation a treaty was drafted that included the *Alabama* claims articles. The United States and Great Britain signed the Treaty of Washington on May 8, 1871, and on May 24 Congress ratified it over last-minute objections. Parliament followed suit several

weeks later, and ratifications were exchanged on June 17, 1871.

In addition to addressing the matter of future responsibilities of neutral governments toward the fitting out, arming, and equipping of vessels by belligerents, the articles of the treaty included an agreement to settle direct claims by arbitration. Accordingly an international commission of jurists was assembled in Geneva in December 1871. After the United States and Great Britain presented their arguments, the process of arbitration almost collapsed owing to the intensity of disagreement over the issue of indirect claims. After heated exchanges the tribunal was charged with consideration of the direct claims and retired to reach a decision. On July 22 the members voted to dismiss outright the claims associated with CSS *Georgia,* but Britain was held responsible for damage done by CSS *Florida,* CSS *Alabama,* and CSS *Shenandoah* after that vessel was permitted to refit and resupply in Melbourne, Australia. A total of $15.5 million was determined to be the amount of damages for which Britain was responsible to the United States. Although the decision met with some dissatisfaction, both sides decided it was acceptable. The precedent set by two nations settling their differences by arbitration rather than war was lost in the power politics of the

twentieth century, but the exercise contributed to a strengthening of Anglo-American relations that helped shape world history.

[*See also entries on the ships* Alabama; Shenandoah.]
— GORDON WATTS

ALEXANDER, EDWARD PORTER

Alexander, Edward Porter (1835–1910), brigadier general. Born on May 26, 1835, in Washington, Georgia, Alexander graduated from West Point in 1857, standing third out of thirty-eight cadets. He received a brevet second lieutenant's commission in the Engineer Corps and remained at the academy as an instructor. Expeditions to Utah and the Washington Territory interrupted his teaching routine. Promotion came slow for Alexander, but on October 10, 1858, he became a full second lieutenant. With his native state out of the Union, followed by Abraham Lincoln's call for troops, Alexander reluctantly tendered his resignation on May 1, 1861. "My people are going to war," he wrote. "If I don't come and bear my part, they will believe me to be a coward."

A captain's commission, dated March 16, 1861, waited for Alexander when he arrived in Richmond the following month. Jefferson Davis placed the Georgian in charge of the Signal Corps in Richmond, and on June 29, he was instructed to perform the same service with the Confederate army at Manassas. From an observation tower that Alexander constructed near the Van Pelt house, he alerted officers to a Federal flanking movement on July 21. In the aftermath of the victory at Manassas, Gen. P. G. T. Beauregard complimented Alexander and his Signal Corps.

Alexander's superiors quickly recognized his wide talents. He consequently shouldered a number of diverse assignments. Not only was he chief of ordnance for Beauregard after Manassas, but he also handled similar duties for Gen. Joseph E. Johnston that fall; William N. Pendleton remained in control of Johnston's Ordnance Department but in name only. Besides his engineering and reconnoitering responsibilities, Alexander found time to create a more efficient supply system and experimented with new weapons ranging from rockets to flaming spears. For his efforts, he received a major's commission on April 18, 1862. After Robert E. Lee took command in May 1862, he instructed Alexander to oversee the operation of an observation balloon during the Seven Days' campaign (June 25–July 1). Alexander earned the confidence of his new superior who promoted him to lieutenant colonel on July 17, to date from December 31, 1861.

After the Army of the Potomac had been repelled outside Richmond, Alexander maintained his varied duties, plus the new chore of training the reserve artillery batteries. Pendleton had proved woefully inadequate as chief of artillery, but Lee could not find a delicate way of dismissing him. Alexander, as a result, consistently handled many of Pendleton's assignments throughout the war. While the fighting raged at Second Manassas (August 29–30) and Sharpsburg (September 17), Alexander busied himself behind the lines with the Ordnance Department. Supported by Lee's recommendation, Alexander received command of Stephen D. Lee's famous artillery battalion on November 7, although he did not relinquish control of the Ordnance Department until December 4. At Fredericksburg on December 13, Alexander insisted that Confederate batteries unlimber on the brow of Marye's Heights so that the guns could blast the infantry, a decision that sealed the fate of the attacking Union soldiers. On March 3, 1863, he was boosted in rank to full colonel.

Alexander constantly strove to enhance the artillery's effectiveness on the battlefield. During the winter of 1862–1863, he helped implement a battalion system that took tactical control of the artillery away from infantry commanders and restored it to ordnance officers. It also corralled batteries into groups of sixteen guns, which made it possible for Lee's artillery to concentrate its firepower. Alexander revealed the potency of this new system at Chancellorsville on May 3, when he massed over thirty guns at Hazel Grove. His skillful direction of Confederate artillery broke the Union defense at Fairview.

After the reorganization of the army following Thomas J. ("Stonewall") Jackson's death, Gen. James Longstreet and Lee wanted Alexander as chief of artillery of the First Corps. Because they did not wish to offend the senior officer, Col. James B. Walton, Longstreet decided on an awkward arrangement that allowed Walton to maintain his post while Alexander directed the tactical operations of the battalions. At Gettysburg on July 3, Alexander not only organized the massive cannonade that preceded Pickett's Charge but was also given the responsibility of determining when the infantry should advance toward Cemetery Ridge. "It was no longer Gen. Lee's inspiration" that would decide the battle, Alexander recalled, "but my cold judgment." Though his missiles proved indecisive, Alexander overall expertly managed the logistical problems that plagued his command during the entire Gettysburg campaign.

Alexander accompanied Longstreet's corps to the West in the fall of 1863 but arrived too late to participate in the fighting at Chickamauga (September 19–20). From October to December, Alexander's battalion saw limited action during the Chattanooga and

GENERAL LEE'S ARTILLERY

Artillery of this period was classified as field, horse, pack, or heavy. Of these, field (sometimes called "light") artillery was the most common, being armed and equipped for service with infantry. In theory, during marches and maneuvers its cannoneers were mounted on their battery's caissons and limbers; in vulgar practice they walked—or when necessary, ran—beside their guns. Horse artillery (also called "flying artillery") served with the cavalry; its cannoneers all had individual mounts. Pack (or "jackass") artillery was used only briefly and unsuccessfully by the Confederates. Heavy artillery (also called "foot artillery") handled siege, seacoast, and fortress guns; they were usually armed and equipped as infantry.

The basic artillery unit was the company. (The modern term battery—which previously had meant only an indefinite number of guns emplaced together in the same position—came into general use during this war.) An ideal Confederate company consisted of a captain; four lieutenants (three serving as section chiefs, one in charge of the caissons); eight sergeants, including an orderly (first) sergeant and a quartermaster (supply) sergeant; twelve corporals; two artificers (blacksmith and saddler); two buglers; a guidon bearer; and approximately ninety drivers and cannoneers. (Confederate regulations set the number of privates at 64 to 125.) Horse artillery needed two extra privates per section to serve as horse holders while their company was in action.

This company would have four guns and two howitzers, each with its accompanying caisson, loaded with ammunition. Gun and caisson together formed a platoon, commanded by a sergeant "chief-of-piece" assisted by two corporals—one the gunner, the other in charge of the limbers and caisson. Two platoons made up a section. In addition, the company was to have a battery wagon for supplies, spare parts, and tools and a traveling forge, which was a mobile blacksmith's shop. (Artillery theory held that each 12-pounder or heavier gun should have two caissons, but this seems to have been followed only rarely in the Federal forces and very rarely, if ever, in the Confederate.) Officers, sergeants, buglers, and guidon bearers were to have individual mounts, and there would be seven to a dozen spare horses to replace casualties.

— JOHN R. ELTING

> *"The only hope
> we had was to
> outgeneral the
> Federals."*
>
> JAMES LONGSTREET
> ON THE WAR IN 1863

AMERICAN PARTY
Southern Know-Nothings

The American party was a secret nativist organization that enjoyed momentary success in the South in the mid-1850s. Growing out of the Secret Order of the Star-Spangled Banner, the party capitalized on hostility to immigrants and Catholics and quickly became a power in the border states and Louisiana where there were significant immigrant populations. Throughout the South, it also attracted a number of ex-Whigs looking for a national conservative alternative to the Democratic party. When questioned, members pretended to know nothing about the party; hence, they became known as Know-Nothings.

A number of prominent Southern political leaders, including John J. Crittenden of Kentucky, Kenneth Rayner of North Carolina, John Bell of Tennessee, and Sam Houston of Texas, joined the party, and by 1855 it was the major rival to the Democrats in the South. The party's defeat that year in the Virginia gubernatorial election, however, coupled with deepening sectional divisions in the national organization over the slavery issue, severely weakened it in the region. In 1856 the Southern-controlled national convention nominated Millard Fillmore for president. Running as a Union candidate, Fillmore made a strong race in the South, polling almost 45 percent of the popular vote; he carried Maryland and only narrowly lost several other Southern states. But Northern desertions left Fillmore a distant third nationally and sealed the fate of the party.

The American party retained a separate organization in some parts of the South until 1860 (New Orleans elected a Know-Nothing mayor that year), but ultimately the bulk of its southern members joined various opposition coalitions and voted for Bell in 1860. The significance of Southern Know-Nothingism lay in its role in opposition to the Democratic party and in sectionalism before the war.

— WILLIAM E. GIENAPP

Knoxville campaigns. The following winter, Johnston asked for Alexander's promotion to brigadier general and his transfer to the Army of Tennessee as chief of artillery. Jefferson Davis refused Johnston's application, confiding to a friend that Alexander was "one of a very few whom Gen. Lee wd [*sic*] not give to anybody."

Davis, however, promised Alexander a brigadier generalship, which he received on February 26, 1864. With the promotion—one of three such commissions awarded to a Confederate artillery officer during the war—came official control of artillery in the First Corps.

The spring of 1864 found Alexander and the rest of Longstreet's troops reunited with the Army of Northern Virginia. When the overland campaign opened in the Wilderness on May 5, Alexander had ninety-one guns under his command. He had little opportunity to use them until June 3 at Cold Harbor where the disposition of his ordnance produced a withering cross fire that doomed the Federal assault. During the siege of Petersburg, Alexander commanded the guns that guarded a twenty-four-mile line between the Appomattox and Chickahominy rivers. Because of Alexander's engineering expertise, Lee relied on him to perfect the mazelike fortifications of the Richmond defenses.

When Lee surrendered at Appomattox on April 9, Alexander had established himself as the army's most prominent artillerist. He recounted his war experiences in *Military Memoirs of a Confederate* (1907). A more revealing look at the Army of Northern Virginia is contained in Alexander's personal recollections, *Fighting for the Confederacy* (1989). This work stands as one of the richest firsthand accounts of Confederate operations in Virginia. Alexander also enjoyed a distinguished postwar career as a railroad president and professor of engineering while serving in a number of appointed government positions. He died on April 28, 1910.

— PETER S. CARMICHAEL

ANDERSON, RICHARD HERON

Anderson, Richard Heron (1821–1879), lieutenant general. The grandson of Col. Richard Anderson, who commanded the Maryland Line in the Revolutionary War, was born on October 7, 1821, near Statesburg, Sumter County, South Carolina. Following his education at Edge Hill Academy, Anderson entered the United States Military Academy. He graduated in 1842, ranking fortieth of fifty-five in a class that also included future Confederate generals James Longstreet, Lafayette McLaws, and D. H. Hill. As brevet second lieutenant of Dragoons, Anderson saw extensive service on the western frontier and was with the troops occupying Texas in 1845 and 1846. During the war with Mexico, Anderson accompanied Gen.

Winfield Scott's expedition from Vera Cruz and was breveted first lieutenant for gallant and meritorious conduct in the engagement at San Augustín. Ten years after the war the young officer was presented a sword by his native state inscribed: "South Carolina to Capt. Richard Heron Anderson, a memorial of gallant conduct in service at Vera Cruz, Cherubusco, Molino del Rey, Mexico."

On the secession of South Carolina in December 1860, Anderson resigned his commission and became colonel of the First South Carolina Infantry Regiment. He was present at the firing on Fort Sumter, and when P. G. T. Beauregard went north to take charge of forces in Virginia, Anderson was placed in command of the defenses of Charleston. He was promoted to brigadier general on July 18, 1861, and a month later was ordered to Pensacola as the top assistant to Gen. Braxton Bragg. In this capacity, Anderson directed the only engagement in the territory, a night attack against the Wilson Zouaves of New York.

Increased activity in Virginia caused the removal of Anderson to that state in early 1862. There he was given command of a brigade in the division of his old West Point classmate, James Longstreet. Anderson's conduct in the Battle of Williamsburg elicited high praise from Longstreet, who reported that the attack "of the two brigades under Gen. R. H. Anderson . . . was made with such spirit and regularity as to have driven back the most determined foe. This decided the day in our favor."

On July 14, following the repulse of the Federals in the Seven Days' Battles around Richmond, Anderson was promoted to major general and given command of a division formerly led by Benjamin Huger. When Longstreet's other units moved northward to combat a new Northern army under John Pope, Anderson remained behind to cover Richmond until it could be determined that the capital was safe from further attack. He rejoined the Army of Northern Virginia in time to participate in the final day's action at the Battle of Second Manassas. In the ensuing Maryland campaign, Anderson's division reinforced D. H. Hill at the Bloody Lane in the Battle of Sharpsburg. Anderson suffered a thigh wound early in the fighting but remained on the field until the victory was no longer in doubt; then, according to a contemporary, he "fell fainting from loss of blood."

Anderson returned to duty before the Battle of Fredericksburg in December. He saw little action in that contest, however, as his division held the left of the Confederate position and was not attacked in the Federals' assault on Robert E. Lee's lines.

In the Battle of Chancellorsville in May 1863, the divisions of Anderson and McLaws held the Federals

in check while Thomas J. ("Stonewall") Jackson made his famous flank march and attacked on the right of the Union line. Later Anderson and McLaws rushed to the assistance of Jubal Early, whose division was under attack by the Union Sixth Corps. Their vigorous action forced the enemy back across the Rappahannock River and closed another Northern "On to Richmond" campaign. For his conduct in this action, Anderson was cited by Lee: "Maj. Gen. R. H. Anderson was also distinguished for the promptness, courage, and skill with which he and his division executed every order."

When Lee reorganized the army in the wake of Jackson's death, Richard S. Ewell and A. P. Hill joined Longstreet as corps commanders. That Anderson was considered for such a post was implied in Lee's message to President Jefferson Davis that "R. H. Anderson and J. B. Hood are also capital officers. They are improving too and will make good corps commanders if necessary."

Anderson's division, one of three in Hill's corps, was at the rear of the column on the first day of the Battle of Gettysburg and saw no action. The next day, in conjunction with two of Longstreet's divisions, Anderson's troops participated in the attack on the Union left. In this maneuver one of Anderson's brigades reached enemy batteries on Cemetery Ridge before they were surrounded and forced back. On July 3 Anderson supported Pickett's ill-starred attack on the Union center.

When Longstreet was wounded seriously in the Battle of the Wilderness, Anderson was placed in charge of the First Corps until "Old Pete" returned. Anderson's most notable achievement during his chief's absence occurred on the night of May 7–8, 1864. Ordered by Lee to begin his march to Spotsylvania Court House at 3:00 A.M. on the second day, Anderson left four hours earlier. Marching through smoke and searing heat caused by burning woodlands on both sides of the road, Anderson attained the strategic road junction ahead of the Federals. Had he failed in his objective, and enemy forces arrived there first, the Federals would have interposed between Lee and Richmond and enjoyed a shorter route to the capital. Commissioned a lieutenant general on May 31, 1864, Anderson led the corps creditably until Longstreet returned in October, at which time the South Carolinian was given command of the divisions of Robert Hoke and Bushrod Johnson.

On the retreat from Petersburg, Anderson's and Ewell's commands were routed at Sayler's Creek on April 6, 1865. Anderson's shattered divisions were subsequently divided between Longstreet and John B. Gordon. As a general without a command appropriate

ANDERSON, RICHARD HERON

Longstreet often lacked finesse when dealing with his fellow officers and civilian officials.

PAGE 330

*Since neither the
Confederacy nor
the Union expected
a long war, both
failed to plan
for the enemy
soldiers they
would capture.*

PAGE 451

to his rank, Anderson was authorized to return home. His name, therefore, does not appear on the surrender rolls of Appomattox.

Trained in the profession of arms, Anderson found no demand for his talents in the postwar era. He tried to make a livelihood as a planter and failed. Ultimately, he went to Charleston and became a day laborer in the yards of the South Carolina Railroad. When his plight was called to the attention of authorities, Anderson was appointed state inspector of phosphates, a position he held until June 26, 1879, when he died of apoplexy in Beaufort, South Carolina. He was buried there in St. Helena's graveyard.

— LOWELL REIDENBAUGH

ANDERSONVILLE PRISON

In November 1863, the Confederate War Department ordered Capt. William Sidney Winder, son of Gen. John H. Winder (the most prominent official in charge of prisons), to locate a site for a new prison in southern Georgia. The Confederates wanted to reduce the problems caused by the accumulation of prisoners of war at Richmond. The younger Winder chose land close to the railroad station at Andersonville, which gave its name to what its creators formally called Camp Sumter (after the county in which it was then located).

The supervisor of the prison's construction was Winder's cousin, Capt. Richard B. Winder, a quartermaster. From the beginning, local opposition and shortage of materials slowed the work. Nonetheless, in January 1864, Richard Winder put impressed

slaves and free blacks to work cutting pine trees and trimming the trunks into twenty-foot posts. The laborers buried the butts of these in a trench and thus formed a stockade surrounding about sixteen and a half acres. There were two gates with enclosures outside. Sentry boxes were spotted along the stockade's top.

Deficient planning paved the way for disaster. On February 18, 1864, before the prison was ready, the Confederates at Richmond shipped the first trainload of prisoners who arrived seven days later at a stockade whose unfinished end was closed only by threatening cannon. Far from providing shelter, the jailors had not even laid out streets or any other organization to facilitate the future cleansing of a camp intended to hold ten thousand men. While the Confederates finished the stockade, the prisoners used bits of scrap wood and pieces of cloth to cover burrows in the ground that served as shelter.

The Confederates at first issued uncooked rations to prisoners who often lacked utensils. By May the bakery and cookhouse were providing a below-standard version of army rations. Meat was often lacking in quantity and quality, and the cornmeal contained so much husk it caused bowel problems. Richard Winder exacerbated the problems by locating the cooking facilities upstream on the brook running through the stockade, so that the waste together with that of the latrines of the guards' camps polluted the already inadequate water supply. Prisoners dug wells from which to drink, but lacking soap in any case they were unable to keep themselves clean. Since from the start no discipline had been enforced in the disposal of human waste, a sewage-filled swamp along the stream rapidly expanded.

On March 27, 1864, Captain Henry Wirz was ordered to Andersonville to take charge of the prison's

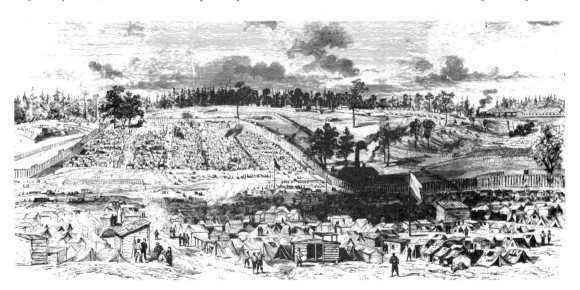

interior. Although he made efforts to impose some order, he had only limited authority over the quartermaster, commissary, and guard forces. The latter, who at first were line units of the Confederate army, were soon replaced by Georgia reserve troops composed of youths and older men whose inefficiency concerned everyone except their own commanders. Nonetheless, they manned the guard posts, called the roll within the stockade, and supervised the paroled prisoners who did an increasing amount of the work outside the walls. In the eyes of the inmates, Wirz was seen as responsible for whatever the others did and for all the deteriorating conditions; he became an object of hatred. One of his few popular actions was his support of a prisoner attempt to stop the robbing and murder of fellow captives by so-called raiders and his facilitating the hanging of six of them on July 11, 1864.

The ultimate responsibility for the executions as well as for all else at Andersonville by then lay with General Winder, who had taken command of the post on June 17, 1864. As in other aspects of his service with prisoners, Winder devoted his primary attention to matters of security. He repeatedly expressed concern about inmates' attempts to tunnel out or otherwise escape, and his warnings to the guards to be more vigilant may well have encouraged some to shoot prisoners who crossed the "deadline," which paralleled the stockade about fifteen feet inside, reducing the land available for prisoners.

Under Winder's command the Confederates enlarged the stockade on the north end in late June to take in an additional ten acres. To forestall Union raids on the prison, Winder recruited slaves to build earthworks and surround the enlarged stockade with a second wall and part of a third. He used this work force to repair the damage done to the stockade by an August flood, which also opened a new source of drinking water that prisoners dubbed the "Providence Spring." The spring's name represented an appeal to God—one of the prisoners' responses to the growing horror of conditions at Andersonville.

By July 1, Richmond authorities had sent 26,367 captives to a prison intended for 10,000. With rare exceptions these were enlisted men, and the bulk lived within the enlarged stockade where—even counting the

HENRY WIRZ

Prison Keeper and War Criminal

WIRZ, HENRY (1823–1865), commandant of Andersonville Prison. Wirz was born Heinrich Hermann Wirz in Zurich, Switzerland, on November 25, 1823, the son of a tailor. He received elementary and some secondary schooling. Although he was interested in medicine, his father insisted on mercantile training. He later claimed to be a physician and assisted doctors in America, but he almost certainly had no medical degree. At the start of the Civil War he was living in Milliken's Bend, Louisiana. He enlisted in the Fourth Louisiana Infantry and became a sergeant. At the Battle of Seven Pines, he incurred a wound above his right wrist, which left him partially incapacitated and in pain for the rest of his life.

On March 27, 1864, Captain Wirz was ordered to Andersonville Prison in Georgia, where he was given command of the prison's interior. Faced with problems largely created by his supervisors, who crammed prisoners into the ill-supplied stockade, Wirz vainly attempted to reorganize the prison. He had only limited authority over most of the personnel, however, and to strengthen his position, he sought promotion. Though supported by superiors and sometimes referred to as "major," he never received that rank. As conditions deteriorated at Andersonville, Wirz was blamed by the prisoners for their suffering. Inmates of earlier prisons had often been amused at his manner, but those at Andersonville described him as a brutal tyrant. Observers commented negatively on his German accent, his frequent use of profanity, and his outbreaks of rage. By war's end, he and General Winder were among the most notorious Confederate prison officials. When Winder died of a heart attack, Wirz was left to bear the brunt of Northern outrage.

Perhaps because of naiveté or lack of understanding of the North's anger over prison conditions, Wirz did not join other prison officers who fled. Instead he stayed on at Andersonville, where he was arrested and taken to Washington, D.C. There, beginning August 23, 1865, he was tried by a military commission on charges of murder and mistreatment of prisoners. The hostile commission permitted Wirz only a limited opportunity to defend himself, and it heard much testimony, often conflicting, against both Wirz and his superiors. The commission found him guilty, and when clemency was denied, he was hanged on November 10 in the yard of the Old Capitol Prison.

The published record of his trial became a leading source for postwar anti-Confederate propaganda. Nonetheless, some former Confederates and even ex-prisoners defended Wirz. In 1909, the Georgia chapter of the United Daughters of the Confederacy unveiled at Andersonville a memorial shaft to the only Confederate executed in the aftermath of the Civil War.

— FRANK L. BYRNE

Both sides tried to house officers separately from enlisted men and usually in different prisons.

PAGE 453

uninhabitable swamp—they had only a bit more than four square yards per man. About 1,355 were in a hospital consisting of a few tents covering five acres. There they received scant treatment for diarrhea, dysentery, and scurvy (the leading killers) and such conditions as typhoid fever, smallpox, and gangrene. The dead were buried in trenches in which locations were marked for 12,912 bodies during the prison's existence.

The prison's population reached a maximum in August 1864 of some 33,000 men. A month later the Confederates began to remove prisoners to camps at Millen, Georgia, and elsewhere. At about the same time, responding to complaints about conditions at Andersonville, the Confederates erected sheds called "barracks." These later were used by the sick as the site became more a hospital than a prison.

When Union invading armies penetrated deeper into the Confederacy, many of the prisoners originally moved from Andersonville were returned, and the prison continued in use until the Confederacy's collapse. Captain Wirz was there paroling prisoners until May 1865, when Union troops arrested him.

After the war, the United States designated the Andersonville graveyard a national cemetery. Union veterans' groups also purchased and preserved the site of the prison yard, where several states erected monuments to their dead. Meanwhile Andersonville's sheer size, high mortality rate, and terrible conditions made it notorious as one of the Civil War's unique atrocities. It became a leading feature in attacks on the memory of the Confederacy, to which Southerners responded defensively. In the twentieth century, Andersonville became a national historic site whose interpreters point out its significance as a memorial to all American prisoners of war.

— FRANK L. BYRNE

ANDREWS RAID

On April 12, 1862, the General, a northbound locomotive on the Western and Atlantic Railroad, pulled into Big Shanty, Georgia (present-day Kennesaw), twenty-five miles north of Atlanta. The crew and most of the passengers ambled to the nearby Lacy House for breakfast, but James J. Andrews lingered near the cars.

Andrews, another civilian, and twenty-two Union volunteers had left Shelbyville, Tennessee, on April 7 with orders from Brig. Gen. Ormsby M. Mitchel to steal a train and burn the bridges south of Chattanooga while Mitchel moved against Huntsville, Alabama. After rendezvousing in Marietta, Georgia, Andrews and nineteen of his men were aboard the train when it

On the eve of the Civil War over 100 companies shared the 9,000 miles of rail in the Confederacy.

PAGE 480

stopped at Big Shanty. While a dazed Confederate sentry looked on, they uncoupled the General, its tender, and three boxcars and sped northward.

Conductor William A. Fuller, engineer Jeff Cain, and shop foreman Anthony Murphy immediately gave chase on foot. Two miles north of Big Shanty, the winded trio borrowed a handcar and, with the help of some section hands, poled northward until the speeding car was derailed by a break Andrews's men had made in the tracks. Righting the car, the railroad men continued to Etowah, where they found the engine Yonah sitting on a siding.

Andrews had stopped several times to cut the telegraph wires, but for fear of arousing suspicion he had failed to disable the Yonah. Keeping to the railroad's timetable, he sidetracked the General upon reaching Kingston to allow a southbound freight to pass. But a second train followed, and a third. Claiming he had imperative orders to deliver a trainload of gunpowder to Confederate Gen. P. G. T. Beauregard, Andrews demanded an explanation for the delay and learned the increased traffic resulted from Mitchel's capture of Huntsville. Sixty-five minutes passed before the General left Kingston.

Five minutes later, the pursuing Yonah encountered the three southbound trains parked on the main line. Abandoning the little engine, Fuller, Murphy, and Cain sprinted to a junction two miles north of Kingston and commandeered the William L. Smith. A broken rail soon stopped the Smith, but Fuller and Murphy, setting out on foot again, flagged down the Texas just after it left the siding at Adairsville. Engineer Peter J. Bracken promptly backed his cars into the station and took up the chase, still in reverse.

Hampered by a lack of tools that made it difficult to pry up rails, the raiders cut loose two boxcars and dropped crossties across the tracks, desperately trying to gain enough time to burn the rain-soaked bridges north of Adairsville. The Texas pushed both cars onto the nearest siding and, avoiding all obstacles, pursued the fleeing General at speeds exceeding sixty miles per hour. Unable to stop for wood or water, the General ran out of steam two miles north of Ringgold.

The relentless Confederate pursuit, bad weather, and just plain bad luck prevented the raiders from doing any lasting damage to the railroad. Captured and tried, Andrews and seven of his men were hanged. Eight others, including two who had missed the train when it left Marietta, later escaped from an Atlanta jail. The six remaining raiders, exchanged as prisoners of war, were the first recipients of the U.S. Medal of Honor.

— DAVID EVANS

ANGLO-CONFEDERATE PURCHASING

In 1861, the wealth of the South consisted chiefly of land and slaves. An agricultural society, it was poor in industrial and manufacturing resources, and its means of transportation were far behind those of the North. Its cities, with the exception of Charleston, Richmond, and New Orleans, were of little importance as trade centers. The states against which the Confederates waged war held roughly two-thirds of the country's population, and their financial and industrial resources were far superior to those of the South.

Despite these circumstances, however, the Confederacy was able to sustain a war lasting four years, largely because of the energetic activities of its commercial agents in Great Britain, who labored steadily to supply the needs of the Southern military forces. Confederate troops were valiant fighters and, in the main, were well led. But they could not fight without arms or supplies, and Southern arsenals and manufacturers could not possibly meet all their needs. The Confederate government, rapidly organized, was quick to appreciate the situation, and very early in the war, before the North had been thoroughly aroused, it dispatched its financial agents and purchasing emissaries to Great Britain.

The Confederate government, however, committed an error by using its available sterling exchange and coin at the outset of the war for procurement purposes. As later events showed, these valuable assets should have been held in reserve and cotton sent to Britain to purchase essential war supplies. The weakness of Confederate purchasing in Great Britain was its reliance on fiat money and its futile funding operation by means of unsecured bonds. These errors of policy eventually destroyed Confederate finance abroad and weakened its purchasing power.

The Civil War stimulated the shipbuilding industry in Great Britain. Altogether about four hundred steamers, many of them iron, and eight hundred sailing vessels were sold to the South, including the cruisers *Alabama, Florida,* and *Shenandoah.* English lawyers advised Confederate agents that ships might be built for the South in British yards, providing three conditions were observed: the Confederate government concealed its ownership; the ship's destination was concealed; and the South adhered to a prohibition against the shipping of war equipment and the enlisting of a crew in British waters. Capt. James D. Bulloch, C.S.N., who expertly planned, coordinated, and controlled Confederate naval activity in Britain, consistently observed these requirements. He always tried to dispatch ships as ordinary sailing vessels.

The difficulties encountered by Confederate officials in Great Britain, however, revealed that the U.S. consular agents had a well-organized and highly developed espionage system, the function of which was to prevent the shipment of goods and materials to the Confederacy. It says a great deal for the tact, diplomacy, and energies of Bulloch and the other agents that so many ships got away and so much equipment and materials were shipped. Although Confederate ships bought and constructed in Great Britain were too few in number to act with effective aggressive power against the U.S. Navy, the commanders of the Confederate ships were able to inflict great injuries upon the merchant vessels of the North and thus drive up insurance rates to a prohibitive degree.

Although the Confederate Congress appropriated large sums for the navy (to be spent in Great Britain), the rate of exchange in the money market always worked against the Confederates, and the Southern navy was always smaller than Congress might have hoped. Jefferson Davis was fairly consistent in his naval policy and clearly understood and strongly supported the need for ship construction in Great Britain.

In the area of ordnance, the Confederate government was never able to equip its forces adequately. The original stock of arms consisted almost wholly of smoothbore muskets, altered from flint to percussion. These disappeared almost entirely during the first two years of the war and were replaced by English rifled and percussion arms of high quality. No official account was kept of the value of the Confederate government's purchases in Great Britain, and records are discouragingly fragmentary. Some statistical data has been collected in an attempt to record the quantity and value of articles that passed through the blockade, but it is difficult, in some instances, to give more than a reasoned estimate. About 1,350,000 bales of cotton were sent to Great Britain during the war, and approximately 600,000 items of equipment were shipped to

BRITISH EQUIPMENT SHIPPED TO THE CONFEDERACY	
Equipment	**Total Value**
small arms	
cannons	
munitions	
clothing	$200 million
hospital stores	
manufactured goods	
luxuries	

Unfortunately for the South, the good relationship with Britain began to deteriorate almost immediately after secession.

PAGE 250

15

ANGLO-CONFEDERATE TRADING COMPANY
The Big Business of Running the Blockade

The Anglo-Confederate Trading Company was a British shareholding blockade-running venture that was formed in early 1862 in Liverpool by members of the shipping firm Edward Lawrence and Company. The supercargo for the company was Thomas E. Taylor, whose zeal and attention to detail was instrumental in establishing a highly successful line of blockade runners that operated primarily between Nassau and Wilmington, North Carolina.

The company also took the lead in the technical development of blockade runners by constructing the steel-hulled sidewheeler Banshee. This was the first vessel built from the keel up as a blockade runner. In April 1863, she became the first steel-hulled vessel to cross the Atlantic. Banshee and her following consorts were hired by the Confederacy to carry in munitions. The contracts were so lucrative that a successful round trip paid the construction cost of a blockade runner and the salary of the crew. Besides the inbound cargo, the company also carried out over ten thousand bales of cotton.

The Anglo-Confederate Trading Company was one of the war's most successful blockade-running firms. Although its total fleet numbered only nine vessels, with no more than four operating at one time, its ships completed forty-nine runs out of fifty-eight attempts. Unlike its competitors, the company did not invest heavily in Confederate bonds and additional steamers. Instead, profits were returned to shareholders. In the fall of 1864, the firm paid dividends that amounted to 2,500 percent over the original cost of a share of stock. Even though at the war's end the company sold off its blockade runners at a substantial loss, these transactions were more than covered by the firm's profits.

— STEPHEN R. WISE

the Confederacy through the blockade (the majority of blockade runners were English vessels).

Goods entering the Confederate States from British ports can be valued at almost $200 million. Agents of the Southern War Department alone spent more than $12,250,000 in Great Britain. Throughout the war, munitions and supplies of all kinds also poured into the North from Europe. In comparison, the South was isolated and had great difficulty equipping and supplying its armed forces. Without these essential imports, the Civil War could have ended possibly in eighteen months.

A careful analysis of the Confederate purchasing agents and their mission in Great Britain reveals that they did nothing that was not justified by the rule of fair and honorable warfare, nothing contrary to English law as construed by English jurists and confirmed by the judgment of English courts. These agents—poorly organized and badly instructed by their superiors (especially during the first thirty months of the war), inexperienced, sometimes guilty of serious errors of judgment, prone to disputes caused by vague orders from senior officers who knew little of the circumstances under which they were working, almost always short of funds, harried by Federal spies, and working for a government unrecognized by Great Britain—made it possible in spite of all their handicaps for the Confederates to sustain a war lasting over four years. Given the crippling difficulties, it is a tribute to their initiative, skill, and energy that they accomplished so much with so little.

[*See also* Alabama Claims; Enchantress Affair; Erlanger Loan; New Plan.]

— RICHARD I. LESTER

ANTISLAVERY

Opposition to the practice of slavery was a long-range movement that began in colonial America. To understand the broad and complicated parameters of antislavery, however, one must distinguish between and among a variety of impulses causing Americans and others in the Western world to oppose the institution of slavery.

Among the first abolitionists were those who objected to the practice on religious grounds. The Society of Friends, or Quakers, in both England and America began to grieve the practice during the eighteenth century, especially in and around the Quaker-owned colony of Pennsylvania. By the time of the American Revolution, Anthony Benezet, a Philadelphia Quaker, was issuing strenuous condemnations of slaveholding and urging Quakers to set an example by ridding themselves of their slaves in works like *A Serious Address to the Rulers of America, on the Inconsistency of Their Conduct Respecting Slavery* (1783).

Close on the heels of Quaker antislavery testimony came the libertarian influences of the American Revolution and other subsequent democratic revolutions in France, Haiti, and eventually Latin America.

As each of these focused on the rights of man and produced various declarations concerning "inalienable" rights to life, liberty, and property, the practice of slaveholding was sharply questioned. In each of these areas and in England there arose an antislavery tide that led first to the abolition of the African slave trade in 1808 in both Britain and America, and then to the emancipation of slaves in Northern American states and in 1833 in the British West Indies.

Religious and political scruples about slaveholding had its effect as well in Southern states. Prior to the 1830s thousands of slaveholders ranging from George Washington to ultraconservative John Randolph of Roanoke voluntarily manumitted their slaves. Viewing slavery as morally wrong or inconsistent with American republicanism, or at best as a "necessary evil," these Southerners were impelled to end slavery—usually through their last wills and testaments.

Southern qualms about slavery and frequently also about the role of African Americans in American society led after the War of 1812 to a spate of efforts to rid the nation both of slavery and of its African population. Manumission societies were formed throughout much of the South, especially in North Carolina and Tennessee, beginning in 1816. By 1827 forty-one organizations devoted to the ending of slavery existed in North Carolina alone. The American Colonization Society, founded in 1817 and headed by such men as James Madison, James Monroe, and John Marshall, also generated antislavery interest throughout the South as it sought to eliminate both slaveholding and Africans from the United States.

With the rise of radical abolitionism in the 1830s, however, the moderate antislavery position of many Southerners became untenable, at least publicly. Indeed, the emergence of American abolitionism, usually identified with William Lloyd Garrison and the founding of his Boston newspaper, the *Liberator*, on January 1, 1831, tended to undermine many moderate antislavery positions in the North and South. Given the view of abolitionists that slavery was a moral evil and that it should be abolished immediately without compensation for slaveholders, abolitionism attacked virtually every other antislavery position. Northern opponents of abolitionist radicalism were quickly labeled "anti-abolitionists," and Southerners found it increasingly difficult to maintain any witness against slavery. Quakers throughout the South grew quiet on the subject, and manumission societies disappeared. Colonization efforts, largely discredited by abolitionists, continued until the Civil War but at a less significant pace. Laws regulating the manumission of slaves were enacted in the South. Other laws forbidding the migration of blacks into Northern states virtually halt-

HARRIET TUBMAN
Abolitionist and Union Spy

Tubman was born on a plantation in Dorchester County, Maryland. One of the eleven children born to her slave parents, Harriet Green and Benjamin Ross, she was given the name Araminta. The young slave girl suffered whippings and beatings and sustained a life-threatening head injury in her teens. At the age of twenty-three she married a free black, John Tubman.

In 1849 when her owner died, she escaped into freedom (leaving her husband behind when he refused to accompany her), took the name Harriet Tubman, and found work in Philadelphia. Within a year, she was involved in rescue attempts to free other family members and became an invaluable asset to the movement organized to assist slaves escaping to freedom. Braving the dangers, Tubman became one of the most intrepid conductors on the Underground Railroad. She moved to Canada in 1852, having made a total of eleven trips in three years, rescuing several dozen slaves.

Given the title "General Tubman" by abolitionist John Brown, Tubman became even more active when the Civil War broke out. For this reason, slave owners put a steep price on her head, and she was perhaps the most wanted woman in the Confederacy. Despite this threat, Tubman made nineteen more trips, leading nearly three hundred runaways out of the South. She worked out of Fortress Monroe, Virginia, before being sent to Beaufort, South Carolina, by the governor of Massachusetts. Under the command of Maj. Gen. David Hunter, Tubman was a scout and spy. During the summer of 1863 she assisted Col. James Montgomery in military campaigns designed to terrorize civilians and stir slaves into rebellion along the Combahee River. They were able to liberate nearly eight hundred slaves and effectively undermine Confederate morale in the South Carolina low country.

Tubman remained relatively impoverished, receiving only three hundred dollars for her three years of service to the Union. After the war she retired to Auburn, New York, and opened a Home for Indigent and Aged Negroes. She died in 1913 in relative obscurity, unheralded as a war hero until the modern era.

— CATHERINE CLINTON

I started with this idea in my head, "There's two things I've got a right to . . . death or liberty."

HARRIET TUBMAN

ed voluntary acts of emancipation. The rise of a militant and sophisticated defense of slavery on religious, philosophical, ethical, scientific, and economic grounds during the 1830s and 1840s eliminated public expressions of antislavery opinion.

Southerners who had strong qualms about slavery found it expedient to move to the North. James Birney moved from Alabama to Kentucky and finally Ohio as he changed from slaveholder to abolitionist. William Henry Brisbane of South Carolina followed the same route until he settled in Wisconsin. North Carolina Quakers such as Levi Coffin followed suit and later helped establish the famous Underground Railroad that aided runaway slaves. Sarah and Angelina Grimke, sisters from a distinguished Charleston family, played key roles in propelling abolitionism in the North after 1835. Angelina's *Appeal to the Christian Women of the South* (1836) and Sarah's *Epistle to the Clergy of the Southern States* (1836) placed them at the forefront of abolitionism and in defining a reformist role for women.

By 1850 abolitionists from the North were no longer welcome or safe to proclaim their message in the South. Two Wesleyan Methodists sent from New York, Adam Crooks and Jesse McBride, were arrested and convicted that year of distributing "incendiary literature" in western North Carolina. Before their appeal could be heard, they were hounded out of the state by a mob. A decade later not even a native Southerner could operate openly as an abolitionist. In 1859 Daniel Worth, former Quaker from Guilford County, North Carolina, and kinsman of governor Jonathan Worth, was arrested and convicted of the same crime as Crooks and McBride.

Interestingly, however, Worth was convicted of distributing a book written by another North Carolinian containing yet another antislavery position. Hinton Rowan Helper, in his sensational *Impending Crisis of the South* (1857), held that slavery was a curse on the South that hampered its economic development. Indeed, he argued, the costs of sustaining slavery had to be borne directly by nonslaveholding whites throughout the South. Though Helper's book was held publicly to be incendiary and was banned in much of the South, it is clear that many Southerners shared his views. Calvin Wiley, North Carolina's first public school administrator, said as much in a pamphlet he titled *A Sober View of the Slavery Question* in 1849. Frederick Law Olmsted encountered the same viewpoint as he traveled throughout the South in the 1850s.

A similar refrain appeared in the extensive writings of Daniel Reaves Goodloe, a native North Carolinian who published the moderate antislavery newspaper *National Era* in Washington, D.C. The title of his 1846 tract reveals his perspective: *Inquiry into the Causes Which Have Retarded the Accumulation of Wealth and Increase of Population in the Southern States: In Which the Question of Slavery is Considered in a Politico-Economical Point of View.* A similar economic comparison of South and North appeared a year later in *Address to the People of West Virginia,* written by Henry Ruffner, clergyman and president of Washington College (present-day Washington and Lee). Such strenuous arguments that were both antislavery and anti-Negro gave a new boost to large-scale colonization schemes in the 1850s.

With the publication of Harriet Beecher Stowe's *Uncle Tom's Cabin* in 1852 and of Helper's *Impending Crisis* in 1857, and with John Brown's raid on Harpers Ferry in 1859, the South became so embattled on the subject of slavery that it was no longer possible for strong antislavery views to be expressed publicly. Nevertheless, private doubts persisted. When the Civil War began, concerns about fighting a war to maintain slavery were expressed in a variety of ways. Antislavery opinion must have been part of the strong antisecessionist vote taken in North Carolina on February 28, 1861, even after seven other states had left the Union. It was probably also a factor in the decision of a hundred thousand men from Confederate states to join and fight in the Union army during the Civil War.

Incipient antislavery opinion loomed in discussions about making use of slaves as Confederate soldiers. In 1864 various proposals were floated by Confederate generals to arm part of the slave population, and in November of that year the matter came before the Confederate Congress. By January of 1865 even Gen. Robert E. Lee was proposing that the Confederacy should consider abolishing slavery. Finally, in March 1865, the policy of arming slaves and giving them emancipation for their service became the law of the Confederacy. By that time, of course, the Confederacy was already doomed, and the question of the fate of antislavery and abolitionism was settled.

[See also Harpers Ferry, West Virginia, *article on* John Brown's Raid; Helper, Hinton Rowan.]

— LARRY E. TISE

APPOMATTOX CAMPAIGN

Beginning on March 29, 1865, and lasting until April 9, this campaign in the concluding days of the Civil War is commonly referred to as Lee's Retreat. Lasting only twelve days, it culminated in the surrender of the largest and most powerful Confederate army.

The movement began on the twenty-ninth when Gen. Ulysses S. Grant sent a force of about 50,000 troops—the Second Corps under Gen. Andrew A. Humphreys, the Fifth Corps under Gen. Gouverneur

K. Warren, and cavalry commanded by Gen. Philip Sheridan—to move around the Confederate right flank west of Petersburg and gain the South Side Railroad. This was Gen. Robert E. Lee's last major supply line into the city, and if captured, he would be forced to withdraw from the defenses of both Richmond, the Confederate capital, and Petersburg.

Lee, realizing the importance of protecting the railroad, dispatched a force under Gen. George E. Pickett to hold a strategic crossroads known as Five Forks. A preliminary series of battles (Quaker Road, March 29; White Oak Road and Dinwiddie Courthouse, March 31) allowed the Union army to maneuver into position to attack Pickett on April 1. Pickett, whose force numbered about 10,000 infantry and cavalry, confronted a similar force of 22,000 men led by General Sheridan at Five Forks. Pickett was defeated with the loss of over 2,000 prisoners, assuring the capture of the South Side Railroad. Federal casualties amounted to 633.

At dawn on the second, Grant issued orders for numerous assaults on the Petersburg lines, and the Sixth Corps under Gen. Horatio G. Wright broke

through at one point. There was more fighting at Confederate Forts Mahone and Gregg and at Sutherland Station where the railroad was seized. Confederate Gen. A. P. Hill was killed in these battles. That night Lee issued orders for his troops to withdraw from both Petersburg and Richmond.

When General Lee left the two cities, his intention was for the scattered contingents of the Army of Northern Virginia, numbering about 58,000 men, to rendezvous at Amelia Court House, located on the Richmond and Danville Railroad. At this point he could replenish his army with needed supplies. The army would then continue into North Carolina and join with Gen. Joseph E. Johnston's force. Successfully bringing his army together at this county seat, Lee found to his dismay that, because of a mix-up in communications, no supplies had been sent. Deciding to remain in the area while his army foraged, Lee allowed General Grant with his force of about 76,000 men (the Army of the Potomac and Army of the James) to begin a pursuit that eliminated the one-day lead Lee held. Consequently, hard riding by Sheridan's cavalry, along with an occasional skir-

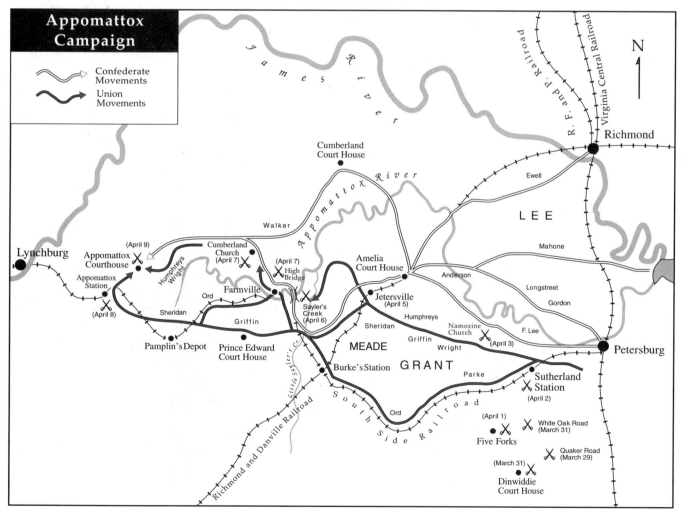

Appomattox
Campaign

Confederate
Movements

Union
Movements

*"The war began in
my front yard and
ended in my front
parlor."*

WILMER McLEAN

mish such as one at Namozine Church on April 3, enabled the Federals to move around and in front of the Confederate army. They then cut the path of Lee's retreat along the railroad at the next station, Jetersville.

The following day, the fifth, when the Southerners pulled out of Amelia Court House, they found not only Federal cavalry blocking their way but fast-marching Union infantry arriving in support. Lee, deciding not to engage in battle at this point, changed his plans and ordered a night march around the entrenched enemy left flank. His destination was the town of Farmville, where he could find rations for his men at the South Side Railroad station.

The Confederate army was able to carry out this plan until dawn on the sixth. Then the Federals spotted the rear of their column near Amelia Springs, north of Jetersville, and immediately gave chase. Traveling along roads parallel to the one Lee's column was moving on, Sheridan's cavalry intercepted his line of march near Sayler's Creek. With the Second and Sixth Corps also close behind, the Confederates had to make a stand to save themselves. In three separate engagements, at the Hillsman farm, Lockett's farm, and Marshall's crossroads (or Harper's farm), the Federal infantry and cavalry put 7,700 men, almost a quarter of Lee's army, out of combat, mainly as prisoners. Those who survived continued on another night march to Farmville, situated on the southern bank of the Appomattox River.

It was also on this day that General E. O. C. Ord, commander of the Army of the James, sent a body of infantry and cavalry to destroy High Bridge so the Confederates could not use it in their retreat. High Bridge was a large trestle by which the South Side

Railroad crossed the Appomattox River. Confederate cavalry learned of the raid and overtook the enemy force near the bridge. In the fight that ensued, most of the Federals were either killed or captured. Union Gen. Theodore Read and Confederate Gen. James Dearing were also mortally wounded.

When Lee's men arrived at Farmville at daylight on the seventh, they found some 40,000 rations of bread and 80,000 of meal in trains at the depot. As allotments were being issued to the troops, word came that Federal cavalrymen were coming into the town from the east. Lee had no alternative but to send the trains off toward Lynchburg. (These were captured the next day at Pamplin's Depot.)

Realizing that the Federals were also moving south of Farmville through Prince Edward Court House to cut off that avenue of escape, the Confederate commander decided to move his army to the north bank of the generally unfordable Appomattox River. If he could get his army safely over and burn all the bridge crossings behind him, including High Bridge to the east, he might delay Grant's men in their relentless chase. Unfortunately for Lee, the plan failed. One of the four bridges spanning the river (the wagon bridge under High Bridge) was not destroyed in time, which allowed the Union Second Corps to cross.

Lee then entrenched his army around Cumberland Church, about three miles north of Farmville, to protect his wagon train. Federal attempts to break the Confederate defense line that afternoon were unsuccessful but held a good portion of the Southern army at bay until darkness fell. The Confederates once again had to make a night march. That evening Grant sent the first of a series of dispatches to Lee requesting the surrender of his army.

HERE IT ENDED

*Wilmer McLean's home,
which served as the
Appomattox Courthouse, was
the site of Robert E. Lee's
surrender to Ulysses S. Grant
on April 9, 1865.*

HARPER'S PICTORIAL
HISTORY OF THE
GREAT REBELLION

CSS ARKANSAS

The 165-foot-long ironclad fought on the Yazoo and Mississippi rivers until Farragut's forces crippled it near Vicksburg.

NAVAL HISTORICAL CENTER, WASHINGTON, D.C.

The next point along the South Side Railroad where Lee could hope to obtain supplies was Appomattox Station, about three miles west of Appomattox Courthouse. To reach that point, the Confederates would have to march thirty-eight miles. A thirty-mile route was available south of the river, but this route, which generally followed the railroad, was open to Grant and his troops.

Lee's army was relatively unmolested on the eighth, the final day of the campaign, although two Federal corps, the Second and Sixth, pursued him north of the river. To the south, with Sheridan's cavalry leading, the Fifth Corps and the Army of the James were taking advantage of the situation. Arriving at Appomattox Station before the van of Lee's column, the cavalry captured the supply trains and, later that evening, a portion of the Confederate artillery and wagon train in the Battle of Appomattox Station. This put a segment of the Union forces directly in front of Lee's force now gathering around Appomattox Courthouse. With the Federals in his rear and cavalry across his line of march, Lee decided to attempt a breakthrough early the next morning.

At daybreak on the ninth, assuming that only Federal horsemen were confronting him, Lee pushed his combined force of infantry and cavalry under Gen. John B. Gordon against the enemy position, forcing them to give ground. But as they fell back, the Army of the James began arriving on the field in support, and it became apparent to Lee that he was about to be surrounded, especially when the Fifth Corps appeared on his flank. The Southerners sent out white flags of truce to suspend hostilities. That afternoon Lee met with Grant at Appomattox Courthouse in the home

of Wilmer McLean to discuss terms of surrender. After four years of bloodshed, the fighting in Virginia was over.

The casualties for the Appomattox campaign totaled approximately 9,000 for the Federal army and 28,000, including desertions, for the Confederates. Lee surrendered close to 30,000 men at Appomattox. All were paroled and allowed to go home.

— CHRIS CALKINS

ARKANSAS

CSS *Arkansas* was laid down at Memphis, Tennessee, in October 1861, built by John Shirley. Before she could be completed, Memphis was threatened by Union forces descending the Mississippi River. The incomplete ironclad was towed down the Mississippi and up the Yazoo River. At Yazoo City, Mississippi, she was completed and commissioned in July 1862.

CSS *ARKANSAS* SPECIFICATIONS

- twin screw propeller ram
- 165 feet long
- 37 feet wide
- 11–12 foot draft
- casement sides perpendicular,
- crew of 200
- ten gun battery: two 64 pounders, two 6-inch rifles, two 32-pounder smoothbores

By 1863 Union blockading squadrons along the Atlantic and Gulf coasts had increased to more than 300 ships.

PAGE 390

On July 15, 1862, as the ironclad descended the Yazoo River, she encountered three Union vessels—*Carondelet, Tyler,* and *Queen of the West.* In the engagement that followed, *Carondelet* was disabled and the other two Union vessels retired downstream with *Arkansas* in pursuit. The chase continued into the Mississippi River where the Confederate ironclad found at anchor the combined naval forces of flag officers Charles Davis and David Farragut, some thirty warships in all. *Arkansas* steamed slowly through the Union force, hit repeatedly by shot and shell. Several of the Union vessels were hit by *Arkansas*'s guns, but only *Lancaster* was seriously damaged.

Arkansas reached Vicksburg and that night came under attack a second time by Farragut's vessels as they ran the Confederate batteries and headed back downstream. The Confederate ironclad, already damaged from the early morning engagement, was hit several times again.

On August 3, *Arkansas,* repairs completed, left Vicksburg to cooperate in an attack on Baton Rouge, Louisiana. Twenty-four hours after leaving Vicksburg, the ironclad's engines began giving trouble, and the ship was anchored while engineers worked on them. The crew got the ship underway again the following morning, but when she was within sight of Baton Rouge, the engines broke down completely. With a Union naval force led by the ironclad *Essex* approaching, the Confederates abandoned *Arkansas* after setting her on fire. She drifted downstream before sinking.

— WILLIAM N. STILL, JR.

ARLINGTON HOUSE

Situated on a knoll overlooking the Potomac River and the city of Washington, Arlington was the Virginia home of Robert E. Lee. The mansion now lies in the heart of Arlington National Cemetery. Composed of a two-story center with flanking one-story wings, Arlington was set on an eleven-hundred-acre tract of land, most of which was wooded. Construction began in 1803 on the north wing, but the entire house was not completed until about 1817 or 1818. It was planned and built by George Washington Parke Custis, step-grandson of George Washington. George Hadfield, second architect of the U.S. Capitol, designed Arlington's portico, which is fronted by six massive Doric columns and modeled on the Greek temple at Paestum. The building is constructed of brick, but its exterior is stuccoed and patterned to simulate cut stone. It is considered one of the finest and

earliest examples of the Greek Revival style in the United States.

Lt. Robert E. Lee married Mary Ann Randolph Custis at Arlington in 1831, and there the family raised seven children. With the outbreak of war in 1861, Lee left Arlington, never to return. The estate was occupied by Federal troops, and it became a training camp. The army felled the forests and ransacked or impounded the family's Washington memorabilia. In 1862 Congress levied a direct tax on all properties in insurrectionary territory and required that the owners personally appear to make payment. The Lees proved unable to cross Federal lines to pay the $92.07 tax. Pursuant to an amendment of the direct tax in 1863, the government purchased the plantation at a public auction.

In May 1864 Secretary of War Edwin Stanton ordered that a national cemetery be created on two hundred acres of the grounds at Arlington. The first burials began that year, and Quartermaster General Montgomery Meigs directed that the lawn and gardens be ringed with burial sites. Shattered by the loss of her family home, Mary Lee mourned that those officials had desecrated Arlington. More than seventeen thousand casualties or veterans of the Civil War were eventually buried there. Emancipated slaves also established Freedman's Village on the grounds. Over a twenty-year period, some two thousand residents lived in the settlement.

Remorseful over losing his wife's estate, Lee attempted to regain Arlington after the war, but failed. President Andrew Johnson proposed returning the Washington relics to the Lee family, but Congress balked. After Lee's death in 1870, his son George Washington Custis Lee pursued the matter, and the Supreme Court finally ruled in 1882 that the government had acted illegally in seizing the house. The Lee family settled the case with the government for $150,000. Arlington still served as headquarters for the cemetery until the late 1920s.

The fate of the mansion changed considerably with the cultural politics of the Southern Renaissance. Thousands of visitors annually paid homage to Lee at Arlington, and proposals were aired to restore the mansion to its earlier appearance. In 1921 author Frances Parkinson Keyes urged the formation of a private preservation society to shepherd the project, but Republican Congressman Louis C. Cramton of Michigan proposed instead that the government establish a national shrine at Arlington. In 1925 Congress unanimously passed legislation that directed the secretary of war to restore the building as "Arlington House, The Robert E. Lee Memorial." Arlington was transferred to the National Park Service in 1933. Today Arlington House displays the history of the Custis-Lee family, as well as upper-class Virginia life.

— JAMES M. LINDGREN

ARMISTEAD, LEWIS A.

Armistead, Lewis A. (1817–1863), brigadier general. Son of an army general, Lewis Addison Armistead was born February 18, 1817, in Newbern, North Carolina. He entered West Point in 1834 but left the academy two years later following an altercation with Cadet Jubal Early of Virginia. In 1839 Armistead joined the army as a lieutenant in the Sixth Infantry. Following active service in the Seminole War, Armistead fought in the Mexican War and received brevet promotion to major for heroism at Chapultepec. He spent the next fourteen years on frontier duty. One of his closest friends was fellow officer Winfield Scott Hancock of Pennsylvania.

With the advent of the Civil War, Armistead resigned his army commission and rushed from Texas to Virginia to offer his sword to the Confederacy. Older than most of his compatriots and thoroughly imbued with army ways, Armistead served the first year of the war as colonel of the Fifty-seventh Virginia. On April 1, 1862, he was promoted to brigadier general. His new command (Ninth, Fourteenth, Thirty-eighth, Fifty-third, and Fifty-seventh Virginia) became one of the most celebrated and battle-hardened brigades in the Army of Northern Virginia. One reason for its success was Armistead's leadership. He regarded obedience to duty, a superior noted, "as the first qualification of a soldier. For straggling on the march or neglect of duty on the part of his men, he held the officer in immediate command strictly responsible. The private must answer to the officer, but the officer to him."

From Seven Pines through Second Manassas, a colleague observed, Armistead increased his reputation—"displaying everywhere conspicuous gallantry, and winning by his coolness under fire, by his stern perseverance and his indomitable pluck, the applause of his superiors and the entire confidence of his men."

Armistead served as provost marshal for Robert E. Lee's army during the Sharpsburg campaign. His brigade then became part of Gen. George E. Pickett's division. Armistead played only a minor role at Fredericksburg and was with James Longstreet's command at Suffolk during the Chancellorsville campaign. He gained immortality at Gettysburg, however.

On July 3, 1863, his brigade was part of the climactic Pickett-Pettigrew assault against the Union center. Armistead received the order to advance and then turned to his drawn-up columns and shouted: "Men! Remember what you are fighting for—your homes, your friends, and your sweethearts! Follow me!"

With his hat on the point of his sword, Armistead led his men forward. Barely 150 of them were left when they reached the Federal lines. Armistead jumped over the enemy obstruction on Cemetery

Ridge and fell mortally wounded among the Federal cannons. He died July 5 in a Federal hospital, after requesting that his watch and other valuables be given to his old friend, Winfield Hancock—whose troops, unknown to Armistead, were the ones who had repulsed the Virginians.

The general is buried in the family plot at St. Paul's Church, Baltimore. Of Armistead and three other brigadiers slain at Gettysburg, Lee wrote that they "died as they had lived, discharging the highest duty of patriots with devotion that never faltered and courage that shrank from no danger."

— JAMES I. ROBERTSON, JR.

It may have been a strategic error to locate the Confederate capital so close to the North.

PAGE 504

ARMY OF NORTHERN VIRGINIA

The principal eastern army (1862–1865) of the Confederate States fought under the direction of Gen. Robert E. Lee with steady and sometimes spectacular success against the Federal Army of the Potomac. With a strength ranging between 35,000 and 85,000 men, the army opened its career by driving away an early threat to Richmond and then defending the cap-

*"Do your duty in
all things. You
cannot do more.
You should never
wish to do less."*

ROBERT E. LEE

DEFENSE OF RICHMOND
The Rise of Robert E. Lee

During the three months beginning with the dramatic events of March 1862, the components of what would become the Army of Northern Virginia played out their roles in the defense of Richmond. Most of Johnston's command moved east of Richmond to the peninsula, where it absorbed Magruder's men into a unified force facing McClellan's slow but massive advance. Johnston fought McClellan on May 5 at Williamsburg and then fell steadily back to the outskirts of the Southern capital. Confederates south of the James River who had been centered on Norfolk eventually moved toward Richmond and by June had augmented the strength of the main army directly defending the capital. Stonewall Jackson retained his independent command as a diversionary force in the Shenandoah Valley and exploited every opportunity he found there to attract the attention of Northern leaders away from the main prize at Richmond. From March 23 to June 9 Jackson fought six battles and marched hundreds of miles, occupying many times his own numbers in fruitless reaction to his daring thrusts.

While Jackson bedazzled a succession of foes in the Valley, Johnston committed his combined forces to battle under promising circumstances on May 31 and June 1, 1862, at Seven Pines (or Fair Oaks). Poor planning and an almost unbelievable degree of confusion among his ranking subordinates, particularly Gen. James Longstreet, dissipated Johnston's golden opportunity. Johnston also lost command of the army when he fell wounded late on May 31. The next day President Jefferson Davis designated Robert E. Lee as Johnston's replacement. Lee never relinquished command, to the intense disgust of Johnston and Longstreet but of almost no one else in the Confederate States.

— ROBERT K. KRICK

around Virginia's northern perimeter resisted Federal threats on several fronts. The largest of these Confederate forces fought the First Battle of Manassas (or Bull Run) on July 21, 1861, when Gen. Joseph E. Johnston's command hurried eastward from the Shenandoah Valley to join with troops under Gen. P. G. T. Beauregard in repulsing an enemy advance southward from Washington, D.C. The unified Southern force, commanded by Johnston, became known as the Confederate Army of the Potomac—a label fraught with confusion because the premier eastern army of the Union became famous under precisely that name.

While Johnston maintained a line near Manassas and along the Potomac below Washington during 1861 and early 1862, Confederate forces concentrated at three other points on the state's military frontier. Gen. John B. Magruder commanded a modest army on Virginia's peninsula; a smaller detachment defended the important naval facilities around Norfolk; and Gen. Thomas J. ("Stonewall") Jackson led a small but aggressive command in the Shenandoah Valley. Pressure from Union forces brought action on all four fronts by the spring of 1862. Johnston felt obliged to abandon northern Virginia—and huge quantities of ordnance and other war matériel—in an awkward movement during March. A mighty Federal army under Gen. George B. McClellan successfully completed a waterborne movement to the peninsula opposite Magruder. Confederates near Norfolk witnessed the revolutionary first duel between ironclad warships as Northern strength became manifest in that area. In the Shenandoah Valley, Jackson launched in March the remarkable campaign that would win him lasting fame.

Lee at once began to sculpt the army into his image of an effective field force. Although the Department of Northern Virginia had existed formally for months, Johnston had continued to call his command the Army of the Potomac. From his post as a nearly powerless military adviser in Richmond, Lee had referred to Johnston's force in March as the Army in Northern Virginia. By the end of that month he had begun, evidently on his own volition, to call the army he soon would make famous "The Army of Northern Virginia."

With Federals in great strength at the very gates of Richmond, Lee had little leisure in which to organize and prepare for the contest that he knew must come almost at once. The general did his best to organize the disparate elements that made up his new command, but his first priority was to entrench the lines it held in order to neutralize to some degree his enemy's preponderance in numbers. Southern soldiers still afflicted with naive notions of chivalry grumbled bitterly about wielding shovels instead of weapons. This stodgy new

ital across a broad arc of northern Virginia through the middle years of the Civil War. In 1864 and 1865 the Army of Northern Virginia was obliged to assume a limited defensive posture in siege lines surrounding Richmond and Petersburg. It surrendered at Appomattox Courthouse on April 9, 1865.

EARLY OPERATIONS IN VIRGINIA. During the war's first year Confederate detachments positioned

commander, they muttered, deserved the derisive title "King of Spades," and he might well blunt their offensive élan by turning them into laborers rather than warriors.

THE SEVEN DAYS' BATTLES. A key element in Lee's planned combination was the triumphant army of Stonewall Jackson in the Shenandoah Valley. Jackson's men rested in the upper valley after dual victories at Cross Keys and Port Republic on June 8 and 9, 1862, and then moved eastward across the Blue Ridge toward Richmond. Confederate cavalry under the daring young Gen. J. E. B. Stuart had ridden all the way around McClellan's ponderous army during mid-June, so Lee knew that the Federal right flank north of Richmond dangled precariously. Jackson's men would approach from that direction and might be able to fall on that point with deadly effect. Lee's new fortifications dramatically increased his ability to secure the approaches to Richmond south of the Chickahominy. He concentrated his strength north of that river and during the last week of June hurled the Army of Northern Virginia against the Federals there.

The opening battles of the new army came to be known as the Seven Days' Battles because they covered a full week from June 25 to July 1, 1862. Stonewall Jackson repeatedly failed during the week in his important role as both the threat to the Federals' flank and the bludgeon to be applied there when necessary. At Mechanicsville on June 26, Gen. A. P. Hill launched a premature attack when Jackson's column arrived tardily and behaved without the wonted aggression once it reached the vicinity. The next day Jackson again failed to perform well as the army's maneuver element, and the result was a ghastly, grinding frontal assault at Gaines' Mill. Despite savage losses, Lee's infantry supplied him with his first major victory when they surged over the enemy line near sunset.

Pursuit of the beaten foe proceeded sluggishly and awkwardly on June 28 to 30, with missed opportunities at White Oak Swamp and another poorly coordinated bloodbath at Frayser's Farm. The week's crowning tactical disaster came at Malvern Hill on July 1, after which McClellan pulled his Federals back under shelter of Northern naval might well downstream from Richmond. Lee had struggled to apply his army to its opportunities and had been failed egregiously by many of his high-ranking subordinates as they all came to grips with the new organization. In the process of its tactical groping, however, the new army had won a great strategic victory by driving McClellan from the edge of Richmond. Jackson never again disappointed Lee and the lessons of the Seven Days' Battles served the army commander well as he prepared to reorganize and move forward. On the basis of his observations during the Seven Days', Lee sent away officers who

had displayed incapacity and promoted promising candidates to fill their places.

Through July and into early August, McClellan's Federals continued to menace Richmond from the new base to which Lee had driven them. Meanwhile another Northern force moved into northern Virginia under the leadership of Gen. John Pope. To counter Pope's threat Lee divided his army and sent Stonewall Jackson toward Gordonsville and Culpeper with a sizable detachment of Confederate troops. A series of draconian anticivilian orders issued by Pope made him a particularly urgent target. With uncharacteristic choler Lee ordered Jackson "to suppress" this belligerent enemy, whom he called "the miscreant Pope." Jackson did just that in a campaign climaxed by a victory at Cedar Mountain on August 9. Soon thereafter Lee began moving the rest of the Army of Northern Virginia away from Richmond, where McClellan's threat had lapsed, to join Jackson.

SECOND MANASSAS. The campaign that ensued represented the first great battlefield collaboration between Lee and Jackson. Although Confederate law did not provide for any military organization larger than a division, nor for any rank higher than major general, Lee readily grasped the truth that his army must have direction at that higher level. Accordingly he assigned Jackson and Longstreet to the leadership of two wings into which the army's infantry was distributed. Stuart commanded all the cavalry and reported directly to Lee. Jackson's wing had been facing Pope for some time when Lee arrived with the vanguard of the remainder of the army. The rest of Longstreet's men reached the front in northern Virginia only in piecemeal fashion during the campaign; some arrived too late to participate in the Battle of Second Manassas. Because his wing was on the scene intact—and because it must have been already apparent that he was infinitely more aggressive than Longstreet—Jackson executed the bold initiatives that marked Lee's late August operations.

After failing to trap Pope between the Rapidan and Rappahannock rivers, Lee slipped Jackson up the right bank of the latter stream looking for an opening. On August 25 and 26 Jackson dashed far behind the Federal army on a march that covered more than fifty miles. Jackson's tattered "Foot Cavalry," as his hard-marching infantry came to be called, captured a vast Federal supply base at Manassas Junction and reveled in the unaccustomed bounty they found there. Jackson's march made Pope's line on the Rappahannock untenable and forced the Federals to fall back hurriedly. When Pope retired toward Manassas, Jackson grappled with him near Groveton on August 28 and then held tenaciously to a position behind an unfinished railroad

*War came a
second time to the
plains of Manassas
in August 1862.*

PAGE 350

In a series of brilliant maneuvers from March 23 to June 9, 1862, Jackson's forces defeated three Federal armies in five battles.

PAGE 539

until Lee and Longstreet arrived in support on August 29.

The Second Battle of Manassas reached its climax on August 30 when Jackson blunted renewed enemy attacks and Longstreet unleashed his wing of the army onto Pope's vulnerable left flank. The resultant rout swept the Federals from the field. Two days later Jackson tangled with an enemy force north of Manassas at Ox Hill (or Chantilly) in a blinding thunderstorm, killing two capable Union generals and compelling Pope's complete withdrawal into the defenses of Washington.

MARYLAND CAMPAIGN. In barely more than one month from its first battle, the Army of Northern Virginia had reoriented the war from the outskirts of the Confederate capital to the vicinity of the Union's capital. Lee eagerly pressed his advantage by ordering his divisions across the Potomac and into Maryland. He was riding the crest of a military tide of impressive proportions and of his own making. Any other strategic decision in the circumstances would have been utterly foolish. Circumstances conspired against Lee once he reached Maryland, however, and he eventually chose to offer battle when his chances had become so slender as to suggest that a return to Virginia without fighting was the only prudent alternative.

By September 10 the Army of Northern Virginia was centered on Frederick, Maryland, well situated to threaten Washington and other points to the north and east; but more than 12,000 Federals menaced the army's flank and rear from their bypassed positions around Harpers Ferry. Lee determined to remove that irritant by capturing the Federals and the bonanza of supplies, armaments, and equipment they held. Jackson's confident veterans received the mission and set out on another of the long marches designed to expend their sweat but not their blood. The operation worked reasonably well, if not as rapidly as Lee had hoped. Jackson captured Harpers Ferry and its garrison with its rich stores on September 15.

Unfortunately for Lee, a copy of his detailed operational order (Special Orders No. 191) fell into enemy hands. General McClellan, who had assumed command of his old army augmented by the troops of the disgraced Pope, knew how thoroughly Lee had dispersed the elements of his army. The eternally cautious Union general frittered away much of the dazzling advantage presented to him, however. Even so, he was able to penetrate westward through the gaps of Maryland's South Mountain, pushing aside the Confederate rear guard and forcing Lee back toward the Potomac.

Late on September 15 Lee took up a position near the village of Sharpsburg, behind Antietam Creek, with the Potomac River at his back. Resisting McClellan there, with an army shrunken by straggling and other causes to the smallest size it would ever number until the end of the war, offered Lee no prospect for a great success and posed the real danger of disaster. Lee nevertheless stayed to fight.

The Army of Northern Virginia staged one of its most impressive performances on the banks of Antietam Creek on September 17, 1862, when it contrived to win a costly draw. Federal dispersion and irresolution served Lee's army well, but even so the Confederates repeatedly stood at the brink of catastrophe. Lee had infected his army with his own sturdy spirit, and the men redeemed their general's poor strategic decision with their personal valor. The army returned to Virginia on the night of September 18, having stood through the day after the battle on its hard-won line.

A RENEWED ARMY. In the aftermath of the Maryland campaign, Lee found time to rebuild carefully the army he had inherited at a moment of crisis. The army enjoyed a halcyon period in the beautiful and bountiful Shenandoah Valley that fall while its commander planned and organized. More than a dozen general officers had fought with the army in Maryland for the last time. In addition to replacing those men with the best available talent, Lee finally was able to formalize his wing system when the Confederate Congress authorized corps units and created the rank of lieutenant general. Jackson and Longstreet received promotions to the new rank that were confirmed on October 11. The new lieutenant generals took command of the Second Corps and the First Corps, which contained all of the army's infantry.

Lee also streamlined the army's support functions that fall as part of perfecting its organization. The acute straggling and near-starvation that had bedeviled the 1862 Maryland campaign never again plagued Lee until the Confederacy verged on collapse late in the war. When the army moved through the same territory during the succeeding summer, en route to Gettysburg, the severe problems that had marked its 1862 operations did not recur.

In mid-November 1862, the Federal Army of the Potomac, now commanded by Gen. Ambrose E. Burnside, moved southeastward toward Fredericksburg, in the process drawing the Army of Northern Virginia away from the Shenandoah Valley and Piedmont Virginia. For three weeks beginning November 20, the Confederates concentrated near Fredericksburg as Burnside's army gathered across the Rappahannock from the city. On the morning of December 11 the Federals opened the Battle of Fredericksburg by bombarding the city and building pontoon bridges across the river against stiff resistance.

Two days later the Northerners marched steadily westward from town against imposing positions held by the Army of Northern Virginia. The result was the easiest major victory won by Lee's army during the war. Confederate riflemen slaughtered enemy infantry, and Confederate artillery found ample targets from elevated positions rising above a shelterless plain. Federal casualties mounted all out of proportion to Southern losses, but Lee was unable to reap any substantial additional fruits of his victory.

The Army of Northern Virginia went into winter camps secure in the knowledge that it had achieved enormous success during its first six months of existence. Within sixty days the army had, almost unaided, relocated the war from its own capital to the environs of the enemy's capital. It had won a startling succession of victories for a nation that had known few. The brilliantly creative collaboration of Lee and Jackson at the army's head, augmented by Longstreet's stalwart defensive aptitude, boded well for the future of the army and of the country it recently had saved. For nearly five months the army sprawled across central Virginia from northwest at Germanna Ford to southeast around Carmel Church, with the Rappahannock and Rapidan as a front-line moat. Stuart's cavalrymen rode daring and exciting raids behind enemy lines, building élan and providing grist for campfire talk if not actually accomplishing much substantive good.

During the winter Lee approved an important reorganization of the army's artillery. Conventional dogma had assigned most batteries to infantry brigades, often turning the artillery, Lee's "long arm," into little more than larger-caliber infantry weapons. Henceforth batteries would be grouped into battalions of sixteen or more guns and directed by artillery officers with enough rank to determine the appropriate employment of their powerful weapons. As campaigning weather approached in the spring of 1863, the Army of Northern Virginia stood at the height of its power and potential.

CHANCELLORSVILLE. Gen. Joseph Hooker commanded the army's familiar foe as it advanced across the Rappahannock and Rapidan west of Fredericksburg in late April 1863. Hooker skillfully stole a march on Lee and concentrated behind the Confederates on April 30 at a country crossroads called Chancellorsville. Lee and Jackson hurried to meet this serious threat (Longstreet was away on a feckless mission in southern Virginia). On May 1 the two leaders blunted Hooker's drive near the edge of a seventy-square-mile body of densely thicketed woodland known as the Wilderness of Spotsylvania. Scrubby undergrowth in the region made maneuver, movement, and fighting difficult except in the clear-

ings and along the roads. That negated much of Hooker's enormous advantage in numbers. Facing a disadvantage of more than two-to-one, Lee fought against the heaviest odds he encountered until the wars' closing weeks. On May 2 Lee and Jackson collaborated on their boldest and most successful—and last—tactical initiative. Lee calmly faced Hooker's legions with a handful of troops while Jackson carefully and secretly led nearly 30,000 men across the front of the Northern army. When Stonewall's troops thundered out of the Wilderness behind Hooker's right, screaming the Rebel yell and driving everything before them, the Army of Northern Virginia stood at its highest tide.

Jackson's mighty flank attack did much to win the battle, but its aftermath cost the Confederacy one of its few absolutely irreplaceable military commodities. Mistaken fire from the muskets of North Carolinians in Gen. James H. Lane's brigade struck Jackson down, mortally wounding him in the darkness of that confused night. When he died eight days later at Guiney Station, Jackson took with him much of the army's and the Confederacy's best hope for success. Back at Chancellorsville the Army of Northern Virginia had put the seal on Jackson's masterful movement by fighting its way stubbornly through the Wilderness on May 3 to sweep the field.

Lee considered the victory at Chancellorsville a springboard for his army to use in taking the war back into enemy country. Before he could use the army in an advance, however, the general faced the necessity of reorganizing it extensively in the absence of Stonewall Jackson. Lee had already considered splitting his infantry into three corps as a means of controlling it more effectively. In the weeks after Chancellorsville he followed that premise when he established a new corps and gave command of it to Gen. A. P. Hill. For Jackson's old Second Corps, somewhat truncated by the creation of the new corps, Lee selected Gen. Richard S. Ewell. Neither officer would begin to fill the enormous gap left by Jackson's death, nor would either of them satisfy even the reduced expectations that their commanding general had for them.

GETTYSBURG AND ITS AFTERMATH. The army shifted northwestward from the vicinity of Fredericksburg in early June 1863. Stuart's cavalry won a stern test at Brandy Station on the ninth, but for the first time their mounted foe had fought on approximately equal terms. That boded ill for a Confederate future that would be affected by declining horseflesh and armaments. Ewell accomplished as much as Jackson could have done around Winchester on June 14 and 15, clearing the way for an advance into Pennsylvania and raising hopes that the Second Corps might continue its invincible record.

At Chancellorsville, Robert E. Lee and Stonewall Jackson came together for their greatest joint victory.

PAGE 91

Jackson's mortal wounding at Chancellorsville by the mistaken fire of his own men was one of the most important military events of the war.

PAGE 91

LEE'S STAFF

*A medallion shows Robert E.
Lee surrounded by his
principal generals, chiefs,
and aides of the Army of
Northern Virginia.*

The meeting engagement that developed on July 1 through 3 at Gettysburg, however, revealed shortcomings in the high command as well as in the new organization. Stuart led his cavalry on another daring adventure en route to Pennsylvania, but this time it left Lee without the screening and reconnaissance support that he badly needed. Ewell equivocated when Lee gave him typically discretionary orders. Longstreet sulked, to the detriment of tactical arrangements on the field, when Lee disregarded his advice. The army commander himself was driven to a desperate and ill-advised attack when better opportunities had evaporated. Stout defense by the old adversary, the Army of the Potomac, now led by the eminently competent Gen. George G. Meade, also must be credited in generous measure for the outcome.

The Army of Northern Virginia actually won a signal victory on July 1 north and west of Gettysburg and then swept into town on the heels of two routed Federal corps, gathering prisoners by the thousands. Bitter fighting on July 2 led to the brink of success, but never beyond. The dramatic and dreadful assault on July 3 directed by Gens. George E. Pickett and J. Johnston Pettigrew is one of the most famous episodes in all of American military history under the familiar—if unfair to Pettigrew—name of Pickett's Charge. The defeated army fell back through Pennsylvania and Maryland to the Potomac in a muddy, bloody, and painful retreat.

Once back in Virginia the Confederates regrouped and soon were ready for further action, but they simply could not replace the skilled officers and brave men buried in Pennsylvania. Lee realigned his cavalry command during this interval, leaving Stuart at its head but for the first time authorizing subordinate divisions under that general's control. Before fighting began anew against Meade's Federals, Longstreet had taken the First Corps to the western theater, where it remained in Georgia and Tennessee until the following spring.

The two remaining corps of the Army of Northern Virginia fought intermittently against Meade's army through the late summer and fall of 1863 in the Piedmont region of northern Virginia. Lee maneuvered the army northward in October and forced the enemy back with considerable success before a grotesque tactical fiasco under A. P. Hill's direction at Bristoe Station blunted the movement. The embarrassment at Bristoe was compounded on November 7 when a Federal storming party captured Lee's fortified bridgehead at Rappahannock Station.

At the end of November Meade crossed the Rapidan west of the Wilderness and attempted to find a means to close with the Army of Northern Virginia. For several days the armies jousted near Mine Run

JACKSON'S STAFF

This medallion shows Thomas J. "Stonewall" Jackson surrounded by his generals, chiefs, and aides.
LIBRARY OF CONGRESS

before Meade recognized that he faced checkmate. The Northern general fell back without launching a major assault because he recognized that it would fail, thus earning the gratitude of his troops but calumny from the Unionist press.

GRANT'S OFFENSIVES. The Army of Northern Virginia wintered in 1863–1864 in Orange County and prepared for the stern test that it knew spring would bring. Gen. Ulysses S. Grant, of western theater prominence, assumed command of all Federal armies in March 1864 and made his headquarters with Meade's Army of the Potomac opposite Lee. At the beginning of May, Grant and Meade put their troops across the Rapidan River into the same Wilderness that had foiled Hooker precisely one year earlier. As the Federal column attempted to slice through the thickets in the direction of Richmond, the Army of Northern Virginia surged into its flanks from the west on two parallel roads about two miles apart. The confusing woods fighting that resulted on May 5 and 6 inflicted enormous casualties on the Federal army but also pushed Lee's army to the verge of destruction. Longstreet's First Corps arrived on May 6 to fight with the army for the first time since Gettysburg, too late to prevent a major Federal success but just in time to avoid complete disaster. In the crisis Lee attempted to lead the famous shock troops of the Texas Brigade in a desperate assault. The men turned Lee back and hurled themselves into the breach, suffering terrible losses in the process.

Although his army had suffered appreciably more than had Hooker's in May 1863 and had hurt Lee

A

At Spotsylvania, the Army of Northern Virginia once again inflicted severe casualties upon its old antagonist.

PAGE 577

During the two weeks of Spotsylvania, 4,600 troops from Ewell's Second Corps became prisoners.

PAGE 577

appreciably less, Grant calmly pushed south from the Wilderness to continue with a war of bloody attrition. His route took him to Spotsylvania Court House—or nearly there, for the Army of Northern Virginia managed to block the Federals' path outside the village with moments to spare. For fourteen days the armies locked in incessant combat, often fighting over imposing lines of breastworks in a first precursor of the trench warfare of later conflicts.

Three more times Lee attempted to lead men personally as his army faced crisis after crisis. On May 10 a Federal frontal assault broke temporarily into the entrenched projection in the Confederate line known as the Mule Shoe Salient because of its shape. Two days later an enormous Northern assault crushed the nose of the salient and came close to breaking the Army of Northern Virginia in half. Lee crafted a new line near the base of the bulge as two brigades of his army sacrificed themselves in hand-to-hand fighting in a delaying action that lasted twenty hours. Their blood christened the curving line of earthworks where they fought as the Bloody Angle. Grant hammered brutally against other earthworks without success, one major attack on May 18 being repulsed by the Confederates so easily that most contemporary writers did not even mention it.

Meanwhile the Army of Northern Virginia suffered a tremendous loss on May 12 when its cavalry chief, J. E. B. Stuart, died in Richmond, victim of a wound suffered in resisting a passing raid on the capital. For the rest of the war, Wade Hampton and Fitzhugh Lee would try to fill Stuart's place.

When the Federal army side-slipped to the southeast again on May 21, leaving the vicinity of Spotsylvania Court House, the history of the Army of Northern Virginia entered a new phase. For nearly eleven months the army would remain locked in steady contact with its foe in a war featuring fortification and attrition rather than the meeting engagements and maneuver at which Lee had excelled since assuming command. The contending forces wrestled their way steadily across Virginia from May 21 to June 10, fighting regularly and sometimes fiercely. The Army of Northern Virginia missed a golden opportunity on the North Anna River May 23 through 27 because all three corps commanders were absent and Lee was ill. The troops next fought with their accustomed tenacity and skill at Totopotomoy Creek and Bethesda Church and then almost effortlessly butchered a mindless frontal assault ordered by Grant at Cold Harbor on June 3. The deterioration in command by this time was affecting the army almost as much as shortages of manpower and matériel. Longstreet had been hit hard in the Wilderness and would not return for five months; Ewell had collapsed and been removed from

his corps command, replaced by Jubal Early; and A. P. Hill remained so regularly incapacitated by sickness as to require frequent relief.

With the army high command in disarray, Lee faced alone the tremendous burden of protecting Richmond. Operations in Virginia took a new and ominous turn when the Federal army succeeded in crossing the James River and attacking Petersburg before Lee had divined their intention. Fortunately for the Confederates, Grant had left the heart and brains of his army dead or bleeding in central Virginia when he destroyed its midlevel command in frontal assaults during May and early June. The Army of Northern Virginia managed to lunge across the James and into the Federals' path just outside Petersburg. Barred from Richmond and foiled at Petersburg, Grant settled into the siege operations that were the next logical extension of the intense but mobile trench war of May.

LEE'S ARMY AT LOW TIDE. The final chapters in the life of the Army of Northern Virginia were written in ten months of often colorless and always deadly trench warfare. Lee endeavored to inject maneuver back into the military equation by sending Jubal Early with the veteran Second Corps back into the Valley where it had won so many laurels in past years. Early used his fragment of the army to good effect in a campaign that swept the Valley from Lynchburg to Harpers Ferry and beyond, reaching in July to the suburbs of Washington, D.C. After a surprising series of successes, however, Early finally fell victim to Federals in overwhelming force during September and October.

Lee's other attempts at movement and fresh initiatives covered less ground and usually met with less dramatic results. Soon after Grant reached the doorsteps of Richmond and Petersburg two immutable strategic verities became apparent: the Confederates could not protect both cities against concentrated forces, so Grant repeatedly sought to concentrate on one or the other; and the railroad lifelines of the Army of Northern Virginia that approached from the south and southwest were vulnerable. In response to the first of those unavoidable issues, Lee deftly moved his dwindling resources back and forth between the two fronts on either side of the James River during the last half of 1864. Bitter battles at such places as Fort Harrison, Fort Gilmer, Darbytown Road, and Deep Bottom captured occasional small tracts of ground for the Federals; more than that, they killed and wounded irreplaceable Southern soldiers. Fighting over the railroads flared at Weldon Railroad, Globe Tavern, and Reams's Station.

None of these affairs accumulated casualties on the scale of the army's great meeting engagements from 1862 through the spring of 1864, but each further enervated the army. The most famous of the bat-

GENERAL ORDERS NO. 9
Robert E. Lee's Farewell to His Troops

Headquarters Army of Northern Virginia,
Appomattox Courthouse, April 10, 1865.

After four years' arduous service, marked by unsurpassed courage and fortitude, the Army of Northern Virginia has been compelled to yield to overwhelming numbers and resources.

I need not tell the survivors of so many hard fought battles who have remained steadfast to the last, that I have consented to this result from no distrust of them, but feeling that valor and devotion could accomplish nothing that could compensate for the loss which would have attended the continuation of the contest, I have determined to avoid the useless sacrifice of those whose past services have endeared them to their countrymen. You will take with you the satisfaction that proceeds from the consciousness of duty faithfully performed, and I earnestly pray that a merciful God may extend to you His blessing and protection. With an increasing admiration of your constancy and devotion to your country, and a grateful remembrance of your kind and generous consideration of myself, I bid you an affectionate farewell.

Robert E. Lee,
GENERAL

"We must look to the rising generation for the restoration of the country."

ROBERT E. LEE
TO GOV. JOHN LETCHER,
AUGUST 1865

tles around Petersburg erupted on July 30 when some soldiers from Pennsylvania mining country blew up several tons of black powder in a tunnel under the Confederate lines. The Battle of the Crater resulted in no change in the military situation—just more casualties.

Lee commanded the Army of Northern Virginia in these closing scenes with the assistance of a new generation of young generals. Some five dozen of the general officers who played a role in the closing months were either new to their ranks or new to the army. Men like John B. Gordon and William Mahone proved to be capable replacements for the famous officers who had fallen, but others could not accomplish what was required of them for lack of ability or lack of experience. Using the dwindling resources in men and officers and supplies available to him, Lee directed the army's operations in early 1865 across a steadily expanding front. The deep reservoir of manpower in the Army of the Potomac allowed Grant to extend around Lee to the southwest and then press westward toward the last roads and railroads. Fighting at Hatcher's Run in February killed Confederate Gen. John Pegram and brought the end closer.

The last offensive gasp of the Army of Northern Virginia came on March 25, 1865, against Fort Stedman near Petersburg. Gen. John B. Gordon led the forlorn hope whose initial success soon disappeared in the face of a horde of Northern reinforcements. A week later the army's tautly stretched lines finally snapped. Federals swarmed into Petersburg and Richmond, and Confederates hurried westward seeking refuge in the direction of Lynchburg, or junction with friendly troops coming up from North

Carolina, or at least food near Farmville. All of those goals proved chimerical. Battered and fragmented at Five Forks and Sayler's Creek, and then hemmed in near Appomattox Courthouse on Palm Sunday, the Army of Northern Virginia ceased to exist when Robert E. Lee put on his best uniform and went to see Ulysses S. Grant in the village about terms of surrender.

Lee wrote a famous epitaph for the army in his General Orders No. 9, reviewing in moving terms the soldiers' "four years of arduous service marked by unsurpassed courage and fortitude," and expressing his "unceasing admiration of your constancy and devotion to your Country." William Swinton, a dedicated foe of the army and the early chronicler of the opposing Army of the Potomac, delivered an equally fitting tribute from across the lines:

Who that ever looked upon it can forget that body of tattered uniforms and bright muskets—that body of incomparable infantry which for four years carried the revolt on its bayonets ... which, receiving terrible blows, did not fail to give the like; and which, vital in all its parts, died only with its annihilation?

[*See also* Appomattox Campaign; Chancellorsville Campaign; Early, Jubal, *sidebar* Early's Washington Raid; Fredericksburg Campaign; Gettysburg Campaign; Manassas, First; Manassas, Second; Peninsular Campaign; Petersburg Campaign; Seven Days' Battles; Sharpsburg Campaign; Shenandoah Valley; Spotsylvania Campaign; Stuart's Raids; West Virginia Operations; Wilderness Campaign; *and biographies of selected figures mentioned herein.*]

— ROBERT K. KRICK

*Albert Sidney
Johnston's former
fellow cadet
Jefferson Davis
appointed him a
full general and
placed him in
command of the
western theater of
operations.*

PAGE 302

ARMY OF TENNESSEE

This army was the major Confederate military force in the area between the Appalachian Mountains and the Mississippi River—a vast region known in the 1860s as the West. The Army of Tennessee was one of some two dozen independent field armies organized by the Confederates. It and the Army of Northern Virginia were the largest and longest-lived of those armies. In a very real sense, they were the Confederacy. They embodied its hope for national independence.

Formation under
Albert Sidney Johnston

By late summer 1861 there were important concentrations of Confederate troops in northern Arkansas and southern Missouri, south central and southeastern Kentucky, western Tennessee, and at Columbus (Kentucky), New Orleans, Mobile, and Pensacola. Realizing the need for centralized control in the West, President Jefferson Davis sent Gen. Albert Sidney Johnston to command all Confederate forces between the Appalachian Mountains on the east and the Ozark Mountains on the west except the troops on the Gulf coast.

Johnston's assignment was the first of three attempts Davis made to establish a centralized military structure in the West. All three efforts failed because the president could never find a general willing or able to exercise such a command. In Johnston's case, the failure came when he established himself at Bowling Green, Kentucky, where he became so bogged down in local matters that he largely neglected other parts of his far-flung command.

To be sure, Johnston's task was difficult. He had far too few men—about forty thousand—to hold the extended frontier line for which he was responsible. Many of his soldiers were untrained and poorly armed and equipped. Johnston was also hampered because his line was pierced by three great rivers—the Mississippi, the Tennessee, and the Cumberland—that provided avenues of invasion for Northern armies. To complicate matters, local political pressure to defend the Mississippi River was so great that nothing could be done about Harris's overcommitment of forces to western Tennessee. Worst of all, Maj. Gen. Leonidas Polk, commanding Southern forces on the Mississippi River, had violated the neutrality of Kentucky by occupying Columbus. Polk's action helped drive the Bluegrass State into the arms of the Federal government and enormously complicated the Confederates' military problems in the West.

In early 1862 Johnston's forces were scattered unevenly along a thin east-west line roughly matching the southern borders of Kentucky and Missouri. The

line was vulnerable, and it was menaced by Federal armies at several points. The position lacked both naturally defensible terrain and good means for the east-west movement of troops. Despite its manifest drawbacks, Johnston's line had to be held. To abandon it and fall back to a better, more defensible position to the south would have given up much of the more valuable, most productive parts of Tennessee as well as all practical hope of having Kentucky and Missouri adhere to the Confederacy.

In January Johnston's line began to unravel. On the nineteenth at Mill Springs in southeastern Kentucky, a Federal force smashed the right of his line, and the

Confederates fled back into Tennessee. In the following month Union forces pushed the Confederates out of Missouri and then on March 7 and 8 at Elkhorn Tavern, Arkansas, defeated the Southerners' effort to regain their old position. Meanwhile, another Federal column began the conquest of Tennessee itself by thrusting up the Tennessee and Cumberland rivers to capture Forts Henry and Donelson near the points where those streams crossed the Tennessee-Kentucky border. Possession of the river forts opened those waterways to the Union navy, enabled the Federals to outflank the massive Confederate fortifications in western Tennessee, and put the Northerners in position to cut off Johnston's force at Bowling Green.

Realizing the magnitude of these defeats, Johnston evacuated Bowling Green, abandoned Nashville and most of western Tennessee, and retreated to Corinth, Mississippi. There he brought together fragments of his command and united them with reinforcements rushed from New Orleans, Mobile, Pensacola, and other points. The force that resulted from this Corinth concentration was known at its March birth as the Army of Mississippi (sometimes the Army of the Mississippi).

Gen. P. G. T. Beauregard was second in command of Johnston's new army, which was organized into four corps. The commanders of these units were men who played leading roles in the war in the West. Polk commanded the First Corps; Maj. Gen. Braxton Bragg, fresh from the Gulf coast, the Second; Maj. Gen. William J. Hardee, who had been with Johnston at Bowling Green, the Third; and Brig. Gen. John C. Breckinridge, a former vice president of the United States, the Reserve Corps. (Although called "corps," these units were, in fact, large "grand divisions.")

The army that Johnston assembled at Corinth was—and would remain—overwhelmingly a western army. Most of its troops hailed from Alabama, Georgia, Mississippi, and Tennessee. Almost all the others were from Texas, Louisiana, Arkansas, Kentucky, and Missouri. Unfortunately for this army, the great majority of Southerners with prewar military education and training came from the eastern states. Virginia, for example, had 104 living graduates of the U.S. Military Academy in 1860; the other ten Confederate states together had only 184. By one 1860 count, more than 70 percent of the U.S. Army officers who came from the soon-to-secede states were from the eastern Confederacy. To make matters worse, the few trained, experienced men available in the West usually joined the first units their states organized in 1861, and most of those units were rushed to Virginia early in the war. The western army usually got the later-organized regiments—those raised after most of the state's trained personnel had gone.

Owing in large part to this maldistribution of militarily knowledgeable Confederates, the Army of Tennessee never had the strength of command that the Army of Northern Virginia enjoyed. The western officers were brave and intelligent enough, but they lacked—especially at the beginning of their service—the familiarity with military weapons and equipment and the knowledge of small-unit drill, tactics, and administration possessed by many of their counterparts in the East.

In early April 1862 Johnston moved his newly organized army out from Corinth to strike a Federal force that had advanced up the Tennessee River to Pittsburgh Landing just north of the Mississippi-Tennessee border. Johnston hoped to destroy that army and regain much of what he had lost in the preceding three months. He had about forty thousand men, and he was hopeful that the Confederate force that had fought at Elkhorn Tavern a month earlier and was now on the way east would join him before the battle.

On April 6 Johnston caught the Federals by surprise. His men overran their camps near Shiloh Church and drove them back to the Tennessee River. That afternoon, however, Johnston was killed. Beauregard, taking command, halted the attack, hoping to regroup and finish the victory on the seventh. That night thirty-five thousand Northern reinforcements arrived, and on the following day the combined Union forces drove Beauregard's men away. The Confederates pulled back to Corinth where they were joined by the men from the Trans-Mississippi. The Federals followed slowly, and at the end of May Beauregard was forced out of Corinth and back to Tupelo, some fifty miles to the south. The Confederate counteroffensive had failed.

The Army under Braxton Bragg

Soon after reaching Tupelo, Beauregard went on sick leave. Davis, who had been displeased by his behavior in Virginia in 1861 as well as by his conduct at Shiloh and his evacuation of Corinth, removed him from command and promoted Bragg to full general to replace him. Davis also reorganized the western command structure, separating eastern Tennessee and the area west of the Mississippi from Bragg's authority. Internally, too, the army was reorganized. Bragg created two wings of two divisions each. One wing was commanded by Polk; the other by Hardee.

Hoping to strike before the Federals in northern Mississippi could resume their advance, Bragg left about thirty thousand men and swung the rest of his army around to Chattanooga. (Most of the men remaining in Mississippi were the New Orleans garrison and the Trans-Mississippi troops who reached the army after Shiloh.) From Chattanooga, the Confederates moved

Beauregard entered West Point at the age of sixteen, already a commited disciple of Napoléon Bonaparte.

PAGE 43

Braxton Bragg became a full general on April 12, 1862, the fifth ranking officer in the Confederacy.

PAGE 69

into Kentucky to reestablish their claim to that state. Confident that thousands of Kentuckians would flock to their ranks, the Southerners advanced in two columns, one consisting of Bragg's army, the other the eastern Tennessee forces under Maj. Gen. E. Kirby Smith.

This second Confederate counteroffensive quickly ran into three major problems. For one thing, Davis—as was his habit—had not created clear lines of command. Assuming that officers of goodwill would cheerfully cooperate, Davis did not give Bragg authority over Smith until such time as their columns were united, when Bragg's higher grade would automatically put him in command of the combined force. Smith wanted to retain independent command, however, and refused to cooperate with Bragg. A second problem arose when the Southerners discovered that very few Kentuckians were sympathetic to the Confederacy or wished to join its army. Most pro-secession Kentuckians had long since left the state. The final problem developed because the two chief subordinates in the army—Polk and Hardee—personally disliked Bragg, resented his authority, often disobeyed his orders, and began what became a campaign to undermine his position and bring about his removal from command. For his part Bragg realized that several of his high-ranking generals—especially Polk—were major liabilities whose presence blocked the promotion of more able men. He urged that he be permitted to rid the army of its "deadwood."

After some early successes—which came mostly from the hard marching and fighting of his troops—Bragg found his campaign dissolving into confusion. Smith was off on his own in eastern Kentucky, and when Bragg left to attend the inauguration of the Confederate governor of Kentucky, Polk, who assumed command, disregarded Bragg's orders to attack the Federals and move on to Harrodsburg.

In the midst of this confusion, the Confederates blundered into the Federals at Perryville on October 8. The outnumbered Southerners won a tactical victory in the battle, but Bragg realized he could not remain in the state without more popular support than he had. He therefore fell back into middle Tennessee and took up a position at Murfreesboro. Bragg's counteroffensive had failed in its major objective, but it did transfer the Confederates' main western operations from Mississippi to Tennessee.

During the lull after Perryville the army acquired its new name—the Army of Tennessee—and was formally divided into two infantry corps. Polk and Hardee were promoted to the newly created grade of lieutenant general and assigned to command them. Smith, also named a lieutenant general, was transferred to the Trans-Mississippi. The army's cavalry, which had previously operated in small units, was consolidated under Brig. Gen. Joseph Wheeler.

Two other post-Perryville developments affected the army. In November Davis again attempted to provide coordination for military efforts in the West, appointing Gen. Joseph E. Johnston to oversee Confederate activities in the area. Davis expected Johnston to provide guidance for both Bragg's army and the Southern forces in Mississippi. Specifically, Johnston was to transfer troops between the two areas to meet a threat to either. This second attempt at coordinated western command eventually failed because of intelligence, logistical, and transportation problems and because Johnston, lacking faith in the scheme, proved unwilling to assume responsibility for deciding when troops should be sent from one area to the other.

Bragg's army also received a visit from Davis himself. The president was pleased with the condition and morale of the troops when he visited their camps in December, but he was unable to curtail the bitter feuding among the generals. He ordered a division of nine thousand men transferred from the army to Mississippi, in effect taking over the command he had assigned to Johnston.

Not long after Davis departed, the Federals ventured out from their base at Nashville against Bragg at Murfreesboro. The two armies met along Stones River on December 31. Bragg attacked and, despite bungling by several of his subordinates, drove back the Federals. The Southerners, however, were too weak to complete the victory, and both armies settled down for the night. New Year's Day was quiet, but on January 2 Bragg launched a foolish attack that was repulsed with great loss of lives. On January 3 and 4, Bragg fell back to Tullahoma. Once again the Confederate troops had fought well and had won a tactical success. The army lacked the strength to complete the victory, however, and the generals were unable to provide the leadership their men deserved.

The army rested at Tullahoma for more than five months. Meanwhile, the Federals were threatening Vicksburg, Mississippi, and the Confederate government urged Johnston to coordinate an effort to save the town. When Johnston proved unwilling to do so, Davis ordered him to take personal command of the forces in Mississippi. Believing that this order ended his responsibility as overall commander in the West, Johnston ceased even to go through the motions of that office. Davis's second attempt at a western command structure had evaporated.

While the Army of Tennessee was at Tullahoma, the sniping between Bragg and the Polk-Hardee coterie intensified. Murfreesboro joined Perryville as a subject of controversy. Bragg proved especially clumsy in the internecine squabbling, exposing himself first to one criticism and then to another. Davis, in fact, seems to have lost confidence in Bragg and desired to replace him with Johnston. The president, however, was unwilling to give a direct order on the subject, and his subtle maneuverings to that end were frustrated by Johnston's refusal to act on presidential hints. In May Johnston went to Mississippi, and the army faced its next crisis with its high command even more weakened than it had been earlier.

The Federal troops did not strike again at the Army of Tennessee until mid-June. When they did, Bragg's position quickly collapsed. Advancing in five columns, the Union forces deceived Bragg and outflanked his position. By the end of the month Bragg realized his predicament and retreated to the south side of the Tennessee River near Chattanooga.

While the army was being maneuvered out of middle Tennessee, it underwent another reorganization. Hardee, sent off to Mississippi, was replaced by Lt. Gen. D. H. Hill. Substitution of Hill for Hardee, however, did nothing to cool the anti-Bragg furor in the army's high echelons. The East Tennessee Department was reunited with Bragg's command, and the troops there under Maj. Gen. Simon Bolivar Buckner were designated a third corps in the Army of Tennessee.

In August and September the Federals crossed the Tennessee River below Chattanooga. By so doing, they threatened Bragg's supply line and forced him back into North Georgia. Meanwhile, an alarmed Confederate government rushed reinforcements to Bragg from Mississippi and Virginia. The troops from Mississippi arrived first, and their presence led Bragg to create another corps. Thus, in early September the army consisted of four corps, each of two divisions, under Polk, Hill, Buckner, and Maj. Gen. W. H. T. Walker.

After some confused maneuvering in North Georgia during which several of Bragg's subordinates refused to obey his orders, the Army of Tennessee met the Federals along Chickamauga Creek late on September 18. Heavy but indecisive fighting went on all the following day. That night reinforcements from Virginia under Lt. Gen. James Longstreet reached the field, and Bragg reorganized his army yet again. He now created two wings—the left under Longstreet; the right under Polk. Longstreet's wing contained some of the troops of Polk's old corps, Buckner's Corps, and the troops from Virginia. Polk's wing contained part of his old corps, Hill's Corps, and Walker's Corps.

On September 20 the Confederates were lucky enough to attack at a time and place where a misunderstanding had created a gap in the Northerners' line. The Southerners broke through and chased about half of the Federals from the field. The remaining Union forces held on until dark and then withdrew to Chattanooga. Bragg followed and occupied the heights east and southwest of the town. He hoped to cut the

RIFT IN HIGH COMMAND

Strains caused by the unsuccessful Perryville campaign brought into the open the rift in the army's high command. Bragg, bitter at the failure in Kentucky, sought scapegoats and blamed Polk for most of the army's troubles. Polk and Hardee—joined by Smith—renewed and intensified their campaign against Bragg. They sent criticisms of their commander to the president and to members of Congress. Hardee, who had great influence within the army, managed to turn many subordinate officers against Bragg and to undermine his support. Polk urged his old friend President Davis to get rid of Bragg. The army soon divided into pro-Bragg and anti-Bragg factions. Much of Bragg's support came from the Pensacola-Mobile units he had brought north to the Corinth concentration. The Polk-Hardee bloc found its strongest adherents among the Tennessee-Kentucky officers. In one form or another this civil war within the army raged until Bragg left in December 1863, and vestiges of it lingered to the end of the war.

— RICHARD M. MCMURRY

In February 1864, Jefferson Davis summoned Bragg to Richmond to serve as his military adviser.

PAGE 70

routes by which food reached Chattanooga and force his enemy to surrender or abandon the area.

Once the army settled down to besiege Chattanooga, the generals renewed their squabbling. Bragg sought to discover why his orders had not been obeyed on so many recent occasions. Polk, Longstreet, Hill, and Buckner all emerged as anti-Bragg critics, joined by several of their subordinates. Bragg sought to deal with the trouble by relieving Polk from command and sending him away to await orders. Far from quieting matters, however, his action only intensified the clamor of his critics who circulated a petition denouncing their commander.

President Davis himself traveled west to intervene in the dispute. At an incredible meeting, Davis and Bragg listened as, one by one, the senior generals of the army declared that Bragg should be removed from command. Davis decided to sustain Bragg, but he made several changes in the army's organization. Polk was sent to Mississippi to replace Hardee who returned to the army to command Polk's Corps. Hill was simply sent away to await orders. Buckner was given command of a division. Many of the units commanded by anti-Bragg generals were broken up and scattered through the army. Bragg also acted to get rid of Longstreet by sending him off to eastern Tennessee to operate against Knoxville. Unfortunately for Bragg, he

INSTABILITY AT THE HELM: THE ARMY OF TENNESSEE

Year	Commander	Fate
1861	Albert Sidney Johnston	Killed at Shiloh
1861	P.G.T. Beauregard	Removed by command of Jefferson Davis
1861–63	Braxton Bragg	Asked to be relieved from command after two tumultuous years
1863	Joseph E. Johnston	Removed by Jefferson Davis
1863	John Bell Hood	Turned over remains of army to Lt. General Richard Taylor

In December 1863, Davis named Joseph E. Johnston commander of the Army of Tennessee because there was no better choice.

PAGE 304

By May 1864, Joseph E. Johnston had done a creditable job of rebuilding the strength and morale of the Army of Tennessee.

PAGE 304

also sent Longstreet's troops off with him. As a result of these changes, the army now consisted of Hardee's Corps and what had been Hill's Corps under the command of its senior officer, Maj. Gen. John C. Breckinridge.

This turmoil helped to destroy the unity of the army and demoralize the troops. All through October and November they sat on the hills around Chattanooga, watching the North pour reinforcements and supplies into the city. At the Battle of Missionary Ridge, November 23 through 25, the Federals attacked Bragg's army. When the Confederates' position collapsed, they fled south to Dalton, Georgia. Bragg asked to be relieved from command, and Davis granted his request.

The Command of Joseph E. Johnston

The Confederate government now faced the daunting task of rebuilding its main western army. The first problem—selecting a new commander—presented a dilemma. Davis had only one army commander of demonstrated ability—Robert E. Lee—and he commanded the main army in Virginia. The Army of Tennessee's new commander had to be selected from the Confederacy's other high-ranking generals, all of whom were political enemies of Davis, or of limited ability, or both. Finally Davis resurrected Joseph E. Johnston as the least undesirable choice and ordered him to Dalton. Lt. Gen. John Bell Hood came to take command of the second corps.

Over the next four months Johnston did a creditable job restoring the army's morale and preparing it for the next campaign. As was his wont, however, he also spent a great deal of time bickering with the government and explaining why he would not be able to accomplish very much. He and the government authorities were unable to reach any agreement about what strategy they should adopt, and when the 1864 campaign opened, the Confederates were working at cross purposes. The government wanted Johnston to launch an offensive; Johnston believed that he was too weak for aggressive action and that he should fall back into Georgia, hoping the Federals would make a mis-

take that would give the Southerners a chance to strike.

When the Federals advanced in May 1864, the Southern government rushed reinforcements, building Johnston's strength up to about seventy-five thousand men. The largest single element of these reinforcements came from Mississippi and was commanded by Polk. Although technically a separate army operating with Johnston, Polk's command evolved into a third corps in the Army of Tennessee. Thus, in the Atlanta campaign, the army consisted of infantry corps under Hardee, Hood, and Polk and a cavalry corps under Wheeler. When Polk was killed on June 14, Alexander P. Stewart, a division commander, was promoted to lieutenant general to replace him.

All through May and June, Johnston sought a position in which he could block the Federal advance into Georgia. Unable to find one and constantly outmaneuvered by his adversary, he fell back toward Atlanta, abandoning valuable territory, exposing the heartland of the Confederacy, and demoralizing many soldiers and civilians. By mid-July Johnston had retreated to the outskirts of Atlanta and had lost some twenty-two thousand men.

THE FINAL OFFENSIVE UNDER HOOD. Johnston's retreat created great alarm in both Georgia and Richmond, but when queried about his plans, Johnston gave only vague replies. Faced with these facts, Davis decided to replace Johnston with Hood who, on July 17, was promoted to the temporary grade of full general and named the Army of Tennessee's fifth commander. Lt. Gen. Stephen D. Lee was ordered from Mississippi to command what had been Hood's Corps.

Hood soon launched three attacks around Atlanta (Peachtree Creek, July 20; Atlanta, July 22; and Ezra Church, July 28). In all three the Confederates suffered tactical defeats, but they managed temporarily to check the Federals' progress. For a while, it seemed, Hood had thwarted the Federal advance and would hold the city.

In early August Hood tried to force the Northerners out of Georgia by cutting their railroad supply line from Chattanooga. He sent Wheeler with much of the army's cavalry north to wreck the railroad. Wheeler made a few half-hearted attempts to rip up the track. He soon abandoned efforts to wreck the railroad and rode off into northeastern Tennessee where, for several weeks, he was effectively out of the war.

With Wheeler gone, Hood was without his best means of gathering intelligence. In late August the Federals swung around southwest of Atlanta and cut the Confederates' rail line. Hood sent Hardee with two corps to drive them away. In a two-day battle at Jonesboro (August 31 and September 1) the Confederates failed to force back the Northerners. With his supply line cut, Hood had to surrender Atlanta. He evacuated the city and shifted to Palmetto. Both armies were exhausted, and both rested for several weeks.

Once again President Davis came west to visit the army. He removed Hardee from command of his corps and sent him to the south Atlantic coast. Maj. Gen. B. Franklin Cheatham, a division commander, took Hardee's place. Davis and Hood agreed that Hood should move the army into North Georgia and threaten the Union line of supply. Such a maneuver, they hoped, would force the Federals to leave Atlanta in order to preserve their connection with the North. The president also created a new command structure in the West, appointing Beauregard to oversee both Hood's army and the Confederates in Mississippi.

The new effort began auspiciously, with Hood slashing at the rail line as he moved north. The Federals followed and even pursued Hood into northern Alabama. Soon, however, they sent part of their army to defend Tennessee while the remainder abandoned its connection with the North and marched off across Georgia to the sea.

This development convinced Hood that he should move into Tennessee—a decision he reached without consulting either Davis or Beauregard. Indeed, Hood had come to resent Beauregard, and he ignored him as much as possible. Beauregard, for his part, decided not to do more than try to keep Hood's army supplied. Hood wandered west along the south bank of the Tennessee River to Tuscumbia. There he was delayed for about three weeks by high water in the river and by his preparations for the Tennessee campaign.

In late November Hood marched north to the Duck River where he found the Federals near Columbia. On November 29 he sent most of his army around to the east, crossed the river, and marched for Spring Hill. If he reached the road there, he would be north of the Federals and in position either to dash on to Nashville or to try to destroy them as they attempted to escape northward.

In one last fiasco, the Army of Tennessee approached Spring Hill and then halted. All night the Southerners sat around their campfires while a few yards to the west the Federals raced past. There have been allegations that some of the Confederate generals were drunk, or using drugs, or spending time with ladies in the area. Certainly, Hood was exhausted from a long day in the saddle and went to bed, leaving no orders to block the road. This collapse of command has never been satisfactorily explained.

The next morning the Confederates followed the Federals north to Franklin. There, Hood threw the army into a headlong assault against a very strong position. In a battle that lasted long into the darkness, the army lost some five thousand men. During the night, the Northerners pulled back to Nashville.

On December 1 Hood followed the Federals northward. For two weeks he kept the army sitting near Nashville while the Unionists brought in reinforcements and built up a mighty force. When the Federals struck (December 15–16) Hood's army collapsed and fled south to Corinth, Mississippi—where it had been born almost three years before—and then on to Tupelo. There, on January 23, Hood turned the battered Army of Tennessee (now only eighteen thousand officers and men) over to Lt. Gen. Richard Taylor.

Taylor soon sent parts of the army to other areas. Some went to Mobile to help defend that city. Others left to join the meager force being assembled in North Carolina in an effort to block the Federals who had crossed Georgia and turned north toward Virginia. Still others remained in Mississippi. Many units were en route to one of these points when the end came in April and May 1865.

Throughout its existence, then, the Army of Tennessee struggled with numerous handicaps. It was defending an area where geography aided the enemy. It did not share equitably in the Confederacy's supply of trained officers. Often the army was neglected by its government, receiving short shrift with regard to supplies and weapons. It was hampered by internal feuds among its generals—by what historian Steven Woodworth has called "the ugly world of Army of Tennessee politics." Its greatest handicap, however, was the absence of a strong, confident, stable hand at the helm. Because of these weaknesses, the Army of Tennessee, in the end, could not hold the West.

[*See also* Franklin and Nashville Campaign; Henry and Donelson Campaign; Shiloh Campaign; *and biographies of selected figures mentioned herein.*]

— RICHARD M. MCMURRY

ARMY OF TENNESSEE

The Command of Joseph E. Johnston

Hood's association with the army in Tennessee became a tapestry woven of intrigue, defeat, humiliation, and near-annihilation.

PAGE 278

B

BALLOON

Confederate experiments with balloons are not well known, unlike those of the Union's Thaddeus S. C. Lowe. An 1862 document on Union aeronautical activity during the Peninsular campaign contains the earliest mention of Confederate ballooning. Confusion exists about the balloon. Although two sites for balloon work are mentioned, the only documented use took place on the James River in 1862. Accounts of Confederate hot-air-filled cotton balloons and later coal-gas-filled silk balloons are unsupported. Another, undocumented, ballooning episode is suggested to have taken place at Charleston, South Carolina. [*See illustration with this article.*]

It is likely there was only a single Confederate balloon. This multicolored airship was constructed by Langdon Cheves and Charles Cevor in Savannah. They purchased silk, which was assembled and treated with gutta-percha dissolved in naphtha to make it gas-proof.

The balloon was filled at the Richmond Gas Works and transported by rail. From about June 27, 1862, the balloon, tethered to either a boxcar or CSS *Teaser*, was used to observe Union troop movements. The Confederates, however, did not attempt to obtain an immediate tactical advantage by using a telegraph to direct artillery fire or troop movements according to the balloon's observations. Both balloon and tug were captured on July 4, 1862, when the tug ran aground.

It is unlikely Cevor and Cheves built a second balloon that was subsequently lost at Charleston; no evidence supports this speculation. Both men worked on the Charleston defenses, and accounts of their Virginia experiment may have been transposed to that city. The best source on Confederate ballooning uses Langdon Cheves's correspondence to show that one balloon was built in Savannah with multicolored silk bought for the purpose. The best descriptions of Civil War-era balloons can be found in the Union army's ballooning papers in the *Official Records*.

— L. E. BABITS

HEIGHT ADVANTAGE

Only one balloon is known to have been constructed by the Confederates. Shown here is the Federal balloon Intrepid, *used to reconnoiter battles in Virginia in 1862.*

LIBRARY OF CONGRESS

BANKING

Prior to the secession crisis, several Southern states had banking systems as solid and sophisticated as those in the North. Northern attempts to coordinate the transmission of financial information and banks' responses to crises had yielded a range of structures and mechanisms from clearinghouses (where bankers met daily to clear their balances with each other) and safety funds (early forms of deposit insurance) to free banking laws that permitted anyone to start a bank.

Several Southern states, however, had developed a much more effective solution to those problems—namely, branch banking, in which a bank could open offices in other locations without separate acts of the state legislature. Branching, which the North ignored, allowed rapid transfer of resources among branches, treating the resources of each individual as part of the whole. Most important, branching allowed for more efficient transmission of information about financial conditions from one branch location to another. At the onset of the Civil War, the South's banking system had emerged virtually unscathed from the panic of 1857 and had seen the culmination of a decade of impressive growth.

Secession, however, changed things immediately. In states that seceded first, banks felt instant effects. South Carolina banks suspended (i.e., ceased paying gold and silver coin, or specie, for their notes) in late 1860; a

number of New Orleans factorage houses with liabilities exceeding $30 million suspended during the first two weeks of December. But Mobile and New Orleans banks continued to redeem notes for specie until fall 1861. In order to do so, they dramatically cut their lending and circulation. Even in the states that did not secede, banks had to reduce circulation and increase reserves. Deposits in Louisiana and North Carolina remained high, and little evidence exists to show that throughout the South bankers gave much thought to the practical problems of a war that would separate them from their Northern correspondents (banks in other locations in which banks regularly kept balances). Some minor expansion of lending occurred to Southern borrowers—attempts to carry friends of business acquaintances—but no coherent policy appears to have emerged. Nevertheless, all major categories of bank statistics showed declines from 1860 to 1861; circulation fell by $12 million, deposits by $5 million, specie by $4.5 million, and loans by $22 million. The number of banks also shrank from 119 to 104.

In addition to the deleterious effects of the secession crisis itself, the Confederacy and the states themselves exacted a toll on Southern banks. Alabama banks had to provide a $2 million loan to the state of Alabama and had to accept Confederate Treasury notes at par. Each bank had to contribute an amount proportional to its capital. At the level of the Confederate government,

BALTIMORE RIOT
Torn Loyalties

Baltimore in the spring of 1861 was a tinderbox. The secession crisis of the winter, complicated by depressed economic conditions, intensified sectional passions in Maryland. The bombardment of Fort Sumter and Abraham Lincoln's call for troops compounded the state's indecisiveness. Torn in their loyalties, Marylanders nevertheless opposed the coercion of the Southern states. Yet troops going by rail to the defense of Washington would have to pass through Baltimore.

On April 18 some Northern troops traveled through the city without incident. Police authorities, either unworried or merely neglectful, failed to make preparations for continued safe passages. On the following day, the public mood was more volatile. The legacy of the Know-Nothing riots in the 1850s, inflamed by the fiery

rhetoric of Southern radicals and compounded by economic suffering, created a highly inflammatory atmosphere in Baltimore. News of the Sixth Massachusetts Regiment's arrival now provoked gathering mobs to obstruct its route. As the railway cars were drawn by horses through the city, crowds began to jeer and pelt the soldiers with stones and missiles. Disembarking from the coaches, the troops continued by marching to Camden Street Station. Despite police efforts to maintain order and Mayor George Brown's symbolic act of walking at the head of the troops, rioting ensued. In the exchange of fire and missiles, four soldiers and a number of citizens lay wounded and dead.

Hysteria gripped Baltimore. A mass meeting that evening evoked extreme state rights statements from Governor

Thomas Hicks. Municipal authorities, fearing the possibility of additional arrivals, cut Northern rail links to the city. A delegation was sent to Washington for consultations with alarmed Federal authorities. Meanwhile, Baltimoreans prepared for a siege. Finally, by April 28 the crisis had passed, and Unionist sentiment reasserted itself in the city. Gen. Benjamin F. Butler sealed Federal control over the city with his occupation of Federal Hill on the night of May 13. Yet the rioting left its scar, as evident in the state song:

Avenge the patriotic gore
That flecked the street of Baltimore,
And be the battle queen of yore,
Maryland, my Maryland!
— RICHARD R. DUNCAN

banks had a twofold obligation. First, they had to support the Confederacy by a direct loan (April 1861) to the government. They accomplished that by redeeming in coin their own notes that the banks paid for the government bonds, which constituted the collateral for the loan. Even though the banks had suspended specie payments, their notes traded at only a slight discount and, at the beginning of the war, were "as good as gold." As a result, the Confederacy did not (and probably could not) insist on receiving specie directly for the bonds. In May 1861, Secretary of the Treasury Christopher G. Memminger contacted a number of banks to ask for further loans from each of them, paying for them with $1,000 and $500 Treasury notes. Banks were expected to pay out in specie at par on the Confederate notes, although some discounted the notes early. At that point, Memminger well knew, as he told Louisiana bankers in September 1861, the value of Confederate notes depended on the public's willingness to accept them as a circulating medium, not on the bankers' attitude.

A second obligation involved gaining the banks' participation in establishing the Confederate Treasury note currency. Achieving that meant convincing the New Orleans banks to participate in the program. But Louisiana's Constitution prohibited specie suspensions, and the New Orleans banks had remained absent from any of the banking conventions. Mobile's banks followed suit, continuing to pay specie. Thus the notion of a unified "national" currency never took hold.

Circulation of bank, local, private, and state issues rose 150 percent above the prewar average. The number of depreciated moneys rose dramatically, with the most discounted notes called shinplasters. Regardless of a bank's prewar position, that inflation would have undermined its notes' credibility even without the other problems brought on by the war. But three separate pressures combined to destroy the Southern banking system.

(1) First, by offering their specie and notes for purchase of Confederate bonds, the banks assumed those bonds as collateral for their assets. When the Confederacy collapsed, the value of those bonds and hence those assets also collapsed.

SHINPLASTERS
Shingles, Red Dogs and Stump Tails

A generic term applied at various times to paper money, especially small-change notes, shinplasters also went by the names shingles, stump tails, red dogs, and wildcat currency. Any term so indiscriminately used probably defies an accurate definition: usually, shinplasters referred to low-value paper money issued by state banks during the free banking era (1837–1863), to virtually all small-change bills, and during the war in the Confederacy to any paper money (except of Confederate notes) that circulated at a high rate of depreciation to gold or silver (specie).

Such money, however, was not unusual prior to the free banking era. The scarcity of circulating coin meant that, despite state laws against small-change notes, they circulated widely. Many antebellum Southern cities circulated notes of all types during emergencies, with lottery and railcar tickets also passing as a medium of exchange. In the most general sense, they too constituted shinplasters.

During panic times, when banks suspended all specie payments, local businesses and governments issued change scrip in order to continue daily commerce.

Specifically, in the Confederacy, the currency of a number of state banks lost credibility as Federal forces closed in and as the bank specie reserves—already turned over to the Confederate government as backing for bonds or hidden from the government as its policies grew increasingly confiscatory—dwindled. Thus the value of many of those notes dropped to nearly nothing.

One other factor accounted for the depreciation of various notes into shinplasters. After the Emancipation Proclamation, Southerners knew that Federal forces would free slaves as soon as the Union armies occupied an area. To banks, that meant that the collateral for many of their loans had disappeared, thus eroding whatever assets the Southern banks still had.

To alleviate the problem that caused some types of shinplasters, the Confederate Senate, in September 1862, passed a bill to authorize Confederate Secretary of the Treasury Christopher G. Memminger to coin copper tokens of one, five, ten, and twenty-five cents. The Confederate House tabled the measure, and no other small-change law was enacted. Before the war, of course, many individual states had laws prohibiting small notes, but those proved ineffectual even in peacetime.

Neither version of shinplasters— small-change notes or depreciated money—developed owing to any inherent instability in the banking system (North or South). Instead, depreciation of such notes resulted from depreciating bond prices. The shinplaster experience reflected both the confiscatory Confederate policy toward banks and the public's reaction to battlefield events as well as the sudden change in the property status of slaves.

— LARRY SCHWEIKART

*Next to the War
Department, the
Treasury was the
most important
arm of the
government.*

PAGE 620

*By 1864, the
Treasury had one
thousand
employees in
Richmond and two
thousand in the
field offices.*

PAGE 620

(2) Some assets would have remained, however, under other circumstances. Most Southern banks held large amounts of collateral in the form of Southern land (plantations) and property (chattel). The Union victories, combined with the perceived effects of the Emancipation Proclamation, eroded the value of those assets as well. That constituted the second process that destroyed the Southern banking system: even if a peace had been negotiated, if it came at the expense of slavery (as in some of the more desperate Southern ideas after 1864), the banks would have had virtually no assets left anyway.

(3) Finally, Confederate and state policies during the war—independent of overall monetary policy and the one-third decline in money values—led to a staggering drain on a Southern bank's resources. One study has shown that a typical bank would have retained barely 36 percent of its assets by 1864, owing to taxation on stock, earnings, and various fees. What would the remainder of that bank's assets be worth if they consisted of slaves and Confederate bonds?

As if these pressures were not enough, banks in the Confederacy also had to deal with personnel problems and with the approach of enemy troops. Employees frequently moved in and out of civilian bank jobs, depending on the demands of the army or their families. Some bankers away at the front received instructions to return to their institutions. More disturbing were the problems associated with the impending arrival of Federal troops. Banks hid specie from the Union armies (as well as the Confederate government), and in one case a Tennessee banker escaped with his bank's specie to England and returned with it after the war to reopen his bank. Under other circumstances, banks saw Union troops issue counterfeit look-alike notes, which only further eroded the public's flagging confidence in paper money.

The collapse of the Southern banking system, although little appreciated by historians, constituted a dual tragedy. First, the dearth of financial institutions in the postbellum South led to major disruptions in commercial and agricultural lending. That, in turn, helped seal the fate of freedmen and whites alike by denying them access to credit under competitive circumstances. With virtually no banks in existence—and certainly no banks at all in direct, close competition—farmers and entrepreneurs either had to seek credit from furnishing merchants or other informal sources or, in the case of farmers, had to sharecrop. The record of black-owned insurance companies and savings and loans in the North suggests that at least *some* black-owned institutions would have appeared in a free market.

When combined with the undesirable and constrictive effects of the National Bank and Currency Acts, the ability of Southerners to start and grow banks almost vanished for decades. The second unappreciated aspects of Southern banking as it related to the Confederacy was that the Confederate experiment killed the extremely viable and healthy branch banking systems, almost unique to the South. Only in a few states—most notably California—did branching develop, and overall it remained absent from the political debates about banking that reformed the American system from the late 1800s to 1913. Thus, in addition to its other less than illustrious accomplishments, the Confederacy, through its failure, saddled much of the United States with an inferior unit banking system for years.

— LARRY SCHWEIKART

BARKSDALE'S MISSISSIPPI BRIGADE

This brigade of four Mississippi infantry regiments won one of the highest reputations as a fighting unit earned by any organization in the Army of Northern Virginia. The Thirteenth Mississippi was made up of companies from the state's east-central counties. Its first and best-known commander was William Barksdale. The Seventeenth came from Mississippi's far northern tier of counties, the Eighteenth was raised in west-central Mississippi, and the Twenty-first included companies from several widely separated regions.

The regiments had separate baptisms of fire at First Manassas and Ball's Bluff before they were united as a brigade under Gen. Richard Griffith in December 1861. After Griffith was mortally wounded at Savage Station, Barksdale became brigadier.

The Mississippi Brigade impressed an admiring Virginia major as "the finest body of men I ever saw . . . almost giants in size and power . . . and . . . almost without exception fine shots." When they screeched the rebel yell, the major wrote, "the volume of sound was tremendous." The men of the brigade performed ably throughout the war as some of Lee's most reliable shock troops. They won special distinction under Barksdale defending the riverfront at Fredericksburg in December 1862 and attacking to and beyond the Peach Orchard at Gettysburg. The brigade's most difficult day came on May 3, 1863, when it was driven from Marye's Heights near Fredericksburg, but because of the circumstances no discredit was attached to the brigade. Gen. B. G. Humphreys, who had been colonel of the Twenty-first, commanded the brigade after Barksdale's death at Gettysburg.

— ROBERT K. KRICK

BEAUREGARD, P.G.T.

Beauregard, P. G. T. (1818–1893), general. Destined for a military career marked by controversy and conflict with superiors and colleagues, Pierre Gustave Toutant Beauregard was born at Contreras Plantation in St. Bernard Parish, Louisiana, just south of New Orleans, on May 28, 1818. Much has been made of his French creole origins, leading some to ascribe his later difficulties to aristocratic haughtiness derived from a fiery Gallic inheritance, but such theorizing stems largely from romantic notions of creole society. One of only eight full generals in the Confederate forces, he would see action in almost every theater of the Civil War, from the firing on Fort Sumter to a final surrender in the Carolinas during the last days of the conflict.

Beauregard entered West Point at the age of sixteen after several years at the French School in New York City, already a committed disciple of Napoléon Bonaparte and the military theorist Henri de Jomini. Immersion in this new Anglo-Saxon milieu led to his abandonment of the hyphen from the Toutant-Beauregard family name, prelude to his eventual discarding of "Pierre" for his favored "G. T. Beauregard." Graduating second in the academy's class of 1838, he received a lieutenant's commission in the Corps of Engineers and quickly distinguished himself in building and repairing coastal fortifications at Pensacola, Florida, and near the mouth of the Mississippi in his native state.

Assigned to Winfield Scott's command at the outbreak of the Mexican War, he won that crusty soldier's praise for skillful reconnaissance missions in the campaign from Tampico to Mexico City, particularly impressing the general with the precision and acuity of his recommendations as to the best line of march against the enemy capital. Despite a brevet as major for bravery in the attack on Chapultepec, Beauregard came away from the war embittered against Scott, resentful that his contributions to victory had not won official commendation greater than that accorded fellow officers like Robert E. Lee and George B. McClellan. A comparable conceit as to his talents and accomplishments would continue to plague his relationships in the years ahead, and his scathing criticism of what he saw as the weaknesses in Scott's generalship revealed what would be an abiding tendency to accept conventional abstract theory rather than imaginative pragmatic execution as the measure of military performance.

From 1848 to 1860 Beauregard served as engineering officer in charge of "the Mississippi and Lake defences in Louisiana," and after 1853 as superintendent responsible for building the Federal Custom House at New Orleans, establishing in both assignments a reputation for superior engineering skills. After an unsuccessful try for the mayoralty of New Orleans in 1858, he enlisted the aid of Senator John Slidell, husband of his wife's sister, to win appointment in 1860 as superintendent of West Point. But his clear secessionist sympathies led to dismissal from the post on January 28, 1861, a mere five days after his installation.

Beauregard resigned his Federal commission effective February 20, 1861, and returned to Louisiana in expectation that he would be made commander of the state's now independent military forces, an appointment that went instead to Braxton Bragg. In resentful pride, he refused any other commission in the state army, enlisting perversely as a private in the Orleans Guards. That unit saw little of him, for Slidell and other influential political leaders had already pressed his claim with Jefferson Davis for appointment in the Confederate army. Convinced that the Louisianan's vaunted gunnery expertise made him particularly suited to the task, Davis commissioned him as brigadier general on February 27, 1861, with command of the Confederate and South Carolina forces aligned against the Federal garrison at Fort Sumter in Charleston Harbor.

Assuming his post on March 6, Beauregard quickly rearranged gun implacements on the Charleston Battery and the islands to its left and right to mount a circle of fire around Fort Sumter in the center, confident that this concentration would keep at bay any Federal vessels attempting to reinforce the fortification and also allow for its destruction should that become necessary. His efforts proved highly effective. When negotiations with U.S. Maj. Robert Anderson, commander of the Federal garrison, failed to secure Union withdrawal from the island stronghold, Beauregard opened fire on Sumter during the early morning hours of April 12, and the fateful years of civil war had begun.

The events at Charleston made Beauregard an immediate Confederate hero, hailed as "Old Bory" and praised as one of the world's great soldiers. President Davis, the Confederate Congress, newspapers across the South, and smitten female admirers showered him with gratitude, while an equally responsive Northern editor placed a price on his head. If all this tended to reinforce an already prickly self-esteem, for the

President Davis ordered P.G.T. Beauregard to Charleston to take command of the harbor and make preparations for the use of force.

PAGE 224

"OLD BORY"   *Proud, fiery, and brilliant, Gen. P.G.T. Beauregard of Louisiana ordered the April 12, 1861, firing on Fort Sumter, Charleston, that ignited the Civil War.*   NATIONAL ARCHIVES

moment at least he gave no time to reveling in applause, but set about buttressing the defenses of Charleston by shifting the target of his batteries from Sumter to the harbor entrance.

Early in May 1861, he testily rejected a suggestion by Davis that he go to Pensacola to take Fort Pickens, thus crossing swords with his superiors for the first but not the last time. However much he might have offended the president, it did not keep Davis from appointing him in mid-May to command of the defenses of the Mississippi from Vicksburg to the Kentucky-Tennessee border. But by May 28 things looked dramatically different. Now the Confederate capital had been shifted to Virginia and new orders sped him on to Richmond.

Federal troops had crossed the Potomac to occupy Alexandria, pointing clearly to an impending attack upon the Confederate railroad junction at Manassas just north of the capital, and it was here that Davis and Robert E. Lee, his personal military adviser, wished Beauregard to take command. He did so on June 3, launching a dizzying round of activity centering on earthworks around Manassas, troop reorganization, and grandiose plans for a full-scale campaign into enemy territory across the Potomac, tactfully but resolutely rejected by his Richmond superiors. With a Federal attack obviously imminent, Davis and Lee ordered Gen. Joseph E. Johnston to move his army from the Shenandoah Valley to reinforce Beauregard. As the senior officer, Johnston had right of command of the joined forces, but recognizing Beauregard's longer presence on the scene and better knowledge of the terrain, he allowed his colleague to retain that prerogative, a courtesy Beauregard eventually repaid by asking Johnston to leave the field when actual fighting began.

Luckily for the Southern cause, Gen. Irvin McDowell's attack upon the Confederate positions just north of Manassas at Bull Run on July 21 preempted Beauregard's battle plan. As presented to a dismayed Johnston, that blueprint reflected many of the weaknesses of Beauregard's generalship. It abounded in a bewildering confusion of orders and lines of authority and gave little attention to possible responses of the adversary. Its implementation might well have spelled disaster for the Southern forces. But despite indescribable disarray and inefficiency in his headquarters, once the fighting began Beauregard revealed his essential strength as a commander, what historian Frank Vandiver has called a "soldier's greatest asset—battle sense." Skillfully countering McDowell's moves, he sent the Federal force reeling back toward Washington.

A grateful President Davis raised him to full generalship on the morning after the battle, confirmed when Congress dated his commission fifth in seniority behind only Adj. Gen. Samuel Cooper, Albert Sidney Johnston, Robert E. Lee and Joe Johnston. Once again he heard his praises sung in all quarters of the South, and for a brief moment he seemed indeed to be what one Richmond editor dubbed him, "Beauregard Felix," favorite of the gods. Mindful of the troubles experienced in distinguishing friend from foe during the fighting at Manassas because of the similarity between the Confederate and Union standards, he added to his honors by designing the famous Southern battle flag, replacing the Stars and Bars.

His universal acclaim proved short-lived. To an old feud with Commissary Gen. Lucius B. Northrop over supposed lack of supplies to his troops, he now added a blustery dispute with Secretary of War Judah P. Benjamin for what he perceived as meddling interference with his command prerogatives. Davis attempted to calm these imbroglios but began to grow more impatient with Beauregard when it became clear that his complaints to opposition members of Congress fed increasing attacks upon administration policy. Disaffection increased with reports that the general had wide backing to contest for the permanent presidency in the coming elections ending the provisional status of the government.

But it was Beauregard's report to Congress on the Battle of Manassas that caused the greatest uproar. Although denying opposition claims that Davis had prevented pursuit of retreating Federal troops, the general implied that the taking of Washington had been nonetheless sacrificed by Davis's rejection of his original invasion plan and by the president's slowness in ordering Johnston's army to join forces with his own. Furious, Davis shot back that no such strategy had ever been presented to him and charged Beauregard with attempting to exalt himself at his superior's expense. Unrepentant, Beauregard countered with a letter to the *Richmond Whig* in which he obliquely chastised Davis anew. His persistence struck many as sheer contumacy, and the heading of his communication—"Centreville, Va., Within hearing of the Enemy's Guns"—made him seem vainglorious and ridiculously pompous.

Whether on the initiative of his congressional friends or at the instigation of the president, late in January 1862, Beauregard was ordered west as second in command to Albert Sidney Johnston. As Johnston's position crumbled along the Tennessee-Kentucky border, he rejected Beauregard's pleas to mount a concentration of all available troops in defense of Fort Donelson against Ulysses S. Grant's certain attack, sending him instead to supervise the withdrawal of Gen. Leonidas Polk's army from Columbus, Kentucky.

B

By July 21, 1861, at First Manassas, Beauregard and Johnston's combined forces totaled 32,000, only 1,000 less than Union Gen. Irvin McDowell's.

PAGE 347

The victory at First Manassas produced several heroes for the Confederates, Johnston and Beauregard foremost.

PAGE 350

Shiloh: A small Methodist church gave its name to the first major land battle in the West on April 6 and 7, 1862.

PAGE 546

Falling back all along their lines, Johnston and Beauregard gathered a force of some 35,000 men at Corinth, Mississippi. From there they moved on April 3 to attack Grant's army in camp at Pittsburg Landing on the west bank of the Tennessee River near a small church called Shiloh. Delay in the deployment of troops and careless noise in the undisciplined ranks convinced Beauregard that the element of surprise critical to his battle plan was now lost, and he urged postponement of the attack. Johnston demurred, and on April 6 the Confederates struck. From his position in the rear of the Confederate troops, Beauregard exercised more general command of the field than did Johnston, who threw himself into the thick of the fray like a corps leader until he fell fatally wounded. With Johnston's death Beauregard assumed full command and at day's end had almost forced Grant's army into the river. But the desperate weariness of his men led him to call a halt, and by next morning Don Carlos Buell's army had arrived to give Grant reinforcement sufficient to push back the exhausted Confederate foe.

Failure to clinch victory when it seemed in his grasp exposed Beauregard to renewed criticism by his enemies and even by one of his subordinates, Braxton Bragg. His own attempts to portray Shiloh as a misrepresented success only further diminished his reputation, an erosion heightened when Gen. Henry Halleck drove him from Corinth south to Tupelo. There, suffering from a chronic throat ailment from which he hoped to seek relief in Mobile, he turned temporary leadership of the Army of the West over to Bragg without authorization from Richmond, giving Davis the pleasure of ordering his immediate dismissal from command.

Determined to keep Beauregard out of the field, Davis next assigned him to head the Department of South Carolina and Georgia, headquartered at Charleston, where he arrived on September 15, 1862. Still convinced that the best way to protect the city lay in concentrating such firepower on the entrance to the harbor that Federal naval vessels would be unable to break through, he successfully hectored Richmond for increased matériel to strengthen his batteries and fortifications. In April 1863, he turned back a Union flotilla of nine ironclads and later that year withstood a siege by combined army and navy forces that inflicted heavy damage on Fort Sumter and surrounding island installations but failed to dislodge his hold on the city. In all, he had effectively managed what has been called "the war's longest and most skillful defense of a land point against attack from the sea."

During that extended standoff some additional opportunities had come his way. Lee wanted him to serve in northern Virginia while he led the campaign into Maryland and Pennsylvania, and Samuel Cooper invited him to aid Joe Johnston by guarding against Union incursions into Mississippi. But with his heart still set on an independent field command, Beauregard stubbornly rejected all such offers, until in April 1864, at Lee's instigation, he was given charge of the Department of North Carolina and Southern Virginia, responsible for holding the southern approaches to Richmond.

The advance of the Army of the Potomac against Confederate forces in northern Virginia made Beauregard's mission vitally important, for loss of the Southern supply lines would spell almost certain collapse of Lee's attempts to hold the capital. When Union Gen. Benjamin Butler in early May moved troops up the James River to Drewry's Bluff, midway between Petersburg and Richmond, Beauregard managed to drive him back into a position bottled up between the James and Appomattox rivers, despite frequent interference from Davis and Bragg, now chief of staff. Again his critics charged that he had allowed an enemy force to escape destruction. His continuing reluctance to send reinforcements to Lee as Grant maneuvered to get his army between the Virginian and Richmond produced even more friction with his superiors.

Whatever his failings, he alone among the Confederate leaders anticipated Grant's move south of

BATTLE OF SHILOH, APRIL 1862

April 6	
Dawn	Johnston, Beauregard and 35,000 troops attack Grant's army near Shiloh, Mississippi Johnston killed in battle Beauregard assumes command
Day's end	Grant's forces retreating Beauregard calls halt to allow Confederate force time to rest
April 7	
Morning	Federal reinforcements arrive, able to repel Confederate forces.

the James after the battle at Cold Harbor. While Lee for almost forty-eight hours remained ignorant of his opponent's whereabouts, Beauregard successfully blocked Grant's advance upon Petersburg until increasingly desperate communiqués convinced his skeptical colleague that it was indeed the full force of the Army of the Potomac pushing against his lines. Lee then moved quickly south and Petersburg was saved. It remains Beauregard's finest hour.

In the ensuing siege of Petersburg, he continued under Lee's direction, restive again in a subordinate position and frequently at odds with the high command. Bragg and Davis persisted in their long established animosity by charging him with various acts of malfeasance. He consequently welcomed assignment in October 1864 to head a new department called the Military Division of the West, with oversight of the armies of Gen. John Bell Hood in Georgia and Richard Taylor in Alabama.

Suggestive that the appointment represented primarily an attempt at political fence-mending by the administration, Davis severely limited Beauregard's authority in this new assignment, restricting him to basically advisory powers. Exploiting this opportunity, Hood won Beauregard's reluctant approval for a push into Tennessee but then proceeded to ignore the department commander in the campaign that led him to disaster at Nashville in December. Beauregard meanwhile proved incapable of divining William Tecumseh Sherman's objectives in his march east from Atlanta, failing to concentrate Confederate forces as the Federal juggernaut moved inexorably toward the sea. With his command widened to the Atlantic coast, he attempted to hold a line from Augusta to Charleston, where he expected the main Federal attack. But again Sherman confounded him, striking instead at Columbia in February 1865 and driving Beauregard's forces back into North Carolina before he could unite with those of Gen. William J. Hardee as they evacuated a now indefensible Charleston.

On the advice of Lee, a dismayed Davis dispatched Joe Johnston to take over Beauregard's command, leaving the Louisianan to direct rear-area troop movements and protect lines of communication. Apparently resigned to the war's inevitable conclusion, he declined appointment to small field commands in western Virginia and eastern Tennessee, preferring to remain under Johnston. When a gloomy April 13 conference with President Davis and Secretary of War John C. Breckinridge in Greensboro confirmed Lee's capitulation to Grant, Johnston surrendered his army to Sherman near Hillsboro, North Carolina, on April 26, 1865, and on May 1 Beauregard headed home to Louisiana.

BEAUVOIR
The Jefferson Davis
Memorial Home

Developed in the late 1840s and early 1850s by Mississippi planter James Brown, this waterfront estate near Biloxi, Mississippi, was home to Jefferson Davis during the final twelve years of his life. The Beauvoir estate was dominated by a raised, single-story Greek Revival cottage and flanking pavilions. Having escaped the ravages of war, the property was purchased in 1873 by Davis family acquaintance and author Sarah Anne Ellis Dorsey, who gave her new home its French name because of the "beautiful view" of the Gulf of Mexico.

Responding to an offer from Mrs. Dorsey, Jefferson Davis decided to write at Beauvoir rather than develop and occupy his own property in the area. By February 1877, Davis was at work on *The Rise and Fall of the Confederate Government* in the east, or library, pavilion. He was assisted by personal secretary William T. Walthall and Mrs. Dorsey. Upon her arrival in 1878, Varina Howell Davis replaced Mrs. Dorsey, whom she disliked. Despite Sarah Dorsey's intention to bequeath Beauvoir to Davis, he purchased the estate in 1879 for $5,500. The Davises, later joined by daughter Varina Anne ("Winnie"), entertained a variety of notables while residing at Beauvoir.

Following the deaths of Jefferson in 1889 and Winnie in 1898, Varina Davis sold the property for $10,000 to the Mississippi Division, United Sons of Confederate Veterans. The organization, in accordance with her wishes, leased the property to the state of Mississippi for a Confederate soldiers' home. The Jefferson Davis Memorial Home, from 1903 to 1957, provided shelter and care for about two thousand residents, including veterans and their wives, widows, and servants. Museum operations at the site were initiated in 1941 with the opening of the main house for tours. Today, the entire eighty-four-acre estate operates as a historic landmark.

— KEITH ANDERSON HARDISON

Unlike most of his fellow Confederate generals, he found the postwar years generally prosperous and rewarding. Occasional moments of dejection in the Reconstruction period led to flirtation with various possibilities of foreign military service in Brazil, Romania, Egypt, Spain, and Argentina, none of

"If it happens again, I shall join one of their camps and share their wants with them; for I will never allow them to suppose that I feast while they suffer."

P.G.T. BEAUREGARD
UPON LEARNING THAT
SOME OF HIS REGIMENTS
WERE WITHOUT FOOD
1861

Jefferson Davis knew that if Republicans won the White House in 1860, it would be tantamount to ending the nation: the South could not live under an abolitionist administration.

PAGE 163

It was only a matter of time before a joint army-navy expedition took aim at the Crescent City.

PAGE 400

which materialized, turning him to his old engineering skills. Appointed superintendent of the New Orleans, Jackson, and Great Northern Railroad late in 1865, he also served as president of the New Orleans and Carrollton street railway from 1866 until he was ousted as part owner of the company a decade later. Recovery from that setback came the next year, when he and Jubal Early began a long stint as supervisors of the drawings of the infamous Louisiana Lottery for reportedly handsome salaries. Some restoration of military status came with his appointment in 1879 as adjutant general and commander of the Louisiana militia, a position he held until 1888, when he was elected commissioner of public works for New Orleans.

Inevitably, passage of the years caught him up in a series of literary clashes with Joe Johnston over events at Manassas, with various promoters of Albert Sidney Johnston as the true hero of Shiloh, and with his old nemesis Jefferson Davis over just about everything, in a flurry of conflicting reminiscences. His chief contributions to the fray appeared in *The Military Operations of General Beauregard,* attributed to a friend, Alfred Roman, but essentially his own creation, and a *Century* magazine article, "The Battle of Bull Run," later expanded into *A Commentary on the Campaign and Battle of Manassas.*

After a brief illness he died in New Orleans on February 21, 1893. He was interred in that city's tomb of the Army of Tennessee in Metairie Cemetery, dominated, ironically, by the equestrian statue of Albert Sidney Johnston.

— JOSEPH G. TREGLE, JR.

BELLE ISLE PRISON

In the summer of 1862, the Confederate authorities at Richmond relieved the overcrowding in their warehouse prisons for Union enlisted men by opening a camp on Belle Isle (or Island), an eighty-acre tract in the James River on which was already located an ironworks and workers' housing. The lower fifteen acres, where the prison was located, were flat and sandy. The proximity of the river's rapids and the connection to the south bank by a single railroad bridge simplified security. By mid-July, the island camp held 5,000 men. Though conditions during the first summer were relatively pleasant, they soon would make the island's name seem ironic indeed.

The opening of the prisoner exchange under the cartel of July 22, 1862, resulted in a rapid reduction of the prison population, and by September 23, the camp had closed. In January 1863, Belle Isle reopened at first as a temporary camp and then, with the breakdown of exchange, as a more permanent facility. In the camp's final form, the Confederates partially surrounded four to five acres with a deadline three feet wide by eight feet deep and with earthworks outside where the guards stood. A fenced walkway led to the river bridge. During the daytime the prisoners used the walkway to reach the river to drink, bathe, and use the sinks (latrines). Outside the prison were guards' quarters and a small hospital. Within the prison camp was a central thoroughfare from which radiated some sixty streets.

During the greater part of its history, the prison's commandant was Lt. Virginius Bossieux, a Virginian of French origin. Under him the prisoners were organized into squads of a hundred, headed by sergeants who called the roll and distributed rations.

By early fall 1863, the prison intended to hold 3,000 had some 6,300 captives. In early 1864, there were 8,000 or more within the camp. The overcrowded prisoners suffered greatly. To reduce escape attempts, they were not allowed access to the sinks after dark, so the ground became filthy. Although the Confederates supplied some tents, there were never enough, and prisoners either improvised shelter with pup tents made of blankets or simply burrowed in the soil. A few fires provided the only heat. The rations consisted of cornbread, rice, and occasional meat. Some prisoners tried to improve their lot by trading with one another and with the guards, using a variety of goods including prison-made jewelry and other souvenirs. Other prisoners stole scarce clothing, blankets, or food from one another.

In the winter of 1863–1864, the United States sent some clothing and food to the prisoners. The captive Union officers who distributed the goods—which many hungry prisoners quickly traded to guards for extra food—reported to their fellows and their government on the sad situation of the enlisted men. Though most sick prisoners were removed to hospitals on the island or in the city, deaths in the prison itself were numerous—ten or more men died each day. Because the prison was in full view of the Confederate capitol building, Union critics charged that Confederate leaders had to be aware of its deplorable conditions. This, together with the physical appearance of occasionally exchanged prisoners, was played up in Union propaganda.

By the end of March 1864, the Confederates had removed all the Belle Isle prisoners to Andersonville, Georgia. During that summer, the temporary cessation of shipments to that equally congested pen caused a renewed accumulation of some 6,000 prisoners on Belle Isle. The worried Confederates supplemented their inadequate guards with two howitzers. In October, the Confederates transferred their new captives to Danville or (mostly) to Salisbury. Once again the Belle Islanders had gone from the frying pan to the fire. On February 10, 1865, the Confederates returned the island to its owners.

In the postwar period parts of the island served industrial functions. By the 1990s the city of Richmond had received title to the island and was contemplating recreational and historical uses for the prison site.

— FRANK L. BYRNE

BENJAMIN, JUDAH P.

Benjamin, Judah P. (1811–1884), U.S. senator, Confederate attorney general, secretary of war, and secretary of state. Born a British subject in the British West Indies on August 6, 1811, Benjamin was taken to the United States in his early youth. The child of Sephardic Jewish settlers, he was descended from families that could be traced back to fifteenth-century Spain.

Judah Benjamin's boyhood was much more steeped in Jewish culture and tradition than either Southern or Jewish historians have acknowledged. He was reared in Charleston, South Carolina, and grew to manhood in New Orleans, two of the largest Jewish communities in the United States in the early nineteenth century. His father was one of the twelve dissenters in Charleston who formed the first Reform Congregation of America. Although the records of Beth Elohim congregation were burned and we cannot know for certain, he probably was one of the first boys confirmed at the new reform temple, which was founded when he was thirteen years old. The character of a Jewish boy reared by a deeply involved Jewish family would be shaped by that experience the rest of his life.

He went to Yale Law School at fourteen, left under mysterious circumstances, and was admitted to the Louisiana bar in 1832. A strategic marriage to Natalie S. Martin, whose family belonged to the ruling creole aristocracy in New Orleans, propelled him into financial success and subsequently into a political career. He participated in the explosive growth of New Orleans between 1820 and 1840 as a commercial lawyer and political advocate for banking, finance, and railroad interests.

Benjamin prospered for a time as a sugar planter, helped organize the Illinois Central Railroad, and was elected to the Louisiana legislature in 1842. As a rising political star in the Whig Party, he was the first acknowledged Jew to be elected to the U.S. Senate (1852; reelected as a Democrat, 1858). In the Senate he was noted as an eloquent defender of Southern interests and has been ranked by some historians as one of the five great orators in Senate history, the equal of Daniel Webster and John C. Calhoun.

In Washington, he met Jefferson Davis (1853) and forged a friendship in an unusual confrontation. They were both intense and ambitious senators—Davis of Mississippi and Benjamin of Louisiana. Varina Howell Davis, the future First Lady of the Confederacy, wrote years later of them during this period, "Sometimes when they did not agree on, a measure, hot words in glacial, polite phrases passed between them." Because of a suspected insult on the floor of the Senate, Benjamin challenged Davis to a duel. Davis quickly and publicly apologized, and the incident of honor defended and satisfied drew them together in a relationship of mutual respect.

His wife had taken his only daughter, Ninnette, and moved to Paris in 1842. She joined him briefly after his election to the Senate, but returned again to Paris because of scandalous rumors about her in Washington. Thereafter Benjamin saw her once a year on trips to Paris. Only a fragment of a letter remains between them: "Speak not to me of economy," she wrote. "It is so fatiguing."

In the Senate, Benjamin was embroiled in the political turmoil leading to the Civil War, and he was frequently attacked on the basis of his religious background. Once in a debate on slavery when Senator Ben Wade of Ohio accused Benjamin of being an "Israelite with Egyptian principles," Benjamin is reported to have replied, "It is true that I am a Jew, and when my ancestors were receiving their Ten Commandments from the immediate Deity, amidst the thunderings and lightnings of Mount Sinai, the ancestors of my opponent were herding swine in the forest of Great Britain." It was a rare reply. Usually, when newspapers, political enemies, and military leaders insulted him with stinging phrases of religious prejudice, he almost never answered, but simply retained what observers called "a perpetual smile."

After secession, President Jefferson Davis appointed Benjamin as his attorney general on February 21, 1861. The president chose him because, in Davis's own words, Benjamin "had a very high reputation as a lawyer, and my acquaintance with him in the Senate had impressed me with the lucidity of his intellect, his systematic habits, and capacity for labor." Since the office of attorney general was a civilian post, the leadership in the capital considered it of little consequence, but this did not deter Benjamin. He plunged into the cabinet policy debates on all aspects of the Confederacy and developed a reputation as one who loved details, complexity, and problem solving. He became the administrator to the president, called by observers "the Poo Bah" of the Confederate govern-

Judah P. Benjamin was appointed, in succession, to Justice, War, and State.

PAGE 83

Benjamin possessed a keen intellect and qualities of statesmanship that earned him the soubriquet "the brains of the Confederacy."

PAGE 658

INDISPENSABLE *It is difficult to imagine Jefferson Davis or the Confederate government managing without Judah P. Benjamin—secretary of state, secretary of war, and attorney general.* NATIONAL ARCHIVES

ment. At his first cabinet meeting, Secretary of War Leroy P. Walker said, "there was only one man there who had any sense, and that man was Benjamin." During his tenure at the Justice Department, Benjamin became a strong advocate of cotton diplomacy (the policy of shipping cotton to Europe as barter for arms and supplies, and of denying cotton to countries that did not support the South).

Davis then appointed Benjamin acting secretary of war in September, making the appointment permanent on November 21. By appointing a brilliant administrator without military experience, Davis could thereby be his own secretary of war, a position he had held in the Franklin Pierce administration. But Benjamin was a failure because when the war went badly on the battlefield, the military turned on him as a scapegoat. Frustrated generals who could not attack the president publicly had a convenient target in his secretary of war. As the Union forces struck back, criticism of Benjamin mounted. He was not a military man, and his orders, though flowing from constant meetings with the president, were treated as originating from him and were resented in the field as interference and amateurism.

Benjamin had highly publicized quarrels with Gen. P. G. T. Beauregard and Gen. Thomas J. ("Stonewall") Jackson. Beauregard called Benjamin in a letter to Davis "that functionary at his desk, who deems it a fit time to write lectures on law while the enemy is mustering at our front." Jackson threatened to resign, writing Davis that "with such interference in my command, I cannot be expected to be of much service in the field." Davis defended his "right hand," as Varina described Benjamin, who was working twelve and fourteen hours a day with Davis and was being blamed by the military for carrying out the president's orders.

Benjamin was berated by Northern generals as well. When Benjamin Butler, who commanded the forces that conquered New Orleans, issued a statement about the city, he said "the most effective supporters of the Confederacy have been . . . mostly Jews . . . who all deserve at the hands of the government what is due the Jew Benjamin."

The anger against Benjamin came to a head after the fall of Roanoke Island in early February 1862. Benjamin had been under intense pressure from Gen. Henry A. Wise at Roanoke and Governor Henry T. Clark of North Carolina to send many more men and arms to the garrison there. He had resisted for reasons that would not be known until twenty-five years after the war, and he accepted the subsequent public condemnation in silence to protect his country. Roanoke was sacrificed because to have done otherwise would have revealed to the enemy just how desperate the South was.

At the dedication of the Robert E. Lee monument in Richmond in 1890, Col. Charles Marshall, an aide-de-camp on General Lee's staff, read part of a letter from Benjamin, which revealed that President Davis had agreed to allow Benjamin to be publicly censured:

I consulted the President whether it was best for the country that I should submit to unmerited censure or reveal to a Congressional Committee our poverty and my utter inability to supply the requisitions of General Wise, and thus run the risk that the fact should become known to some of the spies of the enemy, of whose activity we were well assured. It was thought best for the public service that I should suffer the blame in silence and a report of censure on me was accordingly made by the Committee of Congress.

When Benjamin resigned, Davis, as a reward for loyalty, promptly named him secretary of state.

On the subject of slavery, both Davis and Benjamin were "enlightened" Southerners whose attitudes were evolving. Most Jewish historians have understandably reacted with revulsion to the fact that Benjamin owned 140 slaves on a sugar plantation, and they have been unable to consider the question of his views on slavery with anything but embarrassed dismay. To comprehend Benjamin on this score, one must put him into context as a political figure against a backdrop of planter dogmatism and abolitionist fervor.

Such an exploration leads directly to an extraordinary episode of the war in which Benjamin played a central role: the effort to persuade Davis to issue a Confederate emancipation proclamation, which would promise slaves freedom in exchange for military service. That move, which began to take shape early in the war in the minds of military and political leaders but did not surface until 1864, is usually dismissed as a desperate gamble made at the end of the war to lure Britain into the fight. But as secretary of state, Benjamin's obsession all along had been to draw England into the war. Slavery, however, was a stumbling block because England had abolished slavery in 1833. As the clouds of defeat gathered, Benjamin spoke before ten thousand people in Richmond, delivering a remarkable speech in favor of a Confederate offer to free slaves who would fight for the South. Although the idea of arming slaves as soldiers was supported by Lee, who needed more men in the field, the public and political reaction was fierce. Howell Cobb, the former governor of Georgia, wrote that "if slaves will make good soldiers, our whole theory of slavery is wrong." Nevertheless, the Confederate Congress passed a partial version of the measure on March 13, but by then it was too late. Richmond fell less than a month later.

Benjamin achieved greater political power than any other Jew in the nineteenth century—perhaps even in all American history.

PAGE 53

51

Benjamin's apparent change of personality after the war has puzzled historians. The utter secrecy and privacy of his later life is anomalous, given his earlier hunger for fame. No one can ever know, but certainly one key to understanding his silence after the war is his creation of a Confederate spy ring in Canada and the subsequent proclamation, conceived by the Union's secretary of war, Edwin Stanton, and issued by Lincoln's successor, President Andrew Johnson, for the arrest of Davis and seven Canadian Confederate spies after the Lincoln assassination. History, by means of the trials of the conspirators and by exhaustive investigations, has absolved both Benjamin and Davis from any responsibility. But the psychological and emotional impact on Benjamin of the long period of hysteria that followed the assassination must have taken its toll, especially since Lincoln's death fell on Good Friday and 2,500 sermons were given on Easter Sunday comparing Lincoln to a fallen Christ figure, as the nation acted out a passion play. There is no record of what Benjamin thought of the various published accusations against him.

If Benjamin's role in history has been misjudged by historians and was minimized even by participants, much of the responsibility for that lies with Benjamin himself. He chose obscurity early in the war with the unwavering decision that he could best serve the South by serving Davis and remaining in the presidential shadow. For reasons that have puzzled historians, Benjamin burned his personal papers—some as he escaped from Richmond in 1865 and almost all of the rest just before he died—and he left only six scraps of paper at his death. One historian has called him a "virtual incendiary."

Benjamin fled to England after the war and built a second career as a successful international lawyer. He was called to the bar (June 1866) after only five months' residence and achieved enormous financial success in his new home country. In 1868, he wrote a classic treatise on commercial law in England *(Treatise on the Law of Sale of Personal Property)* known even today to law students as "Benjamin on Sales." In 1872, he became a queen's counsel, practicing with wig and robes in the House of Lords and appearing in 136 major cases.

Although he had been known in the U.S. Senate as an outstanding orator, in England he gave no published speeches on the war. He left no articles, essays, or books about his role in the war or any other aspect of it. Indeed, he made only two public statements in nineteen years that concerned the war. The first was a three-paragraph letter to the *Times* of London in September 1865, just after he arrived in England, protesting the imprisonment of Jefferson Davis. The second was a short letter in 1883 contradicting the charge that millions of dollars in Confederate funds were left in European banks under his control. There were no letters defending strategy or admitting error; nor does history record any war-related conversations with students or scholars. He spent a few evenings at dinner with Davis when the ex-president visited London five times between 1868 and 1883. Otherwise, he avoided nostalgic encounters with friends from the South. It is one of the enduring mysteries that Benjamin chose to erase all ties to his previous life. In fact, he never even returned to the United States.

Late in life, he retired and moved to Paris to be with his family. Benjamin died on May 6, 1884, and was buried in Père Lachaise cemetery in Paris under the name of "Philippe Benjamin" in the family plot of the Boursignac family, the in-laws of his daughter. Three grandchildren died in childhood and no direct descendants survived. In 1938, the Paris chapter of the Daughters of the Confederacy finally provided an inscription to identify the man in the almost anonymous grave:

> JUDAH PHILIP BENJAMIN
> BORN ST. THOMAS WEST INDIES AUGUST 6, 1811
> DIED IN PARIS MAY 6, 1884
> UNITED STATES SENATOR FROM LOUISIANA
> ATTORNEY GENERAL, SECRETARY OF WAR AND
> SECRETARY OF STATE OF THE CONFEDERATE STATES
> OF AMERICA, QUEEN'S COUNSEL, LONDON

In life, as in death, he was elusive, vanishing behind his agreeableness, his cordiality, his perpetual smile. To blend into the culture—whether Southern or English—was bred into him, a matter of the Jewish Southerner's instinct for survival. The public man celebrated on two continents sought a kind of invisibility, not unlike the private man nobody knew. Shunning his past, choosing an almost secret grave, with calculated concealment, he nearly succeeded in remaining hidden from history.

Since his death, Benjamin's life has remained relatively unchallenged in the images that have come down through history. Although historians have routinely called him "the brains of the Confederacy," they know relatively little about him. Many historians of the Civil War have referred to him as President Davis's most loyal confidant, but Davis himself in his 1881 memoir of the Confederacy, referred to Benjamin in the most perfunctory fashion, mentioning his name only twice in the 1,500-page, two-volume work. That is especially odd if, as Varina Davis testified in a letter written in 1889, Benjamin spent almost every day in the office with her husband and was a central figure in events.

Benjamin's image comes down through history as "the dark prince of the Confederacy," a Mephistophelian Jewish figure. Stephen Vincent Benét in *John Brown's Body* reflected the contemporary view of him:

> Judah P. Benjamin, the dapper Jew,
> Seal-Sleek, black-eyed, lawyer and epicure,
> Able, well-hated, face alive with life,
> Looked round the council-chamber with the slight
> Perpetual smile he held before himself
> Continually like a silk-ribbed fan.
> Behind the fan, his quick, shrewd, fluid mind
> Weighed Gentiles in an old balance. . . .
>
> The mind behind the silk-ribbed fan
> Was a dark-prince, clothed in an Eastern stuff,
> Whole brown hands cupped about a crystal egg
> That filmed with colored cloud. The eyes stared,
> searching.
>
> "I am a Jew, What am I doing here?"

Pierce Butler in 1907 and Robert Douthat Meade in 1943 wrote the two standard biographies of Benjamin in the first half of the twentieth century, pulling together the thousands of Civil War orders and letters to friends and family in England, France, New Orleans, Charleston, and elsewhere that he was unable to destroy after the war. Butler interviewed Benjamin's contemporaries, including Varina Howell Davis. Meade spent twelve years traveling—researching diaries, memoirs, and papers and interviewing family members and friends. His book revealed Benjamin to have been a gifted tactician with a philosophical nature and an urbane manner, a gourmet, an inveterate gambler, and a man whom women adored. Still, it acknowledged a paucity of material.

Meade and Butler also drew from the research of the spare beginnings of an unfinished biography by Francis Lawley, the Richmond and Washington correspondent of the London *Times* during the war, who became, according to Meade, "devoted to Benjamin, who doubtless helped to color his vivid dispatches with a sympathetic attitude toward the Confederacy." Benjamin kept up a relationship with Lawley for the rest of his life, but only six pages survive of the biography Lawley planned, along with fewer than a dozen letters.

Meade and Butler were both Southern historians unfamiliar with American Jewish history. Judaism for them represented strange and unsteady territory that they, perhaps too deeply ingrained with the attitudes of their time, were not prepared to explore. Butler, in

1907, treated Jewishness as if it were an unpleasant component of his admiring portrait, one that he was reluctant but duty-bound to include briefly. He referred to Benjamin's father as "that *rara avis*, an unsuccessful Jew" and described Benjamin in England as "this wonderful little Jew from America." Meade, writing during that sensitive period of the rise of Nazi Germany just before World War II, was more circumspect, yet observed that "like so many of Jewish blood today, Benjamin tended to become cosmopolitan." In the late 1930s, no Southern historian could convey the harshness of the anti-Semitism surrounding Benjamin without seeming prejudiced himself. In a steady drumbeat of insults in Richmond, Confederate opponents would later refer to Benjamin as "Judas Iscariot Benjamin," and, according to Mary Boykin Chesnut's diary, "Mr. Davis's pet Jew." The Jewish aspect of Benjamin's life and career was not fully examined until it was taken up in a 1988 biography, almost fifty years after the publication of Meade's book.

Historians have pointed out ways in which Jews and Southerners were alike—stepchildren of an anguished history—and yet different. Whereas the Jewish search for a homeland contrasted with the Southerner's commitment to place, Southern defenders of the Confederacy often used Old Testament analogies in referring to themselves as "the chosen people" destined to survive and triumph against overwhelming odds. Benjamin is fascinating because of the extraordinary role he played in Southern history and the ways in which Jews and non-Jews reacted to him. He was the prototype of the contradictions in the Jewish Southerner and the stranger in the Confederate story, the Jew at the eye of the storm that was the Civil War.

Objectively, with so few Jews in the South at the time, it is astonishing that one should appear at the very center of Southern history. Benjamin himself avoided his Jewishness throughout his public career, though his enemies in the Southern press and in the halls of the Confederate Congress never let the South forget it. The virulence of the times required a symbolic figure as a catalyst for an ancient hostility and perhaps contributed to his intentional elusiveness. As Bertram Korn pointed out in *American Jewry and the Civil War*, the nation both North and South experienced "the greatest outpouring of Judeophobia in its history" during the Civil War, and Benjamin was a convenient target.

Benjamin achieved greater political power than any other Jew in the nineteenth century—perhaps even in all American history. Although he was a nonpracticing Jew, he never attempted to deny his faith and contemporary society treated him as Jewish. Benjamin thus must stand as a symbol of American democracy and its

"The gentleman will please remember that when his half-civilized ancestors were hunting the wild boar in the forests of Silesia, mine were the princes of the earth."

JUDAH P. BENJAMIN
IN REPLY TO A SENATOR

openness to religious minorities. In spite of the bigotry surrounding him, not only was he elected to the U.S. Senate and appointed to three high offices in the Confederacy, but he was also offered an appointment as the ambassador to Spain and a seat on the U.S. Supreme Court. The nineteenth-century emancipation of the Jews, which began in Europe after the French Revolution, was as great a shock to Jews as were the centuries of persecution that preceded it. Benjamin was the main beneficiary of that emancipation and its most visible symbol in America.

In the final years before the war, Benjamin was widely admired nationally in both Jewish and non-Jewish communities for his prestige as a Southern leader and his eloquence as an orator. His election to the U.S. Senate was a watershed for American Jews. Because of the war, he became the first Jewish political figure to be projected into the national consciousness. Jews in the South were especially proud of his achievement because he validated their legitimacy as Southerners. A pivotal figure in American Jewish history, Benjamin broke down the barriers of prejudice to achieve high office. After him, it was more acceptable for Jews to be elected to office and to aspire to service in the councils of national power.

— ELI N. EVANS

BLEEDING KANSAS

The term *Bleeding Kansas* arose from a series of events that followed the passage of the Kansas-Nebraska Act in 1854. The act invalidated the restrictions on the expansion of slavery in the Missouri Compromise of 1820, initiating the struggle to make Kansas a free or slave state under the doctrine of popular sovereignty advocated by Senator Stephen A. Douglas of Illinois.

The conflicts in territorial Kansas from 1854 to 1861 involved much more than the slavery question; also at work were the insatiable hunger for both public and Indian lands, the desire by political parties for patronage appointments, competition for town sites, selection of railroad routes, and at times outright banditry and personal plunder. Yet the struggle between free-state and proslavery elements was evident even in some of these contests, and it was this controversial question that attracted national attention, with newspaper editors and politicians often exaggerating its significance.

Competition between the North and South resulted in organized efforts to encourage migration to Kansas. The New England Emigrant Aid Company was formed in Massachusetts, and more limited efforts were made in the South with the encouragement of such leaders as Col. Jefferson Buford of Alabama. In the subsequent patterns of settlement, proslavery groups were concentrated in the towns of Atchison, Leavenworth, and Lecompton and free-state settlers in Lawrence, Topeka, Manhattan, and Osawatomie.

When the time came to organize a legislature, armed proslavery Missourians crossed the border on election day 1855 to cast some of the 4,968 illegal votes against 1,210 lawful ones. Consequently the legislature and the laws it passed were denounced as bogus. The free-state groups organized separately and held a constitutional convention in Topeka in October 1855, which proposed a constitution that would admit Kansas as a free state without benefit of an enabling act of Congress (usually required) but would provide for exclusion of free blacks and mulattoes from the state. Congress refused admission under this constitution.

A series of acts and threats of violence gave unhappy substance to the term *Bleeding Kansas*. Lawrence as the main seat of free-state activity became the locus of conflict in the so-called Wakarusa War in 1855, triggered when a proslavery settler killed his free-state neighbor over a boundary dispute. A military confrontation was prevented only by the intervention of the territorial governor, Wilson Shannon. A year later the city suffered an attack called the "sack of Lawrence" on May 21, led by the Douglas County proslavery sheriff Samuel J. Jones. Raiders destroyed two free-state presses and burned a hotel occupied by the New England Emigrant Aid Company and the home of the free-state leader Dr. Charles Robinson (later state governor). Upon receipt of this news John Brown, Sr., in the Osawatomie area set out to help protect Lawrence but turned back with his party of six men on May 24 to murder in especially brutal fashion five of his proslavery neighbors along Pottawatomie Creek. Two days before the sack of Lawrence, Senator Charles Sumner of Massachusetts had indicted the South in a speech, "The Crime against Kansas," which so provoked Congressman Preston Brooks of South Carolina that he beat Sumner with a cane on the floor of the Senate. The emerging Republican party thereupon coined the term "Bleeding Sumner."

The turmoil in Kansas had an impact upon the changing scene of political parties and the increased tension between the North and South. The declining Whig party sought to revive its fortunes by protesting the Kansas-Nebraska Act and its impact on the slavery issue. Its efforts between 1854 and 1856, however, were hampered by the increasing nativist opposition to Catholics and immigrants articulated by the Know-Nothing party. Attempts to fuse the interests of the two groups eventually failed. The new Republican party, which had tried to bring together one group of Whigs and Free-Soilers as early as the Jackson,

Michigan, convention in 1854 , had succeeded by 1856 in becoming the major anti-Democratic party in the North. The Know-Nothings, then, can be viewed as a bridge or an intermediate phase between Whiggism and the expansion of Republicanism. The Republican party exploited in the North the proslavery sack of Lawrence and the attack on Sumner by distributing nearly a million copies of the "Crime against Kansas" speech.

National attention, both North and South, continued to focus on Kansas with the Lecompton convention meeting in the territorial capital in 1857. Delegates, elected primarily by proslavery voters (free-state electors abstained), crafted a proslavery constitution. Because it was not voted on by all the people in the territory, Senator Douglas was convinced that the principle of popular sovereignty had been violated. He broke with President James Buchanan in his opposition to the document, thereby losing much of the support once given him by fire-eaters in the South and contributing to the split in the Democratic party in the presidential election of 1860. Congress then passed the English bill, which provided for a popular vote on the Lecompton constitution. But even with the bill's provisions for generous public land grants for Kansas if the constitution were ratified, the document was rejected in the territory by a vote of 1,788 for and 11,300 against. Admission of the state into the Union was then delayed until 1861.

The violence that had flared intermittently in Kansas had caused an estimated fifty to over one hundred deaths. As late as 1858 five free-state men were killed in the Marais des Cygnes massacre by proslavery partisans.

Yet by the time Southern states were seriously debating secession, the Kansas question had become significantly muted. During the controversy over the Lecompton constitution, Governor H. R. Runnels of Texas had asserted that the rejection of Kansas as a slave state would further threaten the South, and he urged military preparations to protect the rights and honor of his state. Governor Joseph E. Brown of Georgia was equally concerned and threatened to call a convention to determine the status of Georgia if Kansas were rejected. But a Georgia citizen writing to Alexander H. Stephens expressed a more widespread view that there was little if any chance of Kansas becoming a slave state and that nothing more should be made of the issue. Many had come to realize that geographical and economic factors discouraged the expansion of slavery into Kansas and had contributed to the fact that there were only two slaves in the territory in 1860. Among the many newspaper editorials concerning secession, the *Charleston Mercury* in February 1860 was one of the very few, if not the only

one, still arguing that the soil and climate of Kansas could sustain slavery. Other newspaper editors and political leaders turned their attention in 1860 and 1861 to different issues.

[*See also* Republican Party; Sumner, Caning of.]

— W. STITT ROBINSON

BLOCKADE

[*This entry is composed of three articles describing the Union strategy to prevent shipping through Southern ports and the Confederate efforts to combat that strategy:* An Overview; Blockade Running; *and* Blockade Runners. *For further discussion of the blockade and responses to it, see* Anglo-Confederate Purchasing; Charleston, South Carolina; Commerce Raiders; Erlanger Loan; New Orleans, Louisiana; New Plan; *Trent* Affair.]

AN OVERVIEW

The Union moved quickly to begin a blockade of the Confederacy. On April 19, 1861, Abraham Lincoln declared a blockade of the ports of South Carolina, Georgia, Alabama, Florida, Louisiana, and Texas, and eight days later extended it to Virginia and North Carolina. This was not intended to be a paper blockade. The object was to station enough ships to block entrance to or departure from Southern ports in order to prevent the South's obtaining essential war materials, to deny it the ability to export its cotton, and to deter Southern privateers and raiders from harassing Union shipping. But it also presented both diplomatic and physical problems for the North. Since the early years of the American Revolution, freedom of the seas and the defense of neutral rights had been an essential ingredient in American foreign policy. In pursuing its blockade of the Southern states, the North wished at the same time to avoid precedents that would hamper its own trade during future European wars. The attitude of Great Britain was helpful in achieving this objective, for the British did not want to insist on a freedom to trade that might be used against them in the future.

To close some 3,500 miles of coastline, the North had fewer than fifty ships in commission at the beginning of the war. Although the temporary Confederate policy of withholding cotton exports in an attempt to influence the British worked to the advantage of the blockaders, the Union navy had too few vessels to mount an effective blockade. So the North bought or chartered civilian vessels to fill immediate needs until more ships could be built. By the latter part of the war, nearly five hundred vessels were taking part in the operation.

As the gateway to the Mississippi valley and the country's second leading port, New Orleans early on felt squeezed by the Union blockade.

PAGE 400

B

BLOCKADE

An Overview

During the first months, blockade runners found it comparatively simple to slip into Southern ports, but the blockade quickly became more effective. As direct entry into Southern ports from Europe became more difficult, goods intended for the Confederacy were sent on neutral vessels to Nassau in the Bahamas, Bermuda, or Havana. There they were transferred to Southern blockade runners who brought in both essential war materials and luxuries.

Dramatizing the possibilities for evading the blockade was the South's announcement in the fall of 1861 that James M. Mason and John Slidell, who were to represent the Confederacy in England and France, would proceed to Europe on a Confederate raider after running the blockade at Charleston. The Union strengthened its blockade off the port, but the two envoys were able to reach Havana on a chartered vessel. From there they attempted to travel to St. Thomas on the English ship *Trent*. *Trent* was stopped by a Union ship, and Mason and Slidell were taken to the North. For a few weeks there was fear of open conflict with England, but the crisis was defused. Neither side wanted war. American Secretary of State William H. Seward indicated that the action had not been authorized by the American government, the stern British protest stopped short of an ultimatum, and the North released the Southern emissaries.

The difficulty of blockading the numerous ports and inlets of the Confederacy and the necessity for better positioned Union bases persuaded the Union Navy Strategy Board that the blockade would have to be tightened by the use of amphibious operations to seize key inlets and provide new bases for Union vessels. The first of these operations was intended to make the blockade of Virginia more efficient. Union ships in the Chesapeake were being evaded by shallow draft vessels that connected Richmond and Norfolk by canal with the sounds of Virginia and North Carolina. Blockade runners made extensive use of this route in the early months of the war. But in late August 1861, a Union force attacked forts guarding Hatteras Inlet and captured Forts Clark and Hatteras. The latter was converted into a Union base.

An advantage for Confederate blockade runners was the distance of the Union bases at Hampton Roads and Key West from many of the ports and inlets that had to be blockaded. The Atlantic Blockading Squadron, based in Hampton Roads, found it difficult to police the whole area, and in the early fall of 1861 it was divided into northern and southern sections. Lincoln and his cabinet also accepted a proposal, presented by Secretary of the Navy Gideon Welles, for an attack on Port Royal. Situated between Charleston and Savannah, Port Royal possessed a fine natural harbor, capable of serving all the needs of the blockaders. In early November, a large Union force of some twelve thousand troops and numerous ships occupied Port Royal after the Confederates abandoned its defending forts. This led to the Union control of a whole string of sea islands and made possible further amphibious operations along the south Atlantic coast.

In the winter of 1861–1862, the Union tried again to make blockade evasion more difficult in the North Carolina –Virginia region. The North Carolina sounds continued to present great opportunities for blockade runners, and early in the new year the Union sent some 11,500 men to attack Roanoke Island. They hoped to capture the island and to move against the towns on Albemarle Sound to disrupt Confederate canal and rail communication. Not all the objects were attained, but Roanoke Island was taken and the noose around the South was drawn a little tighter.

In an effort to break the tightening cord, the Confederacy in March 1862 sent its ironclad CSS *Virginia* (previously the USS *Merrimack*) to try to break the Union blockade at Hampton Roads. *Merrimack* had been partially burned and scuttled by Union forces when Norfolk was taken by the Confederates early in the war. The Confederates had rebuilt it as an ironclad. The Union knew of this potential threat and had built its own ironclad—*Monitor*—to counter it. In trying to break the blockade, *Virginia* at first had some success, but *Monitor* fought it to a standoff, which left the blockade intact. The Confederacy experimented with ironclads and submarines throughout the war, but the North had the resources to counter all such efforts to break the blockade. The submarine CSS *H. L. Hunley* did succeed in sinking a blockading vessel off Charleston in February 1864 but did not return from the engagement.

In the first year of the war the Union had difficulty in mounting an effective blockade of the ports along the Confederate coastline in the Gulf of Mexico. Ultimately, the Union blockade in that region came to depend heavily on amphibious operations. Both New Orleans and Mobile provided great opportunities for Southern blockade runners. Of the two, New Orleans presented somewhat fewer problems for direct assault, and the Union determined to capture this vital Southern port. Preliminary footholds were gained in the fall of 1861, but the main attack was launched early the next year. In April, Flag Officer David G. Farragut combined forces with Commdr. David D. Porter and Gen. Benjamin Butler to capture the city, thereby delivering a powerful blow to Confederate trade. Mobile was too heavily defended to be taken, but Union forces put it under an increasingly stringent blockade. The North also launched a series of attacks against Texas ports.

In the early months of the war, Confederate privateers had caused considerable havoc to Union commerce, but as the blockade tightened in 1862 and 1863, and as neutrals refused to accept Confederate prizes in their ports, the main assault on Union merchant ships was launched by Confederate government raiders. From time to time these succeeded in slipping into Confederate ports. Also, blockade runners continued to bring in much needed supplies, usually sailing from neutral ports in the Caribbean.

A major problem experienced by the Confederacy was that of private owners of blockade runners seeking greater profits by importing scarce luxury goods rather than the necessities needed by Southern armies. The government first urged private blockade runners to carry military supplies, then made use of government-owned ships, and finally, in 1864 decreed that only necessary articles could be imported. Private owners were also ordered to provide half of the cargo space in their blockade runners for use by the Confederate government. Blockade runners continued to operate until the end of the war, but they never met all the needs of Southern armies.

In its efforts to prevent the activities of the blockade runners, the Union was prepared to interpret its maritime rights in ways that it had challenged in earlier years. The Union defended the doctrine of "continuous voyage," which had been used against the United States by Great Britain during the Napoleonic Wars. This doctrine allowed the seizure of ships trading between neutral ports if the cargo was ultimately destined for a blockaded port or, in the case of a ship carrying contraband, if it was destined for any port in enemy territory. American courts upheld the seizure of British ships destined for neutral ports when the cargo was ultimately intended for the Confederacy. In the *Peterhoff* case this doctrine was extended even to goods that were destined to come into the Confederacy overland from the Mexican port of Matamoros. (The Mexican-Texas border was used for widespread evasion of the blockade.)

The situation of both neutrals and Confederate blockade runners became more precarious after September 1862 when the Union Navy Department created a West India Squadron, with the intention of both protecting Union ships from Confederate cruisers and reducing the activities of blockade runners.

In the last two years of the war, evasion of the Union blockade became much more difficult, although runners were still able to enter some of the major Southern ports. Charleston was a heavily used point of entry until September 1863 when Union forces captured Fort Wagner. The city, however, was able to resist attack from the sea and remained in Confederate hands until 1865.

Mobile was another port that presented major problems for Union blockaders; it possessed formidable defenses against amphibious operations. Not until August 1864 did Farragut have the strength necessary to take the Mobile Bay forts, when he pressed ahead relentlessly with his famous cry, "Damn the torpedoes." Mobile itself was not occupied until the very end of the war, but the capture of the forts effectively closed the port to Confederate vessels.

By 1864 Wilmington, North Carolina, offered the most opportunities for blockade runners. It was the vital supply port for Confederate armies in Virginia and was also a port through which the South contin-

The Crescent City's business community, a substantial element of which hailed from the Northeast, was tugged toward Unionism by trade and shipping connections.

PAGE 399

The first Federal attack on Charleston came in June 1862 when six thousand troops landed southeast of the city; casualties were heavy on both sides, and the Union forces retreated.

PAGE 96

ued to export cotton. Access to the port by way of the Cape Fear River was defended primarily by Forts Fisher and Caswell. Until these were taken the port could not be closed. A strong Union attack on Wilmington's defenses failed in December 1864, but in January 1865 a large fleet and some eight thousand troops took Fort Fisher and closed the last major gap in the Union blockade.

The Union, however, never completely sealed the coastline of the Confederacy. Even in the last year of the war, half of the blockade runners were getting through. The Union blockade nevertheless was a success. Southern imports and exports dropped dramatically during the war. This was at a time when the Confederacy desperately needed increased imports to supply its armies and maximum sales of cotton to finance its huge war effort. Largely because of the Union blockade, Southern armies were undersupplied and Southern finances became increasingly chaotic as the war progressed. The South's lack of naval power allowed the North to pursue a relentless war of attrition.

— REGINALD HORSMAN

BLOCKADE RUNNING

Throughout the Civil War, munitions, uniform material, leather, food, and other essential military and civilian goods poured into the Confederacy on board vessels known as blockade runners. These vessels were a vital element in the Confederate supply system. Before the war ended, blockade running would be sustaining the Southern armies, but at the beginning of the conflict few realized the tremendous volume of trade that would eventually exist between the Confederacy and the outside world.

In early 1861, the head of the Confederate Ordnance Bureau, Col. Josiah Gorgas, had three sources of supplies for the Confederate armed forces: goods on hand, home production, and imports. By using the arms seized in Federal arsenals, Gorgas had enough weapons and supplies to outfit the 100,000 men called out by President Jefferson Davis. Unlike others in the South, Gorgas did not believe that the war would be a quick one, and he knew that his on-hand stocks of munitions would soon disappear. In time, he planned to establish munition plants that would make the new nation self-sustaining, but Gorgas realized that until the factories could be completed, certain "articles of prime necessity" would have to be imported from Europe. Imports were supposed to be only a stopgap measure, something to fill the void between the depletion of existing stocks and the beginning of home production. But the Confederates were never able to meet their needs with domestic industry,

and the flow of imports grew until it eventually became the most important element in the Confederate supply system.

In April 1861, in order to gain foreign supplies, Gorgas dispatched Capt. Caleb Huse to Great Britain to serve as a purchasing agent. Huse was later joined by Maj. Edward C. Anderson, and together they began work with Comdr. James Dunwoody Bulloch, the purchasing agent for the Navy Department. To provide funds for their agents the Confederacy contracted with the Charleston firm of John Fraser and Company, who sent bills of exchange to its Liverpool office of Fraser, Trenholm, and Company, from which cash was provided to the War Department's European officials. But even with the funds, the agents still faced two problems: the Confederacy's determination to follow a foreign policy known as "King Cotton," and the Federal blockade.

KING COTTON. The blockade of the Southern coast had been established shortly after the firing on Fort Sumter. Though in the beginning it was enforced by only a handful of vessels and its legality was questioned, it was recognized by the major European powers. At the same time, the British monarch, Queen Victoria, called upon her subjects to avoid giving assistance to either side.

Though disappointed by the European response, the Southerners were not worried because they believed that King Cotton would protect their new nation. King Cotton was an economic and political theory based on the coercive power of Southern cotton. The British textile industry imported 80 percent of the South's cotton. Without the cotton, the theory held, the industry would fail, and the entire economic fabric of Great Britain would collapse. In order to avoid that disaster, the British would have to intervene in the war on the South's side.

It was for this reason that during the summer of 1861, local politicians, merchants, newspapermen, and planters banded together to enforce an embargo keeping the South's cotton at home. Though never sanctioned by the government, the embargo was unofficially approved by Davis and his advisers, who felt it would bring Great Britain into the war. At the same time, in order to aid the financially disrupted planters, the Confederate government purchased over 400,000 bales of cotton. Initially viewed as a white elephant, this cotton eventually played an important role in the blockade-running system.

Though designed to bring the British into the war, the embargo also had the side effect of depriving Anderson, Huse, and Bulloch of a means to transport supplies. No vessels were coming from the South, and for the moment, British shippers were reluctant to go against the wishes of their queen or the guns of the

Union navy. For the moment the purchasing agents were stymied, and for assistance they turned to the firm of Fraser, Trenholm, and Company, the Confederacy's European financial agents, for help in shipping their goods.

Fraser, Trenholm, and Company was a branch of the Charleston-based John Fraser and Company. Both were directed by George Alfred Trenholm. From his Charleston office Trenholm backed the cotton embargo, but at the same time allowed his partner in Liverpool, Charles K. Prioleau, to outfit a steamer to run the blockade. The vessel readied by Prioleau was the screw steamer *Bermuda*, and the voyage was organized as a private commercial venture. Prioleau agreed to sell cargo space to Anderson and Huse.

Though the agents felt the cost to be high, they also realized that this was their best opportunity to deliver their goods. They met Prioleau's price and on September 18, 1861, after an uneventful voyage, *Bermuda* successfully arrived at Savannah, Georgia, becoming the first steam blockade runner to reach the South. After landing its cargo, *Bermuda* returned to Liverpool with over two thousand bales of cotton. Profits were tremendous, and this example soon caused other firms to organize blockade-running ventures. Any hesitation brought on by the blockade or Queen Victoria's proclamation soon disappeared in the quest for money.

Although *Bermuda*'s success inspired additional blockade-running companies, it did little to relieve the problems confronting the Confederate purchasing agents. They still had no government-owned vessels to carry their munitions, and private firms were escalating their rates on government cargoes. Anderson, the senior agent, decided that it was in the best interest of the Confederacy to cut out the middleman and purchase a steamer. With financial help from the Navy Department agents, the steamer *Fingal* was obtained and sent through the blockade, arriving at Savannah in mid-November 1861. Equipment from the vessel was enough to outfit ten regiments. As Bulloch stated, the ship carried "the greatest military cargo ever imported into the Confederacy."

Besides the armaments, *Fingal* also carried Anderson and Bulloch. Anderson went on to Richmond where he pushed the concept of government-owned-and-operated blockade runners, but he found no backers. Neither the War Department nor the Navy Department would consider any involvement with blockade running. Officials preferred to leave it in the hands of private shippers while waiting for British intervention. Disillusioned with the results of his visit, Anderson returned to

WILMINGTON, NORTH CAROLINA
The Hole in the Blockade

During the war Wilmington served as the port not only for the Ordnance Bureau vessels but for all east-coast blockade runners operating under contracts with the Confederacy. It was also used by the vessels owned by the states of North Carolina, Virginia, and Georgia, as well as private companies. During the war numerous Confederate agents passed through Wilmington on their missions, including Rose O'Neal Greenhow, who drowned when her blockade runner, *Condor*, ran aground near New Inlet on September 30, 1864. She was later buried in Wilmington with full military honors.

During 1864, the blockade-running trade at Wilmington greatly increased as the South's demand for overseas goods grew. Though luxury items continued to arrive, the Confederacy placed tighter restrictions on the blockade runners, which resulted in the importation of vast amounts of military goods. Besides munitions, Wilmington was also the receiving point for the Army of Northern Virginia's meat rations. Gen. Robert E. Lee, knowing the reliance of his army on the supplies coming into Wilmington, reported that should the port fall, he would be unable to maintain his troops.

Throughout the war the North attempted to keep Wilmington under a tight blockade, but the port's widely spaced entrances forced the Union navy to split its warships into two squadrons that could not support each other. This division of strength coupled with the power of the Confederate forts stymied any effective blockade. Though active operations against Wilmington had been considered as early as the summer of 1862, the North was unable to put together a combined army and navy expedition against Fort Fisher until December 1864. Two assaults were made against the fort, and it, along with Whiting and Lamb, was captured on January 15, 1865.

The fall of Fort Fisher ended Wilmington's role as a blockade-running port and effectively cut the Confederacy's lifeline to Europe. Though the Confederates, under Gen. Braxton Bragg, continued to resist Northern advances against Wilmington for another month, the city's fate as well as that of the Confederacy was sealed, and on February 22, 1865, while a rear guard destroyed government property and records, Bragg evacuated Wilmington. On March 14, in order to show Wilmington's new loyalty and encourage business, Mayor Dawson organized a mass celebration called the Grand Rally, which celebrated the return of Wilmington to Federal control.

— STEPHEN R. WISE

Private blockade runners were seeking greater profits by importing scarce luxury goods rather than the necessities needed by the armies.

PAGE 57

Savannah, where he served out the war as an artillery officer.

While Anderson began working on Savannah's defenses, Huse continued to purchase supplies in Europe, and since there were still no Southern vessels arriving in Great Britain, he contracted with local firms to carry the goods into the Confederacy. Huse's supplies arrived by two methods. He contracted for direct delivery to the South by British shippers, or he sent cargoes to Havana, Cuba, or Nassau, Bahamas, where they were transferred to steamers for the final run through the blockade. The latter system of transshipping proved more popular, and, by early 1862, vessels owned by British blockade-running companies and Trenholm's firms were operating between Havana and Nassau and the Confederacy. For their services, the private shippers charged the government extremely high rates, which Huse and other Southern agents had to meet.

Assisting Huse were Confederate consuls Charles J. Helm in Havana and Louis Heyliger in Nassau. Besides serving as government representatives, the two consuls had the crucial responsibility of making sure that cargoes received from Huse were properly transshipped. Both performed admirably, but because of the early capture of New Orleans, Heyliger soon found himself overseeing the bulk of the supplies coming from Great Britain.

During the spring and summer of 1862, Heyliger worked with private shippers to deliver vital munitions. The task posed problems. Even though Heyliger paid extraordinary fees for cargo space, he found that many companies refused to work with him, preferring instead to carry more profitable civilian goods rather than the bulky and often dangerous munitions. The best deals were made with Trenholm's firms, who gave the government preferred rates, though their patriotism never cut too deeply into their profit margin.

Although Trenholm's firms were on occasion willing to offer special deals to the Confederacy, British manufacturers cautiously regulated their involvement with Huse, being careful not to overextend their credit. By the end of 1862, the Confederate purchasing agent was £900,000 in debt and his means of payment seemed at an end. The ever-increasing premiums on bills of exchange soon ended their use and Huse had nearly expended his supply of specie. Without some form of exchange, Huse's operations would collapse. Then the Confederacy discovered a new use for King Cotton.

COTTON BONDS. When the South's cotton embargo failed to bring Great Britain into the war, many thought that the hundreds of thousands of cotton bales purchased by the government at the start of the war would become the predicted white elephant, but this was not the case. Cotton, so long an instrument of foreign policy, was now converted to a medium of exchange.

Following the lead of the Navy Department, the government began to use cotton to finance its overseas ventures. Employing the cotton purchased early in the war, the Confederacy issued a variety of cotton bonds. There were two ways to make a profit off the bonds: one could receive interest and redeem the bond at face value after a set length of time, or the holder could bring the bond to the Confederacy and receive cotton.

It was the latter method that made the bonds so popular. Cotton could be obtained in the South at about ten cents a pound and then sold in Great Britain for forty-eight cents a pound, thus making a cotton bale purchased for $50 in Charleston worth nearly $250 on the Liverpool market. There was a wide variety of bonds, or as they were sometimes called, certificates. Even some of the Southern states, such as Georgia and North Carolina, issued them and used them to sponsor their own blockade-running ventures.

The use of the bonds allowed the Confederacy to pay off Huse's debt and provide him with new funds and credit for additional supplies. They were the basis for contracts between the South and its suppliers and were also used to finance the purchase and construction of blockade runners and warships. Private blockade-running ventures used them to guarantee outgoing cargoes for their steamers, because with the bonds and the right type of vessels, blockade running could be an extremely profitable business.

Using the bonds, many War Department bureaus, such as the Subsistence, Quartermaster, and Medical bureaus, withdrew their business from Huse and entered into one-sided partnerships with blockade-running companies—and there was never any shortage of such companies. The largest and most successful were the two companies operated by George Trenholm. Together his firms operated over thirty blockade runners and cargo vessels and grossed millions of dollars, which were reinvested in ships, cargoes, real estate, and Confederate bonds.

Other important firms included the Importing and Exporting Company of South Carolina, the Chicora Importing and Exporting Company, and the Charleston Importing and Exporting Company. These Charleston-based companies paid handsome dividends to their investors. Among the prominent British companies were the highly successful Anglo-Confederate Trading Company and the less lucrative Collie and Company. All these firms delivered civilian and military goods to the Confederacy. The civilian goods were immensely profitable since they were sold at outrageous wartime prices that contributed to inflation throughout the South.

The delivery of military goods also gave a good return, as the firms made extremely favorable contracts with the various War Department bureaus. One bargain, struck between the Confederacy and Crenshaw and Collie and Company, had the government paying 75 percent of all expenses plus the commission fees for the purchasing of ships and supplies, while allowing its civilian partners to use one-quarter of the cargo space for privately owned goods. Though a lopsided venture, the contract was similar to many issued during the war. Because of the need for supplies, most government agencies felt that a bad contract was better than no contract.

THE ORDNANCE BUREAU. The one notable exception to this arrangement was Gorgas's Ordnance Bureau. Like Anderson, Gorgas realized the advantage in using government-owned-and-operated vessels. Instead of making contracts with blockade-running firms, Gorgas had his agents purchase steamers in Great Britain. A depot headed by Maj. Norman S. Walker was established in St. George, Bermuda; from there the goods purchased and shipped by Huse were transferred to Ordnance Bureau steamers and sent to Wilmington, North Carolina, where they were met by Capt. James Sexias.

The Ordnance Bureau's blockade-running operation was under the control of Gorgas's brother-in-law, Maj. Thomas L. Bayne. Bayne supervised not only the landing and distribution of incoming cargo but also the purchasing and loading of government cotton. Initially Bayne's section worked out of Wilmington, but before the war ended, his command was upgraded to bureau status with agents at Charleston, Mobile, and St. Marks, Florida.

The line established by Gorgas and operated by Bayne employed five vessels. The most successful were *Cornubia, Robert E. Lee,* and *Eugenie,* captained by the furloughed Confederate naval officers Richard N. Gayle, John Wilkinson, and Joseph Fry, respectively. A typical cargo consisted of cases of Enfield rifles, cartridges, leather, knapsacks, stationery, sewing thread, lead, saltpeter, and uniform cloth. Though in service only from November 1862 to November 1863, Gorgas's vessels made forty-seven runs through the blockade. They delivered, among other things, nearly 100,000 Enfield rifles, tens of thousands of cartridges, and thousands of pounds of lead and saltpeter, all basic military necessities needed to keep the Confederate army alive.

The vessels operated by Gorgas were products of an ongoing maritime revolution brought about by blockade running. Steam warships had ended the days of sailing ships, and to counter their pursuers, the blockade runners also turned to steam engines. By the time the war ended, blockade running had helped launch a new generation of steam vessels, including the first successful commercial use of twin-screw-propeller ves-sels. The class of steamer that started the revolution was that found in the United Kingdom's coastal and cross-channel passenger trade, known as Clyde steamers. These were later replaced by iron- and steel-hulled vessels built exclusively for blockade running. Designed to carry an immense amount of cargo, these ships could make a profit of $100,000 on a single voyage from the Confederacy.

BLOCKADE-RUNNING ROUTES. The new vessels were needed. By December 1864, all of Gorgas's ships had been lost. At first the Confederate government did not replace them, but instead increased their reliance on private vessels. Operating out of Havana, Nassau, and Bermuda, the steamers delivered their cargoes to Charleston and Wilmington on the east coast and Mobile and Galveston in the Gulf of Mexico.

In the Gulf, Mobile grew in importance as an importation site for government supplies. From there supplies were sent to Selma and other western depots for distribution or use in munition plants. Down the coast, Confederate cargoes delivered to Galveston rarely crossed the Mississippi River. Logistics coupled with political instability in Mexico kept Texas from ever becoming a major landing site. What did come in remained in the Trans-Mississippi Department for use by the local military.

The Confederacy directed the majority of its shipments to Charleston and Wilmington where the goods could be easily transported to depots, factories, and armies. The most popular routes were from Nassau to Charleston and Bermuda to Wilmington. After the attack on Charleston during the summer of 1863, the bulk of the Nassau trade shifted to Wilmington, making it the South's main port of entry and one of the most strategic points in the Confederacy.

The ships carrying supplies to the east coast had a very high success rate. During the war, runners were successful on over 75 percent of their runs, and most of the time the ships passed in and out unseen by the blockaders. The runners had the advantages of speed and surprise over their adversaries. Rarely would a cannon shell find its mark and even then the Union warships did not try to sink the blockade runners; when captured, most blockade vessels were taken north, condemned at prize courts, and sold with their cargoes at auction. The money was divided among the captors, thus making it far more advantageous for Northern crews to capture than to sink the runners.

CONFEDERATE REGULATION OF BLOCKADE RUNNING. Because of the high success rate and resulting profits, private companies dominated the trade until August 1863, when the Confederate government was finally forced to take an active hand in blockade running. Defeats at Gettysburg and Vicksburg had resulted in an increased demand for

The Confederate government tried to convince the Europeans that the Federal blockade was ineffective and illegal.

PAGE 158

The Confederacy failed to acknowledge that Great Britain, as the world's foremost naval power, would desire to let stand any blockade.

PAGE 158

It was not in the vested interests of the neutral powers, particularly Great Britain, to denounce the blockade.

PAGE 158

During the fall of 1862, financial agent Colin J. McRae purchased cotton throughout the South and arranged for its shipment through the blockade to European markets.

supplies and had dealt a severe blow to the Southern bond market, shattering the Confederacy's overseas finances. In order to revive the South's credit and gain new supplies, Secretary of War James A. Seddon turned to an expanded use of cotton. He ordered his commanders at Wilmington, Charleston, and Mobile to requisition cargo space for the shipment of government cotton. The operators of the blockade runners were paid a fair rate for the space, and any refusal would result in their vessels being seized.

This was only the beginning of Seddon's plans. In March 1864 his initial instructions were tightened and, with presidential approval, passed into law. The stricter regulations allowed the Confederacy to take up to 50 percent of a vessel's outgoing and incoming cargo space. This guaranteed that the South would be able to export its cotton to pay for European goods and would have stowage space for incoming supplies. At the same time Gorgas's bureau was expanded to supervise all government overseas shipping. In Europe, operations were consolidated under Colin J. McRae, who, in effect, became the Confederacy's European secretary of the treasury.

The unheralded McRae did a remarkable job in establishing a centralized system in Europe. He also revived Anderson's and Gorgas's plan for a line of Confederate-owned blockade runners. He ordered fourteen vessels in Great Britain and planned eventually to remove all private operators from the business of carrying government supplies.

McRae was soon joined by another official who also realized the importance of government-sponsored blockade running. During the summer of 1864, the Confederacy called upon the director of the largest blockade-running operation, George Alfred Trenholm, to become secretary of the treasury. Trenholm accepted the position, resigned from his companies, and set to work running the government's overseas operations. He promulgated additional, stricter regulations and made plans for the government's fourteen blockade runners being built in Great Britain. Only two of these specialized vessels, however, saw Confederate service before the war ended.

Even without these super–blockade runners, the flow of supplies continued. Under Trenholm's and McRae's guidance the Confederacy received more munitions during their tenure than at any time earlier, but the men were fighting a losing battle. The South, battered by Northern armies and suffering massive desertions from its own ranks, was running out of men. Nor could it keep its vital ports open. In August 1864 Mobile was captured; Wilmington was closed in early January 1865; and a month later Charleston was evacuated. The fall of these harbors cut the Confederacy's lifeline.

Because of the determined work of a few relatively unknown individuals, the economic power of cotton, and specialized steamers, the Confederate military was never without the means to fight. By Confederate records the South imported during the war 60 percent of its arms, 30 percent of its lead for bullets, 75 percent of the army's saltpeter, and nearly all its paper for cartridges. The majority of cloth for uniforms and leather for shoes and accoutrements came through the blockade, as well as huge amounts of metals, chemicals, and medicine. During the last months of the war, the Army of Northern Virginia received the bulk of its food via blockade runners. Though the lifeline was fragile and tenuous, it worked until the ports were captured. Defeat did not come from lack of materials. In fact, by the end of the war, the South had more munitions and goods than men; manpower was the one thing the blockade runners could not supply.

— STEPHEN R. WISE

BLOCKADE RUNNERS

A blockade runner was any vessel that challenged the U.S. Navy's blockade of the Confederate coastline. Though a few Confederate warships such as *Nashville, Sumter,* and *Florida* and some privateers ran the blockade, the vast majority were cargo vessels that carried civilian and military supplies into the South and transported cotton to neutral ports. The motivating factor behind these ships was the profit derived from the sale of their cargoes.

Men served as captains of blockade runners for a variety of reasons. Such Southerners as Thomas Lockwood, Robert Lockwood, James Carlin, Louis Coxetter, and Robert Smith were motivated by both patriotism and the desire for profits. Others such as naval officers John Wilkinson, John Newland Maffitt, Joseph Fry, and Richard N. Gayle operated blockade runners under orders from the Confederate government. British citizens Joannes Wyllie, Johnathon Steele, Augustus Charles Hobart-Hampden, and the Irishman William Ryan ran blockade runners for adventure and profit. Whatever their motive, their skills were an important factor in a vessel's success or failure.

At the start of the war, many shipowners attempted to use sailing vessels, but quickly realized that they would not do. Sailing ships large enough to carry a profitable amount of cargo were easy marks for steam warships, and the small brigs, schooners, and sloops that could slip in and out of harbors and sounds had insufficient cargo capacity. After June of 1862, sailing ship blockade runners virtually disappeared along the east coast. They were used somewhat more often in the Gulf of Mexico, where many operated along the Texas coast; but supplies from east of the Mississippi River rarely crossed the river and imports coming into Texas had no impact on the war's major theaters.

To counter their steam-powered pursuers, the blockade runners turned to steam engines. Early in the war, before the blockade tightened, any steamer had a good chance of reaching a Southern port, and the first vessels to run the blockade were large, deeply laden ships such as the propeller-driven *Bermuda* and *Fingal.* Both were conventional merchantmen with large cargo capacities, but they had short careers because their deep drafts restricted them to main ship channels where eventual capture was inevitable. By the spring of 1862, the large steamers that had escaped capture were relegated to ferrying goods between Great Britain and Nassau, Bermuda, and Havana. From these ports a more elusive style of blockade runner was employed in order to avoid the Federal warships.

The steamship type that first began transshipping cargoes to and from the Confederacy were American-built coastal packets. These paddlewheel vessels were built with a low freeboard which, coupled with a wide beam, gave the steamers a shallow draft. They were sturdy and well adapted to negotiating the shallow southern coastline. Once their staterooms were removed, the vessels could carry between two hundred and five hundred bales of cotton.

Along the east coast such ships as *Gordon, Cecile,* and *Kate* became prominent blockade runners. *Kate,* a 477-ton packet measuring 165 feet by 29 feet, 10 inch-es by 10 feet, 4 inches, was successfully guided through the blockade twenty times by Capt. Thomas Lockwood. In the Gulf the New Orleans-based vessels *Matagorda* and *William G. Hewes* also became renowned blockade runners under the names *Alice* and *Ella and Annie.* Before its capture in 1864 off Mobile, *Alice,* commanded by Robert Smith, made eighteen trips through the blockade.

Though many packets were successful blockade runners, investors continued to seek out ships that could turn an even greater profit, and by early 1862, operators began using a style of paddlewheel steamer that had been developed for the United Kingdom's coastal and cross-channel passenger trade. Since many were built in and around Glasgow on the Clyde River, the ships were called Clyde steamers. Usually built with an iron hull, they were rugged, fast, and maneuverable and had a shallow draft and large cargo capacity that allowed them to carry from five hundred to one thousand bales of cotton. In a short time they became the mainstay of blockade running.

The first Clyde steamer to begin blockade running was *Herald,* a 446-ton iron-hulled sidewheeler that made 24 trips through the blockade before being destroyed off Wilmington. In all, over 80 Clyde steamers were converted to blockade runners. Among their ranks were the war's top runners, including the most

BLOCKADE RUNNERS: A CROSS SECTION

Name	Builder/Place of Construction	Hull and Propulsion/ Dimensions	Tonnage	Successful Runs/ Point of Entry	Fate
Annie	John and William Dudgeon London 1863	iron, twin-screws, 170′ × 23′4″ × 13′4″	687 gross tons	13 runs Wilmington	captured 11/1/64
Denbigh	Laird and Sons, Birkenhead, England	iron, paddlewheel 182′ × 22′ × 8′7″≤	250 gross tons	26 runs Mobile and Galveston	destroyed 5/23/65
Herald	John Reid and Company Port Glasgow, Scotland, 1860	iron, paddlewheel 221.6′ × 22′ × 10.4′	446 gross tons	24 runs Charleston and Wilmington	destroyed 11/18/62
Kate	Samuel Sneden Greenpoint, NY	wood, paddlewheel 165′ × 29′10″ × 10′4″	477 burden tons	20 runs Charleston and Wilmington	destroyed 11/19/62
Margaret and Jessie	Robert Napier & Sons, Glasgow, Scotland 1858	wood, paddlewheel 205′ × 26′ × 14′	950 burden tons	18 runs Charleston and Wilmington	captured 11/5/63
Matagorda	Harlan and Hollingsworth Wilmington, Del., 1858	iron, paddlewheel 220′ × 30′ × 10.5′	1250 gross tons	18 runs Mobile and Galveston	captured 9/10/64
Syren	Builder not listed Greenwich, Kent, England 1863	?, paddlewheel 169.5′ × 24′ × 15.5′	475 burden tons	33 runs Wilmington and Charleston	captured 2/18/65

*More than three-
fourths of the
cotton used in the
textile industries
of England
and France
came from the
American South.*

PAGE 157

successful, *Syren,* which made 33 trips in and out of Wilmington and Charleston. It was followed by *Denbigh* with 26 runs from Havana to Mobile and Galveston. Other ships of this class included *Alice,* with 25 trips; *Fannie,* with 20 trips; and the Confederate Ordnance Bureau's *Cornubia,* with 18 trips. Another well-known ship was *Margaret and Jessie,* which also made 18 trips and was considered the war's fastest blockade runner.

Although these ships were very successful, business interests demanded still better, and soon British dockyards were turning out ships built specifically for running the blockade. The first was *Banshee,* a steel-hulled 533-ton sidewheeler that measured 214 feet by 20 feet by 8 feet. In May 1863, it became the first steel-hulled vessel to cross the Atlantic Ocean. Then, under the command of Johnathon Steele, it became a successful blockade runner operating primarily between Nassau and Wilmington.

At first these ships were designed simply to meet the trade's basic requirements, but soon, seeking to increase profits, builders began to experiment with design and construction techniques, resulting in a revolution in shipbuilding. Engines were placed so that they were surrounded by coal bunkers to protect them from enemy shot. Many of the new runners were built of steel and designed with rounded deck structures, underwater blow-off pipes, hinged masts, and telescoping smokestacks. Builders experimented with paint schemes to camouflage the runners from enemy warships and increased engine size as well as the size and number of boilers. For additional speed, vessels were made longer with extremely narrow beams. Because of their design, the runners contained more cargo space than contemporary merchant ships.

The first generation of these super–blockade runners often suffered from many engineering and mechanical problems. *Banshee,* with steel plates of only $1/8$ inch and $3/16$ inch, leaked badly, and others like the *Flamingo* spent more time being repaired than running the blockade. But builders soon overcame these problems and by the end of the war were producing such vessels as *Chicora, Lucy,* and *Fox,* which between them made fifty-two trips through the blockade without being captured. The epitome of the final generation of runners was *Colonel Lamb,* which was partially designed by Capt. Thomas Lockwood, the war's most successful blockade-running captain and the acknowledged "father of the trade." The 1,788-ton *Colonel Lamb* was the finest vessel built for blockade running. It measured 281 feet by 36 feet by 15.5 feet and could carry 2,000 bales of cotton, which translated into a profit of $100,000 on a single voyage from the Confederacy.

Though most blockade runners were sidewheelers, the war also saw the first successful commercial use of twin-screw-propeller steamers. Some fourteen of these novel vessels attempted to run the blockade, the most successful being *Annie,* which made thirteen trips. The twin screws proved to be sturdy, reliable vessels that combined light draft, speed, and great carrying capacity.

The specialized vessels used for blockade running were, for the most part, owned by private companies. But the Confederate Ordnance Bureau operated a line of blockade runners, and the Treasury Department also owned a few. In 1864, the government ordered fourteen super–blockade runners, but most were unfinished at the war's end.

The Confederate navy made use of some of its outdated Southern-built warships as runners and used the British-built twin-screw *Coquette* to transport cotton and supplies. The navy also employed the British-built *Juno* as a picket vessel at Charleston and in 1864 purchased at Wilmington the twin-screws *Atalanta* and *Edith* for use as commerce raiders. In Great Britain, Comdr. James Dunwoody Bulloch ordered a number of twin-screw vessels that were designed to serve as both blockade runners and commerce raiders, but none was finished in time to see active duty.

In all just under 300 steamers tested the blockade. Out of approximately 1,300 attempts, over 1,000 were successful. The average lifetime of a blockade runner was just over four runs, or two round trips. Some 136 were captured and another 85 destroyed.

By war's end, the blockade runners had evolved into very specialized vessels that carried out their missions with a high success ratio. They were so successful that the Federal navy converted captured blockade runners into gunboats and used them as blockaders, but even this could not stop the blockade runners from delivering their cargoes. Throughout the war, the Confederate military was well served by the runners.

Besides their impact on the war, blockade runners greatly influenced subsequent ship design. They expanded maritime technology by advancing the development and use of steel, twin-screw propulsion, enclosed ship bridges, fast hull forms, and camouflage paint schemes, all innovations that are still used in ship construction today.

— STEPHEN R. WISE

BLUFFTON MOVEMENT

The Bluffton movement, led by Robert Barnwell Rhett, Sr., of South Carolina, aimed to sever connections with the Democratic party, to challenge the leadership of John C. Calhoun, and to advance the cause of disunion. Launched on July 31, 1844, at a dinner in Rhett's honor in the low-country town of Bluffton,

South Carolina, the movement quickly spread to the neighboring Beaufort, Colleton, Orangeburg, and Barnwell districts, enlisting men in the cause of separate state action against a hostile national government.

The causes of the movement were the abolition by Congress of the gag rule—the ban on antislavery petitions presented to Congress—and the tabling of the McKay bill, which would have lowered tariff duties, in the spring of 1844. Suspicious of ties with a national party composed of Northern as well as Southern members, Rhett wanted to repudiate the Democratic party and its presidential nominee, James K. Polk. Unlike Calhoun, who believed that the Democrats would protect Southern interests, Rhett feared that the Northern majority threatened to destroy slavery. Moreover, he was concerned about Northern Democratic equivocation on the annexation of Texas. Though Polk favored annexation and the Democratic platform advocated territorial expansion, Rhett and the "Bluffton Boys" suspected that Northern Democrats could not be trusted to redeem those pledges after the election.

The movement revealed the beginning of a generational split in South Carolina politics. The Blufftonites were largely younger, inexperienced men drawn to the leadership of Rhett, who was twenty years younger than Calhoun. Hoping to secure the presidential nomination in 1848, Calhoun and his allies supported Polk, and their influence first weakened and then ended the Bluffton movement six weeks after it began. Rhett returned to the Calhoun fold. But a rising generation of leaders, too young to have experienced the nullification movement, had received their first schooling in Carolina radicalism. In time, they would be further emboldened to calculate the value of the Union.

— JOHN McCARDELL

BONHAM, MILLEDGE L.

Bonham, Milledge L. (1813–1890), brigadier general and South Carolina congressman and governor. Born in Edgefield District, December 25, 1813, Milledge Luke Bonham graduated from South Carolina College and practiced law in Edgefield. He served in the South Carolina General Assembly from 1840 to 1844 and in the U.S. House of Representatives from 1857 to 1860, filling the seat left vacant by the death of his cousin Preston S. Brooks. He had considerable military experience before the Civil War, commanding the South Carolina Brigade in the Seminole War and serving as lieutenant colonel with the Palmetto Regiment in the Mexican War.

Bonham anticipated the secession crisis as early as 1858, once remarking that Republican success "ought to be and will be the death signal of this Confederacy, come when it may." When the crisis broke in December 1860, he promptly resigned his seat in the House and went home. South Carolina sent him to Mississippi to help persuade that state to follow its action. At the outbreak of the war Bonham commanded the South Carolina militia with the rank of major general. He relinquished this position to accept a Confederate brigadier's commission under P. G. T. Beauregard. He commanded the South Carolina troops moving to the defense of Richmond and led his brigade throughout the First Manassas campaign. Mary Boykin Chesnut reported that an observer told her that "'no general ever had more to learn than Bonham,' when he first saw him in command, and truly he believed no one ever learned more in a given time."

Although he served admirably, Bonham, when he was passed over for promotion, joined several other officers that autumn in protesting Jefferson Davis's policy of ranking officers from the "old army" over militia officers. He resigned his commission on January 29, 1862, having secured election to the First (regular) Confederate Congress. There he questioned Davis's

initial plan for conscription, preferring to rely on volunteers until their numbers proved inadequate. Later, however, Bonham supported the administration's bill authorizing the president to suspend the writ of habeas corpus whenever he believed it necessary to do so.

When Governor Francis W. Pickens's term expired in December 1862, Bonham was chosen by the state legislature to replace him. The new governor inherited

The Bluffton movement threatened nullification and even secession if South Carolina's demands for a lower tariff and an end to abolitionist agitation were not met.

PAGE 497

SEEKING FAIRNESS

Milledge L. Bonham of South Carolina was more cooperative with the Confederate government on conscription than were his neighbors in Georgia and North Carolina.

NATIONAL ARCHIVES

*Tens of thousands
of slaves toiled for
the Confederacy
in a service both
the bondsmen
and their owners
disliked.*

PAGE 561

two major problems from his predecessor: coastal defense and military conscription. In the minds of many South Carolinians the two were closely intertwined. The state had contributed liberally to the Confederate army. Yet most of the South Carolinians were serving on the Virginia front or in the West at a time when the state's coastal region lay threatened. The taking of Port Royal by the Union navy in November 1861 had been a particularly hard blow. Many in the state questioned whether their defense was being neglected. As enlistments fell off, South Carolina adopted conscription even before it passed the Confederate Congress.

For all his previous differences with the Davis administration, Bonham was determined that South Carolina "in every legitimate way should sustain the Confederate authorities." In spite of the continuing drain of Carolina troops to other fronts and the unrelenting shelling and raiding of the Sea Islands in the Charleston area including Fort Sumter, he made good his inaugural promise to cooperate with the Confederacy in contrast to his neighboring governors in Georgia and North Carolina. While they made wide use of their discretionary powers in granting exemptions from conscription for state officers, Bonham refused to follow that course.

In yet another matter of exemptions, which arose shortly after he took office, Bonham worked diligently for compromise. On May 1, 1863, the Confederate Congress repealed the section of the Conscription Act that exempted overseers on large plantations. This threatened to place an economic hardship on South Carolina and ran contrary to state law, which provided for such exemptions. Bonham felt obligated to uphold the state statute. Until he could secure its repeal, which he did in December 1863, he recommended that South Carolinians exempt under state law claim a similar exemption with Confederate enrolling officers. He induced the latter to agree to this arrangement until he could bring the state statute in line with the new Confederate regulations. South Carolina continued on the course of cooperation until the end of 1864, when it reversed its policy of claiming no exemptions because of increasing dissatisfaction with the Davis government's failure to provide adequately for the state's defense and the immediate threat of invasion from William Tecumseh Sherman's army.

Meanwhile Bonham worked closely with his former commander General Beauregard, who had been placed in charge of South Carolina's defenses. When the general ordered the evacuation of Charleston by all noncombatants in February 1863, Bonham reluctantly agreed. When he then called up all white males beyond draft age for the defense of the city, the question arose of alien residents' liability for service. His predecessor

had excused them, but Bonham refused to do so. The legislature backed his position in September 1863, with a law requiring alien residents to serve when needed. President Davis agreed to accept these state troops for three months' service (half the regular time) on the condition that South Carolina arm and equip them. The governor agreed to arm them but reported that resources for their supply were thin because of prior commitments to the Confederacy. For all these difficulties, Union efforts to take Fort Sumter failed twice in 1863, although Charleston continued under intermittent bombardment.

By the fall of 1863 Bonham began receiving reports from enrolling officers in the northwestern corner of the state that they were meeting with widespread resistance to conscription as well as desertion by those who had already served. This could be attributed not only to the Confederate military reverses of that summer but to local conditions as well. This region, which backed up against the mountains of North Carolina where many deserters found refuge, was mostly populated by nonslaveholders who had never been enthusiastic about secession. Bonham dispatched state troops to the area, obtained the cooperation of Governor Zebulon Vance of North Carolina in suppressing the disturbances, and called the legislature into special session. It responded with strong legislation making sheriffs and others liable to fines and imprisonment for failure to cooperate in curtailing draft evasion and desertion. It even agreed to a Confederate proposal to raise a special force from those not liable to conscription for special service against deserters. There was some improvement; but as the military and economic situation deteriorated further by the summer of 1864, conditions in that corner of the state once again worsened. All of Bonham's further efforts to curtail disaffection met with little success.

Yet another manpower problem confronting Bonham in 1863 was the need for slave labor to build and maintain coastal fortifications. This was not a new concern. The impressment of slaves for this purpose had begun early in the war, affecting primarily slave owners in the coastal areas. It met with little opposition initially; but as more slaves were taken for varying lengths of time by both state and Confederate authorities, the mood of the planters changed. Part of the problem lay in the inadequacy of supporting legislation relative to the length of impressment and compensatory pay to the owners. The legislature sought to remedy this by passing a law in December 1862, just as Bonham took office, limiting requisitions for slaves to thirty days' service and providing owners eleven dollars a month compensation. The law was flawed in many respects, however, including one provision that allowed owners to pay a dollar a day instead of furnishing a slave, an option many of them took. Enforcement was difficult, and only a few hundred slaves were recruited by this means in spite of Bonham's efforts to make the process work. Finally, in August 1863, Beauregard announced that his agents would assume responsibility for impressment. Some 3,500 slaves were now secured through impressment and voluntary action by their owners, but this number soon dwindled as planters complained that their blacks were ill treated and not returned promptly and that their labor was needed at home. Enforcement became increasingly difficult, and Bonham was never able to solve the problem adequately.

Bonham was also confronted with popular dissatisfaction over the impressment of provisions and supplies for the Confederate army. This practice had been carried on informally since early in the war, arousing protest in South Carolina and elsewhere. When Congress formalized the procedure in the Confiscation Act of March 26, 1863, it became the new governor's specific problem. As complaints mounted, the governor brought the issue to the legislature's attention in its special session in September 1863. He indicated his displeasure at the frequently high-handed methods being used by Confederate commissioners and secured a legislative resolution supporting his position. While not specifically disavowing confiscation, both governor and legislature expressed concern that the law be administered evenly and fairly and only when absolute necessity dictated. Bonham conveyed these sentiments to Secretary of War James A. Seddon, who replied in a conciliatory fashion that he would investigate any complaints. As these continued to come in, Bonham brought the matter back to the legislature in November. It responded with resolutions asking the state's congressional delegation to work for change in Richmond. The governor was also requested to inform the state's citizens of their rights under the impressment law. Bonham continued to forward complaints to Seddon, but this problem, too, remained unresolved until war's end.

As Bonham's term came to an end in December 1864, it was evident that South Carolina faced imminent invasion. Over the governor's strong protest, the state had been ordered to give up most of its remaining cavalry for duty in Virginia the previous March. Now Bonham asked the legislature for authority to call up all males between sixteen and sixty for militia duty within the state with those between sixteen and fifty being allowed to go to Georgia in view of the menace in that direction. He also sought to have all militia forces and others deemed necessary for the state's defense declared exempt from Confederate service. The legislature promptly approved his request. This was a decided reversal of South Carolina's previous cooperation with the Confederacy, but the state's situation called for drastic action.

Following the completion of his term, Bonham again became a brigadier general of Confederate troops, commanding a cavalry brigade under Joseph E. Johnston until war's end. He then returned to his law practice in Edgefield. He served in the General Assembly during Presidential Reconstruction only to be sidelined during the Republican years. Active in the restoration of white rule, he was appointed state railroad commissioner in 1878 and continued in that position until his death on August 27, 1890.

— WILLIAM E. PARRISH

BOOTH, JOHN WILKES

Booth, John Wilkes (1838–1865), assassin of Abraham Lincoln. Born in Maryland, the son of a slave-owning actor of English birth, Booth followed in his father's footsteps with a successful stage career, but his youth in Maryland made him a slavocrat in lifestyle—riding horses, shooting guns, holding violent opinions in politics, and disdaining blacks. He

seems to have thought of himself as a Northerner but wrote in 1864, "My love (as things stand today) is for the South alone."

Although he left few letters for historians, Booth did compose two long political statements, one in the

"Sic semper tyrannis! The South is avenged!"

JOHN WILKES BOOTH
AFTER SHOOTING
PRESIDENT LINCOLN,
APRIL 14, 1865

ASSASSIN

Sympathetic to the South, Maryland actor John Wilkes Booth feared Lincoln's re-election in 1864 would make the president a dictator.

NATIONAL ARCHIVES

B

winter of 1860–1861 and the other in November 1864. The first justified secession as constitutional and blamed abolitionists for the nation's crisis. "This country was formed for the *white,* not the black man," he wrote in the later statement, and slavery was "one of the greatest blessings (both for themselves and us)" bestowed by "God . . . upon a favored nation." Intense identification with the Confederate cause and fear that Lincoln's reelection in 1864 would make him a dictator led Booth to begin planning that summer to kidnap Lincoln, take him to Richmond, and exchange him for Confederate prisoners of war.

Booth recruited Southern-sympathizing idlers, ex-Confederate soldiers, and a spy in Maryland for his kidnapping scheme and visited Montreal late in 1864, where he may have contacted Confederate agents. He decided very late to murder Lincoln. Acting as a self-styled "Confederate . . . doing duty *upon his own responsibility,*" he shot the president at Ford's Theatre in Washington, afterward shouting the Virginia state motto, "Sic semper tyrannis" [thus always to tyrants].

Confederate sympathizers helped hide him from pursuing soldiers, but he died on Virginia soil twelve days later, shot by a Union cavalryman.

[*See also* Lincoln, Abraham, *article on* Assassination of Lincoln; Espionage, *article on* Confederate Military Spies.]

— MARK E. NEELY, JR.

BRAGG, BRAXTON

Bragg, Braxton (1817–1876), general and military adviser to Jefferson Davis. Bragg was born in Warrenton, North Carolina, on March 21, 1817. He attended West Point, graduating fifth in the 1837 class of fifty. He served in the Seminole Wars, where his health began its lifelong decline, and won two brevet promotions for gallantry during the Mexican War. In 1856, after marrying Eliza (Elise) Brooks Ellis, Bragg resigned from the army to become a successful sugar planter in Louisiana. When the state seceded in

BOOTH EXHUMATION UPDATE
Why we didn't "dig" John Wilkes Booth

An enduring myth of the Lincoln assassination has been that John Wilkes Booth, the president's killer, somehow managed to elude capture in 1865 and live to a ripe old age, wandering the world, siring several children and assuming a variety of bogus identities. In all these stories, an innocent man was killed by Union troops and buried in the Booth family plot in Baltimore.

In 1991 the story reached high velocity following the airing of an episode of NBC television's "Unsolved Mysteries," which profiled what it called the "unlikely controversy." The two pro-escape historians featured on the program were courted by the press and articles appeared in newspapers and journals supporting their position.

A number of us who have been researching the assassination have concluded that there is no merit to these theories. We challenged them in print in newspapers, journals and magazines, arguing that the evidence of an escape is very questionable, that the tale-tellers

were not believable and that there were three separate identifications of Booth's body by people who knew him in life.

This public attention led the pro-escape researchers to join together with two distant relatives of the Booth family in a lawsuit seeking to force Green Mount Cemetery to allow the exhumation of the grave so that the remains could be examined forensically to determine if it was Booth or not. The cemetery opposed the petition saying that Booth's immediate family had been satisfied 130 years ago. The attorney for the cemetery asked several of us to testify in opposition to the suit.

Why oppose an exhumation which could PROVE that it was Booth buried there? The grave had been flooded several times, there was uncertainty in the cemetery records about exactly where in the plot the coffin was buried (at least 12 other family members are buried there) and this all led me to conclude that the odds of a conclusive ID were fairly small.

Six of us appeared in court and laid out the reasons why we believe it WAS

Booth buried there. One of the historians from the "Unsolved Mysteries" show gave his conclusions and the two members of the extended Booth family asked the court's permission to determine whether a stranger was buried among their kinfolk. The hearing lasted four days and attracted much media scrutiny, especially in Washington, Baltimore, and Richmond.

On May 26, 1995, Baltimore Circuit Court Judge Joseph H.H. Kaplan denied the exhumation petition. He said, "the historical evidence which suggests that John Wilkes Booth was captured, killed and positively identified is indeed convincing."

The decision was appealed by the members of the Booth family. On June 5, 1996, the three member Maryland Court of Special Appeals in Annapolis reaffirmed Judge Joseph H.H. Kaplan's decision refusing to order the exhumation, saying that Judge Kaplan made no errors in law.

— STEVEN G. MILLER

January 1861, the governor made Bragg a major general in command of the state's forces.

On March 7 President Jefferson Davis appointed Bragg brigadier general in the Confederate army. Ordered to Pensacola, Florida, Bragg quickly changed the volunteers he found there into drilled, disciplined soldiers. On September 12 Davis, pleased with Bragg's performance, promoted him to major general and on October 7 assigned him command of western Florida and all of Alabama.

In February 1862 Davis directed Bragg to proceed with his troops to Gen. Albert Sidney Johnston's army in northern Mississippi. Here Bragg shouldered two responsibilities—command of the Second Corps and chief of staff of the army—positions he held at the Battle of Shiloh. The Confederates attacked on April 6, slowly advancing throughout the day, despite the dispersal and tangling of corps, divisions, and brigades. Bragg commanded the forces near the center of the battlefield for several hours before moving to the Confederate right where the advance had stalled at the Hornet's Nest. Here he spent five hours directing piecemeal assaults before the Nest fell about 5:00 P.M. As the troops pushed forward, P. G. T. Beauregard, in command of the army since Johnston's death earlier in the day, called off the advance, an action that Bragg believed cost them the victory. By 2:00 P.M. the next day the Confederate line had collapsed before the weight of the reinforced Union army.

Bragg became a full general on April 12, 1862, the fifth ranking officer in the Confederacy. This promotion allowed Davis to assign Bragg to permanent command of the Western Department when Beauregard took an unauthorized sick leave. For a number of reasons, Bragg decided in July that an invasion of Kentucky could reap many benefits for the South. In anticipation of this move, he began an unprecedented transfer of an army by rail on the twenty-third. The move from Tupelo to Chattanooga—776 miles via six railroads—went without a hitch and proved to be the most successful part of the entire enterprise.

Advancing from Chattanooga on August 28 with 27,000 soldiers, Bragg encountered the enemy at Munfordville, where the heavily outnumbered Federal garrison of 4,000 surrendered on September 17. In an attempt to unite forces, Bragg traveled to Lexington to confer with Gen. E. Kirby Smith, leaving the army under his second in command, Gen. Leonidas Polk. As Federal Gen. Don Carlos Buell advanced, Polk disobeyed orders from Bragg, orders that might have enabled the Confederates to concentrate and defeat the Federals. Instead, Polk moved to Perryville where his deployment of the army for battle proved faulty. Bragg rejoined the army on October 8 and, despite Polk's mistakes, managed to push Buell's army back nearly

BRAXTON BRAGG

A close military adviser to Jefferson Davis and the fifth ranking officer in the Confederacy, Gen. Braxton Bragg was a more able administrator than field commander.

LIBRARY OF CONGRESS

two miles before the advance stalled. By midnight, however, Bragg began a retreat that ended in Tennessee. Despite the early promise of the Kentucky campaign, Bragg had achieved nothing of lasting value for the Confederacy.

Bragg next met the Federal army on December 31, 1862, about three miles northwest of Murfreesboro, in open farm country with small stands of thick cedar trees. Bragg ordered the Army of Tennessee, 35,000 strong, to pivot on its right, swinging northeast in an effort to force Gen. William S. Rosecrans back beyond the Nashville Pike and to cut the Federal line of retreat. The grand pivot proved unsuitable on the rough and broken terrain, and, although Bragg managed to surprise Rosecrans, within an hour the Federals rallied, took strong positions, and fought fiercely for ten hours. On January 2, following a day of desultory firing, Bragg ordered an assault on a Union division threatening Polk's position. Eighty minutes of bloody combat convinced Bragg that the Federals could not be dislodged, and at 11:00 P.M. his army retreated from Murfreesboro.

For the next six months Bragg dallied in the Tullahoma area, reorganizing his army, quarreling with his subordinates, and caring for his ailing wife. In late June, Rosecrans again advanced, forcing Bragg to retreat to Chattanooga where he remained for several weeks. By late August Rosecrans began a flanking movement around the city, compelling Bragg to scurry southward in order to cover his line of communications. The Union's three corps were widely

Hoping to strike before the Federals in northern Mississippi could advance, Bragg left about 30,000 men at Tupelo and swung the rest of his army around to Chattanooga.

PAGE 33

*Polk, Longstreet,
Hill, and Buckner
all emerged as
anti-Bragg critics.*

PAGE 35

separated as they maneuvered through the mountainous country, and twice Rosecrans presented Bragg with excellent opportunities to strike the Federal forces in detail. Each time, however, the cowardice or disobedience of Bragg's subordinate commanders allowed the Federals to escape.

Rosecrans, scenting the danger, hurriedly pulled his scattered corps together at Chickamauga Creek. On September 19 and 20 a mighty battle raged as Bragg attempted another grand pivot, hoping to force the Federals into McLemore's Cove and destroy them. The Army of Tennessee held its own through the nineteenth, and advanced at some points. That night the long-awaited Gen. James Longstreet arrived from Virginia, and Bragg reorganized the army into two wings, again hoping that a grand pivot would yield handsome results. Polk, however, attacked hours later than Bragg ordered and then allowed piecemeal assaults to exhaust his resources.

On the left, Longstreet formed his wing and waited for Polk's attack to produce results. Bragg, active on the field all day (contrary to Longstreet's postwar assertions), ordered Longstreet's troops forward at the precise moment a gap inadvertently opened in the Union line, thus initiating the famous breakthrough long credited solely to Longstreet. The timing of the assault and Longstreet's judicious troop deployment proved highly successful. The Union line broke and fled. The last Federal stand took place at Snodgrass Hill where Gen. George Thomas held fast until nightfall, covering the wild retreat of Rosecrans and the Federal army.

Moving the army to the heights overlooking Chattanooga, where Rosecrans had ensconced the Union army, Bragg spent the next several weeks quarreling with his subordinates and frittering away the advantages he had gained over the Federals at the Battle of Chickamauga. While his attention was thus occupied, the Federals replaced Rosecrans with Gen. Ulysses S. Grant. On November 24 Grant's forces easily swept the few Confederate soldiers deployed on Bragg's left off of Lookout Mountain and the following day chased the entire Army of Tennessee down the far side of the seemingly impregnable Missionary Ridge. On November 29 Bragg asked to be relieved from command. To Bragg's chagrin, Davis accepted the resignation with unseemly haste.

In February 1864, however, Davis, ever loyal to his friends, summoned the general to Richmond to serve as his military adviser, an office that allowed Bragg to wield considerable power among his army cohorts. Bragg served Davis and the Confederacy well during the eight months he spent in the capital city. The efficiency of several military institutions improved under his supervision, primarily through changes in department heads. In an extreme case Bragg initiated the dismantling of the Bureau of Conscription after finding it riddled with corruption. Davis relied heavily upon Bragg's understanding of military affairs, often seeking Bragg's expertise or opinion on a variety of matters. Bragg, however, never became a sycophant to Davis; indeed, the two often disagreed. Approaching his responsibilities with a characteristic intensity and devotion to duty, Bragg willingly shouldered censures and criticisms that otherwise would have fallen on Davis or, in at least one instance, Gen. Robert E. Lee. Unfortunately, Bragg's appointment as military adviser came too late in the war for him to make a great impact. Had he been assigned the post earlier, the Confederacy could have profited more from his considerable administrative talents.

In October 1864, while still performing the duties of military adviser, Bragg returned to field command when Davis ordered him to Wilmington, North Carolina, the last Confederate port remaining open to blockade runners. Bragg's performance here was shameful. He failed to prepare properly for anticipated attacks, and when the Federals made a concerted assault against Fort Fisher in January 1865, the commanding general stood by several miles away, wringing his hands and refusing to give credence to desperate appeals for aid from inside the fort. Bragg's explanations for his conduct were pusillanimous and illogical.

Bragg spent the last weeks of the Confederacy's life as a subordinate to Gen. Joseph E. Johnston, who, with the remnants of the Army of Tennessee, unsuccessfully attempted to block Gen. William Tecumseh Sherman's advance through North Carolina. As the Confederate government fled Richmond, Bragg joined Davis just in time to use his influence in convincing the president that the Confederacy had indeed been defeated. On May 10, 1865, as Bragg and his wife wended their way home, Union cavalry caught up with them near Concord, Georgia. Bragg was granted a parole on the spot and received no further trouble from the Federals; he died in Galveston, Texas, on September 27, 1876. He is buried in Magnolia Cemetery, Mobile, Alabama.

Bragg held a greater range of responsibilities than any other Confederate during the Civil War. He began in command of the Gulf coast fortifications at the start of the war; served as corps commander and chief of staff under Albert Sidney Johnston; was promoted to command of the Army of Tennessee, a position he held longer than anyone else, leading the western army to its northern high tide and to its one great victory; was one of only two people (the other was Lee) to serve as military adviser to the president; and ended his Civil War career as a subordinate field commander once again.

As an army field commander Bragg left much to be desired. Many factors contributed to his poor generalship. He suffered from myriad illnesses—migraine headaches, boils, dyspepsia, and rheumatism, to name a few—which frequently were brought on by stress. The diseases alone were enough to debilitate anyone, but the remedies he used to relieve his pain and discomfort may have been as damaging. He failed to inspire loyalty, confidence, or obedience in his subordinates, and he lacked the steadiness, the resolution, and the good luck of a successful field commander. A West Point–trained career officer, Bragg had little patience with his volunteer soldiers, and his harsh efforts to discipline them seemed sometimes to go beyond the bounds of reason and necessity. Bragg also failed to learn from his mistakes, and to the end of the war he remained seemingly ignorant of the technological changes that required corresponding changes in tactics.

His personality may have been Bragg's greatest shortcoming. Although severely criticized and denigrated over the years, during his lifetime he had many staunch supporters, as evidenced by declarations of support and admiration even when he wielded little or no influence. Bragg, however, saw people in either black or white. Those he considered friends received his unwavering support and praise; all others he went out of his way to criticize and annoy. This flaw in his character frequently led to and exacerbated embarrassing quarrels with his subordinates, some of whom on two extraordinary occasions conspired together in petitioning Davis to remove Bragg from command of the Army of Tennessee. While serving as military adviser, Bragg took every opportunity to denigrate or thwart those he disliked, and he carried much of the responsibility for the removal of Joseph E. Johnston, a friend and supporter, from command of the Army of Tennessee in July 1864.

Bragg remains a study in contrasts and illuminates the Confederacy's serious misuse of talent. An able administrator, he spent most of the Civil War as a mediocre (at best) army field commander; although he maintained many loyal friendships, he went out of his way to create lasting enmities; sincerely devoted to the Confederate cause, he contributed greatly to its demise.

— JUDITH LEE HALLOCK

BRANDY STATION, VIRGINIA

This village, some seven miles northeast of Culpeper, Virginia, on the Orange and Alexandria Railroad, bordered the site of a June 9, 1863, battle that witnessed the largest clash of mounted units during the Civil War. By the narrowest of margins, Maj. Gen. J. E. B.

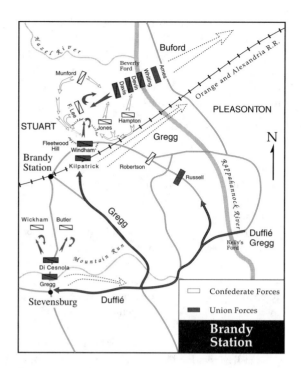

Stuart wrestled a tactical victory from the Union cavalry under Brig. Gen. Alfred Pleasonton. Although they were defeated, Federal troopers demonstrated for the first time that they could hold their own against Stuart's soldiers. Imbued with a new sense of confidence, Union cavalry in Virginia became a formidable opponent for the rest of the war. Never again would Gen. Robert E. Lee's horsemen enjoy the degree of success that had marked their earlier campaigns. Southern casualties at Brandy Station amounted to 51 killed, 250 wounded, and 132 missing; the Federals lost 1,651.

The Rappahannock River divided the two antagonists after the smashing Confederate victory at Chancellorsville (May 1–4, 1863). Planning to launch a second raid of the North on June 9, Lee instructed Lt. Gen. Richard S. Ewell's Second Corps and Lt. Gen. James Longstreet's First Corps to abandon their camps in Culpeper County for the Shenandoah Valley. Stuart's troopers were to cross the Rappahannock the same day and screen the infantry's movements. Six batteries of horse artillery and five brigades of cavalry, totaling just more than 9,500 troopers and gunners, made up the Army of Northern Virginia's cavalry division. Supremely confident, as always, Stuart commanded the largest force of his career.

The night before the scheduled advance, Stuart's brigades were widely scattered along the Rappahannock. He hoped they could cross the river with little delay at dawn. Brig. Gen. Fitzhugh Lee's regiments were seven miles northwest of Stuart's headquarters at Fleetwood Hill, and Brig. Gen. William Henry Fitzhugh ("Rooney") Lee's soldiers bivouacked two

"The Civil War is, for the American imagination, the great single event of our history. . . . Before the Civil War we had no history in the deepest and most inward sense."

ROBERT PENN WARREN
THE LEGACY OF THE CIVIL WAR, 1961

The Battle of Brandy Station was the largest mounted clash of the war, involving some 10,000 cavalry.

PAGE 89

miles west of the Rappahannock River and along the banks of the Hazel River. Brig. Gen. William E. ("Grumble") Jones's troopers spent the night along the Beverly's Ford Road, two miles south of the Rappahannock and not far from Saint James Church. Brig. Gen. Beverly H. Robertson's men rested southwest of Brandy Station on John M. Bott's farm. Brig. Gen. Wade Hampton's command also spent the night southwest of Brandy Station at Stevensburg. Because Stuart had failed to send pickets to the northern banks of the Rappahannock, he had little idea of the enemy's intentions.

Before the Confederates had stirred from their camps on June 9, Maj. Gen. Joseph Hooker had determined that Lee intended to move his army northward. The Northern commander ordered Pleasonton to take 11,000 cavalrymen and 3,000 infantry across the Rappahannock and "disperse and destroy the rebel force assembled in the vicinity of Culpeper." Pleasonton divided his command into two columns: the right wing under Brig. Gen. John Buford would cross at Beverly's Ford while the left wing under Brig. Gen. David M. Gregg would cross at Kelly's Ford. Both commands would reunite at Brandy Station and then push toward Culpeper where Pleasonton mistakenly believed Stuart's cavalrymen were encamped. He hoped to catch his adversary off guard, as Stuart edged his men to the banks of the river during the night of June 8. The Union officer, however, did not confirm reports that placed Confederate cavalry within a few hundred yards of the Rappahannock. A surprise was in store for both Pleasonton and Stuart in the morning.

Under a thick fog, Buford's men stormed past the Confederate pickets at Beverly's Ford around five in the morning. As the Northerners pounded down the Beverly's Ford Road, "Grumble" Jones roused his sleepy troopers, sending the exposed batteries of Maj. Robert F. Beckham a mile behind the lines to Saint James Church. Jones slowed Buford's rushing horsemen, slashing at the sides of the Union column with his nearest units, while Beckham sent canister flying down the road with the one cannon he had left at the front.

Jones reluctantly pulled his advanced regiments back to the high ground around Saint James Church. The entire brigade positioned itself west of the building; the artillerists were east of the church, extending the line just across Beverly's Ford Road. When the Federals raced across the exposed plain that rested below the Confederates, a barrage of shells, followed by a series of mounted counterattacks, sent the Northern cavalrymen scurrying to the woods. Although Jones had stabilized the Southern line, Stuart could not have been pleased by the enemy's fording of the Rappahannock. With his brigades widely dispersed, he frantically called on his subordinates for assistance.

From his camp at Stevensburg, Hampton hurried to the front at 6:00, leaving one regiment at Fleetwood Hill and placing his other three units to the right of Beckham. On the western end of the line, Rooney Lee's brigade connected with the left flank of Jones's brigade. Lee posted his soldiers along Yew Ridge, a hulking eminence near the western tip of Fleetwood Hill. Hampton and Lee extended the line into the shape of a "huge crescent" that overlapped the flanks of Buford's troopers. To relieve the pressure from Hampton's probing skirmishers, Buford sent the Sixth Pennsylvania Cavalry against the Confederate center at Saint James Church. The Union soldiers made a gallant charge, as they fought hand to hand among Beckham's guns, but without sufficient support they were forced to retire. The failed attack brought a period of relative calm over this portion of the field.

The fighting now shifted toward Rooney Lee's position atop Yew Ridge, as Buford realized that the route to Brandy Station, via the Beverly's Ford Road, had been sealed off by the Confederates. Since 8:30 that morning, Buford had tested the enemy's left flank. Lee's troopers stood firm behind a stone wall until noon, when Federal infantry slipped around the end of the Southern line at Dr. Daniel Green's farm. Obliged to withdraw to the northwest end of Fleetwood Hill, Lee's soldiers now faced to the north and west. They waited for Buford to renew his assaults, as gunfire echoed two miles to their southeast. It warned of Stuart's newest threat.

About the time Hampton's men reinforced Jones at Saint James Church, Stuart learned of Gregg's crossing at Kelly's Ford. He sent the First South Carolina to the scene with the promise that Robertson's brigade would relieve them shortly. Gregg discovered that Robertson's troopers were galloping down the same road that he had planned to use to arrive at Brandy Station. Turning his column down a different road just west of Paoli's Mill, Gregg picked a less direct route to the battlefield, but it offered little Confederate resistance along the way. It was close to 9:00 when Gregg's hard-riding troopers passed Mount Dumpling. Fleetwood Hill was only two miles away, and Gregg ordered his men to attack the prominent eminence immediately. Only one Confederate cannon stood in the way of the Northern onslaught—an attack aimed at the rear of the Confederate line around Saint James Church. Stuart had been surprised for the second time that day.

The Southern cavalry chieftain mistakenly believed that Robertson's regiments could handle whatever enemy force had crossed Kelly's Ford. When Jones reported Federal activity around Brandy Station, Stuart quickly dismissed his subordinate's claim, remarking, "Tell General Jones to attend to the Yankees in his front, and I'll watch the flanks." Oblivious to the danger that lurked behind him, Stuart even disregarded the messages of Maj. Henry B. McClellan, a member of his staff, who watched the leading elements of Gregg's division steadily push toward Fleetwood Hill from the direction of Brandy Station. The lone Confederate cannon initiated a duel with three Union field pieces. The banging guns finally convinced Stuart that a potential disaster brewed behind his lines.

Stuart immediately ordered two regiments from Jones's brigade to Fleetwood Hill. Unit formations disintegrated as the troopers made a hard ride from Saint James Church. When Jones's cavalrymen reached the crest of the hill, they launched a ferocious attack that blunted the Union advance. Both sides continued to send reinforcements to the southern end of Fleetwood. Charge and countercharge characterized the next phase of the battle. The clash of sabers, not the ringing shots of pistols, pierced the air. It was a dramatic moment, but one that has created the false impression that the Battle of Brandy Station was limited to the ground surrounding Stuart's headquarters.

Four of Hampton's regiments followed Jones into the cauldron. Just as his troopers surged across the top of the hill, a fresh Union brigade under Col. Judson Kilpatrick struck opposite the terminus of Fleetwood. A confusing melee ensued and most of Kilpatrick's regiments were repulsed. Desperate to salvage the day, he called on the First Maine to make a final charge. The Union cavalrymen swept forward, gaining a temporary hold on Fleetwood Hill, but the momentum of the assault carried the members of the First Maine a mile across the hill where they found themselves "cut off from all support." After their attack, Beckham placed all his available guns along the ridge, as the Confederates established permanent control of Fleetwood Hill.

Two hours of severe fighting had exhausted Gregg's division, and reinforcements were not at hand. His supporting division, under Col. Alfred N. Duffie, stumbled into Col. M. C. Butler's Second South Carolina at Stevensburg. Though Duffie could see Fleetwood, he made little attempt to break through the enemy's thin line. If Duffie had aggressively led his command, he could have aided Gregg at Brandy Station or marched to Culpeper to discover the disposition of Lee's infantry. With only two hundred men at hand, Butler's energetic defense saved Stuart from a potential fiasco.

After Gregg's battered command galloped off the field, heading toward the Rappahannock Railroad Bridge, Stuart consolidated his position along a two-mile front with Hampton on the right, stretched east across the Orange and Alexandria Railroad. Jones occupied the center of the line while Rooney Lee anchored the left flank, which bent around the northern rim of Fleetwood. Stuart wanted to pursue Gregg, but enemy activity on his left made this venture impossible, as Buford and Lee had been hotly engaged for most the afternoon.

Unlike Duffie, Buford tried to assist Gregg by concentrating his forces, mostly dismounted cavalry and infantry, against Lee's refused left flank. Just when Buford's men seized the northern crest of Fleetwood around 3:30, they received the order to retire to Beverly's Ford. Pleasonton had already decided on a general withdrawal. Reports of Confederate infantry, the failure of Gregg's attack, and Buford's slow progress against Rooney Lee convinced Pleasonton that little more could be achieved south of the river.

Although Stuart could claim a tactical victory at Brandy Station, he had been badly surprised by Pleasonton, an incident that tarnished his reputation. After the battle, one Southern cavalryman wrote, "Stuart was certainly surprised and but for the supreme gallantry of his subordinate officers and men in his command it would have been a day of disaster and disgrace." In his official report, Stuart refused to admit that he had not been prepared for Pleasonton's assault but conceded that his troops nearly lost the field to the enemy. Stuart criticized Robertson for failing to block Gregg's advance and chastised Col. Thomas T. Munford, the temporary commander of Fitzhugh Lee's brigade, for his tardy arrival on the battlefield.

Stuart's insatiable need for approbation was not satisfied by his commanding officer, who offered few words of praise after Brandy Station. Lee must have been pleased by Stuart's aggressive leadership on the battlefield, which prevented the Federals from unmasking the location of the Confederate infantry. Nevertheless, criticism came from all circles and wounded Stuart's sensitive pride. A North Carolina woman wrote that "the more we hear of the battle at Brandy Station, the more disgraceful is the surprise." Mindful of public reaction to Brandy Station, Stuart tried to redeem himself in the coming campaign by launching a raid in Pennsylvania that possessed little military value and virtually paralyzed the entire army.

— PETER S. CARMICHAEL

BREAD RIOTS

There is no incident on the Confederate home front more misunderstood than the Richmond bread riot of April 2, 1863, and no civilian subject less studied than that of other food riots, mostly in the springs of 1863 and 1864, although New Orleans experienced a distur-

On June 9, 1863, Union Brig. Gen. Alfred Pleasonton's nearly 10,000 mounted troops surprised Stuart and compelled the Confederates to fight for their lives.

PAGE 594

B

BREAD RIOTS

The April 1863 bread riot was the most serious of the Southern food protests over shortages and high prices.

PAGE 503

bance as early as July 1861. These events have been attributed to wartime inflation and a lack of adequate food supplies at fair prices.

A series of incidents that preceded the April 1863 disturbance in the Confederate capital helped cause it and explain why it occurred when it did. Specific local factors increased demand for shrinking supplies, exacerbating inflation that led to hoarding and speculation. Further irritants to a disgruntled population were the explosion of the Confederate ordnance laboratory on March 13, which killed more than sixty poor women, and a heavy snowfall the next week. The snow quickly melted, making roads nearly impassable and causing flooding of the James River, which shut down the waterworks and public hydrants.

Crime and vice were common in Richmond, especially at night. The bread riot was organized violence on a large scale conducted openly. It was also political protest, planned and led by women, a purposeful rather than a spontaneous event.

Its timing was related to a series of outbreaks elsewhere. Atlanta, Georgia, had a food riot on March 16, 1863, as did Macon, Columbus, and Augusta about the same time. On a main rail link between Virginia and the lower South, Salisbury, North Carolina, witnessed a flour riot on March 18, when soldiers' wives raided merchants. Raleigh, High Point, and Boon Hill in the same state all experienced food riots that month. Mobile, Alabama, had one on March 25 (and a more serious incident in mid-April, as well as disturbances in August and on September 4). In Petersburg, Virginia, there was a bread riot on April 1. Most of these events were reported in Richmond papers, often with favorable editorial comments about the alleged hoarders, speculators, or profiteers who were targeted.

There had been talk about a protest in Richmond for several weeks, but final plans were made at a meeting held in Belvidere Baptist Church the night of April 1. Women from all over the city, particularly poorer neighborhoods, attended, as did some from outlying counties. Their participation indicates prior knowledge that something was about to happen.

The riot began before nine in the morning when Mary Jackson, a painter's wife, left her butcher's stall in the Second Market. Followed by a growing crowd of women and boys she marched to the Governor's Mansion. It is unclear whether Governor John Letcher actually addressed the group. The crowd became a mob when it surged out of Capitol Square, down Ninth Street, and invaded the business district on Main and Cary streets, sacking about twenty stores.

Mayor Joseph Mayo tried to quell the women by reading the Riot Act, but he was ignored. Governor Letcher called out the Public Guard, a state security force for the Capitol and other buildings, under its act-

ing commander, Lt. Edward Scott Gay. There is no reliable evidence for the story that President Jefferson Davis took command of the Guard, ordering the men to prepare to fire while confronting the looters and giving them a deadline to disperse.

Estimates of the mob's size have ranged from a few hundred to twenty thousand, but careful scholars argue for about one thousand actual participants, as distinguished from spectators. Richmond's tiny police force was no match for the rioters. There are a few references in some accounts to bloodshed, shots fired, and injuries suffered, but none has been substantiated. The riot was over by eleven.

Forty-four women and twenty-nine men are known to have been arrested, but not all of them were charged or tried. Court records later burned, so the disposition of many cases is unknown. Only twelve women were convicted, one of a felony. A majority were probably poor women, but others were or had once been members of the middle class, including at least eight of those arrested; a few owned land and even slaves. Male rioters got stiffer penitentiary sentences, four for felonies and two for misdemeanors.

The Confederate government failed in its attempt to censor news of the riot. Telegrams reached Danville and Lynchburg within hours. Reports were carried throughout the South by railroad passengers leaving Richmond and to the North by Union prisoners exchanged soon after the event. Most of the city's editors initially honored a request not to print articles about the incident, but John Moncure Daniel, a bitter critic of the Davis administration, blasted the authorities in his *Examiner* for their lenient treatment of the rioters, calling for a dictator to suppress lawlessness. He also attacked the women with ethnic, sexist, and religious slurs. Ironically, his colorful but distorted accounts are the basis for most historians' descriptions.

Sullen crowds gathered again on April 3, but were promptly dispersed by the City Battalion. Troops under Maj. Gen. Arnold Elzey, commander of the Department of Richmond, who had already withheld reinforcements from Lt. Gen. James Longstreet because of the crisis, strengthened Provost Marshal John Winder's men. Cannon were placed at the edge of the business district amid rumors of another riot planned for the night of April 10. The city moved quickly to enlarge its parsimonious welfare program.

Another rash of incidents the next spring suggests that the pinch of hunger became painful enough to move women to desperate action as their winter food supplies were exhausted. Savannah had a riot on April 17, 1864, and one occurred in Bladenboro, North Carolina, the same month. There are sketchy details about incidents in the last year of the war at Abingdon, Virginia; Lafayette, Alabama; Forsyth,

Thomasville, and Marietta, Georgia; and Sherman, Texas.

Of their importance there can be no doubt. Historian Emory M. Thomas has called the Richmond riot "the best case study of the results of Southern food supply problems." Three levels of government in the capital were shaken, and all took steps to prevent another incident. Morale plummeted throughout the Confederacy. The food riots were a sign of urban unrest, similar to the yeoman discontent expressed in rural areas by women's raids on government storage depots, like that at Jonesville, North Carolina, in 1865. They were also disturbing evidence that the war had become a poor woman's fight, as well as a poor man's. Women who demonstrated in city streets and country crossroads and openly defied civil and military authorities hardly conformed to traditional Southern definitions of patriotism and female roles.

[*See also* Poor Relief; Poverty; Speculation.]

— MICHAEL B. CHESSON

BRECKINRIDGE, JOHN C.

Breckinridge, John C. (1821–1875), U.S. congressman, vice president, and presidential candidate, major general, and secretary of war. Breckinridge, who was born into one of Kentucky's most illustrious families, studied at Centre College, the College of New Jersey (Princeton), and Transylvania University. He practiced law briefly in Iowa and then in his home state. Major of the Third Regiment of Kentucky Volunteers, he arrived in Mexico too late for significant participation in the Mexican War. Breckinridge was elected to the Kentucky House of Representatives in 1849 as a Democrat and to the U.S. House in 1851 and 1853. In 1856 at age thirty-five he was elected vice president of the United States on the Democratic ticket with James Buchanan. In 1859, over a year before his term expired, the Kentucky legislature chose him for the Senate term beginning March 4, 1861. As the slavery controversy developed in the 1850s, Breckinridge had called for "perfect non-intervention" on the part of Congress on the issue of slavery in the territories.

When the Democrats split in 1860, Breckinridge became the presidential candidate of the Southern party. Though he believed that a state had the right to secede, he denied that he was the secession candidate. Breckinridge lost his home state to Constitutional Unionist John Bell, but he carried eleven of the fifteen slave states and won 72 electoral votes to 39 for Bell and 12 for Stephen A. Douglas, the Northern

Democratic candidate. But Republican Abraham Lincoln received 180 votes for a clear majority. As vice president, Breckinridge announced the election of Lincoln on February 13, 1861, when the electoral votes were officially counted.

Breckinridge hoped that some compromise would save the Union, but in the Senate he defended the actions of the Southern states. After the war started, he served on a six-man committee that formulated Kentucky's unique neutrality policy. When that troubled status ended in September 1861, Breckinridge fled to Virginia to avoid arrest. The Senate expelled him on December 2.

Considered an important asset for the Confederacy, Breckinridge was commissioned brigadier general on November 2 and given the Kentucky Brigade in Gen. Simon Bolivar Buckner's Second Division in southern Kentucky. He helped organize the Confederate government of Kentucky, which was admitted into the Confederacy on December 10, 1861. One of the best of the "political generals," Breckinridge won the respect and admiration of most of his peers, with the conspicuous exception of irascible Braxton Bragg.

Breckinridge's first major engagement was at Shiloh where, in command of the Confederates' Reserve Corps, he performed well enough to merit promotion to major general as of April 14. After serving with Earl Van Dorn at Vicksburg, Breckinridge led an unsuccessful attempt to take Baton Rouge. Rejoining the Army of Tennessee, he incurred heavy casualties in his division at Murfreesboro in a charge ordered by Bragg. Several Kentuckians urged Breckinridge to seek a duel with his caustic commander.

Southern Democrats nominated John C. Breckinridge of Kentucky on a platform that demanded federal protection of slave property in the territories until statehood.

PAGE 185

Breckinridge then returned to the Vicksburg area and participated in Joseph E. Johnston's vain efforts to relieve that city. After it fell, he was ordered to rejoin Bragg's army in eastern Tennessee. At Chickamauga on September 19–20, 1863, Breckinridge's division was in D. H. Hill's corps. His assaults on the Federal left flank helped break the Union line but failed to destroy the army. Breckinridge commanded a corps on Lookout Mountain and Missionary Ridge above Chattanooga on November 25, 1863, when the Confederates were overrun. Bragg charged Breckinridge with drunkenness and removed him from command. But Confederate leaders had learned to discount Bragg's frequent accusations, and in February 1864 the Kentuckian was given command of the Department of Southwest Virginia. He built his command from scratch, and on May 15, with the aid of cadets from the Virginia Military Institute, he defeated Gen. Franz Siegel's larger force at New Market. It was perhaps Breckinridge's finest performance of the war.

Soon transferred to the Army of Northern Virginia, Breckinridge helped check Ulysses S. Grant at Cold Harbor. Then, as commander of a small corps, he accompanied Jubal Early on his raid to the outskirts of Washington. When they returned to the Shenandoah Valley, the Confederates were under intense pressure from Gen. Philip Sheridan's much larger force. Gen. John B. Gordon penned a vivid picture of Breckinridge at this stage of the war:

> *Tall, erect, and commanding in physique . . . he exhibited in marked degree the characteristics of a great commander. He was fertile in resource, and enlisted and held the confidence and affection of his men, while he inspired them with enthusiasm and ardor. Under fire and in extreme peril he was strikingly courageous, alert, and self-poised.*

Later, Gen. Basil W. Duke also praised his fellow Kentuckian but added, "His chief defect as a soldier—and, perhaps, as a civilian—was a strange indolence or apathy which at times assailed him. . . . When thoroughly aroused he acted with tremendous vigour, . . . but he needed to be spurred to action. . . . He was at his best when the occasion seemed desperate."

After John Hunt Morgan's death on September 4, 1864, Breckinridge was returned to command of the Department of Southwest Virginia. Despite inadequate resources, he was able to fend off Union attacks against the vital saltworks in that area.

Meanwhile, the Department of War had become one of the most troubled spots in the Confederate government, and in February 1865 President Jefferson Davis appointed Breckinridge secretary of war. In 1861 Breckinridge had doubted that the Confederacy could win the war, and as he viewed the situation from his new position, he soon concluded that the cause was hopeless. He worked to bring the struggle to an honorable conclusion, which, in his view, rejected guerrilla warfare. "This has been a magnificent epic," he declared. "In God's name let it not terminate in a farce." When Richmond fell he was instrumental in preserving many of the military records.

Briefly with Lee, then with Joseph E. Johnston, and finally accompanying President Davis on his flight, Breckinridge made a daring and dangerous escape through Florida to Cuba. He went on to Europe and Canada where he remained in exile until President Andrew Johnson extended a general amnesty on Christmas Day, 1868. Breckinridge returned to his Lexington home in March 1869 after an absence of over eight years. Comparing himself to "an extinct volcano," he practiced law, worked for economic development in the state, and urged national conciliation until his death on May 17, 1875. He was only fifty-four.

— LOWELL H. HARRISON

BROWN, JOSEPH E.

Brown, Joseph E. (1821–1894), Georgia governor and U.S. senator. Born in South Carolina to a middle-class farm family that soon moved into the hill country of North Georgia, Joseph Emerson Brown completed his education at Yale Law School and then prospered in law and land speculation. In 1849 he won election to the state senate. He quickly emerged as a leader of the Democrats and in 1857 was elected governor. A skillful politician who understood the white masses of Georgia, he won reelection in 1859, 1861, and 1863. Generally a domestic liberal, in national affairs he became an ardent secessionist.

Governor Brown directed a strengthening of the militia and other military preparations, and after the election of Abraham Lincoln he warned against abolition, racial equality, and intermarriage as he championed immediate secession. When a convention of delegates was called to consider the issue, he refused to reveal the close vote between secessionists and cooperationists—those who opposed immediate secession and favored cooperation with other Southern states to win redress of their grievances. He ordered the seizure of Federal installations even before the convention formally voted to secede.

Following that vote on January 19 the governor worked forcefully to organize Georgia's considerable resources. He mobilized troops and equipment, but he did not fully cooperate with the new Confederate government, which was trying to mobilize the resources of a whole new nation. First, last, and always Brown was a Georgian, and he consistently defended traditional state rights, individual freedoms, and strict legalism against the encroachments of the Confederacy, no matter how great the emergency.

On April 12 the war began, and six days later, Brown called for volunteers. Thousands of new troops rallied but equipment was scarce, and Brown tried to keep departing Georgia troops from carrying weapons out of the state. He also attempted to maintain control of military units that were being integrated into the Confederate armed forces. This was only the beginning of his clashes with Confederate authorities.

But within the state Brown was a brilliant politician who understood his constituents in all their differences and variations from poor whites on up through wealthy planters. Most of all he understood the yeoman masses who would have to do most of the fighting and sacrificing, and in that respect he had clearer vision than President Jefferson Davis and his principal aides.

Early in the war Governor Brown worked hard to obtain adequate clothing and equipment for Georgia troops, and later he dispatched state purchasing agents all over the South and even abroad in chartered steamships, which often carried out state-owned cotton and brought back blankets, clothing, and medicine. He acted with equal vigor to look after the masses at home. He directed the state penitentiary to produce cotton cards so that thread could be prepared for spinning, and he also organized an efficient system for obtaining and fairly distributing scarce salt so that meat could be preserved. The governor also organized relief for the needy families of soldiers; during the last two years of the war his administration's heaviest expenditures went into an extensive and effective welfare system that assisted the yeoman masses bearing the main burdens of the war. Brown greatly increased taxes during the war, but he made the system more progressive by exempting many of the poor and increasing the burden on the rich. Neither he nor anyone else in the Confederacy, however, could control the raging inflation that was undermining the whole Southern economy. Brown restricted cotton acreage, and the teetotaler Baptist governor further boosted food production by restricting distilling, which was a booming business in his own hill country of North Georgia. Within Georgia, Brown ran an efficient operation; indeed at that level he was very likely the most effective Southern governor, the state leader who got the most out of his beleaguered people.

But Governor Brown could not or would not see the larger picture, and all too often he ignored or rejected the need for Confederate unity, the obligation of the individual Southern states to close ranks behind the central government in Richmond if the rebellion

GEORGIA FIRST

Governor and U.S. Senator Joseph E. Brown led the mobilization of Georgia's military, but was more loyal to his state than to the government of his new nation.

LIBRARY OF CONGRESS

was to have any real chance of success. From the beginning he had chafed at Confederate control, and in April 1862 he challenged the Confederates directly.

At that time the Confederate government, desperately short of troops, enacted the first national draft in American history. Immediately Brown challenged this dramatic but necessary expansion of Confederate power, denouncing it as "at war with all the principles for the support of which Georgia entered into this revolution." He tried to maintain control of all state military forces, but the legislature gave him only limited support, and the state supreme court backed the Confederates. Grudgingly Brown yielded, though he continued to protest as he rebuilt his state military forces with men too young or too old for conscription. Each time the embattled Confederates later expanded the age limits of the draft, the governor waged the same noisy struggle first to hold on to his army and then to rebuild it with older and younger recruits. Also he granted draft exemptions to thousands of state employees, including militia officers, setting a precedent that made it more and more difficult to enforce Confederate conscription throughout the crumbling Southland.

Brown also led his Georgians in opposition to impressment, especially the requisition of slave laborers by the Confederate army. He stopped the imposition of martial law in Atlanta in 1862 and frustrated Confederate efforts to seize the state-owned Western and Atlantic Railroad in 1863 and 1864. He frequently criticized Confederate tax and blockade-running policies. His opposition to the Davis administration reached a peak with his denunciations of arbitrary arrests and the suspension of the writ of habeas corpus, and early in 1864 the war-weary legislature backed him on this issue.

The governor did not always resist the Confederates, but his opposition grew steadily and led to an

In September 1862, Georgia Gov. Joseph E. Brown thundered against the second conscription act, charging that it struck down Georgia's "sovereignty at a single blow."

PAGE 307

About the second conscription act, Brown declared that "no act of the government of the U.S. prior to the secession of Georgia" had been so injurious to constitutional liberty.

PAGE 307

Under the command of Commodore Franklin Buchanan, Virginia sortied March 8, 1862, into Hampton Roads to assault the Union fleet.

PAGE 651

increasingly bitter correspondence with President Davis. Brown had the support of some powerful Georgians like Vice President Alexander H. Stephens and his brother Linton Stephens in the legislature and former secretary of state Robert Toombs and a growing number of planters and other influential people, but his main backing came from the yeoman masses. These were his people; he had sprung from this sturdy stock, and he, not the old planter elite, knew them best. And yet finally, whatever his intentions, he led them down the road to ruin with his state rights extremism.

Even the invasion of Gen. William Tecumseh Sherman's mighty army in 1864 did not dilute Brown's resistance to the fading Confederate government. Just at the time Atlanta fell to the invaders in September, Governor Brown furloughed the ten-thousand-man Georgia militia to keep it from coming under Confederate control. This left his state even more vulnerable to Sherman's devastating march to the sea, and though he rejected Sherman's peace feelers, Brown was soon calling for peace as morale plummeted all over the state.

The Confederates made one last desperate move late in the war by calling for the use of black troops—Southern slaves—in the Confederate army with the promise of freedom for honorable service, and Brown ran true to form. He denounced the plan as another dramatic departure from tradition. Once again, in the last days of the Confederacy, he showed himself unable or unwilling to make the adjustments necessary for victory in total war.

Inevitably defeat came in the spring of 1865 when Robert E. Lee surrendered in Virginia in April and the last scattered Confederates laid down their arms in May. Union troops arrested Governor Brown who was briefly imprisoned in Washington, D.C. Soon paroled, he returned to Georgia and supported the Reconstruction program of President Andrew Johnson who pardoned him in September. Opportunistically Brown supported Radical Reconstruction and served as chief justice of the state supreme court for two years, but when that regime collapsed in Georgia, he swung back to the Democrats. He prospered as a lawyer and businessman and served in the U.S. Senate from 1880 to 1890 when he resigned. Four years later one of Georgia's most successful and enduring politicians died at his home in Atlanta.

— F. N. BONEY

BUCHANAN, FRANKLIN

Buchanan, Franklin (1800–1874), naval officer. Buchanan was born in Baltimore, Maryland, on September 17, 1800. As the child of a prominent Maryland physician, he enjoyed a comfortable life while growing up. He received a commission in the U.S. Navy in January 1815 and served initially under Oliver Hazard Perry. Buchanan was promoted to the rank of lieutenant in 1825 and commander in 1841. Four years later, Secretary of the Navy George Bancroft chose him as the first superintendent of the newly created U.S. Naval Academy at Annapolis, Maryland. Buchanan served in the Mexican War as a sloop commander and later commanded Matthew C. Perry's flagship in the latter's expedition to Japan in 1852. Promoted to captain in 1855, Buchanan then commanded the Washington Navy Yard.

He resigned his commission in April 1861 and offered his services to the Confederacy the following August. Confederate Secretary of the Navy Stephen R. Mallory issued Buchanan a commission as captain on September 5. His first major assignment was as chief of the Office of Orders and Details in the Navy Department, where he made all assignments of personnel, helped to formulate naval policy, and acted as adviser to Secretary Mallory. On February 24, 1862, Buchanan became flag officer in command of the naval defenses on the James River. Moving to Gosport Navy Yard, Buchanan made the new ironclad ram CSS *Virginia* (formerly USS *Merrimack*) his flagship.

Buchanan took *Virginia* into Hampton Roads on March 8, 1862, to attack the Federal squadron there. His first target was the frigate *Cumberland*. After exchanging broadsides with this adversary, *Virginia* rammed it. *Cumberland* began sinking and threatened to take *Virginia* down with it because the ironclad's ram was stuck in its hull. Fortunately for the Confederates, the ram broke off, and the ship was freed to continue the attack. Buchanan turned *Virginia* toward the frigate *Congress,* whose captain ran the ship aground to avoid being rammed. An hour's pounding by *Virginia*'s cannons set *Congress* afire and killed and wounded dozens of its crew. The Federal captain then struck his colors and surrendered. Because fire from Federal shore batteries and sharpshooters prevented Buchanan from receiving the surrender, he ordered his gunners to destroy *Congress*. While supervising this destruction, Buchanan was wounded in the thigh by a rifle bullet. Subsequently, he yielded command of the operation to Lt. Catesby Jones.

Buchanan's wound prevented him from participating in the famous confrontation on the following day between *Virginia* and the Federal ironclad *Monitor*. He convalesced first at Norfolk and later moved to Greensboro, North Carolina. The Confederate Congress confirmed Buchanan's appointment as admiral on August 21, 1862, making him the ranking officer in the Confederate navy. In September, Mallory assigned Buchanan to command the naval forces in

Mobile Bay, Alabama, hoping he would be more active and aggressive than his predecessor, Capt. Victor M. Randolph, had been. At Mobile, Buchanan won the respect not only of his command but of the army officers as well. This resulted in a spirit of cooperation between the two branches not found in other areas of the Confederacy.

Under Buchanan's command, the Mobile squadron had as its primary goal the defense of Mobile Bay rather than the breaking of the Union blockade. Buchanan had under him at first *Baltic,* a weak ironclad, and three wooden gunboats, *Morgan, Gaines,* and *Selma.* Work on two ironclad floating batteries, *Huntsville* and *Tuscaloosa,* and an ironclad ram, *Tennessee,* had begun at Selma, Alabama, that fall. Construction of a second ironclad ram, the sidewheeler *Nashville,* had commenced at Montgomery, Alabama, at about the same time. Buchanan had *Tennessee, Huntsville,* and *Tuscaloosa,* all of which were launched in February 1863, brought to the Mobile Navy Yard to receive their machinery, armament, crews, and iron plating. In June, *Nashville* reached the city to go through the same process of completion. The admiral kept his gunboats in the lower bay near Fort Morgan, Fort Gaines, and Fort Powell to help guard the bay entrances while he pushed for completion of the ironclads.

Buchanan had to endure delays in getting the work done and problems in obtaining cannon, armor plating, and seamen. These difficulties meant that the two ironclads would not reach completion that summer as Buchanan had hoped. When *Tennessee* was finally commissioned February 16, 1864, Buchanan ordered it taken into Mobile Bay, but the ironclad's deep draft prevented it from passing over the Dog River bar. Workmen constructed camels (wooden caissons), which they used to raise the ship and float it over the bar on May 18. Four days later, Buchanan shifted his flag from *Baltic* to *Tennessee.* Later that month, he planned an attack on the Union blockading fleet. *Tennessee* ran aground near Fort Morgan, delaying the strike, and Buchanan soon canceled the offensive because he considered the Federals too strong for his little squadron.

On August 5, 1864, Union Adm. David Farragut led his fleet against the Confederate forts and warships in the Battle of Mobile Bay. The superior Federal vessels quickly dispersed or destroyed the Confederate wooden gunboats, leaving *Tennessee* to face Farragut's squadron alone. Almost all the Union ships joined in the fray. Three gunboats rammed *Tennessee* but caused little damage. Buchanan, however, suffered a broken leg when an enemy shell knocked loose a port cover and it struck him. The Federal fire cut *Tennessee*'s steering chains, making it impossible for the crew to change its position. When the ram's smokestack was shot

MOBILE'S DEFENDER

Maryland naval officer Franklin Buchanan defended Mobile Bay, Alabama, until defeated by Union Admiral David Farragut on Aug. 5, 1864. Portrait by Mathew Brady.

NAVAL HISTORICAL CENTER, WASHINGTON, D.C.

away, the ship filled with smoke, and the crew could not answer the increasing hail of enemy shells. Commander James D. Johnston received Buchanan's permission to surrender the ironclad after an hour-long engagement.

Buchanan was taken to Fort Lafayette, New York, where he was held prisoner until February 1865. After his exchange, he was reassigned to Mobile but did not reach the city before its surrender in mid-April. Buchanan participated in the surrender of the Department of Alabama, Mississippi, and East Louisiana on May 8, 1865.

After the war, Buchanan returned to his home in Maryland. He served as president of Maryland Agricultural College, which later became the University of Maryland, for one year. He then retired to his home at Easton, where he lived until his death on May 11, 1874.

— ARTHUR W. BERGERON, JR.

BURIAL OF LATANÉ

An enduring icon of the Lost Cause, the history and genre painting *The Burial of Latané,* touched the hearts of generations of Southerners despite what may seem to modern eyes only stilted composition and crude rendering.

Its inspiration came on June 13, 1862, when Capt. William Latané became the sole Confederate casualty

"Damn the torpedoes—full speed ahead!"

DAVID GLASGOW FARRAGUT
BATTLE OF MOBILE BAY, AUG. 5, 1864

of J. E. B. Stuart's reconnaissance on the Virginia peninsula. Latané's body was taken to a nearby plantation for burial. When enemy forces barred a local clergyman from the scene, the resident women conducted a funeral service themselves.

The incident inspired a popular poem and then the canvas executed by Richmond portraitist William D. Washington (1834–1870). It showed a pious matron preaching the burial service in an Eden-like bower that suggested the sacred beauty of the Southern landscape. Women gathering about the coffin symbolized the enduring strength of Confederate womanhood. Blacks assisting with the burial gave visual prominence to the Lost Cause myth of slave loyalty. And a well-clothed child decorating Latané's bier contradicted reports of home front poverty. Most important, *The Burial of Latané* offered reassurance to anxious wives and parents that their loved ones in arms would be buried with dignity and respect wherever they fell.

Washington's "touching and impressive scene," in the words of one early critic, caused a sensation when first exhibited in Richmond. And an 1868 engraved adaptation, offered for $1.50 a copy by publisher William Smith of New York, became a huge bestseller in the postwar South, where it was advertised as a "beautiful and appropriate ornament for any parlor."

— HAROLD HOLZER

BUTLER, MATTHEW CALBRAITH

Butler, Matthew Calbraith (1836–1909), major general and U.S. senator. Born in Greenville, South Carolina, Butler attended South Carolina College, but withdrew in 1856 after participating in a student riot. He studied law and was admitted to the South Carolina bar the following year. His marriage in 1858 to the daughter of Governor Francis W. Pickens led to a career in politics, and he was elected in 1860 to the South Carolina House of Representatives as a state rights advocate and Democratic secessionist.

Butler joined the call for a secession convention, and at the outbreak of hostilities, he resigned from the legislature to lead the Edgefield Hussars into Confederate service. An accomplished horseman, he joined Hampton's Legion in May 1861 and commanded a mounted unit at First Manassas. His actions there gained him recognition for his physical courage and tactical skill and earned him a promotion to the rank of major. During the Peninsular campaign, Butler displayed his mastery of cavalry tactics by successfully screening Confederate withdrawals and rapidly shifting to the offensive during the Battle of Williamsburg. He was promoted to colonel in August 1862, fought at Sharpsburg and Fredericksburg, and made a decisive contribution at Brandy Station in June 1863 by repulsing a Union flanking movement. He was wounded during this engagement by enemy artillery, resulting in the amputation of his right leg, but he was appointed brigadier general during his convalescence and returned to command in 1864 with no loss of enterprise or skill. Butler participated with distinction in numerous cavalry engagements including Hawes Shop and Trevillian Station and achieved the rank of major general in September 1864.

Butler returned to his law practice after the war and was again elected to the South Carolina legislature in 1866. Concluding that Republican rule was beyond reform, he joined forces with Martin Witherspoon Gary to return the Democratic party to power and restore the conservative regime. He assisted Gary in organizing the Red Shirt movement, Democratic gun clubs whose purpose was to intimidate and suppress the basic element of Republican power, the black voter. After the Democratic victory of 1876, Governor Wade Hampton appointed Butler to the U.S. Senate, where he served until 1894. Butler died in April 1909 in Washington, D.C.

— ROBERT T. BARRETT

CABINET

The Confederate cabinet consisted of President Jefferson Davis, Vice President Alexander H. Stephens, and the secretaries of the six departments that composed the executive branch of the Confederate government: State, War, Justice, the Treasury, the Navy, and the Post Office. With several important exceptions, each of these departments replicated its counterpart in the prewar Union.

In organizational terms, most of the exceptions involved the offices of the attorney general, which, for the first time in American history, were given departmental status in the new Department of Justice. At the same time, the Confederacy failed to create a Department of the Interior. Its functions, such as the Bureau of Printing, the Patent Office, and territorial affairs, were transferred to Justice, which, as a consequence, was a much larger and more important department than the small suite of offices that served the Union attorney general. Another factor that greatly enhanced the attorney general's office was the decision not to establish a Confederate supreme court. In the absence of a supreme tribunal, the attorney general served as final interpreter of the constitutionality of legislation, a task made easier by the fact that state and Confederate district courts generally upheld war measures. Even so, had the Confederacy survived, these written interpretations of statutory and constitutional law might have provided an enduring basis for administrative centralization.

Although the formal organizational missions of the other departments closely corresponded to those in the prewar Union, most departments found their administrative challenges dramatically altered by the Civil War. For example, the Department of the Navy, under Stephen R. Mallory, began the war without a major vessel and soon lost easy access to international sealanes from Southern ports. Improvisation and, at times, brilliant ingenuity introduced the ironclad to modern warfare, but the construction of a large, or even small, oceangoing fleet was well beyond the material capacity of the South.

The Treasury Department was similarly hamstrung by an underdeveloped banking system, a shortage of gold bullion, and the limited utility of a plantation economy based on the export of cotton as a source of revenue for wartime government operations. In all these respects the challenge facing Confederate Treasury secretaries was very different from that faced by their prewar Union predecessors. Similar shortages of natural resources and productive capacity led the War Department to direct a wide program of confiscation, government-owned industry, and allocation of Southern manpower in order to mobilize men and matériel for the front. As was true of the other departments, these activities broke new ground in their innovative use of government author-

Jefferson Davis named Stephen R. Mallory head of the Navy Department of February 25, 1861.

PAGE 343

FIRST CABINET

From left to right: Benjamin, Mallory, Memminger, Vice President Stephens, Walker, President Davis, Reagan, and Toombs.

HARPER'S PICTORIAL HISTORY OF THE GREAT REBELLION

THE CONFEDERATE CABINET

POSITION	NAME	DATES OF SERVICE[1]
Attorney General	Judah P. Benjamin	Mar. 5–Nov. 21, 1861[2]
	Thomas Bragg	Nov. 21, 1861–Mar. 18, 1862
	Thomas H. Watts	Mar. 18 1862–Oct. 1, 1863
	Wade Keyes	ad interim, Oct. 1, 1863–Jan. 2, 1864
	George Davis	Jan. 2, 1864–Apr. 24, 1865[3]
Postmaster General[4]	John H. Reagan	Mar. 6, 1861–May 10, 1865[5]
President	Jefferson Davis	Feb. 18, 1861–May 10, 1865[6]
Secretary of the Navy	Stephen R. Mallory	Mar. 4, 1861–May 3, 1865[7]
Secretary of State	Robert Toombs	Feb. 21–July 24, 1861
	Robert M. T. Hunter	July 24, 1861–Feb. 22, 1862
	Williams M. Browne	ad interim, Mar. 7–Mar. 18, 1862[8]
	Judah P. Benjamin	Mar. 18, 1862–May 2, 1865[9]
Secretary of the Treasury	Christopher G. Memminger	Feb. 21, 1861–July 17, 1864
	George Trenholm	July 18, 1864–Apr. 27, 1865[10]
Secretary of War	Leroy Pope Walker	Feb. 21–Sept. 16, 1861
	Judah P. Benjamin	Nov. 21, 1861–Mar. 17, 1862[11]
	George Wythe Randolph	Mar. 18–Nov. 15, 1862
	Gustavus Woodson Smith	ad interim, Nov. 17–20, 1862
	James A. Seddon	Nov. 21, 1862–Feb. 5, 1865
	John C. Breckenridge	Feb. 6–May 3, 1865[12]
Vice President	Alexander H. Stephens	Feb.11, 1861–May 11, 1865[13]

[1]Unless otherwise indicated, starting date is date of confirmation by the Senate; ending date is date on which resignation became effective.

[2]Benjamin was appointed acting secretary of war on September 17, but the position was not made permanent and confirmed by the Senate until November 21. During the interim, Assistant Attorney General Wade Keyes ran the Justice Department.

[3]Ending date is that of the last cabinet meeting Davis attended, in Charlotte, North Carolina, after which he resigned.

[4]On February 25, 1861, Jefferson Davis nominated and the Senate confirmed Henry T. Ellet as postmaster general, but Ellet declined the appointment.

[5]Ending date is that of Reagan's capture by Union troops near Irwinville, Georgia.

[6]Starting date is that of Davis's inauguration; ending date is that of his capture by Union troops near Irwinville, Georgia.

[7]Mallory composed and dated his letter of resignation on May 2, following the cabinet meeting at Abbeville, South Carolina, but he did not present it to the president until the following day at Washington, Georgia. Mallory left the cabinet immediately, but Jefferson Davis's letter officially accepting his resignation is dated May 4.

[8]Browne had been running the state department since, at latest, February 22, 1861, but Jefferson Davis did not officially designate him secretary of state ad interim until March 7.

[9]Ending date is that of the cabinet meeting at Abbeville, South Carolina, after which Benjamin left the cabinet and fled the country, reaching Bimini on July 10.

[10]Ending date is that on which Trenholm submitted his letter of resignation. Trenholm left the cabinet immediately, although Davis's letter officially accepting the resignation is dated April 28. Davis then appointed John H. Reagan as secretary of the treasury ad interim, a position Reagan held until his capture by Union troops near Irwinville, Georgia, on May 10.

[11]Benjamin was appointed acting secretary of war on September 17, 1861, and he continued to run the department unofficially until March 24, 1862.

[12]Ending date is that of the remaining cabinet members' arrival at Washington, Georgia. Afterward, Breckinridge and John H. Reagan separated from the president with the intent of rejoining him later, but Breckinridge was unable to do so. He eventually fled to Cuba.

[13]Starting date is that on which Stephens took the oath of office; ending date is that on which he was arrested by Union cavalry at his home in Crawfordville, Georgia.

Source: All dates are taken from Rembert W. Patrick, *Jefferson Davis and His Cabinet*, Baton Rouge, La., 1944.

ity and attempts at centrally directed economic coordination.

The two departments least changed by the war may also have been those least important to the Southern war effort. The Department of State had little to do beyond entertaining foreign representatives and giving advice to largely autonomous commissioners pursuing diplomatic recognition of the Confederacy in European courts. More active but also more mundane was the Post Office, which attempted the most thorough reproduction of prewar Federal organization. Absorbing with little change the antebellum system for delivering the mails, the Confederate Post Office moved letters in that part of the South that remained outside Federal control throughout the war.

As his first cabinet, President Davis appointed Judah P. Benjamin of Louisiana, attorney general; Stephen R. Mallory of Florida, secretary of the navy; Christopher G. Memminger of South Carolina, secretary of the treasury; John H. Reagan of Texas, postmaster general; Robert Toombs of Georgia, secretary of state; and Leroy P. Walker of Alabama, secretary of war. In making these selections, Davis chose men who had been major rivals for the Confederate presidency or those his rivals recommended. He also gave geographical balance to his administration by allocating each of the states that seceded before the attack upon Fort Sumter at least one representative in the first cabinet. (Davis himself represented Mississippi.) As was also true in the Union, administrative ability and personal friendship played but minor roles in these early appointments. As a group, this cabinet lasted only from early March, when Reagan was appointed, until July 1861, when Toombs resigned in order to accept an appointment as brigadier general in the Confederate army.

Jefferson made in all sixteen appointments, aside from acting secretaries, to head the six Confederate departments. One man, Judah Benjamin, accounted for three of these, as he was appointed, in succession, to Justice, War, and State. (He owed his survival to his close relationship with Davis; no other adviser so often or so influentially had the president's ear.) Benjamin, along with Mallory at Navy, Reagan at the Post Office, Davis as president, and Stephens as vice president, served in the cabinet throughout the life of the Confederacy. There was substantial turnover among the others. The War Department alone had five permanent secretaries, Justice had four, State had three, and the Treasury had two. The cabinet that sat between November 21, 1862, and September 8, 1863, had the longest tenure in terms of continuous membership. Along with Davis, Stephens, Mallory, and Reagan, that cabinet had James A. Seddon at War, Thomas H. Watts at Justice, Benjamin at State, and Memminger at

Treasury. Even though these men served together for only ten months, they had the deepest influence upon the performance and development of their respective departments.

Under President Davis, the cabinet met frequently and, when it met, deliberated for hours. Though these meetings were often indecisive, Davis appears to have heeded what advice was given. For the most part, however, the cabinet served the president in other ways. One of these was as a structure for an immense delegation of authority over executive administration of the Southern war effort. With few exceptions, the secretaries, their assistant secretaries, and subordinate bureau chiefs were solely responsible for departmental operations within wide-ranging grants of statutory authority from the Confederate Congress. For the most part, Davis involved himself only in the detailed decision-making of the War Department and, within its sphere, imposed his views only in military operations.

Another way that the cabinet served Davis was as a political lightning rod. Even though most departments were more or less autonomous of both legislative and executive direction, the deteriorating military position of the South and the ever-escalating demands that the war effort imposed upon civilians produced in the Congress repeated and bitter denunciations of executive performance. Although the president resisted many calls for the resignation of department secretaries, most of the turnover in his cabinet in fact reflected timely sacrifices to this congressional clamor.

[*See also* Judiciary; Presidency; State Department; Treasury Department; War Department; *and biographies of selected figures mentioned herein.*]

— RICHARD FRANKLIN BENSEL

CAROLINAS CAMPAIGN OF SHERMAN

On December 22, 1864, Maj. Gen. William Tecumseh Sherman sent the following telegram to President Abraham Lincoln: "I beg to present you as a Christmas gift the city of Savannah." With this communication Sherman brought to a conclusion his dramatic March to the Sea. By all standard rules of strategy, his next move should have been the immediate transfer of his army by water to Virginia, where Lt. Gen. Ulysses S. Grant had the Army of Northern Virginia bottled up behind fortifications at Petersburg. The Federal navy had the ships for this move, and both Lincoln and Grant supported the plan. Sherman, however, did not. He wanted instead to apply total war, as he had done in

In Jefferson Davis's own words, Judah P. Benjamin "impressed me with the lucidity of his intellect, his systematic habits, and his capacity for labor."

PAGE 49

Early in 1865, as a sense of gloom overshadowed much of the Confederacy, Congress recommended that Davis restructure his cabinet in the hope of restoring public confidence in the cause.

PAGE 660

Sherman clamped a siege on Savannah, but, as he had in Atlanta, he allowed the Confederate force to escape when he took the city on December 21.

PAGE 355

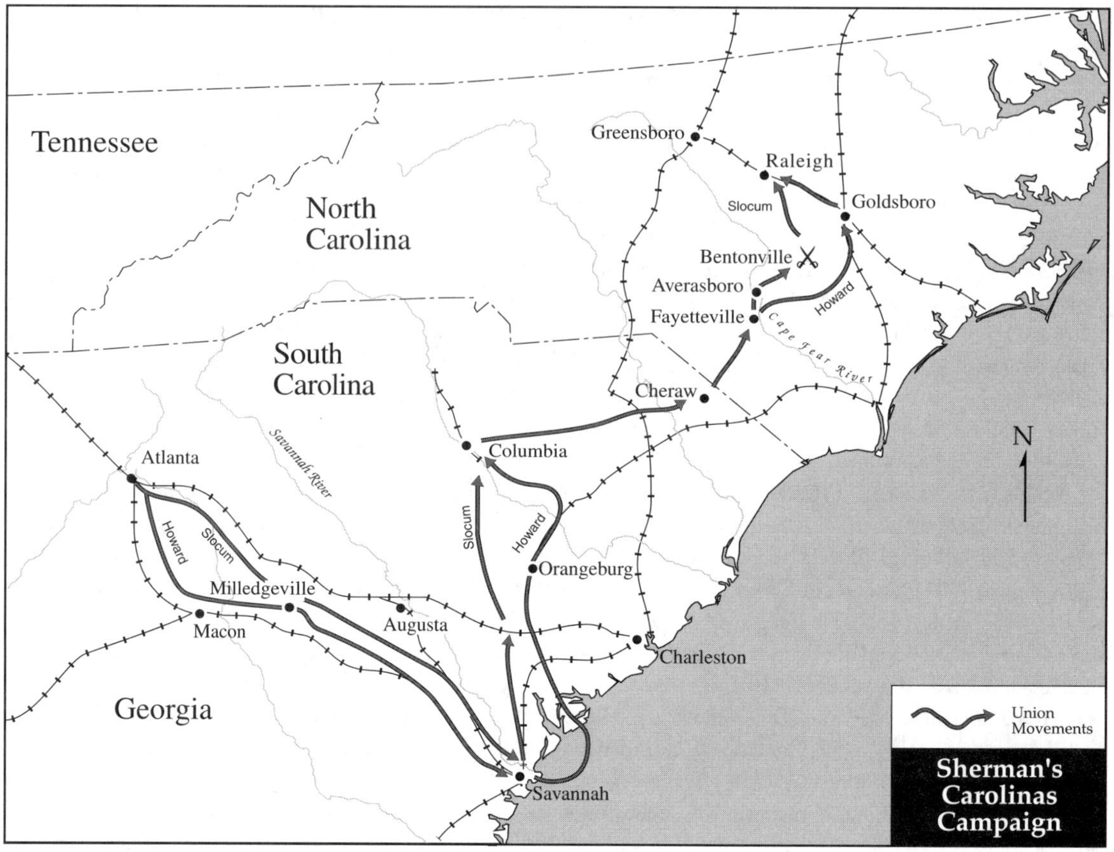

It was a happy Sherman who telegraphed Lincoln on December 22 offering Savannah as a Christmas gift.

PAGE 355

Sherman's Carolinas Campaign

Georgia, to the Carolinas, especially the Palmetto State for its role in bringing on the conflict. He believed that by bringing the war to the Carolina home front, his operations would have a direct bearing on the struggle in Virginia.

Sherman, a very persuasive individual, was granted permission for the Carolinas march, his position having been strengthened considerably by the news of Maj. Gen. George Thomas's near-annihilation of the Confederate Army of Tennessee at Nashville in mid-December 1864.

Sherman's campaign plan called for feints on Charleston, South Carolina, and Augusta, Georgia, followed by a move on Columbia, South Carolina's capital city. From there he planned to march in a northeasterly direction first to Fayetteville on the Cape Fear River in North Carolina and then to Goldsboro, which was connected to the North Carolina coast by two railroads. By this circuit he could cripple the chief lines of communication in the Carolinas as well as destroy all public and industrial property in his line of march. Furthermore, by bringing war to the home front, he felt certain that a defeatist psychology would be instilled in civilians and soldiers alike.

Since Sherman planned to sever all connections with his base at Savannah, the men would have to forage liberally in the countryside to survive. Army wagons could transport only a limited quantity of pro-

visions, and no government supplies could be expected until the army reached the Cape Fear River. In an attempt to regulate the foraging parties, Sherman issued very strict orders, but as had been the case on the March to the Sea, there was a wide discrepancy between the orders and the actions of some of the men. Most of the outrages committed in the Carolinas were the work of "bummers," self-constituted foragers who operated on their own and not under supervision.

By late January 1865 Sherman's sixty thousand veterans had begun crossing the Savannah River into South Carolina. The army was divided into two wings, the left commanded by Maj. Gen. Henry W. Slocum, the right by Maj. Gen. O. O. Howard. Each wing in turn comprised two corps, and each corps followed a different line of advance, forming a front over forty miles wide. Brig. Gen. Judson Kilpatrick was in charge of the cavalry.

When Sherman commenced his Carolinas campaign, the meager Confederate forces that might have opposed him were scattered from Mississippi to Virginia, so by the second week in February the Federal army had penetrated well into South Carolina. On the twelfth, Orangeburg was occupied and five days later Columbia was in Sherman's hands. Much of South Carolina's capital city went up in flames on February 17. Burning cotton, high winds, and drunken Federal soldiers were to blame for this conflagration. "Though I never ordered it," Sherman said, "and never wished it, I have never shed any tears over the event, because I believe that it hastened what we all fought for, the end of the war." Lt. Charles A. Brown of the Twenty-first Michigan commented: "South Carolina may have been the cause of the whole thing, but she has had an awful punishment."

At Cheraw, the army's last stop in South Carolina, Sherman learned that Gen. Joseph E. Johnston had replaced P. G. T. Beauregard as commander of Confederate forces in the Carolinas and Georgia. He now concluded that his antagonist of the Atlanta campaign would somehow manage to unite his forces and give battle at a place of his own choosing. This Sherman had hoped to avoid.

On March 8 North Carolina for the first time felt the full weight of the Federal army. Sherman, assuming a friendly reception from North Carolina's pro-Union element, issued orders for the gentler treatment of the local citizens, but he did nothing to stop the burning of the state's great pine forests. North Carolina's turpentine woods blazed in "splendor as bummers touched matches to congealed sap in notches on tree trunks."

The most formidable obstacle in Sherman's path lay in the swirling waters of the Lumber River and the adjacent swamps. The region prompted him to remark, "It was the damnedest marching I ever saw." Fortunately for him, his engineers by now had become skilled at bridging streams and corduroying roads.

Federal cavalry crossed the Lumber on March 8. Upon learning that Confederate horsemen under Lt. Gen. Wade Hampton were nearby, Kilpatrick set a trap for him, only to have his own camp surprised by the enemy on the morning of the tenth. Kilpatrick escaped capture by hastily departing the bed of a female traveling companion. Eventually the Federals retook their camp. As a result there is some disagreement over who won the cavalry engagement at Monroe's Crossroads, contemptuously tagged by some as "Kilpatrick's Shirt-tail Skedaddle."

By engaging the Federals in battle, the horsemen in gray opened the road to Fayetteville. That night near the city, the Confederate cavalry under Hampton and Maj. Gen. Joseph Wheeler joined forces with Lt. Gen. William J. Hardee's small command, which had been moving north just ahead of Sherman. On the eleventh, as the Federals entered the city from the south, the Confederates withdrew across the Cape Fear, burning the bridge behind them.

At Fayetteville Sherman ordered the arsenal destroyed, along with other properties. He also took the opportunity to clear his columns of the vast numbers of white refugees and blacks following his army. He referred to them as "twenty to thirty thousand useless mouths."

From Savannah to Fayetteville, Sherman had managed his army in an almost flawless manner. From the Cape Fear to Goldsboro, however, it was a different story. He not only mistakenly placed little emphasis on Hardee's delaying action at Averasboro on March 16 but also allowed his own columns to become so strung out that Johnston came close to crushing one of the Federal corps near Bentonville. At this village, twenty miles west of Goldsboro, Johnston had skillfully managed on the nineteenth to concentrate his scattered forces, although a sparse group it was, totaling no more than 21,000 effectives. Seldom in history have so few been led in battle by so many officers of high rank. Present on the battlefield that day were two full generals of the Confederacy, three lieutenant generals, and numerous brigadier and major generals.

Completely ignorant of Johnston's bold move, Sherman allowed his Fourteenth Corps to be caught off guard. For a while it seemed the Confederates would carry the day, but Federal reinforcements in the afternoon blunted Johnston's offensive. More Federal troops reached Bentonville on the twentieth, and by the next day Sherman had his entire army on the field. That night Johnston withdrew to Smithfield, ten miles to the west.

Though Bentonville was the largest battle fought on North Carolina soil (Confederate casualties, 2,606; Federal, 1,527), it was not one of the war's decisive engagements. Nevertheless, it must rank as an important battle. It marked the successful conclusion of Sherman's Carolinas campaign, and it was large in scope: 81,000 men were locked in combat over a three-day period.

At Goldsboro, Sherman's victorious troops linked up with Maj. Gen. John M. Schofield's command, and on March 25 the first train from the coast arrived. This completed the task Sherman had set for himself upon leaving Savannah.

After the war, Sherman commented that he would be remembered for the March to the Sea but that that operation was child's play compared to the Carolinas campaign. He characterized it as "one of the longest and most important marches ever made by an organized army in a civilized country. The distance from Savannah to Goldsboro is four hundred and twenty-five miles and the route embraced five large navigable rivers. . . . The country generally was in a state of nature with innumerable swamps . . . mud roads, nearly every mile of which had to be corduroyed. . . . We had captured . . . important cities and depots of supplies. . . . We had in mid-winter accomplished the whole journey . . . in fifty days . . . and had reached Goldsboro with the army in superb order."

The Federal march was a remarkable logistical feat that brought home to the people of the Carolinas the

Sherman wanted the Confederates to know that he believed in a hard war but a soft peace.

PAGE 355

realities of war. Still, this operation had little direct bearing on Gen. Robert E. Lee's decision to surrender. It was the decisive Confederate defeat at Nashville coupled with the collapse of the transportation system in Virginia that paved the way for Appomattox.

— JOHN G. BARRETT

CAVALRY

The Confederate cavalry reigned supreme for the first two years of the Civil War. Even Philip Sheridan, the cavalry commander for Ulysses S. Grant's Army of the Potomac, wrote in his memoirs, "From the very beginning of the war the enemy had shown more wisdom respecting his cavalry than we. Instead of wasting its strength by a policy of disintegration he, at an early day, had organized his mounted force into compact masses, and plainly made it a favorite."

Part of the Southern superiority was probably due to the caliber of such leaders as J. E. B. Stuart, Wade Hampton, Fitzhugh Lee, and Nathan Bedford Forrest. But there were other reasons. The Confederate cavalry, early in the war, was organized into one independent, autonomous unit and acted as such. The regiments never suffered from the piecemeal detachment to individual infantry units that plagued the Federal mounted arm until 1863, when it too was organized into one unit. Stuart was given command of the cavalry of the Confederate Army of the Potomac (the precursor to

Robert E. Lee's Army of Northern Virginia) in October 1861. In the West, the Confederate Army of Tennessee brigaded its cavalry in November 1862. It consisted of four brigades under Joseph Wheeler, John Austin Wharton, Nathan Bedford Forrest, and John Hunt Morgan.

Given this structure, the Confederates were able to introduce new tactics into cavalry doctrine—making large-scale mounted raids and putting cavalry into the battle to fight dismounted. Stuart conceived of the raid as a viable operation, and other Confederate commanders followed suit, as did the Federals later in the war. The Confederates also introduced the tactic of having the cavalry ride to the strategic point on the battlefield to fight dismounted on a regular basis. Both these innovations rested upon the first—the new, and superior, organization of the Confederate cavalry.

Organization

In the Virginia theater, Stuart, and later Hampton and Fitz Lee, commanded the Army of Northern Virginia's cavalry, and Wheeler commanded the horsemen in the Army of Tennessee. The Army of Northern Virginia's cavalry began with about 1,700 troopers in six regiments in late 1861. By mid-1862 Stuart's division had grown to six brigades under Fitz Lee, William Henry Fitzhugh Lee, Beverly Holcombe Robertson, William Edmondson ("Grumble") Jones, Wade Hampton, and Albert Gallatin Jenkins, and numbered some 4,000 present for duty out of an aggregate of some 7,000. By mid-1863 the cavalry had grown to 10,000 men in

CAVALRY ATTACKS

Confederate horsemen attack a Federal supply train near Jasper, Tennessee.

FRANK LESLIE'S ILLUSTRATED
FAMOUS LEADERS AND
BATTLE SCENES OF THE
CIVIL WAR

seven brigades—much too large a force for its organizational makeup. Because of this, Stuart's division was broken into two divisions under Fitz Lee and Hampton, each with three brigades of two to four regiments.

Stuart's cavalry corps soon numbered 20,000 present and absent. Though the rolls contained nearly 20,000 names, only about a third might be present at any one time because of the way the cavalry had been established. Each trooper provided his own mount and was paid sixty cents a day for its use. When a trooper lost his horse, because of disease or battle wounds, he had to secure another, which usually meant traveling home to get another horse from the farm. As the war dragged on, it became harder and harder to find serviceable mounts, and this added to the number of cavalrymen absent because of sickness, wounds, or desertion.

In May 1864 the Army of Northern Virginia's cavalry was further enlarged organizationally into three divisions, with William Henry Fitzhugh Lee becoming the new major general. After Stuart was killed at Yellow Tavern in May 1864, Hampton was given command of the cavalry corps, and Matthew Calbraith Butler was promoted to take Hampton's place in command of one of the divisions. By mid-1864 the number of cavalry had begun to decline. Of an aggregate of 14,418 in November, only 6,051 were present for duty, and 1,224 were dismounted. By the time of the surrender at Appomattox in April 1865, the cavalry numbered 134 officers and 1,425 enlisted men. It must be remembered, though, that a large portion of the Army of Northern Virginia's cavalry escaped from Appomattox to Lynchburg, some disbanding and riding home, others traveling south to continue the war in the Carolinas with Joseph E. Johnston's Army of Tennessee.

In 1862 the Army of Tennessee's four brigades comprised sixteen regiments in all. By January the next year, Wheeler's division numbered 8,300 men present for duty. In March a true cavalry corps was created for the Army of Tennessee when Wheeler's force was divided into three divisions under Morgan, Wharton, and William Thompson Martin. Each division had at least two brigades (Morgan's had three), with each brigade composed of two to five regiments. The corps' total strength was 6,872 men present for duty from an aggregate of 13,820. Forrest's division had two brigades of four and five regiments. By late 1863 Wheeler's troopers numbered 11,700 present of 28,000 on the rolls. In March 1865 this tally had dropped to 5,105 cavalrymen present of 7,042 on the rolls. On April 26, 1865, 175 officers and 2,331 enlisted men were paroled at Greensborough, North Carolina, when the Army of Tennessee surrendered.

Tactics

In addition to its initial superior organization, the Confederate cavalry's early ascendancy over its Federal opponent stemmed from the less dogmatic approach its commanders took to the employment of mounted forces. Prior to the war, many of the future commanders of both North and South had been trained at West Point and Jefferson, and later Carlisle, Barracks. Their cavalry training revolved around Napoleon's maxims of war and the theories expounded by Henri de Jomini. These two Europeans believed that cavalry served a specific purpose on the battlefield as a supporting arm to the infantry, and that its role within the army was limited. Basically, they thought that the cavalry was best suited for scouting, covering the army's flanks and rear, and charging infantry formations (but only after the main infantry attack) to ensure victory and cause confusion during the enemy's retreat. It was believed that cavalry could not act alone, either offensively or defensively, and that when in action cavalry should rely on the saber. These theories were mirrored in the doctrine and tactics taught within the U.S. Army prior to the Civil War.

The tactics that evolved from these theories were used throughout the war by the Confederate cavalry. At Manassas, independent companies like the famed "Black Horse Troop" of Warrenton and regiments of cavalry were used to seal the Southern victory by pursuing the retreating Federals across Stone Bridge, down the Warrenton Pike, to Centreville, and beyond. Throughout the war the Army of Northern Virginia and the Army of Tennessee used cavalry to scout the enemy's position and determine the intentions of the Union armies, both prior to Southern offensives and during the campaigns. Stuart's cavalry did an excellent job in covering Lee's flanks when the Army of Northern Virginia was marching south to the Rappahannock line in October 1862 after the Sharpsburg campaign. Stuart screened Lee's movements again when the Confederate army marched north on its way to Gettysburg in June 1863.

The cavalry was also used to control the area between the armies and to keep the Southern generals informed about Federal movements, intentions, and positions. In early 1861, prior to First Manassas, Stuart's horsemen did an excellent job of keeping Robert Paterson's Union force in the Shenandoah Valley from knowing the exact whereabouts of Joseph E. Johnston's army until after it had reached Manassas. After Manassas, Stuart set up a line of outposts along the Potomac River to keep Johnston informed of enemy movements before him.

In April and May 1862 the Southern cavalry on the peninsula did another good job of keeping tabs on

The Army of Tennessee was the major Confederate military force in the area between the Appalachians and the Mississippi—a vast region known in the 1860s as the West.

PAGE 32

Southern casualties at Brandy Station amounted to 51 killed, 250 wounded, and 132 missing; the Federals lost 1,651.

PAGE 71

Shenandoah Valley, 1864: In three battles—Third Winchester on Sept. 19, Fisher's Hill on Sept. 22, and Cedar Creek on Oct. 19— Sheridan defeated the Confederates.

PAGE 184

Many Southerners blamed Early for the loss of the Shenandoah Valley, though it is doubtful anyone esle could have prevented it.

PAGE 184

the Federals around Yorktown and covering John B. Magruder's withdrawal to Williamsburg. Throughout the war, whether along the Potomac, Rappahannock, Rapidan, or elsewhere, the Southern cavalry was used to cover the army's front by keeping tabs on the enemy before it, countering any Federal scouting raids, and warning of any major buildups that might signal an attack.

Throughout the war both Stuart's cavalry in Virginia and Wheeler's cavalry in the West were used to obtain supplies for their respective armies. This included everything from wagons, horses, and mules to uniforms, tents, money, and arms—horses and arms probably being the most important.

The charging of infantry formations by cavalry, in the traditional mounted attack, was exemplified by Jubal Early's use of his cavalry at Fisher's Hill on October 18, 1864. As dawn broke, the Confederate cavalry, positioned prior to sunrise on the Federal right flank, stormed into Sheridan's encampment, driving the men out of their camp and back beyond Middletown. After Sheridan's successful counterattack, Early's cavalry covered the army's retreat by holding the pursuing Federals at bay while the infantry moved up the road and past key road and river crossings. From mid-March 1865 until Lee surrendered at Appomattox, covering the Army of Northern Virginia's rear was a full-time job for the cavalry as Grant relentlessly pushed Lee westward. This last campaign saw the Confederate cavalry mix mounted fighting with dismounted rearguard action to protect Lee's wagon trains and infantry formations from being surrounded and cut off.

CAVALRY RAIDS. The most notable change in the use of cavalry, inaugurated by Stuart, was the large-scale mounted raid. Prior to 1862 it would have been thought foolish, and potentially disastrous, to send an army's cavalry force into enemy territory alone. But Stuart's "Ride around McClellan" in June 1862 changed that perception. Taking 1,200 men, Stuart covered 150 miles behind George B. McClellan's army to reconnoiter the Federal right flank and rear. By destroying considerable amounts of stores and capturing prisoners (with very little Confederate loss), Stuart changed the role of cavalry in this American war and established Confederate preeminence, at least until the Federals learned from their mistakes. During 1862 Stuart undertook three more raids, Forrest went on two, and Morgan conducted three.

Other famous raids by Stuart included assaults on Catlett's Station (August 22–23, 1862), Chambersburg (October 9–12, 1862), and Dumfries (December 26–31, 1862). During the raid on Catlett's Station, Stuart took 1,500 men to capture John

Pope's headquarters. Besides destroying Federal stores, Stuart seized a large amount of money as well as Pope's papers, which gave Lee the information he needed to undertake the Second Manassas campaign. For Chambersburg, Stuart led 1,800 men into Pennsylvania to destroy machine shops and stores in the city and to round up about a thousand horses badly needed by the Army of Northern Virginia. The Dumfries raid was the fourth of a series of excursions against Ambrose Burnside's rear during November and December 1862. Stuart and 1,800 troopers destroyed a large amount of property, capturing prisoners, horses, wagons, and arms. But in July 1863 Stuart undertook his disastrous Gettysburg raid. This time he went too far afield with his force, and instead of gaining intelligence for Lee or securing supplies in a quick strike, he got bogged down with his booty and effectively took himself out of the Gettysburg campaign.

Forrest led 1,000 men in July 1862 on his first raid and captured 1,000 Federals at Murfreesboro, along with $1 million worth of stores, destroying important railroad bridges along the way. This action delayed a planned Federal offensive and forced two Union divisions to be diverted from the front to guard the rail lines of the rear. Forrest's second raid, in December 1862, was aimed at the rail line connecting Grant's headquarters at Columbus, Kentucky, and Federal troops in northern Mississippi. Forrest's 2,500 men tore up the Mobile and Ohio Railroad during this foray.

In Morgan's first raid, in July 1862, 800 troopers captured 1,200 prisoners and a number of Federal depots while covering one thousand miles. This raid lowered Northern morale and delayed another planned Federal offensive. Morgan's October 1862 raid against Lexington, Kentucky, involved 1,800 men and resulted in the capture of a number of posts and the destruction of several key railroad bridges. In December 1862 he conducted a raid at the head of 4,000 men; they netted 1,800 prisoners and destroyed $2 million worth of Federal stores. But as had Stuart's raid at Gettysburg, Morgan's July 1863 Ohio raid ended in disaster. His force of 2,400 endured terrible fighting and covered a very long distance before surrendering at New Lisbon (Beaver Creek) on July 26. This failure, too, was the result of a mounted force being gone too long and too far from its main army, thus encountering stronger opposition and critical delays.

The tactic had been proven time and again: an independent body of cavalry could cover long distances in the enemy's rear, capturing stores and prisoners, gathering intelligence, and destroying vital supplies and lines of communication—if it were done quickly and with a force large enough to counter any opposition it might meet. These operations also forced the enemy to dedicate front-line troops to guard the rear from other mounted raiders or guerrilla forces, thus making the cavalry a force multiplier. The success of these raids, then, rested on several factors: the raiders had to be heavily armed (to defeat any opposition encountered); they had to be familiar with the terrain to be traversed; the operation had to be kept secret; and the force had to keep moving at all times.

Raiding continued as a main operation of the Confederate cavalry into the middle years of the war. But after Gettysburg, its usefulness began to ebb. This was due, in part, to the fact that the Federal cavalry had begun to operate as the Confederates had all along—in large, independent bodies moving offensively and not just in reaction to Southern thrusts.

At the Battle of Brandy Station, the largest mounted clash of the war (involving some 10,000 cavalry), the Federal horsemen discovered they could ride and fight against Stuart as equals. On the morning of June 9, 1863, Alfred Pleasonton rode out of Fredericksburg and attacked Stuart's force as it guarded the Rappahannock River line. Under cover of a morning haze John Buford surprised William Edmondson ("Grumble") Jones's force and drove them to Brandy Station. At the same time David Gregg pushed Beverly Holcombe Robertson's men from Kelly's Ford. Just as Fleetwood Hill, the site of Stuart's headquarters, was about to be overrun by the Federals, Wade Hampton arrived and counterattacked, driving the Union force from the battlefield. Though Pleasonton retreated from the field, he had accomplished much. He had learned that Lee was moving north, he had surprised and humiliated the seemingly invincible Stuart, and he had shown his men that the Southern cavalry could be bested. As historian H. B. McClellan wrote, "It made the Federal cavalry. Up to that time confessedly inferior to the Southern horsemen, they gained . . . that confidence in themselves and in their commanders which enabled them to contest" the Southern cavalry from then on. By the time of the Gettysburg campaign, the Federal cavalry was gaining experience, its leaders were becoming bolder, its mounts were improving, and its equipment, superior to the Confederate arms, was at last plentiful. In addition, the numbers of Federal cavalry were growing.

DISMOUNTED FIGHTING. The third important innovation that developed during the war was the large-scale use of dismounted cavalry in battle. By 1864 the Confederates were outnumbered and outgunned by the Federals. Confederate mounts were degenerating in both quality and quantity, and the cavalry could no longer attack en masse Federal cavalry formations—their numbers were too large. Nor could

BATTLE OF THE WILDERNESS
Dismount and Defend

One of the best examples of dismounted cavalry tactics was the role played by Stuart's cavalry in the Battle of the Wilderness in May 1864. The Federal army, under Grant, threw 127,000 troops, 21,000 of which were cavalry commanded by Sheridan, into this campaign. Lee's Army of Northern Virginia was composed of only 54,000 infantry and 9,000 cavalry, and the disadvantage in numbers had to be compensated for somehow. On May 5 Stuart's cavalry rode to Todd's Tavern, where they encountered Federal cavalry coming up a road. Here the Confederates dismounted and held the enemy in check until dark, fighting like infantry. The next day saw similar action near the intersection of the Catharpin and Brock Roads. One Confederate diary entry reads, "Our regiment was moved to the front and dismounted to fight." Sheridan then moved his cavalry to Spotsylvania Court House, where Fitz Lee's men had ridden, dismounted, and erected barricades behind which to fight. This action allowed Lee to rush Anderson's corps to the crossroads and secure the Army of Northern Virginia's flank. The ability of Stuart's cavalry to move quickly to a strategic point, dismount, and hold the ground until reinforcements arrived gave Lee the time he needed to move up a heavier force. The fighting continued on May 8, with the cavalrymen felling trees and building barricades to block the road. As one trooper wrote, "We boys of the cavalry were not much on using spades and shovels, but could use axes very well. We . . . cut down a long line of trees . . . and these made a pretty good obstruction to fight behind." By midmorning Lee's infantry had arrived and replaced the cavalry in the rifle pits.

— KENNETH L. STILES

Brandy Station: By the narrowest of margins, Maj. Gen. J.E.B. Stuart wrested a tactical victory from the Union cavalry.

PAGE 71

"It was as if he couldn't get religion and that galloping cavalry and his dead grandfather shot from the galloping horse untangled from each other, even in the pulpit."

WILLIAM FAULKNER
LIGHT IN AUGUST, 1932

the Confederates ride with impunity around the Federal flanks and through the rear area, for the Southern horses were not up to such arduous tasks. As the Confederate army began to fight an almost exclusively defensive war, the chances to use the mounted arm in offensive charges or to follow up a victory with a mounted pursuit diminished—thus the turn to fighting as mounted *infantry*. Like brigading the cavalry

The Battle of the Wilderness in Northern Virginia pitted Lee against Grant in the opening stage of the overland campaign that eventually led to the siege of Richmond and Petersburg.

PAGE 677

J.E.B. Stuart's most spectacular expedition occurred on June 12–15, 1862, in the Peninsular campaign.

PAGE 594

and raiding, this innovation was eventually copied by the Federals.

The Battle of the Wilderness was the first battle in which the Confederate cavalry fought almost exclusively as infantry, but it was not to be the last. During Early's 1864 Shenandoah Valley campaign, dismounted cavalry was used extensively to slow the pursuit of Sheridan's Federal horsemen. Early's cavalry would fall back to important gaps or crossroads, dismount, and build barricades from which they were able to delay the Union forces. Prominent use was made of dismounted cavalry at Front Royal on September 20, Milford on September 22, and Luray on September 24.

Though true cavalry clashes did occur throughout 1864, dismounted fighting began to occupy more and more of the cavalry's time in battle, and it was the Confederates who adopted the practice first. In late 1863, the colonel of the First Vermont Cavalry ordered his men to charge a dismounted Confederate force in a tree line. His report stated, "To charge into woods with the saber against . . . dismounted cavalry requires high courage, and is against immense odds." The Federals' adherence in the beginning to the traditional European manner of cavalry fighting—mounted with saber in hand—derived, in part, from the philosophical outlook of Union officers, particularly George B. McClellan, who had studied and reported on European mounted training and tactics prior to the war. The Federals emphasized that the strength of the cavalry lay in its spurs and sabers and neglected to train its men in the tactics and weapons of dismounted combat. Their fondness for the saber caused them to be slow to adopt new tactics for fighting. Only after the Confederates used them to their advantage did the Federals follow suit. By war's end, though, after Union cavalrymen had learned to ride into battle, dismount, and fight on foot, the Federals again bested their Confederate adversary. They could put more men with greater firepower (because of their breech-loading repeating carbines) into the battle at a given time. Once again, the Federals had learned from the Confederates and gained the advantage.

Throughout the war, however, the Confederate cavalry was held in awe for its ability to strike quickly and deeply into enemy territory. After the fighting in the Wilderness, the infantry in the Army of Northern Virginia no longer joked about "never having seen a dead cavalryman." As one Southern artilleryman wrote, the Confederate cavalry "had shown itself signally possessed of the quality, that the infantry and artillery naturally admired most . . . obstinacy in fight." The Confederate cavalry became a major player in the army's campaigns. Its place in the history books was assured for the depth it added to the mounted arm.

[*See also* Brandy Station, Virginia; Early, Jubal, *sidebar* Early's Washington Raid; Gettysburg Campaign; Morgan's Raids; Price's Missouri Raid; Shenandoah Valley, *article on* Shenandoah Valley Campaign of Sheridan; Stuart's Raids; Wilderness Campaign; *and biographies of selected figures mentioned herein.*]

— KENNETH L. STILES

CEDAR CREEK, VIRGINIA

Ten miles south of Winchester, Virginia, Cedar Creek was the site of an October 19, 1864, battle that witnessed the destruction of Maj. Gen. Jubal Early's Army of the Valley. Never again would the Confederacy draw provisions from the Shenandoah Valley. Southern casualties amounted to around 2,900 men killed, wounded, or missing; the Federals lost 5,665.

Confederate debacles at Third Winchester (September 19) and Fisher's Hill (September 22) swept Early's troops from the lower Valley and allowed Maj. Gen. Philip Sheridan to lay waste to the region. When the Union army retreated, Early followed, arriving at Strasburg on October 13. A few miles to the north on the hills above Cedar Creek stood Sheridan's Army of the Shenandoah.

Early desired offensive action but realized that without reinforcements and supplies he had little hope of achieving a decisive victory. Gen. Robert E. Lee was not of the same mind. Discounting reports that had placed Sheridan's army at 35,000 to 40,000 men, Lee grossly underestimated the enemy's strength. He demanded that Early take his 10,000 rifles and "move against" Sheridan.

On October 17, Early sent Maj. Gen. John B. Gordon and Jedediah Hotchkiss, a topographical engineer, to Massanutten Mountain. They discovered that the left flank of Sheridan's army was not prepared to resist a sudden assault. The Union Eighth Corps had encamped east of the Valley Turnpike, while the Sixth and Ninth Corps had bivouacked west of the road and around the mansion Belle Grove.

Conferring with his subordinates the next day, Early approved one of the most audacious flanking maneuvers of the entire war. It called for Gordon to take three divisions—those of Brig. Gen. John Pegram, Maj. Gen. Dodson Ramseur, and Brig. Gen. Clement A. Evans—across the north fork of the Shenandoah at Fisher's Hill, skirt the end of Massanutten, cross the river again, and then form for an assault against the eastern flank of the camp of the Eighth Corps. Maj. Gen. Joseph B. Kershaw's division was ordered to move through Strasburg, cross Cedar Creek at Bowman's Mill, and coordinate his attack with Gordon. The remaining infantry division, commanded by Brig. Gen. Gabriel Colvin Wharton, would advance down the Valley Pike in a supporting role, while Brig. Gen. Thomas Lafayette Rosser's horsemen were to protect Early's left flank.

Gordon's column moved out at 8:00 P.M. on October 18, stumbling across a mountain trail that resembled "a pig's path." Because victory depended on surprise, the soldiers removed equipment that might create noise and alert the enemy's pickets. After fording the Shenandoah for a second time, they went into position a half-mile east of the enemy's camp, just before 5:00 A.M. Forty-five minutes later, concealed by a heavy fog, Gordon's troops and Kershaw's division stormed the Union camps. For the next three hours the Confederates drove the Eighth and Nineteenth Corps toward Middletown. Confident that he had attained a remarkable victory, Early told Gordon, "This is glory enough for one day." His soldiers had bagged eighteen pieces of artillery and 1,300 prisoners.

The Federals had formed a final defensive line three miles north of their camps. By 10:00 A.M. Early had edged his way toward the enemy, but the momentum of the Confederate assault had disappeared. Early believed that "it would not do to press my troops further." His men were exhausted, and the famished soldiers abandoned the ranks to plunder Northern camps.

Away from his men when the fighting erupted, Sheridan had rushed to the scene, where he massed his cavalry against Early's left flank. At 3:30 P.M. his troopers pounced on the exposed position. Up and down the line echoed the cry, "We are flanked," as the Confederates fell back in disorder. While trying to restore calm in his command, Ramseur, the youngest West Pointer to achieve the rank of major general in the Confederacy, received a mortal wound.

Early's army retreated to Fisher's Hill, where the general bitterly remarked, "The Yankees got whipped and we got scared." Although his subordinates had flawlessly executed his plan, Early did not have sufficient numbers to compensate for surrendering the initiative to Sheridan. Defeat at Cedar Creek eliminated the Army of the Valley as an effective fighting force for the rest of the war. While Early headed south with his battered army, the morale of the Northern people soared. Together with the capture of Atlanta and Mobile Bay, Sheridan's triumphs in the Valley ensured Abraham Lincoln's victory in the presidential elections that November.

— PETER S. CARMICHAEL

CHANCELLORSVILLE CAMPAIGN

This country intersection in Spotsylvania County, Virginia, became the focal point of a vast battlefield spread across some fifty square miles, on which Robert E. Lee and Thomas J. ("Stonewall") Jackson collaborated on April 29–May 6, 1863, for their greatest joint victory. Chancellorsville was also Jackson's last battle. His mortal wounding by the mistaken fire of his own men was one of the most important military events of the war.

After its resounding and easy victory in the Battle of Fredericksburg on December 13, 1862, Lee's Army of Northern Virginia spent the winter centered in that vicinity, but with flanks spread more than a dozen miles upstream and twice that far downstream. The Rappahannock River served as the military frontier between the contending countries; the Federal Army of the Potomac remained opposite Lee on the river's left bank. In the aftermath of the aptly named "Mud March" in January, President Abraham Lincoln replaced Ambrose E. Burnside with brash and boastful—but politically well-connected—Joseph Hooker. Hooker revamped his army's support functions, inaugurated an efficient intelligence service, and greatly improved morale. As he planned for spring campaigning, Hooker also produced an outstanding scheme designed to force Lee from the heights behind Fredericksburg that had proved so daunting a few months earlier.

Hooker intended to send his revitalized cavalry arm on a raid deep into the Confederate rear and at the same time to move his army far upriver and surprise Lee by crossing well west of Fredericksburg. The cavalry excursion faltered in attempts to get underway during mid-April as a result of bad weather and the lack of energy of its chief. The raiders finally departed on April 29 and spent a week ricocheting through central Virginia, harassed and controlled by a small Southern mounted detachment, while Lee's main cavalry force remained with the army to perform vital screening and reconnaissance duties. A few weeks later during the Gettysburg campaign the same situation prevailed, only in reverse; it was as though the Federals had learned from their experience, while the Confederates ignored the lesson they had taught so skillfully at Chancellorsville.

Meanwhile, General Hooker put into motion his plan to move upriver to get behind Lee. The march covered considerable distance and required heavy logistical support, but it succeeded remarkably well. By the end of April 30 Hooker had moved much of his army nearly thirty miles, crossed two rivers by various fords,

April 30, 1863: U.S. Gen. Joseph Hooker skillfully stole a march on Lee and concentrated behind the Confederates at a country crossroads called Chancellorsville.

PAGE 27

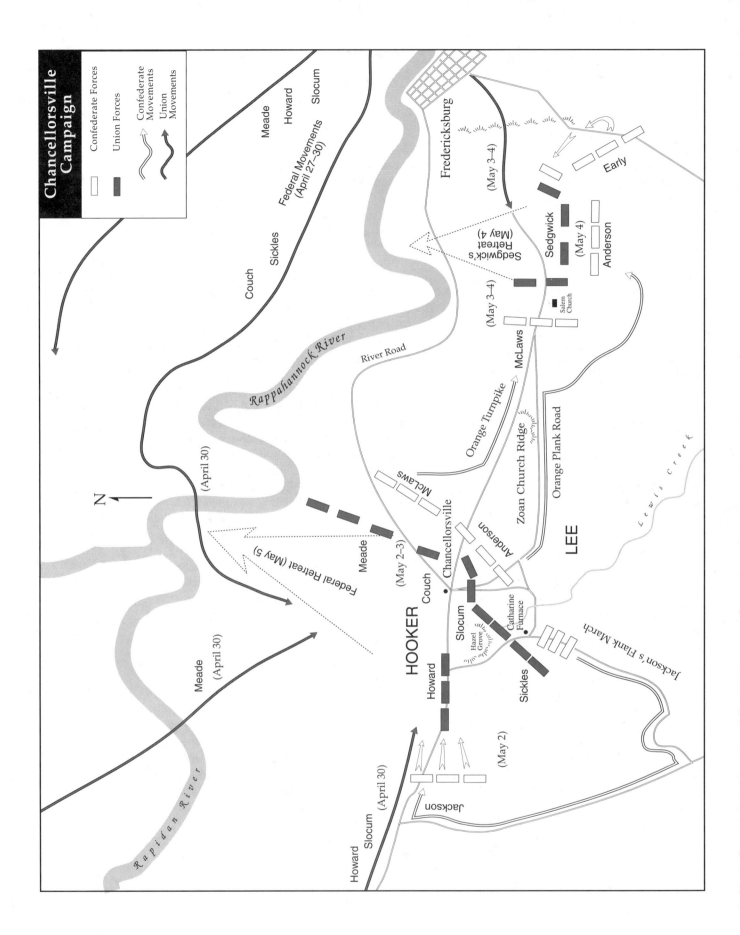

Chancellorsville Campaign

and concentrated in the densely wooded Wilderness of Spotsylvania around the Chancellorsville crossroads. "Chancellorsville" was not a town or even a hamlet, but rather a single building—a half-century-old inn at the intersection of the Orange Turnpike and Orange Plank Road. Hooker was unpopular with most of his high-ranking subordinates for various reasons, but his daring maneuver prompted Gen. George G. Meade to chortle, "Hurrah for old Joe! We're on Lee's flank and he doesn't know it." Hooker clearly was hoping that his coup would force the Confederate army to abandon its position and retire well to the south. He outnumbered Lee by more than two to one, having 130,000 men against 60,000, and could hardly imagine his opponent facing both those odds and the successful opening march by the Army of the Potomac.

By April 30 Lee did know where Hooker was and had boldly determined to gather his own army west of Fredericksburg to fight. The Federals had left a strong detachment feinting toward Fredericksburg, so Lee put Jubal Early in charge of a rear guard to face that threat. He hurried the rest of the Army of Northern Virginia in the direction of Chancellorsville. The few Confederates who had been retiring in the face of Hooker's host held a tenuous grip on the Zoan Church ridge east of Chancellorsville on the morning of May 1 when Lee and Jackson approached with the vanguard of the army. The Zoan ridge was not only strong high ground but also in the open, outside the seventy-square-mile morass known as the Wilderness. In the tangled Wilderness, Hooker would lose much of the advantage of his huge preponderance in numbers, so taking Zoan Church offered him a tremendous opportunity. The campaign turned in that moment when Stonewall Jackson arrived on the scene and ordered the corporal's guard of Confederates on hand to attack. The bravado that had sustained Hooker to this time evaporated in the face of a determined foe. During the rest of the campaign the Federal command story was one of steady spiritual deterioration. There was much talk at the time that Hooker was drunk, but the conventional wisdom soon emerged that he had given up his customary high alcoholic intake on assuming command and that the change had thrown his nervous system out of balance. Some reasonably strong contemporary evidence now available suggests that Hooker may indeed have been in liquor during the campaign.

From the Zoan Church ridge the Confederates pushed Hooker's troops steadily back toward Chancellorsville on May 1. Jackson orchestrated a tangled tactical combination of brigades, assigned in the order they arrived; ignoring divisional lines, they advanced westward on the roughly parallel Plank Road and Turnpike. The Confederates exploited an unfin-ished railroad grade as a third corridor through the Wilderness. Using that route, the Georgia brigade of Gen. Ambrose Ransom ("Rans") Wright slipped past the Federal right flank and forced it to swing northward nearly ninety degrees. The new configuration would be a central feature of the next day's operations.

At night on May 1 the Confederate high command gathered at a crossroads one mile from Chancellorsville to consider its options. Despite the enormous disparity in manpower that he faced, Lee was determined to assume the offensive. He had reconnoitered personally on his right during the day and found the ground there both heavily defended and nearly impassable. A small party of staff officers scouted through the brightly moonlit night directly toward Chancellorsville and came back to report that no opening offered in that direction. Through the night reports came in from a number of sources—a topographical engineer, a local furnace operator, a Presbyterian clergyman who knew the region, and cavalry officers—suggesting that a way might be found to turn the Federal right. For Lee to move a column across his enemy's front, leaving a very small force as a decoy, violated the basic principles of war. To take such a risk when outnumbered more than two to one went beyond that to the verge of folly. Lee decided to go ahead, nonetheless.

When Jackson headed into the Wilderness early on May 2, he took some thirty thousand men with him, leaving Lee only about fifteen thousand with whom to face Hooker. For ten hours Lee feigned attacks and threw forward entire regiments as skirmishers responsible for scouting and screening the line. Tactical doctrine suggested that one or at most two of the ten companies in a regiment should provide a skirmish force in front of the main line of defense. At times Lee had no main line, just skirmishers. While Lee played his desperate game, Stonewall Jackson marched on a long looping route across Hooker's front and toward his right flank. Less than a mile into the march Jackson's men had to cross a high open spot that exposed them to Federal view. They double-timed through the ensuing artillery barrage and continued on their way. Aggressive Federal Gen. Daniel E. Sickles pushed infantry southward to interdict the Confederate movement. The Northern probe clashed with a rear guard near Catharine Furnace but did not deflect Jackson from his purpose.

Jackson rode near the head of his long column as it neared the point at which he and Lee had planned that the attackers should turn toward the enemy. He soon found that the Federal line stretched farther west than had been assumed; carrying through the original intention would not prove very effective. To meet this changed situation, Jackson marched farther north before turning east. Early in the afternoon his advance

Lee calmly faced Hooker's legions with a handful of troops while Jackson carefully and secretly led nearly 30,000 men across the front of the Northern army.

PAGE 27

Stonewall's troops thundered out of the Wilderness behind Hooker's right, screaming the Rebel yell.

PAGE 27

brigades arrived on a high wooded ridge that overlooked the unprotected right flank of the Union army. Hard marching and careful planning and daring had presented Jackson with one of the great opportunities of the war. As his brigades arrived, Jackson arranged them into a mighty attacking force two miles long, straddling the Orange Turnpike and overlapping the Federal line by a mile on each side. When two divisions had arrived, Jackson nodded to division commander Robert Rodes and said quietly, "You can go forward then."

The Confederates pouring out of the woods and screaming the rebel yell routed Federal Gen. O. O. Howard's Eleventh Corps and smashed two miles through the enemy positions. The bravest Northern defender could not stand long against a force that overlapped him on both sides as far as he could see. Flagrant disobedience of attack orders by Confederate Gen. Alfred H. Colquitt neutralized fully 40 percent of Jackson's line, but the rest surged irresistibly forward. The Federal position next beyond Howard's belonged to Sickles's troops, but most of them had marched south to investigate around Catharine Furnace, so Howard's retreat roared unchecked through the vacuum. For the rest of his life Hooker blamed Howard for the disaster (soon after the war he called Howard a "hypocrite . . . totally incompetent . . . a perfect old woman . . . a bad man"). In fact, no force of any sort could have faced successfully so massive a surprise attack in flank and rear.

Darkness and the confusion inherent in the wide-ranging advance stopped Jackson's momentum a mile short of Chancellorsville. As the general returned from a mounted reconnaissance beyond his amorphous front line at about 9:00 P.M., Confederates of the Eighteenth North Carolina Infantry fired in confusion on his party and wounded Jackson in three places. Early the next morning surgeons amputated his shattered left arm in a field hospital tent.

Cavalry Gen. J. E. B. Stuart assumed temporary command of Jackson's corps during the night of May 2–3 and prepared to drive the Federals from Chancellorsville. Southern artillerists identified an open knoll called Hazel Grove as the key to the battlefield, and Stuart prepared to seize it at dawn. Before Stuart could take Hazel Grove, Joe Hooker abandoned it. Confederate guns hurried to the hilltop and opened a steady fire that did much to win the day. Bitter and terribly confused woods fighting on May 3 between Hazel Grove and Chancellorsville exacted more casualties than had the dramatic actions of May 2, but in impenetrable obscurity. A knowledgeable Confederate officer who later wrote of the battle concluded resignedly, "It would be useless to follow in detail the desperate fighting which now ensued and was kept up for some hours." Its net result was gradual establishment of Confederate control around Chancellorsville. When Lee rode into the clearing around the house with his reunited army, the troops hailed him with a celebration so long and heartfelt that a staff officer wrote, "I thought that it must have been from such a scene that men in ancient days rose to the dignity of gods."

Lee's moment of triumph was interrupted when word arrived from near Fredericksburg that Early's rear guard had been penetrated by a Federal force under Gen. John Sedgwick. Lee suspended operations around Chancellorsville and sent reinforcements eastward under Gen. Lafayette McLaws. Near Salem Church, four miles west of Fredericksburg, part of the rear guard brought the Federals to a halt. McLaws handled his role poorly, and Lee went to the area in person on May 4 to arrange the attack that pushed Sedgwick back across the river during the night. The next night Hooker abandoned his position north of Chancellorsville and returned to the left bank of the Rappahannock, ending the campaign. Lee had suffered about thirteen thousand casualties; Hooker, eighteen thousand. The astonishing Confederate triumph under adverse circumstances is often, and aptly, called Lee's greatest victory, but its final act constituted a Southern disaster unequaled during the entire war. On May 10 Stonewall Jackson died at Guiney Station, south of Fredericksburg, removing what might have been the South's best hope for independence by military means.

The spectacular opening of the 1863 campaign at Chancellorsville presented Lee with an opportunity to raid north of the Potomac. He and his army, full of almost unlimited confidence in one another, carried their Chancellorsville momentum into Pennsylvania but found a strikingly different set of circumstances at Gettysburg. There the ultimate consequence of Chancellorsville became apparent at a time "when every moment . . . could not be balanced with gold," in the words of a Confederate staff officer, who could only mutter sadly, "Jackson is not here."

— ROBERT K. KRICK

CHARLESTON, SOUTH CAROLINA

[*This entry is composed of two articles,* City of Charleston *and* Bombardment of Charleston. *See also* Fort Sumter, South Carolina; *H. L. Hunley;* Navy, *sidebar* Davids.]

CITY OF CHARLESTON

Founded in 1670 as Charles Town, the settlement was moved from its original site to a nearby peninsula at the confluence of the Ashley and Cooper rivers, which flowed into the Atlantic. The economy flourished with the export of low-country rice and the import of African slaves. Approximately 40 percent of all Africans involuntarily shipped to America entered across Charles Town's wharves. It became the principal city of the South and the capital of South Carolina. After the Revolutionary War, the city's name was changed to Charleston, and Columbia became the capital of the new state.

Postwar booms in the export of rice and the new staple of cotton sputtered during the 1820s, and Charleston's economy stagnated. The city's poor rail connections westward, its shallow harbor, and the lack of a variety of exports and of a pool of free, educated workers especially hurt small retailers and skilled laborers. The wealthy planter-merchant elite, however, prospered, since the price of rice and luxury Sea Island cotton declined only slightly less than the cost of living.

The city was the economic, social, and cultural capital for the great planters of the low country. Here they built summer homes to escape the isolation and the sickly season on the plantations. They preempted the choice residential sites on the lower peninsula or its flanks, where they could enjoy salubrious sea breezes and proximity to social institutions. They also brought their families to Charleston from January through March to enjoy the annual social season, which featured horse races, balls, concerts, and the theater. The planters' emphasis on family connections, sociability, and conspicuous leisure activities strongly influenced the city's character.

William Gilmore Simms was antebellum Charleston's most famous literary figure, but he was discontented with the city's intellectual life. The few citizens who were interested in ideas met periodically at Russell's Book Store and during the 1850s founded *Russell's Magazine,* the last of the Old South's literary publications. In the same decade the South Carolina Historical Society and the Carolina Art Association were founded. Physicians and naturalists made the greatest contributions to the city's intellectual life. Recognized nationally, Dr. Lewis R. Gibbes of the College of Charleston helped make the city the center of scientific activity in the Southeast.

During the late antebellum period local businessmen used their influence on the City Council to invest municipal money in improving the city's rail connections. They revived its merchant marine and obtained funds to dredge the harbor, helping stimulate an economic boom. By the early 1850s Charleston had become the manufacturing center of the state, but its economy was soon in trouble again. Competing railroads siphoned off traffic, and the city's hinterland dependencies remained too few and too small to promote Charleston's growth. The city continued as a colonial outlier of the northeastern regional system.

The faltering economy, coupled with a steady stream of immigrants, sailors, and vagrants straggling

STANDING GUARD

"Confederate Flag over Fort Sumter, October 20, 1863," by Conrad Wise Chapman shows a lone watchman guarding the site where the war began.

THE MUSEUM OF
THE CONFEDERACY,
RICHMOND, VIRGINIA

C

*Beauregard quickly
rearranged gun
implacements on
the Charleston
Battery to mount a
circle of fire around
Fort Sumter.*

PAGE 43

*Having declared
their state an
independent
republic, the South
Carolinians
resented the
presence of what
was to them a
foreign flag.*

PAGE 224

into the port city seeking work, caused growing unemployment. Prostitution flourished. With a population of 40,522 in 1859—it had declined about 2,500 since the beginning of the decade—the city of Charleston ranked twenty-second in the nation. It was the most populous of the South Atlantic ports and the major distribution center for the state. The out-migration of slaves and the immigration of Irish and Germans transformed Charleston from a city that was 53 percent black to 58 percent white, from a city dominated by a skilled black labor force to one in which two-fifths of the working class were white and 60 percent were foreign born.

The inequality in the distribution of wealth was enormous in comparison to Northern cities: just over 3 percent of the 4,644 free white heads of households owned approximately half of the wealth in Charleston. Most Charlestonians owned neither land nor slaves, and class divisions were as obvious as racial divisions. Economically, most whites living in the city had more in common with African Americans than with the white elite.

An increase in thefts and homicides, and rising Northern antislavery rhetoric, which Charlestonians feared would encourage slave insurrections, alarmed the propertied classes. Faced with these problems of social instability, they embarked on a program of reforms. They inaugurated a public school system, built a larger poorhouse, established a professional police force, and remodeled the jail. Charleston's problems were compounded by its large slave population for which there existed several separate agencies of social control.

In April 1860 the Democratic National Convention met in Charleston only to split quickly into Northern and Southern wings and arrange to reconvene elsewhere. When the national Republican party nominated Abraham Lincoln for president, Charleston became the South's leading publisher of secession pamphlets.

As the crisis worsened, the city's authorities harassed Charleston's 3,237 free blacks, including 122 of the city's mulatto aristocracy, themselves slaveholders. The police began a systematic door-to-door search and interrogation of the African American community. Poor free blacks unable to produce absolute proof of their emancipated status were reenslaved. The mulatto aristocracy was terrified. They faced the same fate. Previously, they had escaped police harassment because of their relationships with the white elite, but as the calls for secession grew louder, their white guardians fell silent. Many of Charleston's mulatto elite considered emigrating from the city but felt that they could not leave successful careers, take enormous losses through sale of their real estate, or even get safe passage out of South Carolina. But hundreds of less prosperous

free blacks sold what they could, packed what they could carry, and fled. Some sold their property at huge losses and felt cheated by whites who took advantage of their predicament.

Following Lincoln's election, delegates from across South Carolina convened in Charleston, where on December 20 they adopted the ordinance of secession from the Union. Bells rang throughout the city, cannons were fired, and volunteers jammed the streets.

On December 26 Maj. Robert Anderson, commanding the U.S. garrison on Sullivan's Island, moved his troops to Fort Sumter in Charleston Harbor. A few days later, in the first military encounter of the war, South Carolina troops seized three local sites occupied by Federal troops. In January the vessel *Star of the West* attempted to reinforce Fort Sumter, but it was fired on by batteries on Morris Island and turned back.

Following the formation of the Confederate States of America, Gen. P. G. T. Beauregard took command at Charleston. He redeployed the troops and rearranged the ring of batteries around Fort Sumter. When Major Anderson refused to surrender the fort, Beauregard ordered its bombardment on April 12, 1861. After Anderson surrendered the following day, his troops embarked for the North, and Confederate soldiers occupied the fort. President Lincoln called for 75,000 volunteers and a blockade of Southern ports.

Gen. Robert E. Lee arrived in Charleston on November 6 to take command of the Military Department of South Carolina, Georgia, and Florida. The following day Hilton Head Island, Port Royal, and Beaufort fell to Union forces. Charlestonians panicked. In December a devastating fire swept across the city, and some suspected slave arsonists.

Union strategists were determined to seize Charleston, "the cradle of secession," to stop the daily manufacture of cartridges there and the building of ironclad vessels. The steam-powered workshops of the former U.S. arsenal located on the western edge of the city produced artillery shells and thousands of cartridges daily for the Confederacy. Construction was nearing completion on the 150-foot *Palmetto State*, commissioned by the Confederate government for harbor defense, and *Chicora*, a vessel protected by 500 tons of iron armor and mounting six guns, the cost of which was funded by the state of South Carolina. The third ironclad built in the city during the war was named *Charleston*. The Federal high command also wanted to stem the flow of vast amounts of military supplies and luxury goods brought in by blockade runners. The first attack came in June 1862, when six thousand Federal troops landed southeast of the city, and a fierce firefight erupted on James Island. Casualties were heavy on both sides, and the Union forces retreated. In April 1863 nine Federal ironclads attacked Fort Sumter, but were forced to withdraw, owing to Confederate fire and the threat of mines or submarine torpedoes, a weapon developed by the Confederate Torpedo Bureau that inaugurated a new era in naval warfare. The third attack, jointly planned by the army and navy, began in July when a large Union force occupied most of Morris Island. When the last Confederate redoubt could not be taken after heroic but costly attacks by black troops, Union forces began a bombardment of the city to force its surrender. The siege lasted for 587 days. Although the harbor defenses remained too formidable for the Union navy, its increased surveillance and the occupation of Morris Island severely curtailed blockade running at Charleston.

Occasionally, daring military exploits boosted briefly the spirits of Charlestonians. In October the Confederate ship *David*, the first combat submarine, disabled a Union blockader off Charleston; in early 1864, the *H. L. Hunley* became the first submarine to sink an enemy vessel.

By this time the city was deserted below Market Street, where the Union shells could reach; above this point, the life and business of the city went on. In December Gen. William J. Hardee redeployed the demoralized troops around Charleston to meet an anticipated attack by Gen. William Tecumseh Sherman. But Sherman's destination was the state capital. In mid-February 1865 General Hardee decided that Charleston was no longer defensible, and it was evacuated. Union troops immediately seized the city. The following September a Northern reporter in Charleston described it as "a city of ruins, of desolation, of vacant homes, of widowed women . . . of deserted warehouses, of weed-wild gardens, of miles of grass-grown streets."

For nearly two centuries Charleston had been the most important city in the vast territory of the Carolinas and Georgia. From about 1837 to 1862 Southern policies had been largely determined by South Carolina, and South Carolina had been largely controlled by Charlestonians. But in three years the city lost forever both its wealth and its influence.

— WALTER J. FRASER, JR.

BOMBARDMENT OF CHARLESTON

Early in the war Union military strategists determined to seize Charleston, the hated symbol of rebellion, to stop the daily manufacture of thousands of cartridges, the building of ironclads, and the flow of military supplies brought in by blockade runners. Following two unsuccessful attempts to take the city in June 1862 and April 1863, the Federals planned a joint army-navy operation. Following the capture of Morris Island and the reduction of nearby Fort Sumter by the army,

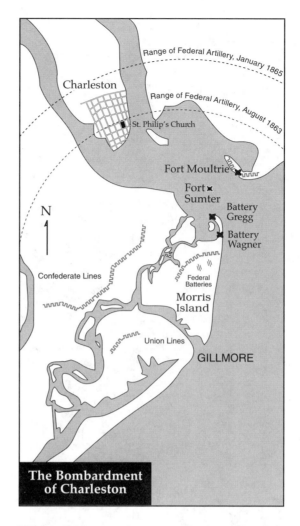

The Bombardment of Charleston

H. L. Hunley *was tested at Mobile and then sent by railroad flatcar to Charleston.*

PAGE 277

Union vessels were to steam into the harbor and demand the surrender of the city.

In July a force of 6,000 Federal troops under Gen. Quincy A. Gillmore quickly occupied most of Morris Island. A heroic and costly attack by African American troops failed to overrun Fort Wagner, the Confederate strong point. This prevented the navy from executing its role in the operation, since the harbor defenses remained formidable. General Gillmore dug in on Morris Island, constructed batteries, and trained his rifled long-range guns on Fort Sumter. One 200-pounder Parrott rifled gun was aimed at Charleston, some four miles away.

On August 21, 1863, Gillmore sent a message to the commanding officer of Charleston, Gen. P. G. T. Beauregard, demanding the evacuation of Fort Sumter and Morris Island within four hours or bombardment of the city would commence. Beauregard dashed off a reply charging that by not giving "timely notice," Gillmore was committing "an act of . . . barbarity." But in the early morning hours of August 22, Gillmore ordered the bombardment to begin. It would continue for 587 days.

*After the attack on
Charleston during
the summer of
1863, the bulk
of the Nassau
trade shifted to
Wilmington,
North Carolina.*

PAGE 61

CHARLESTON SQUADRON

South Carolina's state navy was absorbed into Confederate service in April 1861 under Commdr. H. J. Hartstene. In November Capt. Duncan N. Ingraham assumed command, and in 1862 the Charleston Squadron acquired strength with the addition of the ironclads *Chicora* and *Palmetto State*.

On January 31, 1863, the squadron struck the Union blockade, seeking to open the city to outside commerce. The Charleston command declared the blockade broken, but little damage had been done, and the city remained sealed. Soon after, Captain Ingraham was replaced as commander afloat by Capt. John Randolph Tucker of the *Chicora*.

While the naval command concentrated on ironclads, Charleston was becoming a center for experimentation with mines and torpedoes. A cadre of young officers in the squadron pushed their superiors for action, and expeditions to attack Union monitors were organized. On October 5, 1863, Lt. William T. Glassell attacked the USS *New Ironsides* with the torpedo boat *David*. The damage inflicted kept *New Ironsides* out of action for more than a year.

In late 1863 the ironclad *Charleston* was added to the squadron and became Tucker's flagship. Torpedo expeditions against the blockade continued (the submarine *H. L. Hunley's* successful attack was under army command), but the ships and gunboats engaged in purely defensive operations for the rest of the war, bombarding the Union troops and batteries besieging the city. When Charleston was evacuated, the squadron was destroyed.

— MAURICE K. MELTON

Charlestonians were angry and frightened. Those who could afford to took trains or carriages out of the city to safer communities. The poorer people remained. Authorities moved the post office, banks, and hospitals north of Calhoun Street, beyond the range of the Union artillery, and evacuated the city's orphans to Orangeburg.

The Union occupation of Morris Island and the increased surveillance by the Union navy severely curtailed blockade running while Federal land forces inched closer to the city. Confederate money depreciated and the costs of goods and services soared in Charleston. A few speculators in foodstuffs made huge profits, but destitution was widespread.

The bombardment of the city was sporadic until late 1863, when the shelling began with regularity. During nine days in January 1864, some 1,500 shells were fired into Charleston; occasionally they started fires. St. Philip's Church was hit repeatedly and its interior wrecked, and City Hall and the guard house were punctured with shell fragments. But because the city below Market Street was deserted, few people were killed during the bombardment.

With many of the city's firemen and police doing soldier duty, city services began to break down. Robberies increased dramatically. The bombardment, coupled with declines in student enrollments, severely impaired classroom instruction in the public schools.

General Beauregard was ordered to North Carolina in mid-April 1864, and Maj. Gen. Samuel Jones assumed command of the defenses of Charleston. By this time thousands of Union troops had occupied all of Morris Island, and their artillery was pounding Fort Sumter into rubble. During the summer fierce skirmishes broke out on islands around the city, and the Union artillery increased its shelling. Two of the worst days of the bombardment were September 30 and October 10, when 110 and 165 shells, respectively, fell into the city. During the fall several civilians were killed.

In October Lt. Gen. William J. Hardee arrived in Charleston to replace General Jones and take command of the remnants of the Department of South Carolina, Georgia, and Florida. About 12,500 soldiers—poorly trained, armed, clad, and fed—were concentrated around the city and Savannah. During mid-November Hardee turned over the defense of Charleston to Maj. Gen. Robert Ransom, Jr., and took hundreds of troops with him to defend Savannah against William Tecumseh Sherman, who was marching toward the city with 60,000 battle-hardened troops.

General Hardee evacuated Savannah in December and retreated toward Charleston, where he redeployed 16,000 soldiers around the city. By January 1865 amphibious assaults on the city's defenses were increasing and Union shells were falling onto the Neck north of Calhoun Street. In mid-February Hardee concluded that it was no longer feasible to defend Charleston. During the night of February 17–18, the soldiers and most of the few remaining well-to-do evacuated the city and its defenses. Some 10,000 Confederate troops retreated northward up the peninsula.

On February 18 the Federals took possession of the city. The Union flag was raised over all public buildings and fortifications, and martial law was declared. One Union officer remarked that Charleston had fallen "after a siege which will rank among the most famous in history."

— WALTER J. FRASER, JR.

CHARLOTTE NAVY YARD

The impending evacuation of the Gosport Navy Yard at Norfolk, Virginia, in May 1862 caused Navy Secretary Stephen R. Mallory to order the relocation of the facility's heavy machinery and ordnance stores. Officials chose the southern North Carolina city of Charlotte for the new yard because of its inland location and excellent rail connections with coastal ports. The government acquired a site bordered by two rail lines, and workers erected new structures. By year's end the Charlotte Navy Yard was producing gun carriages, projectiles, and other ordnance equipment. The addition of a large steam hammer permitted the forging of heavy propeller shafts, large anchors, and wrought-iron armor-piercing bolts unobtainable elsewhere in the Confederacy. The navy yard also produced torpedoes and wooden blocks and repaired locomotives. Many of the establishment's employees came with the machinery from Gosport. They were joined by local workmen and, in 1864, by skilled mechanics recruited in England.

Capt. Samuel Barron apparently was the installation's first commander but was replaced in October 1862 by Commdr. Richard L. Page. Page was followed in rapid succession by Capt. George N. Hollins and Commdr. Catesby Jones before again assuming command in May 1863. Chief Engineer Henry Ashton Ramsay superintended the works from the spring of 1864 until the end of the war.

With the rapid disintegration of the Confederacy in April 1865, the Charlotte Navy Yard was abandoned. Symbolic of that end was the destruction at the yard of the records of the Navy Department after their removal from Richmond.

— A. ROBERT HOLCOMBE, JR.

CHICKAMAUGA CAMPAIGN

The Battle of Chickamauga on September 19 and 20, 1863, was a decisive Confederate victory after three defeats—at Gettysburg, Vicksburg, and Knoxville. Although the Confederates did not retake Chattanooga, their objective, the victory brought new life to their cause. Chickamauga was one of the few Civil War battles fought with Southern troops (66,000) outnumbering Union troops (58,000). The victory came at a high price, however, with the Confederacy reporting nearly 18,000 casualties, and the Union, nearly 16,000. Known for its ferocity, the battle was often described by the men who fought it as a soldiers' fight. In many areas, the underbrush would not allow the use of artillery, leaving small units of infantry to do the fighting on their own, and the thick woods and smoke from battle made it difficult for officers to control their commands. But because both armies were composed of veterans by this time, officer control was not as important as it might have been elsewhere.

The Chickamauga campaign began in early summer when the Union Army of the Cumberland moved from Murfreesboro toward Confederate defensive positions around Tullahoma, Tennessee. The Army of Tennessee, commanded by Gen. Braxton Bragg, fell back into the shelter of Chattanooga after the Union army, under Maj. Gen. William S. Rosecrans, carried out a series of skillful maneuvers that threatened the Confederate supply lines.

The Union military objective then became the important railroad hub of Chattanooga. Bragg fully expected to be overwhelmed by a Union force of over 100,000 men as he prepared to defend this vital Confederate position. In addition, the Confederate high command felt Chattanooga, because of the geography, was the last position strong enough to stop the invading Northern army. (The ridges surrounding the city only opened up to possible Union attack at one point, Lookout Valley, west of the town.)

Confederate commanders were slow in establishing a strategy, allowing the Union plan to take shape. From the end of July until September 9, the Union Army of the Cumberland set off on a maneuver that took Bragg by surprise. Rosecrans divided his army, sending two corps south to cross the Tennessee River in Alabama and one corps north. Bragg believed that the corps moving north of Chattanooga was the primary force. The Union plan worked. On September 9 the Confederates abandoned Chattanooga and moved south to block the Union advance into North Georgia by way of LaFayette.

Bragg had trouble determining where the various Union corps were located. Between September 11 and 17, he tried several probing movements in an effort to isolate and destroy the corps one by one in the mountain coves of North Georgia. He was unsuccessful, so on September 17 he decided on a plan that would place the now reinforced Army of Tennessee between Chattanooga and the widely separated corps of the Union army. Bragg selected two crossings over the West Chickamauga Creek—Reed's Bridge and Alexander's Bridge—which he assumed would put him well north of the Union left flank at Lee and Gordon's Mill, about ten miles south of Chattanooga. Once the Confederates were across the Chickamauga, they could use the creek as an anchor on the left, push the Union

"Chickamauga, like all Indian words, is interpreted to mean 'river of death.' God knows what it really means."

SHELBY FOOTE
IN GEOFFREY WARD, THE CIVIL WAR, 1990

A mighty battle raged as Bragg attempted another grand pivot, hoping to force the Federals into McLemore's Cove and destroy them.

PAGE 70

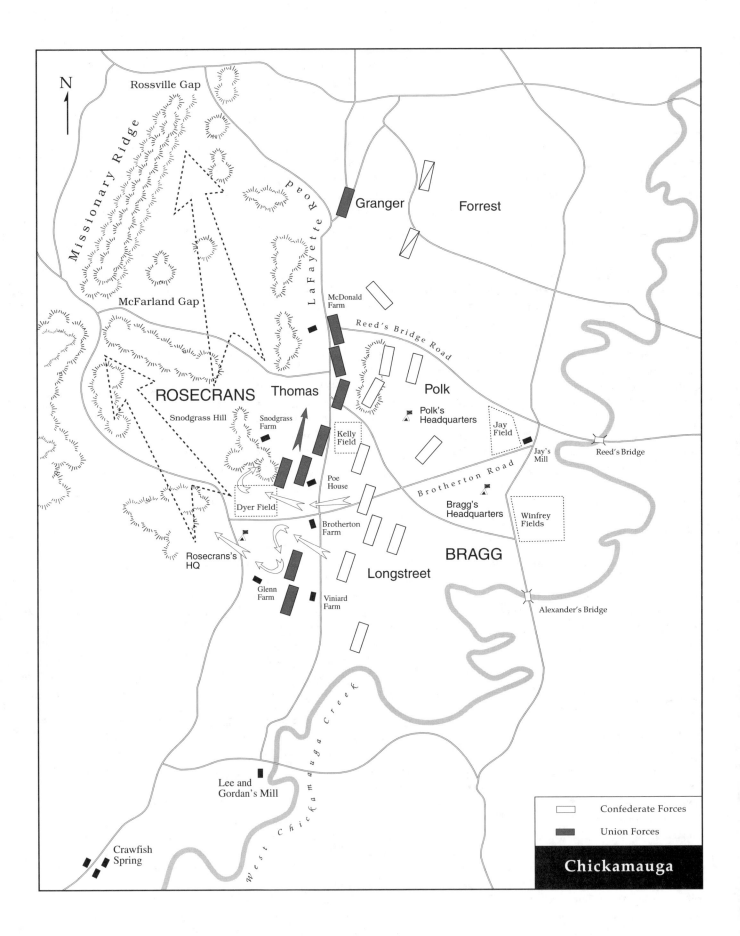

N

Rossville Gap

Missionary Ridge

McFarland Gap

LaFayette Road

Granger

Forrest

McDonald Farm

Reed's Bridge Road

ROSECRANS

Thomas

Polk

Polk's Headquarters

Jay Field

Jay's Mill

Reed's Bridge

Snodgrass Hill

Snodgrass Farm

Kelly Field

Poe House

Dyer Field

Brotherton Road

Bragg's Headquarters

Winfrey Fields

Rosecrans's HQ

Brotherton Farm

BRAGG

Longstreet

Alexander's Bridge

Glenn Farm

Viniard Farm

Lee and Gordan's Mill

West Chickamauga Creek

Crawfish Spring

☐ Confederate Forces

■ Union Forces

Chickamauga

corps back into the narrow mountain coves west of LaFayette, and destroy them.

With his army still widely scattered, Rosecrans now realized he had to concentrate his forces before the Confederates severed his supply lines with Chattanooga. He ordered his two southernmost corps—those of Maj. Gen. George H. Thomas and Maj. Gen. Alexander McCook—to move north as quickly as possible and concentrate at the little town of Crawfish Spring. This maneuver was carried out by the eighteenth. That evening, the Union left was extended three miles north of Lee and Gordon's Mill along the LaFayette Road and north of Bragg's crossing points on the Chickamauga Creek. Union cavalry had attempted to keep the Confederates east of the creek on the eighteenth, but the cavalry was outnumbered, and the Southerners were able to cross at both locations late in the afternoon.

Early on the morning of Saturday, September 19, George Thomas sent Brig. Gen. John Brannan's division east of the LaFayette Road toward Reed's Bridge in order to capture an isolated Confederate brigade reported to be on the west side of the Chickamauga Creek. Brannan met Brig. Gen. Nathan Bedford Forrest's cavalry corps at the edge of the Jay field, just west of Jay's Mill. As Forrest was drawn into battle, he realized he was facing infantry, and he quickly searched out Confederate infantry for help. Soon there was fighting along a mile-long front extending from the Reed's Bridge Road south into the Winfrey fields. As both sides committed additional units to the battle, the woods and fields south of Reed's Bridge Road erupted with fierce fighting that spread south for almost four miles.

Meanwhile, Rosecrans moved his headquarters from Crawfish Spring to a local farmstead, which brought him closer to the center of the fighting.

As the battle on the north end of the field began to subside, assaults intensified on the Union center and right. In the early afternoon, an attack against the Union center by Confederate Maj. Gen. Alexander P. Stewart's division broke through the Union line at the Poe House. Stewart's division pushed that of Brig. Gen. H. P. Van Cleve across the LaFayette Road, west through the Poe fields, and into the North Dyer fields and the Tan yard. Stewart, being unsupported, was forced to retire after heavy losses when he was hit on both flanks.

Around 2:00 P.M., a fierce contest occurred around the Viniard farm less than a mile east of Rosecrans's headquarters and still farther south from where the fighting had begun. Rosecrans ordered Brig. Gen. Jefferson C. Davis forward to seek the Confederate line, and he was soon hotly engaged with Brig. Gen. Bushrod Rust Johnson's division and Col. Robert Trigg's brigade. Davis was forced back across the LaFayette Road into the fields west of the Viniard

house, but he was soon reinforced by two brigades. Facing withering fire from Col. John Wilder's artillery, Johnson and Trigg were forced to retire to the woods east of the LaFayette Road.

As darkness covered the battlefield, fighting broke out in the center of the Confederate line. Maj. Gen. Patrick Cleburne's division, moving west from Jay's Mill along Brotherton Road, struck at the Union line confronting two Southern divisions. Two brigades from B. Franklin Cheatham's division supported Cleburne's men. After an hour of confused fighting, both sides retired with heavy losses. Confederate Brig. Gen. Preston Smith and Union Col. Philemon Baldwin were both killed.

That evening, Braxton Bragg reorganized his army, dividing it into two wings, the right commanded by Lt. Gen. Leonidas Polk and the left by Lt. Gen. James Longstreet. Longstreet, who arrived about midnight, had no time to scout the field and was not familiar with the terrain.

Rosecrans, at his headquarters, held a council of war with his corps commanders and staff. He was advised to withdraw and take defensive positions along Missionary Ridge to protect Chattanooga. But thinking he had won the day, he decided to stay and force Bragg from the field.

Bragg had ordered Polk to strike the Union left at daylight on the twentieth, but the battle did not get underway until midmorning. This so infuriated Bragg that he later ordered Polk's arrest. The delay, however, did give Longstreet an opportunity to look over his wing formations.

When the battle began, the Confederates met with success on their right near the McDonald farm. Two brigades of Maj. Gen. John C. Breckinridge's division enveloped the Union left and gained the rear of the northernmost Union position. Being unsupported in the attack, however, Breckinridge had to retire when faced with a flank attack from the last of the Union reserves. The Confederates, along the center of their line, had three divisions poised in the thick woods east of the Brotherton farm.

Just before noon, as the battle moved south all along the line, about 11,000 Confederates crossed the LaFayette Road on a mile-long front. They caught the Union troops in Wood's division in an administrative marching formation, as they moved from their position in the Brotherton fields north to close up with another division. This unsupported movement of troops (in response to an unverified order by Rosecrans to Wood) and the timing of the Confederate's attack led to the defeat of the Union army at Chickamauga. Longstreet's troops poured through the gap in the Union lines, causing a general rout of the Union center and right.

Chickamauga was one of the few Civil War battles fought with Southern troops (66,000) outnumbering Union troops (58,000).

PAGE 99

"They were the two bloodiest days of American military history. More than a quarter of the 124,000 men engaged were killed, wounded, or missing."

BRUCE CATTON
QUOTED BY FRANK
MANLEY IN CHICKAMAUGA
1989

*Bragg ordered
Longstreet's troops
forward at the
precise moment a
gap inadvertently
opened in the
Union line,
thus initiating
the famous
breakthrough long
credited solely to
Longstreet.*

PAGE 70

Brief but effective countercharges by isolated Union regiments and brigades gave George H. Thomas time to gather retreating units to form a new line facing south around the Snodgrass farm. Thomas's part of the original line east of the LaFayette Road continued to hold through the afternoon of the twentieth. The new line on Snodgrass Hill was in serious trouble when reinforcements under Maj. Gen. Gordon Granger arrived. Because Rosecrans and two of his corps commanders left the field when the Confederate breakthrough occurred, Thomas, a Southerner by birth, was now the ranking Union officer. All afternoon, the Confederates assaulted the Federals on Snodgrass Hill. There were minor successes, but it was not until dark that the Union regiments, under Thomas's orders, began to fall back north through the Rossville and McFarland gaps in Missionary Ridge toward Chattanooga.

The Confederates had won an important tactical victory, but they failed to follow up their success with quick pursuit. Instead, Bragg, feeling he had failed to destroy the Union army according to his plan, decided to lay siege to the defeated Union army in Chattanooga. Over the next two months, the Confederates tried to starve the Union army into submission. But the Federals received supplies and reinforcements until they were strong enough to break the siege in late November 1863 in the Battles of Orchard Knob, Lookout Mountain, and Missionary Ridge.

Twenty-seven years after the Battle of Chickamauga, Union and Confederate veterans returned to create the Chickamauga and Chattanooga National Military Park, the first such park. It was to be used as a place for military and historical study. It was also a place of healing for old bitter feelings between the two sides.

— JOHN F. CISSELL

CITIZENSHIP

The American Constitution recognized dual American citizenship—that of the nation and that of the state. Early Supreme Court decisions gave the state the claim to precedence. It was not until the adoption of the Fourteenth Amendment in 1868 that U.S. citizenship became primary and that of the state derivative. The permanent Constitution of the Confederacy made one significant change in the matter of citizenship. As a concession to state rights, federal jurisdiction was removed from controversies between citizens of different states, leaving such matters entirely to state courts. The Confederacy inherited the remaining U.S. laws and rulings on citizenship when the Confederate Congress ordered the continuation of all U.S. laws not inconsistent with the Confederate Constitution.

The only subsequent change was a law of August 22, 1861, conferring all the rights of citizenship upon noncitizens in the army and promising them full citizenship after the war in any state of their choice if they would renounce all other allegiance and swear to uphold the Confederate Constitution and its laws.

The naturalization laws inherited from the United States required five years of continued residence in a Confederate state, a declaration of intent at least two years before admission to citizenship, a renunciation of past allegiance, and an oath to support the Confederate Constitution and that of the state in which the person resided. Thus Congress implied that allegiance to the state was as important as that to the Confederacy.

Several efforts were made to give the states a stronger role in the process. In January 1862 Congress passed a bill repealing all existing laws of naturalization and putting the process entirely in the states' hands. President Jefferson Davis vetoed it on the grounds that it did not protect the right of foreigners living in the Confederacy and that it violated a constitutional provision that Congress set the rules for naturalization. Several efforts to pass a similar bill were made, but all failed.

Alien enemies residing in the Confederacy suffered the tribulations of wartime. A law of August 8, 1861, required all alien enemies to leave the Confederacy within forty days. Under the sequestration laws, the courts issued thousands of writs of garnishment against their property. Both Confederate and state courts refused to hear cases when the plaintiff was an alien enemy. Those Union sympathizers who kept their sympathies secret and did not resort to treasonable activities, however, seem to have escaped with both life and property intact.

The possibility that Confederates who fell into enemy hands might be treated as rebels never materialized. Though the United States never recognized the Confederacy, it regarded the Southern nation as a belligerency, and captured Confederate soldiers and alien enemies were treated as legitimate prisoners of war. Confederates abroad suffered no discrimination, though Confederate agents could never confer officially with foreign governments.

— W. BUCK YEARNS

CIVIL LIBERTIES

On February 22, 1862, the president of the Confederate States of America proclaimed in his inaugural address that his administration would continue to cherish and preserve the personal liberties of citizens. Protecting individual rights was a paramount reason for secession, and the Confederate Constitution (Article I, Section 9) incorporated all of the guarantees of civil liberties found in the amended U.S. Constitution. Jefferson Davis boasted that, in contrast to the United States of America, which continued to exercise "tyrannical" authority as it had in suppressing civil liberties in Maryland, "there has been no act on our part to impair personal liberty or the freedom of speech, of thought, or of the press."

Events in the next few months demonstrated the great difficulty of maintaining such a position while fighting an unlimited modern war for the Confederacy's survival. This war forced the mobilization of most human and material resources and the centralization of authority, processes that inevitably challenged individual liberties as well as state rights. If the Confederate government assiduously protected civil liberties, its war effort could be undermined by spoken and written criticism, unfettered movement of people and information, and severe shortages of troops. If, however, it restricted the spoken and written word and the activities of its citizens or suspended civil government and the writ of habeas corpus, it risked alienating the public, whose support was essential for military success.

Faced with this dilemma and hard-pressed on the battlefield, Confederate leaders at both the national and the state levels heatedly debated civil libertarian issues. Military necessity ultimately dictated the three areas in which they reluctantly, but legally, restricted civil liberties: declaring martial law, conscripting men into military service, and suspending the privilege of the writ of habeas corpus. In each case, unlike President Abraham Lincoln, President Davis adhered to strict constructionist principles and persuaded Congress to pass appropriate enabling legislation before he approved restrictions on civil liberties.

On February 27, 1862, Congress authorized the president to suspend the privilege of the writ of habeas corpus and to declare martial law in areas threatened by the enemy. Davis immediately placed Norfolk and Portsmouth under martial law so that the military could arrest and detain disloyal individuals. Then on March 1, in a controversial and perhaps excessive attempt to curtail spying and criminal activity in the vulnerable capital, Davis appointed Gen. John H. Winder the military governor of Richmond. Within a year, Congress permitted generals to declare martial law so they could enforce conscription and maintain public order near the front. This was especially detested in Unionist strongholds, such as eastern Tennessee, and in locales with burgeoning peace societies, such as Alabama, northeastern Mississippi, and southwestern

Virginia. Within his own administration Davis faced a harsh and outspoken critic, Vice President Alexander H. Stephens, who repeatedly denounced martial law, conscription, and the suspension of habeas corpus as unnecessary violations of civil rights that undermined the integrity of the Southern republic. These issues further polarized Confederate politics into pro- and anti-Davis factions.

In the spring of 1862, with casualties mounting and one-year volunteers heading home, the Confederacy resorted to conscription. This infringement upon personal liberty incensed many Southerners, including several outspoken generals. Critics recalled the denunciation of forced service in the Declaration of Independence and, ironically, noted its similarity to slavery. Governor Joseph E. Brown of Georgia called Davis an "emperor" and began a lengthy debate on the unconstitutionality of conscription. Citing state rights, Governor Zebulon B. Vance exempted North Carolina officials from the despised draft. Some judges even issued writs of habeas corpus to free draftees.

The widespread opposition to conscription convinced Congress to permit President Davis to suspend the privilege of the writ of habeas corpus three separate times for a total of sixteen months. They justified these suspensions and the repeated use of martial law as necessary for apprehending thousands of draft evaders and keeping them in the ranks. Yet such measures inevitably produced further dissent among Southerners. Georgia's legislature unanimously condemned the third suspension, and state legislators in Mississippi and Louisiana passed hostile resolutions.

Southern newspapers took Davis to task, violently attacking him, his administration, and his generals for interfering with habeas corpus, imposing conscription, and abusively enforcing the Impressment Act. The fiercely independent press undermined morale on the home front and ignored the censorship restrictions intended to protect the military. Congress passed a law in January 1862 making it a crime to publish news about Confederate land and naval forces. Yet neither national nor state authorities ever suppressed such outspoken journals as the *Richmond Examiner,* the *Charleston Mercury,* or the *Raleigh Standard.* Eventually, several prominent generals closed their camps to reporters, and irate troops and vigilantes destroyed a few presses.

Early in 1863 the Confederate Senate considered a sedition bill that would have curtailed freedom of the press and of speech. The measure died because most Southern legislators were avid proponents of free speech. Among the most vociferous was Henry S. Foote of Tennessee, who compiled a "shocking catalogue" of his government's questionable arrests following the suspension of habeas corpus. For example,

Some of the state leaders were no more willing to concede power to the Confederate government than they had been to the Federal government.

PAGE 585

The most serious question was the constitutionality of the conscription acts of April–September 1862 and February 1864.

PAGE 585

General Winder jailed John Minor Botts, a former U.S. congressman, for declaring his neutrality, and the Reverend Alden Bosserman for openly praying for the defeat of "this unholy rebellion." Most preachers and teachers accepted the restrictions on free speech in the South's closed society. But some who merely questioned the course of events lost jobs, and staunch Unionists fled northward. Others secretly supported peace societies, and angry mobs and zealous soldiers forcibly expelled a few. In lieu of specific legislation, the public pressures that had long stifled discussion about slavery now tried to impose loyalty to the Confederacy through intimidation and book burning.

As death and deprivation intensified public disaffection, tighter restrictions upon Southerners proved counterproductive. Disloyal words and deeds became too widespread to curtail. By early 1865, despite presidential pleas, Congress refused to sanction further suspensions of the writ of habeas corpus. De jure and de facto proscriptions of civil liberties repeatedly generated profound controversies, but ultimately they had only marginal impact on the demise of the war-torn Confederacy.

— BLAKE TOUCHSTONE

CIVIL WAR

[For discussion of the course of the war itself, see entries on selected battles, cities, and states.]

NAMES OF THE WAR

With the echo of the first shot in April 1861, Americans began arguing over a name for the conflict. The debate has waned with the passing decades, but it still has not ended. By far the most popular of the titles is "The Civil War." Both sides used the term throughout the four-year struggle. In the South, generals such as Lee, Longstreet, and Gordon, as well as wartime Richmond newspapers, referred to the war by that name. The term's opponents, concentrated in the South, argue that "The Civil War" suggests a rebellion against lawful authority. It also implies that two different sections of the nation were fighting for control of a single government, when in fact the Confederacy was seeking to exist independently. Justifications for the name are that the struggle came within the definition of civil war expounded by many philosophers of that day, that the conflict was indeed a civil war in areas like Missouri, Tennessee, and Kentucky, and that the term is short, convenient, and less controversial than any of the other names.

"War between the States" has been a favorite Southern appellation since the conflict ended. Not used during the war itself, the term came into use with the publication in 1868 of Alexander H. Stephens's *A Constitutional View of the Late War between the States*. It enjoyed its highest boost in popularity during the Spanish-American War, when Americans of North and South joined together in a common cause. Southern congressmen once sought to make the term the official title, but a resolution to that effect was tabled. An objection to this name is that it is long and cumbersome. Further, the Southern nation was a confederation of eleven sovereignties, with much more involved than merely state rights. This title is thus misleading.

The Union counterpart in titles is "War of the Rebellion." Northerners at the time considered the South to be in rebellion, and many Confederates seemed to take pride in being called "Rebels." This name is too long, however, and it is also erroneous because the conflict was a full-scale war, with two organized governments respecting the rules of war. Yet "War of the Rebellion" continues to live as the title of the 128 huge volumes containing the official records of the Union and Confederate armies.

Two names, "Second American Revolution" and "War for Southern Independence," were outgrowths of Confederate beliefs that their struggle paralleled the colonists' fight in the 1770s to break away from British control. Foreign writers often referred to the North-South contest as "The Confederate War," and a Maryland writer proposed "War of Secession." Both terms, however, suggest that secession was the primary cause of the war, which then puts the blame for hostilities solely on the South.

In many parts of the old Confederacy today, "The War" is a phrase that needs no explanation. Other titles with short-lived appearances have included "War of Sections," "The War for Nationality," "Conflict of the Sixties," "The War against Slavery," "The Uncivil War," "The Brothers' War," "War against the States," and "The Lost Cause."

Among the somewhat facetious names given by Southerners are "The Yankee War," "The Southern Defense against Northern Aggression," and "Mr. Lincoln's War." By far the most diplomatic of all the titles for the American struggle is "The Late Unpleasantness."

— JAMES I. ROBERTSON, JR.

CAUSES OF THE WAR

During the Civil War, few people on either side would have dissented from Abraham Lincoln's statement in his second inaugural address that slavery "was, somehow, the cause of the war." After all, had not Jefferson Davis, a major slaveholder, justified secession in 1861 as an act of self-defense against the Lincoln administration, whose policy of excluding slavery from the territories would make "property in slaves so insecure as to be comparatively worthless . . . thereby annihilating in effect property worth thousands of millions of dollars"? And had not the new vice president of the Confederate States of America, Alexander H. Stephens, said in a speech at Savannah on March 21, 1861, that slavery was "the immediate cause of the late rupture and the present revolution" of Southern independence? The old confederation known as the United States, said Stephens, had been founded on the false idea that all men are created equal. The Confederacy, by contrast, "is founded upon exactly the opposite idea; its foundations are laid, its cornerstone rests, upon the great truth that the negro is not equal to the white man; that slavery, subordination to the superior race, is his natural and moral condition. This, our new Government, is

the first, in the history of the world, based on this great physical, philosophical, and moral truth."

Historical Views of the Causes of the War

For at least a half century after the war, this remained the predominant interpretation of its causes. In 1913 the foremost Civil War historian of his day, James Ford Rhodes, declared definitively that "of the American Civil War it may safely be asserted that there was a single cause, slavery." Although no historian today would put it quite so baldly, most of them would agree with the basic point. But during the century and a quarter since the guns ceased firing, dissenters from this viewpoint have provoked many rhetorical battles over the causes of the war.

EARLY DISSENSION. Two of the earliest dissenters were none other than Jefferson Davis and

CIVIL WAR

Causes of the War

NAMING OF BATTLES

Confederates and Federals sometimes differed in their designations of a particular engagement. D. H. Hill, lieutenant general, C.S.A., afterward wrote:

So many battle-fields of the Civil War bear double names, that we cannot believe the duplication has been accidental. It is the unusual which impresses. The troops of the North came mainly from cities, towns, and villages, and were, therefore, impressed by some natural object near the scene of the conflict and named the battle from it. The soldiers from the South were chiefly from the country and were, therefore, impressed by some artificial object near the field of action. In one section the naming has been after the handiwork of God; in the other section it has been after the handiwork of man.

Whether or not Hill's explanation is correct, his observation itself is borne out by a number of examples. Confederates named battles after such man-made objects as towns or settlements (Manassas, Leesburg, Boonsboro, Sharpsburg, Perryville, Murfreesboro) and buildings (Elkhorn Tavern, Gaines's Mill, Shiloh Church). Federals used the names of watercourses (Bull Run, the Chickahominy, Antietam Creek, Stones River) and other natural features (Ball's Bluff, Pea Ridge, Pittsburg Landing, South Mountain, Chaplin Hills).

In quite a few instances multiple names were used indiscriminately by both sides. An extreme example is the June 30, 1862, clash in Virginia that bore the names of a great variety of objects, all of them man made (Glendale, White Oak Swamp Bridge, Frazier's or Frayser's Farm, Nelson's Farm, Charles City Cross Roads, New Market Road, Willis Church). Still other battles always and everywhere were known by but a single name (Gettysburg, for example).

— RICHARD N. CURRENT

BATTLES WITH DUAL NAMES

Date of Battle	Confederate Name	Federal Name
July 21, 1861	First Manassas	Bull Run
Aug. 10, 1861	Oak Hills	Wilson's Creek
Oct. 21, 1861	Leesburg	Ball's Bluff
Jan. 19, 1862	Mill Springs	Logan's Cross Roads
Mar. 7–8, 1862	Elkhorn Tavern	Pea Ridge
Apr. 6–7, 1862	Shiloh	Pittsburg Landing
June 27, 1862	Gaines's Mill	Chickahominy
Aug. 29–30, 1862	Second Manassas	Second Bull Run
Sept. 1, 1862	Ox Hill	Chantilly
Sept. 14, 1862	Boonsboro	South Mountain
Sept. 17, 1862	Sharpsburg	Antietam
Oct. 8, 1862	Perryville	Chaplin Hills
Dec. 31, 1862– Jan. 2, 1863	Murfreesboro	Stones River
Apr. 1864	Mansfield	Sabine Cross Roads
Sept. 19, 1864	Winchester	Opequon Creek

Alexander Stephens. After 1865 slavery was a dead and discredited institution. It no longer seemed appropriate, as it had in 1861, to emphasize it proudly as the reason for secession. To salvage honor and assert a sound constitutional basis for their lost cause, Stephens and Davis now insisted that Southern states had seceded and gone to war not to protect slavery but to vindicate state sovereignty. In *A Constitutional View of the War between the States,* which invented the favorite Southern name for the conflict three years after it was over, Stephens maintained that "the War had its origin in opposing principles" concerning not slavery and freedom but rather "the organic Structure of the Government of the States. . . . It was a strife between the principles of Federation, on the one side, and Centralism, or Consolidation, on the other." And Davis, writing his book *The Rise and Fall of the Confederate Government* in the 1870s, insisted that the Confederates, like their forefathers of 1776, had fought solely "for the defense of an inherent, unalienable right . . . to withdraw from a Union into which they had, as sovereign communities, voluntarily entered. . . . The existence of African servitude was in no wise the cause of the conflict, but only an incident."

THE PROGRESSIVE THEORY. This virgin-birth theory of secession became widely accepted among Southern whites: the Confederacy had been conceived by no worldly cause but by constitutional principle. Thus the Civil War was a war of Northern aggression against Southern rights, not a war to preserve the American nation and, ultimately, to abolish slavery. By the 1920s, though, the notion that a people would go to war over principles had become suspect among historians. Human behavior, most of them thought, was rooted in materialism. The "Progressive school" dominated American historiography from the 1920s to the 1940s. This school posited a clash between interest groups and classes as the central theme of American history: industry versus agriculture, capital versus labor, railroads versus farmers, manufacturers versus consumers, and so on. The real issues of American politics, in this interpretation, revolved around the economic interests of these contesting groups: tariffs, taxes, land policies, industrial and labor policies, subsidies to business or agriculture, and the like.

The Progressive school explained the causes of the Civil War within this interpretive framework. The war transferred to the battlefield a long-running contest between plantation agriculture and industrializing capitalism, and the industrialists emerged triumphant. It was not primarily a conflict between North and South: "Merely by the accidents of climate, soil, and geography," wrote the foremost Progressive historian, Charles A. Beard, "was it a sectional struggle"—the accidental fact that plantation agriculture was located in the

South and industry mainly in the North. Nor was it a contest between slavery and freedom. Slavery just happened to be the labor system of plantation agriculture, as wage labor was the system of Northern industry. For some Progressive historians, neither system was significantly worse or better than the other—"wage slavery" was as exploitative as chattel bondage. In any case, they said, slavery was not a moral issue for anybody except a tiny handful of abolitionists; its abolition was a mere incident of the destruction of the plantation order by the war. The *real* issues between the North and the South in antebellum politics were the tariff, government subsidies to transportation and manufacturing, public land sales, and related questions on which manufacturing and planting interests had clashing viewpoints.

This interpretive synthesis proved a godsend for a generation of mostly Southern-born historians who seized upon it as proof that slavery had little to do with the origins of the Confederacy. The Nashville Fugitives, an influential group of historians, novelists, and poets who gathered at Vanderbilt University and published in 1930 a famous manifesto, *I'll Take My Stand,* set the tone for the new Southern interpretation of the Civil War's causes. It was a blend of the old Confederate apologia voiced by Jefferson Davis and the new Progressive synthesis created by Charles Beard. The Confederacy fought not only for the constitutional principle of state rights and self-government but also for the preservation of a stable, pastoral, agrarian civilization in the face of the overweening, acquisitive, imperialistic ambitions of an urban-industrial Leviathan. The real issue that brought on the war was not slavery—this institution, wrote one of the Nashville Fugitives, "was part of the agrarian system, but only one element and not an essential one"—but rather such matters as the tariff, banks, subsidies to railroads, and similar questions in which the grasping businessmen of the North sought to advance their interests at the expense of Southern farmers and planters. Lincoln was not elected in 1860 in the name of freedom over slavery; rather, his election represented the ascendancy of tariffs and railroads and factories over agriculture and the graces of a rural society. The result was the triumph of acquisitive, power-hungry robber barons over the highest type of civilization America had ever known—the Old South. It was no coincidence that this interpretation emerged during the same period that the novel and movie *Gone with the Wind* became one of the most popular literary and cinematic successes of all time; history and popular culture on this occasion marched hand in hand.

REVISIONISM. An offshoot of this interpretation of the Civil War's causes dominated the work of academic historians during the 1940s. This offshoot came to be called revisionism. The revisionists denied that sectional conflicts between North and South—whether over slavery, state rights, or industry versus agriculture—were genuinely divisive. The differences between North and South, wrote one of the leading revisionists, Avery Craven, were "no greater than those existing at different times between East and West." The other giant of revisionism, James G. Randall, suggested that they were no greater than the differences between Chicago and downstate Illinois.

Such disparities did not have to lead to war; they could and should have been accommodated peacefully within the political system. The Civil War was therefore not an irrepressible conflict, as earlier generations had called it, but *The Repressible Conflict*, as Craven titled one of his books. The war was brought on not by genuine issues but by extremists on both sides—rabble-rousing abolitionists and Southern fire-eaters—who whipped up emotions and hatreds in North and South for their own partisan purposes. The passions they aroused got out of hand in 1861 and erupted into a tragic, unnecessary war that accomplished nothing that could not have been achieved by negotiation and compromise.

Of course, any such compromise in 1861 would have left slavery in place. But the revisionists, like the Progressives and the Vanderbilt agrarians, considered slavery unimportant; as Craven put it, the institution of bondage "played a rather minor part in the life of the South and the Negro." Slavery would have died peacefully of natural causes in another generation or two had not fanatics forced the issue to armed conflict. This hints at another feature of revisionism: while blaming extremists on both sides, revisionists focused most of their criticism on antislavery radicals, even antislavery moderates like Lincoln, who harped on the evils of slavery and expressed a determination to rein in what they called "the Slave Power." This had goaded the South into a defensive response that finally caused Southern states to secede to free themselves from the incessant pressure of these self-righteous Yankee zealots. Revisionism thus tended to portray Southern whites, even the fire-eaters, as victims reacting to Northern attacks; it truly was a war of Northern aggression.

Slavery

Since the 1950s, however, historiography has come full circle to Lincoln's assertion that "slavery was, somehow, the cause of the war." The state rights, Progressive, agrarian, and revisionist schools seem moribund if not actually dead. To be sure, echoes of some of these interpretations can still be heard today. Economic conflicts of interest, for example, did occur between the agricultural South and the industrializing North. These con-

flicts emerged in debates over tariffs, banks, land grants, and similar issues. But these matters divided parties and interest groups more than North and South. The South in the 1840s and 1850s had its advocates of industrialization and protective tariffs and a national bank, just as the North had its millions of farmers and its low-tariff, anti-bank Democratic majority in many states. The Civil War was not fought over issues of the tariff or banks or agrarianism versus industrialism. These and similar kinds of questions have been bread-and-butter issues of American politics throughout the nation's history, often generating a great deal more friction and heat than they did in the 1850s. But they have not caused any great shooting wars. Nor was the Civil War a consequence of false issues trumped up by demagogues or fanatics. It was fought over real, profound, intractable problems that Americans on both sides believed went to the heart of their society and its future.

In 1858 two prominent political leaders, one of whom expected to be elected president in 1860 and the other of whom *was* elected president, voiced the stark nature of the problem. The social systems of slave labor and free labor "are more than incongruous—they are incompatible," said Senator William H. Seward of New York. The friction between them "is an irreconcilable conflict between opposing and enduring forces, and it means that the United States must and will, sooner or later, become either entirely a slaveholding nation, or entirely a free-labor nation." In Illinois, senatorial candidate Abraham Lincoln launched his campaign with a theme taken from the Bible: "A house divided against itself cannot stand." The United States, he said, "cannot endure, permanently, half *slave* and half free. . . . It will become *all* one thing, or *all* the other." The policy of Lincoln's party—and Seward's—was to "arrest the further spread of [slavery], and place it where the public mind shall rest in the belief that it is in the course of ultimate extinction."

SECTIONALISM. When Seward and Lincoln uttered these words, the free and slave states had coexisted peacefully under the same Constitution for seventy years. They shared the same language, legal system, political culture, social mores, religious values, and a common heritage of struggle to form the nation. Yet by the late 1850s, Southern spokesmen agreed with Lincoln and Seward that an irreconcilable conflict within a house divided into free and slave states had split the country into two antagonistic cultures. "In this country have arisen two races," said a Savannah lawyer—and he meant not black and white but Northern and Southern — "two races which, although claiming a common parentage, have been so entirely separated by climate, by morals, by religion, and by estimates so totally opposite to all that constitutes

The price of slaves increased steadily from 1802 to 1860. In 1810, the price of a "prime field hand" was $900; by 1860, that price had doubled.

PAGE 555

C

honor, truth, and manliness, that they cannot longer exist under the same government."

What lay at the root of this antagonism? Slavery. It was the sole institution not shared by North and South. Both had cities, farms, railroads, ports, factories, colleges, literary societies, poets, poverty, wealth, slums, mansions, capitalists, workers, riverboats, gamblers, thieves, racial segregation, immigrants, Protestants, Catholics, Jews, ethnic and class conflict, and almost anything else one might name—but only one had slavery. That "peculiar institution" defined the South. The *Charleston Mercury* stated in an editorial in 1858 that "on the subject of slavery the North and South . . . are not only two Peoples, but they are rival, hostile Peoples." When the members of a South Carolina planter family who contributed four brothers to the Confederate army learned of Lincoln's election as president, they agreed that "now a stand must be made for African slavery or it is forever lost." In going out of a Union ruled by Yankee fanatics, "we . . . are contending for all that we hold dear—our Property—our Institutions—our Honor. . . . I hope it will end in establishing a Southern Confederacy who will have among themselves slavery a bond a union stronger than any which holds the north together."

The defensive tone of much of the proslavery argument was provoked by the rise of militant abolitionism in the North after 1830. William Lloyd Garrison, Theodore Weld, Wendell Phillips, Frederick Douglass, and a host of other eloquent crusaders branded slavery as a sin, a defiance of God's law and of Christian ethics,

immoral, inhumane, a violation of the republican principle of liberty on which the nation had been founded. Although the radical abolitionists did not get far in the North with their message of racial equality, the belief that slavery was an unjust, obsolete, and unrepublican institution—a "relic of barbarism," as the new Republican party described slavery in its 1856 platform—entered mainstream northern politics in the 1850s. "The monstrous injustice of slavery," said Abraham Lincoln in 1854, "deprives our republican example of its just influence in the world—enables the enemies of free institutions, with plausibility, to taunt us as hypocrites."

EXPANSION OF SLAVERY. But it was not the existence of slavery that polarized the nation to the point of breaking apart. It was the issue of the expansion of slave territory. Most of the crises that threatened the bonds of union arose over this matter. The first one, in 1820, was settled by the Missouri Compromise, which balanced the admission of Missouri as a slave state with the simultaneous admission of Maine as a free state and banned slavery in the rest of the Louisiana Purchase territory north of 36°30′ while permitting it south of that line. Paired admission of slave and free states during the next quarter century kept their numbers equal. But the annexation of Texas as a huge new slave state—with the potential of carving out several more within its boundaries—provoked new tensions. It also provoked war with Mexico in 1846, which resulted in American acquisition of three-quarters of a million square miles of new territory in

SLAVES
A Valuable Commodity

Slaves were the principal form of wealth in the South. The market value of the 4 million slaves in 1860 was $3 billion—more than the value of land, or cotton, or anything else in the slave states. It was slave labor that made it possible for the American South to grow three-quarters of the world's cotton, which in turn constituted half of all American exports. But slavery was much more than an economic system. It was a means of maintaining racial control and white supremacy. Northern whites were also committed to white supremacy. But with 95 percent of the nation's black population in the South, the region's scale of concern with this matter was so much greater as to constitute a different order of magnitude

and create a radically different set of social priorities.

The economic, social, and racial centrality of slavery to "the Southern way of life" focused the region's politics overwhelmingly on defense of the institution. Many Southern leaders in the age of Thomas Jefferson had considered slavery a "necessary evil" that would eventually disappear from this land of liberty. But with the rise of the cotton kingdom, slavery had become, in the eyes of Southern whites by the 1830s, a "positive good" for black and white alike. Proslavery pamphlets and books became a cottage industry. Their main themes were summed up in the title of a pamphlet by a clergyman published in 1850: *A Defense of the South against the Reproaches and*

Encroachments of the North: In which Slavery Is Shown to Be an Institution of God Intended to Form the Basis of the Best Social State and the Only Safeguard and Permanence of a Republican Government. The foremost defender of slavery until his death in 1850 was John C. Calhoun, who noted proudly that "many in the South once believed that slavery was a moral and political evil. That folly and delusion are gone. We see it now in its true light, and regard it as the most safe and stable basis for free institutions in the world" and "essential to the peace, safety, and prosperity" of the South.

— JAMES M. MCPHERSON

the Southwest. This opened a Pandora's box of troubles that could not be closed.

Convinced that the "slave power" in Washington had engineered the annexation of Texas and the Mexican War, the "antislavery power" in Congress determined to flex its muscles. In 1846 David Wilmot of Pennsylvania introduced in the House of Representatives a resolution banning slavery in all territory that might be conquered from Mexico. By an almost unanimous vote of all Northern congressmen against the virtually unanimous vote of all Southern representatives, the resolution passed—because the larger Northern population gave the free states a majority in the House. Equal representation in the Senate enabled Southerners to block the Wilmot Proviso there. But this issue framed national politics for the next fifteen years.

The most ominous feature of the Wilmot Proviso was its wrenching of the normal pattern of party divisions into a sectional pattern. On most issues before 1846, Northern and Southern Whigs had voted together, and Northern and Southern Democrats had done likewise. But on the Wilmot Proviso, Northern Whigs and Democrats had voted together against a solid alliance of Southern Whigs and Democrats. This became the norm for all votes on any issue concerning slavery—and most of the important national political issues in the 1850s did concern slavery. This sectional alignment reflected a similar pattern in social and cultural matters. In the 1840s the two largest religious denominations, the Methodists and Baptists, had split into separate Northern and Southern churches over whether a slave owner could be appointed as a bishop or missionary of the denomination.

In addition to a growing conviction in the North that slavery was contrary to the teachings of Christ, a secular free-labor ideology had become the dominant Northern worldview. It held up the ideals of equal opportunity, equal rights, the dignity of labor, and social mobility. Slavery represented the opposite. It denied equal opportunity and rights, degraded the concept of labor, and blocked social mobility. Most important, it afflicted poor but aspiring white men as well as slaves. "Slavery withers and blights all it touches," wrote a free-labor advocate. "It is a curse upon the poor, free, laboring white men. . . . They are depressed, poor, impoverished, degraded in caste, because labor is disgraceful." Wherever slavery goes, said a New York congressman in 1849, "there is in substance no middle class. Great wealth or hopeless poverty is the settled condition."

The national political controversy focused on slavery in the territories because, though the Constitution protected the institution in the states where it existed, Congress could presumably legislate the status of terri-

tories. And equally important, the territories represented the future. In 1850 they constituted more than half of the landmass of the United States. From 1790 to 1850 the territories that became states accounted for more than half of the nation's increase in population. As that process continued, the new territories would shape the future. To ensure a free-labor destiny, Northerners wanted to keep slavery out of these territories. In 1848 a new political party, the Free-Soil party, was founded on this platform. "We are opposed to the extension of slavery," declared a Free-Soil newspaper, because if slavery goes into a new territory, "the free labor of the states will not. . . . If the free labor of the states goes there, the slave labor of the southern states will not, and in a few years the country will teem with an active and energetic population." And eventually, the expansion of free territory and the containment of slavery would make freedom the wave of the future, placing slavery "in the course of ultimate extinction," as Lincoln phrased it.

That was just what Southerners feared. The North already had a majority in the House; new free states would give them a majority in the Senate as well as an unchallengeable domination of the electoral college. "Long before the North gets this vast accession of strength," warned a South Carolinian, "she will ride over us rough shod, proclaim freedom or something equivalent to it to our Slaves and reduce us to the condition of Haiti. . . . If we do not act now, we deliberately consign our children, not our posterity, but *our children* to the flames."

This argument swayed white nonslaveholders in the South as much as it did slaveholders. Whites of both classes considered the bondage of blacks to be the basis of liberty for whites. Slavery, they declared, elevated all whites to an equality of status and dignity by confining menial labor and caste subordination to blacks. "If slaves are freed," maintained proslavery spokesmen, whites "will become menials. We will lose every right and liberty which belongs to the name of freemen." The Northern threat to slavery thus menaced all whites. Nonslaveholders also agreed with slaveholders that the institution must be allowed to go into the territories. Such expansion might increase their own chances of becoming slave owners. The attempt by Northern Free-Soilers to exclude slavery from the territories united Southern whites in a conviction that Northerners were trying to place a stigma on the South of "degrading inequality . . . which says to the Southern man, Avaunt! you are not my equal, and hence are to be excluded as carrying a moral taint." The South could not tolerate such an insult. "Death is preferable to acknowledged inferiority."

The controversy over slavery in the region conquered from Mexico led to a crisis that almost pro-

Most upper South residents considered slavery a temporary evil. They hoped to remove blacks and slaves from their half of the South.

PAGE 202

By 1854, the Compromise of 1850's flaws and new territorial disputes had revealed the failure of this legislation to remove the causes of conflict.

PAGE 138

voked secession in 1850. In the end, the complex Compromise of 1850 narrowly averted this outcome. The essential features of the Compromise admitted California as a free state and divided the remainder of the Mexican Cession into two large territories, New Mexico and Utah, whose residents were given the right to decide for themselves whether or not they wanted slavery. (Both territories subsequently legalized slavery, but few slaves were taken there.)

STATE RIGHTS AND SLAVERY. The Compromise of 1850 also included a concession to the South in the form of the Fugitive Slave Law that gave unprecedented powers to the Federal government. This raises an important point about the state rights theory. State rights, or sovereignty, was a means rather than an end, an instrument more than a principle. Its purpose was to protect slavery from the potential hostility of a national majority. Southern political leaders from the 1820s to the 1840s jealously opposed the exercise of national power for a variety of purposes. "If Congress can make banks, roads, and canals under the Constitution," said Nathanial Macon of North Carolina, "they can free any slave in the United States." Calhoun, the South's leading political philosopher, formulated an elaborate constitutional structure of state rights theory to halt any use of Federal power that might conceivably be construed at some future time as a precedent with negative consequences for slavery.

At the same time, though, Southerners were not averse to using national power in defense of slavery. Indeed, this was a more reliable instrument than state rights. And the South had the power to wield. During forty-nine of the seventy-two years from 1789 to 1861, a Southerner—and slaveholder—was president of the United States. Twenty-four of the thirty-six Speakers of the House and presidents pro tem of the Senate were from the South. At all times during those years a majority of Supreme Court justices were Southerners. This happened because, though the South had only a minority of the national population, it usually controlled the Jeffersonian Republican party and, after 1828, the Democratic party, which in turn usually controlled the government. Southern domination of the Democratic party increased during the 1850s, so that even though both Democratic presidents in that decade—Franklin Pierce and James Buchanan—were Northerners, they were beholden to Southerners and did their bidding.

The usefulness of this national power had been demonstrated in the 1830s when Congress imposed a gag rule to stifle antislavery petitions and the post office banned antislavery literature from the mail in Southern states. But the Fugitive Slave Law of 1850 provided an even more striking example. It was the strongest manifestation of national power thus far in American history. It overrode the laws and officials of Northern states and extended the long arm of Federal law, enforced by the army and navy, into Northern states to recover escaped slaves and return them to their owners. Senator Jefferson Davis, who later insisted that the Confederacy fought for the principle of state sovereignty, voted with enthusiasm for the Fugitive Slave Law. When Northern state legislatures and courts invoked state rights and individual liberties against this Federal law, the U.S. Supreme Court, with its majority of Southern justices, reaffirmed the supremacy of national law to protect slavery.

Calhoun died in 1850, and during the following decade the South moved further away from his principles of state sovereignty and used its leverage in the Democratic party to wield greater national power than ever. Jefferson Davis was one of the principal architects of this process. As secretary of war in President Franklin Pierce's cabinet, he helped persuade a reluctant Pierce to cave in to Southern demands for repeal of the Missouri Compromise restriction on slavery in the territories north of 36°30′. Pierce endorsed repeal as a party measure; so did Senator Stephen A. Douglas of Illinois, who knew that he would need Southern votes if he expected to win the presidency. Patronage and pressure induced just enough Northern Democrats to vote for the Kansas-Nebraska Act in 1854 to obtain its passage.

But this turned out to be the first of several Pyrrhic victories for the South. It drove tens of thousands of angry Northern Democratic voters out of the party and gave birth to the Republican party, which by 1856 had become the second major party in the North. Running on the Wilmot Proviso platform of excluding slavery from the territories, the Republicans carried most Northern states in the presidential election of 1856. James Buchanan won the election only because of Southern support. Open warfare between proslavery and antislavery settlers in Kansas spilled over into the halls of Congress, where fistfights broke out between Northern and Southern representatives, members came armed to the floor of Congress, and South Carolinian Preston Brooks caned Senator Charles Sumner of Massachusetts into unconsciousness at his seat in the Senate. Presidents Pierce's and Buchanan's actions—and nonactions—favored the proslavery side in Kansas. Under heavy Southern pressure, Buchanan in 1858 even went so far as to endorse the fraudulently ratified Lecompton constitution to bring Kansas into the Union as a slave state. Kansas "is at this moment," the president told Congress, "as much a slave state as Georgia or South Carolina." This was too much for most remaining Northern Democrats, who followed Douglas's leadership and broke with the president to defeat the Lecompton constitution.

Each incident in the Kansas controversy propelled more Northern voters into the Republican party. So did the Supreme Court's *Dred Scott* decision in 1857, in which five Southern and one Northern Democratic justice overturned precedents to rule that Congress had no power to prohibit slavery in the territories. This made slavery legal not only in Kansas but in every other territory as well. But this would remain a barren right unless the territorial legislatures enacted and enforced a slave code. In Kansas, where antislavery settlers were in a clear majority by 1858, there was faint chance of that. So Southern politicians, led by Jefferson Davis, made their boldest bid yet to use national power in the interest of slavery. They introduced in Congress a Federal slave code for the territories and demanded its endorsement by the Democratic National Convention in 1860.

Meanwhile the abolitionist John Brown, who had gained experience as an antislavery guerrilla fighter in Kansas, led a quixotic but violent raid to seize the Federal armory at Harpers Ferry in Virginia. He planned to arm the slaves and foment a chain reaction of slave uprisings throughout the South. The raid was a total failure: Brown and most of his followers were captured or killed; Brown was hanged. This affair sent shock waves of fear and outrage through the South. It also confirmed Southern convictions that loss of control of the national government would be fatal. U.S. Marines commanded by Robert E. Lee had captured Brown. But what if the Federal government had been in Republican hands? Southerners equated John Brown with all abolitionists, and abolitionists with the "Black Republicans."

The Brown raid formed the backdrop of a bitter contest for Speaker of the House in the 1859–1860 session of Congress. The Republican candidate gained a plurality but not the necessary majority of votes. For eight weeks the donnybrook went on. Congressmen hurled bitter insults at one another, and one observer reported with perhaps some exaggeration that on the floor of the House "the only persons who do not have a revolver and a knife are those who have two revolvers." A Southerner wrote that a good many slave-state congressmen wanted a shoot-out in the House; they "are willing to fight the question out, and settle it right there. . . . I can't help wishing the Union dissolved and we had a Southern confederacy." At one point during the contest, the governor of South Carolina wrote to one of his state's representatives: "If you upon consultation decide to make the issue of force in Washington, write or telegraph me, and I will have a regiment in Washington in the shortest possible time."

The Speakership fight was finally settled by election of a nonentity. A few weeks later, Southern dele-

gates walked out of the 1860 Democratic National Convention when Northerners refused to accept a platform endorsing a Federal slave code for the territories. All efforts to reunite the severed party failed, and the bolters nominated a "Southern rights" candidate. This ensured the election of Abraham Lincoln, who carried every Northern state and therefore the election. For the South, this was the handwriting on the wall. They had lost control of the government, probably permanently. It was not state rights they had contended for in this contest. It was national power, power that they had held and had used to secure the Fugitive Slave Law, the Kansas-Nebraska Act, the *Dred Scott* decision, and other measures to protect slavery. But every such victory had driven more Northern voters into the anti–slave power camp, which finally elected a president who believed slavery a "monstrous injustice" that should be "placed in the course of ultimate extinction." So seven slave states left the Union and formed the Confederate States of America.

SECESSION. But that did not necessarily mean war. The government could have acquiesced in the division of the United States into two nations. Some Northerners did propose to "let the erring sisters depart in peace." But most were not willing to accept the dismemberment of the United States. They feared that toleration of disunion in 1861 would create a fatal precedent to be invoked by disaffected minorities in the future, perhaps by the losing side in another presidential election, until the United States dissolved into a dozen petty, squabbling, hostile autocracies. The great experiment in republican self-government launched in 1776 would collapse, proving the contention of European monarchists and conservatives that this upstart republic across the Atlantic could not last. "The doctrine of secession is anarchy," declared a Cincinnati newspaper in an editorial similar to hundreds in other newspapers. "If the minority have the right to break up the Government at pleasure, because they have not had their way, there is an end of all government." Even the lame-duck President Buchanan, in his last message to Congress in December 1860, said that the Union was not "a mere voluntary association of States, to be dissolved at pleasure." The founders of the nation "never intended to implant in its bosom the seeds of its own destruction, nor were they guilty of the absurdity of providing for its own dissolution." If secession was legitimate, said Buchanan, the Union became "a rope of sand" and "our thirty-three States may resolve themselves into as many petty, jarring, and hostile republics. . . . The hopes of the friends of freedom throughout the world would be destroyed. . . . Our example for more than eighty years would not only be lost, but it would be quoted as conclusive proof that man is unfit for self-government."

" . . . *the destiny of the land, the nation, the South, the State, the County, was already whirling into the plunge of its precipice . . .* "

WILLIAM FAULKNER
REQUIEM FOR A NUN
1951

The formal withdrawal of individual states from the Federal Union occurred in two distinct phases of separate state actions.

PAGES 514–15

No one held these convictions more strongly than Abraham Lincoln. "Perpetuity . . . is the fundamental law of all national governments," he declared in his inaugural address on March 4, 1861. "No State, upon its own mere motion, can lawfully get out of the Union." Later in the year, Lincoln told his private secretary that

the central idea pervading this struggle is the necessity that is upon us, of proving that popular government is not an absurdity. We must settle this question now, whether in a free government the minority have the right to break up the government whenever they choose. If we fail it will go far to prove the incapability of the people to govern themselves.

But even this refusal to countenance the legitimacy of secession did not make war inevitable. Moderates on both sides sought a compromise formula. Nothing

CIVIL WAR BATTLEFIELDS & MONUMENTS
National Park Services Battlefield Monuments

Name[1]	Location	Date Established
Andersonville National Historical Site	Ga.	Oct. 16, 1970
Antietam National Battlefield Site (redesignated a national battlefield, 1978)	Md.	Aug. 30, 1890
Appomattox Courthouse Monument (redesignated a national historical park, 1954)	Va.	June 18, 1930
Arkansas Post National Memorial	Ark.	July 6, 1960
Brice's Cross Roads National Battlefield Site	Miss.	Feb. 2, 1929
Chickamauga and Chattanooga National Military Park	Ga., Tenn.	Aug. 19, 1890
Colonial National Memorial (redesignated a national historical park, 1936)	Va.	July 3, 1930
Cumberland Gap National Historical Park	Ky., Tenn., Va	June 11, 1940
Fort Donelson National Military Park (redesignated a national battlefield, 1985)	Tenn.	Mar. 26, 1928
Fort Jefferson National Monument	Fla.	Jan. 4, 1935
Fort Sumter National Monument	S.C.	Apr. 28, 1948
Fredericksburg and Spotsylvania County Battlefields Memorial National Military Park	Va.	Feb. 14, 1927
Gettysburg National Military Park	Pa.	Feb. 11, 1895
Glorieta Pass Battlefield Unit (addition to Pecos National Historical Park)	N.Mex.	June 27, 1990
Gulf Islands National Seashore	Fla., Miss.	Jan. 8, 1971
Harpers Ferry National Monument (redesignated a national historical park, 1963)	W.Va., Md.	June 30, 1944
Kennesaw Mountain National Battlefield Site (redesignated a national battlefield park, 1935)	Ga.	Feb. 8, 1917
Manassas National Battlefield Park	Va.	May 10, 1940
Monocacy National Battlefield	Md.	Oct. 21, 1976
Pea Ridge National Military Park	Ark.	July 20, 1956
Petersburg National Military Park (redesignated a national battlefield, 1962)	Va.	July 3, 1926
Richmond National Battlefield Park	Va.	Mar. 2, 1936
Rock Creek Park (includes Fort Stevens)	D.C.	Sept. 27, 1890
Shiloh National Military Park	Tenn.	Dec. 27, 1894
Stones River National Military Park (redesignated a national battlefield, 1980)	Tenn.	Mar. 3, 1927
Tupelo National Battlefield Site (redesignated a national battlefield, 1961)	Miss.	Feb. 21, 1929
Vicksburg National Military Park	Miss.	Feb. 21, 1899
Wilson's Creek National Battlefield Park (redesignated a national battlefield, 1970)	Mo.	Apr. 22, 1960

[1] For a list of battles with dual names, see the sidebar Naming of Battles on p. 105.

availed to stay the course of secession in the seven lower South states. Delegates from these states formed the Confederate States of America in February 1861, elected Jefferson Davis president, and proceeded to establish a new nation with the appearance of permanence. But the other eight slave states were still part of the United States when Lincoln took the oath of office. He hoped to keep them there by assurances that he had no intention or right to interfere with slavery in the states and by refraining from hostile action against the Confederate states, even though they had seized all Federal property and arms within their borders—except Fort Sumter and three other less important forts. By a policy of watchful waiting, of maintaining the status quo, Lincoln hoped to allow passions to cool and enable Unionists to regain influence in the lower South. But this hope was doomed. Genuine Unionists had all but disappeared in the lower South, and Fort Sumter became a flash point of contention.

A large brick fortress on an artificial granite island in the middle of Charleston Bay, Fort Sumter could not be seized by the Confederates as easily as other Federal property had been, even though it was defended by only some eighty-odd soldiers. Lincoln came under great pressure from conservatives and upper South Unionists to yield the fort as a gesture of peace and goodwill that might strengthen Southern Unionism. After leaning in this direction for a time, Lincoln concluded that to give up Sumter would do the opposite; it would demoralize Unionists and strengthen the Confederacy. Fort Sumter had become a master symbol of sovereignty. To yield it would constitute de facto recognition of Confederate sovereignty. It would surely encourage European nations to grant diplomatic recognition to the Confederate nation. It would make a mockery of the national government's profession of constitutional authority over its own property.

So Lincoln devised an ingenious plan to put the burden of decision for war or peace on Jefferson Davis's shoulders. The garrison at Fort Sumter was about to run out of provisions in April 1861. Giving advance notice of his intentions, Lincoln sent a fleet toward Charleston with supplies and reinforcements. If the Confederates allowed unarmed boats to bring in "food for hungry men," the warships would stand off and the reinforcements would return north. But if they fired on the fleet, the ships and the fort would fire back. In effect, Lincoln flipped a coin and told Davis: "Heads I win; tails you lose." If the Confederate guns fired first, the South would stand convicted of starting a war. If they let the supplies go in, the American flag would continue to fly over Fort Sumter. The Confederacy would lose face; Unionists would take courage.

Davis did not hesitate. He considered it vital to assert the Confederacy's sovereignty. He also hoped that the outbreak of a shooting war would force the states of the upper South to join their fellow slave states. Davis ordered Gen. P. G. T. Beauregard, commander of Confederate troops at Charleston, to open fire on Fort Sumter before the supply ships got there. At 4:30 A.M. on April 12, Confederate artillery started the Civil War by firing on Fort Sumter. After a thirty-three-hour bombardment in which the Confederates fired four thousand rounds and the skeleton crew in the fort replied with a thousand—killing no one on either side in the first clash of this bloodiest of wars—the burning fort lowered the American flag in surrender. As Lincoln put it four years later in his second inaugural address: "Both [sides] deprecated war; but one of them would *make* war rather than let the nation survive; and the other would *accept* war rather than let it perish. And the war came."

[*See also* Compromise of 1850; Cornerstone Speech; Declaration of Immediate Causes; Dred Scott Decision; Election of 1860; Expansionism; Fort Sumter, South Carolina; Fugitive Slave Law; Harpers Ferry, West Virginia, *article on John Brown's Raid;* Kansas-Nebraska Act; Missouri Compromise; Nullification Controversy; Secession; State Rights; Sumner, Caning of; Wilmot Proviso; *and biographies of selected figures mentioned herein.*]

— JAMES M. McPHERSON

STRATEGY AND TACTICS

The strategy and tactics of the Civil War reflected the influence of the Napoleonic era, with its appealing popular belief that wars could be won in climactic battles. They also reflected the engineering curriculum at West Point, which helped American officers adapt the products of the Industrial Revolution to local conditions. The curriculum at West Point, which supplied most of the leading officers on both sides, spent little time on European warfare, although Dennis Hart Mahan had organized the Napoleon Club at the academy in order to encourage extracurricular study of the subject. Nevertheless, only a few officers had read any of the work of Antoine Henri de Jomini, the principal interpreter of Napoleon's campaigns. Jomini's allegedly rigid prescriptions for warfare conducted along geometric lines and his emphasis on limited war were not generally accepted doctrine. Technology, training, and the practical engineering education received by the leading Civil War generals, not Jominian influence, determined the limits of thought that would decide wartime strategy (planning the allocation of resources to achieve the military goals of a war or campaign) and tactics (the

The most prominent secessionists were known as the fire-eaters—in particular, Yancey of Alabama, Ruffin of Virginia, and Rhett of South Carolina.

PAGE 518

utilization of those resources when an engagement was pending or actually under way).

Tactics

The tactics employed by the Union and Confederate armies were much the same. During the early months of the war, formations were generally quite irregular, as green officers and their equally green troops were just learning tactics, and outmoded tactics at that. Later, the armies frequently relied mainly on one or two lines of two ranks each, in close order, perhaps a thousand men long, and sometimes followed skirmishers (soldiers who precede the main body to discover or delay the enemy). These lines might attack similar lines in close formation, much as in the days of the inaccurate smoothbore musket. Or they might shoot at or charge lines in entrenchments or behind breastworks.

In either event, the rifle-musket, developed in the 1850s, made such tactics quite obsolete. The invention of the minié ball—a bullet with a hollow base that would expand upon firing so as to catch the rifling grooves in the gun barrel—so improved the accuracy and range of the musket that battles were more deadly than in the past. Properly used, the Civil War rifle-musket made it extremely difficult to destroy an opponent who was comparably equipped and manned. Armies could be defeated and badly crippled, but they would survive to fight another day.

The combination of new weapons technology, frontal assaults, and commonsense use of the ax and spade made the Civil War the bloodiest of American wars. Under such conditions it did not take men in the ranks long to learn to dig in with amazing speed when their safety required it (Union troops approaching Atlanta could entrench for the night in less than an hour). Thus, judicious use of trenches or breastworks gave the defense a significant advantage, sometimes estimated at three to one, over an offense of equal size. The resulting carnage, especially to the attacker, appalled many officers. Union Gen. William Tecumseh Sherman, for example, attempted with some success to employ skirmishers instead of the customary two-rank line as a way to avoid the extraordinary casualties usually suffered by troops attacking a well-protected adversary equipped with rifle-muskets.

Although Civil War officers welcomed new technology, they did not always grasp its significance when applied to the fate of their soldiers. Close-order frontal assaults had become foolish, so tactical turning movements, in which part of one's force was stealthily moved to the flank or rear of the enemy, were often attempted in order to avoid bloody frontal encounters. The commander on the tactical defensive, however, knowing the dangers of frontal assault to the tactical offensive, preferred to receive his enemy from the

fronts. Therefore, the defender either changed fronts, retreated, or kept his flanks so well guarded by troops or features of the terrain that effective tactical turning movements were frequently impossible. Frontal assaults sometimes became inevitable if there were to be any battle at all. Under the circumstances, by the middle of the war, generals on the defensive put much thought into field fortifications and entrenchments and sometimes discovered that the men had thought out the problem for themselves and prepared trenches on their own initiative.

Professional officers on both sides were also receptive to other new technology, notably the steam engine and the telegraph. Steamboats played a vital role, making river supply and combat practical, and one cannot underestimate the role of the rickety Southern rail network in supporting Confederate strategy. Rail movement between main armies in Virginia, Tennessee, and Mississippi facilitated redeployment of small detachments from all over the Confederacy in order to hit the Union army at its perceived weak spots.

Clearly, speedy steam transportation gave new meaning to the Jominian concept of interior lines, which supposed an advantage to a force that was closer to separated enemy contingents than they were to each other, and therefore permitted that force to concentrate first against one enemy contingent and then the other before they would be able to concentrate in response. Steam could provide an advantage equivalent to interior lines to the side that had the most conveniently located railroads. In theory, possession of interior lines could be countered by simultaneous advances of two or more forces of the adversary. The most notable examples of simultaneous advances are the campaigns of Ulysses S. Grant and Sherman during the last year of the war, although Abraham Lincoln and H. W. Halleck had ordered such advances in late 1862. But such movements required swift relay of information and orders. Thus, the telegraph was an essential partner with the steamboat and railroad in permitting coordinated advances or rapid concentrations.

Strategy

The technology of transportation, information, and rifle-muskets, plus extensive use of entrenchments, created the stalemate that marked the Civil War. The major goal of strategy on both sides was to break that stalemate. American generals had learned about the defensive power of entrenchments at West Point and saw the offensive potential of the turning movement in the Mexican War. Indeed, the turning movement was the motif of most Civil War campaigns, because it was a potentially effective means of breaking the impasse by avoiding bloody frontal offensives against entrenchments. Yet armies moved over great distances and still fought bloody battles without decisive results.

OPENING STRATEGIES. Initially the Union considered a logistic strategy, as typified by the proposals of Winfield Scott, the general in chief of the Union army, who had demonstrated the utility of the turning movement in the Mexican War. Scott sought to avoid bloody battles caused by attacking large armies. Instead, he sought to deprive the Confederacy of military resources. A naval blockade would be established along the Confederacy's coastline, and an army of eighty thousand men and another naval force would operate on the Mississippi River to turn Southern positions and bisect the Confederacy. Labeled the "Anaconda Plan" because it was aimed at squeezing the Confederacy to death, Scott's plan was not adopted because of the impatience of Union politicians who expected quick victory.

Nevertheless, progress along the Mississippi was satisfactory, and the Union had substantial control of the river after July 1863. On the other hand, the Union blockade of the Atlantic and Gulf coasts was not particularly effective. Many blockade runners got through the blockade successfully. At the port of Wilmington alone, for example, over 80 percent of Confederate attempts to run the blockade were successful. This result was replicated elsewhere, as the Confederacy purchased vessels with high speeds and low profiles that made it relatively easy to evade the blockade. Moreover, ships of the blockading squadrons were limited by the amount of coal they could carry. Rapid consumption of fuel and frequent breakdowns meant much time spent off-station either recoaling or repairing.

President Jefferson Davis initially attempted a comprehensive defense of the entire Confederacy, as illustrated in 1861 when Albert Sidney Johnston did not concentrate his troops pending possible enemy threats in Kentucky but rather established what historian Archer Jones has characterized as a "system of strong points with troops attached to them," called a "cordon defense." Davis admitted this decision to be wrong after setbacks at Fort Henry, Fort Donelson, and Roanoke Island, because it dispersed Confederate forces rather than concentrated them. The early emphasis on territorial defense, however, not only met the political need to sustain morale but also served the military need to protect Confederate resources. For example, with the only important ironworks in the Confederacy in 1861 located in Richmond—the Tredegar company—that city's defense became vital.

THE NEW CONFEDERATE STRATEGY. Davis soon rejected passive defense and pursued instead an "offensive-defensive" strategy that frequently employed raids. Davis's strategy was also politically motivated: by going on the offensive, he might influence Northern elections and increase the chance of foreign recognition. In this effort time was on the Confederates' side; the longer they could keep armies in the field, the greater the political impact of their offensive victories.

Offensive-Defensive. Davis's strategy called for a defensive posture that would emphasize the strategic turning movement for both offensive and defensive purposes. In the strategic (as opposed to tactical) turning movement, one placed one's own army at a favorable point on the adversary's line of communication, forcing him to recover his communications by attacking on ground of one's choice. In this way, one could seize the advantage of the tactical defensive when on the strategic offensive. Although relying on defense, stressed historian Frank E. Vandiver, Confederates would exploit opportunities for counterattacks. The offensive-defensive enabled the South to take maximum advantage of its vast geography and the supremacy of the defense. Confederates were forced to trade space for time. A retreating force moved faster than its pursuer, for it could hinder pursuit by destroying bridges, blocking roads, or taking up rails, and while it moved toward its base it gathered more troops as it relieved itself of the obligation to guard bridges, junctions, and population centers. Some historians have been critical of the offensive-defensive; E. Merton Coulter, for example, thought that the defensive was a disaster for the Confederacy, and T. Harry Williams believed that a defensive war meant a long war, a disadvantage to the side with inferior resources. Yet it seems difficult to imagine a better strategy, taking all Southern circumstances into account.

The shift to the offensive-defensive was illustrated by the way in which Confederates met the 1862 threat to Richmond posed by the approach of the Army of the Potomac under George B. McClellan. In order to avoid frontal conflict, McClellan himself planned a strategic turning movement. He went around Joseph E. Johnston by moving his troops south on Chesapeake Bay to Union-held Fortress Monroe, at the tip of the peninsula formed by the York and James rivers. By moving up the peninsula and threatening Richmond, McClellan hoped to force Johnston onto the tactical offensive, thereby giving McClellan the defensive advantage. Typically, turning movements failed to trap defending armies, except at Vicksburg and Appomattox, but they frequently forced retreats. They also provoked counteroffensives to regain lost territory or prevent losing more. Thus the threat to Richmond posed by McClellan's turning movement caused Confederates to attack at Fair Oaks and the Seven Days' Battles, where the South lost a larger percentage of forces engaged than the Federals. The affair was a tactical

During the first months, blockade runners found it comparatively simple to slip into Southern ports.

PAGE 56

The Battle of Chickamauga on Sept. 19–20, 1863, was a decisive Confederate victory after three defeats—at Gettysburg, Vicksburg, and Knoxville.

PAGE 99

Robert E. Lee regarded John Bell Hood's men as shock troops to be used in the most desperate situations, and at that assignment they never failed.

PAGE 278

victory for the Union, but Confederates won a significant strategic and political battle when they forced McClellan back, a move that led to his evacuation of the peninsula. The results were not decisive, however, and McClellan's withdrawal only set the stage for future bloody battles.

Southerners also used the railroad, steamboat, and telegraph for counteroffensive concentrations that embraced almost the entire Confederacy, as in the Shiloh and Chickamauga campaigns. Prior to the Shiloh campaign, Halleck, Grant, and Flag Officer Andrew Foote had conducted a grand turning movement in the West, capturing Forts Henry and Donelson in February 1862, driving the Confederates out of Columbus and Nashville and forcing them to abandon their cordon defense. Under the influence of P. G. T. Beauregard, however, Confederates used the railroad, steamboat, and telegraph to prepare a counteroffensive to win back western Tennessee in spring 1862 by concentrating in northern Mississippi troops from all over the middle and western South. This plan was in accord with Davis's offensive-defensive strategy; the goal was to drive back Grant, who was on the Tennessee River, before the army of Gen. Don Carlos Buell could join him. Surprise at Shiloh was complete, and Grant was driven back to the protection of his gunboats. Maneuverable armies with rifle-muskets proved virtually indestructible, however, and when Buell reached Grant the tables were turned. Confederates lost their gains on the second day and withdrew to Corinth, Mississippi, evacuating it a month later when menaced by Halleck's leisurely advance. Since the South lost a greater percent of forces engaged than the North, the campaign proved to be a military defeat, and the loss of territory produced serious political attrition in the Confederacy.

The Confederate counteroffensive concentration at Chickamauga came in response to Gen. Braxton Bragg's retreat from Tennessee to northern Georgia in the summer of 1863. After threatening to turn Buell and forcing the Union general to retreat to the Ohio River, Bragg was himself forced back by Buell's successor, William S. Rosecrans, who conducted a series of turning movements against him. Bragg's retreat, however, provided the Confederates the occasion to implement a long-contemplated offensive plan—to make another concentration by rail. Part of a corps from the Army of Northern Virginia under the command of James Longstreet, plus other troops from eastern Tennessee, Mississippi, and northern Georgia, were sent to Bragg. Longstreet arrived in time to take an important part in the September 1863 Battle of Chickamauga, driving the Union forces into Chattanooga, where they remained under siege for over a month. Although the two most important Confederate

concentrations in space, Shiloh and Chickamauga, did not lead to ultimate Confederate victory, they nonetheless bought time and caused Union planners to prepare their future course of action more carefully than they had before.

Politics and Raids. As the war progressed, Davis added a political element to his strategy. Tentatively in 1862, but definitely in 1864, he sought to influence Union politics, with some limited success, as the peace Democrats illustrated in their 1864 platform. Understanding the political overtones of Davis's thinking helps to understand some otherwise inexplicable Confederate actions, notably the 1862 movements north by Robert E. Lee and Bragg, and the 1864 replacement with the aggressive John Bell Hood of Joseph E. Johnston. Both actions were attempts to undermine Northern morale by inflicting defeats upon the Union Army and thus affect the Federal elections.

Davis's plans to influence the Union elections of 1864 depended upon clear Confederate victories, and Johnston's retreats, however skillful, did not contribute to a political strategy because they were perceived as defeats by Confederate civilians. Johnston was therefore replaced by Hood, who attacked Sherman, failed to drive him back, and retreated into the defenses around Atlanta. Once more Sherman employed a turning movement, forcing Hood's withdrawal from Atlanta on September 2, 1864. Because of Atlanta's symbolic significance, Confederate morale was significantly weakened.

Throughout the war, the Confederate leadership had relied on raids to supplement major offensive and defensive movements. Raids maintained the offensive initiative and involved a minimum of bloody contact with the enemy. They were part of a logistic strategy aimed at crippling the Federals by undermining their supply. For example, in late 1862 Grant, using Memphis as his base, had advanced south along the railroad in an attempt to turn Vicksburg from favorable ground to the east. The Confederates stopped him at Oxford, Mississippi, when Earl Van Dorn raided Grant's supplies at Holly Springs and Nathan Bedford Forrest simultaneously raided Grant's railroad in Tennessee. These raids, involving a minimum of contact with the Federals, temporarily stopped the advance of a 40,000-man Union army. The Confederate raids forced Grant to cope with attacks on his railroads and supply depots by basing his army on the river, keeping limited communications, using interior lines, and living off the land. Grant persisted, until in April 1863 he crossed his troops over to the west bank of the Mississippi, marched south of Vicksburg, and ferried back to the east bank. Grant turned Vicksburg and forced the surrender of the city and 29,000 men on July 4, 1863.

Raids also had political effects. The cavalry raids that defeated Grant's December 1862 march on Vicksburg, frustrated the summer 1863 advance of Buell on Chattanooga, and delayed for months offensive action by Rosecrans against Bragg all raised Southern morale. Although such small raids were very helpful to the Confederate cause, major moves north, such as Lee's raid into Maryland in 1862, Bragg's invasion of Kentucky in 1862, and Lee's raid into Pennsylvania in 1863, proved to be less valuable owing to heavy casualties and the political attrition created by civilians' perceptions of defeat when the Confederate armies withdrew, as raiders inevitably had to do. Although it seemed so to those on the home front, Sharpsburg was not part of an invasion, for Lee aimed not to occupy territory, but rather to supply his troops on Northern soil, gather recruits, encourage foreign recognition, influence the Union's fall elections, and encourage Northern peace movements. Lee's hopes were largely in vain, for although he won a tactical victory at Sharpsburg, Confederates suffered twice the percentage of the Union's casualties and then retreated. Confederate civilians, untutored in the subtleties of military strategy, looked upon the battle as a defeat, perceiving that Confederates had gained territory and then lost it.

Events proceeded no better for Lee in 1863. He planned a second raid across the Potomac into Pennsylvania to secure supplies from Union territory, leaving the resources of the Shenandoah Valley available for the following fall. As in 1862, however, the Confederacy ran a risk. If Lee returned to Virginia too soon after major battle, the public on both sides would assume that he had been defeated. Nevertheless, Lee attacked in a three-day battle at Gettysburg, was twice repulsed, and withdrew. Even if Lee had won a tactical victory, withdrawal, and the consequent drop in civilian morale, would have been inevitable: his foragers were unable to fan out widely in the face of the enemy. Some scholars have seen in Lee's operations an effort to win the war by destroying the enemy army in battle. But his use of raids for supply makes this thesis doubtful. Like so many other Confederates, Lee hoped for victory by political means, expecting the Republican party to be displaced by Democratic peace advocates in the 1864 elections.

THE NEW FEDERAL STRATEGY. Even with the fall of Atlanta in 1864, the war was still in a strategic stalemate. After three years, Tennessee was the only Confederate state to be substantially restored to the Union. The problem of continued stalemate has caused historians such as Archer Jones and Russell F. Weigley to reinterpret Grant's later strategy. Grant understood the importance of river transport, and if he appeared to rely on a strategy of attrition, it was not by choice.

ULYSSES S. GRANT

In Grant, Abraham Lincoln at last found a general he could rely upon to defeat the Confederates and bring the war to an end.

NATIONAL ARCHIVES

Once Grant became general in chief, writes Weigley, he sought "the utter destruction of the Confederacy's capacity to wage war," although he preferred enemy destruction that was due to "capture, not . . . attrition and ultimate annihilation." In the spring of 1864, now General in Chief Grant recognized the difficulties of weakening the Confederates by conquering enough of the South to deprive them of supplies and recruits. Progress was too slow and garrisons in occupied territory absorbed too many men.

Instead Grant planned to use simultaneous advances to counter Confederate interior lines. The telegraph naturally played a vital role in Grant's plans, which called for raids to isolate Confederate soldiers from their supplies by destruction of the railroads and other facilities that provided them. But none of the raids took place until November 1864, when Sherman began his march from Atlanta through Georgia to Savannah. Facing token opposition, Sherman took only a month to devastate an area of Georgia about 50 miles wide and 250 miles long. By February 1865 he had turned north to raid the Carolinas. Sherman saw clearly the tremendous political and military impact such raids would have on Confederate morale and desire to continue the war.

While Sherman was making his way to Atlanta, Grant kept Lee so busy in Virginia that he could not again send Longstreet west, but Grant's efforts to gain decisive victories only forced Lee into the trenches around Petersburg and Richmond, beginning a siege. This dubious achievement cost Grant so many casual-

"I propose to fight it out on this line if it takes all summer."

ULYSSES S. GRANT
DISPATCH TO
WASHINGTON, BEFORE
SPOTSYLVANIA COURT
HOUSE, MAY 11, 1864

SURRENDER

In the front parlor of this house, Robert E. Lee surrendered to Ulysses S. Grant almost four years to the day after the bombardment of Fort Sumter.

ties that Northern morale was seriously compromised. Confederate civilians took heart from Grant's difficulties, but by April 1865 he had finally stretched Confederate defenses so thin that Lee was forced to evacuate Richmond and Petersburg and flee west, hoping to turn south into North Carolina and join Joseph E. Johnston. Lee got as far as Appomattox Courthouse, where he was turned by Union troops and surrendered to Grant on April 9, 1865. The Confederate attempt to unite Lee and Johnston failed.

The military, social, and political will of the Confederacy was drained. The South was not defeated by a strategy of annihilation, for 326,000 men were still available at the end of 1864, but desertion had almost doubled in the previous nine months, and the Southern army was well on its way to exhaustion. Steady attrition destroyed Southern morale, will, and psychological capacity to resist. Events had forced the Union to adopt a raiding logistic strategy, and in the end, as Archer Jones remarks, "political attrition had won the war before the military attrition of Grant's logistic strategy could bring military victory." But Davis's offensive-defensive strategy, supplementing a defensive posture with raids, turning movements, and offensive concentrations, had enabled the Confederacy to fight much longer than anyone could have predicted from a simple comparison of Union and Confederate resources.

— RICHARD E. BERINGER

CAUSES OF DEFEAT

Efforts to explain the causes of the Confederate defeat in the Civil War have generated a great deal of controversy over the past century and a quarter. The debate began with the publication in 1866 of *The Lost Cause* by Richmond journalist Edward Pollard, who blamed Jefferson Davis, and it continues today. Yet despite all the efforts to determine "Why the North Won" or "Why the South Lost"—the difference in phraseology is sometimes significant—there is no consensus among students of the war. The best way to approach the problem is to review the principal explanations for the Confederate defeat with an eye to the defects and virtues of each.

Major Explanations

Most interpretations fall into one of two categories: internal or external. Internal explanations focus mainly or entirely on the Confederacy and usually phrase the question as "Why did the South lose?" External interpretations look at both the Union and the Confederacy and often phrase it as "Why did the North win?" No matter which approach they take, most analyses assume, at least implicitly, that the Union victory was inevitable. But this is a fallacy. The Confederacy had several opportunities to win the war and came close to doing so more than once.

THE UNION'S OVERWHELMING NUMBERS AND RESOURCES. The earliest and perhaps most durable explanation of Confederate defeat is an external one. It was advanced by Robert E. Lee himself in his farewell address to his soldiers at Appomattox: "The Army of Northern Virginia has been compelled to yield to overwhelming numbers and resources." This explanation enabled Southerners to preserve their pride in the courage and skill of Confederate soldiers, to reconcile defeat with their sense of honor, even to maintain faith in the righteousness of their cause while admitting that it had been lost. The Confederacy, in other words, lost the war not because it fought badly, or because its soldiers lacked courage, or because its cause was wrong, but simply because the enemy had more men and guns.

This thesis remains alive and well today. In a symposium at Gettysburg College in 1958 on "Why the North Won the Civil War," historian Richard N. Current reviewed the statistics of Northern demographic and economic preponderance—two and one-half times the South's population, three times its railroad capacity, nine times its industrial production, and so on—and concluded that "surely in view of the disparity of resources, it would have taken a miracle . . . to enable the South to win. As usual, God was on the side of the heaviest battalions." And in 1990 Civil War historian Shelby Foote declared that "the North fought that war with one hand behind its back." If necessary, "the North simply would have brought that other arm from behind its back. I don't think the South ever had a chance to win that war."

Many Southerners, however, began to question this overwhelming-numbers-and-resources thesis soon after the war, and by the twentieth century many of them had rejected it. This explanation did credit to Confederate skill and courage in holding out for so long against such great odds, but it seemed to do little credit to their intelligence. After all, Southerners in 1861 were well aware of their disadvantages in numbers and resources. Yet they went to war confident of victory. Were they naive? Irrational? Inexcusably arrogant?

As they pondered this matter, numerous Southerners—and non-Southerners—concluded that overwhelming numbers and resources were not the cause of the Northern victory after all. History offered many examples of a society winning a war against greater odds than the Confederacy faced. The outstanding example in the minds of everyone in 1861 was the United States in its War of Independence against the most powerful nation in the world. In our own post-Vietnam generation we too are familiar with the truth that victory does not always ride with the heaviest battalions.

To win the Civil War, Union armies had to invade, conquer, and occupy the South and to destroy the capacity of Confederate armies to wage war and of the Southern economy to sustain it. But victory for the Confederacy did not require anything like such a huge effort. Confederate armies did not have to invade and conquer the North in order to win the war; they needed only to hold out long enough to force the North to the conclusion that the price of conquering the South and crushing its capacity to wage war was too high, as Britain had concluded in 1781 and as the United States concluded with respect to Vietnam in 1972. Most Southerners thought in 1861 that their resources were more than sufficient to win on these terms. And even after losing the war, many of them continued to insist they could have won. Former Confederate Gen. Joseph E. Johnston wrote in the 1870s that the Southern people had not been "guilty of the high crime of undertaking a war without the means of waging it successfully." And former Gen. P. G. T. Beauregard wrote in 1884: "No people ever warred for independence with more relative advantages than the Confederacy."

Although Johnston's and Beauregard's memoirs had a self-serving quality—they too blamed Jefferson Davis, partly in order to deflect blame from themselves—their assertions find plenty of echoes in modern studies. Most historians in the twentieth century have rejected the overwhelming-numbers-and-resources thesis as a sufficient explanation for Confederate defeat. Instead, they have advanced a variety of *internal* explanations.

INTERNAL CONFLICTS. One such approach focused on what might be termed the internal-conflict thesis. Several variations on this theme have emerged. One of the earliest and most persistent was spelled out by Frank Owsley in his book *State Rights in the Confederacy,* published in 1925. Owsley maintained that the centrifugal force of state rights fatally crippled the central government's efforts to prosecute the war. Owsley singled out Governors Joseph E. Brown of Georgia and Zebulon Vance of North Carolina as guilty of obstructive policies, of withholding men and arms from the Confederate army to build up their state militias, and of petty political warfare against the Davis administration. On the tombstone of the Confederacy, wrote Owsley, should be carved the epitaph: "Died of State Rights."

A variant on the state rights thesis focuses on the resistance by many Southerners, including Vice President Alexander H. Stephens, to such war measures as conscription, certain kinds of taxes, suspension of the writ of habeas corpus, and martial law. Opponents based their denunciations of these "despotic" measures on grounds of civil liberty, or state rights, or democratic individualism, or all three combined. This opposition crippled the army's ability to fill its

"I have done the best I could do for you. . . . I shall always be proud of you. Goodbye, and God bless you all."

ROBERT E. LEE
LAST WORDS TO HIS
TROOPS, APPOMATTOX
1865

"Seldom has there been such a peace as that which followed Appomattox."

FRANK LAWRENCE
OWSLEY
THE IRREPRESSIBLE
CONFLICT, 1930

ranks, obtain food and supplies, and stem desertions. It hindered the government's ability to curb antiwar activists who divided the Southern people and sapped their will to win. The persistence during the war of the democratic practices of individualism, dissent, and carping criticism of the government caused historian David Donald in 1958 to amend that inscription on the Confederacy's tombstone to: "Died of Democracy."

Three flaws mar the power of the internal-conflict thesis to explain Confederate defeat. First, recent scholarship has demonstrated that the negative effects of state rights sentiment have been much exaggerated. State leaders like Brown and Vance did indeed feud with the Davis administration. But at the same time these governors as well as others took the initiative in many areas of mobilization: raising and equipping regiments, providing help for the families of soldiers, organizing war production and supply, building coastal defenses, and so on. Rather than hindering the efforts of the government in Richmond, the activities of states augmented them. "On balance," concludes a recent study, "state contributions to the war effort far outweighed any unnecessary diversions of resources to local defense."

As for the died-of-democracy thesis, it appears that, on the contrary, the Confederate government enforced the draft, suppressed dissent, and suspended civil liberties at least as thoroughly as did the Union government. The Confederacy enacted conscription a year before the Union and raised a larger proportion of its troops by drafting than did the North. And though Abraham Lincoln used his power to suspend the writ of habeas corpus and to arrest antiwar activists more vigorously than did Jefferson Davis, the Confederate army suppressed Unionists with as much ruthlessness, especially in eastern Tennessee and western North Carolina, as Union forces wielded against Copperheads in the North or Confederate sympathizers in the border states.

This points to a second flaw in the internal-conflict thesis: we might term it "the fallacy of reversibility." If the North had lost the war—which came close to happening on more than one occasion—the same thesis of internal conflict could have been advanced to explain the *Northern* defeat. Bitter divisions existed in the North over conscription, taxes, suspension of habeas corpus, martial law—and significantly, in the case of the North, over emancipation as a war aim. If anything, the opposition was more powerful in the North than in the South. Lincoln endured greater vilification than Davis during much of the war. And Lincoln had to face a campaign for reelection in the midst of the most crucial military operations of the war—an election that for a time it appeared he would lose, an outcome that might well have led to peace negotiations

with an independent Confederacy. This did not happen, but its narrow avoidance illustrates the intense conflict within the Northern polity that neutralized the similar but perhaps less divisive conflicts within the South as an explanation for the Confederate defeat.

Third, one might ask whether the internal conflicts between state and central governments or among different factions and leaders were greater in the Confederacy than they had been in the United States during the Revolution. Americans in the war of 1776 were more divided than Southerners in the war of 1861, yet the United States won its independence and the Confederacy did not. This suggests that we must look elsewhere for an explanation of the Confederate defeat.

INTERNAL ALIENATION. Similar problems taint another interpretation that overlaps the internal-conflict thesis. This one might be termed the internal-alienation argument. Much scholarship recently has focused on two large groups in the South that were or became alienated from the Confederate war effort: nonslaveholding whites and slaves.

The nonslaveholders were two-thirds of the Confederacy's white population. Many of them, especially in mountainous and up-country regions of small farms and few slaves, opposed secession in 1861. They formed significant enclaves of Unionism in western Virginia where they created a new Union state, in eastern Tennessee where they carried out guerrilla operations against the Confederacy and contributed many soldiers to the Union army, and elsewhere in the upland South. Other nonslaveholders who supported the Confederacy and fought for it became alienated over time because of ruinous inflation, shortages of food and salt, high taxes, and a growing suspicion that they were risking their lives and property to defend slavery. Clauses in the conscription law that allowed a drafted man to buy a substitute and exempted from the draft one white man on every plantation with twenty or more slaves gave rise to a bitter cry that it was a rich man's war but a poor man's fight. Many families of soldiers suffered malnutrition as food shortages and inflation worsened. Bread riots occurred in parts of the South during 1863—most notably in Richmond itself. Numerous soldiers deserted from the army to return home and support their families. Several historians have argued that this seriously weakened the Confederate war effort and brought eventual defeat.

The alienation of many Southern whites was matched by the alienation of a large portion of that two-fifths of the Southern population that was black and slave. Slaves were essential to the Confederate war effort. As the South's principal labor force, they enabled the Confederacy to mobilize three-quarters of its white men of military age into the army—compared with about half in the North. Slavery was therefore a source of strength to the Confederacy, but it was also a source of weakness. Most slaves who reflected on their stake in the war believed that a Northern victory would bring freedom. Tens of thousands voted with their feet for the Union by escaping to Federal lines, where the North converted their labor power and eventually their military manpower into a Union asset. This leakage of labor from the Confederacy and the unrest of slaves who remained behind retarded Southern economic efficiency and output.

The alienation of these two large blocs of the Southern people seems a plausible explanation of the Confederate defeat. But some caveats are necessary. The alienated elements of the American population in the Revolution were larger than those in the South during the Civil War. Many slaves ran away to the British, and the Loyalists undoubtedly weakened the American cause more than disaffected nonslaveholders weakened the Confederate cause. It is easy to exaggerate the amount of nonslaveholder alienation in the South; some historians have done precisely that. And though large numbers of slaves ran off to Union lines, this happened only where Union military and naval forces invaded and controlled Confederate territory—an external factor—and the great majority of slaves remained at home.

But perhaps the most important weakness of the internal-alienation thesis is that same fallacy of reversibility mentioned earlier. Large numbers of the Northern people were bitterly alienated from the Lincoln administration's war policies. Their opposition weakened and at times threatened to cripple the Union war effort. About one-third of the border-state whites actively supported the Confederacy, and many of the remainder were at best lukewarm Unionists. Guerrilla warfare behind Union lines occurred in these regions on a larger scale than in Unionist areas behind Confederate lines. The Democratic party in the free states denounced conscription, emancipation, certain war taxes, the suspension of habeas corpus, and other measures. Democrats exploited these issues in an aggressive attempt to paralyze the Lincoln administration. The peace wing of the party—Copperheads—opposed the war itself.

If the South had its class conflict over the theme of a rich man's war and poor man's fight, so did the North. If the Confederacy had its bread riots, the Union had its more dangerous and threatening draft riots. If many soldiers deserted from Confederate armies, a similarly large percentage deserted from Union armies until late in the war. If the South had its slaves who wanted Yankee victory and freedom, the North had its Democrats and border-state whites who strongly opposed emancipation and withheld support from the

war because of it. Internal alienation, therefore, provides no more of a sufficient explanation for Confederate defeat than internal conflict, because the similar—perhaps greater—alienation within the North neutralized this factor, too.

LACK OF WILL. Another explanation for the Confederate defeat overlaps the internal-conflict and internal-alienation theses. This one can be termed the lack-of-will thesis. It holds that the Confederacy could have won if the Southern people had possessed the will to make the sacrifices necessary for victory. In his book *The Confederate States of America,* the North Carolina–born E. Merton Coulter declared flatly that the Confederacy lost because its "people did not will hard enough and long enough to win." And in 1986 the four authors of *Why the South Lost the Civil War* echoed this conclusion: "We contend that lack of will constituted the decisive deficiency in the Confederate arsenal."

The lack-of-will thesis has three main facets. First is an argument that the Confederacy did not have a strong sense of nationalism. The Confederate States of America, it is said, did not exist long enough to give their people that mystical faith called nationalism or patriotism. Southerners did not have as firm a conviction of fighting for a country, a flag, a deep-rooted political and cultural tradition, as Northerners did. Southerners had been Americans before they became Confederates, and many of them—especially former Whigs—had opposed secession. So when the going got tough, their residual Americanism reemerged and triumphed over their newly minted, glossy Confederate nationalism.

This is a dubious argument. If the rhetoric of Confederate nationalism did not contain as many references to abstract symbols or concepts like flag, country, Constitution, and democracy as did Union rhetoric, Southerners felt a much stronger and more visceral commitment to defending land, home, and family from invasion by "Yankee vandals." In this sense, Confederate nationalism was if anything stronger than its Union counterpart. In their letters and diaries, Southerners expressed a greater determination to "die in the last ditch" than Northerners did. As the Confederate War Department clerk John Beauchamp Jones expressed it in his diary in 1863, the Southern people had far more at stake in the war than did Northerners: "Our men *must* prevail in combat, or lose their property, country, freedom, everything. . . . On the other hand, the enemy, in yielding the contest, may retire into their own country, and possess everything they enjoyed before the war began."

A Union officer who was captured in the Battle of Atlanta on July 22, 1864, and spent the rest of the war in Southern prisons, wrote in his diary on October 4 that from what he had seen in the South "the End of

"All times are one time, and all those dead in the past never lived before our definition gives them life, and out of the shadow their eyes implore us."

ROBERT PENN
WARREN
ALL THE KING'S MEN, 1946

the War . . . is some time hence as the Idea of the Rebs giving up until they are completely subdued is all Moonshine—they submit to privations that would not be believed unless seen." The Southern people persisted through far greater hardships and suffering than Northern people experienced. Northerners almost threw in the towel in the summer of 1864 because of casualty rates that Southerners had endured for more than two years. Thus it seems difficult to accept the thesis of lack of will stemming from weak nationalism as a cause of Confederate defeat.

A second facet of the lack-of-will interpretation is what might be termed the guilt theme—the suggestion that many Southern whites felt moral qualms about slavery, which undermined their will to fight a war to preserve it. The South, wrote historian Kenneth M. Stampp, suffered from a "weakness of morale" caused by "widespread doubts and apprehensions about the validity of the Confederate cause." Defeat rewarded these guilt-ridden Southerners with "a way to rid themselves of the moral burden of slavery," so a good many of them, "perhaps subconsciously, welcomed . . . defeat." Other historians with a bent for social science concepts agree that the Confederates' morale was undermined by the "cognitive dissonance" of fighting a war to establish their own liberty but at the same time to keep 4 million black people in slavery.

This also seems doubtful. To be sure, one can turn up quotations from Southern whites expressing reservations about slavery, and one can find statements by Southerners after the war expressing relief that it was gone. But the latter are suspect in their sincerity. And in any event one can find far more quotations on the other side—assertions that slavery was a positive good, the best labor system and the best system of social relations between what were deemed a superior and an inferior race. As one study of former slave owners after emancipation expressed it, "nothing in the postwar behavior and attitudes of these people suggested that the ownership of slaves had necessarily compromised their values or tortured their consciences."

In any case, most Confederates thought of themselves as fighting not for slavery but for independence. If slavery weakened Southern morale to the point of causing defeat, it should have weakened American morale in the Revolution of 1776 even more, for Americans of that generation felt more guilt about slavery than did Southerners of 1861. That sentiment helped produce the abolition of slavery in Northern states and the large number of manumissions in the upper South in the generation after 1776. And it is hard to see that Robert E. Lee, for example, who did have reservations about slavery—and about secession for that matter—made a lesser contribution to

Confederate success than, say, Braxton Bragg, who believed firmly in both slavery and secession.

A third facet of the lack-of-will interpretation focuses on religion. At the outset, Southern clergymen preached that God was on the side of the Confederacy. But as the war went on and the South suffered so much death, disaster, and destruction, some Southerners began to wonder if God was on their side after all. Perhaps, on the contrary, he was punishing them for their sins. "Can we believe in the justice of Providence," asked one prominent Confederate, "or must we conclude that we are after all wrong?" Several historians have pointed to these religious doubts as a source of defeatism and loss of will that corroded Confederate morale and contributed to Southern defeat.

But note the phrase *loss of will* in the preceding sentence: not *lack*, but *loss*. There is a difference—a significant difference. A people whose armies are destroyed or captured, railroads wrecked, factories and cities burned, ports seized, countryside occupied, and crops laid waste quite naturally lose their will to continue the fight because they have lost the means to do so. That is what happened to the Confederacy. If one analyzes carefully the lack-of-will thesis as it is spelled out in several studies, it becomes clear that the real topic is *loss* of the will to carry on, not an initial *lack* of will. The book *Why the South Lost the Civil War*, which builds its interpretation around the *lack*-of-will thesis, abounds with *loss*-of-will phraseology: Union military victories "contributed to the *dissolution* of Confederate power and will . . . *created* war weariness and *destroyed* morale. . . . The loss of Atlanta and Sherman's march, combined with Lincoln's reelection, severely *crippled* Confederate will to win. . . . By 1865 the Confederacy had *lost* its will for sacrifice" (italics added).

This is the right way to put it. The cause-effect relationship is in the correct order: military defeat caused loss of will, not vice versa. It introduces external agency as a crucial explanatory factor—the agency of Northern military success, especially in the eight months after August 1864. The main defect of the lack-of-will thesis and of the internal-conflict and internal-alienation theses discussed earlier is that they attribute Confederate defeat to factors intrinsic to the South and tend to ignore that outside force battering away at the Confederacy. Thus the authors of *Why the South Lost the Civil War* conclude flatly, in the face of much of their own evidence, that "the Confederacy succumbed to internal rather than external causes." The overwhelming-numbers-and-resources interpretation at least has the merit of recognizing the external aspects of Confederate defeat, although the weaknesses of that interpretation remain.

NEAR THE END   *A sheet music cover for a Northern song lampooning the Confederacy's imminent collapse shows Davis asking Breckinridge to disguise him for escape.*   LIBRARY OF CONGRESS

*An estimated
1,166,850
American soldiers
became casualties
in the Civil War,
665,850 of
whom died.*

PAGE 127

INFERIOR LEADERSHIP. Another category of interpretation with an external dimension might seem to resolve the dilemma of explanation. This one focuses on leadership. Numerous historians of both Northern and Southern nativity have argued that the North developed superior leadership that became the main factor in the ultimate Union victory. This literature deals mainly with three levels of leadership.

First, generalship: The Confederacy benefited from better generalship in the first half of the war, particularly in the eastern theater and at the tactical level. But by 1864 a group of generals, including Ulysses S. Grant, William Tecumseh Sherman, and Philip Sheridan, had emerged to top commands in the North with a grasp of the need for coordinated offensives in all theaters, a concept of the total-war strategy necessary to win this conflict, the skill to carry out the strategy, and the relentless determination to keep pressing it despite a high cost in casualties. In this interpretation the Confederacy had brilliant tactical leaders like Lee, Stonewall Jackson, Nathan Bedford Forrest, and others who also showed strategic talent in limited theaters. But the South had no generals who rose to the level of overall strategic ability demonstrated by Grant and Sherman. Lee's strategic vision was limited to the Virginia theater, where his influence concentrated Confederate resources at the expense of the western theaters in which the Confederacy suffered from poor generalship and where it really lost the war.

The second level where numerous historians have identified superior Northern leadership is in management of military supply and logistics. In Secretary of War Edwin M. Stanton, Quartermaster General Montgomery Meigs, Assistant Secretary of the Navy Gustavus Fox, Chief of U.S. Military Railroads Herman Haupt, and many other officials the North developed by 1862 a group of top- and middle-level managers who organized the Northern economy and the flow of supplies to Union armies with unprecedented efficiency and abundance. The Confederacy could not match Northern skill in organization and administration. In this interpretation, it was not the North's greater resources but its better management of those resources that won the war.

Third, presidential leadership: Lincoln proved to be a better commander in chief than Davis. A surprising number of Southern-born historians join Northerners in this conclusion. Two quotations to illustrate the point: Northerner James Ford Rhodes wrote at the beginning of the twentieth century that "the preponderating asset of the North proved to be Lincoln." And in 1960 the Southern-born historian David Potter put it even more strongly: "If the Union and Confederacy had exchanged presidents with one another, the Confederacy might have won its independence."

This may overstate the case. In any event, a broad consensus exists that Lincoln was more eloquent than Davis in expressing war aims, more successful in communicating with the people, more skillful as a political leader in keeping factions working together for a common goal, better able to endure criticism and work with his critics. Lincoln was flexible and pragmatic and possessed a sense of humor that helped him survive the stress of his job; Davis was austere, rigid, humorless, with the type of personality that readily made enemies. Lincoln had a strong physical constitution; Davis was frequently prostrated by illness. Lincoln picked good administrative subordinates (with some exceptions) and knew how to delegate authority; Davis went through six secretaries of war in four years and spent a great amount of time on petty administrative details that he should have left to subordinates. A disputatious man, Davis sometimes seemed to prefer winning an argument to winning the war; Lincoln was happy to lose an argument if it would help win the war. Davis's well-known feuds with two of the Confederacy's top generals, Beauregard and Joseph E. Johnston, undoubtedly hurt the South's war effort.

The thesis of superior Northern leadership seems more convincing than other explanations for the Union victory. But once again, caveats are in order. With respect to generalship, even if the North did enjoy an advantage in this respect during the last year or two of the war, the Union army had its faint-hearts and blunderers, its McClellan and Pope and Burnside and Hooker, who nearly lost the war to superior Confederate leadership in the East, despite what was happening in the West. On more than one occasion the outcome seemed to hang in the balance because of *incompetent* Northern military leadership.

As for Union superiority in the management of production and logistics, this was probably true in most respects. The Northern war effort could draw on a wider field of entrepreneurial skills to mobilize men, resources, technology, industry, and transportation than could the South. Yet the Confederacy could boast some brilliant successes in this area of leadership. Ordnance Chief Josiah Gorgas almost literally turned plowshares into swords, building from scratch an arms and ammunition industry that kept Confederate armies better supplied than had seemed possible at the outset. The Rains brothers, George and Gabriel, accomplished miracles in the establishment of nitrate works, the manufacture of gunpowder, and the development of the explosive mines (then called torpedoes) that were the Confederacy's most potent naval weapon. Secretary of the Navy Stephen R. Mallory's boldness and resourcefulness turned out to be a pleasant surprise. What seems most significant about Confederate logistics is not the obvious deficiencies in railroads and the commissariat—to cite two notorious examples—but rather the ability of some Southern officials to do so much with so little. Instead of losing the war, their efforts went far toward keeping the Confederacy fighting for so long.

Finally, what about Lincoln's superiority to Davis as commander in chief? This might seem self-evident. Yet Lincoln did make mistakes. He went through a half-dozen failures as commanders in the eastern theater before he found the right general. Some of his other military appointments and strategic decisions could justly be criticized. And as late as the summer of 1864, when the war seemed to be going badly, when Grant's forces had suffered enormous casualties to achieve a stalemate at Petersburg and Sherman seemed equally stymied before Atlanta, Lincoln came under great pressure to negotiate peace with the Confederacy. To have done so would have been to admit Northern defeat. Lincoln resisted the pressure, but at what appeared to be the cost of his reelection. If the presidential election had been held in August 1864 instead of November, Lincoln would have lost. He would thus have gone down in history as an also-ran, a loser unequal to the challenge of the greatest crisis in the American experience. And Jefferson Davis might have gone down in history as the great leader of a war of independence, the George Washington of the Southern Confederacy.

That this did not happen was owing to events on the battlefield—principally Sherman's capture of Atlanta and Sheridan's striking victories over Jubal Early in the Shenandoah Valley. These turned Northern opinion from deepest despair in the summer to confident determination by November. This transformation of the Northern will illustrates the point made earlier that the will of either the Northern or the Southern people was primarily the result of military victory rather than a cause of it. Events on the battlefield might have gone the other way on these and other occasions during the war. If they had, the course of the war might have been quite different.

The Factor of Contingency

It is this element of contingency that is missing from generalizations about the cause of Confederate defeat, whether such generalizations focus on external or internal factors. There was nothing inevitable about the Northern victory in the war. Nor was Sherman's capture of Atlanta any more inevitable than, say, McClellan's supposed capture of Richmond in June 1862 had been. There were several major turning points, points of contingency when events moved in one direction but could well have moved in another. Two have just been mentioned: McClellan's failure to capture Richmond and Sherman's success in capturing

Atlanta. The latter, coupled with Sheridan's victories in the Shenandoah Valley, proved to be the final and decisive turning point toward Union triumph. Two earlier moments of contingency that turned in favor of the North were of equal importance, however.

The first occurred in the fall of 1862. Confederate offensives during the summer had taken Southern armies from their backs to the wall in Mississippi and Virginia almost to the Ohio River and across the Potomac River by September. This was the most ambitious Confederate effort to win European recognition and a victorious peace on Union soil. But in September and October Union armies stopped the invaders at Sharpsburg and at Perryville, Kentucky. This forestalled European intervention, dissuaded Northern voters from repudiating the Lincoln administration by electing a Democratic House of Representatives in the fall of 1862, and gave Lincoln the occasion to issue the Emancipation Proclamation, which enlarged the scope and purpose of the war.

The other major turning point came in the summer of 1863. Before then, during the months between Union defeats at Fredericksburg and Chancellorsville, a time that also witnessed Union failures in the western theater, Northern morale and especially army morale dropped to its lowest point in the war. The usually indomitable Capt. Oliver Wendell Holmes, Jr., recovering from the second of three wounds he received in the war, wrote during the winter of 1862–1863 that "the army is tired with its hard and terrible experience . . . . I've pretty much made up my mind that the South have achieved their independence."

But then came the Battle of Gettysburg and the capture of Vicksburg. This crucial turning point produced Southern cries of despair. At the end of July 1863 Ordnance Chief Gorgas wrote:

> One brief month ago we were apparently at the point of success. Lee was in Pennsylvania. . . . Vicksburgh seemed to laugh all Grant's efforts to scorn. . . . Now the picture is just as sombre as it was bright then. . . . It seems incredible that human power could effect such a change in so brief a space. Yesterday we rode on the pinnacle of success—today absolute ruin seems to be our portion. The Confederacy totters to its destruction.

Predictions in July 1863 of the Confederacy's imminent collapse turned out to be premature. More twists and turns marked the road to the end of the war. This only accentuates the importance of contingency. All the factors discussed in this essay—numbers and resources, leadership, will, internal conflicts and alienation—formed the context of the specific events of the war. Separately or collectively, in complex and indirect ways, they influenced the direction that events took at

"The War claimed the Confederate States for the Union, but at the same time, paradoxically, it made them more Southern."

ROBERT PENN
WARREN
THE LEGACY OF THE
CIVIL WAR, 1961

TABLE 1. CIVIL WAR CASUALTIES

Casualties	Union	Confederate	Total
Died of Disease	224,000	140,000[a]	364,000
Died in Prison	30,200	26,000[a]	56,200[a]
Missing, Presumed Dead	6,750	not available	—
Other Nonbattlefield Deaths	34,800	not available	—
Total Nonbattlefield Deaths	**295,750**	**166,000[a]**	**461,750[a]**
Killed in Action	67,100	54,000	121,100
Died of Wounds	43,000	40,000	83,000
Total Battlefield Deaths	**110,100**	**94,000**	**204,100**
Total War-Related Deaths[b]	**405,850**	**260,000[a]**	**665,850[a]**
Nonmortally Wounded	275,000	226,000	501,000
Total Battlefield Casualties[c]	385,100	320,000	705,100
Total Casualties[d]	**680,850**	**486,000[a]**	**1,166,850[a]**

[a]Approximate figure.

[b]Total nonbattlefield deaths plus total battlefield deaths.

[c]Total battlefield deaths plus nonmortally wounded.

[d]Total war-related deaths plus nonmortally wounded.

SOURCE: Data taken from Thomas L. Livermore, *Numbers and Losses in the Civil War in America, 1861–1865*, Boston, 1901, and from E. B. Long and Barbara Long, *The Civil War Day by Day: An Almanac, 1861–1865*, Garden City, N.Y., 1971.

TABLE 2. TEN BATTLES WITH THE HIGHEST CASUALTIES

Battle	Date	Casualties		
		Union	Confederate	Total
Gettysburg	July 1–3, 1863	17,684	22,638	40,322
Seven Days	June 25–July 1, 1862	9,796	19,739	29,535
Chickamauga	Sept. 19–20, 1863	11,413	16,986	28,399
Spotsylvania	May 8–19, 1864	17,500	10,000[a]	27,500
Wilderness	May 5–6, 1864	17,666	7,500[a]	25,166
Shiloh	Apr. 6–7, 1862	13,047	10,694	23,741
Sharpsburg	Sept. 17, 1862	11,657	11,724	23,381
Chancellorsville	May 1–4, 1863	11,116	10,746	21,862
Second Manassas	Aug. 29–30, 1862	10,096	9,108	19,204
Murfreesboro	Dec. 31,1862–Jan. 2, 1863	9,220	9,239	18,459

[a]Approximate figure.

Source: Data taken from Thomas L. Livermore, *Numbers and Losses in the Civil War in America, 1861–1865*, Boston, 1901, and from E. B. Long and Barbara Long, *The Civil War Day by Day: An Almanac, 1861–1865*, Garden City, N.Y., 1971.

crucial points of contingency. To understand why the Confederacy lost, in the end, we must turn from large generalizations that imply inevitability and study instead the contingency that hung over each military campaign, each battle, each election, each decision during the war. The chain of cause and effect from each of these events to the next will enable us, as with the piece-by-piece completion of a jigsaw puzzle, to get the big picture into some kind of focus.

[See also Civil Liberties; Morale; Slavery, article on Slavery during the Civil War; State Rights; Taxation.]

— JAMES M. MCPHERSON

LOSSES AND NUMBERS

The Civil War was the bloodiest war in the history of the United States. An estimated 1,166,850 American soldiers became casualties in this conflict, 665,850 of whom died. Disease killed almost twice as many men as bullets and shot. Inadequate medical facilities and a lack of understanding of the germ theory caused many wounded to perish from infection long after the fighting had ended. Table 1 illustrates the distribution of casualties in both Union and Confederate armies.

Battlefield casualties resulted from a variety of innovations in technology compounded by a profound lack of updated tactics. This gap between technology and tactics—sometimes referred to as the "Tec-Tac Disjoint"—killed many men needlessly. Both armies continued to employ linear tactics even in the face of the withering fire of newly perfected rifled weapons, dooming many of their troops. The Confederate propensity to attack also led to enormous losses that the South could ill afford. Later in the war, however, both Union and Confederate armies increasingly relied on entrenchments. Table 2 lists the war's ten bloodiest battles, which accounted for 38 percent of all battlefield casualties.

The staggering losses were more damaging to the South, since the North had a sizable advantage in population. In part, the war was decided by attrition. Napoleonic tactics, still in use by most Civil War leaders, advocated moving masses of troops into one cataclysmic battle that would decide the war. In the Civil War, however, huge armies constantly bludgeoned each other, but very few decisive battles occurred. In the end, the North's ability to replace losses in the field was a decisive factor in victory.

Not to be discounted was the role of immigrants, African Americans, and whites from the border states. An estimated 178,892 free blacks and former slaves—93,346 from the seceded states—served in the Union army, a manpower resource the South did not have. Nearly 500,000 foreign-born troops also served in the

armies of the North. Furthermore, the majority of white men from the slaveholding border states of Delaware, Kentucky, Maryland, and Missouri fought for the North; only approximately 185,000 served in the Confederate army. But even discounting these blacks, immigrants, and border state whites, the North still enjoyed a tremendous advantage in its reserve of military-age men. In all, two and a quarter million men served in the Union army and approximately 900,000 served the Confederacy.

All of these statistics translate into a Civil War soldier's grim reality. The chances of death or dismemberment were very high, with nearly 30 percent of all Union troops and 48 percent of Confederate troops becoming casualties. As an illustration, consider a typical company of one hundred men. In Federal armies, six would be killed on the battlefield or from wounds, eight would die of disease, and fifteen others would be wounded. In a Confederate company, ten would die as a result of combat, sixteen would fall to disease, and twenty-two would be wounded.

— DONALD S. FRAZIER

CLAY, CLEMENT C.

Clay, Clement C. (1816–1882), congressman from Alabama and Confederate representative in Canada. Clement Claiborn Clay was born on December 13, 1816, at Huntsville, Alabama. He was the son of Clement Comer Clay, an Alabama politician who served as governor in 1836 and 1837 and was named to the U.S. Senate shortly before the expiration of his term. As a result of his outspoken support of the secession movement, Clement Comer Clay was arrested by Federal troops after they occupied northern Alabama and was kept under military arrest for some time. Because of the similarity of the two men's names, Clement Claiborn Clay added Junior to his name and is often referred to as Clement C. Clay, Jr.

Young Clay graduated from the University of Alabama, receiving a bachelor's degree in 1834 and a master's degree in 1837. During his father's term as governor, he served as his private secretary and then studied law at the University of Virginia. He was admitted to the bar in 1840 and joined his father's law practice in Huntsville. Clay also operated a plantation called Wildwood in Jackson County and was the editor of the *Huntsville Democrat* from 1840 until 1842.

A member of the Democratic party, Clay was elected to the Alabama General Assembly in 1842 and was reelected in 1844 and 1845. While completing his last term, Clay was elected by the legislators as judge of the Madison County Court in 1846, serving

The Confederacy could not match Northern skill in organization and administration.

PAGE 124

until 1848, when he resigned. In 1853 Clay ran for the U.S. House of Representatives but was defeated. That winter, the Alabama legislature elected him to the U.S. Senate, and he was unanimously reelected in 1859.

While in the Senate, Clay championed the cause of state rights and supported John C. Calhoun's interpretation of the U.S. Constitution, arguing that Congress had no power over slavery in the states, that the territories were joint property of the states, that Congress had no right to make any law discriminating between the states or depriving them of their full and equal rights in any territory, and that any law interfering with slavery was a violation of the Constitution.

Clay was especially outspoken in his opposition to Justin S. Morrill's land grant act to aid colleges. Morrill's proposal that the Federal government donate public land to support higher education in each state in proportion to its population passed the House of Representatives in April 1858 but was opposed by Clay in the Senate. Basing his arguments on state rights, he declared that the legislation "treats the States as agents instead of principals, as the creatures, instead of the creators of the Federal government." Because of his opposition and that of other Southern senators, it was not until February 1859 that the Morrill Act passed

the Senate, and then it was vetoed by President James Buchanan.

Clay also supported the admission of Kansas into the Union under the provisions of the Lecompton constitution enacted by the proslavery Kansas legislature. The Lecompton constitution called for a vote on slavery by the citizens of Kansas. One article guaranteed the right of property in slaves and specified that should it be rejected by the voters, a constitution without slavery would be enforced but the right of property in slaves who were already in Kansas would not be abolished. The Lecompton constitution first was approved by the voters of Kansas when antislavery forces boycotted the election. Ultimately, however, Kansas was not admitted under the Lecompton constitution, which was later repudiated by a majority of the settlers.

Clay remained in the Senate until Alabama adopted its ordinance of secession on January 11, 1861. He was one of five Southern senators who made dramatic speeches on the floor before walking out of the chamber.

With the formation of the Confederate States of America, Clay was offered the position of secretary of war by President Jefferson Davis, but he declined the post in favor of Leroy P. Walker. Shortly afterward, in November 1861, the Alabama General Assembly elected Clay to the first regular session of the Confederate Senate on the tenth ballot by a vote of 66 for Clay, 53 for Thomas H. Watts, and 5 for George P. Beirne. Clay drew a two-year term and took his seat in February 1862. He was appointed to the Commerce, Conference, and Military Affairs committees. During his career in the Senate, Clay was a strong supporter of Secretary of Navy Stephen R. Mallory and was named chairman of a special joint committee to investigate the administration of the Navy Department. Clay apparently used his influence to exonerate Mallory.

Clay also supported the passage of legislation that would restrict a Confederate supreme court from having appellate jurisdiction over state courts in what was one of the strongest debates on state rights in the Confederate Congress. (A supreme court was never established.) He also authored legislation to conscript foreign nationals into the Confederate army. Clay's state rights stance also was evident when he joined with Alabama's other senator, William Lowndes Yancy, to protest to President Jefferson Davis that they were "mortified" because Alabama troops were being placed under the command of officers from other states.

Much of Clay's work in the Senate was devoted to mobilizing the Confederacy for total war. He became disheartened by what he perceived to be a lack of total support for the war effort on the part of many Southern officials, once writing that he was "sick of the selfishness, demagogism and bigotry that characterize a large portion of those in office." When Clay learned "how many are growing rich in the Commissary and Qr. Masters Departs. by defrauding the Government and the people and yet are unchecked," he said he could hardly stand to continue in public service.

Throughout his term of office, Clay was a staunch supporter of President Davis and often a confidant of Varina Howell Davis, the president's wife. She once wrote to Clay to express her concern over the toll the task of governing the Confederacy was taking on her husband's health, telling him that the "President hardly takes time to eat his meals and works late at night." Clay became one of Davis's closest advisers on foreign policy. In fact, he, along with Benjamin H. Hill, Howell Cobb, and Robert M. T. Hunter, became the chief administration leaders in the Senate.

Clay, however, privately blamed much of Davis's problems with Congress on the Confederate president's personality, which Clay described as being that of a complex and inscrutable man who would not ask for or receive counsel. Davis, said Clay, seemed bound to go exactly the way his friends advised him not to go. Clay lamented that he had difficulty being friends with Davis and regretted that Davis "will be in a minority." Although Clay nevertheless was one of Davis's strongest supporters, he was honest and open in his dealings with other Southern leaders, even the anti-Davis faction, and as such maintained their respect throughout his term of office.

His loyalty to Davis, however, cost him the support of many of his constituents, for Davis's policies were not well received by many Alabamians. When Clay stood for reelection in 1863, he was defeated by Richard W. Walker. Clay then joined his wife in Petersburg, Virginia, where he attempted to negotiate a deal to purchase 100,000 bales of cotton to be sold overseas by the Confederate government. The scheme was never completed.

In late April 1864 Clay and Jacob Thompson were appointed Confederate representatives to Canada, to join James P. Holcombe, who was already there. It was to be a secret assignment that Clay commented he could not enjoy; he accepted it only "with extreme reluctance, thro' a sense of duty to my country, & will do my best to serve her faithfully & efficiently." He left Petersburg on April 30 and traveled to Wilmington, North Carolina, where on May 6 he, Thompson, and their secretary, William W. Cleary, boarded a blockade runner for the trip to Canada via Bermuda. They reached Halifax, Nova Scotia, on May 19 and were joined by Holcombe.

Clay was entrusted with about $100,000 to finance his Canadian operations. One of his primary duties was to disrupt the North's war-making potential by sending secret agents south into the United States to contact Copperheads, pro-Southern sympathizers, and members of the Knights of the Golden Circle and the Sons of Liberty. Two of Clay's most successful agents were Thomas H. Hines and John B. Castleman, who tried to persuade Illinois, Indiana, and Ohio to withdraw from the Union, form a northwestern confederacy, and enter into an alliance with the South. In addition they hoped to purchase several Northern newspapers and to disrupt the North's financial base through the spread of disinformation on the gold market.

Clay and his agents also had been given $25,000 with which to help Confederate prisoners held on Johnson's Island in Lake Erie escape to Canada. From there, they were to be shipped South through the blockade to rejoin their units, or they could remain in Canada to aid the Southern movement. Clay and the others recruited almost a hundred of the escapees who were willing to continue their service to the South.

Neither Clay nor Thompson, however, had the temperament to encourage a revolution. Eventually, they clashed over their objectives, and Thompson moved his base of operations to Toronto, Holcombe settled at Niagara Falls, and Clay moved to St. Catharines, Ontario.

Of more importance were Clay's secret contacts with Northern Copperheads to seek a negotiated end to the fighting. Clay's counterpart in the North was Horace Greeley, who, although an abolitionist, hoped to end the slaughter on the battlefield through negotiations. When Greeley learned that Clay and Charles Francis Adams, whom he referred to as "two ambassadors of Davis & Co.," were in Canada with what he believed to be "full and complete powers for a peace," he pressured President Abraham Lincoln to meet with them. In arguing with Lincoln, Greeley pointed out that "our bleeding, bankrupt, almost dying country also longs for peace; shudders at the prospect of fresh conscriptions, or further wholesale devastations and of new rivers of human blood." Greeley's arguments reflected the growing pacifism and defeatism that by the summer of 1864 had added to the increased demand for a negotiated settlement of the war in the North. Faced with a Democratic call for an immediate cessation of hostilities, Lincoln's prospects for the 1864 election were dimming. Although he had little faith in the success of Greeley's proposal, in reply to his request Lincoln agreed to talk "with any person anywhere professing to have any proposition of Jefferson Davis in writing, for peace, embracing the restoration of the Union and the abandonment of slavery."

Greeley was named the intermediary between Clay and Lincoln and was empowered to inform the Confederate commissioner of the North's intention to enter into talks with responsible negotiators. On July

Some politicians, surprised by the First Lady's astute understanding of contemporary issues, accused her of meddling in the president's decisions.

PAGE 166

C

Europe's recognition of Southern independence would have created diplomatic havoc in Washington.

PAGE 175

15, 1864, Lincoln informed Greeley that "I not only intend a sincere effort for peace, but I intend that you shall be a personal witness that it is made," and he extended to Clay, Thompson, Holcombe, and G. N. Sanders, whom he called Confederate "commissioners," a formal letter of safe conduct to the national capital. Armed with Lincoln's letter, Greeley traveled to Niagara Falls on July 17 to talk with Clay and the others, but he was disappointed when he learned that they were not duly accredited representatives of the Confederate government. The men explained that their presence was unofficial and could not be acknowledged by Southern authorities. They promised, however, that if they were guaranteed safe conduct to Washington, D.C., and from there to Richmond, they could secure the necessary approval. Afterward Lincoln was convinced that Clay and the others were present not to negotiate a peace between the Union and the Confederacy but to incite peace activists in the North to obstruct the war effort. As a result, he declared that he would negotiate only with certified representatives of the South who were willing to restore the peace, preserve the Union, and abolish slavery.

Clay and his colleagues also wanted to influence the Democratic National Convention held in Chicago in August 1864, in the hopes of electing a Democratic president and negotiating an end to the war. The Democrats were badly divided between Copperheads and those supporting the North's war effort, and many Northerners feared that Clay would be able to influence and perhaps even control the Democratic nomination. This rumor was so widespread that some newspapers reported that Clay had prepared a platform to be adopted by the Democratic delegates. It was said to call for the war to be continued only to restore the Union as it was before the fighting started, with "no further detriment to slave property" and permanent slave status for all blacks "not having enjoyed actual freedom during the war."

Seventy Confederate supporters led by Hines and Castleman did infiltrate Chicago during the Democratic convention, but they had to flee the city when the delegates adjourned. Splitting up, a third headed South and a third returned to Canada; the twenty-two remaining Confederates joined Hines and Castleman and traveled to south-central Illinois, where they planned to destroy military supplies and disrupt railroad traffic in the St. Louis, Missouri, area. The plan failed, and in late October and early November, Hines's and Castleman's men returned to Chicago, where they hoped to lead an armed uprising in conjunction with the presidential election; they were discovered, however, and most were arrested. This ended the Northwest Conspiracy.

Another major effort to encourage pro-Southern sentiment in the North took place on November 25, 1864, when eight Confederates led by Col. Robert M. Martin succeeded in setting fire to ten hotels, three theaters, and some vessels in the harbor of New York City. Although this caused much excitement, little actual damage was done and no uprising occurred because ten thousand Federal reinforcements had been sent to the city to discourage Copperhead activities.

In October 1864 Clay gave $2,462 to Lt. Bennett H. Young to underwrite a Confederate raid on St. Albans, Vermont. Planned by Clay and Young, this was one of the most spectacular Confederate raids of the war. Young and twenty men quietly infiltrated St. Albans on October 18 and spent the day reconnoitering its defenses. The following day at 3:00 P.M. the Confederates robbed St. Albans's banks of $200,000 and herded its citizens onto the village green. The Southerners then tried to set fire to several hotels and other buildings, seized horses from the streets and livery stables, and shot up the town, wounding three civilians, one of whom later died. After occupying the village for about forty-five minutes (during which time Young claimed they were Confederate soldiers despite the fact that they were not uniformed or carrying a flag), the Southerners mounted the horses they had seized and rode for the Canadian border fourteen miles away.

Word quickly spread of the attack, and troops were rushed to the region. When the Confederates crossed the border into Canada, they abandoned their weapons and horses and separated. Pursuing Northerners crossed into Canada and captured seven of the troopers as well as Young. Canadian authorities then arrived and took charge of the prisoners. Eventually fourteen of the raiders were captured, and on November 7, 1864, they were brought to trial in Montreal Police Court. Clay paid $6,000 to hire three well-known attorneys to defend Young and the others. The Confederates asked for a delay to secure copies of their commissions from Richmond, and eventually the case was dismissed because the court had no jurisdiction; the arrests had not been made with warrants signed by the governor-general. Five of the raiders were rearrested, released again, and arrested a third time before they were finally released on bail and fled to Europe.

In seven months, Clay and the other Confederate representatives in Canada had spent more than $500,000 but had failed to instigate a northwestern revolution, negotiate a peace, nominate a peace candidate on the Democratic ticket, or seriously disrupt the North's war effort. They did cause much hysteria with their raids and terrorist activities. Realizing he could accomplish nothing more, Clay sailed from Halifax for Bermuda on January 13, 1865. In Bermuda he boarded a blockade runner and sailed to Charleston, arriving on February 2. On the tenth, he rejoined his wife in Macon, Georgia.

After the Confederate surrender, Clay decided to abandon his homeland and started on horseback for Texas. During the journey he learned that President Lincoln had been assassinated and that he had been implicated as one of the conspirators. When he discovered that a reward had been offered for his capture, Clay abandoned his plan to go to Texas and rode 150 miles to surrender to Federal authorities back in Macon. He was arrested and taken to Augusta, Georgia, where he was shipped, along with Davis, to Fortress Monroe, Virginia, and imprisoned.

Although never brought to trial, Clay was not released until May 1866 after his wife pleaded with President Andrew Johnson for his freedom. He returned to Wildwood and resumed his law practice. His health had deteriorated during the war, and he declined to reenter politics. Clay died on January 3, 1882, in Madison County. His papers, which are preserved at Duke University Library in Durham, North Carolina, offer some of the best insights into the inner workings of the Confederate government during the war and shed light on the various personalities involved.

— KENNY A. FRANKS

COBB, HOWELL

Cobb, Howell (1815–1868), congressman from Georgia and major general. Howell Cobb was born at Cherry Hill, Jefferson County, Georgia, on September 7, 1815. He was the oldest of seven children and brother of Thomas R. R. Cobb, who would be the chief designer of the Confederate Constitution. In 1819 the Cobb family moved to Athens, home of Franklin College (the University of Georgia), where Howell acquired a Jacksonian Democratic bias against nullification before graduating in 1834. About a year later he married Mary Ann Lamar, daughter of a wealthy middle Georgia merchant-planter. They settled in Athens.

Admitted to the bar in 1836, Howell's political career began the following year with his appointment as solicitor general of the state's western district. He was elected to Congress in 1842 from the Sixth Georgia District and repeatedly reelected as a Democrat for the rest of the decade. Chosen Speaker of the 31st Congress, he helped steer through that body the Compromise of 1850. The next year his Georgia friends organized the Union party and elected him governor. Meanwhile his leadership in the state Democratic party had gone to others, while his support

of Democratic presidential candidate Franklin Pierce in 1852 infuriated the Unionists. A politician without a party, he resumed his law practice after leaving the governorship in 1853. Two years later, running as a Democrat, he easily recaptured his old congressional

SKILLED NEGOTIATOR

Congressman and Maj. Gen. Howell Cobb of Georgia urged in early 1861 that the seceded states maintain peaceful relations with the North.

LIBRARY OF CONGRESS

seat. Back in Washington, Cobb was soon hobnobbing with Democratic leaders. It paid off with his appointment in 1857 as secretary of the treasury by President James Buchanan. His conflict with the Georgia Democrats had taught Howell that to resonate with folks back home he had to move resolutely toward separatism.

On December 7, 1860, U.S. Secretary of the Treasury Cobb resigned from President James Buchanan's cabinet. A few days later he set out for his home in Athens, Georgia. He had scarcely settled there when he headed for northern Georgia to turn the sentiment among old Unionist friends into passion for secession. But despite the best efforts of this born-again state rights advocate, many Unionist delegates were chosen on January 2, 1861, to attend the mid-January convention in Milledgeville, the state capital.

On the eve of the convention Cobb took his message to a gathering of friends and delegates at the Macon home of his brother-in-law, John B. Lamar. He implored his listeners to mute Unionism, a tactic he believed would permit the convention to take Georgia out of the Union with a minimum of bickering. Although not a delegate, Cobb accompanied Lamar and his guests to nearby Milledgeville and was honored with a chair on the convention floor. On January 19 he wired his son that the ordinance of secession had been adopted. The convention completed its work by nam-

Once invited by presidents to confer on important matters of state, Cobb was to be granted no such courtesy by President Davis.

PAGE 132

C

ing ten delegates to a convention of seceded states to meet in Montgomery, Alabama, on February 4. Cobb and Robert Toombs were chosen delegates-at-large along with eight district delegates. One of the latter was Cobb's younger brother Thomas. The Cobbs had fared well, thanks to Howell's prominence and zeal.

Georgia's delegates to the Montgomery convention assembled with those from South Carolina, Florida, Alabama, Mississippi, and Louisiana. The convention unanimously chose Cobb as its presiding officer. In a short acceptance speech, the incipient Confederacy's first leader announced that separation from the United States was "perfect, complete, and perpetual." He continued by urging a cordial welcome be extended to those Southern states not yet in the fold, adding emphatically that peace must be maintained not only with the late sister states of the North but with the world at large as well. He concluded by predicting for the Confederacy an "era of peace, security, and prosperity."

That Cobb was accorded the distinction of being chosen the Confederacy's first leader was an acknowledgment of his skill as a negotiator. Whether he was being rewarded or punished is not altogether clear. Impassioned secessionists may have been playing a clever game. His plea for peace recalled his dexterity during the drafting of the Compromise of 1850 when, according to his critics, he had given away too much. By electing him president of the Montgomery convention they were withholding the bigger prize, president of the Confederacy. Although Cobb denied he had been the victim of such intrigue, some of his friends believed otherwise.

With the drafting of the Constitution of the Confederate States of America, the Montgomery convention became the Provisional Congress. Cobb was convinced that its crowning achievement was the unanimous adoption on March 11 of the Constitution. None had labored more diligently than his brother in framing the document that Howell proclaimed was the "ablest ever prepared . . . for a free people." Perhaps next in importance to the adoption of the Constitution was Cobb's administration of the oath of office to President Jefferson Davis on February 18. Although pleased with the selection of Davis by the Congress, Cobb was distressed by the choice of Alexander H. Stephens as vice president. Surmounting almost two decades of political rivalry between the two was Cobb's conviction that his fellow Georgian's Unionism had survived the birth of the Confederacy.

Having met twice in Montgomery, Congress moved the capital of the Confederacy to Richmond in late May. It would hold three meetings there. Until it adjourned sine die on February 17, 1862, Cobb was its presiding officer. Meanwhile he began a second career. Assisted by relatives and friends, during the summer of

1861 he recruited the Sixteenth Georgia Infantry Regiment. Congress rewarded him on August 28 by approving his nomination for a colonelcy.

Recruitment received a mighty boost on July 21 from the defeat of Union forces at First Manassas. Cobb agreed with his brother, also a colonel, that it "has secured our independence." Howell predicted the blockade would soon be lifted and peace would follow quickly. His boundless optimism was contagious, and nine hundred Georgians joined the Sixteenth Regiment to celebrate the imminent independence of the Confederacy.

By mid-August Howell's troops were quartered at Camp Cobb, located about a mile from the state house, which was the new headquarters of the Provisional Congress. Cobb's life of political leadership and soldiery continued for eight months. Soldiery promptly presented a litany of woes. Early in September the regiment was ravaged by mumps and measles, about thirty cases proving fatal in five weeks. Meanwhile a special agent dispatched to Savannah to pick up a shipment of Enfield rifles discovered that Governor Joseph E. Brown had confiscated them. When Cobb learned what had happened, he lost his self-control, excoriated Confederate authorities, and demanded such interference cease. His demand produced a thousand rusty rifles. Cleaned and polished, they moved an official of the State Department to congratulate the Georgian on having the best guns in the Confederate army. In mid-October his son boasted that the colonel had progressed enough to shout drill orders from horseback.

On October 18 and 19 Cobb moved his troops to the Yorktown area, where they joined Gen. John B. Magruder's Army of the Peninsula. Cobb quickly developed a liking for "Prince John." Both Cobb and his brother, whose Georgia Legion was encamped nearby, believed the general was competent, though somewhat excitable, and that he was unfairly charged with a weakness for strong drink. The clammy atmosphere of the lower peninsula defied Cobb's morale-boosting improvisations. He felt unappreciated as he prepared to depart for the final session of the Provisional Congress. His brother, likewise beset with gloom, joined him in addressing a letter to the War Department requesting transfer of their commands to Georgia. The request unheeded, Cobb set out for Richmond on October 18. He arrived amid excitement over the seizure by the USS *San Jacinto* of two Confederate envoys aboard the British merchantman *Trent*. Cobb believed this act was a violation of international rights.

Once invited by presidents to confer on important matters of state, Cobb was to be granted no such courtesy by President Davis. Rather, Davis dismissed the *Trent* affair with a single reference before the opening of the final session of the Provisional Congress. As the prospect of England's entering the war faded, Secretary of the Treasury Christopher G. Memminger, lamenting to Cobb that the *Trent* affair had ended as it did, trusted that further complications "between them and England" would yet end the blockade. Cobb was to cling to the hope that England would go after the "cowardly Yankee" government.

The final session of the Provisional Congress lasted about three months. This was a difficult time for Cobb. When he was in Richmond, Magruder urged him to return to Yorktown; when he was with his troops, politicians wanted him in Richmond. Magruder's continual alarms over a likely attack may have been aimed at keeping Cobb on the lower peninsula. They became a routine of camp life, Cobb conceding that without "this amusement" soldiers would forget the war and become unfit. That many of them wished to return home with their arms at the end of their twelve months' enlistment was far more upsetting to Cobb than the general's monotonous alerts. The Georgian expressed his concern to Memminger, urging that Davis instruct all generals to see that discipline was tempered with kindness. Memminger responded that Davis had promised to do all he could to soften the "old habits" of the professionals, concluding on the considerate note that Cobb would soon be "up here" to help legislate on his concern.

When Cobb returned to Richmond in mid-January 1862, the Provisional Congress was entering its final weeks. Its leader was approaching the end of a political career that had spanned over a quarter-century. For the first time he was dejected over the Confederacy's prospects. This was partly due to his presumption that Gen. George B. McClellan was about to deliver a crushing blow. Helping to push him closer to defeatism was a rumor that Savannah was about to be attacked. In desperation Cobb joined three fellow Georgians in urging a scorched-earth reception. Although his fears proved groundless and his call for destruction went unheeded, Confederate reverses in February convinced him of the necessity of putting the torch to homes and fields.

As he arose before the Provisional Congress on February 17 to deliver his valedictory, Cobb lacked his earlier optimism. After excoriating the enemy and extolling the Confederacy as true to the "conservative principles" of the Founding Fathers, he pronounced Congress adjourned. Five days later, on Washington's birthday, he called into session the House of Representatives of the newly elected bicameral Congress of the Confederate States of America, administered the oath of office to Speaker Thomas S. Bocock, and summarily became a warrior statesman without portfolio.

On March 8, 1862, Cobb took charge of the newly formed Second Brigade. Recently promoted to brigadier general, he now commanded over five thousand troops consisting of four regiments, including the Sixteenth Georgia and that of his brother. While conducting a chase after Federals in North Carolina, he was ordered to join Magruder on the peninsula in accordance with a plan prescribed by Gen. Robert E. Lee to concentrate forces near Richmond. His brigade took a position across the Warwick River from the Northerners. There was little action until April 16. Then a short but hot fight took place around Lee's Mill. In this, his first test under fire, Cobb was satisfied he had handled his men well. By late June Confederate forces had withdrawn to within a few miles of Richmond. On the twenty-fifth the Seven Days' Battles began, with Magruder putting on a show of force in front of the capital. Two days later McClellan began his retreat to Harrison's Landing with Southern forces in vigorous pursuit. After losing an artillery duel and failing to overrun a rear guard at Malvern Hill on July 1, the Confederates spent the next day burying their dead. Of Cobb's men engaged in this action, one-third had been killed or wounded.

Cobb needed a rest, but having attended two fruitless parleys with Union officers on the subject of prisoner exchanges, he was asked by General Lee to try again. He refused and went home instead. Within a month he was back with the Second Brigade, now assigned to Gen. Lafayette McLaws's division of the Army of Northern Virginia. Maryland was about to be invaded and Cobb's destination was Crampton's Gap in South Mountain. On September 14 McLaws ordered Cobb to hold the Gap "if it costs the life of every man." A disaster ensued. The Second Brigade was badly mauled and its commander blistered by the staccato expletives of McLaws. Because other passes could not be sealed either, the Battle of Sharpsburg (September 17) was indecisive. Although the invasion failed, the Army of Northern Virginia survived. The hapless Cobb was sent to the Gulf coast.

Acting on instructions from Lee, the War Department ordered Cobb to report to Gen. P. G. T. Beauregard in Charleston. Early in November the Georgian conferred with the general about his assignment to the newly created Military District of Middle Florida, one of seven in Beauregard's department. With headquarters in Quincy, middle Florida was a rich agricultural area fronting on the Gulf of Mexico between the Suwannee and Choctawhatchee rivers. It was formed to defend vital rivers, particularly the Apalachicola and its tributaries, against Federal gunboats, to protect plantations and saltworks from raids, and to discourage collusion between Federal blockaders and Unionist Southerners.

The Confederate Constitution vested the national government with some centralizing powers.

PAGE 149

Cobb planned to secure the coast with troops and seal the important river by filling its channel with obstacles. These operations required more than the thousand troops on duty when Cobb arrived. Warning the War Department in early March against the "delusion of an early peace," he requested five thousand men. Although denied his request, he was permitted to woo volunteers by suspending conscription. When Cobb left for another duty station in September, he had raised about half the number of troops he had requested.

In August 1863 Cobb was in Atlanta conferring with Gen. Braxton Bragg, commander of the Army of Tennessee, planning the defense of Georgia. As he was preparing to return to Quincy, he received orders to tidy up the assorted recruits Governor Brown had assembled in Atlanta. Thus was born the short-lived Georgia State Guard. Until its demise in February 1864, the State Guard supplied a few troops for Bragg and for defense units in North Georgia and Savannah as well. Cobb used it to track down deserters, stragglers, and profiteers. His new assignment made him a participant in the disaster that was unfolding in Georgia, and it enabled him to renew contacts with Richmond. He met with Davis twice in Atlanta, and when he learned that the controversial Bragg was to be replaced, he headed for Richmond to plead for his choice as successor. He was pleased with the appointment of Gen. Joseph E. Johnston.

Having been promoted on December 3, Cobb arrived in Richmond as a major general. He promptly expressed concern over the absence of a comprehensive military plan, conferred with the president, and submitted to the leaders of Congress a plan that would authorize him to recruit from the State Guard a new command. Because immediate action was not taken on his proposal, he conveyed to Vice President Stephens his conviction that Congress was lack-brained.

Cobb was relieved to be back in Georgia. He promptly visited the Army of Tennessee and predicted "Old Joe" Johnston would drive the Federals out of the state. In an unofficial letter to the president, he explained that this could be done by means of a strong drive into Tennessee. Meanwhile enlistments in the State Guard were expiring and with them Cobb's command.

For over a month Cobb was without a unit. Finally Congress acted and on April 5 the War Department braced itself for the Confederacy's last effort in the Southeast by ordering Cobb to Macon to establish headquarters for the Georgia Reserve Force. With the heaviest concentration in Macon, fewer than five thousand troops, many of them part-time soldiers, were strung between Savannah and Columbus to repel hostile forays against railroads south of Atlanta. On July 30 Cobb repulsed Gen. George Stoneman's raiders in a sharp clash east of Macon, thereby setting the stage for

the capture of some six hundred raiders and their commander.

With the fall of Atlanta on September 2, 1864, matters had become critical enough to oblige Davis to visit Georgia. Arriving in Macon on the twenty-fourth, he joined Cobb in paying a visit to the Army of Tennessee encamped about twenty-five miles south of Atlanta. When the two returned to Macon, Cobb was greeted with an additional assignment. Richmond had finally put together an overall military plan, a part of which was a new command known as the District of Georgia. It embraced Macon, Columbus, and Augusta and was responsible to the Army of Tennessee. On the twenty-eighth Cobb received orders to serve as its commander. He now had two commands, but few troops. (Yet, despite this lack of manpower, he opposed recruiting slaves. He would write the secretary of war in January 1865 that "if slaves will make good soldiers our whole theory of slavery is wrong.")

From Macon, Cobb and Davis went to Augusta where on October 2 they conferred with Beauregard, newly appointed commander of the Military District of the West. Cobb returned to Macon hoping to contribute his troops to a general confrontation with the enemy. This hope was destroyed on November 15, when Gen. William Tecumseh Sherman left Atlanta in flames and began his slash-and-burn March to the Sea. Although one of Cobb's plantations became a victim of Sherman's raiders, Cobb believed that they were less devastating than the reverses suffered by the Army of Tennessee. Early in January he confessed to Davis that his despair over Sherman's outrages paled beside his unease over southwestern Georgia, where his family had gone to escape the raiders. He believed that this food basket of the Confederacy was sitting on a potential slave insurrection that could easily be ignited by the inflammable Sumter Prison at Andersonville.

With over twelve thousand "splendidly equipped" troops under Maj. Gen. James H. Wilson rampaging eastward across Alabama, southwestern Georgia suddenly acquired importance. Cobb was ordered to turn Wilson back. He had half as many men, poorly equipped. Before undertaking his final military assignment, he made a fruitless appeal to Davis for more troops.

On April 11 the sinking Confederacy's birthplace caught a glimpse of its first leader, whose devotion and faith were vanishing. In conference with the governor of Alabama it was decided that Cobb would not try to defend Montgomery; rather, he would make a stand at Columbus. Six days later Columbus fell. Cobb escaped with six hundred men under cover of darkness. Upon reaching Macon he was handed a dispatch from Beauregard dated April 20 announcing an armistice. Two days later Cobb surrendered to Wilson, was arrested, and while on the way to prison was paroled by President Andrew Johnson.

After the war Cobb practiced law in Macon, was pardoned on July 4, 1868, and on October 9 dropped dead in the lobby of New York's Fifth Avenue Hotel. He was buried in Athens.

— HORACE MONTGOMERY

COMMERCE RAIDERS

Raiders were naval warships that preyed upon the merchant ships of enemy nations. Commerce raiding, or *guerre de course,* was a strategy employed by weaker naval powers against nations with a large merchant marine. Raiders drove up insurance rates on the enemy's merchant shipping and caused many ships to flee to the protection of other countries' flags. They could be a powerful tool in economic warfare. Successful commerce raiders often forced the enemy to pursue them rather than participate in military actions against home shores. They generally sought to avoid contact with enemy warships because of their light armament.

The Confederacy employed both public (naval) and private (privateer) forms of commerce raiding. Commissioned naval vessels were sent to distant sea lanes to hunt, capture, or destroy traders. Privately owned, government-licensed warships, called privateers, generally sought to capture merchant vessels for profit in waters closer to home. Privateers had nearly become obsolete with the advent of steam propulsion.

The Treaty of Paris of 1856 outlawed privateering and regulated government commerce raiding. The United States and Spain, alone among the major maritime nations, refused to sign. Thus neither the United States nor the Confederate States had renounced privateering when the Civil War began.

One of President Jefferson Davis's first actions in office was his April 17, 1861, call for privateers to be licensed. Letters of marque, the government commission papers of privateers, were issued quickly; within two months over a dozen prizes had been brought into Southern ports. Privateering vessels required speed, minimal armament, and a relatively small crew. Most were small, fast schooners and brigs, although some were steamships. Most privateers operated in the waters around weakly blockaded ports, dashing beyond the safety of friendly coastal defenses to snatch a prize sailing near shore. A few privateers made cruises off the New England coast and in the Caribbean. Several ships were quite successful, but economic considerations led to the demise of privateering. By mid-1863 larger numbers of blockaders patrolling the coast decreased the chance to earn a profit in privateering while the potential profit from blockade running increased.

The naval vessels best suited for commerce raiding could make long cruises, had speed sufficient to run from more powerful ships, and an armament to match any adversary that could catch them. Generally, these vessels had full sailing rigs to minimize coal consumption and steam engines driving a propeller to add speed for chasing and running. Government cruisers generally operated in areas far removed from Southern

The British did not wish to insist on a freedom to trade that might be used against them in the future.

PAGE 55

Commerce-raiding cruisers were a nuisance and a menace to Northern shipping, but they could have no influence on the outcome of the war.

PAGE 662

CONFEDERATE COMMERCE RAIDERS

Cruiser Name	Dimensions	Guns	Prizes
Alabama	L. 220′, b. 31′6.7″ dph. 17′8″	8	69 (58 sunk, 9 bonded, 2 ransomed)
Archer	90 tons	1	1 (sunk)
Chickamauga	L. 174′ 1.2″, b. 25.8″ dph. 14.2′	3	4 (sunk)
Clarence	L. 114′, b.24′ dr. 11′	1	7 (6 sunk, 1 bonded)
Florida	L. 171′, b. 29′11″ dph. 9′6″	8	37 (33 sunk, 4 bonded)
Georgia	L. 212′, b. 27′ dph. 13′9″	5	9 (5 sunk, 4 bonded)
Nashville	L. 271′, b. 62′ dph. 13′	2	2 (sunk)
Shenandoah	L. 230′, b. 32′ dph. 20′6″	8	37 (32 sunk, 3 bonded, 2 ransomed)
Sumter	L. 184′, b. 30′	5	17 (7 sunk, 2 bonded, 8 released)
Tacony	296 tons	1	14 (9 sunk, 4 bonded, 1 recaptured)
Tallahassee	L. 220′, b. 24′ dph. 14′	3	35 (sunk)
Tuscaloosa	500 tons	3	2 (1 sunk, 1 bonded)

*Because many of
the Confederacy's
most effective
commerce raiders
were built in Great
Britain, the U.S.
maintained that
Britain should be
held responsible.*

PAGE 7

*The impact of
commerce raiding
by* Alabama *and
other Confederate
warships was
disastrous for the
U.S. Merchant
Marine.*

PAGE 6

shores; indeed, only five of the twelve most successful commerce raiders were ever in a Confederate port.

Commerce raiders, both naval and private, caused many problems for neutral nations. Foreign governments trod a narrow path to avoid favoring one side or the other in the struggle. Early in the war, as a result of President Abraham Lincoln's proclamation of blockade, Great Britain and France recognized the Confederacy as a belligerent. The recognition of belligerency allowed the infant nation to purchase stores and weapons. Both Great Britain and France, however, forbade the belligerents to recruit or fit out expeditions in their territory. Thus, vessels and their armament could be purchased in Europe, but ordnance could not be fitted, nor the crew engaged, at the time of sailing. This prevented several Confederate raiders from sailing after being purchased in Great Britain and France. Warships of both the Confederacy and the Union were allowed to replenish coal occasionally in neutral ports but could not recruit or engage the enemy while in neutral waters. Violations of the duties of neutrals and of their sovereignty caused a number of diplomatic incidents and led, after the war, to the international arbitration of the *Alabama* Claims.

Neutrality restrictions also prevented Confederate privateers and government warships from bringing prizes into foreign waters. This prohibition led to the slow death of privateering for economic reasons: prizes had to be brought into port and sold for profit. It also led to the destruction, rather than the appropriation, of prizes taken by government cruisers. After seven prizes captured by the raider *Sumter* were allowed to go free from Cienfuegos, Cuba, in 1861, Confederate cruisers destroyed prizes rather than attempting to send them to the South by way of neutral ports.

The first Confederate government commerce raider to prey on Northern shipping was the small steam-auxiliary *Sumter,* which sailed on June 30, 1861. The steamer was converted in New Orleans from a passenger-cargo vessel into an ocean cruiser. Under its talented captain, Raphael Semmes, *Sumter* captured eighteen Union vessels in a seven-month cruise through the Gulf of Mexico and the North Atlantic. Suffering from worn-out engines and boilers, *Sumter* was laid up and later sold at Gibraltar.

The next Confederate raider to sail was the former passenger steamer *Nashville.* It was seized at Charleston, armed with two small 12-pounder cannons, and commissioned the CSS *Nashville.* Under Lt. Robert Pegram it made a voyage in 1861 from Charleston to Southampton, England. The *Nashville* destroyed the U.S. clipper ship *Harvey Birch* in the English Channel on the outward voyage; on the return trip it burned another Union vessel. The Confederate navy sold it as

unsuitable for its use, and the next owner converted the *Nashville* into a blockade runner.

Several exceptional groups of Confederate commerce raiders used whaleboats and small schooners to hunt prizes. Acting as maritime guerrillas, these men employed impudence, stealth, local knowledge, and careful planning to strike at unarmed Union merchant vessels, and occasionally warships, in waters throughout the Confederacy. Three maritime guerrillas were particularly successful: John Taylor Wood, John Y. Beall, and John Clibbon Braine.

Commander John Taylor Wood, CSN, captured seven Union vessels between October 1862 and February 1864. He conducted raids in whaleboats that had been carried to various river landings atop wagons. Wood became President Davis's naval aide and eventually commanded the *Tallahassee,* a more capable vessel. At the war's end, Wood and several other prominent Confederates escaped to Cuba through Florida waters in a stolen small boat.

Master John Y. Beall, CSN, of Matthews County, Virginia, became the "Mosby of the Chesapeake," capturing small Union vessels on the bay. Beall and a party of watermen destroyed four Federal schooners on September 19, 1863. Beall was captured and imprisoned in November 1863 but was paroled in March 1864. He then organized a breakout attempt from Point Lookout Prison, Virginia, that failed. Leading another raiding party, he seized the steamers *Philo Parsons* and *Island Queen* on September 19, 1864. On December 16 of that year, while trying to free seven Confederate prisoners being moved to Fort LaFayette in New York, Beall was captured by Union forces. They hanged him as a spy at Governor's Island, New York Harbor, on February 24, 1865, although he was a warrant officer operating under orders.

Another Confederate commerce raider, John Clibbon Braine, sailed with clandestine parties of Confederates on board passenger steamers. Braine and his companions captured the steamer *Chesapeake* in December 1863, the steamer *Roanoke* in September 1864, and the schooners *St. Mary's* and *Spafford* in March 1865.

The largest Confederate commerce raiding program was based on the work of James Dunwoody Bulloch and other naval officers in Europe. They ordered vessels built for government service in foreign shipyards and arranged delivery of the armament and crew at some remote point. The first of Bulloch's ships completed was the cruiser *Florida.* Built on the plans of a British Royal Navy cruiser at Birkenhead, England, it sailed on March 22, 1862. The *Florida* met the steamer *Bahama* in the Bahama Islands and received guns and crew. The raider was partially armed and commissioned August 10, 1862, but the men discovered that crucial parts of its guns had been left behind. The *Florida* had to run the blockade in and out of Mobile, Alabama, for additional crewmen and ordnance parts. Operating under three captains, *Florida* captured thirty-seven Union merchant vessels. The Confederates converted one of its prizes, the bark the *Clarence,* into a lightly armed cruiser. *Clarence* and a succession of armed prizes, the barks *Tacony* and *Archer,* captured twenty-three further vessels. *Florida* was captured and towed from the harbor of Bahia, Brazil, by USS *Wachusetts* in violation of Brazilian neutrality. The United States promised to return *Florida* to Brazil, but the ship "accidentally sank" before the promise could be kept.

The most successful Confederate raider was CSS *Alabama.* It sailed on July 29, 1862, from Liverpool and met two ships carrying its officers, crew, and armament at Terceira in the Azores. On August 24, Raphael Semmes commissioned the ship CSS *Alabama.* It cruised the North Atlantic and sailed into the Gulf of Mexico where it sank the blockader USS *Hatteras* off Galveston, Texas. *Alabama* captured sixty-nine vessels, sinking fifty-eight of them. In the South Atlantic, Semmes commissioned the captured bark *Conrad* as the subsidiary cruiser CSS *Tuscaloosa.* It in turn captured two vessels. After a cruise through the Indian and Atlantic oceans, *Alabama* met and was sunk by the Union cruiser USS *Kearsarge* in battle off the coast of Cherbourg, France, in the English Channel.

Another purchasing agent, Capt. Matthew Fontaine Maury, CSN, bought the new iron, sail-auxiliary screw steamship *Japan* at Dumbarton, Scotland, for conversion into a cruiser. The ship left Scotland on April 1, 1863, and met the steamer *Alar* off Ushant, France, to receive arms and supplies. Its commander, William L. Maury, commissioned the vessel CSS *Georgia* on April 9, 1863. Maury burned five of the nine ships that he captured during a seven-month cruise in the Atlantic. When the iron hull proved unsuitable for a cruiser, *Georgia* was decommissioned at Liverpool and sold.

Another of Matthew Maury's purchases was not as successful. On November 24, 1863, the former Royal Navy cruiser *Victor* left Sheerness, England, under suspicion of violating British neutrality laws. Outside British territorial waters it was commissioned CSS *Rappahannock.* The ship was to meet *Georgia* off the French coast to receive armament, but severe machinery problems forced it to put in at Calais, France, for repairs. The ship was found unsuitable for service as a cruiser and sat out the remainder of the war as a station ship at Calais.

Union protests to the British government following the successes of *Florida, Alabama,* and *Georgia* led to

the seizure of several vessels on suspicion of their violating British neutrality. The first was a small cruiser, *Alexandra,* being built as a gift for the Confederate government. A second, more substantial cruiser, similar to *Alabama,* was seized in Glasgow for similar reasons. This steam-auxiliary sailing ship, named *Canton* or *Pampero,* might have been a formidable commerce raider had it been commissioned.

When highly suitable vessels could not be found for commerce raiding, the Confederacy pressed other ships into service. In the summer and fall of 1864, two blockade runners were converted into commerce raiders while in Confederate ports. The runner *Atalanta* became the raider CSS *Tallahassee* and later CSS *Olustee;* the runner *Edith* became CSS *Chickamauga.* Navy Secretary Stephen R. Mallory chose John Taylor Wood, who had done well in guerrilla raids on Chesapeake Bay, as *Tallahassee's* first commander. *Tallahassee-Olustee* captured and destroyed thirty-five vessels during two cruises. *Chickamauga* sank four during a single short cruise.

The last Confederate commerce raider to operate was the full-rigged clipper steam-auxiliary ship *Shenandoah.* Formerly the merchant vessel *Sea King, Shenandoah* cruised against the New England whaling fleets in the Pacific and Arctic. It captured thirty-seven vessels and burned thirty-two. Its commander, James Waddell, did not learn that the war had ended until August 2, 1865. *Shenandoah* sailed for the United Kingdom, arriving November 6, 1865, the last Confederate military unit to fly the national ensign.

A number of vessels intended for commerce raiding were nearing completion when the war ended. Four enlarged and improved *Alabama*-type corvettes built in France and six fast twin-screw steamers built in Great Britain were never delivered to the Confederacy. The French government prevented the corvettes from sailing, and the Confederacy sold the ships to raise money for other projects. The six guerrilla raiders built on the *Tallahassee* model were fast twin-screw steamers with a small sailing rig. They were designed to pay for themselves first by running the blockade and then by making dashes against coastal commerce, fishing fleets, and Northern seacoast cities. These ten ships were ultimately dispersed to the Prussian, Brazilian, and Peruvian navies.

Following the end of the war, the United States brought suit against Great Britain, holding that that country was liable for not exercising "due diligence" to prevent the depredations of the commerce raiders purchased there. An international tribunal of arbitration was established in Geneva, Switzerland, to decide the case. Great Britain, found liable for the acts of *Florida, Alabama, Shenandoah,* and their tenders, settled the

During Alabama's *cruise Semmes had captured and burned fifty-five Union merchant vessels valued at more than $4.5 million.*

PAGE 6

case in 1873 by paying the United States $15.5 million in gold.

Confederate raiding of Northern merchant fleets was among the most successful programs of the government. The commerce raiders did great damage to the Northern economy. Over three hundred vessels were destroyed and many hundreds more were sold to foreigners to prevent financial ruin if captured by a raider. It took the U.S. merchant fleet over forty years to recover from the depredations of the Confederate commerce raiders.

[*See also* Alabama Claims; Anglo-Confederate Purchasing; Enchantress Affair; *and entries on the ships* Alabama *and* Shenandoah.]

— KEVIN J. FOSTER

COMPROMISE OF 1850

In the 1840s Americans' enthusiasm for expansion collided with growing antislavery sentiments, and the resulting controversy spurred a search for some formula to resolve the issue of slavery in the territories. The Compromise of 1850 was the most comprehensive effort by Congress to solve territorial and slavery-related problems. For a few years it was applauded and sometimes revered, but by 1854 its flaws and new territorial disputes had revealed the

failure of this legislation to remove the causes of conflict.

President James K. Polk entered the White House in 1845 determined to add territory to the United States, and the war with Mexico expanded the nation's borders to the Pacific Ocean. The Wilmot Proviso, however, offered in 1846 by David Wilmot, a representative from Pennsylvania who belonged to Polk's own Democratic party, exposed the internal dangers of such continental visions. Wilmot proposed that slavery be prohibited from any lands gained from Mexico. Though his idea never became law, it polarized Congress and aroused state legislatures, North and South.

In the 1848 presidential campaign, Democrat Lewis Cass advanced an idea that became known as "popular sovereignty." Although Congress at some point would have to approve statehood for a new territory, Cass suggested that it should "in the meantime" stay out of territorial questions, allowing the people living there "to regulate their own concerns in their own way." This was an attractive formula to many, but it raised doubts among Southern leaders, who insisted that slaveholders had a right to carry slaves into any territory during the territorial stage. Many Northerners, on the other hand, wanted and expected settlers to prohibit slavery before statehood. For political benefit Democrats interpreted Cass's idea differently to Northerners and Southerners, but distrust of Cass in the South helped elect his Whig opponent, slave-owning Zachary Taylor.

The gold rush of 1849 forced these divisive issues onto Congress's agenda, as more than eighty thousand people streamed into California. President Taylor urged them to apply for admission into the Union, and they did so, proposing a state constitution that barred slavery. California's application threatened to end for the foreseeable future the balance between free and slave states in the Senate. Immediately, some Southerners objected that California should be a slave state or that the Missouri Compromise line should at least be extended westward to the Pacific. Nine Southern states sent representatives to the Nashville Convention, which asserted slaveholders' rights and endorsed extension of the Missouri Compromise line. President Taylor remained adamant for California's admission, but his sudden death in July 1850 left the decision to Congress.

In these circumstances the venerable and respected Henry Clay, who had played a prominent part in the compromises of 1820 and 1833, assumed a central role. In January 1850 the Whig leader proposed an overall settlement packaged as one piece of legislation, the "omnibus bill." Stephen A. Douglas of Illinois, a rising star in the Democratic party, assisted Clay. The senators' proposals encompassed five major areas. First, California would enter the Union as a free state. Second, new territories called New Mexico and Utah would be organized in the Southwest with governments empowered to legislate on "all rightful subjects . . . consistent with the Constitution." This ambiguous phrase, interpreted differently by Southerners and Northerners, continued the confusion inherent in Cass's original proposal. In fact, the legislation anticipated disagreement and provided for appeal of a territorial legislature's action directly to the U.S. Supreme Court. Third, Texas would give up its claims to a more extensive western boundary, and in exchange the United States would assume the state's public debt. Fourth, the slave trade in the District of Columbia would be ended. And fifth, a stronger fugitive slave law for the nation would be enacted.

For six months Clay and Douglas worked to arrange support for the omnibus bill, but when it finally came to a vote, it was defeated. The prospect of an overall adjustment had not been attractive enough to overcome sectional objections. With Clay sick and absent from Washington, Douglas devised another strategy. He proposed the five elements of the compromise as five separate bills, hoping to piece together different majorities for each part of the compromise. The strategy worked, and by September 17 the Compromise of 1850 had become law. Each bill had gained a majority, although the bulk of Northern and Southern congressmen voted against each other in every instance but one.

Crowds in the capital celebrated the passage of the compromise, and initially political leaders hailed it as a

settlement of the issues that threatened to divide the nation. In 1852 Franklin Pierce, who pledged to support the compromise, won a smashing victory in the presidential election. The views of his Whig opponent, Winfield Scott, were unknown, and Free Soil candidate John P. Hale openly repudiated the compromise. Thus, this legislation seemed to have won broad acceptance and growing prestige. By 1854, however, the peacemaking properties of the legislation had vanished.

What caused this great reversal? First, the Compromise of 1850 had skirted, rather than settled, the controversy over what rights proslavery and antislavery settlers had in the territories. The ambiguous language of the bill provided no formula to guide the future. Northerners continued to believe that slavery could and should be prohibited from the territories, whereas Southerners insisted that they had the right to carry slaves into any territory before it became a state. In 1850 one witty observer had remarked that Congress was passing a lawsuit rather than a law, and truly the compromise did nothing to settle the status of slavery in the territories. Thus, in 1854, when territorial organization for Kansas and Nebraska was considered, bitter disputes broke out anew. Second, the Fugitive Slave Law contained questionable features that soon fueled controversy. African Americans who were alleged to be escaped slaves had no opportunity in legal proceedings under the law to challenge that claim, and Federal commissioners received ten dollars for each fugitive they returned to slavery but only five dollars for alleged fugitives they set free. These provisions violated the beliefs many held about fair play and the right to a trial by jury. Moreover, under the Fugitive Slave Law, gripping human dramas began to occur in Northern towns and cities as freedom-loving men and women, some of whom had lived in the North for decades, were arrested and remanded to slavery. The Compromise of 1850 had proved, in the words of historian David Potter, to be only an "armistice," not "a true compromise."

[See also Georgia Platform; Bleeding Kansas; Dred Scott Decision; Fugitive Slave Law; Missouri Compromise; Wilmot Proviso.]

— PAUL D. ESCOTT

CONFEDERATE STATES OF AMERICA

[*This entry serves as a general introduction to the history of the Confederacy. For further discussion of the origin of the Confederacy, see* Civil War, *article on* Causes of the War; Secession; State Rights. *For further discussion of*

The Compromise of 1850 included a concession to the South, the Fugitive Slave Law, which gave unprecedented powers to the Federal government.

PAGE 110

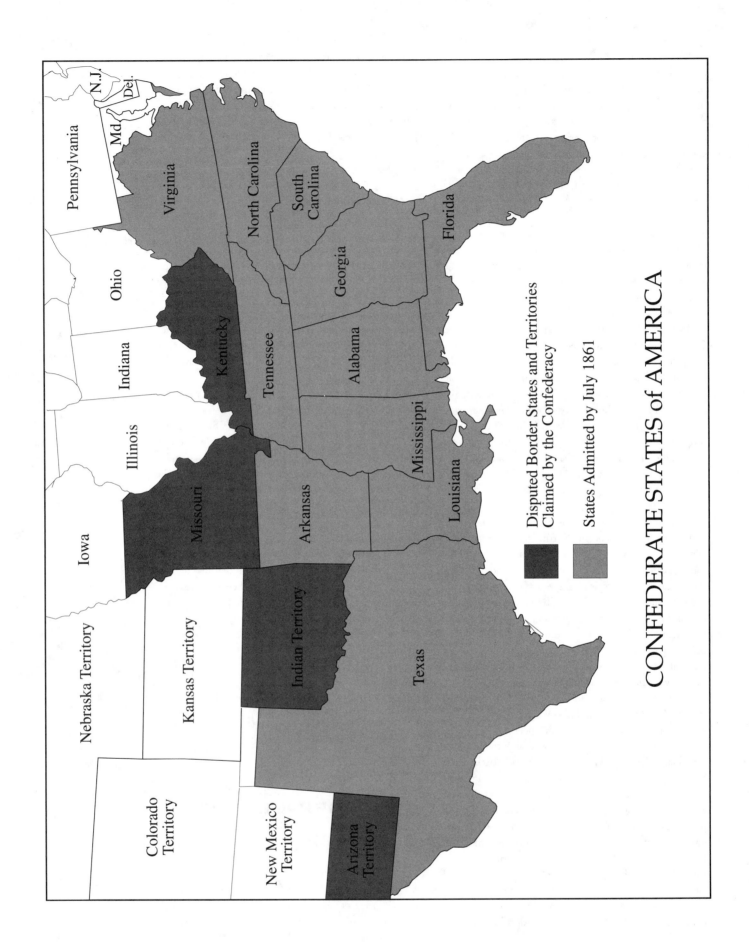

CONFEDERATE STATES of AMERICA

Disputed Border States and Territories
Claimed by the Confederacy

States Admitted by July 1861

Confederate government and politics, see Cabinet; Congress; Constitution; Diplomacy; Judiciary; Politics; Presidency; Public Finance; *and articles on selected states. For further discussion of Confederate society, economy, and culture, see* Slavery; Society. *For further discussion of the Civil War and its effects on the Confederacy, see* Civil War; Morale; Navy; Prisoners of War. *See also selected biographies of numerous figures mentioned herein.*]

Some Southerners came to believe that the South possessed a character quite distinct from that of the North, distinct enough to qualify the region for separate nationhood. They looked upon themselves as constituting a suppressed nationality comparable to the Irish or the Polish, though they could hardly claim a distinctive language, religion, or tribal history.

There were, of course, real differences between the North and the South. The most important consisted of the relatively rapid industrialization of the one section and the persistence of a slavery-based agricultural economy in the other. Cotton and slavery might have provided an adequate basis for Southern nationality and independence—if American nationalism and the spirit of the Union had been less strong than they proved to be. Southern nationalists did not want war, but war came, and as a result their experiment with independence was brief, lasting only from 1861 to 1865.

SECTIONALISM AND SECESSION. Ever since the founding of the American republic, sectionalism had erupted in a Union-threatening crisis from time to time. At the constitutional convention of 1787, the project for a "more perfect Union" was endangered when Northern and Southern delegates disagreed on such questions as the prohibition of slave imports. The Union seemed at risk in 1819 when a controversy arose over the admission of Missouri as a slave state, and again in 1832 when South Carolina nullified Federal tariff laws. An even more serious crisis occurred in 1850; it resulted from a number of sectional disputes, the most serious of which concerned the status of slavery in the territories. Compromises enabled the Union to survive each of these crises.

So long as political parties remained national in membership, partisanship offset sectionalism and made compromise possible. Then, in the 1850s, partisanship gave way to sectionalism as the Whig party disappeared, the Democratic party split, and the new Republican party gained strength. President George Washington had warned in his Farewell Address (1796) that the Union would be imperiled if a time should ever come when parties were organized on a geographical basis, with a party of the North and another of the South. By 1860, that time had arrived. The party of the North, the Republicans, now elected their presidential candidate, Abraham Lincoln, though they failed to win a majority in either house of Congress.

South Carolinians made Lincoln's election the occasion for adopting an ordinance of secession and declaring South Carolina an independent state on December 20, 1860. In doing so, they followed a theory and a procedure that John C. Calhoun had formulated years earlier. According to Calhoun's doctrine of state sovereignty and state rights, secession was a perfectly legal and constitutional process. By February 1, 1861, the other six states of the lower South—Mississippi, Florida, Alabama, Georgia, Louisiana, and Texas—had followed South Carolina's example, though some secessionists justified their action on the basis of a revolutionary rather than a constitutional right, citing the precedent of July 4, 1776.

In the slave states of the upper South and the border, leaders hoped for a compromise that would preserve the Union, and with that object in view Virginia invited the rest of the states, North and South, to a peace convention, which met in Washington, D.C., but accomplished nothing. Meanwhile another convention sat in Montgomery, Alabama, and organized a provisional government for the Confederate States of America.

The seceded states had taken over most of the Federal property within their borders. A few forts remained under Federal control, most conspicuously Fort Sumter in Charleston Harbor. Confederate policy, as set in a resolution of the Provisional Congress, looked to the acquisition of these forts by negotiation if possible and by force if necessary. Lincoln, however, announced his intention to "hold, occupy, and possess" all the forts and other Federal property, and he refused to deal with commissioners from the Confederacy. When a Federal relief expedition approached Charleston Harbor, the Confederates opened fire on Fort Sumter, April 12, 1861, and compelled its surrender on April 14. The next day Lincoln called upon the states remaining in the Union for troops to enforce Federal laws in the states that had withdrawn from it.

The governors of Virginia, Tennessee, Arkansas, North Carolina, Missouri, Kentucky, and Delaware rejected Lincoln's call. Virginia and Tennessee began at once to give military support to the Confederacy, without waiting for the referenda that eventually showed majorities in both states in favor of secession. Conventions in Arkansas and North Carolina soon voted to secede. Extralegal bodies later proclaimed the secession of Missouri and Kentucky, and the Confederacy claimed both of these states also. Both were represented in the Confederate Congress, but their legitimate governments and a majority of their people remained loyal to the Union.

The Missouri crisis of 1819–20 marked the first major sectional confrontation in which the South turned to the doctrine of state rights in the defense of slavery.

PAGE 515

*The first phase of
secession took the
seven states of the
lower South out
of the Union by
Feb. 1, 1861.*

PAGE 515

*In response to
Lincoln's election
in Nov. 1860,
South Carolina
withdrew on
Dec. 20, 1860.*

PAGE 515

CONSTITUTION AND GOVERNMENT. Montgomery remained the Confederate capital until July 1862, when the government moved to Richmond, Virginia. Meanwhile the Montgomery convention performed three functions: it chose a provisional president and vice president, served as a Provisional Congress, and drew up a constitution for the Confederacy.

For president, the convention selected Jefferson Davis, recently a U.S. senator from Mississippi and formerly a secretary of war and a professional soldier. For vice president, the choice was Alexander H. Stephens, long a congressman from Georgia. Both men had been moderates rather than fire-eaters or extreme secessionists. Both were later elected, without opposition, to regular terms in office.

The Provisional Congress reenacted all U.S. laws not inconsistent with the Confederate Constitution, and this document was an exact copy of the U.S. Constitution except for certain significant changes. For instance, the president was given an item veto, and he and the vice president were limited to a single six-year term. Protective tariffs were prohibited. So were slave importations, but the institution of slavery itself was guaranteed. As Stephens declared, the "cornerstone" of the Confederacy was the same as that of slavery—the principle of the inequality of the white and black races.

After the unicameral Provisional Congress (1861–1862), there were two regular Congresses (1862–1864, 1864–1865). Each of these, like the U.S. model, consisted of a House and a Senate. Of the 267 men who, during the life of the Confederacy, served as senators or representatives, almost a third had been members of the U.S. Congress at one time or another, and one had been a U.S. president—John Tyler.

The Confederate Congress established six departments: State, Treasury, War, Navy, Justice, and Post Office. These duplicated the U.S. departments except for Justice, which the United States had not yet created, and Interior, which the Confederacy omitted. The new postal service succeeded the old without a break, the Southern employees of the U.S. government becoming employees of the Confederate government overnight.

Heads of departments changed frequently, so that Davis's cabinet had much less stability than Lincoln's. The most influential of Davis's cabinet advisers was Judah P. Benjamin, successively attorney general, secretary of war, and secretary of state.

The Confederate Constitution provided for a judiciary with a supreme court, but Congress included no such high tribunal when setting up a court system.

DIPLOMACY. At first, the Confederates looked confidently to Europe for assistance that would enable them to establish their independence. They were encouraged by the example of the Revolutionary War, in which France had intervened to help the rebellious English colonies succeed. They were further encouraged by the doctrine of King Cotton: they thought Great Britain and France were so dependent on Southern cotton that the two powers, to maintain their supply, would step in and end the war, with the Confederacy intact.

The Confederates promptly sent missions to Britain, France, Russia, and other countries to seek recognition and aid. It looked for a time as if Britain would go to war with the United States after a U.S. warship seized two of the Confederate emissaries, James M. Mason and John Slidell, from the British steamer *Trent* while they were on their way abroad (November 1861). But neither the British nor any other government ever officially received a diplomat from the Confederacy or recognized it as a member of the family of nations.

Britain did recognize the belligerency, though not the independence, of the Confederacy when Queen Victoria issued her proclamation of neutrality (May 13, 1861). Other countries did the same. This meant that they would extend to the Confederacy the rights of a nation at war under international law.

The British government violated its neutrality to the extent of allowing British shipbuilders to sell the *Alabama* and other warships to the Confederacy. These, constituting the main force of the Confederate navy, engaged in commerce raiding on the high seas. They had access to foreign ports but not to their own, which were shut off by the Union blockade. Arguing that the blockade was ineffective and hence illegal, the Confederates tried unsuccessfully to persuade the British to break it.

When Emperor Napoleon III of France set up a puppet government in Mexico, the Confederates were willing to give it recognition (thus disregarding the Monroe Doctrine) in return for French recognition of their own government, but nothing came of this idea.

In the end, Confederate diplomacy failed partly because the European interest in Southern cotton was offset by other economic interests. More important, the European powers were divided, and Russia was conspicuously friendly to the United States. Neither Britain nor France dared risk intervention so long as the Confederacy had not clearly demonstrated its ability to survive with very little outside help.

THE ARMY. The president of the Confederate States, like the president of the United States, was commander in chief of the army and navy. Except for what coordination President Davis could provide, the Confederacy had no unified command until near the end of the war, when Robert E. Lee became general in chief. Originally, both a Regular Army and a

Provisional Army were contemplated, but the Regular Army never developed, and the Provisional Army fought the war.

Troops were recruited for this army directly as individuals and indirectly as members of state militias, which the governors furnished. From the outset men were impressed, or drafted, into state militias, but the Confederacy in its direct recruiting relied on volunteers until April 16, 1862, when its Congress passed the first national conscription act in American history. This act applied at first to able-bodied men from eighteen to thirty-five and eventually to those from seventeen to fifty. It exempted state officeholders, workers in a variety of presumably indispensable occupations, and one owner or overseer for every twenty slaves. It also exempted men who could provide substitutes. All these provisions were unpopular, and most were modified before the end of the war.

Volunteers continued to enlist and did so in about the same numbers as were conscripted. How many men, altogether, served in the Confederate army can only be guessed at. The most reliable estimate is 850,000 to 900,000, or somewhat less than half as many as served in the Union army, but a much higher proportion of the white population. At any given time the effective strength of the armed forces was considerably less than the numbers on the rolls. Many were absent without leave—as many as two-thirds in late 1864 according to Davis himself. Some deserters joined the enemy, and so did some draft evaders. More than 100,000 such "tories" fought on the Union side.

The Confederacy also lost considerable numbers as prisoners of war. In 1862 the Federal and Confederate authorities agreed to a cartel providing for a regular and large-scale exchange of prisoners. The arrangement soon broke down because Davis refused to exchange black prisoners or their white officers and declared Benjamin F. Butler and his subordinates "outlaws" to be executed if captured. As Union prisoners accumulated, the Confederates were unable to provide suitable facilities for all of them, and terrible suffering resulted at Andersonville and other Southern prisons. Still, Union General in Chief Ulysses S. Grant was unwilling to renew the cartel, since the return of prisoners would benefit the Confederacy more than the Union, the Confederacy being more desperately in need of additional troops.

So desperate were Confederate leaders by 1865 that they finally decided to recruit slaves, but the war ended before any blacks actually served as Confederate soldiers.

STRATEGY. To maintain their independence, the Confederates needed not to win the war but only to keep the Federals from winning it. The Confederacy did not possess sufficient human and material resources to overwhelm the North in any case. Hence Davis adopted an essentially defensive though by no means entirely passive strategy. It was offensive-defensive. Throughout the war, while undertaking to repel Federal advances, the Confederates also made extensive counterthrusts from time to time.

Thus in 1862 Thomas J. ("Stonewall") Jackson sped northward down the Shenandoah Valley to threaten Washington and draw Federals away from beleaguered Richmond. Robert E. Lee and Braxton Bragg made simultaneous movements into Maryland and Kentucky, movements that culminated in the Confederate recapture of Harpers Ferry and in Confederate retreats from Sharpsburg, Perryville, and Murfreesboro.

In 1863 Lee invaded Pennsylvania with the twofold objective of intensifying the war-weariness of the North and relieving the pressure on Vicksburg, which was under siege. He retreated from Gettysburg and the Confederates surrendered Vicksburg on the same day, July 4, 1863.

Again in 1864, when Federals were hemming in Richmond and Petersburg, Jubal Early attempted to divert them by raiding the outskirts of Washington. And finally, after the fall of Atlanta, John Bell Hood attacked the Federals at Nashville, only to be routed.

Meanwhile John Hunt Morgan, Nathan Bedford Forrest, and Joseph Wheeler made cavalry raids into Union-held areas of the South and even into Kentucky, Indiana, and Ohio.

The Confederate strategy did not prevent the steady loss of territory to the Federals. After only a little more than a year of war, the Confederacy had lost control of northeastern Virginia, stretches of the coast from North Carolina to Florida, and a large part of both Tennessee and Louisiana, including the state capitals, Nashville and New Orleans. By the end of 1863 more than half of the original Confederacy had been isolated from the Richmond government because of Federal penetration, and by the end of 1864 no more than three states—most of Virginia and North and South Carolina—remained under the government's control.

This does not necessarily mean that the Davis policy was ill-advised. "If it did not win the war," as historian Frank Vandiver has written, "the offensive-defensive did enable the Confederates to outlast their resources—ample proof of the soundness of the strategy and the strategist."

THE ECONOMY. Far inferior to the Union in both human and material resources, the Confederacy at the start could claim only about two-fifths as many people (a third of them slaves), one-fourth as much bank capital, and one-tenth as great a manufacturing capacity. The Confederacy did produce more corn and livestock

Lincoln devised an ingenious plan to put the burden of decision for war or peace on Jefferson Davis's shoulders.

PAGE 113

*Richmond Bread
Riot, April 1863:
Mayor Joseph
Mayo tried to
quell the women
by reading the
Riot Act, but he
was ignored.*

PAGE 74

*From the
beginning of the
war, military
authorities
impressed slaves
to work on
fortifications or to
serve as teamsters,
nurses, or cooks.*

PAGE 286

per capita, and it had a large potential asset in its cotton crop.

The Confederates failed to make timely and adequate use of the cotton as a basis for foreign credit. Hence financing the war proved difficult. Bullion and coin were relatively scarce, and the Confederates had to rely much more on the issue of paper money and much less on taxation and borrowing than the Union did.

The consequence was extreme inflation. This was made worse by a scarcity of many commodities, a scarcity that was due to the blockade and to extensive hoarding, which in turn was exacerbated by the government's policy of impressment, that is, the seizure of goods at arbitrary prices. Inflation was also intensified by the shrinkage of Confederate-held territory and the resulting increase in the ratio of currency to commerce as people in the occupied areas sent their Confederate money to what was left of the Confederacy, where the paper retained at least a little of its nominal value.

Transportation suffered from the inadequacy of the railroads, which had serious gaps to begin with. True, the Confederates were the first to reinforce an army by rail in the midst of battle, and their railroads gave the presumed advantage of "interior lines" some reality. Still, the government failed to take effective control of the railroad system until late in the war. By then the tracks and rolling stock had deteriorated badly, and the gaps had grown worse with the loss of key junctions such as Chattanooga and Atlanta. River and coastal shipping similarly was obstructed by enemy occupation.

Horses and mules, together with horse-drawn and mule-drawn vehicles, played a larger role in Confederate life, both military and civilian, than did railroad trains or riverboats. In the beginning the Confederacy was well supplied with horses and mules, but these were rapidly used up, and replacements were hard to get. By 1863 there was a serious shortage.

The Confederates acquired some munitions and other war matériel by seizures of U.S. arsenals, purchases abroad, and captures on the battlefield. But they had to depend mainly on expanding their few existing facilities, such as the Tredegar Iron Works in Richmond, and on developing new ones. The government tried to stimulate war-related manufactures by various means, among them the granting of draft exemptions to needed laborers. There were remarkable achievements in the production of salt, nitrates, and other necessities, but not enough to meet all the military and civilian requirements. Even when a surplus of commodities, such as foodstuffs, existed in one place, there were often shortages in other places because of the transportation difficulties.

Economic exhaustion eventually set in. As Charles W. Ramsdell has said, "The Confederacy had begun to break down *within,* long before the military situation appeared to be desperate."

SOCIETY. The war brought significant, if not all of them permanent, changes in Southern society, especially in the role of women, the relationship of classes, and the position of blacks.

Women took up responsibilities that formerly had belonged to men. They assisted the war effort directly by encouraging men to enlist, by sewing for soldiers and nursing them, and by serving as spies, among whom the most famous were Belle Boyd and Rose O'Neal Greenhow. They ran farms and plantations and worked at factory and government jobs. As diarists and memoirists, most notably Mary Boykin Chesnut and Catherine Ann Edmondston, they left the best literature embodying the wartime experience.

At least for the duration, women were liberated from the romantic antebellum stereotype of the lady on the pedestal, though certainly not from family obligations and the necessity of work. The hardships of the farm eventually caused many wives to call their soldier husbands home, thus depriving the army of men instead of inducing them, as earlier, to enlist.

Planters could no longer base their prestige solely on the land and slaves they owned. A heroic war record also counted, and men of no previous high standing, such as Stonewall Jackson, rose to positions of leadership and fame. At the same time, class consciousness grew among small farmers and day laborers, who expressed their feelings in the common saying that it was "a rich man's war and a poor man's fight." Mobs of women occasionally engaged in bread riots, demanding price reductions and looting stores of groceries and other merchandise.

Black men and women, as slaves, kept the plantations going and thus enabled an unusually high proportion of white men to be absent in the army. Blacks also gave direct assistance to the military as construction gangs, teamsters, cooks, and the like. Afterward, members of planter families liked to tell of retainers who had remained loyal to them throughout the war.

Yet the slaves constituted at least as much of a liability as an asset to the Confederacy. They did not revolt, as whites had feared they would, but—especially after Lincoln's Emancipation Proclamation (January 1, 1863)—they flocked to the camps of oncoming Federals and assisted them as spies, guides, and laborers. About 100,000 blacks from the South (and others from the border states and the North) joined the Union army. In short, the slaves themselves contributed mightily to the final defeat of the Confederacy and the destruction of slavery—the institution upon which the Confederacy was based.

POLITICS. Political parties did not emerge in the Confederacy, though there remained in many cases a distinction between old Democrats and former Whigs. Politics, often virulent, nevertheless persisted in the form of rivalries for power and disagreements over governmental methods and even aims. These dissensions seriously weakened the Confederacy.

Politics pitted President Davis, always a Democrat, and his faithful followers against a growing number of opponents, the foremost of whom was Vice President Stephens, once a Whig. Davis, burdened with responsibility as he was, took a fairly broad view of the powers of the central government. Stephens became increasingly extreme in his devotion to state rights. He and other critics of Davis blamed him for practically everything that went wrong in the Confederacy.

Some of the severest critics were state governors. Davis had to contend with especially troublesome resistance from Joseph E. Brown of Georgia and Zebulon Vance of North Carolina. These governors wanted to keep control of their own state militias, and they objected both to Confederate conscription and to its enforcement by suspension of the writ of habeas corpus. Brown kept many Georgia soldiers inside the state, and Vance accumulated stocks of war matériel for the exclusive use of North Carolina troops.

Confederate nationalism had to compete not only with state rights but also with persisting Unionism. This was most pervasive in the Appalachian Mountains and in the adjoining hill country, where slaves were few. Fifty-two counties of northwestern Virginia rejoined the Union as the state of West Virginia in 1863. A third of the counties of Tennessee, those in the eastern part of the state, would probably have rejoined the Union as East Tennessee if Federal armies had established control there as early as they did in northwestern Virginia. From the outset Confederate leaders had worried about popular tendencies toward "reconstruction," and these tendencies increased with military reverses, multiplying casualties, economic hardships, and a consequent lowering of public morale.

Peace movements gained ground, particularly in North Carolina and Georgia. In North Carolina a secret society known as the Red Strings (or Heroes of America) cultivated defeatism, and William W. Holden ran for governor as a peace candidate in 1864. (He was easily defeated by Vance, who called for keeping up the war effort.) In Georgia, Stephens and Brown advocated negotiating with the enemy. Stephens was willing to settle for guarantees of state rights in a reunited nation, but Davis refused to consider anything short of peace with independence. Davis insisted on this as his minimum terms when he authorized Stephens and other envoys to meet with Lincoln and his secretary of state, William H. Seward, in the Hampton Roads conference of February 1865.

Lincoln took the position that the war would end only when the Confederates laid down their arms, and before long they had no real choice except to do so.

— RICHARD N. CURRENT

CONGRESS

Upon voting to secede from the United States, the conventions of the seven original Confederate states sent delegations equal to their 1860 congressional representation to Montgomery, Alabama, to form a new nation. Fearful of delay, they adopted, with only one day's discussion, a one-year Provisional Constitution, which converted the Montgomery convention into the new government's legislative body. Congressmen from states that later seceded were elected by their convention or legislature. Thus, there were no popularly elected Provisional congressmen. In all, the Confederate Congresses had representatives from eleven seceded states and the extralegal Confederate governments of Kentucky and Missouri, plus nonvoting representatives from the Arizona Territory and the Cherokee, Chickasaw, Choctaw, Creek, and Seminole Indian nations.

The average Confederate congressman was well off financially, with a median estate worth $47,000. Sixty-four percent had served in state legislatures and 32 percent in the U.S. Congress. Only 10 percent had had no previous political experience. Professionally they ranged from horse breeder to financier. At least 92 had been Whigs, and most of these had been conservative on secession. At least 138 had been Democrats, and most of them had been early secessionists. Political experience and wealth were greatest in the Provisional Congress, somewhat less in the First, and even less in the Second, though this decline was relatively slight.

THE PROVISIONAL CONGRESS. The Provisional Congress met until February 17, 1862. The Provisional Constitution permitted plural officeholding, so a number of members served both in Congress and in the army, a privilege denied by the Permanent Constitution. Voting was by state, as it had been in the Philadelphia Convention, and a tied vote in a delegation left that state's vote uncounted.

The business of nation building occupied the first months. Congress acquired a body of laws by adopting all U.S. laws consistent with the Confederate Constitution. It elected Jefferson Davis president and Alexander H. Stephens vice president, and then established executive departments much like those of the United States. Other aspects of government, such as a postal system, the judiciary, and citizenship and naturalization systems, were also carried over with little change. Congress contracted for the regular publica-

The preamble to the Confederate Constitution contained an explicit reference to state sovereignty and a direct appeal for the "favor and guidance of Almighty God."

PAGE 150

On July 31, 1861, Congress suspended the supreme court until it could be organized under the Permanent Constitution.

PAGE 306

tion of its laws and had the major laws published in a newspaper in each state. The Senate and House rules were adopted almost bodily from the U.S. Congress, but recording of debates was left to newspaper reporters, with frequent secret sessions making adequate reporting impossible.

The delegates to Montgomery had hoped for a government without political parties, and to a large extent they succeeded. Old habits, however, could not be so easily abandoned. In private correspondence the erstwhile secessionists, Unionists, Democrats, and Whigs expressed distrust of their former political opponents. These feelings were of some importance in determining how people voted in elections, but there is no evidence of any significant voting alignment within Congress based on past politics until the Second Congress. Without specific party lines to guide them, therefore, each congressman had to decide for himself how he would vote.

This political vacuum worked in President Davis's favor. He was never without his congressional critics, but during the first year the war was going well and people were confident of victory. Demands upon them were relatively light. Criticism of the president was therefore mainly personal or doctrinal and did little to affect the course of legislation. Whigs and Unionists argued that Davis denied them patronage. Some secessionists felt that he was secretly a reconstructionist. Scattered armchair experts disliked his military policies. Extreme state rights advocates disliked his frequent vetoes. Meanwhile administration measures went through Congress almost intact, and the newspapers jeered at the legislature as being a "register of Executive decrees." Underneath all this, another factor operated in Davis's favor: during wartime people generally assume that their political and military leaders know best what to do, and that overt opposition borders on treason. Nothing but the firmest conviction would allow the Provisional Congress to tamper with administration requests.

Confederate leaders originally hoped to finance the government on a low tariff income, but as an interim device Congress authorized an issue of $1 million in Treasury notes guaranteed by a tax of $1/8$ ¢ per pound on cotton exported. It also provided for a Provisional Army of 100,000 militia volunteers, ordered the president to arm and equip them as he wished, and established a general staff.

The Fort Sumter affair necessitated a called session of Congress, but there seemed to be no alarm. On May 16 Congress authorized the issue of $20 million in fiat Treasury notes and $50 million in 8 percent bonds for general investment and for money pledged from the sale of agricultural produce—the first produce loan. This quick and easy financing set Congress on the road

to a monetary policy based on Treasury notes and bond issues to absorb surplus currency. Congress now removed all restrictions on the number of volunteers who might be accepted in the army and bypassed the states by letting the president receive independent companies. The president was also given the right to control all telegraphic operations. On May 21 Congress finally established a tariff system that was to last for the duration. The leading rate was 15 percent on most commonplace items, with raw materials paying somewhat less and luxuries somewhat more.

Congress now removed itself from diplomatic strategy and accepted the administration's policy of cotton diplomacy. It prohibited the export of cotton and other staples except through Confederate ports or into Mexico, trying to cut off all supplies going to the United States and to force Europe to break the blockade and come get what it wanted. Some congressmen wished to buttress the policy with a promise of a lower tariff to any nation recognizing the Confederacy, but this movement floundered and was dropped.

The victory at First Manassas did little to influence the next sessions of Congress. It authorized a call for 400,000 volunteers and let the president accept units of specialists and local defense. During the winter it enacted several feeble acts to induce volunteering and reenlistments, none of them very successful. Finally the Provisional Congress ordered a war tax of fifty cents on each one hundred dollars of goods named by the Treasury Department.

The Provisional Congress had spent much of its first month in writing a constitution for the permanent government of the Confederacy. The new Constitution provided for a Congress identical to that of the United States, and elections for representatives were held on the first Wednesday in November 1861. Each state had its former Federal representation and used old election procedures. Most states allowed absentee voting by soldiers and refugees at army camps and other designated places. Traditional politicking would have seemed divisive; candidates usually announced themselves briefly in newspapers and did little personal campaigning. A few districts engaged in vigorous battles over local issues, but national policy was seldom a subject of debate. Voters tended to support men whom they had favored before the war. Democrats and secessionists were popular at this time, and the election returns gave them about a three-to-two majority in the First Congress. Five state legislatures chose one former Whig and one former Democrat, and eight legislatures chose two former Democrats. The overall pattern of those elected seemed basically like that of the Provisional Congress.

THE FIRST CONGRESS. When the First Congress convened on February 18, 1862, it was evident that the one-year volunteers were weary of military service. There was the possibility that more than half of them would not reenlist, and President Davis was compelled to ask for the conscription of all able-bodied men between the ages of eighteen and thirty-five. On April 16 Congress, over the objections of the Atlantic seaboard states above Florida, enacted such a law. It then conferred blanket exemptions on a long list of occupations whose personnel was deemed more important to the home front than to the army. That fall Congress extended the conscription age to forty-five but refused to reduce the number of class exemptions. By the end of 1863 the need for troops was becoming desperate, and on February 17, 1864, Congress set the conscription age from seventeen to fifty and pared the exemption list drastically.

Demands for changes in these laws occupied much of Congress's time. The first law had let eligible men offer substitutes. This obviously favored the wealthy, and Congress finally drafted both the substitutes and those who had hired them. Planters had been allowed one exempt overseer for every twenty slaves they owned, but this elitist practice had severe critics. In the end, Congress exempted only those overseers so employed before February 16, 1862. After a bitter debate, state rights advocates secured the exemption of all state officers certified by their governor as necessary for proper government.

Wedded to conservative financing, Secretary Christopher G. Memminger continued asking for more Treasury notes, backed by faith in the government and payable in specie after the war. He also requested great amounts of bonds into which currency could be invested and which would be exchangeable directly for agricultural products. Congress gave him most of what he requested, but people preferred to spend their rapidly inflating currency quickly rather than buy bonds. Near the end of the First Congress Memminger reported that funding was going badly, and at his suggestion Congress enacted a forced funding law, which set up a schedule by which currency would gradually decline to worthlessness unless funded into bonds. In January 1863, it levied its first significant tax on property, income, licenses, and businesses, plus a 10 percent tithe on slaughtered hogs and agricultural products.

The First Congress dealt with other matters of only slightly less importance. In their need for supplies, army agents often ruthlessly seized them from producers and wholesalers. The Impressment Act of March 26, 1863, permitted the seizure of agricultural products and military supplies at a "fair" price and established a system of arbitration whereby a former owner might negotiate a better price. Congress also permitted the destruction of property if it were in danger of being captured. On February 6, 1864, the legislature ordered that no major

staple crop or military stores could be exported except under regulations established by the president, and it outlawed the importation of luxuries. Despite almost violent debate on the subject, Congress on three occasions gave the president authority to suspend the right of habeas corpus when deemed necessary.

Congress was noticeably reluctant to take any initiative in two areas. It left to the president all decisions about what manufactories were needed for the war effort, but when asked by the War Department it quickly encouraged private individuals to manufacture guns, ammunition, clothing, and other army accoutrements. It also flirted with the idea of price control to stem inflation but never managed more than a vestige of such regulation.

By 1864 an important new alignment had appeared in the legislature. The Confederacy was now divided into what historians Alexander and Beringer term "exterior" and "interior" districts. Exterior districts were those occupied by the enemy and therefore little affected by the legislation of Congress. Their voters naturally preferred congressmen who would support any measure that might help redeem their homes. Interior districts were those still within Confederate jurisdiction and in which its laws could be enforced. They supported congressmen who would heed local grievances as well as tend to issues of national survival.

THE SECOND CONGRESS. Politics reverted to type during elections for the Second Congress during mid-1863. Louisiana, Missouri, Tennessee, and Kentucky—now almost entirely exterior areas—held elections by general ticket, with each voter casting his ballot for one congressman from each district; other states continued to vote as before. The major issue now was the Davis administration and critics were in full cry. Usually they attacked the one or two programs that most closely affected their districts, but in the southeastern seaboard states they arraigned the government on almost everything. Past politics became openly important, and the general aura of discontent and war weariness helped candidates who had urged caution in 1860. In the Second Congress two-thirds of the new men were former Unionists and three-fifths were Whigs. These men, however, were no less loyal Confederates than the two-term congressmen and remained so to the end of the war. They simply did not want a war that demanded further sacrifices.

In the Second Congress, which met on May 2, 1864, a congressman's former party, his secession stand, and the exterior or interior status of his district became ever more important in determining his vote. The First Congress had carried legislation about as far as it could go, and now the administration could ask only for refinements in the laws. The voting alignments, how-

Memminger was a Jacksonian Democrat with a preference for currency comprised solely of gold and silver coin.

PAGE 363

ever, too often took precedence over national survival and made constructive legislation almost impossible. Meanwhile a peace movement was gaining momentum. But the president insisted that the North already knew the conditions on which the Confederacy would make peace and that further negotiations would signal

CONGRESSIONAL BILL

This 1864 bill from the Confederate House of Representatives amends procedures for purchasing rations and clothing from the Quartermaster's Department.

CIVIL WAR LIBRARY AND MUSEUM, PHILADELPHIA

irresolution. The result was that no significant law was enacted during the first session.

The last session of Congress, which began on November 9, 1864, was marked by a legislative stalemate. A majority of congressmen were now from exterior districts, but enough of them were willing to ally with interior-district men on certain issues to block new administrative programs. Until the last week, the administration won only two victories. There was talk in and out of Congress of depriving Davis of his constitutional prerogative as commander in chief and persuading Gen. Robert E. Lee to take full military command. Davis scotched this plan on February 6, 1865, by naming Lee general in chief, knowing that Lee would not exercise a broader command. Davis also virtually ended the peace agitation in Congress at about the same time by sending a commission to meet with Northern representatives, but he instructed them to accept peace only with independence. After the inevitable failure, Congress officially vowed to continue the war until victorious.

Meanwhile other matters were at a standstill. Congress refused all requests for financial reform and on December 28, 1864, merely extended the funding

deadline to July 1, 1865. A few days before Congress ended, so many men had left Richmond that there was barely a quorum in the House and some compromise was absolutely essential. On March 13 Congress let the president call upon the states for as many slaves as he wished to serve as soldiers but left it to the individual state to decide whether such men should be freed. There were 125,000 men still exempt or detailed. Davis wanted all exemptions ended and the men subject to detail to the army or the home front as the president wished; on March 16, 1865, Congress kept a few exemptions and let the president detail the rest. On March 18 Congress ordered that goods impressed must be paid for at market prices. On the same day the legislature gave the president his only outright defeat; it refused to pass a new habeas corpus suspension. All these desperation laws of Congress's last week were of course too late to be of any value.

Confederates generally had a low opinion of their Congress. Those approving President Davis's leadership chided Congress for tampering with administration requests; those critical of the administration considered Congress too submissive. Pragmatically, Congress had little alternative to such submissiveness. Survival of the Confederacy was uppermost in the minds of everyone, even congressmen, and legislative chaos would have been ruinous. As Alexander and Beringer so well demonstrate, past politics, position on secession, economic factors, and local conditions often influenced voting, but until late 1864 there is little evidence of bloc voting. In the Second Congress a definite Whig-Unionist versus Democrat-secessionist alignment began to emerge, as well as the important interior versus exterior district alignment. It was now obvious that the new congressmen were not decisively committed to Southern independence at the expense of their districts. By then, however, the limits of legislation had been reached and no obstructionist alignment had any measurable effect on the conduct of the war.

[*See also* Impressment; Montgomery Convention; New Plan; Poor Relief; Public Finance; State Rights; State Socialism; *and selected biographies of figures mentioned herein.*]

— W. BUCK YEARNS

CONSTITUTION

The states that left the American Union in 1860 and 1861 brought with them a rich tradition of constitutionalism. Many Southern leaders explained their support for secession in terms of the failure of the Federal compact. Most blamed Northerners for failing to live up to their obligations, although some thought it was structural flaws in the U.S. Constitution that made secession necessary.

The Provisional Constitution of the Confederate States of America signed on February 8, 1861, created a compact among six Deep South states. The Permanent Confederate Constitution, signed on March 11, 1861, created a political structure for what became the eleven-state Confederate nation. Both documents were similar to the U.S. Constitution. The differences between the two reflected the political struggles that had led to secession.

THE MONTGOMERY CONVENTION AND THE PROVISIONAL CONSTITUTION. On February 4, 1861, forty-three delegates from South Carolina, Alabama, Mississippi, Georgia, Florida, and Louisiana assembled in Montgomery, Alabama, to write a provisional constitution for the Confederate States of America. The convention finished its work four days later. Such speed was possible because of the "mania for unanimity" among the delegates and because the Provisional Constitution was something of a cross between the Articles of Confederation and the U.S. Constitution and borrowed heavily, in language and concepts, from both documents. Like the Articles of Confederation, the Provisional Constitution created a unicameral Congress in which each state had a single vote. Borrowing from the British system, the Provisional Constitution allowed cabinet members to serve in Congress and stipulated that Congress choose the president. Like the Constitution of 1787, it provided for a president with a veto power and enumerated powers for the Confederate Congress similar to those given to the U.S. Congress. There were also a number of substantive differences between the Provisional Confederate Constitution and the Constitution of 1787.

Under the Provisional Constitution Jefferson Davis became president of the fledgling nation and formed a government. By its own terms the Constitution was to last no more than a year, but it was in operation for only thirty-one days before the delegates wrote and signed a permanent constitution. The preamble of the Provisional Constitution reflected the state rights philosophy and Protestant culture of its framers: "We, the Deputies of the Sovereign and Independent States of South Carolina, Georgia, Florida, Alabama, Mississippi, and Louisiana, invoking the favor of Almighty God . . . ."

THE PERMANENT CONSTITUTION. Under the terms of the Provisional Constitution, the Montgomery convention reconstituted itself as the Provisional Congress of the Confederate States of America until such time as a permanent constitution could be adopted and a permanent congress elected.

There was no serious debate over the name of the new nation—the "Confederate States of America" reflected what the founders thought they were creating.

The delegates who gathered in Montgomery mirrored, in their occupations, their interest in politics, and in their stake in slavery, the elite of the society they represented. In early March when the Texas delegation arrived, their numbers rose to fifty. Of these, forty-two were lawyers and thirty-three described themselves as planters (including twenty-seven of the lawyers). Forty-eight were native Southerners, forty-nine were slaveowners. Twenty-one owned at least 20 slaves and one owned 473. Thirty-eight were college graduates. Almost all had extensive political experience: twenty-three had served in the U.S. Congress; sixteen were former or sitting judges, including two state chief justices; two had been in national cabinets, and a third had been in the cabinet of the Republic of Texas. Oddly, one of the most influential members of the convention had no political experience per se. Thomas R. R. Cobb, the "James Madison" of the Confederate Constitution, had never held an elective office, although he had been the first reporter of the Georgia Supreme Court. He was also one of the South's foremost legal scholars and the author of the influential *An Inquiry into the Law of Negro Slavery* (1858).

On February 9, the day after the signing of the Provisional Constitution, members of the Provisional Confederate Congress appointed a twelve-man committee, chaired by South Carolina's secessionist leader Robert Barnwell Rhett, Sr., to draft a permanent constitution. Other important members of the committee included Thomas R. R. Cobb and Robert Toombs of Georgia; James Chesnut, Jr., of South Carolina; and Wiley Harris, a skilled Mississippi lawyer. On February 28 Rhett presented the Congress with a draft of a permanent Constitution. For the next ten days the Montgomery delegates functioned as a Congress during the morning and as a constitutional convention during the afternoon and evening. On March 11, 1861, the Montgomery convention adopted this document and sent it on to the seceded states for ratification.

Structurally the U.S. and Confederate Constitutions were nearly identical. Both had a preamble and seven articles, and both created a national president, a bicameral legislature, and a court system. The only major structural difference was that the first twelve amendments to the U.S. Constitution were incorporated, almost word for word, into the main body of the Confederate Constitution.

The Confederate Constitution is often seen as a document for a nation based on state rights and limited government. To a great extent this is true, but the document also vested the national government with some centraliz-

From the very start of his public career, Rhett was identified as a firebrand eager to challenge established authority.

PAGE 496

*When delegates
convened in
Montgomery to form
the Confederacy,
Robert Toombs was
a serious candidate
for president.*

PAGE 612

ing powers. Like the U.S. Constitution, the Confederate document had a necessary and proper clause, a supremacy clause, and a clause requiring all state officials to swear allegiance to the national government. Article I, Section 9 of the Confederate Constitution had a habeas corpus suspension provision that was identical to that of the U.S. Constitution. These certainly gave the national government power to act.

In addition, innovations in the Confederate Constitution gave the new government more power in some respects than the U.S. government had. The president was limited to one term, but that term was for six years. Thus he may have had more opportunity to implement his policies than his counterpart in Washington. The Confederate president had a line-item veto and the right to dismiss at will all cabinet members. Incorporating aspects of a parliamentary system, the document stipulated that Congress could grant cabinet officers "a seat upon the floor of either House, with the privilege of discussing any measures appertaining to his department." This gave the administration an advantage in getting its programs through Congress that the U.S. president lacked. Robert Toombs thought these provisions strengthening the executive branch were the most important differences between the two constitutions.

The most significant differences between the two, however, lay in the Confederate provisions limiting the power of the national government, protecting state rights and, most important, protecting slavery.

A limited government. A persistent complaint of antebellum Southerners had concerned the national government's assumption of increased power after 1789. Reflecting the divergent views of state rights advocates and nationalists were the fights over the establishment of a national bank, the 1828 "Tariff of Abominations," the doctrine of nullification, and the constitutionality of the Federal government's funding internal improvements. Thus, the Confederate preamble differed significantly from that of the U.S. Constitution in order to cure what were seen as defects allowing centralization. Unlike its Federal counterpart, the preamble did not state that the central government was to "provide for the common defense" or "promote the general welfare." It also contained an explicit reference to state sovereignty (discussed below) and a direct appeal for the "favor and guidance of Almighty God."

Article I granted the Confederate Congress the legislative powers "delegated" in the Constitution. This was a major limitation on the power of the Confederate government. The enumerated powers clauses (Art. I, Sec. 8) limited taxes to those providing "revenue necessary to pay the debts, provide for the common defence, and carry on the Government of the Confederate States." This clause specifically forbade

any "bounties" or taxes "to promote or foster any branch of industry." Section 8 absolutely prohibited the Congress from appropriating money for "internal improvements intended to facilitate commerce" except for those directly connected to navigation, harbors, and rivers. Under this Constitution there would be no support for national roads, railroads, or other such improvements.

It also provided that the executive branch could propose appropriations and needed only a simple majority in Congress to have them adopted, whereas appropriations originating with Congress needed a two-thirds majority to pass. This particular provision strengthened the president vis-à-vis Congress but generally it made the national government less flexible than that of the United States. The Constitution also required that all appropriations be for exact amounts and declared that there could not be "extra compensation to any public contractor, officer, agent or servant." The absolute prohibition on "impa[i]ring the right of property in negro slaves" limited the use of slaves for war activities. These provisions, combined with the lack of a common defense clause in the preamble, were significant departures from the U.S. Constitution and at least potentially hampered the operations of a government that was about to fight a major war with a far richer and more powerful adversary.

Finally, in a move to eliminate patronage (which could have undermined the president's power to run the government), the Constitution prohibited the president from removing civil servants except for "dishonesty, incapacity, inefficiency, misconduct, or neglect of duty." The president, however, retained the explicit power to fire cabinet members and diplomats without cause.

During the war itself the Davis government was able to overcome some, but not all, of the constitutional obstacles to a strong government. President Davis amassed considerable power, but at great cost to his political capital. During the war the Davis administration often suppressed civil liberties to a greater extent than its counterpart in Washington. Only five days after Davis took office the Confederate Congress adopted legislation allowing the suspension of habeas corpus. Davis sporadically imposed martial law on Richmond and other major cities. In some areas of the Confederacy, like eastern Tennessee, martial law led to the summary executions of a few civilians and the mass incarceration of others. By the end of the war, Vice President Alexander Stephens and other leading politicians no longer supported the administration, in part because of Davis's "betrayal" of Southern Constitutional principles. "Our liberties, once lost," he declared, "may be lost forever."

State rights. Directly tied to the limitations on the national government was a respect for state rights.

Some scholars have argued that the Confederate Constitution was so extreme on this issue that the Confederacy was doomed to lose the war. Others dispute this point. In any event, even a cursory glance at the document shows that in respecting state rights—and simultaneously limiting the power of the central government—the Confederate Constitution created a government that was quite different from that in place in the Union.

The state rights tone was set in the preamble, which added to "We, the people of the Confederate States," the significant phrase "each State acting in its sovereign and independent character." Article I allowed the states to impeach "any judicial or other Federal officer, resident and acting solely within the limits of any state." Such an officer would then be tried by the Confederate Senate. This provision was never implemented during the life of the Confederacy. Nevertheless, the threat of impeachment may have undermined the ability of Confederate officials to enforce unpopular laws and policies in their state. Article I, Section 10, also allowed states to impose their own import and export duties, something prohibited to the states remaining in the Union.

Southern distrust for the national judiciary was apparent in the drafting of Article III of the Confederate document. A key provision of the U.S. Constitution is the clause creating diversity jurisdiction by giving the federal courts the power to hear cases "between Citizens of different States." The Confederate Constitution lacked such a provision, which in practice meant that civil suits between citizens of different states would have to be litigated in state courts. This undermined the nationalization of law and jurisprudence, and had the Confederacy survived, it probably would have led to unnecessary complications in litigation and complaints about the failure of litigants to get a fair trial in a neutral forum. Moreover, in a nation that was predicated on state rights and local interests, the abolition of diversity jurisdiction could have led to a judicial and business climate that would have hampered economic development. The Confederate Constitution also failed to include the phrase "law and equity" in granting jurisdiction to the national courts. This is generally seen as a concession to the civil law system in Louisiana and its vestiges in Texas. A final bow to state rights, and one that could have led to enormous instability, was a provision allowing a constitutional convention to be called on the demand of just three states.

During the war, state judges issued writs of habeas corpus directed against military officers trying to impose Confederate conscription. Without a functioning court system, which the Constitution would have allowed but did not mandate, the Davis administration

and the Confederate military could only respond to these manifestations of state rights with suspensions of martial law.

Slavery. Far from a "peculiar institution," slavery was, as Confederate Vice President Alexander Stephens declared, "the cornerstone" of the Confederacy. As such, it was protected even more in the Confederate Constitution than it had been in the proslavery U.S. Constitution of 1787.

The most obvious difference between the two documents lay in their use of the term *slavery.* In deference in 1787 to some of the Northern delegates who thought their constituents might oppose the Constitution if the word appeared, the framers of the U.S. Constitution substituted such phrases as *other persons, such persons,* and *persons owing service* for the word *slaves.* No such problems arose in the framing of the Confederate document. The blatantly proslavery Confederate Constitution contains the words *slave* or *slavery* ten times in seven separate clauses.

As their predecessors had in the Philadelphia Convention of 1787, the South Carolina delegates in Montgomery wanted to count slaves fully for representation. South Carolina had a larger percentage of slaves than any other state and would have gained by their full representation. The delegates in Montgomery, however, must have understood that a full counting of slaves would have discouraged the other Southern states, with smaller percentages of slaves, from joining the Confederacy. Thus, the convention chose to continue the Federal compromise by maintaining the three-fifths clause for determining congressional apportionment.

The frequent refusal of Northern states to cooperate in the rendition of fugitive slaves had been a major irritant in the antebellum period. The Montgomery delegates did not, however, substantially alter the fugitive slave clause in their Constitution. There were probably two reasons for this. First, they were writing a constitution for a slaveholders' republic, and it was unlikely that any Confederate state would ever adopt legislation similar to the Northern personal liberty laws. Second, a substantial change in the wording of the clause would have undermined the Southern argument that the meaning of the clause in the U.S. Constitution was clear and that secession was justified by the North's refusal to fulfill its constitutional obligations.

The Confederate Constitution also mirrored, but surpassed, the federal Constitution on the issue of the slave trade by absolutely forbidding the operation of the African slave trade. This was done over protestations of South Carolinians, who wanted the matter left to Congress. Prohibiting the trade was not an indication of antislavery sentiment but the result of the distaste for the African trade by some slave owners, fear of Africans

Southerners believed that slavery was a necessary form of race control.

PAGE 553

The Southern states were determined to retain slavery after the Revolution. Thus began the fatal division between "free states" and "slave states."

PAGE 553

C

themselves, and the fear that Europe would not recognize the Confederacy if it did not unequivocally prohibit the trade. Permitting the trade also might have discouraged Virginia and Maryland from entering the Confederacy because of the excess of slaves in those states. Those states might not have wanted foreign competition with their interstate slave trade.

On all other issues the Constitution created a thoroughly proslavery republic. The Constitution authorized Congress to *limit* the importation of slaves from other nations and states but did not prohibit it altogether as current federal law did. The Constitution absolutely prohibited any law "impa[i]ring the right of property in negro slaves." Reflecting Southern states' rejection of Northern states' decisions that had freed the slaves of visitors, Article IV guaranteed that the citizens of each Confederate state "shall have the right of transit and sojourn in any State of this Confederacy, with their slaves and other property; and the right of property in said slaves shall not be thereby impaired." The Constitution's fugitive slave clause reiterated this right. Finally, the Constitution affirmed the proslavery holding of Chief Justice Roger B. Taney in the U.S. Supreme Court *Dred Scott* decision, by declaring that slavery could never be prohibited from any Confederate territory. At the same time, however, the Confederate authors jettisoned Taney's implausible argument that the national government could not regulate the territories. Thus, their territory clause accomplished two proslavery goals. It guaranteed both slavery in the territories and the ability of Congress to counter any antislavery movement that might arise in the Confederate hinterlands.

RATIFICATION. On March 11 the Montgomery convention unanimously adopted the new Constitution. The next day Howell Cobb, president of the convention, sent the Constitution to the states for their approval. The ratification of five states would complete the process. On March 12 the Alabama secession convention debated and ratified the document by a vote of 87 to 5; on March 16 the Georgia convention read and ratified the Constitution by a unanimous vote of 260 to 0; on March 21, after some political maneuvering, Louisiana ratified 94 to 10; on March 23 the Texas Secession Convention approved the Constitution 126 to 2 after almost no debate; and on March 26 Mississippi ratified it by a vote of 78 to 7. The Confederate Constitution was now in force.

Radicals delayed ratification in South Carolina. Robert Barnwell Rhett, Sr., wanted to amend the document to prohibit any free state from entering the Confederacy. But finally, on April 3, South Carolina ratified by a vote of 138 to 21. The negative votes represented not latent Unionist sentiment but the proslavery

extremism in the Palmetto State. After ratification the South Carolina convention proposed amendments to eliminate the three-fifths provision and count all slaves for representation; to prohibit free states from joining the Confederacy; to repeal the constitutional prohibition on the slave trade; and to prohibit the government from going into debt, except in the event of war.

Finally, on April 22, Florida ratified the Constitution with a vote of 50 to 0. By this time fighting between the Union and the Confederacy had begun. By the end of June, North Carolina, Arkansas, and Virginia had joined the Confederacy. Tennessee adopted an ordinance of secession in May and placed the Confederate Constitution before the voters, who endorsed it in August by a vote of 85,753 to 30,863. Rump governments in Kentucky and Missouri also eventually endorsed the Confederate Constitution, but those states remained firmly in the Union throughout the war.

[*See also* Congress; Dred Scott Decision; Fugitive Slave Law; Judiciary; Presidency; *and* State Rights and the Appendix for the text of the Constitution.]

— PAUL FINKELMAN

CONSTITUTIONAL UNION PARTY

Comprising members of the old Whig and American parties, the Constitutional Union party organized for the presidential election of 1860. The party proposed to remove the slavery question from the political arena and adopted an ambiguous platform that supported the Constitution, the Union, and the enforcement of the laws of the United States.

In February 1860, thirty prominent leaders from the old Whigs and Americans—including John J. Crittenden, William C. Rives, and Washington Hunt—issued an appeal to the American people, denouncing both the Democratic and the Republican parties and calling for the organization of a new party. Believing that the public was tired of slavery agitation, organizers of the Constitutional Union party felt they could relieve sectional strife by remaining silent on the slavery issue.

The first Constitutional Union National Convention was held at Baltimore in May 1860. Here party members nominated John Bell of Tennessee for president and Edward Everett of Massachusetts for vice president. Bell's conservatism on the slavery issue and his large slaveholdings made him an appealing candidate both to Northern moderates and to upper South Unionists. Also at the Baltimore convention, Constitutional Unionists declared all party issues secondary to preservation of the Union, and they denounced Breckinridge Democrats as anti-unionist conspirators.

As the November election approached, party members hoped that moderate Republicans, sensing defeat for their candidate, would vote for the Constitutional Union ticket to prevent a Democratic victory. Constitutional Unionists also thought that the division within the Democratic party between Stephen A. Douglas and John C. Breckinridge might convince Democrats that neither nominee would win and thus they would support John Bell in order to defeat Abraham Lincoln. Bell, however, received only 12.6 percent of the popular vote, carrying the three upper South states of Virginia, Kentucky, and Tennessee.

Throughout the secession winter of 1860–1861, Bell and other Constitutional Union party leaders urged Lincoln to adopt conciliatory measures toward the South. The outbreak of the Civil War ended all hopes of a peaceful reconciliation and signaled the demise of the Constitutional Union party.

[See also Whig Party.]

— BRUCE W. EELMAN

CONTRABAND

From early modern times, the Western nations have elaborated increasingly detailed conventions of warfare governing persons and property. During the eighteenth century, the term *contraband of war* came into vogue to designate forbidden articles of commerce—chiefly arms and ammunition—that neutral nations might not furnish to belligerents in time of war. By the nineteenth century the term also applied to such articles captured from one belligerent by another. The Civil War stretched the meaning of the term in new and unforeseen directions.

The process began with the war scarcely a month old, when four escaped slaves forced the issue. The men had been impressed into service to build Confederate fortifications on Virginia's lower peninsula. They sought refuge at Fortress Monroe, the Union-held position at the tip of the peninsula, commanded by Gen. Benjamin F. Butler, a shrewd Massachusetts politician.

Prevailing Federal policy steadfastly supported the property rights of slaveholders, but Butler viewed that principle through the prism of his circumstances. Facing an array of slave-built earthworks, he had no doubt of the military usefulness of impressed slaves. If their masters considered them property, why could not the United States do the same, to deny the Confederacy the benefit of their labor and to turn it to the Union's advantage? On such a basis, he offered protection to the fugitives. Although at first he did not invoke the words *contraband of war*, the designation "contrabands" rapidly gained currency both in his command and throughout the North. In August 1861, Congress ratified the notion into law with the Confiscation Act, which authorized the seizure of all property (slaves included) used for belligerent purposes and freed the affected slaves.

Union soldiers lost no time putting the contrabands to work performing mundane camp chores. But during the spring and summer of 1862, as Union forces advanced into the Confederacy, the army required military laborers more than servants. Congress obliged first by prohibiting members of the armed forces from returning runaway slaves to their masters and second by passing a strengthened Confiscation Act and a new Militia Act, which freed the slaves of all disloyal persons and authorized the wholesale employment of former slaves in the Union war effort.

After President Abraham Lincoln issued the Emancipation Proclamation, the size of the contraband population soared. Concentrated mostly in the plantation regions of the Union-occupied South, it numbered several hundred thousand by the end of the war. Able-bodied men served as soldiers and military laborers; women were put to work as farm laborers under the direction of plantation lessees or army-appointed "superintendents of contrabands." Those incapable of labor took refuge at "contraband camps," where the army and Northern benevolent societies provided food, shelter, clothing, and other amenities. Such assistance provoked a wide-ranging debate over its economic and social implications, strains of which echoed into the twentieth century.

The North's designation of escaped and captured slaves as contraband of war caught the South on the horns of a dilemma. Neither politicians nor ideologues could find a means to undercut the contraband logic, except by continuing to sing the antebellum refrain that slaves loved their masters and had no desire to seek refuge with the Northerners. Although Confederate planners understood the importance of slave labor to their cause, they struggled in vain to halt the transformation of slaves into contrabands.

The popularity of the designation "contraband" arose largely from its wry play upon the contradictory nature of slaves as persons and property. Ironically, it also helped perpetuate an association of other-than-human attributes to the former slaves that lingered in the North as well as the South long after the dust of war had settled.

— JOSEPH P. REIDY

By stimulating the movement of laborers and soldiers to the Union side, the proclamation threatened to worsen the already serious manpower shortage of the Confederacy.

PAGE 189

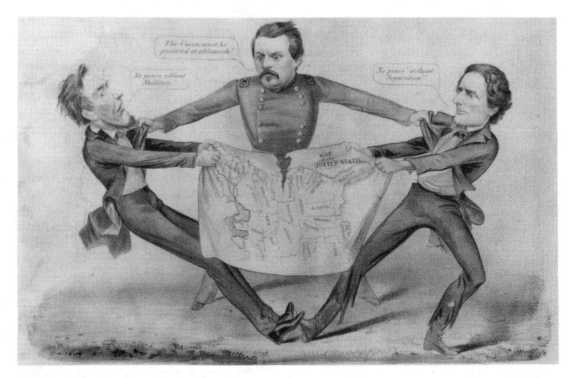

COPPERHEADS

The label was a smear term applied to Democratic critics of the Lincoln administration. Although many dictionaries still define "Copperhead" as "a Northern sympathizer with the South during the Civil War," some recent historians have characterized Democratic dissenters in the North more realistically, discrediting Radical Republican rhetoric and presenting the Copperheads simply as conservative and partisan critics.

Radical Republicans, led by Whitelaw Reid, the editor of the *Cincinnati Gazette,* sought to discredit Democratic dissenters in the upper Midwest by equating them with a poisonous snake that had a brown-blotched body and copper-colored head. After Democratic victories in the fall 1862 election, the Republicans intensified their smear campaign, invariably referring to the Democratic party as the Copperhead party and to its candidates as Copperheads. Some even referred to the conservative members of President Abraham Lincoln's cabinet as Copperheads.

Democratic dissent reached high tide during the first six months of 1863: in Indiana and Illinois the so-called Copperhead state legislatures feuded with their Republican governors; union military failures fostered a sense of defeat; many opposed Lincoln's emancipation measures; and widespread violations of civil rights (including the arbitrary arrest of Clement L. Vallandigham for alleged disloyalty on May 5, 1863) aroused resentment. Moreover, Federal conscription was highly unpopular in many quarters.

But Copperheadism, linked to the peace movement throughout the war, faded during the second half of the year, as Union military victories at Gettysburg and Vicksburg lessened criticism of the Lincoln administration. Propeace Democratic gubernatorial candidates lost several election contests: Vallandigham in Ohio, George W. Woodward in Pennsylvania, and Thomas Seymour in Connecticut. The smear campaign was also instrumental in these defeats inasmuch as it discredited the Copperheads as pro-Southern and traitorous in their outlook.

Besides Vallandigham, Woodward, and Seymour, other well-known Copperheads included Samuel Medary (editor of the *Crisis* in Ohio), Wilbur F. Storey (editor of the *Chicago Times*), Dennis A. Mahony (editor of the *Dubuque Herald*), Daniel W. Voorhees (congressman from Indiana), Horatio Seymour (governor of New York), and Benjamin Wood (congressman and editor of the *New York Daily News*).

Radical Republicans, claiming that the Copperheads belonged to subversive secret societies, transformed three organizations into bogeymen in order to discredit the Democrats, influence elections, and serve as an excuse to organize Union Leagues (Republican-controlled secret patriotic societies). The three were Knights of the Golden Circle, Order of American Knights, and Sons of Liberty.

George W. L. Bickley, while residing in Cincinnati in 1859, had founded the Golden Circle as an agency to convert a part of northern Mexico into a personal fief and perhaps annex it to the United States. Early in the war he lived in Knoxville, Tennessee, where he tried to re-create the Golden Circle and work for the secession of Kentucky. Despite Republican contentions, not a single castle of the Knights of the Golden Circle existed north of the Ohio River during the war years.

The Order of American Knights (O.A.K.), founded by Phineas C. Wright (a former resident of New Orleans) in St. Louis in early 1863, received considerable publicity in the Northern press during the last two years of the war. An "Occasional Address of the Supreme Commander" expressed an abhorrence of President Lincoln's "unconstitutional acts," including emancipation, and glorified state rights. Wright's incompetence and shabby reputation spelled failure for the largely paper-based organization. Col. John P. Sanderson, stationed in St. Louis, wrote "a grand exposé" of the O.A.K. in 1864. Sanderson imagined that the "traitorous organization" had half a million members in the upper Midwest, with Vallandigham as head of the Northern branch and Confederate General Sterling Price commanding the Southern branch. Sanderson's suppositions found their way into Judge Advocate General Joseph Holt's report on subversive societies, printed as political propaganda preceding the 1864 presidential election.

The Sons of Liberty (S.L.), based in Indianapolis, was founded by Harrison H. Dodd in early 1864. "Its objective and purposes, " a booklet printed by Dodd stated, "are the maintenance of constitutional freedom and State's rights, as recognized and established by the founders of our republic." No known chapters existed outside Indianapolis, yet Dodd convinced Vallandigham, at the time an exile in Canada, to accept the nominal headship of the Sons of Liberty. Dodd's actions regarding a New York–to–Indianapolis arms shipment and suggestion of "a revolution" gave Republican leaders the chance to devise a devastating exposé and make arrests that led to two Indianapolis-based treason trials and much adverse publicity for the Sons of Liberty. Some detectives manufactured suppositions that also linked the S.L. to the Camp Douglas conspiracy.

Some Confederate agents in Canada and officials in Richmond accepted the Republican political propaganda at face value and supposed that a northwestern Confederacy was a possibility. Gen. P. G. T. Beauregard, for example, wanted Southern governors to issue a joint statement urging the upper Midwest to set up its own confederacy, promising friendship and free use of the Mississippi River.

[See also Thompson, Jacob, sidebar Northwestern Conspiracy; Peace Movements.]

— FRANK L. KLEMENT

CORNERSTONE SPEECH

Delivered by Confederate vice president Alexander H. Stephens on the night of March 21, 1861, at the Athenaeum in Savannah, Georgia, this speech became notorious for its declaration that the Confederate government's "cornerstone" rested on the inequality of the races and the institution of black slavery.

Delivered extemporaneously, the speech began with praise for the "improvements" the Confederate Constitution had made on the older one, such as the banning of a protective tariff and federal financing of internal improvements. The Constitution also set the slavery question to rest forever, Stephens said, and during the long justification of the institution that followed he uttered the phrase that gave the speech its name. He went on to commend the breadth and wealth of the Confederacy and its wise and conservative Congress and expressed the belief that the new nation would soon be enlarged by the border states. The prospect of war had diminished, but the South, though desirous of peace with all, had to be ready to fight. He warned against factionalism in the South and

EXCERPT

". . .The prospect of war is, at least, not so threatening as it has been. The idea of coercion, shadowed forth in President Lincoln's inaugural, seems not to be followed up thus far so vigorously as was expected. Fort Sumter, it is believed, will soon be evacuated. What course will be pursued toward Fort Pickens, and the other forts on the gulf, is not so well understood. It is to be greatly desired that all of them should be surrendered. Our object is peace, not only with the North, but with the world. All matters relating to the public property, public liabilities of the Union when we were members of it, we are ready and willing to adjust and settle upon the principles of right, equity, and good faith. War can be of no more benefit to the North than to us. Whether the intention of evacuating Fort Sumter is to be received as an evidence of a desire for a peaceful solution of our difficulties with the United States, or the result of necessity, I will not undertake to say. I would fain hope the former. Rumors are afloat, however, that it is the result of necessity. All I can say to you, therefore, on that point is, keep your armor bright and your powder dry."

A persistent complaint of antebellum Southerners had concerned the national government's assumption of increased power after 1789.

PAGE 150

Jefferson Davis regarded Stephens's extolling of slavery as the "cornerstone" of the Confederacy as heedless of the paramount issue of state versus national sovereignty.

PAGE 588

*Farmers in the
Confederacy first
felt the impact of
the war during the
financial crisis of
late 1860 and
early 1861.*

PAGE 213

praised its policy of free trade. If true to itself and its destiny, he concluded, the South would not fail.

The speech was widely reported. Thoughtful Southerners, including Jefferson Davis, deplored Stephens's emphasis on slavery rather than the politically advantageous theme of state versus national sovereignty. Northern reaction was uniformly hostile. The abolitionist press used the speech to demand harsh measures from Abraham Lincoln. The speech's value to the Union cause, one Northern paper later judged, was "incalculable."

[*See also* Confederate Constitution; Montgomery Convention.]

— THOMAS E. SCHOTT

COTTON

In 1858 Senator James Henry Hammond of South Carolina replied to Senator William H. Seward of New York:

> *Without the firing of a gun, without drawing a sword, should they [Northerners] make war upon us [Southerners], we could bring the whole world to our feet. What would happen if no cotton was furnished for three years? . . . England would topple headlong and carry the whole civilized world with her. No, you dare not make war on cotton! No power on earth dares make war upon it. Cotton is King.*

Hammond, like most white Southerners, believed that cotton ruled not just in the South but in the United States and the world. Many economists agreed. In 1855, David Christy entitled his influential book *Cotton Is King*. Cotton indeed drove the economy of the South, affected its social structure, and, during the Civil War, dominated international relations of the Confederacy through "cotton diplomacy."

Cotton in the Antebellum Period

In the early eighteenth century, long-staple cotton was grown in Georgia and on the Sea Islands of South Carolina, but it depleted the soil and proved unprofitable to market. The intensive and laborious hand method of picking out cotton seeds severely restricted the amount of cotton that could be prepared for making into cloth. Cotton could not compete with rice and indigo for commercialization, and Southern colonialists experimented with the crop primarily for domestic use. Despite some increased cotton production during a tobacco depression between 1702 and 1706, few attempted to produce cotton commercially before the Revolutionary War.

Extensive production of cotton awaited the advent of Eli Whitney's cotton gin in the spring of 1793. To separate the seed from the cotton, gins first used spikes placed on rollers and then saws. The influence of the gin was instantaneous; soon Southern mechanics set up gins as far west as Mississippi. By 1804 the cotton crop was eight times greater than it had been the previous decade. The cotton gin made practical the use of the heavily seeded short-staple cotton, which could be grown in upland areas more readily than long-staple cotton. An increase in market demand growing out of England's textile industry ensured favorable prices and spurred the ascension of the short-staple cotton industry.

Cultivation of cotton, on both small and large farms, utilized relatively simple methods. Hoe ridge cultivation was developed after 1800 with ridges set apart about three to six feet, depending on the fertility of the land. After 1830 farmers used V-shaped harrows, which were converted into cultivators, side harrows, and double shovels. (Harrows raked soil with metal teeth to remove debris and smoothed out and leveled the soil once it was broken; cultivators turned the soil under; shovels were used as more traditional plows and also turned the soil over while digging deep furrows.) Cultivation procedures changed little throughout the nineteenth century. A bed for the cotton had to be prepared by clearing out the old stalks from the previous crop. Sometimes these stalks were beaten down with clubs, but if they were large (four to five feet), they had to be pulled by hand. Manure or commercial fertilizer was placed as deeply as possible in the furrow. Usually the cotton bed was built up in February and March. The actual planting of the cotton seed in most areas was in April: early planters risked frost; late planters risked dry spells. Planting was done by hand. In about a month, the plants were thinned. The crop was cultivated with a sweep plowed between the rows four or five times and hoed by hand three or four times. In the middle of June, when they were anywhere from six inches to a foot high, the cotton plants bloomed. Around the last of July or first of August, forty-two to forty-five days after they had blossomed, the cotton bolls opened. Picking usually began about August 20. Most of the crop was ginned immediately after picking.

Cotton prices fluctuated wildly over the years. Prices were high until 1819, then down, up, and down again. In 1837 they hit a crisis low and remained rather low until 1848. Prices rose sharply in 1849 and 1850 but dropped in 1851, though not as low as previously. Throughout the remainder of the 1850s prices rose.

The average amount of seed cotton used to make a 400-pound bale of lint ranged from about 1,200 to 1,400 pounds. The bales had to be transported from the gins to a local market and then on to larger markets. Cotton was shipped to market continually from September through January. Wagons loaded with bales of cotton often lined roads. The moving of cotton demanded better roadbeds, sometimes even plank roads, near market towns. River transportation to seaports was common from market towns located on rivers or canals. Major cities grew up at railroad stations as rail lines began to link the hinterland to ports and then to the Northeast and Midwest.

Improvements in the production and transportation of cotton and the new demand for the fiber led to a scramble for greater profits. To reap the most profits and to provide the labor needed for cotton picking, a large number of slaves were imported into South Carolina and Georgia, and slave labor became a valuable market throughout the South. The way into the Southern aristocracy was through the ownership of land and slaves, and the way to get land and slaves was to grow cotton: the crop provided the cash and credit to buy both. At this time, too, the cotton kingdom pushed ever westward with planters searching for new and richer soils to grow more white cotton with the labor of more black slaves. Ironically, just as abolitionist sentiment was increasing in the United States, the invention of the cotton gin instigated a deeper entrenchment of slavery into the Southern economy and society.

The Southern aristocracy, which slavery created, dominated Southern society and inhibited the development of efficient methods for soil use. In the face of soil exhaustion, Southern planters needed to extend control into the fresh lands of the western territories. Hence, territorial expansion became a sectional issue as both North and South realized that western lands were essential for the survival of the Southern slave culture.

Most discussions of cotton dwell on the short period when cotton did rule as king. This "mature" period of cotton and slavery was not necessarily typical of or relevant to the earlier periods of plantation agriculture that accompanied the emergence of the cotton monoculture. Discussions also tend to treat the South as one unit rather than the large and varied region it was. The cotton kingdom extended west through Texas and north about six hundred miles up the Mississippi River valley.

Antebellum history often seems dominated by scenes of plantations worked by slaves. Although thousands of large plantations employed slave labor and produced most of the South's cotton, numerically there were more small farmers, mostly whites, who cultivated the upland areas. Many of these yeomen were subsistence farmers and produced only a surplus of cotton for market. Southern farmers who did not grow cotton sold some of their foodstuff to the planters. Cotton

could bring prosperity or depression, according to changes in the market, and these fluctuations meant very differing experiences for whites, slaves, and antebellum free blacks of each different region of the South.

When at its peak, the demanding cultivation and transportation of cotton required the labor of the majority of men, women, and children in the rural South. Most Southern life was regulated by the agricultural economy, and more and more over time, this came to mean the cotton economy. Although free workers and slaves pursued a diversity of agricultural and industrial occupations in the antebellum South, by 1850 the routine of taking care of the white-blossomed, white-bolled short-staple cotton plants increasingly typified rural Southern existence.

By 1860, cotton ruled the South, which annually exported two-thirds of the world supply of the "white gold." Cotton ruled the West and Midwest because each year these sections sold $30 million worth of food supplies to Southern cotton producers. Cotton ruled the Northeast because the domestic textile industry there produced $100 million worth of cloth each year. In addition, the North sold to the cotton-growing South more than $150 million worth of manufactured goods every year, and Northern ships transported cotton and cotton products worldwide.

Cotton in the Confederacy

As the U.S. cotton industry developed, other countries became more dependent on cotton produced in the American South. The power of cotton allowed the Confederacy to employ cotton diplomacy as its foundation for foreign relations during the Civil War; Southerners attempted to use cotton to pressure countries such as England and France into the war on behalf of the Confederacy. Southern leaders were convinced that the key to their success lay in gaining international recognition and help from European powers in breaking the blockade that the Union had thrown up around coastal areas and ports and that was increasingly effective as the war went on. (Although the Union blockade never thoroughly sealed the Confederate coastline, it was successful in causing Southern imports and exports to drop drastically at a time when the Confederacy needed to fund its huge war efforts.)

Southerners saw cotton as the great leverage in this effort, and at the time this made sense. More than three-fourths of the cotton used in the textile industries of England and France came from the American South. Between a fourth and a fifth of the English population depended in some way on the textile industry, and half of the export trade of England was in cotton textiles. About a tenth of the nation's wealth was

Trade in farm commodities ground to a halt as banks began to hoard specie after the Union blockade of the Southern coast took hold.

PAGE 213

also invested in the cotton business. The English Board of Trade said in 1859 that India was completely inadequate as a source of raw cotton; England apparently was dependent on the American South for cotton. This concept of King Cotton led many Southerners to believe that England and France would have to intervene in the Civil War in order to save their own economies. The Confederacy began applying pressure on the neutral powers through a voluntary embargo of cotton. Although Congress never formally established the embargo, local "committees of public safety" prevented the shipping of cotton from Southern ports.

To exploit their leverage, the Confederate States sent William Lowndes Yancey, Pierre A. Rost, and A. Dudley Mann to England in the spring of 1861 to confer with Lord Russell, the British foreign secretary. As a result, the British and French granted the Confederacy belligerency status. It was a small victory, probably not very effective in helping the Confederacy. The cotton diplomats failed to arrange with England a denunciation of the blockade or the negotiation of a commercial agreement, let alone diplomatic recognition of the Confederacy.

Regardless of wishful beliefs and England's real economic dependence on cotton, at the time of the outbreak of the Civil War an overabundance of cotton existed in Europe. Furthermore, British hostility to slavery decreased the likelihood of intervention. Moreover, it was not in the vested interests of the neutral powers, particularly Great Britain, to denounce the blockade. The Confederate government attempted to convince the Europeans that the Federal blockade was ineffective and thus illegal under the terms of the 1856 Treaty of Paris. The Confederacy failed to acknowledge that Great Britain, as the world's foremost naval power, would desire to let stand any blockade, regardless of its legality or actual effectiveness. And to make matters even worse, the South's voluntary embargo undercut its own argument that the Federal blockade was porous.

Although the South never succeeded in convincing foreign powers to intervene against the North, cotton diplomacy was successful in obtaining financial help from abroad. This came in the form of loans and bonds, which Confederate Treasurer Christopher G. Memminger guaranteed with cotton. The Confederate Treasury Department issued $1.5 million in cotton certificates during the war for acquisitions abroad. One such loan backed by cotton was the Erlanger loan, signed on October 28, 1862, and modified on January 3, 1863. This loan, amounting to $15 million, was secured by cotton. At the time cotton was worth twenty-four pence a pound, and the Erlanger loan made cotton available to holders at six pence per pound.

This reliance on cotton for the security of loans, bonds, and certificates placed a great deal of responsibility on the Produce Loan Office, whose agents had to ensure that planters would fulfill government subscriptions of cotton at a time when many planters were unwilling to sell to the government. Ultimately, however, cotton enabled the Confederacy to realize $7,678,591.25 in foreign exchange.

The Confederacy also hoped to raise tax revenue on the sale of cotton abroad. On February 28, 1861, Congress passed an act levying an export duty of $1/8$ ¢ per pound on all cotton shipped after August 1 of that year. The government hoped to raise $20 million through the export tax in order to pay a $15 million loan funded by an issue of 8 percent bonds. But because of the tightening blockade and the South's own voluntary cotton embargo, the measure raised only $30,000. When the secretary of the treasury lobbied to have this minuscule tax raised, opposition from the planter class kept Congress from increasing it, even when the Confederacy's finances were desperate.

To a degree, planter opposition also undercut Southern efforts to shift from cotton production to the planting of foodstuffs. The Confederacy was convinced it could become self-sufficient. It would produce all the food and cotton it needed, and revenue from cotton could buy weapons, blankets, and other manufactured goods until the Confederacy started manufacturing its own. Planters believed that the yeomen and poor would fight in the army and that slaves would continue to produce food and the South's greatest weapon, cotton.

By the spring of 1862, however, there was already an abundance of cotton and a shortage of foodstuffs. In April 1862 yeomen soldiers could not go home to plant spring crops, and their families would again have no food. To encourage the growth of foodstuffs, every Southern cotton-producing state attempted to limit the amount of cotton that could be grown. State governors issued proclamations urging planters to reduce their cotton acreage by as much as four-fifths and encouraging them to plant enough wheat, corn, and beans to feed themselves, their slaves, and the armies in the field. The planters responded, cutting their usual acreage of cotton to about half and devoting the rest to food crops. Many planters even had enough surplus foodstuffs to sell to the families of the yeoman poor whose husbands and sons were away in the war. Still, the planters did not reduce their cotton production as much as the state and Confederate governments wanted. Some scholars argue that this is an example of how the Confederacy contributed to its own defeat by refusing to disturb the interests of the planter class.

But even with resistance by the planters, the shift to the production of foodstuffs combined with the drain in manpower and the eventual Union occupation created a drastic drop in cotton production as the war dragged on: 4.5 million bales were grown in 1861; 1.5 million in 1862; 500,000 in 1863; and only 300,000 in 1864. As production dropped, the price of cotton skyrocketed on the world market, and blockade runners decided the risks were worth taking; cotton-exporting corporations formed throughout the cotton kingdom. In addition, Mexico traded cotton directly across the Texas border.

In an attempt to control the flow of cotton to Europe and rectify the declining economy, Southern politicians in late 1863 introduced an approach called the "New Plan." Through this series of administrative actions and congressional laws, the Confederate government became directly involved in blockade running. Rather than making contracts for supplies payable in cotton, the government itself began selling the cotton abroad and buying supplies with the proceeds, thereby cutting out the middlemen. The plan's supervisor, Colin J. McRae, gained direct control over cargo space on blockade runners. Those who refused to accept a fair rate to transport cotton for sale by the government would have their vessels confiscated. The War Department increasingly turned to the sale of cotton to purchase needed supplies, and by the end of 1863 it had reserved fully one-third of all cargo space on blockade runners.

As a result of these measures and other financial consolidations under the plan, Confederate foreign financing was greatly improved and 27,229 bales of cotton were exported for $5.3 million in sales. But because of the Confederacy's early confidence in the diplomatic leverage of King Cotton, it did not institute measures such as the New Plan soon enough to make a considerable impact on the war effort. The South could not keep its vital ports open or continue to endure Northern attacks on the battlefield.

Some scholars have written with hindsight that the Confederacy might have been more successful, had it pursued a different strategy with its cotton. If Confederate leaders had confiscated all the cotton in the South and stored it, they could have used it as a basis to obtain credit from European nations. With credit, some scholars believe, the Confederacy could have bought a navy strong enough to break the Union blockade. Others argue that the Confederate government would have been better served if it had made cotton, not gold, the basis of its currency.

Although the Civil War ended the slave plantation system, it did not end the South's legacy of cotton. Cultivation of the crop had worn out much of the land. Many planted up and down on slopes, which then eroded. The concentration on cotton production meant complete reliance on a one-crop system; crop rotation

UNION COTTON TRADE
Selling to the Enemy

If the Confederate government was able, albeit partially and belatedly, to gain control over the cotton trade with Europe, it had much less success in curtailing the cotton trade with the Union. On May 21, 1861, the Confederate Congress prohibited the sale of cotton to the North. Yet an illicit trade across military lines flourished between Southern cotton farmers and Northern traders. President Abraham Lincoln gave licenses to traders, who followed the Union army into the South. On March 17, 1862, the Confederacy gave state governments the right to destroy any cotton that might fall into the hands of the Union army. Some devoted Confederates burned their own cotton to keep it out of enemy hands. Other Southerners, however, discovered that Union agents were willing to pay the highest prices in over half a century for cotton or offered badly needed supplies as barter. Ironically, valuable currency for cotton from the North saved some small Southern farmers from starvation. But this selling of cotton to the North undermined Confederate nationalism, as did the official Confederate trading of cotton with the North conducted in the last years of the war.

As the price of foodstuffs reached astronomical heights and Confederate currency became worthless with inflation, the smuggling of cotton out of the South to the North increased. Women whose husbands had been killed or were away at the battlefield or in prison were heavily involved in forming these caravans. Rich planters and factors also made large deals with Federal officials. The situation became totally absurd when cotton was sold to Federal troops to get supplies for the Confederate army. Even President Lincoln approved an arrangement to send food for Robert E. Lee's troops at Petersburg in exchange for cotton for New York. Ulysses S. Grant stopped this exchange because he was attempting to cut off Lee's supplies, but other such exchanges occurred throughout the Civil War.

— ORVILLE VERNON BURTON
PATRICIA DORA BONNIN

A severe drought in the summer of 1862 parched the crops and reduced yields for all farmers.

PAGE 214

was uncommon, and farmers did not plow under clover or peas to restore humus to the soil. Diminishing fertility of cotton lands was a major problem farmers continued to face after the Civil War.

[*See also* Blockade, *overview article*; Diplomacy; Erlanger Loan; Expansionism in the Antebellum South; Farming; New Plan; Plantation; Produce Loan; Slavery; Urbanization.]

— ORVILLE VERNON BURTON
PATRICIA DORA BONNIN

CRITTENDEN COMPROMISE

In December 1860 Kentucky senator John J. Crittenden proposed a comprehensive set of resolutions designed to avert secession and war. These resolutions became known as the Crittenden Compromise following their December 18 referral to the Senate Committee of Thirteen, a special committee set up to review methods for diffusing the sectional crisis.

Crittenden, nationally known for his past compromising efforts, offered the South protection by giving slavery in the slave states a permanent constitutional status while simultaneously allaying Northern fears of unchecked slave expansion. The Crittenden Compromise comprised six unamendable constitutional amendments: the first and most important restored and extended the old Missouri Compromise line by protecting slavery south of 36°30′ but prohibiting the institution north of the line, and citizens in territories were to decide for themselves whether new states would enter the Union free or slave; the second amendment prohibited Congress from abolishing slavery on government property in slave states; the third forbade the abolition of slavery in the District of Columbia unless it was abolished in both Maryland and Virginia, and then not without consent of the inhabitants or compensation to the owners; the fourth protected interstate transportation of slaves; the fifth compensated claimants of fugitive slaves rescued by mobs; and the sixth prohibited future constitutional amendments that would overturn these guarantees.

Initially, it appeared as if these resolutions had a real chance for passage. Upper South Unionists embraced the Crittenden Compromise as the only hope of avoiding secessionist victory in their states. Many in the Republican ranks were also sympathetic to conciliatory measures. President-elect Abraham Lincoln, however, made it clear that he would not waver on his commitment to contain slavery where it already existed. Although Lincoln was agreeable to some of the resolutions, his opposition to the restoration of the 36°30′ line made passage of the compromise impossible.

Following its failure in the Committee of Thirteen, Crittenden brought his compromise directly before the Senate on January 3, 1861, and called for a national plebiscite on the resolutions, arguing that the American people supported the compromise. On January 16, however, the Senate voted down Crittenden's appeal 25 to 23. The failure of the Crittenden Compromise ended any hope of halting the secession movement by congressional action. Lincoln's opposition to the compromise was a major setback to Southern Unionism.

— BRUCE W. EELMAN

DAHLGREN PAPERS

Following the aborted Kilpatrick-Dahlgren cavalry raid on Richmond (February 28–March 3, 1864), Col. Ulric Dahlgren was killed while attempting to return to Union lines. Soon after Dahlgren's death young William Littlepage, a local schoolboy, searched Dahlgren's pockets and discovered papers that produced a storm of controversy. They contained various inflammatory statements, including references to burning Richmond and killing President Jefferson Davis and his cabinet.

The publication of the Dahlgren Papers in the Richmond newspapers fanned the flames of hatred and prompted cries for retribution. Eventually Gen. Robert E. Lee wrote to Gen. George G. Meade, asking him if his government had approved or sanctioned the violent actions proposed in the captured letters. Meade disavowed the statements but wrote his wife of "collateral evidence in my possession," suggesting he believed the papers genuine.

Dahlgren's supporters quickly sprang to his defense and insisted the Papers were either forged or planted on the fallen warrior. All those intimately involved in the raid, including its leader Gen. Judson Kilpatrick, denied the published statements concerning the burning of Richmond and the killing of Davis and the Confederate cabinet. Others claimed the transposition of the *h* and *l* in Dahlgren's signature on one of the documents proved they were forgeries.

Any impartial investigation into the controversy became frustratingly difficult because none of the original Dahlgren Papers survived. During the 1950s, however, historian V. C. Jones thoroughly reviewed the issue and refuted theories that claimed the papers were false because of Dahlgren's name being misspelled. He noted that of the three separate papers concerning the raid, the two with the most damning statements had no signature. To establish the Papers' authenticity he documented a chain of possession and offered testimony from virtually every

PLOTS AGAINST LINCOLN

Both Abraham Lincoln and Jefferson Davis functioned as de facto commanders in chief of their respective armies and, as such, exerted tremendous influence on their troops. Under the existing rules of war the president of the opposing government was a legitimate target, due to his position as military commander, even though he was technically a civilian.

In the wake of the controversy over the Dahlgren Papers, Confederates launched several plans to capture Lincoln and bring him to Richmond to either serve as ransom for the thousands of imprisoned rebel soldiers, or else as a hostage to force a negotiated settlement of the conflict.

Evidence now exists of the following capture schemes:

Gen. Bradley T. Johnson and Gen. Wade Hampton—in early 1864 they concocted the idea of a raid to grab Lincoln at his summer retreat, the Soldier's Home, on the northern outskirts of Washington. Gen. Jubal Early "pulled rank" on them and took over the plan for himself.

John Wilkes Booth—beginning summer of 1864, he and a band of followers set up a network of rebel sympathizers who would whisk Lincoln from Washington to Richmond once Booth's group waylaid him. On March 17, 1865, they failed at a capture attempt and the group dissolved.

Capt. Thomas Nelson Conrad—scouted the movements of Lincoln in Washington in the summer of 1864 and reported that a capture attempt could be successful.

Gen. Jubal Early—the Washington Raid of September 1864 was stopped on the outskirts of Washington City. Was it the cover for a lightning swift raid to enter the city and carry off Lincoln? Some modern researchers think so.

Col. John Singleton Mosby—did "the Gray Ghost" organize a bomb attack on the White House when capture was no longer possible? One U.S. army intelligence expert has suggested this recently.

Lincoln seemed to have lived a charmed life during the war; despite determined plotting by his enemies, he was not grabbed and used as a bargaining chip to force an armistice. His assassination, though not a direct outgrowth of military planning, was the only other option Booth felt he had left.

— STEVEN G. MILLER

D

prominent Confederate authority who claimed to have seen the documents. His findings are still valid today.

[*See also* Kilpatrick-Dahlgren Raid.]

— MICHAEL J. ANDRUS

DAVIS, JEFFERSON

Davis, Jefferson (1807 or 1808–1889), U.S. senator, U.S. secretary of war, and president of the Confederate States of America. Davis was born on June 3, probably in 1807 (he sometimes put it in 1808), in Christian County (present-day Todd), Kentucky, the son of Samuel and Jane (Cook) Davis. In about 1811 the family settled near Woodville, Mississippi. After two years at St. Thomas College, near Spring-field, Kentucky, Davis entered Jefferson College in Mississippi and later transferred to Wilkinson County Academy. He joined the junior class at Transylvania University, Lexington, Kentucky, in the fall of 1823.

Influenced by his older brother, Joseph E. Davis, Jefferson entered the U.S. Military Academy in September 1824. Cadet Davis compiled a good academic record as well as a fairly large number of demerits. He ranked twenty-third out of thirty-three in the graduating class and was commissioned brevet second lieutenant of infantry on July 1, 1828.

Routine assignments took him to various frontier posts and to some Indian fighting. In September 1832 he received the surrender of the famed Sauk chief Black Hawk and escorted his prisoner from Prairie du Chien, Wisconsin Territory, to Jefferson Barracks, Missouri. Promoted to first lieutenant of dragoons on May 10, 1834, Davis led several expeditions into hostile Kiowa and Wichita villages. A year later, on May 12, 1835, he submitted his resignation from the army.

Davis married Sarah Knox Taylor (daughter of Zachary Taylor) on June 17 at her aunt's house near Louisville, Kentucky. The couple went immediately to Mississippi, where brother Joseph had provided Jefferson eight hundred acres to clear, build on, and on which to start a planter's life. Both Jefferson and "Knoxie" contracted a severe fever in late August or early September, and on September 15, 1835, she died. Desolate and gravely ill, Davis traveled to Havana, Cuba, in the winter to recover. He returned to Mississippi via New York and Washington. He lived in seclusion—working on his plantation (Brierfield), reading, and learning his brother's views on slave management, which were considered comparatively liberal. Gradually he became a knowledgeable and successful planter whose slaves are reported to have held him in high regard.

Nearly ten years passed before Davis emerged from his seclusion. When he did, he entered Mississippi politics and married again. Varina Howell, a Natchez girl not twenty when she married Davis on February 25, 1845, became the mainstay of his life. Independent, sometimes willful, Varina irritated Davis at first, but after a period of adjustment, she shared his trials and triumphs, fought battles for him, bore him four sons and two daughters, and loved him always.

Davis was elected to Congress that year and when the Mexican War began he was elected colonel of a volunteer regiment from Vicksburg. With it he joined his former father-in-law's army at Carmargo, Mexico. General Taylor advanced against Monterrey, and Davis's Mississippi regiment played an important role in the campaign. Davis and his Mississippians remained with Taylor while much of his army joined Gen. Winfield Scott's campaign from Vera Cruz to Mexico City. Mexico's leader, Gen. Antonio Lopez de Santa Anna, attacked Taylor in the expectation of annihilating a weakened American force. At the victorious Battle of Buena Vista, Davis and his Mississippi riflemen did heroic duty. Wounded, Davis returned to the United States to find himself a hero.

The Mississippi legislature presented him a sword of honor and appointed him in 1847 to fill out an unexpired Federal senatorial term. Reelected in 1850, Democrat Davis went on to prominence in the Senate and in Federal affairs. He became chairman of the

Military Committee of the Senate and proved to be a bureaucrat with remarkably progressive ideas—new weapons always caught his attention and he remembered the success of the new percussion rifles he had provided for his Mississippians. During his term Davis's cultural interests led him to take a leading role in developing the Smithsonian Institution.

Senator Davis could be heard expressing the Southern position on national issues often and eloquently. He disliked the Compromise of 1850 and favored extension of the Missouri Compromise line to the Pacific as a solution to the slavery problem.

In the 1850s Davis came to inherit the mantle of John C. Calhoun as the leading Southern spokesman. But party and doctrinal loyalty led him to resign his Senate seat in 1850 to enter, belatedly, the governor's race in Mississippi against Henry S. Foote. Foote took a moderate stance toward the Great Compromise and seemed to be riding a rising feeling of Unionism. Davis had once before been in a raucous campaign for a forlorn hope but had usually held appointive office and had not really been a cracker-barrel politician; now he disciplined himself to doff his natural hauteur and stump as much of the state as time and his precarious health permitted. He talked of the need for a united South, one committed to protecting its rights within the Union; he reached for votes from the poor whites, a class long ignored under a Mississippi oligarchy. He lost, by barely a thousand votes, and returned, in his words, to "quiet farm-labors, until the nomination of Franklin Pierce, when I went out to advocate his election." Davis became President Pierce's secretary of war.

His penchant for innovation, already seen during his Senate stint, grew with his new position. Convinced by experience that western military operations required new methods, Secretary Davis brought in camels for use in the desert. He introduced new infantry tactics, pushed the substitution of iron for wooden gun carriages, increased the number of rifles and musket-rifles capable of using the new minié cartridge, and modernized the ordnance at some of the coastal forts.

He had long advocated a transcontinental military railroad and, as secretary of war, surveyed various routes for that line. During his secretaryship he had charge of expanding the U.S. Capitol and sometimes served as acting navy secretary.

Mississippi returned Davis in March 1857 to a Senate facing serious national problems. Davis viewed the future with increasing gloom. The Kansas-Nebraska Act of 1854 had repealed the Missouri Compromise and opened lands west of Missouri to local options on slavery. A protracted war between pro- and antislavery settlers in Kansas Territory dragged on through the 1850s until the whole country lamented "Bleeding Kansas." This crisis finally disrupted the party system as the Whig party expired and the anti-South and antislavery Republican party took its place.

Increasingly the cotton South turned to Davis as adviser and defender. He made no apologies for slavery since he considered it the best adjustment of capital to labor, far better than the industrial system of the North where laborers were subjected to "humiliation and suffering." Davis saw slavery in the South as "moral, a social and political blessing." Protecting slavery meant, also, protecting sovereign state rights in the Union. Davis's defense of the South threw him into combat with the "Black Republican" party. Seeking to preserve the Democratic party as the last national forum of compromise between the sections, he opposed Stephen A. Douglas's popular sovereignty doctrine enshrined in the Kansas-Nebraska Act. Initially a proponent of the act, Davis came to see it as a snare and a delusion, since "squatter sovereignty," as he called it, would allow territories to pass laws annulling Southerners' constitutional property rights.

From a constitutional issue, slavery rose to become a moral issue, and political rhetoric inflamed the national conscience. Davis spoke often on the slave issue. And he hewed hard to his love for the Union. As late as the spring of 1860 he thought the Union safe but felt, rightly enough, that danger came not from differences but from politics and politicians.

He knew, after 1858, that preserving the Union would be difficult, especially in 1860, an election year that might see the Republicans winning and ensconcing an "abolition president" in the White House. He considered that tantamount to ending the nation—the South could not live under an abolitionist administration because constitutional protection would disappear.

Jefferson Davis came to his views on Southern rights through reading, discussion, and iron logic. Devoted to the nation by lineage, history, and patriotism, Davis nonetheless believed in the compact theory of the Union, which held that the states were sovereign, that they had yielded sovereignty by joining the Union, and that they could reclaim it by seceding. As pressure built against slavery and against the cotton system through the 1850s, Davis became louder in his calls for Southern rights within the Union, but he urged moderation and restraint to save the Republic.

Appointed in December 1860 to the Senate Committee of Thirteen charged with finding a solution to the crisis, Davis saw little hope and reluctantly advised secession and the formation of a Southern confederacy.

Anguished, ill, and weary, Davis made a farewell speech to the Senate on January 21, 1861, which stated clearly the South's position and reasons for leaving the Union. He and his family left Washington for

At the end, his dream of independence fading, Davis remained first and last the foremost Confederate.

PAGE 165

D

Brierfield Plantation on January 22. Back in Mississippi he accepted a commission as major general of state troops, but at Brierfield he received word of his election as president of the Provisional Government of the Confederate States of America.

He did not want the job. He felt better qualified for military command but dutifully accepted the political post. Why his reluctance about the presidency? He knew the problems ahead for the new Confederacy—the probability of war and the South's unreadiness—and he disliked the kind of politicking the presidency required. Was he the right man? Yes. On balance, the South called its best to lead its quest for independence. Davis had national, even international, renown, the respect of friends and foes, a judiciousness valuable in raucous times, a balancing realism, a need to be needed, and proper presidential probity.

In his inaugural address at Montgomery, Alabama, on February 18, 1861, Davis spoke of his hope for peace, described the South's course to secession, stressed the Confederacy as a product of evolution, not revolution, announced Southern dedication to agriculture and to free trade, and made a firm declaration: "We have entered upon the career of independence, and it must be inflexibly pursued." He urged creation of a national army and navy and spoke prophetically of his own future:

> Experience in public stations . . . has taught me that care and toil and disappointment are the price of official elevation. You will see many errors to forgive, many deficiencies to tolerate, but you shall not find in me either a want of zeal or fidelity to the cause that is to me highest in hope and of most enduring affection.

An expected state rights advocate, Davis became almost immediately an unexpected Confederate nationalist. A constitutionalist, he used that document to strengthen the central government. A national army that superseded the state militias became the main bastion of his administration. When the government took control of military operations within Confederate borders, the states lost more power than they guessed.

Davis picked his cabinet with an eye toward state representation, toward old political lines, and toward ability. His first picks were not uniformly good, notably the secretary of war, Alabamian Leroy P. Walker; the secretary of state, Georgia's Robert Toombs; and the secretary of the treasury, South Carolinian Christopher G. Memminger. His two best appointees were Louisianan Judah P. Benjamin, who as attorney general headed the new Department of Justice, and Floridian Stephen R. Mallory as secretary of the navy. Benjamin would become a close presidential confidant and Mallory an innovative, resourceful navy builder.

Through early negotiations with Abraham Lincoln's government about Federal property in the South, Davis learned quickly that diplomacy, far from being a gentlemanly enterprise, was a practice in deceit. Failure of negotiations led to the Fort Sumter crisis in April 1861. That fort across Charleston Harbor boasted old ordnance and a small garrison, but its Union banner flouted Confederate sovereignty. Davis made a decision, over some cabinet objections, and Confederate guns began firing at Fort Sumter on April 12, 1861. War began.

Davis organized his armies with skill, although critics suggested that he meddled with generals too much and stuck by such controversial cronies as Gen. Braxton Bragg and Commissary Gen. Lucius B. Northrop beyond reason. To some extent Davis served as his own war secretary—that six men filled that title indicates problems—and, like most chief executives, he relied on people he knew to get things done. If he did hold a tight rein on some generals, many of them needed it; to generals he trusted, such as Robert E. Lee, he gave help and scant advice.

He understood morale building and, in order to weld Virginia to the Confederacy, moved the capital to Richmond in late May 1861.

From the start he offered a hard war program to a laissez-faire Congress. His urging produced a Conscription Act in 1862 that saved the Confederate armies as first enlistments expired; he supported an impressment program that generated much public resentment as the armies commandeered supplies for the men and animals; despite his own predilections he urged tough taxes on land, cotton, and slaves, and endorsed a unique tax-in-kind to be paid with food, forage, cloth, or animals; he accepted also the produce loan, which was designed to extract more staples in return for Confederate paper. But neither he nor Congress could condone the truly draconian taxes needed in a new and warring nation.

Necessity brought Davis to varied innovations. As war eroded his country and its people, he forced himself to become a much more public figure, spoke often, made several "swings around the Confederacy" to rekindle flagging faith, and maintained a prodigious correspondence with critics, friends, and restive governors. Toward the last he even proposed limited slave emancipation in return for national service.

Some things he ought to have done he could not bring himself to do. Although Congress provided authority virtually to nationalize the railroads, Davis did not press its enforcement—it smacked too much of federalism. Nor did he deal harshly with an increasingly critical press. Where Lincoln suppressed seditious publications, Davis did not; he stuck by freedom of expression. He suspended the writ of habeas corpus only under congressional authority, never under assumed war powers.

As the war ran against his country, Davis worked harder for longer hours, pushed his wretched health beyond limits, and became estranged from Congress and from most of the public. He found the state rights policies of many governors almost inconceivable in a period of crisis and frowned on cajoling reluctant patriots. Congress often balked at the president's war program but grudgingly followed his lead. His own dedication was sometimes seen as haughty aloofness, but a close reading of his state papers and his letters shows his fiery devotion unflagging to the end.

As president he had the task of devising a national strategy for victory, and he adopted the offensive-defensive as the best way to use interior lines and inferior Southern resources against Northern strength. Under this plan, Southern armies would conserve men and matériel, retreat in the face of superior forces (if state rights governors permitted), and wait for a moment of Southern superiority. He applied this strategy in Maryland and Kentucky in 1862 and in the West. When he found that old-fashioned command structures failed under the vastness of the war, he tried a new theater-command idea that might well have worked had Joseph E. Johnston, the general picked for the command, been bold.

At the end, his dream of independence fading, Davis remained first and last the foremost Confederate. When General Lee evacuated Richmond on April 2, 1865, Davis led a refugee government to Danville, Virginia, and then moved southward in hopes of getting across the Mississippi and continuing the struggle. He was captured at Irwinville, Georgia, on May 10, 1865.

He had done as well as anyone could to create a Southern nation. Although he lacked Lincoln's facility with language, at times he approached eloquence in talking of the cause he nearly won. He created a revolutionary state, and when the dream was lost and his country gone, he could take some consolation in a legacy of honor.

Davis served a harsh two-year prison stint at Fort Monroe while awaiting a treason trial and achieved at last a mite of martyrdom. Varina's ceaseless efforts to free him, combined with those of many others in the North and South, finally succeeded. Released from prison on bail in May 1867 (he was never brought to trial), Davis continued his life in the Confederacy. Never wavering in his belief in the cause, never admitting error, he continued to argue the constitutional right of secession and the legitimacy of the Confederacy. Financially strapped, he worked at tasks that friends provided, tried various business schemes that failed, and at last found refuge at Beauvoir, a charming

house belonging to a lifelong friend near Biloxi, Mississippi. There he spent his last years writing his history of the war and his country. In June 1881, Davis's two-volume *Rise and Fall of the Confederate Government* appeared. A heavy, badly organized book, the product of Davis and several collaborators, it was Davis's view of the whole Confederate experience and decidedly his book as he flayed his enemies and praised his friends: Joseph E. Johnston and P. G. T. Beauregard ranked as villains, while Bragg and Northrop came off well. Davis's second book, *Short History of the Confederate States,* published in 1889, lacked anger, presented a more balanced view of the war, and showed real literary quality.

Personal tragedy dogged much of Davis's life. Not only did he lose his first wife early, but also his four sons died before him. One of them, Joseph Evan, was killed in a fall from a White House balcony in Richmond on April 30, 1864.

In his last years, Davis became a hero, seen as a long-neglected symbol. On his rare public appearances he came increasingly to advocate reunion and reconciliation. He died on December 5, 1889, aged eighty-two, survived by Varina and two daughters, Margaret and Varina Anne ("Winnie").

[*See also* Beauvoir; Presidency.]

— FRANK E. VANDIVER

DAVIS, VARINA HOWELL

Davis, Varina Howell (1826–1906), first lady of the Confederacy. It is one of the Civil War's rich ironies that Varina Howell Davis became First Lady of the Confederacy, for she was unsuited by personal background and political inclination for the role. Born into the planter class in Mississippi in 1826, she received an excellent education at a girls' academy in Philadelphia and at home with a private tutor. Her father, William B. Howell, was an active member of the Whig party, and she grew up in a household where people took politics seriously and discussed them with gusto. She was a straightforward, candid, and outspoken girl, and her personality was always at odds with the role of the Southern "lady."

When she met Jefferson Davis at a Christmas party in 1843, she was a tall seventeen-year-old with large expressive eyes, and she was already known for her dry wit. Davis was a rich widower in his mid-thirties who had only recently recovered from the death of his first wife, Sarah Knox Taylor Davis. Her impressions of Davis were mixed: she thought he was arrogant and

The First Lady got off to a bad start in the summer of 1861 by appearing at public receptions when she was visibly pregnant.

PAGE 166

aloof but also handsome, well spoken, and cultivated. Her initial doubts gradually faded, however, and she fell in love with him. He also fell in love, attracted to her fine mind and good looks. The couple married on February 26, 1845.

The marriage was charged with struggle from the beginning, starting with an inheritance dispute.

Joseph E. Davis, Jefferson's older brother and manager of the family's large estate, devised a will that excluded Varina from inheriting any of the Davis property. She protested immediately, but to no avail—Jefferson told her to accept his brother's decision. She felt further alienated from her husband when he enlisted in the army to fight in the Mexican War without consulting her. It was becoming clear that Jefferson simply accepted the sex roles of his era and expected her to do what he told her to do. By the time he returned from war in 1847, the couple had become estranged. When he was appointed to the U.S. Senate, he left her at home in Mississippi for almost a year to punish her.

Somehow the Davises reconciled and she went to Washington, but other conflicts plagued the marriage, often because Jefferson Davis continued to make arbitrary decisions without consulting his wife. He controlled the family's finances and even decided whether Varina could visit her relatives. In what became a typical pattern in the relationship, she would protest his decisions and then eventually acquiesce. She had no other choice. If she wanted a divorce—which she never mentioned in writing—it would have been almost impossible to obtain under Mississippi law. Moreover, she had no income of her

own, and it would have been difficult to return to her parents, because by the late 1840s her father was going bankrupt. In the 1850s the Davises had four children, but they were never able to resolve their power struggles.

Varina Davis retained her Whiggish sympathies through the 1850s, even though her husband was a Democrat, and like many Southern Whigs she was alarmed by the secession crisis of 1860 and 1861. She told several close friends and relatives that it was foolish for Southern states to leave the Union and that the Confederacy would never survive. After her husband became president, she reluctantly joined him in Richmond to spend what she later called four of the worst years of her life.

Few people seem to have known of her opposition to secession, but she nonetheless became a controversial figure. Members of Richmond's society called her direct manner crude and unrefined; the First Lady was not deemed to be a proper lady. Some politicians, surprised by her astute understanding of contemporary issues, accused her of meddling in the president's decisions. In fact she seems to have exercised little political influence over her husband, but her extraordinary behavior was enough in and of itself to draw criticism.

The First Lady got off to a bad start in the summer of 1861 by appearing at public receptions when she was visibly pregnant, something that very few politicians' wives did in the nineteenth century. She could also be blunt-spoken, according to a man who met her in Richmond in 1862. He described her as "very smart, . . . quite independent, says what she pleases and cuts at people generally." Furthermore, Varina Davis had an acute sense of the ridiculous, which got her into trouble. At a dinner party she attended, a general's wife remarked that the underdrawers for an entire Confederate regiment had mistakenly been made with two right legs. She burst out laughing, much to the horror of the other guests.

As the war ground on, Varina Davis continued to depart from the traditional female role. As early as 1862, she envisioned a hard life after the war and told her husband she would take a paying job outside the home if necessary. She also began selling off her personal possessions—clothing, china, and books—to build up cash reserves. Her personal life was further marred by the tragic death of her young son Joseph, who died in a freak accident in 1864 when he broke his neck in a fall. As she told one of her friends, she was relieved when the Confederacy collapsed and the war ended in 1865.

Yet the postwar era was also filled with challenges for Varina Davis. Her husband served two years in federal prison, and after he was released in 1867 he was never able to support his family. Continually at the edge of destitution, the Davises never again owned a home. Varina Davis gradually took over the management of their household affairs as her husband's health declined. After he died in 1889, she moved to Manhattan, where she lived for the rest of her life. Still fending off poverty, she nonetheless created an interesting life, writing for newspapers and magazines. Many of her publications focused on the war, and they often reflected her conviction that secession had been a terrible mistake. It certainly cast a long shadow over her life, even though she had never wanted to be the Confederate First Lady.

— JOAN E. CASHIN

DECLARATION OF IMMEDIATE CAUSES

The Declaration of the Immediate Causes of Secession was adopted by the South Carolina secession convention to explain the reasons for the state's withdrawal from the Union. The declaration was drafted by a special committee of the convention, chaired by Christopher G. Memminger, a longtime South Carolina congressman and future Confederate secretary of the treasury.

The declaration represented the views of the more moderate members of the convention. Another document, the Address to the People of South Carolina, drafted by a committee chaired by Robert Barnwell Rhett, Sr., reflected the philosophy of the radical faction in the convention.

The declaration stated that South Carolina and other states had asserted their rights of freedom and sovereignty in the Declaration of Independence, the peace treaty signed with Great Britain in September 1783, and the Federal Constitution ratified in 1788. The declaration noted that in recent years the Northern states had refused to fulfill their constitutional obligations to the Southern states, especially in regard to fugitive slaves. The election of a president whose opinions and purposes were hostile to the Southern institution of slavery left South Carolina no recourse but to dissolve the union existing between the states and to resume its position as a separate and independent state.

The declaration was debated by the convention on December 24, 1860. An effort by Maxcy Gregg, a member of the radical faction, to table was defeated by a 124 to 31 vote, and the convention, after some minor amendments, passed the declaration.

— RALPH A. WOOSTER

DEMOCRATIC PARTY

The American party system that emerged in the 1830s took deep root in the South as it did elsewhere in the country. The system was a highly mobilized, deeply divided one, in which Democrats and Whigs regularly confronted each other in intense election and legislative battles. In the Southern states, both parties competed effectively on a regionwide basis (with the exception of South Carolina, where the two-party system never developed). In the 1830s and 1840s the Democrats enjoyed their greatest Southern support in Mississippi, Alabama, Texas, Arkansas, and Florida, but they were closely competitive in the rest of the region as well.

In addition to their electoral strength, Southerners such as James K. Polk, John C. Breckinridge, Howell Cobb, John Slidell, Jefferson Davis, and the editor Thomas Ritchie, also played significant roles in the national party, shaping its outlook, articulating its perspective, managing its activities, and advancing its policies. Between 1836 and 1860, Southerners appeared on every Democratic presidential ticket.

The party's commitment to limited government included nonintervention with slavery where it existed and resistance to demands, when they arose, that slavery be abolished or its extension limited. Although Southerners were a minority within the party as a whole, their interests, when different from those of other Democrats, were safeguarded by such procedural devices as the need of a candidate to garner two-thirds of a national convention's votes before a nomination for president could be made.

When the crisis over the expansion of slavery into the new territories began in the mid-1840s, the Democrats repeatedly demonstrated their commitment to letting the South pursue its own practices in peace and to sustaining its claim to equal treatment in the new territories. Democrats defended Southern rights and values within the Union even at the ultimate cost of Northern votes. And as the party became identified with appeasing Southerners in the matter of slavery extension, some Northerners reacted violently enough to contribute to a fundamental electoral realignment that severely weakened the party as a national force.

Many Northern Democrats resisted Senator Stephen A. Douglas's successful attempt in 1854, at Southern insistence, to repeal the Missouri Compromise prohibition of slavery in the Federal territories above the line of 36° 30′ north latitude. Three years later the Democratic administration of President James Buchanan, again at Southern insistence, demanded that Congress accept Kansas's proslavery Lecompton Constitution. Douglas believed the Lecompton Constitution to be fraudulently ratified and a corrup-

"This momentous question, like a fire bell in the night, awakened and filled me with terror. I considered it at once as the knell of the union."

THOMAS JEFFERSON

With the effective repeal of the Missouri Compromise the national party system collapsed, all the slavery issues came once more to the fore, and secession quickly followed.

PAGE 373

tion of the notion of popular sovereignty, and he refused to accept any further moves by the party to guarantee slavery in the territories. A bitter and devastating internal party fight followed, and a significant number of Northern Democrats left their party in disagreement and disgust.

As a result, while keeping its national status and role, in the 1850s the center of gravity of the Democratic Party shifted South. This meant that, in addition to traditional Democratic policy preferences on economic development and issues of the role and power of government, the Democratic attitude toward slavery expansion became more favorable to Southern interests and more aggressive in its support for them. The Republican party built itself as a major political force by stressing how far the Democrats had become a tool of Southern interests.

There continued to be ideological congruence on a range of traditional Democratic policies among the factions. But they could not resolve their differences over how far to guarantee the right of slaveholders to take their property into new territories under Federal protection. In 1860, the fatal split led to two different Democratic candidates contesting for the surviving Democratic vote: Douglas, the national candidate, and Breckinridge, the candidate of the Southern wing. This catastrophic national breach was the prelude to the secession crisis in which Southern Democrats divided between strong Southern rights men who led the secession movement, on the one hand, and, on the other, various factions of administration supporters and more pro-Union types, including some who still followed Douglas despite his hostility toward the notion of a territorial slave code.

After secession and the establishment of the Confederacy, Democrats played important political roles in the new nation. The Confederacy's top leadership—Jefferson Davis and such cabinet members as Robert M. T. Hunter and Judah P. Benjamin, among many others—were all prominent prewar Democrats who continued to dominate the policies and politics of their homeland. The Democratic commitment to limited government remained a hallmark of their policies as well. Although wartime exigencies inevitably led to the centralization of power in the Confederacy, its very strong state rights tradition more than echoed prewar Democratic advocacy in a way that Whiggery did not.

Political divisions within the Confederacy were persistent and bitter in constitutional conventions and state legislatures, in Congress, and ultimately in the electoral arena. Although formal partisanship and party organization were discouraged and never officially existed, partisan memories and differences, under other names and in fragmented fashion, often affected policies, attitudes, and behavior in the Confederate States. And there was a Whig-dominated revulsion against the Democratic leaders of the Southern nation expressed in state and congressional elections in the upper South in 1862 and 1863. But all of this remained localized and unsustained in the absence of formal national institutions of electoral and policy mobilization and management: caucuses, partisan newspapers, national committees, and regular conventions.

In the North during the Civil War, the Democratic party remained strong and vigorous, although it was now the minority party there, owing to the loss of its Southern wing. Generally, most Northern Democrats supported the war against secession, but though hostile to the Confederacy, they provided continuous and sturdy opposition to the Lincoln administration, challenging what they believed to be Republican lust for revolutionary changes in American society, including the end of slavery. At the same time, an important peace wing in the party fought strenuously to end the war and allow the South to do as it wished. They were strong enough to include a peace plank in their national platform in 1864. Confederate leaders hoped for Democratic victory in the nation, but their hopes were in vain. Although the racism and tenacious, crabbed conservatism of many Democrats attracted hundreds of thousands of votes in the North, their search for peace without victory and their willingness to appease the South allowed the Republicans to brand all Democrats as Southern sympathizers, even traitors to the Union in time of peril. One Republican newspaper, the *New York Evening Post,* blasted them, not untypically, as the party of "Dixie, Davis and the devil."

This war-induced Southern coloration of the Democratic party remained a potent issue in national politics for more than a generation after Appomattox. "Waving the Bloody Shirt" of Unionism against Democrats was standard Republican practice into the 1890s. Although a "solid South" favorable to the Democrats also ultimately was a product of the Civil War and its aftermath, the pro-Southern tone of the party over the course of America's most dramatic and defining episode as a nation severely handicapped Democratic efforts to regain control of national politics until well into the twentieth century.

[*See also* Bleeding Kansas; Copperheads; Election of 1860; Fugitive Slave Law; *and selected biographies of figures mentioned herein.*]

— JOEL H. SILBEY

DIPLOMACY

From the outset of the Civil War, Confederate leaders sought to exercise the prerogatives of nationhood by securing European recognition and, through direct negotiations, to tap whatever foreign interests might exist in the perpetuation of an independent Southern republic. As early as March 1861 President Jefferson Davis, with the approval of the Confederate Congress, appointed William Lowndes Yancey, Pierre A. Rost, and A. Dudley Mann as commissioners to Great Britain, France, Russia, and Belgium, empowering them with the authority to establish diplomatic relations with those countries. Their instructions, prepared by Secretary of State Robert Toombs, emphasized the need to confirm the South's legitimacy as an independent nation—its long and careful deliberations that had led to separation, its constitutional government, its strength and determination to defend its political integrity. The Confederacy's free trade and liberal navigation policies, Toombs added, would ensure accessible and profitable markets for the manufactures of Europe. Toombs instructed the commissioners to propose treaties of friendship, commerce, and navigation with the nations of Europe when they received official recognition.

EARLY OPTIMISM FOR RECOGNITION. Confederate leaders had reason to anticipate the triumph of their diplomacy. Britain's powerful conservative classes, long cynical toward the democratic experiment in America, saw clearly that the Civil War placed democratic institutions on trial. The United States itself had passed beyond the control of the Old World, but if the American people were determined to demonstrate the failure of their political institutions, reactionary Europe could encourage them in their effort so that the work of destruction might triumph. In July 1861 *Blackwood's Magazine* declared: "It is precisely because we do *not* share the admiration of America for her institutions and political tendencies that we do not now see in the impending change an event altogether to be deplored." Even much of Britain's liberal sentiment turned instinctively against the North. Sympathetic to the idea of self-determination, it questioned Washington's right to employ force in repressing the will of a minority that preferred independence. Many British liberals, moreover, were attracted to the South's free trade principles. Edouard de Stoeckl, the Russian chargé d'affaires in Washington, observed that British leaders anticipated the elimination of an Atlantic rival. "The Cabinet in London," he reported, "is watching attentively the internal dissensions of the Union and awaits the result with an impatience which it has difficulty in disguising."

During April 1861 the Confederate objective of securing Europe's recognition seemed propitious. If many in Britain favored the breakup of the American Republic for moral, political, and economic reasons, French emperor Napoleon III understood that his dream of a colonial empire in Mexico would face far less challenge from an independent Confederacy than from a reconstructed Union. Shortly after the Fort Sumter crisis in April, Henri Mercier, the French minister in Washington, proposed to British minister Lord Lyons that they seek authority to recognize the Confederacy at the appropriate moment. The United States had recognized other countries without regard to their revolutionary origins. Lyons agreed in principle but believed that their governments should carry the responsibility for determining the time and mode of the decision, especially since recognition would damage British relations with the government in Washington. For Stoeckl the rupture between North and South was irrevocable; strict impartiality between the warring sections would serve no European interest. "The recognition of the Southern Confederacy by France and England," he wrote on April 14, "will offer us a very natural excuse to follow their example in recognizing a *fait accompli.*"

Conscious of Confederate weakness on the high seas as well as the North's immense shipping trade, President Davis, on April 17, issued a proclamation offering letters of marque and reprisal for privateers to prey on Northern commerce. Two days later President Abraham Lincoln, determined to deprive the Confederacy of all foreign imports, announced a blockade of the entire Southern coast. Lincoln, with the overwhelming support of the North, recognized but one objective: the reforging of the Union. Secession was unacceptable. Unless the North retreated from its demand for Southern capitulation, Confederate vice president Alexander H. Stephens responded, "no power on earth can arrest or prevent a most bloody conflict." Pursuing uncompromisable goals, the North and South after the firing on Fort Sumter faced total war. Lincoln's secretary of state, William H. Seward, reaffirmed the North's determination when, on April 23, he informed the governor of Maryland that the United States, under no circumstances, would permit the issues between North and South to be settled by foreign arbitrament. Any Anglo-French effort at mediation, he warned Mercier and Lyons, would constitute unwarranted intervention calling for total resistance.

Seward had warned Lyons earlier that, if war came, Britain would need to forgo the importation of Southern cotton for a time. The British minister observed that his country required Southern cotton and would obtain it one way or another. With news of the war, however, Queen Victoria, on May 13, issued a proclamation of neutrality, recognizing the South as a belligerent. France, Spain, the Netherlands, Brazil, and other maritime states followed the British lead. The Lincoln administration, joined by congressional lead-

In late 1862 L.Q.C. Lamar was appointed a special commissioner to seek Russian recognition of the Confederacy.

PAGE 318

Toombs wrote out the instructions for the Confederacy's unofficial foreign ministers before they left to try to secure recognition from Europe.

PAGE 612

ers, resented deeply the European recognition of Southern belligerency. Seward responded by informing the British and French governments that the conflict between North and South was not a war but a local insurrection of no legitimate concern to foreign powers. Seward instructed U.S. diplomats abroad to prevent any European recognition of the Confederate States of America. Lincoln added that Confederate privateering was piracy and all engaged in it would be treated as pirates.

Mann reached London on April 15; Yancey and Rost two weeks later. On May 3 they gained an informal interview with British foreign minister Lord John Russell. The commissioners argued the legitimacy of the Confederacy's existence, its determination to survive under its Constitution, and its intention to cultivate peaceful and mutually profitable relations with other countries. Such evidences of nationhood, they said, merited recognition. Russell declared that the matter rested with the cabinet; meanwhile he would not comment. Rost moved on to Paris, where Count de Morny, a confidant of Emperor Louis Napoleon, informed him that France and England had agreed to pursue identical policies toward the Confederate States, but that recognition was merely a matter of time. Britain and France, he said, understood their interests in Southern independence. In mid-July the commissioners reported that British opinion was undergoing an encouraging change, more and more convinced that the North could not subdue the South.

Washington discovered during April that the Confederate government had dispatched commissioners to the European capitals. Seward warned the French government that the United States would regard any communication between it and the Southern agents as injurious to American dignity and honor. When he learned that Lord Russell in London had received the commissioners informally, he prepared a letter, his famed Number 10 of May 21, so menacing that Lincoln modified some passages and eliminated others. Even in revised form the dispatch was little less than an ultimatum, suggesting that the United States would break diplomatic relations if Russell persisted in seeing the Southern envoys. Charles Francis Adams, the new U.S. minister, arrived in Britain on May 13, the day of the queen's proclamation. A few days later, in an interview with Russell, he condemned the British decision. Then on June 10 Adams received Seward's dispatch of May 21. He now informed Russell that any further relations between the British government and the Confederate commissioners, whether official or not, would constitute a manifestation of hostility toward the United States. Russell assured Adams

that conversation was not recognition, and that he had no intention of seeing the Confederates again. Throughout the summer of 1861 Seward condemned the British and French governments for behaving as if the United States were at war. The country, he argued, faced a domestic disturbance that it would dispose of in its own way.

THE FAILURE OF KING COTTON. What gave the South its presumption of success in its quest for European recognition was the alleged power of cotton. Toombs reminded the commissioners in March that the annual yield of British manufacturing based on Southern cotton totaled $600 million. "The British Ministry," he observed, "will comprehend fully the condition to which the British realm would be reduced if the supply of our staple should suddenly fail or even be considerably diminished." *De Bow's Review* predicted that the blockade would be "swept away by the English fleet of observation hovering on the Southern coasts to protect . . . the free flow of cotton to English and French factories." If cotton was king, the South had only to embargo that commodity to force Britain to destroy the blockade. The Confederate Congress refused to establish a formal embargo, but Committees of Public Safety in the Southern seaports effectively halted the export of cotton to Europe. Having burned much of the 1861 cotton crop, the South had little to sell. The Confederacy gambled that the shortage of cotton would destroy British adherence to the blockade. The added realization that the blockade, maintained largely by lightly armed merchant vessels, was ineffective reinforced this conviction. The Treaty of Paris (1856) had declared not only that a neutral flag covered enemy goods, except contraband, but also that a blockade, to be legally binding, must also be effective. Still the British government, ignoring the blockade's weakness as well as its doubtful legality, treated it with great circumspection. The dearth of cotton for shipment not only failed to eliminate the blockade but also created resentment and the unwanted impression that the blockade was effective. The huge surplus of raw cotton in British and French warehouses merely compounded the evidence of King Cotton's weakness.

In September President Davis, with congressional support, assigned separate commissioners to the principal governments of Europe. He appointed Mann to Brussels, James M. Mason to London, and John Slidell to Paris. The new secretary of state, Robert M. T. Hunter of Virginia, instructed Mason to explain to the British government the true position of the Confederate States as an independent, permanent, and constitutional nation. The North, Hunter added, had rejected peaceful separation and then subjected the South to a barbarous, uncivilized war. In taking up

DIPLOMATS SEIZED

James M. Mason, left, and John Slidell, the Confederate commissioners to London and Paris, respectively, were seized by U.S. forces en route to Europe.

HARPER'S PICTORIAL HISTORY OF THE GREAT REBELLION

arms the Confederate States appealed to the world, not for aid and alliances, "but for the moral might which they would derive from holding a recognized place as a free and independent people." Six months of fighting, including the Confederate victory at Manassas in July, had demonstrated the South's capacity and determination to maintain its independence. If recognition must finally come, it appeared the duty of nations to place their moral weight immediately on the side of peace.

THE *TRENT* AFFAIR AND THE U.S. BLOCKADE. Mason and Slidell, with secretaries George Eustis and James Macfarland, left Charleston on October 12, ran the Union blockade, and made their way to Havana. There, on November 7, they embarked on *Trent,* a British mail steamer bound for England. On the following day Capt. Charles Wilkes of USS *San Jacinto* removed them and their secretaries from the British vessel, permitting *Trent* to continue on its voyage. Wilkes took the Confederates to Fortress Monroe and then to Boston. Confederate officials and writers took hope from the realization that Wilkes had defied international law and insulted the British flag. Hunter assumed that the British, in protecting the right of asylum, would avenge the insolence. Britain, declared the Confederate press, would suffer an unmitigated insult or go to war. "If the insult goes unresented," the *Southern Literary Messenger* advised, "another too flagrant to be borne will inevitably follow."

From London the Confederate commissioners reported a wave of anger and resentment. They reminded Russell on November 27 that the Federal action was a violation of international law, not justified under any treaty between Britain and the United States. If Confederate citizens merited the protection of the British flag, the cabinet had no choice but to demand the restoration of Mason and Slidell to their former positions. In his response of December 7 Russell declined to enter into any discussion of the

Trent case, but the British government had already demanded the instant restitution of the captured Confederate leaders; unless the North yielded, Rost observed, war was certain. Seward recognized the justice of the British case, as well as the warlike mood of the British people, and brought the controversy to a deliberate end. With the release of Mason and Slidell, Yancey predicted, the British government would maintain a "frigid neutrality" toward the Confederacy. As the year ended, the Confederate commissioners could only lament the apparent control that Seward and Adams exerted over European policy.

Mason, Slidell, and their secretaries reached London on January 29, 1862. Slidell and Eustis departed for Paris the following morning. Mason found himself surrounded by Confederate sympathizers, but the ministry, he reported, remained reticent on the questions of the blockade and recognition. In late January the British Foreign Office submitted to Europe's governments the Union practice of clogging harbors by sinking ships loaded with stones; all agreed that the damage to Charleston Harbor was an outrage. The British government complained to Washington but in no way challenged the legitimacy of the Federal blockade. On February 7 Mason requested and received an interview with Lord Russell; it resolved nothing. Mason concluded that the British cabinet would act on the blockade if pressed by the House of Commons, but the debates of early March convinced him that Parliament would never force any change in British policy. Indeed, on February 11 Russell informed Lyons that as long as the Federal government maintained ships in sufficient numbers, not to prevent access to any harbor, but merely to render entering or leaving dangerous, Britain would regard the blockade as effectual under international law.

Slidell, on February 5, asked French minister Antoine Édouard Thouvenel for an interview. Thou-

*The sectional crisis
that led to the
Civil War in 1860
fueled British fears
that the U.S. might
resolve its internal
problems through
some form of
international
adventure.*

PAGE 250

venel informed Rost that the French government would welcome a discussion of the blockade but was not prepared to entertain the question of recognition. If the Federal blockade was so ineffective, Thouvenel asked Slidell, why did so little cotton reach neutral ports? French merchants had asked Slidell that same troubling question. Slidell explained that the blockade runners were generally small vessels; for them turpentine provided greater profit than an equal volume of cotton. Slidell acknowledged that the blockade, despite its ineffectiveness, still managed to eliminate large neutral vessels whose owners preferred to avoid risks. In reporting his interview Slidell advised Hunter that "two or three steamers arriving at Havre with cotton on French account, after having run the blockade, would go further to convince people here of its inefficiency than all the certified lists from our customhouses." Slidell added that France was sympathetic to the Confederate cause and would challenge the blockade if Britain, with its greater interests, would take the initiative. Unfortunately, Slidell observed in March, British policy was not promising. Russell's definition of a blockade, he complained to French officials, merely resuscitated the discarded notion of paper blockades.

CONFEDERATE PUBLIC RELATIONS EFFORTS AND PRO-SOUTHERN SYMPATHIES. Confederate leverage in seeking European recognition required not only the power to compel attention but also popular sympathy for the Southern cause. In large measure the Confederate commissioners carried the burden of informing Europe's political and business leaders of the validity, strength, and promise of the Southern independence movement. But in November 1861 Hunter dispatched Henry Hotze, a young and able journalist, to direct the Confederacy's educational program in Europe. In London Hotze detected not only the North's near monopoly of the news but also the strange capacity of its agents to antagonize through exaggerated claims to power. Hotze quickly gained access to the *London Post* and by April 1862 was writing editorials for the *Standard* and the *London Herald,* a leading opposition paper. In May he established his own journal, the *Index.* Determined to influence British leaders, Hotze avoided giving offense. His fair and accurate reporting of battles and commercial opportunities won respect and a wide British following.

Meanwhile President Davis sent Edwin de Leon to France as a Confederate agent. De Leon failed from the outset. Slidell denied him the support required to gain access to French leaders of importance. With de Leon's dismissal in late 1863, Hotze took up the Confederacy's educational program in France. His fairness again gave him access to important news agencies. He won widespread support among French officials, merchants, shipbuilders, and others who favored the

Confederacy, but he could not undermine French liberal attachment to the United States. However pervasive Europe's pro-Confederate sympathies, they had no bearing on the decisions of the European governments.

For many Europeans Northern industrial and financial advantages had at first created doubts that the South could sustain even a defensive war. But the rout of the Union forces at Manassas in July 1861 dispelled the illusion of a certain and easy Northern victory. The Southern commissioners reported that the Confederate triumph produced a powerful sensation in Europe. Benjamin Moran, assistant secretary in the U.S. legation in London, lamented: "This defeat will have a bad effect for the North in Europe, & will raise the hopes of the rebels." On August 14 the commissioners reminded Lord Russell that Britain had recognized countries that had demonstrated far less capacity to maintain their independence than had the Confederacy at Manassas. Russell offered no response.

Yet so lacking in energy and purpose was the Northern war effort that foreign observers now questioned the capacity of the Union to reconquer the South. Not even the Federal capture of Fort Henry, Fort Donelson, and New Orleans between February and April 1862 convinced the British of Northern superiority. "All the successes of the North," Lord Russell observed in April, "do not persuade me they can conquer the South." The Federal capture of New Orleans challenged the illusion of Confederate power, but Gen. George B. McClellan's retreat from Richmond in early July confirmed the widespread conviction among European observers that the Union was doomed. "It is plain," declared the *Times* (London), "that the time is approaching when Europe will have to think seriously of its relations to the two belligerents in the American war." In Parliament William S. Lindsay advocated British mediation to end the apparently interminable and pointless struggle. Lindsay withdrew the motion when Prime Minister Lord Palmerston warned Parliament that mediation meant war.

Mason noted in June that the gradual exhaustion of the cotton supply was driving British sentiment toward the Confederacy. He described the impact on Lancashire:

> *The cotton* famine *(as it is now every where termed), prevailing and increasing in the manufacturing districts, is attracting the most serious attention. Parochial relief . . . is found utterly inadequate to prevent* actual starvation *of men, women, and children, who, from such causes, are found dead in their houses. Private contributions . . . do not and cannot remove the sufferers from the starvation point; and very soon they must be left to die, unless aid is afforded from the treasury.*

Clearly British policies that deprived the mills of Southern cotton were becoming matters of public concern, especially as the Lancashire mills in 1862 began to deplete the stores of raw cotton in British warehouses. By July Britain's stock of 1.2 million bales had declined to 200,000; by September only 100,000 remained, with the mills consuming 30,000 bales a week. This proved to be the climax of the cotton famine, although unemployment and destitution among the mill workers continued. During 1863 both the cotton supply and employment began to recover, partially from successful blockade running in the South and partially from increased imports of raw cotton from India, China, Brazil, and Egypt. In France the cotton famine and recovery corresponded to that of Great Britain.

By July 1862 the high cost of British neutrality and the Confederate successes in the field had convinced Mason and Slidell that the time had come to demand formal recognition as a matter of right. But under strong advice from friends in Parliament, they agreed to await a more opportune occasion. Responding to the news of Confederate successes in Virginia, Slidell, on July 20, gained an interview at Vichy with the French emperor, who stressed his troubles in Mexico and fear of a collision with the United States. Slidell then argued the Confederate case for immediate recognition in a long letter to Thouvenel. The Confederate States, he wrote, now stood before the world as an established nation meriting immediate recognition. During their conversation on July 23, Thouvenel advised Slidell to withhold his demand. "In a few weeks," said the French minister, "when we shall have further news from the seat of war, we can better judge the expediency of so grave a step, and the English Government may perhaps then be prepared to cooperate with us, which they certainly are not now." When Slidell urged mediation and assured Thouvenel that the South would welcome it, Thouvenel responded that both Mercier and Lyons insisted that an offer of mediation would create exasperation in the North and achieve nothing. In London, on July 24, Russell explained British reluctance to offer mediation by observing that neither the North nor the South would compromise its objectives. Mason responded that all Europe understood the finality of the separation; Britain's refusal to grant recognition merely prolonged a ruinous and hopeless war. Russell observed that the ultimate outcome of the American war remained uncertain. When the South had finally resisted all efforts to conquer it, other countries might justly recognize its independence. That time had not yet arrived.

In September Mason and Slidell assured Judah P. Benjamin, Confederate secretary of state since March, that the British and French governments were reconsid-ering their previous decisions to avoid any involvement in American affairs. In mid-September the earl of Shaftesbury, returning from a vacation in the south of France, visited Slidell in Paris to inform him that Britain was fast approaching a decision to intervene. The British ministry, encouraged by the South's victory in the Second Battle of Manassas in late August, had taken up the question of mediation. Palmerston, responding to Second Manassas, penned a note to Russell on September 14: "The Federals . . . got a very complete smashing. . . . Even Washington and Baltimore may fall into the hands of the Confederates. If this should happen, would it not be time for us to consider whether in such a state of things England and France might not address the contending parties and recommend an arrangement upon the basis of separation?"

THE CONFEDERACY'S OPPORTUNITY PASSES. On September 14 and 15 Gen. Robert E. Lee moved his forces into Maryland. When the news of Lee's costly battle at Sharpsburg and the Confederate retreat across the Potomac reached Europe in late September, Slidell predicted that the Northern success in checking the Southern advance would serve as another pretext for British procrastination. Indeed, on October 2 Palmerston reminded Russell that mediation based on separation would benefit the South; the North, therefore, would resist such interference until additional Southern victories compelled it to capitulate. Ignoring Palmerston's caution, William E. Gladstone, chancellor of the exchequer, declared at Newcastle on October 7: "Jefferson Davis and other leaders have made an army, and are making, it appears, a navy, and they have made what is more than either, they have made a nation." Supported by Gladstone, Russell in mid-October prepared a memorandum arguing for mediation; the cabinet, including Palmerston, rejected it.

In Paris Slidell, on October 26, informed the new French minister, Edouard Drouyn de Lhuys, that the British cabinet, except for Gladstone, stood firm against mediation. If the French government favored the Confederacy, as the emperor insisted it did, the time had come for France to act alone. Two days later the emperor called Slidell to St. Cloud and again expressed his sympathy for the South. To act without Britain, however, would render France vulnerable to British policy and expose it to Washington's wrath. He informed Slidell, however, that on October 15 the king of Belgium had advocated a joint French-British-Russian proposal for a six-month armistice with a lifting of the Federal blockade. Slidell doubted that Britain and Russia would accept mediation; nor was he convinced that the emperor would act. Yet on November 8 Mason reported that Britain and Russia had received such a proposal. On that day the Russian government

Relations between Great Britain and the U.S. had frequently been strained prior to the Civil War.

PAGE 626

The gravity of the Trent affair was evident in the creation of a War Committee in the British cabinet.

PAGE 627

informed the British Foreign Office that it had rejected the emperor's strategy. On November 12 the British cabinet, convinced that the North would reject mediation, reached the same decision. With good reason Richmond's dismay over the failure of mediation was profound; never again would the European powers consider such a direct involvement in the American war.

In January 1863 Mason, responding to Benjamin's repeated instructions, pressed Lord Russell on the issue of the blockade. Mason protested the British refusal to explain why, in its modification of the doctrine of blockade, it denied the Confederacy the historic rights of belligerency. Russell repeated what he had written to Lord Lyons in February 1862, that the Declaration of Paris did not demand that a port be blockaded so that no vessel could gain access, whatever its size or the prevailing conditions. Storms and winds, he argued, could not render a blockade nonbinding on neutrals. Mason responded in February that nowhere did the Declaration of Paris refer to winds or storms or the nature and size of vessels engaged in blockade running. One vessel, wrote Mason, had evaded the blockade at Charleston thirty times. Russell terminated the exchange on February 27 by asserting that he had explained the British position and did not care to discuss it further. In Paris Slidell took hope from assurances that French sentiment continued to favor the South. The emperor, he wrote in January, would pursue mediation again, either alone or with the concurrence of Britain and Russia. As the weeks passed, Mann in mid-March expressed his growing disillusionment:

> *So far as I can judge . . . the chances for an early European recognition of our independence, have not increased in the slightest degree. . . . The Emperor of the French seems to be just as far as ever from taking the initiative in this regard.*

No longer did Confederate successes in the field—the victory at Fredericksburg in December or even that at Chancellorsville in May—seem to matter.

NAVAL PURCHASES ABROAD. Even as the British government rejected Southern appeals for recognition or any direct intervention in the American war, it enabled the Confederacy to achieve remarkable successes on the high seas. As early as May 1861 Confederate Secretary of the Navy Stephen R. Mallory instructed James D. Bulloch of Georgia to buy or order six vessels in England to prey on Northern commerce. At the same time the Confederate Congress appropriated funds for the purchase of two ironclads and dispatched James H. North to procure them in France under the assumption that the French government favored the destruction of the blockade. Bulloch, finding no cruisers available, contracted for the construction of two vessels. North discovered that France was not prepared to sell ironclads. Eventually, in May 1862, he arranged for the construction of a giant ironclad by the Thompson works of Glasgow. In July Bulloch contracted with the Laird Brothers of Birkenhead for two rams.

As early as February 1862 the U.S. consul in Liverpool, Thomas H. Dudley, reported to Adams that Liverpool shipbuilders were constructing a Confederate cruiser, *Oreto.* Lord Russell insisted that an Italian company had ordered the ship. *Oreto* cleared for Palermo but sailed to the Bahamas where, armed and equipped, it became the Confederate commerce raider *Florida.* During April Adams learned that another Confederate cruiser, *No. 290,* was under construction in Liverpool. Too late Russell ordered the vessel stopped. It departed suddenly in July, acquired armament in the Azores, and became the famed Confederate raider *Alabama.*

Despite Adams's continued warnings that one day the United States would demand compensation for the damage wrought by British-made Confederate commerce raiders, the British permitted additional vessels to escape during the early months of 1863. But in September Adams threatened the British government with war if it permitted the Laird rams, then in the water, to escape. In seizing them the British government terminated the Confederate acquisition of British-made vessels. Cruisers already in the Atlantic continued their devastating assaults on Northern commerce. Later Russell, in conversation with Adams, condemned the South for making Britain the base of its maritime operations.

FINAL DIPLOMATIC EFFORTS. As late as June 1863 Slidell continued to press the French government for recognition, arguing that the capacity of the Confederate States to maintain their independence was beyond question. He informed the emperor that the British cabinet denied recognition not because it doubted the South's eventual success but because it desired the breakup of the Union and was confident of a Confederate victory. France could stop the prolonged conflict by recognizing the Confederacy. The emperor responded that any proposal for recognition submitted to the London government to stop the war would reach Washington and expose an isolated France to U.S. retribution. At risk was not only French commerce but also the entire French effort in Mexico. France could not afford to move without Britain. Again, during the parliamentary debates of July, Palmerston, supported in his judgment by the Union victories at Vicksburg and Gettysburg, refused to budge. Concluding that Britain would never recognize Mason, Benjamin on August 4 instructed him to conclude his mission and, with his secretary, withdraw from London.

Mason received Benjamin's letter on September 21 and informed Russell of his impending departure. Russell, in a brief note, observed that he had explained the British refusal to recognize him on previous occasions. "These reasons," he concluded, "are still in force, and it is not necessary to repeat them." Having lost faith in Britain, Benjamin turned to France for support in breaking the blockade; the French government, still refusing to act unilaterally, rejected responsibility for Europe's acceptance of the blockade as well as any intention of courting trouble by challenging it.

Throughout 1864 Confederate leaders hoped that their assertions of ultimate victory would still bring the needed European support. By summer the Confederacy's fate in the courts of Europe hinged on the success or failure of Gen. Ulysses S. Grant's assault on Richmond. Mason, now in London under a broad commission to serve the Confederacy wherever he might be effective, reported optimistically in June that a Southern victory in Virginia would still compel the British ministry to act. In Paris Slidell complained that the French emperor was too concerned with his problems elsewhere but still agreed with Mason that a decisive Confederate victory at Richmond would lead to Anglo-French intervention.

To reassure Europe of the South's determination to win, the Confederate Congress, on June 14, issued a manifesto to the governments of Europe, which declared that the South, in its quest for immunity against external interference, committed its cause to "the enlightened judgment of the world." In his final appeal to Europe on December 27, 1864, Benjamin wondered why Britain and France, despite the South's continued resistance, had refused to recognize its independence. Concluding at last that the explanation lay in slavery, he dispatched Duncan F. Kenner, a member of Congress from Louisiana, on a secret mission to convey to Mason and Slidell his offer of emancipation in exchange for recognition. In Paris the emperor informed Slidell that such an offer would not have influenced his decision. Mason returned to London where, on March 14, 1865, Palmerston presented an identical response. Britain's earl of Donoughmore observed that two years earlier the offer might have mattered; in March 1865 Grant's campaign had eliminated the issue.

Lee's surrender terminated the Confederacy's diplomatic effort in Europe. Richmond's perennial pursuit of European recognition and trade was a major element in the entire Confederate war effort. Europe's recognition of Southern independence would have created diplomatic havoc in Washington. European defiance of the Federal blockade would have opened the South to the massive imports the Confederate war effort required. That Washington escaped such potentially costly external challenges was a measure of Seward's success in convincing the European governments that, whatever their interests in Southern independence, they could not intervene diplomatically without risking war. Europe's disinclination to fight the United States bound any European support of the Confederacy to the conviction that the South could triumph on its own. That conviction was never realized.

[*See also* Blockade, *overview article*; Great Britain; Laird Shipyards; State Department; Trent Affair; *and selected biographies of figures mentioned herein.*]

— NORMAN A. GRAEBNER

DIRECT TAX ACT

At the time the Confederacy was established in February 1861, there had been no direct taxation of real estate or personal property in the United States since the War of 1812. Instead, the chief fiscal tool of the Federal government had been import duties. With a view to getting rid of the protective tariffs, some Southerners had proposed the abolition of the customs houses and the imposition of direct taxation. But fearful of any system in which the taxpayers knew how much they were paying, Congress retained the customs dues.

The Provisional Constitution of the Confederacy provided either that direct taxes could be apportioned among the states, each state to pay a fixed amount based on the last census (the old Federal system), or that the Confederacy, in the absence of a census, could levy a tax based on a fixed percentage of the assessed value of all property. Because the Confederacy never took a census of its own and refused to use the Federal census of 1860, and because the Permanent Constitution had no alternative provision for levying and collecting such a tax, the power of levying direct taxes expired to all practical purposes with the end of the provisional government on February 18, 1862.

In the congressional session on May 8, 1861, Secretary of the Treasury Christopher G. Memminger sought authorization to impose a direct tax on the Southern people. But lacking a letter of support from President Jefferson Davis for this radical measure, Congress tabled Memminger's request and asked him to furnish a report on direct taxes at its next session in July 1861.

In preparing this report, the secretary discovered that each state used a system unique to itself, so that Congress would have to devise its own program. He

On the tax side of the state budget, Georgia favored its less wealthy citizens.

PAGE 604

*The Supreme
Court's 1857* Dred
Scott *decision
overturned
precedents to rule
that Congress had
no power to
prohibit slavery in
the territories.*

PAGE III

The Dred Scott
*decision made
slavery legal not
only in Kansas but
in every other
territory as well.*

PAGE III

therefore proposed that $25 million be raised through a tax of fifty-four cents on each hundred dollars of assessed property. To be taxed were real estate, slaves, and personal property such as stocks, bonds, cattle, and merchandise.

Resistance to the war tax authorized by the act of August 19, 1861, was noisy and prolonged. Unable to attack this proposal on legal grounds, opponents claimed that a tax equal to only 2.5 percent of the South's Gross National Product would provoke armed resistance and the collapse of the Confederacy. The plain fact was that both within and outside Congress most owners of large slaveholdings expected to have their $3.5 billion stake in slavery protected without their having to make any sort of contribution for that purpose. They also assumed that the war would be short and Southern independence secured at little or no cost to themselves. Secretary Memminger inadvertently assisted such delusions by failing to make clear the direct connection between inadequate taxation and defeat. Gazeway B. Lamar, a Georgia banker, presciently observed that the Southern people must be prepared to pay heavy taxes. Otherwise, they might as well surrender immediately and hand over their slaves for emancipation by the Federal authorities.

Yet the law as finally enacted was riddled with exemptions that reduced tax yields by a third. Moreover, lacking prior experience in such measures, Congress made numerous drafting errors. Collection and assessment times were put off to too distant a day. No provisions were made for paying the assessors and collectors, for reimbursing them for their expenses, or for securing the cooperation of sheriffs, who held the state tax records. Moreover, in the interest of economy, too few personnel were provided for, so that the effectiveness of the tax depended upon the integrity of the taxpayer.

As finally passed, the act called for the appointment of a chief collector in each state and a collector in each county assisted by at least two assessors. Each citizen was to furnish a list of taxable property by a specified date. The necessity of collecting the tax directly from the public might be avoided if a state assumed the tax. In that case, the state would receive a 10 percent rebate on the amount it paid. Payment had to be in specie or Confederate Treasury notes only.

As a fiscal measure, this tax was not a success. There were long delays getting suitable persons to fill the various posts. The state governments issued their own currency in exchange for Confederate notes, thereby frustrating the whole purpose of the tax, which was to reduce inflation by retiring some of the excess Treasury notes. Assessments and checking the veracity of property declarations were hindered by states' giving encouragement to their sheriffs not to cooperate with

the Confederate assessors. Moreover, because there was no centralized guidance from Richmond, appraisals varied widely from state to state. This was particularly true of slaves, whose average declared prices were much too low.

Texas and Mississippi, in the hope of evading payment entirely, refused to assume the tax, and the Treasury had to collect directly from the citizens. Only South Carolina took the Confederate records and collected the tax from its own citizens. Without doubt, however, the greatest deficiencies of the act were its failure to impose the tax each year for the duration of the war and its failure to demand a larger revenue of at least $40 million to $80 million a year.

— DOUGLAS B. BALL

DRED SCOTT DECISION

As the slave of army surgeon John Emerson, Dred Scott had lived on a military base in Illinois and at Fort Snelling, in the Wisconsin Territory, which was made free by the Missouri Compromise. In 1850 a St. Louis court, following Missouri precedents dating from 1824, found Scott had become free while living outside Missouri, a slave state, and once free, he remained free despite his return to Missouri. In 1852 the Missouri Supreme Court, articulating the proslavery ideology and hostility to the North that would eventually lead to secession, rejected its own long-standing precedents:

> *Times are not as they were when the former decisions on this subject were made. Since then not only individuals but States have been possessed of a dark and fell spirit in relation to slavery, whose gratification is sought in the pursuit of measures, whose inevitable consequence must be the overthrow and destruction of our government. Under such circumstances it does not behoove the State of Missouri to show the least countenance to any measure which might gratify this spirit.*

In 1854 Scott began a new suit in the U.S. District Court against John F. A. Sanford, a New Yorker who had recently become the executor of Emerson's estate after Emerson's widow, and initial executor, had remarried. Scott argued he was a citizen of Missouri and sued Sanford in federal court because there was a diversity of citizenship between the two parties. Sanford answered that blacks, whether free or in bondage, could *never* sue as U.S. citizens in a federal court. Judge Robert W. Wells ruled that *if* Scott was free, then he was a citizen of Missouri for purposes of federal diversity jurisdiction. After a trial, however, Judge Wells ruled that Scott was still a slave. Scott then

appealed to the U.S. Supreme Court. At issue was more than the status of Scott and his family: the Missouri Supreme Court's decision challenged Congress's authority to prohibit slavery in any federal territory. The central political issue of the 1850s was now before the Supreme Court.

The end of the Mexican-American War had left the nation in possession of vast amounts of land (known as the Mexican Cession), including the present-day states of New Mexico, Arizona, California, Utah, and Nevada. Much of this land was below the Missouri Compromise line and thus theoretically open to slavery. With the acquisition of this territory and the rise of proslavery thought and Southern nationalism, Southerners were no longer content to be shut out of the western territories. The Kansas-Nebraska Act (1854), which partially repealed the Missouri Compromise by allowing slavery in the territory immediately to the west of Missouri under a concept of popular sovereignty, led to a mini-civil war in Kansas and the formation of the Republican party in the North. In the 1856 presidential election this two-year-old party, pledged to stop the spread of slavery into the territories, carried all but five Northern states.

The avidly proslavery Chief Justice Roger B. Taney of Maryland used *Dred Scott v. Sandford* [sic] (1857) to decide these pressing political issues in favor of the South. Taney's two most controversial points were (1) that the Missouri Compromise was unconstitution-

al because Congress could not legislate for any federal territories acquired after 1787 and because freeing slaves in the territories constituted a taking of property without due process, in violation of the Fifth Amendment; and (2) that blacks, even those in the North with full state citizenship, could never be U.S. citizens. Taney asked: "Can a negro, whose ancestors were imported into this country, and sold as slaves, become a member of the political community formed and brought into existence by the Constitution of the United States, and as such become entitled to all the rights, privileges, and immunities guaranteed by that instrument to the citizens?" Rigorously applying a jurisprudence of original intent, Taney answered with a resounding no. In an analysis that was historically incorrect and shocking to the North, Taney asserted that when the Constitution was adopted blacks were universally considered "beings of an inferior order, and altogether unfit to associate with the white race, either in social or political relations; and so far inferior, that they had no rights which the white man was bound to respect; and that the negro might justly and lawfully be reduced to slavery for his benefit."

In dissent Justice Benjamin Robbins Curtis of Massachusetts noted that in 1787 free blacks were citizens of five states and thus they were also citizens of the United States when the Constitution was adopted. Curtis also argued that under a "reasonable interpretation of the language of the Constitution," Congress had the power to regulate slavery in the federal territories. This dissent heartened Northerners like Horace Greeley, who wrote that Taney's decision was an "atrocious," "wicked," "abominable," "false," "detestable hypocrisy" built on "shallow sophistries." The *Chicago Tribune* expressed the reaction of many Northerners: "We scarcely know how to express our detestation of its inhuman dicta, or to fathom the wicked consequences which may flow from it."

But not all Northerners opposed the decision. Northern Democrats hoped the decision would destroy the Republican party by essentially declaring its "Free-Soil" platform to be unconstitutional and once and for all end the national debate over slavery in the territories. In the words of the New York *Journal of Commerce*, the decision was an "authoritative and final settlement of grievous sectional issues."

The decision also undermined Northern Democrats, however, whose strength had been grounded in the party's appeal to popular sovereignty. Under popular sovereignty settlers would decide for themselves if they wanted slavery in a territory. This system appealed to American concepts of democratic rule and Northern negrophobia. Northern Democrats hoped popular sovereignty would keep both slaves and blacks out of the territories. At the same time, however, popular sovereignty allowed Northern Democrats to appease their Southern colleagues who opposed restrictions on slavery in the territories.

Just as Taney's decision undermined Republican Free-Soil politics, so it undermined Democratic popular sovereignty. Under *Dred Scott* the settlers of a territory, like the Congress, were precluded from restricting slavery. This made popular sovereignty meaningless and took away from Northern Democrats their most potent weapon. Stephen A. Douglas, the most prominent proponent of popular sovereignty, told his Illinois constituents that settlers could still keep slavery out of most of the territories by not passing laws that would protect slave property. This led Southern Democrats to demand a federal slave code for the territories and helped set the stage for the split within the Democratic party in 1860.

Taney doubtless thought his powerful fifty-four-page decision would finally open all the territories to slavery while undermining the Republican party. "Taney's opinion," historian Don Fehrenbacher has written, "proves to be a work of unmitigated partisanship, polemical in spirit though judicial in its language, and more like an ultimatum than a formula for sectional accommodation. Peace on Taney's terms resembled . . . a demand for unconditional surrender." The decision was, as historian Harry Jaffa has written, "nothing less than a summons to the Republicans to disband."

But instead of disbanding, Republicans successfully made Taney and the decision the focus of their 1858 and 1860 campaigns. In his "house divided" speech (1858) Abraham Lincoln argued that Taney's opinion was part of a proslavery conspiracy to nationalize slavery and a prelude to future proslavery jurisprudence. He warned of "another Supreme Court decision, declaring that the Constitution of the United States does not permit a *state* to exclude slavery from its limits." He told the voters in Illinois, and by extension the entire North, that "we shall *lie down* pleasantly dreaming that the people of Missouri are on the verge of making their state *free;* and we shall *awake* to the *reality*, instead, that the Supreme Court has made *Illinois* a *slave* state."

Such arguments, combined with such other issues of the day, led a majority of Northerners to vote Republican in 1860; that in turn led to secession and the creation of the Confederacy.

[*See also* Bleeding Kansas; Compromise of 1850; Democratic Party; Fugitive Slave Law; Kansas-Nebraska Act; Missouri Compromise; Republican Party; Sumner, Caning of; Wilmot Proviso.]

— PAUL FINKELMAN

DREWRY'S BLUFF, VIRGINIA

Also called Fort Darling, the fortified position atop Drewry's Bluff overlooking the James River played a vital role in defending the water approaches to Richmond, about seven miles away.

As the Union Army of the Potomac under Maj. Gen. George B. McClellan prepared to blast the Confederates out of their defenses at Yorktown in May 1862, Gen. Joseph E. Johnston determined to evacuate the Yorktown line and retreat farther up the Virginia Peninsula toward Richmond. In doing so, however, he compelled the evacuation of Norfolk. To prevent the capture of the Confederate ironclad *Virginia*, its crew destroyed the ship, leaving the James River open to ascent by the Union navy.

The Federals naturally determined to take advantage of *Virginia*'s absence, and in mid-May the Union ironclads *Monitor* and *Galena* escorted three wooden warships upriver. The best place to challenge this small fleet of Union vessels was at Drewry's Bluff. The high ground would afford Confederate artillery a clear field of fire and be difficult to hit from the river below. The narrowness of the river at that point and the installation of sunken vessels as obstructions would further hinder the Federals. Gen. Robert E. Lee sent a brigade of infantry to support the position, while the crew from *Virginia* arrived to serve the heavy guns in the works.

Although the Confederates carried out their improvements in haste, the natural advantages of the position soon became apparent. When the Federal fleet arrived on May 15, 1862, neither of the ironclads could elevate its guns sufficiently to return the Confederate fire. Furthermore, the obstructions prevented them from attempting to run past the fort. As the Southern crews watched from above, all the while pouring fire into the vessels below, *Monitor* and *Galena* maneuvered futilely. As the fighting continued, *Galena* began to suffer damage from the Confederates' heavy shells. After four hours of battle, the Union ships moved off. *Galena* sustained more damage and casualties than any of the other vessel, but limped to safety. Still, the Confederates at Drewry's Bluff had thwarted the Federal attack.

On May 16, 1864, Drewry's Bluff again became the scene of fighting. A Union landing at Bermuda Hundred earlier in the month threatened to leave the Confederate capital and the city of Petersburg below it vulnerable to attack. Union Maj. Gen. Benjamin F. Butler, commanding the 39,000-man Army of the James, failed to press his advantage, however. He lost precious time as he cautiously moved along the peninsula of land between the James and Appomattox rivers. The Confederates had time enough to concentrate their forces and stop Butler's advance, whereupon the Union commander retreated to Bermuda Hundred.

Butler's position was too strong to be attacked directly, but Gen. P. G. T. Beauregard was willing to pit his 20,000 men against them in the open. Hoping to bring Butler out of his defenses, Beauregard sent Maj. Gen. Robert Frederick Hoke to Drewry's Bluff. This was enough to convince the Federals to leave their lines.

On May 12, Butler advanced almost half of his force toward Drewry's Bluff, leaving behind enough infantry to hold his defenses. On the next day, the Federals attacked the Confederate works with some success, but once again, rather than following up his initial success, Butler vacillated. He formed a defensive line with Maj. Gens. Quincy A. Gillmore and William F. Smith on the left and right, respectively.

In the meantime, Beauregard reached Drewry's Bluff and received welcome reinforcements. He hoped to launch an attack of his own, now that he had succeeded in luring Butler away from his defenses. Early on the morning of May 16, Confederates under Maj. Gen. Robert Ransom, Jr., slammed into the Union right flank. The Southerners enjoyed great initial success, but as the fighting progressed in the early morning fog, the attack became disjointed.

The assault soon spread along the broad front of the opposing forces, but the poor visibility continued to disrupt the attacking columns. The Federals managed to launch a counterattack that stymied any further Confederate inroads. By midmorning, the fighting had begun to slacken, and despite a half-hearted attempt by the Southerners to strike at Butler as he retreated to his defenses, the battle was over. The fighting had cost the Federals almost twice as many men as the Confederates—4,160 to 2,506—and had ended Butler's threat to Richmond and Petersburg. By the end of the next day, May 17, Beauregard had put the "cork" in the "bottle" and sealed Butler into his lines at Bermuda Hundred, where he could do no further harm.

— BRIAN S. WILLS

DUKE, BASIL WILSON

Duke, Basil Wilson (1838–1916), brigadier general and historian. Duke was born May 28, 1838, in Scott County, Kentucky. After he earned a law degree at Transylvania University, he opened a law practice in St. Louis, Missouri. In June 1861, he married Henrietta Hunt Morgan, sister of John Hunt Morgan.

Active in the Missouri secessionist movement, Duke was sentenced to death in absentia by a secessionist vigilance committee. He was elected a first lieutenant in Morgan's Lexington Rifles, a part of the Second Kentucky Cavalry; after promotion to colonel, Duke commanded the regiment. He was wounded at Shiloh but recovered to participate in Morgan's great Ohio raid in 1863, where he was captured along with the rest of Morgan's command. A prisoner of war for a year before being exchanged, he returned to Confederate service, was promoted to brigadier general in September 1864, and commanded a cavalry brigade that served in Kentucky and Virginia until Appomattox. With Robert E. Lee's surrender, Duke was ordered to provide Jefferson Davis's escort as he fled Richmond. He was captured during a decoy mission to lead Federal troops away from Davis.

After the war, Duke resumed his law practice in Louisville and was elected to the Kentucky House of Representatives in 1869. He wrote, among other works, *A History of Morgan's Cavalry* (1867) and *The Reminiscences of General Basil W. Duke, C.S.A.* (1911), and edited *Mid-Continent* and *Southern* magazines. Duke died on September 16, 1916.

— PAUL F. LAMBERT

Some historians have speculated that Davis and Johnston had long been personal enemies or that their wives had engaged in a dispute of some sort.

PAGE 303

EARLY, JUBAL

Early, Jubal (1816–1894), lieutenant general. Early was one of the Confederacy's most able corps commanders and an architect of the cult of the Lost Cause. "Old Jube" fought in most of the major campaigns of the Army of Northern Virginia and held an independent command in the Shenandoah Valley late in the war. Although he should be considered just behind Thomas J. ("Stonewall") Jackson and James Longstreet in ability, Early's reputation suffered because of losses to Union Maj. Gen. Philip Sheridan in 1864 and because of a cantankerous personality that won from Robert E. Lee the fond epithet of "my bad old man" but also created friction with fellow officers.

Jubal Anderson Early was born on November 3, 1816, in Rocky Mount, Franklin County, Virginia, the third of ten children. His father was a prominent farmer, his mother from a family with large slaveholdings. Young Jubal entered the U.S. Military Academy at West Point in 1833, performing better in academics than in discipline and graduating eighteenth of fifty in the class of 1837, which included Joseph Hooker, John C. Pemberton, and John Sedgwick. Commissioned second lieutenant July 1, 1837, Early as part of Company E, Third Artillery, participated in the Seminole War in Florida (1837–1838) and then went to Tennessee to assist with Indian removal. Before learning of his promotion to first lieutenant, to date from July 7, 1838, Early had begun the process of resigning from the army, effective July 31, 1838.

Returning to Rocky Mount, Early studied law and set up practice in 1840. He became active in the Whig party, representing Franklin County for a term in the Virginia General Assembly. In 1843, Early was appointed the commonwealth's attorney for Franklin, a post he held until 1852. In between came service in the Mexican War. As major of the First Virginia Regiment, he performed garrison duty in northern Mexico under Zachary Taylor, seeing no combat but contracting the rheumatism that afflicted him throughout his life. He was honorably discharged on August 3, 1848.

When the secession crisis came, Early won a seat as a delegate to the Virginia secession convention, which convened in Richmond on February 13, 1861. Franklin County voters selected Early, a staunch Unionist, pre-

sumably because of the county's tobacco ties with markets in the North. Early's cautious approach earned him the nickname "the Terrapin from Franklin." Even after the climactic events at Fort Sumter and the Federal call for troops to put down the rebellion, Early voted on April 17 with the fifty-five delegates hoping to remain in the Union. When the ordinance passed, he barely hesitated before offering to help with the military defenses of Virginia, claiming that the U.S. Constitution still prevailed but that "that does not prevent our State authorities from repelling invasion." After the war, Early wrote that any doubts about secession "were soon dispelled by the unconstitutional measures of the authorities at Washington and the frenzied clamor of the people of the North for war upon their former brethren of the South."

For the next four years, the man called "Old Jube" or "Old Jubilee" by his troops would assert his forceful character on the battlefield. Named colonel on May 16, 1861, he led the brigade at First Manassas that turned the tide of battle late in the day on the Confederate left. For these efforts he was promoted to brigadier general, to date from July 21. At the Battle of Williamsburg on May 5, 1862, he was severely wounded in the shoulder but recuperated in time to rejoin the

"OLD JUBE"

Ranked with Jackson and Longstreet in ability, lieutenant general Jubal Early of Virginia was one of the Confederacy's most able corps commanders.

LIBRARY OF CONGRESS

At Fredericksburg, Jubal Early and D. H. Hill brought their divisions to reinforce Jackson's corps.

PAGE 230

army at Malvern Hill on July 1. Commanding a brigade under Richard Ewell in Jackson's wing of the army, Early fought at Cedar Mountain, Second Manassas, and Harpers Ferry. Old Jube's performance at Sharpsburg garnered the praise of Lee and Jackson for repelling withering Federal assaults on the Confederate left near the Dunkard Church. At the Battle of Fredericksburg on December 13, Early's men again sealed a breach during a crucial moment in the Union attack on the Confederate right.

By the end of 1862, Early had also proved himself to be one of the true characters in the army. He had a knack for challenging superiors without repercussion. While marching to Fredericksburg in late November, Jackson questioned why he saw so many stragglers in the rear of Early's column. Early cracked that Jackson witnessed the straggling "probably because he rode in the rear of my Division." The severe Jackson reportedly only smiled at the blunt reply. Early also was one of the few people who could swear in front of Lee, who overlooked such indiscretions because of Early's talents for command. Others, however, did not so readily forgive his acerbic nature. Brig. Gen. G. Moxley Sorrel wrote that Early's "irritable disposition and biting tongue made him anything but popular," and Confederate soldier Henry Kyd Douglas found him "arbitrary, cynical," and "personally disagreeable." Both, however, offered high praise for his abilities. Early himself knew the impression he had on others but did not care.

In appearance, Early was considered striking with dark piercing eyes and a gray patriarchal beard broken at times by a smile like that of a possum. He rode into battle wearing a slouch hat topped by a black ostrich plume. Rheumatism bent his six-foot frame, making him appear shorter and older than he was. He punctuated a piping, nasal voice (which one person likened to an old woman's) with streams of tobacco juice and stinging oaths that impressed many with their originality. Arriving at Lynchburg, Virginia, in 1864, he raised himself in the saddle to yell to Federal cavalry: "No buttermilk rangers after you now, you God-damned Blue-Butts!"

Promotion to major general did not come until January 17, 1863. At that time he was also confirmed as permanent commander of Ewell's former division. As Lee and Jackson outmaneuvered Union Maj. Gen. Joseph Hooker at Chancellorsville (May 1–3), Early guarded Marye's Heights above Fredericksburg against Maj. Gen. John Sedgwick. The Union forces proved too much for Old Jube's smaller command, but the Confederates on May 4 regrouped with Lee's army to push Sedgwick back over the Rappahannock.

In June 1863, Lee steered his army northward to conduct a raid that culminated at Gettysburg. With

the death of Jackson at Chancellorsville, Ewell had ascended to command of the Second Corps, which included Early's division. To them fell the task of clearing the Union Eighth Corps under Maj. Gen. Robert H. Milroy from Winchester, Virginia. On June 14, Early's men successfully stormed a Federal fort northwest of town in what became the Second Battle of Winchester. Early's men continued through the Cumberland Valley into Pennsylvania, brushing aside the minimal resistance from emergency militia and traveling to the Susquehanna River at Wrightsville until receiving the call from Lee to concentrate toward Gettysburg. The march fortuitously placed Early's men on the enemy's right flank in the late afternoon of July 1, just in time to help shatter the Eleventh Corps under Maj. Gen. O. O. Howard and chase it through town toward Cemetery Hill.

What happened next became one of the great "what ifs" of the Civil War. Lee ordered Ewell to take Culp's Hill, if practicable. Early and Ewell both believed their men too disorganized to seize the moment. After the war, Early and Longstreet waged a bitter war of words over this and other actions at Gettysburg in some of the most celebrated articles written about the conflict. Each blamed the other for contributing to Confederate defeat. Some historians believe Ewell (and secondarily Early) acted appropriately based on information of the time. Nonetheless, Early overstated Longstreet's culpability in an attempt to absolve Lee from criticism.

Early continued to show promise for higher command, although his progress was not unblemished. He took part in a disaster at the Rappahannock Bridge on November 7, 1863, but performed better in the Mine Run campaign at the end of November, leading the Second Corps when Ewell fell ill. In December, he was sent to western Virginia to disrupt rail lines of the Baltimore and Ohio and canvass the countryside for supplies. At the Wilderness on May 5 and 6, 1864, Early refused to launch a flank attack on the Federal right because he believed an enemy force would prevent the maneuver (despite testimony to the contrary from John B. Gordon). Although Lee needed to prod Early to make the successful attack, he valued his lieutenant enough to give him the Third Corps at Spotsylvania when A. P. Hill fell ill. Early returned briefly to divisional command before taking over the Second Corps when Lee removed Ewell.

The new lieutenant general, with promotion to date from May 31, 1864, shortly received exciting orders. Union forces under Maj. Gen. David A. Hunter were advancing up the Shenandoah Valley with the ultimate destination of Lynchburg. If the railroad link in that town were severed, and the Valley controlled by the Federals, then a vital granary and invasion route would be lost. On June 12, Lee ordered a twofold mission:

EARLY'S WASHINGTON RAID

"The Road to Washington Lay Open"

With about 14,000 men, Lt. Gen. Jubal Early in July 1864 raided Maryland, defeated a small force at Monocacy Junction, threatened to enter Washington, and forced the Union to divert the better portion of two corps that would have been pitted against the Army of Northern Virginia. Early lost about 700 and the Federals 1,300 of their roughly 7,000 men during the major action of the campaign at the Monocacy River on July 9.

Early conducted the raid as the second half of a two-part plan by Gen. Robert E. Lee first to clear the Shenandoah Valley of Union soldiers and then to threaten Washington and Baltimore to compel Ulysses S. Grant to siphon troops from Petersburg. Recently promoted to command the Second Corps of the Army of Northern Virginia, "Old Jube" started for Lynchburg on June 13 to prevent Union Maj. Gen. David A. Hunter from seizing the town and severing a vital east-west rail link. Although Hunter commanded 18,000 men against Early's 12,000, the Union general apparently lost his nerve and retreated to the west on June 19.

Early seized the chance Hunter's departure presented; by July 5, the vanguard of the newly christened Army of the Valley had begun crossing the Potomac at Shepherdstown. Complicating Early's advance was a vaguely defined scheme to free Confederate prisoners of war at Point Lookout, below Baltimore. Early sent cavalry toward Baltimore to cut rail lines and be in position to aid the escaped Confederates—something that never occurred because Federals learned of the escape plan.

Union Maj. Gen. Lew Wallace, meanwhile, had used his own initiative to establish a force at Monocacy Junction, several miles south of Frederick, where he could protect roads leading to Baltimore and Washington as well as a rail line of the Baltimore and Ohio. To bolster his force of reserves, Wallace received last-minute reinforcement from seasoned veterans of James B. Rickett's division of the Sixth Corps. Wallace stationed most of his men where they could guard two bridges—a wooden structure for the Georgetown Road and an iron one for the Baltimore and Ohio rail line a half mile to the north. He also sent a portion of his troops two miles farther to the north to protect the Baltimore Pike from Robert Rodes's Confederate division.

After testing the Union positions with artillery and a demonstration that Wallace repulsed, Early concluded that he would have to ford the Monocacy to flank the Union position. John McCausland's cavalry fortuitously provided the way when the men crossed the river roughly a mile below the bridge and ran into the Union left. Early decided that Dodson Ramseur's division would hold the center while John B. Gordon's division followed the cavalry's path to attack the Federal left. Gordon advanced with three brigades, attacking en echelon from the right under brigadiers Clement A. Evans, Zebulon York, and William Terry. After emerging from woods seven hundred yards from the Union soldiers, Gordon's men needed to mount three charges across a field choked with shocks of wheat and broken by a stream to force the Federals from three positions along wooden fences, a stone fence, and finally the cuts along the Georgetown Road. General Evans went down with a serious wound early in the attacks. By 4:30 P.M. the work was done; Wallace's men retreated toward Baltimore, and the road to Washington lay open to Early's men.

Shortly after noon on July 11, Early scanned the outer defenses of Washington while the remainder of his army finished an arduous march in extreme heat along dust-choked roads. Early correctly judged his men to be too fatigued to attack works manned by 100-day men, invalids, and heavy artillery. The delay, however, proved fateful. During the night, the remainder of the Sixth Corps under Maj. Gen. Horatio G. Wright filed into the defenses. They would soon be bolstered by the Nineteenth Corps under William H. Emory. Wallace's defense at the Monocacy had delayed Early's men just enough to allow reinforcements to arrive.

Early spent July 12 skirmishing with Union soldiers but decided to withdraw rather than risk an attack that would have proved far too costly, even if successful. The Confederates recrossed the Potomac at White's Ford on July 13 and 14, having raided the North successfully and having forced Grant to part with troops that could have helped in the campaign against Lee.

— WILLIAM ALAN BLAIR

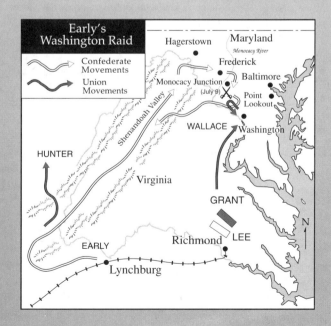

clear Hunter and his army out of the Valley and then head north to threaten Baltimore and Washington in the hope that Ulysses S. Grant would divert troops from the Richmond-Petersburg theater. With his small Army of the Valley, numbering from 8,000 to never more than 14,500, Early from June to November marched more than 1,600 miles while fighting 75 battles and skirmishes. His men chased Hunter from the valley in mid-June, raided Maryland, collected levies of $220,000 from Hagerstown and Frederick, defeated a scratch force under Lew Wallace at Monocacy Junction on July 9, and threatened to enter Washington, on July 11. Many criticized Early for failing to take the city, but the fight at the Monocacy River had delayed the advance, allowing two divisions of the Union's Sixth Corps to file into the defenses and limit the chances of success. Early's campaign nevertheless had caught Grant by surprise and forced the diversion of the Sixth and Nineteenth Corps that would have faced the Army of Northern Virginia.

Grant now ordered Philip Sheridan to assemble an Army of the Shenandoah to deny Lee the Valley's resources. In three battles—Third Winchester on September 19, Fisher's Hill on September 22, and Cedar Creek on October 19—Sheridan defeated the Confederates. At Cedar Creek, however, Early had conducted a surprise flank attack that routed two corps and forced another to withdraw until Sheridan delivered a decisive counterattack later that day.

Many Southerners blamed Early for the loss of the Valley, although it is doubtful anyone else could have prevented it. He made errors in the placement of his troops but overall conducted an excellent campaign that rivaled Jackson's performance of 1862. The fall defeats, however, removed the area from the Confederates and contributed to a turn in Northern morale that ensured President Abraham Lincoln's reelection in November.

After a defeat of his thousand-man force on March 2, 1865, at Waynesboro, Early finally was removed by Lee, who still had faith in his lieutenant but recognized his "bad old man" had lost the confidence of soldiers and authorities. Artillerist E. Porter Alexander after the war wrote that Early had "proved himself a remarkable corps commander," adding that his "greatest quality perhaps was the fearlessness with which he fought against all odds & discouragements."

After Lee's surrender, Early fled first to Texas and then to Mexico, finally arriving in Canada in July 1866, where he wrote his memoirs. He returned to the United States in 1869, after President Andrew Johnson pardoned former Confederates, and settled in Lynchburg to practice law. In 1877 he became a commissioner of the Louisiana State Lottery, which allowed him to pursue his lecture tours and writing for various

Confederate military studies. The former Unionist became an unreconstructed rebel who wore only gray and never apologized for his actions, including the burning of Chambersburg, Pennsylvania, on July 30, 1864, which he ordered as retribution for Union destruction in the Shenandoah Valley.

As an officer in both the Association of the Army of Northern Virginia and the Southern Historical Society, Early had an enormous influence on the writing of Civil War history. He helped fashion the cult of the Lost Cause, elevating Lee to saintlike status and arguing that the agrarian South never lost a battle but only succumbed to overwhelming numbers churned out by a greedy, industrial North. As long as Old Jube lived, wrote historian Robert Stiles, "no man ever took up his pen to write a line about the great conflict without the fear of Jubal Early before his eyes."

Early maintained his cantankerous ways until 1894. On February 16, he took a fall from which he never recovered and finally died on March 2. He was buried in Spring Hill Cemetery in Lynchburg.

— WILLIAM ALAN BLAIR

ELECTION OF 1860

The election of 1860 led to the secession of some of the states that formed the Confederate States of America, but to this day historians are not sure why. The platform of the victorious Republican party dropped its 1856 denunciation of slavery as a "relic of barbarism" comparable to polygamy and instead pledged the "maintenance inviolate of . . . the right of each state to order and control its own domestic institutions." Though the platform opposed slavery's expansion into the territories and the reopening of the African slave trade, many knowledgeable Southerners doubted the West would sustain slave agriculture, and many opposed the slave trade agitation. The Republican candidate, Abraham Lincoln, carried a consistent antislavery record, but he was so little known outside Illinois and so widely regarded as a nonentity sure to be controlled by others that he, personally, could hardly have weighed as a factor. Honoring regnant political custom, he did not campaign or offer any remarks for publication from his nomination on May 18 to his election on November 6.

The Constitutional Union party, embracing conservative Whig remnants, on May 9 had nominated John Bell of Tennessee with no platform. The Democratic party had convened their national nominating convention in Charleston, South Carolina, in April, but no candidate was nominated until June. Southern delegates wanted a platform pledging Congress and the executive to protect slave property in the territories. The minority platform, drafted by Democrats who supported the nomination of Stephen A. Douglas of Illinois, left it to the Supreme Court to decide what power Congress or territorial legislatures held over slave property in the territories. After the minority platform was adopted by the full convention, the Alabama delegation led those of Mississippi, Louisiana, South Carolina, Florida, Texas, Georgia, and some delegates from Delaware and Arkansas out of the convention.

The Democrats reconvened in Baltimore on June 18. When they refused to let bolting Southern delegates back in, the Virginia, North Carolina, and Tennessee delegations withdrew along with parts of the Maryland, Kentucky, Missouri, Arkansas, California, and Oregon delegations. Douglas gained the nomination. On the next day the (mostly) Southern Democrats nominated John C. Breckinridge of Kentucky on a platform that demanded federal protection of slave property in the territories until statehood. It also urged the acquisition of Cuba and the building of a Pacific railroad while condemning the acts of state legislatures that frustrated execution of the Fugitive Slave Act.

The party contest for popular votes that ensued, though lively, did little to inform or educate voters. The political campaign of that summer was bewildering. Despite the critical issues looming in the sectional party split, the Republicans, drawing on their old Whig heritage, somehow set the tone by running a copy of the old Harrison log-cabin-and-hard-cider campaign of the 1840s. The Republicans ran what has been called a "hurrah" campaign, characterized more by spectacle and vociferous cheering for their candidate than by emphasis on or explanation of the planks in their platform. They slighted issues and scoffed at threats of disunion. The other parties scurried to match the Republicans' marching clubs and torchlight parades.

Essentially, the contest boiled down to a Breckinridge-Bell struggle in the South and a Lincoln-Douglas struggle in the North. Voters learned little about the candidates from the other section of the country except what the candidates from their own section wanted them to hear. Perceptions of Lincoln and Douglas in the South were terrifyingly distorted. Breckinridge's image in the North was equally skewed. Breckinridge made one speech in the campaign, breaking with tradition, but Douglas shattered tradition altogether, campaigning throughout the North in the summer and venturing into the upper South late in the summer. After news from the states that held their gubernatorial elections in October showed that Lincoln would win Pennsylvania and Indiana and with them the presidential election, Douglas plunged into the Deep South in the autumn. Most historians have written admiringly of his attempts to save the Union in this campaign by warning the South against secession in the event of Lincoln's election.

PRESIDENTIAL ELECTION OF 1860				
	Republican	Democrat	Southern Democrat	Constitutional Union
Alabama	0	13,651	48,831	27,875
Arkansas	0	5,227	28,732	20,094
Delaware	3,815	1,023	7,337	3,864
Florida	0	367	8,543	5,437
Georgia	0	11,590	51,889	42,886
Kentucky	1,364	25,651	53,143	66,058
Louisiana	0	7,625	22,681	20,204
Maryland	2,294	5,996	42,282	41,760
Mississippi	0	3,283	40,797	25,040
Missouri	17,028	58,801	31,317	58,372
North Carolina	0	2,701	48,539	44,990
South Carolina	Did not hold a popular vote for presidential electors.			
Tennessee	0	11,350	54,709	69,274
Texas	0	Fused with Bell.	47,548	15,438
Virginia	1,929	16,290	74,323	74,681

Like all elections up to that time in American history, the election of 1860 was a collection of state elections, and party strategies varied from state to state. Some Southern radicals hoped for Republican victory in order to bring about secession all the faster. Naturally, in the upper South, an area likely to become the bloody doormat over which armies marched in the event of disunion and civil war, the Breckinridge forces stressed their Unionism (and downplayed its conditional quality). In the Deep South they especially urged Southern unity—perhaps to extract concessions from the Republicans, perhaps to start the process of secession and independence. Motives varied greatly and are difficult for historians to assess. Most Breckinridge leaders seem to have doubted they could win. Few put much faith in achieving victory ultimately by throwing the election into the House of Representatives. And both Bell and Breckinridge forces depicted themselves as the best guarantors of slavery's survival; the former maintained that the best chances lay *within* the Union.

Despite the fatalism of many Southern politicians about the outcome on November 6, voting totals rose in every Southern state—in some by great margins. Estimates of voter turnout are not available for the South, but it appears to have been good there and may have been as high as 82 percent in the North.

Breckinridge carried all the future states of the Confederacy except Virginia (which included the Unionist area that would secede to form West Virginia in three years) and Tennessee, both of which went to Bell. Most historians have been quick to point out, however, that Breckinridge's opposition, if united, carried 55 percent of the Southern vote.

Secessionist Democrats emerged from the election with unity sufficient to take the Deep South out of the Union. Republican victory thus prompted secession in several states, but only the threat of military coercion after the firing on Fort Sumter provoked the secession of some of the states that formed the Confederacy.

[*See also* Constitutional Union Party; Democratic Party; Lincoln, Abraham, *article on* Image of Lincoln in the Confederacy; Republican Party.]

— MARK E. NEELY, JR.

ELECTION OF 1863

This election, coming on the heels of serious Confederate military reverses in the summer of 1863, changed the nature of Confederate politics. On July 4 Gen. Robert E. Lee withdrew from Gettysburg after defeat there. On the same day Gen. John C. Pemberton surrendered his army and the city of Vicksburg to Gen. Ulysses S. Grant. In June, Gen.

Braxton Bragg had been maneuvered out of his base at Tullahoma, Tennessee, and withdrew his army to Chattanooga, which he soon abandoned.

Although the Confederate armies bounced back to win some victories, notably at Chickamauga in September 1863, the morale of the home front deteriorated under the impact of the military setbacks, combined with inflation, conscription, impressment, and long casualty lists. Pathetic letters from home to soldiers at the front painted graphic pictures of starvation, fears of slave unrest, and marauding bands of deserters from both armies. Many soldiers, responding to these letters, returned home and were among the voters in 1863. In some locations, discontent was channeled into action by various peace societies, some of which even ran candidates.

Almost 40 percent of the 137 members of the Second Congress were new to that body, for many incumbents who had been secessionists in 1860 and 1861 were turned out of office. Among the new congressmen, over two-thirds had opposed secession in 1861. The results had party implications: in 1861 Democrats had tended to be secessionists, and former Whigs, Unionists; three-fifths of the new congressmen in 1863 had once been Whigs. These men had gone with the Confederacy once the decision for secession was made; but their initial hesitation seemed to recommend them to the voters in the crisis of 1863. Moreover, some of the new members composed a "peace party," bringing a fresh ideological stance into Congress. Some desired a restoration of the Union; others believed that peace with independence could still be won at the conference table if President Jefferson Davis were not too stubborn to negotiate.

This political change was not confined to Congress. Former Whigs (mostly former Unionists) increased their strength in almost every Confederate state legislature, and some were elected governors. In Alabama the voters picked a former Whig in the gubernatorial election for the first time in the state's history—even though the Whig party itself was long dead.

The Second Congress, meeting in its initial session on May 2, 1864, presented a striking contrast to the First Congress. Almost two-thirds of the members of the first House had been Democratic or secessionist; in the second House the balance was about even. Not counting areas where normal elections could not be held because of the presence of Federal troops, the voters elected former Unionists to replace secessionists in fifteen districts and returned incumbent former Unionists in another sixteen. Most of these thirty-one seats in the second House represented districts in the Appalachians and the adjacent Piedmont.

Much of the change was due to peace sentiment. Jehu A. Orr of Mississippi told the electorate during

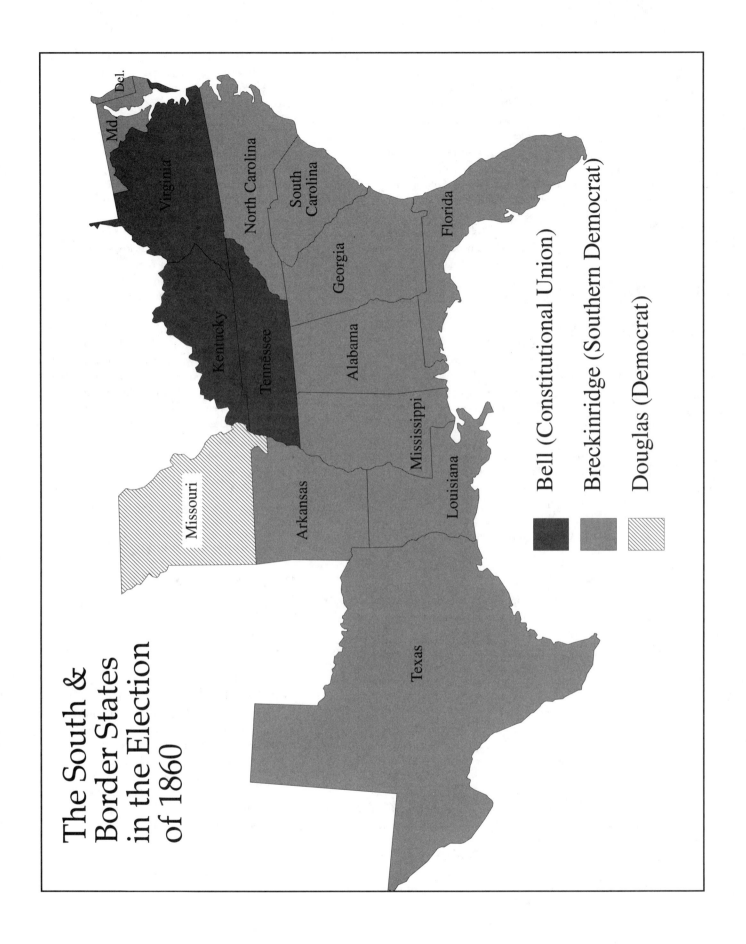

The South &
Border States
in the Election
of 1860

Del.

Md

Virginia

North Carolina

South Carolina

Florida

Georgia

Kentucky

Tennessee

Alabama

Mississippi

Missouri

Arkansas

Louisiana

Texas

Bell (Constitutional Union)

Breckinridge (Southern Democrat)

Douglas (Democrat)

his campaign that he would do his best to achieve an honorable peace and that he believed secession had been a great mistake. The contraction of Confederate-controlled territory also resulted in legislative turnover. Many of the reelected secessionists came from "phantom constituencies," districts that were controlled by the Union army. For such areas, notably Kentucky, Missouri, and much of Tennessee, ballots could be cast only by soldiers and refugee civilians. Had normal elections been held throughout the Confederacy, the result would probably have been a resounding defeat for those who had originally favored secession.

The North Carolina contingent in the Second Congress included eight newcomers, some of them apparently elected through the influence of peace societies. The Tarheel delegation was now composed of ten former Union Whigs and only two former secession Democrats (one a holdover senator and the other an incumbent who reclaimed his seat by a mere ten-vote margin). Some Confederates were so alarmed by Tarheel behavior that they feared a second revolution, and in fact much of the change in voting behavior in the Second Congress was due to bloc voting by the North Carolina delegation. James Madison Leach of North Carolina, for example, declared that he had opposed secession for twenty years; James T. Leach, also of North Carolina, avowed that he was an early advocate of reconstruction; and another North Carolinian frankly admitted that he ran for the Second Congress because he opposed Davis's war measures and wanted to stay out of the military.

For the most part, the Unionists in the Second Congress were opposed to the rigorous policies of the Davis administration, which they thought were encroaching upon their constitutional rights. The new congressmen and their incumbent allies were less willing than other congressmen to curtail draft exemptions and more willing to restrict the zeal of quartermasters who impressed supplies for the army and paid less than market prices for what they took. The impact of the 1863 elections was especially notable on the issue of the suspension of the writ of habeas corpus. By 1864 suspension was being used to prevent the emasculation of the draft law by judges who would issue writs to get soldiers out of the army. Some legislators who opposed conscription attacked it indirectly by appealing to the individual's right to be free of arbitrary detention by government authority. Similarly, the new congressmen were less willing to use slaves as soldiers than were their more experienced colleagues. In contrast, those voting for draconian measures in support of the war effort usually represented occupied districts, notably Missouri, Kentucky, and parts of Tennessee and Virginia. These delegates could vote in full confidence that their constituents would not feel the effects of

harsh impressment, sweeping conscription, or suspension of the writ of habeas corpus.

The turnover in membership also meant that the Second Congress would be less unified than its predecessor. Although political parties never developed in the Confederacy, the change in the composition of the membership in the Second Congress, the legislative issues of the last Congress, and the stress of a losing war effort exacerbated political divisions and led to the development of factions that might have become the basis of a two-party system if the Confederacy had survived. Analysis of legislative voting in the Second Congress reveals deep cleavage between former Union Whigs and former secession Democrats. More important, however, legislative behavior in the Second Congress was closely correlated with the location of a congressman's home in relation to the Union army.

In short, by the fall of 1863, Confederate-controlled territory had diminished and the cost of secession had become apparent to Confederate voters, who turned away from original secessionists. Even so, the new members—though differing in attitude from the old—were generally familiar to the voters. There was no electoral revolution; most of the new members were simply familiar names whose previous behavior was more symbolic of caution than that of the men they displaced.

— RICHARD E. BERINGER

EMANCIPATION PROCLAMATION

In the Preliminary Emancipation Proclamation of September 22, 1862, President Abraham Lincoln declared that, as of January 1, 1863, "all persons held as slaves within any State, or designated part of a State, the people whereof shall then be in rebellion," would be "forever free." In the final Emancipation Proclamation of January 1, 1863, he designated all of the Confederacy as still in rebellion except for certain Louisiana parishes and Virginia counties and the entire state of Tennessee. Most of the excepted areas were those under the presumed control of Federal forces. Eastern Tennessee was not yet under such control but could hardly be considered "in rebellion," since its people were overwhelmingly pro-Union. Lincoln justified the proclamation as "a fit and necessary war measure," and so he could not logically have applied it to the border slave states or to the Federally occupied portions of the South—areas in which his government was not waging war.

Newspapers in the Confederacy ridiculed Lincoln's action. They accused him of leaving the slaves in bondage where he had the power to free them and pretending to emancipate them where he had no power to do so. Yet the papers also denounced the proclamation as a call upon the slaves to revolt. Especially worrisome were its clauses advising freed slaves to "abstain from all violence, unless in necessary self-defense," and stating that "such persons" would be "received into the armed service of the United States."

The Confederate government took steps to retaliate. In a January 12, 1863, message to his Congress, Jefferson Davis characterized the proclamation as "a measure by which millions of human beings of an inferior race" were being "encouraged to a general assassination of their masters." He recommended dire punishment for captured white officers of black troops. Congress responded with a joint resolution containing the following provisions: such officers were to be tried by military courts, which could impose the death penalty; black soldiers, if formerly slaves, were to be handed over to state governments for return to their previous owners.

The Davis government was temporarily strengthened by the popular reaction to Lincoln's policy, which at first had a unifying effect on Confederate citizens. Even the most persistently anti-Davis newspaper, the *Richmond Examiner,* endorsed Davis's stand, charging Lincoln with "the most startling political crime in American history." The preliminary announcement disheartened Unionists in eastern Tennessee and caused Thomas A. R. Nelson and other leaders to switch their loyalty from Lincoln to Davis. Andrew Johnson, the Unionist governor of Tennessee, feared that still others would go over to the Confederate side, and he was much relieved when Lincoln excluded the entire state from the final proclamation.

The Confederacy was seriously weakened, however, by the long-term effects of Lincoln's emancipation policy. Early on, Davis feared that it would handicap Confederate efforts to gain recognition and intervention from abroad. His diplomatic and propaganda agents overseas, aware of "the universal hostility of Europe to slavery," also worried that Lincoln's action would draw European sympathy and support away from the Confederacy. To counteract this threat of the proclamation, Confederate propagandists included in the June 11, 1863, issue of their periodical, the *Index,* an "Address to Christians throughout the World," in which a number of prominent Southern preachers testified that the abolition of slavery would be "an interference with the plans of Divine Providence." Eventually the Confederates indicated a willingness to issue their own emancipation decree if, by doing so, they could be assured of foreign recognition. Their failure to obtain such

recognition was due, at least in part, to Lincoln's proclamation.

For the Confederacy, the proclamation had even more disastrous consequences through its influence on the slaves. Though nearly all of them were illiterate, they soon learned about the promise of freedom to come on January 1, 1863. Some Mississippi militiamen in Confederate service requested permission to go home before then—"as the negroes are making their brags that by the first of January they will be free as we are and a general outbreak is expected about that time." Here and there throughout the South the rumor ran that slaves were preparing to rise on the appointed day. To strengthen control over them, Congress amended the Conscription Act on October 11, 1862, so as to exempt one man as owner or overseer for every twenty slaves on a plantation (the Twenty-Slave Law). Actually, slaves responded to the proclamation not by attempting to revolt but by heading for the nearest Union army camp. They were already fleeing in that direction; now, with freedom as the lure, the numbers increased. Approximately 100,000 from the Confederate states (along with other blacks from the Northern and border states) sooner or later joined the Union army.

By stimulating the movement of laborers and soldiers to the Union side, the proclamation threatened to worsen the already serious manpower shortage of the Confederacy. As early as January 10, 1863, Gen. Robert E. Lee warned the secretary of war about the consequences of the "savage and brutal policy" that Lincoln recently had proclaimed. There is an "absolute necessity," Lee wrote, "to increase our armies, if we desire to oppose effectual resistance to the vast numbers that the enemy is now precipitating upon us." It proved impossible to increase the armies sufficiently, however, and a year later Gen. Patrick Cleburne concluded that the South was losing the war because it lacked the manpower of the North. As a result of the proclamation, Cleburne said, "slavery, from being one of our chief sources of strength," had become "one of our chief sources of weakness." He therefore suggested that the Confederacy take the drastic step of recruiting its own army of slaves. When Congress finally authorized such a step, on March 13, 1865, the earlier joint resolution concerning the proclamation was revised. Instead of warning the North against recruiting "negroes," the resolution now warned only against recruiting "our negro slaves."

At the Hampton Roads peace conference, on February 3, 1865, the proclamation emerged as an issue in the discussion between Lincoln and representatives of the Confederacy. Vice President Alexander H. Stephens (according to his own account) asked

"The Yankee remains to be fully emancipated from his own legends of emancipation."

C. VANN WOODWARD
THE ANTISLAVERY MYTH
1962

Lincoln what permanent effect, if any, the proclamation would have on the slaves. "Would it be held to emancipate the whole, or only those who had, at the time the war ended, become actually free under it?" Lincoln (again, according to Stephens's account) replied that this was a question for the courts. "His own opinion was, that as the proclamation was a *war measure,* and would have effect only from its being an exercise of the war power, as soon as the war ceased, it would be inoperative for the future." Doubting, as he did, the postwar validity of the proclamation, Lincoln helped to bring about the adoption of the Thirteenth Amendment, which made the question moot.

Whether or not the proclamation would have conferred legal and lasting freedom on any slave, it certainly brought at least a degree of practical freedom to the multitudes that it encouraged to escape from bondage. By thus depleting the human resources of the Confederacy, while also helping to deter foreign intervention, the proclamation contributed mightily to the Confederacy's ultimate defeat.

[*See also* African American Troops in the Confederacy; Contraband; Juneteenth; Slavery; Thirteenth Amendment.]

— RICHARD N. CURRENT

ENCHANTRESS AFFAIR

The brig *Enchantress* was taken by the Confederate privateer *Jeff Davis* on July 6, 1861, off the coast of Delaware. A prize master and five seamen from the Confederate vessel attempted to take the prize into a Southern port. But sixteen days after her capture, *Enchantress* was retaken by the Union warship *Albatross.* The six Confederates were imprisoned in Philadelphia, tried for piracy (October 22–28, 1861), and convicted.

When an international conference meeting in 1856 had agreed to declare privateering illegal, the United States had declined to sign the agreement. Nevertheless, in 1861 the U.S. government decided to accept the argument that privateering was piracy, and the *Enchantress* affair gave it the opportunity to do so. The five members of the brig's crew were sentenced to death as pirates.

The sentence, however, was never carried out. Confederate president Jefferson Davis threatened retaliation for what he described as "a practice unknown to the warfare of civilized man, and so barbarous as to disgrace the nation which shall be guilty of inaugurating it." If any Confederate privateersmen were executed, he said, captured Union officers would be treated in accordance with the disposition of the imprisoned crew. Ultimately, the captured privateersmen and the prize muster were declared prisoners of war, and many were eventually exchanged.

The *Enchantress* case was one of several involving captured Confederate privateers that persuaded Lincoln's government to drop its decision to treat their crews as pirates.

— WILLIAM N. STILL, JR.

ERLANGER LOAN

Negotiated between the Confederate States of America and Emile Erlanger and Company of Paris, the Erlanger Loan was issued on March 19, 1863, in five European cities and raised £1,759,894 ($8,535,486 gold value) for Confederate use in Europe. It was secured by government-owned cotton in the Confederacy and provided that cotton would be delivered in the Confederacy to the bondholders on demand.

The Erlanger family had become prominent in banking in Germany in the early nineteenth century under the leadership of Raphael Erlanger. By midcentury, the family, originally Jewish, had converted to Christianity, and Raphael Erlanger had become a baron. He sent his son, Frederick Emile, to establish a branch of the family business in Paris. The firm issued railroad and government bonds, and Emile became friendly with the emperor, Louis Napoleon.

John Slidell, Confederate commissioner to France, cultivated the friendship of many businessmen, bankers, and others with connections to the emperor. Slidell was aware that by mid-1862 the Confederacy was severely restricted in its ability to place funds in Europe to pay for its shipbuilding and munitions-purchasing programs. The Confederacy had, during the first year of the war, sent to Europe nearly all of the bills of exchange that had accumulated in the South before the Federal blockade stopped all normal shipping in early June 1861. Although numerous small vessels ran the blockade, only small amounts of cotton were carried to Europe during the first year to earn new exchange. The Confederate government was slow to develop a blockade-running program of its own and hesitated to risk shipping the limited amounts of gold and silver that it held. Confederate paper money had, of course, no value in Europe. When Emile Erlanger and Company proposed a bond issue for the Confederacy, Slidell highly recommended it, not only as a means of meeting the financial crisis, but also for political purposes, since Erlanger was influential with the emperor. It may have been relevant also that Slidell's daughter and Emile Erlanger were soon to become engaged to be married.

Erlanger's original offer to issue £5 million at 8 percent interest, with the Confederacy receiving 70 percent of the face value and paying a commission of 5 percent to the firm, was rejected by the Richmond authorities as much too expensive. They agreed to allow the firm to issue £3 million, at 7 percent interest, with the South receiving 77 percent and paying a 5 percent commission, only because they hoped that it would increase Slidell's ability to elicit favorable decisions from Louis Napoleon. A provision that bondholders could convert their bonds into cotton in the Confederacy with the right to export it was an important incentive for investors, since the price of cotton in Europe was quite high.

The firm issued the bonds at 90 percent of face value in London, Liverpool, Paris, Amsterdam, and Frankfurt, and the issue was an immediate success. Within two weeks, however, the price sagged to 87, and Erlanger feared that subscribers might not make the remainder of their installment payments. The firm secretly bought in the market to sustain the price and induced the Confederates to provide funds to continue the effort. The price was sustained and all payments were made, but the Confederates had bought back nearly half of the loan. During the next year, Erlanger was able to resell many of these bonds, and the Confederates were able to use many others in payment of debts. In the end, the Confederate government had sold bonds with a face value of £2,391,000 and had raised £1,759,894 in Europe at an effective annual interest rate of a little over 12 percent. The price of the bonds became an indicator of European estimates of the likelihood of Confederate independence.

It is impossible to determine whether the bond issue increased Slidell's influence at the court of Louis Napoleon. The Erlanger loan was successful, however, in providing funds in Europe to continue Confederate military and naval purchases in 1863.

— JUDITH FENNER GENTRY

ESPIONAGE

[*This entry is composed of three articles*: Confederate Secret Service, *which overviews the organization and operations of Southern espionage efforts;* Federal Secret Service, *which discusses Northern espionage during the Civil War; and* Confederate Military Spies, *which profiles notable Southern espionage agents. For further discussion of Confederate attempts to influence the war and Northern opinion through espionage, see* Copperheads; Lincoln, Abraham, *article on* Assassination of Lincoln; *and* Thompson, Jacob, *sidebar* Northwestern Conspiracy. *See also selected biographies of figures mentioned herein.*]

CONFEDERATE SECRET SERVICE

According to records discovered as recently as 1990, the Confederacy spent approximately $2 million in gold on Secret Service activities—a princely sum for those days and many times the amount spent by the Union for similar purposes. The Confederate Secret Service covered a wide range of operations from classic espionage penetration of the Federal government in Washington to the development of secret weapons for use behind enemy lines. Secret Service operations also included assistance to Gen. Robert E. Lee and other field commanders in the collection of tactical intelligence and an ambitious attempt to capture President Abraham Lincoln as a hostage. Most important of all, the Secret Service engaged in a serious clandestine political effort to create a peace movement in the North.

The Confederate Secret Service, like the modern American intelligence community, comprised a group of organizations created at different times for distinct purposes and originally with no unifying concept of operations. Experience, however, was an active teacher, and before the war's end legislation was introduced into the Confederate Congress to bring the diverse activities together into a Special and Secret Service Bureau—the Confederate version of a central intelligence agency.

In early 1861, while the Confederate government was still in Montgomery, Alabama, Jefferson Davis began to employ secret agents for political missions abroad. The most successful early espionage operation, however, appears to have been organized by Virginia before that state had formally joined the Confederacy. The most notorious agent of this effort was a Washington hostess, Rose O'Neal Greenhow, who used her social connections and her sexual attractions to elicit a flow of useful information about Federal military preparations in the Washington area. Her greatest success was to alert the Confederates in northern Virginia to Gen. Irvin McDowell's movement from Washington toward the railroad junction at Manassas, which resulted in the Union defeat at the 1861 battle there.

The Confederate espionage network in Washington that included Greenhow continued throughout the war to supply intelligence in support of the government in Richmond, and the network also provided direct support to General Lee's Army of Northern Virginia. Its information enabled Lee to anticipate General Grant's Wilderness campaign and even informed him of Grant's basic strategy of making a flanking maneuver after each frontal encounter. Lee thus was able to prepare roads in order to get ahead of and stop Grant's moves.

The War Department also assigned skilled Secret Service agents to various Confederate generals for spe-

ESPIONAGE

Confederate Secret Service

In January 1863, Colin J. McRae served as the European manager of the Erlanger loan, negotiated with Emile Erlanger and Company of Paris.

PAGE 340

ESPIONAGE

Confederate Secret Service

Skilled telegraph wire-tappers rode with J.E.B. Stuart and John Hunt Morgan on their famous raids.

PAGE 552

The Signal Corps' special function seems to have been wire tapping—cutting into Federal telegraph lines and reading the messages.

PAGE 552

cific campaigns. For example, Lt. Henry Thomas Harrison was assigned to Gen. D. H. Hill in North Carolina in early 1863 and later to Gen. James Longstreet for the Gettysburg campaign. Harrison was credited with alerting Longstreet to George Meade's movements into Pennsylvania that resulted in the battle.

Conventional wisdom says that the North was industrial and the South agricultural, but the war brought a spate of technical innovations from Southern inventors. Some of these inventions were weapons like underwater mines that could be used more effectively if they and their technology could be kept secret. As a result, a number of activities, like mine laying and the development of timed detonators for sabotage, were considered by the Confederates as Secret Service activities and protected by special security arrangements.

Similarly, the Confederate Signal Corps, another innovation, depended on the security of its signaling and the cipher systems used for important messages. As a result, it did not seem illogical to the Confederates to charge their Signal Corps with the mission of managing a secret courier line between Washington and Richmond for the delivery of important messages from Confederate agents in the North. Once the Signal Corps was involved in clandestine operations via the secret line, it was a small step to have both the Signal Corps and the War Department espionage apparatus managed by the same people.

The idea of using signal flags to send messages over the battlefield was first advanced before the war by surgeon Albert James Myer of the U.S. Army. The Confederates used the system in time to help win the First Battle of Manassas, but the Union army failed to implement the idea until the Confederates had demonstrated its success. The Confederate Signal Corps also ran its secret line between Richmond and Washington continuously throughout the war. It was still in operation when General Lee surrendered on April 9, 1865.

The practical use of underwater explosives was first demonstrated in the James River near Richmond in the summer of 1861 by Comdr. Matthew Fontaine Maury, who had established an enviable reputation as a scientist through his work on oceanography. The use of mines was further developed by the Confederate War Department's Torpedo Bureau, under Gen. Gabriel J. Rains, and by the Navy Department's Submarine Battery Service first under Maury and then under Lt. Hunter Davidson.

The Confederates also organized groups of saboteurs, called Strategic Corps, to plant explosives at depots, factories, bridges, river shipping facilities, and other targets behind Union lines. Their chief success was the destruction of the Union army's main supply base at City Point, Virginia, on August 9, 1864. A Strategic Corps team planted a bomb on a ship at the dock, which caused several other ships loaded with ammunition to explode, showering Ulysses S. Grant's neighboring headquarters with debris and inflicting widespread damage. Other teams burned ships on the Mississippi and Ohio rivers and attacked logistics targets in the rear of Union armies.

The most important Secret Service operation of the entire Confederate effort was the attempt to turn widespread disaffection with the war and the Lincoln administration into an effective peace movement. Preparations for this operation began in 1863, and it was launched in April 1864 when Jefferson Davis approved the allocation of $1 million in gold to Jacob Thompson, a former U.S. secretary of the interior who had been selected to head the operation. Thompson's overt mission was to serve as a Confederate commissioner in Canada to search for peace with the U.S. government. (Since Canada was a British possession and Britain did not recognize the Confederacy, Thompson could not be appointed as a minister or ambassador; therefore, the title "commissioner" meant only that the Confederates had commissioned him to act on their behalf.)

There was a covert side to Thompson's mission, however. If no progress was made toward peace, Thompson was to attack the Union war effort by clandestine operations from Canada. To provide him with the technical means necessary for such operations, Clement C. Clay, a former U.S. senator, was also appointed a commissioner. Clay apparently represented the interests of the War Department.

The Confederates promoted an existing secret political group, the Knights of the Golden Circle, as a means of organizing the opposition to the war. Many local chapters of the Knights operated on a quasi-military basis, and some were armed and willing to consider a revolt to express their disaffection. The Confederates tried to induce the Copperheads, as they were called, to take coordinated action against the war. The primary focus was to be Chicago, where the Copperheads and a cadre of Confederates infiltrated from Canada were to free the thousands of Confederate prisoners of war held there. The target date was August 1864, and the attack was to be accompanied by revolts or demonstrations in other cities in Illinois, Indiana, and Ohio. The copperheads, however, could never be brought to act, and the operation was eventually penetrated by Federal agents who arrested several of the key plotters in November 1864.

In the meantime, other operations were attempted by the Confederates in Canada. One of the leading Secret Service operatives, John Y. Beall, tried to free the Confederate prisoners on Johnson Island in the harbor of Sandusky, Ohio, but was frustrated when his supporting team got cold feet. Another team, led by Lt. Bennett H. Young, tried to burn St. Albans, Vermont, and made off with over $200,000 in U.S. currency and negotiable paper.

The Confederates in Canada also apparently recruited John Wilkes Booth in July 1864 to organize an attempt to abduct President Lincoln. Booth had help from Richmond but appears to have been directed primarily from Canada. He tried once to capture Lincoln in March 1865 but failed. At that point, Richmond apparently decided it was too late to try again and planned instead to blow up the White House to disrupt coordination between Grant and William Tecumseh Sherman. An explosives expert was sent to assist Booth, but he was captured on his way into Washington. In the absence of his technical adviser and unable to contact knowledgeable superiors, Booth apparently decided to approximate the damage that would be caused by an explosion by attacking simultaneously several officials who would likely have been involved in such an explosion. The result of Booth's decision was the assassination of Lincoln and the wounding of Secretary of State William H. Seward on April 14, 1865. None of the other targets was attacked. Booth was assisted in his escape by several elements of the Secret Service, but he was caught and killed by Union cavalry on April 26, 1865.

The end of the war found the Confederate espionage net in Washington and the Signal Corps's secret line still in operation. More important, the

WHEEL OF SECRETS

This coding disk was used by the Confederate Secret Service to code and decipher messages.

THE MUSEUM OF THE CONFEDERACY, RICHMOND, VIRGINIA

Confederate apparatus in Canada, now under the direction of Gen. Edwin Grey Lee, who had replaced Thompson, was still intact and had Secret Service money to operate with. For several months Lee and his colleagues acted almost like a Confederate government in exile, turning out propaganda denying Confederate complicity in the Lincoln assassination and defending individuals accused of crimes by the Federal government.

Like all clandestine operations, the Confederate Secret Service had failures as well as successes, but on

EXECUTION

A photograph by Alexander Gardner shows the July 7, 1865 hanging of Mary E. Surratt, Lewis T. Powell, David E. Herold, and George A. Atzerodt, condemned as conspirators in the Lincoln assassination.

NATIONAL ARCHIVES

Thanks to Edward Porter Alexander, the Confederates had a signal service with their forces at First Manassas, months before the Federals could assemble an effective counterpart.

PAGE 550

the whole, the efforts were imaginative and made contributions to the Confederate war effort that have never been recognized.

— WILLIAM A. TIDWELL

FEDERAL SECRET SERVICE

As in the new Confederacy, intelligence and espionage in the Union emerged more out of necessity, accident, and experimentation than from any organized plan. Indeed, many in the Northern high command still held to the eighteenth-century notion that spying was a contemptible practice beneath the dignity of soldiers. No systematic attempt was made during and immediately after secession to gather reliable military information. Instead, the Union leaders simply relied upon what came to them via rumor and exaggerated newspaper claims. When Gen. Irvin McDowell led his army into Northern Virginia in the campaign culminating in the humiliating defeat at Manassas on July 21, 1861, he did not even have a good map of the countryside.

In fact, the first—admittedly ineffective—attempts to arm Abraham Lincoln's armies with information came from the agents of a civilian detective, Allan Pinkerton. Lincoln had known him prior to the war, and it was Pinkerton who discovered a plot to assassinate Lincoln during his trip to Washington to be inaugurated. Foiling the plot endeared Pinkerton to Lincoln and also called his name to the attention of another former acquaintance, Gen. George B. McClellan. First in western Virginia, and then in Washington, when McClellan replaced the hapless McDowell, Pinkerton was called on to use his stable of "detectives" to provide information on contract. At McClellan's behest, Pinkerton, though always a civilian, organized what he chose to call the U.S. Secret Service, though in fact it never held any official military or governmental status or sanction.

Pinkerton's was a twofold mission: in Washington he was to keep an eye on Confederate sympathizers and ferret out spies; when McClellan's Army of the Potomac was on campaign, Pinkerton would serve on his staff without official rank and manage the efforts of spies and scouts in collecting information about enemy troops. At the former task Pinkerton proved to be rather effective. He caught noted Southern agent Rose O'Neal Greenhow and saw her imprisoned, and had a number of other suspected traitors either arrested or driven out of the city.

In the field, however, Pinkerton proved to be one of the war's notable failures. He knew nothing of military intelligence—few did—nor of how to interpret what information he acquired. From his Chicago detective agency and elsewhere he assembled a small corps of agents, all civilians, whom he sent behind enemy lines charged with learning whatever they could of Confederate numbers, positions, morale, equipment, and anticipated movements. The value of Pinkerton's reports was in the first place predicated on the quality of what was sent to him. His agents were sometimes effective, like Timothy Webster, who operated in the Confederacy for months under cover before being caught and hanged. But they were not trained military men and women who knew the value or import of what they saw. Moreover, they all were prone to accept rumor as fact. And when their reports came back to Pinkerton, he compounded the problem by apparently devising a formula of his own for converting *reported* numbers of troops into *actual* numbers—which always came out much higher. Thus, in April 1862 when only 17,000 Southerners faced McClellan at Yorktown, Pinkerton told the general that there were 120,000! Even when Pinkerton succeeded in enumerating every unit in the army facing McClellan that summer, he still tripled their actual numbers in his reports. In part this may have been because Pinkerton read his man McClellan very well, and the general always preferred to believe himself too heavily outnumbered to risk a fight. When McClellan was finally eclipsed in the fall of 1862, Pinkerton disappeared from the war with him.

Despite the lack of an organized beginning to Federal espionage and intelligence gathering, many generals besides McClellan employed their own agents, though usually for limited times and specific purposes. Moreover, once Union armies began to occupy Confederate territory, information started coming into the camps on its own, chiefly from Union sympathizers seeking protection and from runaway slaves, or "contrabands," who flocked to the Federal banners in the thousands. Each commander dealt with such information as he chose, although most turned responsibility for it over to the army provost marshal general, who was already charged with managing the fugitives themselves.

The first attempt at a systematic military gathering of information emerged in the western theater, under the guidance of Ulysses S. Grant. In October 1862, as he was planning his overland drive toward Vicksburg, Grant selected Brig. Gen. Grenville M. Dodge for command of a division in his army, with authority for organizing and operating a spy network to provide Grant with intelligence on enemy numbers and movements. Dodge was a perfect choice, having already built and commanded the First Tennessee Cavalry, a regiment of mounted scouts operating in Missouri and Arkansas. He also operated another regiment of loyal western Tennesseeans who provided information on the enemy in their region.

Upon receiving the assignment from Grant, Dodge went to work and quickly produced something far more effective and efficient than Pinkerton's dime novel–style operation. Secrecy was a byword. Only Dodge knew the identity of all of his agents, most of them civilians; they were frequently noted in dispatches only by numbers. He equipped them with Confederate money for their work behind enemy lines and paid them for their services with profits from the sale of confiscated cotton. Although the total number of his agents may never be known, at least 117 would serve him at one time or another, and his network would, by the end of the war, include operatives in almost every Confederate state east of the Mississippi except Florida.

Any kind of information was of interest to Dodge. Given the deplorable quality of road and terrain maps of the Southern states, Dodge—himself an engineer—constantly used information from his people to update the charts he provided to Grant. During the Vicksburg campaign itself, Dodge kept Grant constantly informed of Confederate numbers and positions, allowing the Federals to apply numerical superiority where it counted, while ignoring lesser enemy forces that Pinkerton and McClellan would have exaggerated into legions. Dodge even gave his operatives bogus information about Federal movements as gifts for Confederate commanders in order to win their confidence, thus inaugurating counterintelligence and double agents. Not only did Dodge's network gather information. It also collected Southern spies, constantly thwarting Confederate operatives, including the capture and eventual execution of Sam Davis, the boy spy later virtually canonized in the Lost Cause pantheon for dying rather than revealing the names of his fellow spies.

Dodge managed his small intelligence empire, while still leading his combat division, until he was wounded in the Atlanta campaign. Thereafter it functioned largely on its own under the hand of William Tecumseh Sherman, having already set a model for effectiveness as the most widely flung and far-reaching intelligence network of the war.

Meanwhile, spy work in the eastern theater had progressed at a more leisurely and less professional pace. Following the disappearance of Pinkerton in November 1862, espionage floundered without firm management until the spring of 1863, when Gen. Joseph Hooker engaged Col. George H. Sharpe to head the newly formed Bureau of Military Information in March. A Rutgers and Yale graduate, Sharpe was colonel of the 120th New York Infantry, but more likely it was his proclivity for drinking and high living that grabbed the equally fun-loving Hooker's attention. Yet if he was a

bit of a dissipate, Sharpe was also a born spy master. In his first major task, providing Hooker with data on Robert E. Lee's army prior to the Chancellorsville campaign, Sharpe assessed Confederate numbers down to less than one-fourth of 1 percent—a margin of error of only 150 men out of some 60,000. He performed nearly as well during the Gettysburg campaign but then commenced his most dramatic service when Grant came east in 1864.

Through contacts as yet unknown, Sharpe managed to get through to Samuel Ruth, Union-sympathizing superintendent of the Richmond, Fredericksburg, and Potomac Railroad, and Elizabeth Van Lew, both operating in the Confederate capital itself. Ruth furnished information on troop movements, supplies, and the condition of the South's rail network, and helped escaped Federal prisoners find their way to safety. He even sent information for Federal raiding parties who destroyed portions of his own rail line when it carried valuable matériel for the Southern war effort. Van Lew, a woman regarded as odd and therefore not suspected by her high society Richmond friends and neighbors, was Ruth's associate in some of this work. "Crazy Bet" visited Northern prisoners in Richmond's prisons and then conveyed military information gleaned from them through the lines to Sharpe. From these and other sources, many of them Confederate officers whom she flattered into indiscreet revelations, Van Lew derived a mass of information that she wrote in code on onionskin paper and hid inside empty eggshells, sending them in the keeping of her servants to Union lines. Upon the fall of Richmond in April 1865, one of Grant's first calls was at the Van Lew mansion to extend his thanks.

While Sharpe assumed the field intelligence role once performed by Pinkerton, the duty of keeping an eye on traitors and spies within Washington itself, and much of the North, fell to the National Detective Police, created in 1863 under the management of Lafayette C. Baker. His counterintelligence efforts, for the most part effective, were sometimes crude and brutal, including midnight arrests, incarceration without habeas corpus, and involuntary confessions.

Even as late as 1865 there was no uniform coordination of all Union intelligence activities. Baker reported to the secretary of war; Sharpe to George G. Meade or Grant; Dodge's network to Sherman's staff; and a host of other operatives to their individual employers. As a result methods and effectiveness varied widely, but in the main, by mid- or late 1863 Union armies across the map were getting good information and using it well. At the same time they were successfully subverting most Confederate efforts at gathering good intelligence and performing acts of espionage behind Federal lines.

— WILLIAM C. DAVIS

ESPIONAGE

Federal Secret Service

"War is not merely a political act, but also a political instrument, a continuation of political relations, a carrying out of the same by other means."

KARL VON CLAUSEWITZ

Popular Washington, D.C., hostess Rose O'Neal Greenhow joined the spy ring of Col. Thomas Jordan as soon as the war broke out.

PAGE 252

Days before First Manassas, Greenhow sent messages to Beauregard informing him of U.S. Gen. Irvin McDowell's marching orders and troop strength.

PAGE 253

CONFEDERATE MILITARY SPIES

The Confederate spies who were successful at their missions and never bragged about their successes remain largely unknown. We know the most about those spies who either were caught in the act or talked at some point about their wartime experiences.

The men and women who served as spies supporting the Confederate military effort were a diverse group representing many aspects of Southern society. The two attributes that come closest to describing them as a group were their commitment to the Southern cause and their lack of qualification for combat service. Even this second attribute is not completely descriptive, however, for though many of the spies were women, physically disabled men, or wounded veterans no longer able to serve in the field, the young soldiers who served as cavalry scouts proved to be so capable at collecting information under pressure that a number of them were drawn into the clandestine world of espionage.

When the Confederates began to create the institutions that were needed for combat, they had the help of a number of men who knew clandestine operations to the extent that it was known by the U.S. government before the war. In addition, a number of immigrants in both the North and the South had had personal experience in the clandestine activities associated with various republican revolutions in Europe in the decades before the Civil War. The Confederates may also have had some help from British or French intelligence agents who saw the weakening of the United States as one possible outcome of a Confederate victory. The net effect was that the Confederates had available nearly all the know-how then in existence to help them organize the collection of information they needed to defend themselves against the Northern armies.

Confederate spies belonged to a number of different organizations that together formed the Confederate Secret Service. Scholars are still trying to piece together the history of these organizations, but some parts of the story are well known.

ROSE O'NEAL GREENHOW. The first Confederate spy to gain widespread recognition was Rose O'Neal Greenhow, widow of a respected agent of the U.S. State Department. She was noted for her intelligence and had a great deal of political experience—much more than was usual for a woman in those days. She had lived in Mexico and California and had known most of the American presidents and cabinet officers from the time of Andrew Jackson down to Abraham Lincoln's predecessor, James Buchanan. The great spokesman for the Southern point of view, John C. Calhoun, had been her friend and tutor. As an active member of Washington society and a successful hostess, Greenhow knew or was acquainted with nearly everybody of any consequence in the American government before the arrival of Lincoln.

When the leading Southerners left Washington in early 1861 to begin the organization of the Confederate government, it would have been only natural for them to think of Rose Greenhow as somebody who might be able to help them gather information about the activities of the Northerners who remained behind. She was recruited into an espionage organization by Thomas Jordan of the provisional army of Virginia. Jordan taught her a simple cipher system for her communications and arranged a courier network to deliver her reports to the Virginia forces across the Potomac River. When the Virginia forces were incorporated into the Confederate army in June 1861, Jordan became a member of the staff of Gen. P. G. T. Beauregard, the Confederate commander, and continued to manage Greenhow and the other members of the espionage organization to which she belonged.

Greenhow exploited her contacts among government officials, particularly her friendship with Senator Henry Wilson of Massachusetts, who had succeeded Confederate President Jefferson Davis as chairman of the Senate Military Affairs Committee. In July she was able to send a message to Jordan alerting him to the plans of Union Gen. Irvin McDowell for an advance into Virginia. McDowell's venture ended with Union defeat at the First Battle of Manassas, and Greenhow was widely credited in Confederate circles with having provided the information that made victory possible.

Greenhow's chief drawbacks were her flamboyant personality and her ardent belief in the Southern cause. Combined, these attributes kept her from maintaining the low profile that would have been more suitable for a successful spy. She was arrested by Union detectives on August 23, 1861, and kept under house arrest or in prison until mid-1862, when she and two other Confederate women spies were freed and sent to the Confederacy.

Greenhow, while in prison, continued to contact some of her informants and to forward their information, but after her release the Confederates sent her to England to promote sympathy for the Southern cause. On her return to the Confederacy in October 1864, she was drowned while trying to reach shore from her stranded blockade runner.

AUGUSTA MORRIS AND CATHERINE BAXLEY. The other women sent south with Rose Greenhow were Augusta Hewitt Morris and Catherine Virginia Baxley. These two women did not achieve the notoriety that surrounded Greenhow, but they had longer careers in espionage.

Morris apparently returned to the North using the alias "Mrs. Mason" and continued to work for the

Confederacy. One of the leading Confederates in Washington was Thomas Green, who lived in a mansion only three blocks from the White House. In 1863 Green was reported by Union detectives to be working with a Mrs. Mason and traveling to Baltimore two or three times a week in order to mail information to Richmond. (The Confederates used the U.S. mails heavily in their courier system. A report in a double envelope would be mailed to a collaborator who would remove the outer envelope and hand the inner one to a courier who would carry it across the Potomac and deliver it in Richmond.)

On May 3, 1864, Morris was given $10,500 from the Incidental and Contingent Expenditures fund of the Confederate War Department. This was a large sum for those days and probably represented a payroll for an espionage organization such as the one reporting to Green.

Baxley also returned to the North and was provided with a cipher system for communication with the Confederate State Department and the South's clandestine organization in Canada. Her mission probably involved carrying information and messages between Canada and Richmond through Union territory. She was arrested again by the Union in early 1865 and remained in prison until the war was over.

BELLE BOYD. Another woman who achieved some notoriety as a Confederate spy was a young Virginian named Belle Boyd. During 1861 around Martinsburg, Virginia (present-day West Virginia), and in 1862 near Front Royal, Virginia, Boyd served as a courier and spy for the Confederate forces in the area. She appears to have had little or no training in the craft of espionage and exposed herself unnecessarily to arrest by the Federal forces, but she talked her way out of a number of close calls and managed to provide Col. Turner Ashby and Gen. Thomas J. ("Stonewall") Jackson with some extremely useful information on Federal troop movements and strengths. She was arrested in June 1862 and confined in the Old Capitol Prison in Washington. In August of the same year she was sent south in an exchange of civilian prisoners. She returned to Martinsburg, was arrested again, and sent south once more.

On May 8, 1864, Boyd sailed from Wilmington, North Carolina, on a blockade runner, carrying dispatches for Confederate agents in Europe. Her ship, the *Greyhound,* was captured, and Boyd (who had destroyed the dispatches in her care) was sent to the North for interrogation. She was finally released by her captors and sent to Canada.

On June 12, 1864, Miss Belle Boyd and maid checked into the St. Lawrence Hall Hotel in Montreal and were assigned rooms 136 and 137. On June 15, the Reverend Stuart Robinson, a Presbyterian minister

from Louisville, Kentucky, who was assisting the Confederate clandestine organization in Canada, checked into the same hotel and was assigned room 138. It would appear that the Confederates were anxious to keep track of Boyd and to verify her continued loyalty to the Confederacy.

In due course Boyd went on to England, where she was married on August 25, 1864, to Ensign Samuel Hardinge, recently of the U.S. Navy. He had commanded the prize crew that had taken the *Greyhound* into port and had fallen in love with Boyd. Unfortunately, he did not live long thereafter, and Boyd became a widow at twenty-one. After the war, she spent the remainder of her life as an actress and lecturer trading on her notoriety as a former Confederate spy.

OTHER FEMALE AGENTS. There were several other female spies who provided outstanding service to the Confederacy. Early in the war, Antonia Ford of Fairfax County, Virginia, added to the information provided by Rose Greenhow, and later, after the Confederate partisan Col. John S. Mosby began his operations in northern Virginia, Ford provided him with valuable tactical information. Sarah Slater and Josephine Brown worked between Richmond and Canada, mostly during 1864 and 1865. The sisters Ginnie and Lottie Moon were raised in Ohio by a Virginia father. When war came, they went south and found useful employment in gathering information and carrying messages for the Confederates in Kentucky and Tennessee and in the Trans-Mississippi area. After the war, they continued their unconventional activities, working for women's suffrage and other causes.

Still other women worked for the Confederate clandestine effort in a variety of circumstances, but there were also a number of men who provided invaluable information to the Confederacy.

DANIEL LUCAS. A good example of male espionage agents who were not qualified for combat was Daniel Bedinger Lucas of Jefferson County, Virginia (present-day West Virginia). Lucas was a graduate of the University of Virginia and a lawyer. In 1861 he served on the staff of Gen. Henry A. Wise, a former governor of Virginia, in his campaign in western Virginia, but Lucas suffered from a congenital deformity that prevented him from engaging in the physical activity demanded by field duty. He returned to Richmond, where he was active in the management of espionage and other secret operations. In late 1864 he went to Canada to assist Gen. Edwin Grey Lee, who had been sent there to change the direction of the clandestine activities being organized against the North.

After the war, Lucas practiced law in West Virginia, was appointed to a short term as a U.S. senator from that state, and became a justice of the West

Belle Boyd charmed Federal officers into divulging military information that she transmitted through messengers to Confederate leaders.

PAGE 198

Virginia Supreme Court of Appeals. He was discreet in conversation and writings about his wartime clandestine experiences, and as a result, the details of his years with the Confederate Secret Service are not known.

JOHN PALMER. One of the most successful of the Confederate spies was John Williamson Palmer, a correspondent for the *New York Tribune*. Palmer had impeccable credentials and freedom of access behind Union lines. His dispatches, printed under the byline "Altamont," were widely read and exceptionally perceptive concerning Confederate strategy. What was not so obvious was that he was in an excellent position to report on Union strategy and to make sure that his interpretation of Confederate strategy represented the view the Confederates wanted the Union to have. Palmer played this difficult and dangerous game for about two years, but finally he gave it up—possibly because of the nervous strain involved—and spent the final years of the war in Richmond writing letters car-

BELLE BOYD
The Legendary Female Spy

BOYD, BELLE (1844–1900). The most famous of the Confederacy's female operatives, Boyd was born in or near Martinsburg, Virginia (present-day West Virginia). Although most scholars agree that Boyd made important contributions to the Shenandoah Valley campaigns, some of the dramatic details of her memoir, *Belle Boyd, in Camp and Prison*, are still controversial. When Martinsburg came under Union occupation in 1861, Boyd's exploits included shooting at a Federal trooper who broke into her family's home (July 4, 1861) and charming attentive Union officers into divulging military information that she transmitted through secret messengers to Confederate leaders. During the fall of 1861 Boyd served as a courier for Gens. Thomas J. ("Stonewall") Jackson and P. G. T. Beauregard. Early in 1862 she was arrested by Union forces and detained for a week in Baltimore. In mid-May 1862, Boyd claims, she spied on a secret Union strategy session in Front Royal while crouched in a closet above the meeting room and then made a midnight ride of fifteen miles, through Federal sentries, to inform Col. Turner Ashby of her findings.

Boyd's most significant feat came on May 23, 1862, as General Jackson's forces approached Front Royal. Having obtained information on the status of Federal forces in the area, she dashed from Front Royal—on foot—to meet the advance guard of Jackson's troops. Caught in the crossfire of the opposing armies and waving her white bonnet to cheer on the Confederate troops, she reached Maj. Henry Kyd Douglas and reported that Jackson would have to hurry his attack in order to seize the town before retreating Federal forces burned its supply depots and bridges. Her message confirmed Jackson's own intelligence, and the Confederates were victorious.

Her deed sealed her status as a Confederate celebrity and resulted in her arrest on July 30, 1862, and imprisonment in Washington's Old Capitol Prison. She was released as part of a prisoner exchange a month later and sent to Richmond, Virginia, where she spent a few months among her admiring countrymen. Sometime in the winter of 1862–1863, she was appointed an honorary aide-de-camp, with the rank of

BELLE BOYD   LIBRARY OF CONGRESS

captain, by General Jackson's headquarters.

In the summer of 1863 she returned to Martinsburg, only to be arrested again by Union forces. Her second incarceration at Old Capitol Prison lasted until December 1863, when she was released and banished to the South for the remainder of the war. In May 1864, she set sail for England, carrying Confederate dispatches. Her ship was captured by a Union vessel. She was sent to Canada and made her way to England, where, on August 25, 1864, she married Samuel Hardinge, Jr., the Union officer who had been put in charge of the captured blockade runner.

That winter, Hardinge was briefly incarcerated in America under suspicion of treason, and in order to support herself, Boyd wrote and published her memoirs in London. In 1866, after Hardinge's death, she took up acting. Later that year she returned to the United States, where she continued her acting career until 1869, when she married English businessman John Swainston Hammond. The couple was divorced in 1884, and in 1885 she married a young actor, Nathaniel Rue High, Jr., of Ohio. She toured the country giving recitals on her wartime experiences, earning the praise of Union and Confederate veterans alike. Boyd died of a heart attack in 1900 in Kilbourne City (Wisconsin Dells), Wisconsin, and was buried there.

— ELIZABETH R. VARON

rying Confederate propaganda. These letters were put into the Union mail system for delivery, thus appearing to have originated in the North.

THOMAS CONRAD. Another successful Confederate spy was Thomas Nelson Conrad, who operated a boys' school in connection with the Dumbarton Avenue Methodist Church in Georgetown in the District of Columbia. At the beginning of the war, Conrad helped the Confederate clandestine organization in Washington—probably the same one to which Rose Greenhow belonged. In 1862, however, Conrad was arrested and sent south in an exchange of civilian prisoners. Conrad went to work for the Secret Service of the Confederate War Department and made numerous trips into Union territory. In 1863 he was in Montgomery County, Maryland, just north and west of the District of Columbia, and from that point he observed the movements of the Union army north toward Gettysburg.

The youthful Captain Conrad took great delight in devising disguises that would fool enemy detectives, and he chose to try them out on the Confederates protecting Richmond to prove their effectiveness. The Confederate provost marshals, however, did not like being fooled. One of their ledgers, now in the U.S. National Archives, was used to record persons clearing the provost checkpoint on entering or leaving Richmond. It contains a list of aliases known to have been used by Captain Conrad—they were on the lookout for him.

Later Conrad, as a lay Methodist preacher, became a chaplain in the Third Virginia Cavalry and served at the same time as one of Gen. J. E. B. Stuart's cavalry scouts. In the spring of 1864 he was sent by Jefferson Davis to report on the movements and destination of the corps being assembled near Annapolis, Maryland, by Northern Gen. Ambrose Burnside.

The following September he was sent to Washington as head of a small team to observe the movements of President Lincoln and determine if it would be feasible to capture Lincoln as a hostage. While in Washington, Conrad stayed at the home of Thomas Green, who had worked with Augusta Morris. Conrad reported that Lincoln's capture was possible. In November 1864 he was sent back to the Potomac River to organize an espionage line, paralleling the existing secret line of the Confederate Signal Corps, in order to report information pertinent to the operation to abduct Lincoln. He was captured by the Union navy on the night of April 16, 1865, and kept in prison for some weeks.

After the war, Conrad held various teaching positions and served as the first president of the institution that later became the Virginia Polytechnic Institute and State University.

HENRY HARRISON. Another highly successful Confederate spy was Henry Thomas Harrison of Mississippi, who worked as a scout and spy against Ulysses S. Grant's forces in Tennessee and Mississippi. For a time he operated under the direction of Thomas Jordan, who had directed Rose Greenhow before being transferred to the Confederate Army of Tennessee.

Later Harrison moved to the eastern area to work against the Union forces in North Carolina and Virginia. He was particularly successful in providing information to Gen. James Longstreet during the Gettysburg campaign. Harrison was subsequently assigned to duty behind Union lines in New York City, but the nature of his mission there is not known.

SAM DAVIS. A less successful Confederate scout in the Army of Tennessee was young Sam Davis of the First Tennessee Infantry. He was recruited by Capt. Henry Shaw, who operated under the alias of Coleman, to join a group of scouts collecting information for Gen. Braxton Bragg, then in command. The group successfully collected a great deal of important information behind Union lines and then scattered to make their way individually back to Confederate territory. Davis was picked to carry the essential papers; the other members of the group would not have anything incriminating on them if caught.

As it transpired, Davis, Shaw, and other members of the group were captured, but only Davis could be proved to be working for the Confederate Secret Service. His Union captors pressed him to identify "Coleman," but he refused. He was tried as a spy, although he had been captured in uniform. He was sentenced to be hanged and at the last moment was offered a pardon if he would tell where Coleman could be found. Although Coleman was a fellow prisoner, Davis refused to point him out and gave his life for the cause.

JOHN WILKES BOOTH. Another ardent supporter of the Southern cause was John Wilkes Booth, whose sister, Asia Booth Clark, wrote that her brother had told her that he was a spy for the Confederacy. A good deal is known about Booth's activities in 1864 and 1865 while he was trying to organize the capture of President Lincoln as a hostage, but very little is known about his activities before he was drawn into that plot.

Booth appears to have been recruited to head the team for the capture operation in late July 1864. He abandoned his other activities for the Confederate Secret Service and in August and September wound up an oil venture and other personal affairs. He recruited several people to help in the operation and in October 1864 went to Canada, where he met leading members of the Confederate Secret Service in Montreal. A trip to Washington in November overlapped with Captain

John Wilkes Booth planned to kidnap Lincoln, take him to Richmond, and exchange him for Confederate prisoners of war.

PAGE 68

Conrad's stay for a few days. In late November and December Booth made trips to southern Maryland to organize the route his team would take when they had captured Lincoln. Finally, in March 1865, the team set out to seize the president but were frustrated when Lincoln changed his itinerary.

The Confederates then sent Lt. Thomas F. (Frank) Harney, an explosives expert, to Washington in a scheme to blow up the White House during a meeting of key officials in order to disrupt coordination between Grant's and Sherman's armies. Harney, however, was caught on his way into Washington, and Booth took it upon himself to approximate the damage that would have been caused by an explosion. He tried to organize simultaneous attacks against Lincoln, Vice President Andrew Johnson, Secretary of State William Seward, and Secretary of War Edwin Stanton. As it turned out, only Lincoln was murdered and Seward injured by his attacker.

Booth escaped through southern Maryland, but Union troops caught and killed him on April 26, 1865. Four of his associates were hanged in June of that year, and several others served prison sentences of varying lengths.

P. C. MARTIN. A Confederate spy of a radically different type was P. C. Martin, an importer and liquor dealer from Baltimore. Martin left Maryland early in the war to escape arrest for his pro-Southern activities. He settled in Montreal, where he became the leader of the Confederate clandestine activity in that city.

He helped organize an ambitious plan to free the Confederate prisoners of war held on Johnson Island in the harbor of Sandusky, Ohio, but the plan was frustrated when word of it got out. After Booth's departure in October 1864, Martin took the actor's theater wardrobe on a ship down the St. Lawrence to run the blockade into the Confederacy. The ship was wrecked and Martin was drowned. Booth's wardrobe was recovered in 1865.

WALTER BOWIE. One of the most intriguing Confederate spies was Walter Bowie of Prince George's County, Maryland. Bowie was a prominent young lawyer in Upper Marlboro, Maryland, when the war broke out. He went south to volunteer his services to the Confederacy and served for some months in a staff position in Richmond. In 1862, he returned to Maryland to take charge of the courier and reporting system supporting the Confederate espionage organization in Washington that Rose Greenhow had belonged to. He was apprehended and imprisoned in the Old Capitol Prison in Washington, but he managed to escape with the help of the Confederate underground organization in that city.

Bowie acquired a reputation as a guerrilla operating in southern Maryland and eventually joined the parti-

san unit in northern Virginia commanded by John S. Mosby, but his reputation appears to have been based on a confusion of identities. There were three Walter Bowies in the Confederate army in Virginia, and their records were sometimes mixed up (they still are today). During the Civil War when news was often circulated by word of mouth, there was ample opportunity for one Walter Bowie to be credited with the actions of another. One of the other Walter Bowies, for instance, was a graduate of the Virginia Military Institute and spent several months operating in southern Maryland as the head of a raiding team belonging to the Confederate volunteer navy. It is likely that his activities were credited to the Walter Bowie from Prince George's County.

One of Bowie's duties in managing the espionage network was to prepare summaries of information collected by the entire organization. A summary that has survived among the papers of Col. Charles Venable of Robert E. Lee's staff shows that in April 1864 Bowie reported to Lee about General Grant's preparations for the campaign of 1864. Bowie's report was quite accurate and even outlined the tactic of repeatedly moving to the flank of Lee's army that Grant employed when the campaign opened in May 1864.

Mosby's force had become well established in northern Virginia, and Bowie was sent to join his unit, where he found that Walter Bowie of the volunteer navy had preceded him. Mosby took over the task of maintaining contact with the Confederate clandestine organization in Washington, while the Maryland Bowie, as a lieutenant of one of Mosby's companies, was sent with a small team to southern Maryland with the ostensible mission of seizing the governor of Maryland. This mission coincided in time with Conrad's mission to investigate the possibility of capturing Lincoln and was probably related to it.

Bowie moved through southern Maryland, passed around Washington to the north, and tried to return to Virginia through Montgomery County north and west of the District of Columbia. In the course of that passage Bowie's party was ambushed by local citizens, and Bowie was killed.

ROBERT COXE. A different type of agent was Robert Edwin Coxe of Georgia. Coxe was a wealthy planter who had lived in Europe for several years before the war. In 1863 he moved his family to Canada and established himself in St. Catharines, Ontario, near Niagara Falls. The proximity to Niagara provided excellent cover for the meeting of clandestine agents. A museum (which still exists) on the Canadian side of the falls kept a book in which visitors recorded their signatures. An agent could visit the museum and sign the book without attracting attention. Somebody at the museum or another visitor would inspect the book periodically and, when an expected signature appeared, send word to St. Catharines. In due course a representative of the Confederate Secret Service would turn up to meet the visiting agent at a prearranged location. Under cover of tourist traffic, this arrangement lasted through the remainder of the war without being discovered.

In June 1864, the former U.S. senator Clement C. Clay, one of the Confederate commissioners in Canada, moved into Coxe's house in St. Catharines along with the former U.S. consul Beverly Tucker. Clay and Tucker conducted a number of clandestine operations from this location while Coxe went to Maine, then to Poughkeepsie, New York, and finally to Washington, D.C. After the assassination of Lincoln, Coxe was arrested, but he was later released for lack of evidence.

In addition to the people mentioned above, there were a number of others known to have been involved in Confederate clandestine operations, but we have little information about them. These include Benjamin Franklin Stringfellow, who served as a cavalry scout and was in Washington to deliver a diplomatic message when the war ended; Channing Smith, another cavalry scout, who was commissioned in late 1864 and sent for some special assignment with Mosby; Emile Longmare, who worked with the Copperheads in the North to promote an antiwar movement; Vincent Camalier, who worked as a smuggler of contraband and crossed the lines with word of impending Union movements; Augustus Howell of Prince George's County, Maryland, who was almost caught up in Booth's assassination operation; and Thomas Harbin, an agent of the Confederate War Department, who worked with Booth and his team.

The dedication of these and other Confederate spies is obvious. Many of them received no money for their pains, and most who were paid received little more than their expenses. They were individuals doing what they could for the cause in which they believed.

— WILLIAM A. TIDWELL

EWELL, RICHARD S.

Ewell, Richard S. (1817–1872), lieutenant general. One of seventeen men to attain the rank of lieutenant general in the Confederate military, Richard Stoddard Ewell was a key figure in the eastern campaigns. He served as a division commander under Gen. Thomas J. ("Stonewall") Jackson early in the war and then replaced Jackson after his death as head of the Second Corps in Gen. Robert E. Lee's Army of Northern Virginia.

A native of Virginia, Ewell graduated thirteen in the West Point class of 1840 and served mostly in the Far West with the cavalry during the twenty years prior to the Civil War. He saw limited action in the Mexican War.

Ewell entered Confederate service in April 1861. He commanded a brigade at the Battle of First Manassas but was not directly involved in the combat.

In March 1862 Ewell (now leading a division) went to the Shenandoah Valley to join Jackson in his campaign against Union Gen. Nathaniel Banks. Though Jackson was the overall commander, Ewell's men did most of the fighting. His troops engaged and routed the Federals in the opening battle at Front Royal on May 23, 1862. Two days later, moving against Banks at Winchester, Ewell made the initial attack, and one of his brigades under Gen. Richard Taylor led a final charge that routed the enemy. After Jackson retreated to avoid a pincer by Federal Gens. John C. Frémont and James Shields that threatened his rear, Ewell personally planned, directed, and won a battle with Frémont at Cross Keys on June 8, 1862. When Jackson attacked Shields early the next morning, Ewell led the men who captured a Federal artillery battery on the coaling ground above Port Republic, resulting in a Southern victory.

In June 1862, Ewell moved with Jackson to Richmond to join Lee in defending the Confederate capital under siege by Union Gen. George B. McClellan. He fought in only one of the five battles (Gaines's Mill, June 27, 1862); after taking terrible losses in an unsuccessful attack against an entrenched enemy, he held his tenuous line until Southern reinforcements came up to make the final, victorious charge.

Ewell moved north with Jackson after the Seven Days' Battles to confront Federal Gen. John Pope and led the newly formed Army of Virginia. After defeating the main Union element under Banks at Cedar Run on August 9, 1862, Jackson and Ewell raced north on a flanking march to Pope's rear. They opened the Battle of Second Manassas at Groveton on August 28, 1862, where Ewell was shot in his right knee. The wound resulted in the amputation of his leg.

While Jackson continued the campaign, moving with Lee into Maryland, Ewell returned to Richmond to recuperate. He was nursed by the sweetheart he had lost to another during his youth, Lizinka Campbell Brown, who was now a wealthy widow.

In May 1863, just as Ewell was well enough to return to duty, Jackson was wounded at Chancellorsville. Jackson died on May 10, 1863, and Ewell was named as his replacement to head Lee's Second Corps. Prior to his rejoining the army, Ewell married Lizinka on May 24, and they enjoyed a brief honeymoon. He then led his corps north toward Pennsylvania.

Marching down the Shenandoah Valley, Ewell stopped to engage Union Gen. Robert Milroy at

Horace Greeley was named the intermediary between Clement C. Clay and Lincoln.

PAGE 129

"The road to glory cannot be followed with much baggage."

RICHARD S. EWELL
1862

Winchester. He gained a spectacular victory on June 14, 1863, and then moved northward, intent on capturing Harrisburg, the capital of Pennsylvania. Just prior to his attack, Lee recalled Ewell to Gettysburg, where the enemy under Gen. George Meade was concentrating.

Ewell attacked the Northern flank on July 1, 1863, and drove the Federals from the field. Although Ewell has been criticized by some for not continuing to assault the enemy, who had retired to Cemetery Hill, this assertion ignores the facts. The Federals' position was strongly manned. Had he charged the heights, Ewell would have been easily repelled and would have suffered devastating losses to his command. The next day Lee attacked the Union left with Gen. James Longstreet's corps. Late in the day, when Meade drew men from his right (fronting Ewell) to hold off this threat, the chance arose for Ewell to drive a wedge into the Northern line. But he was not ready, and his delayed charge, mounted piecemeal, failed.

RICHARD EWELL

After Stonewall Jackson's death in May 1863, Robert E. Lee appointed Richard S. Ewell as head of the Second Corps in the Army of Northern Virginia.

HARPER'S PICTORIAL HISTORY OF THE GREAT REBELLION

Following their defeat at Gettysburg, Lee and his army retreated back to Virginia. Ewell spent the winter of 1863–1864 along the Rappahannock River. Not completely recovered from the amputation of his leg, he considered relinquishing command, but Lizinka (who had joined him that winter) would not hear of it. She took the unprecedented step of assuming charge of his affairs while he rested to regain his strength.

In May 1864 Gen. Ulysses S. Grant led the Federals south against Lee. Ewell made initial contact with the enemy in the Wilderness on May 5, 1864, showing consummate skill as he fought off the repeated Federal charges. Grant, facing a stalemate, took his army around Lee's right, and the two met again at Spotsylvania. At first the battle was inconclusive. Thinking that Grant would once again maneuver, Lee started to withdraw Ewell's artillery just as the

Northerners renewed their assault at sunrise on May 12, 1864. Without his guns, Ewell was quickly overrun, losing half his corps before he finally restored his line. He was so distraught over the casualties to his command, however, that he became sick and was forced to go on leave. When he reported for duty on May 31, Ewell found that Lee had replaced him with Jubal Early.

Assigned to Richmond, Ewell managed the city's defenses above the James River. After repeated unsuccessful attempts to regain a field command, Ewell became so disillusioned that when Lizinka proposed in late December that she take the oath of allegiance to the Union in order to regain her properties in the North, Ewell agreed to assist her in committing treason. She left Richmond for St. Louis on March 24, 1865. Less than two weeks later, Ewell led his ragtag assortment of troops after Lee toward Appomattox. He was captured on April 6 during the Battle of Sayler's Creek and imprisoned at Fort Warren in Boston Harbor.

Released in July 1865, Ewell retired to Spring Hill, Tennessee, where Lizinka owned a large plantation. He became a gentleman farmer. During the winter of 1872, Ewell fell ill with pneumonia. When his spouse attempted to nurse him back to health, she contracted the disease and died on January 22. Forty-eight hours later, Ewell joined his wife in death.

— SAMUEL J. MARTIN

EXPANSIONISM IN THE ANTEBELLUM SOUTH

The myth of a monolithic, unchanging slave South distorts the history of the slavocracy. Thus the Civil War supposedly matched the entire South against the North. But, in fact, the four border states never left the Union, West Virginia seceded from Virginia, and over 100,000 Confederate residents joined Abraham Lincoln's army. So too, before the Civil War, the South supposedly massed unanimously behind the so-called positive good of perpetual slavery. But, in fact, most upper South residents considered slavery a temporary evil. They hoped to remove blacks and slaves from their half of the South. Meanwhile, important lower South clergymen considered slavery short on Christian blessings. They urged state legislatures to protect slaves' families and access to Christianity. Most owners derided such suggestions as meddling interference, not proslavery Christianity.

These divergent viewpoints within the South, involving the pivotal matters of whether slaveholders' absolute power should be perpetuated, limited, or removed to other locales, put into perspective another fundamental Southern intramural contest, that concerning whether slavery should be expanded into new territories. According to the standard account, Southerners combated only Northerners in pre-Civil War controversies over territorial expansion, with "expand or perish" the Southerners' persistent motto. So when Abraham Lincoln won the presidency in 1860 pledging no expansion of slavery, Southerners supposedly concluded that the Union, not slavery, must perish.

The expand-or-perish interpretation, while concentrating the causes of secession into three vivid words, actually reduces a complex phenomenon to a caricature. The oversimplification is useful only to warn all who study Southern slaveholding that variations over time and space must be noticed. Southern beliefs about the *economic* necessity for expansion especially fluctuated. Convictions about slaveholders' *political* need for expansion flourished more consistently—with some important exceptions. The exceptions predominated in the climactic 1850s, when expand-or-perish thinking was particularly erratic. As the Civil War approached, South Carolina's planters, who feared they might perish without disunion, worried that Southern territorial expansion, especially into the Caribbean, might remove slavery from their state. In contrast, New Orleans merchants, who thought they might perish without Caribbean expansion, believed that disunionism could cripple expansionism. The border South's prosperous residents, who often supported territorial expansion as a way to remove slavery from their area, still hoped that expansionism would perish if disunion resulted.

Just as Southern attitudes about territorial expansion changed from one place to another, so the expansion issue changed from one era to another. Southern drives for more territory accelerated from 1793 to the mid-1830s, met opposition in the 1840s, and turned around again in the 1850s, as the Southern economy veered from half recession to unrelieved depression to almost universal prosperity. A paradox illuminates the point: the fallacious myth of universal Southern enthusiasm for expansion during the era of sectional controversy, from 1844 to 1860, fits the facts—*before* 1844. As for the period before 1793, Southern zeal for expansion could scarcely be found.

From 1793 to 1843, Southern expansionists were making up for earlier Southern generations' characteristic lack of desire for new territorial acquisitions, but they had not yet developed the fears of later generations that exotic territorial adventures could destroy old cultural stabilities. During the eighteenth century, the slave South had been predominantly a seaboard civilization, usually (though not always) uninterested in spreading west of the coastal colonies. Native Americans—Creeks, Choctaws, Seminoles, and Cherokees—had cultivated some of what became upland South Carolina and Georgia, northern Mississippi and Alabama, and western Tennessee. Non-English peoples had controlled the rim of the Anglo lower South, including the French-owned areas of what became Louisiana and Arkansas, and the Spanish-owned areas of what became Texas, Florida, and southern Alabama and Mississippi.

Eighteenth-century entrepreneurs did not yet covet what became the southernmost tier of the United States, because they could not conceive of a lucrative crop suitable for North America's westward, noncoastal tropics. They considered lower South latitudes too tropical for the upper South's staple crop, tobacco, and not tropical enough for South America's staple crops, sugar and coffee. Only the South Carolina and Georgia coastal malarial swamps could support the colonial lower South's most coveted crop, rice; and only the Sea Islands near the coast could support the secondary staple, silky Sea Island cotton. West of the coast, some colonial South Carolinians grew indigo for a limited market, lost after the American Revolution. Other Carolinians produced the cheaper grades of cotton, also commercially limited without a yet-to-be-invented gin to separate seeds from fibers. So while black slaves outnumbered white citizens more than eight to one in Georgia and especially South Carolina coastal areas, almost four out of five North American slaves toiled north of the future cotton kingdom. Slaves especially peopled the upper South tobacco belts, although whites still outnumbered blacks.

Southern Consensus for Expansionism

Eli Whitney's invention of the cotton gin in 1793 at last sent lower South entrepreneurs swarming to southwestern frontiers that were soon densely populated by slaves. Two simultaneous economic and political developments accelerated the population surge from the older South to the new cotton frontier. Almost at the moment when the cotton kingdom required more slaves, Congress abolished the African slave trade (1807). And almost at the moment when the newer South's economy ascended, the older South's economy declined. In upper South tobacco belts, debilitated soil and poor prices produced chronic stagnation. In South Carolina's coastal rice swamps, land was more worn and profits less fabulous than in colonial times; and in that state's up-country area, the first cotton spree had yielded the first cotton-exhausted soil. Throughout these eastern locales, struggling planters needed to shrink their operation or lose their property. Out in the southwestern cotton kingdom, buoyant developers,

Southern planters needed to extend control into the fresh lands of the western territories.

PAGE 157

Imperialism played a role in the origins of the Confederate States of America.

PAGE 285

EXPANSIONISM IN THE ANTEBELLUM SOUTH

Southern Consensus for Expansionism

Confederate imperialism derived from the Southern expansion movement of the 1850s.

PAGE 285

Many Southerners concluded that American extension into Latin regions would benefit their section.

PAGE 285

now legally barred from buying slaves from Africa, competed for contracting slaveholders' unneeded bondsmen. As a result, some 750,000 blacks were relocated from 1790 to 1860. The lower South's share of slaves in the United States leapt from 21 to 59 percent over these years.

In the wake of slavery's spread over previously uncultivated tropical regions, slave sellers in older areas had the cash to finance a modest postboom survival economy. Slave buyers in new cotton areas had the laborers to produce a post–eighteenth-century bonanza. The process of paying leaner Peter to fatten hungry Paul, however, served more than economic desires. Among planters who wanted to preserve slavery, slave buying was the key to consolidating slavery's lower South empire. Among Southerners who wanted to remove slavery and blacks from their area, slave selling was the key to producing an all-white upper South. That antislavery rationale for an expansion of slavery even came to appeal to some Southern opponents of slavery who had earlier opposed slaveholder expansionism. In the eighteenth century, before the cotton expansion, Thomas Jefferson of Virginia had considered slavery's expansion wrong. But by 1820, after the cotton kingdom was well established, Jefferson called expansionism right. If slavery were to be bottled up in old areas, he thought, fearful whites would never free the densely concentrated blacks. If slavery were to be "diffused" into new areas, on the other hand, whites would more readily emancipate the scattered slaves. "Diffusion" was the key word. It united Southerners who hoped to remove all slaves from their declining area with Southerners who wanted more slaves to proceed toward their advancing area.

That unanimity imperiled both Native American landowners inside the lower South's domain and foreign landowners just outside. Newly expansive slave owners, while wishing the lower South swept of alien whites and Native Americans, especially sought to remove neighbors who encouraged slave resistance. The most menacing resistance came not from the few groups of slave insurrectionists, who always were quickly quashed, but from the more numerous individual runaways, who ultimately helped defeat Confederate armies. During the Civil War, runaways increased when slaveholders' enemies massed close by; and in the early nineteenth century, foreigners and Native Americans were uncomfortably close to the new cotton kingdom.

In Spanish Florida, for example, some Spaniards, Seminoles, and an occasional Englishman encouraged Georgia and South Carolina slaves to flee. In the face of this unrest, slaveholders argued that either the government must protect property or property holders must protect themselves. Farther north, on the

Tennessee frontier, Andrew Jackson had become a vivid symbol of that maxim. In 1818 President James Monroe ordered General Jackson to chastise some Seminoles who were troubling whites on the United States side of the Spanish Florida border. Jackson did more. He chased Seminoles over the Spanish border, seized their fort, killed several of their chieftains, hanged two Englishmen said to be their accomplices, and expelled a Spanish garrison from Pensacola.

Southern statesmen, in a pattern that would become crucial in the 1850s, divided along geographic lines on the wisdom of such adventuring as Jackson's. Southwestern frontiersmen cheered Jackson's raid. But South Carolina's John C. Calhoun (privately) and Kentucky's Henry Clay (publicly) deplored private raids that arguably exceeded governmental authorization. Nevertheless, southwesterners, South Carolinians, and border Southerners alike urged public governments to oust aliens and make private assaults unnecessary. After the Missouri controversy of 1819 through 1821, slaveholders' motivations were increasingly political as well as economic. More lower South land would mean more Southern states and thus more defenders of slavery in Congress.

Safer Southern frontiers would also mean safer American frontiers. That nationalistic reason for expansion southward especially prevailed before the Missouri controversy but lingered long after. Such patriotism enabled Southern leaders to rally a national consensus to evict foreigners and Native Americans from the entire lower South during the first four decades of the nineteenth century. In 1803 President Thomas Jefferson, as part of the Louisiana Purchase, bought the future slave states of Louisiana, Arkansas, and Missouri from the French. In 1819 another Virginian president, James Monroe, taking advantage of the Spanish weakness that Jackson's raid had revealed, purchased the future state of Florida and southern areas of Mississippi and Alabama from Spain. In the 1830s yet another Southern president, Jackson himself, deported Native Americans to reservations across the Mississippi River. And in 1844 the last antebellum president from Virginia, John Tyler, brought four decades of unanimous Southern zeal for expansion to a climax—and to an end—with his insistence that the Union annex Texas. That republic had secured its independence from Mexico in 1836, which had secured its independence from Spain in 1819.

President Tyler sought a national consensus to make the United States the latest nation with sovereignty over the vast Texas acreage. He thus did not emphasize one aim of fellow Southern expansionists: increasing the South's power in Congress. He did, however, reemphasize slaveholders' problems with neighbors perceived as hostile. If neighboring enemies incited slaves, Jackson had said and Tyler now repeated, slaveholders must be able to control the contiguous land. Jackson had worried about allegedly slave-inciting Spaniards, Englishmen, and Seminoles in Spanish Florida, which abutted Georgia. Tyler thought that English antislavery influence might eventually prevail in the Texas Republic, which abutted Louisiana and Arkansas. Better to annex another area contiguous to the lower South, Tyler declared with the aging Jackson's support, than to expose the slavocracy to anti-slavery neighbors.

Tyler reiterated not only Jackson's determination to take over contiguous areas but also Jefferson's desire to acquire outlets for the relocation of slaves. A new economic slump throughout the South, moreover, lent urgency to Jefferson's old argument for diffusing slaves away. In the 1840s the adolescent southwestern cotton kingdom, no less than the aging colonial South, endured economic crisis. Cotton prices, which had averaged 16.4 cents a pound in 1835 and 1836, plunged in the 1840s, after the devastating panic of 1837, to an average of 7.9 cents a pound. Only an exorbitant yield could compensate for these 50 percent lower prices, and only virgin lands could spawn 50 percent higher yields. Not even the relatively undeveloped Southwest now seemed sufficiently unscarred. An unspoiled Texas would provide an economic safety valve, said Tyler, to drain redundant slaves away from decaying slaveholding areas.

This newest safety valve argument continued to promise racial as well as economic relief. If no Texas outlet was secured, annexationists warned, the black population would swell in states suffering economic decline. If economic depression then persisted, whites would flee from excess blacks. Were Texas to be annexed, on the other hand, slaveholders would be able to sell unneeded slaves through the outlet. Here, in pristine form, was the agrarians' expand-or-perish argument. Unless slavery could spread into new areas, the slaveholders' depressed economy would collapse and the South's racial order would crumble. Add to this formula for disaster the possibility that English abolitionists in Texas, right across the Louisiana-Arkansas border, would incite blacks to flee or pillage or worse. This logic yielded a clear choice: increase the number of Southern congressional seats and double the lower South's land by adding Texas to the Union or expect a racial inferno. That exclusively Southern reason for national expansion, however, made Northerners increasingly resistant to American Manifest Destiny, slaveholder-style.

Collapse of the Southern Consensus

If the Southern expand-or-perish argument had remained unchallenged in the mid-1840s and had per-

vaded the 1850s, no historian would be able to deny that a monolithic South had been united behind slave diffusion. But in the period of the Texas annexation, the expansionists' diffusion argument inspired, in dialectical fashion, the first Southern breach over the question of slavery's expansion. In 1844 Southern Democrats, with rare border South exceptions, massed behind the expand-or-die thesis. When Southern Democrats thus insisted, reluctant Northern Democrats almost had to appease their party brethren, for the Democratic party was always stronger in the South than in the North. In contrast, when Northern Whigs insisted, Southern Whigs could hardly defy their party allies, for Whiggery was always stronger in the North than in the South. In 1844, after Southern Democrats relentlessly demanded Texas and after Northern Democrats reluctantly acquiesced and Northern Whigs contemptuously disapproved, Southern Whigs were driven to ask whether slavery would in fact perish unless the institution could diffuse into Texas.

That query undercut lower South unanimity on the expand-or-perish dogma. How, after all, could the single new slave state of Texas save slavery, in or out of Congress, if the institution drained out of eight border and upper South states and out of South Carolina too? Furthermore, how could cotton production in virgin Texas rescue the cotton South from a depression caused by cotton overproduction? Annexation, warned Whig South Carolina Congressman Waddy Thompson, would "very soon" remove slavery from "Maryland, Virginia, North Carolina, Tennessee, and Kentucky." Even in aging South Carolina, he feared, slavery would become "an incumbrance which we shall be glad to get rid of; and . . . it will afford me very little consolation in riding over my fields, grown up in broom-sedge and washed into gullies, to be told that . . . slavery still exists and is prosperous" in Texas.

Kentucky's Henry Clay, Whig nominee for president in 1844, reversed Waddy Thompson's lower South logic. Although a large border South slaveholder himself, Clay looked for the day when the South could rid itself both of slaves and of free blacks. He declared Texas annexation desirable in the abstract, because more slaves would then be diffused from the upper South. But he saw diffusion as not worth either a foreign war or a sectional controversy. A statesman's "paramount duty," he declared, was "preserving the Union," not saving slavery, a "temporary institution."

Slavery a "temporary institution"! Preserving the Union the "paramount duty"! With those four words, Henry Clay underscored, as if in Civil War blood, the difference between the border and lower South in their priorities about slavery, expansionism, and Unionism. But if the lower South's Waddy Thompson, hoping to keep slaves in South Carolina, and the border South's

Native Tennessean William Walker conquered and ruled Nicaragua in the mid-1850s.

PAGE 285

Mississippi secessionist John A. Quitman agreed to lead a filibuster army against Spanish forces in Cuba.

PAGE 285

Territorial expansion became a sectional issue as both North and South realized that western lands were essential for the survival of Southern slave culture.

PAGE 157

Henry Clay, hoping to keep all Americans in the Union, rejected annexation for contrary Whig reasons, the Whigs' alliance against Texas almost killed expansionism. Three months after the Democrats' ultra-expansionist James K. Polk defeated Clay in the November 1844 presidential election, the U.S. Senate nearly rejected the admission of Texas into the Union. The margin for Texas was thin, 27–25, because only three of fifteen Southern Whigs joined with the unanimously pro-Texas Democratic senators. Despite continued Whig opposition, the Democrat–led administration and Congress annexed Mexican territories from Texas to the Pacific, including California, in the Mexican Cession of 1848.

In the half-century since the invention of the cotton gin, U.S. expansionism in lower South latitudes had swept across the continent. That omnivorous territorial expansion, achieved in the 1840s despite increasing Southern opposition and greater Northern opposition, bid fair to override all obstacles once again in the 1850s. During that presecession decade, Southern attempts to control Kansas, California, New Mexico, Arizona, Cuba, Nicaragua, and Mexico periodically convulsed the nation, helped provoke the election of Abraham Lincoln in 1860, and helped lead to the formation of the Confederacy. Yet all latter-day Southern expansion efforts failed, in part because Northerners massed powerfully against them, and in part because Southerners failed to mass unanimously for them.

The lack of unanimous Southern zeal for expansion in the 1850s stemmed, first of all, from expansionism's very success. During the presecession decade, there was no way slaveholders could cultivate all the Texas, Arkansas, and California acres previously acquired. There was also no way most Southerners could still think that the slave South would perish economically. As the 1840s ended, so did the post-1837 depression. The prosperity of Southerners in the 1850s, with the exception of South Carolina rice farmers, exceeded pre-1837 levels. Cotton prices, which had averaged under 8 cents a pound in the 1840s, averaged 11 cents a pound in the 1850s. The lower South now needed more slaves to exploit unused land, not more outlets for unneeded slaves. Meanwhile, the upper South, also enjoying better times, no longer needed to sell slaves to survive. So lower South demand for slaves exceeded the supply, and the price of slaves soared 70 percent between 1850 and 1860.

One remarkable proposed solution demonstrated how completely times had changed. In the 1840s, many declining Southerners, growing too much cotton on too many tired acres, had sought fresh lands as a way to export excess blacks. In the 1850s, some booming Southerners, growing too little cotton with too few laborers, sought to import Africans as a way to develop excess land. A lower South movement to reopen the African slave trade grew with stunning rapidity in the mid-1850s. By buying slaves from Africa, ran one rationale for the proposed panacea, the lower South could expand its cotton kingdom continually without contracting the upper South's number of slaves counterproductively. With the upper South keeping its slaves while the lower South consolidated a hemisphere-wide empire, went the dream, Southern states, ever more numerous in Congress, would transcend the debilitating divisiveness of Texas annexation.

But the proposal caused a worse divisiveness. In the upper South, angry slave sellers noted that by seeking to reopen the African slave trade, slave buyers in the lower South were seeking to slice prices, even to cut U.S. sellers out of the market altogether. Reopening the trade would also defy Federal laws, enrage the North, and lead to disunion. After this upper South outcry, the lower South proposal sank almost as fast as it had arisen. But by urging that the South had overly abundant territory and insufficient slaves, the lower South finished off the Texas-outlet logic.

In yet another indication that the economic side of the planters' expand-or-perish rationale had become past history, the only remaining group of economically perishing planters tended now to oppose territorial expansion. South Carolina's coastal rice aristocrats suffered through a crippling economic slide in the 1850s, with the value of the rice crop sinking 25 percent below 1840s levels. South Carolina up-country cotton producers fared better, but their economic recovery was less spectacular than Southwesterners'. Some 7,000 whites and 70,000 South Carolina blacks departed for the cotton frontier in the 1850s, preserving that stagnating state's distinction as the only slave-exporting lower South state. The state also retained its distinction as the only declining eighteenth-century locale of slavery that exported slaves and still crusaded to keep slavery forever.

That singular determination to retain departing slaves turned most South Carolinians against tropical meccas. Waddy Thompson had put it well in Texas times: who would stay in depleted Carolina if they could go to virgin El Dorados? John C. Calhoun came around to a similar attitude in 1846, opposing a southwestern drive to acquire all of Mexico. Leading South Carolinians continued to harbor such views of proposed Caribbean expansion in the 1850s. Mexico seemed full of non-American peons, Cuba full of free blacks, and the Southwest full of coarse frontiersmen. "It is not by bread alone that man liveth," intoned South Carolina's revered Francis Sumter in 1859. "We want some stability in our institutions."

Many South Carolinians opposed a supposedly destabilizing Caribbean empire because they favored a supposedly stabilizing disunion revolution. These disunionists hoped that outside the Union and beyond unsettling Northern attacks, a settled South could flourish. They feared that if the Union did acquire vast tropical lands, restless southwesterners would never decide to secede. Still, a taste for staying home and distaste for expansionism swept up the powerful South Carolina Unionist, U.S. Senator James Henry Hammond, just as it did the secessionists. "I do not wish," said Hammond, "to remove from my native state and carry a family into the semibarbarous West."

While South Carolinians, the most avid disunionists, usually considered slaveholder expansion into raw land the semibarbarous road toward extinction, New Orleans businessmen, the most important proponents of Caribbean expansion, also cared little about acquiring new agricultural land. These avid imperialists instead longed for new urban markets. New York City and other northeastern urban centers were routing New Orleans in the competition for midwestern trade. In response, New Orleans merchants dreamed of commanding South American trade from U.S. ports in the Caribbean. It was not planters but the South's most expansive merchants who feared they might perish unless the North American republic spread over South America.

New Orleans merchants, as capitalist as any Northerner, and South Carolina planters, more anti-capitalist than any other Americans, clashed not only over whether capitalistic hustle was salutary but also over the most effective means of Southern survival. Most South Carolinians favored disunion as a way to escape the materialistic North. Most New Orleans capitalists favored the Union as a means to acquire a materialistic empire. If we exert enough pressure on Northern Democrats, New Orleans newspapers editorialized, the party will use the Union's power to acquire first Cuba's harbors and then other lucrative Caribbean ports. If we fail to leave the Democratic party and the Union, responded many South Carolinians, we will be left hopelessly behind in a riotously expansive nation.

That climactic Southern intramural war undercuts an important latter-day explanation for slaveholder expansionism. The Southern slave labor system, runs some historians' argument, generated less efficient laborers and less entrepreneurial owners than the Northern free labor system; and hence, without constant expansion to fresh lands, Southerners supposedly feared that their allegedly anachronistic system would perish. Evidence for that interpretation derives from the Texas annexation struggle in the 1840s, when the cotton South was staggering economically. But during the climactic struggle over Caribbean expansion in the 1850s, when cotton growers were booming, up-to-date New Orleans capitalists became the avid Southern territorial expansionists, South Carolina's not very

Most slave owners believed that slavery would not work well in an urban industrialized environment.

PAGE 558

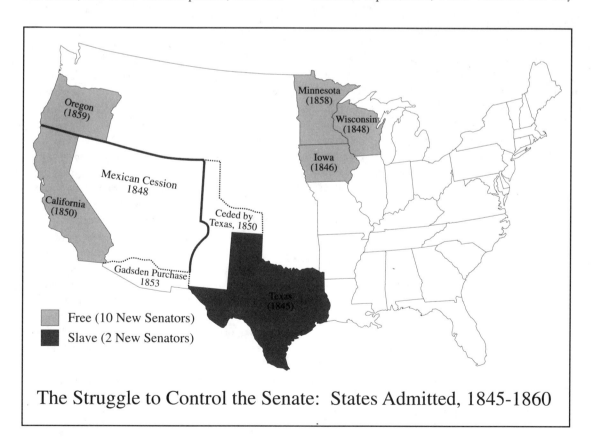

Free (10 New Senators)
Slave (2 New Senators)

The Struggle to Control the Senate: States Admitted, 1845-1860

EXPANSIONISM IN THE ANTEBELLUM SOUTH

Collapse of the Southern Consensus

Northerners found the Fugitive Slave Law outrageously un-American and tyrannical, particularly in requiring all free citizens to hunt down a brave escapee from despotism.

PAGE 232

capitalistic planters generally became anti-expansionists, and southwestern slaveholders, whatever they thought of Cuba, were seeking more slaves so they could pile up higher profits than Northern employers of free laborers could muster.

With the economic aspect of agrarians' expand-or-perish conception now vanished, and with economic expand-or-perish imperatives now impelling only the nonagrarian merchants, the political taproot of Southern agriculturalists' expansion became preeminent. Throughout the eras when Southerners sought more land, then more safety valves, and then more markets and more slaves, defensive defiance was these slaveholders' political style. Slaveholders' aggressive defensiveness usually took the form of drives for more congressional seats and especially for more secure borderlands, lest Northerners overwhelm slaveholders from without and corrode hinterlands from within. The old concern about slaveholders' vulnerable outposts, however, shifted in the 1850s from lower South to border South latitudes. True, near the Mexican border, lower South expansionists continued to complain about Mexican seduction of fugitive slaves. That argument helped impel abortive efforts to acquire Mexico in the 1850s. Near the Gulf of Mexico, other lower South expansionists focused on Cuba. They claimed that English abolitionists wished to emancipate (or, as the word went, "Africanize") Cuba, just as Englishmen had wished to emancipate Texas. An "Africanized" island commanding the Gulf, ninety miles from Florida, could not be tolerated. But Southerners farther from the Gulf considered English-inspired "Africanization" less creditable than in Texas times.

With a lower South reaching from the Atlantic to the Pacific now acquired, the greater border menace seemed to be northward, where more Northerners seemed to be helping slaves escape from the border South. This shift in the direction of greatest Southern concern created a revealing phenomenon: Southern congressmen cared less about California and Cuba, on the one hand, than about the Fugitive Slave Law and Kansas, on the other. During the crisis of 1850, Southerners demanded the opportunity to make California a slave state; and especially in southern California, cotton plantations would have enjoyed fabulous yields. But Southerners in Congress surrendered California to the North in exchange for a new Fugitive Slave Law. That edict was especially designed to protect the border South, where less plantation slavery was possible. Four years later, Southern drives to acquire Cuba and to open up Kansas to slavery came to a climax at practically the same moment. Cuba, already a slave island and more tropical than the most tropical lower South, possessed even more fertile land for slaveholders than did California. In contrast, Kansas, diffi-

cult to win for slavery and located northward in the border South temperate zone, could never sustain cotton and offered less potential for other plantation crops as well. Yet in 1854 Southern congressmen fought harder for the Kansas-Nebraska Act than for Cuba. Subsequently, Southern congressmen more insistently demanded that the Union admit Kansas than that the nation acquire Cuba.

These Southern priorities exasperated William Marcy, a New York Democrat and Franklin Pierce's secretary of state. The South's demand for Kansas, wrote Marcy, "has sadly shattered our party in all the free states," depriving "it of that strength which . . . could have been more profitably used for the acquisition of Cuba." Marcy's irony could as easily have been applied to 1850, when the South's insistence on a dubiously enforceable Fugitive Slave Law ruptured Southern sympathy in the North and deflected Southern energies from southern California, which was so highly adaptable to slaveholding.

Such priorities were less bizarre than Marcy thought. A now land-rich South understandably put lower priority on the acquisition of California and Cuba, both lush but neither located on a slaveholder's porous border. The higher priority involved consolidation of the vulnerable border South. Inside that embattled middle ground between the free labor North and the heavily slaveholding South, many inhabitants often hoped that their relatively few slaves would drain southward. Meanwhile, some Northern neighbors hoped to entice border fugitive slaves northward. The border slave state of Missouri, already surrounded on two sides by free labor Illinois and Iowa, could not save slavery, so Missouri slaveholders said, if a free labor Kansas menaced it from a third border. With this critical argument for the Kansas-Nebraska Act, Missourians reemphasized one constant in the changing story of Southern expansionism. Whether in Louisiana in 1803 or Florida in 1819 or Texas in 1844 or Kansas in 1854, Southerners feared slaves would flee from borderlands unless land could be seized from enemies over the border.

But if the entire South put its highest priority on controlling the Kansas borderlands, southwestern congressmen continued to support the lesser priority of Cuba. As U.S. Senator Albert Gallatin Brown of Mississippi put it, "I want Cuba, and I know that sooner or later we must have it, . . . for the planting or spreading of slavery" and to expand slaveholders' congressional power. Presidents Franklin Pierce (1853–1857) and James Buchanan (1857–1861), both Northern Democrats, tried to meet this demand by buying Cuba from Spain. When Spain would not sell, Pierce's ministers to Spain, England, and France issued the famous Ostend Manifesto (1854), warning that if

208

Spanish possession of Cuba endangered America, "by every law, human and divine, we shall be justified in wresting it."

Spain would not be bullied, whereupon Caribbean expansionists embraced so-called filibustering. Antebellum Americans used that term (linguistically derived from *freebooter*) to connote private armies that hoped to sail from a U.S. port, land in a Caribbean nation, lead an allegedly popular revolution, and annex the supposedly liberated nation to the United States. Such private invasions, which arguably culminated in John F. Kennedy's Bay of Pigs fiasco in Cuba in the 1960s, bore a resemblance to Andrew Jackson's incursion into Florida in 1818. A disproportionate percentage of 1850s filibusterers came from Jackson's Tennessee frontier. The most successful filibusterer, Tennessee's William Walker, briefly captured Nicaragua in the mid-1850s. The Jackson-Walker raiding spirit found its perfect financial complement in the New Orleans mercantile community's worried imperialism.

The combination of New Orleans cash and Tennessee adventurism might have been lethal to Caribbean nations—if the U.S. government had failed to enforce the Neutrality Law of 1818, which forbade U.S. citizens from invading foreign nations. But Northerners would have condemned any president who allowed lawless Southerners to capture a slaveholder's empire (and hence gain more congressional votes). Northern Democrats always preferred to appease the South a good deal while standing firm against Southern demands a little, thus keeping the party electable in the North and overwhelming in the South. In pursuit of that politic goal, Northern presidents sought the legal purchase of Cuba while imprisoning illegal filibusters. Only a relentlessly unified South might have budged Presidents Pierce and Buchanan from that seemingly balanced statecraft.

Southerners could not muster unanimous support for illicit private raids on Caribbean nations any more than they could for reopening the African slave trade or for Jackson's 1818 strike on Florida. Just as John C. Calhoun had considered Jackson an enemy of hierarchy and order, so most South Carolinians usually considered the filibusterers to be disorderly pirates who were seeking to seize disorderly nations. Just as Henry Clay had feared that Jackson's raid (and, later, Texas annexation) would disrupt the Union, so many upper South Democrats declared piracy in Cuba not worth disunion in America. With Southerners fighting Southerners, Northern Democratic presidents could follow Northern constituents' desires. Thus, Federal judges and naval officers blocked critical filibuster expeditions before invasions reached the targeted nations, aborting especially the plot of former Mississippi governor John Quitman to capture Cuba in

1855 and the assault by William Walker on Nicaragua in 1857.

Although Southerners were as badly divided on filibustering as on reopening the African slave trade, they were more united on the issue of Kansas. Yet irresolution plagued even this main Southern expansionist effort of the 1850s. By securing the Kansas-Nebraska Act in 1854, Southerners acquired the right to race Northern settlers to Kansas. Instead of speeding to Kansas, however, most migrants to the Southwest headed for more tropical virgin lands in Texas and Arkansas. With more Northerners peopling Kansas, not even determined Southern congressmen could pressure enough Northern Democrats to admit Kansas as a slave state in defiance of most Kansans' wishes.

Not enough Northerners appeased the South because too many Southerners deserted. In 1858, the House of Representatives rejected Kansas as a slave state by a vote of 120–112. If the six upper South ex-Whigs who voted "no" had voted "yes," the South would have had its sixteenth slave state. Southern opposition, having almost defeated Texas, had blocked the acquisition of Kansas for the South. The only southward expansion to triumph in the 1850s was the Gadsden Purchase (1853) of a strip of lower California—an acquisition aimed at building railroads, not planting cotton.

The frenetic Southern expansion efforts of the 1850s, which upset most Northerners yet acquired not one slave state, contrasted dismally with the sustained expansion efforts of 1793 to 1843, which had distressed few Northerners and had secured a lower South empire. But back in the heady pre-Texas days, all Southerners had cherished expansionist objectives, even if some had winced at Jackson's methods. With Southern unanimity over expansionist goals dissolving and Northern protests rising, Southerners were fortunate that Texas squeaked through; and no luck could thereafter win further expansion of the slavocracy. Even in Kansas, despite the Kansas-Nebraska Act, late antebellum slave society's demands eventually outran its power. Disunited Southerners could not forever successfully defy the more numerous and, in the end, equally resolute Northerners.

Northern Republicans of the 1850s would have dismissed the notion that Southern division hindered Southern expansion. They believed in that decade that everywhere they looked, whether toward Cuba or Nicaragua or Kansas or Mexico, Southerners were seeking to take over the Union and the hemisphere. Moreover, whenever Republicans called slavery too immoral to be allowed to spread, Southerners responded that Republicans must silence their hateful slander.

Republicans were right that *some* Southerners wanted every inch of New World space in the 1850s

Secession and the Civil War only gave Northerners more power to aid more fugitives— a slaveholders' problem that no Union or Confederacy could solve.

PAGE 232

In 1803, President Thomas Jefferson, as part of the Louisiana Purchase, bought the future slave states of Louisiana, Arkansas, and Missouri from the French.

PAGE 204

and that *no* Southerner could abide Northern insult. By calling slavery too barbarous to spread, Republicans took the expansion issue beyond pragmatic considerations, such as whether Caribbean acquisitions would depopulate South Carolina, to patriotic considerations, especially whether Southerners were respectable people. Republican moral condemnation generated a charged Southern vocabulary: would Southerners "submit" or "resist"? In this white man's egalitarian nation, white males could not "submit" to charges of moral inferiority without surrendering their self-respect and honor. Indeed, a failure to "resist" moral condemnation itself had practical consequences in a Southern world still divided on the morality of permanent slavery. If border Southerners submitted to Republican insult, these disbelievers in slavery's permanence would be lost to the slavocracy. Waverers must instead be rallied to resent the Republicans. If clergymen who criticized slaveholders' Christian imperfections saluted Republicans' antislavery morality, no Southerner would listen to them. Internal reformers must instead castigate outside agitators. All factions of Southern opinion thus had a pragmatic stake in condemning Northern critics.

This verbal aggressiveness once again illuminated the most constant aspect of Southern expansionism, whatever the changing economic motives: besieged Southerners' defiance of detractors, whether by rebutting insult or by seeking additional congressional seats or by fortifying vulnerable hinterlands. And curse the Republicans they constantly did. Along with their scorn came expansionist proposals, each more extreme than the last, and all of them, taken together, giving off the illusion of a consolidated civilization, even of a conspiratorially united slavocracy. But if resentment of Republican condescension was almost universal, support of filibusterers or endorsement of reopening of the African slave trade or a move to Kansas was not. So, too, in the secession crisis, while the necessity of resisting Lincoln's antislavery criticism was acknowledged almost universally, the necessity of resisting only outside the Union was not. After anti-expansionist South Carolinians precipitated disunion, pro-expansionist Louisianians felt compelled to follow their lower South brethren. But border Southerners felt a countervailing compulsion: to save the Union. Here again, the Southern politics of the 1850s, so often aimed at making border areas more Southern than Northern, had failed.

The resulting Southern disunity would prove to be even more fatal to Confederate armies than it had been to Caribbean filibusters, the reopening of the African slave trade, and the securing of Kansas. In war even more than in peace, the infuriated Southerner was an awesome force. But not even the South's fabled courage could ultimately defeat the more numerous Northerners, plus the border South third of Southern white folk, plus the runaway sixth of Southern black folk. And fugitive slaves, by fleeing toward Northerners during the Civil War, proved that prewar Southern expansionists' fears of nearby "aliens" had been all too prescient.

[*See also* Bleeding Kansas; Compromise of 1850; Democratic Party; Fugitive Slave Law; Imperialism; Kansas-Nebraska Act; Missouri Compromise; Wilmot Proviso.]

— WILLIAM W. FREEHLING

EXTORTION

As part of their effort to unite the South around a coherent set of ideals, Confederate cultural and political leaders struggled to identify the particular virtues of the South and to purge themselves of any accompanying vices. Wanting to consider themselves morally superior to the greed they claimed had overwhelmed the economic system of the North, leading Confederates hoped to root out their own greediest practices.

Foremost among those was what Southerners called extortion. As historian Drew Gilpin Faust has pointed out, since the eve of secession, "southerners had been citing the growing materialism of American, and especially northern, society as a fundamental justification for independence." Religious and political speakers drew on the South's heritage of republican ideology to claim that special economic privilege threatened to undermine the region's particular virtues of self-sufficiency, personal independence, and mutual respect among the classes. Southerners defined extortion as using a position of power to make unfair profits. Under this heading fell such practices as creating monopolies on goods, speculating on cotton and food crops, hoarding goods to raise prices, and setting prices on necessities beyond reasonable limits. To Southerners who believed that their society adhered to values of personal integrity and respect rather than those of a faceless marketplace, these were offenses against public morality and suggested that the South was becoming too much like the North. The practices mocked Southerners' claim to have a country based on religious principles and to understand the basic truths of political economy.

People who manipulated the economy for selfish purposes had long faced criticism in the South, but the opportunities the war presented for both production and marketing intensified economic developments that were well underway. In the 1850s far more Southerners than ever were turning to commercial agriculture, and those with money were investing in a wide range of commercial ventures, especially manufacturing and the railroads. Accusing fellow Southerners of extortion was a way to raise general concerns about the growing importance of a commercial economy, and then to blame the problem on the region's most obvious offenders. Accusations of extortion could thus serve a cathartic function for much of society.

The issue became most heated over food shortages and increases in food prices. Households unable to support themselves were newly dependent on local stores. A main problem with food supplies was impressment by the military. After the Confederate Congress passed the impressment law, farmers lived in fear of getting less than market prices for crops seized by the government. The impressment agents then became the enemies, appearing to work in tandem with corrupt marketers to deprive farmers of a just return on their goods and consumers of a just price. General store owners who hoarded food and raised prices seemed especially offensive in a time of sacrifice. In towns and cities from Richmond to Mobile, women mounted protests and then riots against the unfairness of high food prices and the unavailability of basic items. As historian Paul Escott has noted, the general popularity of the goals of these riots shows how fully most Southerners had accepted the idea that government and financial interests were working together unfairly.

As the war dragged on and Confederate troops met failure after failure, Southerners looked in many directions for scapegoats. With unseen forces apparently sapping the region's economic fortunes, many Southerners blamed Jewish bankers and immigrant merchants. This tendency continued the long-standing fear held by native-born Protestant Southerners that outsiders came to the South only to cheat them out of their money. Jews offered obvious targets for numerous reasons. Along with their historical stereotype as Shylocks, many did not work in the fields, many owned stores, and they were not part of the Protestant churches that were so important as agents of community life. Congressman Henry S. Foote wildly estimated that Jews made up nine-tenths of the region's merchants and speculated that they would own most of the wealth in the South by the end of the war.

Southerners generally agreed that too many were taking advantage of the war. As a Montgomery, Alabama, newspaper noted, "the whole country is ringing with denunciations of the extortioners." Some claimed that the profiteering followed economic logic and saw no reason to try to stop it, but they were the minority. The difficulty lay in what to do about extortion. The Confederate Senate debated a bill to restrict overpricing and excessive speculation, and seven states passed laws against those practices. A law in South Carolina set a 75 percent limit on the amount of profit resalers could make, and other states passed similar laws. The vagueness of the issue and the fear of stifling production limited such laws to symbolic importance, but that should not minimize their significance. By condemning the various forms of extortion so frequently, Southerners could believe that they were fighting for ideals far higher than money.

[*See also* Bread Riots; Speculation.]

— TED OWNBY

FARMING

On the eve of the Civil War, farming in the South had assumed a patchwork quality. There were, of course, thousands of large plantations employing mainly slave labor in the river bottoms of the Old Southwest and on the South Atlantic coast. But tens of thousands more small farmers, mostly white, cultivated the uplands, some of whom farmed for a subsistence and a surplus of cotton, corn, tobacco, or hogs, while still others were content to avoid markets altogether. Within these crop cultures, there labored many others, not properly called farmers, but without whom crops could not be planted or harvested. Most conspicuously, women labored in the home to raise children, make cloth, prepare food, and produce commodities for local trade in their truck gardens, milking barns, and chicken pens.

These various kinds of farming arose not from personal preference but from a conflict over the shape of Southern agriculture that had begun in the 1830s and would end only with the Populist revolt in the 1890s. As plank roads, river improvements, and later railroads connected the Southern interior to northeastern and midwestern markets, large farmers seized the opportunity to make ever greater profits. In some but not all parts of the South, they used the power of state and local government to require others to fence their animals in place of enclosing crops and to hunt game and range hogs only in designated places, thus limiting access to what had been common lands. Developers also required by means of cash taxes that small farmers help build and pay for an infrastructure of roads, cotton weighing platforms, and other public buildings that made commercial farming profitable. In the early 1840s, these development measures had begun to place commercial growers and subsistence farmers in conflicting positions.

By 1860, then, three kinds of farmers labored on the land in the Old South:

1. large planters who produced a staple crop, mostly cotton, with slave labor, for sale in distant markets;

2. large commercial farmers who employed tenants and day laborers to produce livestock, corn, and wheat, also for distant markets;

3. smaller farmers and the women and children in their households who produced a subsistence for themselves and sometimes a surplus, usually for sale or for barter in the neighborhood.

This tripartite social formation also produced two distinct classes of dependents, slaves on the one hand and poor white tenants and laborers on the other. When the war began, secessionists supposed that the South's farmers would rise as one to defend the new nation, but that was not the case. The war, in fact, exacerbated differences among farmers as well as disrupting the production of agricultural products.

Farmers in the Confederacy first felt the impact of the war during the financial crisis of late 1860 and early 1861. As secession became nearly a certainty, creditors began to call in their debts due from Southern commercial farmers, both large and small, and after secession credit disappeared entirely. At the same time, trade in farm commodities ground to a halt as banks began to hoard specie after the Union blockade of the Southern coast took hold. Cotton and wheat lay on docks and in barns, and a new Confederate war tax on property forced farmers to either borrow scarce money or sell crops at ruinously low prices. Those farmers who had most thoroughly committed themselves to supplying markets outside the South took the first blow in the conflict.

Smaller semisubsistence farmers did not begin to feel the pinch until the fall of 1861. By that time, the first wave of volunteers had served in summer campaigns after having taken care to plant their crops the previous spring. In the fall, however, as the fighting continued, soldiers could not return home to help harvest those crops. The task fell to women and children, who found themselves both shorthanded and without animals to haul crops from the fields to barns or to markets; the Confederate army had purchased or impressed thousands of horses, mules, and oxen in the summer of 1861. Moreover, it became nearly impossible to preserve pork in December because the price of salt had skyrocketed—by a factor of twelve in Savannah between May and October 1861. Before the war, salt had been imported mainly as ballast in ships that would carry away cotton, ships that in 1861 remained blockaded in Southern ports. The result was a subsistence crisis on many Southern farms during the first

By the spring of 1862, there was already an abundance of cotton and a shortage of foodstuffs.

PAGE 158

Many farmers found that impressment and the tax-in-kind hurt them, so they withheld food from the market or planted less.

PAGE 575

Cotton drove the economy of the South, affected its society, and, during the war, dominated the Confederacy's international relations through "cotton diplomacy."

PAGE 156

winter of the war. Between November 1861 and March 1862, six Confederate states approved legislation for the relief of indigent families left behind by men serving in either state militias or the Confederate army.

In April 1862 the Confederate government's Conscription Act began a massive and forced removal of labor from the countryside at the worst possible moment. But the act did not effect everyone equally. On small farms, young men between the ages of eighteen and thirty-five, both heads of households and agricultural laborers, were unable to plant spring wheat and corn, thereby leaving their families at the mercy of local markets in foodstuffs. At the same time, large planters, being exempt themselves from the draft, instructed their slaves to plant corn and wheat and beans instead of cotton, thus ensuring not only a subsistence for slaves but also a large marketable crop in foodstuffs that would command premium prices among the poor during the next fall and winter. Moreover, a severe drought that summer parched the crops and reduced yields for all farmers, and the Confederate army itself consumed a large portion of the South's foodstuffs and cloth. It also commandeered much of the best pasture land in the Shenandoah Valley and the Tennessee River basin to graze horses used by the cavalry and the quartermaster corps. Finally, the war itself disrupted planting in many parts of the Confederacy, especially on the South Atlantic coast, where Union raiders regularly penetrated one hundred miles or more inland, and in parts of middle Tennessee, the Mississippi delta, and southern Louisiana occupied by Union armies.

By the fall of 1862 the price of corn, produced now mainly on large plantations, had risen to $2.50 per bushel, well beyond the purchasing ability of ordinary farm families. Confederate soldiers received only about eleven dollars per month, and part of that paid the soldiers' own expenses: a uniform, shoes, and tobacco. Not surprisingly, many of those soldiers deserted and returned home to harvest what little had been planted the previous spring. As one farmer in Mississippi wrote in December 1862, "We are poor men and are willing to defend our country but our families first and then our country." The crops had failed, however, and many were forced to purchase corn at inflated prices. In a Mississippi county, for example, one local notable wrote that six hundred families there had a father or son in the army and could not afford to eat. "The Bread is here," he argued, "but owing to the High price is beyond the reach of these poor people."

Many blamed speculators for the scarcity and high price of foodstuffs, but small farmers themselves had contributed to the inflated prices, especially of corn. Confederate taxes, unlike most local taxes, had to be paid in cash, and therefore many converted their corn, rye, wheat, and barley into liquor, which, being easily transportable and in great demand as usual, could be sold in distant cities and to Confederate soldiers for specie. Yet the Confederate government remained the real culprit in these difficulties. Its conscription laws had confiscated the labor supply on small farms and its new taxes had the effect of converting foodstuffs into a marketable luxury.

As a result, many small farmers began to organize actively against not only military service but also the Confederacy itself; both had undercut the independent economy that they had gone to war to preserve in the first place. Farmers in the mountains barricaded themselves in hollows; others in Piedmont North Carolina closed the borders of several counties against Confederate recruiting agents; and many in Tennessee, Arkansas, and northern Alabama organized themselves into guerrilla bands. Moreover, many Southern communities included disaffected yeoman families who hid male relatives by day and fed and comforted them by night. But that strategy only preserved the men; it did not make their labor available to their families.

In 1863 inflation destroyed any hope the Confederate government might have had of mobilizing smaller farmers in its favor. The continued absence of labor on small Southern farms meant that little had been planted in the spring of 1863, and less harvested the following fall. Farmers in Virginia harvested only about one-third of their normal crop. In addition, the spring wheat in Georgia and Alabama suffered from rust and the corn from a severe drought. The price of corn rose that summer from three dollars to ten dollars per bushel. Moreover, the supply of cloth dwindled in the countryside. Southern textile mills diverted all their efforts to the production of uniforms, blankets, and tents for the army, leaving little or nothing for a population that was still wearing clothing manufactured three years earlier. Farmers' wives found it impossible to make their own cloth, mainly as a result of a shortage of cards with which to straighten cotton and wool fibers. For small farmers and their families food and clothing had become not just pricey, but impossible to obtain or even to produce at home.

In the spring of 1863 poor women in the South took the matter directly to the authorities. In a dozen or more places in the Confederacy, women rioted for fair prices that would enable poor men and women to acquire the common necessities of everyday living. In Salisbury, North Carolina, women working in government textile mills invaded stores and offered what they called "government prices" for flour, bacon, and molasses; these were prices that had been set by a local board under the terms of the Impressment Act and had lagged behind inflation. When their demands were refused, the women simply seized the items they needed. In Richmond more than a thousand women met at the capitol building and then looted downtown stores for food and clothing. Poor men and women in the countryside did much the same when they threatened "to organize and commence operations" if food and clothing did not soon become available. As one farmer in Bladen County, North Carolina, put it: "Some of us has been traveling for the last month with the money in our pockets to buy corn & tryd men that had plenty & has bin unable to buy a bushel." Planters were "holding on for a better price . . . so as to take all the soldiers wages for a fiew bushels," and that was not fair. "The time has come," he concluded, "that we the comon people has to hav bread or blood & we are bound boath men & women to hav it or die in the attempt."

But the worst was yet to come. In 1864 inflation placed all commodities of any kind out of the reach of ordinary farmers. In February of that year, flour sold in Richmond for $250 per barrel, corn for $30 per bushel, and bacon for $6.50 per pound. Moreover, the Confederate government began to impress at a government price much below market prices all goods of any use to the army. Farmers located near railroads typically lost all their grain and livestock, and large portions of eastern North Carolina were commandeered as pasture for the Army of Northern Virginia's cavalry because pastures in the Shenandoah Valley were now both worn out and vulnerable to Union attack. The final blow came with Union advances into southern Virginia, the Mississippi delta, Tennessee, and northern Alabama, and with William Tecumseh Sherman's march through Georgia and the Carolinas. The devastation of farms in the Confederacy was complete.

In the end, the war to preserve the Southern countryside had transformed it. It had bankrupted commercial farmers and destroyed their capital for a generation. It had turned many poor white farmers against both the Confederate government and neighboring planters. And it had freed the slaves who, after the war, would compete with white farmers for scarce land and credit and later flood the Southern market for agricultural labor, thereby driving down wages. But the war had also created new possibilities. Southern farm men and women who had protested the imposition of unjust prices during the war would do so again in the Southern Alliance and the Populist party. And Southern commercial farmers who had struggled against the deadweight of slavery before 1860 would seize the opportunity to produce a New South rooted in highly commercialized investment agriculture.

[*See also* Bread Riots; Cotton; Impressment; Plain Folk; Rice; Slavery; Substitutes; Sugar; Taxation; Tobacco.]

— WAYNE K. DURRILL

FAST DAYS

Jefferson Davis proclaimed nine days of fasting between June 1861 and March 1865. Along with national fasting days, the governors and legislatures of several states proclaimed occasional days of either thanksgiving or humiliation. Most stores closed, and, when possible, military companies suspended drills. With roots deep in American religious history, fast days have long sounded a call for sacrifice and unity in the name of a high religious goal. Denying themselves food to show religious and political unity may well have held a special meaning for people being asked to sacrifice food for the war effort. Fast days were also times for collecting money for the cause: the call for self-denial served as a call for contributions.

Official days of fasting were part of the effort by Confederate leaders to create the national unity necessary to fight a long and difficult war. Fast-day preachers and secular speakers proclaimed that Southerners were fighting a holy war that pitted a people of high moral standards against a people driven by greed and consumed by immorality. Linking the religious mission of the Confederacy to the stories of the Old Testament, they claimed to represent a new chosen people. One church periodical asserted that military success at Manassas, Chancellorsville, and Chickamauga had followed specific days of fasting.

Preachers used the occasion to castigate Southerners for a host of sins that seemed to stand in the way of the military effort and of the purity of their cause. Drunkenness and adultery seemed especially tempting to men away from their homes, dishonest financial dealings seemed too available with the economic disruption of the war years, the possibility of corruption among political officials seemed more likely with the new powers the government was assuming, and the abuse of slaves seemed more of a problem with opportunities for escape increasing.

On days of fasting, Southerners were urged to examine whether they were living up to the highest of their ideals and to consider the consequences of failure. As Georgian Charles Colcock Jones, Jr., wrote from an army camp, "the nation must be brought to feel their sins and their dependence upon God, not only for their blessings but for their actual salvation from the many and huge dangers which surround us."

It is not easy to determine how fully white Southerners answered the calls for fasting and humiliation. Discussions of the fasts appear often in the letters and diaries of the wealthy, but they are much harder to find in the documents left by the ordinary folk. For example, the diaries of South Carolina farmer David Golightly Harris mentioned the first of the Confederacy's nine fast days, but not the other eight. The call for

The food riots were disturbing evidence that the war had become a poor woman's fight as well as a poor man's.

PAGE 75

public fasting ran up against two important Southern traditions. One was a religious tradition that stressed individual conversion rather than group rituals. The second was a political tradition that stressed personal independence rather than obedience to central authority. Despite their less than complete acceptance, however, the fast days were important examples of calls for self-examination and sacrifice.

— TED OWNBY

Robert Barnwell Rhett was a classic Southern fire-eater whose uncompromising devotion to Southern independence earned him the title of "the father of secession."

PAGE 496

FIRE-EATERS

Southern proslavery and state rights extremists were termed fire-eaters in the two decades before the Civil War. The image evoked by the term was that of swaggering hotheads intent on breaking up the Union in their defense of slavery and Southern rights. The most famous of the fire-eaters were Edmund Ruffin of Virginia, an agricultural reformer; Robert Barnwell Rhett, Sr., of South Carolina, an editor and low-country planter; and William Lowndes Yancey of Alabama, a lawyer and gifted orator.

The fire-eaters were the ideologues of secession. They identified the ownership of slaves as the most fundamental of all Southern rights and insisted that Southern honor and equality could accept no outside interference with the institution of slavery. They pushed traditional state rights doctrines to the logically extreme position that states could peacefully withdraw from the Union.

Too impatient and scornful of compromise to be entrusted with positions of political power, the fire-eaters turned to agitation to spread their message that Southern honor and security demanded separate nationhood. Through speeches, pamphlets, editorials, and committees of correspondence they popularized

secession as a constitutional right among the Southern white masses.

Although blocked in their secessionist efforts during the sectional crisis over the Compromise of 1850, the fire-eaters played a key role in the secession movement of 1860 and 1861. They were instrumental in the breakup of the national Democratic party over the issue of Federal protection of slavery in the territories and fully exploited Southern fears over Abraham Lincoln's election. Nevertheless, they were soon shunted aside as more moderate politicians assumed control of the new Confederate government.

— WILLIAM L. BARNEY

FLOYD, JOHN B.

Floyd, John B. (1806–1863), politician and brigadier general. Born on June 1, 1806, in Montgomery County, Virginia, John Buchanan Floyd served as governor from 1848 to 1852. His political service to the Democratic party secured his appointment as President James Buchanan's secretary of war (1857–1860). After bitter criticism by Northern politicians and the press for the alleged transfer of arms and equipment from Northern to Southern arsenals and contractor indiscretions within the War Department, he was commissioned a Confederate brigadier in 1861. He served in the West Virginia campaign under Robert E. Lee, being involved in small battles at Cross Lanes, Carnifix Ferry, and Gauley Bridge. Sent west in December 1861 with his brigade of Virginia troops, he joined Albert Sidney Johnston's forces in western Kentucky.

As senior brigadier, Floyd assumed command on the Cumberland River at Fort Donelson, Tennessee, in February 1862, just as Ulysses S. Grant's joint army-navy expedition invested the work (having captured nearby Fort Henry on the Tennessee River a week before). Although hampered by divided leadership (there were three brigadiers besides himself), unclear and conflicting orders from Johnston, a jealous but largely untested army of over fifteen thousand men, and an untenable static defense position, Floyd stymied Union forces for three days while Johnston conducted a retreat of the main army from Bowling Green to Nashville. Nonetheless, in a comedy of errors, fouled communications, amateurish tactical bungling, and loss of nerve, Floyd and his fellow officers (Gideon Pillow, Simon Bolivar Buckner, and Bushrod Rust Johnson) relinquished the initiative, failed to extricate their army, and were forced to surrender to Grant. In a famous opéra bouffe scene of passing command, Floyd and Pillow fled with the Virginia brigade (and miscellaneous portions of the garrison), thereby earning the

POLITICAL GENERAL

Senior brigadier John B. Floyd is remembered for a humiliation at Fort Donelson, Tennessee; his political skills surpassed his military contributions.

LIBRARY OF CONGRESS

enmity and scorn of friend and foe alike for the remainder of the war.

Floyd subsequently escaped to Nashville and aided in restoration of order and transfer of army supplies from the city. But because he had deserted his command, he was subsequently removed from other positions of command in the Confederate service. Active as a Virginia militia major general in southwestern Virginia, Floyd organized partisan bands to combat Union incursions, but his health broke, resulting in his early death in August 1863 near Abingdon, Virginia. Known to posterity for the Fort Donelson disaster, Floyd represented the typical nineteenth-century political general whose ambitions exceeded his military talents, to the detriment of the Confederacy.

— B. FRANKLIN COOLING

FOOTE, HENRY S.

Foote, Henry S. (1804–1880), Tennessee governor and congressman. Historians who have mentioned Henry Stuart Foote at all have not been kind to his memory. Charles S. Sydnor viewed him as the Clement L. Vallandigham of the South, and E. Merton Coulter said he was "choleric," "excitable," "incorrigible," "eccentric," "irascible," "voluble," and "restless." Clement Eaton described him as "a little man, always barking and snapping, . . . a consummate demagogue." But worse still, most historians have done what Foote would have abhorred: they have ignored him. Thomas Hart Benton swore not even to mention his name in his *Thirty Years' View.* When others have referred to him, the comments have been negative. His only biographer, John Edmond Gonzales, suggests that he was a "political chameleon"—aligning himself with first one political party and then another.

Contemporaries had little better to say of him. Jefferson Davis, a fellow Mississippian, found him a thorn in his side in both the U.S. Senate and the Confederate presidency; Davis, who fought him physically and verbally, denounced him as "a constitutional liar." A colleague in the Confederate Congress described him as a "nuisance" whose conduct on the floor of Congress often was "disgraceful," and a Richmond newspaper editor said he was a "loose and inaccurate thinker."

On the other hand, his Nashville postwar law partner, Arthur S. Colyar, saw him as "one of the brightest intellects on the American continent" but also observed that he was "the most changeable of men." A Mississippian, writing some fifteen years after Foote's death, regarded him as a "foeman worthy of the steel of the ablest opponent of whatever cause espoused." No one questioned his skill at debate and repartee. He had

a good basic knowledge of law; indeed, the Nashville Bar Association declared at the time of his death that he had had no equal as a trial lawyer. As a journalist, lawyer, writer, and lawmaker, he was successful. As a politician, he won—perhaps—his share of the contests. Always on the move, he was respected if not loved, whether in Alabama, Mississippi, California, Texas, Tennessee, Richmond, or Washington.

Foote was born in Fauquier County, Virginia, on February 28, 1804. After graduation from Washington College at the age of fifteen, he studied law and was admitted to the bar at Richmond when nineteen. During his lifetime he established residence and practiced law in half a dozen states and the District of Columbia, in addition to residing for some months in exile in England and Canada.

Foote first settled in Tuscumbia, Alabama, in 1823, where he married, practiced law, and edited a newspaper. His vitriolic journalistic style soon led to a duel with John A. Winston, later governor of Alabama. Neither man was hurt, but Foote was barred from the practice of law in Alabama for three years. Undaunted, he gathered up his family and moved to Mississippi, living and practicing law successively in Jackson, Natchez, and Vicksburg. His support of Andrew Jackson made him known throughout much of Mississippi, and he was elected to the legislature in 1837. At about the same time, he developed a strong interest in the independence movement in Texas and, after paying an extended visit to that new republic, published in 1841 a two-volume work, *Texas and the Texans.*

But his primary interest was politics, not law and journalism, and he aligned himself with the Democratic party in Mississippi, becoming one of the party's most respected leaders. He served, with Jefferson Davis, as a presidential elector in 1844 and vigorously supported James K. Polk because of Polk's willingness to annex Texas. In 1847 he was elected to the U.S. Senate.

In Washington Foote became one of the architects of the Compromise of 1850, although his colleague Davis, and indeed all of the Mississippi House delegation, bitterly opposed the measure. But he saw the compromise as a means of preserving the Union; as a strong Union supporter in a state where secession already was being discussed, he risked his political future to work for the measure's passage. In 1851, boldly heading the Union Democrats, he announced for governor and was elected by a small majority over Davis, a state rights Democrat—a feat attributable to his oratorical abilities and his powers of persuasion.

He was unhappy as governor because his interests lay primarily in national politics. He had supported Franklin Pierce for president and hoped for a cabinet post but received "a cruel blow" when the president ignored him and appointed Jefferson Davis secretary of

"*In Mississippi, Henry S. Foote, who favored [the Compromise of 1850], defeated Jefferson Davis, who was opposed, for the governorship.*"

FRANCIS BUTLER SIMKINS
A HISTORY OF THE SOUTH
1958

"*The Compromise
of 1850 proved to
be not only
temporary but
from the Southern
viewpoint a tragic
mistake.*"

FRANCIS BUTLER
SIMKINS
A HISTORY OF THE SOUTH
1958

war. He offered his candidacy for U.S. Senate in 1854, but the legislature, controlled in large measure by state rights Democrats, elected Albert Gallatin Brown. Soon, in typical Foote fashion, he resigned the governorship a few days before he had finished one term and moved to San Francisco, where he joined his two sons-in-law in the practice of law. By the end of the decade, however, he had returned to Mississippi and again entered politics with vigor. In 1859 he announced for Congress, but because of his Unionist proclivities, he received little encouragement. He withdrew and by midsummer had established a residence and law practice in Nashville.

Foote had been in Nashville less than six weeks when he became aligned with the Democratic party with a view to exerting influence in the presidential election of 1860. Months before Democrats assembled in Charleston to nominate a presidential candidate, Foote had announced his support for Stephen A. Douglas. Alarmed at the Republicans' gains in 1856 and viewing that party as a prime instigator of disunion, he predicted that the Southern states would secede should a Republican be elected. The Illinois Democrat, he said, was the only person who could satisfy all sections and maintain peace.

Douglas's defeat was upsetting to Foote, and he confidently predicted that Abraham Lincoln would bring secession and war. Remembering the Southern convention of 1850, he urged Governor Isham G. Harris and other Tennessee Democrats to call a conference of representatives from the Southern states to meet in Nashville. The fifteen slaveholding states should attempt to secure certain guarantees from the Republicans, he said; that failing, they should declare the Union at an end and withdraw in concert. The last thing they should do, he asserted, was to secede in piecemeal fashion. But these efforts failed, and Foote

turned his attention to Tennessee. He worked with Governor Harris and the secessionist Democrats to accomplish separation in the Volunteer State, becoming one of the many former sincere Unionists who gave up hope for a peaceful settlement after Lincoln was inaugurated.

In the early fall of 1861, Foote became a candidate for the Confederate Congress from the Fifth District. He won handily over two opponents, and in early February 1862 he departed for Richmond. He wasted no time in leading the opposition to the administration and soon was at war with Davis and most of the cabinet. He accepted with difficulty the fall of Forts Henry and Donelson and the occupation of Nashville, calling for the dismissal and censure of Secretary of War Judah P. Benjamin and Naval Secretary Stephen R. Mallory. Benjamin, he said, was unfit to hold a cabinet post and Mallory was "utterly incompetent." But he saved most of his invective for his old nemesis, President Davis; he was a person, Foote said, who would establish a dictatorship to serve his own ends, who had only "power for mischief," who was basically corrupt, and who might best serve his country if placed in a mental institution. (He had characterized Thomas Hart Benton in roughly these same terms a decade earlier when both served in the U.S. Senate.)

Foote's propensity for fighting anyone and everyone got him into serious trouble in Richmond, and he occasionally despaired of his life. He had remembered Washington as a place where he had been threatened with fists and guns, but men of the Deep South also fought with knives and clubs. He had only to refer to Alabama Congressman E. S. Dargan as a "damned rascal" when the Alabamian lunged at him with a bowie knife. When Foote ridiculed a congressman from Arkansas, the two came to blows before being separated. When a Richmond editor called upon Congress to censure and expel him for his general conduct, he reacted in such a manner that the editor threatened to kill him. The editor persuaded Congressman William G. Swan to carry a written challenge to Foote, but the irascible Nashvillian responded so violently that Swan stabbed him with the only weapon at hand—an umbrella. The two were arrested and placed under a peace bond by a Richmond magistrate.

Foote referred to himself as the champion of the people against the aggressions of a selfish administration. As such, he boasted that he carefully read all bills introduced, and he presented a large number himself. He bitterly opposed the suspension of the writ of habeas corpus by Earl Van Dorn around the Vicksburg area and attacked Braxton Bragg for imposing martial law in Atlanta. He insisted upon a careful investigation after each battle the Confederacy lost, and he frequently criticized the Davis administration for withholding information on the conduct of the war. He investigated the commissary and cited the waste and profiteering he uncovered. Generally anti-Semitic, he wanted to expel all Jewish traders from the South and constantly urged Davis to dismiss Benjamin from his cabinet. He urged people to accept Confederate paper money, wanted Congress to make it legal tender, and publicly declared that anyone who refused to accept Confederate notes was "deserving of the Penitentiary."

Foote was disturbed that the new government was not accepted in Europe, and on this matter he and President Davis agreed. Davis was critical of both France and England because they appeared to be "unfriendly," and Foote introduced a resolution urging Davis to recall the Southern envoys from every country that had not granted recognition by May 1, 1863.

Foote and Davis also agreed on the wisdom of trying to persuade the states of the Old Northwest to withdraw from the war. Southern Illinois, Indiana, and Ohio, in large measure, had been settled by migrants from Confederate states, and their sentimental attachment to the land of their birth remained strong. The Northwest was tied to the South by the vast Mississippi River system and common economic bonds. Also, the peace element in the Democratic party in those states had won important victories in the fall 1862 elections. Both Foote and Davis urged leaders in those states to force Lincoln to make peace and recognize the independence of the South. The matter became one of the many subjects upon which Foote repeatedly addressed Congress.

If there was one characteristic that Foote consistently displayed, it was his inconsistency. Invariably, in matters affecting his political life he fled when the going got rough. So it was with his relationship with the Confederacy. Early in his congressional career he had predicted a short war and an early victory for the South. Always impatient, he urged that the war be taken to the enemy; he would expend a million men and $2 billion, if need be, to take the war into the North and rake those states with fire and sword. It was the Northern people who must be made to feel the harshness of war, he said; their "cupidity" and "semi-barbarous and insatiable lust for . . . domination had started the war," and they must be made to suffer.

He rejoiced in his first few months in Richmond that the Southern people daily became "more enthusiastic and resolute and far more confident as to the ultimate outcome of the struggle." So encouraged was he with victories in the East in the late fall of 1862 that he suggested that commissioners be sent to Washington to propose terms of a just and lasting peace guaranteeing Southern independence. He believed the South had so much support among the common folk of the North that a refusal by the administration would result

in a revolt of such magnitude that Lincoln would be deposed. But as Northern armies took Tennessee, the West, and much of the Southwest and ultimately closed in on Atlanta and on Lee in Virginia, he turned to Washington to beg for peace at almost any price.

When Congress convened in November 1864 after a brief recess, Foote expressed a belief that the Confederacy could not hold on beyond spring of the next year. He had given up on Southern independence but believed that a negotiated peace might at least preserve slavery. Congress, however, published a manifesto declaring that the Confederacy would never give up short of independence and then enacted a measure making negotiation with the enemy punishable by fine and imprisonment.

Foote nevertheless was determined to sound out the Federal authorities. He and his wife secretly fled toward Union lines but were overtaken on January 10, 1865, by Confederate troops some thirty-seven miles beyond the picket lines and within five miles of Union troops. Mrs. Foote was permitted to proceed, but Foote was briefly confined in Fredericksburg and then permitted at his request to return to Congress in Richmond. As his colleagues debated censure and expulsion, he fled again—this time successfully—and on January 28 was received across enemy lines and imprisoned. Although he wrote letters to Lincoln, the press, and some of the cabinet members, he was in large measure ignored.

When Andrew Johnson became president, he ordered Foote to either leave the country within forty-eight hours or stand trial for treason and rebellion. Foote fled to Montreal, from where he wrote numerous letters pleading not for the Confederacy but for his own liberty and the right to live in the United States. He wrote Johnson of his hope for peace and prosperity for America and to affirm that he was ready to take the oath of allegiance. To fellow Tennesseans, he wrote advising them to ratify the Thirteenth Amendment and swear allegiance to the United States. Finally, in late August 1865, Johnson permitted him to return to the country. By that time he had taken the oath of allegiance, publicly endorsed black suffrage, and assured all that he would not become involved again in politics.

After Foote paid an extended visit to his daughter and her husband, William M. Stewart, a U.S. senator from Nevada, he lived in St. Louis for a year, writing and speaking. By the summer of 1867, he was back in Nashville and had become affiliated with the conservative Democrats. He campaigned for the Democratic presidential candidate in 1868, and, though the Radical Republicans won the presidency, the conservatives in Tennessee were returned to power. Foote apparently had little confidence in Ulysses S. Grant, but he urged

"If agents of the Confederate government had the right to go in and take the men belonging to that state, how were states' rights and state sovereignty to be maintained?"

HENRY S. FOOTE

Tennesseans to support the president—another instance of his ambivalence and opportunism.

Writing had been not only a profitable venture for Foote but therapeutic. Early in 1866 Harper and Brothers published his *War of the Rebellion*, a lengthy work covering the colonial period through 1864 but emphasizing the past fifteen years. He saw nothing "irrepressible" about the conflict but attributed it to a "blundering generation" of the fifties and sixties—the "sectional factionists." In 1873 he moved to Washington, where he practiced law and wrote a series of articles for a Washington newspaper. These were collected and published as *Casket of Reminiscences* in 1874. Then, in 1876, he published his last book, *The Bench and Bar of the South and Southwest*; critics complimented the "new" Foote for the absence from this work of the usual vitriolic comments about people he did not like.

By the time his last book circulated, he was back in Tennessee and affiliated with the Republican party, the same party he had vilified since its formation in 1854. Republicans composed the minority party in the Volunteer State, and leaders welcomed him gladly. They named him an elector for the state at large, and he used his position to describe Democrats repeatedly as "unscrupulous men," dishonest and corrupt. Rutherford B. Hayes's victory in 1876 was pleasing to Foote, who for the next four years divided his time between Nashville and Washington. In 1878 he was elected permanent president of the Republican State Convention, and a few men even talked of him for governor. He was seventy-four by that time, however, and a Nashville newspaper described him as "a decrepit old gentleman with a fiery red head, almost entirely bald, . . . leaning heavily on a stout gold-headed cane."

Late in 1878, Hayes appointed him superintendent of the U.S. Mint at New Orleans, where he was well received. By the end of the following year he had become seriously ill and departed in April 1880 for Nashville, where he died on May 19. Former governor Joseph E. Brown of Georgia attended his funeral, and Gen. William Brimage Bate and former Confederate congressmen Robert Looney Caruthers and Arthur Colyar were pallbearers. He was buried in Mt. Olivet Cemetery.

— ROBERT E. CORLEW

FORD, ANTONIA

Ford, Antonia (1838–1871), spy. The daughter of a prominent merchant in Fairfax Court House, Virginia, Ford began her career as a spy in 1861 by passing information she gathered from Union forces in her hometown to Confederate leaders Col. J. E. B. Stuart and Gen. P. G. T. Beauregard. Although the exact nature of Ford's espionage activities is unclear, they seem to have been appreciated by Stuart, who rewarded Ford, on October 7, 1861, with a commission as an honorary aide-de-camp.

Gen. Lafayette C. Baker, chief of Union counterintelligence, was aware of Ford's reputation: in March 1863, in the wake of Col. John S. Mosby's famous capture of Gen. Edwin H. Stoughton in Fairfax Court House, Baker placed a female counterspy in Fairfax to entrap Ford. Ford allegedly revealed to the counterspy that she had aided Mosby, and as a result, she was arrested on March 13, 1863, and committed to Old Capitol Prison in Washington, D.C. A few months later, Ford was released and sent on to Richmond as part of a prisoner exchange. Mosby in later years adamantly maintained that Ford had nothing to do with the Stoughton incident.

A year after Ford's arrest, on March 10, 1864, she married the Union officer who had arrested her, Maj. Joseph C. Willard. The couple settled in Washington, D.C., where Antonia Ford died in 1871.

— ELIZABETH R. VARON

FORREST, NATHAN BEDFORD

Forrest, Nathan Bedford (1821–1877), lieutenant general. Forrest was born in Chapel Hill, Tennessee, on July 13, 1821. Although he had barely six months' formal education, Forrest assumed responsibility for his family at the age of sixteen following his father's death. Life in the Southern backcountry, the demands of Southern honor, and a constant struggle for control conditioned his life.

Forrest supported his family until 1842, when he moved to Hernando, Mississippi, to go into business with an uncle. In 1851, he relocated to Memphis, Tennessee, where he engaged extensively in the slave trade, establishing one of the largest such operations in the region. With the money he obtained, he rose from semisubsistence to planter status, acquiring substantial plantation property in Coahoma County, Mississippi. Throughout his prewar years, Forrest held various public offices and positions of authority: constable in Hernando; coroner in DeSoto County, Mississippi; lieutenant in the DeSoto Dragoons (Fifty-first Regiment, Mississippi Militia); and alderman in Memphis from 1858 to 1859 and in 1860.

Following Tennessee's secession from the Union, Forrest enlisted as a private in Capt. Josiah White's Tennessee Mounted Rifles (Seventh Tennessee Cavalry) with his youngest brother and fifteen-year-old son. Shortly afterward, the governor of Tennessee summoned him to Memphis and authorized him to raise a battalion of mounted troops, which later became known as the Third Tennessee Cavalry Regiment. As a lieutenant colonel, Forrest recruited and equipped his command, mostly at his own expense. In his first substantial combat experience at Sacramento, Kentucky, on December 28, 1861, he demonstrated the traits that characterized him as a soldier throughout the war by employing envelopment tactics and engaging the enemy personally.

In February 1862 Forrest established a reputation for boldness when he led his men out of Fort Donelson before its surrender, after having participated actively in its defense. Following his election as colonel, the cavalry commander fought at Shiloh, suffering a severe wound during the final phase of that battle. Subsequently, he assumed a new command, later known simply as Forrest's cavalry brigade, and promptly won promotion to brigadier general following a daring raid against the Union garrison at Murfreesboro, Tennessee, on July 13, 1862.

In mid-December 1862, Forrest crossed the Tennessee River into the western part of the state on a raid designed to sever Maj. Gen. Ulysses S. Grant's supply lines. For two and a half weeks, Forrest's cavalrymen used bluff and bluster to capture railroad depots, burn supplies, and disable miles of track and trestlework. Forrest succeeded in eluding his pursuers until December 31, when he fought a pitched battle at Parker's Crossroads. He was on the verge of winning the battle when a second Union force appeared, at which point he was fortunate just to extricate the bulk of his command. Nevertheless, Forrest succeeded in crippling Grant's supply lines and thwarting that general's initial assault against Vicksburg, Mississippi.

On February 3, 1863, Forrest's command suffered a defeat at Dover, Tennessee, while under the overall command of Maj. Gen. Joseph Wheeler. Then, following redeeming victories at Thompson and Brentwood, Tennessee, Forrest successfully halted a raid in April and May 1863 by Union Col. Abel Streight against the Western and Atlantic Railroad. In the climax to his pursuit, the Confederate cavalryman again used psychology and deception to compel a numerically superior force to surrender to him. Forrest was a master of this kind of warfare. In the case of his confrontation with Abel Streight, he employed false couriers from phantom units and moved the minimal number of troops at hand so as to artificially inflate his command.

Forrest's cavalry participated in Braxton Bragg's retreat from central Tennessee, his evacuation of Chattanooga, and the subsequent battle along Chickamauga Creek, Georgia. Following the victory over William S. Rosecrans's Federals at Chickamauga, Forrest urged but failed to convince Bragg to pursue the defeated enemy. Angry at his superior's ineptitude and resenting Bragg's previous treatment of him, Forrest bitterly

denounced Bragg and won a transfer to an independent command in Mississippi.

For the third time in his military career, Forrest raised a command, known simply as Forrest's cavalry corps, with new recruits and conscripts joining a small nucleus of veterans. Promoted to major general on December 4, 1863, he led raids against Federal communications and supply lines in Tennessee and Alabama and blunted various Union raids into Mississippi throughout 1864. In April he conducted a raid into western Tennessee that culminated in the capture of Fort Pillow. In the latter stages of that battle, Forrest lost control of his men, who killed members of the black Tennessee Unionist garrison who should have been spared.

In June Forrest ably defeated and routed a superior force of Union infantry and cavalry at Brice's Cross Roads. In July he helped turn back another Federal invasion force at Tupelo, although he suffered a temporarily disabling wound while directing the pursuit of the retreating Union troops. After recovering from his wound, Forrest engaged in a generally successful effort to destroy the railroads of northern Alabama and central Tennessee and decimated the river supply depot at Johnsonville, Tennessee. He cut short the Johnsonville expedition to march with John Bell Hood in that general's disastrous Tennessee campaign in November and December 1864. Forrest's outstanding conduct of the rear guard in Hood's retreat from Nashville, Tennessee, saved the Army of Tennessee from further destruction.

Forrest returned to Mississippi to reorganize his cavalry command. During this period he received a promotion to lieutenant general to date from February 28, 1865. In the closing months of the war, Forrest attempted to restore the condition of his command to resist further Union advances. Despite his preparations, he was unable to prevent a vastly superior force

FORREST, NATHAN BEDFORD

CAVALRY LEADER

Nathan Bedford Forrest rose from humble beginnings to a brilliant career as cavalry raider whose men vexed Federal supply lines in Tennessee and disrupted Grant's first assault against Vicksburg.

NATIONAL ARCHIVES

"If you ever again try to interfere with me or cross my path, it will be at the peril of your life."

NATHAN BEDFORD FORREST
TO BRAXTON BRAGG

FORREST'S RAIDS

Gen. Nathan Bedford Forrest conducted three principal cavalry raids against Federal garrisons and supply lines in his native state of Tennessee during the Civil War. He undertook forays behind Union lines throughout his career, but those in July 1862 against the Union garrison at Murfreesboro, in December 1862 and January 1863 against Union lines in western Tennessee, and in November 1864 against the Union depot and storage facility at Johnsonville, established his reputation as one of the South's foremost cavalry raiders.

The first of these raids occurred in July 1862, when Colonel Forrest, already recommended for promotion to brigadier general for his conduct at Fort Donelson and Shiloh, took his cavalry command across the Tennessee River. At McMinnville he received reinforcements and prepared for a push on the Union garrison at Murfreesboro. Arriving at the town early on July 13, Forrest divided his men into three groups. The first was to attack the nearest Union camp of the Ninth Michigan Infantry and the Seventh Pennsylvania Cavalry, the second was to storm the town, and the third was to hit the camp of the Third Minnesota on the farthest side of Murfreesboro.

Forrest expected the operation to proceed smoothly, but complications developed. The Federals in the town surrendered, but the others quickly rallied after the surprise attack and put up a stubborn defense. Forrest led his men against the Minnesotans, capturing their camp and some prisoners.

Through the astute use of bluff, Forrest soon convinced both of the remaining Union commanders to surrender. His victory netted the Confederates 1,200 prisoners and substantial stores of weapons and equipment. He had inflicted casualties of 29 killed and 120 wounded while sustaining losses of 25 killed and 40 to 60 wounded.

Forrest's second major raid into Tennessee took place between December 11, 1862, and January 2, 1863. In compliance with orders to destroy the Union supply lines in western Tennessee, Brigadier General Forrest set out from Columbia, Tennessee, on December 11 to wreck the track and trestlework of the Mississippi Central and the Mobile and Ohio Railroads.

The Southerners reached the Tennessee River, crossing at Clifton on December 15, pushing across the river on flatboats by late the next night. As the Confederates moved toward Jackson, Tennessee, they encountered Union troops under Col. Robert G. Ingersoll. The two forces clashed, with the Southerners routing and capturing much of Ingersoll's command, including the colonel, 147 men, and two 3-inch Rodman cannons.

Forrest then used several ploys to deceive Brig. Gen. Jeremiah C. Sullivan into believing that the Confederates were in front of Lexington in superior numbers. Sullivan obliged Forrest by concentrating his forces and conceding the countryside to the Southerners. Forrest seized the opportunity to dispatch forces to attack depots and destroy track and bridges north and south of the town. He left a thin screen of horsemen to maintain the deception and rode on to capture Humboldt and Trenton.

On December 23, Forrest took Union City and continued to destroy rail lines in the region. In his December 24 report, he noted with satisfaction: "We have made a clean sweep of the Federals and [rail]roads north of Jackson." On Christmas Day, Forrest moved his command to the southeast, with an eye to returning to Confederate lines. Finding that Federal gunboats and burned bridges on the Obion River blocked his path, he located an old, unstable bridge the Federals had ignored, had his men shore up

the structure, and pushed his command across the river.

Coupled with Brig. Gen. Earl Van Dorn's capture of Maj. Gen. Ulysses S. Grant's forward supply base at Holly Springs, Mississippi, Forrest's actions crippled Grant's initial assault on Vicksburg.

The third of his Tennessee raids began on October 24, 1864, when Major General Forrest's cavalry command left their base at Jackson, Tennessee. On October 28 the Confederates reached the Tennessee River near Fort Heiman and placed batteries along the bank, concealing them from view. For the next two days, their artillery sparred with Union gunboats and steamers. The Southerners succeeded in capturing and temporarily converting the Union gunboat *Undine* and the steamer *Venus* to Confederate service. Although Forrest lost both ships in subsequent fighting, his crews managed to escape capture, and his plans for an attack on the massive depot and storage facility at Johnsonville remained intact.

In the meantime, Forrest began to deploy his troops and artillery across the river from the depot. His cannoneers wrestled their guns into place and concealed them. By 2:00 p.m. on November 4, all was ready. The Confederate gunners, their weapons targeted from as close a range as the terrain would permit, blasted the Union supply base with devastating effectiveness. By nightfall, the entire bank was ablaze.

In the Johnsonville raid Forrest's men had destroyed four Union gunboats, fourteen transports, twenty barges, and an estimated $6.7 million worth of Federal property. Sherman noted stoically, "That devil Forrest was down about Johnsonville, making havoc among the gunboats and transports." Forrest was also, as in his previous Tennessee raids, enhancing his reputation as a raider.

— BRIAN S. WILLS

under Brig. Gen. James Harrison Wilson from dispersing his command and capturing Selma, Alabama, in March and April 1865. Forrest regrouped his men a final time before surrendering them at Gainesville, Alabama, in May.

Following the war, Forrest struggled to regain control over his life during Reconstruction and in the face of a series of business failures. For some years, he served as president of and worked diligently to promote the Selma, Marion, and Memphis Railroad. Contrary to his avowal at the end of the war to remain quietly at home, he embraced the budding Ku Klux Klan and assumed the role of first grand wizard of the secret organization. Never completely adjusting to the new realities of the postwar years, Forrest helped restore white Conservative Democrats to power and sought to reassert white supremacy in the South. He died in Memphis on October 29, 1877, having failed to recoup his prewar fortune.

Nathan Bedford Forrest stands as one of the foremost cavalry raiders of the war. His ferocity as a warrior was almost legendary. His claim to have slain one more enemy soldier in personal combat than the twenty-nine horses killed beneath him only added to the legend. Forrest fought by the simple maxim "Forward men, and mix with 'em." He understood, perhaps better than most, the basic premise of war: "War means fighting and fighting means killing."

— BRIAN S. WILLS

FORT PILLOW MASSACRE

The Confederates originally constructed the earthwork fortification on the Mississippi River, north of Memphis, to protect the water approaches to that city. Fort Pillow was situated on a high bluff on the eastern bank, overlooking the river. After the Confederates evacuated the fort in 1862, it became part of the chain of Federal garrisons employed to protect communications and supply lines in the region. In 1864 Maj. Lionel F. Booth commanded a garrison there, variously estimated at between 557 and 580 black and white troops of the Thirteenth Tennessee Cavalry, the Eleventh U.S. Colored Troops, and Battery F of the Fourth U.S. Colored Light Artillery.

In March and April 1864 Maj. Gen. Nathan Bedford Forrest determined to attack the isolated Union garrison as part of a raid into western Tennessee and Kentucky. The first Confederates arrived before Fort Pillow in the early morning hours of April 12, under the command of Brig. Gen. James R. Chalmers.

Chalmers succeeded in driving the Federals into their innermost entrenchments and deployed his men. Forrest arrived at 10:00 A.M. to find Fort Pillow virtually surrounded, with Confederate sharpshooters situated on high ground, enabling them to fire directly into the fort. Forrest reconnoitered and placed additional sharpshooters.

These sharpshooters had already profoundly affected the fighting at Fort Pillow. At 9:00 A.M., Confederate fire had struck Booth in the chest as he stood near one of the earthwork's portholes. Maj. William F. Bradford assumed command, although he continued to use Booth's name in negotiations with the Confederates.

Under this covering fire, Forrest's men seized a row of Union barracks and outlying rifle pits. This success convinced the Confederate general that he was now in a position to storm the fort. But, typically, Forrest preferred to take the fort through negotiation, if possible. To that end, at 3:30 P.M., he sent in a demand for the unconditional surrender of the garrison, warning, "Should my demand be refused, I cannot be responsible for the fate of your command."

Bradford insisted upon having an hour to consult with his officers. Forrest, worried that he might use the time to obtain reinforcements, granted him twenty minutes. The Confederate commander also dispatched troops to the riverbank to prevent an approaching Union transport vessel from landing and impatiently rode to the scene of the truce negotiations. Finally, Bradford declared that he would not surrender. Forrest rode back to his lines and issued orders for an assault.

The Confederates rushed across the relatively short distance to the fort and scaled the parapet. As they swarmed into Fort Pillow, firing point-blank into the defenders, the Federal garrison retreated. In such an eventuality, the Union commanders had planned to rely upon the gunboat *New Era* to drive off the pursuing Southerners and thereby enable the garrison to escape. As the garrison broke for the riverbank below, however, the fighting became chaotic and Bradford was unable to execute the plan. Many of the Federals tried to surrender. Others ran for their lives. Still others fired as they withdrew, apparently hoping to prolong the defense until help could arrive.

Remaining outside Fort Pillow, Forrest lost control of events inside the fort and on the riverbank below. Pent-up anger and racial animosity led some of the Confederates to give their opponents no mercy. Casualty figures demonstrate that members of the fort's garrison, especially black troops, suffered an inordinately high number of deaths. Although the Confederates were the attacking party, they lost just 14 killed and 86 wounded, while the Federal defenders lost 231 killed, 100 wounded, and 226 captured. The victorious

"Civil war, such as you have just passed through, naturally engenders feelings of animosity, hatred and revenge. It is our duty to divest ourselves of all such feelings."

NATHAN BEDFORD FORREST
FAREWELL ADDRESS TO HIS MEN, MAY 9, 1865

FORT SUMTER

The Confederate Stars and Bars waves over Fort Sumter on April 14, 1861, only days after the bombardment that drove out the Federal forces and ignited the war.

NATIONAL ARCHIVES

The events at Charleston made Beauregard an immediate Confederate hero, hailed as "Old Bory" and praised as one of the world's great soldiers.

PAGE 43

Southerners took prisoner only 58 of the 262 black troops engaged.

The Northern press immediately labeled the events at Fort Pillow a "massacre." A U.S. congressional committee investigated the affair, calling witnesses and accumulating often gruesome testimony. The committee determined that a massacre had occurred at the fort. Forrest denied the charges, but the exertions that he and other Confederate officers had to take to prevent unnecessary killings are the most telling testimony that such slaughter took place and that, for however long, he was powerless to prevent it. In any event, as commander of the troops on the scene, Forrest was responsible.

— BRIAN S. WILLS

FORT SUMTER, SOUTH CAROLINA

The scene of the opening battle of the Civil War, Fort Sumter was located on an artificial island inside the entrance to Charleston Harbor. A pentagon, with brick walls about three hundred feet long, forty feet high, and eight to twelve feet thick, the fort was still under construction in 1860. To it, on the night of December 26, Maj. Robert Anderson moved his garrison of U.S. troops from Fort Moultrie at the edge of the harbor entrance, where he and his men had been exposed to the threat of attack by South Carolinians.

Having declared their state an independent republic, the South Carolinians resented the presence of what was to them a foreign flag, and they looked upon Anderson's move to Fort Sumter as an act of aggres-

sion. They considered it another hostile act when, in January 1861, the Buchanan administration sent the unarmed merchant ship *Star of the West* with reinforcements for the fort. As the ship approached Charleston Harbor, South Carolina shore batteries opened fire and compelled it to turn back.

The Confederate government early on established its policy with regard to the two principal forts remaining under Federal control in the seceded states. On February 15, 1861, the Provisional Congress in Montgomery secretly resolved that "immediate steps should be taken to obtain possession of Forts Sumter and Pickens . . . either by negotiation or force." President Jefferson Davis thereupon sent to Washington three commissioners—Martin J. Crawford, John Forsyth, and A. B. Roman—to try negotiation. He ordered P. G. T. Beauregard to Charleston to take command of the harbor and make preparations for the use of force.

In Washington the Confederate commissioners failed to get an audience with any member of the Lincoln administration, but Secretary of State William H. Seward communicated with them through a go-between. The commissioners thought it a great diplomatic victory for the Confederacy when Seward pledged that his government would not, without notice, undertake to change the situation at Sumter. As Commissioner Crawford reported, the Confederate States "were not bound in any way whatever to observe the same course" (but were left free to continue their preparations for attack). "We think, then, that the policy of 'masterly inactivity,' on our part, was wise in every particular."

Such inactivity displeased Governor Francis W. Pickens and his fellow South Carolinians, who demanded immediate action. "The President shares the feeling expressed by you that Fort Sumter should be in our possession at the earliest possible moment," Secretary of War Leroy P. Walker assured Governor Pickens on March 1, but cautioned: "Thorough preparations must be made before an attack is attempted, for the first blow must be successful."

General Beauregard proceeded to extend and enlarge the batteries surrounding and targeting the fort. His preparations practically complete, he advised the Davis government on March 27 that the expulsion of Anderson from Sumter "ought now to be decided on in a few days." Davis gave Beauregard the following instructions on April 2: he should be ready to strike whenever the commissioners withdrew from Washington, and meanwhile he should cease to allow Anderson the privilege of buying groceries in Charleston.

On April 8 the Davis government heard from the commissioners that they had met a final "refusal" and considered their mission at an end. This news alone would have been sufficient to trigger an assault on Sumter, but even more ominous news arrived in Montgomery on the same day. A telegram from Beauregard said Governor Pickens had just received a message from President Abraham Lincoln to the effect that "provisions would be sent to Sumter peaceably, otherwise by force." Secretary Walker immediately replied to Beauregard: "Under no circumstances are you to allow provisions to be sent to Fort Sumter."

Davis and his cabinet decided not to wait for the arrival of Lincoln's expedition but, instead, to risk the onus of firing the first shot. On April 10 Walker on behalf of Davis ordered Beauregard to demand immediate evacuation of the fort and, if refused, to "reduce" it. Anderson the next day rejected the demand but said he and his men would be "starved out in a few days." Walker then authorized Beauregard to "avoid the effusion of blood" if Anderson would state a time for his withdrawal and would agree meanwhile not to fire unless fired upon. Beauregard sent James Chesnut, Roger A. Pryor, and two aides by boat to present this offer to Anderson after midnight. Anderson promised to hold his fire and to evacuate in three days—unless he should receive "controlling instructions" or "additional supplies." Chesnut and Pryor told him his reply was unsatisfactory and a bombardment would begin in an hour.

The bombardment began at 4:30 on the morning of April 12, 1861. Anderson was unable to make much of a response, completely outgunned as he was. He received no assistance from Lincoln's expedition, which proved a fiasco. The leading warship *Powhatan* had been misdirected to Fort Pickens, other vessels had been delayed by a storm, and the rest stood helplessly offshore. Cannon balls battered the brick walls of the fort while hot shot set fire to the wooden buildings inside. Anderson surrendered at noon on April 14. All

his eighty-four soldiers and forty-three laborers had survived, but two men died as a result of a gun explosion during the surrender ceremonies.

Among Confederate leaders it had been an axiom that a clash at Sumter would induce Virginia and other states of the upper South and the border to secede. None of these states did so immediately, but Virginia, Tennessee, Arkansas, and North Carolina seceded in consequence of Lincoln's call for troops on April 15. Southerners generally rallied to the support of the Davis government. Northerners did the same with respect to the Lincoln administration. Most of them believed the Confederates had convicted themselves of war guilt, but the Confederates accused Lincoln of having deliberately provoked the attack. Davis, in *The Rise and Fall of the Confederate Government* (1881), still felt called upon to explain: "He who makes the assault is not necessarily he who strikes the first blow or fires the first gun."

In 1863 U.S. forces made two unsuccessful attempts to retake Sumter and capture Charleston. The U.S. flag was not again raised over the fort until April 14, 1865, exactly four years after the surrender.

— RICHARD N. CURRENT

FRANKLIN AND NASHVILLE CAMPAIGN

In early September 1864, after the close of the Atlanta campaign, the Confederate Army of Tennessee camped at Palmetto, Georgia, a few miles southwest of Atlanta. The army was exhausted and, like its opponents, needed to regroup before beginning the next round. While the soldiers rested, Southern leaders developed plans to pry the Federals out of Atlanta and to get them out of Georgia.

The Confederate strategy was hammered out between September 25 and 27, during a visit to the army by President Jefferson Davis. The chief executive and Gen. John Bell Hood, the army's commander, reasoned that operations against the railroad connecting the Federals occupying Atlanta with their base at Chattanooga, Tennessee, would compel them to withdraw northward to protect their line of supply. If all went well, the Southerners would eventually lure their enemy into an area where the Confederates could fight at an advantage. A Southern victory in North Georgia would go far to offset the past summer's defeats; if it came in time, it might also affect the 1864 election in the North.

In early October Hood moved into northwestern Georgia, striking eastward against the railroad as he

Smitten female admirers showered Beauregard with gratitude, while an equally responsive Northern editor placed a price on his head.

PAGE 43

F

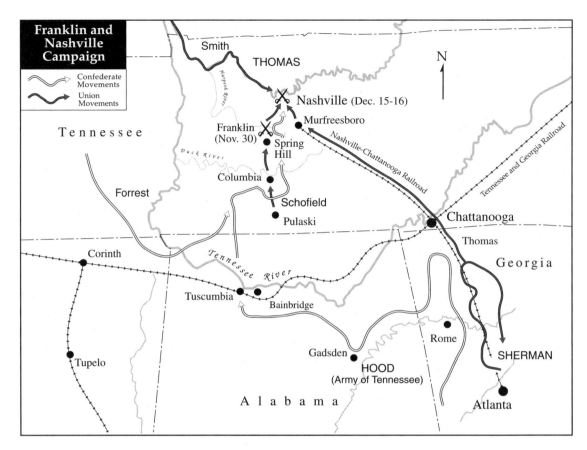

went. His army—about 40,000 men—was divided into three infantry corps (commanded by Lt. Gen. Alexander P. Stewart, Stephen D. Lee, and Maj. Gen. B. Franklin Cheatham), a cavalry corps (under Maj. Gen. Joseph Wheeler), and an independent cavalry division (under Brig. Gen. William Hicks Jackson). After doing extensive damage to the railroad, Hood moved west. He reached Gadsden, Alabama, on October 20.

The Federal army followed Hood, but one Northern corps was left to hold Atlanta. When Hood moved into Alabama, the Union commander, Maj. Gen. William Tecumseh Sherman, posted his army just west of Rome, Georgia. Sherman refused to be drawn farther westward. Instead, he soon detached part of his force to protect Tennessee and with the rest returned to Atlanta. On November 15 he' marched off across Georgia for Savannah on the Atlantic coast.

Realizing that Sherman was not going to chase him across Alabama, and that it was unlikely he could move fast enough to head off the Federals in Georgia, Hood hatched the idea of marching into Tennessee. A threat to Nashville should force the Unionists to abandon Georgia. If it did not, the mere presence of a Southern army in middle Tennessee might confuse the Union plans. A Confederate victory in Tennessee would restore Southern morale and prestige. It might even be possible, Hood fantasized, for the Confederates to win in Tennessee and then move to Virginia and join the

army there for one great battle that would bring Confederate independence. Hood decided upon this scheme without consulting either the government or Gen. P. G. T. Beauregard, his immediate military superior. When informed of Hood's intentions, Beauregard insisted that Wheeler's cavalry be detached to oppose Sherman. To replace Wheeler, Beauregard promised Hood the cavalry of Maj. Gen. Nathan Bedford Forrest, then with Southern forces in Mississippi.

Execution of Hood's plan depended on speed. Every hour's delay gave the Unionists more time to prepare for his coming. Over the next several weeks a combination of poor planning and administration, logistical problems, and the need to link up with Forrest forced Hood to drift westward to Tuscumbia. Not until November 20 did Hood get all of his army across the Tennessee River, and on the twenty-first the Southerners started for middle Tennessee.

Maj. Gen. George H. Thomas commanded the Federals defending Tennessee. His force consisted of the Fourth Corps (Maj. Gen. David Stanley), the Twenty-third Corps (Maj. Gen. John M. Schofield), and assorted cavalry and garrison units. In all, there were about 65,000 Federal troops in the area, but many of them were posted along the railroad between Nashville and Chattanooga. Reinforcements from the Mississippi Valley and other points were on the way to Nashville. Thomas stationed Schofield with 30,000 men at Pulaski to observe Hood and delay his march while he assembled the rest of his force at Nashville.

When Hood moved forward, Schofield pulled back to the Duck River at Columbia. There the Southerners found him when they arrived on November 26. On the next day, the Federals crossed the river and destroyed the bridges, but they remained in position to block Hood's direct route to Nashville.

Hood decided to swing east of Columbia, cross the river at a ford, and then march northwest to Spring Hill, where he would regain the road to Nashville. Historians have usually depicted Hood as maneuvering to cut Schofield off from Nashville and destroy his force. It seems more likely, however, that Hood was thinking only in terms of getting to Nashville ahead of Schofield, not in terms of destroying him.

Whatever his intent, Hood moved to execute it during the night of November 28–29. Forrest's cavalry, that of Cheatham and Stewart, and one division of Lee's corps marched off to swing around to Spring Hill. The rest of Lee's corps, almost all of the artillery, and the wagons remained in front of the Federals at Columbia.

By noon on November 29, Forrest's horsemen were near Spring Hill, where they encountered small groups of Northerners east of the town. Throughout the afternoon Confederate infantry arrived and deployed in the fields east of the road. Meanwhile, the Federals—aware of Hood's maneuver—were gradually pulling out of their river line and marching northward.

Confusion reigned among the Confederates. Units moved back and forth. The generals, without clear orders, did not know how their units were deployed, where they were, or what they were doing. Hood's staff—there was no chief of staff—simply broke down, and his control of the army dissolved. Messages from Hood were sometimes not delivered to corps commanders. Many reports from the field did not reach army headquarters. Hood made a few ineffective attempts to get some of his units onto the Columbia-Franklin road, but an almost total misunderstanding of how his army was aligned frustrated his efforts. (Hood believed that his men were deployed facing westward; they, in fact, faced to the north.) Finally, an exhausted Hood fell asleep in a nearby house. Confederate soldiers settled down for the night east of the road, and the Federals marched north to safety.

The Confederate breakdown at Spring Hill has never been satisfactorily explained. Some historians have thought that one or more of the Southern generals were drunk, under the influence of drugs, or off visiting some local ladies. More likely, Hood's own weaknesses as a commander (he typically did not ensure that his orders were obeyed), his poor administration of the army, his apparent lack of any definite plan, the absence of a functioning staff, and the fact

that he had been up for more than twenty hours and was simply too tired to go on all combined to produce the chaos.

On November 30 Schofield had his men in position at Franklin while his engineers worked to prepare crossings over the Harpeth River. Hood's Confederates followed the Federals north. Late that afternoon Hood threw his army into a massive frontal assault on Schofield's position at Franklin. The Southerners overran an advanced Federal work and then continued on to smash into the very strong Union line. In places Hood's men broke through, but Northern reserves poured into the fight and eventually pushed the Southerners back. Many of the Confederates then rallied and attacked again and again. Some Federal officers reported a dozen separate attacks on their positions. Not until nine or ten at night did the fighting fade away. Schofield then crossed the river and continued his march to Nashville.

The Federals reported 2,326 men (of some 28,000 engaged) lost at Franklin. Hood lost about 5,000 (of 28,000), including 12 general officers and 55 regimental commanders. The leadership of the army had been shot away. Two Southern brigades were commanded after the battle by captains. One regiment numbered only thirty men.

Despite his heavy losses at Franklin, Hood decided on December 1 to follow Schofield northward. In truth, he had little choice. He obviously could not overtake Sherman, who was far across Georgia, and to withdraw southward would be to abandon middle Tennessee, demoralize the army, and admit defeat. To remain at Franklin would not accomplish anything. Perhaps Hood could get reinforcements from the Trans-Mississippi; perhaps the Federals at Nashville would be content to wait out the winter; perhaps they would attack and give him and his men a chance to reverse the situation that had existed at Franklin. Nashville itself was too strongly fortified for the weakened Confederates to assault, but they could build their own works and perhaps hold them against an attack.

In early December Hood's crippled army deployed outside Nashville on a long east-west line to cover most of the major roads running south from the city. While the Southerners worked to fortify their position, Thomas continued to build up his army in the city. The Federals were joined by the Sixteenth Corps (Maj. Gen. A. J. Smith) as well as by some 5,200 men brought up from garrison posts in Tennessee and new troops shipped from the North. Thomas, a systematic officer, wanted to prepare a force that would do a thorough job of wrecking Hood's army. Meanwhile, Hood made the Confederate situation even more desperate by sending off most of his cavalry and some infantry

Confederate military history records no rout more thorough than that sustained by John Bell Hood at Nashville.

PAGE 279

to Murfreesboro to operate against the Nashville-Chattanooga railroad.

The task of organizing the cavalry, and then bad weather, delayed the Federal attack until December 15. When Thomas struck, his plan was brilliant. He distracted Hood with an early probe against the right of the Confederate line and then launched an overwhelming assault against its left. Enveloped on their left, the Southerners fell back to a new, shorter line along the Brentwood Hills a few miles to the south.

On the afternoon of December 16, Thomas assaulted Hood's new line. While Union infantry attacked at several points, a massive artillery barrage pulverized the Southerners. Late in the day Northern cavalrymen were again able to envelope the Southerners' left, and the Confederates there found themselves under attack from three directions. At about 4:00 P.M., Hood's line collapsed, and his men fled southward.

For the next several days the Confederate army moved toward the Tennessee River with Union cavalry nipping at its heels. Lee's corps, the least beaten Southern unit (it had been on the Confederate right on December 16 and had not been involved in the debacle on the left of Hood's line), covered the retreat. Things were a bit easier for the Confederates after December 18, when they got across the Duck River at Columbia. On Christmas day the leading units reached the Tennessee near Bainbridge, Alabama, and by December 28 the last of Hood's men had crossed. The Confederates moved west to Corinth, Mississippi, and then south to Tupelo.

Thomas lost 2,562 men in the Battle of Nashville out of about 50,000 engaged. Hood had an estimated 23,000 troops in the battle. His losses are not known. The best estimates put his killed and wounded at about 1,500. The Northerners reported that they took 4,500 prisoners during the battle and while the Southerners were retreating to the Tennessee River. Doubtless, many other Confederates deserted and went to their homes. On December 31 Hood's army reported 18,708 officers and men "present for duty."

Hood's Franklin and Nashville campaign, in the words of one Confederate officer, was "a complete and disastrous failure." It was the worst-managed major military operation of the war. For all practical purposes, it destroyed the Army of Tennessee. Hood himself was relieved from command on January 23, 1865, and the army never again fought as a unit. Parts of it were sent off to help defend Mobile; other units set out for North Carolina to reinforce the Confederates there. Some arrived in time for the final skirmishes in the East; others were strung out all across Mississippi, Alabama, Georgia, and the Carolinas when the war ended.

— RICHARD M. MCMURRY

FREDERICKSBURG CAMPAIGN

The town of Fredericksburg, Virginia, at the falls of the Rappahannock River, numbered 5,022 inhabitants in 1860; it was the site of a victory for the Army of Northern Virginia on December 13, 1862, that must be reckoned its easiest major triumph of the war. Ambrose E. Burnside assumed command of the Federal Army of the Potomac on November 7 and at once determined to move it southeast toward Fredericksburg, hoping to interpose between Robert E. Lee and Richmond and thereby to gain either tactical or strategic advantages. Lee's army at the time was scattered in the lower Shenandoah Valley and in Piedmont, Virginia, taking advantage of the harvest season while recuperating from the difficult Maryland campaign. Burnside promptly sought information about Southern strength around Fredericksburg by means of a cavalry reconnaissance. On November 8 Capt. Ulric Dahlgren, later notorious for a controversial raiding scheme around Richmond, led several dozen Union horsemen into the town. They surprised a handful of Confederate cavalrymen in Fredericksburg but found no other defenders.

The Federals advanced down the left bank of the Rappahannock toward Fredericksburg, while Lee with forward elements of his army attempted to keep pace across the river. Burnside had divided his army into three "grand divisions," an innovation that did not survive his tenure in command. Gen. E. V. Sumner, leading the grand division at the head of the army, reached the heights opposite Fredericksburg on November 17. With most of Lee's regular infantry still two days away, Sumner looked across the river at a tiny Confederate detachment consisting of a few artillery pieces and a few hundred untested infantry. The shining opportunity for the Federals came to naught, however, as they equivocated about crossing, even though a broad and rocky stretch of river at the north edge of town was readily negotiable.

Burnside arrived on the scene on November 19. So did Confederate Gen. James Longstreet. On the twentieth Lee reached Fredericksburg, and the Northern chance to take uncontested control of the strong ground west of town had vanished. With that position in Federal hands, Lee would have been obliged to head southward another twenty miles to the next strong point. Burnside had called for a pontoon train with which to effect his river crossing, but it did not come for weeks. The orders that reached the train's operators had not conveyed any sense of urgency. Meanwhile, the Federals had threatened to bombard the city of Fredericksburg on the premise that its cover was useful to

Lee's army. The civilians evacuated the town in bitter cold weather amid haunting scenes of suffering that moved the Army of Northern Virginia to sympathy and eventually to an outpouring of donated funds to help support the refugees.

The bombardment of Fredericksburg finally came soon after the pontoons arrived. Early on December 11 Burnside sent engineer troops down to the river, which was more than four hundred feet wide, to build pontoon bridges at three points. The bridge builders had little difficulty at the crossing a mile below town; they eventually put down three spans there. The two crossing points in town proved to be far more dangerous for the engineers. Veteran riflemen of William Barksdale's Mississippi brigade held the waterfront in town, enjoying ample protection in basements and behind walls. The virtually unopposed crossing below town doomed any Confederate hope that the Federals could be held beyond the river permanently—indeed, why should they not be allowed into the city to try their luck on the killing plain beneath the heights where Lee's army waited in supreme confidence? Lee had left two divisions far downstream, however, and until D. H. Hill and Jubal Early could bring those troops up to lend a hand, the Confederates needed to buy some time. Barksdale's men provided a day's delay for that purpose.

Burnside's engineers pushed their first boats into the icy river (the thermometer read 24° at 7:00 A.M. in a nearby city), anchored them, and began to lay boards for the bridge flooring. Before they had reached midpoint in the stream, the growing light allowed the Mississippians to find them in their rifle sights and drive them away. After repeated costly and frustrating efforts, Burnside ordered that some 150 cannon on the heights above the river be fired on the town to clear away the opposition. Within an hour the artillery hurled several thousand rounds into Fredericksburg's buildings. "I believe," one of the Mississippians wrote, "there was not a square yard in the city which was not struck by a missile of some kind." After the guns ceased, the bridging teams attempted to resume work, but the Confederates met them with fire not at all diminished by the heavy shelling. The turning point at the river crossing came when three Northern regiments jumped into the pontoon boats and turned them into assault craft, crossing the river in the face of steady losses in order to drive away the Confederates and establish what apparently was the first literal bridgehead in American military history.

Barksdale's troops fell back reluctantly through the streets of Fredericksburg, contesting each block and ensuring the completion of their task. They had earned a full day for Lee to use in consolidating his position. The rest of the army, which had been watching Barks-

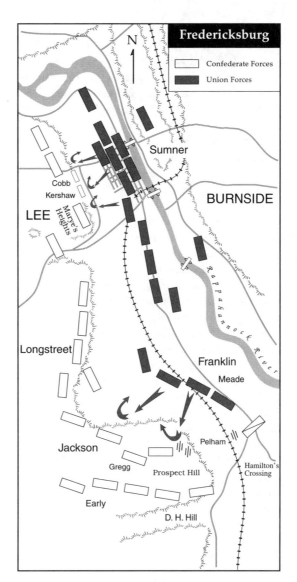

The Federals opened the Battle of Fredericksburg on December 11, 1862, by bombarding the city and building pontoon bridges across the Rappahannock.

PAGE 26

dale's men from the amphitheaterlike high ground around the city, cheered them as they came back from their hard day's work.

Burnside did not attack on December 12. He occupied the day in moving his troops across the river and laying plans. Those Federals in the city on the twelfth indulged in a carnival of looting and destruction of civilian property entirely unprecedented in the Virginia theater of the war. By 1864 such behavior would become a tacit Federal war policy, but in December 1862 it was new, and it embarrassed some Northern officers while outraging the Confederates who looked on helplessly. Their chance for revenge was not long in coming.

Lee's line at the foot of the high ground behind Fredericksburg ran for seven miles along irregular contours carved out by geological forces. Immediately west of the city a commanding ridge rose sharply from an open plain. Farther to the Confederate right the ground sloped up from the river much more gradually.

On Lee's right center the ridge lay a good deal farther west than it did on his left or on his far right. As a result, a deep reentrant angle in the line (a deep bulge swerved away from the attackers) created a zone in which Burnside could not consider attacking. Lee's position was really not vulnerable to frontal assault at all, but if one had to be made (and politicians and newspapers were pressuring Burnside to move), it would have to come against the shoulders of the reentrant. Burnside determined to attack directly out of town against the ridge there and at the same time to move against Lee's far right near Hamilton's Crossing.

December 13 dawned foggy, but the mist cleared by midmorning and an Indian summer day (56° at 2:00 P.M.) burst upon nearly 200,000 soldiers approaching mortal combat. Lee had almost 80,000 men arrayed on his strong line, and Burnside brought about 115,000 troops to battle. Gen. William B. Franklin, commanding on the Federal left, followed the army commander's vague orders about moving against the enemy by organizing an attack westward from the Bowling Green Road. His first alignment fell prey to one of the most famous individual feats of the war. Maj. John Pelham of Alabama and a small detachment moved rapidly from spot to spot firing a single cannon and managed by means of a daunting enfilade fire to confuse the Federal effort for nearly an hour.

When the Northern assault finally rolled forward, it came under intense artillery fire from Confederate guns emplaced on Prospect Hill, near the right of Stonewall Jackson's line. After extensive counterbattery fire, the Union attack went forward again. This time it found an unguarded point on the line, and a division of Pennsylvanians poured through. For the second consecutive battle Jackson had allowed a curious lethargy about defensive matters to land him in trouble. The Pennsylvanians, who were commanded by Gen. George G. Meade, penetrated deep into the Confederate position and mortally wounded Gen. Maxcy Gregg of South Carolina. The success of the breakthrough, however, was temporary and largely illusory. Jackson was holding the Confederate right with roughly one-half of Lee's strength, yet his line covered only about one-fifth of the army's front. That alignment resulted not from Confederate prescience but from simple good fortune. When Early and D. H. Hill brought their divisions back to the army's position from far downstream, using the time bought by Barksdale's defense of the riverfront, they piled them up behind their comrades in Jackson's corps. There was no time to juggle the entire front. Meade's men ran into more Southern reserves than they could hope to deal with, and soon the Northerners were obliged to retrace their steps under pressure from pursuing Confederates.

Franklin's brief success with Meade's division constituted the only marginally bright spot of the battle for the Union army. While Meade and his men advanced and retreated, their comrades several miles to the north had opened a series of attacks that turned into one of the most one-sided and hopeless butcheries of the war. The ridge just behind Fredericksburg included a stretch six hundred yards long through which the deep Sunken Road traversed its base. The road had a retaining wall of stone on the town side that became famous enough to be treated as a proper noun. Confederate infantry behind the Stone Wall enjoyed protection as thorough as any devised later in the war by military engineers. For a half-mile toward town from this ready-made fortress, the ground lay bare, broken only by a few fences and a half-dozen houses. A pronounced swale around a canal ditch offered the attacking Union soldiers a bit of cover, but the ditch was bridged poorly and in few places. Northerners moving across that bare plain would face terrible punishment from Confederate artillery on Marye's Heights (as the ridge above the road was known, after the family that owned part of it). The attackers might form under a little protection in the swale, but they would have to move toward the Stone Wall without cover of any sort. The only possible result would be a bloody disaster, with casualties in the thousands, the fatal multiplier being how many doomed brigades Burnside fed into the carnage.

That brief early winter afternoon, on one of the shortest days of the year, must have seemed an eternity to the thousands of Northern boys who took their turns lining up and then plunging bravely over the crest toward the Sunken Road, without a hope of success. Confederates in the road and on the hills behind it shot about eight thousand of the attackers without losing more than a thousand men. Gen. Thomas R. R. Cobb of Georgia commanded the brigade that opened the battle defending the Sunken Road. He fell mortally wounded early in the action. Joseph B. Kershaw's South Carolinians joined the Georgians in the road, and other Southern units participated—almost unnecessarily—from nearby vantage points. When darkness put an end to the slaughter, no man of the attacking force had come close to the wall.

The Confederate command, apparently unaware of the degree of havoc wreaked upon their foe, expected a renewal of the attacks the next day. Burnside was of the same mind and even proposed leading a desperate assault in person, but wiser counsels prevailed. Southerners entrenched portions of their infantry line on December 14, the first such extensive field fortifications on a Virginia battlefield, but they found no occasion to use them until fighting resumed the following spring in the same location. Burnside recrossed his hard-won pontoon bridges under cover of a noisy storm on the night of December 15–16 and ended a campaign that had been an unmitigated disaster for the Union cause. Burnside had lost nearly thirteen thousand men while inflicting fewer than five thousand casualties on his enemy. The Battle of Fredericksburg closed the 1862 campaign in Virginia on an extremely high note for Lee's army and the South. For nearly five months the winter season would suspend active campaigning. When the war resumed in the spring of 1863, Lee's army would show tremendous confidence, based on its success at Fredericksburg, as it faced a new Federal commander.

— ROBERT K. KRICK

FUGITIVE SLAVE LAW

A revealingly unanswerable question illuminates blacks' influence on whites' history. Did fugitive slaves disrupt the Union more before 1860 or the Confederacy thereafter? During the Civil War, approximately one in six slaves fled to Union armies or territories. Approximately one in six of these runaways joined the Union's ultimately liberating army. The fugitives undermined the Confederacy's racial order, damaged its economic production, and swelled the ranks of its armed assaulters. Black runaways also created the Union's contraband problem, for although Lincoln's armies fought to secure obedience to Federal laws, which included the Fugitive Slave Law of 1850, could soldiers fight the slaveholders and also return slave property? Finally, the fugitives complicated the issue of the purpose of the war. A war effort at first aimed only at preserving the white people's Union came to need those 100,000 black soldiers. But would ex-slaves fight for exclusively white liberty? The 600,000 self-liberated fugitives, by raising these issues, helped cause a war initially fought on other grounds to spawn black emancipation.

Before the Civil War, too, black fugitives had disrupted white people's controversies. Without runaway slaves, the explosive fugitive slave issue would not have existed, and the equally explosive territorial expansion issue would have been more manageable. Southern expansionist drives were aimed, to a large degree, at deterring fugitive slaves. Southerners feared that if antislavery proponents controlled the other side of the slavocracy's borders, whether in Texas or Kansas or Florida, more slaves would flee toward freedom. If one can imagine a South without a fugitive slave problem, a much-longer-enduring antebellum Union becomes conceivable.

But this slaveholders' republic without fugitive slaves is ultimately unimaginable. American dreams of freedom inspired blacks, too, and flight was the slaves' most promising avenue to liberty. One black betrayer, by alerting whites to an insurrection plot, could destroy a group revolt, but a single fugitive could run as far as skill and luck allowed. A slave escaping from the border states, especially, shortened the long odds against successful flight and heightened the impact of the escape. Border blacks who freed themselves dampened the border South's not-so-great enthusiasm for slavery and challenged the North's not-so-serene compliance with the slaveholders. Successful fugitives could also become inspiring orators and writers, celebrating blacks' journey toward freedom, as did Frederick Douglass in his magnificent speeches and autobiography.

With the Fugitive Slave Law of 1850, the white establishment sought to abort the black slaves' major method of including themselves in white aspirations and history. An earlier Federal fugitive slave law, passed in 1793, had fallen victim to *Prigg v. Pennsylvania* (1842), wherein the U.S. Supreme Court had declared that state authorities need not help enforce a Federal law. That Fugitive Slave Law depended on state enforcement, for few Federal judges and policemen yet existed.

The new Fugitive Slave Law, the South's major gain from the Compromise of 1850, established one-man bureaucracies. A commissioner, appointed by Federal judges, received total authority over runaway slaves; a commissioner could demand that any Northerner help capture alleged fugitives; and subsequently, a commissioner was judge and jury of last resort. Accused fugitives had no right to testify in their own behalf or to secure writs of habeas corpus. The commissioner was paid five dollars if he freed the alleged fugitive, ten dollars if he extradited the black to the South. Extra paperwork for extradition supposedly justified the extra payment, but many Northerners considered it a bribe—the symbol of an unspeakably despotic law.

In exchange for Northern acquiescence in allegedly despotic Federal machinery to return fugitives, Southerners agreed to the admission of free-labor California into the Union. After that Compromise of 1850 trade-off, slaveholders demanded that their theoretical gain, the return of fugitive slaves, be realized. Contrary to popular myth, then and now, they largely received their due. Ninety percent of the 322 fugitives tried under the Fugitive Slave Law were remanded to their owners. But the other 10 percent made the headlines, and well-publicized stories of successful defiance weakened the law's deterrent effect on potential fugitives. The notoriety of the few who escaped the commissioners also poisoned Southern opinion of the North, just as the dispatching of blacks southward, without judge or jury, lowered the North's opinion of the South. Seldom has a law 90 percent successful failed so dismally.

"No man can put a chain about the ankle of his fellow man without at last finding the other end fastened about his own neck."

FREDERICK DOUGLASS

Some famous exceptions to the usual, but ultimately less important, smooth return of fugitives included the rescue by Boston blacks in 1851 of Shadrack, a Virginia slave, from a courthouse; he was then sent to freedom in Canada. That same year a Syracuse mob rescued Jerry, a Missouri slave, from a police station, with the same eventual result: freedom in Canada. Also in 1851, a Maryland slaveholder, Edward Gorsuch, went with his son to Christiana, Pennsylvania, in pursuit of his fugitive slaves. A local black leader, William Parker, barricaded the fugitives in his house, with largely free blacks standing guard. When Gorsuch persisted, gunfire cracked, and the master was slain and his son badly wounded. The slaves got away to Canada, as did William Parker. Gorsuch's murderers remained at large.

A still more publicized fugitive slave incident involved a black returned to enslavement. In 1854 a Virginia fugitive, Anthony Burns, was arrested in Boston and ordered remanded to the South. Important intellectuals plotted to spring the literate slave from jail, but their plan failed and a policeman was killed. Fifty thousand angry Bostonians flooded the streets, demanding that Burns be freed. But at a cost of $100,000, a phalanx of policemen plus a U.S. infantry company and a detachment of artillery sliced a path through the protesters, and Anthony Burns set sail for Virginia. He soon voyaged back north, after Bostonians purchased his freedom.

Those huge numbers—$100,000, 50,000 Bostonians—did overwhelm in Southern memories the 290 slaves peaceably returned. Northern states' personal liberty laws also helped pave the Southern path toward secession. These laws affirmed that Northern state officials could not cooperate with Federal Fugitive Slave Law enforcers. Some personal liberty laws also reaffirmed free blacks' legal rights, including the right to secure a writ of habeas corpus. But states had no authority over Federal legal processes, and personal liberty laws never liberated a fugitive from a commissioner. The personal liberty laws chiefly served to express Northerners' sense of the Fugitive Slave Law: that it was outrageously un-American and tyrannical, particularly in requiring all free citizens to hunt down a brave escapee from despotism. Southerners ultimately tried to secede in part from that insulting opinion. But secession and the Civil War only gave Northerners more power to aid more fugitives—a slaveholders' problem that no Union or Confederacy could solve.

[*See also* Compromise of 1850; Contraband; Dred Scott Decision.]

— WILLIAM W. FREEHLING

G

GALVANIZED YANKEES

Although the origin of the term "Galvanized Yankees" is obscure, it has two exactly opposite meanings—both are correct. The primary meaning refers to the 6,000 Southern soldiers who deserted the Confederate cause, joined the Union army as the First through Sixth Regiments, U.S. Volunteers, and spent the rest of the war fighting Indians on the western frontier. The second meaning refers to Northern soldiers who deserted the Federal army and joined the Confederate army, although these soldiers were sometimes referred to as "Galvanized Rebels."

Both groups of Galvanized Yankees were usually recruited from prisoner of war camps. There they chose to fight against their former flag rather than undergo the deprivation and possible death the camps offered. Many, however, changed uniforms only as a ruse to return to their former colors. Consequently, the Galvanized Yankee units experienced high desertion rates (one in seven) when they were in the vicinity of their former comrades. Desertion rates notwithstanding, the turncoat soldiers often fought well for their new country, as in the case of Northerners fighting for the South at Egypt Station, Mississippi, and of the U.S. Volunteer Regiments in the West.

— P. NEAL MEIER

GARLAND, AUGUSTUS HILL

Garland, Augustus Hill (1832–1899), congressman from Arkansas and postwar governor, U.S. senator, and U.S. attorney general. Born on June 11, 1832, in Tipton County, Tennessee, Garland was educated at St. Mary's College in Lebanon, Kentucky, and St. Joseph's College in Bardstown, Kentucky. While in school he was strongly influenced by his admiration for Henry Clay.

Returning to Washington, Arkansas, in 1852, Garland began reading law and formed a law firm with his stepfather, Thomas Hubbard, and worked for Simon T. Sanders, the county and circuit court clerk for Hempstead County. In 1856 he moved to Little Rock, where his law practice became one of the most prestigious in the state.

The defeat of the American party candidates in the 1856 election left the Democratic party, led by the Johnson "Family," in control of Arkansas politics. When the 1860 election began, Garland participated in an opposition convention, assembling the group generally recognized as the successor to the Whig-American party coalition. In the national election that fall Garland was an elector for the Constitutional Union party.

At the January 1860 term of the Arkansas Supreme Court, Garland lost a series of appeals dealing with the taxation of swamp and overflowed lands, and he spent the summer preparing to carry his appeal to the U.S. Supreme Court. On the day after Christmas, he was enrolled as an attorney before the Court.

By the time Garland returned to Little Rock late in January 1861, the state was full of excitement over the coming election that would decide whether to call a secession convention. Garland immediately announced his candidacy for one of Pulaski County's two seats in the convention. With no time to publish his thoughts on secession, he declared that he agreed with the views of Joseph Stillwell, another candidate in Pulaski County.

Garland was a conservative Unionist. He opposed separate state secession and urged cooperation with the border states. He suggested calling a convention of all slaveholding states to adopt the Crittenden Resolutions. As the only cotton-growing state left in the Union, Arkansas would benefit from a monopoly on trade, he argued, and he urged the people to make the state one of the strongest in the Union instead of one of the weakest in the Confederacy.

In February the people of Arkansas voted to call a convention to consider the question of secession, but the convention had a strong Unionist contingent. Garland and Stillwell were elected by 550 votes over their secessionist opponents. The secession convention began on March 4, 1861, the same day that Abraham Lincoln was inaugurated. The Unionist leaders—Garland, his brother Rufus Garland, Hugh F. Thomasson, and W. W. Watkins—adopted a two-part strategy. They worked to defeat efforts to draw up a secession ordinance and suggested waiting to see what Lincoln would do. After agreeing to submit the ques-

In October 1865 Garland filed a petition asking that he be allowed to return to practice before the Supreme Court without taking the Iron-clad Oath.

PAGE 236

Garland argued that all laws requiring an oath are repugnant to the Constitution and are therefore null and void.

PAGE 236

tion of secession or cooperation to the voters, the convention adjourned on March 21.

The convention reconvened on May 6, however, in reaction to Lincoln's call for troops and immediately adopted a secession ordinance. Garland voted for the ordinance reluctantly in the hope of continuing to influence the course of events. Next the convention considered whom to send to the Confederate Congress. The first nomination went to former senator Robert Ward Johnson; the second to Garland. He was elected on the first ballot. While the convention turned to rewriting the state constitution, Garland headed for Montgomery to join the Provisional Congress. When he took his seat he was the youngest member of that body; he would become one of only twenty-eight men to serve in all three Congresses.

After Congress reconvened in Richmond, Garland was appointed to the Public Lands and the Finance committees. It was in committees that Garland built a reputation for hard work and scholarship. His first major motion was a resolution calling on the Finance Committee to investigate the expediency of declaring Treasury notes and bonds legal tender. This resolution was the beginning of a long controversy over legal tender that was never resolved. By the time discussion of the matter was dropped in 1864, notes were accepted as legal tender though they had never been designated as such.

Congress adjourned in August, and Garland returned to Arkansas to seek election to the First Congress as a representative of the Third District. His main opponent was Jilson P. Johnson of Desha County, an early secessionist and part of the Johnson Family. Garland waged a vigorous campaign, and, certain he had won when the unofficial totals were announced, he left for Virginia for the final session of the Provisional Congress.

By the time he reached Richmond, Congress was already in session. Garland was appointed to the Judiciary Committee in addition to his other assignments, which was in keeping with his interest in constitutional law. During this session the committee was dealing with issues relating to the seizure of property. Resolutions introduced by Garland led this inquiry in two directions. He proposed allowing citizens whose goods or property had been confiscated by Federal authorities to recover their losses by seizing land owned by U.S. citizens, and amending the Sequestration Act to exempt the property of free blacks who had been forced to leave the slave states. Garland accepted the absolute right of a government to seize alien enemy property, but he sought to protect property owners from loss.

Meanwhile a problem had developed over the November election. Arkansas Governor Henry Rector had announced the results of the election on the basis of official returns sent to the secretary of state by the county clerks. According to these returns Garland had received 2,157 votes, Jilson Johnson, 2,125 votes, and four other candidates, fewer numbers of votes, giving Garland a plurality. But Johnson announced that he was contesting the election because of problems in the returns from Arkansas County. Garland at first ignored Johnson's challenge, but the House of Representatives accepted it and sent the matter to the Committee on Elections. The committee, deeply divided along party lines, was determined to work slowly and carefully. During the course of the controversy it issued a number of reports and asked the principals to provide evidence several times.

Although the status of his congressional seat was uncertain, Garland decided to run for the Senate. When Confederate senators were chosen in 1861, R. W. Johnson had used his influence as head of the Family to ensure his own selection, but he had drawn a short term and had to seek reappointment in 1862. Garland had gotten more votes than Johnson in the balloting for seats in the Provisional Congress, so he apparently felt the time was ripe to remove the Family from power.

Garland, Johnson, and a third candidate were invited to address the General Assembly. Garland, in his speech, put special emphasis on the financial difficulties facing the Confederacy, referring to the need to make notes and bonds legal tender and discussing a bill for new taxes. He then turned to the topic of ending the war. Garland argued that the cost of the war to both sides in men and money was such that it should end soon. He urged that the Confederacy stay ready for war but make an offer for peace. The final vote came two days later: Johnson received forty-six votes on the twelfth ballot, and Garland forty-two.

Garland had better luck with his congressional seat. When the third session of the First Congress convened in January 1863, more evidence concerning the contested election was sent to the Committee on Elections. Jilson Johnson, however, decided to withdraw his suit, the committee was dismissed, and Garland retained his seat.

He was now able to immerse himself in committee work. In addition to the Judiciary Committee, he was a member of committees on Enrolled Bills and on the Medical Department. He also served on various committees dealing with matters ranging from homesteads for disabled veterans to plans for retaliation against the United States for attempts to enforce the Emancipation Proclamation.

At the close of the First Congress, Garland sent a report to his constituents outlining major legislation and focusing on financial matters. The last part of the report was directed at boosting morale. Calling on civilians to support the government and the army, Garland mentioned in passing that he felt the conventions being held to organize a Unionist government for Arkansas were of no importance.

When the Second Congress convened in May 1864, Garland was made chairman of the Committee on Territories and Public Lands and was again appointed to the Judiciary Committee. He also served on the Special Committee to Inquire into the Charges against W. R. W. Cobb.

The climax of Garland's summer came with his election to the Confederate Senate. Taking his seat in November 1864, Garland was appointed to the Committee on Post Offices and Post Roads. In the next month he introduced twelve bills, resolutions, and memorials on subjects ranging from the salaries of civil officers to limiting the number of slaves employed by the army.

Garland was increasingly concerned about the Confederacy's ability to maintain itself. His ideas on the economy reached final form in January 1865, when he offered a resolution calling for the Judiciary Committee to study the need for a Home Department. Such a department, he urged, should have broad powers for the development, management, and control of the South's internal resources. But the growing military crisis did not make an expansion of government powers attractive, and this resolution died in committee.

Garland brought to Congress his belief in constitutionalism and his faith in a strong central government. He supported the Davis administration on most issues. In letters to his constituents he always emphasized money and military matters and explained them in detail, for he felt these were the things of greatest interest to the people. But his own primary interests lay in two other areas—the suspension of the writ of habeas corpus and the establishment of a supreme court.

In 1862 Congress gave President Jefferson Davis the power to suspend the writ of habeas corpus and declare martial law in areas threatened by invasion. Although the law was applied sparingly nationwide, in Arkansas Gen. Thomas C. Hindman, and later Lt. Gen. Theophilus H. Holmes, exceeded this authority by issuing a series of directives curtailing the power of the civil authorities, establishing price controls, suspending the writ of habeas corpus, and declaring martial law. Garland was horrified.

With this firsthand knowledge of how martial law and suspension of habeas corpus could be misused, Garland was absolutely opposed to the extension of the law when it expired in February 1863. A new, more limited law for the suspension of habeas corpus was passed in February 1864. When the Second Congress convened in May, several members felt they had a

mandate to repeal the law even though it was about to expire, and the matter was sent to the Judiciary Committee. The majority of the committee supported renewing the law, but in a minority report issued on May 28, 1864, Garland and Burgess Sidney Gaither of North Carolina favored letting the law expire. Garland gave three major reasons the law should be allowed to lapse: first, the law allowed too much discretion about whom to arrest; second, it violated judicial independence by allowing the president to appoint investigating committees for matters normally handled by the courts; and finally, it tended to lower civilian morale. Neither the majority nor the minority report recommended any action, and the law was allowed to expire.

The effort to establish a supreme court for the Confederacy also preoccupied Garland. The Judiciary Act of March 16, 1861, defined the powers of a supreme court, but its organization was suspended in July 1861, delaying its operation without destroying its proposed authority. Bills introduced in 1862 to organize the court never came to a vote.

In April 1863, in a report written by Garland, the House Judiciary Committee recommended the passage of the Senate supreme court bill, with an amendment to give the court appellate jurisdiction over state courts. Garland felt this jurisdiction was essential for the stability of the South in that it would ensure the equal enforcement of Confederate laws. Although his viewpoint was well received, the House postponed action on the bill, and it died when Congress adjourned in January 1864.

By late 1864 Garland knew that the war had been lost. Disgusted with the Senate for spending its time and energies fighting with President Davis, Garland left Richmond in late February 1865 to return to Arkansas.

In May Confederate Governor Harris Flanagin authorized him to confer with Federal authorities to arrange terms for the restoration of peace and order. Garland accepted the commission and went to Little Rock, where he met with Gen. J. J. Reynolds and Unionist Governor Isaac Murphy. When Garland presented Flanagin's plan for unifying the state, Reynolds and Murphy went as far as they could in being conciliatory. They agreed to give the army a chance to disband and promised not to arrest the Confederate civil officers unless ordered to do so. But they refused to recognize the county officers in southern Arkansas.

With the war over, Garland turned his attention to personal matters. He prepared an application for a pardon to be sent to President Andrew Johnson. He stressed that he had been elected to the Confederate Congress as a conservative, that he never called for harsh measures against the Unionists, and that he was always opposed by the secessionists. He included let-

Henry S. Foote asserted he would "never consent to the establishment of a supreme court of the Confederate States so long as Judah P. Benjamin shall continue to pollute the ears of majesty Davis with his insidious counsels."

PAGE 307

> *"[In 1874] a conflict
> developed in
> Arkansas between
> rival claimants for
> the governorship;
> known as the
> Brooks-Baxter War,
> it resulted in the loss
> of some 200 lives. A
> compromise ended
> in a constitutional
> convention and the
> election of Governor
> Augustus H.
> Garland."*
>
> FRANCIS BUTLER
> SIMKINS
> A HISTORY OF THE SOUTH,
> 1958

ters of recommendation written by an impressive array of prominent officials, all of whom backed his pardon as a way of securing conservative support for the government and as a step toward restoration of peace and order. The pardon was granted July 15, 1865.

Next Garland sought to reestablish his law practice. Among the matters needing attention was the case of *McGee v. Mathis* and related cases, which he had filed with the U.S. Supreme Court during the December 1860 term. When Garland checked the records in July 1865, he discovered that the cases were still on the docket. This posed a dilemma. He wanted to attend to the cases, but he could not take the Iron-clad Oath, which required all federal officeholders, including lawyers practicing in federal courts, to swear that they had neither supported nor served in any government that was opposed to the U.S. government.

In October 1865 Garland filed a petition asking that he be allowed to return to practice before the Court without taking the oath. The case, titled *Ex parte Garland,* challenged the oath's constitutionality. It was the first attempt by a Southerner to use the judicial system to ameliorate punishment of the ex-Confederates. In his petition Garland reminded the Court that he had been sworn as an attorney of the Supreme Court in December 1860 and that he had filed briefs and arguments in a number of cases that were pending when Arkansas seceded. He wanted to resume the duties he had taken on before the war, but he could not take the oath without committing perjury. He argued that all laws requiring an oath are repugnant to the Constitution and are therefore null and void; he further argued that if the oath was valid, his presidential pardon relieved him of having to take it. On January 14, 1867,

the Court ruled that the law requiring the oath was unconstitutional. The decision restored to Garland, but only Garland, his right to practice before the Supreme Court without taking the oath. As a practical matter, other Southern lawyers could have petitioned the Court for readmission, basing their argument on Garland's victory; but the oath was quietly dropped to avoid the continuing litigation.

Garland now turned to the political arena. In 1868 he led Arkansas conservatives in an unsuccessful fight to prevent the ratification of a new constitution. He was also chairman of the Arkansas delegation to the Democratic National Convention. But as the final measures of Congressional Reconstruction were put into place, Garland withdrew from public affairs.

An adviser to Arkansas Democrats throughout Reconstruction, Garland returned to public life in 1874 when Joseph Brooks and his supporters tried to oust Elisha Baxter from the governor's office. During the Brooks-Baxter War that followed, Garland was a leader of the Baxter forces, devising a strategy that led to the reaffirmation of Baxter as the rightful governor and to the calling of a constitutional convention. When the new constitution was ratified, Garland was elected governor. Hampered by economic and political pressures, he reestablished conservative government and was the symbol of the end of Reconstruction in Arkansas.

In 1877 Garland was chosen for a seat in the U.S. Senate. While there he worked for legislation of both regional and national impact, including federal aid to education, relief for disaster victims, construction of a levee system, and establishment of a national health agency.

The high point of Garland's public life came with his appointment as U.S. attorney general in 1885. Long noted for his legal scholarship, he issued meticulously written opinions dealing with matters ranging from land patents to federal appointments. Garland returned to private life in 1889, establishing a law practice in Washington, D.C. On January 26, 1899, he died while arguing a case before the Supreme Court.

— BEVERLY WATKINS

GARNETT,
RICHARD BROOKE

Garnett, Richard Brooke, (1817–1863), brigadier general. A member of Tidewater aristocracy, Garnett was born on November 21, 1817, at the family mansion in Essex County, Virginia. In 1841 he and his cousin, Robert Selden Garnett, graduated in the same West

Point class. Dick Garnett fought against the Indians in Florida and the West.

In May 1861 the handsome officer with blue eyes, wavy hair, and closely cropped beard accepted appointment as a Confederate major. Promotion to brigadier general in the Provisional Army came in November. When Gen. Thomas J. ("Stonewall") Jackson moved up to command of the Shenandoah Valley defenses, Garnett succeeded him at the head of the Stonewall Brigade.

His first battle, at Kernstown in March 1862, was Garnett's undoing. With his troops low on ammunition and Federals threatening both flanks, Garnett on his own sought to save his brigade by ordering it to fall back from the front. This withdrawal caused Jackson's whole force to abandon its position. Jackson promptly removed Garnett from command and initiated court-martial proceedings. They were never held because of the press of war. A staff officer who knew Garnett well remarked that he "was ever thereafter anxious to expose himself, even unnecessarily, and to wipe out effectually by some distinction in action, what he felt to be an unmerited slur upon his military reputation."

Garnett campaigned zealously to get a new command and soon was given a brigade in Gen. George E. Pickett's division. He led it well in the 1862 Sharpsburg campaign. On July 3, 1863, Garnett's brigade was in the front rank of the Pickett-Pettigrew charge at Gettysburg. Extremely ill, the general was wearing a heavy overcoat in spite of the heat. Garnett got to within twenty yards of the Federal lines when he disappeared in the gunsmoke and confusion. His riderless horse soon galloped toward the rear. Presumably, Federal soldiers stripped his dead body of its sword and other insignia before burying Garnett in one of the mass graves on the battlefield.

— JAMES I. ROBERTSON, JR.

GEORGIA PLATFORM

The Georgia Platform was adopted in December 1850 by a special convention called to consider the state's response to the Compromise of 1850. The Platform announced that, although Georgia did not approve of the Compromise, the state would "abide by it as a permanent adjustment of this sectional controversy." It further specified that Georgia "will and ought to resist, even (as a last resort) to a disruption of every tie which binds her to the Union," any congressional act that repealed or altered the Fugitive Slave Law, that restricted or suppressed the slave trade, or that abolished slavery in the District of Columbia.

Since these were all matters settled by the Compromise, the effect of the Platform was to admit Georgia's acquiescence in the Compromise's principal provision, namely, the admission of California to the Union as a nonslaveholding state. It was this provision that had so excited the Southern states, since it upset the balance of slave and free states in the Senate. Many Southern political leaders feared that the Compromise represented an attempt to enact the Wilmot Proviso, which sought to ban slavery from territories acquired as a result of the Mexican War, and which had passed the House of Representatives but failed in the Senate.

By introducing the slavery question at the national level, the Compromise disrupted party lines in the South and began the formation of new alliances. In Georgia Whigs, led by Robert Toombs, and Democrats, led by Howell Cobb, joined ranks to form the Constitutional Union party. Highly respected and safe on the slavery question, these men gave repeated assurances that the Compromise did not threaten slavery. They stood in opposition to fire-eaters led by Governor George W. Towns, who sought to precipitate secession of the Southern states. Though less vocal or numerous than in other states, especially South Carolina and Mississippi, the secessionists in Georgia posed a serious threat to the supporters of the Union in that state. And since Georgia was the first state to hold a convention to determine a position on the Compromise, all eyes were focused on Milledgeville when the convention assembled.

The position of "conditional Unionism" as articulated in the Georgia Platform quickly found support in the states of the upper South as well as in Alabama and Louisiana. Thus isolated, secessionists in South Carolina and Mississippi had little success in advancing their cause. The Georgia Platform therefore lessened sectional tensions. It also stated clearly the consequences of further congressional interference with slavery, giving warning that any renewal of the slavery question would put the Union at risk.

[See also Compromise of 1850; Fugitive Slave Law.]

— JOHN McCARDELL

GETTYSBURG CAMPAIGN

Following the Union defeat at Chancellorsville in May 1863, Robert E. Lee sought approval from the Confederate government to mount an invasion of Maryland and Pennsylvania with his Army of Northern Virginia. The North was becoming increasingly despondent over the progress of the war with the

The engagement that developed on July 1 through 3 at Gettysburg revealed shortcomings in the high command as well as in the new organization.

PAGE 29

"Gettysburg was the price the South paid for having R. E. Lee."

SHELBY FOOTE
IN GEOFFREY WARD, THE CIVIL WAR, 1990

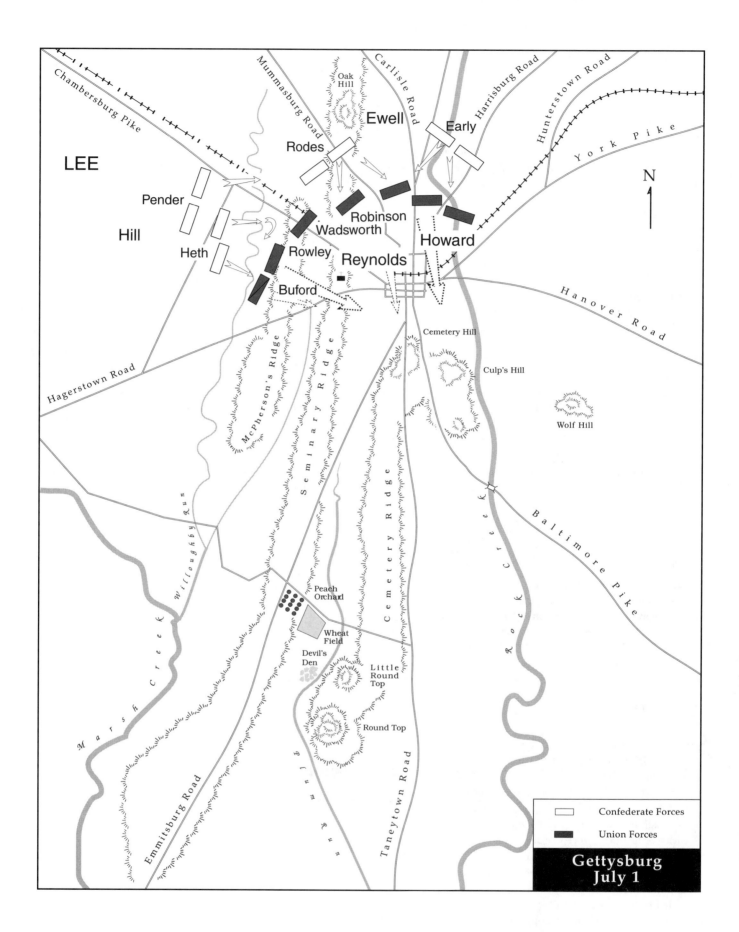

Chambersburg Pike

Mummasburg Road

Carlisle Road

Harrisburg Road

Hunterstown Road

York Pike

Oak Hill

Ewell

Rodes

Early

LEE

Pender

Robinson

Wadsworth

Howard

N

Hill

Heth

Rowley

Reynolds

Buford

Cemetery Hill

Hanover Road

McPherson's Ridge

Culp's Hill

Hagerstown Road

Seminary Ridge

Wolf Hill

Willoughby Run

Cemetery Ridge

Rock Creek

Baltimore Pike

Peach Orchard

Wheat Field

Devil's Den

Little Round Top

Marsh Creek

Round Top

Emmitsburg Road

Plum Run

Taneytown Road

☐ Confederate Forces

■ Union Forces

**Gettysburg
July 1**

repeated failures of the Northern armies and their attendant high casualties. Lee believed he could build momentum for the growing Northern peace movement by shifting his army to Northern soil and inflicting a defeat upon the Federal Army of the Potomac. Operations in Pennsylvania would also allow Lee to provision his army from the rich agricultural areas of Pennsylvania's Cumberland Valley, while relieving Virginia from the destructive presence of contending armies. Finally, Harrisburg, the Pennsylvania capital, could be threatened or perhaps temporarily captured, adding further embarrassment to the Lincoln administration and fuel for the peace movement.

Lee's proposal initially met with opposition in Richmond. There was concern over the security of the Confederate capital while Lee moved north. Some thought was also given to detaching elements of Lee's army to help break the siege of Vicksburg, Mississippi, by the Federal army of Ulysses S. Grant. It was also discussed whether Lee himself, with major elements of his army, should be shifted to Tennessee to mount an offensive against the Federal army under William Rosecrans. Lee's opinion ultimately prevailed, and it was agreed the invasion should take place. It was hoped that by taking the offensive in the east, the Federal forces threatening Vicksburg and Chattanooga would be forced to detach troops to drive Lee out of Pennsylvania.

In preparation for the invasion, Lee reorganized his army into three corps of approximately 20,000 men apiece. The First Corps remained under Gen. James Longstreet's command. The Second Corps (Stonewall Jackson's old corps) was placed under Gen. Richard S. Ewell. The Third Corps, under Gen. A. P. Hill, was formed with elements of Jackson's old corps and with new troops from outside the army. The cavalry division, under Gen. J. E. B. Stuart, was reinforced to six brigades. Lee's total strength was approximately 75,000 men and 280 guns.

The leading elements of Lee's army left their camps near Fredericksburg, Virginia, on June 3. Ewell and Longstreet's corps led the way, screened by Stuart's cavalry, while Hill remained behind temporarily to observe and deceive the Federals.

The Union Army of the Potomac, under Gen. Joseph Hooker, was aware that Lee was on the move but was uncertain of the Confederate's intentions. On June 9 he ordered his cavalry commander, Gen. Alfred Pleasonton, to conduct a reconnaissance in force, with 11,000 men, across the Rappahannock in the direction of Brandy Station. Pleasonton surprised the Confederate cavalry, and the largest cavalry battle of the entire war ensued. Although Stuart recovered from his initial surprise and forced Pleasonton back, the battle caused him great embarrassment. Stuart's

losses were 523 out of approximately 10,000, while Pleasonton lost 837.

Brandy Station failed to check the movement of the Army of Northern Virginia, and the leading elements of the army entered the Shenandoah Valley on June 12. Hooker received definite intelligence concerning this on the thirteenth and promptly issued orders for his army to withdraw from the line of the Rappahannock and march north to a new point of concentration around the Centreville, Virginia, area.

While Hooker's army repositioned itself and Hill and Longstreet marched toward the Valley, Ewell's Second Corps arrived before Winchester, Virginia. Garrisoning Winchester was Gen. Robert Milroy's Second Division of the Eighth Corps, numbering approximately 9,000 men. Ewell launched a skillfully conducted attack late on the fourteenth and penetrated Milroy's defenses. That night, at 2:00 A.M., Milroy attempted to retreat but ran into a trap laid by Ewell. The Federals were routed and Milroy lost 4,443 men, most of whom were captured. Ewell's losses were 269.

INTO PENNSYLVANIA. On June 15 the leading elements of Lee's army entered Pennsylvania. By the twenty-fourth Ewell's entire corps was bivouacked near Chambersburg, Pennsylvania. Hill's corps crossed the Potomac into Maryland on the same day with Longstreet's corps a day's march behind. In what proved to be one of the crucial decisions of the campaign, Lee gave discretionary orders to Stuart to take three of his brigades and march north, crossing the Potomac either east or west of the Blue Ridge Mountains, and eventually to take position on Ewell's right in Pennsylvania. Given the choice, Stuart chose to cut across the rear of the Federal army, crossing well east of the Blue Ridge.

Stuart's raid encountered numerous obstacles in its effort to circuit the Union rear. Powerful infantry columns forced him to make time-consuming detours in his march, and an improved and aggressive Federal cavalry engaged him in several skirmishes that caused further delays and detours. Stuart captured a supply train of 125 wagons and 400 prisoners, but it was small compensation for Lee, who was deprived of his best cavalry during the critical days of the campaign. Stuart would not rejoin the army until July 2.

By June 28 both Longstreet's and Hill's corps were camped in the vicinity of Chambersburg. Ewell's corps pushed farther east to threaten Harrisburg. Robert Rodes's and Edward Johnson's divisions occupied Carlisle, while Jubal Early's division marched to York, Pennsylvania. On the morning of the twenty-eighth, troopers of Albert Gallatin Jenkins's cavalry brigade advanced to within four miles of Harrisburg. This was to be the deepest Confederate forces penetrated into Pennsylvania, for Lee was forced to cancel the opera-

"If I had had Stonewall Jackson with me, so far as man can see, I should have won the battle of Gettysburg."

ROBERT E. LEE

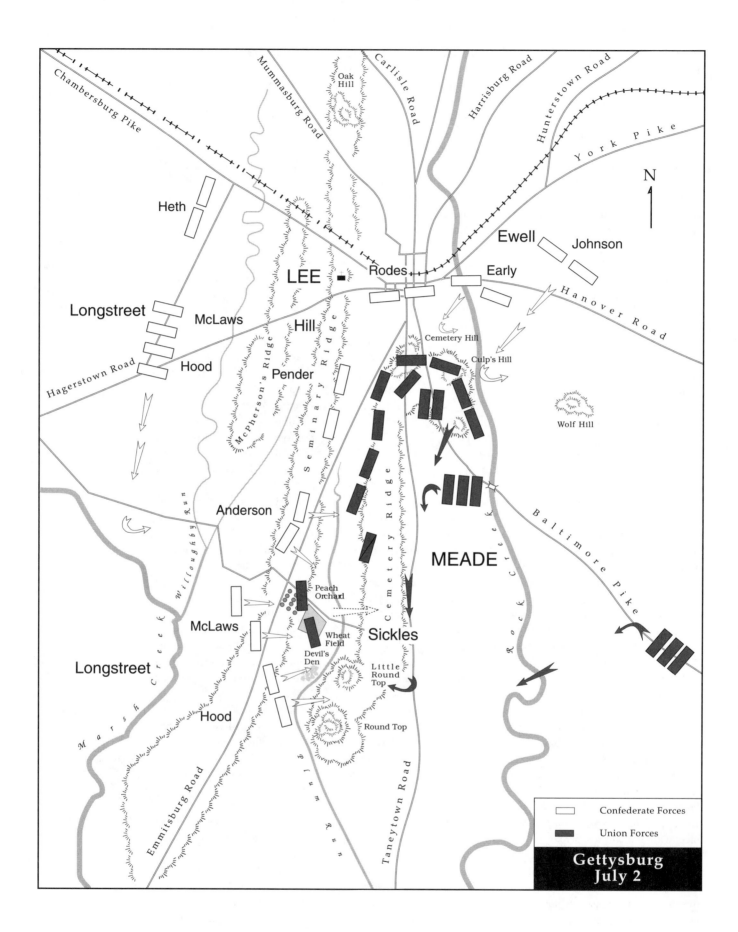

Chambersburg Pike

Mummasburg Road

Oak Hill

Carlisle Road

Harrisburg Road

Hunterstown Road

York Pike

N

Heth

LEE

Rodes

Ewell

Johnson

Early

Hanover Road

Longstreet

McLaws

Hill

Cemetery Hill

Culp's Hill

Hood

Pender

McPherson's Ridge

Seminary Ridge

Wolf Hill

Hagerstown Road

Anderson

Willoughby Run

Cemetery Ridge

MEADE

Baltimore Pike

Rock Creek

Peach Orchard

McLaws

Wheat Field

Sickles

Longstreet

Marsh Creek

Devil's Den

Little Round Top

Hood

Round Top

Plum Run

Taneytown Road

Emmitsburg Road

| | Confederate Forces |
| | Union Forces |

**Gettysburg
July 2**

240

tions against Harrisburg and order Ewell to withdraw from his advanced positions, owing to alarming news about the Federal army.

Without Stuart to provide him with timely and accurate information about the enemy, Lee was uncertain of the exact position of the Federal army. He believed it was still south of the Potomac. But on June 28 he was startled to learn through a spy, James Harrison, that the Federal army was massed in the vicinity of Frederick, Maryland, thirty miles south of Gettysburg. If the Federals moved west across South Mountain, they would be on Lee's line of communications to Virginia. To prevent this, Lee issued instructions to bring about a concentration of his army east of the mountains in the vicinity of Cashtown, Pennsylvania, about ten miles west of Gettysburg. By positioning his army east of the mountains, Lee posed a threat to both Harrisburg and Baltimore, and he believed this would keep the Federals off his line of communications.

By the twenty-eighth, the Federal army was under new leadership. Hooker had resigned over differences with the War Department regarding the Harpers Ferry garrison. In his place Lincoln appointed Gen. George G. Meade to command. Meade pushed his 93,000 men north from Frederick on a broad front. The left brushed the Catoctin Mountains, while the right stretched nearly thirty miles east. Meade's plan was to cover Baltimore and relieve Harrisburg. When this was accomplished, he would seek battle on the most favorable terms. During the final days of June, Meade's numerous cavalry, which was skillfully screening the front of his advancing army, provided him with strong evidence that Ewell had withdrawn from Harrisburg and that Lee's army was concentrating west of Gettysburg. In response to this Meade shifted the weight of his army to the left and began a gradual concentration of his army toward the Pennsylvania crossroads town. On June 30 John Buford's division of Federal cavalry marched to Gettysburg to secure the town and scout the region. They encountered a Confederate infantry brigade, which withdrew westward without an engagement.

The Confederate brigade belonged to Henry Heth's division of Hill's corps. Its commander reported the presence of Buford in Gettysburg, but Hill was skeptical. The Federal army was still believed to be in Maryland. Nevertheless, Hill planned to investigate. Heth and William Dorsey Pender's divisions, approximately 13,000 men, were ordered to march on Gettysburg on July 1. Their orders were to drive the Federal cavalry away but to halt if infantry was encountered. Lee did not want a general engagement to be precipitated with his concentration east of the mountains uncompleted.

The Federals also planned to move powerful forces to Gettysburg on July 1. Both the First and Eleventh Corps were under orders to march to Gettysburg to Buford's support, and four other corps were to move within supporting distance. The stage was set for the meeting of the opposing armies.

DAY ONE. Contact was made at 5:30 A.M. on July 1, when the advance of Heth struck a picket post of Buford's division. Heth pushed on and encountered a dismounted line of Federal cavalry about two miles west of Gettysburg. Believing it was infantry, Heth deployed two brigades of infantry and pressed rashly ahead. About this time, Maj. Gen. John F. Reynolds, commander of the Union First Corps, arrived on the battlefield. Exercising the discretion Meade had provided him, Reynolds decided to commit his First Corps and the Eleventh, as they arrived, to the engagement.

Between 10:30 and 11:00 A.M. a meeting engagement between Heth and James Wadsworth's division of the First Corps took place. Heth was soundly beaten, losing several hundred prisoners and the opportunity to seize Gettysburg cheaply. The Federals, although victorious, lost Reynolds, who was killed early in the fighting. They had, however, gained room and time to arrange a defense from which they could delay the Confederates and screen the strong defensive terrain that rose up south of Gettysburg.

Learning of Heth's contact with the enemy, Ewell diverted the march of Early and Rodes to approach Gettysburg from the north. At 1:30 P.M. the action was renewed, with Rodes launching an uncoordinated attack upon the First Corps. Lee had arrived on the battlefield and attempted to prevent the battle from escalating out of control. It was soon evident, however, that this was impossible, and at 2:30 P.M. he permitted Heth's division to advance to Rodes's support. Early arrived from the north and attacked around 3:00 P.M., inflicting a crushing defeat upon the Eleventh Corps. Heth and Rodes had a more difficult time with the First Corps and lost heavily in their attacks. Late in the afternoon, Hill sent Pender in to relieve Heth, and he and Rodes cleared the First Corps from their positions west of town. The Federals fell back in considerable disorder through Gettysburg to Cemetery Hill, immediately south of town, where they were rallied and reorganized by Generals O. O. Howard and Winfield Scott Hancock.

Hill's corps was too exhausted to attempt to complete the Southern victory by attacking Cemetery Hill. Lee therefore sent Ewell directions to carry the hill if it was "practicable" to do so. But Ewell had his own problems and was unable to mount an attack before night brought an end to the fighting. Out of approximately 42,000 men engaged, over 9,000

Ewell equivocated when Lee gave him typically discretionary orders. Longstreet sulked when Lee disregarded his advice.

PAGE 29

"The brave men, living and dead, who struggled here, have consecrated [this ground] far above our poor power to add or detract."

ABRAHAM LINCOLN
ADDRESS AT GETTYSBURG
NOV. 19, 1863

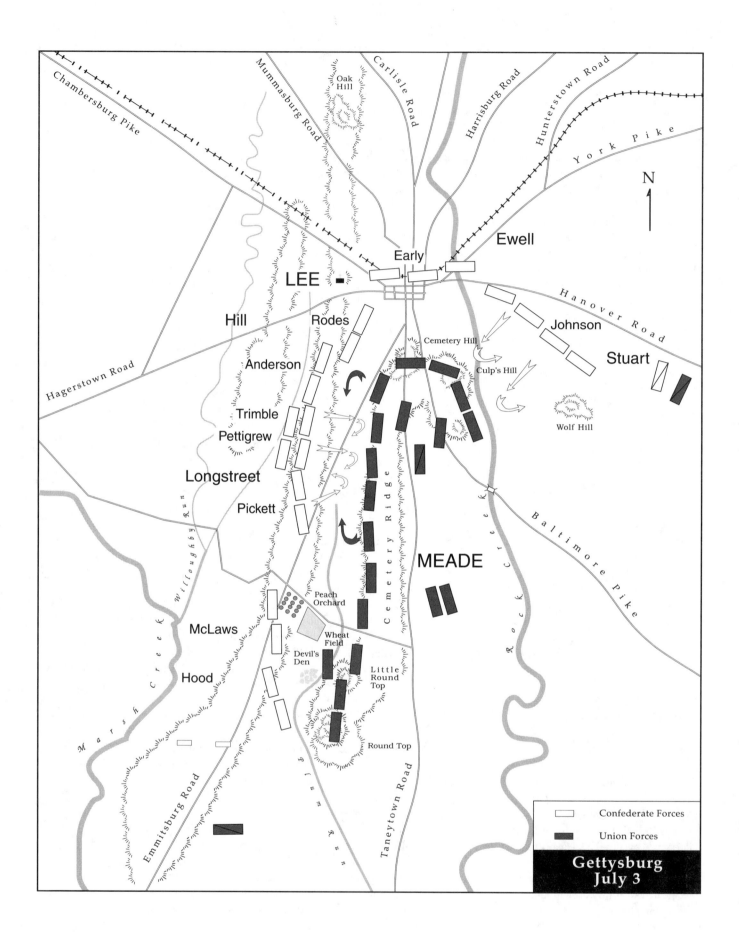

Oak Hill

Chambersburg Pike

Mummasburg Road

Carlisle Road

Harrisburg Road

Hunterstown Road

York Pike

N

Ewell

Early

Hanover Road

LEE

Johnson

Hill

Rodes

Stuart

Anderson

Cemetery Hill

Culp's Hill

Trimble

Wolf Hill

Pettigrew

Longstreet

Pickett

MEADE

Cemetery Ridge

Rock Creek

Baltimore Pike

Willoughby Run

Hagerstown Road

Peach Orchard

McLaws

Wheat Field

Devil's Den

Little Round Top

Hood

Marsh Creek

Round Top

Plum Run

Taneytown Road

Emmitsburg Road

☐ Confederate Forces

■ Union Forces

Gettysburg July 3

242

Federals and approximately 6,800 Confederates were casualties.

Although a Confederate tactical victory, the first day of fighting had been a strategic Union victory. The Federals had gained the advantage of position on ground they had selected. Lee, still without Stuart, was thrust into the role of the attacker, over ground he did not know. But battle had been joined, and Lee was determined to exploit his victory of July 1 by renewing the battle the next day.

DAY TWO. The early morning of July 2 was spent in reconnoitering the Federal position. Lee was uncertain how heavily the Federals had been reinforced during the night. They were found to be holding a horseshoe-shaped position, running from Culp's Hill to Cemetery Hill and down Cemetery Ridge, where Lee was told the Federal left flank rested. Upon this information he developed his battle plan. Longstreet was directed to take John Bell Hood's and Lafayette McLaws's divisions and conduct a covered march to gain a position that would place them upon the Union left flank. Their attack would be supported by Richard Heron Anderson's division of Hill's corps. It was believed at Lee's headquarters that these three divisions, numbering approximately 20,000 men, would crush the exposed Federal flank. Ewell's orders were to demonstrate against Culp's Hill and Cemetery Hill to pin the Federal defenders in place. If the opportunity were offered, however, he was given the discretion to deliver a full-scale attack. Longstreet was opposed to the operation and offered his opinion that the Confederates should attempt to outmaneuver the Federals to gain a position from which Lee could fight on the defensive. Lee was unmoved, and the offensive was set in motion over Longstreet's objections.

Unknown to Lee, nearly the entire Army of the Potomac was in his front. By forced marches Meade had concentrated his army during the night. Only the Sixth Corps, thirty-five miles distant at Manchester, Maryland, was absent, and it was en route and expected by mid- to late afternoon. Meade had skillfully deployed his army to take advantage of the natural strength of the terrain. His left, contrary to the report of Lee's reconnaissance officers, rested not on Cemetery Ridge but on Little Round Top, nearly three-quarters of a mile south of where Lee believed the Federal flank to be. This sector of the Federal front was to be held by the Third Corps. But its commander, Gen. Daniel E. Sickles, was dissatisfied with his position and shortly after 2:00 P.M. he advanced his entire corps nearly one-half mile in advance of the army's general line. The line Sickles occupied extended for nearly one mile and formed a vulnerable salient angle at the Peach Orchard.

Longstreet's flank march occupied the entire morning and was further delayed when Longstreet discovered Sickles's corps in a completely unexpected position. Not until nearly 3:00 P.M. was Longstreet prepared to open his pre-assault bombardment. A sharp artillery duel ensued for nearly one-half hour. At 3:30, Longstreet's infantry stepped off. Devil's Den and Little Round Top were struck first. The efforts of Meade's chief engineer, Gen. Gouvenour K. Warren, managed to avert disaster on Little Round Top by seeing that infantry from the Fifth Corps was sent to its defense. It arrived not a moment too soon. The battle ebbed and flowed, but ultimately the Federals prevailed.

From Devil's Den the battle spread north to the Wheatfield and then the Peach Orchard. Meade hurried the Fifth Corps to Sickles's aid and stripped troops from elsewhere on his line. The heavy blows of Longstreet's and Anderson's brigades proved too much, however, and around 6:00 P.M. Sickles's line collapsed and streamed east in retreat. Uncommitted elements of the Fifth Corps, a division of the Twelfth Corps from Culp's Hill, and the Sixth Corps, which was beginning to reach the field, managed to stabilize the situation and check the victorious Confederates.

On Lee's left, Ewell had opened an artillery bombardment the moment he had heard the sound of Longstreet's guns. Federal guns responded and an hour-long duel ensued, the result of which was that Ewell's guns were completely silenced. Nearly two hours later Ewell sent his infantry forward. Johnson's division assailed Culp's Hill while two brigades of Early's division attempted to storm Cemetery Hill. Johnson's troops gained abandoned Federal entrenchments near the southern base of Culp's Hill, but the summit was defended by a brigade of New York troops who could not be dislodged. On Cemetery Hill, Early's brigades stormed up the hill, routing several regiments of the Eleventh Corps and getting in among some of the Federal artillery. But they were counterattacked by a brigade of the Second Corps and other Eleventh Corps regiments and driven off the hill. This action marked the end of the second day's fighting. At least 16,500 men or more were casualties.

After the war controversy developed over the cause of the Confederate failure to realize victory on July 2. Former Confederate Gens. William Dorsey Pendleton and Jubal Early selected James Longstreet as the scapegoat. Pendleton published an account affirming that Lee had actually instructed Longstreet to attack the Federals at daylight. Longstreet was also accused of deliberately dragging his feet out of opposition to Lee's plan during his corps flank march into position.

Although Longstreet did not support Lee's plan of attack and was guilty of a sulky and obstinate demeanor on July 2, Pendleton's and Early's charges were inaccurate and without substance. There was no

"I do not want to make this charge. I do not see how it can succeed. I would not make it now but that General Lee has ordered it and is expecting it."

JAMES LONGSTREET
TO GEN. E. P. ALEXANDER,
JULY 3, 1863

early morning attack order, and although Longstreet's flank march was in some respects poorly managed, there is no evidence that Longstreet attempted to sabotage Lee's plan by delaying his corps march into position.

DAY THREE. Lee's confidence was unshaken by the failures of the second, and he determined to continue the struggle on July 3. "The general plan was unchanged," wrote Lee. Longstreet, reinforced by George E. Pickett's division, which had been guarding wagon trains in Chambersburg, was to renew the attack, apparently at daylight. Johnson's division, heavily reinforced during the night, was to storm Culp's Hill at the same time. Stuart's cavalry, which had at last found the army, was instructed to march beyond the army's left flank and position itself to threaten the Federal rear.

Unfortunately for Lee, his plans were never realized. Meade seized the initiative and counterattacked on Culp's Hill at 4:30 A.M. Longstreet, who may have misunderstood what Lee wished, had prepared orders around sunrise for his corps to attempt to maneuver around the round tops and gain the Federal flank. Under the circumstances, concerted action was now impossible, and Lee was forced to modify his plan of attack. He now determined to launch a massive frontal assault designed to break the Federal center on Cemetery Ridge. A preattack bombardment by nearly 140 guns would cripple the Federal defenders, and then the divisions of Pickett and Pettigrew and one-half of Trimble's (slightly over 12,000 men) would advance over one mile of open ground and smash through the Union defenses. It was a bold, daring plan, and Longstreet, who was given the task of directing the attack, was adamantly opposed. Lee, however, was determined to make the effort, and Longstreet was compelled against his better judgment to carry out the plan.

At 1:00 P.M. the artillery cannonade opened. Between 80 and 100 Federal guns responded, and one of the largest artillery duels of the war ensued. Thick clouds of smoke covered much of the field and hindered the view of the artillerymen on both sides, causing gunners of both armies to overshoot their targets. After nearly one and one-half hours of intense firing, the Federal artillery ceased fire under orders to conserve their ammunition. By the time the bombardment stopped at 3:00, the Confederate artillery had exhausted its supply of long-range ammunition and was unable to support the infantry.

The Southern infantry emerged into view shortly after 3:00. Their perfectly preserved lines of battle extended for nearly one mile. The Federal artillery reopened at this time and inflicted terrible losses on the attackers but failed to check them. As the Southern infantry loomed nearer, the Federal infantry added its small-arms fire to the canister of the artillery and the

Confederates fell by the hundreds. Federal infantry swung out on both Confederate flanks, which were exposed and unsupported, inflicting more losses and chaos. A small group of men, principally from Pickett's division and led by Gen. Lewis A. Armistead, managed to penetrate the Federal position briefly, but they were quickly overwhelmed. By 4:00 P.M. the attack had been repulsed with tragic loss. Between 5,500 and 6,000 Confederate soldiers were casualties, with perhaps as many as 1,000 being killed.

Elsewhere on the field, Johnson's division, after sustaining heavy losses, had retired from Culp's Hill by late morning. Stuart fared no better. His march east was detected, and powerful Federal cavalry units moved to engage him. Several miles east of town a cavalry action ensued that was indecisive, but it was successful in checking Stuart's forward progress.

The Army of Northern Virginia was spent and exhausted. Imperfect casualty figures give its losses at 4,427 killed, 12,179 wounded, and 5,592 missing. Its losses were undoubtedly higher, probably as many as 28,000. The Army of the Potomac had likewise suffered dreadfully: 3,155 killed, 14,529 wounded, and 5,365 missing.

Lee maintained his position on July 4 in hopes that Meade would attack him. He did not, and that night the army commenced its retreat under a heavy rain that helped slow the Federal pursuit. Lee's advance guard arrived at Williamsport, Maryland, on the sixth and discovered the Potomac swollen by rains and impassable. Lee entrenched his army on strong terrain and went to work building a pontoon bridge. Meade had brought his army up by the thirteenth and contemplated an assault but called it off when the majority of his senior officers advised against it. That night, the pontoon bridge had been completed and the Potomac had fallen so that it was fordable, and Lee withdrew to Virginia. A rearguard action took place on the fourteenth between Buford's cavalry and elements of Heth's and Pender's divisions. The Confederates lost 719 prisoners and General Pettigrew, who was mortally wounded.

The Gettysburg campaign was over. On July 4 Vicksburg surrendered to Grant. The South, with its limited resources and manpower, was faced with a continuing struggle. The North's sagging morale was encouraged by the Union victories, and the peace movement lost its momentum. Although Lee's army had survived to fight another day, it had suffered crippling losses from which it never fully recovered. One Confederate lieutenant may have summarized best what Gettysburg meant for the South when he wrote, "we gained nothing but glory and lost our bravest men."

[*See also* Brandy Station, Virginia; Winchester, Virginia.]

— D. SCOTT HARTWIG

GORDON, JOHN B.

Gordon, John B., (1832–1904), major general, U.S. senator, and governor of Georgia. The descendant of Scottish immigrants and of a Revolutionary War soldier, Gordon was born in Upson County, Georgia, on February 6, 1832, and for more than forty years was one of the most celebrated citizens of the state.

Gordon attended the University of Georgia but did not graduate. In 1854 he studied law in Atlanta and by the end of the year had passed his bar examination and was a partner in an established law firm. When the legal profession failed to provide the income he expected, Gordon moved to the state capital of Milledgeville in November 1855. There he obtained employment as a newspaperman covering the general assembly. By the end of the decade, however, he was in northwestern Georgia working with his father in developing coal mines.

Shortly after the bombardment of Fort Sumter, Gordon helped organize a company of volunteers from Georgia, Alabama, and Tennessee that styled itself the "Raccoon Roughs." On May 15 the company was mustered into Confederate service as part of the Sixth Alabama Infantry Regiment, with Gordon as major and his brother Augustus as captain. After training in Corinth, Mississippi, the regiment departed for Virginia. There it occupied the extreme right of P. G. T. Beauregard's line on July 21. While other regiments routed the Federals at First Manassas, however, the Sixth Alabama only waited, marched, and countermarched.

Gordon's rise in the command structure was spectacularly rapid. He was promoted to colonel on April 28, 1862; to brigadier on November 1, 1862; and to major general on May 14, 1864.

Gordon fought valiantly whenever his command was engaged. At Seven Pines, where he lost 60 percent of his troops, he was placed in temporary command of Robert Rodes's brigade when that officer was incapacitated by wounds. Gordon's brigade led Robert E. Lee's vanguard into Maryland in September 1862 and engaged the enemy at South Mountain. In the words of Rodes, Gordon fought in a "manner I have never heard or seen equalled during the war." D. H. Hill, the division commander, added: "Gordon excelled his former deeds at Seven Pines and in the battles around Richmond. Our language is not capable of expressing a higher compliment."

Gordon's brigade was in the thickest of the fighting at Sharpsburg, a battle in which the general was wounded five times, once in the head. Only a bullet hole in his hat prevented him from drowning in his own blood as he lay unconscious on the ground. He was nursed back to health by his wife, who had left

"RACCOON ROUGH"

Maj. Gen. John B. Gordon of Georgia rose rapidly through the ranks and fought with distinction at Seven Pines and in battles around Richmond.

NATIONAL ARCHIVES

their two sons with her mother-in-law in Georgia to accompany the general to the war. "I owe my life to her incessant watchfulness night and day," said Gordon, "and to her tender nursing through weary weeks and anxious months."

By the spring of 1863 the general, of "striking appearance and commanding presence . . . six feet tall, thin and straight as a rail but muscular and powerful of build," was back in action, commanding a brigade under Jubal Early at Chancellorsville. In the Gettysburg campaign he led Early's column to York and Wrightsville. Rejoining the main Confederate force at Gettysburg, Gordon took an active part in the first day's engagement north and west of the town. An officer who glimpsed Gordon riding a black stallion that day called the sight "the most glorious and inspiring thing . . . standing in his stirrups bareheaded, hat in hand, arms extended, and, in a voice like a trumpet, exhorting his men. It was superb, absolutely thrilling." Gordon did not consider his actions the next two days "of sufficient importance to mention."

At Spotsylvania Gordon's men shouted their famous "Lee to the rear!" order to the commanding general, while Gordon rode to the front of his troops and reestablished the Confederate line, thereby turning imminent disaster into victory.

In June 1864 Gordon's brigade was detached from the forces around Richmond and participated in Early's Shenandoah Valley campaign. Gordon's men helped drive David O. Hunter from the Valley and delivered a crushing blow to Lew Wallace at Monocacy on the aborted raid on Washington. Gordon then took

In 1889 the United Confederate Veterans formed and chose as its leader John B. Gordon, a Confederate general committed to reconciliation with the North.

PAGE 334

Sharpsburg was the twelve bloodiest hours in American military history. In one day, almost 23,000 Union and Confederate casualties had fallen along the Antietam Creek.

PAGE 537

part in the Battles of Third Winchester, Fisher's Hill, and Cedar Creek before rejoining Lee in the defense of Petersburg.

His last major action occurred on March 25, 1865, when he directed a predawn attack on Fort Stedman, hoping to breach the Union lines and permit some of Lee's troops to escape to North Carolina and join Joseph E. Johnston. Initially, the attack carried the works, but lack of support and confusion in the darkness eventually doomed the venture. The thirty-three-year-old lawyer who possessed "the personality and genius for war" commanded the Second Corps on the retreat from Petersburg and surrendered at Appomattox.

Returning to Georgia, Gordon resumed the practice of law, this time in Atlanta, and entered Democratic politics. He lost a gubernatorial bid in 1868 but was elected to the U.S. Senate in 1873. Shortly after his reelection in 1879, Gordon resigned to enter the employ of a major railroad company. He served as governor from 1886 to 1890, after which the legislature again elected him to the Senate.

The popular soldier-statesman served as commander-in-chief of the United Confederate Veterans from the inception of the organization in 1890 until his death on January 9, 1904. He was buried in Oakland Cemetery, Atlanta.

— LOWELL REIDENBAUGH

GOSPORT NAVY YARD

Located across the Elizabeth River from Norfolk, Virginia, Gosport was the largest and best equipped naval yard in the United States in 1861. Norfolk was an important port and shipbuilding center from the colonial period, and Gosport was chosen as the site for a naval yard in the years after the War of 1812. In 1830 the navy opened its first stone dry dock at the yard. By 1861 the yard occupied a rectangular area about three-quarters of a mile long and a quarter of a mile wide. Yard facilities included a granite dry dock, two large ship houses, a third ship house under construction, riggers and sail lofts, sawmills, timber sheds, spar and mast storage sheds, foundries, machine shops, boiler shops, an ordnance magazine, and an ordnance laboratory. The Gosport Navy Yard also served as the storage site for over three thousand naval cannons, most important of which were some three hundred new Dahlgren shell guns.

Commandant of the yard in 1861 was Commo. Charles S. McCauley, a fifty-two-year-old navy veteran. Either under repair or anchored off the yard that spring were the sailing sloops *Plymouth* and *Germantown,* the brig *Dolphin,* ships-of-the-line *Delaware* and *Columbus,* and two frigates, *Columbia* and *Raritan.* Former ship-of-the-line *Pennsylvania* served as an unarmed receiving ship, and the ship-of-the-line *New York* was still on the stocks. The most important vessel at Gosport was the five-year-old steam frigate *Merrimack,* in dry dock for repairs. In March, the steam sloop-of-war *Cumberland* anchored off the yard.

In early April 1861 Federal Secretary of the Navy Gideon Welles, concerned over the fate of *Merrimack,* requested that McCauley make it ready for departure as quickly as possible. When McCauley replied that this would take a month, Welles ordered the U.S. Navy's engineer-in-chief, Benjamin F. Isherwood, to make the repairs. Isherwood went to Gosport with Commdr. James D. Alden, who was to command *Merrimack* when the repairs were finished; they arrived on April 14. He had *Merrimack* ready by the seventeenth, but McCauley refused to let him raise steam. Isherwood later charged that McCauley was drunk; other sources suggest that he was simply confused and indecisive.

Isherwood had *Merrimack's* boiler fires alight the next morning, but he could not persuade Commdr. Alden to sail the ship out in defiance of McCauley. Both officers returned to Washington. Secretary Welles promptly sent Commo. Hiram Paulding to relieve McCauley.

Although the gates into the yard were locked, a loud mob had gathered just outside them, convincing McCauley that thousands of Virginia troops were about to attack. On April 20 he ordered all the ships in the yard burned and scuttled. Upon his arrival, Paulding confirmed these orders and extended them to include the entire yard.

The destruction was not fully effective. Civilians and Virginia soldiers raced into the yard as soon as the defenders abandoned it and extinguished most of the fires. Although all the vessels at the yard, with the exception of *Cumberland* and *Pawnee,* were set afire, *Plymouth, Delaware,* and *Columbus* sank with little damage. Neither powder charges at the dry dock nor those at the powder magazine exploded. The sail loft, rigging loft, gun carriage depot, and two of the ship houses were totally burned, but all the other buildings were saved intact. Confederate naval authorities seized over a thousand guns, thousands of tons of supplies, and even uniforms from various storehouses within the yard and recovered some four thousand shells from the harbor waters. Most important, in the undamaged dry dock, *Merrimack* sank with fire damage confined to its rigging and upper deck. Not only was the hull of the ship salvageable; within a watertight magazine below decks were over two thousand 10-pound cartridges.

Union forces recaptured the navy yard in May 1862. Despite extensive destruction of the yard's facilities by the retreating Confederates, the yard formed an important part of Union naval control of the Hampton Roads area for the remainder of the war.

— ROBERT S. BROWNING III

GOVERNORS

By 1860 all Southern states had governors elected by those citizens eligible to vote for members of the lower house of the general assembly except South Carolina, whose governor was elected by the assembly. All American governors under the first state constitutions had little authority, but the practical matter of efficient government compelled gradual change. By 1860 Southern governors had gained considerable independence from the legislatures, but they were not yet as powerful constitutionally. The power they had gained lay not so much in a strengthened executive branch as in their ability to curb legislative authority. The typical governor could delay legislation passed by the assembly but had little appointive power. It is true that every state that entered the Confederacy named the governor as its commander in chief, but this power was almost untested.

When the Confederacy began its war for independence, the old practice of decision making by legislatures proved inadequate. The citizenry had to be persuaded to make great sacrifices and consider defeat unthinkable; producers and merchants had to be induced to give the war their first priority; soldiers had to be supplied. A central government could provide the basic war measures and some methods of implementing them, but the South was not yet ready for this degree of central authority. And even if it had been, geography and the state of the economy would have prevented the imposition of much more centralism than actually occurred. To wage a successful war, the Confederate government had to have the full cooperation of the states. The extent of each state's cooperation can largely be measured by the actions of its governor.

CHARISMA AND LEADERSHIP. In any struggle for independence against great odds, strong leadership is pivotal. All the first Confederate governors except John Letcher of Virginia had been secession leaders who obviously had the respect of their people. As their responsibilities increased during war, so did their visibility. How dedicated each of them was to victory offered guidance to their people, who usually responded to the war as their governor seemed to respond. With certain exceptions, then, the governors represented the collective sentiment of their constituents.

Twenty-eight men served as Confederate governors. Most were in their forties, and only Charles Clark of Mississippi and Harris Flanagin of Arkansas

were Northern-born. All who were governor during secession were Democrats, and all but three of these had advocated secession upon Abraham Lincoln's election. In the last years of the Confederacy, when discontent was rampant, voters turned mainly to ex-Whigs and former Unionists. Most governors had been lawyers, and half of them had college or university degrees. Most were politically experienced, and six had had military experience. As a whole, they were quite representative of mid-nineteenth-century American political leadership.

Alabama, Florida, Louisiana, Kentucky, Mississippi, Tennessee, Texas, and Virginia began their Confederate years with governors clearly intent upon success. They made sound preparations for war, and when it came they acted decisively. They publicly sought to preserve state and individual rights but also accepted the need for sacrifice. Possibly J. J. Pettus of Mississippi was overzealous in his support of wartime legislation, but he was reelected overwhelmingly; and Andrew B. Moore of Alabama had malcontents from the first whom he could not beguile. These eight governors were no better or worse managers than the other five original Confederate governors, but they had a symbolic quality that established their states' rapport with the Confederate war program.

The other secession governors failed to become charismatic pro-Confederate leaders. Joseph E. Brown of Georgia did so deliberately; Claiborne F. Jackson of Missouri was politically inept; John W. Ellis of North Carolina was too retiring; Francis W. Pickens of South Carolina was too inert; and Henry M. Rector of Arkansas was apparently too scatter-brained.

Only seven of the postsecession governors served long enough for their image to be of much consequence. John G. Shorter of Alabama and John Milton of Florida became governors early in the Confederacy and established themselves as protagonists of both state and nation. Henry W. Allen of Louisiana, Milledge L. Bonham of South Carolina, Francis R. Lubbock of Texas, and William ("Extra Billy") Smith of Virginia took office midway through the war. They were fair-minded, dedicated officials, and it would be difficult to imagine executives operating under such difficulties to have been more successful. None of them had a compelling personality, but all projected a grim determination that would be the last hope of the Confederacy. Zebulon Vance of North Carolina quickly became the paradigm of a state and individual rights fanatic, and both he and his state actually appeared to be anti-Confederate despite their enormous contributions to the war.

The quality of leadership of the eight remaining governors varied much but mattered little. The tenure of Henry T. Clark of North Carolina was very brief.

Just at the time Atlanta fell to the invaders in September 1864, Gov. Brown furloughed the 10,000-man Georgia militia to keep it from coming under Confederate control.

PAGE 78

Although Gov. Zebulon Vance of North Carolina never repudiated his support of the Confederacy, he was more than willing to defend his state and challenge Confederate policies.

PAGE 643

As late as October 1864, Zebulon Vance was a moving force in the Confederate governors' conference held in Augusta, Georgia, that reaffirmed the states' allegiance to the Confederacy.

PAGE 644

South Carolina Gov. Milledge L. Bonham indicated his displeasure at the frequently high-handed methods being used by Confederate commissioners.

PAGE 67

Thomas H. Watts of Alabama served the last seventeen months of the war and made serious efforts at leadership, but by 1864 disaffection was so great that he seemed too pro-Confederate for Alabamans and too pro-Alabama for Richmond. Richard Hawes of Kentucky, Clark of Mississippi, and Thomas C. Reynolds of Missouri made valiant efforts to do something constructive, but their states were largely in Federal hands. Flanagin of Arkansas, Andrew G. Magrath of South Carolina, and Pendleton Murrah of Texas took office near the end of the war and were both inactive in and sometimes obstructive to the war effort.

COOPERATION WITH RICHMOND. Though the image that a governor projected was important to the morale of his state, what he did was even more important. There was a vast uncertainty regarding the proper course of action. Bred under state rights doctrine, he now had to accept the exigencies of war. Upon the enactment of Confederate laws on conscription, impressment, and suspension of habeas corpus, most governors protested automatically. Some—Brown of Georgia and Vance of North Carolina—complained so stridently that they were condemned more for their words than for their deeds. But after making their protests, and occasionally forcing slight compromises, the governors were generally cooperative.

An examination of the careers of the Confederate governors indicates that fifteen of them cooperated effectively with the war policies of the central government. Some were more nationalistic than their legislatures and suffered politically for their zeal. These men were Smith and Letcher of Virginia, Pickens and Bonham of South Carolina, Perry and Milton of Florida, A. B. Moore and Shorter of Alabama, T. O. Moore of Louisiana, Pettus of Mississippi, Clark and Lubbock of Texas, Jackson of Missouri, George W. Johnson of Kentucky, and Isham G. Harris of Tennessee. Certain inevitable obstacles often hampered good execution of Confederate policies in a state, but within recognized limits these governors deserve good marks for nationalism.

Several others would like to have been more effective Confederates but were unable to do so. Ellis and Clark of North Carolina were too passive; Allen of Louisiana and Rector of Arkansas were cut off from Richmond by enemy occupation; Hawes and Reynolds were refugee governors. Five governors came to office when the war was already lost. Watts of Alabama, Magrath of South Carolina, Murrah of Texas, and Charles Clark of Mississippi hoped to salvage something either by separate state action or by continuing the war in the Southwest, but none of their desperate efforts succeeded. Flanagin of Arkansas simply gave up and did nothing.

Only Brown of Georgia and Vance of North Carolina significantly hampered the war effort. Both were fanatical state righters, and their constant carping undoubtedly fed the discontent developing in their states; both men willingly shouldered this resentment. Brown was the more destructive. Vance won the right to exempt state employees from military service and other, smaller victories, but on most matters he cooperated, albeit grudgingly. Brown differed with Richmond more, quarreled more violently, and won more victories over the central government.

MANAGEMENT. Equally important as charisma and the degree of cooperation with Richmond was a governor's executive ability. What power the Southern governors had acquired by 1860 was largely in negative control over legislation. But legislatures at this time were basically conservative, disliking taxation and preferring to interfere as little as possible in the state economy or the personal affairs of the citizens. This system could not operate effectively under the strain of constant demands from Richmond and ever-increasing problems at home. State governors now had to initiate virtually all the necessary legislation and to expand their power as commander in chief to unprecedented levels.

To exercise these new powers, governors often found themselves vying more with their own legislatures than with Richmond. The Florida and South Carolina legislatures even created a plural executive to diffuse executive power, though this worked badly in Florida, and it soon returned to a single executive. But the need for emergency action usually prevailed. There would be a need for a law, the governor would specify what was needed, and generally the legislature would comply. Thus the national pattern also became the state pattern.

The first major duty of the governors was to raise volunteers for the Confederate provisional army. They had started doing so even before secession and soon had far more volunteers than the War Department could accept. The governors protested bitterly when so many volunteers were encamped at home at state expense; nevertheless, these men were available to Richmond at a moment's notice. Legislatures all wanted local defense forces and these the governors provided, though they never proved to be effective defenders.

One of the greatest contributions the states made, even under Brown and Vance, was in matériel for the army. The work in this area was ad hoc and improvisational. Governors found themselves suddenly saddled with a variety of duties without precedent: collecting weapons, manufacturing ammunition, negotiating contracts for the manufacture of all sorts of army needs, sending out purchasing agents and blockade runners to buy everything from meat to muslin, and begging clothing from churches and ladies' organizations. Moreover, they had to compete with Confederate purchasing agents. Selfish localism naturally dictated that one's own volunteers had first call upon such goods, leaving the War Department to outfit less fortunate soldiers.

CIVIL WAR-ERA GOVERNORS OF SOUTHERN STATES

State	Governor	Dates of Service
Alabama	Andrew B. Moore	Dec. 1, 1857–Dec. 2, 1861
	John G. Shorter	Dec. 2. 1861–Dec. 1, 1863
	Thomas H. Watts	Dec. 1, 1863–Apr. 12, 1865
Arkansas	Henry M. Rector	Nov. 15, 1860–Nov. 4. 1862
	Thomas Fletcher	Nov. 4, 1862–Nov. 15, 1862
	Harris Flanagin	Nov. 15, 1862–May 28, 1865
	Isaac Murphy	*Apr. 18, 1864–July 3, 1868*
Florida	Madison S. Perry	Oct. 5, 1857–Oct. 7. 1861
	John Milton	Oct. 7, 1861–Apr. 1, 1865
	Abraham K. Allison	Apr. 1, 1865–Sept. 1865
Georgia	Joseph E. Brown	Nov. 6, 1857–May 9, 1865
Kentucky	George W. Johnson	Nov. 20, 1861–Apr. 8, 1862
	Richard Hawes	Apr. 8, 1862–Spring 1865
	Beriah Magoffin	*Aug. 30, 1859–Aug. 18, 1862*
	James F. Robinson	*Aug. 18, 1862–Sept. 1, 1863*
	Thomas Elliott Bramlette	*Sept. 1, 1863–Sept. 3, 1867*
Louisiana	Thomas O. Moore	Jan. 23, 1860–Jan. 26, 1864
	Henry W. Allen	Jan. 26, 1864–June 6, 1865
	George F. Shepley	*June, 2, 1862–Mar. 4, 1864*
	Michael Hahn	*Mar. 4, 1864–Mar. 3, 1865*
	James Madison Wells	*Mar. 3, 1865–June 25, 1868*
Mississippi	J. J. Pettus	Nov. 21, 1859–Nov. 16, 1863
	Charles Clard	Nov. 16, 1863–May 22, 1865
Missouri	Claiborne F. Jackson	Jan. 3, 1861–Dec. 6, 1862
	Thomas C. Reynolds	Dec. 6, 1862–Apr. 1865
	Hamilton Rowan Gamble	*June 31, 1861–Jan. 31, 1864*
	Willard Preble Hall	*Jan. 31, 1864–Jan. 2, 1865*
	Thomas Clement Fletcher	*Jan. 2, 1865–Jan. 12, 1869*
North Carolina	John W. Ellis	Jan. 1, 1859–July 7, 1861
	Henry T. Clark	July 7, 1861–Sept. 8, 1862
	Zebulon Vance	Sept. 8, 1862–May 13, 1865
	Edward Stanly	*May 26, 1862–Jan 15, 1863*
South Carolina	Francis W. Pickens	Dec. 14, 1860–Dec. 1862
	Miledge L. Bonham	Dec. 17, 1862–Dec. 1864
	Andrew G. Magrath	Dec. 18, 1864–May 28, 1865
Tennessee	Isham G. Harris	Nov. 3, 1857–Aug. 1863
	Robert Looney Caruthers	Aug. 1863
	Andrew Johnson	*Mar. 3, 1862–Mar. 3, 1865*
	E. H. East	*Mar. 3, 1865–Apr. 5, 1865*
	William G. Brownlow	*Apr. 5, 1865–Feb. 25, 1869*
Texas	Edward Clark	Mar. 16, 1861–Nov. 7, 1861
	Francis R. Lubbock	Nov. 7, 1861–Nov. 5, 1863
	Pendleton Murrah	Nov. 5, 1863–June 11, 1865
Virginia	John Letcher	Jan. 1, 1860–Jan. 1, 1864
	William ("Extra Billy) Smith	Jan. 1, 1864–May 9, 1865
	Francis H. Peirpoint	*June 1861–Apr. 16, 1863*

This table includes governors of state governments allied with the Confederacy as well as those allied with the Union. Names and dates in italics denote a Union alliance; those not in italics denote a Confederate alliance. Often a single state was represented simultaneously by a government allied with the Confederacy and a government remaining in, occupied by, or restored to the Union. Dates of service vary widely in historical sources. The dates given here reflect the best available consensus based on various state records, state histories, military histories, and biographies.

The Confederacy was able to sustain a war lasting four years largely because of the energetic activities of its commercial agents in Great Britain.

PAGE 15

The difficulties encountered by Confederate officials in Great Britain revealed that the U.S. consular agents had a well-organized and highly developed espionage system.

PAGE 15

All governors took seriously their position as commander in chief of state forces. They seized Federal installations on their own initiative, and those outside the main battle zones unwillingly took charge of their own defenses. They impressed slaves and free blacks for labor; they obtained from their legislatures or simply arrogated to themselves the right to restrict cotton planting, to arrest peace activists, to ban distilling, to restrict hoarding and speculation, and even to declare martial law. The governors of Georgia, South Carolina, and Texas even ventured into foreign diplomacy.

Some of the new policies were startlingly modern. All tried to allocate money or food to soldiers' families. Arkansas failed in this, but Georgia succeeded magnificently: its welfare expenditures dominated the state's budget for the last two years of the war. Salt was a vital preservative and every governor had carte blanche authority to acquire it. Cotton and wool cards were vital and scarce, and governors either imported them or ordered their manufacture. As unimportant as these efforts may seem, the home front could not have survived as long as it did without them.

To finance this work, conservative antebellum practices had to be abandoned. The financial history of each state shows regular demands by governors for appropriations and almost immediate responses by the legislatures in the form of fiat money and bond issues or new taxes. The Georgia state budget exceeded the state's appropriations for the entire decade of the 1850s. Refugee governors virtually carried their state treasury in their saddlebags and spent it at their own discretion. Thus with rare exceptions the governor asked and the legislature complied—an illustration of executive dominance during wartime. Obviously many of these expenditures were for military purposes, but events were creating such distress among civilians that for the first time in American history individual welfare was considered a government responsibility. The Civil War was indeed putting the Southern states and their governors through a revolutionary experience.

[*See also* State Rights *and selected biographies of figures mentioned herein.*]

— W. BUCK YEARNS

GREAT BRITAIN

Prior to the Civil War, nineteenth-century relations between the United States and Great Britain were influenced by mutual resentments that had festered since the American Revolution and had been amplified during the War of 1812. Those historic antagonisms were reinforced by a series of crises that developed with disturbing regularity. Britain and the United States confronted disagreements over the Canadian rebellion, fishing and trade agreements, and disputed boundaries with Maine and Oregon. American efforts to annex California and Texas and control Central American nations brought the prerogatives of both countries into conflict and left the British with the impression that Americans were "most disagreeable fellows" at best. British officials and elements of the ruling gentry maintained a jaundiced view of Americans and harbored suspicions that the country was capable of all manner of international mischief.

The sectional crisis that led to the Civil War in 1860 fueled British fears that the country might resolve its internal problems through some form of international adventure. Britons and Canadians were both apprehensive about the fact that Americans openly expressed designs for the annexation of Canada to compensate for the loss of the Southern states. Those reservations appeared to be reinforced by President-elect Abraham Lincoln's choice of the aggressive William H. Seward as secretary of state. Seward was often outwardly antagonistic toward the British and had been a supporter of annexing Canada, which he considered "ripened fruit which must fall." Lord Lyons, British minister to the United States, reported that he thought that Seward would be "dangerous," as he frequently employed the Anglo-American relationship as "good material" for his brand of politics. Lyons considered Seward typical of American politicians of "second rate station and ability."

British perception of the Southern United States appears to have been somewhat different from the view held of the North. Though English evangelists soundly condemned the slaveholding South, many Britons felt a close, if only economic, relationship with the American Southeast. Southern cotton had become an essential element of the British textile economy, and manufacturing concerns found ready markets for industrial products in the agricultural South. The cotton-related industry in Great Britain had grown to approximately 80 million pounds sterling in the decade prior to the Civil War, and the mills of Lancashire and West Derbyshire consumed more than 2.5 million bales annually. By 1860 a large percentage of the British population was dependent upon the textile industry, and most recognized the implications of any disruption of the cotton trade. Unlike the general attitude toward the North, where problems with Canada were focused, British attitudes toward the South and Southern attitudes toward Britain were based on mutually beneficial economics and were characterized by a spirit of friendliness and even admiration.

Unfortunately for the Confederacy, that relationship began to deteriorate almost immediately after secession. In April 1861 President Lincoln proclaimed a blockade of Southern seaports. The blockade, designed to isolate the Confederacy politically and economically, threatened the cotton trade. A month later Queen Victoria issued a proclamation of neutrality. In spite of a highly antagonistic reaction in the North, the British proclamation assisted the United States: it forbade British subjects to engage in sympathetic activities on behalf of the Confederacy, forced recognition of the Union blockade, and prevented the fitting out of warships in British ports. The United States was quick to point out, however, that the declaration benefited the Confederacy by recognizing the South's status as a belligerent. That recognition undermined the United States' position that the South's secession from the Union was an internal affair. It also provided a degree of protection for Confederate military personnel by making it difficult for the United States to treat them as criminals or pirates.

Although Victoria's proclamation proved to be important to Confederate survival, Southerners were also convinced that Great Britain's need for cotton would ultimately lead to its supporting the Confederate cause. In response to the Union blockade the Confederacy declared a cotton embargo. Southerners shared a firm belief in King Cotton diplomacy. By starving the mills of Lancashire and West Derbyshire, the South could create sufficient economic and political pressure to force Great Britain to recognize the Confederacy and perhaps even provide military assistance. The *Charleston Mercury* summed up the argument in June 1861, reminding the South that "the cards are in our hands and we intend to play them out to the bankruptcy of every cotton factory in Great Britain and France or the acknowledgement of our independence."

The Confederate cotton embargo had a predictable impact on the British textile industry. In Lancashire the dwindling supply of cotton resulted in the closing of mills and the loss of thousands of jobs. That economic disaster resulted in considerable pressure to recognize the Confederacy and no small amount of interest in active British military intervention in America. But in spite of the pressure, British politicians stoically refused to be drawn into the conflict and even adopted measures designed to ensure that war materials were not shipped from Great Britain to either belligerent. Britain wanted no part of a war with the United States. The impact of the "cotton famine" would be nominal compared to the effect of an embargo on wheat from the United States. It would be cheaper to subsidize the cotton industry than to go to war and perhaps risk internal strife or revolution. In fact, while the cotton industry suffered, the woolen industry advanced. Shipbuilding, too, benefited from Confederate and speculative demands for British vessels. British resistance to

involvement in American affairs was also based on the belief that the Confederacy could win its independence without assistance—a belief held until it was too late to provide assistance. For the Confederacy, King Cotton diplomacy proved to be a bitter disappointment, and

"DIXIE'S NURSE"

An illustrated sheet music cover mocks Queen Victoria as an obese Britannia, expressing Northern resentment over Britain's support for the Confederate war effort.

LIBRARY OF CONGRESS

British failure to recognize or assist the South elicited open expressions of resentment in the Confederacy.

Although the cotton embargo failed to have the desired political impact on Britain's policy toward the Confederacy, the Union navy provided an incident that almost achieved the Confederate political objective of provoking war between the United States and Great Britain. On November 8, 1861, Capt. Charles Wilkes forcibly removed newly appointed Confederate commissioners James Mason and John Slidell from the royal mail steamer *Trent* and took them as prisoners to Fort Warren in Boston Harbor. News of Mason's and Slidell's capture was received with public enthusiasm in the United States, but Britons were outraged by Wilkes's contempt for the sovereignty of a British vessel. The British press demanded release of the prisoners and an apology. The gravity of the *Trent* affair resulted in the creation of a War Committee in the cabinet. The committee mulled the options and after determining that Wilkes had acted illegally, considered preparing for war with the United States. Confederates were also indignant, but at the same

The Civil War stimulated the shipbuilding industry in Great Britain.

PAGE 15

*The most
successful early
espionage
operation appears
to have been
organized by
Virginia before
that state had
formally joined
the Confederacy.*

PAGE 191

ROSE THE SPY

*Rose O'Neal Greenhow,
shown with one of her
daughters, was a prominent
Washington hostess who used
her social connections to elicit
a flow of military secrets
helpful to the Confederacy.*

NAVAL HISTORICAL CENTER,
WASHINGTON, D.C.

time they were elated over the possible international consequences of Wilkes's actions. Southern newspapers reflected the general sentiment that the United States would not back down and that Britain would not stand for the violation of its neutrality. In spite of the high level of tensions between the United States and Great Britain, war was averted when Secretary of State Seward issued an apology and confirmed that Mason and Slidell would be released. The passions subsided, but the affair reinforced the British perception of Northern animosity.

The equitable resolution of the *Trent* affair was another disappointment for the Confederacy—a disappointment compounded by the reception that Mason and Slidell received, once they arrived in Europe. Slidell was able to gain a sympathetic audience with Napoleon III, but Lord John Russell refused to officially recognize Mason and treated his overtures with an indifference that surprised the Confederate State Department and angered Southerners. Throughout 1862 Mason attempted to achieve recognition for the Confederacy without success. Regardless of the impact of the Union blockade, the *Trent* affair, and the Confederate cotton embargo, Great Britain was not willing to be drawn into America's internal conflict. Although many Britons were openly sympathetic to the Confederate cause, the government refused to intervene. By the summer of 1862 the British refusal to

recognize the Confederacy or its envoys had produced open resentment in the South. Southern newspapers called for the expulsion of British consuls residing in the Confederacy and the recall of Confederate commissioners in Great Britain. The *Richmond Enquirer* in April 1863 labeled Great Britain "our worst and deadliest enemy" aside from the United States. After being continually rebuffed by Lord Russell, Mason left London for Paris in August 1863, and the Confederacy

broke off efforts to establish official relations with Great Britain.

Although Great Britain denied the Confederacy recognition, the South received valuable, if clandestine, assistance from the British. In spite of the declaration of neutrality, Confederate agents in Great Britain worked effectively to secure military supplies and equipment. To a great degree the industrial capacity of the Confederacy was enhanced by weapons and war matériel obtained from Great Britain in exchange for cotton and other marketable agricultural products. British shipbuilders supplied vessels for a variety of Confederate purposes. The majority were employed in running cargoes through the Union blockade. In spite of the efforts of the U.S. Navy, fast steamships maintained limited Confederate foreign commerce throughout the war. Other vessels were acquired to be fitted out as commerce raiders. Ships like the *Alabama*, *Florida*, and *Shenandoah* put to sea from English shipyards and destroyed hundreds of U.S. merchant vessels.

During the postwar arbitration of claims against Great Britain for the destruction inflicted by Confederate commerce raiders, it was estimated that British war matériel and unofficial support for the Confederacy extended the rebellion for as much as two years. Had it not been for the efforts of Charles F. Adams, U.S. minister to Great Britain, the amount of support would have undoubtedly been greater. Adams employed every device at his disposal to ensure the strict maintenance of British neutrality. Although he was not always successful, his efforts contributed significantly to frustrating Confederate diplomacy and procurement. His relentless pursuit of U.S. objectives at the Court of St. James was in no small way responsible for the lack of success registered by Confederate foreign policy and the ultimately unsatisfactory nature of relations with Great Britain.

[*See also* Alabama Claims; Anglo-Confederate Purchasing; Blockade, *overview article;* Trent Affair.]

— GORDON WATTS

GREENHOW, ROSE O'NEAL

Greenhow, Rose O'Neal, (1815–1864), spy. A popular Washington, D.C., hostess, the Maryland-born Greenhow joined the spy ring of Col. Thomas Jordan, Gen. P. G. T. Beauregard's adjutant general, as soon as the war broke out. Greenhow, whose late husband had worked for the State Department, assiduously mined her contacts in the U.S. government for military secrets that might be helpful to the Confederacy. Her greatest accomplishment came in the days before the Battle of First Manassas (July 21, 1861), when she sent cipher messages via secret couriers to General Beauregard, informing him of Gen. Irvin McDowell's marching orders and troop strength. Her information influenced Jefferson Davis to send Gen. Joseph E. Johnston to reinforce Beauregard; Johnston's men turned the tide of the battle.

On August 23, 1861, Greenhow was arrested by Allan Pinkerton, head of the Union army's secret service. Though incarcerated in her home, Greenhow managed, through visitors, to transmit information on Union forces to Jordan. She was transferred to Old Capitol Prison in January 1862 and paroled that June on the condition that she not return to the North during the war. In August 1863 Greenhow went abroad as an unofficial diplomat for the Confederacy in England and France; her prison chronicle, *My Imprisonment and the First Year of Abolition Rule at Washington,* was published in London that year. Greenhow drowned on October 1, 1864, when the British steamship carrying her back to the Confederacy ran aground off North Carolina. She was buried in Wilmington, North Carolina, on October 2, 1864, with full military honors.

— ELIZABETH R. VARON

GUERILLA WARFARE

Historically, guerrilla wars have been brutal, savage affairs waged by small groups of men among the mountains, forests, and swamps. The irregular conflict that occurred in the Confederate States of America during the years 1861 through 1865 was no exception. For pro-Confederate Southeners guerrilla warfare was a way of disrupting Northern invasion and occupation. Pro-Union Southerners, on the other hand, engaged in the "little war" to resist Confederate domination. Although it never achieved decisive military results, partisan activity enabled thousands of civilians behind the lines to strike at the enemy while retaining a semblance of their former peaceful lives.

EARLY GUERRILLA ACTIVITY IN THE BORDER STATES. The first large-scale guerrilla actions took place on the western border even before the Civil War started. From May 24, 1856, when a group of abolitionists led by John Brown murdered five Southern settlers in Kansas, guerrilla warfare had raged on the frontier. Bands of Free-Soil and proslavery marauders burned, robbed, and killed in an effort to drive the other from "Bleeding Kansas." When war officially came in 1861, many on the Kansas-Missouri border were already veterans of irregular warfare.

Although Missouri, a slave state, remained technically in the Union, an active minority led by Governor Claiborne F. Jackson worked hard for secession. Consequently, hundreds of Kansas Unionists, fearful of being cut off from the North and nervous over a potential Confederate invasion, joined in bands and marched over the state line. Clad in blue and flying the U.S. flag, the Kansas jayhawkers showed virtually no restraint in their zeal to crush rebellion in Missouri. Jayhawking soon became synonymous with brigandage.

In the autumn of 1861, Senator James Lane led a small army of fellow Kansans into Missouri and left a trail of death and desolation in his wake. The climax came on September 23, when the jayhawkers looted and burned the city of Osceola. Smaller bands of Kansans led by James Montgomery, Marshall Cleveland, and others also roamed western Missouri, stealing slaves and livestock, burning homes, barns, and crops, and murdering any man who protested.

The most notorious gang of jayhawkers was that led by Charles Jennison. Composed largely of antislavery militants, horse-thieves, and common criminals, Jennison's regiment lent savagery to an already bloody border war. In addition to theft, arson, and murder, torture and probably rape joined the list. As a warning to others, Jennison personally sliced off the ears of his victims.

It was largely the vicious, indiscriminate forays of Jennison that finally compelled Federal authorities to force the jayhawkers from the border. By the winter of 1861–1862, however, much of western Missouri was a wasteland, and hundreds, perhaps thousands, of Missourians who might otherwise have remained loyal to the Federal government suddenly became bitter, and often active, enemies.

Although Missouri rebels made several thrusts into Kansas in response to jayhawker raids, it was not until the following year, 1862, that full-scale guerrilla warfare reached the state. Led by William Clarke Quantrill, a twenty-four-year-old Ohio schoolteacher, Missouri partisans, called bushwhackers, launched a series of strikes into Kansas that all but paralyzed the state. On March 7, Aubrey was raided, in September, Olathe was looted, and a month later Shawnee was destroyed. Other bands as well as Quantrill's terrorized Unionists in Missouri, skirmished with cavalry patrols, and harassed Federal garrisons in the western part of the state. Although numerically superior, the Unionists were no match for the better-mounted, better-armed guerrillas. Hence, while blue-clad troops held the towns, colorfully dressed bushwhackers ruled the countryside.

Throughout the rest of Missouri a similar situation existed. In the northeast, Joseph Porter recruited hundreds of men and then laid ambuscades for his Federal

In early 1861, while the Confederate government was still in Montgomery, Alabama, Jefferson Davis began to employ secret agents for political missions abroad.

PAGE 191

*In January 1863,
with J.E.B.
Stuart's approval,
John S. Mosby
began guerrilla
operations in
northern Virginia.*

PAGE 381

pursuers. Farther south, the dashing "Swamp Fox of the Confederacy," M. Jeff Thompson, operated in the bootheel of Missouri, surprising Northern patrols and sniping at Union gunboats on the Mississippi.

Across the river the pattern was repeated. Although Kentucky was a slave state, most of its citizens remained neutral or loyal to the Union. As the regular conflict moved south, however, many of those left behind engaged in a bitter contest to gain control of the state. Unionist home guards, ill disciplined and vengeful, scoured their communities testing the loyalty of neighbors and settling old scores. As a result, numerous bushwhacking bands sprang up.

In an attempt to tap the growing discontent behind enemy lines, both in Kentucky and elsewhere, the Confederate government legitimized guerrilla organizations by passing on April 21, 1862, the Partisan Ranger Act. Many guerrilla leaders, including Quantrill, officially enrolled their men. Federal commanders, however, refused to extend such recognition, and although there were exceptions, Southern partisans were to be hanged or shot when captured. "Pursue, strike, and destroy the reptiles" ran a typical Union decree.

In May 1862 Maj. Gen. John C. Breckinridge sent a number of men, including Adam Johnson, back into Kentucky to recruit troops for the Confederacy. After skirmishing with Federals in the streets of his hometown, Henderson, and surprising a Union detachment near Madisonville, Johnson led his recruits on a raid across the Ohio River. There, on July 18, he seized the arsenal at Newburgh, Indiana. Johnson's act spread panic across southern Indiana and neighboring Ohio. Throughout the summer Johnson remained in Kentucky, employing his men as guerrillas to burn bridges, attack garrisons, and eventually pin down enough Federal troops to facilitate the invasion later that year of a Confederate army led by Gen. Braxton Bragg.

EARLY GUERRILLA ACTIVITY IN THE DEEP SOUTH. Although most guerrilla activity was centered in the disputed border states and was waged largely by Confederate partisans, increasingly the Deep South became a scene of irregular Unionist operations. Stretching from the Ohio River to northern Georgia, the Appalachian Mountains rose like an island of discord in the heart of the new nation. Isolated and long ignored, many of the impoverished mountaineers of the region saw little to gain from secession and much to lose in a "rich man's war and a poor man's fight." After passage of the Confederate Conscription Act on April 16, 1862, with its numerous exemptions that favored the wealthy, their fears seemed justified.

The rugged Shelton Laurel region of North Carolina became a stronghold of anti-Confederate activity where deserters, draft dodgers, and Unionist guerrillas found refuge. After partisans made an unusually bold raid on nearby Marshall on January 8, 1863, Brig. Gen. Henry Heth, commander of the Department of East Tennessee, sent in a regiment. Subjected to sniper fire the moment they entered Shelton Laurel, the angered soldiers flogged and tortured several women to gain information. Then, on January 18, the troops rounded up over a dozen men and boys and shot them the following day. Though intended as a warning, the killings did little to curb mountain bushwhacking.

Elsewhere throughout the South, pockets of revolt and lawlessness materialized as the war dragged on. In the panhandle of Florida, gangs of deserters, criminals, and other "lay-outs" roamed the hardscrabble hills, raiding farms for food, loot, and liquor. On the west coast of the state, William Strickland led a band of freebooters who, emerging from their sanctuary in the swamps, spent the nights prowling nearby plantations and carrying off slaves, food, and plunder. In 1863 Strickland organized his gang into the Union Rangers, and in exchange for arms and equipment, he supplied Federal gunboats with food and information. Farther south, near Tampa, small bands of partisans sparred with Southern troops and drove off cattle intended to feed hungry Confederates to the north.

Although most Southerners had welcomed secession, many slaveless farmers in the uplands of Alabama and Mississippi, in the rural parishes of Louisiana, and in the German settlements of northern Texas had quietly opposed it. After passage of the Conscription Act, however, simple indifference to the Confederate cause in these regions often erupted into antigovernment violence. Secret societies sprang up, loyalist neighbors were threatened, and when enrollment officers tried to enforce the draft, they were chased, beaten, and sometimes killed. In Winston County, Alabama, Unionists worked to form their own Free State, and other Tories in the northwest corner of the state considered merging with the mountain regions of Tennessee and Georgia to create the nonslave commonwealth of Nickajack. When Col. A. D. Streight led a Federal cavalry raid through Alabama and Georgia in April 1863, companies of local Unionists eagerly served as guides.

Farther west, not only did pockets of pro-Union sentiment exist in the poorer parishes of Louisiana, but after the Federal capture of New Orleans early in 1862, pro-Confederate guerrillas also became active. When a Northern landing party was fired upon by a band of bushwhackers at Baton Rouge on May 28 of that year, Adm. David Farragut ordered his gunboats on the Mississippi to shell the town. Several months later Farragut's cannon also opened on Donaldsville for a similar occurrence. Organized gangs of criminals, runaway slaves, and deserters from both armies also preyed upon the state, robbing, raping, and murdering indiscriminately. One group operated from the Atchafalaya Swamp, where the Teche region to the west and the Lafourche country to the east were equally accessible to their forays.

Like its neighbor to the south, Arkansas was also beset by guerrillas of both flags. In the east, Confederate bushwhackers led by James McGhee and Joseph Barton harassed traffic on the Mississippi and burned half a dozen Federal steamers. To the northwest, bands of Unionists clashed with Confederate partisans in the Ozark Mountains.

Similarly, guerrillas under John McNeill and John D. Imboden in rugged western Virginia fought savagely against both Unionist partisans and Federal troops.

WILLIAM CLARKE QUANTRILL. By the spring of 1863 Quantrill was on the minds of all Kansans. Because of his success the year before, the people of the state saw no reason to be optimistic about the coming summer. Already several ominous incidents had occurred, including a daring raid on Diamond Springs in May by Richard Yager's bushwhackers. Consequently, Federal Brig. Gen. Thomas Ewing, Jr., recently appointed to the border command, instituted a series of tough policies.

In an effort to prevent raids into Kansas, Ewing first established a system of stations along the state line. At each camp the general placed over one hundred well-armed and equipped cavalrymen. Next, Ewing recruited a number of spies who successfully infiltrated the partisan ranks. Finally, to deny support to the guerrillas, the general rounded up "several hundred of the worst" sympathizers in western Missouri and prepared to send them south. This last act would have tragic consequences. Hunted like animals themselves, the bushwhackers were outraged at the mistreatment and exile of their families and plotted retaliation. When a brick guardhouse collapsed in Kansas City on August 13, 1863, killing five of the women and children, their thirst for revenge mounted.

No place in America was more hated by Quantrill's followers than Lawrence, Kansas. Not only had the city served as a Free-Soil citadel during the 1850s, but the New England colony was also home to Senator James Lane, the jayhawker who had burned Osceola two years before. In addition, Lawrence was a sanctuary for runaway slaves and headquarters of the Red Legs, a gang of Unionist guerrillas.

One week after the prison disaster, on the morning of August 21, Quantrill and over four hundred bushwhackers, including Frank James and Coleman Younger, halted at the edge of Lawrence. Not only had Federal spies been unable to warn Ewing of the guer-

rillas' plans, but a captain commanding the border station at Aubrey, Kansas, offered no serious opposition when they crossed the state line. The officer also failed to send any word west. Hence, at 5:00 A.M. the three thousand people of Lawrence were asleep when Quantrill charged into the town. For the next several hours the guerrillas roamed Lawrence unhindered, robbing stores, burning homes, and murdering unarmed citizens. Although Senator Lane escaped and the Red Legs were absent that day, the second largest city of Kansas was in ashes and over 150 men and boys lay dead when the Missourians finally left. Thousands of Federal troopers and Kansas militiamen pursued the bushwhackers, but by skillful management Quantrill led his command to the woodlands of Missouri and safety the following day.

Four days after the massacre, on August 25, 1863, Thomas Ewing issued General Order No. 11. In part, the edict decreed that all Missourians residing in three of the counties bordering Kansas were to be expelled from the land and their crops and forage destroyed. Two weeks later the order had been carried out, as one officer put it, "to the letter." The suffering and hardship imposed on innocent and guilty alike were extreme, and Order No. 11 proved to be the harshest military act of the war aimed at a civilian population. Because most troops enforcing the edict were Kansans, it was also certain that the ensuing death and destruction in Missouri would equal, if not greatly surpass, that of Lawrence.

In mid-September, Ewing sent thousands of Federal cavalrymen on a massive sweep through the woodlands of western Missouri in a bid to crush the guerrillas. Several skirmishes occurred and a number of partisans were slain, but once again Quantrill eluded his pursuers.

On October 6, 1863, as he was passing through the southeastern corner of Kansas, Quantrill halted to attack the Union fort at Baxter Springs. Although several defenders were killed, the assault was soon repulsed. A short time later, however, the guerrilla leader encountered a Federal wagon train just north of the fort. Unaware of partisans in the area, Maj. Gen. James Blunt and his escort paused to watch the blue-clad bushwhackers, assuming they were troopers from the fort. Before Blunt realized his mistake, the guerrillas charged and quickly overwhelmed his command. Although the general and several of his men escaped, eighty-five others were killed, including the band musicians and James O'Neal, an artist for *Frank Leslie's Illustrated Newspaper*.

A wave of horror swept the North upon learning of the events in Kansas. For the first and only time the guerrilla war in the West overshadowed the battlefields of the East.

Quantrill gathered about 450 guerrillas and, on the morning of August 21, 1863, burst into Lawrence, Kansas in a raid that gained him national notoriety.

PAGE 475

Wounded three times, John S. Mosby forged his Rangers into one of the war's finest commands.

PAGE 381

JOHN S. MOSBY. In January 1863 Confederate Gen. J. E. B. Stuart detached a private from his command, John S. Mosby, and directed him to take nine volunteers into Union-occupied northern Virginia and engage in irregular operations. Opposed to secession initially and an "indifferent soldier" at first, the twenty-nine-year-old Mosby, after joining Stuart's cavalry, had proven himself to be a daring trooper, courier, and scout. As a guerrilla leader, the former lawyer displayed a talent for war that soon became legendary. By the time his career ended he had achieved the rank of colonel and his field of operations, the region between the Blue Ridge and Bull Run mountains, had become known to friend and foe alike as "Mosby's Confederacy."

Immediately after crossing enemy lines, Mosby's tiny band went on the attack, harassing Union outposts, stealing horses, destroying equipment, and capturing surprised Federal soldiers by the score. On March 9, 1863, at Fairfax, Mosby gained national attention when he roused from bed and captured Brig. Gen. Edwin Stoughton. The embarrassment to the Union army was compounded when Mosby brazenly retreated with his prisoner in full view of the Federal fortifications at Centreville. The feat won Mosby a captaincy and enabled him to officially organize his growing company into the Forty-third Battalion of Partisan Rangers.

Later that month, near Chantilly, Mosby's Rangers were pursued by a force more than twice as large. Again, on April 1, while they were camped along the

Potomac River, a similar Federal column surprised them. In each instance, however, the captain turned on his attackers, inflicting heavy casualties and taking more than a hundred prisoners.

In addition to hit-and-run raids and almost continuous skirmishing, the Virginia partisans burned bridges on the Orange and Alexandria Railroad and tore down miles of telegraph wire. On May 30, 1863, with the aid of a small fieldpiece, Mosby ambushed a locomotive near Manassas and set the cars on fire. As a result, Federal troops needed on front lines were detailed to guard railroads, patrol highways, and serve as escorts.

Unlike guerrillas in the West, Mosby's Rangers normally wore Confederate uniforms, paroled or sent their captives south, and generally conducted themselves according to the rules of warfare. But, as in the West, a large and sympathetic population in northern Virginia provided the guerrillas with food, shelter, information, and recruits. A wide variety of men were attracted to Mosby's company. Discharged veterans, soldiers on furlough, even convalescents, were drawn by the informal come-and-go nature of the command. Local farm boys from Virginia and Maryland were swept up by the romance associated with independent cavalry. A considerable number of deserters and freebooters also joined, lured by the prospect of easy plunder. Under Mosby's leadership, however, the conglomerates were honed into a highly effective fighting force.

Because of atrocities committed by bushwhackers in the West, as well as the penchant for plunder all

MOSBY'S RANGERS

Confederate guerrillas photographed at Fairfax, Virginia, where they captured Brig. Gen. Edwin Stoughton in 1863. Col. Mosby is left of center in the middle row.

NAVAL HISTORICAL CENTER, WASHINGTON, D.C.

guerrilla bands displayed, including Mosby's, powerful Southern voices were raised calling for a repeal of the Partisan Ranger Act, arguing that irregular warfare was barbaric, uncontrollable, and injurious to the cause. Even Robert E. Lee, whose own father had fought the British as a partisan, harbored doubts. Finally, in February 1864, the Confederate Congress revoked the act and a short time later Secretary of War James A. Seddon ended government sanction of all guerrilla groups—with two exceptions. Only John McNeill's partisans in western Virginia and Mosby's in the north were to remain officially recognized by Richmond.

In mid-May 1864, as Ulysses S. Grant pushed south on his great spring offensive against Lee, Mosby's men struck railroad bridges and supply trains in the Federal rear. Then when Confederate Gen. Jubal Early began a diversionary thrust toward Washington, Mosby joined him and soon succeeded in severing rail and wire communications between the U.S. capital and Harpers Ferry for two days.

Returning south, Mosby attacked a pursuing Union column at Mount Zion Church and all but annihilated it, taking over fifty prisoners and leaving another fifty dead and wounded. On the morning of August 13, as Union Gen. Philip Sheridan and his army were invading the Shenandoah Valley, Mosby and three hundred Rangers surprised a section of his supply train near Berryville. Seventy-five wagons were seized or destroyed, almost a thousand head of livestock stolen, and over two hundred Federals taken prisoner.

Later, in an effort to construct another supply line for Sheridan's army, labor gangs set to work rebuilding the Manassas Gap Railroad. Mosby's men attacked furiously, tearing up rails, driving off work crews, even derailing two construction trains. Thousands of Federal troops soon arrived, however, making further raids suicidal. Nevertheless, in a brilliant counterstroke, Mosby raced north and struck Sheridan's "secure" supply line, the Baltimore and Ohio Railroad. On October 14, 1864, the guerrillas derailed a train near Harpers Ferry and stole $170,000 in U.S. payroll funds. Admitting defeat, the Federals suspended all work on the Manassas Gap Railroad.

Various stratagems were devised to crush Mosby. One plan called for the organization of an elite body of sharpshooters, armed with Spencer repeating rifles, to hound Mosby's trail until he was destroyed. On November 18, 1864, Mosby's lieutenant, Adolphus Richards, ambushed and wiped out the one-hundred-man unit. Another antiguerrilla tactic was to arrest the populace in Mosby's Confederacy and destroy their mills, barns, and crops. This caused terrible suffering, but Mosby continued to operate freely. An even more severe measure was the execution of captured Rangers. Although it proved the most difficult decision of his life, Mosby, in an effort "to prevent the war from degenerating into a massacre," ordered captured Federals hanged in retaliation. Summary executions on both sides then ceased.

On January 30, 1865, while visiting Richmond, Mosby was honored by the Confederate House of Representatives. A few days later the Senate paid a similar tribute, making the "Gray Ghost" the only partisan of the war accorded such recognition.

JOHN JACKSON DICKISON. After the Federal occupation of eastern Florida early in the war, Capt. John Jackson Dickison of the Second Florida Cavalry withdrew his command across the St. Johns River. Although isolated and far from lines of support, Dickison chose to fight rather than retreat. Utilizing the swampy environment deftly, Dickison's company staged a series of amphibious assaults, sweeping up Federal pickets, scattering Union raiding parties, and returning runaway slaves. Although he seldom led more than a hundred men, the captain's ceaseless guerrilla attacks ultimately prevented the Northerners from extending their control over central Florida.

On the night of May 19, 1864, Dickison's men crossed the St. Johns and captured nearly sixty Federals at Welaka and Fort Gates. Several nights later, near Palatka, the guerrillas ambushed the Union gunboat *Columbine* as it was passing downriver, capturing or killing one hundred Federals and destroying the boat. Later that summer Dickison audaciously attacked a large Union force at Gainesville, killed, wounded, or captured over two hundred men, and then pursued the rest for miles. Once again, on the night of October 24, 1864, the Confederates surprised a Federal raiding party near Magnolia, inflicted heavy casualties, and chased the survivors into the swamps.

WILLIAM ANDERSON. Probably no guerrilla anywhere waged war more ruthlessly than William Anderson, known to later generations as Bloody Bill. A native of Missouri, he was living in Kansas when the war began. In 1862, after Unionists murdered his father, Anderson returned to Missouri and joined the bushwhackers. When one of his sisters was killed in the Kansas City prison disaster the following year, the twenty-four-year-old guerrilla dedicated the remainder of his short life to the slaughter of Unionists. Several days after his sister's death, Anderson rode to Lawrence with Quantrill, where he reportedly shot fourteen men in cold blood. Six weeks later he killed perhaps as many in the massacre at Baxter Springs.

On June 12, 1864, Anderson and his company, clad in blue uniforms, rode up to a fourteen-man Federal patrol near Kingsville, Missouri, and killed or captured all but two. The prisoners were shot, the bodies were stripped, and one man was scalped. Two days later the bushwhackers attacked a wagon supply train and killed

In January 1863, Mosby and fifteen men undertook guerrilla operations in the Virginia counties south and west of Washington, D.C.

PAGE 382

Mosby's Rangers operated from a base in the Virginia counties of Fauquier and Loudoun, which became known as "Mosby's Confederacy."

PAGE 382

*Mosby's Rangers
became the most
effective and feared
partisan command
in the Confederacy.*

PAGE 382

eight more Federals. The following month Anderson's gang crossed the Missouri and in succession shot or hanged eight men and slashed the throat of a ninth. On July 15, Anderson raided Huntsville, Missouri, killed one man, and stole between $30,000 and $100,000. A week later the bushwhackers burned the railroad depot at Renick and pulled down miles of telegraph wire. The following day Anderson ambushed a Federal patrol, killed two, and then mutilated them.

Throughout the summer Anderson's gang roamed Missouri, burning bridges, bushwhacking patrols, and committing uncounted atrocities. Many, including Anderson himself, adorned their bridles with scalps. Some wore necklaces of human ears.

On September 27, 1864, Anderson and eighty bushwhackers, including Frank and Jesse James, raided Centralia, Missouri. Shortly before noon a train pulled into the station. Among those on board were over twenty Union soldiers, many returning home on furlough. The troops were stripped, lined up, and shot. With the depot and train in flames Anderson and his men rode south a few miles to a stand of timber where several hundred bushwhackers were camped. Shortly after Anderson left, over one hundred Union militiamen entered Centralia. Viewing the carnage and destruction, the militia immediately set off in pursuit. Aware of the Federals' presence, a squad of guerrillas lured them into ambush where they were surrounded and hopelessly outnumbered. The fight became a massacre in minutes. Those who surrendered were subjected to terrible torture. Some were clubbed to death, and others were pinned to the ground with bayonets. Wounded men had their throats cut and many were scalped. Some were beheaded. Throughout the ordeal, those waiting their turn were forced to watch. In all, over 150 Federals died at Centralia. "The war has furnished no greater barbarism," wrote a horrified Union general.

OTHER GUERRILLA ACTIVITIES LATE IN THE WAR. Elsewhere throughout the South, because their loved ones had suffered death, injury, or outrage at the hands of Unionists, a number of guerrillas now waged remorseless vendettas. Sam Hildebrand stalked the forests of southern Missouri, dealing out death to dozens. Similarly, Champ Ferguson of Tennessee haunted the Cumberlands, shooting, stabbing, and mutilating Unionists wherever he found them. Before he was finally hanged, Ferguson claimed over one hundred victims.

The response to guerrilla warfare had also become more brutal. Unlike most commanders, who were content to simply shoot or hang captured bushwhackers out of hand, William Tecumseh Sherman believed the punishment should fit the crime. When torpedoes (land mines) laid along the track threatened to sever his rail communications as he fought south toward Atlanta in the summer of 1864, the general authorized his commanders to place prisoners in a car and pull it forward with a rope to test the track for additional mines. In the event no prisoners were available, suspected Southern civilians would do. "Make somebody suffer" summed up Sherman's response to partisans and their abettors.

By 1864 the situation in Kentucky verged on anarchy. Because of the Emancipation Proclamation and the Federal enlistment of black troops, slave owners loyal to the Union felt betrayed. Many who had formerly favored the Federal government now went to war against it. Guerrilla bands led by Ike Berry, Marcellus Clarke, and a score of others sprang up overnight. In an attempt to suppress the revolt, Maj. Gen. Stephen Burbridge issued a series of draconian laws, including confiscation of property and the execution of five guerrillas for every loyalist killed. Except for adding to the death and destruction, however, the acts accomplished little.

Of all the states that suffered from guerrilla warfare, however, none suffered more than Missouri. By 1864 few counties had been spared. Gangs of vengeful Unionist militia scoured the state, beating, torturing, and murdering Confederate sympathizers. Equally vicious bands of bushwhackers led by John Thrailkill, George Todd, and others roamed almost at will, ambushing Federal patrols, terrorizing the populace, and bringing life in Missouri to a standstill. Trains were attacked, stage lines stopped, and steamboats that braved the rivers subjected to almost constant sniper fire. To run the gauntlet on the Missouri, pilots in St. Louis asked and received a thousand dollars for a single trip to Kansas. Terrified Unionists fled their farms and huddled in garrisoned towns that, for all practical purposes, became little more than islands surrounded by vast killing fields. "The very air seems charged with blood and death," wrote a Kansas City editor.

The last significant guerrilla actions of the war occurred in Virginia. While Mosby was recovering from a serious wound, Adolphus Richards remained active throughout the winter. In addition to sparring with Federal patrols, Richards's men in late January 1865 destroyed a fifteen-car train on the Baltimore and Ohio near Ashby's Gap. An even more spectacular success came on February 21, when partisans under Jesse McNeill slipped into Cumberland, Maryland, and captured Union Gens. Benjamin Kelley and George Crook.

With the war reaching its climax in the spring of 1865 and the South facing imminent defeat, many, including Jefferson Davis, suggested that the Confederate army should disperse and wage guerrilla war. But General Lee forbade it. Drained by four years of desperate fighting, his nation in ruins, Lee ordered his men to lay down their arms and return home. With the partisans scattered in remote regions, it took weeks before some ceased operations. Many drifted home and tried with varying degrees of success to live normal lives. Others, fearing retaliation, moved elsewhere. A few, like Frank and Jesse James, either could not or would not surrender.

On April 21, 1865, twelve days after Lee's surrender, John Mosby disbanded his Rangers. Three weeks later, in one of the last skirmishes of the war, William Quantrill was shot near Bloomfield, Kentucky. Ironically, the career of perhaps the best-known partisan on either side was ended by Federal guerrillas.

The hatred engendered by the irregular war lingered long after hostilities ceased. Thousands who had never heard a cannon had been touched by the guerrilla conflict. The bitterness could be partly measured in the postwar years by the severity of Federal Reconstruction, and it could be seen in newspaper headlines describing bank robberies, train holdups, and murders committed by former bushwhackers. In the Appalachians, the Ozarks, and other regions, generations would be required to heal the wounds inflicted by the guerrilla war.

[*See also* Bleeding Kansas; Mosby's Rangers; *and selected biographies of figures mentioned herein.*]

— THOMAS GOODRICH

G

GUERILLA WARFARE

*Other Guerrilla Activities
Late in the War*

H

HAMPTON, WADE

Hampton, Wade (1818–1902), lieutenant general, governor of South Carolina, and U.S. senator. Born in Charleston to a family of great wealth and distinction, Hampton spent his early years at Millwood Plantation and graduated from South Carolina College in 1836. He studied law but returned to Millwood as a planter and also acquired vast land holdings in Mississippi.

Hampton considered public service more as an obligation than an opportunity and served in the South Carolina house of representatives from 1852 to 1857 without distinction. His election to the state senate in 1858, however, coincided with events that stirred him, and his was a voice for moderation and restraint amid a rising chorus calling for secession and Southern independence. Although the Hamptons were among the largest slaveholders in the South, he opposed reestablishing the African slave trade and believed that the South could resolve its differences within the Union. Nevertheless, when appealing for Southern unity and respect for constitutional law, he declared from the floor of the state senate in December 1859, "Unless every patriot in our land strikes once more for the Constitution, I see not how the Union can be or should be preserved."

Hampton had little influence on the events that followed, and at the outbreak of war he resigned from the state senate and volunteered for Confederate service as a private soldier. Recognizing the power and influence of the Hampton name, Governor Francis W. Pickens instructed Hampton to raise a military command and secured for him the rank of colonel in the Confederate army. Hampton's call to arms was enthusiastically answered by the sons of the master class, and within days Hampton's Legion was formed.

Tall and powerfully built, Hampton epitomized the Southern ideal of a gallant warrior, and, in his first engagement, in July 1861 at First Manassas, was praised for his contribution to the Confederate victory. Promoted to brigadier general the following year, he was successful in reducing the enemy threat in actions preliminary to Seven Pines. Hampton was heavily engaged in this battle and sustained a wound that forced him from command.

During his convalescence in South Carolina, he came to realize that the Federal advantages in both men and matèriel were a fatal combination and became convinced that the South could not sustain a prolonged war. With this in mind, he returned to his command in June 1862 determined to press for an early victory and participated in the decisive stage of the campaign to

sweep enemy troops from the approaches to Richmond. Maneuvering in the vicinity of White Oak Swamp, Hampton found himself behind the enemy's right flank and prepared to exploit this unexpected position. Gen. Thomas J. ("Stonewall") Jackson hesitated, however, and Hampton waited with growing anger and frustration as the advantage passed from Confederate hands and the main battle developed at Malvern Hill. Out of loyalty to Jackson, Hampton kept his counsel but felt that a decisive defeat of the Army of the Potomac had been within their grasp and that they had lost a strategic opportunity.

While harassing the ensuing Union retreat from Virginia, Hampton was transferred to the cavalry, where he served as senior brigadier to Maj. Gen. J. E. B. Stuart. Stuart and Hampton were contrasts in temperament and leadership. Their military success masked their differences, which nevertheless broke through the surface when Hampton on one occasion wrote, "I suppose Stuart will as usual give all the credit to the Va. brigades. He praises them on all occasions, but does not often give us credit." Hampton fought at Sharpsburg in September 1862 and the following month returned with Stuart to Maryland, where they humiliated the Army of the Potomac with a series of bold maneuvers. After the Battle of Fredericksburg, Hampton led a series of daring raids behind enemy lines, which secured his fame as a leader of cavalry.

Hampton participated in some of the bloodiest fighting of the war during the spring and summer of 1863. In June he charged with his cavalry at Brandy Station, where his brother Frank was killed by enemy infantry. Less than a month later, Hampton sustained heavy losses to his command and was himself severely wounded in hand-to-hand fighting at Gettysburg. He expressed a tempered optimism when he wrote from the hospital at Charlottesville, "I am doing well. . . . Our army is in good condition after its horrible and *useless* battle." He returned to the field in November with a promotion in rank to major general and assumed divisional command of the cavalry under Stuart.

With the initiative shifting to the enemy, Hampton spent the early months of 1864 defending Confederate lines and recruiting fresh troops in his native state. In early May he was engaged in the Wilderness campaign when Stuart, protecting Richmond's outer defenses, was killed by enemy cavalry. With Stuart dead, Hampton reported directly to Robert E. Lee, and in August he was given overall command of the cavalry. Hampton reorganized his troops and led them in defense of Petersburg. It was during a heavy engagement in late October that his son, Preston, temporarily assigned to his staff, was fatally wounded while charging the enemy. This personal loss transformed the war for Hampton: he no longer hoped for an honorable peace but now sought to avenge his son's death.

In January 1865 Hampton was ordered to South Carolina to rally defenses against the threatened enemy invasion. Soon after his arrival he was promoted to lieutenant general, one of only three general officers without formal military training to achieve this rank. Hampton, unable to deter the enemy advance, evacuated his troops to North Carolina, where he was among the last of the Confederate high command to surrender.

After the war Hampton returned to South Carolina, where he led the efforts to defeat the Reconstruction government and restore the conservative regime to power. Rejecting the extremes of racial politics, he campaigned as a moderate Democrat and was elected governor in 1876 and again in 1878. After resigning the governorship, he was elected to the U.S. Senate, where he served from 1879 to 1891. Hampton died in April 1902.

— MARK E. NEELY, JR.

HAMPTON ROADS CONFERENCE

Held on the U.S. steamer *River Queen* off Fort Monroe at Hampton Roads, Virginia, on February 3, 1865, this four-hour conference between ranking officials of the Federal and Confederate governments failed to achieve any tangible results despite hopes on both sides. President Abraham Lincoln and Secretary of State William H. Seward represented the United States; the Confederate delegation included Vice President Alexander H. Stephens, Senator Robert M. T. Hunter, and John A. Campbell, a former Supreme Court justice now serving as assistant secretary of war.

The meeting originated in a peace initiative proposed in late 1864 by Francis P. Blair to Lincoln, that both sides cease fighting and join forces against Napoleon III's troops in Mexico. Lincoln had no interest in this idea, but he was willing to talk to the Confederates and allowed Blair to explore the possibility. In several trips to Richmond, Blair secured Jefferson Davis's agreement for the conference. Though he held little hope for its success, Davis had political reasons of his own for sanctioning the meeting. He hoped what he regarded as the conference's inevitable failure would blunt the burgeoning peace movement in the Confederate Congress and in several states. The conference was almost aborted by a protracted disagreement on the diplomatic language of the Confederate commissioner's instructions. But Gen. Ulysses S. Grant's unabashed enthusiasm for the conference and his personal plea to Lincoln succeeded in removing this difficulty.

The mutually incompatible aims of both sides, not to mention the near-hopeless military situation of the Confederacy, guaranteed failure even before the talks began. Reunion and an end to the rebellion were for Lincoln sine qua non. Davis's instructions to his delegation spelled out its mission as "an informal conference" for "securing peace between the two countries." Stephens, who knew the only chance for the Confederacy was an armistice, tried several times to bring up Blair's Mexican plan. Lincoln rebuffed the suggestion each time, as well as Hunter's bid for an armistice. Nothing without reunion, he said. Blair's had been an unofficial mission.

Turning to the subject of slavery and the treatment of Confederate leaders, Lincoln promised leniency. He also held out the possibility of compensation—up to $400 million—to slave owners for their confiscated slaves. There would be no backing down on the Emancipation Proclamation: the courts would have to sort out tangled questions of its applicability that the Confederates raised. In any event, Seward said, the

Thirteenth Amendment had just passed the U.S. Congress, thereby rendering such questions moot upon its ratification. Since both slavery and the rebellion were doomed, Lincoln urged the Confederates to lay down their arms and return to their former allegiance to save further bloodshed. On this note the conference ended.

The failure of the conference to achieve peace served the Davis administration in two ways. Southerners took Lincoln's insistence on reunion as a humiliating demand for unconditional surrender, and this rekindled momentarily a fierce war spirit across the ravaged Confederacy. The conference's failure also muffled the administration's many congressional foes.

— THOMAS E. SCHOTT

HAMPTON'S LEGION

"Legions" were permitted and organized only in the early stages of the Civil War. A legion was a miniature army in that it contained all three military components: infantry, artillery, and cavalry. Ten such units existed in the Confederate armies. The most famous in the group was the South Carolina legion of Wade Hampton.

One of the wealthiest planters in the antebellum South, Hampton had known a life of splendid luxury. He was a state legislator and ardent Southern nationalist when the war began. Hampton promptly diminished his fortune by recruiting a legion that, if necessary, could fight independently. In less than a week after his initial call, thirty South Carolina companies volunteered for Hampton's unit. This was more than twice the number that could be accommodated. Hampton's Legion came to consist of six infantry companies, four cavalry companies, and a battery of artillery sporting six new and revolutionary Blakely guns.

The highest-born of the Palmetto State served as privates in such companies as the Columbia Zouaves and Edgefield Hussars. Officers came exclusively from the socially elite class. The legion also boasted a veritable platoon of black servants who prepared meals and attended to other tasks.

Hampton trained and splendidly equipped his unit at Camp Hampton, a few miles outside Columbia. The legion received a royal welcome upon its early summer arrival at Richmond, Virginia. One of its field officers boasted that the unit was "by all odds the finest looking and best drilled body of men that has left" South Carolina.

When battle became imminent at Manassas, Hampton speedily boarded his unit on a train and rushed northward. The companies marched three miles from the railroad depot straight into the war's first major battle. Hampton's second-in-command, Lt. Col. Benjamin J. Johnson, was killed almost immediately. This left the legion with no experienced field officer. Federals enfiladed the Carolinians' position and soon had Hampton's force surrounded on three sides. Legion officers did not possess enough military knowledge to know when to retreat. Hence, the legion stubbornly maintained its position and fought gallantly until superior officers persuaded Hampton to retire to a less exposed sector. The unit suffered casualties of 121 of the 600 engaged. Among the wounded was Colonel Hampton, who barely escaped death when a bullet grazed his skull.

In November 1861 Hampton received promotion to brigadier general. His legion then became part of Gen. James Longstreet's division. It fought in the 1862 Peninsular campaign. The legion ceased to exist shortly thereafter, when the infantry companies were merged with the brigade of Gen. John Bell Hood, the cavalry units became part of Col. Thomas Lafayette Rosser's command, and the artillery was redesignated as Hart's South Carolina Battery. Four officers in Hampton's Legion eventually became Confederate generals.

[*See also* Hampton, Wade.]

— JAMES I. ROBERTSON, JR.

HARPERS FERRY, WEST VIRGINIA

[*This entry is composed of three articles:* Arsenal and Armory, *which discusses the establishment and contents of the U.S. installation;* John Brown's Raid, *which discusses the 1859 raid by abolitionist John Brown; and* Battle of 1862, *which discusses the battle won at the site by Thomas J. ("Stonewall") Jackson.*]

ARSENAL AND ARMORY

President George Washington recommended that Congress establish federal armories and arsenals to ensure adequate arms production for self-defense for the fledgling United States. Congress approved the legislation in 1794, and Washington selected Springfield, Massachusetts, as the site of the first national armory and Harpers Ferry, Virginia, as the site of the second. Washington favored Harpers Ferry because of the water power generated at the confluence of the Potomac and Shenandoah rivers; the abundance of raw materials, such as iron ore for gun barrels and timber for stocks; its location in Virginia, which would provide a Southern armory in Washington's home state

Probably the outstanding Civil War example was Hampton's Legion—organized, uniformed, armed, and equipped by Wade Hampton of South Carolina.

PAGE 287

Hampton recruited his infantry up to regimental strength and transferred the cavalry and artillery to regiments of their respective arms.

PAGE 287

and an economic boost to the Potomac valley; and its proximity to the new federal capital, located only sixty-two miles down the Potomac.

Production of small arms at Harpers Ferry did not begin until 1800, however, because of difficulties with land purchases and inadequate skilled labor to construct the factory and water power works. From 1800 to 1861, the armory produced over 620,000 rifles and muskets, with annual employment ranging between 250 and 425 workers. With the exception of the period from 1841 to 1854, when ordnance officers ran the Harpers Ferry establishment, a civilian superintendent managed the armory's overall operations, and a civilian master armorer supervised weapon designs and day-to-day production of the small arms. Both the armory (the factory complex where weapons were manufactured) and the arsenal (the warehouse for weapons' storage) fell under the auspices of the Ordnance Bureau, a branch of the government within the War Department under control of the secretary of war.

Harpers Ferry weapons accounted for numerous innovations in federal arms manufacturing. The 1803 model was the first military rifle produced at a federal armory, its handsome half-stock, octagonal barrel, and brass fittings reflecting the influence of Pennsylvania rifle artisans. Percussion technology replaced the antiquated flintlock with adoption of the 1842 model percussion smoothbore musket. The first percussion rifle produced by the government was the 1841 model "Mississippi" rifle. Improvement upon the individual percussion cap system occurred with development of the 1855 model rifle and 1855 model rifle-musket. These weapons utilized a Maynard primer system, which advanced a percussion tape onto the breech cone each time the weapon was cocked. Although the Maynard primer saved loading time by eliminating the fumbling percussion cap, the tape jammed easily and often was ruined by moisture; hence this system saw no use during the Civil War.

Interchangeable parts manufacturing also was pioneered at Harpers Ferry. John H. Hall, a Maine inventor who contracted with the government in 1819 to produce one thousand breech-loading rifles, developed a system of tools, machinery, and gauges in his rifle works along the Shenandoah River that "succeeded in establishing methods for fabricating arms exactly alike, and with economy, by the hands of common workmen." By developing precision machinery that produced uniform parts, Hall doomed craft-oriented production. His American System of manufacturing, he believed, "formed the taproot of modern industrialism."

Another Harpers Ferry invention that changed the character of warfare was the Burton bullet, better known as the minié ball. James H. Burton served as master armorer at Harpers Ferry from 1849 to 1854,

and during his tenure, he perfected a hollow-based, conical-shaped lead bullet that expanded and gripped the rifling of a gun barrel upon discharge of the powder. Since the bullet was slightly smaller than the barrel's interior caliber, for the first time an infantryman could load a rifle as quickly as a musket (three times per minute). As a result, the Burton bullet antiquated the inaccurate musket and enabled the U.S. Army to adopt the much deadlier rifle as its primary small arm.

Despite these innovations at the Harpers Ferry armory, production consistently lagged behind its sister armory at Springfield. Reasons include persistent droughts, which reduced water power and shut down machinery; an infirm work force that was constantly battling disease; inept managers who practiced political patronage and promoted the regional economy above the national interest; and craft-oriented workers who resisted the introduction of machine technology. In an attempt to correct these problems, the Ordnance Bureau between 1841 and 1854 replaced the civilian superintendents with professional ordnance officers who rebuilt and retooled the armory, transforming it, according to historian Merritt Roe Smith, into one of the five "most progressive manufacturing establishments of its type" in the country.

Abolitionist John Brown eyed the Harpers Ferry armory for its products rather than for its progressive manufacturing. Approximately 100,000 weapons were stored at the arsenal in 1859—weapons Brown intended to seize and distribute throughout the South in an attempt to end slavery. On Sunday night, October 16, 1859, Brown and his eighteen followers captured the undefended armory and arsenal, but Brown failed to escape. Local militia soon surrounded the government buildings, and at dawn on October 18, U.S. Marines, under command of Lt. Col. Robert E. Lee, charged the armory fire engine house and captured Brown, ending the raid. Although Brown's men had removed a few guns, these were soon recovered, and the bullet-damaged armory buildings were quickly repaired.

Sixteen months following Brown's raid, Virginia seceded from the Union. Seizure of the Harpers Ferry armory and arsenal became a primary target of a group of secessionists led by former Virginia governor Henry A. Wise and including Turner and Richard Ashby, John D. Imboden, and former armory superintendent Alfred M. Barbour. On April 17, 1861, the date of Virginia's official secession vote, these secessionists received permission from Governor John Letcher to advance the state militia to seize the armory and arsenal. The following day, Barbour arrived in Harpers Ferry and announced Virginia's intention. His public pronouncement also warned Lt. Roger Jones and his small garrison of forty-five U.S. regulars guarding the federal property. Subsequently, Jones ordered gunpowder placed throughout the armory and arsenal buildings as he prepared for their destruction. At 10:00 P.M. on April 18, with three hundred Virginia militia only one mile from Harpers Ferry, Jones torched the federal property and withdrew his force into Maryland. The flames totally consumed the two arsenal buildings, destroying fifteen thousand small arms. Most of the armory was saved, however, as local residents extinguished the fires before much damage occurred.

With Harpers Ferry now located on the border between North and South, Virginia officials decided to dismantle the armory and ship its machinery south to Richmond, Virginia, and Fayetteville, North Carolina. Col. Thomas J. ("Stonewall") Jackson, who commanded at Harpers Ferry, superintended the transfer of most of the machinery. When the Confederates abandoned Harpers Ferry on June 15, 1861, the armory buildings were burned, leaving only brick skeletons as a reminder of the once-thriving small arms factory.

Federal armies occupied Harpers Ferry in 1862 and reroofed some of the armory buildings for quartermaster and commissary storage. The armory also housed Confederate prisoners and served as Gen. Philip Sheridan's primary supply depot during the 1864 Shenandoah Valley campaign. Following the war, the United States decided not to reestablish its armory at Harpers Ferry, and the property was sold at public auction in 1869.

— DENNIS E. FRYE

JOHN BROWN'S RAID

John Brown's attack on the Harpers Ferry armory and arsenal (October 16–18, 1859) sent shock waves throughout the North and South. In a violent attempt to rid the country of slavery, Brown chose Harpers Ferry as his initial target because of the 100,000 weapons stored in the U.S. arsenal. He planned to seize these rifles and muskets for his army of slaves—an army Brown would recruit, train, and use to conduct guerrilla warfare throughout the Southeast. Slaves emancipated by his forces would find safe refuge in the strongholds of the Appalachian Mountains, where Brown intended to establish his own nation, backed by a constitution that would guarantee freedom for all.

Brown launched his bold scheme on a dreary Sunday evening, October 16, 1859. At 10:00 P.M., he and eighteen followers began marching from the Kennedy farm, their isolated headquarters in Maryland five miles north of Harpers Ferry. By midnight the raiders had possession of the armory and arsenal and the bridges leading into Harpers Ferry. With these initial targets secured, Brown sent raiding parties to seize hostages and slaves from prominent estates in the vicinity. One of these hostages was Lewis Washington,

the great-grandnephew of George Washington, whom Brown wanted as a symbol of his revolution. In the opening hours, no shots had been fired and no opposition encountered. The attack had surprised the community and the U.S. government.

About 1:00 A.M., however, Heyward Shepherd, a free black baggage porter for the Baltimore and Ohio Railroad, panicked when confronted by Brown's men and was shot as he tried to escape. The gunfire awakened Dr. John W. Starry, who resided near the railroad; upon investigation, he discovered Shepherd's mortal wound and learned of the raiders' intention to free the slaves. Brown's men then made a critical error. Instead of retaining Starry, they allowed him to slip away into the Monday morning darkness. Starry quickly galloped to nearby Charles Town, where he sounded the alarm and alerted local militia. Within hours, hundreds of militiamen from Virginia and Maryland were descending upon Harpers Ferry, blocking all avenues of escape for Brown and his men.

Brown compounded his problems by allowing an eastbound passenger train to proceed through Harpers Ferry. The conductor telegraphed notice of the raid, and word quickly arrived in Washington of the trouble. President James Buchanan then ordered a contingent of ninety Marines from the Washington Naval Yard to Harpers Ferry. Lt. Col. Robert E. Lee, at home on leave at Arlington, received instructions to proceed to the town and take command of the situation. Lt. J. E. B. Stuart, who delivered the War Department orders to Lee, accompanied the colonel. By the early morning of October 18, Marines had surrounded John Brown, now trapped within the small brick fire-engine house of the armory.

> "*I, John Brown,
> am now quite
> certain that the
> crimes of this guilty
> land will never be
> purged away but
> with Blood.*"

JOHN BROWN
BEFORE HANGING

> "*I hear many
> condemn these men
> because they were
> so few. When were
> the good and the
> brave ever in a
> majority?*"

HENRY DAVID
THOREAU
PLEA FOR CAPTAIN JOHN
BROWN, 1859

Just before dawn on the eighteenth, Lee sent Stuart to the barricaded doors of the engine house to demand Brown's surrender. Brown refused and then stated his terms of safe passage into Maryland and Pennsylvania for himself, his few remaining men, and his eleven hostages. Instructed not to parlay, Stuart backed away from the door and waved his hat, signaling the Marines to attack. The first attempts to beat down the doors with a sledgehammer failed. A dozen Marines then used a ladder as a battering ram, and a door was penetrated. Marine Lt. Israel Greene quickly dashed into the building and, confronting Brown, badly wounded him across the head and neck with his saber. Two raiders were bayoneted and killed; two others were captured. No hostages were injured during the attack.

The episode exacted a heavy toll. Ten of Brown's raiders had been killed or mortally wounded, including two of his sons. Four townspeople had died, including the Harpers Ferry mayor. One Marine had been mortally wounded during the attack on the engine house.

Brown was transported to Charles Town, the seat of Jefferson County, Virginia, where he was tried for murder, treason, and inciting slave insurrection. His trial commenced on October 27 and lasted over three days. A jury found him guilty of all charges, and on November 2, Judge Richard Parker sentenced him to be hanged. One month later, on December 2, 1859, with his gallows surrounded by thousands of Virginia militiamen, Brown was executed. Then the silence of the moment was broken by the voice of J. T. L. Preston of the Virginia Military Institute: "So perish all such enemies of Virginia! All such enemies of the Union! All such foes of the human race." Yet, just before his death, Brown had handed his jailer a note, with a prophecy: "I, John Brown," it opened, "am now quite certain that the crimes of this guilty land will never be purged away but with blood."

Reactions to Brown's raid, the trial, and his execution propelled the country into a fervent emotional debate over the issue of slavery. Leading Southerners, alarmed by Brown's "direct stab at the peculiar institution" and dismayed by Northern support for Brown's overt violence, warned of the impending breakup of the Union. Jefferson Davis, speaking to the U.S. Senate, declared, "Have we no right to allege that to secure our rights and protect our honor we will dissever the ties that bind us together, even if it rushes us into a sea of blood?" The *Charleston Mercury* announced, "The day of compromise is passed. . . . The South must control her own destinies or perish." And the *Richmond Enquirer* dolefully noted, "The Harpers Ferry invasion advanced the cause of Disunion more than any other event . . . since the formation of the Government."

Influential Northerners, in contrast, praised John Brown as a martyr. Ralph Waldo Emerson described him as "the Saint" whose death made "the gallows glorious like the cross." Henry David Thoreau elevated him to "an angel of light," and Louisa May Alcott called him "Saint John the Just." Church bells throughout the North tolled in Brown's honor on his execution day, and public prayer meetings and gun salutes proclaimed a pro-Brown sentiment. Incensed by the Northern reaction, South Carolina invited the Southern states to a secession meeting, but the convention failed to materialize, in part because the governor of Texas declared the South Carolina response premature and certain to lead to the destruction of the Union.

John Brown and his failed thirty-six-hour raid upon Harpers Ferry drove the nation to the brink of civil war. His martyrdom in the North and the intense hatred for him in the South led a Kansas paper, the *Lawrence Republican*, to observe, "It is safe to say that the death of no man in America has ever produced so profound a sensation."

— DENNIS E. FRYE

BATTLE OF 1862

Harpers Ferry was the site of a battle on September 13 through 15, 1862, in which Thomas J. ("Stonewall") Jackson captured 12,500 prisoners, the largest surrender of U.S. troops during the Civil War. Jackson's success at Harpers Ferry enabled Robert E. Lee to cease his withdrawal from Maryland and fight the Battle of Sharpsburg on September 17.

Lee and the Army of Northern Virginia commenced the first invasion of the North on September 3, 1862, when thirty-five thousand bedraggled Confederates began splashing across the Potomac River at White's Ford northeast of Leesburg, Virginia. When the army arrived unchallenged at Frederick, Maryland, twenty miles north of the Potomac, Lee halted the advance to rest his troops and to monitor Northern reaction to his incursion into Union territory.

While at Frederick, Lee became particularly concerned about the fourteen thousand Federals who remained south of his army at Harpers Ferry and Martinsburg, blocking access to vital communication and supply lines into the Shenandoah Valley. To remove this threat from his rear, Lee on September 9 issued Special Order 191, a bold and complicated strategic move designed to eradicate the Union garrisons in the lower valley.

Special Order 191 divided the army into four parts. Three columns, comprising six divisions and totaling twenty-three thousand men, would march upon Harpers Ferry from three directions, seize the three mountains surrounding the town, and hence trap the Federals between the hills. Lee and the remainder of the army, meanwhile, would await reunion of the scattered Confederates at Boonsboro, Maryland, twenty miles north of the Ferry. Lee selected Maj. Gen. Thomas J. ("Stonewall") Jackson to direct the Harpers Ferry mission, and he allowed only three days for its completion.

Although the division of his army in enemy territory posed a hazard, Lee considered the risk minimal. His primary opponent, Maj. Gen. George B. McClellan and the Army of the Potomac, had moved cautiously and slowly toward Rockville, Maryland; but Lee considered this a defensive posturing for the protection of Washington and Baltimore, not an aggressive march toward the Confederates operating around Harpers Ferry. If and when McClellan appeared on the horizon, Lee intended to have his army reunited on a battleground of his choosing.

On Wednesday morning, September 10, implementation of Special Order 191 commenced. Maj. Gen. John G. Walker and his division of two thousand men waved farewell to Maryland and recrossed the Potomac into Loudoun County, Virginia, where eyes turned northwest toward their target—Loudoun Heights—a steep bluff overlooking Harpers Ferry from the south bank of the Shenandoah River. Maj. Gen. Lafayette McLaws and the seven thousand soldiers comprising his division, along with Richard H. Anderson's division, marched southwest from Frederick toward Maryland Heights, the high ridge dominating Harpers Ferry from north of the Potomac. Stonewall Jackson, with fourteen thousand men from his own division and the divisions of Richard S. Ewell and A. P. Hill, pushed west from Frederick. Jackson marched through Middletown and Boonsboro to Williamsport, where he crossed the Potomac and promptly frightened the Union garrison at Martinsburg into a hasty retreat south toward Harpers Ferry. From all directions of the compass, Confederates were tramping across the countryside in a three-pronged pincer movement directed at Harpers Ferry.

The Federals knew they were coming. Col. Dixon S. Miles, commander of the Harpers Ferry garrison, had received scout reports and telegraph messages informing him of the danger. Consequently, at the outset of the invasion, Miles had deployed his forces in anticipation of a Confederate attack. But Miles had badly miscalculated. The fifty-eight-year-old West Point graduate believed an infantry attack against Bolivar Heights—a low-lying ridge one mile west of Harpers Ferry—would be the main Confederate target. Miles thus placed the bulk of his garrison, or nearly eight thousand men, upon Bolivar Heights. This number increased to ten thousand when the Martinsburg garrison arrived on September 12. Another poor

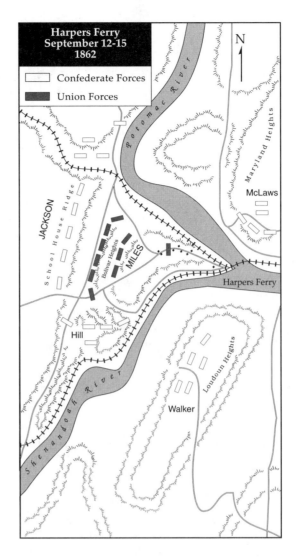

"At times he regarded the wounded soldiers in an envious way. He conceived persons with torn bodies to be peculiarly happy. He wished that he, too, had a wound, a red badge of courage."

STEPHEN CRANE
THE RED BADGE OF
COURAGE, 1895

judgment by the Harpers Ferry commander involved enemy artillery. Miles did not believe the Confederates could drag long-range cannon over a thousand vertical feet to the crests of Maryland and Loudoun Heights. Hence, the Union commander defended Maryland Heights with only two thousand men and placed no Federal soldiers on Loudoun Heights. Even if Maryland and Loudoun Heights fell to the Southern infantry, Miles considered these positions relatively harmless, since Confederate small-arms fire from the ridge tops would be too far removed and isolated to cause damage to his garrison.

Miles's miscalculations proved fortunate for the Confederates, who were experiencing their own problems. River crossings and mountain gaps had slowed the Confederate march toward Harpers Ferry and had further debilitated infantrymen already suffering from lack of shoes and a paucity of food. In addition, Jackson's circuitous and fatiguing march through western Maryland and the lower valley encompassed fifty-one miles in seventy-two hours. Further complicating

H

In 1861, Stonewall Jackson, West Virginia's most distinguished Confederate officer, harassed Federal troops and destroyed tracks between Harpers Ferry and Martinsburg, appropriating the rails to Southern use.

PAGE 667

the situation were time constraints. Special Order 191 stipulated that the Harpers Ferry mission be completed by September 12, but the twelfth arrived and passed without any Confederates reaching their targets. Because the Southerners had fallen behind schedule, McClellan's accidental discovery of Special Order 191 on September 13 further aggravated Lee's problems as the Federal commander boasted he had "all the plans of the Rebels" and would "catch them in their own trap."

Finally, on September 13, Confederates began taking their Harpers Ferry objectives. Walker occupied Loudoun Heights without firing a shot. Jackson's fourteen thousand men blocked escape from the west by settling upon School House Ridge, a linear rise paralleling the main Federal position on Bolivar Heights. The brigades of Joseph B. Kershaw and William Barksdale, both of McLaws's command, waged a six-hour battle on the crest of Maryland Heights before the Federals finally withdrew. By dusk on the thirteenth, Confederates completely encircled Harpers Ferry, and their artillerymen began clearing roads and hauling artillery to the crests of Maryland and Loudoun Heights.

Union commander Miles, recognizing his predicament, desperately sent couriers searching for McClellan and assistance. McClellan responded on September 14 by attacking three gaps in South Mountain to "cut the enemy in two and beat him in detail." Confederate resistance stalled the Union advance, however, and provided Jackson with one additional day to conquer the Harpers Ferry position.

Confederate cannoneers began bombarding Miles's garrison at 2:00 P.M. on Sunday the fourteenth. Although the hail of shell demoralized the Federals, most found refuge in deep ravines, and few were injured by the ironstorm. To ensure a quick end to the siege, Jackson, during the night of the fourteenth, transferred fifteen guns to a plateau on Loudoun Heights to enfilade the ravines sheltering the Federals. Stonewall also ordered Hill's three thousand men to flank the Union left on Bolivar Heights by attaining a position on the Chambers Farm. With his garrison now outflanked and outgunned, Colonel Miles surrendered shortly after 8:00 A.M. on September 15.

The fruits of victory for Jackson included seventy-three pieces of artillery, thirteen thousand small arms, two hundred wagons, and 12,500 prisoners—the largest capitulation of U.S. troops during the Civil War. Jackson's loss included 39 killed and 247 wounded. The Confederate victory at Harpers Ferry temporarily halted General Lee's retreat from Maryland and allowed him to stand at Sharpsburg, where Jackson's forces reunited with the army on September 16 and 17.

— DENNIS E. FRYE

HARRISON, HENRY THOMAS

Harrison, Henry Thomas (1832–?), scout and spy. A native of Tennessee, Harrison entered Confederate service in early 1861 as a civilian scout in northern Virginia and became a scout in Mississippi in 1862. He signed reports there as "H. T. Harrison, Secret Agent." One picture shows him in the uniform of a second lieutenant, holding a revolver and pointing to a simple numerical cipher printed on cardboard.

Called to Richmond in January 1863, he reported to Secretary of War James A. Seddon and was assigned to Gen. James Longstreet. While on temporary duty with Gen. D. H. Hill in North Carolina, Harrison was captured near New Bern by a Union patrol on March 21, 1863. He was released on April 13 when his complex cover story held up. No longer able to spy in North Carolina, he was sent back to Longstreet.

On June 2, 1863, Col. Moxley Sorrel of Longstreet's staff furnished Harrison with two hundred dollars in U.S. currency and ordered him to Washington to track Union troops as they set out to counter Robert E. Lee's invasion of Maryland and Pennsylvania. Harrison reached Longstreet near Chambersburg, Pennsylvania, on the night of June 28. As Longstreet wrote later, Harrison brought "information more accurate than a force of cavalry could have secured." This is generally credited with changing the disposition of Lee's army before the Battle of Gettysburg. During the last year of the war, Harrison was in New York City engaged in undisclosed clandestine activities.

In a letter from Baltimore, dated April 7, 1866, Harrison told his wife, Laura: "I write on the eve of a journey, and will not see you for some time, perhaps never." Later she learned that he was in the gold fields of Montana Territory. The last word of him there came in the spring of 1867. Thinking her husband dead, Laura remarried. After an absence of over thirty-four years, Harrison unexpectedly showed up on November 20, 1900, seeking to see his two daughters. Turned away, he went to Cincinnati. From there he wrote to Laura's brother in March 1901 that he was going to San Francisco. Then Harrison disappeared for good.

— JAMES O. HALL

HEISKELL, J.[OSEPH] B.[ROWN]

Heiskell, J. B. (1823–1913), a congressman from Tennessee. The eldest of nine children of the editor and publisher of the *Knoxville Register*, one of the most respected and influential newspapers in the region, Joseph Brown Heiskell graduated from East Tennessee College (1840), read law under Finley Gillespie of Madisonville, and commenced his practice in Monroe County before relocating in Rogersville and marrying a daughter of John A. McKinney, a prominent member of the Rogersville bar. Like his father and uncle before him, Heiskell occupied a seat in the Tennessee legislature (1857–1859), where he chaired the committee that prepared the first legal code for the state.

A staunch Whig, Heiskell opposed secession but joined the rebellion after Abraham Lincoln's call for volunteers and ran on a pro-Confederate ticket for the Provisional Congress. Although he lost the August 1861 election for the First District of Tennessee by an overwhelming margin to Unionist T. A. R. Nelson, he was elected to the First Confederate Congress three months later, after the legislature had redistricted the state and many Unionists stayed away from the polls.

Taking his seat in Richmond on February 18, 1862, the opening day of the first session, Heiskell served continually and rarely missed a vote through the end of the second session in mid-October later that year. A member of the Judiciary and War Tax committees, he introduced as many as twenty-one bills and resolutions. Most had to do with fiscal matters, though one measure sought to facilitate the production of small arms, another called for an investigation of ordnance factories in Richmond, and another would have allowed draft exemptions to persons engaged in the manufacture of iron, lead, and copper, of whom there was a considerable number in upper eastern Tennessee.

During his first two sessions in office, Heiskell proved to be decidedly proadministration, arguing and voting in favor of two conscription bills and the suspension of the habeas corpus writ. At the same time he firmly believed that it was the duty of the Confederate government to remunerate its citizens for losses sustained during the war, and he supported regulating by law the seizure and impressment of private property for the use of the military. Undoubtedly the most intriguing (and controversial) proposal introduced by Heiskell was his resolution of September 10, 1862, in which he advocated the taking of hostages in retaliation for the capture and imprisonment of Southern citizens and other noncombatants—that is, to arrest for the purpose of later exchanging not mere farmers and mechanics but "men prominent in their respective neighborhoods for their adhesion to the anti-slavery, black republican, anti-Christian government in Washington."

In the third and fourth sessions, from January 1863 to February 1864, Heiskell sponsored another twenty bills, distinguishing himself as one of the more active members of the Tennessee delegation, despite obtaining

a leave of absence so that he could return home, where he served conspicuously as a voluntary aide-de-camp for Confederate forces in the area. Back in Richmond, Heiskell remained concerned about military affairs in eastern Tennessee, as witnessed by his calls for investigations of the Confederate disaster at Fishing Creek, Kentucky (in which his brother, Carrick W. Heiskell, then a captain of the Nineteenth Tennessee Infantry, had participated), and the operations of Gen. John S. Williams at Blue Springs, Tennessee. Perhaps the most curious measure he brought forward during this period was a January 1864 resolution that instructed the congressional doorkeeper to regulate the heating in the House "so as to preserve a temperature not higher than sixty-two degrees Fahrenheit." On major issues he generally stood by the president, voting in favor of a direct tax, the third Conscription Law, and the abolition of the practice of hiring substitutes for military service. He also assumed a hard-line position on a proposed prisoner of war exchange, approving (though in the minority) Jefferson Davis's refusal to recognize Gen. Benjamin F. Butler as a legitimate Federal exchange agent. Congress's vote on this issue prompted Heiskell's resignation in February 1864, some ten days before Congress adjourned.

Reelected unanimously to the Second Confederate Congress, Heiskell assumed increased responsibilities by serving on as many as five committees. Contrary to what has been written, he continued to play an active role in government, contributing ten additional pieces of legislation during the first session. For example, in May 1864, in the midst of the Wilderness campaign, he was the chief sponsor in the House of a bill authorizing President Davis to suspend the writ of habeas corpus and declare martial law in Richmond. Yet he also differed with Davis by criticizing the inequality of prices paid under impressment laws, complaining bitterly about the performance and abilities of the postmaster general, and, in his last recorded action in Congress, voting with the majority on June 14, 1864, against turning over control of the railroads to the Confederate military.

By the time Congress reconvened in November 1864 for what turned out to be its final session, Heiskell was in the enemy's hands, having been captured some three months earlier while at home. The details of his surrender are sketchy, but according to published reports it appears that he walked to meet the Federals before they entered Rogersville, prompting President Abraham Lincoln to question whether Heiskell "was scared and wanted to save his skin." The object of intense, high-level negotiations for a special prisoner exchange that never materialized, Heiskell remained confined in Camp Chase, Ohio, until the end of hostilities. In the meantime arrangements were

"Such was the war. It was not a quadrille in a ballroom. Its interior history will not only never be written—its practicality, minutiae of deeds and passions, will never even be suggested."

WALT WHITMAN

*Heavily
outnumbered and
indecisive in his
early moves,
Johnston lost
Forts Henry and
Donelson in
February 1862 to a
Federal offensive
led by Grant.*

PAGE 302

made for his salary and mileage per diem to be drawn by his wife, Sarah, to help care for their five children.

Following the war, Heiskell moved to Memphis, where he reestablished his legal practice and was joined by his brother Carrick and fellow congressional colleagues Landon Carter Haynes and William G. Swan, among other eastern Tennessee émigrés. Although he was excepted from Andrew Johnson's amnesty proclamation of May 1865, there is no record that he requested a pardon or ever received one. Nevertheless, this unreconstructed Confederate who early in the war had vowed never to "affiliate with a people who are guilty of an invasion of [Southern] soil" eventually held public office again, serving as a delegate to the state constitutional convention in 1870 and as attorney general and court reporter of Tennessee (1870–1878), before rejoining his Memphis law firm. Interestingly, one of Heiskell's sons, Frederick, an 1872 graduate of Washington and Lee University, married a daughter of Senator Lucius Q. C. Lamar of Mississippi, a New South spokesman.

— R. B. ROSENBURG

HELPER, HINTON ROWAN

Helper, Hinton Rowan (1829–1909), abolitionist. Helper was born in the North Carolina up-country, the son of a small farmer. In the mid-1850s, after writing a book about his failed attempt to strike it rich in California's gold fields, he wrote *The Impending Crisis of the South: How to Meet It,* a 413-page tome that attacked slaveholders for forcing onto nonslaveholders a political economy that enriched the few while preventing economic development in the South as a whole. In the book Helper called for uncompensated emancipation of all slaves and for their subsequent colonization outside the United States.

When the *Impending Crisis* was first published in New York in 1857, it provoked little stir in either the North or the South, much to Helper's disappointment. He therefore moved to New York and sought to market the work through a variety of schemes. All were unsuccessful, although he did manage to persuade Horace Greeley to give the book a favorable review in the *New York Tribune.* During the presidential campaign of 1859, Greeley also raised $19,000 to pay for about 100,000 copies of a shorter edition of the book, *The Compendium of the Impending Crisis,* which was then distributed widely by the Republican party as a campaign document. The book, however, first came to national attention during the contest for Speaker of the

House of Representatives in January 1860, when John B. Clark, a Democratic congressman from Missouri, presented a resolution calling *The Impending Crisis* "insurrectionary and hostile to the domestic peace and tranquility of the country." Clark argued that no one who endorsed its principles, as had Republican nominee John Sherman of Ohio, was "fit to be Speaker of this House." The ensuing controversy gave the Democrats, the minority party in the House, a means by which to brand the Republicans a party of disunion and thereby defeat Sherman's bid for the Speaker's chair. Thereafter, Southern Democrats pointed to *The Impending Crisis* as proof that the Republicans planned to abolish slavery immediately and destroy the South.

Helper realized little profit from *The Impending Crisis* or the controversy that it produced, however, and spent the remainder of his life working in poorly paying civil service jobs, serving as a collection agent for private debts, and writing four other unprofitable books, three of them violently racist in tone. He died by his own hand, bitter and virtually penniless, in Washington, D.C.

— WAYNE K. DURRILL

HENRY AND DONELSON CAMPAIGN

The Tennessee and Cumberland rivers in western Kentucky and middle Tennessee from February 3 through February 16, 1862, witnessed the creation of a vital link in the ultimate Union victory. Joint operations between land and naval forces on these rivers proved capable of surmounting Confederate position defense and indecisive leadership to capture Forts Henry and Donelson. In this campaign Ulysses S. Grant, together with his naval colleague Andrew Hull Foote, effected the first major penetration of the Confederacy in the West. Drawing upon antebellum perception of western rivers as valuable travel arteries of communication and commerce, Union authorities settled on the Mississippi valley with its tributary rivers like the Tennessee and Cumberland as the proper avenues of advance. The Confederate theater commander, Gen. Albert Sidney Johnston, was virtually powerless to blunt such an advance, although command mistakes on his part accelerated the opportunity.

Political, economic, and military strategic goals of the Lincoln administration in the West ultimately rested upon reopening western rivers. Johnston, whose responsibilities stretched from the Appalachian Mountains to beyond the Mississippi River, had neither

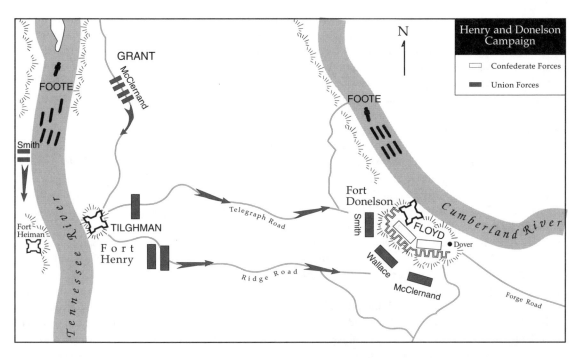

men nor matériel to conduct a proper defense of such a vast area. He concentrated his poorly trained, mostly sick, and inadequately supplied force of forty thousand men at strong points like Columbus, Kentucky, on the Mississippi, and Bowling Green, Kentucky, astride the Louisville and Nashville Railroad. He relied upon two earthen fortifications, constructed by the Tennessee state government about twelve miles apart in frontier-like Stewart County, Tennessee, to hold where the twin rivers bisected his defense line. Inadequately sited, constructed haltingly by slave gangs and soldiers, neglected by the high command, Forts Henry and Donelson were overlooked by Johnston and senior Confederate officials until the moment of crisis. Yet these forts guarded the vital upper heartland, where rich mineral and agricultural resources and important cities like Clarksville and Nashville, the Tennessee state capital and munitions center, lay directly behind Johnston's forward defenses. The rivers held the key to unlocking this treasure for the Union.

Northern ownership of most of the steamboat fleet on western rivers denied this resource to the Confederacy. But during the autumn of 1861 the Union government saw the merit in forging a gunboat flotilla. When teamed with steamboats as troop transports, the means of mounting a strike force to crack Johnston's line became apparent. Henry W. Halleck, Federal commander of the Department of Missouri, balked at first, fearing Johnston's perceived strength and the inadequacies of his own subordinates, and having misgivings about Grant. But Grant and Foote finally secured Halleck's grudging support for a rapid attack via the rivers.

The Union expeditionary force of fifteen thousand men, supported by seven gunboats, some armored, departed river staging areas like Cairo, Illinois, and Paducah, Kentucky, on February 3. Riding floodwaters of the swollen Tennessee, they moved virtually undetected to within striking distance of Fort Henry by February 6. Here, Kentuckian Lloyd Tilghman tried desperately to finish an uncompleted Fort Heiman on high ground across from a flooded Fort Henry and ready his defenses. He was unprepared when Grant and Foote struck and only barely ordered his infantry to escape overland to Fort Donelson. Tilghman remained behind with a "forlorn hope" of about a hundred artillerymen to conduct an "honorable" defense against the gunboats. Meanwhile, Grant's soldiers became mired in the mud as his divisions under Generals John Alexander McClernand and Charles Ferguson Smith attempted to move on the forts by country roads.

Foote refused to be slowed by the army. Under orders from Grant to effect a coordinated attack, the gunboats pushed forward and engaged Tilghman's heavy seacoast fortress guns by early afternoon on February 6. The ensuing battle proved no contest. The Confederate gunners damaged several of the gunboats before virtually all their cannon were rendered inoperable and carnage was widespread among the gunners. Foote demanded unconditional surrender (the first rendering of that phrase), and Tilghman had no choice. Federal naval personnel simply rowed through the fort's sally port onto a flooded parade ground to take the Confederate's sword. Fort Henry cost the Union forces eleven killed, thirty-one wounded, and five missing. Tilghman suffered five killed and eleven

"No terms except an unconditional and immediate surrender can be accepted. I propose to move immediately upon your works."

ULYSSES S. GRANT
TO GEN. S. B. BUCKNER,
FORT DONELSON,
FEB. 16, 1862

The loss of Forts Henry and Donelson forced the evacuation of parts of middle and western Tennessee by the Confederate army commanded by Gen. Albert Sidney Johnston.

PAGE 546

*After the surrender
of the forts, the
gunboats of the
Union navy
effectively
controlled the
Tennessee from its
mouth to Muscle
Shoals, Alabama.*

PAGE 546

*"The test of merit in
my profession, with
the people, is
success. It is a hard
rule, but I think
it right."*

ALBERT SIDNEY
JOHNSTON
AFTER THE LOSS OF FORTS
HENRY AND DONELSON
1862

wounded, with the rest of his force remaining at the fort captured.

The effect of the Union victory was electric. As Grant consolidated his position on the high ground around Fort Henry in preparation for moving on to Fort Donelson, the navy again took the initiative. A flotilla under Comm. S. L. Phelps raided 150 miles up the Tennessee River, cutting the railroad bridge above Fort Henry, spreading havoc along the way, and destroying quantities of war matériel. Before being stopped near Muscle Shoals, Alabama, this demonstration of Union naval power sent shock waves among Confederate military and the public alike. Lincoln's gunboats had become a "superweapon." Meanwhile, on February 7, Johnston realized his Bowling Green position was no longer tenable and ordered a retreat to Nashville. He sent subordinates with their commands to cover his flank at Fort Donelson.

Johnston eventually dispatched John B. Floyd, Gideon Pillow, Simon Bolivar Buckner, and Bushrod Rust Johnson, together with upwards of eighteen thousand Confederates to defend Fort Donelson. His instructions were vague, but, in his mind at least, the army was to conduct a holding action long enough for the main Army of Central Kentucky to retire behind the Cumberland at Nashville. With Floyd (the most inexperienced of the generals) as senior commander, and none of the four a leader of first rank at this point in the war, the stage was set for disaster. Unit commanders and their men, while equally untried, were more combative, but with the exception of cavalry led by an unknown Tennessee colonel, Nathan Bedford Forrest, no Confederates contested Grant's march from Fort Henry on February 12. Union forces moved into position virtually without opposition, while Foote's flotilla steamed back down the Tennessee, up the Ohio, and thence up the Cumberland to help.

Action at Fort Donelson began on February 13. While awaiting Foote's arrival, Grant issued instructions to McClernand and Smith to move into position but avoid any general engagement with the Confederates. Contrary to orders, both McClernand and Smith nudged forward in probing attacks that were repulsed. At one point, with the weather warm and balmy, dry leaves in front of a battery position caught fire, threatening Union wounded with horrible death. Their adversaries leaped from their rifle pits to help save them in a touch typical of later scenes in this war between brothers. By nightfall Grant realized that Fort Donelson would be no easy repetition of the earlier victory. He ordered reserves forward from Fort Henry to form a third division under Lew Wallace and awaited Foote to make a naval attack the next day.

The youthful Union soldiers had jettisoned blankets and overcoats during the warm overland march

from Fort Henry, but now the spring weather turned bitterly cold and blizzardlike overnight. Fires were forbidden on both sides, and everyone suffered. February 14 found two shivering armies capable of little more than sharpshooting and skirmishing. That afternoon, however, the Union navy approached Fort Donelson's two water batteries. This time the battle proved no contest for the gunboats. Confederate artillerists occupied commanding heights and had had weeks of training. Foote chose to run his ironclads close in toward the enemy guns, and the Southern gunners exacted a terrible toll. Virtually all the Union gunboats suffered damage, Foote was wounded, his flagship a shambles, and the myth of Lincoln's gunboats was shattered forever. Amid shouts of victory by the Confederates, their generals decided to escape the Fort Donelson trap.

At dawn the next day, Pillow's and Buckner's divisions went forward with a rush through the frozen countryside in an effort to beat back McClernand's division blocking the roads to Nashville and freedom. They succeeded handsomely. By noon not only was McClernand routed, but the roads lay wide open. Grant remained unaware of the impending disaster, having left headquarters that morning to consult with the wounded Foote aboard his flagship. McClernand's calls for help finally caused Lew Wallace to wheel his command into a blocking position to stymie the Confederate drive. Grant received word of the defeat and returned to rally his army. He told McClernand and Wallace, "Gentlemen, the position on our right must be retaken" and left it to them to accomplish the mission. Summoning his old West Point mentor, C. F. Smith, he explained that the Confederates had undoubtedly evacuated some of their lines to conduct the assault and ordered Smith to drive forward and capture the fort. More anxiously, he sent a dispatch to Foote saying that the army was in danger and asking for naval intervention.

Meanwhile, the Confederate generals dithered, argued, misread one another's concept of mission, and lost the initiative and hence the battle. Floyd and Buckner understood that once victory had been attained, the army would march off, leaving artillery and rear-area troops to the mercy of the enemy. Pillow demurred, wanting to hold Tennessee soil as long as possible and to evacuate the whole garrison. In the end, with the hour late and Union counterattacks beginning to press the tired Confederates, the four men decided to retire for the night, gather up supplies, wounded, artillery, and the like, and evacuate at dawn on February 16. But C. F. Smith's division had knifed forward and captured Buckner's outer defense line, thus breaching Confederate fortifications and causing the Kentuckian to have grave reservations about further defense.

Confederate scouts searched for avenues of escape that night. Army doctors counseled that the men could not survive crossing frozen creeks and the long trek to Nashville. Buckner became gripped by battle fatigue and fears of Smith's division; Pillow urged continued resistance; Floyd vacillated. Time was wasted, and in a midnight council that has since defied understanding, a decision was made to surrender to Grant on the morrow. Forrest stalked angrily into the night, vowing to escape. Floyd and Pillow, fearing punishment at the hands of Union authorities, similarly deserted, passing command to Buckner in the famous opéra bouffe episode derided by subsequent generations. Floyd's three-thousand-man Virginia brigade, Pillow's personal staff, and uncounted hundreds of others evaded the Union dragnet over the days after the surrender. But when Buckner sent a flag of truce to his opponent that night, the Confederate fighting men became enraged and nearly mutinied at this betrayal by their leaders.

Eventually, Buckner met with his old army friend Grant in the hamlet of Dover, within Confederate lines. Grant demanded unconditional surrender, and Buckner, though aghast at such treatment from an old colleague, was powerless to refuse. Grant telegraphed Halleck later that day: "We have taken Fort Donelson and from 12,000 to 15,000 prisoners including Generals Buckner and Bushrod Johnson; also about 20,000 stand of arms, 48 pieces of artillery, 17 heavy guns, from 2,000 to 4,000 horses, and large quantities of commissary stores."

When this news reached Johnston at Nashville, he was shocked, since all previous news from the fort indicated victory. Nashvillians rioted and fled the city in droves, with Buell's army eventually occupying the capital on February 24. Johnston could provide no defense. Aided by Floyd, Pillow, and Forrest, his forces evacuated as much Confederate property as possible, but his retreat did not stop short of northern Alabama and Mississippi. Union forces stood poised to end the rebellion all over the upper South. But, as fatigued and battered in victory as the Confederates were in defeat, Grant's men could not move quickly. Moreover, their generals fell to bickering, and momentum slipped from their grasp. Johnston was able to regroup to fight another day.

Still, a Confederate field force was swept into Northern prison camps. Western and much of middle Tennessee as well as all of Kentucky were reclaimed for the Union. Hopes of early European recognition of the Confederacy were dashed, and Johnston's reputation as the South's greatest warrior was destroyed. The fall of Forts Henry and Donelson changed the war in the West overnight. Flagging spirits in the North were revived, and a deep wedge was driven into the South.

The Southern home front began its wavering trend toward eventual collapse in a war of attrition.

— B. FRANKLIN COOLING

HEROES OF AMERICA

A secret, underground, pro-Union organization (often called Red Strings because a piece of red string in a lapel or on a window or door served as a secret sign of membership) composed of militant Unionists, deserters, and draft dodgers—and, to some extent, slaves and free blacks—the Heroes of America (HOA) existed in North Carolina, Virginia, West Virginia, Tennessee, the District of Columbia, and possibly other states during the Civil War. Its main mission was to protect its members from Confederate authorities. The HOA also provided needy members with food and other necessities, maintained an underground railroad on which members could be spirited to the Union lines, encouraged disloyalty on the home front and desertion in the ranks of the Confederate army, fostered the formation of armed, anti-Confederate guerrilla units, provided military intelligence to Federal troops, and promoted class conflict in the Confederacy by inducing the poor to join by promising a postwar distribution of the property of wealthy planters.

During the war it was rumored that the HOA originated within Union lines and was introduced into the Confederacy by special Federal agents. But the balance of the evidence now available suggests that the secret society was founded in central North Carolina, probably in Davidson County (the environs of present-day Lexington), where so many of its known leaders lived. It likely had its roots in a secret underground association of approximately five hundred armed Unionists who mustered under the U.S. flag in Davidson and the adjoining counties of Forsyth, Guilford, and Randolph. Witnesses reported that this band of militant Unionists, headed by John Hilton of Davidson County, favored the "coercion policy of Lincoln" and were prepared to "strike for the old Union." In July 1861 Confederate troops aborted this threatened insurrection of disloyalists.

One of the main leaders and organizers of the HOA was Dr. John Lewis Johnson, a druggist and physician, who lived in the Abbotts Creek community in southern Forsyth County. Perhaps because he was pressured by Confederate authorities to volunteer for the army or face charges of disloyalty, he joined the ranks as a substitute in 1862. By 1863 Johnson was serving in a Confederate hospital in Raleigh. The Tarheel capital, where the Grand Council of the

"I did not come here for the purpose of surrendering my command."

NATHAN BEDFORD
FORREST
FORT DONELSON, 1862

The Northern peace movement precipitated a Southern peace movement, especially in North Carolina, where strong peace sentiment already existed.

PAGE 413

Heroes of America was first organized, thereafter became a center of HOA activity.

In the summer of 1863 William W. Holden, editor of the influential Raleigh *North Carolina Standard,* embarked on his campaign for peace. Holden and his Peace party followers—influenced by the movement of some Northern Democrats for peace and reunion with a constitutional guarantee of slavery for the returning Southern states—demanded that Confederate authorities, or the states acting in convention together, make a permanent peace with the North.

The HOA supported the peace movement. Johnson is on record as having taken part in a Peace party rally near Raleigh in July 1863. Many other disloyalists took part in peace meetings, especially in the central and western Piedmont. The U.S. flag was hoisted at peace meetings in Wilkes and Rowan counties.

The 1863 phase of the peace movement culminated in an insurrection of deserters and draft dodgers across the central counties in September. A brigade of Confederate troops was sent in to suppress the uprising. The Heroes of America, through a clever network of secret dugout caves, managed to conceal hundreds of the men from the hunters. When the troops left a neighborhood, the men in hiding emerged from their dens and returned to aid their families and to offer protection and support to those whose husbands or sons had been captured.

A raid by Confederate soldiers in September left Holden's press in ruins, but the redoubtable editor renewed his activities in January 1864. President Jefferson Davis reacted by suspending the writ of habeas corpus. Undaunted, Holden challenged the incumbent, Zebulon Vance, in the 1864 gubernatorial contest on a peace platform.

In July, as a tactic to cow Holden supporters, newspapers backing Vance exposed the Heroes of America to the public for the first time during the war. Prompted by a promise from Vance to be lenient with those who voluntarily came forward, dozens of men publicly confessed their membership in the society and asked pardon from the governor for allowing themselves to be "misled" into joining it. The press revealed the secret signs, passwords, and rituals of the HOA. Holden was accused of being a leader of the society. With most of his supporters fearing reprisals, including arrest for disloyalty, few showed up at the polls to vote for him, and Vance won by a landslide. After Holden's loss to Vance, the HOA ceased to play a role in the politics of Confederate North Carolina.

In October 1864 Johnson, who had been ordered to duty at the front (probably as punishment for his Peace party activities), decamped with a company of Confederate troops to the Federal lines. He then went to Washington, D.C., where he initiated into the HOA Daniel Reeves Goodloe (a Republican and abolitionist from North Carolina), Benjamin Sherwood Hedrick (a Patent Office examiner and native Tarheel who had been fired in 1856 from his professorship at the University of North Carolina for expressing pro-Republican and antislavery sentiments), and John G. Barrett (the commissioner of patents). A National Grand Council of the Heroes of America with Hedrick at its head was established in Washington. In 1870 Goodloe testified before a Senate committee that during the war Johnson had also initiated Abraham Lincoln and Ulysses S. Grant into the Heroes of America. If this is true, it is likely that Lincoln and Grant kept their membership quiet because the Republican party, alarmed at the tendency of many Southern Heroes to identify politically with the Northern Democrats, was wary of granting publicity to the Heroes of America or to the peace movement that many of them supported.

In the fall of 1864 an investigation by Confederate detectives revealed that the HOA was widespread and powerful in southwestern Virginia. An informant reported that the secret order had been introduced into the area in the fall of 1863 by one Horace Dean of North Carolina. Montgomery County alone was said to harbor eight hundred members, including the sheriff, several justices of the peace, and other local government officials. By the winter of 1864 bands of deserters and disloyal county officials, many of whom belonged to the HOA, controlled southwestern Virginia.

During the Civil War the Heroes of America played an important role in the demise of the Confederacy. At first composed solely of die-hard Unionists, the ranks of the order by midwar had become swollen by the addition of thousands of disaffected citizens, especially deserters and draft dodgers. Together, they spread dissension, disorder, and disloyalty in the army and on the home front.

— WILLIAM THOMAS AUMAN

HILL, A. P.

Hill, A. P. (1825–1865), lieutenant general. Considered the finest division commander in Confederate service, and Lee's principal lieutenant in the last year of the war, A. P. "Little Powell" Hill has become the personification of the life and death of the Army of Northern Virginia. Both Robert E. Lee and Stonewall Jackson called for him on their deathbeds.

Ambrose Powell Hill was a product of Piedmont, Virginia landed gentry. Born on November 9, 1825, near Culpeper, he received a private education before his 1842 appointment to West Point. While on summer furlough from the academy in 1844, the tragedy of Hill's life occurred. He contracted gonorrhea. The disease's bacteria, unknown to anyone, lodged in his urinary tract and created strictures that eventually would bring debilitating illness.

An eight-month sick leave forced Hill to drop back a year at West Point. At his 1847 graduation he stood fifteenth in his class. The new artillery lieutenant arrived too late in Mexico to see action. Seven years of duty assignments followed in Mexico, Texas, and Florida. In 1855 Hill transferred to the U.S. Coastal Survey Service in Washington. His 1859 marriage to Kitty Morgan McClung would produce four daughters.

With the outbreak of civil war, Hill became colonel of the Thirteenth Virginia. He saw no major action for a year. Nevertheless, his proven talents in organization, drill, and discipline led to his promotion on February 26, 1862, to brigadier general. His baptism in battle came on May 5 at Williamsburg. Hill's successful attack at a critical moment swept Union forces from his front, and he won praise as the most conspicuous brigadier on the field. On May 26 he received promotion to major general and command of the largest division (six brigades) in all of the Confederate armies.

It was in the Seven Days' counteroffensive by Lee that the Powell Hill of history emerged. Directed to attack the Federal right flank in concert with Stonewall Jackson's forces, Hill grew impatient at Jackson's tardiness and assaulted on his own. His division took heavy casualties at Mechanicsville and equally severe losses the next day at Gaines's Mill. On June 30 the divisions of Hill and James Longstreet fought a bloody but inconclusive engagement with Federals at Frayser's Farm. Hill blamed all three defeats on Jackson's failure to provide necessary and expected support.

A post–Seven Days' argument with Longstreet resulted in the latter placing Hill under arrest. Lee intervened and transferred Hill to Jackson's command. An even stronger clash of wills developed. On August 8 Jackson criticized Hill for poor marching procedures on the move to intercept Gen. John Pope's advance. But Hill's timely arrival the following day in the Battle of Cedar Mountain was instrumental in the Southern victory. Similarly, Hill's steadfastness in beating back repeated Union attacks at Second Manassas elicited high praise.

By then, "Little Powell" was a familiar figure in the ranks. Five feet, nine inches tall, he weighed but 145 pounds. His curly hair was chestnut-colored and worn long. Hazel eyes flashed during battle or anger. Disdaining uniform and insignia, Hill customarily wore calico shirts—his favorite being bright red in color.

Lee's army was marching into Maryland on September 4, when Jackson's patience with Hill's casu-al marching style snapped. He placed Hill under arrest for insubordination. Hill obtained temporary release a week later and participated dutifully in the capture of Harpers Ferry. On September 17, in one of the most dramatic moments of the war, Hill's Light Division

"LITTLE POWELL"
Lt. Gen. A. P. Hill, who clashed repeatedly with Stonewall Jackson, was considered the South's finest division commander. Both Jackson and Robert E. Lee called for him on their deathbeds.

NATIONAL ARCHIVES

dashed into battle at Sharpsburg after a seventeen-mile forced march and saved Lee's army from almost certain destruction.

For seven months thereafter, Hill and Jackson waged an increasingly bitter exchange of charges and countercharges that did credit to neither man. An inexplicable gap in Hill's lines at the Battle of Fredericksburg added fuel to the controversy. The quarrel ended with Jackson's death following Chancellorsville. On May 26, 1863—a year to the day of his last promotion—Hill was assigned as a lieutenant general in command of the newly formed Third Corps in Lee's army. It was Hill's troops who opened the Battle of Gettysburg. Sickness limited the general's activities, and his debut as a corps commander was less than spectacular.

Hill partially redeemed himself on the retreat to Virginia with a smashing repulse of Federals at Falling Waters, Maryland. Yet on October 14, he suffered his worst defeat when he precipitately launched an attack against powerfully entrenched Federals at Bristoe Station. Hill was a central figure in Lee's attacks the following May against Ulysses S. Grant's army in the Wilderness. Illness then forced him to relinquish command for two weeks. Lingering effects from gonorrhea had produced a slow blockage of the kidneys.

The general prematurely struggled back to duty and performed badly in the May 23 fighting at the North Anna River. With his health somewhat improved by the end of the month, Hill made a speedy arrival at Petersburg on June 18 and helped prevent

Uncharacteristically, Stonewall Jackson failed to arrive [at the Seven Days' Battles], and an impatient A. P. Hill started the attack prematurely.

PAGE 533

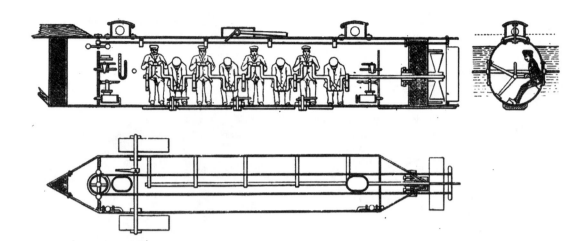

H

SOUTHERN SUB

An 1863 cutaway plan by William A. Alexander shows the Confederate submarine H. L. Hunley, *the first undersea warship to sink an enemy vessel in combat.*

NAVAL HISTORICAL CENTER, WASHINGTON, D.C.

"He is now at rest, and we who are left are the ones to suffer."

ROBERT E. LEE
ON THE DEATH OF A. P. HILL, PETERSBURG, 1865

that gateway city to Richmond from falling into Union hands. Throughout the long besiegement that followed, Hill commanded the southern half of Lee's defenses. He did so brilliantly. One high-ranking officer observed that from June 1864 through March 1865, "every Federal effort to break Lee's right was met and defeated by General Hill with promptness and without heavy loss on his part."

Victories, always against heavy odds, came after engagements at Jerusalem Plank Road, Weldon Railroad, the Crater, Reams's Station, Peeble's Farm, Jones's Farm, and Burgess's Mill. Lee relied heavily on the little general throughout the months of entrapment. Not once did Hill disappoint him.

These accomplishments came in spite of worsening health. Malfunctioning kidneys slowly produced uremia. For most of February and March 1865, Hill was unable to perform his duties. The general tried to regain his strength with rest at the James River estate of a kinsman. He painfully returned to the front only two days before Grant's all-out assault on April 2 against Lee's position. It was barely dawn that morning when Hill was fatally shot through the heart while trying to reestablish his lines. He is buried in Richmond beneath a statue to his memory.

A Richmond newspaper stated in 1864 that Hill was "the abiding strength and dependence of Lee's army." Gen. William Mahone later said of him: "A more brilliant, useful soldier and chivalrous gentleman never adorned the Confederate army."

— JAMES I. ROBERTSON, JR.

H. L. HUNLEY

The Confederate submarine *H. L. Hunley* was the first undersea warship to sink an enemy vessel in combat. Despite the importance of the act and the fame that resulted, many details of the submarine's history are uncertain. The submarine was the last in a series of privateer submersibles built by a consortium of investors and engineers in New Orleans, Louisiana, and Mobile, Alabama. To reward private initiative, the Confederacy offered prize money equaling 20 percent of the value of any Union warship sunk. The submarine partners planned to earn prize money sinking Federal warships.

The partners originally included James R. McClintock and Baxter Watson, machinists and engineers; Robert Ruffin Barrow, financier; and Horace L. Hunley and Henry J. Leovy as surety on the privateer bond. The men first built a submarine called *Pioneer* in New Orleans in 1862. The submarine received a privateering commission but apparently never saw action before being destroyed when the city fell.

Hunley, McClintock, and Watson moved to Mobile, Alabama, and built another submarine there. The machine was constructed in the shop of Thomas B. Lyons and Thomas W. Parks and may have been named *American Diver*. Hunley financed the construction of the hull and research to develop an "electromagnetic engine" to propel it. An effort to produce an electric engine for it failed, and instead a hand-operated crank turned by four men was installed. *American Diver* was lost, without loss of life, in rough seas off Fort Morgan in an attempted attack on the Federal fleet.

Hunley lost little time in building another submarine. He retained one-third interest and sold the remainder to E. C. Singer, R. W. Dunn, B. A. Whitney, and J. D. Breaman. Constructed as a larger version of *American Diver*, the new submarine was propelled by nine men, with one man steering and controlling depth and the other eight turning a crank propeller. The new vessel apparently was first called *Fish Boat* but was later renamed *H. L. Hunley*. The boat was described as about thirty feet long, four feet wide, and five feet deep. The submarine would sink an enemy ship by passing beneath it and allowing a towed explosive "torpedo" to detonate *H. L. Hunley* against the ship's side. Control of the towed torpedo proved too uncertain, and it was later mounted on a spar projecting beyond the bow.

H. L. Hunley was tested at Mobile and then sent by railroad flatcar to Charleston, South Carolina. Large Union naval targets, and chances for helping the Confederacy and earning prize money, were more plentiful off that port. McClintock, operating as skipper, took the submarine on several trips against the blockaders off Charleston Harbor but failed to meet the enemy. In late August 1863 the Confederate government seized the submarine and replaced the crew with naval volunteers from the ironclads *Chicora* and *Palmetto State*, under Lt. John A. Payne. On August 29, 1863, while learning to operate the submarine, Payne accidentally sank it, killing five men.

The sub was raised, repaired, and placed under Horace Hunley and Lt. George E. Dixon of the Twenty-first Alabama Volunteers. The two men trained another naval crew in September, but a second accidental sinking on October 15 killed Hunley and seven crewmen. Dixon persuaded Gen. P. G. T. Beauregard to allow another attempt against the steam sloop USS *Housatonic*. The sub was raised a second time, refitted, and a new crew trained. On February 17, 1864, Dixon and a mixed navy and army crew attacked *Housatonic*. The torpedo sank the blockader but may have also sunk *Hunley*. The submarine did not return from its raid and has never been found.

Two modern reconstructions of *Hunley* have been built by local groups working with city museums and technical schools, one in Charleston in 1966 and 1967, and one in Mobile in 1990. Each is located at the city museum. They were based primarily on a painting by Conrad Wise Chapman, now in the Museum of the Confederacy at Richmond, and on somewhat hazy recollections of the builder and various witnesses. No contemporary plans are known to exist. Both modern ships were of welded construction with simulated rivet detailing. Neither should be termed an exact replica, but a conjectural reconstruction, as accurate as research and modern techniques allowed at the time of its construction.

— KEVIN G. FOSTER

HOOD, JOHN BELL

Hood, John Bell (1831–1879), lieutenant general. Born in Owingsville, Bath County, Kentucky, on June 1, 1831, Hood spent his boyhood years in neighboring Montgomery County. His parents were descendants of pioneer stock and solid members of Kentucky society.

H. L. HUNLEY RESURFACES
The Mystery of the "Peripatetic Coffin"

Did the *H. L. Hunley* sink as a direct result of the torpedo attack on the USS *Housatonic* (and therefore lies nearby), or did something else happen while she was returning to port? Either way, the answer was buried beneath the cold waters of Charleston Bay, seemingly forever.

The debate had gone with no apparent end in sight, until May 4, 1995, when a group calling itself the National Underwater Marine Agency (NUMA) revealed that they had located the ship in the silt off Sullivan's island. This independent organization, founded by American best-selling adventure author Clive Cussler, had previously located a number of other famous shipwrecks.

Immediately there were claims and counterclaims of earlier discovery and charges that NUMA had used someone else's research, but these were overshadowed by the matter of ownership. NUMA had been working with the permission of the University of South Carolina's Institute of Archaeology and Anthropology (I.A.A.), and it was in South Carolinian waters. It looked like South Carolina had a strong claim. However, ocean wrecks come under federal control and Washington took notice immediately. To some it began to look like a case of South Carolina "state rights" versus "Yankee coercion" again.

Soon the cast of characters included the U.S. Navy, the Smithsonian Institution, the General Services Administration, the State of South Carolina, NUMA, the University of South Carolina's I.A.A., the Sons of Confederate Veterans, and other claimants. All were in agreement that, if stable enough, it would be raised, studied, and displayed in an appropriate setting. However the groups began squabbling almost at once.

A commission was set up to coordinate the effort and ensure cooperation between the various groups. In 1996 an agreement was finally worked out: the Federal Government would legally own the wreck, but South Carolina would retain possession of it. In early 1997 it was announced that studies of the wreck indicate that it is strong enough to be raised intact. As of 1998 efforts were being made to raise the estimated $10,000,000 needed to resurrect what was once called "The Peripatetic Coffin."

Plans include recovery and honored burial of the final crew and a full study of the design and technology of the boat. Once the salvage is complete, the mystery of the sinking should be solved

— STEVEN G. MILLER

His father attended medical school, and though he did not take a degree, he opened a practice in Bath County. After the members of his family moved to Montgomery County in 1835, their fortunes were reversed when Hood's maternal grandfather died and left them 225,000 acres of land and a sum of cash. As a result young Hood thereafter led a comfortable life.

FIERCE FIGHTER

Lt. Gen. John Bell Hood quickly established a reputation as a fighting general; he and his Texas Brigade served with distinction at the Seven Days' Battles, Second Manassas, and Fredericksburg.

NATIONAL ARCHIVES

Hood won appointment to West Point on February 27, 1849, and graduated in 1853, finishing forty-fourth in a class of fifty-two. He was appointed brevet second lieutenant in the Fourth U.S. Infantry and was stationed in the West. Later, he was transferred to a detachment of dragoons and appointed second lieutenant in the Second U.S. Cavalry. The dragoons were stationed in Texas, and it was at this time that Hood formed his lifelong attachment to the Lone Star State, especially appreciating its rough pioneer spirit. Although he spent relatively few years there, he came to identify strongly with Texas. For the most part his duties on the frontier were uneventful, though he was once wounded while campaigning against the Indians.

With the secession of Texas, Hood resigned his commission in the U.S. Army on April 17, 1861, and headed east to Richmond, where he volunteered his services to the Confederate government. Assigned to the rank of captain and then major, Hood rose rapidly in command until he was given charge of the newly organized Fourth Texas Infantry, which he whipped into shape with stiff discipline and organization. As a young officer, Hood was a splendid physical specimen. He stood six feet, two inches, was broad at the shoulders, narrow at the hips, and had a full head of blondish auburn hair with a provocative off-color

"Major, send a shell first over their heads and let them get in their holes before you open with all your guns."

JOHN BELL HOOD
ADVANCING UP THE
RAPPAHANNOCK, 1863

cowlick. He had a long, lean face and great sad eyes of a hypnotic blue.

His service record with the Confederate army in the East, especially after First Manassas and the Peninsular campaign, reads like a history of the Army of Northern Virginia. He quickly established a reputation as a fighting general and demonstrated that quality on many fields. Hood served with distinction at Williamsburg, the Seven Days' Battles (especially at Gaines's Mill), Second Manassas, Sharpsburg (Antietam), and Fredericksburg. He missed the Confederate victory at Chancellorsville in May 1863 but fought at Gettysburg, where he was severely wounded in the left arm. Although he recovered sufficiently to resume command, he never regained the full use of his arm. Hood was promoted to brigadier general to rank from March 3, 1862, and to major general to rank from October 10, 1862.

At times brilliant as a brigade and divisional commander, Hood was always a fierce fighter. Robert E. Lee regarded Hood's men as shock troops to be used in the most desperate situations, and at that assignment they never failed. Hood fought with an intensity he passed on to his men. His unit, though he commanded it for less than six months, was known throughout the war as Hood's Texas Brigade and was composed mostly of Texans who came east at the beginning of the war.

In the fall of 1863 Lee transferred an entire corps of his army, including Hood, to Tennessee, where it joined the Army of Tennessee under the command of Braxton Bragg in an attempt to defeat the Federal army under William S. Rosecrans. This move ended Hood's association with Lee and the army in the East. Hood's command arrived from Virginia in time to participate in the greatest battle fought in the West, Chickamauga, where Hood lost his right leg. Not expected to recover from his wound at first, he survived but was never the same physically and perhaps emotionally. Recovery was slow, but by early winter of 1864 he was fit to return to duty.

Promoted to lieutenant general on February 1, 1864, with date of rank set at September 20, 1863, Hood was ordered to return to the Army of Tennessee as a corps commander under Bragg, a man whom he neither liked nor trusted. Hood's association with the army in Tennessee became a tapestry woven of intrigue, defeat, humiliation, and near-annihilation. Shortly after Hood's return to the army, Joseph E. Johnston replaced Bragg as commander, largely as a result of a series of squabbles within the high command. Hood was directly involved and was accused of having undermined his old commander in an attempt to ingratiate himself with his superiors. Johnston, consequently, never quite trusted Hood, and Hood returned the favor by continuing the criticism he had leveled at Bragg. When Johnston was relieved from command of the Army of Tennessee, Hood succeeded him on July 17, 1864. He was promoted to full general with temporary rank on July 18, 1864.

Having begun the war commanding about a thousand men, Hood now found himself in charge of an entire army numbering many thousands. Though he had succeeded at the previous level, he was not equal to his new task. Against the advice of many, Hood attacked William Tecumseh Sherman's army in a series of battles around Atlanta, and he continued these assaults until he had seriously crippled his army. Successive losses at Peachtree Creek, Ezra Church, and Jonesboro cost Hood the fighting edge of his army as well as the city of Atlanta, which was evacuated on September 1. Instead of attempting to block Sherman's March to the Sea, Hood turned north into Tennessee to threaten Sherman's rear and cut his line of supply and communication. Sherman, however, refused to take the bait and turn northward, leaving Hood instead to contend with Federal troops under John M. Scofield

and George H. Thomas (both classmates of Hood's at West Point).

In a series of rash and ill-prepared battles, Hood succeeded in nearly destroying what was left of his army. After much maneuvering through middle Tennessee, he attacked the well-entrenched Federals under Scofield at Franklin on November 30, 1864. Despite staggering losses and the demoralization of much of his army, Hood pushed his troops on to Nashville, where he deployed and awaited attack from both Scofield and Thomas. When it came, the Federal assault was delivered with such weight of numbers and ferocity that it was over in a matter of hours. Confederate military history records no rout more thorough than that sustained by Hood at Nashville. A despondent Hood was now relieved from command at his own request. In May 1865 he surrendered at Natchez, Mississippi, having never been returned to command.

As a soldier, Hood was without peer in the Confederate army as a leader at the brigade and divi-

HOOD'S TEXAS BRIGADE

This brigade was organized on November 1, 1861, at Dumfries, Virginia, from thirty-two volunteer infantry companies recruited in Texas. The original brigade included the First, Fourth, and Fifth Texas Infantry and the Eighteenth Georgia Infantry. These three Texas regiments were the only units from that state to serve in Robert E. Lee's Army of Northern Virginia.

In all, Hood's Texas Brigade fought in thirty-eight engagements. After the Battle of Seven Pines on May 31, 1862, the eight infantry companies of Hampton's South Carolina Legion were added to the brigade. The Texans became famous at the Battle of Gaines' Mill on June 27. In this battle, the brigade was credited with breaking the Union line and putting the enemy to flight. The unit continued its heavy fighting at Second Manassas and Sharpsburg. In October 1862, the Third Arkansas Infantry replaced the Eighteenth Georgia and Hampton's Legion, giving the brigade its final organization. As part of Lt. Gen. James Longstreet's corps, the unit fought at Gettysburg, Chickamauga,

and Knoxville. At the Battle of the Wilderness, the brigade stemmed the Federal assault at the Widow Tapp farm, earning the unit lasting glory but at the cost of half its men. The Texas Brigade participated in the battles around Petersburg before surrendering with Lee's army at Appomattox.

The brigade holds a number of records for its staggering loss rate. In six major battles—Gaines's Mill, Second Manassas, Sharpsburg, Gettysburg, Chickamauga, and the Wilderness—the unit lost 3,470 killed, wounded, or missing. The most terrible period for casualties, however, came early in the brigade's career, when it suffered 1,780 casualties in the eighty-three days between Gaines's Mill, on June 27, 1862, and Sharpsburg, on September 17, 1862. Through recruitment and replacements, an estimated 4,500 men served in its ranks. At Appomattox only 476 were left to surrender.

Regiments within the brigade also suffered record losses. The First Texas Infantry is credited with having the highest percentage loss for a Confederate unit on a single day: 82.3 percent. Over

150 men of this regiment fell in twenty minutes of heavy fighting in Miller's Cornfield at Sharpsburg. Overall, the brigade lost 64.1 percent casualties for the day, ranking it third of any brigade in the war for a single day's loss.

During the war Hood's Texas Brigade was commanded by several officers. The original commander was Louis T. Wigfall, who resigned to join the Confederate Senate early in 1862. He was replaced by Brig. Gen. John Bell Hood, a West Point graduate and veteran of the Texas frontier. Hood received promotion to division command in midsummer, leaving Col. William Tatum Wofford in command of the brigade. Brig. Gen. Jerome Robertson led the brigade through the fall of the year and throughout 1863. Then Brig. Gen. John Gregg commanded the brigade until his death at Darbytown Road on October 7, 1864. Command then fell to a succession of regimental officers including Col. C. M. Winkler, Col. Fredrick S. Bass, and Col. Robert H. Powell.

— DONALD S. FRAZIER

H

In early August
1864, Hood tried
to force the
Northerners out of
Georgia by cutting
their railroad supply
line from
Chattanooga.

PAGE 36

sional levels. He was able to inspire his men and make them follow him despite the odds. His troops, man for man, were judged perhaps the best combat troops in the Army of Northern Virginia. Above the divisional level, however, Hood was a failure. As an administrator he lacked the most basic of skills, and as a strategist he was rash, impulsive, and inappropriately aggressive. To be sure, he suffered from physical handicaps after the loss of his arm and leg, although to his credit, he never used this as an excuse for failure. Hood demonstrated both distressing traits—shifting responsibility to subordinates and intriguing against superiors, to name but two—and attractive qualities—courage, dash, devotion to an ideal, gallantry, and charm. In the end, however, it was his inability to recognize his own weaknesses and to make realistic adjustments to the changing circumstances of war that brought about his downfall.

After the war he made his home at New Orleans, where he engaged in the cotton business and married Anna Marie Hennen. Shortly before Gettysburg Hood met and fell deeply in love with Sally ("Buck") Preston, daughter of John S. Preston of South Carolina. After at least two refusals of marriage, Sally finally agreed to an engagement, despite strenuous objections from her family. This was after Chickamauga. By the time the Franklin and Nashville disaster had come and gone, so had their relationship. The union between Hood and Sally Preston was never consummated, and the two parted company at war's end never to see each other again. His business thrived and his family lived well. Yet for all his apparent happiness, Hood spent the remaining years of his life writing his war memoir, *Advance and Retreat,* which was full of apologies, bitterness, and hostility. Before Hood found a publisher for the book, a final calamity befell him. In 1878 and 1879 a yellow fever epidemic in New Orleans forced the closing of the cotton exchange and brought ruin to a number of local businessmen, Hood among them. He lost his wife and a daughter to the fever in August 1879, and on August 30, he too died of the disease. He left behind heavy debts and ten orphaned children for whom no financial provision had been made. Friends had his memoirs published and sold for the benefit of the children. Hood was laid to rest in Metairie Cemetery, New Orleans.

— TERRENCE V. MURPHY

HUNTER, ROBERT M. T.

Hunter, Robert M. T. (1809–1887), secretary of state, congressman from Virginia, and commissioner to the Hampton Roads peace conference. The second Confederate secretary of state was born on April 21,

1809, at Mount Pleasant in Essex County, Virginia. After graduating from the University of Virginia in 1828, he studied law and was admitted to the Virginia bar in 1830.

From 1834 to 1837 Hunter served in Virginia's House of Delegates. Though elected as an independent, he allied himself with the anti-Jackson state rights Whigs. As an opponent of Old Hickory, he voted against legislative efforts to instruct Virginia's senators to support Thomas Hart Benton's expunging resolution and opposed Virginia's endorsement of the specie circular. On the other hand, to the dismay of the Whigs, he refused to endorse state internal improvements or the enlargement of banking establishments.

In 1837 Hunter, running as a "Sub-Treasury, Anti-Clay, state rights Whig," was elected to the U.S. House of Representatives. To the distress of the national Whigs, he consistently supported Martin Van Buren's subtreasury plan. Hunter's peculiar political independence proved advantageous after the Twenty-sixth Congress convened in December 1839. When the House deadlocked over the election of a Speaker, each party saw enough of its own principles in the Virginian to elect him as a compromise candidate, and at the age of thirty, Hunter became the youngest man ever to fill the position. But by attempting to act as a nonpartisan Speaker, he pleased neither party and let pass an opportunity to build a base of political support.

During the presidential campaign of 1840, Hunter issued a public letter stating that he would support neither President Martin Van Buren nor the Whig, William Henry Harrison, in the autumn election. Virginia Whigs were offended at what they considered yet another act of rebellion from a renegade who was nominally in their party. In 1841, when Hunter sought reelection with the endorsements of both parties, the Whigs repudiated him. Local Democrats nominated Hunter and he retained his seat in Congress, but he had effectively ended his association with the Whig party. The Whigs retaliated by voting him out of office in 1843.

In the race for the presidency in 1844, Hunter, acting with a group of Virginia colleagues, tried to engineer a victory for John C. Calhoun by attempting to change the rules of the national nominating convention to favor minority candidates. Although they failed to win the nomination for Calhoun, they managed to deny Van Buren the party's nod. Instead, dark horse James K. Polk was nominated for and won the White House.

In March 1845 Hunter returned to the House of Representatives, where he led the fight for the retrocession of Alexandria County (later Arlington County) from the District of Columbia to Virginia. In 1847 the Virginia legislature sent Hunter to the U.S. Senate. As chairman of the Senate Finance Committee, he steered through Congress the tariff of 1857.

During the crisis over the settlement of the Mexican Cession, Hunter stood in opposition to the Clay compromise proposals. He ultimately voted for the Fugitive Slave Law and the organization of New Mexico and Utah; he opposed the admission of California, the abolition of the slave trade in the District of Columbia, and the settlement of the boundary dispute between Texas and New Mexico. After the death of Calhoun during the compromise debate in March 1850, Hunter, along with Jefferson Davis of Mississippi and Robert Toombs of Georgia, took over the direction of the Southern Democrats. The three came to be known as the "Southern Triumvirate."

Hunter was widely mentioned as a possible Democratic nominee for president in 1860, and his native state supported him when the party convened in Charleston. After a deadlock developed, however, and the delegates reconvened in Baltimore, Hunter threw his support to John C. Breckinridge, the eventual nominee of the Southern branch of the party.

As conditions deteriorated after the election of Abraham Lincoln, Hunter was one of three senators from the border states chosen to sit on the Committee of Thirteen that ultimately proposed the Crittenden Compromise. In an attempt to defuse the situation at Fort Sumter, on January 2, 1861, he introduced a resolution that would have required the president to retrocede any fort, dockyard, arsenal, or other such Federal installation upon proper application by a state legislature or convention. In response to Republican obstinacy, Hunter joined his senatorial colleague James M. Mason and eight Virginia congressmen in calling for a convention to avert sectional crisis by redrawing the Constitution.

Hunter presented his own proposals for restructuring the Federal government in a speech before the Senate on January 11, 1861. In a plan derived directly from principles enunciated by John C. Calhoun during the debate over the Compromise of 1850, Hunter called for constitutional amendments declaring that Congress had no power to abolish slavery in the states, the District of Columbia, or Federal dockyards, forts, and arsenals and that Congress could not abolish, tax, or obstruct interstate slave trade. He demanded a constitutional guarantee that fugitive slaves would be restored to their rightful owners or that the state providing refuge would compensate the slave owner for his lost property. To prevent a president from fomenting insurrection and circumventing the Constitution through patronage, Hunter called for a dual executive. One president would be elected from each section. While one president served in the White House for four years, the other would sit as president of the

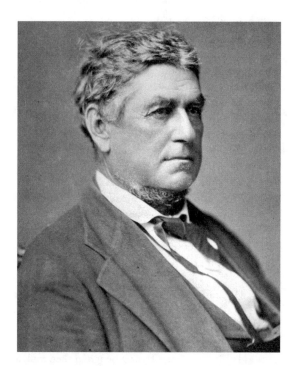

Senate; at the close of four years, they would switch offices. No bill could be passed without the consent of both.

He also proposed restructuring the Supreme Court. The chief executive from each section would appoint five justices. These justices would have the power to call before them any state that did not fulfill its constitutional obligations, including the return of fugitive slaves. If a state were found guilty, the rights of its citizens would be abrogated, and any other state in the Union could tax their property or commerce.

Hunter's plan had no support, and he resigned his Senate seat in March. After the Old Dominion seceded from the Union, the Virginia secession convention named Hunter one of its five delegates to the Provisional Confederate Congress, then meeting in Montgomery. Once he had taken his seat, he lobbied intensely for the removal of the Confederate capital to Richmond or another Virginia city.

After the resignation of Robert Toombs, Hunter accepted appointment as secretary of state, a post he held from July 24, 1861, until February 22, 1862. One of his first acts was to adopt the principles of the Paris Conference of 1856 governing privateering, neutral flags, and blockades. Refusing to recognize a paper blockade, he insisted that blockades must be effective to be in force.

Displeased with the progress that the three Confederate commissioners to Great Britain—A. Dudley Mann, Pierre A. Rost, and William Lowndes Yancey—were making in winning recognition for the Confederacy, Hunter recalled Yancey and reassigned Mann and Rost. He dispatched his old colleague James

*A state rights
Democrat, Mason
moved in the
congenial company
of his fellow
Virginia senator
Robert M. T. Hunter
and South
Carolinian John C.
Calhoun.*

PAGE 357

M. Mason to England with instructions to stress that the Confederacy would offer low tariffs to the industrial giant. Mason was directed to recall to the British that they had in the past extended diplomatic recognition to other break-away nations, including the South American colonies that declared independence from Spain, and Greece, when it declared itself free of the rule of the Ottoman Empire. Hunter sent John Slidell to France with similar instructions. Both representatives were seized from the British mail packet *Trent* shortly after the ship departed Havana on November 8. Although Hunter and other members of the administration hoped that the *Trent* incident would offer Britain an excuse to declare war on the United States, the English did not seize the opportunity. Hunter initiated a mission to Spain that proved similarly unsuccessful.

A slow and ponderous man, Hunter might have made an admirable secretary of state in ordinary times, but he was not suited for policy-making in a revolutionary emergency. In February 1862 he yielded his post as head of the State Department and then took a seat in the Confederate Senate, where he was elected president pro tem. He continued to dabble in diplomatic affairs by serving on the Foreign Relations Committee; he also sat on the Conference and Finance committees.

In the Senate Hunter took a keen interest in the Confederacy's financial woes, especially attempts to limit inflation. Recognizing the need to restrict the amount of unsecured paper money, he preferred selling Treasury bonds below par over issuing depreciated currency. At one point he proposed that each taxpayer, in exchange for a bond, should contribute one-fifth of his total income to the Confederate government to finance the war; this measure failed to pass the House. During the next session, Hunter proposed a tax-in-kind, which was enacted. He also introduced a bill on January 23, 1863, gradually reducing interest rates on Treasury bonds from 8 percent to 6 percent and limiting the amount of bonds the secretary of the Treasury could issue monthly to $50 million. The miserable condition of the Confederacy's finances by March 3, 1865, forced Hunter to defend his economic vision in the Senate, where he blamed the failure to halt rampant inflation on "impaired publick confidence."

As 1864 closed, Hunter objected to a bill exempting cargoes of vessels owned by individual states from restrictions on imports and exports; he feared that all trade would pass from the national government to the states. Instead, he proposed lifting all restrictions on importation. He also offered an amendment to a bill to provide supplies to the army that would have allowed commanding generals to impress whatever supplies they required for the use of their armies.

In general, Hunter supported the Davis administration until the matter of freeing and arming the slaves came up in February 1865. Hunter opposed the move as unconstitutional and a blatant violation of state rights, but he was forced to vote in support of the measure because of strict directions to do so from the Virginia General Assembly.

Early in 1865 Francis Preston Blair, a political colleague of Hunter's since the Jacksonian period, appeared in Richmond to urge a meeting between the warring sides to conclude a peace. Blair warned that if the conflict continued much longer, the United States would be forced to overwhelm the South by offering its forfeited lands to the people of Europe. Under Blair's initiative, a peace conference was arranged for February 3 on board the steamboat *River Queen* in Hampton Roads. Davis commissioned Hunter, Vice President Alexander H. Stephens, and Assistant Secretary of War John A. Campbell to meet with Lincoln and Union Secretary of State William H. Seward. The Confederate commissioners were instructed by Davis to begin discussing "the issues involved in the existing war, and . . . securing peace to the two countries."

Stephens expected to improve the Southern bargaining position by suggesting that the two sections reunite to revive the Monroe Doctrine and force Napoleon III out of Mexico, although Hunter thought this a feeble suggestion. Lincoln refused to negotiate on any basis other than reunion and abolition, although he held out a small hope that the abolition might be a compensated one. He also categorically refused to discuss anything further while the South was in arms. Hunter reminded Lincoln that Charles I had treated with the Parliamentarians during the English Civil War. According to the Virginian, the president "laughed, and said that 'Seward could talk with me about Charles I, he only knew that Charles I had lost his head.'" Hunter could not accept such "an absolute submission both as to rights and property, . . . a submission as absolute as if we were passing through the Candine forks," and the conference broke up.

Although he believed the South's defeat was inevitable, Hunter returned to Richmond and in a public address urged greater prosecution of the war. In March, however, after a consultation with Robert E. Lee on the military situation, he seized an opportunity to seek a cease-fire during which questions about slaveholders' property rights and the status of the rebellious states could be answered. On this occasion he worked with William A. Graham, John A. Campbell, James L. Orr, and William C. Rives to introduce a resolution in the Confederate Senate calling on Davis to propose through Lee an armistice to reestablish peace and union and to settle whether the seceded states would retain their former rights and privileges if they returned to the Union. Sympathetic members of the Senate, however, determined that Davis's mind was set against suing for peace and that the resolution would do no good. They had not acted on the peace resolution when Congress adjourned for the last time.

At the conclusion of the war, Ulysses S. Grant called for Hunter's arrest, and he was imprisoned in Fort Pulaski, Georgia, until January 1866. During Hunter's incarceration, Benjamin F. Butler took great delight in devastating the Virginian's lands in Essex County. Upon being paroled, Hunter returned to Fonthill, his 3,100-acre plantation near Lloyds, Virginia, and again took up farming and the practice of law.

In 1867 and 1868 Hunter served as a delegate to Virginia's Underwood convention. He supported the resulting new state constitution minus its two clauses that disfranchised all former state and local Confederate officials and that required a loyalty oath as a qualification for public office. (As a result of a compromise engineered by the Committee of Nine, these two clauses were separately voted on by the electorate and defeated.) Under the new order, he served as state treasurer beginning in 1874 and grappled with the problem of the payment of Virginia's enormous prewar debt. He was defeated for reelection in January 1880 by one of William Mahone's Readjuster candidates.

As vice president of the Southern Historical Society, Hunter engaged in heated public correspondence with Jefferson Davis over the reasons for the calling of the Hampton Roads peace conference and the policy of conscripting and emancipating blacks. The dispute was made all the more bitter because the point of contention was so small. Davis maintained he had agreed to the meeting only because Blair had asked for it and produced a corroborative letter from Judah P. Benjamin to back his argument. Hunter stressed the public pressure to bring the war to an end because of the rapidly diminishing resources of the South and backed his recollection of the peace conference with letters from the other two commissioners. Hunter also produced an account of the "Origin of the Late War," published in 1876 in the *Southern Historical Society Papers*, which defended the South's decision to secede as the only possible response to repeated Northern aggression. At the urging of Calhoun's children, he gave serious consideration to writing a full-scale biography of the South Carolinian to enshrine his principles and protect his memory but decided that such a work from his hand would hurt rather than help his former mentor and colleague.

In his declining years Hunter was named collector of the port of Tappahannock by Grover Cleveland. Two years later, on July 18, 1887, he died at Fonthill and was interred in the family cemetery at Elmwood.

— SARA B. BEARSS

I

IMPERIALISM

Imperialism played a role in the origins of the Confederate States of America. When dis-Unionists argued the case for secession, they sometimes voiced predictions that an independent Southern nation would grow into a vast empire for slavery—that the new country would extend its domain and institutions southward into Mexico, Central America, the islands of the Caribbean Sea, and even the farthest reaches of South America. Such pronouncements, in many instances, were merely rhetoric designed to persuade Southerners that the potential benefits of secession outweighed its risks. However, Article IV, Section 3, of the Confederate Constitution, with its provision that the Confederacy could acquire new territory and that slavery was to be legal in such acquisitions, suggested that the new nation might follow an imperialistic course.

Confederate imperialism derived from the Southern expansion movement of the 1850s, when many Southerners reached the conclusion that American extension into Latin regions would benefit their section. They looked southward for new slave states that would enhance their political power in Washington. They also anticipated other advantages from southward expansion, including plantation opportunities, the elimination of northern Mexico as a haven for fugitive slaves, wealth from control of isthmian transit routes, improved Southern trade with the Pacific coast and Asia, and an outlet for the surplus black population of the upper South. Virginian Matthew Fontaine Maury, who as superintendent of the U.S. Naval Observatory helped plan an expedition by two U.S. naval officers to explore the Amazon River, hoped that Virginia planters would one day take their slaves to Brazil, thus relieving his state of the danger of race war. Some Southern expansionists anticipated that U.S. acquisition of the Spanish colony of Cuba, which already had slavery, would enhance the competitive position of the South's sugar planters in world markets: since U.S. acquisition of the island would terminate the African slave trade to Cuba, labor costs there, and thus the price of Cuban sugar, would rise.

Southern pressure for America's territorial and commercial expansion southward influenced American diplomacy. President Franklin Pierce completed the Gadsden Purchase from Mexico and tried to pressure Spain into selling Cuba. President James Buchanan sought land cessions from Mexico, asked the U.S. Congress to authorize an American protectorate over Mexican Chihuahua and Sonora, supported the efforts of the Louisiana Tehuantepec Company to procure transit concessions across Mexico's isthmus, and tried to purchase Cuba. Southern politicians, diplomats, and entrepreneurs played key roles in these projects. From 1849 to 1860 the slave states provided much of the leadership, manpower, and support for the era's illegal filibustering (that is, private, military) expeditions. The most important of these expeditions attacked Cuba, Mexico, and several of the states of Central America. Native Tennessean William Walker conquered and ruled Nicaragua in the mid-1850s. Even though Walker had no intention of seeking Nicaragua's annexation to the United States, many Southerners rallied to his cause, especially after he legalized slavery there in September 1856.

Prominent Southern radicals became involved with the filibusters. Edmund Ruffin met with Walker during the Southern Commercial Convention at Montgomery, Alabama (1858). William Lowndes Yancey, C. A. L. Lamar, Roger A. Pryor, Albert Gallatin Brown, and John A. Winston aided filibusters in a support capacity. Mississippi secessionist John A. Quitman agreed to lead a filibuster army against Spanish forces in Cuba. Such contacts between notorious radicals and the filibusters attracted attention from the nation's press. This publicity, combined with the secrecy that necessarily cloaked planning for illegal military expeditions, gave rise to charges by antislavery Republicans, Southern anti-imperialists, and foreign observers that the whole tropical expansion movement was part of a secessionist conspiracy. The Knights of the Golden Circle, a filibuster organization that aspired to create a new slave empire with Cuba at its center and embracing the Deep South, most of the border slave states, Central America, the West Indies, and parts of Kansas and South America, conformed to this conspiracy interpretation. Southern imperialism, however, was less an agenda for separate nationhood than a program to avert the necessity of a separate nation. It enjoyed broad public support throughout the South, especially in the Gulf states. Important Southern politicians who did not favor immediate secession,

The expand-or-perish interpretation, while concentrating the causes of secession into three vivid words, actually reduces a complex phenomenon to a caricature.

PAGE 203

Just as Southern attitudes about territorial expansion changed from one place to another, so the expansion issue changed from one era to another.

PAGE 203

including Jefferson Davis, Alexander H. Stephens, John Slidell, and Judah P. Benjamin, advocated slavery's southward extension and worked toward that end, sometimes in collaboration with the filibusters.

The frustration of Southern imperialism intensified the alienation of the slave states from the Union and thus became a contributing cause to Southern secession. Northern Presidents Pierce and Buchanan, though willing to acquire territory through diplomatic channels, enforced U.S. neutrality statutes against filibustering expeditions. Their efforts prevented Quitman's planned strike against Cuba in 1854 and 1855, and contributed to Walker's downfall in Nicaragua in 1857 and his inability to reconquer that country in the years that followed. Antislavery Republicans in Congress opposed legislation to facilitate the purchase of Cuba. Many Southerners interpreted Northern obstruction of tropical expansion projects as evidence that the South's population was being reduced to second-class status within the Union; Northern hostility to slavery's southward extension appeared to be an indictment of their way of life. One of the last prewar efforts to resolve sectional strife, the so-called Crittenden Compromise, addressed these perceptions. This proposal (December 1860) would have reinstated the Missouri Compromise line and extended it to the Pacific Ocean, protecting slavery in any territory "hereafter acquired" south of the 36°30′ parallel latitude—a seeming invitation to slavery's future thrust into the tropics. President-elect Abraham Lincoln and the Republican party rejected the plan.

Had the Confederacy established its independence, it likely would have attempted expansion into the tropics. Warfare with the North, however, precluded such initiatives. Confederate armies did invade vulnerable areas of the Union with hopes of incorporating those areas into the new nation. But Confederate penetration of the New Mexico Territory and the states of Kentucky, Missouri, and Maryland was hardly an example of imperialism—which implies rule over subject peoples. The Confederacy made part of New Mexico into the Confederate territory of Arizona, under the expectation of eventual statehood, and recognized Missouri as its twelfth state. Southern imperialism, with its dream of a vast slave empire, died at the beginning of the Civil War.

— ROBERT E. MAY

IMPRESSMENT

The Confederacy's need for supplies prompted the Congress to enact an impressment law on March 26, 1863. As with other initiatives passed in an effort to

obtain goods for the war effort, the Impressment Act created severe dissension on the home front.

The act established state boards of commissioners throughout the South. President Jefferson Davis and the state governors were each entitled to appoint one person to the board. This board served two functions: it mediated disputes between impressment agents and the individual whose property was to be impressed, and it fixed prices for goods set to be impressed by government agents. The board published the list of prices frequently so as to keep in step with fluctuations on the markets. Still, the lists rarely reflected the prevailing market price.

Local impressment agents administered the law. They traveled throughout the South and surveyed the stocks of farmers, merchants, and others with products deemed necessary for the government. The agent and the farmer or merchant would assess the value of the property chosen for impressment. The individual whose property was impressed was either paid in full in Confederate scrip at the time or was issued a certificate entitling him to payment upon redemption later.

Apparently, the civilian population voiced little opposition to the impressment measure until the summer of 1863. Then the floodgates of protest opened. With the nation reeling from the military debacles at Gettysburg and Vicksburg, and with Confederate currency rapidly depreciating in value, Southerners were less than pleased to see impressment price lists that set prices well below market values. These rates—which were often 50 percent below the market price for the goods—infuriated farmers and small businessmen alike who were squeezed by inflation and government demands. It came to be assumed that if the government impressed your goods for the army's use, you would take a loss. Southerners were also bothered by the haphazard way impressment agents enforced the law. Moreover, the burden of impressment was not distributed equally: those living near the Confederate field armies or near transportation depots were hit hardest. Similarly, Southerners were preyed upon by fake impressment agents who used counterfeit certificates as licenses to steal from neighbors. These were real problems, but for many, what irked them most about the law was its wastefulness: too often impressed foodstuffs, supposedly destined for the field armies, rotted at depots because agents failed to obtain transportation prior to the impressment or because transportation could not be found.

From the beginning of the war, military authorities also impressed slaves to work on fortifications or to serve as teamsters, nurses, or cooks. As with the impressment of foodstuffs and other supplies, this impressment was administered by local military authorities—Congress did not regulate impressment procedures until the 1863 law. After 1863 Congress insisted that the impressment of slaves and military goods conform to the laws of the state where the slave was impressed.

The owners of impressed slaves were paid thirty dollars a month or whatever wage may have been agreed upon in advance. In the event the impressed slave was killed while working for the government, the owner was entitled to be reimbursed in full. Masters nonetheless were often resistant to allowing impressment agents to spirit off their slaves. Planters found that impressed slaves were not treated well and were kept past the time specified in the government contract. In addition, the government was slow to pay, and when it did, it always paid in worthless Confederate currency. In short, many owners found impressment to be an economic liability. Nonetheless, military authorities found slave labor to be imperative for the war effort, especially as the tide turned against the Confederacy. By February of 1864 the government wanted to hire a minimum of twenty thousand slaves; if the slave owners did not volunteer their chattels, the government reserved the right to impress them.

Scholars have been unable to calculate the amount of goods impressed. Authorities on the Confederate financial system, however, have speculated on the amount. Since Treasury notes were issued largely to pay for impressed goods, the amount of notes issued during the course of the Impressment Act's existence provides a rough estimate of what impressment brought to the Confederate government. Over $500 million worth of vouchers and notes were still unpaid as late as March 1865.

The unpopularity of the impressment system and the inequities it represented almost preordained its demise. By the end of the war the Impressment Act was a dead letter, and the government found itself forced to pay for goods at market prices.

— MARY A. DECREDICO

INFANTRY

During Gen. Philip Sheridan's victorious 1864 Shenandoah Valley campaign, a veteran Federal officer noted that, though outnumbered and repeatedly defeated, the Confederate infantry often inflicted more casualties than they took. They were better shots, he decided, than his own men and more skilled in taking cover, fighting like Indians or hunters. Also, in emergencies their regiments could move rapidly in an apparently disorderly swarm without losing their cohesion, offering less of a target than the orderly ranks the Federals tried to maintain. (It must be noted that this

difference was most pronounced in the eastern theater, in actions between the Army of Northern Virginia and the Army of the Potomac; in the west, where Federal soldiers often had much the same civilian backgrounds as their opponents and Federal leadership was more aggressive, it was less evident.)

Several major factors contributed to this combat efficiency of the Confederate infantry. The government wisely attempted to keep its existing regiments filled with volunteers and conscripts rather than allowing them to dwindle away from battle casualties and sickness while raising more new regiments (as was done in the North for political reasons). Mixed in with veterans under experienced officers, these replacements quickly learned both the formal and the practical aspects of soldiering. The combat efficiency of Confederate infantry regiments therefore remained generally constant, as compared to the U.S. forces, which were a mixture of badly under-strength veteran units and fat newly raised regiments, green as gourds from colonel to drummer boy.

Organization

The basic Confederate infantry organization was the regiment. Its organization was practically identical with that of a U.S. regiment: ten companies (each consisting of three officers and approximately ninety-five enlisted men); a small regimental headquarters (colonel, lieutenant colonel, major, adjutant, quartermaster, surgeon, assistant surgeon, sergeant major, quartermaster sergeant, commissary sergeant, hospital steward, and two "principal musicians"); and sometimes a band. The major noticeable difference between the two sides was that each Federal regiment had its own chaplain.

During the first year of the war, the Confederate infantry included a number of odd units—separate companies and battalions (formations with three to eight companies), and so-called legions. These last were inspired by famous Revolutionary War formations, such as "Light-Horse Harry" Lee's legion of light infantry and light dragoons, which had proven highly effective in the irregular warfare waged in the Southern states. Probably the outstanding Civil War example was Hampton's Legion—organized, uniformed, armed, and equipped by Wade Hampton of South Carolina—an eight-company battalion of infantry, four companies of cavalry, and two of artillery. It soon proved impossible, however, to employ such legions as units in large-scale warfare. Hampton therefore recruited his infantry up to regimental strength and transferred the cavalry and artillery to regiments of their respective arms. Some separate battalions remained in existence throughout the war, but many of them were added to existing regiments or combined to form new ones.

In less than a week after his initial call, thirty South Carolina companies volunteered for Hampton's unit— more than twice the number that could be accommodated.

PAGE 263

When battle became imminent at Manassas, Hampton speedily boarded his unit on a train and rushed northward.

PAGE 263

BATTLE-READY

Standing at attention in April 1861 are the Sumter Light Guards, Company K, 4th Regiment, of the Georgia Volunteer Infantry.

LIBRARY OF CONGRESS

A varying number of regiments—usually four or five—formed a brigade, a basic tactical formation at this time. Brigades were made up of regiments from the same state (a notable exception in the Army of Northern Virginia was its lone Arkansas regiment, which was lumped into its Texas Brigade); whenever possible they were commanded by an officer from that state. Brigades were frequently identified by name—usually that of the commander under which it originally won distinction—rather than by its number. Thus the Virginia Brigade, which Gen. Thomas J. Jackson led at First Manassas, was known as the Stonewall Brigade for the rest of its much-battered existence. The Texas Brigade referred to itself as Hood's Texans, even after John Bell Hood had left the Army of Northern Virginia. Sometimes the practice became confusing: at Gettysburg, for example, McGowan's Brigade was first commandeded by J. Johnston Pettigrew and then by J. K. Marshall; Archer's Brigade was led by Birkett Davenport Fry. A different type of nickname was that adopted by some Kentucky troops after the Federal occupation of their home state—the Orphan Brigade.

Until the winter of 1862–1863 the Army of Northern Virginia's infantry brigades might include a company of artillery, a practice that continued for approximately a year more in the western Confederate armies.

Several—usually four or five—brigades of infantry, with several companies of artillery, constituted an infantry division. (In contrast, until February 1863 most Federal divisions also included a regiment or more of cavalry.) An average of four infantry divisions and additional artillery made up a corps; several corps (with cavalry, reserve artillery, engineers, and service troops) formed an army. Thanks to the Confederate practice of keeping existing infantry regiments as near to full strength as possible, their infantry formations usually were stronger than their Federal equivalents; a Confederate infantry brigade of 1862 through 1864 could put approximately as many rifles into line as a whole Federal division. Only when the Confederate conscription could no longer furnish sufficient replacements did their infantry units dwindle away like the veteran Federal regiments.

Though most of the Confederate states raised separate battalions of sharpshooters, there is little evidence that many of these were trained, armed, or employed as such. Instead, like other separate battalions, they frequently were later consolidated to form standard infantry regiments. However, during the 1864 campaign many infantry brigades of the Army of Northern Virginia organized 180-man corps of picked soldiers for outpost service, sniping, and patrolling. These corps were divided into four-man groups, each of which lived and fought as a team. These organizations proved highly useful, especially for fighting in thick woods such as the Wilderness.

Mounted infantry were infantrymen given horses or mules for greater mobility; they moved mounted but dismounted to fight. In the East they appeared largely in the more irregular Confederate forces in the Shenandoah Valley, but in the West they were relatively common. Though useful in raids and in advance or rearguard actions, especially in broken country, Confederate mounted infantry had two major weaknesses. Being armed with unhandy, long muzzle-loading muskets, it was relatively helpless if caught while mounted by Federal cavalry: dismounted, with every fifth man detailed to hold horses, it seldom could stand off attacks by superior numbers of enemy infantry for any great length of time—a mission that Federal mounted infantry units armed with Spencer repeating rifles could accomplish handily.

Clothing and Equipment

Though the first year of the war saw gentlemen's companies with smart uniforms, elaborate camp equipment, and black body servants for each private, the average Confederate infantryman of 1861–1862 could be only sketchily equipped. This became something of a virtue, for he soon preferred to travel light. Knapsacks (packs) were discarded as too cumbersome; most soldiers substituted the traditional American "horseshoe roll," rolling their blankets up lengthwise (inside an oilcloth or rubber blanket if they had one), slinging it over the left shoulder, and fastening its ends together behind the right hip. Extra articles of clothing could be rolled up inside the blanket. Alternatively, the soldier might make a short roll of his blanket and sling it across the middle of his back on a narrow strap or thong. A shortage of suitable material made blankets a difficult item to procure. Northern observers reported Confederates using varicolored quilts or strips of carpet, the latter sometimes with a central slit cut in them so they could be worn as ponchos. Captured U.S. blankets and civilian ones in all colors were also common.

The haversack (a plain canvas bag, roughly a foot square, with a flap cover and often a removable inside bag for small articles) slung at the soldier's left hip held his rations and few personal possessions. Over it would hang his canteen. His leather cartridge box with its forty rounds of ammunition usually was worn on the waist belt, handy to his right hand; between it and the belt buckle was a small leather pouch for percussion caps. The bayonet was carried in a leather scabbard suspended from a frog on the left side of the waist belt, under the haversack and canteen.

Confederate equipment as a whole showed great variety—prewar militia issue, obsolete U.S. material found in seized arsenals, different European models smuggled in through the blockade, captured material, and various domestic manufactures. Soldiers frequently added two practical items, a large tin cup and a "side" (bowie) knife, which was more of a tool than a weapon. Some veterans claimed that Confederate infantrymen tended to discard their bayonets (which were seldom actually bloodied in combat) and even their cartridge boxes and cap pouches, preferring to stuff cartridges and caps into their pockets. Considering the limited pocket space the Confederate jacket and trousers provided, this last story should be regarded with suspicion.

Recent research, confirmed by contemporary photographs, indicates that the Confederate infantryman was, contrary to received tradition, generally well supplied with clothing. Quartermaster Department records show a steady issue of clothing, if not smart uniforms, to the troops. Perhaps the Army of Northern Virginia's most ragged period was during the Second Manassas and Sharpsburg campaigns of August through September 1862, when its first locally procured uniforms (especially shoes) were wearing out and the Quartermaster Department was just beginning to develop an efficient supply system. By 1865 raggedness reemerged in troops from states such as Florida, which could not provide adequate support. Other states, such as North Carolina, however, had a surplus of uniforms on hand in 1865. Clothing supply for the Confederate western armies was less reliable but appears to have been generally adequate. America was rough campaigning country: after a few weeks in the field new uniforms would be showing heavy wear and tear.

The standard infantry uniform was a gray forage cap, a short, single-breasted gray jacket, sky-blue trousers, and heavy shoes. Naturally there were many variations, especially in the shades of gray cloth available. A frequent substitute for gray was "butternut," yellowish-brown shades obtained by dyes made from walnut hulls and copperas. Trousers were often gray or butternut, instead of blue, and many soldiers replaced their issue caps with soft slouch hats of many patterns. The showy zouave uniforms of 1861 soon disappeared, though one or two Louisiana regiments may have retained theirs for some time. The Second Alabama and Fourth Arkansas infantry in 1863 wore reddish homespun and broad-brimmed wool hats. The Forty-seventh Georgia had uniforms

"*The soldiers know their duties better than the general officers do.*"

ROBERT E. LEE

of blue-striped brown ticking. Requiring uniforms in a hurry before the Battle of Shiloh, the Second Texas received undyed clothing that reminded them of shrouds. Some prisoners taken in 1863 had English-manufactured jackets and overcoats of excellent dark-blue cloth. In the Wilderness in 1864, a North Carolina brigade in new uniforms of unusually dark gray were mistaken for Yankees and shot up—along with Lt. Gen. James Longstreet—by another Confederate unit.

Shoes were a major problem. Imports from England were gradually throttled, and domestic production was seriously hampered by a shortage of leather. By 1863 shoes were being made with canvas uppers, which came apart in wet weather. By 1864 some unfortunate infantrymen were receiving shoes with iron-bound wooden soles. In consequence, dead or captured Northerners were frequently stripped of their footgear.

Parts of Federal uniforms, which might also be taken from captured supply depots, were commonly worn. Although sky-blue trousers were regulation for Confederates, the use of blue coats and overcoats was considered a violation of the laws of warfare, and Confederate commanders usually ordered such articles redyed or discarded. It could result in unfortunate incidents. A. P. Hill's attack on the Federal left flank at Sharpsburg probably owed part of its success to the fact that his men had replaced their tattered outfits with blue uniforms they had just captured at Harpers Ferry, and the Federals could not readily distinguish friend from foe.

The general appearance of Confederate infantry was marred by a thriftless element that neglected its clothing and equipment, preferring to go ragged rather than care for it or carry a change of shirts and underwear. A good many of them (like some Federal soldiers) seem to have had a personal aversion to soap and water; in 1864 a Federal cavalryman described prisoners from the Eighth South Carolina Infantry Regiment as having the aroma of aged billy goats. Ironically, such men became the "ragged rebels" of Confederate tradition—supposedly the epitome of the Confederate infantryman and one of the South's most beloved myths.

Tactics

The rifle-musket's increased range and accuracy forced considerable changes in tactics. American officers—Confederate and Federal—whose last combat service had been in 1846 and 1847 against Mexican troops armed with smoothbore flintlock muskets with an effective range of barely two hundred yards, now found themselves in a new, far more deadly sort of

WEAPONS
Rifles and Rifle-Muskets

The Confederate infantryman's standard weapon was the rifle-musket, a long-barreled, muzzle-loading, percussion-ignition, rifled weapon that fired the so-called minié ball. Besides the rifle-musket, there was the rifle, a weapon with a shorter, heavier barrel, usually equipped with a sword bayonet. The Confederates also had a few special sharpshooters' rifles, the most prized of which seems to have been the short, English-manufactured, caliber .45 Whitworth. When fitted with a telescope sight, it was reportedly accurate up to eight hundred yards.

The first Confederate infantry organized in 1861 were haphazardly armed with weapons taken from seized U.S. arsenals in their territory, those already in the possession of their state militias, and whatever could be purchased in Europe or the Northern states before hostilities began. (It is estimated that approximately 600,000 small arms were brought into the South by blockade runners.) Such sources were later supplemented by the hastily developed Confederate arms industry and by captured weapons.

Though some Confederate infantry, especially in the West, were initially armed with flintlock muskets, smoothbores, shotguns, and hunting rifles, by late 1862 and early 1863 the average Confederate infantryman had received a modern rifle-musket or rifle. The English-made caliber .557 Enfield rifle-musket and short rifle were reportedly the most popular, but various U.S. models—either captured or Southern-manufactured—were also common. Some 100,000 good Austrian Lorenz caliber .54 rifle-muskets added variety. It should be noted that Federal infantry were not much better armed than the Confederates during the war's first two years; even in 1863, at Vicksburg and Gettysburg, some Federal soldiers turned in their obsolete smoothbore muskets and replaced them with captured rifle-muskets.

In general, these weapons were accurate at up to six hundred yards and could kill at one thousand. Their percussion firing mechanism functioned even in bad weather, which had left the flintlock musket useless except as a long handle for its bayonet. Their major weakness was a comparatively slow rate of fire. A fresh, well-trained soldier with a clean rifle-musket could fire three rounds a minute, but as continued firing fouled its barrel, the rate of fire would drop to two rounds a minute, or less.

— JOHN R. ELTING

war. Artillery could no longer attempt to unlimber within three hundred yards of enemy infantry and demolish it with canister without quickly taking prohibitive losses. Cavalry charges against unbroken infantry became next to impossible, and infantry attacks were risky, costly affairs. In short, the infantryman with his rifle-musket dominated the battlefield; the effectiveness of his fire led to the increasing use of field fortifications.

Both opponents began the war with the same drill manuals and the same tactics, modifying the latter to fit the improvements in infantry weapons. If the changes seem slow and insufficient to modern readers, it must be remembered that it probably was late 1862 before the majority of infantry on either side had modern rifle-muskets and the need for change became apparent. Also, the rifle-musket's relatively slow rate of fire made it necessary to use masses of men in both the attack and the defense. At Fredericksburg, Robert E. Lee's defensive line in the Sunken Road at the foot of Marye's Heights was four men deep, each line firing in turn and then passing to the rear to reload. An attacking army normally expected heavy losses and so commonly adopted deep formations, to be certain of getting enough men into its objective to hold it against counterattacks. At Shiloh in 1862 Confederate Gen. Albert Sidney Johnston's initial attack on the Federal left flank was delivered by two corps, one behind the other, with two more corps held in column as reserves. At Gettysburg the right flank of Pickett's charge was three brigades deep; at Atlanta in 1864 John Bell Hood formed his brigades with their regiments in column (one behind the other), thus giving them a depth of eight to twelve men.

The common formation used by an infantry regiment in action throughout the war was the "line of battle"—its companies abreast in a two-deep line, with the regimental colors in the center. One company usually would be deployed as skirmishers from one hundred to three hundred yards in front of their regiment, depending on the terrain. In wooded or broken country, this skirmish line would be strengthened, sometimes with half the regiment being so engaged. During prolonged fighting in such areas, whole regiments might be deployed in heavy lines of skirmishers, individual soldiers taking cover and firing at will.

A typical infantry division attack formation was in three lines, each composed of one or more brigades. (The composition of each line would be based on the number of brigades present, their relative strength, and the tactical situation.) The leading brigade would be in line of battle, its regiments advancing abreast, preceded by one or two lines of skirmishers who probed forward to locate and develop the enemy position. The second line, also deployed in line of battle, followed approximately 250 yards behind. The third line might be similarly deployed or held in "column of fours" for rapid movement to a point of danger or opportunity.

Once hostile contact was made, the first line pushed up to absorb the skirmishers and attacked. This seldom was a dashing bayonet charge; instead, it often broke down into an "advance by rushes," elements of the first line working forward, sometimes gradually, from one bit of cover to the next, with pauses to build up the fire superiority to cover the next rush. If the first line stalled, the second line would be fed in to restore the momentum of the attack, followed if necessary by the third line. The assaulting force, at the moment of collision with the enemy, would thus consist of two or three lines merged into one heavy, disorderly wave, the individual regiments badly intermixed. Only forceful personal leadership by officers and noncommissioned officers of all grades could keep it under the necessary minimum of control to ram the attack home. Even then, it might fail, especially if the enemy had had time to entrench and so was sheltered from infantry and artillery fire.

Perhaps the most marked tactical feature of the Civil War was the employment of hasty entrenchments, made of whatever materials were available. These were little used before late 1863, but after experiencing the protection afforded by sunken roads at Fredericksburg and Sharpsburg and stone farm fences at Gettysburg, the average soldier on both sides concluded that it was wise to dig in. Through 1864 and 1865, unless utterly exhausted, troops in the vicinity of the enemy, even if they were under orders to attack, would habitually entrench as soon as they halted, using their tin cups, halves of discarded canteens, and knives.

In action, infantry officers of all grades had to be quick to detect gaps in the enemy's front and to maintain tight contact with the friendly units to their front and flanks. A gap of any size between units might allow the enemy to wedge into their front and roll up their line in both directions, while an open flank not covered by alert patrols was an invitation to disaster, troops in line formation being very vulnerable to attacks from the flank and rear.

Though his war ended in defeat, the Confederate infantryman had won an outstanding reputation for hard fighting, swift marching, endurance amid hardships, and sheer pugnacity. He nevertheless had remained a thorough individualist, much given to straggling, unauthorized foraging, absence without leave, and general indiscipline.

Officers whom the Confederate infantryman trusted could lead him against any danger. But such trust

"I am sending you the guns, dear General. This is a hard fight, and we had better all die than lose it."

JAMES LONGSTREET
TO GEN. ROGER PRYOR,
SHARPSBURG

was hard earned, the Southern infantryman being persnickety and demanding of his officers. He disliked strict West Pointers (particularly officers below the grade of general), regarded men from other states as unreliable foreigners, and scorned any tendency toward pomp and circumstance. Above all, he expected nothing less from every officer, whether new lieutenant or general, than unhesitating, outstanding courage and personal leadership. Both victory and defeat killed or disabled large numbers of such officers; eventually, it became impossible to replace them with men of equal courage and competence. A British observer concluded that Confederate infantry could accomplish wonders—but at a cost the South could not afford.

[*See also* Civil War, *article on* Small Arms; Uniforms.]

— JOHN R. ELTING

JACKSON, THOMAS J. ("STONEWALL")

Jackson, Thomas J. ("Stonewall") (1824–1863), lieutenant general. Stonewall Jackson ranks among the most brilliant commanders in American history. Even though his field service in the Civil War lasted but two years, his movements continue to be studied at every major military academy in the world. He was an artillerist who excelled in infantry tactics, a devout Christian merciless in battle, a man of eccentricities but one motivated by an inflexible sense of duty. Jackson's death at the midway point of the war was the greatest personal loss that the Confederacy suffered. Many writers then and now insist that had he lived, the outcome of the South's attempt at independence might have ended differently.

No general ever rose from humbler beginnings. Jackson was born on January 21, 1824, at Clarksburg deep in the mountains of what is now West Virginia. Although Jacksons were longtime residents of the area, his father was a struggling attorney with mounting debts. Jackson was only two years old when his father and an infant sister died of typhoid fever. For four years the widow and three children were virtual wards of the town. Mrs. Jackson remarried, but her new husband was unable financially to care for the children. They were sent individually to live with relatives. Jackson's mother died a year after the breakup of the family.

The lad grew up under the care of an uncle who ran lumber and grist mills in Lewis County, south of Clarksburg. Jackson developed into a sturdy youth accustomed to hard work and outdoor activities. The absence of parents also made him withdrawn and introspective in personality. Local tutors, plus a love of reading, provided him with a limited education.

Jackson went to the U.S. Military Academy in 1842 only after the first appointee from his congressional district decided not to pursue a military education. Few cadets ever entered West Point with less scholastic preparation than Jackson. Moreover, the mountain lad was introverted, awkward, and lacking in social graces. He made few friends during the four years at the academy. Using impassivity as a protection, Jackson concentrated all of his energies on learning. Determination, patience, and hours of studying by day and night accomplished his goal. Rising from near the bottom of his class at the start, Jackson ranked seventeenth of fifty-nine cadets at his 1846 graduation.

War had already been declared with Mexico when Jackson entered the army as a lieutenant in the Third U.S. Artillery. He proceeded at once to Mexico. His battery saw no action for six months, and Jackson openly despaired of getting into battle. In March 1847, however, he participated in the assault on Vera Cruz; other engagements followed, with Jackson cited for gallantry at Contreras and Chapultepec. By the end of the war, Jackson held the rank of brevet major. None of his West Point classmates had done as well in Mexico.

Jackson returned to the States and reported for duty at Fort Hamilton on Long Island, New York. By then he had developed an increasing interest in religion. (In Mexico, he had had several discussions about Catholicism with the bishop of Mexico City but found the services too formal.) In September 1848 Jackson received baptism and attended a number of communions at an Episcopal church adjacent to Fort Hamilton. His duties as assistant quartermaster and occasional member of courts-martial left Jackson free

THE PROFESSOR

An 1851 portrait of Thomas J. "Stonewall" Jackson, around the time he joined the Virginia Military Institute as a professor of artillery tactics.

NATIONAL ARCHIVES

to pursue his fondness for reading. History was his favorite subject. Jackson also maintained a steady correspondence with his beloved sister, Laura, who was married and lived in Beverly, Virginia. He continued through the years to make periodic visits to this only surviving member of his immediate family.

"My religious belief teaches me to feel as safe in battle as in bed. God has fixed the time for my death. I do not concern myself about that."

STONEWALL JACKSON

Unlike West Point, VMI focused first on leadership in civil life, but also trained its cadets for service as citizen-soldiers in time of war or national emergency.

PAGE 652

"Always mystify, mislead and surprise the enemy; and when you strike and overcome him, never let up in the pursuit."

STONEWALL JACKSON

Apprehensions over health were an ongoing concern to Jackson. Chronic discomfort, especially with his stomach, liver, and kidneys, soon convinced him that his troubles were punishment from God for his sins. Jackson sought relief from several New York physicians. When hydrotherapy seemed to ease his pain, Jackson became an ardent devotee of water treatments and thereafter regularly visited spas whenever possible. He likewise made physical exercise a part of his daily routine. Although many of his problems may have been the result of hypochondria, his weak eyesight and poor hearing were real and plagued him after his Mexican service.

In December 1850 Jackson's company transferred to Fort Meade in the remote interior of Florida. The artillerist uncharacteristically became embroiled in arguments with his commanding officer, Maj. William H. French. Jackson was soon under arrest for accusing French of having an affair with his maid. Meanwhile, Jackson had received an offer to become professor of artillery tactics and optics at the Virginia Military Institute (VMI) in Lexington, Virginia. The academy was small, having been in existence barely a dozen years; nevertheless, it offered Jackson both a challenge and a change of scenery. He resigned his army commission and reported to the institute on the eve of the 1851–1852 school year.

"The Major" spent a fourth of his life at VMI. Only three months after his arrival in Lexington, Jackson joined the Presbyterian church and rapidly became one of the most devout Calvinists of his age. He found solace in constant prayer and strength through an inflexible faith. He attended every service at the Lexington Presbyterian Church. To the amusement of the congregation, Jackson slept through at least part of every service. He always sat bolt upright, his back never touching the pew. In that way, Jackson said, the pain of discomfort was punishment for his disrespectful naps.

Jackson's name and that of VMI are permanently intertwined—but not because of the professor's classroom performance. He was too skilled in artillery principles to be able to present it effectively. Having no background in the other subjects he taught—acoustics, analytical mechanics, astronomy, and physics—Jackson was forced to study as he taught. Memorizing lectures the night before he gave them, he was unable to expand upon or deviate from presentations. A question from a cadet, and Jackson could only repeat verbatim what he had previously said on the subject.

At the same time the professor was a disciplinarian who tolerated nothing less than absolute attention and response from cadets in class. Jackson was personally responsible for the expulsion of a half-dozen cadets from VMI. At least two of them challenged him to

duels; one threatened to kill him on sight. Cadets called him "Major Jackson" to his face. Behind his back, he was "Tom Fool," "Old Blue Light," "crazy as damnation," "the worst teach that God ever made," and similar derogations.

Giving credence to many of those disparagements were a number of eccentricities that Jackson regularly exhibited. He would often thrust his arm into the air without warning and then make several pumping motions with it (in order to make his blood circulate better, he explained). Jackson on occasion would forget to eat; he seemed always wrapped in inner concentration; his reticence sometimes led him to stare in darkness at a blank wall; he ate only foods he disliked; he walked with exaggerated strides; on the few occasions when he laughed, Jackson threw back his head, opened his mouth widely, and emitted no sound whatsoever. He was unquestionably a "town character," Lexingtonians said with a shake of their heads.

On the other hand, Jackson displayed a number of qualities that impressed those who knew him well. Devotion, duty, and determination were his bywords. He was honest to a fault, extremely conscientious, and pleasant in the confines of small, private gatherings; his dependability won friends just as his piety won respect. In the latter years of the 1850s, Jackson organized and taught a black Sunday School class for slaves and freedmen, in open defiance of a Virginia law that forbade blacks from congregating in public.

Jackson married twice, both times to daughters of Presbyterian ministers. His first marriage, to Elinor Junkin of Lexington in 1853, ended when she died in childbirth fourteen months later. In 1857 he married Mary Anna Morrison of Davidson, North Carolina. That union, extraordinarily bound by Christian love, produced one surviving daughter.

Thoughts of a possible civil war began with Jackson in December 1859, when he and part of the VMI cadet corps were among the witnesses at the execution of abolitionist John Brown. Jackson remained a strong Unionist until he thought his beloved Virginia threatened by Federal coercion. At the secession of his state, he dutifully offered his services to the Confederacy. He left Lexington on April 20, 1861, never again to see his adopted town.

When Jackson and a contingent of cadets arrived in Richmond to serve as drill instructors for thousands of recruits gathering for military service, the ex-professor hardly resembled an impressive soldier. It had been fourteen years since Jackson had last seen combat. He was then thirty-seven, five feet, ten inches tall, with extended forehead, sharp nose, thick beard, and high-pitched voice. Unusually large hands and feet were the extremities of a 170-pound frame. Jackson rode a horse awkwardly, body bent forward as if he were leaning

"LIKE A STONE WALL"   *This portrait by George W. Minnes, from the Mathew Brady collection, was taken two weeks before Jackson's death on May 10, 1863.*   NATIONAL ARCHIVES

*Jackson tendered
his resignation on
Jan. 31, 1862,
protesting, "with
such interference
in my command I
cannot expect to
be of much service
in the field."*

PAGE 333

*"In advance, his
trains were left far
behind. In retreat,
he would fight for
a wheelbarrow."*

LT. GEN. RICHARD
TAYLOR
ON STONEWALL JACKSON

into a stiff wind. His uniform for the first year of the war consisted of battered kepi cap pulled down almost to his nose, the well-worn blue coat of a VMI faculty member, and boots that reached above his knees.

Appearance was deceiving. Jackson swept into war with cool professionalism and complete confidence in himself. Something else was there that molded Jackson into an outstanding general. He reduced his burning faith to military logic. The great national catastrophe that had descended was a trial ordained by God to test the faith of man. Therefore, as Jackson viewed it, the Civil War was a religious crusade to regain the Almighty's favor. Christian faith and the Confederate cause were, for Jackson, one and the same. He proved to be demanding, steel-cold, even pitiless, in the field because he was fighting on the order of Joshua, Gideon, and other commanders of Old Testament fame.

His field dispatches, official reports, and home correspondence all contained references to "the blessings of God" and "an all-wise Providence." At the height of one of his greatest victories, Jackson turned to an aide and exclaimed joyfully: "He who does not see the hand of God in this is blind, sir, blind!"

Appointed a colonel of infantry on April 27, 1861, Jackson's first orders were to return to the Shenandoah Valley and take command of gaudily dressed militia and inexperienced volunteers rendezvousing at Harpers Ferry. The new commander assumed his duties with a stern and heavy hand. Units theretofore accustomed to parades underwent hours of daily drill; incompetent officers were sent home; all liquor in the town was poured into the streets; artillery emplacements and picket posts quickly ringed the area. Jackson taught the ignorant, corrected the errant, and punished the insubordinate. An officer who returned to Harpers Ferry after Jackson took command stated in wonder: "What a revolution three or four days had wrought! I could scarcely realize the change."

In less than a month fresh troops swelled the Confederate garrison to such a size that Gen. Joseph E. Johnston assumed command. Jackson's accomplishments, however, bore personal dividends. On June 17, 1861, he was promoted to brigadier general and given a brigade of five infantry regiments from the Shenandoah Valley. His first duty as a general was to help destroy railroad property at nearby Martinsburg. ("If the cost of the property could only have been expended in disseminating the gospel of the Prince of Peace," Jackson observed.) On July 2 Jackson and one of his regiments easily repulsed a Federal probe near Falling Waters, Virginia.

The most famous nickname in American history came to Jackson and his brigade on July 21 at Manassas. When a Union army moved into Virginia to seize the railroads at Manassas Junction, the forces of Johnston and P. G. T. Beauregard combined to resist the advance. The all-day battle was actually a collision between two armed mobs seeking to become armies. Jackson's brigade was posted back of the crest of Henry House Hill, an eminence that commanded the Confederate left. In early afternoon Federals broke through the first lines of the defenders and swept up the hill in anticipation of victory. Jackson ordered his men to the hilltop. Gen. Barnard E. Bee, seeing the force in position, shouted to his faltering South Carolina troops: "Look, men! There stands Jackson like a stone wall! Rally behind the Virginians!"

Stonewall Jackson's line held fast in hours of vicious combat. A late-afternoon counterattack by fresh Confederate regiments sent exhausted Federals in retreat toward Washington. The South had gained a victory and found a hero.

In the next three months Jackson and his Stonewall Brigade lay quietly encamped near Centreville. Promotion to major general (retroactive to August 7) came with orders in November for Jackson to take command of the defenses of the Shenandoah Valley. He established his headquarters at Winchester, organized his small force, and obtained the use of Gen. W. W. Loring's small Army of the Northwest. On New Year's Day, 1862, Jackson embarked on an expedition to clear Federals from nearby railroad stations and Potomac River crossings. Owing primarily to sleet storms and wretchedly cold weather, the ensuing Romney campaign achieved little but underscored Jackson's always-present determination to strike the enemy.

Jackson returned with his men to Winchester after ordering Loring's troops to remain in the field at Romney. Loring complained to the War Department. Secretary of War Judah P. Benjamin ordered Jackson to recall Loring. Jackson did so and then submitted his resignation from the army because of what he regarded as unwarranted interference with his authority. Governor John Letcher and other friends succeeded in persuading Jackson to remain in command. Secretary Benjamin yielded, and Loring was transferred elsewhere.

This affair demonstrated that like all mortals of unswerving purpose, Jackson was convinced of his own infallible judgment. "Old Jack," as his troops affectionately called him, was nevertheless exceedingly contentious with many of his immediate subordinates. These prickly relationships—with such officers as Gens. Turner Ashby, Richard Brooke Garnett, Charles S. Winder, and A. P. Hill—often marked, and marred, Jackson's career. He was never apologetic about wounding the pride of others. "Through life," Jackson insisted, "let your principal object be the discharge of duty."

His greatest achievement was the 1862 Shenandoah Valley campaign. That spring, Jackson's responsibilities were twofold: to block any Union advance into the valley, and to prevent Federals there and at Fredericksburg from reinforcing George B. McClellan's army moving on Richmond. When Jackson began his offensive, a Federal officer later commented, the Confederate general "began that succession of movements which ended in the complete derangement of the Union plans in Virginia."

Rebuffed at Kernstown on March 23, Jackson retired up the valley. He appeared suddenly at McDowell on May 8 and sent a Federal force in retreat. Then his "foot cavalry" marched rapidly northward down the valley. On May 23, Jackson overpowered the Federal garrison at Front Royal, drove the main Federal army from Winchester two days later, and then fell back when three Federal armies totaling 64,000 soldiers began converging on Jackson's 17,000 Confederates. On June 8 and 9, Jackson inflicted defeats on his pursuers at Cross Keys and Port Republic. He had thwarted every Union effort made against him. He did so through a combination of hard marches, knowledge of terrain, unexpected tactics, singleness of purpose, heavy attacks concentrated at one point, and self-confidence arising from the belief that God was on his side.

Jackson shifted his army to Richmond to assist Robert E. Lee in the counterattack against McClellan. "Old Jack's" role in the Seven Days' Battle was critical and became controversial. He failed to make his expected June 26 arrival at Mechanicsville and the battle that exploded there; he was also late the next day in reaching the field at Gaines' Mill. On June 30, whether from fatigue or lack of directives from Lee, Jackson remained inactive at White Oak Swamp while conflict raged a few miles away at Frayser's Farm. It was a less-than-sterling performance by the general who had brilliantly whipped Union armies in the Shenandoah Valley.

Thereafter, Jackson won new laurels with every engagement he fought. On August 9, at Cedar Mountain, he defeated the vanguard of Gen. John Pope's army. Later that month, Jackson executed the flank movement for which he became both feared and famed. He swung his men almost sixty miles around Pope's right, captured the main Federal supply depot in the rear of Pope's army, launched an attack of his own at Groveton, and then held off Pope's army at Second Manassas until Lee's forces arrived and sent the Union forces reeling in defeat. In Lee's Maryland campaign the following month, Jackson's troops overwhelmed the large Federal garrison at Harpers Ferry before rejoining Lee's army for the Battle of Sharpsburg. Jackson successfully withstood heavy Federal assaults

GEN. "STONEWALL" JACKSON TIMELINE

1824, January 21
Born Clarksburg, Virginia. His father died when Thomas was two, and he was raised by relatives.

1846
Graduated from U.S. Military Academy, West Point, NY. Received commission in the artillery.

1847
During the Mexican War he received two brevets for bravery at the battles of Contreras and Chapultepec.

1851
Resigned from the army to accept a position at Virginia Military Institute (VMI), teaching artillery tactics.

1859
Commanded VMI cadets acting as guards during the hanging of John Brown at Charles Town, Virginia.

1861, April
Led a company of VMI cadets to Richmond, where they acted as drill instructors for the new volunteers. He was appointed Brigadeer General and was sent to Harpers Ferry to organize troops.

1861, June
Led a brigade at First Bull Run (Manassas). He attained his nickname for his stubborn defense of Henry House Hill.

1862, Spring
Took part in the Shenandoah Valley Campaign, where men under his command captured the Union garrison at Harpers Ferry, the largest surrender of U.S. troops until World War II.

1862, December
Led a brigade at Battle of Fredericksburg, where his men easily repulsed Union attack.

1863, May 2
Accidently shot by his own troops, he died eight days later. He was the most famous martyr of the Southern Confederacy.

"There is Jackson standing like a stone wall. Let us determine to die here, and we will conquer."

GEN. BARNARD
E. BEE
ON JACKSON'S BRIGADE AT
FIRST MANASSAS, 1861

"Colonel Walker, did it ever occur to you that General Jackson is crazy?"

RICHARD S. EWELL

throughout that morning and gave affirmation to the nickname "Stonewall."

Reorganization of the Army of Northern Virginia came in the autumn. On October 10, 1862, Jackson was appointed lieutenant general and placed in command of

*"I know not how
to replace him."*

ROBERT E. LEE
AT STONEWALL JACKSON'S
FUNERAL

half of Lee's forces. Jackson spent weeks polishing his corps: reshuffling officers, replenishing men and supplies, and personally seeing that religious services, Bibles, and tracts were present in the ranks. A widening disagreement with one of his division commanders, A. P. Hill, overshadowed much of that period.

Jackson's forces repulsed with comparative ease a major Federal assault at the December Battle of Fredericksburg. Four months of inactivity followed, in which Jackson oversaw the preparation of his 1862 battle reports, worked hard at enkindling a deeper religious spirit in his soldiers, and knew genuine happiness when Anna Jackson visited her husband with the five-month-old daughter he had not seen.

Spring 1863 brought a new advance from the Federal army. In the tangled confusion of the Virginia Wilderness, Jackson performed his most spectacular flanking movement. A twelve-mile circuitous march brought Jackson and 28,000 men opposite Gen. Joseph Hooker's unprotected right. Late in the afternoon of May 2, Jackson unleashed his divisions in an attack that drove routed Federals some two miles, before darkness brought the battle to a standstill. Jackson was anxious to continue pressing forward. For the only time in the Civil War, he rode out to make a personal reconnaissance of the enemy's position. He was returning through thick woods to his own lines when Confederates mistook the general and his staff for Union cavalry and opened fire.

Three bullets struck Jackson. One shattered the bone in his left arm below the shoulder. Following amputation of the limb, Jackson was taken to the railhead at Guiney's Station for possible transfer to a Richmond hospital. Pneumonia rapidly developed. Jackson had always expressed a desire to die on the Sabbath. Around 3:15 on Sunday afternoon, May 10, 1863, he passed away quietly after saying: "Let us cross over the river and rest under the shade of the trees."

The general is buried beneath his statue, the centerpiece in Stonewall Jackson Cemetery, Lexington, Virginia.

[*See also* Loring-Jackson Incident.]

— JAMES I. ROBERTSON, JR.

*Buchanan took
Virginia into
Hampton Roads
on March 8, 1862,
to attack the
Federal squadron
there.*

PAGE 78

JAMES RIVER
SQUADRON

Created in the spring of 1862, the James River Squadron served as a crucial part of the Confederate defenses on the James River below Richmond until its vessels were destroyed by their own crews in the spring of 1865.

Aware of the possibility of a Federal attack up the James River, the Confederates built a number of shore batteries along the river and supplemented them with several small civilian steamers converted into gunboats. The first of these was the gunboat *Patrick Henry*, a former river steamer commanded by Capt. John R. Tucker. Added later was the former screw-tug *Teaser*, armed with a single 32-pound gun. In early 1862, with the ironclad CSS *Virginia* nearing completion, Secretary of the Navy Stephen R. Mallory combined the vessels on the James River to form the James River Squadron commanded by Flag Officer Franklin Buchanan aboard *Virginia*. Buchanan's squadron was supplemented by the addition of the wooden gunboats *Jamestown*, *Raleigh*, and *Beaufort*, which escaped to the James River after the Federal capture of Roanoke Island in the Carolina sounds. The unarmored vessels supported *Virginia* during its epic struggle with USS *Monitor*. In May, after the Confederates were forced to abandon Norfolk and scuttle *Virginia*, the remaining vessels took refuge above the batteries and river obstructions at Drewry's Bluff. Several were stripped of their armament for additional shore batteries. The remaining gunboats joined the shore batteries in repelling a Union foray up the river on May 15, 1862.

Aside from minor raiding sorties, the squadron participated in no major operations during the rest of 1862 or 1863. Capt. French Forrest, former Confederate commander of the Gosport Navy Yard, succeeded Buchanan as squadron commander and played a role in having *Patrick Henry* turned into the home of the Confederate Naval Academy in October 1863. Although the Federals captured *Teaser* in late 1862, the strength of the squadron was increased by the addition in 1862 of the ironclad *Richmond* and in 1863 the ironclads *Fredericksburg* and *Virginia II*. Like *Richmond*, these newer ironclads were shallow-draft, casemated vessels. They mounted four guns in varying calibers and configurations, but typically two of these were large-shell guns and two were large-caliber rifled pieces. Along with the ironclads, the wooden gunboats *Nansemond*, *Hampton*, and *Drewry* and the small steam launches *Torpedo*, *Scorpion*, *Wasp*, and *Hornet* had joined the squadron by the start of 1864. The gunboats were armed with a variety of cannons, but the launches had only a single spar torpedo apiece for armament.

With a nucleus of three strong ironclads, the James River Squadron was the most powerful group of vessels ever assembled by the Confederacy. Disappointed by Forrest's apparent lack of initiative, Mallory replaced him with Commdr. John K. Mitchell in January 1864. By this time, however, the Federals had effectively blocked the river just above

THE REBEL IRON-CLAD FLEET FORCING THE OBSTRUCTIONS IN JAMES RIVER.—[SKETCHED BY A. R. WAUD.]

IRONCLAD FLEET

The shallow-draft ironclads Fredericksburg, Richmond, *and* Virginia *are shown forcing obstructions in the James River on Jan. 23, 1865.*

NAVAL HISTORICAL CENTER, WASHINGTON, D.C.

City Point with a combination of submersible mines and sunken hulks. Led by the ironclads, Mitchell's squadron fought a series of engagements in the summer of 1864, driving off Union working parties and assisting in the defense of shore installations. When flooding carried away some of the river obstructions in January 1865, Mitchell seized the chance to attack the Federal supply city at City Point. In the darkness, though, both *Virginia II* and *Richmond* ran aground and came under fire from Union shore batteries. Supported by the wooden gunboats and *Fredericksburg,* the stranded vessels eventually got free. *Virginia II,* however, was damaged, and the small gunboat *Drewry* was blown up after being abandoned by its crew. Mitchell's foray thus failed, as did a bold attempt in early February to put the small launches on wheels and move them overland to attack the Union ships at City Point.

On February 18, 1865, Rear Adm. Raphael Semmes, former captain of *Alabama,* took command of the squadron. Morale was low. Many officers and men served as gunners ashore. Semmes and the squadron were powerless to prevent the fall of Richmond, and on April 3 he ordered the ships scuttled to prevent capture. With the remaining crewmen, Semmes fled inland to Danville, Virginia. There the remnant of the James River Squadron dissolved on May 1 after receiving word of the surrender of Gen. Joseph E. Johnston. Among the last to surrender were the naval cadets of *Patrick Henry.* After serving as guards of the final gold supply of the Confederacy, the young officers were given forty dollars a piece and sent home.

[*See also entries on the ship* Virginia.]

— ROBERT S. BROWNING III

JOHNSON, ANDREW

Johnson, Andrew (1808–1875), military governor of Tennessee, and vice president and president of the United States. Johnson, the only member of the U.S. Senate from a seceding state to remain loyal to the Union, was born the son of a Raleigh, North Carolina, innkeeper whose death left the family in poverty. Bound out as an apprentice tailor, Johnson learned his trade and the rudiments of reading and writing at the shop. He broke his apprenticeship articles after three years, ultimately settling in Greeneville, Tennessee, where he practiced his trade and became active in local politics. Between 1829 and 1842 Johnson served as alderman and then mayor of Greeneville and as a state legislator. From 1843 to 1853 he served in Congress.

Johnson cultivated a reputation as a radical Democratic representative of the workingmen, artisans, and small farmers who predominated in the hilly country of eastern Tennessee. As he sought statewide office, however, Johnson became a strong advocate of the rights of slaveholders in the Union. A united Democratic party elected him governor for two terms (1853–1857) and then to the U.S. Senate in 1857, where he took a firm

Semmes's objective was to draw U.S. warships from blockade duty by sinking U.S. merchant ships.

PAGE 530

proslavery stand. In the presidential election of 1860 he supported the Breckinridge-Lane ticket of the proslavery wing of the Democratic party. Nonetheless, Johnson was not comfortable in the extreme proslavery camp. He did not agree that a state had a constitutional right to secede, and it would become clear that he bore a powerful emotional attachment to the Union.

When the states of the Deep South began to secede after the election of Abraham Lincoln to the presidency, Johnson took a much firmer pro-Union stand than most upper South and border-state congressmen. As Southern senators resigned their seats, he assailed them and was bitterly denounced in return. His course was controversial in Tennessee, where he emerged as the leading Unionist, but it made him a hero in the North and gave him a national reputation.

Johnson defeated his state's secessionists at first, but he could not dam the wave of secessionism that swept Tennessee after the firing on Fort Sumter and Lincoln's call for troops. Johnson was driven from Tennessee and took an active role in devising war measures in the Senate.

By 1862 Union forces had occupied Nashville and surrounding areas of central Tennessee. Hoping to make the state an example that would undermine support for the Confederacy among reluctant secessionists, Lincoln designated Johnson a brigadier general of volunteers and appointed him military governor of the state, with instructions to establish a loyal civil government to take its place in the Union.

Johnson immediately set to work creating a political organization to serve as a vehicle for restoration, but a variety of factors frustrated his efforts. Unlike eastern Tennessee, central Tennessee was firmly secessionist. The few Unionists were conservative Whigs, deeply committed to slavery and suspicious of the radically

Democratic Johnson. Only after sullen resistance did central Tennesseans obey orders requiring all who had aided the rebellion to take oaths of loyalty or to promise to desist from disloyal action. Despite eastern Tennessee's strategic importance, Johnson was unable to persuade the Union military commanders in Tennessee to secure a political base for loyalism by liberating his home region. Nor could he get Lincoln or the War Department to intercede. The commanders proved unwilling even to commit the resources necessary to make Nashville itself secure militarily. Few people were willing openly to espouse Unionism when Confederate troops might return at any time. Moreover, the commanders refused to recognize Johnson's final authority over matters of civil government, insisting that they retain ultimate control of law enforcement and other matters of military concern. Bickering took up a good deal of Johnson's energy.

The uncertain future of slavery also inhibited the establishment of a Unionist political organization. Johnson himself had defended slavery, and he doubted he could secure much support for antislavery Unionism in Tennessee. When runaway slaves gathered around the Union military encampments in Tennessee, Johnson favored using them as military laborers but opposed organizing them as fighting units. But proslavery Unionists turned out to be lukewarm in their condemnation of disloyalty and reluctant to act to restore loyal government. Johnson gravitated toward more radical Unionists, who began to attack slavery and to demand that only ardent Unionists participate in the restoration process. After Lincoln issued the preliminary Emancipation Proclamation in the fall of 1862, Johnson endorsed emancipation in Tennessee and the recruitment of African Americans as soldiers. With this, conservative Unionists repudiated both Johnson and Lincoln. The divisions among Unionists, who probably remained a minority in central Tennessee, rendered establishment of a Unionist government impossible.

In December 1863 Lincoln took reconstruction matters into his own hands, promulgating proclamations offering amnesty to Southerners who took an oath of loyalty and outlining a procedure whereby they could restore civil governments whenever their number equaled 10 percent of the 1860 presidential electorate in their states. Lincoln's proclamations galvanized Johnson into action, but he insisted upon a more rigorous oath and a more limited electorate. As a result his efforts sputtered once more.

As he attempted to restore Tennessee's state government on a radical basis, Johnson also undertook extensive speaking tours in the North to help Union election campaigns. He proved a popular political attraction and reconfirmed his position as the leading Unionist of the South. As such, and because he was more radical than Lincoln and a Democrat, Johnson seemed an ideal running mate for Lincoln in 1864. The party convention nominated him in June, and he was elected in November.

Johnson was determined to complete restoration of the state government before ascending to the vice presidency in March 1865. An irregularly chosen constitutional convention met in January and proposed amendments to the state constitution that abolished slavery and made key state offices appointive by the governor. These were to be submitted to the people for ratification, with election of a governor and state legislature to follow. On February 22, 1865, 25,000 voters—compared to 145,000 who had voted in the 1860 presidential election—ratified the amendments almost unanimously. Johnson resigned his military commission and governorship on March 3, 1865, and was inaugurated vice president of the United States the following day.

Johnson succeeded to the presidency upon the death of Lincoln on April 15, 1865. As president he undertook a more lenient program of Reconstruction than he had followed as military governor. Where Lincoln had not already appointed provisional governors, Johnson issued proclamations doing so. The governors were to appoint temporary state officials and to recommend persons for appointment to Federal offices. They were to call constitutional conventions, insisting only on the abolition of slavery, nullification of ordinances of secession, and repudiation of Southern war debts. By an amnesty proclamation Johnson pardoned nearly all Confederates who would take a loyalty oath. Pardoned Confederates were permitted to participate in the Reconstruction process and often took leading roles in the reestablished governments.

As president Johnson opposed extending voting privileges to black Americans, vetoed Federal legislation to protect their civil rights, and worked to defeat the Fourteenth and Fifteenth Amendments to the Constitution. The bitter conflict Johnson's course engendered with the Republican-controlled Congress led to his impeachment in 1868. He was acquitted by one vote and served out his term, retiring in 1869. In 1875 he was again elected senator from Tennessee, but he died the same year.

— MICHAEL LES BENEDICT

JOHNSON,

BRADLEY TYLER

Johnson, Bradley Tyler (1829–1903), brigadier general. Johnson graduated from Princeton University in

1849 and was admitted to the Maryland bar in 1851. A leader in the state Democratic party, Johnson fervently worked for self-determination in Maryland. His sense of honor and devotion to his state led him to form a militia company in his hometown of Frederick, Maryland, which became part of the First

STONEWALL'S MAN

Col. Bradley Tyler Johnson of Maryland fought at First Manassas and served under Stonewall Jackson during the 1862 Shenandoah Valley campaign.

NATIONAL ARCHIVES

Maryland Infantry. Johnson was elected major and later was promoted to lieutenant colonel (July 1861) and to colonel (March 1862). The First Maryland fought at First Manassas, served under Gen. Thomas J. ("Stonewall") Jackson during the 1862 Shenandoah Valley campaign, and participated in the Seven Days' Battles. In August 1862 the unit was mustered out of service, and Johnson joined the staff of Stonewall Jackson.

Johnson was assigned temporary command of Gen. John Robert Jones's brigade during Second Manassas and acted as provost marshal of Frederick in the Sharpsburg campaign. He next served on a military court in Richmond. In November 1863 Johnson assumed command of the Maryland Line and in June of the next year was promoted to brigadier general to replace Gen. William E. ("Grumble") Jones, who was killed in the Battle of Piedmont. In Gen. Jubal Early's raid on Washington in July 1864, Johnson led an aborted attempt to liberate Confederate prisoners at Point Lookout, Maryland. Johnson and Gen. John McCausland led the raid on Chambersburg, carrying out Early's orders to burn the town. After Johnson's brigade was routed at Moorefield, West Virginia, in August, he and McCausland disputed responsibility for the disaster. Johnson requested a court of inquiry, but none was ever convened. Johnson's brigade participated in the 1864 Shenandoah Valley campaign, and in November he was relegated to command a prison at Salisbury, North Carolina, where he served until the close of the war.

After the war Johnson practiced law in Richmond and served in the Virginia state senate. He wrote and spoke frequently on the war, demonstrating his eloquence, humor, and passion for the South. Johnson died at Amelia, Virginia, and is buried in Loudon Park Cemetery, Baltimore.

— JOHN E. OLSON

President Davis sent Johnston to command all Confederate forces between the Appalachians and the Ozarks, except the Gulf coast.

PAGE 32

"We shall attack at daylight tomorrow. I would fight them if they were a million."

ALBERT SIDNEY
JOHNSTON
SHILOH, 1862

JOHNSTON, ALBERT SIDNEY

Johnston, Albert Sidney (1803–1862), general. Johnston, a distinguished soldier of three republics, was born on February 2, 1803, in Washington, Kentucky, and was educated in private schools and at Transylvania University. He graduated from the United States Military Academy in 1826, standing eighth in his class.

Johnston had an unusually versatile military career. He served in the Black Hawk War as adjutant to the commanding general, as senior general, and, later, as secretary of war of the Republic of Texas, as a staff officer in the Battle of Monterrey in the Mexican War, as paymaster of U.S. troops stationed in the frontier forts of Texas, as colonel of the elite Second Cavalry Regiment, and as the commander of the U.S. force sent to quell the incipient Mormon rebellion in the Utah Territory.

Upon the secession of his adopted state, Texas, Johnston resigned his U.S. commission and joined the Confederacy. His former fellow cadet and now close friend, Jefferson Davis, immediately appointed him a full general in the army of the Confederacy and placed him in command of the western theater of operations. Heavily outnumbered and indecisive in his early moves, Johnston lost Forts Henry and Donelson in February 1862 to a Federal offensive led by Brig. Gen. Ulysses S. Grant, thereby opening the region to Union penetration along the Tennessee and Cumberland rivers. But Johnston redeemed himself two months later by concentrating his forces at Corinth, an important rail center in northern Mississippi, and surprising Grant in the Battle of Shiloh, April 6 and 7. Johnston was killed the first day of the engagement while his lines were still advancing. He was buried in the Texas State Cemetery in Austin.

— CHARLES P. ROLAND

JOHNSTON, JOSEPH E.

Johnston, Joseph E. (1807–1891), general. Johnston was the son of Peter Johnston, a distinguished soldier in the command of "Light-Horse Harry" Lee in the War for Independence. From this association came a long friendship between the two veterans' sons— Joseph E. Johnston and Robert E. Lee.

Joseph Eggleston Johnston was born February 3, 1807. When he was four the family moved from Prince Edward County, Virginia, to the southwestern part of the state, near Abingdon, where Peter Johnston was a circuit judge. Both the new location and the family's kinships gave young Joseph ties to what was to become a powerful, informal network of prominent Confederates called the "Abingdon bloc."

Johnston graduated from the U.S. Military Academy in 1829, thirteenth in a forty-six-man class. His friend Robert E. Lee stood second. For most of the rest of his life Johnston would place behind Lee, and there are hints that, despite their friendship, Johnston experienced twinges of jealousy toward his more distinguished classmate.

Except for a few months when he was employed as a civil engineer, Johnston remained in the service until he resigned in 1861 to join the Confederacy. Johnston's story for those thirty-two years was the usual one of a career military officer whose assignments took him from New York to Florida to Mexico. Meanwhile, he steadily made his way up through the grades of the army's hierarchy while acquiring a reputation as a brave, competent officer. Commissioned into the Fourth Artillery as second lieutenant in 1829, Johnston served in the Mexican War and was named lieutenant colonel of the First Cavalry in 1855. Wounded in the wars against the Seminole Indians in Florida and in the Mexican War, he won frequent praise for heroism.

In 1860 Johnston's career took an upward turn when the position of quartermaster general of the army became vacant. Johnston was selected for the coveted post, which carried with it promotion to the staff grade of brigadier general. He was now both a brigadier general (staff grade) and a lieutenant colonel (permanent grade). For once, he had surpassed Lee, who remained a lieutenant colonel. On April 22, 1861, Johnston resigned to go with Virginia into the Confederacy.

When Johnston reached Richmond, he found Robert E. Lee a major general in command of the state army. The governor named Johnston to the same grade. Soon, however, the state decided that it needed but one major general, and Johnston was reduced to brigadier general.

Displeased with his demotion in the state army, Johnston transferred to Confederate service as a brigadier general (then the highest grade in that army).

Johnston was sent to command the Southern forces gathering at Harpers Ferry, Virginia. He was to organize and train the troops and defend the town. Almost immediately, however, Johnston concluded that Harpers Ferry could not be held. After a brief squabble with the government, he evacuated the town and fell back to Winchester.

In July Johnston took his army to reinforce the Confederates at Manassas. There, in the first great battle of the war, the South won a victory. As the senior officer present, Johnston commanded the victors, and after the battle, he remained in command of all Confederate troops in the area.

In September Johnston fell into a row with the Southern government about his rank. He and four other officers had been named to the new grade of full general. Confederate law stipulated that former army officers joining the Confederacy would be ranked within each grade by the relative rank they had held in the U.S. Army. Johnston believed he would be ranked by his staff grade of brigadier general and would therefore be the highest-ranking Confederate officer. To his dismay, he found himself ranked fourth, after Samuel Cooper, Albert Sidney Johnston, and Lee.

President Jefferson Davis later justified the placement on the grounds that Johnston was ranked by his permanent grade of lieutenant colonel, not by his staff grade of brigadier general. The reasons for Davis's decision are unknown. Some historians have speculated that Davis and Johnston had long been personal enemies or that their wives had engaged in a dispute of some sort. Others have argued that Davis had supported another candidate for the quartermaster general vacancy in 1860 and used the matter of Confederate rank to strike back at Johnston. It is also possible that Davis simply distrusted Johnston's abilities and wanted to make sure that he would never exercise command over Albert Sidney Johnston or Lee.

Whatever the reason for this action, Davis's decision was unfair to Johnston and probably illegal. Cooper was ranked by his staff grade. (Cooper, however, was in a staff position in both armies; the others were in command of troops in the Southern army.) Fair and legal or not, Davis's decision stood. It was wise because it meant that Johnston would never be in position to hamper Lee. The real problem, of course, was that Confederate law made no provision for the different types of grade that existed in the U.S. Army.

Throughout the winter of 1861–1862 Johnston carried on an increasingly bitter correspondence with Davis and other officials about his rank, the organization and supply of his army, and the general war policy that the Confederacy should follow. As the differences between the general and the president grew more heated, many of Davis's political and mili-

IN LEE'S SHADOW

Long a rival with Robert E. Lee, Gen. Joseph E. Johnston fought with Jefferson Davis over his ranking, resisted directions, and lost the president's confidence.

NATIONAL ARCHIVES

tary enemies realized that Johnston made a good point man for their attacks on the administration. Increasingly Johnston became identified with the opponents of the president. At the same time Davis began to lose whatever confidence he had in Johnston's ability to handle an army.

On May 31, 1862, at the Battle of Seven Pines, Johnston was seriously wounded. Because he would be incapacitated for some months, Davis on June 1 named Lee to take his place. Lee soon won such a string of victories that there would never be a question of any other officer commanding the main army in Virginia.

Johnston was able to return to duty in November. By then the South had suffered several disasters in the area between the Appalachian Mountains and the Mississippi River, then known as "the West." Davis decided to send Johnston to the West as an overall commander for Confederate forces in Tennessee and Mississippi. The president hoped that Johnston would be able to coordinate those two armies and, by transferring troops from one to the other, combine their resources to defeat a Union threat to either.

Unfortunately for the Southerners, the Federals were strong enough to mount simultaneous operations against more than one point, and the Confederates were usually unable to ascertain what their enemy was doing. Johnston lacked faith in Davis's scheme to shift troops around to defeat the enemy, and he was unwilling to assume responsibility for ordering such movements. Instead, Johnston offered the impracticable proposal of shifting troops from west of the Mississippi to help defend Vicksburg.

All through May and June 1864, Johnston sought a position in which he could block the Federal advance into Georgia.

PAGE 36

The result was a disaster for the South. By mid-May one Confederate army was cooped up in Vicksburg and was slowly being starved into surrender. Davis ordered Johnston to Mississippi to assume personal command of the effort to raise the siege. Johnston was either unable or unwilling to take any meaningful action, and on July 4 the city and its army surrendered.

From the Confederate point of view the Vicksburg campaign was a debacle from start to finish. As soon as it was over, Davis and Johnston fell into an unseemly squabble over who was responsible for the loss of the city, its army, and enormous quantities of invaluable railroad equipment. Johnston, his wife, his staff officers, and his political and military friends exchanged letters among themselves in which they expressed the belief that Davis's hatred for Johnston had become so great that the president would do anything to disgrace him. It is hard to escape the belief that the Johnston coterie was becoming at least mildly paranoid about the government's attitude toward the general. Johnston also made available to Davis's critics, such as Senator Louis T. Wigfall, information about the campaign that they were able to use in their attacks on the president.

For several months after the loss of Vicksburg, Johnston was in what amounted to exile in Mississippi. There Davis doubtless would have been glad for him to remain. In December 1863, however, Davis had to find a new commander for the Army of Tennessee, the Confederates' major military force in the West. After considering several alternatives, he had to name Johnston to the post because there was no better choice. At the end of the year Johnston reached Dalton, Georgia, and assumed his new command.

By May 1864 Johnston had done a creditable job of rebuilding the strength and morale of the Army of Tennessee. The old mistrust of the government remained, however, and he and the Richmond authorities were never able to agree on a plan for the summer's campaign. Davis wanted Johnston to advance and reestablish Confederate control over Tennessee. Johnston thought he was not strong enough for such an offensive move. Johnston also believed that Davis was withholding supplies and reinforcements. He would not tell the government what he intended to do, and he constantly complained about whatever suggestions were made to him.

When the Federals advanced against Johnston at Dalton, he was unable to hold his position and fell back into the heart of Georgia. By mid-July, Johnston had backed his army south to Atlanta. He had lost more than twenty thousand men, given up valuable territory in North Georgia, abandoned the right bank of the Chattahoochee River (thereby exposing the great Confederate industrial complex in central Alabama), demoralized many of his soldiers, and thrown some Southern political figures into a near panic. The government was still in ignorance of whatever plans he may have had to defend Atlanta.

In mid-July Davis, his patience finally exhausted, removed Johnston from command of the army and replaced him with Gen. John Bell Hood. Johnston, with a small group of loyal officers, retired to Macon, Georgia. For seven months he and his wife traveled about the fast-shrinking Confederacy while his political allies continued their assaults on the Davis administration for its handling of the war in general and its treatment of Johnston in particular.

In February 1865 Davis recalled Johnston to active service—mostly at the request of Lee, who had been named general-in-chief of the Confederate armies. Johnston was ordered to assume command of troops in the Carolinas and halt the advance of a Union force that had marched across Georgia and was heading north toward Virginia. The effort was hopeless, and on April 26 in North Carolina, Johnston surrendered his army.

In the years after the war Johnston lived in Virginia, Alabama, and Washington, D.C. He worked in the transportation ("express") business, as a railroad president, and later as a commissioner of railroads. From 1879 to 1881 he served in the U.S. House of Representatives from Virginia. He devoted much of his time and energy to writing. His chief work, *Narrative of Military Operations Directed during the Late War between the States,* was published in 1874. Like almost all Civil War generals' memoirs, it is self-serving and presents a one-sided view of events. Johnston died on March 21, 1891. He was buried in Baltimore.

Johnston's reputation has probably changed more drastically than that of any other Confederate general. For decades historians who based their work on postwar memoirs praised his military abilities. Recent writers, using more reliable sources, have revised that opinion, and as a result his reputation has precipitously declined.

— RICHARD M. MCMURRY

JONES, CATESBY

Jones, Catesby (1821–1877), naval officer. Born April 15, 1821, in Fairfield, Virginia, Catesby ap Roger Jones entered the U.S. Navy as a midshipman in 1836. He was promoted to lieutenant in 1849 and remained in that rank until he left the service in 1861. His career in the U.S. Navy was characterized by the normal ship-to-shore rotation. In the 1850s he worked with Lt. John A. Dahlgren in experiments with naval ordnance. This experience would result in his appointment to similar work in the Confederate navy.

Upon the secession of Virginia, Jones resigned his commission and was appointed a captain in the Virginia State Navy. On June 10, 1861, he was commissioned a lieutenant in the Confederate navy and assigned to command naval batteries on Jamestown Island. Jones's experiments with the effect of naval gunfire on sloping iron armor led to his appointment as executive officer of the ironclad CSS *Virginia*. As second in command he participated in the March 8, 1862, engagement in which USS *Cumberland* and *Congress* were destroyed by *Virginia*. When Capt. Franklin Buchanan was wounded, Jones assumed the command and was in charge the following day when the Confederate armorclad fought USS *Monitor*. He resumed the position of executive officer when Buchanan's replacement took command.

After the destruction of *Virginia* in early May 1862, Jones commanded, successively, river batteries at Drewry's Bluff on the James River near Richmond, the wooden gunboat *Chattahoochee* on the Chattahoochee River near Columbus, Georgia, and the naval ordnance works at Charlotte, North Carolina. On May 9, 1863, he was ordered to take charge of the Confederate Naval Iron Works at Selma, Alabama. Under his direction this facility cast more than a hundred large naval guns. Jones commanded the ironworks until they were captured by Union forces on April 2, 1865.

After the war Jones established residence in Selma and formed a partnership with John M. Brooke and Robert D. Minor, fellow Confederate naval officers, to purchase war supplies in the United States for foreign governments. The company was never successful despite extensive travel by Jones in the United States and a trip to Peru. On June 20, 1877, Jones died after being shot by a neighbor over a quarrel between their children.

Jones was highly respected by his peers both in the Confederate and the U.S. navies. Adm. David Dixon Porter remarked after the war that he had regretted the loss of only two officers from Union service, Jones and Brooke.

— WILLIAM N. STILL, JR.

JONES, J. B.

Jones, J. B. (1810–1866), writer. Born in Baltimore on March 6, 1810, John Beauchamp Jones grew up in Kentucky and Missouri. He became a successful novelist—his *Wild Western Scenes* (1841) sold 100,000 copies—but he achieved greater recognition as a journalist. In the 1840s Jones settled near Philadelphia, where he wrote many novels portraying frontier society and in 1857 established the *Southern Monitor*, a weekly journal that defended Southern rights within the Union.

In *Secession, Coercion and Civil War* (1859), Jones sought to temper the passions of secession, but the Fort Sumter crisis caused him to move to the new Confederate capital at Montgomery. Here he was hired by the War Department as a clerk and began to compose his important diary. "At fifty-one I can hardly follow the pursuit of arms; but I will write and preserve a diary of the revolution. . . . To make my diary full and complete as possible is now my business," he wrote on April 29. He made almost daily entries until April 19, 1865. Early the next year *A Rebel War Clerk's Diary* was published in two volumes—his supreme achievement, the most consulted and quoted primary source for events in wartime Montgomery and Richmond.

Jones's *Diary* presents portraits of Jefferson Davis and other leaders that are among the best contemporary likenesses in Civil War literature. His daily record of activities in the War Office, under five secretaries and numerous bureau chiefs, colonels, and generals, provides much of the inner history of the Confederacy. Also important to social and economic historians are his observations on inflation and the daily prices of necessities; military historians value his faithful reports of weather conditions.

From Jones's pages one can discern the pain and privations of the common people, the self-interest and narrowness of politicians and military men, and the anguish accompanying a failing cause. Using terse, direct language, often colored by anger, stereotypes, and prejudice, Jones is a personal and lively chronicler. He lacks the literary qualities of Mary Boykin Chesnut, however, and the objectivity and deeper perception of Robert Garlick Kean, whose diary, *Inside the Confederate Government*, was published in New York in 1957. Jones's style—tough and combative—masks the fears of a father of a large family eking out survival on a small salary in Richmond's wildly inflationary economy.

With the fall of Richmond Jones moved back to Philadelphia, where he oversaw the publication of his book. In October 1865 he gave testimony in the Henry Wirz trial in Washington, defending the commandant of Andersonville from charges of willful neglect and starvation of Union prisoners of war (and defending the Confederate administration as well). Soon after, he succumbed to declining health and died in Burlington, New Jersey, on February 4, 1866, while the *Diary* was in press. It enjoyed a large publication and has been reprinted, in whole or part, at least three times. A mod-

Lost Cause icons came pouring off the presses in New York, Philadelphia, Boston, and Chicago after 1866.

PAGE 336

ern scholarly edition is a major need of Confederate historiography.

— JOHN O'BRIEN

JUDICIARY

The Confederacy's judicial system was a subject of controversy from the start, and Congress never established in full the system called for by the new nation's constitutions. In a departure from the Federal system, circuit courts were never created. Subsequently, bitter divisions over principle and personalities prevented organization of both a supreme court and a court of claims, which had been planned. The court of claims would have heard lawsuits against the Confederate government in the same way that the U.S. Court of Claims—established in 1855—handled suits against the U.S. government. Nevertheless, a judicial system resting on state courts and Confederate district courts functioned without paralyzing confusion or variances in rulings. State courts, following precedents established in the U.S. system, customarily upheld the powers of the central government.

The judicial clauses of the Provisional Constitution sought to continue cases interrupted by secession by extending judicial powers to all cases in law and equity arising under the laws of the United States. (Most Southern states had both law courts and courts of equity; the latter, following English practice, supplemented law courts by applying general principles of justice in circumstances not covered by the law.) But other features, beyond this practical provision, soon occasioned controversy. The Provisional Constitution called for a single judicial district in each state, which meant that the number of district courts that had existed under the United States was reduced by more than half. This undesirable situation produced the only amendment made to either Confederate constitution, when in May 1861 Congress received the authority to define districts as it deemed appropriate.

The Provisional Constitution also called for a supreme court, and the Judiciary Act of March 16, 1861, envisioned that this high court would exercise appellate jurisdiction over state courts—a disturbing idea to many. The supreme court was to consist of all the district court judges assembled together. Experience in the states had shown that this was not a satisfactory procedure, and observers pointed out that western judges would have difficulty traveling to Richmond in a timely manner. Consequently, on July 31, 1861, Congress suspended the supreme court until it could be organized under the Permanent Constitution.

Battles over the role of the judiciary grew more heated as the Provisional Congress debated a permanent constitution. To radical state rights thinkers in the Congress, the court system had been one of the chief engines of centralization and usurpation under the United States. One senator declared that if John Marshall's abilities had not made the U.S. Supreme Court so powerful, the Union would still be in existence. Questions of state versus Confederate authority presented themselves in almost every clause of the section on the judiciary, and changes adopted for the Permanent Constitution foreshadowed subsequent controversy.

First, state rights radicals, in March 1861, succeeded in eliminating the jurisdiction of Confederate courts over disputes between citizens of different states. Failing in several other limitations of central authority, they attacked the most important point: appellate jurisdiction for the Supreme Court over decisions rendered in state courts. On this point the radicals nearly prevailed, but a divided delegation from Florida denied them a majority, and thus the Permanent Constitution called for a supreme court that was not explicitly restricted and crippled as the state rights men wished. Battles over the nature of the court, however, would continue in the First Congress.

Another change made to Article III of the Provisional Constitution eliminated language giving the Confederate judiciary power over all cases of law and equity. This deletion respected state rights, since Louisiana and Texas operated under the Roman legal tradition, which lacked separate courts of equity. The distinction between law and equity, however, remained for most of the states, and Congress could have given its district courts power over cases of law and equity there. Instead, it eventually prevented them from entering cases of equity wherever "plain, adequate remedy may be had at laws."

The Permanent Constitution called for a court of claims, but Congress never established one. In the absence of that court the executive departments, the Board of Sequestration Commissioners, and the district courts handled the relevant work. Provision was made for a court of admiralty to sit in Key West, but since the Confederacy never controlled that city, the admiralty court never became a reality.

In accordance with the Permanent Constitution, President Jefferson Davis asked the First Congress on February 25, 1862, to establish a supreme court. Although Congress considered the matter in 1862 and 1863, it failed to act. Soon after Davis's request, bills were introduced calling for a supreme court consisting of one chief justice and three associate justices. Senator Benjamin H. Hill of Georgia argued that a government without a supreme court would be "a lame and

The last session of Congress, which began on Nov. 9, 1864, was marked by legislative stalemate.

PAGE 148

Structurally the U.S. and Confederate Constitutions are nearly identical.

PAGE 149

limping affair," but both houses let the matter drop without a vote in 1862. The next year Hill proposed a similar bill, and the conflicts that had stalled consideration came out into the open.

Supporters of a supreme court argued that the nation needed clarity and consistency in its laws and sought to allay concerns that there would be a usurpation of state power within the Confederacy. On that point, however, many legislators—led by men such as Clement C. Clay, William Lowndes Yancey, Louis T. Wigfall, and Robert W. Barnwell—were extremely sensitive. The key question was whether a supreme court would be free to enforce Confederate law as the supreme law of the land. Without appellate jurisdiction over state courts, a supreme court was superfluous, yet appellate jurisdiction seemed likely to Clay to "favor the consolidation of the government." Yancey warned that it would "chain" the states to central authority. According to historian W. Buck Yearns, all but four senators wanted a supreme court, but only six of them were willing to grant the appellate jurisdiction that would make it meaningful.

Politics and personalities also played a role in the battle over a supreme court. With elections approaching in 1863, some congressmen were reluctant to go on record as giving the central government any additional power. Other congressmen thought they knew who would be appointed to the court if it were established, and their opposition to certain individuals became opposition to the court. Tennessee's representative, Henry S. Foote, asserted that he would "never consent to the establishment of a supreme court of the Confederate States so long as Judah P. Benjamin shall continue to pollute the ears of majesty Davis with his insidious counsels." Others feared that Assistant Secretary of War John A. Campbell, a former justice of the U.S. Supreme Court and a very able lawyer, would become chief justice and promote central power in the Confederacy just as John Marshall had done in the United States. In the end, the Senate passed a bill for a watered-down supreme court, but the House let the matter drop, and the Confederacy had to proceed without the highest court called for by its Constitution.

Confederate district courts were organized and judges appointed. Under the Judiciary Act they were instructed to follow state laws and state court practices as well as enforce Confederate laws. But they were often busy with traditional civil and criminal matters and especially with habeas corpus cases involving soldiers seeking to avoid military service. Because the Confederate judicial system was so weak and truncated, it was the state courts that proved to be most influential.

In a striking irony, the Davis administration turned to and relied upon state courts to uphold the powers of the central government. No issue presented the question of central versus state power more sharply or elicited more angry threats from governors than conscription. On this question President Davis and several state governors thoroughly debated the powers of the Confederacy and brought strongly opposed viewpoints into the open. In the absence of a supreme court, Davis took the contested questions into state courts, where Confederate authority was affirmed.

In September 1862 Governor Joseph E. Brown of Georgia thundered against the second conscription act, charging that it struck down Georgia's "sovereignty at a single blow." Brown even declared that "no act of the government of the United States prior to the secession of Georgia" had been so injurious to constitutional liberty, and he obtained resolutions from his legislature to support him. In similar fashion South Carolina's governor and executive council insisted that any man exempted by state law from the militia was also exempt from conscription and threatened to issue a "countervailing order" against any Confederate conscription officer who tried to enroll such individuals.

In response Jefferson Davis was unbending on principle and conciliatory on procedure. He defended the constitutionality of the conscription law at length to Governor Brown, and he bluntly wrote South Carolina's leaders that "if a State may free her citizens at her own discretion from the burden of military duty, she may do the same in regard to the burden of taxation, or any other lawful duty, payment or service." That would deny the Confederacy the right "to enforce the exercise of any delegated power and would render a Confederacy an impracticable form of Government." Yet Davis also promised the Palmetto State's leaders that he would release any soldier whose exemption was upheld by South Carolina courts, and he assured Senator Benjamin Hill that he relied "on the decision of the Supreme Court of Georgia to remove the difficulties."

In these two states, as well as in Virginia, Alabama, Texas, Florida, and Mississippi, President Davis won his tests of the constitutionality of conscription. In Georgia the decision of the state supreme court was unanimous and was greeted by spectators with an outburst of applause that forced the chief justice to call for order. The decision of the Texas Supreme Court declared that the "power to raise and support armies is an express constitutional grant to the Congress of the Confederate States, and there is no limitation as to the mode or manner of exercising it. When Congress calls for the military service of the citizen . . . the right of the State government must cease or yield to the paramount demand of Congress." Thus state courts upheld the supremacy of Confederate law on a vital question and continued to do so. Although individual judges, such as Richmond Pearson of North Carolina, sometimes caused much concern, the South's judicial system

Georgia Gov. Joseph E. Brown could not or would not see the larger picture, and all too often he ignored or rejected the need for Confederate unity.

PAGE 77

The Judiciary Act of March 16, 1861, defined the powers of a supreme court, but its organization was suspended in July 1861.

PAGE 235

proved to be "fragmented in structure but centralized in substance," in the words of historian Emory Thomas.

There were undoubtedly several reasons for this surprising outcome. The facts that the administration's measures were necessary and that opponents offered no alternatives may have had some influence. Perhaps more salient was the fact that the permanent Constitution authorized Congress to "make all laws which shall be necessary and proper for carrying into execution" the powers granted to the national legislature. The power to make war and the power to raise and support armies were among those grants of authority. Even in a confederation whose members were historically jealous of state prerogatives and state sovereignty, the logic of having a central government to wage war against external enemies remained clear.

In addition, the judges who staffed the courts of the Southern states had learned their law in the judicial system of the United States. They, as well as the attorneys general of the Confederate States, referred to past decisions in U.S. history for guidance and often cited decisions of U.S. courts as precedents. Although Southern jurists may have believed that the Federal government had usurped state authority, they were not unfamiliar with the idea of a central government supreme in its defined sphere. The crisis of war surely called out for such a government in the South. It was fortunate for the Confederacy that the absence of a supreme court did not greatly multiply the problems under which it already labored.

[*See also* State Rights.]

— PAUL D. ESCOTT

JUNETEENTH

June 19 (or "Juneteenth") is observed by African Americans in Texas to commemorate the official emancipa-tion of slaves in the Lone Star State following the end of the Civil War.

Although Gen. Robert E. Lee capitulated to Gen. Ulysses S. Grant at Appomattox Courthouse on April 9, 1865, the Trans-Mississippi Department did not surrender until June 2, and a shortage of transport vessels delayed for over two weeks the arrival of Union forces in Texas. On June 19, 1865, Gen. Gordon Granger landed in Galveston and proclaimed the freedom of the state's slaves. Subsequently, African Americans in Texas have celebrated June 19 annually as their true emancipation day.

During the late nineteenth century, the typical Juneteenth celebration was a day-long event commencing with a parade complete with brass bands and representatives of the leading African American churches, fraternal orders, and social clubs. A barbecue, speeches, sporting events, and dancing (sometimes concluding with an evening ball) would follow.

Although the popularity of the celebration diminished after World War II, it never completely died out. Employers complained that many of their African American employees used Juneteenth as an excuse to take the day off, and some civil rights activists preferred that their constituents pay more attention to contemporary efforts to gain full equality. The growing interest in African American history during the late 1960s and early 1970s fueled public recognition for Juneteenth commemorations. In 1972 the Texas legislature passed a resolution proclaiming June 19 to be a "holiday of significance to all Texans and, particularly, to the blacks of Texas." As such, this event fosters community spirit among blacks and also serves as a source for racial interaction in communities throughout the state.

— JAMES M. SORELLE

KANSAS-NEBRASKA ACT

In 1854, Congress passed the Kansas-Nebraska Act, repealing part of the 1820 Missouri Compromise. That previously sacrosanct agreement had divided Federal territories acquired in the Louisiana Purchase (1803) at the 36°30´ geographic line, with slavery permitted southward (including south of the slave state of Missouri) but prohibited northward (including west and north of Missouri) whenever Congress authorized settlement of these areas. In 1824, Illinois, to Missouri's east and outside the Louisiana Purchase area, banned slavery after a historic struggle. In 1846, Iowa, carved out of Louisiana Purchase territory to Missouri's north, extended the 36°30´ ban from the territorial to the statehood stage by entering the Union as a free-labor state. If Congress had authorized settlers to enter the Louisiana Purchase territory to Missouri's west without repealing the 36°30´ proscription of slavery, Missouri, with only 10 percent of its population enslaved, would have been guaranteed a third nonslaveholding neighbor.

In 1854, Missouri's very powerful Senator David R. Atchison warned several equally powerful Southern Democrats, living with him in a Washington, D.C., boardinghouse, that slavery in Missouri could not then endure. Its neighbors would both inspire Missouri slaves to flee and stimulate Missouri's 88 percent majority of nonslaveholders to rout the slaveholders. Congress, declared Atchison, must instead repeal the 36°30´ ban when opening the area for settlement. Then, he promised, Missouri slaveholders would seize their western hinterlands and consolidate their regime.

The final form of the Kansas-Nebraska Act, drawn to Atchison's specifications, repealed the Missouri Compromise ban on slavery in Kansas Territory, located west of Missouri, and in Nebraska Territory, located north of Kansas Territory. The majority of settlers in each, decreed Congress, would decide slavery's fate. An area previously reserved for one section was here turned into a prize for the winner of an endurance race, involving which section would send more settlers to the two territories.

Most Northerners loathed having to compete for an area previously declared theirs. Congress nevertheless passed the minority section's law, for first Atchison's boardinghouse mates, then almost all Southern Democrats, and then most Southern Whigs supported the Missourian—and because Northern Democrats could not then defy Southern Democrats. Particularly, Illinois Senator Stephen A. Douglas, the Northern Democrats' congressional leader, wished to open Kansas and Nebraska Territories to settlers, for he wanted whites and railroads to develop the West. He also hoped to win the presidential nomination of a revitalized Democratic party. These objectives required Southern Democrats' support, and the price of their support was legislation that allowed settlers rather than congressmen to determine a locality's institutions—precisely Douglas's popular sovereignty principle. So after Southern Democrats insisted, Douglas made repeal of the Missouri Compromise his cause, as did President Franklin Pierce, another Northern Democrat.

The ensuing law helped inspire the rise of Douglas's Illinois rival, Abraham Lincoln, and more broadly, the rise of the Democratic party's new rival, the Republican party. The Kansas-Nebraska Act also provoked armed combat in what became known as Bleeding Kansas. Although proslavery Missourians reached that pre–Civil War battleground first, more antislavery Northerners ultimately arrived. Yet in 1857 and 1858 Southerners demanded that Douglas support the admission of Kansas into the Union under the Kansas proslavery minority's proposed Lecompton constitution, which protected slavery. When Douglas balked at this defiance of what the majority of Kansans wanted, Southerners blamed him for the congressional decision that rejected the Lecompton constitution. After Douglas won the Democratic party's presidential nomination in 1860, most Southern Democrats seceded from the party. With the Democrats split, the Republican Lincoln won the presidency, and a Southern Confederacy beckoned.

[*See also* Bleeding Kansas.]

— WILLIAM W. FREEHLING

KEITT, LAWRENCE

Keitt, Lawrence (1824–1864), congressman from South Carolina and colonel. Keitt, one of South Car-

The Kansas-Nebraska Act in 1854 turned out to be the first of several Pyrrhic victories for the South.

PAGE 110

The Act drove tens of thousands of angry Northern Democratic voters out of the party and gave birth to the Republican party, which by 1856 had become the second major party in the north.

PAGE 110

The Declaration of Immediate Causes was adopted by the South Carolina secession convention to explain the reasons for the state's withdrawal from the Union.

PAGE 167

olina's most outspoken advocates of secession, was elected to the U.S. House of Representatives in 1852. While in Congress, he twice resigned his seat. In 1856, he accompanied fellow South Carolinian Preston Brooks to the U.S. Senate chamber where Brooks beat Senator Charles Sumner senseless. During the fray,

Keitt used his own cane to keep away others who tried to come to Sumner's defense. A special House committee recommended expelling Brooks and censuring Keitt. When Northern congressmen couldn't muster the votes to expel Brooks, they turned their wrath on Keitt. He was censured and promptly resigned his seat. In a special election, the voters of his district turned out in record numbers and voted overwhelmingly to return him to Congress.

By the summer of 1860, with Abraham Lincoln's election a certainty, Keitt was in the forefront of those calling for South Carolina's secession. Like Robert Barnwell Rhett, Sr., he was strongly radical on the question and had little patience for Cooperationists and none for Unionists. Some have interpreted his behavior as a reaction to the murder of his ill brother by slaves in Florida. His speeches and correspondence do contain numerous references to slave insubordination, plots, and conspiracies.

Keitt was in Columbia when news of Lincoln's election came. He was a popular figure in the state capital and was serenaded by the excited crowds. On at least one occasion, in response to the clamor, he addressed a throng gathered outside his hotel. Elected a delegate to South Carolina's secession convention, he resigned his seat in Congress the day the convention met in Columbia.

In the convention, he remarked that he had "been engaged in this movement" since the day he first embarked on a political career. And when the ordinance of secession was adopted, he said that he was

pleased that the convention had "carried the body of this Union to its last resting place, and now we drop the flag over its grave." When the convention was preparing its "Declaration of the Immediate Causes which Induce and Justify the Secession of South Carolina," Keitt was among those who refused to shy away from the question of slavery as a primary cause. "It is," he said, "the great central point from which we are now proceeding." He was defeated in a bid to be one of the commissioners to confer with the government in Washington over the status of Federal property in South Carolina, but he was elected to be one of the state's eight delegates to the Montgomery convention.

Keitt, like Rhett, found in Montgomery that his reputation had preceded him. For most of his political career he had played a negative role. After years of criticizing the existing central government, he found it difficult to participate in creating a new one for the Confederacy and seldom spoke. According to Alexander H. Stephens, Keitt said his wife had advised him "to keep his mouth shut and his hair brushed." Whether because of his reputation as an obstructionist or his wife's admonition, he played only a modest role in the convention.

Keitt was named to a five-person committee to draft the rules governing the convention. Other than that, his contributions centered on efforts to amend the proposed constitution. He led the South Carolina delegation's attempts to eliminate the three-fifths clause for taxes and representation. South Carolina was willing to pay more taxes (it could well afford to) in return for a larger congressional delegation. Initially, the amendment passed, but later the convention reversed itself and the three-fifths clause remained. He also supported an amendment giving Congress the authority to reopen the slave trade, a measure that was defeated.

In the maneuvering for the presidential election, Keitt and James Chesnut torpedoed Rhett's candidacy. Keitt and W. W. Boyce strongly favored Howell Cobb of Georgia and worked for his election. With persuasion, the South Carolina delegation went for Jefferson Davis, but Boyce and Keitt were openly reluctant. On the evening of the election, a crowd gathered at the Exchange Hotel to serenade Vice President Stephens. He spoke to the jubilant crowd, and then Keitt was called upon to make some remarks. As a radical secessionist he assured the assemblage that the new government was in good hands with Davis and Stephens. Above all else, he noted, the Union was dead!

Back in South Carolina's convention, Keitt argued against ratification of the Confederate Constitution. He was part of a very small minority, however, and when the vote was taken, both he and Rhett were recorded as voting yes.

Upon his return to Montgomery for the second session of the Provisional Congress, Keitt resumed his role as government critic. Later, en route to Richmond with the Chesnuts, he pronounced "Jeff Davis a failure—and his cabinet a farce." Needless to say, it did not take long for these Davis loyalists to spread the word. By July, Richmond gossips were already talking about the "coalition against Davis." Keitt and Boyce were rumored to be among the leaders "of the party forming against Mr. Davis."

Lawrence Keitt was an unhappy man. As one of the earliest and most ardent secessionists, he had expected to become a power broker in the new government. His reputation as something of a Hotspur and his impolitic criticism of Davis doomed him to a minor role at best. Realizing the futility of his situation and dreaming of military glory, the congressman refused to stand for election to the First Congress.

Back home, he raised a regiment of eight hundred men, the Twentieth South Carolina Volunteers. He was elected colonel, and from mid-January to March 1862, he organized and trained the unit. Keitt was excited about being in uniform and wrote glowing letters to his wife, Sue. In June 1862, when John C. Pemberton reorganized the Department of South Carolina, Georgia, and Florida, Keitt was given command of the defenses of Sullivan's Island in Charleston.

Four months later, Davis replaced Pemberton with P. G. T. Beauregard. The new commander enhanced Keitt's command to include the area between the Cooper and South Santee rivers. It was a difficult area to defend. The coast was riven with innumerable inlets, creeks, and tidal marshes. Most of the white population had abandoned the area. Keitt wanted to divide his command to defend several potential invasion sites, but Beauregard ordered him to keep his forces concentrated in the Charleston area. In May and June 1863, the Twentieth South Carolina was chasing Union raiding parties south of the port city.

On July 18, Union troops attacked Fort Wagner on Morris Island. Following the failure of the Fifty-fourth Massachusetts to take the Confederate position, a six-week siege commenced. On August 1, Fort Wagner was added to Keitt's command. He visited the island on several occasions to view the ever more successful Union attempts to breach the works. On September 5, he sent a message to Beauregard from Fort Wagner that the fortifications were no longer tenable. Beauregard told him to hold. The situation was desperate. Union sappers (specialists in field fortifications) were literally at what was left of the walls. Constant shelling kept the defenders in their bombproofs. When they ventured out to try to repair the parapets or get some fresh air, they usually became casualties. On September 6, Keitt wrote, "The retention of the post after to-night involves the sacrifice of the garrison." He added that if he could not withdraw his forces, he intended to assault the enemy at first light the next day. Late in the afternoon, Beauregard agreed to the abandoning of Wagner.

As soon as darkness fell, Keitt began evacuating his men. He remained with the rear guard and was among the last Confederates to leave Morris Island early on the morning of September 7. The withdrawal was done so stealthily that as close as the Union forces were, they did not realize it had taken place. There were only a few glitches. The powder magazines failed to blow up because of faulty fuses, and two barges of men were captured. Nevertheless, it was a successful operation and more than one thousand men were saved for further Confederate service. Beauregard commended him for his actions. With Sullivan's Island now within reach of Federal guns, the Twentieth South Carolina was moved to Mount Pleasant on the mainland opposite the city.

In the fall of 1863, Keitt, who had long dreamed of becoming a general officer, decided to take matters into his own hands. He obtained leave and journeyed to Richmond to press his case in person. He was on a quixotic quest. He had never tempered his early criticism of Davis and continually expressed such sentiments as "to be a patriot, you must hate Davis," or "His [Davis's] imbecility has been as mischievous as treachery." Such comments circulated in government circles and further damaged what was already a lost cause. Nor did Keitt's champions—Major General Pemberton and Congressmen Boyce and Louis T. Wigfall—help matters. All were known Davis critics. In addition, the superintendent of conscription reported that the number one violator of the Conscription Act of 1862 was Col. Lawrence M. Keitt. Keitt accepted volunteers in excess of his unit's authorized strength. This was a clear violation of the law that was designed to raise as many men as possible for front-line units. The South Carolinian tap-danced on this issue and maintained that he had done nothing illegal.

In his meeting with Davis and War Department officials, Keitt agreed to raise a second regiment (this one to be cavalry) in the hopes that this would bring him a star. Back home he found recruiting far more difficult in late 1863 than it had been eighteen months earlier. The promotion was not forthcoming. The president, through channels, always found a reason to say no. Keitt seemed to accept that but was offended that Davis had neither the good manners nor the manly courage to answer him personally.

In May 1864, the Twentieth South Carolina was ordered to Virginia. Twice, Keitt loaded his men on trains only to have his order rescinded and his unit sent to James Island to repel possible Union advances. After

When Keitt became the acting commander of Kershaw's Brigade, the brigade's veterans "felt and saw at a glance" Keitt's "inexperience and want of self-control."

PAGE 312

At the very time news of Brooks's caning of Sen. Sumner reached the North, word came from Kansas that a proslavery mob had attacked free-state advocates' shops and newspapers in Lawrence, Kansas.

PAGE 601

a week of this uncertainty, the tired and exhausted unit boarded railroad cars for the northern front. On May 30, Keitt met with Davis and asked that the Twentieth South Carolina be assigned to Kershaw's Brigade. The president granted his request, and much to his surprise and delight, Keitt found himself the senior colonel in the brigade. As such, he became its acting commander. Keitt was pleased, but the brigade's veterans "felt and saw at a glance" Keitt's "inexperience and want of self-control."

The Army of Northern Virginia was maneuvering near Cold Harbor. On June 1, Keitt was directed to do a reconnaissance of the area along the brigade's front. Instead he formed his entire brigade along an old road. He ordered the line to advance. Astride his iron-gray charger with saber held high, the brigade's acting commander led the charge. The left side of the line broke under Federal shelling. In trying to rally his troops, Keitt was an inviting target for enemy marksmen. Felled by a musket ball in the liver, he lingered a day and died on June 2.

At Cold Harbor, Colonel Keitt's inexperience and impetuousness resulted not only in his own death but also in that of many brave men of Kershaw's Brigade. Historian Douglas S. Freeman singled out Keitt in the introduction to his third volume of *Lee's Lieutenants:* "The competent Generals who escaped bullets and disease were hampered in almost every action by some man who, like Keitt at Cold Harbor, . . . was unable to meet the exactions of the field." It's a scathing indictment of the secessionist who sought glory on the battlefield and found only death.

Keitt's body was returned to South Carolina, and he was buried in Orangeburg during a downpour of rain. There were the usual tributes in the press, but one contemporary source was noticeably silent. Although in South Carolina at the time of Keitt's death, Mary Boykin Chesnut makes no mention of it in her famous diary. Earlier she had written that Keitt was "quick as a flash. No one gets the better of him." And when he was in Richmond in 1863 lobbying for promotion: "Our old tempestuous Keitt breakfasted with us yesterday. I wish I could remember half of the brilliant things he said." "Quick," "tempestuous," "brilliant," are words that capture the spirit of the man who was in the vanguard of the movement to break up the Union. They are a fitting epitaph.

— WALTER B. EDGAR

KEMPER, JAMES LAWSON

Kemper, James Lawson (1823–1895), major general. A native of the Virginia Piedmont, Kemper was born June 11, 1823, in Madison County. He graduated in 1842 from Washington College in Lexington, saw limited service in the Mexican War as a captain of Virginia volunteers, and then established a law practice in his home area. Elected five times to the Virginia General Assembly, Kemper also chaired the state committee on military affairs and was president of the board of visitors of the Virginia Military Institute. In 1861 he resigned as Speaker of the House of Delegates to enter the Confederate army.

Appointed colonel of the Seventh Virginia, he led the regiment from First Manassas through Seven Pines. On June 3, 1862, Kemper received a brigadier's commission and took command of a Virginia brigade formerly led successively by James Longstreet, Richard S. Ewell, and A. P. Hill. That unit became part of George E. Pickett's division. Kemper won praise for gallantry at Second Manassas and Sharpsburg. A man of "solid qualities and sound judgment," he became known for high-flown oratory before and after battles.

On July 3, 1863, Kemper and his troops were on the extreme right in the first line of the Pickett-Pettigrew attack at Gettysburg. Kemper was captured after being shot in the groin. Subsequently exchanged, he was unable to resume field service. Kemper was promoted to major general on September 19, 1864, and commanded Virginia's reserve forces for the remainder of the war.

He resumed his law practice in Madison County, became a postwar orator of renown, and in 1874 was elected governor of Virginia. After his April 7, 1895, death in Orange County (where he is buried), a eulogist said of Kemper: "A Virginian, he loved his State with all the force of an ardent and earnest nature."

— JAMES I. ROBERTSON, JR.

KERSHAW, JOSEPH B.

Kershaw, Joseph B. (1822–1894), major general. Descended from forebears prominent in military and political arenas, Kershaw was born at Camden, South Carolina, January 5, 1822. His grandfather, also named Joseph, had emigrated from England and played an active role as a colonel in the Revolutionary War. His father, John, served several terms as mayor of Camden, was a county judge, a member of the state legislature, and a one-term member of Congress.

Orphaned at seven, Joseph Kershaw attended local schools and the Cokesbury Conference School in the Abbeville District. Leaving after a brief period there, Kershaw went to Charleston where he clerked in a dry goods store. The job paled quickly, and he returned to Camden, read law, and was admitted to the bar in 1843. At the start of the Mexican War Kershaw wore the uniform of a first lieutenant with the DeKalb Rifle Guards of his hometown. His stay in Mexico was cut short by a fever that forced his early return to Camden where he resumed his law practice and was elected to the state legislature in 1852.

Kershaw was a member of his state's secession convention and in February 1861 was elected colonel of the Second South Carolina Infantry, which he had recruited. The regiment occupied Morris Island during the bombardment of Fort Sumter. Kershaw led the regiment at First Manassas as part of Milledge L. Bonham's brigade. Promoted to brigadier general, February 13, 1862, and given command of the brigade following Bonham's resignation, Kershaw fought in the Peninsular campaign and Seven Days' Battles and helped capture Maryland Heights during the reduction of Harpers Ferry. While defending the Sunken Road at Fredericksburg, he displayed "great coolness and skill," in the words of E. Porter Alexander. The South Carolinian also fought with distinction at Chancellorsville. On the second day at Gettysburg, as Lafayette McLaws's division embarked on its assault against Little Round Top, Kershaw appeared "cool, composed and grand, his steel-gray eyes flashing the fire he felt in his soul," wrote D. Augustus Dickens, brigade historian.

Transferred west with James Longstreet in September 1863, Kershaw arrived at Chickamauga in time to help crush the Federal right flank. He also participated in the Knoxville campaign before the corps was recalled to Virginia.

On May 6, 1864, Kershaw was riding with Longstreet and Micah Jenkins through the Wilderness when a mistaken volley from William Mahone's troops across the Plank Road ripped through the group. As his men prepared to return the fire, Kershaw dashed to the head of the column, shouting "They are friends!" His prompt action averted further bloodshed, although Longstreet was severely wounded and Jenkins was killed.

On May 18, shortly after he took part in the Battle of Spotsylvania, Kershaw was promoted to major general. He joined Jubal Early in the Shenandoah Valley campaign of 1864 but was ordered back to Richmond in September. While en route to the capital, he received news of Early's defeat at Winchester. He hastened back to the valley where he opened the attack at Cedar Creek. Kershaw eventually moved into the defenses of Petersburg and marched westward in April 1865. He was captured at Sayler's Creek and imprisoned at Fort Warren until August 12.

Returning to his law practice in Camden after the war, Kershaw was elected to the legislature in 1865 and became president of the senate. In later years he was elected judge of the Fifth District, a position he held until failing health intervened. He was appointed postmaster of Camden in 1893 and died April 13, 1894. He was buried in Quaker Cemetery, Camden.

— LOWELL REIDENBAUGH

KILPATRICK-DAHLGREN RAID

This raid, named for Union Gen. Judson Kilpatrick and Col. Ulric Dahlgren, began on February 28, 1864, with the avowed purpose of freeing Union soldiers held in Richmond's Libby Prison and Belle Island. Over the next four days, 4,000 handpicked Federal cavalrymen clashed with a scattered force of 500 Southern soldiers and home guard units to the west and north of Richmond. In the end, the Federals lost 340 men, 583 horses, and much equipment and never reached close proximity to either of the two prisons.

In mid-February 1864 Union intelligence reported that the Confederate capital's meager defenses left it especially vulnerable to a cavalry raid. The boisterous and ambitious H. Judson Kilpatrick sought the approval of President Abraham Lincoln for a surprise raid that would free prisoners and wreak havoc on the Confederate capital. Lincoln gave his enthusiastic sup-

At Cold Harbor, Col. Keitt's inexperience and impetuousness resulted not only in his own death but also in that of many brave men of Kershaw's Brigade.

PAGE 312

The publication of the Dahlgren papers in the Richmond newspapers fanned the flames of hatred and prompted cries for retribution.

PAGE 161

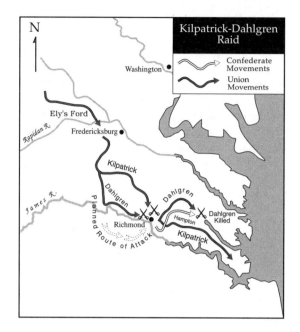

Kilpatrick-Dahlgren Raid

⟶ Confederate Movements
⟶ Union Movements

N

Robert E. Lee wrote to Gen. George G. Meade, asking him if his government had approved or sanctioned the violent actions proposed in the captured Dahlgren papers.

PAGE 161

port, hoping that Kilpatrick would bring some positive results to the Union war effort.

On the night of February 28, Kilpatrick set out with his men toward Ely's Ford on the Rapidan River. Included in his force was young Ulric Dahlgren. The earnest son of navy officer John Dahlgren was to lead a detachment of cavalry across the James River and attack from the south, while Kilpatrick's main force entered the city from the north. Gen. Robert E. Lee had predicted such a raid four months earlier and was well prepared for this one. As sleet and rain fell in torrents, Confederate spies spread the word of the Union plans and alerted city defenses of the enemy approach. By the time Kilpatrick's men arrived, the Confederates were ready.

The Federals first sensed trouble soon after Dahlgren split away from Kilpatrick's main force on February 29. Kilpatrick unexpectedly met strong resistance five miles north of Richmond. After fighting several hours, he withdrew to the east and then, after hesitating, turned to resume battle. Maj. Gen. Wade Hampton and his small force of three hundred cavalrymen came from behind. In the ensuing darkness Kilpatrick's exhausted men doggedly fought the Confederates, but the Union general's fighting spirit was gone and he again turned to retreat eastward toward Federal lines.

Meanwhile, Dahlgren with his detachment of five hundred men found the James River swelled from the recent rains. When Dahlgren tried instead to enter Richmond from the west, he met stiff resistance from G. W. Custis Lee's local defense brigade. This force of armory workers and government clerks blocked Dahlgren's planned approach. In the confused retreat, Dahlgren and one hundred of his men became separated. Trying to reach the safety of Union lines, Dahlgren

stumbled upon an ambush in King and Queen County. He was killed instantly, and most of the remaining Federals surrendered.

Papers found on Dahlgren's body by a teenaged boy revealed that the raiding cavalrymen planned more than simply freeing prisoners. The papers detailed Federal intentions to burn the city and kill Jefferson Davis and his cabinet. Richmond newspapers soon published the papers, and Southerners were outraged. They demanded an investigation and explanation from Federal authorities. Union officials first claimed that the papers were forgeries and later admitted only to Dahlgren's guilt.

The extent of Union involvement in the plans to burn Richmond and kill Confederate civilian leaders remains unclear. But in March 1864, the mere allegation of such dark intentions was enough to strengthen Southern resolve to persevere in the war.

[*See also* Dahlgren Papers.]

— LESLEY JILL GORDON-BURR

KNOXVILLE AND GREENEVILLE CONVENTIONS

The Knoxville Convention of May 30 and 31, 1861, and the Greeneville Convention of June 17 through 20, 1861, represented eastern Tennessee Unionists' challenge to the state's secession crisis. Although they failed to prevent Tennessee's alliance with the Confederacy or to establish a separate pro-Union state, they gave powerful voice to anti-Confederate sentiment, provided leadership for those opposed to the Southern cause, and required the Confederate government to allocate precious resources to Tennessee's mountain districts. Because of its dependence upon the strategically vital East Tennessee and Virginia Railroad to carry troops from the Deep South to the eastern theater of war, the Confederacy had to retain the region regardless of its inhabitants' expressed wishes.

A people with scant commitment to slavery or commercial agriculture, eastern Tennesseans had long felt alienated from planter-dominated middle and western Tennessee. On February 9, when the entire state had voted against Governor Isham G. Harris's call for a secession convention, eastern Tennesseans with a negative vote of 81 percent were far more emphatic than western Tennesseans at 65 percent and middle Tennesseans with only 51 percent. But the bombardment of Fort Sumter and Abraham Lincoln's subsequent call for volunteers galvanized the Ten-

nessee legislature to declare separation from the Union on May 6 and to schedule a plebiscite for June 8.

Reacting to this in mid-May, fifteen prominent Knox County Unionists, including William G. Brownlow and Oliver Perry Temple, met in Temple's law office and called for a Union convention. Whigs in politics, they found common cause with their longtime Democratic party foe Senator Andrew Johnson. Emboldened by editorials in Brownlow's *Knoxville Whig* and Johnson's passionate rhetoric, over 400 delegates assembled at Knoxville's Temperance Hall on May 30 and 31 and chose Congressman Thomas A. R. Nelson as their presiding officer. Though a nondelegate, Johnson addressed the convention, which thereafter passed resolutions condemning the June plebiscite, urging Tennesseans to reject secession, and empowering Nelson to convene a second convention should events warrant.

On June 8, middle and western Tennesseans overwhelmingly endorsed secession, but eastern Tennesseans rejected it by a 68 percent vote. Arguing that the referendum had been won by force and fraud, Nelson called a second convention at Greeneville on June 17, but only 285 delegates gathered. Some earlier supporters had reluctantly accepted the plebiscite's verdict, and others—most notably Andrew Johnson—had fled the state. Transient Confederate troops constantly threatened the delegates, and a passing Louisiana regiment ate the conventioneers' breakfast. Nonetheless, the convention entertained truculent proposals advocating armed resistance and eastern Tennessee statehood, but eventually it passed calmer resolutions expressing an "earnest desire" that eastern Tennessee remain neutral territory and requesting the Nashville government to allow the region separate statehood. Not surprisingly, the convention's three-man commission to the Tennessee legislature found an unsympathetic audience.

Whatever the conventions' lack of success, they served notice of eastern Tennessee's resistance to joining the Confederacy. Over thirty thousand of its inhabitants would enroll in Union regiments, others fought as guerrillas, and when Ambrose Burnside's Union army marched into the region in 1863, his soldiers were greeted as liberators.

— FRED ARTHUR BAILEY

L

LAIRD SHIPYARDS

The William Laird and Sons Company was founded by John Laird, Jr., and William Laird, who had a history of successful construction of merchant and military ships. Located on the English River Mersey, across from the harbor of the city of Liverpool, the company was one of the earliest shipyards to build iron ships and by 1842 had built forty-four. In 1839 it constructed the iron paddle packet *Dover* for the British navy and in 1842 the iron paddle frigate *Guadalupe* for the Mexican government. At 788 tons *Guadalupe* was the largest iron vessel that had ever been constructed.

During the American Civil War the Lairds contracted with Confederate navy agent James Dunwoody Bulloch for the construction of *Alabama* and two ironclad rams. The *Alabama* contract was signed on August 1, 1861, and the ship was completed on June 15, 1862. The shipbuilders, following Bulloch's design, constructed a unique vessel for its day: it was powered by both steam and sail, and it had a device to lift the propeller out of water when under sail only, large storage areas for provisions to enable the ship to stay at sea for long periods of time, passages for the passing of ammunition to the deck guns, and a condenser to convert seawater into drinking water.

During its cruise of twenty-three months under Capt. Raphael Semmes, the ship destroyed more enemy vessels than any other ship in naval history. Its destructive cruise raised the question of British culpability, which in turn led to the Geneva Arbitration Tribunal that in 1873 ordered Great Britain to pay $15.5 million to the United States for failure to prevent delivery of the ship to the Confederate navy.

The two ironclad rams Bulloch contracted for were formidable ships designed to operate in the shallow American coastal and river waters in order to raise the Union blockade and even to lay siege to certain Northern cities. The ships were 230 feet long, 42 feet at the extreme width, with a draft fully loaded of 15 feet. Made of wood with iron siding, they were powered by both sail and steam. Their most distinctive feature was a seven-foot iron ram protruding from the bow below the water level.

Largely because of the destructive *Alabama* cruise, the British government had become sensitive to Washington complaints and to reports submitted to it by the U.S. consul in Liverpool. Before the rams were completed, the British government seized them in 1864, thus preventing delivery to the Confederate navy. The Laird rams served well and long in the British navy as *Scorpion* and *Wivern*. Because the British domestic law to impose its neutrality on British subjects was outdated, the Lairds were not punished, despite the later decision of the Geneva tribunal.

The William Laird and Sons Company still operates on the Mersey River and maintains a Confederate museum that concentrates on *Alabama* and the Laird rams.

[*See also* Alabama Claims; *and entry on the ship* Alabama.]

— WARREN F. SPENCER

LAMAR, L. Q. C.

Lamar, L. Q. C. (1825–1893), framer of Mississippi's ordinance of secession, lieutenant colonel, diplomat, U.S. congressman, and Supreme Court judge. Lucius Quintus Cincinnatus Lamar, a native of Georgia, graduated from Emory College at Oxford, Georgia, in 1845. He married the daughter of Augustus Baldwin Longstreet, president of Emory College. When Longstreet resigned to become the president of the University of Mississippi, Lamar followed, taking a job as a mathematics professor despite his legal education and his preference for the law.

By 1851, Lamar had become an advocate of state rights, speaking out publicly in opposition to California's admission as a free state and earning a reputation as an eloquent and forceful speaker. Lamar was elected from Mississippi to the U.S. House of Representatives in 1857 and reelected in 1859. By this time, he was a vigorous spokesman for Southern interests, though he denied being a secessionist. As a delegate to the Charleston Democratic National Convention in 1860, Lamar sided with moderate Southern Democrats, opposing Southern withdrawal over the issue of territorial rights. Yet when the representatives of the Southern states withdrew, Lamar joined them. The election of Abraham Lincoln convinced him that secession was inevitable, and he began planning for a Southern nation. He resigned

As early as February 1862 the U.S. consul in Liverpool reported that Liverpool shipbuilders were constructing a Confederate cruiser. It became the famed Confederate raider Alabama.

PAGE 174

Toombs stressed the need to confirm the South's legitimacy as an independent nation.

PAGE 169

his seat in Congress and as a member of Mississippi's secession convention drafted the ordinance of secession.

At the beginning of the war, Lamar helped raise a regiment and became a lieutenant colonel. He insisted

The Confederacy's free trade and liberal navigation policies would ensure accessible and profitable markets for the manufactures of Europe.

PAGE 169

that the time for speeches and statesmanship was over. He was, nonetheless, depressed over the prospects of a long and bloody war, and while encamped at Richmond, he began to suffer attacks that left him temporarily unconscious and paralyzed on one side. After recuperating in Mississippi, he returned to Richmond and fought in the battle at Williamsburg, taking command of his regiment upon the death of Col. C. H. Mott. One-fifth of the regiment's men were casualties. Afterward, Lamar suffered another attack and was again forced to return home.

In late 1862 Lamar was appointed a special commissioner to seek Russian recognition of the Confederacy. He traveled as far as London and France, where he was received and entertained as a diplomat. The Confederate Senate realized, however, that Russia was unlikely to recognize a nation that advocated slavery. It did not confirm Lamar's commission, and he returned to Richmond.

Near the end of 1863, Lamar was sent by the Davis administration to Georgia to quell growing opposition to Confederate policies. Again, he suffered the poor health that would recur the rest of his life. In December 1864 he was commissioned judge advocate of the military court of the Third Army Corps, Army of Northern Virginia.

After the war, although disfranchised, Lamar worked in Mississippi to promote conciliation, and in 1866 he returned to the university as a professor of ethics, metaphysics, and law. In 1870, during Republican rule, Lamar was forced to resign his professorship and to return to the practice of law.

The remainder of his life proved to be the most important and productive of his career. Pardoned from the disabilities imposed on Confederate officials, he served in the U.S. House of Representatives from 1872 to 1877 and in the U.S. Senate from 1877 to 1885. In 1885 he became President Grover Cleveland's secretary of the interior, and in 1888 Cleveland appointed him to the Supreme Court. He served until 1892 and died a year later.

— RAY SKATES

LEAD

A Confederate government of highly limited resources often had to utilize blockade runners and contracts with private firms in order to obtain badly needed war supplies. Lead was among the most vital of these commodities. Without it, weapons had no ammunition.

So scarce was lead in the wartime South that soldiers would collect bullets from battlefields and send them to arsenals in the rear to be melted down and recast. Southern officials issued appeals requesting citizens to strip their homes of all lead articles such as pipes, roofs, window weights, and common utensils. Blockade runners did a brisk business in lead importation: over 1.5 million pounds entered the Confederacy by this means in one thirteen-month period.

Small lead mines existed in eastern Tennessee and Arkansas. But as Col. William Broun of the Confederate Ordnance Department later stated: "Our lead was obtained chiefly, and in the last years of the war entirely, from the lead mines at Wytheville, Va. The mines were worked night and day, and the lead converted into bullets as fast as received. The old regulation shrapnel shells were filled with leaden balls and sulphur. The Confederacy had neither lead nor sulphur to spare, and used instead small iron balls and filled with asphalt."

Wytheville's state-owned mines had supplied George Washington's army with bullets in the American Revolution. After the new nation came into being, Virginia sold the mines to two Austin brothers. (Stephen F. Austin, the "Father of Texas," was a son of one of the owners.) The mines at Wytheville—the quarries themselves were at Austinville, seven miles away—were a thriving business when civil war came.

Of the three types of lead mined there, sulphuret (or "blue ore") was the most abundant. It was either crystalline or granular in structure and easily recognizable from the carbonate and oxide varieties of lead. The C.S. Niter Corps monitored production, with Gen. Josiah Gorgas of the Niter and Mining Bureau in overall charge of operations. When conscription drained manpower from the mines, Confederate officials impressed slaves to continue the work. Output at the Wytheville mines averaged about 80,000 pounds monthly. In all, these mines produced 3,283,316 pounds of lead for the Confederacy.

By 1864 Union officials regarded the Wytheville quarries as the most important target in southwestern Virginia. Federal raiding parties went into action as soon as the Virginia and Tennessee Railroad and nearby points were secured. Gen. William W. Averell made a stab at Wytheville on May 11 but was driven off by Confederate cavalry under Gen. John Hunt Morgan. On December 17, several mounted regiments of Gen. George Stoneman's force captured the mines, poured oil on the equipment, and set fire to the works before returning to their base.

Persistent miners repaired the damage and, on March 22, 1865, resumed operations. Confederates managed to repulse an April 5 attempt by Federals to seize the mines. Two days later, however, a heavier assault by Union cavalry routed the defenders. The lead works were destroyed a second time, only two days before Robert E. Lee's surrender at Appomattox.

In all the Confederacy consumed 10 million pounds of lead in the manufacture of the 150 million cartridges used by its armies.

— JAMES I. ROBERTSON, JR

LEE, FITZHUGH

Lee, Fitzhugh (1835–1905), major general, postwar governor of Virginia, and U.S. diplomat. Born at Clermont, in Fairfax County, Virginia, Fitz Lee was the grandson of Henry ("Light Horse Harry") Lee and great-grandson of George Mason. Lee attended the U.S. Military Academy from 1852 to 1856, while his uncle, Robert E. Lee, was superintendent. Graduating forty-fifth out of forty-nine, he excelled in horsemanship. His equestrian skills earned him a position with the Second U.S. Cavalry in Texas. For two years, he served on the frontier fighting Comanches, where he received a critical wound to his lungs that nearly cost him his life. He returned to West Point as an instructor in 1860.

In May 1861, Lee resigned from the U.S. Army and returned to Virginia. In September, after serving as adjutant to Brig. Gen. Richard S. Ewell during the Battle of First Manassas, he received a commission as lieutenant colonel of the First Virginia Cavalry. Lee led scouting and raiding parties against the Federals picketed in northern Virginia and often left taunting notes for former comrades in the U.S. Army.

Serving under Maj. Gen. J. E. B. Stuart, he received high praise from his commander and was promoted to colonel in the spring of 1862. He joined Stuart for the Ride around McClellan during the Peninsular campaign and was cited for his "zeal and ability." In July, Lee was promoted to brigadier general in command of the Second Brigade. He continued to serve with the Army of Northern Virginia, seeing limited action at Second Manassas and Sharpsburg. During the winter of 1862–1863, he made successful hit-and-run attacks against the Federal army.

On March 17, 1863, one of Lee's taunting messages drew a response from Gen. William Averell, who launched a raid across the Rapidan River at Kelly's Ford. Fitz Lee's small command outside of Culpeper, Virginia, drove the larger invading force across the river for a marginal victory.

At Chancellorsville, Lee's reconnaissance provided key information that the Federal right flank was "in the air" and vulnerable to an attack. This prompted the renowned flank attack led by Gen. Thomas J. ("Stonewall") Jackson on May 2 that resulted in the Confederates' strategic victory. In September, Lee was promoted to major general commanding the Second Division of the cavalry corps.

In 1864, Lee distinguished himself at Spotsylvania, Yellow Tavern—where he assumed command after Stuart was mortally wounded—and Trevilian's Station. During the battle at Winchester on September 19, Lee received a serious wound to his thigh, which kept him out of service until January 1865. At Five Forks, Lee's military reputation was tainted when his attendance at the notorious shad bake (a fish fry given by a fellow officer some distance from his force's position) resulted in his absence from the battle front. He redeemed himself by delaying Gen. Philip Sheridan's pursuit of the retreating Army of Northern Virginia.

After the war, Lee tried farming at his home, Richlands, in Stafford County, Virginia, but he soon turned to politics and was elected governor of Virginia in 1886. He was the U.S. consulate general in Havana, Cuba, from 1896 to 1898. During the Spanish-American War, Lee served as a major general in the U.S. Army. He died on April 29, 1905, in Washington, D.C., and was buried in Hollywood Cemetery in Richmond, Virginia.

— KAREN G. REHM

LEE, GEORGE WASHINGTON CUSTIS

Lee, George Washington Custis (1832–1913), major general. Born September 16, 1832, at Fort Monroe, Virginia, the first child of Mary Custis Lee and

Robert E. Lee, Custis Lee spent much of his life coping with the burden of his father's fame. At West Point he graduated first in the class of 1854, exceeding his father's record (second in the class of 1829). Commissioned in the Corps of Engineers (like his father), Custis Lee served on several construction projects before resigning May 2, 1861, in response to the secession of Virginia.

Lee secured a place on the military staff of President Jefferson Davis and spent most of the war in Richmond. Rewarded with promotions for faithful service, Lee became a brigadier general on June 25, 1863, and a major general on October 20, 1864.

By turns eager for command in the field but unsure of his capacity to lead in combat, Lee was often ill during the war. He remained on Davis's staff because the president wanted him and because his father needed him. The elder Lee relied upon his son to express his views to the president and to keep him informed about policies and politics within the administration.

Lee finally did command a reserve regiment of industrial workers on the retreat from Richmond, but had to surrender himself and his men at Sayler's Creek on April 6, 1865. After the war Lee taught engineering at the Virginia Military Institute in Lexington. Following his father's death, Custis Lee became president of Washington and Lee University from 1871 to 1897. He died on February 18, 1913.

— EMORY M. THOMAS

LEE, ROBERT E.

Lee, Robert E. (1807–1870), general. Born at Stratford, Westmoreland County, Virginia, on January 19, 1807, Lee was the fourth of five children (the third son) of Ann Hill Carter Lee and Henry ("Light-Horse Harry") Lee. Two children of Harry Lee's first marriage also lived with the family. Robert Lee did not remain very long at Stratford. His father had been a hero in the Revolution, governor of Virginia, and a member of Congress; but by the time of Robert's birth, Lee's fortunes were in serious decline. Harry Lee's debts forced him into prison in 1809 and compelled the family to move to Alexandria, Virginia, in 1810. Then in 1812 Harry Lee sustained serious injuries in Baltimore helping an editor defend his newspaper against a mob outraged over editorials opposing the War of 1812. In May 1813, he sailed away to the Caribbean, ostensibly to recoup his fortune and recover his health, leaving family and creditors behind. Light-Horse Harry Lee died on Cumberland Island, Georgia, in 1818 without having seen his family again.

Ann Lee raised her children in very modest circumstances and tried to teach them standards of conduct in the hope that they would avoid their father's mistakes. After attending schools in Alexandria, Robert Lee managed to secure an appointment to West Point. Rather suddenly he left the company of his mother and sisters, for whom he had cared during his adolescence, and in 1825 entered the exclusively male society at West Point.

His mother's precepts, his academic background, and his quick, precise mind all served Lee well at West Point. He finished second in the class of 1829 and garnered not one demerit during his four years at the academy. Lee's success earned him an appointment in the Engineer Corps at a time when the U.S. government was willing to support public projects. His first assignment was at Cockspur Island in the Savannah River preparing the foundation of what much later became Fort Pulaski.

Approximately a month following his graduation from West Point, Ann Lee died, and Robert Lee began his career in the military with a small inheritance (about ten slaves) and roots in his extended family. Although Lee made friends in Savannah, he spent his leaves in northern Virginia increasingly in the company of Mary Custis, the only child of Mary Fitzhugh Custis and George Washington Parke Custis, the adopted son of George Washington. Lee was extraordinarily handsome then, and throughout his young manhood and middle age people called him the best-looking man in the army. He was about five feet, ten or eleven inches tall, with a fit, medium build and nearly perfect posture. A guest at his son's wedding in 1859 claimed that Lee outshone the entire company, and those who saw him on horseback insisted that he appeared even more imposing riding than afoot.

Mary Custis and Robert Lee married in July 1831 at Arlington, the Custis estate just across the Potomac from Washington. The young couple began life together in officers' quarters at Fort Monroe, Virginia, Lee's second duty assignment. They had seven children between 1832 and 1846. The Lees and their children often lived at Arlington while Lee served in the Engineer Department in Washington, and Mary Lee remained with the children at Arlington when duty called Robert Lee to St. Louis and later to the Mexican War.

Lee served on the staff of Winfield Scott during the campaign from Vera Cruz to Mexico City in 1847. He became a member of Scott's "little cabinet," his inner circle of advisers, and Lee's talent, energy, and daring were especially conspicuous at Cerro Gordo and Chapultepec. He emerged from the war with Scott's unabashed admiration and the brevet (temporary) rank of colonel.

THE GENERAL *This April 20, 1865, photograph by Mathew Brady was taken at Lee's home near Richmond shortly before he became president of what is today Washington and Lee University.* NATIONAL ARCHIVES

LEE MEMORIAL ASSOCIATION

The Robert E. Lee Memorial Association is a nonprofit organization that owns and operates Stratford Hall Plantation, Lee's birthplace in Westmoreland County, Virginia. It was formed in 1929 under the leadership of Mrs. Charles D. Lanier to purchase Stratford. The Great House and outbuildings at Stratford were restored under the direction of noted architect Fiske Kimball. The all-female governing board has a member from each state of the Union, the District of Columbia, and Great Britain. A leading benefactor and board member was Mrs. Alfred I. duPont, in whose honor a research library was named at its inception in 1980.

Stratford was built by Thomas Lee about 1738. Two signers of the Declaration of Independence, Richard Henry Lee and Francis Lightfoot Lee, grew up there. A later resident was General Lee's father, Henry ("Light Horse Harry") Lee, the brilliant Revolutionary War cavalry leader. His wife, Ann Hill Carter Lee, gave birth to their fourth son, Robert Edward, at Stratford on January 19, 1807. Lee lived at Stratford for only three and a half years, however. The plantation was sold by the Lee family in 1822 and remained in other private hands until purchased by the association.

The mission of the association today is to preserve and interpret Stratford and to educate the public on the historical significance of Robert E. Lee and other family members. In 1981 the association initiated an annual summer seminar for history teachers. It sponsors special events and annual open houses on General Lee's birthday and July 4. Special tours include one on Children's Days. Others concern architecture, the farm, gardens and decorative arts.

— C. VAUGHAN STANLEY

In 1852 Lee returned to West Point as superintendent, and in 1855 he transferred from staff assignments to command of cavalry troopers on the Texas frontier. When his father-in-law died in 1857, Lee began a protracted leave as executor of Custis's estate.

Custis had dabbled in many enterprises and had done none of them very well. Unfortunately for Lee, Custis had not done a very good job of making his will either. So Lee attempted to unsnarl affairs associated with Custis's estate, a task he never quite completed in his lifetime.

Lee was still working at Arlington in October 1859 when reports of a slave insurrection sent him hurriedly to Harpers Ferry in command of a detachment of marines. He confronted John Brown and a few of his followers barricaded in a fire engine building with thirteen hostages. The situation was tense, but Lee managed to capture Brown and put down his raid without harming Brown's hostages.

In 1860 Lee returned to Texas and duty, having had his fill of farming on his father-in-law's estates. In February 1861, he returned to Arlington in response to the secession crisis. He rejected an opportunity to command the principal field army charged with suppressing the rebellion, choosing instead to offer his services to Virginia and the Southern Confederacy. Lee resigned his commission in the U.S. Army on April 20, 1861, and on April 23 accepted command of the armed forces of Virginia. In this capacity Lee organized the mobilization of Virginia troops and on June 10 surrendered his men and equipment to the Confederate government for the national army and navy. Thereafter Lee served as informal adviser to President Jefferson Davis and remained for the most part in the new capital at Richmond.

On August 31, 1861, Lee became a full general in the Confederate army. By this time he was in western (present-day West) Virginia attempting to unscramble egos and thwart a Union campaign in the Kanawha Valley. Lee failed in both undertakings and returned to Richmond on October 31. Less than a week later Davis sent Lee to command the Department of South Carolina, Georgia, and Florida and to confront Federal incursions along the Southern coast.

Lee arrived in South Carolina on the very day a Federal combined arms force captured Port Royal. Subsequently he worked to contain the enemy invasion and to organize the defense of the coastal region. He concluded that the Confederacy lacked the ships, men, and guns to defend the barrier islands and so contracted the chain of defensive positions up rivers to sites where the guns available would have some chance of stopping Union gunboats. Lee's plans were sound, but his design forced coastal residents to flee inland with their slaves and thus made refugees of some rich and powerful Confederates.

In March 1862, Davis recalled Lee to Richmond and made him, in effect, his chief of staff. Lee was again an adviser while others commanded armies. He did perform a valuable service as buffer between the president and Joseph E. Johnston, who commanded the primary Confederate army in Virginia. In the process of countering Union Gen. George B. McClellan's Peninsular campaign, Davis and Johnston seemed overconcerned about personal prerogatives, and Lee was able to filter some of the vitriol out of communications between the two men. Otherwise, though, Lee worked hard at thankless tasks while McClellan's blue host came steadily closer to Richmond.

Then on May 31, 1862, Johnston committed his army to what became the Battle of Seven Pines, and as the inconclusive fighting wound down, Johnston was seriously injured. On June 1 Davis gave Lee command of Johnston's army and in so doing placed Lee in charge of the Confederacy's tottering fortunes.

Lee withdrew the army into the outskirts of Richmond and ordered the men to prepare elaborate field fortifications. So in the public mind, Lee became "the King of Spades" as well as "Granny Lee" for his supposed overcaution. Lee, however, was already making plans that were anything but defensive and cautious. He reorganized Johnston's army and renamed it the Army of Northern Virginia—all while in the face of the enemy. He sent J. E. B. Stuart and the cavalry to scout McClellan's right flank, a reconnaissance that became known as Stuart's "Ride around McClellan" because he circled the entire Federal army. Lee shifted divisions of troops to attack the Federal right flank and summoned Thomas J. ("Stonewall") Jackson's Shenandoah Valley army to strike the Federal rear. The result of these actions was the Seven Days' Battles (King's School House, Mechanicsville, Gaines's Mill, Frayser's Farm, White Oaks Swamp, and Malvern Hill) from June 25 through July 1, 1862. After the nearly constant and always bloody fighting, the Federals lay inert under cover of their gunboats at Harrison's Landing on the James River, twenty-three miles from Richmond. Lee was suddenly a hero, and the Confederacy seemed saved. But Lee was frustrated: he had wanted not merely to drive the enemy away but to destroy McClellan's army altogether.

The Seven Days' Battles began a year of success for Confederate arms. Lee continued to seek his enemies' destruction and marched to the old battlefield at Manassas to strike the forces of John Pope. While Jackson fixed Pope's attention and fended off Federal attacks, Lee maneuvered James Longstreet and the other half of the Confederate army to strike Pope's flank. Second Manassas was a resounding Confederate victory, but still less than Lee's dream of annihilating a major Union army.

In the hope of fighting a decisive battle on Northern soil, Lee led his army into Maryland as part of a dual offensive in that state and in Kentucky. En route, however, a copy of Lee's invasion order fell into Union hands and under the eyes of McClellan, who was once more in command of the primary Union army in the East. Lee scrambled to reconcentrate his forces while McClellan moved cautiously to strike Lee's divided command. The armies met at Sharpsburg, Maryland, across Antietam Creek, and the battle became the bloodiest single day of the war. The Army of Northern Virginia barely survived a tactical draw, but Lee abandoned his invasion and retreated back into Virginia.

The campaigns of 1862 in Virginia concluded on the Rappahannock River at Fredericksburg on December 13. Ambrose E. Burnside, next to command the Federal Army of the Potomac, attacked Lee's army entrenched south of the city. The result was a massacre of Federal troops, who never breached Lee's lines.

The spring of 1863 brought a new Federal commander to challenge Lee. Joseph Hooker attempted to sweep across the Rappahannock and strike Lee's flank and rear. Lee set most of his army in motion to meet Hooker, and the armies collided in a sparsely settled region near a crossroads called Chancellorsville. Then Lee learned that Hooker's flank was unsecure, and he dispatched Jackson with his entire corps to envelop the Federals. Jackson's attack was devastating, but in the wake of the success, Jackson himself fell, accidentally wounded at the hands of some of his own troops. With J. E. B. Stuart in charge of Jackson's corps, Lee was able to unite the two wings of his army and press Hooker severely. But even at Chancellorsville in what many consider Lee's greatest battle, the Army of Northern Virginia was unable to destroy the Army of the Potomac.

Still hoping for a climactic victory, Lee once more marched north, this time into Pennsylvania. He met the Federals and the new commander George G. Meade at Gettysburg. On July 1, 1863, the Confederates captured the town and drove their enemies onto Cemetery Hill and Ridge. But Richard S. Ewell, in command of one of Lee's three corps, stopped, following to the letter Lee's orders against a general engagement before the entire army arrived. The next day, July 2, Longstreet's corps sought the Federal left flank, found it, and fought a desperate but drawn battle at Little and Big Round Tops and within Devil's Den. Late in the day Stuart arrived with news of his raiding, but with no reliable reconnaissance reports of the strength and disposition of Meade's army. Nevertheless, Lee determined to attack again—to make one last attempt at a battle of annihilation. He decided to try to break the center of the Federal lines on Cemetery Ridge.

Pickett's Charge was a debacle reminiscent of Malvern Hill. Lee took the risk because he believed he had to in order to achieve victory. He had come too far, worked too hard, to shrink from what he perceived to be the moment of truth. He lost.

After the Army of Northern Virginia had limped back into northern Virginia in August, Lee submitted his resignation to the president. He pointed out that he

"[Lee] knew how to put himself in another man's mind. He knew what Grant was going to do because he could make himself Grant long enough to figure out what Grant would do in the situation."

SHELBY FOOTE
IN GEOFFREY WARD,
THE CIVIL WAR, 1990

L

LEE MONUMENT ASSOCIATION

The Lee Monument Association, which played an important role in ensuring the prominent place of Robert E. Lee among the heroes of the Lost Cause, first organized in 1870 shortly after the general's death. At the behest of Jubal Early, veterans of the Army of Northern Virginia met in Richmond, resolved to erect a monument to Lee in the former Confederate capital, and began a regionwide fund-raising campaign. Initially the association competed with similar groups, including the Lee Memorial Association that dedicated a statue to Lee at Washington and Lee University in 1883.

In 1886, Virginia Governor Fitzhugh Lee, a veteran and nephew of the Confederate commander, reorganized the Lee Monument Association under a board composed of state officials and representatives from Richmond's Ladies' Lee Memorial Association, which had raised more money than any other group. With Fitzhugh Lee's leadership and contributions from Early and Lee Camp, a newly formed Confederate veterans' group in Richmond, the reorganized Lee Monument Association raised the remainder of the necessary funds. Its board selected a sculptor, Frenchman Marius-Jean-Antonin Mercié, chose a site on the edge of one of Richmond's growing suburbs, and dedicated the statue's base in 1887. Three years later, on May 29, 1890, a crowd of over 100,000 gathered to watch the unveiling of Mercié's majestic mounted Lee and to celebrate not only the general but the Confederacy. Later, when statues to other Confederate leaders were erected near that of Lee, Richmond's Monument Avenue became a major shrine to the Lost Cause.

— GAINES M. FOSTER

victory and still capable of stratagems designed to lay waste his enemy.

Throughout the winter of 1863–1864 Lee labored to conserve his resources and himself. He ordered rigorous inspections throughout his army to ensure that men and equipment would be ready for the spring and to emphasize the need to husband their dwindling supplies. His new opponent was Ulysses S. Grant, now commander in chief of Union armies. Grant elected to exercise his far-flung command from a headquarters in Meade's army opposite Lee.

During the first week of May in 1864 Grant crossed the Rapidan River and plunged into an area known locally as the Wilderness. Lee let the Federals cross the river and waited to strike until the Wilderness compelled the Federals to disperse their superior numbers and even the odds. From a tactical perspective Lee won in the Wilderness; but Grant did not withdraw and lick his wounds as other Union commanders had done. Grant put his army in motion, east and south, to try to force his way between Lee and Richmond. Lee was just resourceful enough to block Grant's march at Spotsylvania Court House. There the armies again came to grips, and again Grant recoiled and resumed his drive to the east and south. Lee continued his canny counterpunching until the armies came near Cold Harbor, very close to the site of the fighting two years before at Gaines' Mill. Then Grant tried to break through the center of Lee's long line and failed disastrously.

In the wake of Cold Harbor, however, Lee lost his enemy: Stuart was dead, and his cavalry was unable to determine Federal intentions. When Grant's army reappeared, it was south of the James marching on Petersburg, a crucial railroad junction south of Richmond. Inspired fighting and blind luck held Petersburg long enough for Lee to reinforce the defenders. Then Lee again became the "King of Spades." He used trenches to compensate for his inferiority in numbers and held his lines around Petersburg and the line of forts north of the James, east of Richmond, for the next nine and a half months.

Both commanders attempted to break the trench stalemate. For his part Lee dispatched Jubal Early to Lynchburg, down the Shenandoah Valley, and to the outskirts of Washington in hopes of fighting Federals outside of prepared fortifications. And Lee attempted to break the Federal lines and trap his enemies in their holes on several occasions. Ultimately, though, he was himself trapped in a war of attrition that he had worked to avoid. Eventually, on April 1, 1865, Lee's lines became too thin and too short; he had to evacuate his works and Richmond on April 2.

The Army of Northern Virginia survived in flight for only one week. On April 9, 1865, Lee surrendered

had been ill the previous spring (likely with the heart disease that eventually killed him) and had never really recovered. He argued that because he had not been successful, the president should install another in his place. Davis declined to accept the resignation and told Lee that he knew no one better to command the army.

Lee, however, was still unwell. He was compelled to conduct his abortive Bristoe Station campaign (October 9–22) from a wagon instead of horseback. Yet Bristoe Station and Mine Run, which followed in November, demonstrated that Lee was still intent on

to Grant at Appomattox Courthouse. The Confederacy lived little longer than Lee's army.

In peace Lee stood for sectional reconciliation. He accepted the presidency of Washington College in Lexington, Virginia, and attempted to educate a new generation of Southerners to cope with an altered reality in the South. He established a balance in the curriculum between the traditional classical education and the more practical disciplines in science and engineering. He introduced elective courses and supplanted the many rules governing student conduct with one: students should conduct themselves as gentlemen. In Lee's mind conducting oneself as a gentleman was essentially a matter of selfless concern for other people. "The great duty in life," he once wrote, "is the promotion of the happiness and welfare of others."

Even as he lived, Lee became a legend. Southerners needed Lee to prove that good people can and do lose and to demonstrate that success in battle or elsewhere does not necessarily denote superiority. Lee became something of a Christ figure for the defeated Southern Confederates.

Cardiovascular troubles, probably dating from the war period, increasingly plagued Lee in Lexington. During the spring of 1870 he took an extended trip into the Deep South, ostensibly for his health, more likely as a farewell tour. Because he knew or sensed that he was dying, he agreed to sit for a portrait and pose for a statue, acts he had loathed in the past, during the summer of 1870.

Then one evening in the fall Lee came home late from a vestry meeting and suffered a stroke as he attempted to bless his supper. He lingered a time in a passive state, and on October 13, 1870, he died.

[*See also* Arlington House; Army of Northern Virginia.]

— EMORY M. THOMAS

LEE, WILLIAM HENRY FITZHUGH

Lee, William Henry Fitzhugh (1837–1891), major general and U.S. congressman. Born May 31, 1837, to Mary Custis Lee and Robert E. Lee at Arlington, "Rooney" Lee attended Harvard, inspired a damning passage in classmate Henry Adams's *Autobiography* ("the Southerner has no mind"), and left without graduating to accept a direct commission in the U.S. Army in 1857. Lee resigned his commission in 1859 to marry and become a farmer at White House on the Pamunkey River in Virginia.

After Virginia seceded, Lee enlisted in the Confederate army, initially as a captain of cavalry. He served with W. W. Loring in western (present-day West) Virginia during the summer and fall of 1861. By early 1862 he was at Fredericksburg in command of the Ninth Virginia Cavalry. He led this regiment on J. E. B. Stuart's Ride around McClellan in June 1862 and served with Stuart in the Army of Northern Virginia thereafter. Promoted to brigadier general for bravery at South Mountain, Lee participated in raids and reconnaissance during the period in which Confederate cavalry dominated in the East. Then at Brandy Station on June 9, 1863, Lee suffered a wound in his leg and was captured soon after while he recuperated at his wife's home near Richmond.

Imprisoned at Fort Monroe and Fort Lafayette until exchanged in March 1864, Lee afterward resumed active service. On April 23, 1864, he became at the age of thirty-six the youngest major general in the Confederate army. By the time his father surrendered at Appomattox, Lee was second in command of cavalry in the Army of Northern Virginia.

After the war Lee rebuilt his farm and his life. His first wife had died while he was a prisoner of war, and in 1867 he remarried. Lee became president of the Virginia Agricultural Society, state senator (1875–1878), and U.S. congressman (1886–1891). Likely the most successful of the Lee children, Rooney Lee died October 15, 1891.

— EMORY M. THOMAS

LETCHER, JOHN

Letcher, John (1813–1882), governor of Virginia. Letcher grew up in the comfortable middle class in Lexington, Virginia, in the Shenandoah Valley. Optimistic and gregarious, he became a lawyer and for a while edited a local newspaper. Politics was his real calling, and Letcher gradually rose as a moderate Jacksonian Democrat. As a delegate to the state convention of 1850–1851, he helped write a more liberal constitution for Virginia, and in return the voters in his district elected him to Congress for four consecutive terms from 1851 to 1859. There he was a moderate conservative as the South came under increasing pressure from the rising Republican party. In 1859 he won the governorship in a close contest with the disintegrating Whig party.

On January 1, 1860, forty-six-year-old Letcher and his large family moved into the governor's mansion in Richmond to begin his four-year term as the nation stumbled toward civil war. Still a moderate, he championed "prudence and moderation . . . conciliation and

"Strike the tent!"

Matthew Fontaine Maury was immediately appointed by Virginia Gov. John Letcher to serve on an advisory council charged with mobilizing state defenses.

PAGE 360

compromise" and only grudgingly went along with increased military preparations. In the November presidential election he supported Stephen A. Douglas, the Northern Democratic candidate, and after Abraham Lincoln's victory, he unsuccessfully resisted the calling of a state convention. Only after war erupted, Lincoln called for troops, and the Virginia convention voted to secede did Letcher lead his state out of the Union and into the new Confederacy.

Now Governor Letcher was the wartime leader of the most powerful state in the Confederacy; he had a new role to play. Working frantically to mobilize Virginia for total war, Letcher performed efficiently, and even many secessionists conceded that he was finally doing well. He appointed Matthew Fontaine Maury and other able men to his Advisory Council, and aware of his own lack of military experience, he often followed their suggestions. Letcher appointed Robert E. Lee to command the Virginia forces, and among the many other officers he commissioned was Thomas J. Jackson, soon to be known as "Stonewall."

Virginia's rapid mobilization produced more volunteers than weapons, but even so the governor loaned some scarce equipment to other states. A practical man, he knew the Southern states had to cooperate to win. Even more important, he realized that they would have to close ranks behind the Confederate government, which was now moving to Richmond. Letcher's confidence in President Jefferson Davis encouraged his cooperation with the Confederates as did the presence of massive Federal forces on Virginia's borders. But mainly common sense told him that old concepts of state rights, individual freedoms, and strict legalism would have to yield to the immediate demands of the war effort. This pragmatic acceptance of Confederate leadership was the hallmark of his administration.

Soon the war became a grinding battle of attrition, and the Confederacy in April 1862 acted to hold its one-year volunteers in the ranks and to mobilize able-bodied civilians by enacting the first national draft in American history. A storm of protests arose, and some states never fully cooperated with this radical but necessary measure. In private correspondence with other Southern governors Letcher denounced the new draft as unnecessary and unconstitutional, naively assuming that each state would effectively mobilize its own manpower, but he also advised his fellow governors to support Confederate conscription for the duration of the war and only then to challenge it in the courts. Again Letcher followed a win-the-war-first policy, and publicly he ordered Virginia officials to enforce the new draft.

He also cooperated with Confederate call-ups of Virginia's rapidly dwindling militia forces, despite protests from affected counties. Uneasy about vulnerable areas of the state, he backed a small, independent state force, the Virginia State Line, which did not accept men eligible for the draft. Despite Confederate complaints the governor uncharacteristically continued to support this inept little "army" until the legislature disbanded it in February 1863.

Letcher wanted the Line to protect vital saltworks in the southwestern part of the state. The South needed this essential preservative, and Virginia had some of the main sources. In the fall of 1862 the legislature passed the problem of fair distribution at reasonable prices on to the governor and gave him sweeping new powers. Letcher became the salt czar of Virginia, but he failed to establish an efficient statewide system. He hesitated to seize uncooperative saltworks and to fix prices, and he often got tangled in red tape. Early in 1863 the legislature transferred his powers to another state agency, but the salt program continued to falter.

At every level Southerners had difficulty establishing sweeping new administrative policies, and they failed to control inflation. Governor Letcher often denounced "speculators" and "extortioners," but neither he nor the legislature nor any Confederate officials could long check soaring prices that were undermining the South's economy.

Letcher also failed to prevent the Northwest's secession from the state of Virginia, but this too was a problem beyond his or the Confederates' control; the Unionists in that region were too powerful. He also failed to rouse his people with stirring oratory; his speeches were usually loaded with tedious accumulations of facts and statistics.

Clearly he had weaknesses as a popular leader, but he seldom wavered in his selfless support of the Confederate war effort, even as attacks on the Davis administration escalated. Letcher tolerated Confederate impressment of civilian property, a practice he detested and had hesitated to employ in his salt program. Even the impressment of slaves, which infuriated many planters, gained the resigned support of the governor who wanted above all to win the war.

Letcher's continuing cooperation with the Confederates became increasingly unpopular with the conservative people of Virginia. The legislature moved from complaints to actual investigations of his salt program, his support for impressment, and especially his call-ups of militia units. Letcher defended himself ably—he was handling difficult programs that were vital to the war effort—and he was never officially censured. Nevertheless, the legislators' message was clear: do not be so quick to put Confederate needs before the traditional rights and privileges of Virginians.

An experienced politician, Letcher understood, and he did ease up a little, but basically he continued to support President Davis's administration. During 1863, the last year of his governorship, the Confederates and to a lesser extent the Virginia legislature took over many of Letcher's responsibilities as he planned to continue his career by running for the Confederate Congress in his old congressional district. His supporters conducted a brief campaign, but on May 28 he lost to the incumbent. The voters had spoken: Letcher had been too much a Confederate and not enough a Virginian. Shaken by this first major defeat at the polls and economically hurt by the raging inflation in Richmond, he completed his term of office, still hoping that President Davis and General Lee could achieve victory.

Early in January 1864 Letcher and his family returned to Lexington where he continued to support the Confederate war effort as a private citizen. In June a Union army briefly occupied Lexington, and the Northern troops destroyed a few mills and salt supplies, the Virginia Military Institute, and Letcher's home—another crude but clear recognition of his service to the Southern cause.

Early in the spring of 1865 the battered Confederacy finally collapsed, and on May 17 Letcher was arrested and taken to Washington where he remained in prison for almost seven weeks. Paroled on July 10, he returned to Lexington, championed sectional reconciliation, and resumed the practice of law. In the mid-1870s he served a term in the state legislature, but his health declined rapidly. On January 26, 1882, he died at home, once again an American, a Southerner, and a Virginian.

— F. N. BONEY

LIBBY PRISON

In March 1862, the Confederates required the Richmond, Virginia, firm of Libby and Son, ship chandlers and grocers, to vacate its premises so that it could be used to hold prisoners. The Libbys left behind their business sign, which gave their name to one of the Confederacy's better known prisons. Located on Cary Street with the James and Kanawha Canal and the James River itself in the rear, it was a brick building about 300 feet long and 103 feet deep. Although it seemed to be one structure, interior brick walls divided it into thirds. It had three floors plus a basement. Barred windows, many of them unglazed, provided ventilation. City water drawn from the James provided for drinking and washing and also flushed primitive water closets, a rare amenity in Civil War prisons.

Libby's commander during most of the war was Thomas P. Turner. A Virginian who had attended but not completed both West Point and Virginia Military Institute, he began as a lieutenant and ended as a major. He also supervised other Richmond prisons. The jailer under him was an enlisted man, the unrelated Richard R. Turner. A prewar overseer, Dick Turner was a large, often angry and violent man whom most prisoners came to despise and in their recollections often confused with his superior. Prisoners also tended to dislike the officious clerk, Erasmus Ross. The staff came to include blacks captured from the Union who were made to do cleaning and other menial work. The guards were drawn from local military companies.

Because of its division into several parts, it was possible to segregate several types of prisoners within Libby. At first a few political prisoners were held there,

The opening of the prisoner exchange under the cartel of July 22, 1862, resulted in a rapid reduction of Belle Isle's population.

PAGE 48

LIBBY PRISON

This Richmond institution was one of the better known—and less inhumane—Confederate prisons, used mainly to house Federal officers taken as prisoners of war.

FRANK LESLIE'S ILLUSTRATED FAMOUS LEADERS AND BATTLE SCENES OF THE CIVIL WAR

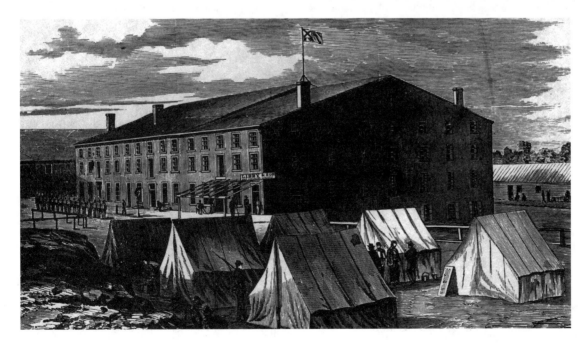

but soon it was used exclusively for prisoners of war. Although some privates were occasionally held in certain rooms later in the war, the Confederates used Libby almost entirely as an officers' prison. Because the headquarters of the Richmond prisons was in the building, many men who were being taken elsewhere were brought in to be registered, and thus a large number of prisoners later recalled having been "in Libby." During the war perhaps 125,000 prisoners actually stayed in Libby, of whom about 40,000 to 50,000 were held for a prolonged time.

The prison was most crowded between May 1863, when regular exchange of officers ceased, and May 1864, when the Confederates transferred most of the officers, using Libby thereafter mainly for transients. During the congested period, over three thousand officers complained of lack of space, cold, vermin, and short rations. Most of the officers, however, had access to money with which they purchased additional comforts, and their hardships never approximated those of the enlisted men imprisoned at Richmond nor did more than a handful die. Nonetheless, because many were highly literate they were able to circulate their understandable complaints about their imprisonment and quickly made Libby infamous.

Unhappy prisoners sometimes escaped individually, and on February 9, 1864, 109 made the Civil War's best known escape through a tunnel, with 48 being recaptured. Correctly believing that some of the others had been helped by sympathizers in the city, the Confederates attempted to stop signaling through hand gestures and cloths by shooting at prisoners who appeared at windows. In March 1864, in an effort to intimidate the prisoners and prevent an uprising in support of the Kilpatrick-Dahlgren raid on Richmond, the Confederates buried several hundred pounds of gunpowder in the basement. They later claimed that since they had informed the prisoners, this was simply a bloodless warning, but the Federals effectively featured it in their propaganda during and after the war. At the war's end, the United States used Libby for a time to confine Confederates, including Dick Turner. After reverting to commercial uses, the building was dismantled in 1888 and 1889, reerected as a museum in Chicago, and later demolished. There are remnants of it still in that vicinity.

— FRANK L. BYRNE

LINCOLN, ABRAHAM

[*This entry is composed of two articles,* Image of Lincoln in the Confederacy, *which discusses Confederates' views of the Republican ticket in the 1860 presidential election and of Abraham Lincoln himself, and* Assassination of Lincoln, *which discusses John Wilkes Booth's plot to assassinate Lincoln. For further discussion of Confederates' views of Lincoln, see* Election of 1860 *and* Republican Party. *For further discussion of the plot to assassinate Lincoln, see* Booth, John Wilkes, *and* Espionage, *articles on* Confederate Secret Service *and* Confederate Military Spies.]

IMAGE OF LINCOLN IN THE CONFEDERACY

The presidential election of 1860 did little to educate voters of the South about Abraham Lincoln, the Republican candidate. The campaign was waged in the North as a contest between Northern Democrats and Republicans, and in the South, between Southern Democrats and Constitutional Unionists; little dialogue between the sections occurred. The distorted image of Lincoln as an abolitionist (which he had never been) carried over into the Confederacy. Once war broke out, Confederates added to this core image of radicalism the usual scurrilous allegations made by one belligerent about the other.

The Confederates' descriptions of Lincoln in the press and popular literature mostly constituted perverse opposites or antic caricatures of his genuine traits. A teetotaler, Lincoln was assumed by Confederates to be a habitual inebriate. Although he had little formal education, their depiction of him as an ignorant illiterate would repeatedly be refuted by public letters and speeches of memorable eloquence and clarity. Lincoln may have seemed a coward to swaggering and militant secessionists because of his unfortunate decision to heed advisers' fears of assassination and to travel in secret through Baltimore to Washington for his inauguration in 1861. Yet from youthful tests of physical strength on the frontier to reckless exposure to enemy fire when Confederates neared Washington in 1864, Lincoln proved generally oblivious to problems of personal safety. Likewise, to depict Lincoln as a corrupt profiteer, as Confederates occasionally did, was to run counter to his consistent personal honesty in money matters. All such images were quite off the mark.

A more durable accusation focused on alleged atrocities committed by Union soldiers in the South during the war. Jefferson Davis himself initiated this tactic even before First Manassas. On July 20, 1861, the Confederate president jeered at Lincoln's recent message to the U.S. Congress and denounced to the Congress in Richmond as "rapine" the destruction of "private residences in peaceful rural retreats," the "outrages [i.e., rapes] committed on defenseless females by soldiers," and the "deliberate malignity" of denying medicines to "the sick, including the women and children" by declaring them contraband of war—in short, "waging an indiscriminate war upon. . . all, with a savage ferocity unknown to modern civilization." William Tecumseh Sherman's image would come to bear the brunt of these accusations, levied from 1861 to this day in the South, while in the end Lincoln's would by and large escape them.

One Confederate accusation, also raised early by Jefferson Davis, would stick: that the North's president was a tyrant who crushed civil liberties and rode roughshod over the U.S. Constitution. This charge, consistent with Southern antebellum complaints about Northern policies, also served Davis well, as historian Paul Escott has shrewdly observed, in keeping the focus of the Confederate citizenry on preserving white liberty from Northern aggression rather than on defending black slavery, an institution whose profits were not enjoyed equally by all classes of Southern citizens. Finally, unlike the demonic pieces of character assassination and popular billingsgate, this charge had some substance. Denouncing Lincoln's arrogation to himself of the power to suspend the privilege of the writ of habeas corpus, Davis said in the summer of 1861, "We may well rejoice that we have forever severed our connection with a government that thus tramples on all the principles of constitutional liberty."

When Lincoln announced the preliminary Emancipation Proclamation on September 22, 1862, he fulfilled Southern fears of his abolitionism. On this issue popular vituperation could hardly be distinguished from the criticism by high-ranking Confederate officials. Virtually all regarded it as a monstrous and criminal invitation to slaves to murder their masters. Davis said in his January 12, 1863, message to Congress, that the document "encouraged [slaves] to a general assassination of their masters," but he added the sophisticated argument that emancipation would mean "extermination" of the black race in America, as they would surely die out in hopeless competition with the allegedly superior white race.

Eventually Davis himself embraced emancipation (as a reward for black military service), but the desperate idea came too late in Confederate history to be put into effect. Davis's increasing difficulties in quelling dissent, desertion, and draft resistance also led him to adopt a policy on civil liberties that Confederate critics in the press likened to Lincoln's. In other words, Davis and Lincoln came to fight the war in similar ways, as historian David Donald pointed out in 1978, using conscription and avoiding realistic taxation. Yet to this day most historians retain images of Davis and Lincoln as opposites.

The notion, born of Lincoln's reputation for personal charity and forgiveness, that Lincoln would not have reconstructed the Southern racial order had he lived contained genuine power to soften Lincoln's image in the South after the war was over. Eventually, Davis's reputation would fall, even among Southerners, and Lincoln's would rise.

In truth, the Confederate view of Lincoln contained little beyond what Northern Democrats said of Lincoln during the Civil War. For example, Roger B. Taney's decision in *Ex parte Merryman*, declaring Lincoln's suspension of the writ of habeas corpus illegal, became Confederate propaganda when it was reprinted in Jackson, Mississippi, and New Orleans during the war. And *Abraham Africanus I,* a political pamphlet published in New York in 1864, would have found a welcoming audience in the Confederacy. Only the intensity of feeling against Lincoln was greater among Confederates than among his determined Northern critics—and even the intensity was finally matched by John Wilkes Booth and his little band of Confederate sympathizers.

— MARK E. NEELY, JR.

ASSASSINATION OF LINCOLN

"Damn the rebels! This is their work," exclaimed U.S. Secretary of the Navy Gideon Welles when he first learned of Lincoln's assassination. Many other Northerners naturally leaped to the same conclusion, and President Andrew Johnson issued a proclamation on May 2, 1865, offering rewards for the arrest of Jefferson Davis along with Jacob Thompson, Clement C. Clay, Beverly Tucker, and George N. Sanders, identified as "rebels and traitors . . . harbored in Canada," for conspiring to procure the murder of President Lincoln. These prominent Confederates escaped prosecution, but the military trial of Booth's co-conspirators and Maryland associates was guided by the theory that the assassination was a Confederate plot.

That now seems very unlikely, though many persons active at one time or another in the Confederate cause were involved with John Wilkes Booth, the actor who shot Lincoln and who identified himself as "a Confederate . . . doing duty *upon his own responsibility.*" Booth's original idea, hatched in the overheated election summer of 1864, was to kidnap Lincoln, take him to Richmond, and perhaps exchange him for Confederate prisoners of war. Late in the year Booth visited Montreal, where he stayed in a hotel notorious as a haunt of Confederate agents. In Maryland and Washington he recruited for his political crime two former Confederate soldiers, Samuel Arnold and Michael O'Laughlin; an escaped Confederate prisoner of war, Lewis Payne; a Confederate spy, John H. Surratt; and at least two other men.

By the time he gathered the conspirators, Booth had lost his opportunity (he planned to capture

"*It has long been a grave question whether any government, not too strong for the liberties of its people, can be strong enough to maintain its existence in great emergencies.*"

ABRAHAM LINCOLN
NOV. 10, 1864

Lincoln as he rode to the Soldiers Home, where the president slept during Washington's hot summer months). When he decided instead to kidnap Lincoln from a theater—the president's appreciation of drama was well known—several men dropped out of Booth's plot. Very late he decided on assassination rather than kidnapping. He shot the president on April 14, 1865, and Payne gravely wounded Secretary of State William H. Seward. Apparently the conspirators hoped, by

killing high government officials, to bring about a change that would yet save the Confederacy.

Booth escaped for a time after the murder and was aided by the Confederate spy Thomas A. Jones of Maryland, who years later wrote a book about these experiences. A Union cavalryman finally shot the assassin dead against orders.

Attempts by the U.S. War Department to implicate Confederate officials stumbled conspicuously in 1866 when a congressional committee discovered that government witness Sanford Conover and others had given perjured testimony. The cooling of Civil War passions caused further decline in belief in the existence of a Confederate assassination plot. Gradually, the theory triumphed that the crime was entirely Booth's inspiration, and even his pro-Confederate political motivation was soft-pedaled by (unconvincing) assertions that he was a deranged actor whose career was faltering.

Eventually some sentimentalists emphasized the expressions of dismay heard in the states of the Confederacy at the time of Lincoln's assassination. In truth, plenty of joy was also expressed in the South, and there exists no systematic, statistical evaluation of the evidence for Southern feelings about the murder of the Confederacy's nemesis, Abraham Lincoln.

— MARK E. NEELY, JR.

> *"Bring me Longstreet's head on a platter and the war will be over."*
>
> ABRAHAM LINCOLN

LONGSTREET, JAMES

Longstreet, James (1821–1904), lieutenant general. Born January 8, 1821, on his grandparents' plantation in the Edgefield District, South Carolina, Longstreet spent most of his youth outside Gainesville, Georgia. After his father died in 1833, his mother sent him to live with his uncle, Augustus Baldwin Longstreet, humorist, minister, and an ardent secessionist in 1860, while she relocated in Alabama. James received an appointment to West Point from Alabama (Georgia's slots were filled) and entered the academy in 1838. His academic record was hardly impressive; he graduated fifty-fourth of sixty-two in the class of 1842.

With a brevet second lieutenant's commission in hand, Longstreet served with the Fourth U.S. Infantry at Jefferson Barracks in Missouri and in Louisiana. Transferring to the Eighth Infantry in 1845, he was stationed in Florida until the outbreak of the Mexican War. From 1847 to 1849, Longstreet served as regimental adjutant and fought under Gens. Zachary Taylor and Winfield Scott. Always brave and alert, Longstreet was wounded while charging the Mexican bastion at Chapultepec. His gallant behavior earned him brevets as captain on August 20 and major on September 8, 1847. After the war, Longstreet saw duty in Texas where he received a captain's commission on December 7, 1852. On July 19, 1858, he was promoted to major in the Paymaster Department in Albuquerque, New Mexico Territory. Longstreet tendered his resignation from the U.S. Army on June 1, 1861.

Longstreet (called "Old Pete" by his men) was made a brigadier general, dated June 17, and led a Virginia brigade near Manassas Junction. He did not see action at First Manassas on July 21, but he had been engaged three days earlier at Blackburn's Ford where he repelled an advancing Federal brigade. The fight at Blackburn's Ford demonstrated the superiority of the defense and probably influenced Longstreet's tactical thinking for the rest of the war. He almost always preferred receiving the enemy's assault and then striking back with a well-directed counterattack.

Longstreet often lacked finesse when dealing with his fellow officers and civilian officials. Though he received a promotion to major general, dated October 7, 1861, he risked his career by supporting Gen. Joseph E. Johnston in his dispute with Jefferson Davis over strategy and by blaming the president for the army's failure to capture Washington after Manassas. His arrogant manner and strong opinions rankled subordinates and superiors alike. Longstreet became moody and withdrawn after he lost three of his four children to scarlet fever in January 1862.

When Johnston shifted his forces to the peninsula in the spring of 1862, Longstreet directed many of the complex movements and handled responsibilities beyond his rank. During a rearguard action at Williamsburg on May 5, Longstreet tenaciously held his ground, allowing the bulk of Johnston's force to continue its retreat. He did not, however, enjoy success at Seven Pines on May 31. Johnston's confusing orders resulted in an argument between Longstreet and Maj. Gen. Benjamin Huger, which delayed the Confederate advance. Longstreet made matters worse by swinging his troops farther south than Johnston had intended, but he redeemed himself by aggressively fulfilling his orders during the Seven Days' campaign (June 25–July 1). Longstreet especially impressed his new commander, Gen. Robert E. Lee, who told Davis that "Longstreet is a Capital soldier."

When Lee reorganized the Army of Northern Virginia after the Seven Days' Battles, he gave Longstreet the right wing, which included five divisions, while giving Maj. Gen. Thomas J. ("Stonewall") Jackson only three. At Second Manassas Longstreet arrived on the field on August 29, just to the right of Jackson. Although urged by Lee to launch an attack immediately, Longstreet warned that a premature assault would not allow him to concentrate his forces. Lee acquiesced, permitting Longstreet to bring his entire command to bear on the enemy the next day, when he drove the Federals off in confusion.

Longstreet further enhanced his reputation at Sharpsburg, Maryland, on September 17. Conspicuously wearing a pair of carpet slippers because of a foot injury, Longstreet was omnipresent, encouraging his men and even holding his staff officers' horses so they could operate the cannon of a depleted battery. One of his subordinates remembered that Longstreet was "like a rock in steadiness when sometimes in battle the world seemed flying to pieces." Throughout the day he brilliantly shifted his troops to meet each Union threat. When Longstreet returned to headquarters that night, Lee embraced him and exclaimed, "Ah! here is Longstreet; here is my old *war-horse*" (which led to Longstreet's being called "Lee's War Horse" on occasion). Lee pushed for Longstreet's promotion to lieutenant general, which was approved, dated October 9. With the boost in rank, he also received command of the First Corps.

The Battle of Fredericksburg on December 13, 1862, must have confirmed Longstreet's faith in superiority of the defense. In repulsing over 25,000 Federals at Marye's Heights, he not only took advantage of the natural terrain but improved it with entrenchments. Longstreet, in fact, deserves credit as one of the first officers to demonstrate the decisive advantage in constructing fieldworks. During the winter, he ordered the use of traverses—earthen walls that cut across a trench and protected the flanks of the men inside.

Unable to feed his army adequately at the beginning of 1863, Lee dispatched Longstreet with two divisions of the First Corps to the area south of the

James River. Although he furnished his troops with sufficient supplies, Longstreet cautiously besieged Suffolk and decided against a major assault. Controversy surrounded Longstreet's decision, since he himself had admitted that the place could be captured. Some detractors point to this failure as proof that he was not aggressive. A British observer, however, wrote that Longstreet "was never far from General Lee, who relies very much upon his judgement. By the soldiers he is invariably spoken of as 'the best fighter in the whole army.'" Because Longstreet was on detached service, he missed the Battle of Chancellorsville but marched with the army into Pennsylvania.

Longstreet and Lee collided over strategy during the Gettysburg campaign. Longstreet had favored a concentration of forces in the West, but Lee insisted on a raid into the North. Longstreet felt comfortable with his superior's plan as long as Lee would retire to a strong defensive position and force the Federals to assault the Army of Northern Virginia. When Lee decided to attack the Northern position south of Gettysburg on July 2, Longstreet felt betrayed. Lee, in fact, rejected Longstreet's suggestion to flank the Union left that day, instructing his subordinate to press straight ahead. Unusually apathetic and sluggish in his movements, Longstreet nevertheless launched a fierce assault through the Peach Orchard and Wheat Field which nearly captured Little Round Top.

"OLD PETE"

Lt. Gen. James Longstreet's delay in carrying out Robert E. Lee's orders to attack has been blamed for the Confederate loss at Gettysburg.

HARPER'S PICTORIAL HISTORY OF THE GREAT REBELLION

"He is the first general I had met since my arrival who talked of victory."

JOHN BELL HOOD
ON LONGSTREET'S
ARRIVAL AT
CHICKAMAUGA

GEN. JAMES LONGSTREET TIMELINE

1821, January 8
Born in South Carolina, but raised in Georgia.

1842
Graduated from West Point. Received commission in U.S. Army (Infantry) and saw service in Louisiana, Missouri, and Florida.

1847–1849
Service in the Mexican War where he received two brevets and was wounded at the Battle of Chapultepec.

1861
Resigned commission in U.S. Army. Appointed Brigadier General, C.S.A. Brigade commander at Battle of First Manassas.

1862
Corps commander under Robert E. Lee. Longstreet took part in the battles of Yorktown, Williamsburg, Seven Days' Battles, Second Manassas, Chickamauga and the Wilderness. Promoted to Lt. General after Battle of Antietam. Fought with distinction at Battle of Fredericksburg.

1863, July 3
Troops under his command took part in Pickett's Charge during the final day of the Battle of Gettysburg. Pickett's men were repulsed with heavy losses. The battle ended in a stalemate.

1864
Accidentally wounded by his own men during the Wilderness Campaign.

1865
Army of Northern Virginia surrendered at Appomattox.

1880
Appointed U.S. Minister to Turkey.

1897
Became Commissioner of Railroads, a post he held the rest of his life.

1904, January 2
Died near Gainesville, Georgia.

Lee continued his frontal assaults the next day against Cemetery Hill. Longstreet adamantly opposed such a move, desiring a flanking maneuver instead. Lee held firm, however, and ordered Maj. Gen. George E.

Pickett's division and elements of the Third Corps to strike the Union center. Before the attack, Longstreet told artillerist Col. Edward Porter Alexander that "I do not want to make this charge. I do not see how it can succeed." Alexander thought Longstreet "obeyed *reluctantly* at Gettysburg, on the 2nd and 3rd. But it must be admitted that his judgment in both matters was sound and he owed it to Lee to be reluctant, for failure was *inevitable*." After the battle, Longstreet privately expressed the hope that all of Lee's subordinates would share responsibility for the army's defeat and that Lee would still enjoy the South's full support.

Longstreet and two of his divisions were detached to the Army of Tennessee after Gettysburg, a plan consistent with Longstreet's strategic view that emphasized a concentration of Confederate forces in the western theater. At Chickamauga on September 20, 1863, Longstreet exploited a gap in the enemy's line, routing the entire Union army, an accomplishment that earned him a new nickname—"Bull of the Woods." He followed this triumph with a poor showing during the siege of Chattanooga when he allowed the Federals to gain a foothold at the base of Lookout Mountain at the end of October.

Longstreet also became embroiled in the feud surrounding Gen. Braxton Bragg that fall. Longstreet fueled divisiveness among the officers in the Army of Tennessee by openly criticizing Bragg. Rumors surfaced that Longstreet would replace Bragg as the army's new commander, but Jefferson Davis suggested that Longstreet receive an independent command and move toward Knoxville, which he did on November 5. A few weeks later the mission ended in failure, marking the nadir of Longstreet's career as he feuded with his subordinates, notably Maj. Gen. Lafayette McLaws, while his men suffered from a lack of rations and clothing.

Longstreet and his two divisions returned to Virginia in April 1864, a welcome addition to the Army of Northern Virginia. One of Lee's staff officers wrote to Longstreet: "I really am beside myself, General, with joy of having you back. It is like the reunion of a family."

Longstreet recaptured his former glory at the Battle of the Wilderness on May 6 by completing a forced march and then directing a counterattack that saved the Confederate right flank. In circumstances remarkably similar to the wounding of Stonewall Jackson the previous year, Longstreet's own men fired at the general and his staff, hitting the First Corps commander in the throat and right arm—a serious injury that required an extended period of absence. Because his officer corps had been thinned, Lee desperately needed the services of his lieutenant for the rest of the Overland campaign and beginning of the siege of Petersburg. One Confederate staff officer felt "very anxious that Genl. Longstreet should get back to the army . . . Genl. Lee needs him not only to advise with, but Genl. Longstreet has a very suggestive mind and none of the other Lt. Genls. have this."

With a husky voice and a paralyzed arm, Longstreet returned to the First Corps in October. The general's condition presented Lee with a perfect opportunity to reassign his subordinate to a less critical post, but Lee immediately gave Longstreet command of the army's left flank, a line that stretched north of the James River. After the Federals broke through the Petersburg defenses on April 2, 1865, Longstreet guided his own troops as well as remnants of the Third Corps during the retreat to Appomattox. When a fellow officer suggested that Longstreet impress upon Lee the need to surrender, Longstreet sharply rebuked him, saying that only Lee could make that decision and that he would follow the general to the end.

Longstreet's reputation declined precipitously after the war, largely owing to the efforts of a cadre of Southern officers headed by Jubal Early. Through the *Southern Historical Society Papers*, these men blamed Longstreet for the loss at Gettysburg and characterized him as a sulky, insubordinate officer who consistently undermined Lee's operations. Longstreet's published criticism of Lee's actions at Gettysburg in the *Philadelphia Weekly Times* of November 3, 1877, and February 28, 1878, and his affiliation with the Republican party after the war made him a convenient scapegoat for the South's defeat. Edward Porter Alexander, who had been at Gettysburg, noted that "Longstreet's *great* mistake was not in the *war,* but in some of his awkward and apparently bitter criticisms of Gen Lee." The negative sentiments held against Longstreet are reflected in an 1876 letter written by Early: "He [Longstreet] is sincerely purporting to lay claim to the chief glory for the seven days around Richmond, but the rebut I gave him on that head has taken the wind out of his sails."

Nevertheless, although Longstreet did not always agree with Lee's decisions, they maintained a warm relationship and respected each other professionally. Lee frequently camped next to Longstreet, and a British observer noted in 1863 that the friendship between the two officers was "quite touching—they are almost always together." Longstreet exhibited shortcomings as an independent commander and lacked delicacy in dealing with subordinates. In combat, however, he had few equals. Unlike Stonewall Jackson who frequently attacked in a piecemeal fashion, Longstreet delivered well-coordinated assaults by concentrating his forces against a specific point.

Pardoned on June 19, 1867, Longstreet, through connections with the Republican party, obtained a number of governmental appointments, including sur-

veyor of the port of New Orleans in 1869; postmaster at Gainesville, Georgia, in 1879; U.S. minister to Turkey in 1880; and Federal marshal for northern Georgia in 1881. President William McKinley appointed him U.S. commissioner of railroads in 1897. Longstreet spent the remaining years of his life near Gainesville where he died on January 2, 1904.

— PETER S. CARMICHAEL

LORING-JACKSON INCIDENT

In the winter of 1861–1862 Maj. Gen. Thomas J. ("Stonewall") Jackson conducted a controversial winter campaign in the mountains and the Shenandoah Valley of northwestern Virginia. After receiving reluctant approval for his plans, Jackson was reinforced by troops under Brig. Gen. William W. Loring.

The small Army of the Valley left Winchester on New Years' Day, 1862, and occupied the town of Romney two weeks later, after difficult marching and countermarching in snow and sleet. Jackson's troops fought the bitter weather, widespread illness, and each other more than they did the Federals and were in no condition to continue the campaign. Loring and his men, to make matters worse, were near mutiny over Jackson's supposed incompetence and favoritism toward his own brigades. Jackson, however, ordered Loring to occupy Romney for the winter while the rest of the army returned to Winchester and operated from there.

When Loring complained to Secretary of War Judah P. Benjamin, Benjamin ordered Jackson to send Loring back to Winchester immediately. Though Jackson complied with Benjamin's order, he tendered his resignation on January 31, 1862, protesting, "with such interference in my command I cannot expect to be of much service in the field."

A host of allies, including Governor John Letcher of Virginia, pressured Jackson to stay and persuaded him to withdraw his resignation in mid-February. The Romney campaign was overshadowed by the bitter Loring-Jackson dispute, with the result that Confederate civil authorities would not overlook Jackson's insistence on military authority again.

— J. TRACY POWER

LOST CAUSE

[*This entry is composed of two articles,* An Overview, *which discusses changing Southern interpretations of the*

War Secretary Benjamin ordered Jackson to recall Loring. Jackson did so and then submitted his resignation.

PAGE 296

"Lost things are always prized very highly."

SHELBY FOOTE
IN GEOFFREY WARD,
THE CIVIL WAR, 1990

L

LOST CAUSE

An Overview

> "Only at the moment when Lee handed Grant his sword was the Confederacy born; or to state matters another way, in the moment of death the Confederacy entered upon its immortality."
>
> ROBERT PENN WARREN
> THE LEGACY OF THE CIVIL WAR, 1961

J. B. Jones's A Rebel War Clerk's Diary (1866) presents portraits of Davis and other leaders that are among the best contemporary likenesses in Civil War literature.

PAGE 305

Civil War and Confederate defeat, and Iconography, which discusses graphic and sculptural depictions of Confederate heroes and military incidents. See also Burial of Latané; Civil War, articles on Causes of War and Causes of Defeat; Juneteenth; Memorial Organizations; Volck, Adalbert.]

AN OVERVIEW

The Lost Cause, the title of Edward A. Pollard's 1866 history of the Confederacy, first referred to the South's defeat in the Civil War, but in time it came to designate the region's memory of the war as well.

Appomattox brought defeat, desolation, and despair to the white South. Almost at once, Southerners began to memorialize their failed cause, establishing Confederate Memorial Day and dedicating funeral monuments to the Confederate dead. These activities, usually held in cemeteries, evoked mourning and melancholy even as they honored the soldiers. They formed part of a larger process through which white Southerners assimilated defeat. Former Confederates reexamined their defense of slavery and decision to secede from the Union and judged both legal and moral. To explain their defeat, some Southerners pointed to the Confederates' personal sins, such as drinking or swearing. But most Southerners proclaimed the South blameless, sought solace in biblical promises that God tested those whom he loved best, and concluded that God had chosen the South for some great destiny. Having decided God had not abandoned them, white Southerners sought other explanations for their defeat. A few leaders blamed each other; others questioned the unity, discipline, or commitment of the Southern people. Almost no one criticized the fighting mettle of Confederate soldiers; rather, their heroism was praised.

In the 1870s the process of coming to terms with defeat entered a new phase. Jubal A. Early and a few other former Confederate leaders organized the Southern Historical Society (SHS), which, through its publications and the other Southern writings it endorsed, established certain "truths" about the Confederate cause: the South had not fought to preserve slavery; secession was a constitutional and justifiable response to Northern violations of the national compact; and Robert E. Lee and Thomas J. ("Stonewall") Jackson were perfect heroes whose very existence testified to Confederate nobility. When explaining Confederate defeat, Early and the SHS offered two not altogether consistent explanations: James Longstreet's tardiness at Gettysburg led to the loss of the war, and the Confederate armies succumbed only to overwhelming numbers and resources.

Beginning in the late 1880s, the mourning and self-examination of the early postwar years gave way by the turn of the century to a popular celebration of the war. Communities throughout the South dedicated Confederate monuments. A few of these statues memorialized generals or other leaders, but most honored the common soldiers and took the form of a lone soldier, often at rest, atop a tall shaft on the courthouse square or a central street. In 1889 the United Confederate Veterans formed and chose as its leader John B. Gordon, a Confederate general committed to a New South and reconciliation with the North. Within a decade, the United Daughters of the Confederacy and the Sons of Confederate Veterans organized. All three groups participated in annual reunions of Confederate veterans, which became regional festivals that drew huge crowds. Some scholars argue that this turn-of-the-century Confederate celebration expressed a civil religion that preserved a distinctive regional identity and Lost Cause mentality. It did indirectly foster white supremacy, state rights, and Democratic party solidarity, as well as incorporate most of the positions held by the SHS. But its rituals primarily celebrated the sacrifice and heroism of the soldiers and vindicated the honor of the South. The celebration thereby rendered the Lost Cause a glorious memory with much of the war's pain, passions, and such issues as slavery or independence expunged. In fact, it did little to revive wartime ideology or forge a distinctively regional identity, but instead reinforced Southerners' deference to leaders and loyalty to country, now the reunited nation.

In 1898 the Spanish-American War allowed the South to demonstrate its loyalty and honor under fire. In the war's wake, and amid a national resurgence of racism that rendered reconciliation among whites easier, most Northerners joined in the celebration of the Confederate soldiers. Robert E. Lee became a national hero, and Blue-Gray reunions demonstrated the North's respect for its former foes. With Northern acknowledgment of Southern honor and with regional confidence restored, the Confederate celebration lost much of its intensity. As the twentieth century progressed, fewer Confederate monuments were erected. As the veteran generation died off, Confederate reunions became less spectacular, and in 1932 the old soldiers held their last major review. Sons' and daughters' organizations persisted, but neither assumed the central role in Southern society the veterans had held. With this decline of the organizations and ceremonies of the Lost Cause, no one interpretation of the war dominated Southern culture as it once had.

Southern academics and other intellectuals developed independent, conflicting interpretations of the war. In their 1930 manifesto, *I'll Take My Stand,* the Nashville agrarians sought to counter both New South commercialism and the ills of modern industrial society by promoting an image of an agrarian South, although one that all but ignored the existence of slavery. Thereafter a few conservative Southern intellectuals similarly evoked the memory of the Old South and the Confederacy in opposition to modern developments they disdained. A larger number of Southern intellectuals, however, rethought their society's celebration of the Confederacy. Novelist William Faulkner, journalist W. J. Cash, historian C. Vann Woodward, and others saw slavery as central to the sectional confrontation, stressed the Civil War's devastating effects on the South, and claimed that defeat helped create a distinctive regional mentality characterized by guilt and an appreciation for human limitations. By the 1960s, a few historians influenced by this tradition even attributed Confederate defeat to guilt over slavery which had led to a failure of Confederate nationalism. Not all historians embraced such explanations; over the course of the century scholars attributed the war to a conflict of civilizations, a blundering generation, the collapse of the political party system, and a host of other factors. They offered myriad explanations of Confederate defeat, although perhaps the overwhelming-numbers-and-resources argument remained preeminent. Most Southern historians and intellectuals, though, emphasized the importance of slavery to the conflict and viewed the war as more tragic than did the Confederate celebration or twentieth-century popular culture.

A few scholars find popular acceptance of failure, guilt, and human limits, which they label the Lost Cause mentality, in twentieth-century country music. Such sentiments appeared in many country songs, but that probably reflected the hard realities of Southern rural and lower-class life rather than any influence of the Lost Cause. The popular memory of the Civil War more often took heroic form. Novels and films—especially the silent classic *Birth of a Nation* and one of the most popular movies of all time—*Gone with the Wind*—portrayed the Old South as a conservative but romantic place that suffered a terrible defeat. Yet in most, as in *Gone with the Wind*, Confederates appeared as heroic figures who survived, if not triumphed, in the end, and slavery seemed a benign if not beneficial institution. Once again, an absence of concern about the plight of African Americans made it easier for both Northern and Southern whites to honor the heroes of the Southern cause. With twentieth-century popular culture's glorification of the Confederacy, following its celebration at the turn of the century, many white Southerners even joked that the South had not actually lost the war, which suggested that the heritage of defeat had ceased to be very important to or even very real for them. Rather than displaying some special caution or wisdom rooted in defeat, white Southerners

became among the most patriotic of Americans; the Lost Cause had primarily fostered respect for the military and unquestioning patriotism.

The Civil War Centennial, more a Northern than a Southern celebration, did little to reverse the decline of interest in the Lost Cause or to reshape its definition. Rather, the centennial further demonstrated the increasing commercialization and trivialization of the memory of the war. During the civil rights revolt of the 1950s and 1960s, many white Southerners did revive the use of Confederate symbols, especially the Confederate flag and "Dixie," in behalf of segregation and white supremacy. They thereby did much to reverse what the turn-of-the-century Confederate celebration had done to render them symbols of honor and loyalty to country. In the 1980s continued display of the Confederate flag exacerbated tensions between white and black Southerners. By then blacks who objected to Confederate symbols as an assertion of white supremacy probably reacted more to the battles of the 1960s than to those of the 1860s. But with few exceptions, black Southerners had never participated in or embraced the Lost Cause. For them the Civil War brought not defeat but deliverance from slavery. They gloried not in Confederate legions but in their ancestors' participation in a Union army that brought emancipation, which many black communities after the war, and into the present, celebrated on January 1, June 19, or various other dates.

These conflicts over Confederate symbols exposed, more than anything else, the nation's failure to establish a biracial society after it emancipated the slaves, but they also revealed that the Civil War remained important for some Southerners. Even in the 1970s and 1980s, many people, not just Southerners, reenacted Civil War battles. The Daughters of the Confederacy and Sons of Confederate Veterans persisted; many of their members continued to interpret the war much as the SHS had. But only a small minority of Southerners participated in reenactments or descendants' organizations; for the majority, Confederate symbols and evocations of the Lost Cause had little fixed meaning and little clear relationship to the issues that motivated Confederates from 1861 through 1865. When a neoconservative Harvard student flew the Confederate flag out her window to challenge liberal calls for cultural diversity on campus; when a country-music singer bragged that if the South had won the war, murderers would be hanged and the day Elvis Presley died would be a national holiday; and when an advertisement for an Atlanta hotel featured William Tecumseh Sherman's picture and told patrons "Say Sherman sent you" to receive a discount, then defining any specific ideological or cultural content to the Lost Cause became difficult, if not futile.

L

LOST CAUSE

An Overview

"*The War gave the South the Great Alibi and gave the North the Treasury of Virtue.*"

ROBERT PENN
WARREN
THE LEGACY OF THE
CIVIL WAR, 1961

"*The past is never dead. It's not even past.*"

WILLIAM FAULKNER
REQUIEM FOR A NUN, 1951

335

Moreover, in the 1980s most white Southerners displayed limited knowledge of or interest in the history of the Civil War. One survey found that just 39 percent of white Southerners claimed to have had an ancestor in the Confederate army; another 37 percent did not know if their ancestors had fought or not. Only 30 percent of the same respondents admitted they had a great deal of interest in Southern history, though another 51 percent claimed to have some interest.

By the 1990s the memory of the Civil War had not totally disappeared from Southern culture, but certainly the specificity and power of the Lost Cause had dramatically declined.

— GAINES M. FOSTER

ICONOGRAPHY

One of the great ironies of Confederate iconography is that while the cause lived, it was rarely depicted in the popular arts, but after it was lost, it was widely celebrated in postwar graphics. In yet a further irony, much of this retrospective Lost Cause parlor art was created not by Southern publishers but by Northern ones eager to profit from the reopening of the Southern marketplace, where the native print industry had all but died during the war.

Lost Cause icons—engravings and lithographs of the Confederacy's great heroes and most famous mili-

ICONS

"The Last Meeting of Lee and Jackson," painted by E.B.D. Julio in 1869, one of many Lost Cause icons the North was eager to print and sell to Southerners.

THE MUSEUM OF
THE CONFEDERACY,
RICHMOND, VIRGINIA

tary incidents—came pouring off the presses in New York, Philadelphia, Boston, and Chicago after 1866. So did sentimental genre scenes illuminating Southern defeat and suffering, typified by Currier & Ives's litho-

graph of a Confederate veteran returning to a war-ravaged home, a print aptly titled *The Lost Cause*. A landmark example of the Lost Cause icon was the print of William D. Washington's painting, *The Burial of Latané*, published in 1868 and popular for generations. As late as 1863 the Virginian who owned the original canvas noted that throughout his life he had seen "many of the steel engravings hanging on the walls of this county and neighboring counties," adding, "I really believe that these engravings helped to hold the Southern People together as one after the war."

Another important Lost Cause icon celebrating two wartime generals, *The Last Meeting of Lee and Jackson*, first appeared in a print adaptation in New Yorker Frederick Halpin's 1872 engraving. It won far greater acclaim and acceptance than the original E. B. D. Julio painting on which it was based.

Robert E. Lee and Thomas J. ("Stonewall") Jackson, together with Jefferson Davis, constituted a Lost Cause "trinity" of icons portrayed more often in prints than any other Confederate heroes. Jackson, surprisingly, proved an object of fascination for Northerners, perhaps because this "Cromwell in Gray" seemed more comprehensible to the Puritan Union culture than cavaliers like Lee. Currier & Ives even celebrated Jackson's martyrdom in a reverential deathbed print granting him a wholly military setting for his final moments, when in fact Jackson had died in a house, not a tent.

Davis had a checkered career in Lost Cause art. At first he was mercilessly lampooned in caricatures that vivified the story that he had donned hoopskirts to evade capture by Union troops. But Davis recovered from this symbolic emasculation when he was shackled at Fortress Monroe. Overnight he became a living martyr of the Lost Cause, and his reemergence was celebrated in engraved and lithographed tributes from then until his death in 1889.

No Confederate hero inspired as many prints—or as consistently reverential ones—as did Robert E. Lee. Although the enfeebled Confederate print industry had been unable to produce a single Lee portrait while the war raged, Northern publishers filled the void once the war ended, first portraying him nobly in defeat in an array of Appomattox prints in 1865. Lee's death in 1870 ignited demand for his image, and when competing memorial associations organized fund-raising appeals to erect statues in Lexington and Richmond, both offered Lee prints as premiums. "A grateful people," one observer reported, "gave of their poverty gladly" to purchase the prints—one of which showed Lee in beatific close-up, the other astride his beloved horse, Traveller.

Lost Cause prints proliferated as long as the fashion for home art itself endured. A journalist visiting a

Mobile home in 1871 noted what had become true of innumerable Southern dwellings after the war: "Upon the walls were portraits of Gen. R. E. Lee, and Stonewall Jackson, and Jefferson Davis." Added the eyewitness: "Indeed, the first two mentioned I see everywhere in the South, in private as well as in public houses."

Financed in part by the sale of popular prints, Edward Virginius Valentine's recumbent statue of Robert E. Lee was installed in 1883 atop the general's tomb in the chapel of Washington College in Lexington, Virginia. In 1890, the Lee Monument Association's heroic equestrian statue of Lee by sculptor Marius-Jean-Antonin-Mercié was unveiled before a throng of 100,000 in Richmond. An orator for the occasion declared it a blessing that "future generations may see the counterfeit presentment of this . . . bright consummate flower of our civilization."

Completion of these two Lee monuments ushered in a golden age of Confederate statuary. The city of Richmond, in particular, was soon crowded with dazzling sculpture, including a series of large equestrian statues of Jackson, J. E. B. Stuart, and others, crowning the same broad avenue where the Mercié Lee had been installed.

Atlanta, too, became an important outdoor gallery of public icons. The installation of one such tribute, Solon Borglum's sculpture of Gen. John B. Gordon, may best be remembered because it ushered in the saga of the most ambitious of all Confederate sculpture memorials—and also the most disastrous.

Around 1915, a journalist named John Graves and the president of the national United Daughters of the Confederacy, Mrs. Helen Plane, conceived of the idea of a Confederate Memorial for one of the South's grandest vistas: the face of Stone Mountain, Georgia. Appropriately, they turned to Solon Borglum's brother, Gutzon Borglum, who would later sculpt Mount Rushmore.

Borglum's plans proved even more ambitious than Graves's and Mrs. Plane's. Dismissing their proposal for a mere Lee portrait as nothing more than a "stamp on a barn door," Borglum conceived of a far grander monumental frieze that would portray artillery and infantry, and colossal sculptures of Lee, Jackson, and Davis. He began work in 1915, but was interrupted by World War I. Work resumed in 1922, and on January 19, 1924—Lee's 117th birthday—the Stone Mountain Monumental Association unveiled the massive head of Lee.

This proved the apex of the movement to create Confederate memorial statuary. Soon after, Borglum began feuding with the Monumental Association over artistic details and money. When the Association fired him, he destroyed all his models, leaving Stone

Mountain permanently unfinished—a monument not only to Lee but to the passionate, three-generation-long effort to create permanent sculpted tributes to Confederate heroes.

— HAROLD HOLZER

LOUISIANA TIGERS

The name "Louisiana Tigers" derived in 1861 from the Tiger Rifles, a Zouave company in Roberdeau Wheat's Battalion. Wheat's men became so notorious for thievery, brawling, and drunkenness that the battalion soon became known as the Louisiana Tiger Battalion. When other Louisiana commands showed similar behavior, the name was applied to all the Louisiana troops in the Army of Northern Virginia. Almost without exception the units that became notorious for

FIGHTIN' TIGER

A Louisiana Tiger depicted while not engaged in the thievery, brawling, and drunkenness for which Louisiana soldiers became infamous. (They were noted, too, for ferocity in battle.)

NATIONAL ARCHIVES

White men in New Orleans rioted, and women sporting secessionist insignia turned up their noses and drew aside their skirts when passing Federal soldiers on the street.

PAGE 399

Butler's New Orleans "Woman Order" was typical of his sternness in suppressing the disorder that greeted his troops' arrival.

PAGE 399

bad behavior were New Orleans commands. The fact that hundreds, if not thousands, of Tigers could not speak English made them even more conspicuous. In fact, many units drilled completely in French for the first year of the war.

There were the approximately thirteen thousand infantry from the Pelican State who served in the Army of Northern Virginia. Originally comprising nine regiments and five battalions, the Tigers were eventually consolidated into two brigades in the Second Corps. The First Louisiana Brigade was composed of the Fifth, Sixth, Seventh, Eighth, and Ninth Louisiana Volunteers; the Second contained the First, Second, Tenth, Fourteenth, and Fifteenth Louisiana Volunteers.

The Tigers fought in every major battle of the eastern theater and at times played a crucial role in them. At First Manassas, Wheat's Battalion first engaged the enemy and delayed them for a crucial time. Under Richard Taylor the First Louisiana Brigade marched through the Shenandoah Valley in 1862 with Thomas ("Stonewall") Jackson, who gave it much of the credit for winning the battles of Front Royal, Winchester, and Port Republic. At Second Manassas, William Edwin Starke's Second Louisiana Brigade earned fame by holding the famous railroad cut with rocks after running out of ammunition. Starke was later killed at Sharpsburg, where the First Louisiana Brigade, now under Harry Thompson Hays, lost 60 percent of its men in thirty minutes. Francis Nicholls led the Second Louisiana Brigade at Chancellorsville and lost his foot during Jackson's celebrated flank attack. Hays's brigade aided Jubal Early in holding the enemy at Fredericksburg and gained acclaim for winning some temporary success at Salem Church.

During the Gettysburg campaign, Hays's brigade made the critical charge that captured Winchester, and the Second Louisiana Brigade captured six hundred Federals at Stephenson's Depot, Virginia. At Gettysburg, Hays's men helped rout the Northerners on the first day and briefly broke the Union line and captured two batteries on Cemetery Hill on July 2. The year ended in disaster when over six hundred of Hays's men were captured during a surprise attack on their position at Rappahannock Station on November 7. Both brigades suffered heavily in the Wilderness, where Leroy A. Stafford, commanding the Second Louisiana Brigade, was mortally wounded.

Because of the heavy losses, the two brigades were consolidated under Hays but kept their separate organizations. Hays was wounded at Spotsylvania on May 9. The Second Louisiana Brigade was mostly overrun and captured at the Mule Shoe, but Hays's brigade played a crucial role in containing the Union breakthrough on the Confederate left. The consolidated brigade, under Zebulon York, accompanied Early to the Monocacy and Washington and fought well throughout the Shenandoah Valley campaign of Sheridan. When York was wounded at Third Winchester, William Raine Peck took command until early 1865. In the last days of the war, the Louisiana Brigade, under Col. Eugene Waggaman, led the attempted breakout of Petersburg at Fort Stedman and was among the last troops to leave the city. At Appomattox only 376 Tigers remained. During the war about 3,300 Tigers had died and at least 10 percent deserted.

— TERRY L. JONES

MCCAUSLAND, JOHN

McCausland, John (1836–1927), brigadier general. Born in St. Louis, Missouri, September 13, 1836, the son of Irish immigrants, McCausland graduated from the Virginia Military Institute in 1857. While a professor at VMI, he went with a number of cadets to witness the hanging of John Brown in Charlestown.

Upon Virginia's secession he formed the Rockbridge Artillery but declined its command. Later, however, he organized troops in the Kanawha Valley and assumed command of the Thirty-sixth Virginia Infantry with the rank of colonel. He was present at the surrender of Fort Donelson, Tennessee, in 1862 but escaped with his troops to safety. After serving with the infantry in southwestern Virginia until May of 1864, he was promoted to brigadier general and given command of a cavalry brigade.

McCausland saved Lynchburg, Virginia, by delaying David Hunter's advance until reinforcements could arrive. He then led a gallant charge at Monocacy, Maryland, and took his cavalry to the suburbs of Washington, D.C., at the head of Jubal Early's army.

In July of 1864 he was ordered by General Early to Chambersburg, Pennsylvania. He demanded $500,000 as retribution for damage caused by Hunter in the Shenandoah Valley. When the townspeople refused to pay, McCausland ordered the town burned. On the retreat from Chambersburg, his cavalry was surprised at Moorefield and many of his men were captured.

McCausland served throughout the Shenandoah Valley campaign and was present at Appomattox. Once again he refused to surrender; instead he cut his way through the Union lines and returned home.

Threats arising from the episode at Chambersburg caused him to flee to Europe and Mexico for two years. After his return, McCausland spent the rest of his life farming in Mason County, West Virginia. At his death on January 22, 1927, he was survived only by Felix Robertson as the last Confederate general.

— J. L. SCOTT

MCRAE, COLIN J.

McRae, Colin J. (1812–1877), Mississippi governor and congressman, and chief financial agent for the Confederacy in Europe. McRae was born in Sneedsboro (present-day McFarlan), North Carolina, on October 22, 1812. In 1817 his family moved to Mississippi where his father became a well-established merchant and trader. Eventually the family settled in Pascagoula, Mississippi, on the Gulf coast; however, as his father's business expanded, the family maintained another home in Mobile, Alabama. McRae, although he was a Presbyterian, attended the Catholic College of Biloxi, Mississippi, for one year.

McRae's father died in 1835, and he took over the operation of the family's extensive mercantile business and assumed responsibility for his ten brothers and sisters. McRae quickly became a respected cotton commissioner and was one of the most successful businessmen along the Gulf coast, where he operated a fleet of coastal trading vessels. He also invested heavily in railroad development and real estate. He was one of the founders of Mississippi City, located about eighteen miles west of Biloxi. In addition he owned thousands of acres of land and many slaves.

Active in Mississippi politics, McRae was appointed a general of militia, and in 1838 he was elected to the Mississippi legislature. In 1840, he moved his base of operations to Mobile and entered into a partnership with Burwell Boykin as a commission merchant. He also became involved in Democratic politics during

Through a series of administrative actions and laws, the Confederate government became directly involved in blockade running.

PAGE 159

NO SURRENDER

Brig. Gen. John McCausland, after fighting in Virginia and Maryland, refused to surrender at Appomattox; he cut his way through Union lines and returned home.

LIBRARY OF CONGRESS

Colin J. McRae in effect became the Confederacy's European secretary of the treasury.

PAGE 62

this period. During the 1840s, McRae formed a business arrangement with his brother John J. McRae to promote the Mobile and Ohio Railroad and later the Mobile and New Orleans Railroad. The brothers also became slave dealers, real estate brokers, and land speculators. John McRae went on to become a U.S. senator from 1851 to 1852, governor of Mississippi from 1854 to 1858, a member of the U.S. House of Representatives from 1858 until secession, and a member of the Confederate House of Representatives from 1861 to 1863.

Colin McRae was a staunch secessionist, and in January 1861 he was elected to represent Mobile County in the Provisional Congress of the Confederacy. He was named to the Finance Committee as well as the Engrossment and Enrollment, Buildings, and Naval Affairs committees. He was also appointed to the Special Committee for the Inauguration of the President and Vice-President.

Because of his vast mercantile interests, McRae was concerned with keeping the port of Mobile open and argued strongly for its defense, pointing out its value as a major shipping point in correspondence with Confederate officials. He suggested that the Confederate navy construct four patrol boats to protect Mobile's harbor area. In addition he opposed transferring large numbers of Alabama troops to the regular army, insisting that they remain under state control and be used to protect Alabama. Because he understood the importance of commerce to the Federal government and realized that one way to weaken the North's war effort was to cripple its overseas trade, McRae also pushed for the issuance of letters of marque to Southern privateers who would scour the oceans in search of Northern shipping.

McRae did not stand for reelection. Instead he became involved in equipping the Southern military and entered the arms and munitions business. In 1861, he became an agent of the Confederate Ordnance Bureau, working in an unofficial capacity until July 16, 1862, when he was appointed an Ordnance Bureau agent for the Confederacy and the state of Alabama.

In 1861 he became interested in the construction of a major arms foundry at Selma, Alabama. Selma offered an ideal location: it was inland and therefore safe from a seaborne assault, it had excellent river and rail connections, and it was close to the coal and iron deposits of central Alabama. In addition, there existed in the city a small foundry and machine shop, the Selma Manufacturing Company, which the Confederacy could purchase for $35,000. In March 1865, President Jefferson Davis approved McRae's plan and authorized the purchase of the Selma company and the construction of an arms and munitions center. In addition to his official connection with the Selma ordnance

works through his Confederate and Alabama commissions, McRae had a personal financial interest in the operation.

McRae spent much time putting the plan into effect, traveling to New Orleans to purchase equipment. The Selma operation developed into one of the largest iron manufacturing centers in the South, second only to the Tredegar Iron Works in Richmond, Virginia. Eventually the entire operation was taken over by the Confederate War and Navy departments. At the peak of its production, the Naval Arms Foundry at Selma employed three thousand workers and specialized in casting heavy cannons as well as operating an arsenal, powdermill, ironworks, and navy yard. It was at Selma that the Confederacy built the machinery and hulls for its naval vessels.

During the fall of 1862, McRae purchased cotton throughout the South and arranged for its shipment through the blockade to European markets, where it would be sold or exchanged for arms and munitions. The operation was so successful that during the first two years of the conflict European arms dealers were the principal source of Confederate weapons and military equipment.

In January of 1863 McRae served as the European manager of the Erlanger loan, negotiated with Emile Erlanger and Company of Paris, France. In return for Confederate bonds backed by cotton, Erlanger agreed to market a loan of 5 million pounds sterling in Europe for a fee equal to 5 percent of the bond issue. At the time cotton was considered an excellent financial investment for Europeans, and bond purchasers were offered two options for redeeming their investment: they could take possession of the cotton that backed the loan in New Orleans at the close of the war for a price of six pence a pound, or if they wanted their cotton before the war ended, they could demand that it be delivered to points within the Confederacy not more than ten miles from a railway or navigable stream for shipment at the bondholders' risk and expense.

The bonds were discounted 40 percent, and Erlanger was secretly allowed to take over the bonds at 77 percent and sell them in foreign financial markets at 90 percent of face value. Although the rates were exorbitant, they were not out of line with the interest charged on other loans of the period. The arrangement also allowed Erlanger and Company to repurchase the bonds, with Confederate capital, as a means of supporting the market and preventing their value from plunging. Because the bonds were backed by cotton, their successful distribution depended on the willingness of purchasers to speculate on the price of cotton.

The agreement allowed Erlanger and Company to make an enormous profit of about 13.5 million francs. The arrangement was criticized by many; however, the

THE QUEST FOR
SOUTHERN CREDIT

In October 1863, McRae suggested a plan to Confederate officials to reestablish Southern credit. First, he proposed the revoking of all contracts in which profits or commissions were allowed. Second, he demanded that a single contracting or purchasing officer be appointed for the War Department and another for the Navy Department. Third, he wanted to appoint a general agent in Europe with broad discretionary powers who would control all Southern credit, raise money, and take charge of all contracting and purchasing agents abroad. Fourth, McRae wanted the Confederate government to take control of all exports and imports, allowing nothing into or out of the South unless it was on a government account or an account of a bondholder demanding cotton. Finally, he urged that Confederate officials seize all cotton and tobacco in the South at a price fixed by Congress. This, he pointed out, would allow the government, rather than speculators, to make a profit. The plan was approved by President Davis and his cabinet and enacted into legislation in January 1864. McRae hoped that through these measures the Confederacy could restructure its credit by maintaining a monopoly on the shipping of cotton. It came too late in the war effort, however, to have much effect.

— KENNY A. FRANKS

loan and subsequent bond issue provided the South with $15 million with which to continue the war effort, and it proved to be the mainstay of Confederate purchasing power in Europe. In spite of its drawbacks, the loan underwrote most of the arms purchases made by the Confederacy abroad until 1864, and at the time its terms were about the best that McRae could have negotiated. The value of the bonds fluctuated greatly during the war years, and the price of cotton rose and fell as the Federal blockade restricted trade and new cotton-producing areas were opened in Egypt. When the war ended the bonds became worthless, but their holders continued to scheme for their redemption for several years.

McRae returned home briefly in 1863 to complete the transfer of the Selma operation to the Confederate government. That same year he was named the chief Confederate overseas financial agent and devoted most of his time and energy to maintaining the South's credit, an increasingly difficult task as the North began to assert its supremacy on the battlefield and the Union's navy tightened its blockade of Southern ports.

At first the blockade was enforced by only one warship responsible for approximately three hundred miles of coastline. It had little effect on Southern trade with Europe and caused McRae little trouble. By 1864, however, the Federal navy had grown from 42 warships to 671 vessels, and their stranglehold on the South threatened to cut communications with other countries. Although McRae did everything possible to maintain trade, his efforts failed, and with the fall of Wilmington, North Carolina, which was evacuated by Southern forces on February 11, 1865, his task became impossible.

In the fall of 1864, at the urging of Secretary of State Judah P. Benjamin, McRae embarked on a secret mission to recruit Poles, who had unsuccessfully rebelled against Russia earlier that year, into Confederate service. In August 1864, four Polish officers had run the Federal blockade and offered their services to President Davis in return for the Confederacy setting aside an area in which the exiles could settle. Davis agreed and authorized the Poles to organize their own military units. On September 1, Benjamin ordered McRae to oversee the arrangements to ship the exiles to Mexico and from there into the Confederacy. He was not to induce any Poles to volunteer; they had to offer their services on their own. McRae was given 50,000 British pounds from the Secret Service fund to carry out the plan. The project failed to generate support among exiles, and in February 1865, McRae admitted to Benjamin that the recruitment effort had not succeeded.

With the downturn in Confederate military fortunes, several holders of Southern bonds in Europe sued McRae in an effort to force payment of their notes. In every instance the courts ruled in McRae's favor and acquitted him of any legal obligation. At the end of the war McRae returned to Mississippi and reestablished many of his former businesses.

When Davis was indicted for treason in 1867, McRae was among those supplying funds for the defense. Although Davis was charged under a statute enacted in 1790, Federal prosecutors never brought the matter to trial, as the defense maintained that the Fourteenth Amendment precluded any further punishment of ex-Confederates. After numerous delays the charges were dropped, and Davis was released under the provisions of a presidential proclamation of general amnesty in December 1868.

In the fall of 1867, McRae joined a group of Confederate expatriates to form a colony of exiles in Central America. He purchased a plantation and mercantile establishment at Puerto Cortès in Honduras. Applying his business talents to the new endeavor, McRae quickly became involved in the cattle and

Slidell highly recommended Erlanger's proposed bond issue, in part because Erlanger was influential with the emperor of France.

PAGE 190

By the time the
Seven Days'
Battles ended, the
Army of the
Potomac was
thirty miles from
Richmond.

PAGE 533

mahogany trade and expanded his mercantile business. He was joined in Honduras by his brother John and one of their sisters. John died in British Honduras (present-day Belize) while visiting Colòn in May 1868 and was buried there. Colin McRae also died in British Honduras in February 1877 and was buried beside his brother.

— KENNY A. FRANKS

MAFFITT, JOHN N.

Maffitt, John N. (1819–1886), naval officer and commander of blockade runners. Maffitt enlisted in the U.S. Navy in 1832 and resigned his commission in 1861 after twenty-nine years of service, including fourteen in the coastal survey. This latter service was probably responsible for the success of his blockade running.

Maffitt was commissioned a lieutenant in the Confederate navy in May 1861. His first command was *Savannah,* flagship of Josiah Tattnall's squadron, which tried to prevent the capture of Port Royal. His next assignment was as captain of a blockade runner. At Nassau on May 6, 1862, Maffitt took command of *Oreto,* which soon became *Florida.* Unable to begin his cruise immediately because of an inadequate crew, incomplete armament, and yellow fever among his men, he began an odyssey in Cuba that eventually took the ship on a spectacular run through the Union blockade in full daylight at Mobile, a feat he accomplished by disguising *Florida* as an English warship. He finally began his first cruise on January 17, 1863. Although he constantly encountered difficulty in supplying his ship, Maffitt captured twenty-five merchant ships. His auxiliaries seized another twenty-two, making the captures attributed to *Florida's* first cruise a total of forty-seven.

After leaving *Florida* Maffitt returned to duty as a blockade runner and briefly commanded the ram *Albermarle* in 1864. His superiors, fearing that the aggressive Maffitt would lose *Albermarle,* had him removed. He climaxed his career by running the blockades at Wilmington, Charleston, and Galveston with *Owl.* Maffitt served for a time in the British merchant service before returning to his home in North Carolina, where he spent his remaining years on a small farm near Wilmington.

— FRANK LAWRENCE OWSLEY

MAGRUDER, JOHN B.

Magruder, John B. (1807–1871), major general. Born in Port Royal, Virginia, Magruder graduated from West Point in 1830. Serving in the First United States Artillery, he earned distinction in the Mexican War. Magruder, who became known as "Prince John," was fond of finery, drink, and revelry, which made him a conspicuous figure but raised questions about his competency among his superiors. On April 20, 1861, shortly after Virginia seceded from the Union, Magruder resigned his brevet lieutenant colonel commission in the U.S. Army. He received a Confederate commission as colonel on May 21, 1861, to date from March 16, 1861. Promotion came rapidly: he became a brigadier general on June 17 and a major general on October 7, 1861.

Command of the Confederate troops on the peninsula in May 1861 offered Magruder a critical assignment. He defeated the Federals at Big Bethel, a minor skirmish on June 10, which won him acclaim throughout the South. A more serious threat materialized in the spring of 1862, when Gen. George B. McClellan's Union army plodded up the peninsula. To slow the Federal advance, Magruder brilliantly disguised the numerical weakness of his force. His subterfuges stalled McClellan at Yorktown for an entire month. This allowed Gen. Joseph E. Johnston to shift his forces to the peninsula and assume overall command there. Magruder's performance, however, did not impress Johnston. His criticisms reached Jefferson Davis whose estimation of Magruder fell considerably.

Magruder's part in the Seven Days' Battles remains the most controversial aspect of his career in Confederate service. While Gen. Robert E. Lee concentrated the bulk of his forces on the Confederate left, Magruder and Gen. Benjamin Huger were left with 25,000 men to stave off more than 65,000 Federals south of the Chickahominy River. Repeating his tactics on the peninsula, Magruder deluded McClellan into believing that he faced a superior force. As Lee chased the retreating Federal army, Magruder joined the pursuit on June 28. The dapper Virginian suddenly became lethargic, punctuated by occasional outbursts of anger. Physical exhaustion, an allergic reaction to some medicine, and the mental strain of holding Lee's thin right flank had taken a toll on Magruder. He did not handle his troops energetically at Savage's Station on June 29 or the next day at Frayser's Farm. At Malvern Hill on July 1, Magruder fell apart. One Confederate officer observed that there was a "wild expression" in Magruder's eyes and "his excited manner impressed me at once with the belief that he was under the influence of some powerful stimulant."

The press singled out Magruder for the failure to destroy McClellan's command while Lee and Jackson largely escaped criticism. Persistent rumors of his drunkenness largely explains why Magruder became a scapegoat of the Seven Days' Battles. Shortly thereafter, he was transferred to the Trans-Mississippi and assigned to Texas in October 1862. Magruder protected the state's coast and launched a successful raid against Galveston on the first day of 1863. In 1864, Magruder detached most of his troops to Gen. Richard Taylor in Louisiana. He stayed in Texas with his small force until the end of the war.

After the war, Magruder emigrated to Mexico, where he served in the army of Maximilian. Magruder returned to the United States after Maximilian's regime fell. He died in Houston, Texas, on February 18, 1871.

— PETER S. CARMICHAEL

MALLORY, STEPHEN R.

Mallory, Stephen R. (1811–1873), U.S. senator and Confederate secretary of the navy. Mallory was born at Port of Spain on the island of Trinidad, British West Indies. His father was a construction engineer from Connecticut, and his mother was Irish. The Mallorys left Trinidad when Stephen was about a year old and lived at several places before settling in Key West in 1820. Stephen's formal education was rudimentary, consisting of six to twelve months in a country school near Blakely, Alabama, at age nine and about three years at a Moravian academy at Nazareth, Pennsylvania. He helped his mother run her boarding-house at Key West after his father's death. In 1833 he became inspector of customs at Key West and read voraciously to improve himself. Having decided to become a lawyer, he studied law under Judge William Marvin from 1830 to 1834 and was soon admitted to the Florida bar. He commanded a small vessel in campaigns against the Seminoles in the Everglades (1836–1838). In July 1838, he married Angela Moreno, a Spanish woman from Pensacola. From 1837 to 1845, he was county judge of Monroe County and was named collector of the port at Key West in 1845.

In 1850, the Florida legislature elected Mallory (a Democrat) as a U.S. senator, and he was reelected in 1856. Appointed chairman of the Naval Affairs Committee in 1853, he unsuccessfully supported appropriations for the development of an ironclad floating battery that was something of a forerunner of Confederate armorclads. His Naval Retiring Board removed Matthew Fontaine Maury from active duty in 1855, prompting much criticism. This board and other reforms designed to streamline the navy's personnel became the model for the Union Navy Department's reorganization during the Civil War. In 1858, President James Buchanan offered to appoint

Mallory minister to Spain, but he declined the appointment.

Although he had been a strong supporter of the South while in the Senate, Mallory opposed secession.

NAVY SECRETARY

Though often criticized during the war, Stephen R. Mallory performed well in building a navy from scratch and is regarded as one of the best in the Confederate cabinet.

NAVAL HISTORICAL CENTER, WASHINGTON, D.C.

Nevertheless, he resigned on January 21, 1861, after Florida left the Union. Offered the post of chief justice of the state's Admiralty Court, he turned it down. Mallory's political enemies accused him of preventing the Florida authorities from seizing Fort Pickens in January 1861, but he had conferred with and received support from senators from other Southern states in advising against bloodshed at that time. Mallory did use his influence with Buchanan to keep warships from entering Pensacola Harbor and to prevent reinforcements from being landed at the fort.

Jefferson Davis named Mallory head of the Navy Department on February 25, 1861. He had not sought the office and was unaware of his nomination. One reason for his appointment was that he came from Florida, which was allotted a prominent cabinet position because of the date of its secession. Mallory had also had experience in naval affairs during his long career, and he had shown great interest in innovations and improvements in both ship design and naval ordnance. The Florida delegation to Congress opposed his nomination because of their misunderstanding of his actions involving Fort Pickens. Mallory's was the only appointment delayed in the Congress, though he was ultimately confirmed on March 4. He and Postmaster General John H. Reagan were the only two men who remained in their cabinet positions throughout the conflict.

Mallory's department at the beginning of the war consisted of approximately twelve small ships and some three hundred officers who had left the U.S. Navy. Although he allowed these officers to retain their

*The Department of
the Navy, under
Stephen R.
Mallory, began the
war without a
major vessel and
soon lost easy
access to
international sea-
lanes from
Southern ports.*

PAGE 81

*Clement C. Clay
was a strong
supporter of
Mallory, and
apparently used
his influence to
exonerate the
Navy secretary.*

PAGE 128

Union ranks, he based promotions entirely on gallant or meritorious conduct. In May 1863, Mallory persuaded Congress to create the Provisional Navy. Through it, he could promote young and energetic officers, which was a significant reform. One of Mallory's major accomplishments as secretary was recruiting and training sailors for the navy. Many of these men transferred to their vessels from the army, despite some opposition by several secretaries of war.

To create a navy, Mallory had to purchase ships built abroad or have them built there. The department also issued thirty-two contracts from June 1861 to December 1862 for construction of gunboats and other vessels within the Confederacy. He emphasized the building of several powerful ironclads. Mallory wrote in May, "I regard the possession of an iron-armored ship as a matter of the first necessity." He hoped to use ironclads to break the Union blockade of the Southern coast. After Mallory called for acquisition of an ironclad, Congress appropriated $2 million to purchase or construct such ships in Europe.

Capt. James D. Bulloch was sent to England to purchase ironclads that could sink the wooden block-aders, and fast commerce raiders that would clear the oceans of Northern merchant ships. Mallory hoped the activities of the commerce raiders would draw blockaders away from the Southern ports. Bulloch succeeded in having *Florida* and *Alabama* constructed by the Laird shipyards and turned over to Confederate commanders. Lt. James H. North also went to Europe to purchase one or more existing ironclads. Although he failed to buy such a vessel, he did have construction of an ironclad ram *(Stonewall)* started in Scotland. It was eventually sold to Denmark before its completion and was acquired by the Confederacy from that country, though too late to participate in the conflict. Bulloch's efforts to obtain two additional ironclad rams from the Laird shipyards in Liverpool failed when the British government gave in to Union diplomatic pressure and seized them in October 1863 before they were completed.

To help pay for these activities, Mallory sent other agents to Europe with the authority to promise cotton for ship construction. This use of cotton bonds set a precedent, and the government authorities in Richmond tried to make better use of their large cotton reserves. In 1863, after the Navy Department's funds began dwindling, Mallory became involved in blockade running and ordered Bulloch and Comdr. Matthew Fontaine Maury to buy a speedy runner to take cotton to Europe. Eventually Bulloch acquired three vessels, which brought him sufficient amounts of cotton to finance his work. Mallory kept these operations small so that they would not interfere with those

of the War Department, which conducted most of the blockade running.

Mallory put some of his best officers, men like Raphael Semmes and John N. Maffitt, aboard the commerce raiders because of the importance he attached to their activities. The efforts of his raiders failed to secure one of the objectives for which he had obtained them. Though these vessels destroyed millions of dollars of Northern shipping, the Union government chose to accept the loss of its merchant ships rather than weaken or abandon the blockade. The warships that did go in search of the raiders were mostly older and heavier vessels that would have been of little use in patrolling the coastline.

To create a navy in the South, Mallory acquired gunboats through purchase, construction, and capture. He set up workshops for producing naval supplies and machinery and foundries for casting cannons and projectiles. As with his overseas program, the naval secretary stressed construction of ironclads. The design he preferred was that of a casemated, armor-plated wooden vessel similar to the floating battery he had supported in the 1850s. Mallory intended for the first of his ironclads to attack the Union blockading ships and open Southern ports. He also hoped that his gunboats would be seagoing vessels that would take the war to the North. None of them, however, was seaworthy, nor did any possess adequate engines for such ambitious projects.

Confederate work crews at Norfolk raised the frigate *Merrimack* from where it had been scuttled. It was converted into an ironclad ram and renamed *Virginia*. Mallory contracted for construction of four armored vessels on the Mississippi River, two at New Orleans and two at Memphis. Various delays prevented completion of all of these gunboats. At New Orleans, *Louisiana* had to be used as a floating battery because its machinery could not propel it against the flow of the river. Memphis fell before the two vessels there were finished, but one, *Arkansas,* was taken up the Yazoo River in Mississippi and completed there. That ship, too, had problems with faulty engines, which led ultimately to its being blown up by its crew to avoid capture.

After the summer of 1862, however, Mallory changed both the mission and the size of his new ironclads. Their primary duty became the defense of the Confederacy's rivers and harbors by supporting the masonry and earthen fortifications that guarded those areas. Instead of the large, deep-draft vessels designed by Lt. John M. Brooke, Mallory switched over to smaller and lighter ironclads based upon the plans of John L. Porter, chief naval constructor. The loss of Norfolk and New Orleans forced Mallory to establish new shipyards at various places in the interior. In addition to facilities at Richmond and Charleston, ironclad construction was started or completed at:

- Selma, Mobile, Oven Bluff, and Montgomery, Alabama;
- Columbus, Georgia;
- Shreveport, Louisiana;
- Yazoo City, Mississippi;
- Whitehall and Edward's Ferry, North Carolina.

Despite their weaknesses, the presence of vessels such as *Tennessee* at Mobile Bay caused Union naval authorities to delay or even cancel attacks on Southern ports.

At first, the Confederate navy could obtain new cannons only from the Tredegar Iron Works in Richmond. Mallory sent Lt. Catesby Jones to Selma, Alabama, in the spring of 1863 to assume control of a foundry there that had been converted to produce heavy ordnance, armor plate, and projectiles. From January 1864 to March 1865, the Selma works turned out fifteen rifled and banded cannons designed by John Brooke. With the rifled pieces produced in Richmond, the Selma guns meant that the navy never had a shortage of modern armament for its vessels. Naval ordnance works at Atlanta, Richmond, Charleston, and Charlotte manufactured gun carriages and other equipment. A powder mill established originally at Petersburg, Virginia, was moved to Columbia, South Carolina, and after 1864 it was producing all the navy's needs.

Mallory played an active and early role in the development and use of torpedoes, or mines. The use of these devices became one of the most successful aspects of the navy's activities during the war. Confederate minefields helped keep the Union navy from entering Charleston Harbor and delayed the attack on Mobile Bay. By the end of the war, torpedoes had sunk or damaged forty-three enemy vessels, including four monitors. These devices destroyed more Federal warships than did all the Confederate gunboats. Mallory also supported the development and employment of torpedo boats and submarines. One of the first submarines was *Pioneer,* which was built at New Orleans. It was scuttled upon the fall of the city, having never had an opportunity to attack the enemy. *H. L. Hunley* became the first submarine in history to attack and sink an enemy vessel, the steam sloop *Housatonic.* A number of semisubmersible torpedo boats called Davids were constructed at Charleston, and the Confederates were planning to build a model that could venture into the open sea. Because of this latter development, one historian has stated that the Davids might have become a more prominent offensive weapon if the war had lasted longer.

The construction of the Eads ironclads at St. Louis for the Union navy concerned Mallory greatly. Because of them, he decided that it was more important to defend New Orleans from the north than from the Gulf of Mexico. In early April 1862, Flag Officer George N. Hollins at Memphis received a message from Cmdr. William C. Whittle at New Orleans that Flag Officer David G. Farragut's Union squadron had entered the Mississippi River. Whittle asked Hollins to come to his assistance. Hollins did so and telegraphed Mallory asking permission to order his vessels southward. He felt that his wooden gunboats would be more effective against Farragut's wooden ships than against the ironclads. Mallory declared that it was more important to oppose the latter, and he even proposed sending the ironclad *Louisiana* northward. He thought that the forts on the lower river would be able to stop Farragut.

When the Federal squadron steamed past the forts, forced the destruction of the ironclads *Mississippi* and *Louisiana,* and captured New Orleans, Mallory was virtually incapacitated by the distress he suffered as a result of these disasters. He came under severe criticism not only for the fall of the Crescent City but also for the loss of Norfolk, Memphis, and *Virginia,* which all occurred about the same time. In August 1862, the Confederate House of Representatives called for an investigation into the Navy Department's role in these events, and a joint committee conducted hearings for about a year and a half. In its report, however, the committee exonerated Mallory from any guilt and praised him for the achievements his department had accomplished so far.

Occasionally, Mallory directed his subordinates to attempt unusual or unrealistic schemes. His message to Capt. Franklin Buchanan in March 1862 suggesting that *Virginia* sail into the Atlantic Ocean and attack New York City was one such order. In February 1863, he proposed an expedition whereby sailors would use small boats to carry them at night to Union monitors stationed off the coast. Once aboard, the men would douse the ironclads with flammable substances and set them afire. A lieutenant went to Charleston to set up such a force, but the project was stopped by the naval commander there in favor of using spar torpedoes. This small unit was called the Special Service Detachment, and ten boats were acquired for it. By September, the force had been broken up and the project abandoned without any attacks on the blockaders.

Mallory and his wife were well liked by Richmond society, even though they were not well known there when the war started. One historian has written of the Floridian that "his wit, his powers as a raconteur, his

The torpedo sank the blockader Housatonic *but may also have sunk* Hunley. *The submarine did not return from its raid and has never been found.*

PAGE 277

genial manners and frank courtesy soon won general esteem." The Mallory home accommodated a number of distinguished visitors to the capital during the course of the war. Mallory was not only adept at spinning tales and flattering the ladies, but he cooked well and mixed excellent mint juleps. Despite the long hours he devoted to his job, he found time to relax with his family.

In mid-January 1865, Mallory urged his naval commander at Richmond, Flag Officer John K. Mitchell, to sortie down the James River with his squadron and attack the giant Federal base at City Point. He hoped that, if they were successful in destroying the base, the Confederates would force Ulysses S. Grant to break off his siege of Richmond and Petersburg. Mitchell delayed sending his vessels downstream, and when they finally moved, their attempt failed. This plan of Mallory's had a fair chance of succeeding. If it had, it might have delayed Grant's operations for some months. Disappointed with Mitchell's handling of this affair, Mallory soon replaced him with Adm. Raphael Semmes.

Mallory accompanied Jefferson Davis and the cabinet in the retreat from Richmond to Danville in early April. They then spent a week at Greensboro, North Carolina. At Charlotte, Davis asked his cabinet about

TORPEDOES AND MINES

*T*orpedo is a generic term for a variety of naval and land mines employed mainly by the Confederacy. The word derived from the Latin name for an electric ray fish whose sting numbs its prey; it was first used to describe a weapon in 1776. Disapproved on moral grounds because targets were struck without warning, the torpedo satisfied the Confederacy's urgent need to make technology compensate for its inferior strength of arms.

Torpedoes destroyed more Union vessels than all other actions: forty-three were sunk or damaged, according to the best estimate. The psychological effect in naval and military action is incalculable. Yet only one Confederate vessel fell victim to a Union torpedo: the ironclad *Albemarle* in Lt. William B. Cushing's famous raid.

As early as June 1861, Matthew Fontaine Maury initiated experiments to design and test torpedoes in the James River. Working with him were Lt. Hunter Davidson and Lt. William L. Maury. As with other naval technologies that the Confederacy refined, primitive torpedoes had been used as early as the Revolution and the Crimean War.

In addition to major factories such as Tredegar in Richmond and the Augusta Powder Works, many small facilities around the South were engaged in manufacturing torpedoes. In Atlanta, wives of naval personnel at the Atlanta Naval Arsenal were employed in this work. An array of moorings, floats, kegs, boilers, springs, triggers, and levers was utilized in various torpedo manufactures. Each type presented three basic design problems—how to deliver the torpedo to the target, how to keep the powder dry, and how to detonate the charge—problems that were addressed in a variety of ways.

Some torpedoes were set adrift in a river current or on a rising tide to strike a ship's hull in random collisions. Others were anchored by grapnels or on weights to float just beneath the surface. In more shallow waters in slower currents, stationary frames held "plantations" of torpedoes. On one such frame, the torpedoes were set at a 45-degree angle facing downstream. This arrangement gave Confederate vessels unobstructed passage over the frame, but Union ships traveling upstream would trigger explosions on contact.

The crux of torpedo design was the triggering device. Some were detonated mechanically by means of a percussion fuse or a trigger pulled on a lanyard. Detonating a torpedo on a thirty-fathom lanyard or a ten-foot spar involved considerable danger. Setting torpedoes adrift or planting an unmanned stand of torpedoes involved a considerable element of chance. A ship might not collide with the weapon or might "sweep" and destroy them. Powder and fuses deteriorated swiftly in the water, or live torpedoes created a peril for Confederates.

Torpedoes were to take many configurations, for their production was limited only by ingenuity and available supplies. The term was applied not just to floating mines studded with percussion fuses; the "coal torpedo," for instance, could probably be classified as a booby trap, for it was a bomb disguised as a lump of coal and hidden in coal bunkers. Shoveled into a Union ship's boiler, it had a devastating effect. A "clock torpedo" smuggled aboard a ship at City Point on the James functioned like a time bomb to create one of the most spectacular and costly explosions of the war.

Ships, military and naval personnel, and civilians were imperiled by stray torpedoes after the war. But by 1865 they had become an established and accepted mode of warfare.

— MAXINE TURNER

CONFEDERATE TORPEDO. Wooden torpedo recovered from Light House Inlet, Charleston, South Carolina. Photographed at the U.S. Military Academy Museum, Highland Falls, New York, 1950. NATIONAL ARCHIVES

accepting the agreement signed by Gen. Joseph E. Johnston and Maj. Gen. William Tecumseh Sherman. With four other cabinet members, Mallory advised Davis to accept the convention's terms, rejecting a proposal that the Confederacy turn to guerrilla warfare. He did not believe that it would succeed and recognized that the Southern people no longer supported the war effort. Mallory went with Davis as far as Washington, Georgia, where, on May 3, 1865, he resigned and left the party to join his family at LaGrange. Mallory did not intend to try to escape from the South.

Most historians have treated Mallory's performance as secretary of the navy better than did many of his contemporaries. The press, public, and politicians criticized him frequently for inefficiency, lack of aggressiveness, and, in some cases, doing too much himself. Given the gigantic difficulties under which he worked, Mallory accomplished a great deal and can be ranked as one of the best Confederate cabinet members. He was intelligent and not reluctant to heed the advice of his staff and his naval officers. Mallory worked well with Davis and most of his fellow cabinet members. His imagination, hard work, and enthusiasm for his job all contributed to his success. Joseph T. Durkin, Mallory's chief biographer, concluded, "He was by no means a great administrator, but he was a conscientious, methodical, and generally reliable one."

After leaving Davis's entourage, Mallory went briefly to Atlanta and then traveled on to LaGrange. On the night of May 20, he was arrested with Senator Benjamin H. Hill in the latter's home and was imprisoned at Fort LaFayette in New York Harbor. Mallory was released on parole on March 10, 1866, and joined his family at Bridgeport, Connecticut. His health had deteriorated because of the pressures of the war years and the months he had spent in prison. Mallory returned to Pensacola in July 1866 and resumed his law practice. He opposed black suffrage and Radical Reconstruction, expressing his views in numerous editorials in the *West Florida Commercial*. Mallory died at his home early on November 12, 1873, and was buried in St. Michael's Cemetery.

[*See also* Navy, *article on* Navy Department.]

— ARTHUR W. BERGERON, JR.

MANASSAS, FIRST

Ten hours of combat near Manassas, Virginia, on July 21, 1861, changed the way a nation viewed war. Both Federals and Confederates came to these fields confident of swift, relatively bloodless victories. They left behind more than 800 dead and 2,700 wounded.

They also left behind any illusions that the war could be won or lost on a single Sunday afternoon. Wrote Confederate Samuel Melton: "I have no idea that they intend to give up the fight. On the contrary, five men will rise up where one has been killed, and in my opinion, the war will have to be continued to the bloody end."

At the confluence of the Orange and Alexandria and the Manassas Gap railroads, Manassas Junction assumed preeminent importance for the Confederates in the summer of 1861. Defending at Manassas were 22,000 Confederates under the command of P. G. T. Beauregard. Beauregard knew his force to be insufficient to stop a Union overland advance on Richmond. Instead, Confederate success depended on the ability of a second Confederate army (10,000 men) in the Shenandoah Valley under Joseph E. Johnston to move swiftly to Beauregard's support when the Federals advanced. Johnston's army would move to Manassas Junction via the Manassas Gap Railroad.

On July 16, 1861, Union Gen. Irvin McDowell led 33,000 slightly trained soldiers out of Washington and Alexandria toward Manassas. Beauregard quickly sent word to Johnston and then assumed a defensive position along Bull Run. His line extended for nearly eight miles, from the Stone Bridge on the north to Union Mills on the south.

On July 18 the Federals tested the Confederate center at Blackburn's Ford. In a sharp skirmish that left 83 Union troops killed or wounded, Confederates under James Longstreet repulsed the Federals. Convinced that he could not force his way across Bull Run, McDowell, at Centreville, spent the next two days searching for an undefended ford. The Confederates made good use of the Union delay. Johnston's army slipped away from a Union force under Robert Patterson in the Shenandoah Valley and took the trains to join Beauregard at Manassas Junction. By July 21, Beauregard's and Johnston's combined forces totaled 32,000, only 1,000 less than the Federals.

McDowell's search along Bull Run uncovered an undefended crossing at Sudley Ford, about two miles north of the Confederate left at the Stone Bridge. On Sunday morning, July 21, McDowell's army moved forward in three columns. Two of them were diversionary—one toward Blackburn's and Mitchell's Ford in the Confederate center and the other toward the Stone Bridge. At 6:00 A.M. a Union 30-pounder Parrott rifle, drawn to its position near the Stone Bridge by a team of ten horses, fired the first shot of the first major land battle of the Civil War.

Meanwhile the main Union column (13,000 men with five batteries) marched northwestward toward Sudley Ford, bent on crossing the stream and sweeping southward behind the Confederates. The march pro-

"Now, gentlemen, let tomorrow be their Waterloo!"

P.G.T. BEAUREGARD
FIRST MANASSAS, 1861

"We have taught them a lesson in their invasion of the sacred soil of Virginia."

JEFFERSON DAVIS
FIRST MANASSAS, 1861

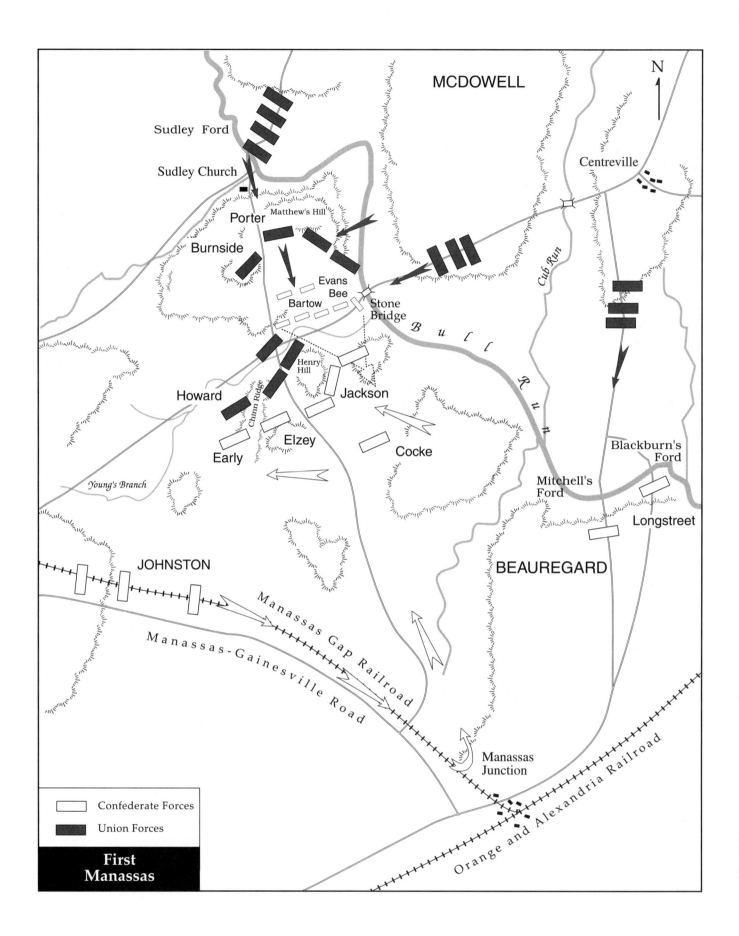

N

MCDOWELL

Sudley Ford

Sudley Church

Centreville

Porter

Matthew's Hill

Burnside

Cub Run

Evans
Bee

Bartow

Stone
Bridge

Bull

Run

Howard

Henry
Hill

Chinn Ridge

Jackson

Blackburn's
Ford

Early

Elzey

Cocke

Mitchell's
Ford

Young's Branch

Longstreet

JOHNSTON

BEAUREGARD

Manassas Gap Railroad

Manassas-Gainesville Road

Manassas
Junction

Orange and Alexandria Railroad

	Confederate Forces
	Union Forces

**First
Manassas**

STONE BRIDGE

An 1861 photograph shows a war-torn field and what was left of an old stone bridge after the Battle of First Manassas.

NATIONAL ARCHIVES

ceeded slowly but without incident until about 8:30 A.M. At that time Confederate signal officer E. P. Alexander, on the Wilcoxen farm about eight miles south of the Stone Bridge, by chance spotted the Union column. Alexander immediately sent warning to Col. Nathan Evans, whose two regiments had charge of defending the Confederate left: "Look out for your left, you are turned." At the same time, Evans received warning of the Union flanking movement from his pickets near Sudley. Leaving 200 men to defend the Stone Bridge, Evans moved with his remaining 900 to block the Union flanking column. His job: delay the Federals long enough for Confederate reinforcements from the center and right to arrive.

Evans met the head of the Federal column on the slopes of Matthew's Hill. For perhaps thirty minutes his two regiments fought alone, while the Federals piled troops from Ambrose Burnside's and Andrew Porter's brigades into the fight. At about 11:00 A.M. Confederate reinforcements arrived. Four regiments under Barnard E. Bee and Francis S. Bartow moved up on Evans's right. Along fence lines and in pine thickets the battle raged. But the Federals, outnumbering the Confederates by nearly 10,000 men, soon lapped around both Confederate flanks. The Southern lines gave way. Soon nearly 3,000 Confederates were streaming rearward to the heights of Henry Hill.

Had McDowell continued his assault at this moment, the battle might have ended as a crushing Confederate defeat. But the Federal advance stopped on Matthew's Hill. The delay gave Beauregard and Johnston the time they needed to rush reinforcements to Henry Hill to stabilize the shattered Confederate line. Thomas J. Jackson's Virginia brigade arrived first and formed behind a thirteen-gun line of artillery on the southeastern edge of Henry Hill. Behind these Virginians the fugitives from Matthew's Hill rallied. By 2:00 P.M. the Confederates on Henry Hill were presenting a strong front. It was a rejuvenation made possible only by Union delay.

At about 2:30 the Federals moved against Jackson's line on Henry Hill, first with Charles Griffin's and James B. Ricketts's batteries of artillery and then with infantry. Jackson's regiments met the Federals with a fire that routed the infantry and devastated Ricketts's battery. Later Griffin moved two of his Union cannons to within two hundred yards of the Confederate line. The Thirty-third Virginia lunged forward and captured them—the first tangible Confederate success of the day. Then the Second and Fourth Virginia of Jackson's brigade charged and captured Ricketts's battery, too. The tide of the battle turned.

For the next ninety minutes the fighting surged across Widow Henry's farm. The Confederates captured and recaptured the Union cannons three times. In this fighting General Bee and Colonel Bartow became the two highest-ranking Confederates to die in the battle. Beauregard and Johnston haphazardly threw

"Your little army . . . has met the grand army of the enemy, routed it at every point, and now it flies, inglorious in retreat before our victorious columns."

JEFFERSON DAVIS
FIRST MANASSAS, 1861

regiments into the battle as they arrived; a frantic procession of crises allowed for little coordination. McDowell, too, fed regiments into the fight singly, or at best in pairs, until by 4:00 he had few regiments left to send forward (about half the Union army remained east of Bull Run and never joined the battle). A final advance by the Eighth and Eighteenth Virginia of Philip St. George Cocke's brigade drove the last Federals off Henry Hill into the valley of Young's Branch.

Foiled in his efforts to dislodge the Confederates from Henry Hill by direct attack, McDowell tried finally to flank the Confederates by sending a brigade under O. O. Howard over Chinn Ridge, around the Confederate left. But before Howard could manage the movement, Johnston had directed two fresh brigades under Jubal Early and Arnold Elzey to Chinn Ridge. When Howard's four regiments crested the ridge, they found themselves caught in a pocket of Confederate fire. Elzey attacked. Howard's regiments broke after a brief fight. With that, from right to left, McDowell's lines began to crumble.

Harassed by Confederate artillery fire, disorganized Union regiments retreated the way they had come— some northward across Sudley Ford, a few eastward across Stone Bridge. The Confederates followed and opened fire on the Federals as they struggled across the bridge over Cub Run, about a mile east of Bull Run. A shell overturned a wagon on the bridge. The Federals panicked. "Before the third shell struck near us, every man as far as the eye could see seemed to be running for very life," recorded one Federal. For hours, frightened Union soldiers and a few hundred civilians who had come out from Washington to catch a glimpse of the battle jammed the roads leading to the Union capital. The Confederates, nearly as disorganized in victory as were the Federals in retreat, did not pursue beyond Cub Run and later returned to their bivouacs along Bull Run.

The battle produced several heroes for the Confederates. Johnston and Beauregard were foremost. Evans received just praise for his delaying action in the morning, and Elzey garnered much notice for his decisive attack on Chinn Ridge in the afternoon. But the most famous would be Jackson. His brigade had provided a focal point for rallying the fugitives from the morning fight on Matthew's Hill. And in the afternoon, his regiments had engineered the initial capture of Ricketts's and Griffin's guns. On these fields Jackson won his sobriquet "Stonewall."

The 387 Confederate dead and 1,582 wounded initially did little to dim Southern euphoria over the victory. One Southern soldier told his wife, "Sunday last . . . was the happiest day of my life, our wedding-day not excepted. I think the fight is over forever." But

Confederate glee soon yielded to the realization that the Federals had no intention of giving up. Strategically, the battle changed little in the Virginia theater; each side simply returned to its starting point to prepare for the next campaign. And people North and South soon realized that the next campaign would be infinitely larger and bloodier. It would be shown that First Manassas elevated the war to a higher, more awful and costly level. The next campaign would involve not 30,000 Federals but almost 130,000. And by 1864 the hundreds lost at Manassas would pale in comparison to the thousands lost at Gettysburg, the Wilderness, and a dozen other fields. But no battle of the war—perhaps no battle in American history— would have so dramatic an emotional impact as First Manassas.

— JOHN J. HENNESSY

MANASSAS, SECOND

War came a second time to the plains of Manassas in August 1862—this time in a form bigger, bloodier, and strategically more significant than in 1861. More than 100,000 troops participated in the battle, leaving behind more than 23,000 casualties (9,000 Confederate). Robert E. Lee's decisive victory over Federal Maj. Gen. John Pope and the Army of Virginia here laid the groundwork for his first raid into the North. Conversely, it brought the Union war effort to a dangerously low ebb. The aftermath of Second Manassas represented perhaps the South's best opportunity to win the war.

After his successful repulse of Union Gen. George B. McClellan's Army of the Potomac in the Seven Days' Battles around Richmond, Lee turned his attention northward to a second Union threat: the newly formed Army of Virginia, commanded by Pope. Fearful that Pope would menace the Virginia Central Railroad—Richmond's communications with the Shenandoah Valley—or, worse, move on Richmond from the northwest, Lee on July 15 dispatched a force under Thomas J. ("Stonewall") Jackson to confront Pope. Jackson and Pope eyed each other across the Rapidan River until August 9, when Jackson attacked an exposed part of Pope's army near Cedar Mountain, just south of Culpeper. Though a Confederate victory, after the battle Jackson had to retire across the Rapidan in the face of increasing Union numbers.

On August 15, confident that McClellan intended no further trouble in front of Richmond, Lee and James Longstreet joined Jackson near Gordonsville. Anxious to force Pope out of central Virginia before McClellan's army, now retiring from the Virginia

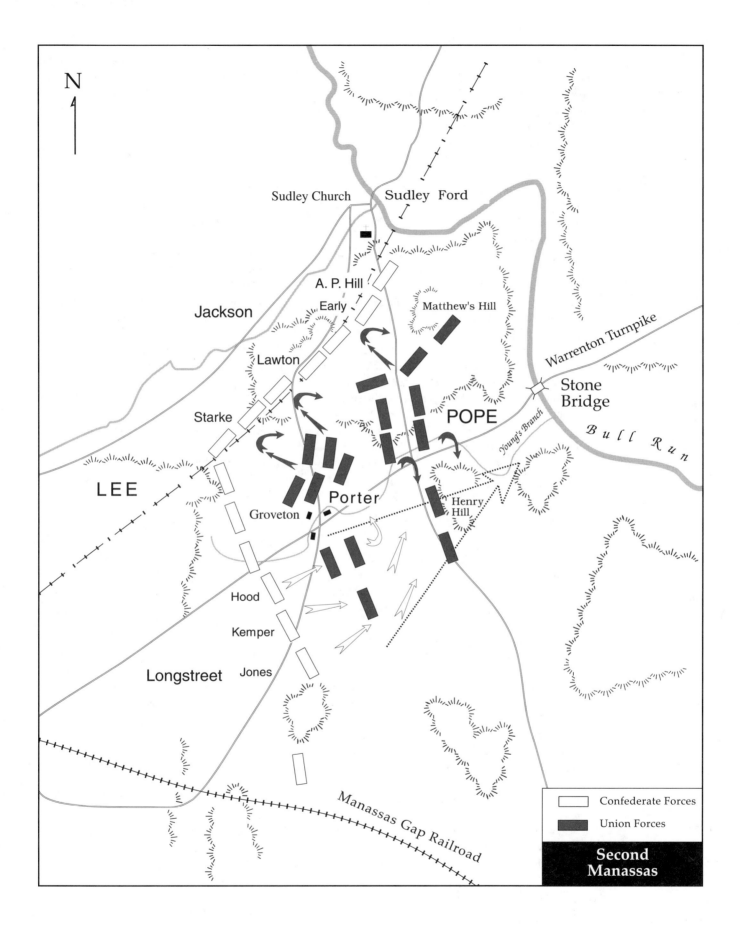

N

Sudley Church   Sudley Ford

A. P. Hill

Jackson

Early

Matthew's Hill

Lawton

Warrenton Turnpike

Starke

Stone
Bridge

POPE

Young's Branch

Bull Run

LEE

Porter

Groveton

Henry
Hill

Hood

Kemper

Longstreet   Jones

Manassas Gap Railroad

☐ Confederate Forces

■ Union Forces

**Second
Manassas**

At Second Manassas Longstreet arrived on the field on August 29, just to the right of Jackson.

PAGE 331

Peninsula, could join him, Lee hunted for a chance to strike Pope or at least drive him back. From August 17 until August 25 the armies sparred, first along the Rapidan and then, after a short retreat by Pope, along the Rappahannock.

On August 25, 1862, Lee found an opening. Holding Longstreet with 30,000 men in front of Pope, Lee sent 24,000 men under Jackson (about half the army) on a wide flanking march around Pope's right flank. They first marched northward to Salem and then turned to the southeast, through Thoroughfare Gap and Gainesville. On the evening of August 26 Jackson's troops cut the Orange and Alexandria Railroad—the Federal supply line—at Bristoe Station and Manassas Junction. In thirty-six hours Jackson's men had marched fifty-four miles to the rear of the Union army. Few strategic maneuvers of the war would surpass this one in nerve and effectiveness.

Surprised and outmaneuvered, Pope turned away from the Rappahannock and fanned out in search of Jackson's command. Jackson spent August 27 pillaging the stores at Manassas and beating back two mild Union advances. That night he set fire to the remaining plunder and marched northward to elude Pope. On August 28 he assumed a position in woods and behind ridges north of the Warrenton Turnpike near Groveton. There, Jackson knew, he could monitor the Federal march and perhaps lure Pope into battle. At the same time he would be in position to await the arrival of Lee and Longstreet, then marching to join him with almost 30,000 men.

Jackson and his troops passed a quiet day on August 28 until about 5:30 P.M. Then Jackson received word of a Union column (Rufus King's division) marching eastward on the Warrenton Turnpike, only a few hundred yards in front of his position. After watching the Union troops march unwarily by for several minutes, Jackson ordered an attack. Soon shells burst above the Federal column. Union brigade commander John Gibbon ordered his regiments to turn off the road and move against the Confederates. For the next ninety minutes the fighting raged on the Brawner and Dogan farms. Though Jackson outnumbered the Union division in front nearly three to one, he was unable to launch a coordinated assault sufficient to overwhelm the Federals. Instead the battle amounted to a brutal, largely static musketry fight waged from behind fence lines. Darkness brought an end to the indecisive fighting. Among the Confederate casualties was Richard S. Ewell, who would lose his leg and be absent from the army for nine months.

Though Jackson had failed to destroy King's division, he had revealed his position to Pope, who responded by ordering his entire army to converge on Jackson's position. The next morning, August 29, Jackson discovered that King had retreated but that additional Union troops had arrived on Henry Hill to the east. He deployed his troops along the cuts and fills of an old unfinished railroad and prepared for battle.

Meanwhile, the rest of the Confederate army, led by Lee and Longstreet, moved to join Jackson. Following Jackson's earlier route, Longstreet on August 28 pushed aside a Union force at Thoroughfare Gap. Resuming the march the next morning, the head of Longstreet's column reached the battlefield at about 10:00 A.M. Longstreet formed on Jackson's right, extending his line southward across the Warrenton Turnpike for more than a mile. Once formed, the Confederate line resembled a huge pair of jaws, ready to snap shut.

John Pope knew nothing of Longstreet's presence south of the turnpike on August 29. Instead he focused all his attention on Jackson. During the morning Franz Sigel's corps and John F. Reynolds's division moved against Jackson along a two-mile front. In what amounted to a protracted heavy skirmish, the Federals managed no progress against Jackson's lines. During the afternoon Pope intensified his efforts. At 3:00 Cuvier Grover's brigade launched a violent bayonet attack that threatened to dislocate part of A. P. Hill's division on the left of Jackson's line. Only hard fighting by Maxcy Gregg's brigade of South Carolinians and Edward L. Thomas's Georgia brigade drove the Federals back.

An hour later another Union charge, this by Col. James Nagle's brigade, plunged into Alexander Lawton's (formerly Ewell's) division, in Jackson's center. The Federals maintained their position for minutes only, until an advance by two brigades of Starke's division to Lawton's right relieved the pressure against Jackson's center and forced the Federals back.

The largest Union attack of August 29 came at 5:00 P.M., and it came against the most beleaguered part of Jackson's line: A. P. Hill's division on the left. Parts of three Union brigades surged against Gregg's brigade on a knoll southeast of Sudley Church. In an episode that would become part of Confederate lore, General Gregg unsheathed his grandfather's Revolutionary War sword and paced his line: "Let us die here, my men, let us die here," he said. Despite Gregg's urgings, his men yielded. The left of Hill's line bent back more than three hundred yards. Only the timely arrival of Jubal Early's brigade restored the Confederate front and forced the Federals to retreat.

Lee had little to do with the fighting on Jackson's front this day. Instead, he focused on launching an attack against Pope's dangling left flank. But in this he was frustrated. First Longstreet prudently requested time to examine the ground to his front. Then Lee received word of a threatening Union force hovering opposite Longstreet's right flank (this was Fitz John Porter's corps along the Manassas-Gainesville road). Not until almost 5:00 would Lee decide this force meant no trouble. But by then it was too late to launch an attack. Instead, Longstreet mounted a reconnaissance in force that ran into strong Union resistance near Groveton. Based on this, Lee canceled all plans for an attack against Pope's left.

The repulses of August 29 did nothing to dissuade Pope from continuing the battle. Indeed, on the morning of August 30 he concluded that the Confederates were retreating. At noon he launched a pursuit—one of the shortest of the war. Lee, Longstreet, and Jackson had, of course, gone nowhere. Pope decided to renew his attacks against Jackson's line. He remained unaware of Longstreet's presence opposite his left.

At 3:00 P.M. Pope launched his largest attack of the battle: more than 5,000 men under the command of Fitz John Porter surged against Starke's division on Jackson's right. In the battle's most intense burst of fighting, Jackson's men clung tenaciously to their position on the unfinished railroad, though in places the Federals closed to within ten yards. After thirty minutes of fighting many Confederates ran out of ammunition. Some met the Union attack with stones. This was, wrote one Federal, "an unlooked for variation in the proceedings." The rock-throwing episode would become the most famous incident of the battle. It lasted only moments, however, until Confederate reinforcements from Hill's division arrived. The Federals retreated, pelted all the while by the cannon of S. D. Lee's battalion, a few hundred yards to the west.

Porter's retreat threw the Union line into a spasm of disorganization. Lee and Longstreet simultaneously sensed the opportunity. Lee ordered Longstreet to attack—to seize Henry Hill and cut off the Union retreat. At the same time, he ordered Jackson to "look out for and protect Longstreet's left." Less than thirty minutes after receiving orders to advance, Longstreet had more than 20,000 soldiers moving forward toward the Union left. Less than 3,000 Federals stood in their path.

John Bell Hood's division, along the Warrenton Turnpike, led Longstreet's assault. Near Groveton the Texas Brigade struck and demolished a brigade of New York troops commanded by Gouverneur K. Warren. One Union regiment, the Fifth New York, had more men killed here than any other infantry regiment in any other battle of the war.

Next, Hood's men routed a Union brigade just west of Chinn Ridge, capturing a battery in the process. Then, joined by Nathan Evans's brigade, Hood ascended the west slope of Chinn Ridge into the face of Col. Nathaniel McLean's brigade of Ohioans. Soon the division of James Lawson Kemper arrived on Hood's right. Col. Montgomery Corse's Virginia brigade wheeled left down the crest of the ridge and crashed into the flank of the Union line. The Federals resisted stoutly, buying time for reinforcements to arrive. For the next hour both sides piled troops into the most intense sustained fighting of the battle. The fighting here would be decisive; it would determine the magnitude of the Union defeat.

While the combat raged on Chinn Ridge, Jackson stood still on the north flank. This in turn allowed Pope to pull troops from the right of his line and put them into position on Henry Hill. By the time the Federals yielded on Chinn Ridge—which they did only after buying precious time and extracting heavy Confederate casualties—four brigades of Union troops were waiting on Henry Hill. David Rumph Jones's division led the Confederate advance against Henry Hill, joined soon by Richard Heron Anderson's division and Cadmus Wilcox's brigade. But an hour of assaults left the Federals unmoved. Darkness brought an end to the fighting. The beaten but intact Union army retreated from the field that night.

The next day Lee moved again to cut off Pope's retreat to Washington by again sending Jackson on a flank march. This time, however, Pope responded promptly. He blocked Jackson's march near Germantown and then attacked him with two divisions. The resultant Battle of Ox Hill on September 1 ended in stalemate after two hours of combat in a driving rainstorm. The battle, which claimed the lives of Union Gens. Isaac Stevens and Philip Kearny, marked the end of the campaign.

The Second Manassas campaign helped chisel the identity of the Army of Northern Virginia. The army's three dominant figures assumed the roles they would henceforth play. Lee showed himself to be the master strategist—patient, trusting of subordinates, and incredibly bold. It would be his most successful campaign. By swift marching and unmatched daring, Jackson showed himself to be the master creator of opportunities. His strategic brilliance during the last week of August 1862 was second only to his Shenandoah Valley campaign. And Longstreet showed himself to be cautious—prudently so, it would prove—but swift, strong, and decisive once moved. On no other battlefield would he contribute more to Confederate victory.

Bringing a Union army to the brink of destruction—and indeed the Union cause to the edge of collapse—cost Lee some 9,000 casualties. More than 16,000 Federals fell or were captured during the campaign. The victory at Second Manassas bared the strategic table for Lee. From here he moved unfettered into Maryland, where what was perhaps the Con-

Although urged by Lee to launch an attack immediately, Longstreet warned that a premature assault would not allow him to concentrate his forces.

PAGE 331

Lee acquiesced, permitting Longstreet to bring his entire command to bear on the enemy the next day, when he drove the Federals off in confusion.

PAGE 331

federacy's greatest hope for victory perished on the banks of Antietam Creek.

— JOHN J. HENNESSY

MARCH TO THE SEA, SHERMAN'S

Union Gen. William Tecumseh Sherman completed the Atlanta campaign with the capture of that Georgia city on September 2, 1864. He allowed the Confederate Army of Tennessee under Gen. John Bell Hood to escape destruction, however, and on October 3 found himself chasing Hood back toward Chattanooga over the same ground he and Gen. Joseph E. Johnston had contested during the recently completed campaign. Frustrated, Sherman reached back to a lifetime of civilian and military experiences and decided to undertake something different. Instead of continuing to try to protect his railroad supply line by chasing Hood all over Georgia, he would send Gens. George H. Thomas and John M. Schofield with some 60,000 troops to Tennessee to handle Hood, while he cut loose from his supply line with approximately 62,000 of his best troops and marched across Georgia to the Atlantic Ocean.

In later years, Sherman called his action nothing more than a change of military base from Atlanta to Savannah, but actually he implemented psychological warfare, demonstrating to Confederate soldiers and the civilian population that the Confederacy could not defend its home front and therefore was doomed. He saw his raid as the only way to end the war quickly. It was much more effective and humane, he believed, than slaughtering troops in conventional warfare.

As he had done in his raid on Meridian, Mississippi, in early 1864, Sherman divided his invading force into two approximately equal wings (under O. O. Howard and Henry W. Slocum) with Hugh J. Kilpatrick's cavalry protecting the flanks. Since he had no supply line, the army was to consume the twenty-day rations it carried with it and the three thousand beef cattle driven along behind. For the rest, it would live off the countryside. The army left Atlanta on November 15, destroying the city's war-making capacity but leaving many of its structures standing. Opposing it was a varied collection of Confederate troops numbering perhaps 8,000: mainly Joseph Wheeler's cavalry corps and Gustavus W. Smith's Georgia militia. On November 17, William J. Hardee became overall Confederate commander in Georgia, but he could do little to stop Sherman and concentrated his small military force on fortifying Savannah. Hood and his Army of Tennessee were far away to the rear, still hoping to draw Sherman into Tennessee.

The March to the Sea covered about fifteen miles a day. The two columns traveled along separate paths, sometimes as far as fifty miles apart, throwing out foragers (bummers) in all directions to supply the troops.

"You cannot qualify war in harsher terms than I will. War is cruelty, and you cannot refine it."

WILLIAM TECUMSEH SHERMAN
LETTER TO JAMES M. CALHOUN, MAYOR OF ATLANTA, SEPT. 12, 1864

The normal daily flow of supplies to the 100,000 men and 35,000 animals in Sherman's army consisted of sixteen trains, each composed of ten cars (10-ton capacity).

PAGE 484

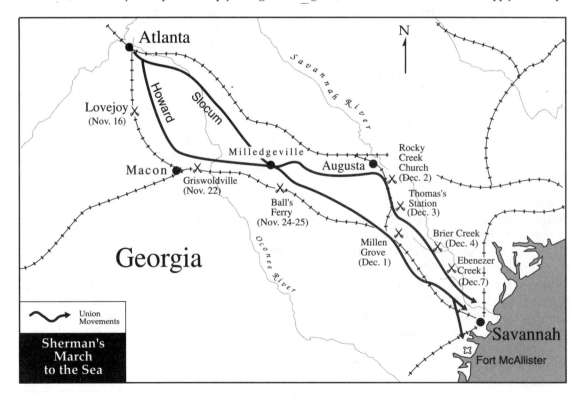

Sherman tried to make it appear that he was moving against Macon, Augusta, or Savannah and then brought his wings together to capture Milledgeville, the wartime state capital, on November 23. This indirect approach confused the outmanned Confederates and made their task even more impossible.

There were a number of skirmishes during the march, including those at Lovejoy on November 16; Griswoldville on November 22; Ball's Ferry, November 24 through 25; Millen Grove, December 1; Rocky Creek Church, December 2; Thomas's Station, December 3; Brier Creek, December 4; and Ebenezer Creek, December 7. The most memorable encounter of the march occurred on November 22 at Griswoldville, ten miles outside of Macon. Union troops brushed aside the attacking Georgia militia and to their horror found that the dead were young boys and old men. Wheeler and Smith could never offer any significant opposition to the advancing Union force. Sherman's casualties for the entire campaign were only around 2,200 men.

As the troops marched, they terrorized the countryside. Physical assault against civilians was rare, but destruction and confiscation of property was widespread. Food was regularly taken, though at times Southerners in need were helped. Clothes and household furnishings were often carried away or destroyed. It was not a scorched earth policy, however, because everything in the path of the invaders was not routinely burned. Only property connected with slavery and Union prisoners of war was systematically destroyed. For example, dogs were killed because of their use in chasing fugitive slaves and escaping Union prisoners.

There was a great deal of destruction in Georgia during the March to the Sea, but Sherman's troops were not the sole perpetrators. Ironically, Confederates helped him create the terror of war on civilians. The plundering by Confederate deserters and elements of Wheeler's cavalry, as well as runaway slaves and Union deserters, intensified the havoc. Sherman regularly wished there was some other way to end the conflict, but he was convinced there was none.

Slaves played an important role in the march. Many ran away from their masters and acted as spies for the army, and even those who simply stood by the roadside and cheered the advancing troops buoyed the soldiers with their exuberance. Sherman, whom the slaves viewed as a conquering messiah, found them an encumbrance to his army, though he treated them with respect on the personal level.

Union officers and men as a rule agreed with their commander's position that the thousands of fugitives following the army were a nuisance. There were some soldiers who were kind to the slaves, but military attitudes were usually racist at worst and condescending at

DEVIL IN GEORGIA

Still reviled—in Georgia and South Carolina especially— William Tecumseh Sherman and his March to the Sea formally introduced the South to the realities of total war.

HARPER'S PICTORIAL HISTORY OF THE GREAT REBELLION

"The legitimate object of war is a more perfect peace."

WILLIAM TECUMSEH SHERMAN 1865

best. On December 9, Gen. Jeff C. Davis, commander of the Fourteenth Corps, demonstrated army attitudes with his actions at Ebenezer Creek. Davis's unit, with black fugitives to the rear and Joe Wheeler's Confederate cavalry not far behind, was crossing the creek on pontoon bridges. As soon as the troops had crossed, the bridges were removed, and the blacks were left stranded. Fearing for their lives at the hands of Wheeler's approaching cavalry, the fugitives made desperate attempts to cross the creek. Many tragically drowned in the effort. Davis and Sherman never admitted any blame.

By December 10, only Savannah and nearby Fort McAllister stood in the way of Sherman's reaching the sea. He chose his old division from Shiloh, now under William B. Hazen, to assault the fort, and this force easily overran the garrison on December 13. William J. Hardee still held Savannah, and on December 17 Sherman demanded its surrender. He clamped a siege on the city, but, as he had in Atlanta, he allowed the Confederate force to escape when he took Savannah on December 21. Meanwhile, John M. Schofield defeated John Bell Hood at Franklin, Tennessee, on November 30, and George H. Thomas finished the job at Nashville on December 15 and 16. It was a happy Sherman who telegraphed Abraham Lincoln on December 22 offering Savannah as a Christmas gift.

Upon entering the city, Sherman continued his psychological warfare, but now he put his troops on their best behavior to show the populace the benefits of returning to the Union. He wanted Confederates to know that he believed in a hard war but a soft peace. He wanted them to quit fighting so that more death and destruction would be unnecessary.

The March to the Sea confused, frustrated, frightened, and angered the people of the Confederacy. At its start, Georgians were encouraged to rise up in opposition and burn what they could not carry away from the invaders. In the midst of the campaign, rumors were rife about the size, location, and activities of the invaders. Their arrival in an area created panic and helplessness. Throughout, Confederate newspapers predicted imminent disaster for the Federals and criticized Sherman for raiding rather than fighting, but desertions increased in Robert E. Lee's army in Virginia and the optimism of the Confederate populace plummeted. From Savannah, Sherman marched through the Carolinas during the early months of 1865, moving toward a juncture with Ulysses S. Grant against Lee in Virginia. The March to the Sea was a harbinger of modern total war, and it created the fodder for later Lost Cause arguments that Sherman was a villain and the Confederate leaders were corresponding exemplars of virtue.

— JOHN F. MARSZALEK

MARINE CORPS

Section 5 of "An Act to provide for the organization of the Navy," passed by the Provisional Congress of the Confederate States on March 16, 1861, established a Corps of Marines, commanded by a major and consisting of six companies. An amendatory act, passed May 20, 1861, expanded the corps to ten companies and elevated the grade of the commanding officer to that of colonel. All laws and regulations of the U.S. Marine Corps not inconsistent with these acts were applied to the government of its Confederate counterpart.

Lloyd J. Beall, former paymaster in the U.S. Army, was appointed colonel of the Confederate States Marines on May 23, 1861. Colonel Beall served throughout the war as the first and only commanding officer of the corps. Fifty-six officers were appointed to the corps during the war period. Nineteen were formerly officers of the U.S. Marine Corps, four had served in the U.S. Navy or Coast Survey, three were appointed directly from civilian pursuits, one, the commandant, with service in the U.S. Army, and the rest came from the ranks of the Provisional Army of the Confederate States.

The Confederate States Marines served in many of the coastal operations of the war:

- Pensacola, 1861–1862;
- Port Royal, November 5–7, 1861;
- Hampton Roads, March 8–9, 1862;
- New Orleans, April 24, 1862;
- Drewry's Bluff, May 15, 1862;
- Charleston Harbor, 1863–1865;
- Mobile Bay, August 5, 1864;
- Fort Fisher, December 24–25, 1864, and January 13–15, 1865.

Marines also served ashore at:

- Second Drewry's Bluff, May 13–16, 1864;
- Fort Gaines, August 5–8, 1864;
- Savannah, December 11–20, 1864;
- Sayler's Creek, April 6, 1865;
- Spanish Fort (Fort Blakely), April 9, 1865.

Marine Guards served aboard many of the warships of the Confederate States Navy including the commerce raiders CSS *Sumter, Georgia, Tallahassee (Olustee), Chickamauga, Stonewall,* and *Shenandoah.* One solitary Marine, Capt. Becket K. Howell, cruised aboard CSS *Alabama.*

The headquarters of the marines was located at Richmond, Virginia. Three companies garrisoned the post at Drewry's Bluff from May 1862 until the evacuation of Richmond in April 1865. Companies were regularly assigned to the naval stations at Mobile, Alabama, and Savannah, Georgia, with detachments on duty at various times at the navy yards at Richmond, Charleston, South Carolina, and Wilmington and Charlotte, North Carolina.

The marines were utilized on numerous occasions as a rapid deployment force, being called upon for missions to Charleston Harbor in February 1862 and the proposed attack upon the Federal prisoner of war compound at Point Lookout, Maryland, in July 1864. Marines also assisted in the capture of USS *Underwriter* at New Berne, North Carolina, February 2, 1864, and USS *Waterwitch* off Ossabaw Island, Georgia, June 3, 1864.

The irresistible tide of Federal ground and naval forces eliminated the Confederate naval bases at Savannah, Charleston, and Wilmington during late 1864 and early 1865. Contingents of Marines from those stations made their way to the post at Drewry's Bluff, where they were organized with sailors into a naval battalion under the command of Capt. John R. Tucker. The majority of marines were killed or captured at the Battle of Sayler's Creek on April 6, 1865. A few managed to escape, only to surrender at Appomattox on April 9, 1865. Others, components of a naval brigade made up of shipless crew from the James River Squadron, surrendered at Greensboro, North Carolina, on April 28, 1865. The last organized force of Confederate Marines, the remnant of the Mobile Company, surrendered north of that city on May 10, 1865.

— DAVID M. SULLIVAN

MASON, JAMES M.

Mason, James M. (1798–1871), congressman from Virginia and diplomat. Though by middle age James Murray Mason had attained the high office his prominent Virginia family had raised him to expect, he could not have anticipated that he would be remembered most because of the actions of others rather than his own. As the grandson of Revolutionary giant George Mason, he grew up with the arrogant confidence of a member of the Virginia gentry. He was born in the northern corner of the state that was then part of the District of Columbia, and he graduated from the University of Pennsylvania. After studying law at William and Mary, he settled in Winchester, Virginia, on a modest estate called Selma.

Mason served in the Virginia legislature in the 1820s and sat in the state's constitutional convention of 1829 and 1830, where he upheld backcountry interests against those of the Tidewater. After a single term in the U.S. House of Representatives (1838–1839), he won election in 1847 to the U.S. Senate and remained there until the secession crisis.

A state rights Democrat, Mason moved in the congenial company of his fellow Virginia senator Robert M. T. Hunter and South Carolinian John C. Calhoun. He served as chairman of the Senate Foreign Relations Committee and drafted the Fugitive Slave Law that was part of the Compromise of 1850. Like Calhoun, whose constitutional views he admired, Mason viewed sectional antagonism as something too deep to be assuaged by palliative measures. For him, Abraham Lincoln's election spelled the end of the Union. He left the Senate on March 28, 1861—nearly a month before Virginia seceded—and served briefly in the Provisional Congress in his old role as Foreign Relations chairman.

Mason's greatest challenge came when Jefferson Davis appointed him the fledgling Confederacy's diplomatic commissioner to Great Britain. Mason's letter of instruction came from his fellow Virginian Hunter, whose own Confederate reincarnation in 1861 was as secretary of state. Hunter told Mason to go to London immediately and present the South's request for diplomatic recognition not as "revolted provinces or rebellious subjects" but as a "new Confederacy and a new Government." In words hardly suited to such a proud nation, he suggested that Mason remind the English—erroneously thought to be in great need of cotton—that the supply of that staple to Britain from an independent South "would be as abundant, as cheap and as certain as if these States were themselves her colonies."

On his way to Charleston in search of a ship to run the blockade, Mason traveled in the company of another former U.S. senator, John Slidell, a Louisianan

sent by the Confederacy as emissary to France. Slidell took his family with him and, like Mason, was also accompanied by a secretary of legation. At first they planned to take the steamship *Nashville*, but an unexpected increase in activity by the blockading Northern ships made them consider going to Mexico before embarking. When they concluded that the overland

route would unduly delay their mission, they found another ship, a privateer with a shallower draft than the *Nashville* and a better chance of eluding the blockading vessels. On the evening of October 11, 1861, *Gordon* slipped out of Charleston in a driving rain and proceeded through the blockade without incident. "Here we are," Mason wrote his wife, "on the deep blue sea; clear of all the Yankees."

The ship arrived in the Bahamas three days later. On learning that the only regularly scheduled British vessel leaving from Nassau stopped, inconveniently, at New York, the commissioners decided to continue on to Cuba where they expected to find passage to the West Indies and then to London. When they reached Havana they were feted by sympathetic Spanish citizens and introduced by the obliging British consul general to Cuban authorities as diplomats of the Confederacy. They made no attempt to keep their mission a secret. Capt. Charles D. Wilkes of the warship USS *San Jacinto* learned of their presence when he put in at a port down the coast. He quickly cast off for Havana in hopes of capturing them when their ship put out to sea. The common knowledge in the Cuban capital that the Southerners had booked passage on the British mail packet *Trent* eliminated guesswork for Wilkes. On November 8 *San Jacinto* intercepted *Trent* on the high seas, and Wilkes, ignoring the cautions of his executive officer not to spark an international incident, did just that.

AMBASSADOR

James M. Mason of Virginia, the Confederacy's ambassador to Great Britain, is remembered chiefly for his role, along with John Slidell, in the Trent *affair.*

NATIONAL ARCHIVES

M

MASON, JAMES M.

Secretary of State Robert M. T. Hunter dispatched his old colleague James M. Mason to England with instructions to stress that the Confederacy would offer low tariffs.

PAGES 281–82

Mason was directed to recall to the British that they had in the past extended diplomatic recognition to other break-away nations.

PAGE 282

After firing shots across the mail packet's bow, Wilkes sent across a boarding party to take prisoner the two Confederate diplomats whose names would ever after be linked in history. For Mason and Slidell, their diplomatic role was beginning much sooner than expected. After much glowering, brandishing of bayonets, and hurling of insults between members of the boarding party and the largely Southern company of passengers, *Trent* gave up its soon-to-be-famous passengers. Though the Northern sailors did not search the British ship for papers or take it as a prize, seizing the two commissioners and their assistants was enough. While Slidell was gathering his bags to leave the mail packet, his wife asked who commanded *San Jacinto*. When told it was someone she knew, she blurted out the bald truth before Mason could stop her: "Captain Wilkes is playing into our hands!"

The incident lasted less than three hours but reverberated across the ocean for weeks to come. As *San Jacinto* sailed up the coast, often within sight of Confederate territory, Mason while pacing the decks lectured his secretary on how this act of "piracy" would force the British to join hands with the South. On November 24 *San Jacinto* dropped anchor in Boston Harbor and turned over its captives to the prison at Fort Warren. Mason and Slidell were ushered into their spartan but clean and warm quarters—an eighteen-by-eighteen-foot room that the two men shared. It was not an uncomfortable arrangement. Far from eating prison gruel in a damp cell, the Southerners enjoyed professionally cooked meals replete, as one disgusted Bostonian reported, with "champagne, fruit, cigars, English papers and letters of sympathy." "Indeed," Mason admitted, "we have a better daily table than any hotel affords."

While Mason and Slidell languished in enforced idleness, the diplomatic furor raged outside the walls of Fort Warren. Learning that Confederate emissaries had been taken at gunpoint from a British ship, the cabinet in Westminster wrestled with a way to avoid war, but as a precaution postponed planned reductions in military spending. Outside the corridors of Whitehall the British press concluded that the government could do no less than demand release of the commissioners and a formal apology from the American government. Some London editors (including one Karl Marx) argued that any war between Britain and the North would suit only the slave owners' purposes and for that reason must be avoided. But reinforcements sent to the British garrison in Canada reminded everyone that the incident could indeed lead to the result Mason so fervently prayed for in his cell in Boston Harbor. While in prison, the Virginia diplomat wrote afterward, he bet a fellow Southern inmate fifty barrels of corn that the British would demand his freedom.

When the American press learned of the outrage the *Trent* affair was causing in England, newspapers spread the fear of imminent conflict with Great Britain throughout the North. A prominent British correspondent in Washington wrote that if war broke out between his country and the North, "Old Nick will be unchained for some time to come." In Fort Warren, Mason and his companions read with enjoyment these reports on the apparent slide toward war their arrest had triggered.

The British cabinet finally composed an ultimatum demanding release of the diplomats and an apology. But as one of his last public acts, Prince Albert, consort of Queen Victoria, altered the text to soften it and provide the Americans with a face-saving retreat by saying the British government hoped Wilkes had not acted on higher authority. Formal presentation of the ultimatum to Secretary of State William H. Seward did not take place until December 23. A hint of the American response had been contained in earlier denials by Abraham Lincoln that his government had ordered Wilkes's action. On December 27 the crisis passed when Seward told the British ambassador that Mason and Slidell would be released without condition.

The Confederate detainees were surreptitiously bundled out of Fort Warren and transferred to a British warship that took them away in an icy gale to Bermuda and then on to London. Mason arrived to a hero's welcome in the Mayfair town houses and country homes of influential British sympathizers. Ominously, though, the government officially ignored him. Though he cultivated all the right elements in industry, press, and Parliament, Mason could not effect the goal he came to achieve—recognition of the Confederacy. In July 1862 he complained that "the Government here is tardy and supine" but hoped the success of Confederate arms and a shortage of cotton would change their minds. He wrote frequently to Lord Russell, secretary of state for foreign affairs, but could not gain an audience. Russell turned aside Mason's entreaties by writing rather offensively that if the Confederacy ever achieved "stability and permanence" it would be recognized: "That time, however, has not, in the judgment of Her Majesty's Government, yet arrived." Late in the war Mason did meet with Lord Palmerston but went away disappointed each time.

Perhaps the Confederate emissary could have achieved the diplomatic recognition Richmond desired, but Mason seems to have accepted defeat too easily. Certainly he could have shown more energy and more tenacity in pursuit of an admittedly difficult goal. Had he done so, his explanations for his failure would have sounded less like attempts to blame others for his own shortcomings.

By autumn 1862 Mason had abandoned his purely diplomatic approach and helped secure loans and facilitate commercial transactions for the South. The next August President Davis decided that because the British had refused his request for recognition, Mason should consider his mission "at an end" and leave London. Mason did as instructed but wrote a plaintive dispatch after he reached Paris saying he was "at some loss to know whether it was intended that I should remain for the present in Europe." He wrote his wife from his flat near the Arc de Triomphe, "I am plodding on in this Babel, but with little in it to interest me. . . . I have seen nothing in Paris. . . . In truth I have not the heart or spirit to gaze after new things." In the fall of 1863, however, he was appointed the Confederate commissioner on the Continent and traveled back and forth between London and Paris. He despaired of ever convincing the British of the rightness of his cause: "The so-called antislavery feeling seems to have become with them a sentiment akin to patriotism."

Up to the end of the war, even when the last Atlantic ports had fallen to Northern assaults, Mason continued to send his forlorn dispatches by blockade runner to Nassau and Bermuda in hopes that they would get through. In March 1865 he was still corresponding with Secretary of State Judah P. Benjamin about such irrelevancies as the missing Confederate seal he had dispatched the previous year. Even after learning of the evacuation of Richmond, he wrote that "the war will go on to final success." A last semiofficial act was to publish in the London *Index,* a news sheet subsidized by Confederate money, a refutation of Secretary of War Edwin Stanton's charge that the Lincoln assassination was engineered by the Confederate government.

Mason planned to sail for Canada in September 1865 after seeing Benjamin, who escaped from Richmond and made his way to London and eventual success as a barrister there. Mason did not leave as expected, however, and was not reunited with his family in Canada until the following April. Under the aegis of President Andrew Johnson's amnesty, the diplomat returned to Virginia in 1869, visibly older, his step slow and heavy. He could not return to Selma. Like the homes of many Southerners, it had been put to the torch during the war. After a long, gradual decline, Mason died on April 28, 1871, in Alexandria, Virginia.

[*See also* Trent Affair.]

— NELSON D. LANKFORD

MASON-DIXON LINE

Because of disputed boundaries between English colonies in America, arising from conflicting statements in colonial charters issued by various kings of England in the seventeenth and eighteenth centuries,

English surveyors and astronomers were sent to North America to locate and establish legal boundaries.

During the years 1763 through 1767, Charles Mason and Jeremiah Dixon surveyed the boundaries of three colonies, Delaware, Maryland, and Pennsylvania. The line of the latter two was surveyed westward 244 miles. Opposition by Indian tribes delayed its completion until 1784. The survey cost $75,000 and was paid by William Penn and Lord Baltimore. An eight-foot-wide vista was cut through the forests and small stone markers placed at each mile post, with larger stone markers bearing the coats of arms of Penn and Baltimore at five-mile intervals. In ensuing years many markers fell or were appropriated by settlers. In 1900 through 1902 the line was resurveyed and stabilized.

Between the Revolution and the Civil War, the line acquired additional significance as the border between Northern states that had eliminated African slavery and Southern states that retained the institution. In 1820 Missouri, west of the Mississippi River, was admitted as a slave state, with slavery prohibited in the remaining territory north of 36°30′.

Immediately prior to the Civil War, Southern slaveholding states were called "Dixie," presumably derived from the word Dixon, and popularized in a minstrel show song in 1859. The term Mason-Dixon Line has continued in use in the twentieth century to distinguish between Northern and Southern states of the American Union.

— PERCIVAL PERRY

MAURY, D. H.

Maury, D. H. (1822–1900), major general and U.S. diplomat. Educated at the University of Virginia and West Point, Dabney Herndon Maury had fifteen years' experience in the U.S. Army by the time the Civil War began in 1861. He had served with distinction during the Mexican War, published a tactics manual for mounted rifles, taught as an instructor at West Point, and fought Indians on the frontier. When his native state of Virginia seceded from the Union, Maury submitted his resignation papers to the U.S. Army. The army refused to accept his resignation and Maury found himself instead dismissed for his traitorous request. Nonetheless, he quickly left his post in New Mexico and arrived in Richmond in July 1861 to offer his military services to the Confederacy.

Maury's first assignment was as a cavalry captain. After a brief stint stationed on the Rappahannock River under Gen. Theophilus H. Holmes, Maury went west to join Gen. Earl Van Dorn's Trans-Mississippi Department. Maury once wrote that his

Mason and Slidell assumed their voyage on Trent *would be protected by international laws, so they made no effort to conceal their plans.*

PAGE 625

only "application for services ever made during the war was for service in the field of the Army of Northern Virginia." The Confederate army never granted that request, and Maury spent the entire war far west of his native state.

At the Confederate defeat at Elkhorn Tavern, Arkansas, in March of 1862, Colonel Maury's performance in the face of failure greatly impressed Van Dorn. Promotion to brigadier general came within a week.

As a brigadier general in the Army of the West, Maury competently led Confederates through the Battles of Iuka and Corinth. During the winter of 1862–1863 he won promotion to major general. In late December 1862 his division went to the aid of Stephen Dill Lee at Vicksburg, Mississippi. On April 15, Maury received new orders to go to Knoxville, Tennessee, as commander of the Department of East Tennessee. He hoped this would keep him closer to home, but in six weeks he changed posts again.

In May 1863, Maury became commander of the District of the Gulf with headquarters in Mobile, Alabama, and he and his family settled in Mobile for the duration of the war. Maury later described this assignment as an "interesting and agreeable command." It was not an idle one. For the next two years he devoted his energy to keeping Mobile and its important bay free from Federal control. He was also responsible for diverting enemy raids sent into Mississippi and Alabama. In April 1864, Federals managed to take control of Mobile Bay, but Maury stubbornly fought to defend the city until the following spring. In April 1865 he finally acquiesced to superior forces and surrendered his command. For Dabney Maury, as for other Confederate officers, his years as a soldier had come to a bitter end.

Maury's postwar years were varied, taking him from Virginia to Louisiana before he served as the U.S. minister to Colombia. Most pertinent to the history of the Confederacy, Maury was one of the founding members of the Southern Historical Society and served as its chairman for twenty years. As part of this organization Maury joined other Southerners in working to recover and make available for publication Confederate records of the war.

— LESLEY JILL GORDON-BURR

MAURY, MATTHEW FONTAINE

Maury, Matthew Fontaine (1806–1873), naval officer. Appointed an acting midshipman at the age of nineteen, Maury served for over thirty-six years in the U.S. Navy, during which time he won international recognition for his pioneering work in the fields of navigation, hydrography, and meteorology. Following Virginia's secession from the Union, Maury resigned his commission to serve in defense of his native state. He was immediately appointed by Governor John Letcher to serve on an advisory council charged with mobilizing state defenses. On April 23, 1861, Maury was commissioned a commander in the Virginia State Navy. He retained this rank when the state navy was incorporated into the Confederate navy on June 10.

In late spring 1861, Maury began a series of experiments with torpedoes, or underwater mines. He believed that, for a nation lacking the resources to construct a large navy, torpedoes offered a cheap and effective alternative for defending Southern waterways from Union warships. Although initially skeptical, Confederate Secretary of the Navy Stephen R. Mallory came to endorse Maury's ideas, and in the fall of 1861 the Confederate Congress appropriated moneys for a torpedo development program. Maury's researches led to building a torpedo with an improved electric detonator, the first used successfully in warfare.

Maury also advocated the construction of steam-powered gunboats to protect Southern waters. The gunboats he envisioned were shallow-draft and highly maneuverable, and mounted large-caliber rifled guns. Such vessels, Maury argued, could be quickly and economically built and, in large numbers, would be capable of driving Federal ships from the South's rivers and bays. The Confederate Congress was impressed enough with his proposal to appropriate $2 million to build one hundred of these gunboats. Yet Maury had scarcely begun supervising work on these craft when the program was abruptly canceled. The success of CSS *Virginia* against the Union blockading fleet at Hampton Roads had convinced the Confederate government that it should apply its limited resources to the building of ironclad warships.

In late summer 1862, Maury was ordered to England as a special agent with instructions to purchase ships for the Confederate government. Over the next two and a half years, he used his worldwide fame as a scientist to promote publicly the cause of Southern independence among the British people. In addition, he continued his experiments on electric torpedoes, the results of which were forwarded to the Navy Department. He also arranged for the purchase of two ships to serve as commerce raiders. One of these vessels, the screw steamer *Georgia*, made nine captures.

On May 2, 1865, knowing that the collapse of the Confederate government was imminent, Maury set sail for Texas with $40,000 worth of torpedo equipment in a last-ditch effort to help the Southern cause. Arriving in Havana twenty days later, he learned that the war was over. Because he fell into three of the six categories of Confederates exempted from the Federal government's 1863 amnesty proclamations (he was a U.S. Navy officer who had resigned and aided the South, an agent of the Confederate government, and a Confederate naval officer above the rank of lieutenant), Maury was unable to return to Virginia until July 1868. He was then appointed a professor of physics at Virginia Military Institute, a position he held until his death.

— CHARLES E. BRODINE, JR.

MEDALS AND DECORATIONS

Medals and decorations, as they are understood today, had no real tradition in the American military at the time of the Civil War. Although the Congress had periodically voted to award special presentation swords or gold medals to high-ranking officers and rewarded officers' bravery with brevet rank, there were no badges of recognition for enlisted men. The Medal of Honor, the first U.S. decoration, was not established until 1862. The Confederates, raised in this tradition, which in part stemmed from American disdain of what was considered to be aristocratic European foppery, therefore had no particular reason to establish medals or decorations. As a result, although the Confederate Congress authorized the president to bestow "medals with proper devices" and "badges of distinction," little was actually done to recognize individual bravery, and the few systems that did exist were largely locally created.

A "Roll of Honor" system was implemented within the various armies, with the intention of recognizing valor and serving as a substitute until medals were issued, but the medals were in fact never struck and the Roll of Honor tended to become a quota system in which companies voted on a prescribed number of recipients for the honor. Since, in many cases, far more men were deserving of the honor than received it, most companies refused to vote at all, and the system was largely a failure.

The only medals known to have been actually presented to Confederate soldiers were what was known as the "Davis Guard Medals." This was a small round silver medal, made out of Mexican silver dollars, with "Sabine Pass . . . Sept 8th . . . 1863" engraved on one side and "DG" and a Maltese cross on the other. President Davis presented forty-two of these medals to the members of the Davis Guard, a company of the First Texas Heavy Artillery, for their defense of the fortifications at Sabine Pass, Texas, in 1863.

Medallions were struck in France during the war for presentation to the members of the Stonewall Brigade, but they did not reach this country until after the war was over. They were offered for sale at veterans' reunions after 1895. All other Southern decorations, such as the United Daughters of the Confederacy's Southern Cross of Honor, were postwar decorations awarded to veterans or their families.

— LES JENSEN

MEDICAL DEPARTMENT

[This entry discusses the organization of medical services in the Confederate army.]

FOR VALOR

Front and back of a Davis Guard medal, designed by Charles Gottschalk and inscribed: "Wm Bailey, Sabine Pass, Sept. 8th, 1863."

THE MUSEUM OF THE CONFEDERACY, RICHMOND, VIRGINIA

*The Treasury
Department was
hamstrung by an
underdeveloped
banking system
and a shortage of
gold bullion.*

PAGE 81

Organization of the Confederate States Medical Department began in March 1861, with the appointment of a surgeon general, four surgeons, and six assistant surgeons. The woeful inadequacy of this staff became quickly apparent, and the department was soon enlarged to meet the needs of both the field armies and the general hospitals.

The first surgeon general, David Camden De Leon, served only from May 6 to July 12, 1861. On July 30, Dr. Samuel Preston Moore, a career military surgeon, replaced him. Moore presided over the Medical Department for the remainder of the war. The surgeon general was assigned the rank of colonel (later brigadier general); surgeons, the rank of major (later colonel); and assistant surgeons, the rank of captain. Medical officer uniforms consisted of a cadet gray tunic with black facings and a stand-up collar. Trousers were dark blue with a black velvet stripe, edged with gold cord, running the length of the leg. White gloves, a star on the collar, a green silk sash, and a cap with the letters "M.S." completed the uniform. Surgeons rarely wore this dress in the field, however.

The surgeon general was responsible for the administration of the Medical Department and the hospitals; he appointed medical officers and directed their work. During the rapid expansion of the Medical Department in the early months of the war, some incompetent physicians entered the service. Moore devised a system of examinations to remove many of these dangerous individuals. He also oversaw and encouraged the publication of professional texts for use by medical personnel.

Units of the Medical Department paralleled those of the military departments. Each army had a medical director who reported to his military commander and to the surgeon general. The chief surgeon of each army division, who was free of regimental medical duties, reported to the army medical director. Brigade surgeons, who retained regimental responsibilities, reported to the chief surgeon. Finally, each regiment had a surgeon and assistant surgeon; the first reported to the brigade surgeon.

Hospital administrative districts were not necessarily the same as those of the military departments. Each hospital was supervised by a surgeon, who reported to one of eight medical directors of hospitals, who in turn reported to the surgeon general. Confusion existed during the first two years of the war because the local military commander or army medical directors could also issue orders to the hospital surgeons. But the interlocking lines of authority were separated in March 1863, so that hospital surgeons reported solely to the medical directors of hospitals who reported solely to the surgeon general.

The general hospitals, located in cities behind the lines of active campaigning, were organized so that state residents could be kept together. Although hospitals usually occupied both fixed structures and movable pavilions, in times of heavy fighting, churches, hotels, and private homes were pressed into service. Under optimal conditions, the Medical Department tried to maintain a ratio of one surgeon for 80 patients, but this sometimes had to be stretched to one surgeon for up to 250 patients. The department also established a system of "wayside hospitals" along railroads for use by furloughed and discharged soldiers returning home.

During the course of the war approximately 1,200 surgeons and 2,000 assistant surgeons served in the Confederate army, and 26 surgeons and 93 assistant surgeons served in the Confederate navy aboard ships and at five naval hospitals.

— HERBERT M. SCHILLER

MEMMINGER, CHRISTOPHER G.

Memminger, Christopher G. (1803–1888), secretary of the treasury. Christopher Gustavus Memminger was born at Neyhinger in the Duchy of Württemberg on January 9, 1803; he was one of two foreign-born members of the Confederate cabinet. Brought to the United States in 1806, when he was orphaned, he was admitted in 1807 to the Charleston, South Carolina, Orphanage.

In 1814, he came to the attention of Thomas H. Bennett, a trustee of the orphanage and an antebellum governor of South Carolina. Bennett took Memminger into his home, assumed his guardianship, and later adopted him into his own large family. This arrangement was highly beneficial to Memminger, who gained thereby not only a happy home but the patronage of a powerful benefactor and the support of his able sons. Memminger could never have prospered to the same degree in his legal, political, and business careers or gained access to Charleston's closely knit, aristocratic society without this connection.

In 1819, Memminger graduated from South Carolina College in Charleston. Subsequently, he studied law with his uncle, Joseph Bennett, and was naturalized as an American citizen and admitted to the bar in early 1824. In his youth, Memminger displayed not only a considerable ability for hard work but also strong religious convictions. Even as a student he demonstrated a tendency toward the strict observance of rules and devotion to principles that both helped and hindered his effectiveness in public life.

Once launched on his legal career, Memminger, with his ability to present complicated legal matters in a lucid manner, soon became a leading member of the South Carolina bar. By 1860, he was a director of several companies and the owner of at least fifteen slaves, a large Charleston house, a plantation, and a summer home in Rock Hill, North Carolina. His estate, worth over $200,000, made him a Southern aristocrat.

His political career started with his serving one term as alderman in Charleston (1834–1836). During that period, he visited New England to study its educational system and on his return instituted a school board (on which he sat for many years) and free public schools for his own city. Subsequently, he served almost continuously as a member of the South Carolina Assembly (1836–1860). In that capacity he played an innovative role in promoting state support of public education, particularly the College of South Carolina.

During the nullification crisis of 1832 and 1833, Memminger had been a moderate Unionist. But he steadily became disillusioned with the Union, and by early 1860, after John Brown's raid on Harpers Ferry, he had become an advocate of secession on the basis of unified Southern action. In keeping with this plan, the South Carolina legislature sent him to Virginia to solicit the commonwealth's support for a simultaneous withdrawal of all the slave states from the Union. Because the Virginians were too badly divided to make a decision, the mission was a failure. It was significant that this reverse was attributed to Memminger's alleged lack of oratorical skills and his less than ingratiating manner.

In 1860, South Carolina seceded and Memminger was selected to go to Montgomery, Alabama, as part of the state's delegation. Before his departure, he had given some consideration to the legal needs of an independent Southern nation and had published his conclusions in "Plan of a Provisional Government for the Southern Confederacy." On the strength of this, Memminger at Montgomery was elected chairman of the committee to draft a provisional constitution. His work on that project was finished on February 8, 1861.

On February 18, Jefferson Davis arrived in Montgomery and took the oath of office as president. The next day he appointed Memminger as secretary of the treasury. The appointment was a surprise, particularly as Davis and Memminger were not acquainted. Mary Boykin Chesnut, in an addendum to her famous diary, claimed that Davis had planned to make Robert W. Barnwell, of South Carolina, secretary of state and Robert Toombs, of Georgia, secretary of the treasury. Barnwell declined the proffered honor and told Davis that the South Carolina delegation wanted Memminger at the Treasury. Davis shuffled his cabinet accordingly, moving Toombs to the State Department. Only after the appointment was announced was it dis-

TREASURER

Christopher G. Memminger, appointed Treasury Secretary by an apparent misunderstanding, combined a fear of strong central government with an inclination to laissez-faire economics.

NAVAL HISTORICAL CENTER, WASHINGTON, D.C.

covered that the South Carolina delegation was allegedly "mortified." He was not, after all, a leading figure in South Carolina.

The new secretary's professional qualifications for his office were very limited. He was honest, hardworking, and genuinely devoted to the new country. He had been a director of the Farmers Exchange Bank of Charleston for many years and had served as a member or chairman of the South Carolina Assembly's Finance Committee from 1836 to that date. But South Carolina's finances offered an atypical experience for a man about to face record deficits, for the state budget was practically always balanced and the tax assessments on land had been frozen since 1840. Memminger thus had no experience with a modern internal revenue system of the sort that the Confederacy would need if it were to have an effective fiscal program.

Memminger was also a Jacksonian Democrat with a preference for a currency comprised solely of gold and silver coin. In two cases during the 1840s, Memminger had tried to strip some of the South Carolina banks of their charters for not paying gold or silver on their notes during a panic. His opposition to irredeemable bank notes included an emphatic distaste for a legal tender currency put out solely on the central government's credit. Yet Memminger swiftly found himself, contrary to his wishes, compelled to use Treasury notes to cover a considerable part of his expenditures.

Near the end of the first Congress, Treasury Secretary Memminger reported that funding was going badly.

PAGE 147

*Secretary
Memminger
designed the tax-
in-kind to serve as
an alternative to
the impressment of
agricultural
products.*

PAGE 605

*The tax system
simply failed to
absorb a sufficient
quantity of the
Treasury notes
from circulation.*

PAGE 603

Moreover, he had a fundamental fear of a strong central government and passionately believed in laissez-faire. He himself had voted for or moved amendments to the Constitution removing the general welfare clause and inserting a provision against government aid to any group. These restrictions were later to thwart plans for the government acquisition of or control over the cotton crop.

No less serious were his personality deficiencies. As a lawyer, he believed that all actions were either legal or illegal without any ambiguities. Still worse, he would declare a proposed solution to a problem illegal without exploring alternative approaches. When one of his proposals was rejected, he would passively accept defeat and fail to pursue the matter further. If the South were to succeed in its bid for independence, it needed to approach its problems in a pragmatic and innovative manner and with a will to persevere in the face of resistance.

Moreover, though witty and friendly within his family circle, Memminger in public life exhibited an austere personality that soon got him into trouble. He offended many members of Congress by insisting that they make appointments to see him and not just drop by. He told department employees to attend to their duties and not engage in idle conversations. His demands were reasonable enough, but he put them so tactlessly as to create much ill will.

More seriously, Memminger also quarreled with members of the cabinet. He refused to refund to Postmaster General John H. Regan the gold the post office had deposited in the Treasury until President Davis ordered him to do so. Memminger also upbraided the secretaries of war and the navy for their failure to use bonds to make payments and for their habit of making sudden demands for funds on the Treasury.

Other government officers complained that Memminger was overly preoccupied with legal technicalities, was slow and uncooperative in meeting their needs, and ungraciously acted as if he had been imposed upon whenever they requested his assistance. He also shared the public delusion that the war would not last long and was convinced therefore that no extraordinary measures were needed. His administration of the Treasury met with little approval and much condemnation both during and after the war. In retrospect he was clearly miscast for the role he was called upon to play.

Many of these problems would have been mitigated had Memminger exploited an important asset—his cordial personal relationship with the president. But Memminger apparently hesitated to invoke his chief's aid—to secure orders from Davis to other members of the cabinet requiring that they cooperate with him or support his financial proposals on the floor of Congress.

The secretary had no sooner organized his department with the help of former Washington officials than hostilities commenced on April 12, 1861. When Congress reconvened in May, Memminger laid before it a war finance plan based on suggestions made by John C. Calhoun in 1816. This program called for financing the war through the issue of Treasury notes, whose value would be sustained by making them fundable into bonds paying interest in coin. As a means of checking any redundancy of the currency thus emitted, not only would the circulation be limited by funding, but direct internal taxes were to be levied sufficient to pay the interest and the maturing principal.

The success of this plan required certain administrative actions. Among the most important was procuring the necessary Treasury notes and bonds from the printers. Memminger knew that the number of local printers was inadequate for the country's needs. Nonetheless, he opposed the creation of a Southern equivalent of the Bureau of Engraving and Printing on the doctrinaire ground that such a body would encourage the use of Treasury notes after the war, a policy he adamantly opposed. He also felt that the rights of the printers as independent contractors took precedence over the Treasury's needs. Under these circumstances, the printers were practically encouraged to do slipshod work and to be late in making deliveries. This left the entire government, particularly the army, without funds for paying the soldiers or furnishing them with essential supplies. This in turn directly promoted desertion.

Besides needing an ample supply of currency to pay the government's bills, the secretary needed a stock of coin with which to pay the interest on the public debt. Memminger failed to accumulate a reserve and refused to borrow for public use the idle coin in the banks' vaults. As a result, not only did coin payments on the debt go into default after July 1862, but bond prices in terms of gold fell, making the funding of notes financially unattractive. Thus one of the key means of sustaining the value of the Treasury notes was improvidently lost. Bond sales also depended upon opening offices to make bond purchases easy for the public. Yet prior to 1863, wanting to avoid unnecessary expense, Memminger failed to use the legal authority given to him to establish more offices. As a result, note funding and bond sales were significantly diminished.

To ensure the circulation of the Treasury notes, Memminger called together a bankers' convention in Richmond on July 24, 1861. At his suggestion, the banks agreed to receive and pay out such notes, thus making them the currency of the country. Thanks to this wise measure, the secretary secured credit for his issues without having to resort to a legal tender law as was the case in the North. This gain was unfortunately offset by the secretary's refusal to follow the advice of some bankers and others to curtail by coercion or voluntary means the issuance of rival currencies. Here again, Memminger refused to pursue the matter because it would impinge on the banks' state-granted privilege of issuing their own notes.

Another important matter was procuring from Congress adequate internal revenues. Memminger knew that the blockade would diminish customs receipts and that the cotton export duty would provide little revenue. Taxes on real estate, personal property (including slaves), incomes, and sales were clearly required.

In May 1861, Memminger asked for a direct tax, but since the president sent no message backing him, Congress put off consideration of this unpopular step until July. Then, again without support from the president or the cabinet, Memminger tried to secure the passage of a modest $25 million tax bill. Congress, after bitter debate and opposition from the large slaveholders, reluctantly complied.

Despite ample warnings from the bankers that the war tax of August 19, 1861, needed to be doubled or quadrupled in order to provide even minimal revenues, Memminger did not request any new levies in 1861. Nor did he assert himself during all of 1862. Instead, he made only weak tax proposals in very general terms. Still worse, he wasted precious time on an abortive forced-loan plan (in essence a 20 percent income tax in return for which the taxpayer would be given 6 percent bonds) and a scheme calling for a state guarantee of the Confederate debt. He did not force the tax issue until January 1863, when he belatedly procured a supporting message from President Davis. Even then, his proposals were of questionable legality and were not accompanied by draft legislation.

In consequence, the tax law of April 24, 1863, enacted two years after the war began, was seriously deficient. It did not tax slaves, despite the secretary's observation that the war was being fought to protect their $3.5 billion investment in slavery. The law also taxed other items far too lightly and ordered few collections before January 1864. As a result the currency grew to nearly $900 million and the country was overwhelmed by a disastrous inflation.

Several other economic matters also required Memminger's attention. The blockade had rendered the export of the South's cotton crop difficult, and the public was clamoring for a scheme that would harness Southern staples to the war effort.

For a while, Memminger temporized, opposing and then supporting proposals that would have the government buy the cotton crop. In October 1861, the secretary finally decided, at the behest of the bankers, to declare such a plan illegal. Had the question been reformulated as a loan by the planters to the government (the Treasury was purchasing with bonds the goods and services needed by the army), then something could have been done. As it was, a cotton purchasing operation was put off until April 1862. This resulted in planter resistance to taxation, added to the costs of acquisition, and seriously delayed shipments abroad on the government's account.

A closely related question was whether, under the King Cotton doctrine, cotton shipments should be withheld with a view to coercing Great Britain and France to recognize the Confederacy. Memminger opposed the vigilante committees that were trying to prevent cotton exports, but did so solely on legal grounds. He made no effort to check their activities and refused to make a public issue of the question. As a result, they seriously inhibited the export of cotton, which Memminger knew to be essential.

A third cotton-related question was whether the government should take an active role in organizing blockade-running operations. At George A. Trenholm's suggestion, the secretary proposed to the cabinet that the Confederacy buy two available shipping lines to promote direct trade with Europe. Thwarted by the opposition of the cabinet and his own inability to convince the president of the necessity of making this purchase, Memminger dropped any further effort to buy or lease ships on the Treasury's account. The abdication of responsibility in this area to the War Department greatly delayed cotton shipments.

Finally, given the shortage of foreign exchange from the sale of produce abroad, the secretary, who had to cover War and Navy department expenditures, realized early on that a foreign loan was urgently needed. He requested and received authority to sell bonds abroad by the act of May 16, 1861. But he failed to pursue the matter, and by 1863, when the so-called Erlanger loan was floated in Europe, the tide of battle had turned against the South. As a result, the Treasury had to borrow money on onerous terms and the funds realized were too little and too late to maintain the government's credit in London or to meet the Confederacy's pressing economic and military needs.

By February 1864, after three years in office, Memminger found himself a discredited man. Congress paid little or no attention to his recommendations. The currency had practically lost its value, the government's credit at home and abroad was badly damaged, and the tax structure was unfair and ineffective.

In May 1864, the House of Representatives passed a resolution of no confidence in the secretary, and Memminger, weary of his thankless task, promptly resigned in July after Congress adjourned. He was succeeded by his good friend and fellow South Carolinian George A. Trenholm.

As one Mississippi soldier wrote his governor, "we are poor men and are willing to defend our country but our families first and then our country."

PAGE 604

State and local authorities demonstrated that they acted with one eye on the home front and one eye on the battlefront.

PAGE 605

William Faulkner, W. J. Cash, C. Vann Woodward and others claimed that defeat helped create a distinctive regional mentality characterized by guilt and an appreciation for human limitations.

PAGE 335

With Charleston under siege and his home within the range of Union guns, Memminger retired to his summer home at Rock Hill, North Carolina, where he remained for the duration of the war. His home in Charleston was captured and pillaged in February 1865 and the property confiscated and later used as an orphanage for black children.

Unlike many of his fellow Confederate leaders, Memminger was neither arrested nor imprisoned. He procured a pardon in 1867 and resumed his business activities and law practice. He also participated in the bitter debates that followed the war, defending himself against unfair or inaccurate accusations regarding his role in the Confederacy's defeat.

In 1876, he was once again elected to the South Carolina Assembly. As part of the first legislature since the overthrow of the Radical Republicans in Columbia, he played a key role in reorganizing the state's finances. He was instrumental in preventing the government from abolishing the statewide public school system, which had been one of the major accomplishments of Reconstruction in the state. Overcoming bitter resistance, he also established with state support a college for blacks.

Retiring from public life in 1879, Memminger died in Charleston on March 7, 1888.

[*See also* Public Finance; Treasury Department.]

— DOUGLAS B. BALL

MEMORIAL ORGANIZATIONS

Efforts to honor the Confederate dead began shortly after the war ended. Although several groups claimed to be first, probably the earliest memorial organization was founded in Columbus, Georgia, in March 1866 by a group of women determined to decorate the graves of soldiers; in July of the same year, the women of the Soldiers' Aid Society of Wilmington, North Carolina, formed the Ladies' Memorial Association of Wilmington for the same purpose. Similar local groups developed in all parts of the South, with goals limited to decorating graves with flowers, often on a day set aside for the purpose. These efforts eventually became Confederate Memorial Day, an annual event whose date varies from state to state.

More widespread memorial organizations were founded in the later 1860s and the 1870s. Some of the organizations were military in nature, such as the Association of the Army of Northern Virginia and the Association of the Army of Tennessee. A variety of local and state organizations were formed, especially in Richmond and other cities. These groups held annual reunions, arranged for burial of soldiers, and provided benevolence for needy veterans and families. They celebrated Confederate Memorial Day throughout the South; memorials were also held on the death of Jefferson Davis and other Confederate leaders. They were joined by the Southern Historical Society (1869) and the Lee Memorial Association (1870), whose goals included preserving the Southern past and glorifying its heroes.

The Confederate Veterans, an umbrella organization of local groups, was founded in 1889 in New Orleans and quickly became a prominent Southern organization. Its first commander in chief was Gen. John B. Gordon, who retained his post until 1904. This group, which restricted membership to veterans, sought both to memorialize the war and to provide needed services to its increasingly elderly membership. Several other umbrella organizations were also formed, including the Sons of the Confederacy (1896), which allowed male descendants of veterans to join, and the United Daughters of the Confederacy (1895), which included any female relative of men who had served. The United Daughters of the Confederacy created the Children of the Confederacy (1896), a group committed to keeping the memory of the Confederacy alive among young people. The official organ for these groups and others was the *Confederate Veteran,* a periodical started in Nashville in 1893 by Sumner A. Cunningham, who remained its editor for twenty-one years.

The United Confederate Veterans was a large-scale organization: its peak membership was 80,000, about one-third of the surviving veterans in 1903. Organized along military lines, it sponsored local meetings of individual camps and annual national reunions. The organization devoted its attention to organizing public ceremonies such as dedications of monuments and Memorial Day celebrations, relief efforts for veterans and their families, drives to persuade Southern state governments to provide pensions and establish soldiers' homes, and burial societies to bury the dead from battlefields, locate and mark graves, care for cemeteries, and pay for funerals. It also boasted a Historical Committee (1892) to oversee the writing of Confederate history, aid state historical associations, and help support Confederate museums. The United Confederate Veterans met jointly with the Grand Army of the Republic in 1913 at Gettysburg, where they reenacted Pickett's charge. The group's last reunion was held in Selma, Alabama, in 1950, with one veteran in attendance.

The United Daughters of the Confederacy (UDC) shared many of the concerns of the United Confederate Veterans and added new activities of their own. Because lineal descendants of Confederate women and nieces of soldiers were included, the organization continues to the present day. In addition to raising money for monuments, caring for graves, engaging in relief work, and sponsoring local, state, and national meetings, the UDC has worked to ensure that Confederate history is taught according to its convictions. To this end it has sponsored scholarships, raised funds for libraries at home and abroad, opened "relic rooms" throughout the South to preserve Confederate artifacts, and led in the development of the Confederate Museum in the old White House of the Confederacy in Richmond. The UDC also offered the Cross of Honor beginning in 1900; this was a medal bestowed for their endurance on men who had served in the Confederate army or navy. Later, they offered the Cross of Military Service to lineal descendants of Confederate veterans who served in other U.S. wars.

The UDC had a notable ability to raise funds for monuments. Many towns owed their courthouse statue of local Confederate leaders to the UDC, which also developed many national projects, alone or in conjunction with other groups. One monument was a memorial to "the faithful slave," a massive boulder placed at Harpers Ferry in 1931 to commemorate former slave Heyward Shepherd, who refused to join John Brown's raid. Another, sponsored jointly with the United Confederate Veterans, was a memorial to the women of the Confederacy. The two groups disagreed about whether women's martial or nurturing aspects should be celebrated in the design, but the conflict was ultimately decided in favor of the men's design for a nurturing figure. The monument was dedicated in 1906. Monuments were also erected in honor of Varina ("Winnie") Davis, the original daughter of the Confederacy; Thomas J. ("Stonewall") Jackson; Robert E. Lee; Jefferson Davis; Henry Wirz, the Andersonville commandant who was executed as a war criminal; other military leaders; and various battlefields.

[*See also* Lee, Robert E., *sidebar* Lee Memorial Association; Monuments and Memorials.]

— MARLI F. WEINER

CONFEDERATE MEMORIAL DAY

The celebration of Confederate Memorial Day, an annual ceremony honoring the Confederate dead, began in the spring of 1866. That January women in Columbus, Georgia, issued a public call to decorate Confederate graves, and for this they are sometimes credited with establishing the holiday. Jackson and Vicksburg, Mississippi, along with several other Southern communities, have challenged Columbus, Georgia's, claim. Most likely, several communities acted independently. The idea apparently grew out of the private decoration of soldiers' graves, though Southerners also borrowed from similar customs in other cultures.

During the next fifty years, more and more Southern communities celebrated the holiday, usually under the charge of a ladies' memorial association or, later, the United Daughters of the Confederacy. The date of the observance varied from place to place. In the Deep South most communities celebrated April 26, the anniversary of Joseph E. Johnston's surrender; in South and North Carolina towns more commonly chose May 10, the date of Thomas J. ("Stonewall")

Jackson's death and Jefferson Davis's capture; towns in Virginia and other areas celebrated on still different dates. After Davis's death in 1889, some communities and a few states began to observe the holiday on his birthday, June 3.

As with the date, the nature of the celebration took various forms in different communities and changed over time. In the early years, citizens in some towns simply went together to the cemetery and decorated the graves. In others they held more formal programs that included hymns, prayers, and speeches in defense of the soldiers' honor and the nobility of the Southern cause. In either case, the central ritual was the placing of greenery or flowers on the Confederate graves. These ceremonies both honored the fallen soldiers and allowed survivors to mourn, thereby distancing themselves from the cause but still expressing hope for its, and their, eventual vindication. As a sense of vindication developed in the 1880s and 1890s, the tone of the celebration changed. The central ritual remained the decoration of the graves, but the occasion became somewhat less funereal and more fes-

tive. Bands now participated, often playing "Dixie," and speeches became more common. During the same years, a few cities invited Union veterans to participate with the former Confederates. The new practices reflected changes in the Lost Cause. The passions and issues of the war had begun to dissipate, and Confederate soldiers had come to serve as symbols not of rebellion but of loyalty to leaders and country.

As the veterans died and interest in the Lost Cause faded during the twentieth century, the holiday became less important in Southern culture. By the end of World War II, many communities no longer held celebrations; today only a few do. Eight Southern states still recognize Confederate Memorial Day, although not all of them close state offices on that day. Florida and Georgia observe April 26, South and North Carolina May 10, and Kentucky and Louisiana June 3. Alabama and Mississippi, making concessions to modern practices, celebrate the fourth Monday in May as Confederate Memorial Day.

— GAINES M. FOSTER

MILITARY JUSTICE

*Most Southern
states had both
law courts and
courts of equity.*

PAGE 306

*Military courts
and provost
marshals, as
authorized by the
Articles of War in
March 1861,
accompanied some
armies even before
First Manassas.*

PAGE 466

The Confederate Constitution empowered Congress to establish rules for the government of Confederate soldiers. Soon there arose a system of military justice based almost entirely on the Articles of War and the army regulations of the United States, which had been derived from the system of Great Britain.

Initially, the Confederate War Department's Adjutant and Inspector General's Office was charged with review and custody of documents pertaining to military justice, but in February 1864, a new bureau, the Judge Advocate's Office under Maj. Charles H. Lee (after April under Maj. William S. Barton), assumed responsibility.

The main topics of the Articles of War adopted on March 6, 1861, were military offenses and the courts of inquiry and courts-martial that were the disciplinary procedural bodies available to deal with them. These offenses included common crimes such as insubordination, drunkenness, fighting, absence without leave, and desertion, and less common ones such as mutiny, threats or violence against superiors, cowardice, and misbehavior in action.

Courts of inquiry were fact-finding bodies ordered by President Jefferson Davis, or convened at the request of an accused, to investigate the responsibility of officers for affairs or accusations or imputations against officers or men. These courts, composed of up to three officers, plus a judge advocate to act as recorder, could summon witnesses and administer oaths, but they could not initiate an opinion and could punish only for contempt. Court findings sometimes led to the convening of courts-martial.

General courts-martial, composed of five to thirteen officers, all senior in rank to the accused, tried officers and men, as well as sutlers, drivers, and all others paid by the army. Initially, only general officers commanding field armies and colonels commanding departments could convene these courts, but by 1865 generals commanding cavalry forces not directly part of an army command, officers commanding separate departments, and generals commanding reserve forces had this authority.

Special or regimental courts-martial consisted of three officers convened to try noncapital offenses committed by soldiers or persons paid by the army. Convening authorities were officers commanding regiments or corps, or garrisons, forts, barracks, or other places where the troops were from different arms of the service.

Judge advocates prosecuted, summoned witnesses, swore in the members of the court, and were then sworn in by the court president who kept order and conducted court business. Convictions were wrought by simple majority, except death sentences which required a two-thirds majority. Sentences were carried out upon approval of the convening authority who could mitigate or suspend sentence. Only President Davis could approve sentences passed on general officers.

Once the army was on the march an expedient was the drumhead court-martial, which executed its judgments immediately. In addition, for noncapital offenses, commanding officers meted out summary justice without reference to formal judicial process. Sentences were often unfair and capricious, usually involving some form of corporal punishment, extra duty, confinement, or reduction in rank.

By 1862 Robert E. Lee and many other commanders had become convinced that the existing system was not ensuring prompt and certain punishment of offenders. The legal necessity to convene each court-martial, not always an easy or timely task during active operations, meant delays, which often resulted in witnesses being unavailable. More delay resulted from the requirements to forward charges to general headquarters before the accused could be ordered to trial and to return the findings to the convening authority for review before sentences could be executed. These shortcomings led to a sharp increase in offenses as offenders mistook the system's slowness for immunity.

The response, embodied in an act of October 9, 1862, was a new type of tribunal: a permanently open military court for each army corps in the field. These courts had three members (colonels) and a judge advocate (captain) appointed by President Davis, plus a court-appointed provost marshal to execute orders and a clerk to record decisions. By 1864, twelve corps, cavalry divisions, all military departments, northern Alabama, and each state had courts. Judges and courts could be transferred as required, and corps and department commanders could detail field officers as members. Although it was not the intent that military courts eliminate courts-martial, their inherent advantages caused a lessening of courts-martial jurisdiction.

Military courts could try all offenses against the Articles of War and the customs of war, crimes against Confederate or state law, and all cases of murder, manslaughter, arson, rape, robbery, and larceny committed by military personnel and prisoners of war outside the Confederate States, where military courts exercised powers equal to Confederate States district courts. They could summon civilian witnesses, for example, and hold them until they agreed to testify. In the case of treason, ambiguity about the applicability of the Articles of War to civilians caused disputes about the jurisdictions of civil and military courts. Military courts (and courts-martial) were not subject to appellate jurisdiction of civil courts.

One shortcoming that could not be legislated for was the tendency to leniency shown by tribunals. The long-term effect was a tide of straggling and desertion that by 1864 threatened to engulf the army. Nor did leniency help instill the desired respect for and obedience to orders that would have made best use of the experience, tenacity, and courage of the Confederate soldier. As Lee observed, many opportunities were lost and many lives uselessly sacrificed because of indiscipline.

[*See also* Provost Marshal.]

— KENNETH RADLEY

MILITARY TRAINING

The turning of raw recruits into soldiers for the Confederacy virtually mirrored the same activity in the Union, both being based upon the system of the pre-war U.S. Army. Drill and weapons training were designed to instill subordination in the soldiers, produce instant and unquestioning obedience to commands, and facilitate the orderly movement of large numbers of men quickly and effectively on the battlefield. Most officers relied on either Winfield Scott's 1835 *Infantry Tactics* or the simpler and more popular *Rifle and Infantry Tactics* written by William J. Hardee (now a Confederate general) and known simply as *Hardee's Tactics.*

Although details varied in these and the other manuals used (in volunteer regiments it was often left up to individual officers to choose whichever manual they preferred), virtually all shared features in common. Men were expected to learn to obey commands as given by bugle or drum, since a voice would not carry far in battle. As many as fifty different such commands had to be learned, not all of them applicable to all soldiers and units.

The basic drill unit was the company, though practice in squad and battalion drill was also required. Regimental drill was as large as most evolutions went, but a few brigades actually practiced full brigade drill early in the war before discovering its impracticability. In his early months in uniform, a Johnny Reb might expect to spend several hours a day practicing his evolutions. This did not include just parade ground maneuvers. Practice in line of march—usually four abreast—was also required. Separate branches like the artillery and cavalry had their own distinctive drill and training regimens.

In the early days, weapons training also occupied much time and practice until handling them became second nature. Silas Casey's 1862 *Infantry Tactics* reduced the loading and firing of the rifled musket to a dozen commands and twenty discrete actions, and Confederate manuals did much the same. Of course, the men quickly learned how to load and fire, but the object of the drill was to have them do so in unison in order to deliver a shattering volley at the command to fire. Even more time was devoted to bayonet practice, with dozens of commands and positions being studied for using the bayonet as virtually a saber at the end of the rifle. Ironically, the bayonet saw almost no practical combat use and inflicted fewer than four wounds out of a thousand.

Attempted almost universally at the outset, all but the most basic and rudimentary training disappeared from most of the Confederate forces after 1863, especially when regiments were reduced by casualties from nearly a thousand to only two hundred or so and with whole companies numbering a mere thirty to forty. Still, though haphazard and ersatz like so much else in the Southern war effort, training in the Confederate forces definitely left its mark in producing one of the most effective groups of fighting men in history.

— WILLIAM C. DAVIS

MINING

In the Confederacy, mining was largely conducted in Virginia where large amounts of iron, coal, and limestone fed the many iron furnaces along the Allegheny frontier, the Shenandoah Valley, Wythe County, and Richmond. Coal and iron mined in Alabama supplied the ironworks at Selma, at Dade City in Georgia, and at Sewanee in Tennessee. Coal fueled railways, steamboats, and factories. Gold mined in the Appalachian field in South Carolina, Virginia, North Carolina, Georgia, and Alabama supplied mints at Charlotte, North Carolina, and Dahlonega, Georgia. Copper mined at Copper Hill, Tennessee, was used in electrical wire for telegraph lines.

Mines, operated like plantations with slave miners and white overseers, were usually pits dug around surface outcrops. But some mines were more deeply sloped tunnels, and in the Richmond coalfield at Dover, Midlothian, and Clover Hill, slaves dug vertical shafts as deep as six hundred feet. Material was broken by miners wielding picks and bars or exploding black powder in holes drilled into the mine face with hand augers. Breakings were shoveled into carts and hauled from the mine by mules.

Without these mines, supplies of coal, iron, gold, and copper would have been limited to imports through the blockade and amounts seized at the beginning of the war. Union campaigns through Tennessee, Georgia, and down the Shenandoah Valley left only

The Confederate government wisely attempted to keep its existing regiments filled with volunteers and conscripts.

PAGE 287

Mixed in with veterans under experienced officers, replacements quickly learned the formal and practical aspects of soldiering.

PAGE 287

Richmond as the source of iron and coal. The Tredegar Iron Works at Richmond cast over a thousand cannons, in addition to armor plate, shells, shot, and components for arms, machinery, and railways. The Richmond coalfield supplied over 100,000 tons of coal annually.

[*See also* Railroads; Telegraph; Tredegar Iron Works.]

— WALTER R. HIBBARD, JR.

MISCEGENATION

The etymological roots of *miscegenation* are *miscere* (Latin, "to mix") and *genus* ("race"). Practically speaking, however, miscegenation has occurred in all civilizations whenever two different peoples have encountered each other. Genetic blending is as much a part of history as is cultural exchange, as evidenced by the triracial (Caucasian, Semitic, and Negroid) origins of such African groups as the Mandingo.

In the recorded history of North America, racial mixing occurred first between Europeans and Native Americans and then between both groups and the transplanted Africans. Although sexual relations with both the indigenous population and the enslaved blacks were overtly discouraged by most European officials, such taboos were impossible to enforce. With time, white-Indian mixing was gradually to lose its stigma, leaving white-black relations as the primary target of the cursed term *miscegenation*.

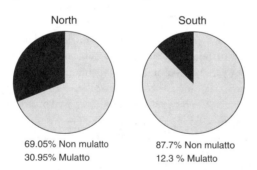

North   South

69.05% Non mulatto
30.95% Mulatto

87.7% Non mulatto
12.3 % Mulatto

The earliest European-Americans attempted to make ethnic terminology a fairly exact science, but precision proved impossible. The Spanish reportedly developed over a hundred words (reputed numbers vary) denoting different racial mixtures. The French colonials had far fewer such designations, and the English even less. Within the bounds that became the continental United States, the most common terms were *mulatto* (half-black and half-white), *quadroon* (one-quarter black and three-quarters white), *octoroon* (one-eighth black and seven-eighths white), *mestizo* (part-Indian, part-white in Latin-oriented communi-

ties), *half-breed* (in British-oriented societies), and *griffe* (part-black, part-Indian, perhaps part-white). The ethnic composition of racially mixed individuals could be cited with presumed certainty in the first two or three generations, but the identification system collapsed with the intermingling of subsequent offspring. Officials often guessed, as demonstrated by records that describe nonwhites as "mulatto in color," or *pardo* (light-skinned mixed race). The inevitable result was the general absorption of Indian mixtures into one of the three dominant cultures and the general categorization of all black-white people as mulatto, regardless of exact composition.

Miscegenation is popularly associated with the American South, that being the area in which slavery survived the longest and in which most blacks resided. The rate of miscegenation was highest in states to the north, however. The percentage of mulattoes amid the enumerated African-American population of the free states in 1850 was 28.96 percent; in the South that year, mulattoes constituted only 10.14 percent. In 1860, the corresponding figures were 30.95 percent (North) and 12.30 percent (South).

To some extent, the Northern numbers were inflated by Southern white fathers who sent mixed-race children to the free states after Southern manumission laws were tightened. Economics and demographics, however, appear to have played a stronger role. Both domestic servants and craftsmen were more likely to be of mixed race, and most Northern blacks lived in towns and cities where their skills were the most marketable. By contrast, the South's free mixed residents were as likely to be rural as urban. Their tendency to intermarry within their caste—as a means of maintaining what was considered to be prestige in a prejudicial social system—created a highly visible brown class that has led casual observers to assume more Southern mixing than actually occurred.

The latest studies on miscegenation in the slave regime also belie some other traditional conclusions. The sexual use of female field hands by white planters and overseers was not the common pattern, nor were instances in which several black slaves on a single plantation bore mixed-race children. More at risk was the household servant, and the typical scenario was likely to be a long-term relationship that bore the characteristics of a common-law marriage. The most detailed study yet available, focusing upon Anglo-Alabama (which excludes the French and Spanish influence of the Gulf coast), has documented a high incidence of bachelorhood or widowerhood among the white fathers of mixed-race children.

Other figures speak to greater family stability among the mixed-race population than has been previously assumed. The fact that 60 percent of antebellum

"Boys on and about the plantation inevitably learned to use [the Negro woman], and having acquired the habit, often continued it into manhood and even after marriage."

W. J. CASH
THE MIND OF THE SOUTH
1941

**PERCENTAGE
OF MULATTOS
AMONG AFRICAN
AMERICANS**

Figures taken from the 1860 census.

U.S. CENSUS BUREAU

RACE-MIXING

A Northern print from 1864 satirizes the supposed consequences of racial equality. Bowing, at left, is Lincoln, faced by Sen. Charles Sumner; Republican editor Horace Greeley is seated at table, center.

LIBRARY OF CONGRESS

Alabama's free mulattoes had mulatto parents is a seemingly obvious but nonetheless needed reminder that every mulatto was not the result of a new incident of miscegenation. Among the remaining 40 percent, the fact that exactly half had white fathers and exactly half had white mothers clearly exposes another carefully nurtured myth: that black-white mixing was the result of male white licentiousness and that all white females abhorred the thought of interracial alliance. In Alabama, where interracial marriages were not penalized until 1852, unions of white wives and mulatto husbands can be documented in all corners of the state.

Less quantifiable is the extent to which white wives tolerated, even encouraged, miscegenous concubinages both during and after slavery. Current studies on child spacing and marital relations, as well as the observations of nineteenth-century census takers North and South, point to a spreading effort by white females to limit the size of their families—abstinence being the method of choice before modern manufacturing and medicine offered other options. Among those who could afford it, concubinage was a practical alternative. As expressed by one Southern farm wife of the early twentieth century: "Why should I mind if my husband has that child every other year by a nice colored woman?"

The offspring of such congenial or tacitly tolerated concubinages were likely to be accorded special treatment by both the family and the community. Under the slave regime, they were often freed, educated, or trained in a trade, or given favored positions on the plantation if manumission was not possible. The conspicuous concu-

binage of Richard Mentor Johnson, vice president under Andrew Jackson, and the more discreet affair attributed by some to Thomas Jefferson are frequently cited examples. Innumerable others exist, such as the lifestyle of the Revolutionary era Indian trade czar and war financier George Galphin, of whom a contemporary (General Thomas S. Woodward, himself part Indian) wrote: "Of the five varieties of the human family, he [Galphin] raised children from three, and no doubt would have gone the whole hog, but the Malay and Mongol were out of his reach." Like Johnson, Galphin provided well for his offspring. His legitimate white daughter wed Georgia's Governor John Milledge. One half-black daughter, Barbara Galphin Holmes, was handsomely endowed at the time of her marriage to Galphin's British-born partner. It is not surprising that contemporary census takers were color-blind—perhaps they saw "green" better than "black"; when they visited the Holmes household, they recorded the widowed Barbara as the white mistress of a number of black slaves. Her quadroon son became a prominent doctor, marrying and living as white in the antebellum South. As with most such families, however, not all lines of descent prospered. By the close of the antebellum era, the free, mixed-race Galphins had proliferated, but most who bore that well-known surname lived in exceedingly modest circumstances.

Less studied by the historical community—and less understood—are the triracial (white, black, and Indian) isolate groups that have peopled both the North and the South. Anthropological scholars have long analyzed their culture. Genealogical literature is

> *"Efforts to build up a taboo against miscegenation made little real progress."*
>
> W. J. CASH
> THE MIND OF THE SOUTH
> 1941

now documenting their origins. From the Carmels of Ohio and the Moors of Delaware to the Cubans of Virginia, the Lumbees and Haliwas of North Carolina, the Melungeons and Ramps of Appalachia, the Brass Ankles and Turks of South Carolina, and the Redbones who scattered their clusters from South Carolina to Texas, these groups have certain characteristics in common. Specific families are usually traceable back to a miscegenous incident in the 1600s or 1700s, from which time they were accorded a nebulous but intermediate social status between black and white. Most members of these groups maintained that status by intermarrying with other black-white or Indian-white people.

With time, as black-white miscegenation became more common and the social order felt more threatened, African ancestors were likely to be forgotten by these families, Indian forebears would be only vaguely remembered, and swarthiness became commonly attributable to "Portuguese" descent. In some regions, the revised family trees were accepted by the larger social order; elsewhere they were not. Public recollection of a family's African ancestry was commonly influenced by a subjectively complex consideration of economic status, physical features, and social behavior. Even the lightest descendants of well-known triracial groups—though they voted, served in local militia companies, and married whites—were likely to find that their communities had long memories whenever someone wished to embarrass or discredit them.

Being of mixed racial ancestry was obviously no guarantee of success, although most successful free blacks were mulattoes. Perhaps their better education and training, their close relationship to whites, their distinguishing color, and the financial benefits provided to some by their parents combined to give them an advantage in life. Such cities as Philadelphia, Charleston, and New Orleans developed highly cultured and respected communities of free mulattoes. Rural areas such as Natchitoches Parish, Louisiana, and Horry County, South Carolina, spawned free people of color who earned wealth and status through the slave plantation system. As a generality, however, antebellum families who acknowledged their mixed origins and operated within the socially approved sphere were more apt to be successful than those who denied their past in an effort to live as white.

In post–Civil War America, the "mulatto elite" or "brown aristocracy" lost its niche as a separate caste, falling—politically and legally, if not always socially—to the top level of a subordinate class generically termed *black*. The efforts of these families to maintain themselves as a distinct stratum within the black subculture provided the educated leadership that African America needed to progress—even though many non-mixed blacks resented the perceived superiority of browns and tans. In retrospect, it is not surprising to find that a majority of "black" politicians during and after Reconstruction were of visibly mixed ethnicity. Ultimately, it is ironic that so many of the modern civil rights leaders have been descended from black-white relationships of earlier centuries. The dominant white race in America sowed, itself, the seeds of leadership that would overthrow its own concept of white supremacy.

— GARY B. MILLS

MISSOURI COMPROMISE

When Missouri applied for statehood in 1819, Representative James Tallmadge of New York moved to amend the new state's constitution to eliminate slavery. Excepting only Louisiana itself, Missouri would be the first state to be carved out of the vast expanse of the Louisiana Purchase. Its disposition would tip the existing balance of slave and free states. Of even graver potential consequence for the South, the amendment if passed threatened to "dam up Southerners in a sea of slaves" and abrogate the understanding that underpinned the Union, that the Federal government had no constitutional right to interfere with slavery in the states.

The proposed amendment gave rise to a firestorm of public controversy, evoked virtually all the pro- and antislavery arguments that would subsequently wrack the Union, illuminated the potential of the slavery issue to divide political parties along sectional lines, and brought threats of secession. "This momentous question, like a fire bell in the night, awakened and filled me with terror," Thomas Jefferson wrote; "I considered it at once as the knell of the union." Tempers cooled only after a compromise made possible by the adept legislative maneuvering of Henry Clay: Missouri and Maine entered the Union without restriction, one slave and one free; and slavery was prohibited in the great bulk of the Louisiana territory north of 36°30′.

The controversy gave rise to a resurgent "Old Republicanism" in the South in the 1820s that helped to bring Andrew Jackson to power in 1828 and to usher in the "second party system." Dependent on support from both North and South, the Jacksonian party worked to quiet discussion of the slavery question for a generation. When abolitionist pressure and the desire to build a transcontinental railroad through the unorganized area north of 36°30′ made this no longer possible, latter-day Jacksonians repealed the territorial prohibition with the Kansas-Nebraska Act (1854), and in 1857 the Supreme Court declared in the Dred Scott decision that the prohibition had never been constitutional, ruling that Congress had no power to prohibit slavery in the territories. With the effective repeal of the Missouri Compromise the national party system collapsed, all the slavery issues came once more to the fore, and secession quickly followed.

[*See also* Dred Scott Decision; Kansas-Nebraska Act.]

— RICHARD H. BROWN

MOBILE SQUADRON

This was the Confederate naval force that defended Mobile from 1862 to 1865. It was commanded by Como. Victor M. Randolph until August 15, 1862, when he was replaced by Adm. Franklin Buchanan who served until his capture on *Tennessee* August 5, 1864. Como. Ebenezer Farrand then commanded the squadron until it surrendered May 5, 1865.

The vessels in the Mobile Squadron were either converted merchant ships or among those built in Selma and Mobile. In 1862 it included five vessels. *Baltic* was a partly armored sidewheel river towboat armed with four guns and scrapped in July 1864. *Morgan* and *Gaines,* wooden sidewheel gunboats carrying eight guns, were built in 1862. *Selma,* originally named *Florida,* was a coastal packet steamer built in Mobile in 1856. Cut down, reinforced, and partly armored, it joined the squadron in 1862. *Tennessee,* added to the squadron in July 1864, was probably the strongest ironclad built by the Confederacy. It carried six heavy guns and 6-inch armor set at a 30-degree angle.

These vessels, except for *Baltic,* formed the squadron that fought at Mobile Bay. Only *Morgan* escaped either capture or destruction. The ship's captain, Como. George W. Harrison, claimed that *Morgan* grounded in shallow water and could not rejoin the battle. As a result of this action, Adm. Franklin Buchanan accused Harrison of cowardice. He was, however, exonerated and was still in command of *Morgan* in March 1865. Other ships, most of them also built at Selma and Mobile, which joined the squadron after this were *Tuscaloosa,* a four-gun ironclad; *Huntsville,* an incomplete ironclad used as a floating battery; and *Nashville,* a heavily armored sidewheel ironclad built in Montgomery and Mobile. These vessels defended Mobile until the squadron's surrender on May 4, 1865.

— FRANK LAWRENCE OWSLEY

MORALE

Like an army that cannot fight on without rations, a new nation fighting for its very existence cannot maintain the struggle without strong, sustaining morale among its military and civilian populations. Thus morale was of vital importance to the Confederacy. The Southern nation obviously possessed spirit enough to engage in four years of a war that was the bloodiest and most destructive in U.S. history. Yet it can be said that Confederate morale proved deficient. During the Civil War the South's morale underwent a disastrous decline until ultimately, as historian Charles Wesley argued long ago, the collapse of the Confederacy came from within. Although no single factor by itself explains the South's defeat in a massive, complex, and multifaceted struggle, morale lay at the heart of the Confederacy's demise. Many scholars today view morale as the Achilles heel of the South in the grinding war it had to fight.

Before the first guns fired on Fort Sumter, Confederate morale was high, but a closer examination reveals that popular sentiments were neither uncomplicated nor untroubled. The South had traveled a long, rough, and somewhat unlikely road to secession. Throughout the 1850s only a small minority of radicals had desired the breakup of the Union, and their calls for a united stand by all the Southern states were ignored. After Abraham Lincoln won the presidential election in 1860, the strategy of separate state secession unfolded. Led by South Carolina, six Deep South states left the Union and formed a new confederacy. But even in the Deep South public opinion had been closely divided in states such as Georgia and Louisiana, and strong Unionist feelings existed elsewhere, as in Alabama. Moreover, crucial upper South states had refused to join the new nation.

Scholars have drawn different conclusions about this situation, but its significance for Confederate nationalism and unity should not be missed. Charles Roland, after surveying the secession of the lower South states, declared that they were "swept out by a great emotional folk movement. Notwithstanding the presence of large Unionist minorities in some of the states, it is doubtful that any similar political rupture in modern history has been supported by as high a proportion of the population."

Roland is probably right, yet in July of 1861 the *Richmond Examiner* stated a different and equally valid view. "Loyal as the great mass of our people are," wrote the *Examiner*'s editors, "there is yet no doubt that the South is more rife with treason to her own independence and honour than any community that ever engaged before in a struggle with an adversary." The Confederate States were in the process of forming a

Defeatism, by early 1864, was rampant in many parts of the South.

PAGE 659

As Charles W. Ramsdell has said, "The Confederacy had begun to break down within, long before the military situation appeared to be desperate."

PAGE 144

373

*Much scholarship
recently has
focused on two
large groups in the
South that were or
became alienated
from the
Confederate war
effort:
nonslaveholding
whites, and slaves.*

PAGE 120

new government and nurturing new loyalties. Those profoundly committed to a Southern nation were few, whereas those who loved the Union and left it reluctantly were many. The solidification of Southern nationalism still lay ahead.

Regional Loyalty versus Confederate Nationalism

With the outbreak of hostilities, a large portion of the slaveholding upper South quickly entered the Confederate fold. Yet the accession of Virginia, North Carolina, Tennessee, and Arkansas to the cause only made the task of building Confederate nationalism more challenging. These states, faced by the necessity of choosing sides, had acted upon a strong sense of regional loyalty. Identification with the South, however, was not the same thing as dedication to a Confederate nation. In the upper South and elsewhere, moderate and substantially Unionist sentiments had to be turned in a new direction and harnessed for a new cause. A Confederate identity had to evolve from Southernness, and devotion to a new nation had to replace loyalty to revered American traditions.

These facts dictated the selection of moderate leaders and conservative policies at Montgomery. Fire-eating radicals, such as William Lowndes Yancey of Alabama who had pioneered in Union-hating and calls for secession, were omitted from high positions. Their day was over, and the task of consolidating a much more diverse and moderate public opinion, marked by historic affection for the Union, was at hand. President Jefferson Davis took the essential first step toward building a sense of Confederate nationalism by portraying the new Southern nation as the true carrier of American traditions. In the face of a degenerate, aggressive North, Davis argued, the Confederacy had become the guardian of the Founding Fathers' legacy. The purpose of the new Southern nation was to "perpetuate the principles" of American constitutional liberty.

This appeal to traditional national values helped unite a region faced with imminent invasion. After Lincoln called for troops, Unionists and secessionists joined together in defense of their threatened home, the South. An outpouring of regional loyalty produced 500,000 volunteers for military service in the summer of 1861—more men than the Confederate government could arm or equip and more than it would subsequently field at any one time. Morale was strong and robust.

The Phases of Morale

Yet the spirit of Confederate nationalism needed further development, or its weakness might become apparent. Events on the battlefield, on the home front, and in the halls of government would have a great effect on national unity and popular morale. To understand this process, one must consider both the phases of Southern morale and the forces that affected it positively or negatively.

EARLY OPTIMISM. In the summer of 1861 the morale of the Southern people was running at high tide. Swept along by the strong wave of loyalty to their region, Southerners joined the army and prepared for their first battle. The Confederate victory at First Manassas produced jubilation and some unrealistic expectations. By fall the massive preparations of the enemy had tempered overoptimistic emotions, and some disputes had arisen within the Confederacy that pointed to future difficulties. But the government of the new nation was becoming an organized fact, the South had fielded impressive armies of its own, and no major disaster had befallen the cause. Unfortunately for Confederate patriots, however, this period of enthusiasm and high hopes lasted only until the spring of 1862.

THE REALITY OF WAR INTRUDES. Around April of 1862 a second phase of Confederate morale began, one that would last until July 1863. In this phase unpleasant realities began to crowd out initial high hopes, and totally unexpected aspects of life in the Confederacy made themselves felt. Conscription signaled the beginning of these new facts. For the first time in American history, the central government passed laws to compel its citizens to serve in the armies. Necessity required Confederate leaders to take this step because bounties, furloughs, and other inducements had failed to lure new enlistments. Ordinary citizens who had joined the army for a year now wanted to return home and plant their crops. "The spirit of volunteering had died out," admitted Secretary of War James A. Seddon.

In this second phase other internal and external problems of fundamental importance to morale appeared. Bitter disputes over questions of policy arose, as the potent issue of state rights reared its head. A growing, activist central government displeased both planters and leaders who had expected something very different in a Southern government. At the same time, Confederate policies generated deep divisions in the population along class lines. Financial and economic difficulties deepened, and the first food riots occurred in Southern cities.

On the battlefield Southern troops won some victories, but Union forces made significant territorial gains, especially with the fall of New Orleans and Forts Henry and Donelson. Any hope for a brief war was fading, and reasons to doubt the Confederacy's staying power were multiplying. When Confederate offensives into Maryland and Kentucky both failed in the fall of

1862, Jefferson Davis had cause to remark that Southerners were entering "the darkest and most dangerous period we have yet had."

Thus from April 1862 to July 1863 the skies over the new nation were darkening. Yet in this period the Confederacy also marshaled its strength and resisted the forces weakening it. Government measures largely stemmed desertion from the armies, and the military situation was far from hopeless. On occasion, a notable success, such as the victory at Chancellorsville, stimulated hopes for a revival of Confederate fortunes. The decline in morale had not become uncontrollable.

IMPACT OF VICKSBURG AND GETTYSBURG. A third and far more ominous phase in Confederate morale arrived with the shocking defeats at Vicksburg and Gettysburg in July 1863. It took some days for accurate news of these disasters to reach the population, but once they did, no one could deny their depressing significance. Robert E. Lee's defeat in Pennsylvania shattered all hopes of winning Confederate independence through successful offensive action. The strongest Southern army had been driven back and had no option thereafter but to assume a defensive posture. Any realistic hope of foreign recognition and aid, long sought but already unlikely, had to be given up. With the capture of Vicksburg, the Confederacy itself was cut in two. The resources of the Trans-Mississippi West fell out of reach, and the Gulf states lay open to Federal invasion from armies in Mississippi or Tennessee. Jefferson Davis admitted that these defeats submerged him "in the depths of . . . gloom," and so dedicated a Confederate as Josiah Gorgas confided to his diary, "Today absolute ruin seems our portion. The Confederacy totters to its destruction."

After this turning point, internal forces of disintegration outpaced the government's efforts to hold the Confederacy together. On the home front, resistance to conscription and impressments grew rapidly. As poverty deepened, thousands of suffering yeoman families quietly withdrew their support from the cause, and more politically active Confederates, particularly in North Carolina and Georgia, began to agitate openly for peace. The army's strength, which had already begun to fall, now plunged sharply downward as the flow of deserters widened into a racing stream. The government began using detachments of seasoned troops to round up concentrations of deserters, but without permanent effect.

The words of Confederate officials documented this increasingly desperate, third phase of morale. Assistant Secretary of War John A. Campbell asked on July 25, 1863, whether "so general a habit" as desertion should be considered a crime when some 40,000 to 50,000 men were absent without leave and 100,000 evaded duty in some manner. On November 26, 1863, Secretary of War Seddon reported that "the effective force of the Army is generally a little more than a half, never two-thirds, of the numbers in the ranks." By the middle of 1864 the army's strength had fallen to 195,000 present out of 316,000 enrolled. Senator Herschel Johnson of Georgia advised Jefferson Davis in 1864 that "the disposition to avoid military service is . . . general," and Maj. S. B. French reported at the end of this period that "in all the States impressments are evaded by every means which ingenuity can suggest, and in some openly resisted."

Morale was very low, but the Confederate cause was not yet seen as hopeless, for the North also was war-weary and staggering beneath the conflict's heavy burdens. Abraham Lincoln sometimes despaired of his reelection, and pro-peace elements in the Democratic party were working hard to control their party's platform and presidential nomination. Jefferson Davis pursued a strategy of encouraging Northern peace advocates while doing everything that could be done to present the stiffest possible resistance on the battlefield. State leaders joined Davis in predicting extermination and degradation at the hands of a depraved enemy unless the South prevailed. The end of this policy, and of the third phase in Confederate morale, approached as William Tecumseh Sherman's troops neared Atlanta.

MORALE AT LOW TIDE. "Our all depends on that army," wrote Mary Boykin Chesnut. "If that fails us, the game is up." Unfortunately for Confederates, she was right. Atlanta fell, and the Richmond war clerk J. B. Jones lamented that "our fondly-cherished visions of peace have vanished like a mirage of the desert." Although Jefferson Davis exhorted his countrymen to fight on, he had to admit that "two-thirds of our men are absent . . . most of them absent without leave." Not long after Sherman's strategic breakthrough, Lincoln won reelection, and Southerners knew that Confederate defeat was only a matter of time.

In this final phase in the level of morale, most sources of support for the Confederacy were evaporating. Only the central government and those determined soldiers who stayed with the armies remained resolute. For a few more months the government tried desperate expedients and brave men in gray fought on, but most Southerners were resigned to defeat before Lee arrived at Appomattox.

Forces Affecting Morale

The spirit of Confederates was tested in many ways during the Civil War. Events naturally affected morale as Southern armies met defeats in battle and as Union pressure helped damage a mismanaged economy. But internal forces also had a serious impact on morale.

All agricultural indicators in the South spelled decline, while prosperity reigned in the fertile regions of the Midwest.

PAGE 431

The South's declining agriculture created a dilemma. The army needed fresh troops, but the home front required care as well.

PAGE 431

Morale was at a low ebb and hopes were being steadily dashed against the shoals of wartime reality.

PAGE 431

It became apparent to Lee that he was about to be surrounded. The Southerners sent out white flags of truce to suspend hostilities.

PAGE 21

Opposition to the government flourished among both planters and small farmers, and class resentments among the poor caused a steadily increasing number to withdraw their support from the war effort.

THE EFFECT OF THE WAR. It is self-evident that defeats on the battlefield worked powerfully to depress Confederate morale. The Confederacy was a beleaguered new nation, and after the first year no Southerner could deny that the cause was losing ground. As time went on, the lengthening litany of defeats eroded confidence among even the stoutest patriots. The connection between military reverses and declining morale is manifest in the correlation between key defeats and trends in desertion. Moreover, it was inevitable that the human cost of the South's struggle for independence would produce a reaction. As the world marveled at the unprecedented carnage Americans were inflicting on one another, hundreds of thousands of Southern homes went into deep mourning. In America's bloodiest war, the South bore the brunt of destruction.

There was another, paradoxical side, however, to the effects of war. Armed conflict strengthened Southern morale by creating an intense and unifying hatred of the enemy. War always forces its combatants to depersonalize the foe in order to cope with the psychological trauma of killing, and civilians share in this process. Moreover, hostile images of the Yankee had long been current in Southern culture. The Civil War provided reason to magnify these negative images enormously. Cultural conceptions of honor contributed to the process, as Southerners judged their opponents by standards the latter did not share.

Confederate political leaders did all they could to intensify these attitudes. From the first days of the Confederacy, Jefferson Davis depicted the United States as a consolidated despotism where corruption reigned and freedom was extinguished. Soon after the fighting started, he began a steady practice of denouncing the Union as an uncivilized, inhuman, and brutal foe. Governors and state legislators added bitter criticisms of the "ruthless barbarity" of an enemy that intended to impose the vilest forms of subjugation upon the South. To the *Charleston Mercury*, Northerners were "civilized savages . . . plunderers, liars, fanatics." When other newspapers, such as the *Richmond Enquirer*, spoke of Northerners' "extreme malignity toward us," they were accelerating a potent social process. Southerners were unifying themselves by defining their foe as so hateful and despicable that no thought of reunion could be entertained. In this way, the war generated feelings that supported Confederate morale and endured long after the Confederate government disappeared.

CONFEDERATE POLICY AND PLANTERS. Another factor affecting morale involved fundamental problems related to the class system and the economy.

These caused so much frustration and resentment that many questioned whether the government deserved their support. An indicator of the severity of the Confederacy's social problems is the fact that dissatisfaction appeared from an early date at the two extremes of the social scale. For differing reasons, both wealthy planters and small yeoman farmers became alienated from the cause.

The large plantation owners discovered that life under the Southern government was shockingly different from their expectations. They had sought to insulate their holdings from change, to guard their world against the intrusions of "Black Republicans." In order to shield slavery and plantation agriculture, they had embarked on a quest for independence that involved them in a massive war. But soon it became evident that the necessities of fighting the war clashed radically with the ends they pursued.

Davis's administration sought firmly and resolutely to build the strong central government needed to fight the North. Control of the armies, conscription of men, impressment of supplies, and suspension of the writ of habeas corpus showed by early 1862 that the Confederate government was going to lead with a strong hand. Davis sincerely believed that all his measures were constitutional, especially given the government's powers to make war and raise armies. But such steps surprised many in the planter class. They had expected a weak and limited central government in a nation devoted to state rights. Instead they saw a behemoth in Richmond whose bureaucracy became larger, in proportion to population, than the government of the North.

Moreover, this central government adopted policies that intruded directly into the affairs of each plantation. Not content with impressing goods, the Confederacy began to impress slaves. Despite the fears of slave owners concerning the treatment of their valuable property, the government commandeered slave labor to dig trenches, build fortifications, and otherwise assist the armies. Davis supported efforts to change what the planters grew by urging them to shift from cotton to food crops. Whenever Federal forces moved deeper into the Confederacy, army officers confiscated planters' stores of cotton and burned it to keep it from falling into the hands of the enemy. By 1863 the tax-in-kind was taking from planters and other farmers a portion of all their food crops. In 1864 new legislation required planters, as a means of keeping their overseers, to promise under bond to provide one hundred pounds of bacon and one hundred pounds of beef for each able-bodied slave. The government had become directly involved in plantation affairs.

These policies caused consternation and provoked harsh attacks on the government in the political arena.

Early in the war representatives of the planter class began to express profound ideological dissatisfaction with the central government. Georgia's governor, Joseph E. Brown, who charged that conscription controverted "all the principles for which Georgia entered into this revolution," was the policy's most outspoken critic, but he was not the only one. Congressmen and newspaper editors joined in denouncing the South's new government as traitorous to the Confederacy's basic purposes. The *Charleston Mercury,* for example, quoted Linton Stephens with approval in 1862 when he condemned conscription as "the very embodiment of Lincolnism, which our gallant armies are today resisting."

Jefferson Davis defended his policies and put them into operation despite the opposition. Eventually, as the Confederacy's situation became more desperate, a few critics realized that Davis and the South had no alternative and dampened their criticism. But much damage had been done to Confederate morale. Leaders of public opinion had questioned the legitimacy of their new government and argued, in effect, that it was unworthy of the people's allegiance. Such criticism did more than express planters' dissatisfaction. It depressed morale generally and impeded the process of building support for the new nation.

THE DETERIORATING ECONOMY. The serious financial and economic problems of the Confederacy also damaged morale for common citizens as well as planters. The government held little specie, raised very little revenue through taxes (partly because planters objected to them), and printed far too much money. As a result uncontrollable inflation ravaged the economy. Moreover, shortages of many commodities that the South was accustomed to buy from Europe or the North quickly developed. Hoarding made shortages worse, and profiteering aggravated the inflation of prices. The economic situation deteriorated steadily and caused many in disgust to condemn the government.

If these economic setbacks were inconvenient for wealthy planters, they were devastating to poorer white citizens. Although small farmers were largely self-sufficient in normal times, most needed a few essential items they could not produce. Salt was a vital preservative for meat, and most families also purchased such items as coffee, sugar, some clothing, and tools. Inflation and shortages quickly drove prices of these commodities out of reach, and instances of hoarding enraged the citizenry. The governors of several states denounced speculation, and newspapers joined in the outcry over greed and the lack of patriotism. In 1861 the *Richmond Examiner* declared, "This disposition to speculate upon the yeomanry of the country . . . is the most mortifying feature of the war." One year later it judged "native Southern merchants" as worse than Yankees and lamented, "The whole South stinks with the lust of extortion." The Rome, Georgia, *Weekly Courier* quoted the Bible against extortioners, and the *Atlanta Daily Intelligencer* warned that because of extortion, "want and starvation are staring thousands in the face."

In fact, the causes of hunger went beyond hoarding and profiteering. Drought or crop failures occurred in years of war as well as peace and naturally depressed morale. But in addition the Confederacy itself some-

It was the policy of the Confederate army to burn cotton whenever Federals moved within striking distance.

PAGE 431

THE SHORTAGE OF FAMILY LABOR

Even more serious was the shortage of labor on small farms caused by volunteering and conscription. An early warning sign of this problem was the flood of letters in 1861 from rural districts lamenting the absence of blacksmiths and other artisans. Soon thereafter many more non-slaveholding families began to appeal for exemptions or furloughs of the husbands or sons who were their chief source of labor. Increasingly on one-man farms, wives and children found that they could not keep up the work of cultivation unaided. As the Edgefield, South Carolina, Advertiser explained, "The duties of war have called away from home the sole supports of many, many families. . . . Help must be given, or the poor will suffer." A desperate woman named Elizabeth Leeson wrote to Secretary of War Seddon in 1863: "I ask [you] in the name of humanity to discharge my husband[;] he is not able to do your government much good and he might do his children some good. . . . The rich has aplenty to work for them." The suffering of soldiers' families was a critical danger to the Confederacy. Military and political officials agreed that letters from suffering loved ones led to many desertions. As an anonymous Virginian wrote to Secretary of War Seddon, "What man is there that would stay in the armey and [k]no[w] that his family is sufring at home?"

Hunger and speculation were destroying people's morale. One acquaintance of Jefferson Davis advised the president that speculation was "the cause of thousands of good men leaving their posts." In 1863 an enrolling officer reported from the hill country of South Carolina that previously loyal citizens were supporting deserters. Citing "the speculations and extortions so rampant throughout the land," he wrote that these civilians "swear by all they hold sacred that they will die at home before they will ever be dragged forth again to do battle for such a cause."

— PAUL D. ESCOTT

"*If this war had smashed the Southern world, it had left the essential Southern mind and will . . . entirely unshaken.*"

W. J. CASH
THE MIND OF THE SOUTH
1941

times seemed responsible for suffering, as families were victimized by impressment or abuses by the military. Florida's governor complained that soldiers had taken the last milk cows from starving families of soldiers, and in 1864 Secretary of War Seddon admitted that "the most scandalous outrages" had occurred in Mississippi. One woman wrote that the troops camped on her land had not hesitated to "catch up the fowls before my eyes." Commenting in 1862, the *Richmond Enquirer* reported, "We often hear persons say, 'The Yankees cannot do us any more harm than our own soldiers have done.'"

CLASS RESENTMENT. The most corrosive factor in the decline of yeoman morale was class resentment, a sense of class injustice. Elizabeth Leeson had voiced the feeling that her family was sacrificing heavily while rich slaveholders had "aplenty to work for them." Perhaps this aspect of "a rich man's war and a poor man's fight" was unavoidable, given the fact that most Southern whites did not own slaves. But Confederate laws and policies magnified the advantage possessed by slaveholders and convinced many non-slaveholders that they were being asked to do much more than their fair share. Nothing damaged Confederate morale more than this conviction of class discrimination and social injustice. The outcry against unfair government policies was intense.

Objections to favoritism in the raising of troops arose in the summer of 1861. After volunteers began to exceed the Confederacy's supply of arms, the government announced that it would arm and accept only long-term volunteers. Companies that could arm and equip their own men, however, were still allowed to enroll for only twelve months' service. In practice, only wealthier men could bear the costs of raising twelve-month units. This policy, admitted Albert T. Bledsoe, chief of the Bureau of War, created "no little dissatisfaction in the country." William Brooks, the presiding officer at Alabama's secession convention, reported that leading men had struggled to encourage enlistments among nonslaveholders in Perry County. Just when leaders had "partially" changed the sentiments of men who "not unfrequently declared that they will 'fight for no rich man's slaves,'" the Confederacy declared its new policy. These "poor laboring men," Brooks pointed out, compared their lot to "slaveholders [who] can enter the army and quit it at the end of twelve months. . . . I leave you to imagine the consequences."

Angry feelings proliferated with the adoption of conscription. The law provided for exemptions for the disabled or unfit and for a variety of occupations, such as transportation workers, miners, and state and Confederate officials. Complaints of favoritism in the application of the law arose almost immediately. Officeholders tended to be from the upper classes, and

some states declared that thousands of them were essential to the operation of the government. Careless administration of the law also produced inequities. An anonymous Georgian, for example, complained to the War Department that it was "a notorious fact if a man has influential friends—or a little money to spare he will never be enrolled." Judge Robert S. Hudson of Mississippi warned President Davis that incompetence or favoritism by enrolling officers had created much "disloyalty, discontent, and desertions." In 1864 Congressman Robert Henry Whitfield of Virginia urged an investigation of exemption boards in the name of "common justice to the poor and uninfluential."

Far more serious was the resentment created by two other features of the conscription law: substitution and the exemption of overseers. The government permitted a conscript, if he had the means, to hire someone to go to war in his place. To the *Richmond Examiner* this ability to pay for a substitute was "the best proof of the citizen's social and industrial value," but, needless to say, many poorer citizens regarded it as an unjust privilege for the rich. Mary Boykin Chesnut wrote in her diary about planters' sons who had "spent a fortune in substitutes," and Confederate documents recorded that at least fifty thousand men escaped the dangers of battle by hiring a substitute. As early as 1862 Secretary of War George Wythe Randolph condemned the "great abuses" of substitution, which had become "a regular business," but not until the beginning of 1864 did Congress end this divisive and unpopular system.

The exemption of overseers, which had been demanded by planters and state officials, created an even greater storm of protest. Because Congress, in October 1862, exempted one white man for every twenty slaves under his supervision, this statute soon was denounced as the "twenty-nigger law." Many nonslaveholders already believed that the war's benefits would accrue primarily to slaveholders; now it seemed that slaveholders would also avoid the war's dangers. "Never did a law meet with more universal odium," observed one congressman, "than the exemption of slave-owners. . . . Its influence upon the poor is most calamitous, and has awakened a spirit and elicited a discussion of which we may safely predict the most unfortunate results." The legislature of North Carolina soon bowed to popular pressure and protested to Congress about the "unjust discrimination" of the law, but Congress enacted only mild restrictions on the exemption of overseers. Planters gladly paid a tax imposed on overseers, who thus continued to enjoy safety in a war that was killing unprecedented numbers of Southerners. The situation fed a popular impression, as Senator James Phelan of Mississippi observed, that "nine tenths of the youngsters of the land whose relatives are conspicuous in society, wealthy, or influential obtain some safe perch where they can doze with their heads under their wings."

Meanwhile, the families of nonslaveholding soldiers faced grinding poverty and suffering. The Confederate government, struggling against enormous problems, was not providing the essentials of economic or physical security. Moreover, as the conviction spread that government policies were discriminatory and unjust, the Confederacy's demands for sacrifice increased. These pressures on morale became insupportable. Coupled with growing evidence of defeat on the battlefield, class resentments and the sheer difficulty of surviving in the Confederacy caused hundreds of thousands of citizens to withdraw their active support from the war effort.

In March 1864, an impressment officer in South Carolina encountered an uncooperative and frustrated citizen. "The sooner this damned Government [falls] to pieces," he said, "the better it [will] be for us." He was ready to compromise and "get back into the old Union." Like most Southerners, this man had sacrificed much for the cause, and he probably had little love for Yankees. But he was one of many whose patience was exhausted. He was angered by the unexpected or unfair policies of his government and disgusted by its inability to provide basic economic or physical security. For him, as for most Southerners, loyalty to his region had not grown into a sustaining devotion to Confederate nationalism. The corrosive and depressing forces that sapped morale had proven too great.

[*See also* Bread Riots; Extortion; Impressment; Poverty; Speculation; Taxation.]

— PAUL D. ESCOTT

MORGAN, JOHN HUNT

Morgan, John Hunt (1825–1864), brigadier general and guerrilla raider. Born June 1, 1825, in Huntsville, Alabama, Morgan grew up in Lexington, Kentucky, where he attended Transylvania University. In the Mexican War he fought as a first lieutenant in the Kentucky cavalry, participating in the Battle of Buena Vista, February 23, 1847. A manufacturer of hemp in Lexington, Morgan organized and commanded an artillery company in the state militia from 1852 through 1854. In 1857 he formed the Lexington Rifles, a volunteer infantry company that joined the pro-Southern state guard militia in 1860. A Confederate from the beginning, he wired President Jefferson Davis on April 16, 1861, offering to serve as a recruiter. He raised a Confederate flag on his woolen

factory, declaring that henceforth he would sell only uniforms of Confederate gray. When Kentucky decided to stay in the Union, he and the Lexington Rifles left for the war on September 20, 1861, rendezvousing with two hundred other men at Bloomfield, Kentucky.

The group elected Morgan to lead them to Confederate lines in western Kentucky.

From October 1 to October 27, 1861, he conducted raids behind the lines on his own authority. Then, on October 27, he was sworn in and elected captain of a cavalry company. Continuing guerrilla warfare, he had, by March 1862, achieved many small victories that made him a famous folk hero, the "Francis Marion of the war." To many Southerners he represented the ideal of the romantic cavalier. His success inspired the popular movement for guerrilla war that culminated in the Partisan Ranger Act of April 21, 1862, which authorized the president to commission companies, battalions, and regiments to conduct guerrilla war behind enemy lines.

Promoted to colonel on April 4, 1862, he commanded a squadron at Shiloh. Gen. P. G. T. Beauregard increased his command to 325 men, and by the time of Morgan's promotion to brigadier general on December 11, 1862, it had grown to a division of 3,900. Discarding the saber, Morgan armed his raiders with infantry rifles and Colt revolvers. They lived off the land and traveled light; their only wheels were two mountain howitzers for each brigade. He used horses to provide mobility, to hit and run. In skirmishing, he deployed the artillery and dismounted the men to fight as infantry. For intelligence, he sent out scouts and intercepted telegraph messages. On the march, he used a system of rolling guards protecting the flanks and leapfrogging to the front when the column passed. He usually kept his

Historically, guerrilla wars are brutal, savage affairs waged by small groups of men among the mountains, forests, and swamps.

PAGE 253

For pro-Confederate Southerners, guerrilla warfare was a way of disrupting Northern invasion and occupation.

PAGE 253

Wounded men had their throats cut and many were scalped. Some were beheaded. Throughout the ordeal, those waiting their turn were forced to watch.

PAGE 258

opponents confused by sending out feints and fake telegrams.

In the first two years of the war, Morgan's raids made a mockery of Federal attempts to protect border state Kentuckians. After the first Kentucky raid, General in Chief Henry W. Halleck admitted, "The stampede among our troops was utterly disgraceful." Andrew Johnson, military governor of Tennessee, concluded that Morgan's raids undermined Federal authority and the efforts to strengthen loyalty to the Union. William Tecumseh Sherman proclaimed that Morgan and the other Confederate raiders were the most dangerous men of the war and would have to be killed or captured.

In reaction to a raid at Gallatin, Tennessee, Union Gen. Don Carlos Buell concentrated his entire cavalry force of 700 men under Gen. Richard W. Johnson and ordered them to seek out and destroy Morgan. Johnson boasted that he would return "with Morgan in a bandbox." On August 21, 1862, he located Morgan near Gallatin, but after two mounted assaults with sabers, the Union cavalry scattered in wild retreat, losing 21 dead, 47 wounded, and 176 missing, including General Johnson, who was captured by his prey.

Morgan's greatest contribution to the Confederate war effort was the diversion of Union troops and resources to defend against his raids. By mid-December 1862, the Union army had 20,357 men guarding communication lines and supply depots in the West. Morgan and other raiders forced the Union to channel men and resources into the construction of stockades to defend railroad trestles and the reconstruction of tunnels, bridges, track, and telegraph lines. But because of Morgan, the Union commanders strengthened their cavalry and organized mounted infantry, and by the summer of 1863, the stronger Union cavalry ended the advantage the Confederate raiders had enjoyed. Morgan's men now suffered a series of defeats.

Attempting to restore morale and efficiency, Morgan marched into Indiana and Ohio without authority and was captured and imprisoned. Many Southerners nevertheless praised him for carrying the war to the enemy. He escaped from the Ohio penitentiary on November 27, 1863, and served as commander of the Department of Western Virginia and East Tennessee from June to August 22, 1864. He was killed on September 4 in Greeneville, Tennessee, attempting to escape from Federal cavalry under Gen. Alvan C. Gillem. Given a state funeral in Richmond, Virginia, he was buried in Hollywood Cemetery and then reinterred with honor in 1868 in Lexington, Kentucky.

[*See also* Guerrilla Warfare; Morgan's Raids.]

— JAMES A. RAMAGE

MORGAN'S RAIDS

Col. John Hunt Morgan, with a brigade of 867 cavalrymen, marched from Knoxville, Tennessee, to Cynthiana, Kentucky, on the first Kentucky raid, July 4 through 28, 1862, recruiting 300 men and eluding a Union force of 3,000 under Gen. G. Clay Smith. President Abraham Lincoln wired: "They are having a stampede in Kentucky. Please look to it!" Morgan exaggerated Southern sympathy and encouraged the Confederate high command to assume that the people of Kentucky would rise in support of an invading Confederate army.

In early August 1862 civilian informers reported that the twin tunnels behind enemy lines on the Louisville and Nashville Railroad seven miles north of Gallatin, Tennessee, were weakly guarded by 375 infantrymen under Union Col. William P. Boone. Morgan prepared for a raid on Gallatin by sending teenage couriers to arrange for food and forage along the seventy-five-mile passage from Sparta to Gallatin. Marching light and under cover of darkness, the raiders reached Gallatin before dawn on August 12, and learned from civilians that Boone's 124 guards were asleep on the courthouse lawn and Boone was sleeping in the hotel with his wife. Morgan's men surprised the Federals and captured them, including Boone, without firing a shot. The soldiers defending the tunnels surrendered with no resistance, and civilians participated in the destruction of the tunnels. The Louisville and Nashville Railroad was Gen. Don Carlos Buell's main artery of supply, and this, the most strategic guerrilla raid of Morgan's career, shut it down, suspending Buell's advance on Chattanooga for ninety-eight days and giving the initiative to Gen. Braxton Bragg for the invasion of Kentucky.

Morgan commanded 2,140 men in a raid on Union Col. Absalom B. Moore's brigade of 2,100 at Hartsville, Tennessee. In a frontal assault on December 7, 1862, Morgan lost 21 men and another 104 were wounded, but the raiders killed 58, wounded 204, and captured 1,834. The purpose of the Christmas raid, December 22, 1862, to January 1, 1863, was to destroy the two Louisville and Nashville Railroad trestles north of Elizabethtown, Kentucky. Morgan's division of 3,900 succeeded, closing the railroad for five weeks and diverting 7,300 troops from the Union army in the Battle of Murfreesboro.

On the "Great Raid," July 1–26, 1863, Morgan's 2,500 men raided through Indiana and Ohio. On July 19, at Buffington Island, Ohio, the pursuing Union cavalry organized by Gen. Ambrose Burnside and commanded by Generals Edward H. Hobson and Henry M. Judah, captured 700 of Morgan's men. Morgan retreated and was captured on July 26 near West Point, Ohio. The raid delayed Burnside's advance

**MORGAN'S
RAIDERS**

*William Tecumseh Sherman
declared that John Hunt
Morgan and company were
the most dangerous men of
the war and must be killed or
captured.*

HARPER'S PICTORIAL
HISTORY OF THE
GREAT REBELLION

into East Tennessee for one month and boosted Southern morale.

Morgan was incarcerated in the Ohio State Penitentiary. He escaped on November 27, 1863, and with two thousand men, raided from southwestern Virginia into Kentucky from May 30 to June 12, 1864, confiscating horses in Lexington and advancing to Cynthiana. There, on June 12, his command was defeated by the cavalry brigade of Stephen G. Burbridge.

Discipline broke down, and after the raid the Confederate War Department charged Morgan with allowing "excesses and irregularities" relating to the armed robbery of the Farmer's Bank of Kentucky in Mount Sterling and other banks. The men who robbed the banks distributed the money among themselves. Robbery of nongovernmental funds was illegal, as was withholding stolen funds from the Confederate government. Morgan was charged with allowing bank robbery in the Union state of Kentucky, and on August 30, 1864, he was suspended, pending a court of inquiry scheduled for September 10. Six days before the inquiry was to commence, Morgan was killed in Greeneville, Tennessee, while attempting to escape from Union cavalry that had surrounded his headquarters and separated him from his men.

[*See also* Morgan, John Hunt.]

— JAMES A. RAMAGE

MOSBY, JOHN S.

Mosby, John S. (1833–1916), partisan officer. Enlisting as a private in the First Virginia Cavalry in May 1861,

Mosby eventually became a scout for J. E. B. Stuart. In January 1863, with Stuart's approval, Mosby began guerrilla operations in northern Virginia. For the next two years the Forty-third Battalion of Virginia Cavalry, or Mosby's Rangers, waged partisan warfare against Union troops and supply lines.

A small, thin, restless man of absolute fearlessness, Mosby, called the "Gray Ghost," was a natural guerrilla leader. He recruited and organized his command, disciplined its youthful members, and plotted the raids. He possessed a keen intellect, an untiring energy, and an iron will. Few, if any, Confederate units reflected its leader more than Mosby's Rangers.

Mosby operated from the counties of Fauquier and Loudoun that became known as "Mosby's Confederacy." From this base, the Rangers attacked Union wagon trains, railroad lines, and troop detachments. His mission, as he said, was "to weaken the armies invading Virginia by harassing their rear."

Wounded three times, Mosby forged the battalion into one of war's finest commands. Robert E. Lee regarded him highly and cited him more often in reports than any other officer. Mosby provided Lee with valuable information and seized hundreds of prisoners and large quantities of arms, equipment, horses, and supplies.

Mosby rose to the rank of colonel and, at war's end, commanded two battalions of eight companies. Refusing to surrender, he disbanded his command on April 21, 1865. His record was unmatched by any other Confederate partisan officer.

Unlike many Southerners, Mosby accepted the defeat of the Confederacy. He resumed his legal practice and eventually worked in the Federal government. He served under Republican administrations as

*A wide variety
of men were
attracted to
Mosby's company.*

PAGE 256

M

MOSBY'S RANGERS

John S. Mosby and his mounted guerrillas conducted lightning-quick raids in Northern Virginia, harassing Union forces and providing Robert E. Lee with valuable intelligence.

LIBRARY OF CONGRESS

Opposed to secession initially and an "indifferent soldier," the twenty-nine-year-old Mosby displayed a talent for war that soon became legendary.

PAGE 256

a consul in Hong Kong, in the General Land Office, and as an attorney in the Department of Justice. Mosby died in the nation's capital and was buried in "Mosby's Confederacy," in Warrenton, Virginia.

[*See also* Mosby's Rangers.]

— JEFFRY D. WERT

MOSBY'S RANGERS

Officially designated the Forty-third Battalion of Virginia Cavalry, Mosby's Rangers was a guerrilla unit under the command of John S. Mosby; it operated in northern Virginia from the winter of 1863 until the end of the war. During that twenty-eight-month span, the rangers became the most effective and feared partisan command in the Confederacy.

In January 1863, Mosby, a cavalry officer, and fifteen men undertook guerrilla operations in the Virginia counties south and west of Washington, D.C. Within five months, so many volunteers had joined the unit that Mosby received permission to organize the command into a unit of the Army of Northern Virginia. At Rector's Cross Roads on June 10, Mosby organized Company A, Forty-third Battalion of Virginia Cavalry. By war's end, the command consisted of two battalions of eight companies, and at least 1,900 men had served in the unit.

Mosby's Rangers operated from a base in the counties of Fauquier and Loudoun, which became known as "Mosby's Confederacy." There civilians concealed, sheltered, and fed the rangers while acting as an information and warning network. From this base, the guerrillas operated eastward toward the Union capital, westward across the Blue Ridge Mountains into the Shenandoah Valley, and northward across the Potomac River into Maryland.

From Mosby's Confederacy, the rangers stood across the supply and communication lines of invading Union armies. Union wagon trains, railroad cars, outposts, and troop detachments became the rangers' targets. Each raid was plotted carefully by Mosby, and when his men struck, they did so swiftly in daylight or darkness. By forcing Federal officers to guard the wagons and railroads, the rangers drained the strength of the invading enemy and became a constant factor in Union campaign strategy.

Although Mosby had hundreds of men at hand, he seldom took more than several dozen with him on a raid. The nature of the warfare demanded secrecy and celerity, and small bodies of mounted men were most effective. Raids lasted usually two or three days, with the rangers returning to their base before dividing the spoils and disbanding. The unit's successes came at a high cost, however: the rangers incurred casualties of between 35 and 40 percent, with nearly five hundred rangers spending some time in Federal prisons.

Their various exploits and raids brought the rangers wartime fame and an enduring legacy—the capture of a Union general at his headquarters; the seizure of a railroad train and $178,000 in Union greenbacks; and the relentless campaign against Philip H. Sheridan's Union army in the Shenandoah Valley.

On April 21, 1865, Mosby disbanded the command, refusing to surrender it. The rangers had provided Robert E. Lee with valuable intelligence and captured hundreds of enemy soldiers and hundreds of thousands of dollars worth of material, but they did not lengthen the war in Virginia or alter its basic nature.

— JEFFRY D. WERT

MUSEUMS AND ARCHIVES

Studying and interpreting Confederate history is a fascinating and time-consuming process. Important research collections are housed in numerous archives, libraries, and museums across the United States, many of which are located in the Southern states that once formed the Confederacy. Resources such as manuscripts, printed works, photographs, other artwork, and contemporary physical artifacts are equally important components in the research process. To contact the public or private facilities that specialize in Confederate history, consult the published directories that describe historical agencies in general, or consult any of the several published catalogues and guides to specific collections.

The largest and most important archival collections are housed in the National Archives and the Library of Congress, both of which are located in Washington, D.C. These facilities have vast quantities of materials related to Confederate civil and military affairs, as well as the papers of prominent politicians and military leaders. Both institutions have published guides to their collections, Henry Putney Beers's *The Confederacy: A Guide to the Archives of the Government of the Confederate States of America* (1968, 1986) and John R. Sellers's *Civil War Manuscripts: A Guide to Collections in the Manuscript Division of the Library of Congress* (1986). Another essential access tool is the *National Union Catalog of Manuscript Collections (NUCMC)* and its index, copies of which are at all major research libraries around the country.

Visual images of the Confederacy, including photographs, paintings, prints, drawings, and portraits, are available at the National Archives, the Library of Congress, and the National Portrait Gallery. Access to the latter two collections is available through Hirst D. Milhollen and Donald H. Mugridge's *Civil War Photographs, 1861–1865: A Catalog of Copy Negatives Made from Originals Selected from the Mathew B. Brady Collection in the Prints and Photographs Division of the Library of Congress* (1961) and the Smithsonian Institution's *National Portrait Gallery Permanent Collection Illustrated Checklist*. Other important photograph collections are housed at the United States Army Military History Institute, Carlisle Barracks, Pennsylvania, and the Valentine Museum in Richmond, Virginia. In addition, numerous examples of Confederate artwork are housed in other facilities in the United States. For an example, consult Virginius C. Hall, Jr.'s, *Portraits in the Collection of the Virginia Historical Society: A Catalogue* (1981).

Maps, atlases, and related cartographic items are especially important to the study of military history. Guides to the collections in Washington, D.C., are Richard W. Stephenson's *Civil War Maps: An Annotated List of Maps and Atlases in the Library of Congress,* 2d ed. (1989), and *A Guide to Civil War Maps in the National Archives* (1986). Other maps are more readily available in the *Atlas to Accompany the Official Records of the Union and Confederate Armies* (1891–1895) and in the numerous secondary sources that are at most research facilities.

State-run libraries and archives and historical societies in those states that once formed the Confederacy also have significant collections. An overview of this level of the study of Confederate history is found in James C. Neagles's *Confederate Research Sources: A Guide to Archive Collections* (1986). Many of the state-run collections have individually published guides; for an example, see the Florida Department of State, Division of Library and Information Services, Bureau of Archives and Records Management, *Guide to the Records of the Florida State Archives* (Tallahassee, Fla., 1988).

Other materials at state facilities concentrate on the Confederate period of individual state governments, the state military regiments that constituted the Confederate army, and the compiled service and pension records of individual soldiers and their widows. The state of North Carolina, for example, has an extensive regimental history and troop roster publication begun in 1966, *North Carolina Troops, 1861–1865,* covering the artillery, cavalry, and infantry. State facilities often contain the papers and diaries of prominent citizens and military men as well as those of ordinary citizens. Many house collections of wartime newspapers and Confederate imprints. Their collections of related photographs and artwork capture the wartime life and surroundings of the individual states.

Other important primary source collections are in the custody of major state and private university libraries, large city or county governments, independently operated historical societies and libraries, or in private collections.

The Southern Historical Collection, which covers the whole of Southern history, is housed at the Wilson Library at the University of North Carolina at Chapel

Oral historical traditions preserve information not available in written sources.

PAGE 405

Oral historical narratives often preserve what is psychologically true, and that can be as important as what is factually true.

PAGE 406

*Accounts of
families living for
weeks on roasted
cottonseed or
killing their only
mule for food
make the difficulty
of the times
more vivid.*

PAGE 406

INTERNET RESOURCES
Johnnie Reb on the
World Wide Web

Museum of the Confederacy
http://www.moc.org/
This archive is based in the former Confederate White House.

U.S. Civil War Center
http://www.cwc.lsu.edu/civlink.htm
Contains much research information and "jump site" links.

Sons of Confederate Veterans Home Page
http://www.scv.org/
Information concerning the descendants' organization.

Gettysburg Welcome Center
http://www.gettysbg.com
Home page for America's most famous battle.

Civil War Trust
http://www.CivilWar.org/
Up-to-date news about the plight of Civil War battlefields.

Civil War Soldier/Sailor Search System
http://www.itd.nps.gov/cwss/
This massive effort hopes to create a data base of 1 million+ names.

Charleston Civil War Information Center
http://www.awod.com/gallery/probono/cwchas.main.html
The city where the war began.

Shiloh National Battlefield Park
http://www.nps.gov.shil/
The National Park Service maintains this web site.

Chickamauga/Chattanooga National Battlefield Park
http://www.nps.gov.chch/

Abraham Lincoln On-line
http://www.netins.showcase/creative/lincoln.html
This site has a lively discussion of "Old Abe", both pro and con.

Civil War Units File
http://funnelweb.utcc.utk.edu/~hoemann/cwarhp.html
A list of researchers with info on regiments of the North and South.

Hill. It features *A Guide to Manuscripts* (1970) and a supplement (1976).

The Virginia Historical Society in Richmond, the center for the study of Virginia history, features Waverly K. Winfree's *Guide to Manuscript Collections of the Virginia Historical Society* (1985). The society's Confederate collections include the bulk of Robert E. Lee's papers and papers of military notables Thomas J. ("Stonewall") Jackson, J. E. B. Stuart, A. P. Hill, and Jubal Early, and materials on various Virginia military regiments.

Items related to Jefferson Davis, Albert Sidney Johnston, and postwar veterans' organizations are on deposit in the Howard-Tilton Memorial Library at Tulane University and are accessed through the *Inventory of the Louisiana Historical Association Collection* (1983).

The Huntington Library in San Marino, California, houses a valuable Civil War collection including papers of Joseph E. Johnston and Stuart that are described in the *Guide to American Historical Manuscripts in the Huntington Library* (1979).

The Eleanor S. Brockenbrough Library at the Museum of the Confederacy in Richmond has an important postwar collection of Davis materials; papers of Lee, Jackson, and Stuart; regimental items pertaining to the theater of operations of the Army of Northern Virginia; and a fine collection of Confederate currency and bonds.

The William Stanley Hoole Special Collections Library at the University of Alabama has a collection of Davis papers, the diaries and papers of Josiah Gorgas, the records of the Shelby Iron Works, and materials related to the wartime history of the state as a whole.

The Hargrett Rare Book and Manuscript Library at the University of Georgia houses the Permanent Constitution of the Confederacy, the papers of Howell Cobb, and a large collection of Confederate imprints.

Confederate artifacts reflecting the material culture of the wartime South are housed in museums throughout the United States. In some instances institutions that are not formally designated as museums, such as state-run historical agencies, will have collections of three-dimensional objects that date from the Confederate years. In addition, there are fine collections in the possession of private citizens.

Some Confederate museums have direct ties to the wartime years, in that the particular facility may have served as a residence of a prominent citizen, a military headquarters, or a postwar veterans' meeting hall. In turn, this added significance often helped with the acquisition of artifacts. During the 1890s, certainly prompted by the twenty-fifth anniversary of the war years, Confederate museums were established in

Richmond, New Orleans, Charleston, and other cities. Former Confederates, from individuals in the top ranks of government down to ordinary soldiers or their descendants, began donating wartime possessions to these and other custodial institutions for posterity. The practice continued well into the twentieth century, and the verbal anecdotes that often accompanied the donations add as well to the store of narrative histories concerning the Confederate experience. Today, the museums that study the Confederacy are more than relic halls, and they are actively engaged in the preservation, study, and interpretation of the wartime South for national audiences.

The Museum of the Confederacy in Richmond houses one of the nation's largest Confederate collections. Founded in 1890 and opening in 1896, the museum features collections of flags, uniforms, edged weapons, firearms, and a variety of other wartime military and domestic effects. Also housed there are personal effects of Davis, Lee, Jackson, and Stuart. The monumental oil painting *The Last Meeting of Lee and Jackson,* by E. B. D. Julio, is on display. Adjacent to the museum is the White House of the Confederacy, the wartime residence of Davis and his family. Fully restored to its mid-nineteenth-century appearance, the building features a fine collection of furniture and decorative arts, many of which were used by the Davis family. In addition, the museum also houses the Eleanor S. Brockenbrough Library, which is its research facility.

Other important and historic buildings associated with the Confederacy include the First White House of the Confederacy and the Alabama Capitol, both in Montgomery. Jefferson Davis's last home, Beauvoir, in Biloxi, Mississippi, is where he wrote his two-volume memoir, *The Rise and Fall of the Confederate Government.*

The Confederate Museum in New Orleans was founded in 1891 and is located in the former meeting hall of the city's United Confederate Veterans. The featured holdings include possessions of Davis, uniforms of P. G. T. Beauregard and Braxton Bragg, flags, weaponry, and oil paintings. The museum's archival and manuscript holdings are on deposit at the Howard-Tilton Memorial Library at Tulane University.

The Confederate Museum in Charleston was opened in 1894 by Confederate veterans, and today the

facility is operated by their descendants. The museum's holdings include both military and civilian artifacts from the firing on Fort Sumter to William Tecumseh Sherman's March to the Sea.

The Virginia Historical Society in Richmond, founded in 1831, houses the Maryland-Steuart Collection, one of the nation's finest collections of Confederate firearms, edged weapons, and military accoutrements. The *Four Seasons of the Confederacy,* a series of military murals painted by Charles Hoffbauer, is another of the society's many treasures. The research arm of the society is nationally renowned for its holdings on the Civil War in Virginia.

The Confederate Naval Museum in Columbus, Georgia, houses the remains of CSS *Jackson (Muscogee)* and the remains of CSS *Chattahoochee.* Both vessels were in active service before being destroyed to avoid capture by Union forces. The museum holds other naval artifacts and ship models and features exhibitions on the Confederate navy and marine corps.

[*See also* Memorial Organizations.]

— GUY R. SWANSON

NEW SOUTH

A view of the very modern exterior of the Museum of the Confederacy in Richmond, Virginia, one of the nation's largest Confederate collections.

THE MUSEUM OF THE CONFEDERACY, RICHMOND, VIRGINIA

NAVAL STATIONS

Confederate naval stations were administrative and logistical units occupying specific geographical areas defined by the secretary of the navy. The station commander, often assisted by an ordnance officer, a surgeon, a paymaster, and an engineer, was responsible for recruiting, ordnance works, naval storehouses, hospitals, marine detachments, and sometimes naval construction in his district. He also inspected commissioned vessels in port and reported their conditions to the department, and he received all reports and requisitions from the commanders of vessels within the limits of his station. By regulation he exercised no authority or control over the commanding officer of a navy yard without the express permission or order of the secretary of the navy. In practice, however, the administrative distinction between station and yard was often ambiguous, and many stations and yards within the same area were under the command of a single officer.

Prior to the spring of 1863 the station commander had operational control of warships within his territorial limits. Afterward, in an effort to have younger, more aggressive officers in control of the naval forces afloat, he was taken out of the operational chain of command and placed in a logistical support role.

Although the imprecise terminology used in contemporary records often makes it difficult to distinguish between various types of naval establishments, the Confederate navy operated at least fourteen stations during the course of the war: Richmond, Virginia; Halifax, Kinston, Charlotte, and Wilmington, North Carolina; Marion Court House and Charleston, South Carolina; Savannah and Columbus, Georgia; St. Marks, Florida; Mobile, Alabama; Jackson, Mississippi; and New Orleans and Shreveport, Louisiana. Additionally, some sources consider the installations at Little Rock, Arkansas; Selma, Alabama; and Yazoo City, Mississippi, as naval stations.

— A. ROBERT HOLCOMBE, JR.

NAVY

[*This entry is composed of four articles:* Confederate Navy, *which overviews the creation and activities of the* Confederate Navy; Navy Department, *which discusses the organization and leadership of the cabinet-level department overseeing the navy;* Manpower, *which discusses the demographic makeup of the navy; and* African Americans in the Confederate Navy, *which examines the role of African Americans in the construction, maintenance, and operations of the navy. For further discussion of naval ordnance, shipbuilding, and ships, see* Blockade, *article on* Blockade Runners; Shipyards; Submarines. *See also* Anglo-Confederate Purchasing; Marine Corps; Naval Stations; State Navies; Uniforms, *article on Navy and Marines Uniforms;* Waterways.]

CONFEDERATE NAVY

On February 20, 1861, delegates from the seven Southern states that had proclaimed their secession from the Union passed an act to establish a Navy Department. The act provided for the appointment of a secretary, a chief clerk, and other minor officials. The following day Stephen R. Mallory of Florida was designated secretary of the Confederate States Navy. The organization of the Confederate navy was patterned after that of the U.S. Navy. A congressional act created four bureaus: Ordnance and Hydrography, Orders and Details, Medicine and Surgery, and Provisions and Clothing. The act also established a Marine Corps. Later a chief constructor and chief engineer were added.

BUILDING THE NAVY. The newly organized navy needed ships and personnel to man them. Some 343 officers, approximately 24 percent of the 1,554 officers who were serving in the U.S. Navy as of December 1, 1860, resigned their Union commissions and joined the Confederate navy. Of this number about a third would in time actually serve. The majority of the remainder accepted appointments with the Confederate army or state military forces or were too old and unfit for active duty. The navy's officer corps would reach a maximum number of 753.

Enlisted personnel were more difficult to acquire. Few left the U.S. Navy for Confederate service. Through volunteering, conscription, and transfer from the army, 3,674 were on active duty by the beginning of 1865.

Confederate Marines numbered 539 officers and men in October 1864. Detachments served on various warships including commerce cruisers, as well as stations and other shore facilities and fortifications.

Mallory wrote in May 1863, "I regard the possession of an iron-armored ship as a matter of the first necessity."

PAGE 344

MEN WANTED FOR THE NAVY!

All able-bodied men not in the employment of the Army, will be enlisted into the Navy upon application at the Naval Rendezvous, on Craven Street, next door to the Printing Office.

H. K. DAVENPORT,
Com'r. & Senior Naval Officer.

New Berne, N. C.,
Nov. 2d, 1863.

To create a navy in the South, Mallory acquired gunboats through purchase, construction, and capture.

PAGE 344

Ships were equally scarce. The Confederate navy inherited five small vessels from the seceded states. In addition, four revenue cutters, three slavers, two privately owned coastal steamers, and *Fulton,* an old side-wheeler laid up in the Pensacola Navy Yard, were purchased or seized. As a stopgap measure the Navy Department continued purchasing merchant steamers for conversion, but Secretary Mallory determined to initiate a warship construction program at home and abroad.

In May 1861 naval agents were sent to Great Britain and France to obtain vessels that could be used for commerce raiding. Later the department contracted for the construction of armored warships. *Stonewall,* however, was the only one of these ironclads to reach Confederate hands. The South was more successful in obtaining wooden cruisers. Commerce raiding has traditionally been a strategy of nations with weak navies, and the Confederacy, with its limited warship building expertise and facilities, could not create a navy strong enough to challenge Union seapower. Also, Mallory hoped to weaken the blockade by forcing the Union navy to convoy merchant ships and seek out and destroy the raiders in various parts of the world. Finally, commerce raiding might disrupt Union shipping to the point where Abraham Lincoln's government would have to negotiate an end to the conflict in order to prevent economic disaster.

The Confederate government built or purchased at home and abroad more than a dozen raiders includ-ing *Alabama, Florida,* and *Shenandoah.* Together they destroyed some 5 percent of the Union merchant fleet and seized or destroyed millions of dollars in cargo. For every vessel the Confederate raiders destroyed or seized, the Union merchant fleet lost eight others as an indirect result. Exorbitant insurance rates caused by war risks resulted in hundreds of vessels remaining in port. In addition nearly a thousand were transferred to other flags, principally British. Altogether, more than 1,616 vessels, with a total tonnage of 774,000 tons, were lost to the American merchant marine during the war. Nevertheless, the Confederate raiders had little of the hoped-for influence on Union policy; the blockade was not weakened and Lincoln and his advisers gave no thought to a negotiated peace.

In contrast to the raiders, ironclad warships built by the Confederate government played a more useful role in the war. Secretary Mallory emphasized armored vessels in his construction program. On May 9, 1861, he wrote: "I regard the possession of an iron armored ship as a matter of the first necessity . . . inequality of numbers may be compensated by invulnerability; and thus not only does economy but naval success dictate the wisdom and expediency of fighting with iron against wood." Initially, the secretary concentrated on obtaining armored warships in Europe but in the summer he ordered the conversion of *Merrimack* into *Virginia* and contracted for the building of two ironclads in New Orleans (*Mississippi* and *Louisiana*), and two in Memphis (*Arkansas* and *Tennessee*). These five ironclads were all unusually large and were designed to operate on the open sea as well as on inland waters. They were intended not only to break the blockade but also, as Secretary Mallory wrote, to "traverse the entire coast of the United States . . . and encounter, with a fair prospect of success, their entire Navy."

By 1862 Mallory abandoned his decision to build large seagoing ironclads within the Confederacy and instead concentrated on small, shallow-draft, harbor-defense armored vessels. Various factors influenced this change in policy: the apparent unseaworthiness of *Virginia* and the ironclads built in New Orleans and Memphis, the belief that the South would be able to obtain powerful seagoing armored ships in Europe, and the pressing need for defensive vessels. Because of the continuing success of the Union's combined operations along the Southern coastline as well as the ineffectiveness of the blockade, Confederate naval strategy emphasized defense. Naval forces were organized to guard ports and rivers and inlets that opened the interior to invasion. The small ironclads were designed to be the nucleus of these naval forces.

TORPEDO BOAT

Named for its size relative to the Goliaths of the Union Navy, the successful David *inspired construction of similar torpedo boats.*

NAVAL HISTORICAL CENTER, WASHINGTON, D.C.

Approximately forty were laid down within the Confederacy and half of them completed and placed in operation. The James River Squadron included:

- *Virginia II, Richmond,* and *Fredericksburg;*
- the Wilmington Squadron, *North Carolina* and *Raleigh;*
- the Charleston Squadron, *Chicora, Palmetto State, Charleston,* and *Columbia;*
- the Savannah Squadron, *Atlantic, Georgia,* and *Savannah;* and
- the Mobile Squadron, *Tennessee* (II), *Nashville, Tuscaloosa,* and *Huntsville.*

A number of ironclads were constructed on the rivers: *Albemarle* on the Roanoke, *Neuse* on the Neuse, *Jackson* on the Chattahoochee, and *Missouri* on the Red. In cooperation with wooden gunboats, forts, and other land and water defenses, these armored warships played a major role in Confederate defense efforts, and they contributed significantly to the defense of Richmond, Charleston, Savannah, and Mobile. *Albemarle* was instrumental in the recapture of Plymouth, North Carolina, in April 1864.

The Confederate government also contracted for a large number of wooden gunboats, many of which were completed and joined the various squadrons. Several experimental vessels such as the submarine *H. L. Hunley* and the semisubmergible *David* were completed. Both *Hunley* and *David* successfully attacked Union warships. Other vessels similar to *David* were laid down but never became operational.

Gun foundries, machine shops, rolling mills, and other manufacturing facilities needed to outfit warships were established in the Confederacy, but these industries were severely handicapped by the lack of labor. Nevertheless, ordnance works in Richmond and Selma, Alabama, cast hundreds of guns, the majority designed by John Mercer Brooke, chief of the Bureau of Ordnance and Hydrography. Armor plate was rolled by Tredegar in Richmond, the Shelby Iron Works in Alabama, and the Atlanta Rolling Mill. Machinery was manufactured in Columbus, Georgia.

THE NAVAL WAR. The Confederacy suffered setbacks before the new warships were ready for active service. In November 1861, a combined Union army and naval force captured Port Royal, South Carolina, despite Confederate defenses including a small naval squadron of converted steamers. In the winter and spring of 1862, Federal forces occupied much of coastal North Carolina, defeating a number of small Confederate gunboats in the process. During this period Confederate naval forces were also involved in combat in Virginia waters.

The James River Squadron was established in 1861 and consisted of the small gunboats *Patrick Henry, Jameston, Teaser, Raleigh,* and *Beaufort.* In early March 1862, the ironclad *Virginia* converted from *Merrimack* joined the small naval force. *Virginia* encountered the Union ironclad *Monitor* in an indecisive engagement that lasted nearly four hours. Both vessels, damaged but intact, withdrew. In May with the capture of Norfolk by Union forces, *Virginia* was blown up by its crew, and the remainder of the James River Squadron withdrew up the James.

In the West, the year 1862 was equally disastrous for Confederate naval forces. On April 24 a Union fleet under Flag Officer David Farragut ran past two forts guarding the Mississippi River below New Orleans and engaged more than a dozen Confederate vessels. All were destroyed or surrendered including the ironclad *Manassas. Mississippi* and *Louisiana,* two large ironclads under construction in New Orleans, were

In October, the confederate ship David, *the first combat submarine, disabled a Union blockader off Charleston.*

PAGE 97

NAVY

Confederate Navy

also destroyed by the Confederates to prevent their capture.

Although the Confederate government would lay down additional warships in the Yazoo and Red rivers, including the ironclad *Missouri* at Shreveport, Louisiana, none would be combat-tested. By late 1862, however, the first of the harbor defense ironclads were approaching completion. *Palmetto State* in Charleston and *Georgia* in Savannah, were commissioned in the fall. Sixteen additional armored vessels would be added to the fleet in the following two years and would become the nucleus of the various Confederate squadrons. More than a dozen would never be completed because of the lack of iron and the scarcity of workers.

Newly built wooden gunboats were also joining the fleet. *Morgan* and *Gaines* in Mobile and *Hampton* and *Nansemond* in Norfolk, Virginia, were completed and commissioned in the fall of 1862. The latter two were "Maury gunboats," named after Matthew Fontaine Maury, famous oceanographer and father of hydrography in the U.S. Navy, who resigned his commission to join the Confederate navy. One hundred of these small wooden gunboats were planned, but very few were actually finished. *Chattahoochee* was completed on the Chattahoochee River in 1863, and the *Pee Dee* on the Pee Dee in 1864.

By 1863 Union blockading squadrons along the Atlantic and Gulf coasts had increased to more than three hundred ships including several of the recently

DAVIDS
To Tame the Union Naval Goliath

The torpedo boat *David* gave its name to other torpedo boats of the same or similar specifications. The name derived from its size relative to Goliath-sized Union ships. Its mission was to glide in under the guns of a blockader and detonate a spar torpedo beneath the waterline. Using such a ship was exclusively a Confederate tactic—though Union Lt. William B. Cushing destroyed *Albemarle* from a launch carrying a spar torpedo. The psychological effect of the Davids upon Union blockaders and the resulting restriction on their movements greatly outweighed actual losses.

The prototype *David* was built in Charleston in 1863 by the Southern Torpedo Company, a group of private investors who later gave control of the ship to the Confederate navy. Its mission determined the design. A 50-foot keel, 6-foot beam, and 5-foot draft satisfied requirements for a small craft. The essential design feature was a 10-foot metal spar extending from the prow; to this was fixed a spar torpedo armed with 60 or more pounds of powder capable of damaging or sinking the largest ship.

A steam engine propelled the cigar-shaped hull at five to seven knots as the ship darted through the Union fleet, seeking its target. Iron plating furnished

protection both from attacking ships and from its own exploding torpedo. *David* offered a very low profile because tanks in the hold could be filled to submerge the hull up to the pilot's cabin and smokestack; thus the ship could be almost entirely concealed beneath the water's surface.

On October 5, 1863, *David* attacked the 3,486-ton ironclad *New Ironsides*, a ship of immense symbolic significance to the entire Union as well as the Charleston blockading fleet. Lt. William Glassel commanded, Engineer James H. Tomb manned the engines, Seaman James Sullivan managed the spar, and Walker Cannon piloted *David* to the target. *New Ironsides* was not sunk, but the exploding torpedo badly damaged both the ship and the fleet's morale. The design and its initial success drew praise from U.S. Adm. John A. Dahlgren.

David's success fueled interest in manufacturing more such ships. In a construction system where standardized design and parts were virtually unknown, some attempt was made to issue uniform specifications for a David: 30-, 46-, or 50-foot length and 5- to 6-foot draft. The one exception was a 160-foot David "Number Six" at Charleston. Of about fifteen vessels built, most were at least partially ironclad. The spar on later ver-

sions was usually longer by several feet than *David*'s 10-foot spar.

Of four wooden Davids built at Richmond for service on the James—*Hornet*, *Scorpion*, *Wasp*, and *Squib*—the latter was made famous when Lt. Hunter Davidson commanded an attack on USS *Minnesota* at Newport News. He failed to sink the ship but was promoted to commander for his daring.

At Charleston in March and April 1864, Engineer Tomb commanded a David against USS *Memphis* and USS *Wabash*. Though neither attack inflicted damage on the ships, the psychological effect was devastating. As ships in Charleston anchored close alongside within protective nets, blockade runners moved more freely. *Torch*, *Midge*, and eight unnamed Davids were also laid down at Charleston.

In January 1865, *St. Patrick*, built at Selma, Alabama, seriously alarmed the crew of USS *Octorara* and other blockaders at Mobile. At the Columbus (Georgia) Naval Iron Works, *Viper* transported men fleeing the last battle of the war in April 1865. Victorious Union men captured numerous Davids, regarding them as a curiosity. *Midge* was transported to the Brooklyn Navy Yard and another to Annapolis as trophies of war.

— MAXINE TURNER

completed monitors. Confederate military officials in Charleston determined to attack the Federal naval force off the port before it was closed. On the last day of January 1863 two Confederate ironclads, *Chicora* and *Palmetto State,* steamed out of the harbor and forced the surrender of two blockaders, *Mercedita* and *Keystone State.* Efforts to bring other Union warships under fire were unsuccessful, and in fact the two that surrendered took advantage of the confusion to rejoin the retiring Union naval force. The two Confederate ironclads returned to the harbor. For the remainder of the war the Charleston Squadron guarded the channels and cooperated with the forts and batteries in defending the port. The Confederate vessels were destroyed by their crews as Gen. William Tecumseh Sherman's army approached the city.

In the spring of 1862 Federal forces took Fort Pulaski, guarding the river entry to Savannah, Georgia. The combined forces, however, were unable to capture the port. Confederate defenses included a squadron of ironclads and wooden gunboats. The first ironclad in the squadron, *Georgia,* was moored in the Savannah River where it could fire down either channel. Later the ironclad *Savannah* and the wooden gunboats *Isondiga* and *Macon* reinforced *Georgia.* The squadron included a third ironclad, *Atlanta.* It was converted from the blockade runner *Fingal* and when completed was probably the most powerful armored warship in Confederate service. In July 1863 it attempted to evade blockaders off the port but ran aground in the river and surrendered to two monitors. As in Charleston the approach of Sherman's army resulted in the destruction of the Confederate naval vessels by their crews.

Richmond, Virginia, the capital, was also defended by a Confederate naval squadron. After the fall of Norfolk in May 1862, the James River Squadron retired up the James above obstructions at Drewry's Bluff. There the ships remained throughout the war, venturing below the obstructions only twice. The nucleus of the Confederate naval forces in the James were the ironclads *Virginia II, Richmond,* and *Fredericksburg.* This force exchanged gunfire with Federal land batteries and warships below the obstructions until Richmond was evacuated in April 1865. The decision to evacuate led to the destruction of the ironclads, the wooden gunboats, and the training ship *Patrick Henry* by their crews. They then joined other naval personnel and Marines who had manned batteries along the river and retired from the abandoned capital.

In North Carolina Flag Officer William F. Lynch commanded the naval forces. His force consisted of a small squadron of ironclads and wooden vessels in the Cape Fear River guarding Wilmington and two ironclads constructed on the Neuse and Roanoke rivers. These two warships were built to cooperate in the recapture of eastern North Carolina including the sounds. In April 1864 *Albemarle,* constructed on the Roanoke River, successfully cooperated in a combined attack against Federal forces at Plymouth. The Confederate attempt to enter the sound was repulsed by Union warships. Later *Albemarle* was sunk at its moorings by a Union raiding force in a small boat. In May the ironclad *Raleigh* attacked blockaders off the Cape Fear River. After a futile effort to destroy the Union ships, the Confederate ironclad grounded while attempting to reenter the river. With the exception of

After the summer of 1862, the ironclads' primary duty became the defense of the Confederacy's rivers and harbors.

PAGE 344

Albemarle, which was raised and towed to Norfolk by Union personnel, all Confederate naval vessels in North Carolina waters were destroyed by their own crews, the Cape Fear Squadron upon the fall of Fort Fisher in February 1865 and the ironclad *Neuse* in the Neuse River in April.

The Mobile Squadron was commanded by Adm. Franklin Buchanan. In 1864 it consisted of four ironclads and wooden gunboats. On August 5, 1864, units of the squadron engaged a Federal fleet under Adm. David Farragut. Buchanan's force was defeated: the ironclad *Tennessee* and wooden gunboat *Selma* were captured, the gunboat *Gaines* ran aground, and the gunboat *Morgan* escaped. In the months that followed, *Morgan* along with the ironclads *Huntsville, Tuscaloosa,* and *Nashville* defended the river approaches to Mobile in cooperation with land forces. The capture of Mobile on April 12, 1865, resulted in the destruction of these ships by their crews.

Mobile was the last important port in the Confederacy to surrender. In all the ports, except Galveston, naval units contributed to their defense. Nonetheless, the Confederate navy had limited success against Federal warships. Only a half-dozen Union vessels of war were actually sunk in action by Confederate warships. This includes *Underwriter,* destroyed in a small-boat engagement. Torpedoes (mines) proved to be the most successful weapon used against Union ships. More than sixty ships including armored vessels were sunk by Confederate torpedoes during the war. In the final analysis, however, the Confederate navy had little chance against its more formidable opponent.

[*For further discussion of particular naval squadrons, see* Charleston Squadron; James River Squadron; Mobile Squadron; River Defense Fleet; Savannah Squadron.]

— WILLIAM N. STILL, JR.

NAVY DEPARTMENT

On February 20, 1861, the Confederate Congress meeting in Montgomery enacted legislation creating the Confederate Navy Department. To head this department President Jefferson Davis turned to Stephen R. Mallory. Born on the island of Jamaica, Mallory moved as an infant to Key West, Florida, a place he would always cherish as home. A successful lawyer, he entered the U.S. Senate in 1851 and served on the Naval Committee, becoming chairman in 1855. Thanks to his position, Mallory was without doubt well informed on naval matters. When Florida left the Union in January 1861, Mallory resigned from the Senate and returned home until summoned by Davis to his new post.

Under the legislation of February 20 the Navy Department's administrative structure consisted of the secretary, two chief clerks, three additional clerks, and a messenger. Initially the department had its offices in Montgomery, but during May and June 1861 it moved with the rest of the Confederate government to Richmond. The Navy Department's offices were located in the Mechanics Institute on Ninth Street between Main and Franklin. Here Mallory and his staff wrestled with the problems of creating and managing a navy.

For the most part matters of policy and strategy were decided by the secretary and his two chief clerks, French Forrest and E. M. Tidball. Forrest was an old navy veteran who had joined the service shortly before the War of 1812. He detested bureaucratic routine, and after importuning the secretary, he was assigned to more active duty. Tidball was not an officer but a bureaucrat who brought to the office political and managerial skills the secretary would find useful.

Despite the tidal wave of problems the department encountered, its employees were fortunate in one respect: they did not have to contend with constant meddling from the president. As a West Point graduate and former secretary of war, Jefferson Davis felt competent to intrude into matters of Confederate military policy and strategy, a habit that often proved troublesome. Having virtually no background in naval matters, however, he rarely interfered in that department's affairs. On the other hand, although this hands-off policy was generally positive, it did have some negative impact. Davis's lack of appreciation for naval power bordered at times on indifference, a common characteristic among Confederate leaders. As secretary, one of Mallory's chief tasks was simply to make the president and his colleagues aware of the value of the Confederate navy in order to garner support.

Organization

To assist the secretary in formulating and executing policy, four offices were created, all located at the general headquarters on Ninth Street. The organization closely resembled the one Mallory had helped fashion to administer the Federal navy in the antebellum years.

J. K. Mitchell was in charge of the Office of Orders and Detail, which held primary responsibility for matters of personnel, including the recruiting, promotion, and assignment of officers and crews. The office also had logistical responsibilities that included procurement and distribution of coal and operations at the naval ropewalk in Petersburg.

The Office of Ordnance and Hydrography was in the hands of John M. Brooke, an Annapolis graduate. As its name implies, Brooke's department was responsible for obtaining and distributing to the fleet ord-

NAVAL LEADERS
Seated, from left: Franklin Buchanan, Josiah Tattnall, and Matthew Fontaine Maury. Standing, from left: George N. Hollins, Raphael Semmes, and Secretary Stephen R. Mallory.

nance and munitions. It was also the duty of this office to provide navigational equipment including instruments and charts as well as to oversee the maintenance of docks and yards.

Medicine and Surgery was under the direction of W. A. W. Spotswood and was charged with providing medical service to the navy. The department administered a hospital in Richmond and smaller institutions at various ports. Providing sufficient quantities of drugs was a particular problem: the department was forced to place an inordinate reliance on costly supplies delivered by blockade runners.

The fourth principal office was that of Provisions and Clothing under the command of John De Bree. Acting much like a quartermaster corps, the men under De Bree were responsible for delivering food, clothing, and other such items to the men in the fleet. Key to the functioning of this office were the paymasters and assistant paymasters, who dealt both with officers and enlisted men of the navy and with civilian contractors and suppliers.

Although these four offices handled the bulk of the affairs of the Navy Department, there were other places of power that, because they did not fall neatly under these offices, enjoyed a fair degree of autonomy. Among them were Steam Engineering, Naval Constructor, Torpedo Bureau, and the Marine Corps. In addition there were floating forces under army command, most notably the Mississippi River Defense Force in 1862 and the Texas Marine Department.

Mallory's organization had much to recommend it, but it suffered from two chronic weaknesses of the Confederacy itself: poverty and state rights, or decentralization. Problems arising from an inadequate budget were compounded by the independent attitudes of the Confederate states. Having left the Union in the name of state rights, the members of the Confederacy were reluctant to grant another central government,

this one in Richmond, power over them. The result for the navy was a high degree of decentralization that often resulted in poor planning and control.

Outfitting the Navy

Although shortages of nearly everything would greatly hamper the Confederate navy, at the beginning of the war it was ironically a surplus that proved nettlesome. When confronted with the need to decide where their loyalty lay—with the Union or with their home state—many Federal naval officers chose their state. These men who "went south" either wrote to or showed up at the offices on Ninth Street to offer their services. To accommodate these officers, at least on paper, the Confederate Congress in April 1862 authorized the appointment of nine admirals, six commodores, twenty captains, twenty commanders, twenty first lieutenants, sixty-five second lieutenants, and sixty masters.

Finding berths for all these men was impossible, and few of these billets were actually filled. At its height the Confederate navy never had more than forty vessels in service. Most of the officers who volunteered their services either ended up on furlough awaiting orders or were directed to the army where they were often attached to a heavy ordnance unit. Those for whom berths were found, however, generally proved to be able and courageous officers.

Under Mallory's direction, the department focused on three strategic goals:

1. the harassment of Union shipping;

2. protection of the Atlantic and Gulf ports;

3. defense of the Mississippi and its southern tributaries.

Each of these tasks presented special problems, but they shared a common requirement—ships.

By 1864, the Federal navy had grown from 42 warships to 671 vessels.

PAGE 341

Mallory contracted for construction of four armored vessels on the Mississippi River, two at New Orleans and two at Memphis.

PAGE 344

From the outset Mallory appreciated that it would never be possible for the Confederacy to outbuild the Union; Southerners had neither the shipyards nor the resources to win a race against the North. Driven by that constraint, Mallory opted to build ironclads, hoping that a superior weapons system would compensate for numbers. His prescience in this matter helped make the Confederate States Navy far more effective than it might otherwise have been. Despite critical shortages of nearly everything necessary for the construction of modern ironclad warships, the South managed to launch a goodly number, enough at least to keep a vastly superior Union navy busily engaged. Altogether during the war the Confederate Navy Department built at least twenty ironclads.

Some of the ironclads, as well as conventional vessels, were built at private yards in the South. Others, however, were built in facilities under direct Department of the Navy control. During the war the department had in operation at one time or another twenty yards, one powderworks, two shops for constructing marine engines, five ordnance manufactories, and the ropewalk in Petersburg. Given the general lack of shipbuilding resources, the Confederacy did remarkably well to build as many warships as it did.

Because Mallory understood the domestic limitations on construction, he looked abroad for assistance. In May 1861 he dispatched a secret naval agent, James Dunwoody Bulloch, to England to procure suitable war vessels. Over the next four years Bulloch played a central role in the intrigue designed to evade laws of neutrality so that the Confederacy might obtain warships. Although Bulloch did contract for the construction of two ironclad rams with which Mallory hoped to attack Union blockaders, his work for the secretary for the most part was aimed at obtaining fast vessels designed to raid Union commerce. In this he was very successful.

Mallory believed that by sending raiders to sea he could accomplish two tasks—wreak havoc on Union commerce and at the same time force the Federal navy to withdraw vessels from blockade duty to chase down *Alabama, Florida,* and their sister ships. This did not prove to be the case. The raiders provided an aura of adventure and romance, but the damage they inflicted, although harmful to Union commerce, was nonetheless tolerable. Furthermore, the Union navy had sufficient vessels available to both chase the raiders and maintain the blockade. Eventually, because no European nation was willing to risk the wrath of the Union, they allowed the raiders to remain in their ports only long enough to make essential repairs and to take on enough fuel to reach the next port. Alone and isolated, unable to find safe ports for resupply and refitting, the raiders found themselves hunted down and either captured or destroyed.

Mallory believed that large ironclads were indispensable for defending Southern ports, a conviction that was reinforced in November 1861 when Port Royal, South Carolina, was attacked by a Federal fleet commanded by Samuel Francis DuPont. Confederate Commodore Josiah Tattnall sortied to defend the port with an assortment of ragtag converted wooden gunboats. A few Federal broadsides sent them scurrying. Unless the Confederacy built vessels more substantial than these cockleshells, Tattnall's rout was likely to be repeated at every Confederate port.

Under the secretary's direction, considerable resources were gathered at New Orleans to build ironclads. The money seems not to have been well spent, however, and during the summer of 1861 the Navy Department was being heavily criticized for its wasteful practices by, among others, Louisiana's governor. Mallory dispatched officers to the Crescent City to clear up the mess and get the ironclads built. Adding to the department's woes was the difficulty of securing sufficient funds for construction from the Confederate Treasury Department and a disagreement within the local army command as to responsibilities for the defense of the city.

The fall of New Orleans in April 1862 sparked numerous investigations within the Confederate government. The Navy Department was not spared. For more than six months a congressional committee took testimony in its inquiry into the administration of the department. In the end Mallory was exonerated from any misconduct; nonetheless, it was a humiliating experience and one that damaged his and the department's reputation.

With New Orleans in Union hands, the Confederate Navy Department was deprived of its only significant shipbuilding facility on the Mississippi. Although the department was able to take into service a variety of rivercraft, these were lightly built vessels that would prove no match for the heavily armed and armored Union squadrons. Mallory's greatest success on the rivers was *Arkansas,* an ironclad built at Yazoo City. It came down the Yazoo in July 1862 and blazed its way through the somnolent Union fleet at anchor near Vicksburg. But it later suffered engine problems and had to be scuttled to avoid capture. The Confederate navy had little impact on the war in the West.

The Navy in Action

Mallory's commitment to ironclads could be most clearly seen along the Atlantic coast. The appearance of *Virginia* on March 8, 1862, demonstrated his belief that large ironclads could both aid in defending the ports and on occasion interrupt the Union blockade. Under his authority other ironclads were built to defend Savannah, Charleston, and the North Carolina sound. At each of these ports Mallory's ironclads posed a threat that the Union forces could not ignore. At the same time, however, with the exception of those at Charleston these ironclads remained only a potential force and never succeeded in attacking and inflicting damage on the enemy. Their inactivity was the object of considerable criticism.

At Charleston Mallory endured an uncomfortable relationship with the army commander Gen. P. G. T. Beauregard. Under the Navy Department's direction two ironclads, *Palmetto State* and *Chicora*, had been built at Charleston for the defense of that port. (In 1864 they were joined by a third, *Charleston*.) To the dismay of Mallory and his department, these ironclads in practice came under the operational authority of Beauregard. At the general's orders in January 1863 these two vessels steamed out of the harbor and drove off the blockaders. It was only a temporary victory, however, for soon the Federals were back with a force sufficient to demolish the Confederates should they make a similar attempt again. Despite the danger, Beauregard urged repeatedly that the ironclads sortie. Mallory would not permit it. The same situation existed at Savannah where the ironclads *Atlanta* and *Savannah* were stationed. Mallory's argument was that sending these vessels out to engage a vastly superior Union force was suicide. He was right; however, the fact that the navy's ironclads remained snug in the harbor angered some and presented a sorry picture to the Southern public. *Atlanta* was run aground and then captured by Union forces in Wassaw Sound, while *Albemarle* was destroyed by Union Navy Lt. William Cushing in one of the great tales of the war. All the Confederate ironclads on the Atlantic coast were destroyed or captured.

One of the arguments Beauregard persisted in making was that the Navy Department ignored the value of torpedoes (underwater mines). Under Mallory's direction the department had established a Torpedo Bureau. Although often unreliable, these weapons had been employed with success on the western rivers, but the department was slow to use them to advantage in the East.

It was at Charleston that the Confederate Navy employed *H. L. Hunley*, a submarine built at Mobile but brought to Charleston in the summer of 1863 on the orders of Beauregard. *Hunley* proved exceedingly unreliable. On two dives it failed to return to the surface with a heavy loss of life. Desperate to find some way to drive the blockaders away, the Confederates on the night of February 17, 1864, sent *Hunley* to attack the Union frigate *Housatonic*. It succeeded in its mission but then went down with all hands lost.

On the Gulf coast at Mobile, the Navy Department placed under construction four ironclads for that port's defense. It was an overly ambitious program that went beyond what local resources could sustain. Only one of the ironclads, *Tennessee*, was completed to the point where it could play a role in defending against the Union attack in August 1864 commanded by Adm. David Farragut. The Confederate naval forces under Franklin Buchanan put up a stiff resistance against a much superior Federal force. *Tennessee* steamed bravely into the middle of the fray only to be sent to the bottom. The remaining unfinished ironclads played no role in the fight.

In addition to building and managing fighting ships, the Navy Department also had under its jurisdiction several blockade runners. Many of these were specially built for the trade under the direction of Bulloch operating under various guises. Altogether about twenty of these vessels served the Confederacy, bringing in much needed supplies, particularly munitions and medicines. On the outward voyage they generally carried cotton. The success of the department's blockade runners is attested to by the fact that Bulloch seemed always to have sufficient cash and credit to carry on his business of ship buying and building. His principal source of income was the sale of cotton run out of the South.

As the war dragged to its climax, Mallory watched unhappily as his ships were captured, scuttled, or destroyed. Some of his vessels participated in the defense of Richmond by trying to hold on to the James River. But the situation was hopeless, and on Sunday evening April 2 Mallory joined Jefferson Davis and the remainder of his cabinet on a train out of Richmond. The withdrawal of the Confederate government soon turned into flight. On May 2 Mallory resigned from the government and a few days later was captured. After an imprisonment of less than a year he was released. He returned to Florida and settled in Pensacola where he remained until his death in November 1873.

Given the resources at hand, the Confederate Navy Department accomplished a great deal. Although Mallory may be faulted for too heavy a reliance on large ironclads and high seas raiders, and inattention to torpedoes, overall he and his department were remarkably effective under the circumstances.

— WILLIAM M. FOWLER, JR.

MANPOWER

From the very beginning of the Civil War, Southern naval authorities struggled to acquire adequate personnel, for the navy had no pool of trained seamen to augment its enlisted force. Throughout four years of war, and in the face of overwhelming personnel and material shortages, the navy nevertheless amassed an honorable record. By 1864, its strength was almost four thousand officers and men.

The firing on Fort Sumter led Admiral Semmes to realize that "it was time to leave the things of peace to the future."

PAGE 530

In six months Semmes captured eighteen ships, seven of which he destroyed.

PAGE 530

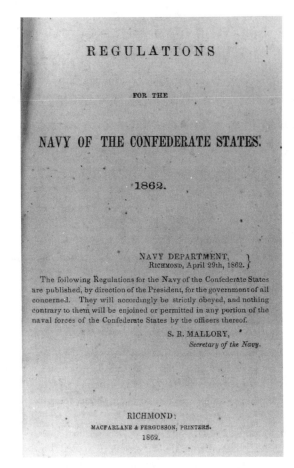

REGULATIONS

FOR THE

NAVY OF THE CONFEDERATE STATES.

1862.

NAVY DEPARTMENT,
RICHMOND, April 29th, 1862.

The following Regulations for the Navy of the Confederate States are published, by direction of the President, for the government of all concerned. They will accordingly be strictly obeyed, and nothing contrary to them will be enjoined or permitted in any portion of the naval forces of the Confederate States by the officers thereof.

S. R. MALLORY,
Secretary of the Navy.

RICHMOND:
MACFARLANE & FERGUSSON, PRINTERS.
1862.

President Jefferson Davis in his inaugural address called upon the Provisional Congress to establish a navy to protect the harbors and commerce of the Southern states, and on February 20, 1861, the Confederate States Navy came into being. Stephen R. Mallory of Florida was appointed secretary of the navy and given a clerical force consisting of a chief clerk, a correspondence clerk, and a messenger. The secretary was charged with administering the various bureaus, which included Ordnance and Hydrography, Orders and Details, Medicine and Surgery, and Provisions and Clothing.

On March 16, an act of Congress established manpower limits for the navy and authorized President Davis to create the posts of four captains, four commanders, thirty lieutenants, five surgeons, five assistant surgeons, six paymasters, and two chief engineers. He was also empowered to employ as many as three thousand masters, midshipmen, engineers, naval constructors, boatswains, gunners, carpenters, sailmakers, warrant and petty officers, and seamen. The act made provisions for a marine corps to consist of one major, one quartermaster, one paymaster, one adjutant, one sergeant major, and six companies of marines. In turn, each company was to have a captain, a first and a second lieutenant, four sergeants, four corporals, one hundred men, and ten musicians.

The navy benefited from the 332 officers who resigned from the Federal navy and returned to their native states. Eventually, they transferred from state service to the Confederate States Navy, carrying the same rank they had held in the "old" service. To accommodate this large increase in officers, the Amendatory Act of April 21, 1862, increased the number of officers authorized for the navy.

To train additional officers the navy founded an academy on March 23, 1863, at Drewry's Bluff, Virginia, on the James River. The steamship *Patrick Henry* was the school's ship. Cabins were built on shore for the midshipmen, who were expected to spend half their time ashore and the other half aboard the training ship. The academy did not have sufficient longevity to graduate any cadets; the first class of 1863 contained fifty acting midshipmen.

The experience of naval administrators in obtaining qualified officers was duplicated in their attempts to recruit enlisted men. The South's lack of a seafaring tradition limited opportunities for finding trained seamen. To encourage enlistments, the navy opened rendezvous stations (recruiting stations) in all major Southern cities and towns, a practice long followed by the U.S. Navy. At the rendezvous, the recruit was interviewed and given a physical. Upon passing the tests, the recruit signed shipping articles that corresponded with the descriptive roll used by the army and was assigned to a receiving ship for training.

The navy also followed the U.S. Navy practice of stationing receiving ships at major ports. These ships served as barracks and training areas for the sailors before they shipped off to a regular assignment. Each receiving ship had a small complement of officers and petty officers to act as instructors. Here the new sailor literally "learned the ropes." The basic rank assigned a raw recruit was landsman; after some training he was promoted to ordinary seaman and then to seaman—the same enlisted rank structure used by the Union navy. The initiate received instruction in seamanship, gunnery, naval regulations and discipline, and a seaman's life in general. The Confederate navy had receiving ships, at one time or another, at Wilmington, North Carolina, Mobile, Alabama, Charleston, South Carolina, Savannah, Georgia, New Orleans, Louisiana, and Norfolk, Virginia.

In an effort to increase its strength, the navy frequently requested men from the army, but the army was reluctant to release any. In early 1862, the navy offered a bounty of fifty dollars to any man who enlisted for three years. This offer met with only limited success. One source of manpower overlooked by the navy was the slave population. The Confederate navy did not enlist African Americans in any large numbers, unlike the Federal navy, which recruited nearly nine thousand black sailors.

The Confederate conscription acts of April 1862, October 1862, and May 1863 allowed men with seafaring experience who had enlisted in the army to transfer to the navy. In March 1864 Congress passed the General Conscription Law, which ordered the army to release 1,200 men to the navy; 960 men were transferred. By the end of 1864 the Confederate navy had reached its manpower peak of 3,674 enlisted men, but more were still needed, and convicts were ordered to serve aboard warships.

The one area in which recruitment went well was the oceangoing navy. The raiding cruisers that sailed the high seas interdicting Union shipping had little trouble acquiring personnel. Most of these seamen were of foreign birth and signed on for the prize money.

The navy had started with a dearth of men and ships, but within four years it had made some progress in creating a viable naval force. The officers and men served their cause well and earned the respect of their adversaries.

— DAVID L. VALUSKA

cent of the Federal navy was black. These men could be recruited in the ranks of landsman, ordinary seaman, and seaman, and by 1863, they were also receiving pay equal to that of white shipmates. There was no similar program in the Confederate navy, and any blacks brought on board were slaves. It is difficult to find any record of free blacks serving aboard ship.

The Southern navy employed slaves in many different ways within the service: they worked in navy yards and armament factories, constructed naval land batteries, and filled noncombat roles on board ships. In an act passed on February 17, 1863, the Confederate Congress authorized the rental of 20,000 slaves for service in workshops and hospitals run by the military. The Selma Naval Ordnance Works, among other such plants, augmented their work force with rented slaves.

On March 13, 1865, less than a month before Appomattox, President Jefferson Davis signed an act providing for the recruitment of 300,000 slaves into the military. But it was too late for the Confederate navy to benefit from the act.

— DAVID L. VALUSKA

AFRICAN AMERICANS IN THE CONFEDERATE NAVY

The Confederate navy never adopted a policy comparable to the Federal navy regarding the utilization of blacks in the naval service. From the outset of the war the Union navy employed African Americans aboard ship in an integrated fashion, and approximately 9 per-

NEW MARKET, VIRGINIA

The little town of New Market was the site of an important Confederate victory on May 14, 1864, that kept the vital Shenandoah Valley in Southern hands most of the last summer of the war. Federal plans for

DOCKHANDS

A crew gathers for a photograph by Mathew Brady at a quartermaster's wharf on the James River in Alexandria, Virginia, c. 1863.

NATIONAL ARCHIVES

the spring of 1864 called for a three-pronged operation against Confederate positions in Virginia. While large Union armies moved on the Southerners in southeastern and central Virginia, a third invasion menaced the strategic Shenandoah Valley, an agriculturally important area between the Blue Ridge and Allegheny mountain ranges.

This third thrust into the Old Dominion consisted of two parts. One force would move from West Virginia into the upper (southern) Shenandoah Valley to cut the Virginia and Tennessee Railroad, damage the saltworks at Saltville and the lead mines at Wytheville, and then move on Lynchburg or Staunton. Meanwhile, another column, some 9,000 men under Maj. Gen. Franz Sigel, would march into the lower (northern) part of the valley to distract the Confederates, keep them from sending reinforcements to other points, and perhaps meet the column from the west. Sigel's advance got underway in late April.

The Confederates defending the area were also divided. Brig. Gen. John D. Imboden commanded 2,000 men in the lower Shenandoah Valley; Maj. Gen. John C. Breckinridge with 6,700 men was charged with defending the upper valley. In early May Breckinridge was given authority over all Confederates in the valley. Wisely, the Southerners chose to concentrate the bulk of their available forces against Sigel. His advance menaced the lower and middle valley, and he might turn east, cross the Blue Ridge, and join in the attack on the main Southern army in central Virginia.

Leaving some of his men to guard key areas in southwestern Virginia, Breckinridge hurried to unite with Imboden. As he went, he called out local reserve forces, including the 250 members of the Corps of Cadets from the Virginia Military Institute in Lexington. When he got all his available force together, Breckinridge had about 5,300 men with whom to meet Sigel's column. On the rainy day of May 15 the two forces collided at New Market.

The battle was a simple one, fought in a small area between the North Fork of the Shenandoah River on the west and Smith's Creek to the east. Breckinridge deployed his small army on an east-west line across the southern part of the battlefield. The Federals occupied a parallel line to the north, though not all their units had reached the field.

Breckinridge originally planned to fight a defensive battle. He hoped to lure Sigel into attacking a strong fortified position and trusted that the usual advantage enjoyed by the defense over the offensive would offset the numerical superiority of the Federals. When they refused to take the bait, Breckinridge decided to strengthen the left of his line and attack at the spot where the terrain offered some advantage to his men. At about 11:30 A.M. the Confederate advance lurched

forward. By that time Sigel had begun to pull back to a position north of New Market.

In midafternoon, as Breckinridge pushed ahead, his men began to take heavy casualties. A gap opened in his line, and the Southerners feared that Sigel would see it and launch a countercharge. The only reserve was the Corps of Cadets, and Breckinridge reluctantly threw it into the line. The gap was plugged, and Confederate fire soon halted feeble Federal efforts at a counterblow. Sigel began to withdraw from the field. By 3:00 P.M. momentum had shifted to the Southerners, and they began the final charge of the day. As the Federals withdrew, the Confederates occupied the field.

About 6,300 Union troops had fought at New Market; 96 had been killed, 520 wounded, and 225 captured or missing. Breckinridge had sent about 4,100 men into the fight. Partial reports indicate that he lost at least 43 killed, 474 wounded, and 3 captured.

After the battle Breckinridge transferred most of his little command across the Blue Ridge to reinforce the main Confederate army then engaged in desperate fighting north of Richmond. By the time the Federals in the Shenandoah Valley managed to get themselves organized for another advance, the situation near Richmond had stabilized, and the Southerners were able to dispatch enough reinforcements to hold the valley through the summer of 1864.

Had New Market been a Federal victory, the Confederates would have lost control of the Shenandoah Valley in the spring of 1864. Deprived of the valley and its agricultural produce, they probably would have been unable to hold out as long as they did. Because it enabled the Southerners to retain possession of the valley, New Market has been called "the biggest little battle of the war."

— RICHARD M. MCMURRY

NEW ORLEANS, LOUISIANA

[*This entry includes two articles,* City of New Orleans, *which profiles the city during the Confederacy, and* Capture of New Orleans, *which discusses the Federal capture of the city in 1862.*]

CITY OF NEW ORLEANS

The South's largest and most cosmopolitan city, New Orleans had the briefest of stints under Confederate authority. Fifteen months after Louisiana seceded, the

Crescent City was back under Union rule after Adm. David G. Farragut dropped anchor outside the levee on April 25, 1862.

Pinched into a shallow clay saucer between Lake Pontchartrain and the Mississippi, New Orleans derives its nickname from the huge crescent bend that the river describes near the French Quarter. Most of the city's 168,000 residents in 1860 hugged the high ground near the river levee, on either side of Canal Street, which historically separates Gallic downtown and Anglo uptown. It was a population of infinite ethnic variety and romantic charm. To the original white creole population (of mixed French and Spanish ancestry) were added, during the antebellum period, heavy infusions of Protestant Americans from both North and South, continuing inputs of foreign French—often refugees from the French and Haitian revolutions—and a huge influx of German and Irish immigration. Even driblets of Italian settlement had reached the Crescent City prior to the Civil War. Comprising nearly 40 percent of the 1860 population, New Orleans's foreign-born community loomed larger than any other Southern city's at the time. Although only one-sixth the size of the white population, the black population in 1860 was also ethnically diverse. In addition to slaves, New Orleans was home to the most prosperous and sophisticated free black community in the United States, which itself was split between the more numerous Francophone Catholics and a small coterie of Protestant African Americans.

New Orleans's heterogeneity, plus the city's historic trade ties with the upper Mississippi valley, rendered secession difficult. John C. Breckinridge, the Southern rights candidate in 1860, ran third in every district of the city. John Slidell, one of New Orleans's two Democratic U.S. senators, blamed Breckinridge's poor showing on the fact that "here in the city seven-eighths of the vote for [Stephen] Douglas were cast by the Irish and Germans." The Crescent City's business community, a substantial element of which hailed from the Northeast, was also tugged toward Unionism by trade and shipping connections with the free states. But for the hysteria aroused by well-organized Southern nationalist groups—helped by Presbyterian minister Benjamin M. Palmer's fire-breathing Thanksgiving Day sermon—the city's immediate secessionists, in the January 7, 1861, election, might not have won a 52 to 48 percent victory for their delegate slate to the state's secessionist convention. Voter turnout was noticeably lower than it had been in the presidential election two months earlier.

BUTLER'S WOMAN ORDER
How the "Beast" Tamed Southern Belles

Issued on May 15, 1862, from the headquarters of the Department of the Gulf in Union-occupied New Orleans, General Order No. 28 declared in part that "when any female shall, by word, gesture, or movement, insult or show contempt for any officer or soldier of the United States, she shall be regarded and held liable to be treated as a woman of the town plying her avocation." No other action during Gen. Benjamin F. Butler's controversial seven-month command of southern Louisiana raised more outcry than his eighty-two-word "woman order."

The directive was typical of the sternness with which Butler suppressed the disorder greeting his troops' arrival in New Orleans. While white men rioted, women sporting secessionist insignia turned up their noses and drew aside their skirts when passing Federal soldiers on the street. Others left streetcars

and church pews whenever blue-clad conquerors entered. One woman emptied her slop jar on Adm. David Farragut's head as he walked beneath her balcony. Butler's patience snapped when another woman spat in the face of two Federal officers. The woman order followed hard upon this incident. Its implied authorization to treat demonstrative women as though they were streetwalkers struck a raw nerve in a community where harlotry had historically been widespread.

At home and abroad, the outcry against the woman order was loud and abusive. New Orleans's own creole general P. G. T. Beauregard was characteristic of Confederate commanders in using Butler's order to arouse his troops: "Men of the South! shall our mothers, our wives, our daughters and our sisters be thus outraged by the ruffianly soldiers of the North?" The Confederate state gov-

ernor called on Southern soldiers to avenge this "foul conduct." Later in the year President Jefferson Davis branded Butler a common felon and ordered his immediate execution should he ever fall into Confederate hands. Meanwhile, on the floor of the British House of Commons, the prime minister, Lord Palmerston, called Butler's proclamation "infamous."

Butler imprisoned Mayor John Monroe for assailing the directive as uncivilized and un-Christian, but neither the Massachusetts general nor his troops ever executed the woman order. Local women thereafter behaved more circumspectly toward occupying troops, except for the prostitutes who reportedly pasted Butler's likeness in "the bottom of their tinklepots."

— LAWRENCE N. POWELL

VIEUX CARRÉ

A mid-nineteenth-century view of the French Quarter, New Orleans, looking down Orleans Street toward St. Louis Cathedral.

HARPER'S PICTORIAL HISTORY OF THE GREAT REBELLION

In 1867, Beauregard and Jubal Early began a long stint as supervisors of the drawings of the infamous Louisiana Lottery for reportedly handsome salaries.

PAGE 48

Although divided in secession, New Orleans was momentarily united in war. Some of the contagion of the city's being a troop-mustering center spread to the local population. Uptown New Orleans's famed

Washington Artillery, which traced its military tradition back to the Mexican War, entrained for Virginia in May to a citywide send-off. A variety of privately outfitted Zouave units also enlisted in the Confederacy. So did assorted ethnic regiments: the French and creole populations set the pace, but various German and Irish units followed close behind. Polyglot New Orleans also furnished a Garibaldi Legion, a Spanish Legion, a Scandinavian Guard, a Polish Brigade, a Scotch Rifle Guard, a Belgian Guard, two companies of Slavonian Rifles, and a company of Greek citizens wearing the national Albanian uniform. Tracing its military tradition back to the colonial period, the city's Franco-African population also offered its services to the Confederacy, but because the idea of black soldiers contradicted Confederate racial nationalism, their Native Guard was mustered into the state militia only.

As the gateway to the Mississippi valley, the country's second leading port early on felt squeezed by the Union blockade. After May 26, 1861, when the USS *Brooklyn* anchored off the mouth of the Mississippi, ocean vessels ceased docking in the Crescent City, although some coastal shipping slipped into the city through the lake. From the summer onward, trade stagnated, prices soared, and necessities like coal and food grew scarce. The city council tried to fend off destitution by establishing a free market in the new ironworks building at the foot of Canal Street, where foodstuffs supplied by local planters were distributed to poor families. In September the banks, by order of the Confederacy, suspended specie payments, drying up the supply of small change and giving rise to a variety of makeshift expedients (like streetcar tickets). Meanwhile,

military recruiters siphoned some of the unemployed, mainly the Irish poor, into Confederate armies.

Because the Union brass was determined to split the Confederacy by seizing the Mississippi, it was only a matter of time before a joint army-navy expedition took aim at the Crescent City. The War of 1812 had made local authorities conscious that such an attack was likely, but work on local defenses lagged under Maj. Gen. David Twigg, who was in command of New Orleans and vicinity until October 1861. Twigg's replacement, Mansfield Lovell, who had been a New York City street commissioner only weeks before moving to the South (he was an unpopular choice because favorite sons like P. G. T. Beauregard had been passed over), invigorated the work of military preparedness, creating powder works, helping local foundries convert to armament production, supervising naval shipbuilding, and completing work on exterior entrenchments. The press extolled his "restless activity." One item of local defense that Lovell pushed to conclusion was the cypress log raft, tied together with chains and huge timbers, that reached between opposite banks of the Mississippi, near Fort Jackson and Fort St. Philip, seventy-five miles downriver from New Orleans.

This manmade invasion barrier proved porous. Proceeding from their staging area at Ship Island (which guarded the approaches to the lake), Union Adm. David G. Farragut's seventeen-ship fleet, together with twenty mortar schooners under Como. David Porter, and a fifteen-thousand-man army recruited in New England by Maj. Gen. Benjamin F. Butler, reached the two forts by mid-April, and, after a five-day mortar bombardment, cut the river chain and ran the gauntlet on April 24. The following day Farragut's naval guns were peering over the levee of a panic-stricken city, many of whose defenders had just been sent to reinforce the collapsing Confederate line in Tennessee and Mississippi.

For a few days Mayor John Monroe defied Farragut's surrender order, galvanizing some of the nativist thugs whose votes and fists had put him into office. "We don't want you here, damn it!" a menacing mob yelled at the first Union officers to come ashore. Farragut threatened to cannonade the city into submission, despite pleas from foreign consuls. In the meantime, General Lovell had evacuated his troops from the city, and drayloads of cotton and sugar, corn and rice, were brought to the riverfront and set afire. Monroe capitulated when word arrived that the downriver forts had surrendered on April 28 (in part because immigrant troops from New Orleans had mutinied). When Ben Butler's troops clambered down the gangplank on May 1, 1862, New Orleans joined New York as one of only two major cities in U.S. history to undergo enemy occupation for an extended period. For the next three years Union-occupied New Orleans served as the nerve center of the newly formed Department of the Gulf.

Because the Crescent City was a command headquarters in a combat zone, military security took first priority, and Ben Butler wasted little time in bringing the turbulent population to heel. He hanged a professional gambler, William Mumford, for lowering the U.S. flag that Farragut had hoisted over the Federal mint. He silenced females who acted insultingly toward Union soldiers by issuing an edict directing that they be treated as streetwalkers—and acquired the nickname "Beast." (The Davis government in retaliation placed a bounty on Butler's head.) He seized newspapers, censored sermons, and made schoolteachers swear allegiance to the Union. He even threatened to confiscate the hotel where he made his headquarters when the proprietor refused to serve him breakfast. And when Mayor Monroe kept up his obstructionism, Butler had him incarcerated for the duration of the war. Thereafter New Orleans's municipal affairs were administered by a succession of military-appointed mayors.

In local legend Butler was also known as "Spoons" for allegedly helping himself to family silver (the corruption charge is probably truer of his brother). But historians better remember Butler, a skillful Massachusetts politician, for sponsoring a new political and social order in the Crescent City. President Lincoln looked on New Orleans as a promising location in which to field-test various emancipation and Reconstruction experiments. Butler galvanized working-class immigrant Unionism by putting destitute Irish and Germans to work cleaning canals and streets, which he financed by taxing wealthy Confederates. He accommodated the slaves' yearning for freedom by ordering that they be paid wages. He accepted the military services of a black creole regiment (the Corps d'Afrique, which was disbanded by Butler's successor), thereby encouraging the city's influential free people of color to follow the lead of its philosophical radicals, men like the Roudanez brothers, Charles and Louis, and Paul Trevigne. By the time Butler was replaced seven months later, the nucleus of an interracial political party called the Free State movement had taken shape in New Orleans.

A Massachusetts politician like his predecessor, Maj. Gen. Nathaniel P. Banks extended and modified Butler's race and Reconstruction policies after taking command of the Department of the Gulf in December 1862. But Banks sought to conciliate upper-class conservative Unionists by clamping down on the black population, both freeborn and slave, and dampening the indigenous drive to extend the vote to creoles of color. When Lincoln's Ten Percent Plan took effect in December 1863—

restoring civil government whenever one-tenth of the 1860 voting population resumed their Unionist allegiance—Banks helped ensure that a top-down coalition of white Unionists took control. Although the state was returned to civil rule (albeit under military supervision) in 1864, New Orleans continued to be administered by occupying authorities for the duration of the war.

New Orleans's status as an occupied city officially ended when John Monroe was reelected mayor in March 1866. It was under Monroe's administration that the police massacre known as the New Orleans Riot of 1866 occurred. Many of the policemen were probably the same plug-uglies who had jeered Farragut's officers when they first stepped ashore four years earlier.

— LAWRENCE N. POWELL

CAPTURE OF NEW ORLEANS

Despite the strategic and commercial importance of New Orleans, Union authorities did not turn their attention to the Crescent City until November 15, 1861. Although his Southern heritage raised doubts about his loyalty, Capt. David G. Farragut was assigned to command the naval forces; Maj. Gen. Benjamin F. Butler led the army contingent. Union forces first concentrated on Ship Island in the Gulf of Mexico, which led Confederate officials to conclude that their objective was Mobile or Pensacola, not New Orleans. By early April 1862, when Farragut's ships entered the Mississippi River, troop transfers had reduced the defenses of New Orleans to little more than 4,500 militia scattered among the masonry forts that protected the city.

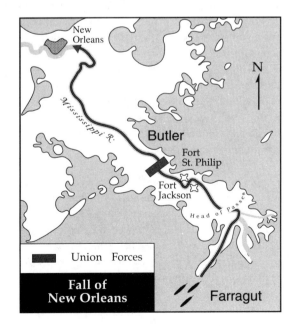

"'Nothing afloat could pass the forts,' a New Orleans citizen remembered believing, 'and nothing that walked could get through our swamps.'"

GEOFFREY WARD
THE CIVIL WAR, 1990

Two forts, eighty miles downriver, guarded the Mississippi: Jackson on the west bank and St. Philip, eight hundred yards north, on the east bank. A chain floated on barges barricaded the river, although high water had partially destroyed this obstacle in late February and again on April 11. An unusual fleet supported the five hundred men and eighty cannon in the forts: three ironclads (the ram *Manassas,* the underpowered *Louisiana* anchored above St. Philip as a floating battery, and the unfinished *Mississippi*), fire barges, and nine other vessels divided among the Confederate navy, the Louisiana navy, and the river defense fleet.

Just above Head of Passes on April 8 Farragut assembled twenty-four wooden vessels, mounting about two hundred guns, and Commdr. David D. Porter's nineteen mortar schooners, each carrying one 13-inch mortar. On April 18 the mortars began a bombardment that Porter believed would silence the forts, thus permitting Farragut's ships to pass them safely. During an eight-hour period that day, Porter fired 2,997 rounds into Fort Jackson. But Farragut, lacking faith in the mortars, had his vessels open a channel through the barricade during the night of April 20. Although the mortars failed to silence Jackson, at 2:00 A.M. on the twenty-fourth, Farragut's fleet steamed upriver. By dawn, twenty-one of his vessels had successfully passed the barricade and the forts. Then, in a free-for-all, Farragut's ships avoided the bull-like charges of *Manassas* and the fire rafts and destroyed the enemy's flotilla. Farragut lost the converted merchantman *Varuna,* and 171 sailors were killed or wounded. The forts' defenders had sustained fewer than 50 casualties.

Leaving two gunboats above the forts to support Butler's troops marching overland from their gulf landing toward the rear of St. Philip, Farragut continued upriver to New Orleans. The city, now undefended since Confederate Maj. Gen. Mansfield Lovell had evacuated it, fell on April 25. Civilian authorities formally surrendered on the twenty-eighth. With the city lost and Union infantry closing in, most of Brig. Gen. Johnson Kelly Duncan's men in the forts mutinied, and he surrendered the same day. Butler occupied New Orleans on May 1. A court of inquiry cleared Lovell on July 9, 1863, of any responsibility for the loss of the city. The onus fell upon the Richmond government for having stripped the garrison of its troops and having failed to place Lovell in command of all naval forces. In all, the Federals had lost 39 men killed and 171 wounded while taking the city. The Confederates had lost 85 men killed, 113 wounded, and approximately 900 captured.

— LAWRENCE L. HEWITT

NEW PLAN

The *New Plan* was the name given to a series of administrative actions and congressional laws whose object was to evade the blockade and put Confederate finances abroad on a cash basis. President Jefferson Davis authorized this program in 1863 and 1864. The indispensable first step was the appointment of an agent to supervise fund-raising abroad. Colin J. McRae, a former Confederate congressman, accepted this appointment and went to Paris. In September 1863, after carefully surveying the situation, he sent President Davis a series of recommendations that became the New Plan.

- First, McRae suggested that he be given full authority to allocate scarce Confederate funds abroad among the conflicting claims of the War and Navy departments' procurement offices. In addition, no agents were to sign contracts without securing McRae's approval for the payment terms.
- Second, the government should stop making contracts payable in cotton. The Confederacy was spending six hundred dollars in cotton to get one hundred dollars worth of goods. If the contractors could ship cotton out of the country, there was no reason the government could not do so on its own account.
- Third, McRae urged that the government employ its powers over foreign commerce to regulate imports and exports. The practice of blockade runners bringing in luxury goods and refusing to take government cotton cargoes had to be stopped.
- Fourth, McRae asked that he be appointed a Confederate Depositary at Paris and that as bursar he alone be authorized to make payments for goods purchased by government procurement agents.

McRae's suggestions met with President Davis's approval. Davis then authorized Secretary of State Judah P. Benjamin to arbitrate the differences among the War, Navy, and Treasury departments and to formulate a specific program to implement McRae's recommendations. Meanwhile, in late 1863, the War Department empowered its officers to preempt a third of all outbound cargo space for the export of government cotton.

Secretary Benjamin swiftly carried out his mandate. Acting on the suggestions of John Slidell, the Confederate commissioner to Paris, which largely coincided with McRae's views, he armed McRae with full powers to supervise other agents, to coordinate their actions, and to control all payments. Benjamin then drafted an agreement and got his cabinet colleagues' assent to coordinate their policies and not to enter into any more agreements with private contractors. It then proved an easy matter to induce a lameduck Congress to enact other key parts of the government plan.

By one act passed on February 6, 1864, Congress empowered the president to prohibit the exportation of staple produce except under regulations of his own devising. The only exemption (in deference to state rights sentiment) was for state-owned blockade runners. A second act, passed the same day, expressly prohibited the importation of items "not of common necessity and use." This put a stop to the cargoes of brandy, silks, and jewelry that did little to feed or clothe the army or the people.

Finally, President Davis promulgated a whole series of regulations to put the plan into effect. All government cotton became the property of the Treasury Department, and the War Department was empowered to collect Treasury cotton and export it. To finance this effort, $20 million was appropriated, Lt. Col. Thomas L. Bayne was made bureau chief, and half of all incoming and outgoing cargo space was reserved for the government. In addition, McRae was authorized to purchase a fleet of blockade runners.

These measures encountered considerable opposition. Resistance centered on the government's control of cargo space. State rights advocates were alienated because state sovereignty did not protect ships leased by state governments. Blockade-running firms attempted to exempt themselves from the regulations by leasing their ships to the states or by refusing to sail. President Davis, however, remained adamant. Ships not authentically operated under state authority were compelled to follow the new rules, and ultimately the shippers yielded.

Government finances abroad were greatly improved. By December 1864, James Seddon, the secretary of war, reported that over 27,299 bales of cotton had been exported, for $5.3 million of sales. Only 1,272 bales were lost, despite the fact that exports were largely limited to the port of Wilmington. In addition, the government had added fourteen steamers to its fleet.

Given the effectiveness of this program in 1864 and 1865, and the fact that the government had entertained such ideas since early 1862, the question arises as to why the New Plan was so long delayed. One problem was the Confederates' aversion to innovations that would augment the government's power. Another factor was the early hope that, because of foreign intervention, the war would be short. By the time the Confederates realized that they must fight on alone, it was too late to realize the benefits that would have accrued from an earlier implementation of this plan.

— DOUGLAS B. BALL

NORTHERNERS

One would not expect to find a significant number of Northerners in either the antebellum or the Confederate South. Yet the census of 1860 indicates that there were approximately 360,000 Northerners residing in the Old South; some estimates place that number as high as 500,000. Many Northerners, of course, found an inhospitable environment in the South and returned to their native states. But a surprising number of Northerners remained in the South and made their life's work there.

Northerners living in the South spanned the entire socioeconomic spectrum. Some were farmers, planters, or overseers; others were common laborers or skilled artisans; many became merchants, shippers, bankers, industrialists, or railroad magnates. A number of Northerners found a rewarding professional life in the South as tutors, college professors or presidents, lawyers, doctors, ministers, and scientists; still others became journalists, politicians, and diplomats.

Some fifty Northern-born men rose to the rank of general in the Confederate army, and many others filled the muster rolls at lesser ranks. Indeed, some of the most vituperative comments directed at Northerners were a consequence of their successful status in the Confederacy. For example, a Richmond editor charged in 1862 that "all the officials, who constitute the very pivot on which the whole war hinges are either Yankees, or foreigners, or Jews."

Several months later, that same editor spoke for many of his fellow Southerners when he became more specific in his vitriol. Judah P. Benjamin, a man who would occupy three cabinet-level positions (in the War, State, and Justice departments) was a "foreigner and a Jew"; Adj. Gen. Samuel Cooper was a "New Yorker"; Secretary of the Navy Stephen R. Mallory was "born in the West Indies of Yankee parents, and educated in Connecticut"; Quartermaster General Abraham C. Meyers was a "Pennsylvanian and a Jew"; and Chief of Ordnance Josiah Gorgas was "a Northern man of an unknown state."

Although they had resided in the South for quite some time, the most prominent native Northerners to become generals in the Confederate army were Gorgas, Cooper, Mansfield Lovell, John C. Pemberton, Daniel Ruggles, and Samuel G. French. Antipathy toward important Northerners in the Confederacy was exacerbated when Lovell and Pemberton, commanding the defenses of New Orleans and Vicksburg, respectively, were forced to surrender to the Federals.

In this regard, President Jefferson Davis became a focal point for criticism of southernized Northerners by appointing them to office and command. Davis and

The Confederate Congress authorized Treasury Secretary Memminger to purchase cotton with bonds under the act of April 14, 1862.

PAGE 622

others, however, defended the contributions of the Northerners to the Confederate war effort. "Casting imputations of disloyalty upon those of Northern and Foreign birth because of that fact alone," wrote the editor of the *Macon Telegraph*, "is a poor way of displaying zeal in behalf of the Southern Confederacy." The editor went on to remind his Southern brethren that there had "been as many traitors to our cause of Southern birth as of Northern birth."

In short, Northerners in the Confederacy exerted an influence on Confederate life far more than hitherto believed and certainly disproportionate to their numbers.

— JASON H. SILVERMAN

NULLIFICATION
CONTROVERSY

During the late fall and winter of 1832 and 1833, the nullification controversy, the most important constitutional crisis between the adoption of the Constitution and the secession of the South, took place.

The controversy had its origins in the passage of the highly protective Tariff of Abominations in 1828, which many in South Carolina believed to be unconstitutional. Over the next several years, radicals led by James Hamilton and Robert Barnwell Rhett, Sr., effectively organized and enlarged their following. When President Andrew Jackson refused to push very hard for a reduction of the tariff and in 1832 signed into law a new measure that only partially reduced duties and did not abandon the principle of protection, South Carolina proceeded to implement the doctrine of nullification as it had been developed by John C. Calhoun in his "South Carolina Exposition and Protest" (1828) and in several important speeches.

Governor Hamilton convened a special session of the state legislature on October 22, 1832, which immediately called a convention to meet at Columbia on November 19. This convention adopted an ordinance declaring the tariffs of 1828 and 1832 unconstitutional and prohibited the collection of Federal duties within the state beginning on February 1, 1833. It also prescribed a test oath for all military and civil officers of the state, except members of the legislature, and forbade any appeal to the U.S. Supreme Court in cases arising under the ordinance. The convention also warned that any attempt by the Federal government to use force would be cause for South Carolina to secede from the Union. The legislature immediately adopted laws to enforce the ordinance, which included the establishment of a military force and the distribution of weapons.

As these events unfolded, President Jackson's rage mounted. Throughout his first term in office he had made clear his dislike of nullification: it was an illegitimate form of state rights, an assault on the doctrine of majority rule, and a threat to the continued existence of the Union. On December 10 he issued his "Proclamation to the People of South Carolina" making clear his intention to uphold the supremacy of the Federal government even if it meant the shedding of blood. Jackson then ordered a variety of military activities and on January 16, 1833, sent a special message to Congress asking for a Force Bill authorizing him to use the military to collect the Federal revenues.

Most people believed South Carolina had acted rashly. No other state formally endorsed the doctrine of nullification and many condemned it. But there was also, especially in the South, widespread opposition to Jackson's desire to use force and to hang the nullifiers for treason, and a number of states rejected the nationalist principles contained in the president's nullification proclamation. Fearful of civil war, Congress, under the leadership of Henry Clay, formulated a compromise: a new tariff that provided for a gradual reduction of duties over the next decade and that abandoned the principle of protection. As a sop to the president the Force Bill was also adopted. Jackson signed both into law on March 2, 1833.

Upon learning that a compromise was likely, South Carolina suspended its ordinance on January 21. Shortly after the adoption of the congressional compromise, the state reconvened its convention and rescinded its ordinance, but in a final act of defiance it nullified the Force Act. Both sides claimed victory. The most important result of the controversy was that over the next three decades the idea of secession became increasingly enmeshed with the doctrine of state rights and the South's defense of slavery.

— RICHARD E. ELLIS

OATH OF ALLEGIANCE

One of the primary problems facing the Federal government when the Civil War began was ensuring that its employees and military men were loyal. Over three hundred U.S. officers resigned to join the Confederacy, as did numerous government clerks and officials. Fearful of disloyalty among those who remained, President Abraham Lincoln on April 30, 1861, ordered all military personnel to retake an oath of allegiance. And Congress, on August 6, 1861, passed legislation requiring civil servants also to take or retake an oath of allegiance.

Even though these regulations were rigidly enforced, fears of disloyalty remained, and numerous ad hoc oaths of allegiance were used as a means of testing and ensuring loyalty. By the summer of 1862, most of the oaths, civil and military, were combined under one oath, the Ironclad Test Oath of Loyalty. The Ironclad Oath was so named because it required the oath taker to swear that "I have never voluntarily borne arms against the United States." In addition, the person had to forsake any allegiance to state authority and swear to "support and defend the Constitution of the United States against all enemies foreign and domestic; . . . bear true faith and allegiance to the same."

An oath of allegiance rapidly became a test of loyalty for common citizens. Maj. Gen. Benjamin F. Butler as military governor of New Orleans required that after October 12, 1861, anyone who wanted to do business in the city or with the U.S. government had to take an oath of allegiance to the United States. As stated by Butler, "It enables the recipient to say, 'I am an American citizen,' the highest title known."

Butler's practice became commonplace as the war progressed, and the Ironclad Oath or a variant thereof was required of thousands of Federals and Southerners. People who wanted to do business with the government, Confederate prisoners of war who wanted parole, Southerners who wanted to be reimbursed for goods taken by foraging Federal troops, and Union sympathizers in the South who wanted to govern themselves—all took the oath. Some took it numerous times: the record might have been set by Robert J. Breckinridge who took the oath nine times between June and December 1865.

After the war the oath presented an immediate problem for both the North and the South. Since its provisions remained in effect, no former Confederate soldier or any Southern citizen who had assisted in the South's war effort could hold a Federal, state, or local office or serve in the military. To evade the "ironclad" portion of the oath concerning bearing arms against the United States, former Confederates had to petition the president of the United States for a pardon, and the

presidents immediately after the war approved many such requests.

In 1884 Congress removed all the iron from the Ironclad Oath when it passed into law a new Oath of Allegiance. The 1884 oath removed all the restrictive portions of the older oaths and left it in its current form—an oath to support and defend the Constitution.

— P. NEAL MEIER

ORAL HISTORY

Oral history is a term used to refer to both a topic of study and the methodology used to record the information studied. Examples of this technique are the seven interviews collected by Kate Cashman Conway from survivors of the Civil War and published in the *Vicksburg Evening Post* in 1906. All those who lived in the South during the Civil War are long dead, of course, but in most instances, their families still exist and are prime conduits through which historical traditions concerning the war have survived to the present.

There are several reasons oral history is valuable for researchers interested in the Confederacy. Chief among these is that oral historical traditions preserve information not available in written sources. For example,

Garland wanted to resume the duties he had taken on before the war, but he could not take the oath without committing perjury.

PAGE 236

the activities of Beanie Short, a guerrilla active in the Cumberland region of northern Tennessee and southern Kentucky, would be unknown today if it weren't for oral tradition. No newspapers in the area recounted his exploits, and there is no mention of him in court records, because few guerrillas stood trial for their crimes during the war. Oral historical narratives also often preserve what is psychologically true, and that can be as important as what is factually true. A South Carolina family still tells a story about two ancestors that explains why they left the Confederate forces to join the Union side. The brothers were part of a band of Confederates traveling through Virginia during the first half of the war. Although they were starving, they were given strict orders by their commanding officer not to steal apples from a nearby orchard. One of the brothers disobeyed, and the commander shot him in the arm. As a result the brothers left and joined the opposing side. Whether or not such an incident ever occurred is less important than the fact that the family today thinks it did. The story enables family members to regard their ancestors in a positive light rather than think of them as merely deserters.

Information gleaned from oral history interviews often humanizes the Civil War. One may read accounts of noted generals and battles without understanding what life during the conflict was like for most people. Orally preserved accounts of families living for weeks on roasted cottonseed or killing their only mule for food make the difficulty of the times more vivid.

Oral histories also often provide a source for popular beliefs and attitudes. A legend common in the southern Appalachians maintains that Abraham Lincoln was the illegitimate son of a Southerner—in some accounts of John C. Calhoun, in others of an unheralded North Carolina mountaineer named Abraham Enloe. Although those who keep such traditions alive take them seriously, they are probably dismissed by most professional historians. They remain alive mainly because of the mountaineers' pride in having Lincoln as one of their own. Another traditional account preserved in some areas is that Lincoln and Jefferson Davis were half-brothers, which can be seen as symbolizing the healing of political divisions among the American people. Moreover, for some people Lincoln's illegitimacy explains his presumed persistent melancholy.

Other positive features of oral history include the possibility of verifying incidents and the provision of information concerning minority groups who, during the war, were more dependent on the spoken than on the written word. Yet, despite its advantages, oral history and the related field of folklore have not been used to their fullest potential by historians studying the Confederacy.

— W.K. MCNEIL

The verbal anecdotes that often accompanied the donations add as well to the store of narrative histories of the Confederate experience.

PAGE 385

ORDNANCE BUREAU

The Ordnance Bureau of the Confederate army functioned as a subsection of the Artillery Corps, but achieved status as one of the most important and successful supply agencies in the Confederacy. The tasks facing the bureau were formidable. All war munitions would have to be provided as state and Confederate forces came into being, but each state worked to provide for its own troops, so that the bureau encountered proprietary and patchwork efforts across the country.

Fortunately for the bureau, Maj. (later Brig. Gen.) Josiah Gorgas, a Pennsylvanian turned Southerner, became its chief on April 8, 1861. A sober, quiet man, Gorgas after graduating from West Point had distinguished himself in the U.S. ordnance service for his ability, although he chafed at his subordinate role. While serving at Mount Vernon Arsenal in Alabama, he met his future wife, Amelia Gayle, daughter of a former Alabama governor, and became converted to the Southern way of life.

With characteristic energy, Gorgas surveyed his bureau and his new country. On May 7, 1861, he reported to Congress that the South had 164,010 small arms ranging from U.S. rifled muskets to .69-caliber muskets, new and altered percussion and flint muskets, Harpers Ferry rifles, Colt rifles, Hall rifles, varied carbines, and Colt and percussion pistols. He discovered some 3.2 million small arms cartridges, along with 168,000 pounds of musket and rifle powder—enough for another one and a half million cartridges. Cannon powder was located at permanent fortifications. Percussion caps, a vital ingredient in modern weaponry, numbered about 2 million, with "a good many at the arsenals and bundled with the cartridges." Georgia was rumored to have 150 tons of saltpeter, with sulphur enough to make another 200 tons of powder. The question was, would fervent state rights Governor Joseph E. Brown contribute these ingredients to the Confederacy?

Gorgas knew many of the arsenals in the South well, and he worked quickly to revamp and modernize several. Charleston's arsenal received steam power; Montgomery's shops were upgraded to repair small arms and manufacture leather goods. Small works were established at Knoxville, Tennessee, Jackson, Mississippi, and Dublin, Lynchburg, and Danville, Virginia. Nashville had extensive shops already, and they became a mainstay for forces assembling under Gen. Albert Sidney Johnston.

From the beginning, the Ordnance Bureau faced serious procurement, collection, and distribution problems. Gorgas decided early to try to centralize manufacturing in Georgia and use the Atlanta rail hub as well as river arteries to distribute the products. Major manufacturing plants were established at Augusta and Macon. The Augusta Powder Works became one of the best in the world, and the Macon Arsenal and Armory ranked among the most efficient installations, along with that town's Confederate States Central Laboratory.

The success of these plants derived from Gorgas's leadership. Because he himself did not work well under authority, he understood the need for freedom in others. And as high responsibility soothed his own abrasiveness, he cherished independence in his subordinates. Careful searching found the right men. From the start he knew that a gifted scientist was needed in the bureau, and he found John W. Mallet, an Englishman serving on the field staff of Brig. Gen. Robert Rodes. Mallet, a member of Great Britain's Royal Society, had been chemist to the Alabama Geological Survey when the war started. His appointment filled a vital niche in the ordnance technological staff. Assigned as chief of the Central Laboratories, Mallet brought standardization to the maze of calibers in small arm ammunition production, invented new and impressive weapons (the "polygonal shell" broke into a predetermined number of pieces), and worked to institutionalize quality in ammunition production.

James H. Burton, who became superintendent of armories, possessed a complete set of English Enfield rifle plans and put them to good use in making a passable Confederate copy. But George Washington Rains stands out as the most successful of Gorgas's stellar subordinates. On April 10, 1862, his Augusta Powder Works began operations. Rains had found the site, secured the Confederate title, and supervised construction of a plant to rival the famous Waltham Abbey Works in England. The Augusta facility, plus others directed by Rains, provided sufficient powder for the war.

Niter was an essential ingredient in powder manufacture, but neither Gorgas nor Rains could devote time to locating sources of the component. Gorgas pushed for a separate Niter and Mining Bureau, attached to the Ordnance Bureau, to find this necessity. Maj. Isaac M. St. John took charge of this bureau in April 1862, and it grew into an indispensable agency. St. John used human urine to leach niter beds across the South.

Ordnance officers became involved in all kinds of activities. Since they served the artillery, leather harnesses, traces, and caissons were among their concerns. Moreover, supplies for ordnance workers increasingly had to come from ordnance establishments. So the bureau became a small "vertical combine," supplying its workers with food, clothing, shoes, medical services, and other needs.

From the outset ordnance officers counted on three sources for arms and munitions: battlefield captures, home manufacturing, and blockade running. Captures provided early supplies; manufacturing, heavily pressed, took time and resources to reach production; and though organization of blockade running also took time and resources, the Ordnance Bureau—chiefly because of Gorgas's personal attention—quickly assumed a key role in importing supplies from abroad. Relying as always on talent, Gorgas sent Maj. Caleb Huse to Europe, charged with the purchase and shipment of arms and munitions. Energetic, sometimes recklessly eager, Huse did admirable work—his astronomical debts were the best proof of his ability.

Funds were always a problem in foreign purchasing, and Gorgas, working with the quartermaster general and the surgeon general, sought innovative ways to provide money. The best system proved to be the exportation of Confederate cotton for exchange in England or other European countries. Various private firms were involved as cotton brokers. Among the most important were Saul Isaac, Campbell and Co.; Collie, Crenshaw, and Co.; and Fraser, Trenholm, and Co. These and other firms not only traded cotton for funds, but many bought and ran blockade runners to and from the embattled South. Gorgas and other supply chiefs tried various schemes for exporting government bales: space on runners was usually purchased on a bale-for-bale basis—that is, one government bale transported along with one bale paid for the privilege.

Complaints of high costs abroad, even of fraud in the blockade-running business, were hardly unexpected. So profitable a business (a successful run might well pay for a private vessel twice over) and so vital a venture for the Confederacy could not escape some excesses. But gradually Gorgas and other bureau chiefs managed the effort efficiently. A new system went into effect in 1863 when Colin J. McRae, an Alabama businessman, went abroad to take charge of foreign purchasing under proceeds of the $15 million Erlanger loan. Although not as helpful as hoped, the loan nonetheless did finance the purchase of blockade runners as well as myriad supplies.

Once purchased, supplies had to reach the South. Freighters could not elude the Federal blockade, so they took their cargoes to transshipment harbors in Nassau, Bermuda, and Cuba. From those ports swift, light-draft blockade runners took the cargo on to the Confederacy. These vessels were always at high risk. The derring-do of blockade runners fills some of the most exciting pages of Civil War history. The Ordnance Bureau shared some five runners with the Quartermaster and Medical Departments.

As private vessels entered the trade, Gorgas took charge of managing the government's program. He

"It seemed to Quentin that he could actually see them: the ragged and starving troops without shoes, the gaunt powder-blackened faces looking backward over tattered shoulders, the glaring eyes eyes in which burned some indomitable desperation of undefeat."

WILLIAM FAULKNER
ABSALOM, ABSALOM! 1936

In early 1861, the Confederate Ordnance Bureau had three sources of supplies for the armed forces: goods on hand, home production, and imports.

PAGE 58

Munitions, uniform material, leather, food, and other essential military and civilian goods poured into the Confederacy on board blockade runners.

PAGE 58

shifted the duty to Maj. Thomas L. Bayne, head of the Bureau of Foreign Supplies in 1862, but kept pushing foreign operations. He achieved a complete change in government blockade running early in 1864 with the passage of two important laws that partly nationalized space on outgoing and incoming vessels and limited importation of luxury goods.

Blockade running proved highly successful, despite increased captures. In the course of the war the Ordnance Bureau imported no less than 330,000 arms, mostly Enfield rifles (state and private ventures brought in at least 270,000 more) and from December 1863 to December 1864, 1,933,000 pounds of saltpeter and 1,507,000 pounds of lead.

Domestic production grew apace but suffered the vagaries of poor transportation, enemy incursions, and dwindling supplies of lead, powder, copper, and saltpeter. By the end of 1862 monthly small arms ammunition production from eight important arsenals totaled 170,000 rounds. But as the war continued, shortages increased. Copper became so scarce that whiskey stills in mountain country were confiscated, and when lead ran short, window weights were taken from buildings in major cities.

As conscription tightened across the South, skilled ordnance workers often were called up for general service or for local defense. Gorgas pointed out the damage done by the loss of one barrel straightener at the Richmond armory—production dropped 360 rifles per month! Ordnance workers were national resources and the bureau chief strenuously fought to keep them at work.

The various makeshifts did the job. The Ordnance Bureau continued providing munitions to Confederate forces until the end of the war. No other Southern supply bureau achieved so much with so few resources. Gorgas ranks as a logistical genius and a management wizard who picked the right men for the field armies and for production, distribution, and foreign operations.

On April 8, 1864, Gorgas wrote in his diary an assessment of his bureau:

> *It is three years ago today since I took charge of the Ordnance Department.... I have succeeded beyond my utmost expectations. From being the worst supplied of the Bureaus of the War Department it is now the best. Large arsenals have been organized at Richmond, Fayetteville, Augusta, Charleston, Columbus, Macon, Atlanta and Selma, and smaller ones at Danville, Lynchburgh, and Montgomery, besides other establishments. A superb powder mill has been built at Augusta.... Lead smelting works were established ... at Petersburgh.... A cannon foundry established at Macon for heavy guns, and bronze foundries at Macon, Columbus, Ga., and Augusta;*

> *a foundry for shot and shell at Salisbury, N.C.; a large shop for leather work at Clarksville, Va.; besides the Armories here [Richmond] and at Fayetteville, a manufactory of carbines has been built up here; a rifle factory at Ashville (transferred to Columbia, S.C.); a new and very large armory at Macon, including a pistol factory, built up under contract here and sent to Atlanta, and thence transferred under purchase to Macon; a second pistol factory at Columbus, Ga.;—All of these ... have borne such fruit as relieves the country from fear of want in these respects.*

Gorgas was right. When Robert E. Lee took his army toward Appomattox Courthouse in April 1865, he stuck to a rail line looking for a ration train. No ration train came, but an ammunition train did.

— FRANK E. VANDIVER

ORPHAN BRIGADE

Officially designated the First Kentucky Brigade, this most famous of Confederate organizations from the Bluegrass State had its origins in the pro-secessionist prewar state guard. In the spring and summer of 1861, while Kentucky remained neutral, secessionist sympathizers gathered across the line at Camp Boone, Tennessee, to enlist with the Confederacy. The Second Kentucky Infantry organized on July 13, followed by the Third Infantry a few days later. The Fourth Infantry followed on September 1, along with Edward Byrne's battery of artillery. That fall, through an administrative confusion, two Fifth Kentucky Infantries were organized, one later being designated the Ninth. On November 19, 1861, the Sixth Infantry organized, and two more batteries, H. B. Lyon's and Rice E. Graves's, were added. For a time the First Kentucky Cavalry and a squadron of horsemen led by John Hunt Morgan were also a part of the brigade, making it more of a "legion" in the then-current definition. During the course of the war there would be several cases of tampering with the brigade's organization, but eventually it came down to the Second, Fourth, Fifth, Sixth, and Ninth Infantries, and Robert Cobb's and Graves's batteries.

Simon Bolivar Buckner briefly commanded the brigade as it was forming, but John C. Breckinridge soon superseded him, commencing a long association with the Kentuckians. In turn, he yielded command to Col. Roger W. Hanson, who was captured along with the Second Kentucky in the fall of Fort Donelson. Thus Col. Robert P. Trabue led the men in their first battle at Shiloh, where they distinguished themselves in the taking of the Hornet's Nest. After covering the

Confederate retreat from Shiloh, the Kentuckians went on to serve at Vicksburg that summer and then participated in the August 5, 1862, attack on Baton Rouge.

They probably acquired their nickname in the carnage of the abortive January 2, 1863, assault on the Federal left at Murfreesboro. Breckinridge, now division commander, opposed the attack, as did Hanson, who had been exchanged and was back in command of the brigade. Hanson took a mortal wound, and the brigade suffered more than 25 percent casualties. Breckinridge wept, crying "My poor Orphans! My poor Orphan Brigade!" He was presumably referring to the fact that Kentucky never left the Union, leaving its Confederate soldiers cut off from succor and support, material and moral, from home. The nickname stuck, acquiring limited use during the war and universal adoption by the 1880s.

Following Murfreesboro, the brigade returned to Mississippi in the failed attempt to relieve Vicksburg and then fought with the Army of Tennessee at Chickamauga, where commander Ben Hardin Helm fell and Col. Joseph Lewis took command for the balance of the war. The Orphans served through the Atlanta campaign until heavy losses at Jonesboro on September 1, 1864, practically destroyed the brigade. Some of those left were given horses to finish out the war as mounted infantry, operating with Confederate cavalry in Georgia and South Carolina. Of the four thousand who had enlisted in 1861, barely six hundred were left to give their parole at Washington, Georgia, on May 7, 1865.

Joseph E. Johnston, William J. Hardee, and other leading generals pronounced the Orphans the finest brigade in the Army of Tennessee. Even allowing for hyperbole, the Kentuckians remain one of the most colorful, hard-fighting, and dedicated units of the Confederate service.

— WILLIAM C. DAVIS

ORR, JAMES L.

Orr, James L. (1822–1873), South Carolina congressman and postwar governor, and U.S. diplomat. Born in Craytonville, Pendleton District, in up-country South Carolina on May 12, 1822, Orr sprang from an Irish family that had settled first in Pennsylvania and then moved eventually to northwestern South Carolina in the 1790s. His father, who owned twenty-five slaves, moved to the village of Anderson in 1830 where he operated a hotel and a store. Orr entered the University of Virginia in 1839 to study law. After two years he returned home, read law, and in 1843 was admitted to

the bar. He became editor of the *Anderson Gazette* and a farmer and slaveholder.

In 1844 Orr was elected to the state legislature as a follower of his neighbor John C. Calhoun and served

JAMES ORR

One of Jefferson Davis's bitterest critics, South Carolina congressman James L. Orr spoke out forcefully for individual and state rights.

NATIONAL ARCHIVES

two terms. He supported efforts to make the state government more democratic. In 1847 Orr narrowly defeated Unionist Benjamin F. Perry for Congress and entered the House in 1849 as the sectional crisis deepened. He denounced the Compromise of 1850, but he opposed the movement for single state secession in South Carolina in 1851.

The following year Orr became convinced that the South could remain safely in the Union. From 1852 to 1860 he was the leader of the National Democrats in South Carolina. He was elected a delegate to the Democratic National Convention in 1856, although he did not attend because of illness. It was the first national party convention to which South Carolina sent a delegation. When Congress assembled in December, Orr was elected Speaker of the House. Because of ill health, he retired from Congress in 1859 and returned to Anderson.

Orr was not a delegate to the Democratic National Convention in Charleston, but he opposed the candidacy of Stephen A. Douglas. In July he publicly opposed single-state secession, but he saw joint secession as the only alternative to Lincoln's election. He was elected to the secession convention, was an unsuccessful candidate for president of the convention, and served on the committee to draft the ordinance. He was named one of three state commissioners to treat with James Buchanan on the matter of

Orr opposed the Fourteenth Amendment but supported limited black suffrage.

PAGE 411

*In the Second
Congress, past
politics became
openly important,
and the general
discontent and
war weariness
helped candidates
who had urged
caution in 1860.*

PAGE 147

Federal property and was a commissioner to the state of Georgia.

After the firing on Fort Sumter in April 1861, volunteer companies were organized all over South Carolina. Orr organized the South Carolina First Regiment, known as Orr's Rifles. It was mustered into Confederate service and was assigned to protect Charleston. Meanwhile Orr continued to serve in the state convention, which met periodically. It created the Executive Council to govern the state, and when the council became unpopular, Orr signed the request to reconvene the convention to abolish it.

While he was stationed in Charleston, Orr became a contender for a seat first in the Provisional Congress and then in the Confederate Senate. It was a three-way contest for two seats. Orr was opposed by two former U.S. senators, Robert W. Barnwell and James Chesnut. Orr's supporters joined forces with those of Barnwell, and together they carried the election. The "Hotspur State" was represented in the Senate by two former moderates.

Orr took his seat on February 17, 1862, the last day the Provisional Congress was in session, and served until the end of the war. In the Senate he headed the Foreign Affairs Committee and also served at times on the Commerce, Finance, and Printing committees. Unlike Barnwell, who supported Jefferson Davis, Orr became one of the president's bitterest critics.

In the Senate Orr supported individual and state rights, sometimes with rancor. When the Senate was considering a bill to give members of Congress certificates to allow them to travel without annoyance, Orr complained that he and another senator on their way to Richmond were almost ejected from a train carrying soldiers. He bitterly denounced the abuse of military power, but Louis T. Wigfall of Texas called the incident an oversight.

Orr defended the traditional system of having soldiers in the ranks elect their officers. In September 1862, the Senate was debating a bill allowing the president to fill a vacancy when the next in line for promotion was incompetent. James Phelan of Mississippi stated that many units elected the least competent men as officers. Orr responded that he hoped such instances were rare, but that any group that elected a fool or a thief knew better than an examining board or the president.

Orr was one of five senators to vote against the Conscription Law of 1862. He suggested a requisition system for the states, but his proposal was defeated. He opposed the seizure of persons who evaded conscription as well as those whose substitutes had deserted. But when the Senate failed to exempt those who had hired substitutes, Orr was one of two dissenters. He always supported liberal exemptions from

the draft. When the Exemption Law of 1862 passed, Orr supported it because it exempted state officers except those specified by the state as subject to militia duty. When the law was criticized because it favored plantation owners or overseers that supervised at least twenty slaves or plantations that required a white man's presence by state law, Orr denounced the notion of class favoritism. Had it been intended, he said on February 12, 1863, the law "would never have received a vote in the Senate."

Orr opposed Confederate regulation of transportation. When the Senate approved partial Confederate operation of the railroads in an emergency in April 1863, Orr attacked the plan. He maintained that private management was more effective. On November 15, 1864, Orr introduced a bill to exempt vessels owned by the states from national restrictions on imports and exports. On December 2, he widened the prohibition to include any vessel in which a state had an interest. The Senate never acted on his bill.

In matters of Confederate law, Orr consistently supported state rights. Early in 1863 he backed the creation of a supreme court, but he voted with the majority to deny the court appellate jurisdiction over state courts. He unfailingly voted against suspending the writ of habeas corpus and punishing conspiracy against the Confederacy.

Generally Orr supported the power of the legislative branch over the executive. In March 1863 he favored giving seats in the Senate to cabinet members. Questioning by Congress would make the cabinet more accountable, Orr believed. On June 6, 1864, he opposed providing forage, fuel, and lights for the president on constitutional grounds. The Constitution, he said, provided that the chief executive's salary could not be raised during his term of office. In February 1865 Orr opposed allowing the War Department to employ a solicitor on the ground that the measure would grant too much power to the secretary of war.

On military matters, Orr usually opposed Jefferson Davis. Along with Representatives William Porcher Miles and W. W. Boyce of South Carolina, Orr warmly supported Gen. P. G. T. Beauregard with whom Davis disagreed. When the general asked for additional artillery to defend the Carolina coast, Orr introduced a bill to grant the request and increase the size of South Carolina infantry and artillery units on February 6, 1863. Davis vetoed the bill on the ground that such reorganization was within executive jurisdiction. Orr frequently attacked Gen. Braxton Bragg whom Davis liked. He also supported Gen. Joseph E. Johnston and criticized Davis for removing him.

As debate on the use of blacks in the Confederate cause grew more heated, Orr supported the use of free black laborers in the army, but not black troops, slave or free. As the military situation deteriorated, he backed an impressment act in March 1863 and on January 30, 1864, introduced a bill to use free blacks. But in February 1865 he suggested a ceiling be placed on the number of such laborers and said that the use of black troops and their resulting emancipation would ruin the Confederacy. When the Senate finally approved arming the slaves by one vote, Orr voted in the negative.

As chairman of the Foreign Affairs Committee, Orr constantly asked Davis to inform the Senate on foreign policy, but Davis almost never honored his requests. Orr joined the peace movement when it seemed that Davis's policies were leading to disaster. In early 1864 in private correspondence, he denounced "a weak incompetent President and an imbecile cabinet . . . [and] a truculent and indecisive Congress."

On March 18, 1865, when the Senate adjourned, Orr returned home. He fell ill with typhoid fever as the war was ending, and his home was ransacked by Union troops. After Robert E. Lee's surrender, Orr urged renewed loyalty to the United States.

When Andrew Johnson appointed Benjamin F. Perry provisional governor of South Carolina on June 30, 1865, Orr accompanied Perry to Washington. Orr was subsequently elected a member of the 1865 state constitutional convention, and Johnson granted him a pardon. When former Confederate general Wade Hampton refused to run for governor, Orr was narrowly elected. He took a paternalistic attitude toward African Americans and signed the Black Code into law. He opposed the Fourteenth Amendment but supported limited black suffrage. A new state constitution was adopted under Congressional Reconstruction, and in July 1868 Orr's term ended.

Orr was elected a state circuit judge by the legislature and soon joined the Republican party. He was associated with the "railroad ring" that took control of the Greenville and Columbia Railroad, but by 1872 he had joined the reform Republicans. When they were defeated, Orr accepted President Ulysses S. Grant's appointment as minister to Russia. On May 6, 1873, he died in St. Petersburg, and his body was returned to Anderson for burial.

— A.V. HUFF, JR.

OVERSEERS

Employed on virtually all rice and sugar plantations, on most cotton plantations with twenty or more adult field hands, and on many smaller units in the tobacco and grain regions, overseers were essential functionaries in managing Southern plantations and controlling the slave population. The overseer, usually a white man of yeoman farmer antecedents, was the link in the managerial chain between the plantation owner or his agent and the black slave drivers. Chiefly responsible for slave welfare and discipline as well as crop production, he assigned gangs to work, apportioned tasks, supervised field labor, administered punishment, enforced curfews, distributed food and clothing, periodically inspected slave cabins, treated minor medical ailments, and maintained various record and account books. In areas of the plantation South where blacks heavily outnumbered whites—most notably along the rice coast of South Carolina and Georgia and in the Yazoo, Mississippi, delta—overseers provided the sparse white population with its principal security against slave misconduct and possible insurrection.

With the continuing expansion of the plantation system into the Southwest along with a concomitant trend toward consolidation of existing units, the number of overseers doubled during the decade of the 1850s, reaching a total of nearly 38,000 on the eve of the Civil War. Of that number, more than two-thirds were located in the leading plantation states of Alabama, Georgia, Louisiana, Mississippi, North and South Carolina, and Virginia. Although the incidence of overseer utilization was highest on the vast sugar and rice estates of Louisiana and South Carolina, respectively, the majority of plantation superintendents were employed on cotton plantations from southern Virginia to eastern Texas. The ratio of overseers to total slave population within different staple regions ranged from a low of one overseer for every seventy-five to one hundred slaves in the cotton, grain, and tobacco counties to a high of one manager for more than three hundred slaves in the heavily black rice districts between Charleston and Savannah. Clearly, the presence of white overseers in such areas as the latter became more crucial than ever following the outbreak of the Civil War.

When hostilities erupted in April 1861, the relative youth and physical hardiness of overseers made them prime candidates for military service. Although many plantation managers responded enthusiastically to the call of their nascent country, their employers manifested almost universal reluctance to dispense with their services. Indeed, efforts by Confederate authorities to enroll overseers in the military provoked a veritable storm of protest from members of the planter class, who, ironically, had previously berated their subordinates for a variety of alleged shortcomings and transgressions. Now they were suddenly considered indispensable—not only to individual proprietors but to the entire white community. Praising "the Overseer system as the best civil police system that can be invented," South Carolina rice magnate James Barnwell Heyward pleaded for the exemption of over-

"Virtually unlimited power acted inevitably to call up, in the coarser sort of master, that sadism which lies concealed in the depths of universal human nature."

W. J. CASH
THE MIND OF THE SOUTH
1941

Drivers were slaves responsible for plantation field production and labor discipline.

PAGE 557

seers in his district both to police the slave population and to render the plantations more effective in furnishing "supplies for the army." Such appeals, with similar reasoning, became general throughout the South.

The exemption of plantation managers proved to be one of the most controversial domestic issues during the war, spawning bitterness and disaffection among small farmers and nonslaveholders. Surprisingly, overseers were not among the occupational groups initially exempted from military service under legislation enacted by the Confederate Congress pursuant to the Conscription Act of April 1862. But in October of that year, in order "to secure the proper police of the country," Congress provided for the exemption of "one person, either as agent, owner or overseer" on each plantation with twenty or more slaves. Subsequent revisions of this statute in May 1863 and in February 1864 substantially reduced the number of overseer exemptions. Thus, by the end of 1863 the number of overseers exempted by authority of Congress had dwindled to approximately three hundred in South Carolina and a mere two hundred each in Georgia and Virginia. It should be noted, however, that regulations governing the exemption of overseers varied considerably from state to state, and additional exemptions were granted by governors and local military commanders as circumstances dictated.

Despite efforts by both Confederate and state officials to respond to planters' concern for the security of their chattel, a severe shortage of overseers developed during the war. Various expedients were devised to combat this shortage. Perhaps the most obvious was that of simply getting along without an overseer, a viable option for many smaller planters. On other units women assumed the unaccustomed role of superintending planting operations, frequently with inauspicious results. In some localities proprietors joined forces and entrusted a single overseer with the oversight of multiple properties. Other planters hired novice overseers from other occupational groups or retained in their employ mediocre managers who, in normal times, would have been summarily discharged. As the war continued, the deficiency in experienced

plantation managers became more acute, and Southern agricultural production suffered accordingly.

Malingering as well as more serious violations of plantation regulations became more common in the absence of an overseer, who had enforced discipline primarily through close surveillance of the slave force and by administering corporal punishment to offenders within parameters specified by his employer. Although violent acts of insubordination were rare, at least before Federal troops arrived in their immediate vicinity, slaves took advantage of relaxed supervision to work at a more leisurely pace, to demand additional privileges, and to augment their food supply with more frequent raids upon their owners' larders.

Even for those planters able to secure competent overseers, the war exacerbated long-standing animosities and rendered more difficult the control of the slave population. Always ready to exploit to their own advantage the inherent conflict between the interests of owner and overseer, the slaves found wartime conditions particularly congenial to such efforts to ameliorate their situation. Moreover, relations between overseers and slaves, at best tenuous in normal times, were further inflamed during the war. The problems became most critical in those portions of the plantation South—especially Virginia and Louisiana—that were subjected to repeated Federal incursions. The presence of Union troops frequently engendered disruptive conduct by overseers and slaves alike, thereby resulting in a total failure of agricultural operations in the occupied area.

It seems fair to conclude that Southern agriculture was severely impaired during the war by a scarcity of able plantation managers, by the unsatisfactory performance of their substitutes, and by the resulting insubordination of the laboring force. This failure to solve the problem of controlling slaves had a demoralizing impact on the home front and was therefore a significant factor in the demise of the Confederacy.

[*See also* Slavery, *sidebar* Slave Drivers.]

— WILLIAM S. SCARBOROUGH

P

PEACE MOVEMENTS

Movements for peace began in the Confederacy soon after hostilities began. They were led by diehard antisecession Unionists, usually old-line Whigs who, unable to accept secession, went underground and formed secret societies dedicated to the overthrow of the Confederacy and the return of the states to the Federal Union. Such societies appeared throughout the Confederacy, but most notably in central North Carolina (the Heroes of America), eastern Tennessee (the Heroes of America and the Peace Society), northern Alabama (the Peace Society), and north-central Arkansas (the Peace and Constitutional Society). Members of these peace societies constantly urged that the fighting end and a peace be made with the North.

In March 1862, the first overt political demonstrations for peace in the Confederacy occurred in central North Carolina. Protesting a state draft of one-third of the militia, some fifty members of the Randolph County militia marched under a white flag and prayed for peace. In neighboring Davidson County, a "Union meeting" was held in which leaders denounced the Confederacy and advocated reunion. Three hundred troops (who were later reinforced by a regiment) were rushed into the central counties to arrest draft resisters and disloyalists.

Bryan Tyson, one of the reunionists, published two works in September 1862—a book entitled *A Ray of Light* and a one-page circular—that influenced the peace movement that would emerge in the Tarheel State in 1863. Tyson argued that a Confederate defeat was inevitable. To avoid that as well as emancipation of the slaves, Southerners should declare an armistice and offer to return to the Union on the basis suggested by the Northern Democrats—with all their rights protected, including a constitutional guarantee of slavery.

In January 1863, a peace movement was launched in the U.S. Congress by Northern Democrats. Led by Clement L. Vallandigham of Ohio, the Democrats demanded that Abraham Lincoln stop the bloodletting by arranging an armistice and working out a compromise that would bring the South back into the Union.

The Northern peace movement precipitated a Southern peace movement, especially in North Carolina, where strong peace sentiment already existed. In May 1863, James T. Leach, a planter and owner of 150 slaves, wrote a letter to the *Weekly Standard* (Raleigh) in which he suggested that the South consider returning to the Union on the basis offered by the Northern Democrats. That fall, Leach was elected as a peace candidate to the Confederate House where, until war's end, he remained the most outspoken advocate of peace in the Congress.

Leach's letter marked the beginning of the peace movement that swept North Carolina in the summer of 1863. Across the state over a hundred peace party political rallies were held in which speakers expressed their discontent with Confederate rule and advocated various proposals for peace. The U.S. flag was hoisted by ardent reunionists at a few of these meetings. Many wanted the authorities in Richmond to arrange a peace. Others blatantly called for reunion on the basis offered by the Northern Democrats. The most prominent among these was Lewis Hanes, a farmer who published a lengthy justification for reunion in the *Standard* on July 31, 1863. The movement inspired an insurrection among deserters, draft dodgers, and militant Unionists in the central counties. It took hundreds of Confederate troops five months to quell the uprising. In September they destroyed the press of William W. Holden, editor of the *North Carolina Standard* and leader of the peace faction in the state. Thus did the 1863 peace movement in North Carolina end in military repression.

Holden's movement influenced the development of peace factions in other Confederate states, especially in Alabama and Georgia. In the fall of 1863, several candidates advocating an honorable peace were elected to Congress, most of them from North Carolina and Georgia. They exerted constant pressure on Jefferson Davis and other congressmen to open negotiations for peace with the North.

At the instigation of Holden and Leach, a new series of peace meetings was held in North Carolina in the early months of 1864. Advocates urged that separate state conventions or a convention of all the Southern states treat for peace with Northern officials or possibly with a convention of Northern states. This would bypass congressional and presidential authorities who, restrained by Davis's intransigence, refused to negotiate for peace on terms that did not include Confederate independence. Intimidated by Davis's suspen-

The 1863 phase of the peace movement culminated in an insurrection of deserters and draft dodgers across the central counties of North Carolina in September.

PAGE 274

"I've got no respect for a young man who won't join the colors."

NATHAN BEDFORD FORREST

P

sion of the writ of habeas corpus in February, Holden's convention movement, and his subsequent bid for the governorship in the August gubernatorial election, failed.

In March 1864, a peace movement emerged in Georgia led by Governor Joseph E. Brown, Confederate Vice President Alexander H. Stephens, and Stephens's half-brother, Linton. The trio introduced peace resolutions into the legislature, calling for Davis to initiate peace negotiations with the North after every Southern military victory. In the fall, they endorsed the call by Northern Democrats for a convention of all the states, North and South, to discuss peace.

In September, the peace faction in Congress, led by W. W. Boyce of South Carolina, proposed that an armistice be arranged and a convention of all the states hammer out a permanent peace. Encouraged by Robert E. Lee's victories from the Wilderness to Cold Harbor and by the peace initiatives proposed by the Northern Democrats at their convention in Chicago, Boyce's supporters tried to force Davis to start peace negotiations or step aside and let someone else do so. Their efforts, however, were to no avail.

Francis Blair, prominent journalist and political confidant to Lincoln, traveled from Washington to Richmond in December 1864 and spoke to congressional peace leaders. He urged them to try to return the seceded states to the Union based on a plan of gradual emancipation. To satisfy those who responded to Blair's proposal, Davis agreed to send delegates to the Hamp-

ton Roads conference in January 1865. Alexander Stephens and two congressmen met with Lincoln and Secretary of State William H. Seward. The meeting failed because Lincoln insisted on reunion, and the Southerners, faithful to Davis's instructions, demanded Confederate independence. Thus ended the last major

effort by Confederate officials to make peace prior to military defeat.

By this point, however, the peace movement had already seriously compromised morale and encouraged defeatism, reunionism, and desertion. Consequently, those who spoke out in favor of peace were usually denounced in the press and by political leaders as disloyal or traitors. In spite of its negative image, the peace movement continued to grow in popularity during the last two years of the war, especially among those who saw reunion on the Democratic basis as preferable to defeat and emancipation. By late 1864, a substantial minority of Southerners favored peace, even if it were based upon reunion; but by then, the question had become moot.

[*See also* Hampton Roads Conference; Heroes of America; *and selected biographies of figures mentioned herein.*]

— WILLIAM THOMAS AUMAN

PEGRAM, JOHN

Pegram, John (1832–1865), brigadier general. Pegram was born in Petersburg, Virginia, on January 24, 1832. After graduating from West Point in 1854, he saw frontier duty in California and Kansas, where he was commissioned second lieutenant of Dragoons.

Pegram resigned from the U.S. Army on May 10, 1861, and accepted a commission as lieutenant colonel of the Twentieth Virginia. His unit took part in the Rich Mountain campaign that summer, serving under Gen. Richard S. Garnett. Forced to retreat from Rich Mountain by an attack from Gen. William. S. Rosecran's troops, he surrendered his command at Beverly on July 13.

Upon his return to the army after being paroled, Pegram was promoted to colonel in July 1862 and assigned to Braxton Bragg's staff at Tupelo, Mississippi, as chief of engineers. Later he became chief of staff for Gen. E. Kirby Smith, with whom he participated in the invasion of Kentucky.

Appointed brigadier general to rank from November 7, 1862, Pegram was assigned to lead a cavalry brigade in Nathan Bedford Forrest's corps, and with him he fought at Murfreesboro and Chickamauga. Pegram was then transferred to the Army of Northern Virginia and was assigned an infantry brigade in Jubal Early's division of the Second Corps. At the Battle of the Wilderness, he was seriously wounded in the leg, but participated later in the Shenandoah Valley campaign. After the death of Gen. Richard Rodes at Winchester, he was assigned to command his division. Pegram returned to Petersburg in December 1864. In the battle of Hatcher's Run, February 6, 1865, he was killed near Dabney's Sawmill.

He was buried at Hollywood Cemetery in Richmond, Virginia.

— CHRIS CALKINS

PEMBERTON, JOHN C.

Pemberton, John C. (1814–1881), lieutenant general. Born August 10, 1814, in Philadelphia, Pennsylvania, John Clifford Pemberton's marriage to a Virginia woman influenced him to fight for the South. By war's end, he had become one of the Confederacy's most controversial generals.

An 1837 graduate of the U.S. Military Academy, Pemberton saw action in the Second Seminole War and was decorated for bravery in the Mexican War. In peacetime, he proved to be an effective administrative officer. Though his defenders would later claim that Pemberton frequently exhibited antebellum pro-Southern sentiments, there is much evidence to the contrary. When war broke out in 1861, he agonized for weeks before coming to Virginia to fight for his wife's native land.

Pemberton's first significant duty came in March 1862, when he was promoted to major general and took command of the Department of South Carolina and Georgia. Always adept at military politics, he had moved rapidly upward in rank despite a lack of accomplishments.

The new commander soon was embroiled in controversy. Many South Carolinians feared that the Northern-born general was not dedicated to an all-out defense of the department. Pemberton added to their fears by declaring that, if he had to make a choice, he would abandon the area rather than risk losing his outnumbered army. When state officials complained to Robert E. Lee, Pemberton's predecessor and now adviser to Confederate President Jefferson Davis, Lee told Pemberton that he must defend the department at all cost. Pemberton was eventually relieved from command, but he had learned a fateful lesson from Lee.

Despite Pemberton's preference for administrative duties and his problems in South Carolina, Davis promoted him to lieutenant general and gave him arguably the most difficult command in the Confederacy. Pemberton was to defend Vicksburg, a Mississippi city standing on high bluffs above the Mississippi River. Its defenses were the last major river obstacle to Union shipping.

Taking command of the Department of Mississippi and East Louisiana on October 14, 1862, Pemberton immediately set to work solving supply problems and

improving troop morale. For several months he enjoyed remarkable success, defeating attempts by Union Gen. Ulysses S. Grant to take Vicksburg in the winter of 1862–1863.

In the spring, however, Grant confused Pemberton with a series of diversions and crossed the Mississippi below Vicksburg practically unnoticed. Grant was free to maneuver because Pemberton had remembered Lee's admonishment and had fought to hold Vicksburg at all cost. Jefferson Davis reinforced Pemberton's thinking with an order not to give up the river city "for a single day." Now that Grant had successfully crossed the Mississippi, Pemberton determined to stay close to Vicksburg. Davis complicated matters by sending Gen. Joseph E. Johnston to Mississippi to try to reverse declining Confederate fortunes. Johnston ordered Pemberton to unite his forces and attack Grant, if practicable, even if that meant abandoning the defense of Vicksburg.

Torn by conflicting orders, Pemberton marked time while Grant swept inland scoring a series of quick victories at Port Gibson, Raymond, and Jackson. Pemberton finally tried to please both Davis and Johnston. He moved his army east from Edwards Station, all the while maintaining close contact with Vicksburg. A new order from Johnston forced Pemberton to reverse his course and unite with Johnston's forces that had been defeated at Jackson. Before the order could be carried out, Pemberton's army bumped into Grant's forces at Champion's Hill and suffered a major defeat. Pemberton retreated to the Big Black River where he suffered more heavy losses. Remembering Lee's and Davis's orders, Pemberton chose to ignore another

For Pemberton, the flurry of Federal activity across the river in early April was indicative of a withdrawal.

PAGE 648

P

Pemberton, who had never commanded an army in combat, received conflicting instructions and chose to comply with the president's and his own preference for holding fortifications.

PAGE 648

order from Johnston to evacuate Vicksburg. He would try to save the city even if that meant risking the loss of his army. He retreated into the city where he and his men endured a forty-seven day siege before surrendering on July 4, 1863. Pemberton became a pariah in the South and was accused by his immediate superior, General Johnston, of causing the Confederate disaster by disobeying orders.

John Pemberton might have made a positive contribution to the Confederate war effort had his talents been properly used. An able administrator, he was uncomfortable in combat. He had demonstrated his weaknesses in South Carolina, yet Davis had sent him to Mississippi anyway. A few months after Vicksburg, Pemberton displayed his loyalty to the Confederate cause by requesting a reduction in rank. He served the remainder of the war as a lieutenant colonel of artillery in Virginia and South Carolina.

After the war, Pemberton lived in Virginia and Pennsylvania. He died August 14, 1881, and is buried in Laurel Hill Cemetery in Philadelphia.

— MICHAEL B. BALLARD

PENDER, WILLIAM DORSEY

Pender, William Dorsey (1834–1863), major general. Pender was born February 6, 1834, in North Carolina and was educated at the U.S. Military Academy. He graduated nineteenth in the class of 1854. As a lieutenant of artillery and then of dragoons, Pender served on frontier duty in New Mexico and on the west coast. He saw enough fighting to be able to report with pride having been "mentioned three times [in reports] for conduct in Indian engagements."

Lieutenant Pender resigned from the U.S. Army in March 1861 and immediately received a Confederate commission as captain of artillery. Two months later Pender was elected colonel of the Third (later the Thirteenth) North Carolina Infantry. He assumed command of the Sixth North Carolina in August 1861 and led that regiment with such élan at Seven Pines the following spring that President Jefferson Davis commended him on the field and promoted him to brigadier general to date from June 3, 1862. General Pender took command of a brigade of North Carolina regiments, including his old Thirteenth, in A. P. Hill's division. He led the brigade through the heaviest fighting during the Seven Days' Battles with notable success and suffered in the process the first of a series of slight wounds incurred in battles. Pender and his men also fought at the heart of the battles of Second Man-

assas and Ox Hill and participated in the Maryland campaign. At Fredericksburg his North Carolinians stood on the far left of Hill's division.

Pender earned a reputation for stern, even brutal, discipline as a result of his ardent efforts to reduce the desertion rate that bedeviled North Carolina units. According to J. R. Boyles, a Confederate soldier at the time, troops of adjacent brigades "had a perfect horror" of Pender "as being such a strict disciplinarian." Although Pender was of very slight build (about 135 pounds), a member of J. E. B. Stuart's staff declared that the North Carolinian was one of the two "most splendid looking soldiers of the war." His ability to hold his troops to their duty appealed strongly both to units that served near them and to the army high command. Late in 1862 Hill commended Pender as "one of the very best officers I know" and in January 1863 again recommended promotion for him. In the reorganization after Chancellorsville, where he had again performed brilliantly, Pender won promotion to major general.

Pender's new division included the best troops of Hill's old command. The men who had feared him soon discovered Pender to be "quite humane, [he] treated us kindly," as long as no one deserted. Major General Pender's only day in combat was July 1, 1863, when he pushed his command through bitterly contested ground just west of Gettysburg and onto Seminary Ridge at the climax of that day's fighting. The next day a piece of shell wounded Pender in the thigh, though not in a fashion to prompt concern for his recovery. A sudden hemorrhage, however, led to amputation of the leg on July 18, and the general died a few hours later. Pender's solid contributions to the Army of Northern Virginia as one of its most able brigadiers are a matter of clear record. His further potential seemed large, as attested by several wistful comments by both Hill and Lee after Pender's death.

— ROBERT K. KRICK

PENINSULAR CAMPAIGN

The Peninsular campaign lasted nearly four months, from March to July 1862, and stretched across the southeastern Virginia Peninsula from the Chesapeake Bay to the suburbs of Richmond. Union Maj. Gen. George B. McClellan had planned to advance his Army of the Potomac triumphantly up the stretch of land between the York and James rivers and capture Richmond. With the Confederate capital taken, the Federal government hoped to bring the year-old Civil

War to a swift and decisive end. Throughout the spring and early summer months of 1862 approximately 60,000 Confederates doggedly fought nearly double that number of Federals. After several weeks of mud-drenched marches and siege warfare, several bloody battles ensued, which cost the Union army over 15,000 soldiers; the defending Confederates lost 20,000 men killed, wounded, and missing. Richmond was free from capture, the Union suffered another embarrassing setback, and the war dragged on for three more years.

Two divisions from McClellan's army landed at Federally held Fort Monroe at the tip of the peninsula in mid-March. As scores of bluecoats debarked from vessels onto Southern soil, Maj. Gen. John B. Magruder, commander of the Confederate defenses at Yorktown, readied his scanty force of 10,000 men for combat. Magruder's Army of the Peninsula lay directly in McClellan's path up the peninsula. Luckily for the Confederates, McClellan severely overestimated Confederate strength—he thought it to be nearly ten times as strong as it was. Magruder added to the Federals' confusion by marching his men through clearings in circles to give the impression of many more troops. Instead of attacking frontally, which would have crumbled Magruder's meager force, McClellan began to amass artillery to pound Yorktown into submission. All through April, McClellan pressed his siege of Yorktown.

Meanwhile, Joseph E. Johnston and his Army of Northern Virginia had lain idle following the Confederate victory at the Battle of Manassas in July 1861. Johnston did not wish to engage McClellan's formidable forces head on and remained content waiting for the enemy's attack. But on April 14, Confederate President Jefferson Davis held a special council of war to determine Johnston's next move. For fourteen hours, Johnston, Maj. Gen. James Longstreet, Secretary of War George Wythe Randolph, Maj. Gen. Gustavus W. Smith, and Davis's military adviser, Gen. Robert E. Lee, discussed how to deal with the growing Union threat at Yorktown. Johnston suggested that his army move inland and await McClellan's approach to Richmond before fighting. Lee, fearful to allow this undetermined force of Federals to move so close to the capital, argued that the peninsula offered numerous defensive positions from which the Confederates could derive advantage. At 1:00 A.M. on April 15, President Davis came to a decision. He ordered Johnston to move his army to Yorktown to reinforce Magruder and fight back the enemy on the peninsula. Johnston abandoned central Virginia to the Union and grudgingly joined Magruder at Yorktown. His men settled into the flooded trenches, unsure how long they would have to remain.

On May 4, McClellan deemed himself ready to do battle. But on that same day, Johnston left, intending to follow his original plan to fight outside of Richmond. On May 5, 1862, the rear guard of Johnston's retreating army turned to fight pursuing Federals near the old colonial capitol of Williamsburg. Six brigades of James Longstreet's division fought to gain needed time for the fleeing Confederates. The Battle of Williamsburg yielded 2,239 Federal casualties and 1,603 Confederate. Many more would soon follow.

Johnston's movement up the peninsula required the abandonment of the seaport town of Norfolk, Virginia. The famed Southern ironclad CSS *Virginia* would be without a port. Rather than leave the ship to the enemy, Confederates burned the vessel. Soon Union troops moved in and spread to nearby Suffolk. Seven miles of the James River below Richmond were now open to Federal forces. A Union fleet attempted to move up the James, but on May 15, Confederates fired on the Federal ships at Drewry's Bluff. The orphaned crew of *Virginia*, a detachment of infantry, and a slew of heavy artillery guns mustered enough resistance to spoil the enemy's plans.

Outside of Richmond, three corps of McClellan's large force positioned themselves south of the swollen Chickahominy River; the other two were on the northern side. When word reached Johnston that McClellan might soon receive reinforcements from Maj. Gen. Irvin McDowell's corps, he concluded that quick, decisive action was in order. On May 31 incessant rains washed away bridges connecting McClellan's corps, leaving two isolated and vulnerable corps north of the Chickahominy. The Battle of Seven Pines was an embarrassing Confederate failure. Johnston's officers bungled orders and moved sluggishly. When fighting finally began, it was heavy but the Southerners failed to gain any ground. Johnston fell severely wounded and Gustavus W. Smith briefly took command. The next day a renewed offensive by the Confederates again failed. By afternoon Robert E. Lee had arrived on the field to take command and order a withdrawal. The Confederate failure cost over 6,000 casualties; the Federals suffered over 5,000. During the next three weeks both armies waited and watched for new bloodletting.

Lee's first concern as commander was to bolster Richmond's defenses. He soon had his men digging field fortifications outside the city. On June 12, Lee sent Maj. Gen. J. E. B. Stuart on a reconnaissance mission into Union lines to determine enemy strength. Stuart rode entirely around McClellan's army in a dramatic cavalry sweep. In the process his troopers discovered that the right flank of McClellan's army stood vulnerable to attack. Upon receiving this information, Lee quickly laid plans to strike at McClellan's weakness. But the Federals were not unaware; Stuart's ride

Stuart's semicircular route had carried him thirty-five miles from Richmond and behind McClellan's army.

PAGE 594

"Once you get them running, you can stay on top of them, and that way a small force can defeat a large one every time."

STONEWALL JACKSON

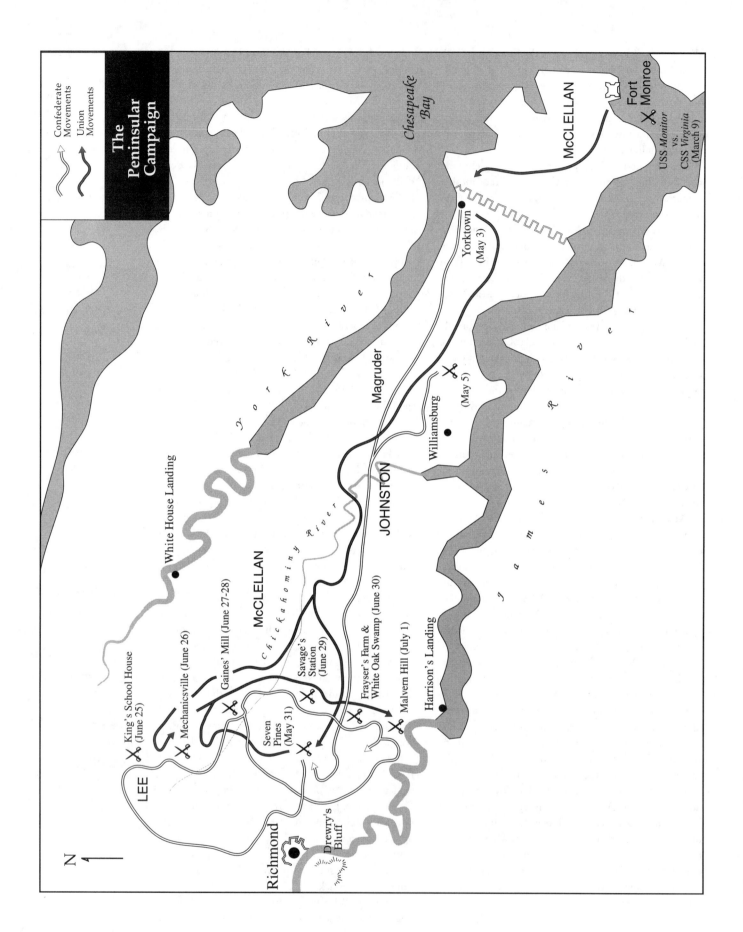

The Peninsular Campaign

Confederate Movements
Union Movements

N

USS *Monitor*
vs.
CSS *Virginia*
(March 9)

Fort Monroe

McCLELLAN

Chesapeake Bay

Yorktown
(May 3)

Magruder

Williamsburg
(May 5)

York River

James River

White House Landing

McCLELLAN

Chickahominy River

JOHNSTON

King's School House
(June 25)

Mechanicsville (June 26)

Gaines' Mill (June 27-28)

LEE

Seven Pines (May 31)

Savage's Station
(June 29)

Frayser's Farm &
White Oak Swamp (June 30)

Malvern Hill (July 1)

Harrison's Landing

Richmond

Drewry's Bluff

prompted McClellan to execute a "change of base" southward from his vulnerable position on the York to the James River.

Lee hurried to attack. Leaving a mere 25,000 men between Richmond and the Federal army, Lee moved his remaining 47,000 soldiers to assault the Union flank. With the aid of Maj. Gen. Thomas J. ("Stonewall") Jackson's Army of the Valley, Lee planned to surprise the exposed Federals. The subsequent battles at Mechanicsville on June 26 and Gaines' Mill on June 27 were indecisive. Unfulfilled was Lee's primary objective of destroying the isolated corps and seriously damaging McClellan's strength. Stonewall Jackson's poor performance was especially disappointing. At both of these engagements his delay undeniably contributed to the Confederate failures. But Lee was undaunted. The next day he continued in bold pursuit while McClellan, stunned by the Confederates' continued aggressiveness, retreated. He was now even more convinced that his men faced superior numbers.

Beginning with a brief engagement at King's School House on June 25, the Seven Days' Battles consisted largely of Lee's dogged attempts to corner and destroy pieces of McClellan's army. Mechanicsville and Gaines' Mill were followed by Savage's Station on June 29, Frayser's Farm on June 30, and finally Malvern Hill on July 1. Similar to Johnston's mishap at Seven Pines, Lee's ambitious plans went awry owing to failed coordination between units, misunderstood orders, and poor staff performance. Savage's Station yielded 626 Confederate casualties and 1,590 Federals; Frayser's Farm cost 2,853 Federal casualties and 3,615 Confederate. At Malvern Hill, Lee suffered a severe defeat when he ordered his troops to charge the enemy's nearly impregnable position atop the hill. When Union artillery unmercifully poured into the infantrymen attempting to charge forward, 5,355 Confederates were lost; Federal casualties numbered 3,214. Confederate Maj. Gen. D. H. Hill later remarked that Malvern Hill was "not war—it was murder."

With this Union victory, McClellan completed his retreat to Harrison's Landing on the James River. He soon turned north to Washington, and the threat to Richmond had passed.

General Lee did not write his report of the Peninsular campaign for two years. Citing a lack of maps and information, he admitted his failure to destroy or even weaken the Union army. But Lee had successfully managed to take advantage of McClellan's overcautiousness and halt the enemy movement toward Richmond. For two full years the Federals would not attempt such an operation again. The Peninsular campaign also cemented Lee's reputation as an aggressive and stubborn fighter. For the next two years of war, Lee showed this ability again and again in the face of Union commanders more talented than McClellan.

[*See also* Drewry's Bluff, Virginia; Seven Days' Battles; Stuart's Raids.]

— LESLEY JILL GORDON-BURR

PETERSBURG CAMPAIGN

For ten grinding months—from June 15, 1864, to April 3, 1865—Confederate forces under Gen. Robert E. Lee conducted the longest sustained defensive operation of the war in the works surrounding Petersburg, Virginia. All but one of the railroads that connected Richmond to remaining Confederate supplies passed first through Petersburg. Both Lee and Lt. Gen. Ulysses S. Grant, commander of all Federal armies, recognized that Union possession of the city would force the evacuation of Richmond and shorten the war.

By early June, Grant's strategy had failed to capture Lee's army northeast of Richmond. Maj. Gen. Benjamin Butler's Army of the James was ignominiously bottled up by Confederate forces near Bermuda Hundred, unable to threaten either Richmond or Petersburg. Maj. Gen. George G. Meade's Army of the Potomac incurred huge casualties in the Overland campaign, leaving the Army of Northern Virginia damaged but not destroyed. In an effort to break the stalemate near Cold Harbor, Grant looked south to Petersburg. If he could sever Confederate supply lines, Lee's army would have to leave entrenchments for open combat.

On June 12 Grant's army slipped away from Cold Harbor and began an audacious turning movement. Maj. Gen. William Smith's Eighteenth Corps went by ship to Bermuda Hundred while the Army of the Potomac marched through fifty miles of enemy territory to the James River. Transports and the 2,100-foot-long James River pontoon bridge, a marvel of combat engineering, placed Federal units a day's march from Petersburg.

Through rapid movement and a convincing feint against Richmond, Grant had frozen Lee north of the James. In Petersburg, Brig. Gen. Henry A. Wise's patchwork force of 2,200 Confederates faced the arrival of Smith's 12,500 men. Despite delays and command mistakes, Union attackers quickly overwhelmed three and one-half miles of the imposing Dimmock Line that surrounded the city. As darkness fell on June 15 and Maj. Gen. Winfield S. Hancock's Second Corps arrived, Smith exercised caution and stopped his advance within sight of Petersburg's spires. Confeder-

Richmond was the main goal of the Army of the Potomac for four years.

PAGE 504

A. P. Hill made a speedy arrival at Petersburg on June 18, 1863, and helped prevent that gateway city to Richmond from falling into Union hands.

PAGE 275

Throughout the long seige of Petersburg, Hill commanded the southern half of Lee's defenses. He did so brilliantly.

PAGE 275

ate Gen. P. G. T. Beauregard took advantage of this delay to reinforce Petersburg with units from the Bermuda Hundred lines. By June 16 Beauregard had marshaled 14,000 men to face Federal troops that would number between 63,000 and 80,000 men on June 17.

On June 16, 17, and 18, Federal forces continued pouring into the Petersburg area. Each day witnessed piecemeal Union attacks against strongly entrenched Confederate lines. Petersburg might have fallen on June 17 when Confederate lines were twice shattered, but heroic Confederate counterattacks by Maj. Gen. Bushrod Rust Johnson's division closed the gaps when Union reinforcements failed to arrive.

Beauregard fought his finest battle at Petersburg, while the Union army suffered from a combination of poor leadership and extreme combat exhaustion. After four days of fighting, Federal losses totaled 10,586 compared to an estimated 4,000 Confederate casualties. With the arrival of Lee's forces on June 18, Grant halted frontal attacks and chose instead "to use the spade."

On June 19 Lee and Grant found themselves in a position neither wanted. For Grant, siege tactics meant slow progress and dwindling morale, something Abraham Lincoln's party could ill-afford in an election year. Lee likewise recognized that the offensive skills of his smaller army would mean little in a campaign of attrition. By late June, Lee's 50,000 men had covered a twenty-six-mile line from Richmond to Petersburg and faced a Federal host that hovered around 112,000 troops.

Drawing upon his Vicksburg experience, Grant began a two-pronged strategy designed to encircle Petersburg while cutting Lee's supply lines. On June 22 through 24, the Second and Sixth Corps challenged Maj. Gen. A. P. Hill's corps for possession of the Weldon Railroad. Hill, however, exploited a gap that developed between the two corps and inflicted 2,962 casualties while maintaining control of the railroad. The Battle of Jerusalem Plank Road (or Weldon Railroad) foreshadowed the coming nine months of action. With each Federal movement westward, Lee launched increasingly desperate counterattacks to prevent the extension of earthworks while preserving connections with Southern supplies.

In late July, Grant hesitantly moved the focus of his strategy from the left flank to an attack in the center of the Confederate line opposite Maj. Gen. Ambrose Burnside's Ninth Corps. Coal miners from the Forty-eighth Pennsylvania tunneled 511 feet to the Confederate line and packed eight thousand pounds of black powder into a gallery under Brig. Gen. Stephen Elliot's salient. Brig. Gen. Edward Ferrero's large, fresh division of black soldiers had been carefully trained to

spearhead the attack through the breach made by "springing the mine." Meade, however, had reservations about the black division's inexperience and about potential political fallout should heavy casualties lead to charges that the army deliberately sacrificed black soldiers. With Grant's approval, Meade ordered an enraged Burnside to choose a new lead division only one day before the assault. The job fell by lot to the division of Brig. Gen. James Ledlie, an incompetent officer who was to spend the attack hiding in a bombproof.

At 4:40 A.M. on July 30 a spectacular explosion blasted a hole 170 feet long, 60 feet wide, and 30 feet deep in the Confederate line. Defenders were thrown into disarray, and despite a late start more than 15,000 troops from the Ninth Corps rushed into the Crater and adjacent works. Lacking leadership, the men milled about in the captured line and failed to gain the high ground just beyond.

Confederate counterattacks, led by Brig. Gen. William Mahone's division, drove Federal troops from the captured works and slaughtered those trapped in the Crater. By 1:00 P.M. the attack was over. The Union army lost an estimated 4,000 men against just 1,500 for the Confederates in a fiasco that prompted a congressional investigation and a military court of inquiry. Grant called the Battle of the Crater "the saddest affair" of the war and resigned himself to a strategy of exhaustion.

In mid-August Federal forces moved again to extend their lines westward. On August 18, as the Union Second and Tenth Corps attacked north of the James near Fussell's Mill, Maj. Gen. Gouverneur Warren's Fifth Corps struck the Weldon Railroad near Globe Tavern, about four miles south of Petersburg. Warren's soldiers moved north from the tavern for a mile, ripping up track as they marched. Two Confederate brigades under Maj. Gen. Henry Heth responded promptly to contest the railroad's destruction. The next day Hill's corps joined the fight and captured more than 2,500 prisoners while driving the Federal line south. Warren's corps regrouped and dug in around Globe Tavern, and on August 21 Hill's men attacked but failed to carry the Union line. Lee then arrived on the field from north of the James and called a halt to assaults against the Union position. Federal losses in the Battle of Globe Tavern (or Weldon Railroad) totaled 4,455, well in excess of the Confederate's estimated 1,600 casualties, but the railroad was cut. Confederate teamsters now had to supply Petersburg by wagon from Stony Creek Depot, twenty miles south of Petersburg. In December a Federal raid at Hicksford destroyed another sixteen miles of the Weldon Railroad and forced an even longer wagon supply route.

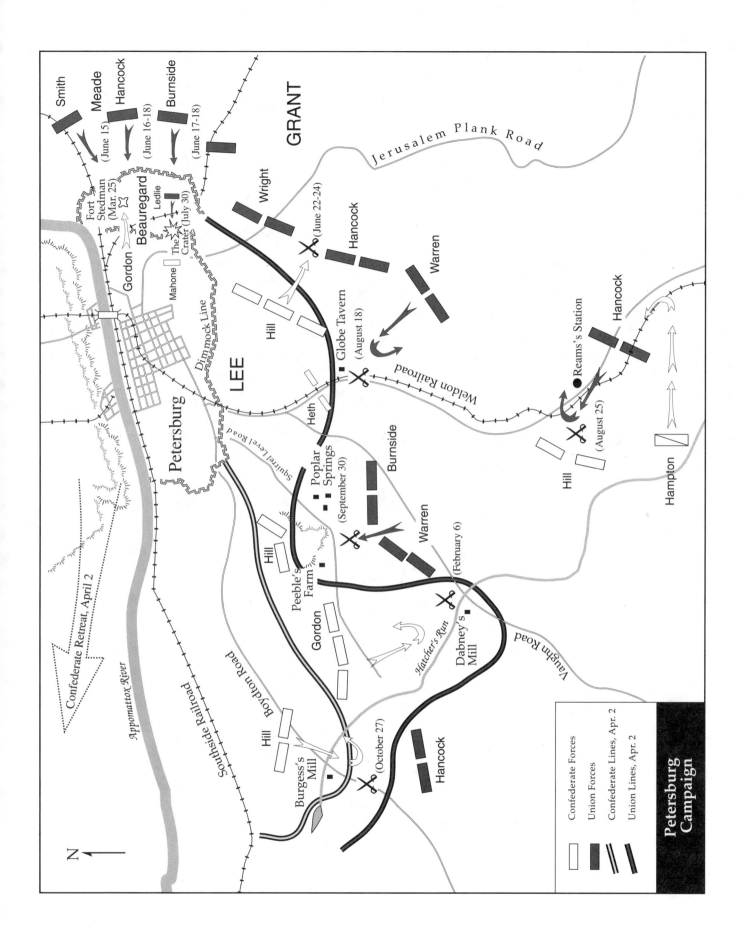

Smith
Meade
Hancock
(June 15)
Burnside
(June 16-18)
(June 17-18)

GRANT

Jerusalem Plank Road

Fort Stedman (Mar. 25)
Beauregard
Ledlie
The Crater (July 30)
Gordon
Mahone
Dimmock Line

Wright
Hancock
(June 22-24)
Warren

Hancock
Reams's Station
(August 25)
Hill

LEE

Hill

Petersburg

Heth

Globe Tavern
(August 18)
Weldon Railroad

Hampton

Squirrel Level Road

Burnside
Poplar Springs
(September 30)

Warren
(February 6)

Hill

Gordon
Hatcher's Run
Dabney's Mill

Peeble's Farm

Confederate Retreat, April 2

Appomattox River

Southside Railroad

Boydton Road

Hill
Burgess's Mill
(October 27)

Vaughn Road

Hancock

N

Petersburg Campaign

Confederate Forces
Union Forces
Confederate Lines, Apr. 2
Union Lines, Apr. 2

421

A. P. Hill painfully returned to the front only two days before Grant's all-out assault on April 2; it was barely dawn that morning when Hill was fatally shot through the heart.

PAGE 276

Confederate forces did enjoy some success in late summer. On August 25 Hancock's Second Corps was five miles south of Globe Tavern, destroying track at Reams's Station, when a vigorous attack by Hill's corps stampeded raw Union recruits and crumpled Hancock's left. Confederate forces captured 9 guns, 12 flags, and more than 2,150 men. And between September 11 and 17, Maj. Gen. Wade Hampton's horsemen rode into the rear of the Union army and captured about 300 men and 2,400 head of cattle. Reams's Station and the Beefsteak Raid improved Confederate morale, but the Federal army missed neither the men nor the meals.

Grant's inexorable strategy continued in late September. As part of a major thrust north of the James at Fort Harrison, elements of the Fifth and Ninth Corps near the Weldon Railroad staged a reconnaissance in force north and west toward the Southside Railroad. On September 30 Union forces captured trenches and a Confederate redoubt at Peeble's Farm near Squirrel Level Road. With characteristic combativeness, Hill attacked the Union position with two divisions and temporarily drove the Federals south. Union counterattacks reestablished the line near Peeble's Farm, and by October 2 Federal troops had extended their line more than a mile west of Globe Tavern. The Battle of Peeble's Farm (or Poplar Springs Church) cost Grant another 2,889 casualties, but it forced Lee to match the extended line or risk envelopment.

In a final attempt to capture the Southside Railroad before winter, Grant employed elements of three corps and on October 27 gained control of the Boydton Road near Burgess's Mill. Hill responded immediately. Confederate infantry on the left flank and cavalry on the right drove back Hancock's Second Corps. Hill's men were driven back themselves by a Union counterattack, but when difficult terrain, slashing, and strong earthworks stopped the Fifth and Ninth Corps from joining the Second Corps, Grant ordered Hancock's men withdrawn. As a result, the road remained in Confederate hands. Federal losses in the Battle of Hatcher's Run (also called Boydton Plank Road and Burgess's Mill) totaled 1,758; Confederate casualties were not reported.

By December 1864 the well-supplied Federal army totaled about 110,000 men. Lee counted 66,000 gaunt and poorly equipped men to protect a thirty-five-mile line from Richmond to Hatcher's Run, southwest of Petersburg. Desertion, disease, sniping, unreliable supply, and sinking morale further weakened Lee's army throughout the winter, and every extension west threatened to cause the collapse of the Richmond-Petersburg line.

On February 5 through 7, 1865, in the middle of what had become a miserable winter, Grant launched the Second and Fifth Corps, elements of the Sixth Corps, and a cavalry division to secure the Boydton Plank Road, one of the last remaining Confederate supply routes into Petersburg. On February 6, Maj. Gen. John B. Gordon's corps struck the Fifth Corps near Dabney's Mill, driving Warren's men away from the road. Union forces halted Gordon's attack, but only after Warren had lost more than 1,300 men. Federal leaders suspended the effort to secure the road when Union cavalry determined that the Confederates were no longer using it as a supply route. After the Battle of Hatcher's Run (or Dabney's Mill), Federal soldiers extended their works to the Vaughn Road crossing over Hatcher's Run. Confederate forces matched the line with their own, which now reached about thirty-seven miles.

By March 1865, Lee recognized that the Richmond-Petersburg line could not be held once Union armies under Maj. Gens. William Tecumseh Sherman and Philip Sheridan, then in North Carolina and the Shenandoah Valley, respectively, arrived to join Grant. Consequently, Lee decided upon a preemptive strike and ordered Gordon to plan an attack on Union lines. If it was successful, Grant might shorten his Petersburg lines, allowing Lee to reinforce Gen. Joseph E. Johnston for an attack on Sherman in North Carolina. If the attack failed, Lee would retreat and join Johnston for a final stand.

Gordon selected Fort Stedman, only 125 yards from the Confederate lines, as the site of Lee's last offensive. Although the March 25 predawn attack was well conducted and met with early success, Union troops soon rallied and recaptured Fort Stedman and adjacent works that Gordon briefly held. The Battle of Fort Stedman cost Lee between 4,400 and 5,000 casualties and made clear his only remaining option: retreat.

Lee awaited only supplies and dry roads before marching to join Johnston. His plans for an April 10 move were upset by the arrival of Sheridan's forces. Augmented by the Fifth and Second Corps, Sheridan concentrated on the Confederate right near Dinwiddie Court House and Five Forks. Lee gave Maj. Gen. George E. Pickett command of 19,000 infantry and cavalry and charged him with protection of the Southside Railroad, Petersburg's single remaining rail link with the south. On March 31, Federal forces were driven back in the Battle of Dinwiddie Court House, but this minor Confederate victory did not change strategic dispositions.

Late on March 31, Pickett withdrew to Five Forks, which Lee ordered him to hold "at all hazards." Sheridan's attack at Five Forks was delayed until 4:00 P.M. on April 1, but before dusk Pickett's left flank had collapsed under the weight of Fifth Corps attacks as his right was enveloped by cavalry. At least 4,500 Confederate troops became casualties including 3,200 captured. Federal losses numbered under 1,000. The Battle of Five Forks convinced Grant to launch an all-out effort to capture Petersburg.

At 4:40 A.M. on April 2, a Union gun signaled the final assault on Petersburg. Federal troops met with stout resistance, but Maj. Gen. Horatio Wright's Sixth Corps broke through on the Confederate right and drove southwest along the line. Much of Lee's right withdrew in a fighting retreat toward the city. By midday, Federal troops had reached the Appomattox River west of Petersburg, and most of the outer line south and west of the city was in Union hands. Lee informed President Jefferson Davis that he would hold Petersburg until nightfall to allow for Richmond's evacuation. Confederate forces fought delaying actions and launched counterattacks that stopped Federal forces short of city streets. By 8:00 P.M. the Confederate retreat toward Amelia Courthouse had begun. The Petersburg final assault had cost Grant between 3,300 and 4,100 men; Confederate losses are not known but included A. P. Hill, who had served the Confederacy so well at Petersburg and was killed in its defense.

The next day, April 3, 1865, Federal forces entered the city unchallenged. Several hours later Richmond fell; within a week Grant forced Lee's surrender at Appomattox Courthouse. The end of the Confederacy had come at a frightful cost though; from June 15, 1864, to April 3, 1865, the Petersburg campaign claimed an estimated 42,000 Federal casualties. Confederate losses—irreplaceable owing to the South's limited manpower—totaled at least 28,000.

The Petersburg campaign heralded more than the Confederacy's death; it also marked the birth of a new type of warfare. Both sides used complex trench systems replete with abatis, fraise, covered ways, bombproofs, and second lines. The United States Military Railroad snaked just behind Federal lines and provided rapid resupply from the massive City Point supply depot on the James River. Grant continually extended and strengthened his lines, knowing that superior numbers and the debilitating effects of attrition, desertion, and starvation would eventually destroy Lee's army. Most important, Grant held the Confederacy's most powerful army and its masterful commander in a static position while his subordinates devastated the South's ability to make war and destroyed its remaining armies piecemeal. Grant at Petersburg demonstrated the keys to success in modern war: superb organization and a genius for doing the obvious.

Lee adjusted to his defensive role with equal skill, marshaling forces to meet threats both north and south of the James, ordering attacks to prevent line extension and the capture of supply lines, and aiding those forces

outside Petersburg when practicable and possible. In the end, however, Petersburg was about matériel and men, and Lee was, at last, drained of both.

—THOMAS J. HOWE

PETTIGREW, J. JOHNSTON

Pettigrew, J. Johnston (1828–1863), brigadier general. Johnston Pettigrew is best known for his role in the first and third days' battles at Gettysburg and his death two weeks later after an insignificant action on the retreat. Douglas Southall Freeman wrote, "for none who fought so briefly in the Army of Northern Virginia was there more praise while living or more laments when dead."

Born in Tyrrell County, North Carolina, on July 4, 1828, Pettigrew graduated first in the class of 1847 at the University of North Carolina. He later moved to South Carolina, where he practiced law, served in the legislature, and was an officer in the militia.

After serving as military adviser to the governor and colonel of a state regiment from South Carolina's secession to the fall of Fort Sumter, Pettigrew became colonel of the Twenty-second North Carolina Infantry in July 1861. He was promoted to brigadier general in February 1862. At Seven Pines, on May 31, 1862, Pettigrew was severely wounded and captured in his first battle.

When he returned to duty Pettigrew commanded a newly formed brigade which saw service on the North Carolina and Virginia coasts and joined the Army of Northern Virginia for the Gettysburg campaign. On July 1, 1863, his brigade suffered heavy casualties but fought brilliantly. Pettigrew, in temporary command of the division on July 3, led it and was wounded in the assault popularly known as Pickett's Charge. On July 14, during the retreat through Maryland, Pettigrew was mortally wounded at Falling Waters; he died July 18, 1863.

He was one of the best educated and most intellectual Southern generals. Lee called him "an officer of great promise" and observed, "his loss will be deeply felt by the country and the army."

— J. TRACY POWER

PHOTOGRAPHY

When the Civil War commenced, there were in the United States more than 3,100 ambrotypists, daguer-

Graphic art was rare in the Confederacy, plagued by shortages of skilled craftsmen, inadequate paper supplies, and a more pressing need for stamps and currency.

PAGE 442

P

PHOTOGRAPHY

reotypists, calotypists, melainotypists, and others, all of whom were, by one process or another, photographers. Of their number, only a fraction practiced their trade in the seceded states. New York City alone boasted more artists than almost the entire Confederacy. Arkansas, by contrast, had a mere nineteen. Moreover, while the number of photographers grew in the North during the war, it shriveled in the South, where demands for manpower took many artists into the armies and the ever-increasing shortage of chemicals, paper, and other necessaries simply put others out of business.

Still the Confederate photographers did create and leave behind an indelible record of several aspects of their side of the conflict. Indeed, the first war photographer was a Confederate, J. D. Edwards. A thirty-year-old New Hampshire native, he was working in New Orleans when the secession crisis erupted. Perhaps as early as January 1861 he was taking images of local volunteers, including excellent outdoor group portraits of members of New Orleans' colorful Washington Artillery (local artist J. W. Petty would also do a series on this unit). Then in April he took his camera to Pensacola, Florida, to produce what still remains the finest body of outdoor work by any Southern photographer. He made at least sixty-nine images of Fort Pickens, Fort Barrancas, Fort McRee, the navy yard, and the dozens of volunteer units there mustered. Many have since been lost, but about fifty are known to

survive, constituting nearly half of the extant body of Confederate outdoor views.

Edwards, like all other artists at the war's outset, viewed his work as a commercial enterprise, not a historical record. He advertised his prints in the New Orleans press and sold copies, as did other artists as long as their supplies held out. While Edwards worked in large format, the South's other war artists took another direction. Just three days after the fall of Fort Sumter, the business team of James M. Osborn and F. W. Durbec of King Street, Charleston, took a camera and portable darkroom inside the still smoldering ruins of the fort to make over forty images of it and the Confederate batteries that forced it to submit. Theirs is still the most complete contemporaneous record of any Civil War event, North or South.

Edwards worked in the wet plate process, making a negative in emulsion on glass. Osborn and Durbec made stereo views, nearly duplicate images placed side by side that, when viewed in a stereo viewer, gave a three-dimensional effect. They were probably the only Confederate photographers to do so. Virtually all the rest used the wet plate process, or else made tintypes on sensitized iron plates. None was successful in marketing this work extensively. The real demand in the Confederacy was for soldier portraits, and consequently, the photographers husbanded their precious raw materials for this more lucrative trade. By comparison with barely more than 100 outdoor views of scenes and soldiers

in the field that are known to have been taken, probably 100,000 or more studio portraits were made of individual Confederates.

The Confederates rarely attempted to put the camera to military use. A. D. Lytle of Baton Rouge has long been believed to have made images of Federal troops to send to Confederate leaders, but there is nothing in his surviving images that would have any military value. Richmond's David Rees did make a few 1863 images of the infamous Libby Prison, and on August 17, 1864, Georgia photographer A. J. Riddle made a series of photos of Camp Sumter at Andersonville. None of this work appears to have been inspired by anything more than commercial motivation or curiosity.

George Cook, who lived in Charleston at the beginning of the war, eventually moved to Richmond, but not before making a memorable series of prints of the interior of Fort Sumter on September 8, 1863, while the Northern fleet bombarded the garrison. He caught the only known image of a shell bursting and soon afterward made an image of three Union ironclads as they were firing. They are the only action images of the war, North or South.

By the last months of the war, most photographers were out of materials and out of business. Those who continued to operate were located in areas occupied by the Federals. With a free flow of supplies to these areas, such artists could resume their craft, and many made a lucrative business from their one-time enemies, especially in New Orleans, Baton Rouge, Nashville,

Memphis, and other larger cities. Ironically, then, the largest remaining output from the Confederate photographers as a whole is pictures of Union soldiers and officers. Some of their work even found its way into the North's illustrated press via woodcuts. The Confederacy's one such newspaper, the *Southern Illustrated News*, died early and made little use of Confederate photographers' work.

Unfortunately, after the war hundreds—maybe thousands—of Confederate images disappeared, lost or destroyed as baleful reminders of defeat and devastation.

— WILLIAM C. DAVIS

PICKETT, GEORGE E.

Pickett, George E. (1825–1875), major general. George Edward Pickett was born into the Virginia aristocracy on January 28, 1825, and grew up on the family plantation on the James River. He attended Richmond Academy and in 1824 received an appointment to West Point. Four unhappy years later, he graduated at the bottom of his class but fought the Mexican War with the Eighth Infantry Regiment and received two brevets for bravery. From 1849 through 1861 he served on frontier duty, first in Texas and then in Washington Territory, where in 1859 he helped provoke a near-war with the British over the possession of San Juan Island.

> *"I was convinced that he would be leading his troops to needless slaughter, and did not speak. I bowed my head in answer."*
>
> JAMES LONGSTREET
> ON GEN. PICKETT'S
> REQUEST TO ADVANCE,
> JULY 3, 1863

P

Both Stuart's and Pickett's charges failed; had they succeeded, Stuart would certainly have shared the glory of having slashed Meade's army into fragments.

PAGE 594

When the Civil War started, Pickett resigned his commission in the U.S. Army and returned to Virginia. His first commission in Confederate service was as a captain of infantry in the Provisional Army. He was quickly promoted to colonel and posted on the Rappahannock front under Theophilus H. Holmes. Although he was the most junior of all the colonels in his district, he was promoted to brigadier general in 1862, reflecting more the need for experienced officers than a high regard for his services.

The spring of 1862 found him on the peninsula as part of Joseph E. Johnston's army, James Longstreet's division. Pickett led his brigade ably at Seven Pines and (after Robert E. Lee took over) during the Seven Days' Battles, where he reported "quite severe" losses. In the Battle of Gaines' Mill, Pickett suffered his first wound, a severe shoulder injury that put him out of combat for three months. When he returned in October 1862, he became a major general in Longstreet's First Corps. His division was in reserve at the Battle of Fredericksburg. In the spring of 1863 when two of Longstreet's divisions were detached for service in the Suffolk campaign in southeastern Virginia, Pickett went along but spent more time courting LaSalle Corbell than fighting Yankees.

Pickett did not reach the battlefield at Gettysburg until late on the second day. The next afternoon he led his division forward as part of the assault that bears his name. Three-fourths of his command became casualties in less than an hour, although Pickett himself emerged unscathed, raising questions about his whereabouts at the height of the charge. His moment of glory had come and gone.

After the army returned to Virginia he was assigned to garrison duty south of Richmond during the early part of 1864. He organized an unsuccessful attack on New Bern, North Carolina, in February 1864, which led to charges of murder of Carolina Unionists. Twenty-two prisoners from the Second U.S. North Carolina Volunteers were accused of being deserters from Confederate service and were hanged under Pickett's orders. After the war when the U.S. secretary of war and the judge advocate recommended filing formal charges against Pickett, only Ulysses S. Grant's personal intervention prevented any action from being taken.

In May 1864 Pickett distinguished himself for the last time in the war by helping "bottle up" Gen. Benjamin Butler at Bermuda Hundred. After stopping Butler, he seems to have suffered a mental breakdown in May 1864, for he took to his bed for a week or more and was relieved of duty. He returned to his command in June, after the siege of Petersburg had already started, but little was heard of him until March 1865 when Gen. Robert E. Lee sent him to hold the strategic junction at Five Forks. On April 1 his division was destroyed while he was enjoying himself at an impromptu shad-bake with Gens. Fitzhugh Lee and Thomas Lafayette Rosser two miles behind the lines. In the confusion of the retreat to Appomattox he remained with the army, although Gen. Robert E. Lee pointedly dismissed him just one day before the surrender.

After the war he fled to Canada to escape prosecution for war crimes. He returned to Virginia in 1866, sold life insurance, and participated in veterans' activities. He died suddenly on July 30, 1875, in Norfolk, Virginia, a prematurely old and embittered man. He is remembered as a giant of Confederate history, but that mythic reputation rests on the events of one afternoon, July 3, 1863. His career up to that date had been unremarkable, and afterwards it was marred by disasters and doubts.

— RICHARD SELCER

PLAIN FOLK

Plain folk formed the core of the South's rural middle class. Neither rich nor very poor, they were the self-sufficient farming and herding families that defined Southern agriculture. Their social and economic condition ranged from tenant farmers to middling landowners who might own as many as two hundred acres. Few plain folk owned or rented slaves, and those who did generally kept fewer than six.

Most plain folk inhabited three distinct parts of the South: the upper South, where they benefited from agricultural diversification; Piedmont regions of the lower South, where they did not have to compete directly against low-country planters; and the backwoods, areas particularly suited to open-range herding and subsistence farming. Everywhere they lived in log or plank dwellings, sparsely furnished and largely unkempt. Most houses contained only one or two rooms, although a few ambitious people had as many as seven or eight. A farmer in the latter group might even own a clock, a half dozen books, or a piano. Most plain folk achieved only an elementary ability to read and write. Their schools operated on a subscription basis, tuition often payable in farm products. The school year lasted only a few months during the winter, when it would not interfere with planting and harvesting. Socially, plain folk exhibited a cordiality and friendliness that bade all welcome to bed and board, whether strangers or neighbors. Dancing (to fiddles and banjos), drinking, gambling, and storytelling constituted their favorite social activities.

Depending on whether they relied more heavily on crops or livestock for a living, some plain folk enjoyed more leisure than others, but none seemed to labor very hard. Plain folk—and to some degree all Southerners—prized their freedom and leisure time. Most were not acquisitive, and they worked only enough to secure life's necessities. Those dependent largely on livestock let their hogs and cattle run free most of the year while they devoted minimal energy to their crops. Corn reigned as the universal crop, but, where geography allowed, tobacco or cotton also served personal and market needs. Only those plain folk who lived in regions dominated by planters had very strong ties to a market economy. Nearly all plain folk tended small vegetable patches in addition to their tilled fields, and they spent a good deal of time hunting and fishing. Some farmers achieved this balance between leisure and survival by owning or hiring slaves. Others planted only enough land to meet their needs and secure some ready cash. Even at that, much rural trade utilized barter rather than money.

Political and social tensions existed between planters and plain folk, but they were not intense or terribly divisive. The strong kinship bonds that defined Southern society preempted much potential class tension. Also, Southern families frequently ran the gamut from nonslaveholder to planter, a circumstance that produced some degree of sympathy and understanding between social classes. Equally important was the communal power of rural society. In mixed planter-plain folk neighborhoods, landholdings and wealth varied widely, and ties of mutual political and economic dependency generally outweighed class resentment. Most rural Southerners, particularly in up-country and backwoods neighborhoods, remained geographically isolated from regions dominated by the plantation economy. The resulting sense of independence and liberty defused tensions and minimized the threat of planter dominance.

White Southerners also enjoyed a common ethnic heritage and a number of shared cultural traits, including heightened sense of honor, the Protestant religion, and an interest in black slavery. Slaveholders prized the latter institution for its economic benefits, but even nonslaveholders viewed slavery as a means of controlling a potentially dangerous portion of the South's population. As abolitionist attacks increased after 1830, and as political reform provided nearly all white adult males with the vote by the 1850s, most white Southerners could rally together in a common cause.

Plain folk played a pivotal role in the history of the Confederacy, beginning with the secession crisis. Plain folk divided on that heart-wrenching issue, as did planters, poor whites, merchants, and craftsmen. Allegiance to class or vocation became less important than kinship, age, economic interests, political affiliation, and a community's racial composition when deciding whether to support or resist disunion. For instance, in those parts of the South where railroads, a market economy, and industry had gained a foothold, many plain folk endorsed secession because they believed Northern economic imperialism threatened their independence. On the other hand, the strongest resistance to secession came in the upper South, where plain folk did not believe that Abraham Lincoln's election posed an immediate threat to local autonomy and security. They became alarmed only when Lincoln, following the attack on Fort Sumter, declared the South to be in rebellion. Upper South plain folk then cursed Lincoln for embarking on "a war of conquest" and forcing them to choose between the Union and the South. Interestingly, 52 percent of the Confederacy's white population, and the majority of its plain folk, resided in the upper South states of Arkansas, North Carolina, Tennessee, and Virginia, the last four states to secede. It is thus conceivable that war could have been avoided, or vastly shortened, had not those key states been driven out of the Union.

Plain folk initially flocked to the Stars and Bars, but their loyalty became severely tested. Young men spoke excitedly about maintaining Southern honor, defending their homes, and preserving the Southern way of life. Their enthusiasm stemmed, in part, from a romantic image of war, but they also believed that the war would be short and hugely successful. As the war bogged down and as common soldiers witnessed the slaughter and suffering of the battlefield, they lost much of their zeal. Once experiencing the exhaustion, discomfort, and sickness of campaigning and camp life, some men declined to reenlist and drifted home.

Others received pitiful pleas from their families, begging them to return. Southern women spun cloth, tended crops, and did all they could to further the war effort, but their resilience had limits. "Unless you come home," warned one hard-pressed soldier's wife, "we must die. Last night I was aroused by little Eddie's crying . . . 'O mamma! I am so hungry!'" Such laments naturally affected soldiers. One Confederate wrote in 1863, "Our men have stayed here till they are very anxious to go home and anxious for the war to end a heap of them says there famileys is out of provisions."

Regions of the South first scorched by the flames of war—Tennessee and northern Virginia in particular—suffered much destruction, confiscation, and social upheaval. Black and white refugees flooded the South as slaves fled their masters and whites fled contesting armies. Whether staying or fleeing, plain folk lost much of their property. "In every direction there appeared a frightful scene of devastation," confessed a Union cavalryman as he surveyed the wreck of one Virginia farming community. "Furniture" was mutilated and defaced; beds were defiled and cut to pieces"

" . . . the men of '65 returning to find themselves alien in the very land they had been bred and born in and had fought for four years to defend . . . "

WILLIAM FAULKNER
REQUIEM FOR A NUN, 1951

P

windows were broken, doors torn from their hinges, houses and barns burned down." Federal forces "plundered" another farmer "of all he had, his corn, wheat, and pork, killed his hogs, drove off his beef cattle and even his milch cows." As a Northern policy of "total war" emerged after mid-1862, Southern civilians suffered increasingly greater deprivation over an ever-broadening area.

The growing centralization of the Confederate government also sapped confidence. By 1863, military conscription, suspension of habeus corpus, increased taxes, impressment of farm products and livestock, and a passport system for travel seemed to make a mockery of the doctrine of state rights. Likewise, local communities, jealous of their autonomy, believed the authority of state government far exceeded prescribed bounds. Conscription became a particular sore point as plain folk saw many professional people, skilled urban workers, and planters exempted from military service. Cries were heard of a "rich man's war and a poor man's fight."

Making matters worse was a belief that government sought greater power while shirking its responsibility. Neither state nor national government seemed to concern itself with the suffering and privation of civilians. Complaints about hunger, labor shortages, and insufficient military defenses seemed to draw little sympathy from the governments the plain folk supported with their blood and toil. As more areas of the South fell under Federal control, discontent, caused by physical suffering and hardship, produced widespread grumbling. Politicians seemed unable or unwilling to shore up the Confederacy's flagging economy. Rampant inflation, price gouging, and illegal hoarding wreaked havoc on plain folk.

Some parts of the Confederacy populated largely by plain folk became notorious Unionist strongholds. Northwestern Arkansas, eastern Tennessee, western Virginia, and the upcountry of North Carolina, Georgia, and Alabama opposed Confederate rule throughout the war. Many communities in those places offered havens to deserters, conscripts, and tax evaders. West Virginia rejoined the Union, and vocal peace organizations thrived in Arkansas and North Carolina.

Yet, despite the steadily declining fortunes of the Confederate nation and the increased suffering of families and soldiers, most plain folk supported the Confederacy to the bitter end. The explanations are several. First, plain folk became not so much disloyal as disillusioned and discouraged, not so much anti-Confederacy as anti-authoritarian. Thousands of men deserted the Confederate army, particularly after 1863, and, insofar as plain folk comprised most of the army, it is safe to say that they supplied most of the deserters. They left the army in response to pleas from their families, and

because they were worn out and discouraged. "I have a very large family of whites consisting of a wife and 10 children," wrote a Virginian seeking exemption from further military service. "I feel that I am willing to bear my full part in this struggle but having served 16 mos . . . I feel that I am worth more to the government at home to raise meat and bread." The principal complaint of this man and many like him was the power of the government to interfere in his life and challenge his independence.

Plain folk also remained loyal advocates of slavery, the existence of which was starkly challenged after 1862. Plain folk became increasingly resentful of slaveholders as the war progressed, yet they seldom renounced slavery or advocated its abolition. They supported slavery for the same reasons they had always supported it; it was part of the Southern way of life, and plain folk were not social revolutionaries. They feared that should the Confederacy fail, over 3 million freed blacks would lead the South to chaos and ruin.

Thus plain folk played a critical role in the life and death of the Confederacy. Without their consent, secession would have failed. Without their presence in army ranks, the Confederacy would have collapsed far sooner. A sense of class resentment emerged as the war dragged on, a more visible and divisive variety than anything that had preceded the war, but this was not the ultimate reason that plain folk loyalty wavered. Their will to fight faded only after they and their families had been battered into submission by hunger and a stronger military force, and after their own government had initiated policies that left little to choose between the Confederate States and the United States.

[*See also* Farming; Morale; Poverty.]

— DANIEL E. SUTHERLAND

PLANTATION

A large plantation was not just cotton fields and a stately mansion approached along an oak-lined drive. A plantation included many other buildings: the smokehouse where meat was preserved, the henhouse where poultry was raised, stables where thoroughbreds were tended, the barn where dairy cows and work animals were housed, and sheds and silos for tools, grain, and other farm necessities. In workshops scattered near the barnyard, slave artisans might craft barrels, horseshoes, furniture, and cloth for use on the plantation. Gardens were cultivated to supply herbs and vegetables. Larger plantations might also maintain a schoolhouse for white children. Some planters built chapels for family worship, and some allowed religious services for slaves as well. More commonly, large plan-

---

"I have been up to see the Congress," Lee told his son, *"and they do not seem able to do anything except eat peanuts and chew tobacco, while my army is starving."*

GEOFFREY WARD
THE CIVIL WAR, 1990

tations included slave infirmaries and nursery facilities where older slave women tended the children of women who worked in the fields. As a safety precaution, almost all plantations had kitchen structures separate from the "big house," the main mansion that housed the planter family.

The big house, usually a two or three-storied mansion, was a visible symbol of the planter's wealth. Coming in from the front porch, a wide entrance hall might lead into a dining room, a parlor, a library, and one or more sitting rooms. In these rooms a planter could display his wealth with European furnishings and imported artwork. On the upper floors, bedrooms for family members and guests were maintained with the most comfortable and luxurious decor available. Nurseries for planters' children were located on the uppermost floors and could be reached by the servants' stairs at the back of the house.

The big house, the centerpiece of the entire plantation, might have formal flower gardens, like the famed plantings at Middleton Place outside Charleston, which took nearly ten years to complete. A separate office for the planter or overseer might be attached to the main house. Slave cabins were often built not far from the big house. Overseers sometimes lived on the plantation, in which case their modest homes might also be found not far from the slave cabins, especially in the case of absentee planters. But economic studies indicate that fewer than 30 percent of planters employed white supervisors for their slave labor. Although not all plantations contained every element listed above, the crucial components were the master's home and the slaves' domiciles, reflecting the difference in status between the black and white worlds on the plantation.

PLANTATIONS MOBILIZE FOR WAR. From Abraham Lincoln's election onward, secession fever propelled the South into war. Once South Carolina broke with the Union and the rest of the Southern states fell like dominoes in the early part of 1861, war appeared inevitable. Mary Boykin Chesnut saw the handwriting on the wall: "These foolish, rash, harebrained southern lads . . . are thrilling with fiery ardor. The red-hot Southern martial spirit is in the air," she wrote in her diary.

Southern gentlemen, especially the young, knew their choices and, buoyed by secessionist bravado, enlisted when the war broke out. Confederate manhood ironically required husbands and fathers to leave the very home and loved ones they were pledging to protect. Slave-owning patriarchs had to abandon their beloved plantations. Loyal Confederate plantation mistresses had to hammer home the necessity of fighting, in case men might falter in their duty. The press and private correspondence overflowed with parables

PLANTATIONS IN ANTEBELLUM SOCIETY

These large plantations were not the average, but the model to which the majority of white Southerners—owners of small slaveholdings and yeomen farmers—might aspire. On the eve of the Civil War, approximately 400,000 masters owned slaves, but only 50,000 boasted plantations—farms with 20 slaves or more—and only 2,300 planters owned holdings of over 100 slaves. Yet almost all slave owners followed the planters' lead and subscribed to the cash crop system, devoting a majority of arable land to a single crop to be sold at market. And in the case of the Confederate South, cotton was king. In the border states as well as Virginia, tobacco cultivation still employed slave labor. In Missouri and Kentucky hemp growers also supplied an eager market, but these crops involved only a small proportion of slave labor. More commonly, coastal planters in the Deep South might plow and irrigate rice fields to harvest their profitable crop, and Louisiana planters could and did put slaves to use in the backbreaking cane field to produce sugar. In all areas, corn was grown to supplement these cash crops and to feed the slave work force.

Because slaves were considered property, the per capita wealth of Southern whites was nearly double that of Northern whites in 1860. With only 30 percent of the nation's free population, the South boasted 60 percent of the nation's wealthiest men. Income levels were lower for Southern whites than for Northern whites, however, and many economists continue to wrangle over the figures and their meaning.

— CATHERINE CLINTON

of strident patriotic females: the belle who broke an engagement because her fiancé did not enlist before the proposed wedding day, the sweethearts who sent skirts and female undergarments to shirkers.

The formation of many Confederate units demonstrated the resolve of the planter class to serve. In Selma, Alabama, the Magnolia Cadets assembled, manned entirely by local gentry. In Georgia, the Savannah Rifles, the Blue Caps, the Rattlesnakes, and many other colorful groups closed ranks against the charge that the battle would be a "rich man's war and a poor man's fight."

When the war began, secessionists expected the South's farmers would rise as one to defend the new nation, but that was not the case.

PAGE 213

The war exacerbated differences among farmers as well as disrupting the growing of crops.

PAGE 213

P

PLANTATION

Planters and Conscription

"Our all depends on that army," wrote Mary Boykin Chesnut. *"If that fails us, the game is up."*

PAGE 375

Class solidarity was built on the bedrock of white superiority to which most white Southerners subscribed. As contemporary Southerner William Cabell Rives proclaimed, "It is not a question of slavery at all; it is a question of race." Therefore planters necessarily blurred class lines for whites by engaging in cooperative ventures during wartime. Parthenia Hague described the way in which Alabamians forged alliances during war: "We were drawn together in a closer union, a tenderer feeling of humanity linking us all together, both rich and poor; from the princely planter, who could scarce get off his wide domains in a day's ride, and who could count his slaves by the thousand, down to the humble tenants of the log cabin on rented or leased land."

The blockade, of course, threw all within the Confederacy's borders back on their own resources. Plantations were not the hardest hit, but they did have to modify long-established patterns of production and consumption. Most significantly, the Confederate government wanted planters to switch voluntarily from the cash crop system to a more diversified subsistence strategy, which would include the planting of crops that could feed the army and civilian populations. A slogan that appeared in the press captured Confederate philosophy: "Plant Corn and Be Free, or plant cotton and be whipped."

Many planters in the Deep South, which was more dependent upon food imports than the upper South border states, adopted the "corn and bread" ideology early on. Cotton production was severely curtailed, dramatically so in the first year of the war. The South's output, 4.5 million bales in 1861, was cut to 1.5 million in 1862. Some states complied more than others; indeed, Georgia reduced its cotton output by nine-tenths from 1861 to 1862. In the coastal regions, especially Louisiana, sugar planters responded to the call, with a decline from 459 million pounds in 1861 to 87 million in 1862.

Many planters were concerned about this move and wondered how they could keep their slaves occupied and afford their upkeep under such conditions. The more conservative decided to reverse the traditional proportion of cash crops to foodstuffs; instead of the usual 600 acres of cotton to 200 acres of corn, they planted 200 acres of cotton to 600 acres of corn. A high rate of cotton production was nevertheless maintained by a minority of planters who refused to toe the patriotic line. As private speculators sought out cotton to store for future sale, a number of planters were happy to supply them, viewing war as an opportunity for profit. Indeed, many smuggled their cotton to Europe through Texas and Mexico, ignoring the government proscription. A handful of planters, oblivious to the charge of treason that could be brought against them,

sought out Northern buyers. They hid their bales in remote warehouses or buried the cotton on their plantations until safe passage might be secured.

One such manipulator, James Alcorn, whose plantation was in the fertile Mississippi Delta, owned a hundred slaves and property worth nearly $250,000. When war broke out, Alcorn sent his family to Alabama and continued his prosperous trade in cotton, hiding and selling it, and avoiding both armies. In 1862 he reported that he had sold over a hundred bales, with another ninety ready to ship. Greed was his motive: "I wish to fill my pockets," he said, and boasted, "I can in five years make a larger fortune than ever. I know how to do it and will do it." At war's end, however, Alcorn decided to cater to loyalist dictates rather than side with the enemies with whom he had collaborated in matters of business. Although he had traded with Northerners, after the surrender at Appomattox he refused to take the oath of allegiance to the Union and was credited with being a great Southern patriot, much to the mystification of his former slaves.

PLANTERS AND CONSCRIPTION. Planters were divided on the subject of cotton policy and many other issues, but the question that seemed to dominate the Cotton Planters Convention in Memphis during their meeting in February 1862 was not agriculture but politics. And many expressed doubt that their revolution, Confederate independence, would succeed. The intertwining of economics and politics was too tied to the fortunes of war.

When in September 1862 the Confederate Congress raised the upper age limit of conscription from thirty-five to forty-five, heads of many poor families were for the first time subject to the draft. This legislation appeared just at a time when that summer's drought had ruined most harvests. Compounding the difficulties, the Confederate Congress in October passed an even more unpopular statute that became known as the Twenty-Slave Law, which exempted from army service any white man who could demonstrate that he was in a managerial role on a plantation with twenty slaves or more; both owners and overseers qualified. This law was intended ostensibly both to control the slave population and to keep the Confederacy fed. But the argument that the law would benefit all whites stuck in the craw of most white Southerners. Even when in May 1863 exempted slaveholders were taxed $500 (to fund the distribution of food for soldiers' families), civilians and especially soldiers were not mollified.

Throughout the war, only 4,000 to 5,000 men received exemptions under this law; indeed, only 3 percent of those men who claimed exemptions took them on the basis of the Twenty-Slave Law. On 85 percent of those plantations that qualified for exemptions, none was taken. Nevertheless, the perception of favoritism rankled. Members of the planter class already could afford to buy substitutes, and now any choice to sit out the war was ratified by government legitimation. Attitudes may have been regionalized: within the Deep South more planters perhaps took advantage of the system, sparking more resentment. There were 1,500 exemptions issued in Alabama alone and of the nineteen categories of exemption, only medical disability was employed more often than the Twenty-Slave Law. Thus, the law was a public relations disaster, to say the least. Mississippian James Phelan wrote a warning to Jefferson Davis: "It has aroused a spirit of rebellion in some places, I am informed, and bodies of men have banded together to resist; whilst in the army it is said it only needs some daring men to raise the standard to develop a revolt."

White women, too, voiced their alarm over conscription. Many left behind in parishes and counties without adequate male assistance appealed to their government. Late in the war a group of women in South Carolina sent a plaintive letter to the governor:

We are personally acquainted with Erwin Midlen for over three years and do no that he is a sickly and feeble man and we do Believe that he is not able for service in the field. We are informed that he is in the 56th year of his age. And we do further sware that he has done all our hawling for the last three years and attended to all our domestic business as we could not Procure any other man to do—see to our hawling and other business as our Husbands are all in the army and some of them killed and some died in service.

The seventeen women who signed begged that Midlen be spared military service. The governor's ruling on the matter remains unknown.

THE DECLINE OF PLANTATION AGRICULTURE AND PLANTER MORALE. Even more disheartening to both the Confederate government and the Southern farmer was the fact that all agricultural indicators in the South spelled decline, while prosperity reigned in the fertile regions of the Midwest. Although over 75,000 farm boys left Iowa for Union service and over 90,000 came from Wisconsin, Northern agriculture did not suffer. Iowa and Wisconsin both reported improved acreage and grain production as well as a rise in farm income during the war.

The South's declining agriculture created a dilemma. The army needed fresh troops, but the home front required care as well. President Davis, among others, harped on the dangers of deserted or unproductive plantations; these Cassandras were unpopular yet prophetic. One advised: "We are today in greater danger of whipping our selves than being whipped by our

enemy." Sinking morale and declining food supplies contributed to gloomy predictions of further degradation. The crippling of cotton production undermined the ruling elite's sense of mastery and helped pave the way for defeat. There were countless examples of reduced fortunes: by 1864 James Heyward of South Carolina planted only 330 acres in rice and 90 in provisions; a mere one-tenth of his land holdings were under cultivation.

Heyward at least was able to continue planting. Many slave owners were driven off their plantations, losing homes and livelihoods in one fell swoop. Some former mistresses, hoping to elude Federal troops, were reduced to living in cabins in the woods. In the first few months of the war, Confederates feared the unknown threat of a Union army, but by 1862 too many Southerners knew firsthand the toll such an invasion extracted. In December 1863 the Confederate Congress railed against the enemy:

Houses are pillaged and burned, churches are defaced, towns are ransacked, clothing of women and infants is stripped from their persons, jewelry and momentoes of the dead are stolen, mills and implements of agriculture are destroyed, private salt works are broken up, the introduction of medicines is forbidden.

Indeed, plantation mistresses turned to the woods as "nature's drugstore" and for other necessities of life. One woman reported that after the enemy left her home she was "forced to go out into the woods nearby and with my two little boys pick up fagots to cook the scanty food left to me." The scorched-earth policy of William Tecumseh Sherman and other Union generals reduced many plantations to ashes and permanently impaired the planters' ability to recover.

Morale was at a low ebb and hopes were being steadily dashed against the shoals of wartime reality. Those planters who stockpiled their cotton crop were in as much danger of losing it to the Confederate cause as to invading Northerners. It was the policy of the Confederate army to burn cotton whenever Federals moved within striking distance. This was an unpopular measure, to say the least, especially at a time when planters were pressing the government to buy their unsold crops. To have their hopes go up in smoke at the hands of soldiers in gray rather than the hated Federals created conflicting loyalties.

Some of these policies alienated planters to the point of political disaffection. In the 1870s the Southern Claims Commission was empowered to rule on the petitions of planters who declared both their pro-Union sympathies during wartime and the destruction of property by Union troops. Of the 700 claims filed to obtain damages of over $10,000, only 191 were suc-

Not long after Sherman's strategic breakthrough, Lincoln won reelection, and Southerners knew that Confederate defeat was only a matter of time.

PAGE 375

cessful, and a mere 224 of the 800 and more who complained of property losses of less than $10,000 were granted.

Perhaps no more than 5 percent of the planter class were Union loyalists during wartime. But many more simply resisted the entreaties of the Confederate government to perform patriotically. As many as 25 percent of the slaveholders in Virginia refused to comply with the government's requisition of their property—slaves—in 1864. Both the loss of labor and the strong resistance combined to weaken the Confederacy's ability to win its war for independence.

THE END OF SLAVERY AND THE PLANTATION SYSTEM. The dangers within arose not only from recalcitrant planters but from the omnipresent threat of slave resistance. John Edwin Fripp of Saint Helena Island off the coast of South Carolina was able to write: "I am happy to say my negroes have acted orderly and well all the time, none going off excepting one or two Boys who accompanied the yanks for plunder but have returned home and appear quite willing to work." Nevertheless, Fripp's experience was the exception rather than the rule. The majority of planters made careful notations in their logs about African Americans deserting plantations. Whenever Union troops moved into a region, slaves fled behind enemy lines. Many, if not most planters, felt wounded when their slaves abandoned the plantation for "Lincoln land." They were especially angered by those African Americans who led Federal troops to storehouses of food and buried treasure—the family silver and other heirlooms. Even after the issuance of the Emancipation Proclamation in January 1863, slave owners mistakenly placed their faith in paternalism. As one woman complained bitterly, "Those we loved best, and who loved us best—as we thought—were the first to leave us."

Planters who feared insurrection, however, were pleasantly surprised, in contrast to those whose cherished notions of slave loyalty were disappointed. Historian James Roark has suggested: "Slavery did not explode; it disintegrated . . . eroded plantation by plantation, often slave by slave, like slabs of earth slipping into a Southern stream." Some planters responded by moving their slaves away from approaching Federal troops, but as the war dragged on, there was nowhere left to hide and hundreds of thousands of African Americans made their way to freedom.

During the fall of 1863 over 20,000 slaves were recruited for service in the Union army in the Mississippi valley alone. Jane Pickett, a plantation mistress and a refugee, recounted the planters' predicament: "The negroes in most instances refused to leave with their masters, and in some cases have left the plantations in a perfect stampede. Mississippi is almost depopulated of its black population." By the winter of 1864–1865, slave owners were reduced to a lengthy process of negotiation with those African Americans who remained. Emma LeConte of Berkeley County, South Carolina, lamented: "The field negroes are in a dreadful state; they will not work, but either roam the country, or sit in their houses. . . . I do not see how we are to live in this country without any rule or regulation. We are afraid now to walk outside of the gate."

The fall, then, came from within, as historian Armstead Robinson has argued, as well as from without. The plantation South simply crumbled, unable to withstand African American challenges to slavery as well as the burdens of blockades, wartime production, and invading armies. The superhuman task of retaining the illusion of white superiority in the face of black resistance, African American independence, and the final blow—the full-blown glory of black manhood in the form of African American Union soldiers—combined to destroy Confederate dreams. Economic ruin further eroded the fragile leadership of the struggling nation. Confederate wealth (excluding slave property) declined nearly 45 percent during the war.

In February 1864 the Confederate Congress authorized impressment of free blacks and slaves for noncombatant military roles, and by November 1864 President Davis was advocating gradual emancipation and military use of African Americans. Davis wrongly assumed that Southerners would choose to give up slavery rather than go down to defeat. But slaveholders stuck to their guns. The Confederacy had been founded because of the perceived threat that Northern Republicans presented to the institution of slavery, and proslavery stalwarts stayed the course: "We want no confederate Government without our institutions." These and other sentiments have prompted historian David Herbert Donald to suggest that the Confederacy might ironically have "died from democracy." Whatever the cause, the plantation system, with its fortunes so tied to black labor, died along with slavery.

The surrender at Appomattox triggered a long, slow process of recovery, but planters never actually recovered. Rather, they devoted their time and energies to promoting romantic legends of the Lost Cause—seeking historical justification rather than economic recovery. Planters' devotion to an imagined past was embodied in Margaret Mitchell's mythic re-creation of Tara and Twelve Oaks, perhaps the most famous plantations of all, in her 1936 novel, *Gone with the Wind*. Despite such fictional exaggerations, most plantations were scarred visibly by the war. And even those not damaged by wartime destruction indisputably suffered a permanent stain—the psychic blight of Confederate defeat.

[*See also* Conscription; Cotton; Impressment; Planters; Rice; Slavery; Sugar; Tobacco.]

— CATHERINE CLINTON

PLANTERS

Although plantation slavery never dominated the entire South, the plantation belt contained the region's best farmland, the major portion of its wealth, and the majority of its slaves. It gave rise to a planter class that, though less than 5 percent of the white population, dominated local and state governments and shaped regional institutions in its own interests. The sprawling plantation South was vast enough to encompass a variety of planter types and personalities. Whether old money or new, paternalist or pure capitalist, planters (owners of twenty or more slaves) formed a distinctive and self-conscious elite that was united in its commitment to preserving slavery as the basis of its power, wealth, and identity. From the moment of secession to the end of the Civil War, plantation slavery remained the touchstone of planters' existence.

During the secession crisis of 1860 and 1861, planters divided on whether the defense of slavery required the destruction of one national government and the creation of another. Those who resisted Southern independence showed no less dedication to slavery. They argued that slavery was safer—for the moment, at least—within the Union than out of it. Still, there was a strong correlation between slavery and support for secession. In general, the greater the density of slaves and slaveholders in a state's population, the greater the support for Southern independence. By spring 1861, planters had led eleven states out of the Union. The Confederate States of America became home to some 43,000 planters (plus those in Arkansas, for which the census returns are incomplete), and no more than a tiny fraction, perhaps one in twenty, remained loyal to the United States.

Planters greeted war with a burst of Confederate patriotism. They rushed to buy Confederate bonds and marched off at the head of regiments they organized and often outfitted with their own money. They eagerly assumed prominent positions in their new nation's government. Confident that cotton was king, they looked forward to bringing the North to its knees and cotton-importing Europe to their side. Victory would secure both the preservation of slavery and Southern independence. To planters, it was obvious that slavery and Southern nationhood went hand in hand.

But mobilization for war required that the government in Richmond build armies and regiment the home front. Government, which traditionally had borne lightly on the people, reached more and more deeply into civilian life, restricted personal freedom, imposed unprecedented burdens, and demanded unimaginable sacrifices. As the war lengthened, Richmond grew increasingly single-minded in its commitment to political independence and more and more willing to subordinate all other interests to that goal. Confederate action forced planters to reveal that they assigned different values to independence and slavery.

At first, Richmond was sensitive to the interests of the planter class, which had brought the new nation into being. A raft of class legislation favored the elite. The Conscription Act of 1861 provided for hiring substitutes, but the cost put the option beyond the reach of most nonslaveholders. The Twenty-Slave Law exempted one able-bodied white male from military service for every twenty slaves on a plantation. Nonslaveholders were quick to point out that the provision allowed many overseers and planters' sons to escape the fighting. The gentry defended the government's favoritism, arguing that without white men to supervise slaves, they would refuse to work, run off, and threaten white women. Only well-ordered plantations could provide the Confederacy with the food and fiber necessary for victory.

In time, however, the elite experienced the rigors of war and the sting of intrusive Confederate policy. Large slaveholders suffered less than plain folk, but they yelled louder. At first, privation meant no more than learning to live without luxuries, but in time necessities such as salt and medicines grew scarce. Planters tolerated privation better than the growing government intervention into plantation affairs. Before the war, as the daughter of a Mississippi planter put it, "each plantation was a law unto itself." Laws had existed to regulate slaves, rarely planters. But as Richmond centralized power in order to fight efficiently, it increasingly ran roughshod over prewar notions of the proper relationship between government and citizens. Jealous of their prerogatives, large slaveholders fought fiercely to maintain their authority, even against their own government, the cornerstone of which, Vice President Alexander H. Stephens had said, was slavery.

Early in the war, state governments and public opinion demanded that planters cease growing cotton, perceived as a selfish act, and start growing corn, vital to the Confederate war effort. Some complied voluntarily, but others resisted. Later, when the Federal blockade choked cotton exports, planters had little choice but to switch to food production. With most white men away at war, responsibility for supervising the transformation often fell to white women. Female planters were not unknown before the war—thousands of women legally owned plantations—but few actually managed their estates. Planters kept up a heavy correspondence with their wives, and plantation women

In North Carolina, perhaps the leading issue in state politics in the 1850s had been whether slave property should carry a larger share of the state tax burden.

PAGE 605

On the eve of the war, small farmers had finally succeeded, they thought, in demanding that planters carry a larger share of the tax burden.

PAGE 605

In Virginia in 1861, planters from the eastern half of the state offered the small farmers of the west a major concession—higher taxes on slaves—in hopes of cementing their support for the Confederacy.

PAGE 605

successfully oversaw the formidable adjustment from staples to food crops. But without cotton, planters' incomes shriveled.

With every passing month, Richmond became more entangled in plantation affairs. Confederate officials told planters what and with whom they could trade and took or burned the cotton or sugar crops when they deemed it prudent. Officials dragged white men away from the plantation and impressed food, livestock, tools, animals, and wagons, paying whatever prices they saw fit in notes. The government created currency and tax systems that planters perceived as discriminatory, even though Richmond never taxed slaves. Confederate troops raided plantations, picking them as clean as Federal soldiers did. Hatred of the North soared, but with few Southern military victories or diplomatic successes, love of the Confederacy did not blossom correspondingly. Instead, planter support for Richmond faded.

Planters found Confederate impressment of slaves particularly troubling. Although slaves were barred from combat, they were theoretically available for military labor. But slaveholders resisted giving up their bondmen to build fortifications, standing on principle—they felt a man had a right to control his slave property—and complaining that the military mistreated slaves and returned them in poor health and recalcitrant. Planters believed they had enough difficulty maintaining control without the government adding to their troubles. When the war began, they made every effort to tighten controls over slaves and those who came into contact with them. They buttressed slave patrols and canceled exemptions from duty. They called home slaves who were on hire in cities and voided their passes to travel and visit families. But nothing they could do restored the stable order upon which slavery depended.

When the war reached the plantations, it sent slavery into a spiral of disintegration. As traditional routines crumbled, planters complained that slaves were "demoralized," a generic term that referred to every sort of misbehavior from rudeness to outright rebellion. Accustomed to respect and obedience from servants they had convinced themselves were loyal and loving, planters were beset by insolence, disobedience, theft, and malingering. Moreover, whenever proximity to Union soldiers made escape possible, the slaves ran away. As their owners' power eroded, they claimed their freedom bit by bit. On many estates, effective control shifted from the "big house" to the slave quarters. Before the war ended, the master-slave relationship was in tatters.

Slavery died for many reasons, but planters pointed the finger of blame at Richmond almost as often as at Washington. On January 1, 1863, Abraham Lincoln issued the Emancipation Proclamation, which planters denounced as an invitation to slaves to rise up in bloody

A BREAK IN TIME

Planters understood that defeat and emancipation meant a revolution in their lives. They were painfully aware of what Jefferson Davis called a "break in time." The old order was gone, but the new had not yet emerged. Proslavery doctrine had predicted that emancipation would lead to racial warfare, social anarchy, and economic collapse, and, indeed, planters found themselves surrounded by devastation. Northern radicals demanded even more: confiscation and perhaps banishment to stamp out the South's aristocratic "traitors." Planters welcomed peace, but they found little reason for optimism. In their minds, defeat had not invalidated the basic assumptions that had undergirded their belief in slavery: that blacks were inherently and immutably lazy, that without total subordination they were dangerous and destructive, and that without coercion they would not work. "Nothing could overcome this rooted idea," a visiting newspaper man noted in 1865, "that the negro was worthless, except under the lash." Unwilling to admit that they had been wrong about slavery or about the nature of the Union, planters had little choice but to give up their dream of an independent slaveholders' republic and to go on farming in a slaveless South.

— JAMES L. ROARK

"servile insurrection." Less than two years later, Jefferson Davis, in an equally revolutionary move, proposed that the Confederacy itself arm and free its slaves. The government had concluded that only by sacrificing slavery could the South win its independence. Planters branded Richmond's plan an outrageous betrayal. A partial version of the plan became law on March 13, 1865, but planters gave up their slaves only when Union soldiers appeared at their gates.

In parts of the Confederacy, however, Federal troops arrived long before the war ended, freeing the slaves in each area they occupied. Planters often fled before their arrival, taking their slaves with them to refugee elsewhere. But in the lower Mississippi valley, many stayed and participated in federally sponsored wartime experiments with free black labor. Union officials sought to resurrect the devastated sugar and cotton economies and to restore the link between planter self-interest and political loyalty. Because the system of contract labor they initiated resembled the South's prewar labor system, some planters found reason for hope.

But Federal efforts to maintain control of blacks and to stabilize agriculture did not revive planters' material fortunes. Most plantation owners saw little value in free black labor and no reason to pledge allegiance to a government that had made black freedom a war aim.

On the other hand, planters no longer sympathized with Richmond either. They were unwilling to defend a government that, for whatever reason, did not defend them. Indeed, complying with government policy meant collaborating in their own destruction. Yeomen also felt alienated from their government, but they believed that Richmond favored the wealthy and failed to make them carry their fair share of the burden. Planters judged the matter of sacrifice differently. No longer loyal to Richmond and unable to transfer loyalty to Washington, they withdrew to their plantations and did what they could to help themselves. They grew increasingly ready to evade conscription, desert from the army, plant cotton rather than corn, and engage in cotton trading with whomever would buy. In the end, they chose the homestead over the homeland.

By the time of the surrender at Appomattox, the planters' world lay in shambles. The North had triumphed over the South, free labor had triumphed over slave labor, and industrial capitalism had triumphed over the political economy of slavery. Because of remarkable miscalculation, the South's planters went from being one of the strongest agrarian classes in the western world to being the weakest. War had destroyed the very institution that secession was intended to secure. Armies had turned plantations into battlefields, hospitals, barracks, feed and fuel centers, and labor pools. Large slaveholders had been devastated physically, economically, and psychologically. Thousands had died; thousands more had lost their sons, their slaves, their life savings. A few planters weathered the storm—those who had extensive Northern investments, those who had hidden away cotton and could reap dollar-a-pound prices, those who could attract rich Northerners to lease their plantations. But war had impoverished the overwhelming majority. Stripped of slaves, wealth, and power, hundreds fled the region, although most saw no choice but to remain.

[*See also* Cotton; Impressment; Plantation; Rice; Slavery; Sugar; Taxation; Tobacco.]

— JAMES L. ROARK

POINT LOOKOUT PRISON

After the Battle of Gettysburg, the United States provided for the sudden increase of prisoners by opening a depot on Point Lookout, Maryland, the peninsula formed where the Potomac River joins Chesapeake Bay. The land was flat, mostly sandy with some marsh, and barely above the water. Because of the Point's proximity to the eastern battlefields, the government had already found it convenient to lease this prewar resort locale for a hospital that was subsequently used, in part, for wounded Confederates.

In late July 1863, quartermaster officers opened a camp for 10,000 men to be housed in old tents. Though the War Department rejected later proposals for barracks, there were wooden cookhouses. The camp consisted of two pens surrounded by fourteen-foot high fences, one for enlisted men of about twenty-three acres and a smaller one for the officers infrequently and temporarily held at the prison. With 14,489 inmates in July 1864 and an exceptionally large population of 19,786 during the exchange of prisoners in May 1865, this was the largest Union prison and with its overall total of some 52,000 was probably the largest prison of either side. Officially called Camp Hoffman after Commissary General of Prisoners William Hoffman, the prison was usually referred to by the name of its location.

Point Lookout's first commander was Brig. Gen. Gilman Marston. There were complaints, even from Union inspectors, about physical conditions under his and his successors' management. In July 1864, Brig. Gen. James Barnes, a Massachusetts-born West Pointer, took command, and he and his provost marshall, Maj. Allen G. Brady, made some improvements. The guard force at first consisted of troops drawn from the field, but these were rapidly succeeded by white semidisabled troops from the Veteran Reserve Corps and newly recruited blacks, often recent slaves. To the latter the Confederates usually reacted contemptuously and hostilely, feelings frequently returned by the black soldiers. With occasional exceptions, relations between the races were unfriendly. Partly because of the prisoners' unhappiness, the Federal authorities were able to recruit over a thousand of them who became "galvanized Yankees" to fight the western Indians.

Far more prisoners continued to endure the hardships of a pen unshaded in summer and frigid in winter. The wood needed to heat the tents was limited in quantity as were blankets and clothing. The United States attempted simply to prevent nakedness and often discouraged outsiders from sending such items. The official ration of food was also limited, and prisoners caught crabs and made jewelry, fans, and even pictures of the prison to trade for additional food. A particular grievance concerned the quality of the water. Some was shipped in, but much came from

By the 1850s, greatly improved sugar-making apparatus had been designed by Norbert Rillieux, a distinguished black creole of Louisiana who had studied physics and mechanics in France.

PAGES 599–600

Jubal Early forced the Union to divert the better part of two corps that would have been pitted against Lee's Army of Northern Virginia.

PAGE 183

shallow wells that rapidly became polluted by sewage from the camp's surface. This contributed to diseases, which, along with less common causes like shootings by guards, accounted for 3,584 deaths, according to Federal records, or in the opinion of a recent historian, over 4,000. Such mortality and the hunger and cold experienced by the prisoners left a postwar legacy of bitterness.

Inevitably some prisoners attempted escape. Prior to the completion of the fence it was possible with luck to run the sentry line at night and get away with help from the strongly pro-Southern inhabitants of the vicinity. After the prisoners were surrounded by boards, the river offered an alternative for those willing to risk swimming with the help of some form of flotation device. From the beginning, Federal authorities stationed naval vessels in the river to forestall any attempt to use boats for escape or rescue.

The accessibility of the equivalent of a small army of reinforcements tempted the Confederates to try to recover the captives. In the winter of 1863–1864, Robert E. Lee formulated a scheme to throw across the Potomac a force of Marylanders drawn from his army to free the prisoners. In July 1864, he added the release of the prisoners to the mission of Jubal Early's Maryland raid. But the partial failure of Early's raid caused the abandonment of the plan. The alarmed Federals immediately built earthworks mounting cannons and a stockade to cut off either attack from the mainland or an uprising from within the prison. They also reduced the temptation for a rescue by moving half of the prison population farther north.

The prison camp continued to operate on a reduced scale until February 1865, when exchange resumed. Union authorities wished to send troops from western states to be exchanged in the East (believing that these would be least likely to retake the field for the Confederates) and hence began to accumulate such troops at Point Lookout. When the fall of Richmond disrupted exchange, the Union retained additional prisoners at Lookout, crowding the prison to its utmost. But the end of the war produced a speedy exodus of prisoners who took the oath of allegiance. By July 1865, the last were gone and the prison was abandoned.

The government preserved the camp's graves, which were moved several times to a nearby national cemetery containing both U.S. and Maryland monuments. The prison site reverted to recreational purposes with considerable portions vanishing through erosion. The remainder is today a Maryland state park.

[*See also* Early, Jubal, *sidebar* Early's Washington Raid.]

— FRANK L. BYRNE

POLITICS

Like most aspects of life in the South, politics underwent profound changes during the Civil War. The predominant issues of the prewar period, secession and union, were supplanted by war-related controversies. Parties disappeared, replaced by a wartime unity that only barely masked a continuation of antebellum partisan hostility. Elections changed as well, as politicians adopted new standards of campaigning that seemed more appropriate for a nation at war. The electorate, of course, remained the same, as did most of the prominent personalities involved in politics. But even these groups would be permanently altered by the War between the States.

Political Issues

The greatest political changes in the South during the Civil War concerned issues debated by politicians and voters. In the 1840s and 1850s, a variety of national and local issues determined the tenor of Southern political discourse. Most Southerners in the antebellum period believed that state rights were paramount, that the right to hold slaves in the territories could not be abridged by Congress, and that tariff rates ought to be lower. They disagreed, however, about issues such as temperance, government subsidies for railroads, and whether secession was the best way to guarantee the South's rights.

The creation of the Confederacy rendered these issues either moot or insignificant. At first, there were no questions of importance to fill this void. Believing it necessary to present a united front to the enemy, candidates in the elections for the First Confederate Congress conducted virtually no campaigns. Office seekers often placed notices in the local press informing the public of their candidacy, but these announcements rarely differed from one aspirant to another. They uniformly proclaimed themselves to be ardent supporters of Southern independence, proponents of a vigorous prosecution of the war, and so forth.

After the Confederate war effort began to falter, differences concerning the conduct of the war became the focus of political contention. One of the most hotly debated issues concerned the Confederate government's conscription system. Sensing their constituents' displeasure with this "horror of conscription," many candidates running for seats in the Second Congress condemned the policy. Some did so on the grounds that it detracted from state and local defense efforts, while others argued that it placed too much power in the hands of President Jefferson Davis. Even more controversial was the provision added to the law in September 1862 that exempted from military duty one white man on every plantation containing twenty or more slaves. Administration defenders insisted that the clause was necessary in order to maintain agricultural production as well as to prevent disciplinary problems with slaves. Nonetheless, by pointing out that the exemption provisions of the conscription law "made a broad and degrading line of distinction between . . . the silken son of pleasure and the hardy son of the soil," many candidates for the Second Congress were able to defeat incumbents who supported the administration's conscription policy.

Another issue that sparked controversy was the suspension of habeas corpus. Local judges were enabling army deserters to avoid prosecution by issuing writs for those held under Confederate authority. Congress attempted to eliminate this practice by granting Davis the power to suspend the writ and declare martial law as well if necessary, and it was primarily a perception of the overzealous use of this latter proviso that brought about the preponderance of disaffection. As with the conscription issue, most of the outcry against suspending habeas corpus came from radical state rights advocates. Among the most vociferous critics of the suspension were Georgia Governor Joseph E. Brown, North Carolina Governor Zebulon Vance, and Vice President Alexander H. Stephens. "Away with the idea of getting independence first, and looking for liberty afterwards," Stephens declared. "Our liberties, once lost, may be lost forever." Davis, however, suspended the writ for only sixteen months in all, and his abridgments of civil liberties were never as frequent or severe as those carried out by his counterpart in Washington.

The government's taxation policies also caused political divisions. Runaway inflation had by the spring of 1863 forced Congress to find alternative means of financing the war. Although a variety of taxes was imposed, the one that generated the most discontent was the 10 percent tax-in-kind levied on agricultural products. Poor yeoman farmers complained that it was unfair for the government to take 10 percent of their meager surpluses, while city dwellers such as clerks and teachers paid only 2 percent of their income. Moreover, the legislation left the principal possession of the wealthy—slaves—untaxed. The administration's advocates argued that slaves could not be taxed without a census, something that could not be undertaken during a war, but this provided little comfort to the impoverished farmer whose produce was hauled away while his rich neighbor's slaves escaped taxation. The army's impressment policy, by which it purchased whatever supplies it wanted from nearby farmers in exchange for worthless promissory notes, also bred resentment toward the Richmond government. Many Southerners harboring political ambitions used opposition to the tax-in-kind and impressment policies to unseat incumbents in the 1863 elections.

As the war grew longer and hopes of victory became increasingly remote, peace became the overriding political issue in the Confederacy. At first, peace proponents sought to win independence simply by negotiating with the U.S. government. They asserted that Davis was stubbornly continuing the fighting even though the South might gain its sovereignty at the negotiating table. The president argued, however, that a peace overture would be fruitless and would irreparably damage public morale as well. Later on, and especially after the defeats at Gettysburg and Vicksburg, the peace movement became a haven for a wide variety of politicians. Some, such as W. W. Boyce of South Carolina, merely believed that a well-defined peace policy would bring about Southern independence more quickly by making it easier for Peace Democrats in the North to oust Abraham Lincoln. Others, such as William W. Holden of North Carolina, seemed to favor peace even if Southern independence had to be sacrificed, and he proposed that North Carolina initiate its own negotiations if Davis refused to do so. "We would prefer our independence, if that were possible," one of Holden's followers stated, "but let us prefer *reconstruction* infinitely to *subjugation*." Campaigning primarily on this issue and holding election rallies that administration supporters characterized as treasonous (the Stars and Stripes were supposedly flown at some of these gatherings), Holden's "Conservative party" won widespread support, especially in western North Carolina, and captured at least five, and perhaps as many as eight, of the state's ten seats in the 1863 congressional elections. In Georgia and Alabama, as well as the more isolated up-country regions of other states, candidates for the Second Congress managed to defeat incumbents by stressing the peace issue.

Disappearance of Parties

Ordinarily, political parties would have served as the conduit through which voters would express their opinions on these issues. In the Confederacy, however, there were no formal parties. This resulted in part from the belief that a political process unencumbered by partisan squabbling would best aid the war effort. Yet while the same belief pervaded the North, partisanship there subsided only temporarily, and the parties themselves never ceased operations. Why, then, did parties so abruptly disappear in the Confederacy?

The answer lies primarily in the decline of the two-party system in the South during the 1850s. After the demise of the Whig party in 1854 and 1855, Southerners who opposed the "Democracy" sought alternative affiliations. At first, it appeared as if the anti-immigrant Know-Nothing movement, which eventually became known as the American party, might win the loyalty of former Whigs, but the dismal

In 1848 the Free-Soil party was founded to keep slavery out of the new territories.

PAGE 109

Open warfare between proslavery and antislavery settlers in Kansas spilled over into the halls of Congress, where fistfights broke out between Northern and Southern representatives.

PAGE 110

performance in 1856 of its presidential candidate, Millard Fillmore, doomed that party to extinction. The Constitutional Union party captured a respectable 39 percent of the Southern vote in the presidential election of 1860, but because that organization had opposed secession as a means to guarantee the South's rights, it too disintegrated soon after the canvass. Recognizing no further reason to continue operations and believing that the energy previously exerted on its behalf would better serve the war effort, the Democratic party ceased functioning soon after the completion of the secession process.

Southerners were proud of the fact that their nation contained no political parties. Like those who had started the previous American revolution, most Southerners believed that in an ideal society there would be no parties, because more often than not these organizations degenerated into self-serving associations that placed the perpetuation of their own power ahead of the public good. Thus, the president pro tem of the First Confederate Congress congratulated legislators that "the spirit of party has never shown itself for an instant in your deliberations." Parties were not merely absent from the floors of Confederate legislative bodies. Party offices closed and officials found new work. In addition, no caucuses were held, no fund-raising took place, no propaganda was distributed, and no party committees directed communications from the electorate to the officeholders and back.

Although Southerners were proud that their nation lacked partisan political organizations, there were drawbacks to this state of affairs that became clear only in retrospect. For example, the lack of parties created a major impediment to the smooth and successful implementation of Davis's legislative agenda. In the North, Republican congressmen and governors understood that publicly opposing Lincoln's policies would make them pariahs within the Republican party and doom their political careers, convincing most of them that they should support the president even if they privately harbored doubts about his proposals. For the same reasons, party members were obligated to support their organization's policies after the legislation was implemented. In the South, however, obstructionist governors such as Brown and Vance were able to paralyze the war effort because, as historian James M. McPherson has noted, "the centrifugal tendencies of state's rights were not restrained by the centripetal force of party."

Despite the absence of formal political parties, historians have noted an "unconscious spirit of party" in the national and state governments of the Confederacy. Each of Davis's original cabinet nominees, for example, had been Democrats before the war. Furthermore, many states made deliberate decisions to send one ex-

NO ONE TO ARGUE AGAINST

The lack of organized parties created other difficulties as well. For example, without the existence of a unified opposition party, Davis could not convincingly argue that his policies were superior to the program of his opponents, because he could not focus on a single opposition agenda with which to compare his own. In addition, the absence of parties created frustration for voters, because they could not identify those responsible for the government's program and register approval or disapproval on election day by voting a party's ticket. Finally, without parties to oversee the distribution of patronage, these appointees could no longer be used as a means to mobilize support for either the administration's policies or friends.

— TYLER ANBINDER

Democrat and one ex-Whig to the Confederate Senate. Nonetheless, statistical studies of the Confederate Congress have demonstrated that an officeholder's stance on secession and the proximity of his district to the war zones tended to play a larger role than prior party affiliation in determining the representative's stance on the measures before him. Yet even these factors were far from reliable predictors of congressional voting behavior. To a much greater extent than perhaps at any previous time in American history, congressmen seem to have genuinely voted according to their consciences on most issues before the Confederate Congress, and as a result no single consistently identifiable opposition grouping ever emerged.

Nonetheless, the public noticed the formation of a number of small opposition factions in Congress. One, which concentrated its attention on the peace issue, coalesced around the leadership of Boyce. The bulk of the Second Congress's North Carolina delegation, which seemed to oppose virtually everything proposed by the administration, was another such faction. The single individual most commonly identified as the leader of the opposition in Congress, however, Senator Louis T. Wigfall of Texas, belonged to neither of these groups. Formerly a fire-eating Democrat, Wigfall had initially supported Davis's most controversial proposals. It seems to have been a perceived insult concerning Wigfall's advice on a cabinet selection, combined with his admiration for another emerging foe of Davis, Gen. Joseph E. Johnston (under whom Wigfall had served during the first year of the war), that pushed the Texan into the opposition

camp. Outside of Congress, many of Davis's opponents took their cues from a triumvirate of Georgians: Stephens, Brown, and ex-general and Confederate secretary of state Robert Toombs, who did everything in their power to embarrass the president and discredit his policies. These groupings, however, never assumed the official trappings of prewar political organizations; they more closely resembled the cliques and factions of the pre-Jacksonian era.

These opposition groups always constituted a small minority in the Confederate Congress. The administration's supporters, like the Southern Democratic party that had preceded them, were dominated by the same prominent personalities and families that had taken the lead in politics before the war. Robert M. T. Hunter of Virginia and Robert Barnwell Rhett, Sr., of South Carolina, as well as Stephens and Toombs, continued to play leading roles as they had before secession. These personalities remained in the forefront of Southern politics in part because ambitious young men who would ordinarily have entered politics instead chose to make their names in the military. Consequently, newspapers complained throughout the war that the state legislatures were filled with amateurs and incompetents, and although this resulted to some extent from the press's dissatisfaction with the legislators' inability to remedy the problems caused by the war, such comments also reflected a very real vacuum of experience and talent in state and local politics.

Other Political Voices

Although prominent politicians and families continued to dominate national political life in the Confederacy as they had in the antebellum period, the war did provide some unique opportunities for poor whites to exert political influence. For example, the belief that the conflict represented a "rich man's war and a poor man's fight" prompted many poor whites to funnel their energy into electing representatives who better reflected their socioeconomic outlook. In addition, poor yeoman farmers dominated the Unionist organizations that began proliferating in the up-country in late 1863. These associations, such as the Heroes of America in western North Carolina and eastern Tennessee, the Peace Society in northern Georgia and northern Alabama, and the Peace and Constitution Society in Arkansas, served as incubators for the Southern Republican party, in which poor whites would exert far more influence than they had in the South's prewar parties. Poor whites did not necessarily have to wait until after the war to wield this political power. The eventual Union occupation of areas such as West Virginia, eastern Tennessee, the Sea Islands of South Carolina, and Louisiana enabled poorer politicians such as Andrew Johnson to gain significant political clout in these regions well before the war had ended. With the reconstruction of each state government in the South, poor whites gained power that had

WOMEN'S POLITICAL MIGHT

Like the South's poor white inhabitants, women also enjoyed increased political power during the Civil War. The most common method by which women made their influence felt in politics was still, as it had been before the war, through their politically active husbands. The diary of Mary Boykin Chesnut documents the efforts of these "female politicians" to have their concerns addressed by their male counterparts. Yet these well-to-do women were not the only ones whose voices were heard in political circles during the war. The correspondence of wartime governors contains an unprecedented number of letters from women, especially those running family farms while their husbands served in the army, concerning political issues. These women often explained in their letters that although they preferred to avoid politics, conditions in the countryside had become so unbearable (usually because of the tax-in-kind or impressment policies) that they felt obligated to inform government officials of the situation and seek redress.

Women may have exercised the most political clout during the Civil War through their participation in civil unrest. On April 2, 1863, for example, several hundred women in Richmond marched to the state capitol to complain that the price and supply of bread had reached intolerable levels. When Governor John Letcher told the protesters that he was incapable of remedying the situation, the crowd took matters into its own hands. Pulling knives, hatchets, and a few pistols from their skirts and pocketbooks, the women proceeded to loot the commercial district of whatever bread and other food items they could find. The events in Richmond were far from unique, as bread riots instigated wholly or in part by women also broke out in Atlanta, Macon, Augusta, Mobile, and a half-dozen other towns. Although the bread riots accomplished little in terms of increasing the supply of food in urban areas, they served as a warning that even without the vote, women were determined to make politicians act upon their concerns.

As the unprecedented role of women in the civil unrest in Richmond demonstrates, politics underwent significant change during the Civil War. Issues were transformed, parties disappeared, and many constituencies learned to wield unprecedented political power.

— TYLER ANBINDER

P

POLLARD, EDWARD A.

By the fall of 1862 alarming cries of hunger were being heard in the South.

PAGE 444

"What shall we do for something to eat?" asked a paper in the hill country of Georgia in 1863.

PAGE 444

been unattainable under a political system previously weighted in favor of slaveholders.

Although it might be argued that the political revolution wrought by Reconstruction would prove even more profound, it was during the Civil War that Southern politicians abandoned the two-party system of politics, and this innovation laid the groundwork for the one-party system that would characterize the region's politics for the succeeding century.

[See also American Party; Bread Riots; Congress; Constitutional Union Party; Democratic Party; Election of 1863; Judiciary System; Peace Movements; Presidency; Public Finance; State Rights; and selected biographies of figures mentioned herein.]

— TYLER ANBINDER

POLLARD, EDWARD A.

Pollard, Edward A. (1832–1872), journalist and contemporary historian of the Confederacy. Pollard, a descendant of the Rives family, grew up on its Oakridge estate in Nelson County, Virginia. Educated at Hampden-Sydney College and the University of Virginia, he was expelled from law school at the College of William and Mary for misconduct. In the early 1850s he prospected for gold in California, became a journalist in San Francisco, and traveled in eastern Asia. Returning to the eastern states in 1856, he became a publicist for Southern rights causes, including William Walker's projects in Nicaragua and reopening of the African slave trade. In *Black Diamonds* (1859), he combined such arguments with sketches of plantation life and master-slave relations.

The attempt to resupply Fort Sumter in 1861 impelled Pollard (then living in Washington) to join the Southern Confederacy. After a brief advocacy of secession in Maryland, he and his brother H. Rives Pollard joined the staff of the *Richmond Examiner*. Many have had the mistaken impression that Pollard was its wartime editor. He was acting editor only in the summer of 1862 during the absence of editor John Moncure Daniel. He and others contributed draft editorials, but Daniel thoroughly rewrote them before publication. Pollard shared the *Examiner*'s extreme Southern-rights views and its animus against Jefferson Davis's administration.

Pollard resolved in 1861 to be the contemporary historian of the war for Confederate independence. He published *The First Year of the War* in 1862 and followed it with annual volumes thereafter. In 1864 the Federal navy captured him trying to travel through the blockade to Europe. He was imprisoned in Boston, then paroled in Brooklyn and exchanged from Fortress

Monroe in January 1865. Back in Richmond, he exhorted Confederates to fight on until victory.

After the surrender, Pollard continued his laudatory histories of the Confederacy. He completed his annual series and published it as *Southern History of the War* (1865) and followed it with his most famous work, *The Lost Cause* (1866), and *Lee and His Lieutenants* (1867). Those works embroiled him in historical controversy with D. H. Hill and other Confederate generals and with admirers of Jefferson Davis about those leaders' wartime performance.

In 1868 Pollard, who had hoped for a renewed Confederate struggle, became reconciled to the national conservative politics of President Andrew Johnson and the Northern Democrats. In *The Lost Cause Regained,* he interpreted their effort for white supremacy and state rights as the substance of what Southerners had sought in the Confederacy. That winter he returned to Richmond to seek judicial vengeance for the murder of Rives Pollard there. In 1869 he wrote his hostile *Life of Jefferson Davis, and Secret History of the Southern Confederacy.*

After that Pollard settled with relatives in Lynchburg and (except for a travel guide) directed his writing to articles. He continued to discuss Confederate history but became a "reconstructed" Southern conservative, urging national reconciliation, economic development, and benevolence toward blacks. He died in 1872, but his writings continued to influence Southern thought about the Lost Cause.

— JACK P. MADDEX, JR.

POOR RELIEF

The unexpected and unprecedented poverty that afflicted the Confederacy provoked innovative but inadequate responses. In a region that had never employed extensive means of poor relief, substantial new initiatives came from individuals and from local and state governments. Ultimately, however, the scope of the war effort required Confederate involvement if aid to the poor was to be effective. Despite some relief activities by the Richmond administration, the problems of poverty and hunger remained unsolved and severely eroded support for the government among the common people.

Poor relief had been a modest affair before the war. The states employed a variety of means to assist the poor, but all were on a small scale. A stigma attached to the recipients of aid; healthy children usually were apprenticed rather than supported as paupers. Government-sponsored poor farms or poorhouses sheltered many of the destitute, and local authorities entrusted others (often elderly persons) to the care of some responsible person who agreed to maintain them for a modest fee. The counties of North Carolina, for example, practiced all these methods and levied taxes at varying levels to defray costs. In Southern cities charitable organizations had developed to give some aid to the destitute. In the words of one writer, poverty was "associated in public opinion with illness and petty crime." An antebellum North Carolinian observed that "the poor will suffer almost any privations before" accepting public relief.

The war forced enormous changes in these practices and public attitudes, but the experience of poverty remained physically harsh and psychologically painful for thousands of yeoman families. In the early days of the conflict there was a widespread recognition that soldiers and their families might need—and deserved—support. Governor Joseph E. Brown of Georgia appealed in May 1861 for contributions to aid soldiers' families and offered prizes to recognize those citizens who did the most to contribute. Artisans, such as tanners or millers, offered their services free to soldiers' families, and some merchants invited local troops to select the goods they needed. Many companies and factories contributed money or donated some of their products. As the war went on, "free markets" came into being in the cities. Tickets were distributed to the poor in New Orleans, Mobile, Charleston, and Richmond; ticket holders then could visit the market to obtain free supplies. Macon, Atlanta, Savannah, Shreveport, and other cities had stores that sold goods to the needy at cost. In Richmond the Union Benevolent Society received aid from the city government and fed 4,500 people by the end of the war.

As the size of the conflict became apparent, local and state governments became more heavily involved. Most states passed laws early in the war to suspend the collection of debts ("stay laws") or exempt soldiers' families from certain taxes. Between November 1861 and March 1862, seven states formulated relief laws, which typically gave county governments responsibility for using the funds raised by a special tax. With hunger spreading, a corps of county officials came into being who scoured their region, or even distant areas, seeking to buy foodstuffs and distribute them to the poor. To assist the county officials, state lawmakers appropriated as much as $6 million at one time for poor relief, in addition to buying and distributing items such as salt, medicines, cloth, and cotton and wool cards. In 1863 the Georgia legislature bought 97,500 bushels of corn for the poor in sixteen suffering counties of that state.

These impressive efforts did not solve the problem, however. Many of the larger state appropriations never existed except on paper, and county purchasing agents increasingly came into competition with the Confederacy's efforts to supply the armies. Only the Confederate government was large enough to cope with the problem of hunger. What, then, did the Confederacy do?

Occasionally the Confederate government cooperated with private charities by exempting their goods from impressment or encouraging the railroads to arrange transportation. In especially deserving cases, under the Exemption Act of May 1, 1863, the Davis administration allowed individual soldiers to return home to their families. Under the Exemption Act of February 17, 1864, Congress required planters who wished to retain their overseers to promise under bond to raise stated amounts of meat and food for the government. These foodstuffs were sometimes sold to soldiers' families at below-market prices. In August 1864, the War Department instructed its commissaries to leave one-half of the surplus raised by bonded planters for "persons who purchase on behalf of the families of soldiers." Records of bonded farmers also show that a small proportion of them were small farmers exempted for "Care of Private Necessity."

The greatest potential for relieving hunger, however, lay with the Confederate tax-in-kind. In 1863, as the central government began to collect large quantities of crops in depots, county relief agents sought help, asking to buy back the crops from poverty-stricken counties at the low prices set by local boards under the Impressment Act. Records show that for a year the Confederacy extended some aid in this way, but the military's needs soon precluded assistance to civilians.

Thus the problem of poverty in the Confederacy remained unsolved. It brought physical and mental suffering to proud, independent yeoman families that had never before needed aid. In 1862 some nonslaveholding citizens of Smith and Scott counties, Mississippi, had petitioned Congress for a law to aid the poor. Although they expressed a willingness to defend slave property, these petitioners warned that they were "not willing to sacry fize our wives and children and leave them to starve for bread and clothing." As poverty spread and poor relief proved inadequate, discontent, disaffection, and desertion grew. Commanders recognized that despairing letters from home caused many men to leave the armies. Poverty influenced many others to turn against the cause. The inadequacy of poor relief, and the fact that it had become necessary, did great damage to the Confederacy.

[*See also* Poverty; State Socialism; Tax-in-Kind.]

— PAUL D. ESCOTT

POPULAR CULTURE

In September 1861 the *Southern Literary Messenger* pointed with excitement to the "splendid opening

Residents of Richmond and Atlanta saw the cost of foodstuffs grow prohibitive: in 1864, sweet potatoes cost $16 a bushel, and meat commanded over $2 a pound.

PAGE 574

which the impending Revolution secures to every Southern enterprize," not the least of which was the evolution of a Confederate popular culture. Not necessarily distinct from that of the antebellum South's, it at least "should occupy, in some respects," as an 1864 broadside remarked, "a different sphere of usefulness." Thus traditional pastimes, fetes, and other entertainments were adapted to wartime civilian and military society, particularly so "for the benefit of the soldiers" and "their wives and children."

Enormously popular, for example, were cartes de visite, small photographic images mounted on heavy card stock usually measuring two and a half by four inches. Easily carried in a pocket or haversack and cheap to produce—created from a negative from which any number of reproductions could be made—they provided accessible and affordable mementos or keepsakes for soldiers and their families. Despite paper shortages, photo studios such as Minnis and Cowell in Richmond and the Metropolitan Gallery in Nashville did a brisk business in marketing carte de visite likenesses of famous individuals as well. Period scrapbooks thus abound with pictures of family members alongside images of Robert E. Lee, Jefferson Davis, and other Confederate leaders. Somewhat more expensive

were daguerreotype, ambrotype, and ferrotype images. An ambrotype, for example, cost from one dollar for a small image to several dollars for a larger one. Whereas the cards could be copied in any number, the more elaborate likenesses were one-of-a-kind positive images, often hand-tinted, mounted under plush velvet in elaborate decorative frames, and available in a variety of sizes.

Prints and engravings proved far more difficult to produce. With the fall of New Orleans, the South lost much of its printing expertise. And whereas Northern printers produced several Confederate scenes—a Baltimore firm, for example, published a series of pro-Confederate etchings by Adalbert J. Volck in 1863 and 1864—such pictures remained largely unseen in the South until after the war. Plagued also by shortages of skilled craftsmen, inadequate paper supplies, and a more pressing need for stamps and currency, graphic art thus remained rare in the Confederacy. There were exceptions, though. In 1861 both Pessou and Simon, of New Orleans, and R. H. Howell, of Savannah, issued handsome lithographs of early Confederate scenes; Tucker and Perkins of Augusta, Georgia, that same year published a finely rendered print of Jefferson Davis, copied from a prewar Mathew Brady pho-

CONFEDERATE THEATER AND DRAMA

Confederate theaters offered artwork of a sort. One Richmond playhouse featured the "Southern Moving Dioramic Panorama," a canvas eight feet high and seventy-five feet long filled with historical scenes. The nearby Metropolitan Theater presented a massive "scenic and automatic spectacle" of wartime illustrations, accompanied by animated "miniature moving, life like figures" and an explanatory lecture. Usually the plays alone were enough to bring in large audiences. Theater provided a vibrant source of entertainment in each of the Confederacy's major cities, although, after the fall of New Orleans in 1862, Charleston's Hibernian Hall and Richmond's Metropolitan, New Richmond, and Varieties theaters remained the most active. Besides Charles Morton, the "most versatile and popular Comedian and Vocalist in the Confederacy," and Ella Wrenn, the "accomplished Tragedienne and Prima Donna," other popular actors

included E. R. Dalton, Walter Keeble, D'Orsay Ogden, Harry Macarthy, Mary Partington, Jennie Powell, and Ida Vernon. Easily the most famous of the many traveling companies was the W. H. Crisp troupe, its male members all honorably discharged Confederate veterans.

In the press of wartime, however, performances often degenerated into rowdy brawls. Soldiers on leave, civilian workers, and drunken troublemakers all eager for a good time filled the cheaper seats, often firing pistols and otherwise disturbing the more cultured theatergoers in the lower tiers. So bad did the situation become that the gentler sort regularly urged theater owners to close down their saloons and upper tiers—hardly a likely prospect in the face of an overwhelming demand from all quarters for entertainment. Theaters presented an array of productions, from traditional operas such as *Il Trovatore* and Shakespearean plays to the melodra-

matic *Corsican Brothers* and *The Marble Heart*.

Many more dramas—such as *The Ticket-of-Leave Man*, *The Capture of Courtland, Alabama,* and *Miscegenation; or, A Virginia Negro in Washington*—reflected the times. In 1864, the New Richmond Theater introduced *The Ghost of Dismal Swamp; or, Marteau, the Guerrilla* with special effects so realistic that critics called it "the great Spectral wonder of the nineteenth century." Most of the productions were abysmally written but were at least presented with unflagging enthusiasm; actors often perceived of themselves as charged with a patriotic duty to bolster morale. Minstrels such as Tom Morris, "the renowned negro delineator," and his Iron-Clad Ethiopian Troupe were especially popular, although keeping any acting company intact was always difficult. Morris and his minstrels were drafted in 1864.

— EDWARD D. C. CAMPBELL, JR.

tograph; and Ernest Crehen in Richmond as late as 1863 published a striking portrait of J. E. B. Stuart. By and large, however, popular prints were infrequent and poorly produced. Hoyer and Ludwig's highly fanciful 1861 lithograph of an oddly uniformed Jefferson Davis is far more representative. Cartoons were somewhat more forgiving of style and quality. The four lithographed *Dissolving Views of Richmond,* published by Blanton Duncan in Columbia in 1862, ridiculed George B. McClellan's Peninsula campaign, and Richmond's George Dunn and Company issued a biting series of caricatures aimed at shirkers, hoarders, and doomsayers.

Painters, too, suffered from scant supplies. With no canvas available, artist John R. Key, nephew of Francis Scott Key, resorted to using burlap for his painting of Fort Sumter. Such topical work was nevertheless eagerly awaited. In Richmond, William D. Washington attracted considerable attention with his masterwork, *The Burial of Latané,* depicting Southern women and their slaves mourning the death of the sole Confederate casualty of Stuart's 1862 ride around McClellan's army. In 1865, soldiers and civilians crowded through the Virginia capitol to view Edward Caledon Bruce's monumental portrait of Lee, since disappeared. Bruce, deaf since the age of fourteen and thus unable to enlist, was unique. Louis M. Montgomery, of the famed Washington Artillery, completed nearly two hundred sketches of military life, but like most other Southern artists—Conrad Wise Chapman, John Elder, Alan Christian Redwood, and William Ludwell Sheppard, for example—he was unable to exhibit much work while actively serving in the army.

Music attracted the broadest possible audience. In the first year of the war alone the public could buy the eighteen-page *New-Orleans 5 Cent Song-Book,* the sixteen-page *Original Songs of the Atlanta Amateurs* ("containing more truth than poetry"), or, the next year, the massive two-hundred-page *War Songs of the South.* Until 1865, despite the shortages that so plagued every printer, song sheets and collections remained available. A Charleston publisher as late as 1864 issued a monthly pocket-size *Taylor's Southern Songster.* As expected, many of the titles honored the ordinary Confederate soldier, various generals, or Southern sentiments. There were nearly fifty musical selections published on Stonewall Jackson's death alone. Popular music titles included "Dear Mother, I'll Come Home Again," "Boys, Keep Your Powder Dry," "The Murmur of the Shell," and "Adieu to the Star Spangled Banner Forever."

Although attracting a smaller segment of the Confederate public, magazines were also part of wartime popular culture. But of the approximately one hundred Southern periodicals in business in 1861, only a few

survived the war. The *Southern Literary Messenger* lasted until 1864, as did the *Southern Literary Companion* and *Southern Field and Fireside,* both published in Georgia; *De Bow's Review,* except for a single issue, suspended publication in 1862 until after the surrender. The *Southern Monthly,* with hopes of becoming a Confederate *Harper's,* lasted only for several issues. Richmond's *Southern Punch,* Mobile's *Confederate Spirit and Knapsack of Fun,* and Atlanta's *Hard Tack* were game attempts at Confederate, especially military, humor. Two new periodicals published in Richmond, the *Southern Illustrated News* and *Magnolia,* a literary magazine, by 1863 were forced to charge twenty dollars for a year's subscription; neither lasted out the war. One that did, the *Countryman,* published in Eatonton, Georgia, employed a young typesetter and writer named Joel Chandler Harris. For children, there were the *Portfolio,* published in Charleston and later Columbia, and the *Child's Index,* printed in Macon.

Popular fiction fared little better than the magazine. Printers issued barely more than a hundred literary titles during the war years. In 1861 Strother and Marcom in Raleigh published a collection of poetry, Hunter Hill's *Hesper;* a Charleston printer that same year issued Claudian B. Northrop's *Southern Odes.* West and Johnston in Richmond and Goetzel and Company in Mobile produced nine literary titles each, the most of any single printer. Both issued editions of two of the war's most popular titles, Victor Hugo's *Les Misérables* (1863–1864) and Augusta Evans Wilson's stilted romance, *Macaria* (1864). Sigmund Goetzel's firm also published two stories by Charles Dickens, George Eliot's *Silas Marner,* and Julian Fane's *Tannhauser.* It was Goetzel too who, faced with the shortage of paper, resorted to printing book covers on sample sheets of wallpaper. Some Confederate fiction, such as Sallie Rochester Ford's *Raids and Romance of Morgan and His Men,* proved popular enough to be pirated in the North. Other works—such as W. D. Herrington's *The Captain's Bride* or Braxton Craven's *Mary Barker*—were but cheap novelettes, worthy of only a moment's attention.

The same might be said of many Confederate broadsides, posters, newspaper notices, and other forms of advertising. While educational, religious, and civic organizations usually struck a serious tone, many merchants and other entrepreneurs were seldom timid in touting their products. A grocery in Cold Springs, Texas, for example, boasted of its "largest and best" inventory, adding that "If you want the worth of your money, call and see us!" In Greensboro, North Carolina, the locally produced Tarpley Rifle was "the best . . . introduced in the country." Some notices were practical: a New Orleans company in late 1861 finally bowed to the

Women gathering about Latané's coffin symbolized the enduring strength of Confederate womanhood.

PAGE 80

Blacks assisting with the burial gave visual prominence to the Lost Cause myth of slave loyalty.

PAGE 80

inevitable and agreed to accept Confederate currency in order "to facilitate the efforts of our customers."

That some vestiges of Confederate popular culture were less than ideal was not significant, however. As the editor of a leading Southern newspaper put it, for many citizens it was equally important that the South "along with her political independence" achieve an "independence in thought and education, and in all . . . forms of mental improvement," whether they were extraordinary or mundane.

[*See also* Lost Cause, *article on* Iconography of the Lost Cause; Photography.]

— EDWARD D. C. CAMPBELL, JR.

POVERTY

Poverty became a serious problem in the Confederacy and ultimately deprived the struggling Southern nation of the active allegiance of many individuals. Though initially unexpected, poverty was so widespread by 1862 that thousands of private persons and officials of state and local government labored to alleviate it. Eventually even the Confederate government became involved in relief efforts. Yet the scope of the problem was so great that it overwhelmed relief activities. Poverty exacerbated class resentments, and hunger caused many Southerners to put the welfare of their families above loyalty to the cause.

A variety of factors contributed to the poverty that descended on the Confederacy. The South had always depended on the North or foreign suppliers for manufactured goods. As the war and blockade disrupted trade, shortages developed in diverse commodities such as iron rails and sewing needles, nails and scythe blades, glass and medicines, cloth and coffee. Salt, an essential preservative, became scarce and remained so, despite large-scale Confederate efforts to acquire it.

Shortages grew worse as a result of hoarding. Merchants and panicky citizens often bought large quantities of potentially scarce items. The *Richmond Enquirer* reported that one man purchased seven hundred barrels of flour, and another planter carted in wagon loads of supplies until his "lawn and paths looked like a wharf covered with a ship's loads." Early in the war speculators hoarded salt, bacon, and leather, and six men gained control of the Confederacy's two nail factories. Newspapers and citizens hotly denounced known instances of speculation and extortion, but deficiencies in the Southern transportation network also hampered distribution of those commodities that were available. As a result, Confederates had to develop an ersatz economy, employing their ingenuity to substitute for many items.

Most Southerners assumed that food would not be a problem for their agricultural nation. Why, then, were shortages of food the primary cause of poverty and suffering? Some food rotted in depots, never reaching soldiers or urban markets. Civilians also lost food to the government through policies such as the tax-in-kind and impressment. Secretary of War James A. Seddon called impressment "a harsh, unequal, and odious mode of supply," yet the War Department depended upon it to supply the armies. Impressment aroused intense anger among the people, as did unauthorized foraging by soldiers, especially troops of cavalry. The *Richmond Enquirer* reported in August 1862 that people were saying, "*The Yankees cannot do us any more harm than our own soldiers have done.*" Drought and crop failures also affected crops in some sections of the Confederacy. But the greatest cause of food shortages was also the most general: the presence in the army of hundreds of thousands of yeoman farmers.

Slave owners could keep their unfree labor force at work while they fought, but non-slave-owning soldiers had to rely on their wives and children or other relatives to cultivate the fields. For many families this burden proved too great, especially as the war dragged on. In a typical plea to the War Department, a Georgia woman wrote, "I can't manage a farm well enough to make a surporte," and an elderly man in Virginia said of his son, "if you dount send him home I am bound to louse my crop and cum to suffer." Zebulon Vance, governor of North Carolina, informed President Jefferson Davis in 1863 that conscription had carried away "a large class whose labor was, I fear, absolutely necessary to the existence of the women and children left behind." Similarly, Governor Milledge L. Bonham of South Carolina opposed a call-up of troops in 1864 on the grounds that it would cause "great suffering next year, and possible starvation." The absence of key artisans, such as blacksmiths who could repair farming tools, aggravated the labor shortage, and the files of the War Department contain hundreds of letters appealing for the detail or exemption of blacksmiths and other artisans.

By the fall of 1862 alarming cries of hunger were being heard in the South. "Want and starvation are staring thousands in the face," declared the *Atlanta Daily Intelligencer*. "What shall we do for something to eat?" asked a paper in the hill country of Georgia in 1863. Tens, even hundreds of thousands of yeoman families, who had always prided themselves on their independence, fell into poverty and suffering. The dimensions of the problem are indicated by the governor of Alabama's admission at the end of the war that more than one-quarter of the white citizens in his state were on relief. A study of surviving records from several counties in North Carolina found that from one-

A rash of incidents in the spring of 1864 suggests that the pinch of hunger became painful enough to move women to desperate action as their winter food supplies were exhausted.

PAGE 74

fifth to two-fifths of the white population depended on government relief efforts for cornmeal and pork.

The South's response to this unprecedented social problem was significant but ultimately inadequate. In the Confederacy's straitened circumstances, not enough food, clothing, and other necessary items were available to serve the armies and the civilian population. The resulting poverty had significant effects. An anonymous Virginian wrote to the War Department in 1863 and asked a critical question: "What man is there that would stay in the armey and no that his family is sufring at home?" Later that year W. S. Keen, a provost marshal in Allegheny County, Virginia, answered the question in a letter to the secretary of war. "When our brave and true men, shall hear that their wives and little ones are actually suffering for bread," he warned, "they will naturally become restless and dissatisfied, and mutiny in our army will result, as naturally and as certainly as gravitation."

Provost Marshall Keen's prediction proved to be correct, as poverty stimulated desertion and caused many frustrated and suffering people to withdraw their cooperation or their allegiance from the government. Thus the problem of poverty was a crucial internal problem for the Confederacy.

[*See also* Bread Riots; Extortion; Impressment; Morale; Poor Relief; Salt; Speculation; State Socialism; Substitutes; Tax-in-Kind; Transportation.]

— PAUL D. ESCOTT

PRESIDENCY

The office of the chief executive officer of the Confederacy derived its powers from the Provisional and Permanent Constitutions. Both documents prescribed an office almost exactly like the presidency of the United States, though they gave the Confederate president the item veto in appropriation bills. The Permanent Constitution gave him direct removal power over department heads and diplomats.

Since the Confederacy was at war, the powers of the presidency were used mainly to sustain military activities. President Jefferson Davis noted impending martial problems in his inaugural address, and in shaping his administration turned his attention first toward creating armies and a navy. Civil functions were not neglected, but were harnessed finally to sustaining a besieged nation.

As "commander-in-chief of the army and navy . . . and of the militia or the several States, when called into the actual service of the Confederate States," Davis found his responsibilities growing with the conflict. His concerns extended from raising and supporting armies and navies to providing supplies, providing commanders for soldiers and sailors, commissioning all Confederate officers, and devising a national strategy for victory. Fortunately for the Confederacy, the president had considerable military experience and knew how to begin.

He picked a cabinet with care, and it was part of the presidency. For war secretary Davis selected Alabamian Leroy P. Walker, whose apparent incapacity led to a long line of succeeding secretaries—but Davis really served as his own war minister. For secretary of the navy Davis picked Floridian Stephen R. Mallory and left most sea operations in his highly capable hands. Christopher G. Memminger took the treasury portfolio.

Judah P. Benjamin, regarded as the brilliant man of the cabinet, had an uncanny ability to get along with an increasingly besieged president. Benjamin cruised through several departments—Justice, War, finally State—and his management of secondary diplomacy (blockade running, foreign purchasing, diplomatic negotiations for increased belligerency) was sound. The Treasury Department, late in the war, came under George A. Trenholm, a South Carolina banker possessed of toughness and acumen.

While organizing military departments, the president considered strategy in a state rights context: governors were jealous of state territory and authority, and any national strategy had to be shaped around that reality. Davis adopted the "offensive-defensive" as the Confederacy's war plan. Weaker Southern forces would stand on the defensive when necessary to husband resources; when the right chance came, they would concentrate against smaller or isolated enemy forces. A look at Confederate operations from First Manassas to the end of the war will show the president's adherence to his strategy. There were those who argued for a more defensive posture—Braxton Bragg, Joseph E. Johnston, and P. G. T. Beauregard, for instance. And clearly the idea of standing on the defensive and receiving attack had an important precedent in American revolutionary history. But it is doubtful that such a strategy would have been better, given the growing strength of Union forces. Davis's plan probably best fitted the Southern situation.

Davis recognized that power came to his office from the Constitution, and he used the supreme law of the land to centralize war government—to secure Confederate assumption of all military operations (taking them out of state hands), to create a strong national army (the best prop for federal authority over the states), and to frame a national tax structure to underwrite the war.

Taxation proved the most difficult problem for the presidency. Secretary Memminger had hard-money penchants in a soft-money environment. And a laissez-

"*As soon as the war was concluded and had established that that foreign country couldn't be foreign after all, the barren fields, ruined cities, and collapsed economy of the South became a national liability.*"

ROBERT PENN
WARREN
THE LEGACY OF
THE CIVIL WAR, 1961

Davis gave most of his cabinet members wide latitude in running their offices.

PAGE 527

The president sought his cabinet members' advice and tolerated opinions contrary to his own.

PAGE 527

faire Congress could never quite face up to the harsh decisions war demanded. Land, cotton, and slaves were the Confederacy's wealth resources, and the president urged their taxation. Congress dodged that necessity for a time with bond issues, loans, and some fairly innovative measures such as the tax-in-kind, the produce loan, and other levies. Finally a tough value-added tax came, along with an income tax, an excise tax, and taxes on virtually everything. But it was too late; expenses ran away with the currency. By early 1864 the Treasury Department did not know how many notes were circulating.

As Confederate money lost value, so did the foreign credibility of the cause. The president sponsored the important loan through Emile Erlanger and Co. in 1863 for $15 million. Discounted almost from the outset, the loan actually produced somewhere between $6 million and $10 million. More would have been lent by the Erlangers, but a conscientious, if whimsical, Congress did not want to encumber future generations.

A recent scholar, Douglas Ball, in *Financial Failure and Confederate Defeat* (1991), echoes a lingering theme in showing that financial chaos might have been avoided and lays the blame for failing to come to a modern financial system on the executive branch. Davis and Memminger, he says, had every reason to know better. That is probably true, but blame needs softening with sympathy. These men were caught up in the daily rigors of war; they were pushing an agrarian system into modern times and trying to shove a reluctant Congress the same way. That anything was done to sustain the currency is a triumph for the presidency and its branches.

Davis embodied the presidency. He is flayed often for aloofness, for petty defense of incompetent friends—General Bragg, Commissary Gen. Lucius B. Northrop, Gen. John Pemberton—and, like most presidents, he did rely on cronies. But he deserves much credit for changing himself from a private to something of a public man. Though he thought politicking distasteful, and surely unnecessary in a warring nation, he took several "swings around the Confederacy" to speak about the war, to sustain public morale. He lacked Abraham Lincoln's language in persuasion, but he had a zealot's fiery eloquence at times when he talked of the cause he tried to win.

War powers expanded from the moment the war began. The role of the commander in chief enlarged by necessity as Davis pushed military organization, recruiting, strategy, and logistics. Davis did not, despite later accusations, overcommand his forces. Some field commanders received special direction if the chief executive thought they needed it, but trusted ones like Lee, Albert Sidney Johnston, Bragg, and E. Kirby Smith enjoyed wide discretionary powers. Presidential attention went to strategical and logistical support of major campaigns (Albert Sidney Johnston's operations in Tennessee in 1862, for instance), but tactics were left to battle commanders.

Confederate affairs increasingly involved the presidency in state affairs. State rights supporters frayed Confederate nationalism and President Davis conducted wide correspondence with various governors in an effort to prop up their commitment to the war. Governors Joseph E. Brown of Georgia and Zebulon Vance of North Carolina worked almost openly against the cause, and Davis fought them with letters, speeches, and proclamations. State rights governors hampered a national strategy by forcing the president to fragment concentration of forces in defense of particular states. As the executive branch grew in power, it confronted these governors with increasing zeal but uneven results. Important legislation aimed at increasing national power (conscription, impressment, partial commandeering of space on blockade runners, heavy taxation) received presidential support before a fractious and reluctant congress.

Acutely aware of the need for centralized national power, the president fought for a strong war program. He expanded war powers by giving authority to the military departments and supported patriotic governors with such aid as a beleaguered executive could give. Congress followed the executive lead in much war legislation. But it balked at suspending habeas corpus by fiat and grudgingly moved toward a federalism that seemed too much like Abraham Lincoln's Union.

The presidency intruded into almost every phase of Confederate life as regulations abounded to manage the draft, impressment, taxation, manufacturing, transportation, even state legislative matters affecting the war. A presidential hand increasingly touched logistics. Influenced by such able logisticians as Gen. Josiah Gorgas, the chief of ordnance, the president worked to improve roads and railroads and to break or elude the blockade.

That the war lasted for four years is largely the result of Davis's expansion of the powers of his office. Presidential zeal transformed a fragmented feudalism into a small, modern martial nation. Because that happened, the Confederate executive is worth examining as an important facet of the American presidency.

[*See also* Cabinet; Davis, Jefferson.]

— FRANK E. VANDIVER

PRICE, STERLING

Price, Sterling (1809–1867), U.S. congressman, antebellum governor of Missouri, and major general. Born in Virginia to a wealthy, slave-owning family, Price moved with them to Missouri in 1830. Elected to Congress in 1844, he left his seat to lead a regiment in the Mexican War, during which he received promotion to brigadier general and became military governor of Chihuahua. After he had served one term as governor of Missouri, his popularity and moderate Unionist stance earned him election as president of the 1861 state convention charged with deciding the issue of secession; the convention voted against it. But Price became angered by radical Unionists in St. Louis, in particular Congressman Frank P. Blair and Federal army captain Nathaniel Lyon, who were working to forestall secessionist efforts in the state. As a result, Price offered his services to secessionist Governor Claiborne F. Jackson as commander of state militia forces.

In an effort to prevent war in Missouri, Price signed an agreement with Federal Western Department commander William S. Harney that both sides would maintain neutrality. Blair and Lyon promptly abrogated the agreement by persuading President Abraham Lincoln to remove Harney from command. After a famous conference with Union leaders on June 11 at St. Louis's Planters' House Hotel, Price mobilized his state troops to oppose the Federal force Lyon was leading toward the state capital. Defeated at Boonville (Price was not present), the state troops retreated with Price to the southwestern corner of the state, where he collected and trained nearly 10,000 state guard recruits. While there, Price traveled to Arkansas and persuaded Confederate commander Ben McCulloch to enter neutral Missouri and join forces to attack Lyon, encamped at Springfield. On August 10, at Oak Hills, the Southern forces defeated Lyon's Federal troops in a battle that resulted in Lyon's death and a Union withdrawal. Buoyed by his ensuing popularity, Price in September marched northward, besieging and capturing 3,000 Federal troops and supplies at Lexington. Pressed by troops under John C. Frémont, he then retreated into Arkansas.

In March 1862, Price (called "Old Pap" by his men) again joined forces with McCulloch in the newly formed Army of the West, under overall command of Earl Van Dorn, to drive Federal forces from northern Arkansas. After being defeated at Elkhorn Tavern, he and his troops officially joined the Confederate army, and Price was commissioned a major general. Against the Missourian's wishes, Van Dorn transferred the army to northern Mississippi to assist Confederate defensive operations in the area against Federal forces under Ulysses S. Grant. Angered by this apparent abandonment of the Trans-Mississippi theater, Price twice traveled to Richmond and confronted President Jefferson Davis, engendering poor relations between the two. Davis called Price the vainest man he had ever met.

"OLD PAP"

Maj. Gen. Sterling Price, antebellum governor of Missouri, led Confederate forces in Missouri, Arkansas, Kansas, and the Indian Territory (now Oklahoma).

LIBRARY OF CONGRESS

Price led forces in successive defeats at Iuka and Corinth before receiving transfer again to Arkansas in the spring of 1863. After leading a mismanaged attack on Helena, Price wintered his troops at Camden. The following spring he and E. Kirby Smith took part at Jenkins' Ferry in successful defensive operations against Union forces under Frederick Steele in the Red River campaign. In an effort to liberate his home state and raise recruits, Price invaded Missouri in the fall of 1864 with a force of 12,000, mostly cavalry. While advancing on St. Louis in September, Price fought a bloody engagement at Pilot Knob and then headed west along the Missouri River pursued by a large Union force. After being defeated in a battle at Westport, he retreated in late October with his troops as far as Texas before turning back to Arkansas.

After the war, rather than surrender, Price escaped to Mexico, where he founded Carlota, a colony of ex-Confederates. When Maximilian's Mexican empire collapsed, Price returned to Missouri in early 1867, where he died suddenly less than a year later.

— CHRISTOPHER PHILLIPS

PRICE'S MISSOURI
RAID

This grand though ultimately unsuccessful cavalry raid in September and October 1864 was conducted by Sterling Price, major general and commander of the District of Arkansas and Missouri, and E. Kirby Smith, commander of the Trans-Mississippi Department. They planned to capture St. Louis and recover Missouri, controlled by Union troops since the fall of

P

1861, for the Confederacy. In July 1864, when transfer of two Union corps to Mississippi weakened Federal strength in Louisiana, exiled Missouri Governor Thomas C. Reynolds wrote Price proposing a cavalry raid into Missouri. Eager to lead an expedition into his home state, Price met with Smith at Shreveport, Louisiana, in early August. Price had become convinced by members of the Order of American Knights, a secret organization loyal to the Confederacy, that such an invasion would cause thousands of recruits to swarm into the Southern ranks. Moreover, Price believed that a successful raid would exacerbate Northern dissatisfaction with the war and contribute to Abraham Lincoln's defeat in the upcoming presidential election. Then Lincoln's Peace Democrat successor, George B. McClellan, would recognize the Confederacy and sue for peace.

On August 4, 1864, Price received orders to make arrangements to invade Missouri, providing him with command of all cavalry west of the Mississippi. Three weeks later, he turned over command of his district to Maj. Gen. John B. Magruder and ordered Brig. Gen. Joseph O. Shelby to attack DeVall's Bluff, Arkansas, located on the White River, to divert the attention of Federal forces at nearby Helena. On August 28, Price left Camden, Arkansas, assuming command of cavalry divisions under Maj. Gens. John Sappington Marmaduke and James F. Fagan the next day. Proceeding to the Arkansas River, the column crossed on September 6 at Dardanelle. On September 12, the force made its way over the White River and the next day rendezvoused with Shelby's force at Pocahontas. While there, Price organized the Army of Missouri into three divisions under Marmaduke, Fagan, and Shelby, totaling 12,000 men and fourteen guns. Over 4,000 of his troops were unarmed, since Shelby had only recently conscripted them from northeastern Arkansas. Price hoped to obtain supplies and arms in Missouri.

Traveling in three parallel columns in order to gather forage and provisions, the force entered Missouri on September 19 and arrived at Fredericktown five days later. There Price received word that 1,500 Federals under Brig. Gen. Thomas Ewing lay poised at Ironton, twenty miles west. Moreover, he learned that a Union infantry corps under Maj. Gen. A. J. Smith had been diverted from Mississippi and was now encamped south of St. Louis. Price dispatched Shelby's division to Mineral Point to wreck railroad bridges between Ironton and St. Louis in order to prevent Smith from reinforcing Ewing. Price himself advanced toward Ironton on September 26. His force encountered slight resistance at Arcadia and quickly pushed Federal troops into Fort Davidson, a hexagonal earthen structure at nearby Pilot Knob.

The fort was armed with sixteen cannon and protected by nearly 900 yards of open meadow. But rather than position artillery on the mountains surrounding it and shelling it into submission, Price unwisely ordered a frontal assault at 2:00 P.M. Within twenty minutes, the Southern troops suffered more than 1,000 casualties, many from Price's most experienced brigades who had advanced several times to the very walls of the fort. Dismayed, he canceled further assaults, opting to use artillery from the heights. During the night, Ewing blew up the powder magazine and escaped with his command to Potosi, 25 miles distant, leaving the fort, cannons, and supplies to the Confederates. In all, the Federals had suffered less than 100 casualties. Discovering the following morning that Ewing had escaped, Price sent Shelby and Marmaduke in pursuit. When they learned that 4,500 Federal cavalry under Brig. Gen. Alfred Pleasonton were advancing from St. Louis to reinforce Ewing, both units withdrew.

The decimation of his best troops at Pilot Knob and the arrival of Smith's 8,000-strong veteran corps at St. Louis convinced Price that any hope of capturing the city had passed. Yet, despite the obvious setback, Price believed that the continued presence of a large, supplied army would not only entice volunteers but might yet stir public opinion and affect the outcome of the November election. On September 30, after sending Shelby's cavalry as a feint toward St. Louis, Price began a slow march westward along the south bank of the Missouri River, hoping to gain recruits and foraging for supplies. As they moved toward the state capital, Jefferson City, the columns destroyed bridges and miles of the Pacific Railroad's track, avoiding all conflict other than minor skirmishes. Despite the supreme commander of the Order of American Knights' calling on members to enlist in Price's Army of Missouri, recruits proved sparse and many of those taken were unwilling to be disciplined. Moreover, Price's languid pace allowed nearly 7,000 Federal militia and regular troops to fortify the capital, rendering its capture difficult. On October 5, Price occupied Hermann, but shaken by the debacle at Pilot Knob and harassed by Pleasonton's cavalry, he bypassed Jefferson City and proceeded toward Boonville, which he occupied four days later.

At Boonville, Price added some 2,000 recruits, bringing his total force to 15,000, though many were unarmed and untrained. Moreover, looters and pillagers, including seasoned guerrillas and bushwhackers, abounded among new recruits. Their exploits had become so notorious that Governor Reynolds wrote Price in disgust, claiming that his troops' ravaging of the river counties would make it difficult to supplant the state's provisional Unionist government. Desperate for arms, Price on October 14 sent Shelby with a brigade to Glasgow, where locals reported that Federals had stored a large cache of weapons. Though Shelby captured more than 500 troops, the Union soldiers were able to destroy the arms before surrendering. Meanwhile, the rest of the army took up the march westward, with a detachment under Confederate partisan leader M. Jeff Thompson raiding Sedalia and capturing the militia there. Throughout, Union elements skirmished with Price's rear guard, which was protecting his cumbersome five-hundred-wagon supply train loaded with booty.

As Price plodded through the center of the state, Maj. Gen. William Rosecrans, commander of the

Department of Missouri, mobilized forces to trap and destroy the invading army. In addition to instructing Pleasonton to dog Price in an effort to slow him, Rosecrans sent A. J. Smith's infantry to Sedalia in pursuit of the Confederate column and ordered 4,500 veterans under Maj. Gen. Joseph A. Mower to move from Arkansas to assist. Finally, he tried to communicate with Maj. Gen. Samuel Curtis, commander of the Department of Kansas, and have him send troops to trap Price between the converging Federal forces. Though ignorant of Rosecrans's plan, Curtis was well aware of Price's whereabouts and massed more than

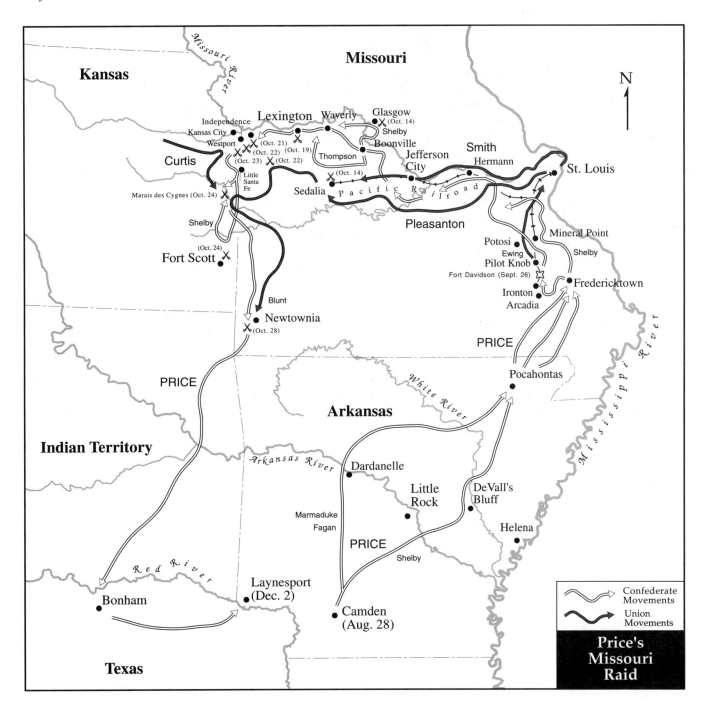

Against Price's wishes, Van Dorn transferred the army to northern Mississippi to assist in defending against Federal forces under Grant.

PAGE 447

15,000 militiamen and regulars near the border. On October 15, he ordered forward three brigades under Maj. Gen. James G. Blunt to Lexington, Missouri. Because most of Blunt's force were militia and would go no farther than the Big Blue River, six miles east of Kansas City, only 2,000 regulars reached Lexington.

Price's army reached Waverly, Missouri, on October 18 and the next day moved toward Lexington. Shelby encountered Blunt's lead units and pushed them back easily. Now aware that separate Union forces numbering more than twice his own were encircling him, Price moved quickly both to prevent Smith and Blunt from effecting a juncture and to leave himself an avenue of escape. He turned southward, planning to position his men between the two Union forces and defeat each in turn, and then to confront Curtis. On October 21, at the Little Blue River, Price encountered 400 dismounted horsemen with two howitzers, a token contingent of Blunt's troops. Blunt's main force had fallen back on the Big Blue, where Curtis's militia was entrenched on the steep west bank of the river. After a sharp skirmish, Price's men forced the small group of Federals to retreat to the hills behind the river. But as the Confederates continued their assault, Blunt returned with the rest of his infantry and artillery, most of whom were armed with repeating rifles and breechloaders. The Federals' superior firepower pushed back the advancing Confederates briefly, but Price's superior numbers soon threatened to turn both of Blunt's flanks, forcing the Union troops to retreat. That night, Blunt rejoined Curtis at the Big Blue.

On October 22, Price sent Marmaduke's division to the east to keep Pleasonton at bay and sent one brigade of Shelby's division to feint against Curtis at the main crossing ford of the Big Blue. Price's major thrust, made by brigades under Thompson and Sidney D. Jackman, came at Byram's Ford, the next upstream crossing, but in three hours of hard fighting, they were unable to prevail. Late in the afternoon, Alonzo Slayback's regiment found an uncontested crossing farther upriver. Taking that route, they fell upon the exposed right of Curtis's line. As the Union line withdrew, Shelby pushed his entire division across and drove the Federals toward Westport. With nightfall, the Confederates were forced to break off the attack before they could complete the victory, allowing Curtis to reform his line just south of Westport.

While Price successfully forced a crossing of the Big Blue, Marmaduke in the rear experienced defeat. Pleasonton crossed the Little Blue and mauled William L. Cabell's brigade, taking nearly 400 prisoners and two cannons. Fighting through Independence, Pleasonton's cavalry pushed Marmaduke's division almost to the Big Blue. Marmaduke fell back to the west side of the river at nightfall and sent word to Price

that the army was in danger of being trapped and destroyed. Fearing the loss of his men and his valuable wagon train, Price made preparations for a fighting withdrawal to the south.

At daybreak on October 23, Price sent Shelby's division, supported by two of Fagan's brigades, to attack the Federals at Westport. During two brutal hours of fighting, the opposing lines of horsemen charged and countercharged in the rolling woodlands along Brush Creek. Meanwhile, Pleasonton hurled a savage assault against Marmaduke at Byram's Ford, both sides taking heavy losses. By noon, Marmaduke's troops had spent all their ammunition, and they broke into a rout across the prairie, with Federal horsemen thundering after and capturing hundreds of them. Simultaneously, Blunt launched an attack on Shelby's line, nearly breaking the Confederate right. Learning of the collapse of Marmaduke's division, Price ordered all troops to retreat southward while Shelby fought for time. As Marmaduke and Fagan streamed toward Little Santa Fe, only Shelby's dogged withdrawal saved Price's army from complete destruction. The Battle of Westport proved to be Price's high-water mark, the last major action to take place in the Trans-Mississippi region. The exact number of casualties is unavailable, but Shelby estimated he had left at least eight hundred dead and wounded on the field. Price fled southward with a disorganized mass of horsemen, cattle, refugees, wagons, and unarmed men.

Curtis failed to order a pursuit for twelve hours, enabling Price to escape the Union pincers and secure his wagon train. Ultimately Price would regret this decision, for the ponderously slow wagons retarded his mounted forces' retreat, allowing the Federals to overtake them just one day later at the Marais des Cygnes River, sixty miles south. While Marmaduke and Fagan held off the advancing Federals, Shelby returned with his command from a foray to Fort Scott, Kansas, surprising Pleasonton and allowing Price to cross the river. In the fray, Marmaduke was captured. That night, Price burned nearly a third of his wagons. Skirmishing continued the entire next day and night, and on the afternoon of October 28, Blunt (now leading the pursuit) caught up with Price's retreating column near Newtonia, Missouri. Again, Shelby managed to drive off the advancing Federals before assistance could arrive. On October 29, Rosecrans recalled all troops belonging to the Department of Missouri, leaving Curtis with just 3,500 cavalry to continue the chase.

Before the situation could be rectified, Price had crossed the Arkansas River and dispersed his forces, marching into Indian Territory. On November 23, they arrived at Bonham, Texas. When the column returned to Laynesport, Arkansas, on December 2, 1864, Price's army had marched an incredible 1,488 miles. Though it had destroyed miles of railroad in Missouri and had diverted a corps of Federal infantry destined for William Tecumseh Sherman in Georgia, Price's raid had failed largely to achieve any of its objectives, and his army had lost an estimated 4,000 casualties, mostly to desertion.

— CHRISTOPHER PHILLIPS

PRISONERS OF WAR

Since neither the Confederacy nor the Union expected a long war, both sides failed to plan for the enemy soldiers they would capture. There were in existence U.S. Army regulations known to both combatants, which placed upon the quartermaster general the duty of taking charge of prisoners and provided for a commissary general of prisoners to carry out responsibilities for them. Such an officer had served during the War of 1812, providing a precedent familiar to North and South. But people on both sides also knew that the War of 1812 and the Revolutionary War had been characterized by charges of atrocious treatment of American captives. Confederates and Federals therefore were suspicious from the start of how their foe would treat prisoners.

Before the outbreak of fighting, the two sides released most potential enemies whom they took into custody. The Confederates, though they held enlisted men as prisoners, paroled U.S. Army officers captured in Texas upon their promise not to serve against the South. The Union similarly paroled captured Missouri militia.

Once fighting began both the Confederacy and the Union improvised arrangements for prisoners. The United States was the first to create a formal system, naming in 1861 Lt. Col. William H. Hoffman as commissary general of prisoners. Hoffman, who was one of the paroled prisoners from Texas, was a veteran army officer with experience only in managing the limited number of men in the peacetime army as economically as possible. Like his Confederate counterpart, John H. Winder, who during most of the war was the officer principally responsible for prisoners, Hoffman was preoccupied with preventing prisoners from escaping. To hold his captives, Hoffman began by leasing Johnson's Island on Lake Erie near Sandusky, Ohio. Though Hoffman originally intended it to be the main depot for Confederate prisoners, the rapid expansion of the war outstripped the capacity of the barracks, and it came to be used mainly to hold officers.

Hoffman then pressed into service Union training camps at Camp Randall (Madison, Wisconsin), Camp Douglas (Chicago), Camp Butler (Springfield, Illinois), Camp Morton (Indianapolis), and Camp Chase (Columbus, Ohio). Existing barracks were fenced in and new ones hastily constructed. The Union also used vacant buildings in St. Louis and seacoast forts such as Delaware on that river and Warren in Boston Harbor. Meanwhile the Confederates commandeered empty warehouses and similar structures for prisons. Both sides selected sites in considerable part because of proximity to transportation facilities, including rivers, bays, and especially railroads.

Prisoner Exchanges

As prisoners accumulated, they and their relatives pressed for their release on parole and exchange. An impediment was the insistence of the United States that it would take no action that recognized the legitimacy of secession or the legality of the Confederate States government. The Federals tolerated the generals in the field making exchanges with their opponents, and they permitted an informal system under which captured officers went on parole to the opposing capital and sought to arrange special exchanges for particular (often influential) captives.

But the Union declined to recognize the authority of the Confederates to license privateering by their people, and it proceeded in 1861 to bring captured privateers to trial as pirates. The Confederates, however, had captured at First Manassas over a thousand Union prisoners, putting the South in a position to retaliate if the privateers were executed. In November 1861, General Winder selected by lot high-ranking prisoners to undergo the same fate as the privateers. Although the Federal authorities concluded that exchanging privateers for hostages would not be equivalent to recognizing the Confederate government, and the Confederates for their part wanted even the limited recognition implicit in a plan for general exchange, the respective army commanders were unwilling to make this special exchange.

Since both sides had an incentive to end the controversy and be relieved of the growing burden of providing for prisoners, they agreed on July 22, 1862, to a cartel modeled on that between the United States and the British in the War of 1812. Gen. D. H. Hill on behalf of the South and Gen. John A. Dix on behalf of the North made an arrangement whereby all prisoners were to be paroled within ten days and sent to their own lines; a formal exchange would take place as soon as equivalent numbers had reached the lines. Agents for both sides were to administer the cartel, keeping records for an elaborate system under which men who could not be exchanged for enemies of equal rank would be matched according to a sliding scale of equivalents. (For example, a general commanding in chief or

Prisoners sometimes escaped individually from Libby, and on Feb. 9, 1864, 109 made the Civil War's best-known escape through a tunnel, with 48 being recaptured.

PAGE 328

*The Confederacy
lost considerable
numbers as
prisoners of war.*

PAGE 143

admiral equaled sixty privates or common seamen.)
The cartel stated that it would continue during the war
regardless of which side held the most prisoners and
that no "misunderstanding" would interrupt the release
of prisoners on parole. After the exchange began, both
sides closed all but a few transient prisons.

But the belligerents discovered that they would
have to create parole camps to house their men awaiting formal exchange, and sometimes they adapted
facilities previously used for enemy prisoners. Both
sides had difficulty in maintaining discipline among
these idle men, who were prohibited from doing military duty, and they feared the likelihood that some of
their soldiers in the field would readily surrender in
order to obtain a vacation from combat. Moreover, a
system resting on mutual trust was difficult to carry out
between combatants who had gone to war partly
because of their mistrust. Almost from the start,
Robert Ould, the Confederate agent of exchange, was
embroiled in a controversy with his Union counterparts characterized by interminable bickering letters.

One issue that arose in these disputes involved a
Confederate protest against Gen. Benjamin F. Butler's
execution of William B. Mumford for hauling down
the U.S. flag at New Orleans. Believing that the threat
of retaliation had forced the United States to back
down in such episodes as that of the imprisoned privateers, Ould's superior, President Jefferson Davis, made
a major tactical blunder. On December 24, 1862, he
issued a proclamation declaring Butler to be an outlaw

and ordering that no captured U.S. commissioned officer should be released on parole until Butler had been
caught and hanged. At the same time he ordered that
black troops when captured should be turned over to
the authorities of the state in which they were taken.
He and the Confederate Congress subsequently
resolved that captured white officers of black units
were to be tried and put to death. The Confederates
thus had taken actions that effectively ended the
release of officers under the cartel, after May 25, 1863.
Moreover, Confederate threats to retaliate against captured Union officers for the execution of two Confederates captured while recruiting, allegedly behind the
Union lines, proved ineffective. Although the Confederates held another lottery among their prisoners, they
found that the Federals by capturing Brig. Gen.
William Henry Fitzhugh Lee, son of Robert E. Lee,
had obtained a hostage that could not be topped in the
game of threatened retaliation.

Meanwhile the exchange of noncommissioned officers and privates had continued. But the belligerents'
exchange agents became involved in controversy over
the legality of paroles of prisoners associated with the
great battles of the summer of 1863, and in July the
United States decided to cease further deliveries of
prisoners. Butler, despite his status as an outlaw
imposed by President Davis, claimed that he could
break the deadlock over exchange, and in early 1864
the Union authorities permitted him to try. He succeeded only in exchanging two experimental boatloads

of prisoners. In March 1864, he and Ould came to a final parting of the ways over the status of black soldiers. Ould agreed that those blacks who had been free before the war would be treated as prisoners of war but refused to grant such status to those who had been slaves. Inconsistent with this declaration, however, the two navy departments exchanged several naval prisoners without raising questions of race or slave status.

Indeed, though the new Federal general in chief, Ulysses S. Grant, urged Butler to insist on equal treatment for black troops, he privately raised several objections to exchanges. He indicated that ceasing exchanges would have the effect of discouraging easy surrenders and desertions to the enemy. He also pointed out that the Confederate conscription system permitted them to put into the field anyone released by the United States. "If we commence a system of exchange, which liberates all prisoners taken," he argued, "we will have to fight on until the whole South is exterminated." Instead of openly acknowledging this brutally realistic argument, Butler and Grant repeatedly demanded that the Confederates agree that their proposals for a man-for-man exchange include ex-slaves as well as other prisoners. Regular exchanges were not resumed during the 1864 campaign season.

Prison Conditions

As the unexchanged prisoners accumulated, both sides crowded more men into existing prisons and built new ones. The Union opened camps at Rock Island, Illinois, and Point Lookout, Maryland (the latter being the only Federal facility to use tents exclusively), and in July 1864, began to move prisoners into a fenced camp at Elmira, New York, which quickly became one of the more overcrowded and deadly Union prisons. Meanwhile, the Confederates had built a stockade at Andersonville, Georgia, which grew into the largest and most notorious Civil War prison. The overflow was sent to several smaller prisons. By the end of 1864, the incidence of deaths at one of these, the camp at Salisbury, North Carolina, began to rival that at Andersonville.

OFFICERS. The inmates of both sides' prisons, new and old, henceforth experienced for a prolonged period conditions that previously had been mostly temporary. A prisoner's treatment was strongly affected by whether or not he was a commissioned officer. Both sides tried to house officers separately from enlisted men and usually in different prisons. One reason was the military tradition that officers had every interest in upholding—they were to be treated as gentlemen. Moreover, segregation of imprisoned officers from enlisted men had the practical effect of disrupting enemy military organization and discipline, facilitating control of the prisoners. (Indeed, the relatively few instances in which officers and men were temporarily

held close to one another resulted in their increased plotting to escape, which convinced authorities of the importance of separation according to rank.)

Since officers were less numerous than enlisted men, their prisons were always smaller, which made for better sanitation. Moreover, because officers usually came from above average economic backgrounds and were better paid, they could buy additional food and comforts, and during most of the war both sides permitted them to do so. Thus, though mortality was high among officers on Civil War battlefields, it was relatively low in the prisons. Nonetheless, highly literate officers, resentful of their captivity, often wrote complaints about their treatment, which added to the notoriety of the Confederates' Libby Prison and the Union's Johnson's Island.

One of the few areas in which officers might suffer more than enlisted men was in that of retaliation. As mentioned above, their status made them obvious targets when either side wished to put pressure on the other. The most notorious instance of their literally becoming targets occurred in the summer of 1864. The Confederate commander at Charleston proposed to discourage the Union bombardment of the city from Morris Island by confining in it fifty high-ranking Union prisoners. With the approval of President Davis, the men were taken into the city. When the local Union commander learned of this and requested that fifty Confederate hostages be sent to him for the same purpose, the Confederates disingenuously denied that they had intended to place captives under fire and agreed to a special exchange of the two groups. Grant, upon learning of this violation of his suspension of exchanges, forbade its repetition.

Thus the Confederates did not succeed in an attempt to reopen exchanges by sending six hundred more captured officers to Charleston. Instead, Union officers, believing that the Confederates intended to place these prisoners under fire, ordered six hundred Confederate officers to be confined after September 7 in a hastily built stockade near the batteries on Morris Island. Housed in crowded tents on short rations, they were guarded by those men of the black Fifty-fourth Massachusetts who had survived the previous year's assault on Battery Wagner. Though most of the Confederates here and elsewhere resented and reacted hostilely to black guards, a few got along better with their keepers than their fellows liked. In October, the Federal authorities had the hostages transferred to Fort Pulaski, Georgia. For many years, this group of ex-Confederate officers recalled their sufferings as the objects of retaliation and proclaimed themselves "The Immortal Six Hundred."

PRISONERS' LIVES. Their physical setting contributed to the captives' misery. The Union usually

As Union prisoners accumulated, the Confederates were unable to provide suitable facilities for all of them, and terrible suffering resulted.

PAGE 143

housed its prisoners in flimsily built, scantily heated barracks. The Confederates used some warehouses and similar buildings but far more camps, with tents for only a minority of the prisoners. Large numbers were forced to burrow into the earth with little or no shelter from the weather. When critics of the Confederacy asked why the prisoners could not have been permitted to cut timber to build their own huts, a partial explanation was the inability to guard working parties. A further problem at all of the larger prisons was the lack of facilities for disposing of human waste if the prison was not located along a large stream (as at Salisbury) or authorities were unwilling to spend money to build sewers (as at Chicago and Elmira). Inadequate shelter and sanitation contributed to the diseases that filled the insufficient hospitals.

Lack of clothing made conditions worse. Confederates often reached Northern prisons in garments badly worn and unsuited to winter weather. Federal commanders issued limited amounts of substandard clothing and sometimes permitted prisoners to receive clothing from relatives and friends. Confederate prison keepers, on the other hand, supplied no clothing to

their captives whose distress mounted as their uniforms wore out. Neither side provided prisoners with more than a limited number of blankets, and the plight of Northern prisoners was worsened by the Confederates' policy of systematically stripping newly captured men of bedding and other equipment. The typical prisoner was ragged and cold.

The most controversial aspect of the treatment of prisoners was the matter of food. Both the Confederacy and the Union claimed that they provided their prisoners with the same rations issued to their own troops; yet their captives claimed to be hungry and in many cases demonstrably lost weight. These contentions were less contradictory than they might seem. Although controversialists would later argue in precise terms about the ounces issued of various foods, the wartime records make it clear that the actual amounts were approximations. Moreover, both sides deducted a portion of the ration to create a so-called camp or hospital fund, theoretically for the prisoners' benefit. The keepers diverted additional rations to those captives willing to work around the prison. Thus no individual prisoner could count on receiving the officially

PRISON SECURITY PROBLEMS

Like the Confederate officers on Morris Island, prisoners of both sides and of all ranks often complained about their guards and the arrangements for security. As might be anticipated in a war involving strong popular emotion, the prisoners were often the focus of animus. As they were marched through enemy cities, civilians mocked and insulted them. In the prisons, officers and guards often treated them as despised enemies. Yet, though clearly some prison personnel acted the part of brutes and sadists, there is abundant evidence that many on both sides behaved with perhaps surprising kindness toward the men under their control. In several instances, clergymen, nuns, and members of the Masonic Order ministered to prisoners.

The problems of prison security that proved so controversial on both sides stemmed less from sadism than from the prison authorities' lack of confidence in their ability to maintain control. Neither side was willing to use first-class

officers or men to run prisons. By 1864 when the prisons were especially crowded, they were guarded in the Confederacy mostly by reserves composed of boys and old men, and in the United States by men on short-term enlistments or unfit for field service. Commanders on both sides complained of their guards' lack of training and discipline. These outnumbered, mediocre guards were expected to keep throngs of prisoners within often flimsy fences and stockades. Should any number of prisoners break out, it was unlikely that guards armed with single-shot muskets could intimidate them. To discourage outbreaks, several prisons directed artillery pieces at their inmates, and Johnson's Island issued revolvers to its guards. But the most common security precaution was to lay out "deadlines" along the fences, which prisoners were forbidden to cross. Considering the quality of many of the guards, it was probably inevitable that some shot on almost any pretext at prisoners near the

deadline. Neither side made any serious effort to enforce discipline in such cases.

Like prisoners in all times, those of the Civil War thought much about and often attempted escapes. The largest and best known was the exodus of 109 Union officers from Libby through a tunnel on February 9, 1864. Inmates of other prisons, Southern and Northern, also dug tunnels, sometimes successfully. Given the inadequacies of the guards, some prisoners found it possible to pass out in various disguises. At the unfenced camp at Columbia, South Carolina, some 373 prisoners simply ran the guard lines. Once out, prisoners on both sides often received help from sympathetic civilians, with Union escapees receiving assistance from mountain whites and slaves. Organized uprisings were less common, but a large one occurred on November 25, 1864, at Salisbury. Most prisoners simply endured prison life.

— FRANK L. BYRNE

announced quantity. And when the food available for the army as a whole was insufficient, as in the Confederacy, the needs of the guards were met first.

Ultimately, however, quantity was only part of the food problem. The basic ration of both sides consisted mainly of bread and meat. Unless supplemented with vegetables, the diet resulted in nutritional deficiencies and such diseases as scurvy. Guards could supplement from several sources; prisoners had only severely limited opportunities to buy vegetables. The Confederates issued none; the Union mainly did so only when scurvy actually appeared. As the cornbread issued by the Confederates was very rough and caused diarrhea, it is not surprising that their captives sickened and that many died.

Despite their hardships, most prisoners had an overabundance of leisure. Neither side attempted to compel them to work. The men read, participated in classes and religious meetings, and wrote diaries and letters. Many made jewelry or other small items as souvenirs for relatives or for sale to their captors. A significant minority seeking better treatment gave their paroles not to escape and agreed to do physical or clerical work for the prison keepers. Both sides thereby reduced the cost of running their prisons.

The prison life of blacks was very different. As the Confederacy declined to recognize them as legitimate soldiers, they often did not survive to reach the prisons; in several well-documented cases Confederate soldiers refused to give them quarter. But hundreds of black soldiers and civilian employees of the United States did reach the Confederate prisons where they were required to perform the more menial tasks. Others were sent to labor in niter works or to construct fortifications. Some were advertised in the newspapers in an effort to return them to slavery.

Prisoners as Manpower

White as well as black prisoners seemed to offer a source of manpower to both belligerents in the desperate year of 1864. The numerically inferior Confederates could gain particular advantage because their more rigorous conscription made it likely that they could return to the field a higher proportion of any exchanged prisoners. Hence the Confederates permitted prisoners in their hands to publicize their sufferings in Southern prisons and petition their government for an exchange. Grant and the Union leadership, however, believed that this would play into the hands of the South. Privately the Union commander admitted, "It is hard on our men held in Southern prisons not to exchange them, but it is humanity to those left in the ranks to fight our battles. Every man we hold, when released . . . becomes an active soldier against us. . . . If we hold those caught they amount to no more

than dead men." He persistently asked the Confederates whether their proposed man-for-man exchange included equal treatment for black prisoners. As the Confederates were unwilling to agree to this, they were unable to obtain reinforcements through exchange.

The Confederates then concocted schemes to recapture their soldiers in Northern prisons. Rebel agents in Canada with the aid of Northern sympathizers devoted considerable time and money to plots to release prisoners in Camps Douglas and Morton. All their plans proved abortive, including an attempt to capture a Federal warship and then release the Confederate officers imprisoned on Johnson's Island. Also futile were hopes of conducting a naval expedition against Point Lookout and an attempt as part of Jubal Early's 1864 raid on Washington to continue to that prison.

Unable to retrieve their own men, the Confederates in desperation attempted to recruit soldiers from the Union prisoners in their camps. The War Department authorized recruiting foreign-born soldiers whose loyalty to the United States was presumed to be relatively low. In the summer and fall of 1864, Confederate recruiters visited the Eastern prison camps for enlisted men, told the inmates their government had abandoned them, and offered extra rations and pay if they joined the Confederate army. They were able to persuade about 4,500 men, not all foreign-born, to join several battalion-sized units led by Confederate officers. The Southerners hoped to use these men behind the lines and for peripheral military operations. Unsurprisingly, their record was mixed and sometimes disastrous, though some did labor effectively as engineers for the Confederacy.

It was as workers rather than soldiers that the prisoners supplied the Confederates with additional manpower. As mentioned above, the South, like the Union, used parolees to help run their prisons. Without such aid the Confederate system could not have functioned. General Winder estimated that the services of some eight hundred captive workers at Andersonville alone saved the Confederacy a million dollars yearly. And the Confederates recruited skilled men for a variety of enterprises besides prison-related work. They attempted to run shoemaking shops at several prisons. At Richmond over one hundred prisoners worked in the quartermaster shops, making shoes, clothing, and other equipment for the Confederates. Others worked for public and private manufacturers of a wide variety of war-related goods.

Although the Union with its abundance of skilled labor made little attempt to use its prisoners thus, it recruited even more Confederate prisoners for combat duty. Confronted with an outbreak of Indian warfare on the Great Plains, the Federals met part of their need

At Andersonville, deficient planning paved the way for disaster.

PAGE 12

While the Confederates finished the stockade, the prisoners used bits of scrap wood and pieces of cloth to cover burrows in the ground that served as shelter.

PAGE 12

JAIL SPORTS

A lithograph from a drawing by Maj. Otto Boetticher shows a baseball game between Union prisoners at Salisbury, North Carolina, in 1863.

NATIONAL ARCHIVES

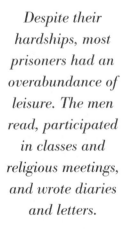

Despite their hardships, most prisoners had an overabundance of leisure. The men read, participated in classes and religious meetings, and wrote diaries and letters.

PAGE 455

for troops by enlisting prisoners to fight there rather than against their fellow Confederates. Organized into six regiments under Northern officers, the United States recruited about six thousand men, including several hundred recaptured Union prisoners who had previously joined the Confederates. Both sides tended to refer to their prisoner recruits as "Galvanized Yankees," verbal evidence of the suspicion that their new loyalty represented a thin coating. But those who fought for the United States for over a year after the war's end often rendered effective service.

The Effects of Politics

As unexchanged prisoners accumulated on both sides, the belligerents exploited their treatment for political purposes. In 1864 both the U.S. Congress's Committee on the Conduct of the War and a committee of the U.S. Sanitary Commission interviewed returned Union prisoners about conditions in Southern prisons. In addition to their verbal descriptions of horrors, both committees' reports included ghastly pictures of individual returnees.

The Lincoln administration used charges of mistreatment of prisoners to arouse bitter feeling against the South. Arguing that Confederate prisoners should be subject to the same treatment, the War Department reduced rations and forbade the sending of parcels from friends. Meanwhile Democrats and other opponents of the administration blamed Abraham Lincoln and Secretary of War Edwin M. Stanton for the lack of exchange and sought to use the prisoners' suffering as an issue in the 1864 presidential election.

The Confederates attempted to rebut Union propaganda and counterattacked with their own. To remind the world that Confederates also were spending long months in prison, President and Mrs. Davis proudly displayed in their White House objects made by time-killing prisoners. In October 1864, English sympathizers held a Southern Bazaar at Liverpool to publicize the sufferings of Confederate prisoners and raise money for their relief. In March 1865, a joint congressional committee denounced the Union reports of prisoner mistreatment as mere sensationalism. It claimed that the reports' illustrations showing almost skeletal men were not typical of the prisoners, and though not furnishing pictures of returned Confederates, the committee asserted that many of them were in as bad or worse condition as the Federals.

The Confederates denied any deliberate mistreatment of their prisoners and attributed any shortages of supplies to the uncivilized nature of the warfare being waged by the United States against the Confederate economy, citing such operations as Gen. Philip Sheridan's devastation of the Shenandoah Valley. Moreover, they sought to attribute the sufferings on both sides to the Union's refusal to exchange prisoners. The Confederates' belated reply to Northern charges, however, received only limited circulation before or after the war's end.

Meanwhile, the warring powers had agreed upon measures to mitigate the prisoners' condition. To reduce political pressure for a general exchange, the Union authorities agreed to release the sick. In September 1864, General Butler proposed the exchange of men believed to be unfit for field service within sixty days. Reports of the bad condition of the several thousand men released under this arrangement built pressure to relieve the remaining prisoners. Confederate exchange agent Ould suggested and Grant agreed to an arrangement whereby each side would be allowed to forward food and clothing to be distributed by paroled officers to its own prisoners. To make this possible for the Confederates, they were permitted to send through the blockade a shipload of cotton for sale in the North. One load was sent and both sides distributed large amounts of goods early in 1865.

NO GAMES

Life was harder—usually inhumane—at Andersonville Prison, Georgia. Prisoners line up for rations in this photograph by A. J. Riddle, Aug. 17, 1864.

NATIONAL ARCHIVES

At almost the same time, general exchange resumed. Beginning the process in January 1865, Grant accepted a previous Confederate proposal to exchange all prisoners being held in close confinement under various attempts at retaliation. The Confederates—so unable to care for their prisoners that General Winder had unsuccessfully suggested paroling them and simply sending them across the lines—now again attempted to reopen exchange. On February 11, Ould proposed to Grant the delivery of "all the Federal prisoners now in our custody" if the Union would deliver an equal number of Confederates. Grant quickly agreed and both sides notified their overjoyed captives that they would be released.

Why was the Union now willing to exchange? With the administration under increasing attack in and out of Congress for the failure to exchange, Grant had been given personal public responsibility for the controversial matter. He knew that the resumption of active campaigning was still weeks away and that the approach of William Tecumseh Sherman who was about to capture Columbia, South Carolina, made reinforcements for the collapsing Confederate armies a less critical concern. But what of the black prisoners whose plight the Federals had used to explain the earlier refusal to exchange anyone? Did the Confederate offer to free all prisoners include ex-slaves? Previously the Federal authorities had pressed the Confederates to be specific regarding the fate of former slaves. In 1865, the Union did not raise the question, and though the Confederates exchanged several hundred blacks, they never acknowledged returning one who had been a slave before the war. Lincoln's reelection and the anticipat-

ed end of the war had reduced the immediate political significance of the status of imprisoned former slaves.

Even as the war entered its final days, both sides continued to manipulate the prisoners for maximum advantage. Grant, correctly believing that his opponents were putting released prisoners into their ranks as quickly as possible, ordered that when possible physically unfit men should be sent first and that prisoners whose homes were in the West should be sent to the East. The Confederates, while too disorganized and harried to discriminate effectively, sought to send Union men who were sick or whose enlistments had expired. Like the Union, the dying Confederacy anticipated taking new prisoners and improvised facilities to hold them. As the surrender of Robert E. Lee marked the beginning of the end, however, the bulk of the remaining Confederate armies were paroled in the field without being held as prisoners of war.

Postwar Issues

It fell to the United States to provide for the repatriation of the prisoners on both sides. Federal prisoners released in the South were fed, reclothed, and returned either to their units or to their home states to be mustered out. As for the imprisoned Confederates, the Union authorities on May 8 ordered the release of all below the rank of colonel who were willing to take the amnesty oath of future allegiance to the United States, a privilege subsequently extended to all prisoners. Out of practical necessity, the Federals paid for their transportation home. The abandoned facilities that had held prisoners on both sides mostly disappeared except for the graves for which the United States ultimately assumed responsibility.

By July 1, 1864, Richmond authorities had sent 26,367 captives to a prison intended for 10,000.

PAGE 13

The Federal authorities also took charge of investigating alleged mistreatment of Union soldiers while in Confederate hands and of attempting to punish those responsible. The principal official in charge was Brig. Gen. Joseph Holt, judge advocate general. This Kentucky Unionist, moved by a passionate animus against the Confederates, ordered the arrest of a number of prison keepers and through his Bureau of Military Justice collected evidence and supervised trials by military commission. The flight from the country of several of the accused and the difficulty of finding witnesses after the demobilization of the Union army limited Holt's success. The best-known outcome of his efforts was the trial of Andersonville commandant Capt. Henry Wirz. After a military trial at Washington whose outcome was all but predetermined, Wirz was convicted of conspiring with "others unknown"—presumably the Confederate leadership—to mistreat Union prisoners and was hanged. More fortunate was the commander of Salisbury Prison, Major John H. Gee. After trial in the field, he was acquitted.

The trials came quickly to an end, but the government continued to make its case in the forum of public opinion. In the published records of the Wirz trial and other proceedings such as the trial of the Lincoln assassins, high Confederate officials from Jefferson Davis on down were linked with prison atrocities. In 1869 under Republican auspices, a committee of the House of Representatives investigated conditions in the former Confederate prisons, seeking evidence of Southern "barbarism" stemming from slavery. After hearing some three thousand witnesses, the committee produced a voluminous and highly negative report.

Ex-prisoners often drew upon these government documents to supplement their own recollections and diaries as they wrote memoirs of their prison days. Though a minority believed that their keepers had done their best, most were convinced that they had been the victims of a deliberate plot to destroy the prisoners. Some of them reflected the political partisanship of Reconstruction; others tried to make a case for pensioning the ex-prisoners.

Apologists for the Confederacy struggled against the tide. In memoirs, Jefferson Davis and others sought to show that they had tried to care for the prisoners. Minimizing their own roles in the attempts at retaliation, they blamed the Federal officials for the breakdown of exchange and the resultant suffering of prisoners of both sides. Former Confederates imprisoned in the North also wrote complaints about how they had been treated. No Northern prison, however, could equal the unique horror of Andersonville; moreover, fewer of the nation's publishers and readers of books were in the South. Thus the Confederacy's defenders were never able effectively to answer the Northern prisoners' charges.

The Confederacy's case fared somewhat better in the hands of professional historians. The Ohioan James Ford Rhodes, while doing research for his history of the Civil War, sought from the U.S. adjutant general statistics on the mortality rates in the prisons. He was told by Gen. Fred C. Ainsworth in 1903 that according to the best information obtainable, 211,411 Union soldiers were captured in the Civil War, of whom 16,668 were paroled in the field and 30,218 died in captivity; on the other hand, 462,634 Confederates were captured, of whom 247,769 were paroled and 25,976 died in prison. Rhodes concluded that the prison mortality rate was a bit over 12 percent in the North and 15.5 percent in the South, a difference less than he had expected. Though these percentages rested on admittedly incomplete records, they have been repeated by scholars ever since. Thus historians, including William B. Hesseltine, author of an old but still useful history of Civil War prisons, have not judged harshly the Confederacy's treatment of its captives.

Such has not been true of the popular literature. Even after the deaths of the prisoners, their memoirs and diaries have continued to appear in print to heap shame on their captors. After World War II, MacKinlay Kantor's widely circulated novel *Andersonville* (1955), based on the familiar charges against the Confederacy, suggested a contrived comparison with the horrors of the Nazi death camps and the culpability of their keepers. Interest in the treatment of American prisoners in later wars has helped keep alive the memory of those of the Civil War, ensuring that this topic will remain one of the more controversial aspects of the Confederacy.

[*See also* Andersonville Prison; *Enchantress* Affair; Galvanized Yankees; Prisons, *sidebar* Johnson's Island Prison; Libby Prison; Point Lookout Prison; Prisons; Provost Marshal.]

— FRANK L. BYRNE

PRISONS

The Confederate prisons began and ended more as a series of improvisations than as a systematic organization. Even before the outbreak of fighting, the Confederates held in temporary camps enlisted men of the U.S. Army taken prisoner in Texas. After the war began, the Confederates captured over a thousand Unionists at their victory at First Manassas and shipped them to Richmond. These they housed in Ligon's Warehouse and Tobacco Factory and in several similar structures. The officer responsible for these captives as well as for the Confederate soldiers and civilians held in other Richmond prisons was the city's provost marshal, Brig. Gen. John H. Winder. Winder had attended West Point and served in the U.S. Army. Because of his age (he was sixty-one when the war started) and probably because he had been lieutenant governor of Vera Cruz during the Mexican War, Winder received his behind-the-lines assignment and quickly became commander of the District of Henrico which surrounded the capital. Stern and unsympathetic, his attempts to regulate civilian life soon made him an object of hatred. Although at first some prisoners found him acceptable, his concern for security combined with the hardships of prolonged captivity in time caused the Union captives to blame him for their woes.

To reduce crowding, the Confederates almost immediately began to disperse their prisoners. They had acquired a cotton factory building in Salisbury, North Carolina, which they put into use. They housed others at Castle Pinckney in Charleston Harbor and at jails there and in Columbia, South Carolina. Seeking yet more space, the Confederates also used an abandoned paper mill at Tuscaloosa, Alabama, and the parish prison at New Orleans. Winder remained generally responsible for all these men, although on a rather vague basis. Unlike the Union, the Confederacy did not then have an office of commissary general of prisoners.

In 1862, Winder expanded his Richmond prisons. He took possession of the brick storehouse of Libby and Son, which became notorious as Libby Prison. Besides housing prisoners, it provided office space for Winder's subordinates who managed the local prisons. By midsummer, Winder had found additional space on Belle Isle in the James River on which he opened a rapidly growing camp. Besides the facilities for Union captives, Winder controlled Castle Thunder, a group of tobacco factories used to confine Confederate deserters, civilians, and political prisoners.

Feeding and providing for all these prisoners presented problems the Confederates very much wanted to eliminate. Hence on July 16, 1862, they agreed with the Union army authorities on a cartel providing for prompt paroling and exchange. They rapidly released the inmates of their prisons and closed or abandoned many of them. For some months, Winder was able to make do with a few temporary holding places (notably Libby) while retaining Castle Thunder and Salisbury as prisons for limited numbers of Confederate offenders. But by 1863, quarrels over the execution of the cartel had led to a breakdown of the exchange, and captives were again accumulating. The Confederates still did not appoint a central authority, and Winder continued to improvise prisons.

Because so many prisoners were in or near Richmond when exchange ceased, the Confederate capital became increasingly crowded. Winder converted Libby into a prison mainly for Union officers. To hold enlisted men, he impressed additional warehouses and

---

JOHNSON'S ISLAND PRISON
The "Northern Andersonville"

In October 1861, Lt. Col. William Hoffman, the U.S. commissary general of prisoners, examined the Lake Erie islands for a prison site and selected as the most practicable a three-hundred-acre island in Sandusky Bay, some two-and three-quarters miles from Sandusky, to which prisoners could be brought by rail and from which they could be moved by boat. On the island, half of which Hoffman leased from its owner and namesake, Leonard B. Johnson, there was a forty-acre clearing on which Hoffman had buildings for guards and prisoners erected. For the latter there were ultimately thirteen two-story barracks in a fifteen acre enclosure surrounded by a high plank fence with platforms for guards and two blockhouses with small cannons. At this early stage of the Civil War, the U.S. authorities thought that Johnson's Island would hold all their prisoners.

The prison almost immediately began to be used mainly for officer prisoners up to the rank of general, with the first arriving on April 10, 1862. The highest number held before the commencement of regular exchange was 1,462 at the end of August 1862. After a temporary reduction, exchanges broke down and the total rose to 2,763 by the end of 1863 and to a peak of 9,423 by January 1865.

Inevitably, escape was a preoccupation of the prisoners. Attempts at tunneling were almost never successful, but it was sometimes possible to deceive the guard at the gate or to scale the wall at night and then cross to the mainland on winter ice. Even then, rewards posted for escapees often induced recapture; still, a few prisoners reached Canada and were able to run the blockade into the Confederacy.

In 1865, first the resumption of exchange and then the end of the war rapidly emptied the prison. In September, the handful of remaining prisoners was transferred. By the following June, the buildings had been sold and the post abandoned. Parts of the site were used for orchards, quarrying, and summer resorts. In the mid-twentieth century a causeway was built to connect the island and the shore. Though remnants of the fortifications remain, the only publicly owned memorial is the cemetery whose 206 graves attest to the fact that this prison for officers was less fatal than many. A statue of a Confederate soldier gazes toward the South.

— FRANK L. BYRNE

enlarged the camp on Belle Isle. The presence of thousands of prisoners added to the war-swollen population of Richmond and made it difficult to provide food for all. By the winter of 1863–1864, soldiers and prisoners alike complained of hunger, and the prison authorities worried whether they could control their embittered charges. Moreover, they realized that so many enemies within the capital created a security problem, the gravity of which was underscored by a cavalry raid on February 28 to March 4, 1864, which reached the city's outskirts. To reduce the prison population, the Confederates removed hundreds to six tobacco warehouses in Danville, Virginia.

Seeking a more substantial solution, Winder sent several officers to Georgia to locate sites for additional prisons. He hoped to reduce the difficulty in obtaining food and simultaneously to move the prisoners as far as possible from Union forces who could free them. Andersonville was chosen for a stockade (officially named Camp Sumter for its county) that became the most heavily populated and notorious Confederate prison for enlisted men. In February 1864, the authorities at Richmond began shipping trainloads of prisoners to the still unfinished stockade. In May, they moved the imprisoned officers from Richmond to a camp at Macon, Georgia. Enclosed by a high board fence, the camp had only one small building, which was used as a hospital and as housing for generals; the rest improvised as best they could. Some fifteen hundred officers were at Macon in the summer of 1864.

To control the new prisons, the Confederacy sent General Winder who had been relieved of his Rich-

mond command. Setting his headquarters at Andersonville, he showed some concern over the wretched conditions of the pen and its inmates but devoted most of his attention to worry over its security, fearing breakouts, treachery by local residents, and Union rescue attempts. In July 1864, he was placed in command of all prisons in Georgia and Alabama, including an unfinished cotton warehouse surrounded by a fence on the Alabama River at Cahaba. Set up in 1863 as a temporary holding facility, the Cahaba Prison, which prisoners often informally called "Castle Morgan," held at one time over two thousand enlisted men. Though its prisoners were transferred several times, the Alabama facility remained in use until the war's end. It was less well known than others in the postwar period because of its smaller size and because a large number of its released inmates were killed in the destruction of the Mississippi steamboat *Sultana.*

At the same time Winder took charge of the Deep South prisons, Gen. W. M. Gardner was put in command of prisons in the other states east of the Mississippi. A Georgian who earlier had been wounded, Gardner, from headquarters at Richmond, supervised prisons in Virginia and North Carolina, which continued to be used largely for transients. When the Confederate War Department ordered the suspension of shipments to overcrowded Andersonville, the prisons farther north again began to overflow. Considering the deteriorating conditions, it is not inappropriate to compare the prisons to ill-constructed, partially blocked sewers.

Meanwhile conditions were slightly better in the Trans-Mississippi region of the Confederacy where

LIBBY PRISON

Over the course of the war, about 125,000 prisoners were held in this Richmond building commandeered from ship chandler and grocer Libby and Son.

IN THE PIT

Federals taken prisoner at First Manassas are contained by Confederates, top, at Castle Pinckney, South Carolina.

prisons, like every other aspect of life, were run independently of the Richmond authorities after 1863. The Confederates selected as sites for prisons training camps in Texas, which offered a supply of guards. One was Camp Groce at Hempstead; another and more important one was Camp Ford at Tyler. Its stockade enclosed five acres and was later enlarged to ten. As at Andersonville, the prisoners had to improvise their own shelter and received no clothing from their captors. They were issued rations of cornmeal and beef. Unlike most prisons, Camp Ford confined both army officers and enlisted men, as well as navy men and enemy civilians. At maximum it held over 4,500 prisoners at one time, but because of its abundant water, only 286 died out of a total of 6,000.

Meanwhile, General Winder struggled to create new prisons and to shift captives to more remote locations. In August 1864, at a site near the railroad at Millen, Georgia, he ordered work to begin on a stockade enclosing forty-two acres, which he called Camp Lawton after the Confederate quartermaster general, Alexander R. Lawton, a Georgian. With a strange pride, Winder remarked, "I presume it is the largest prison in the world." Although the interior was laid out

in a more orderly fashion than was Andersonville (from which most of its inmates were transferred), the prisoners again were left to improvise shelter. By November 8, 1864, some 10,299 prisoners had been incarcerated there under the command of Capt. D. W. Vowles. But a week later the approach of Gen. William Tecumseh Sherman's raiding troops forced the hasty abandonment of Millen. Winder had some of the prisoners shifted to temporary camps at Blackshear and Thomasville in southern Georgia and then returned some to Andersonville, where the Confederates belatedly erected a few sheds to shelter a minority of the inmates.

When the Confederates had sent some Andersonville prisoners to Millen, they had dispersed others to Savannah where they were held in a fenced camp. Still others were transported to a similar encampment at the fairgrounds in Charleston, with some crowding into the yard of the city jail. Earlier in the summer, the Confederates had moved the imprisoned officers at Macon to the same two cities. At Charleston the officers gave their paroles not to escape and were lodged comfortably in the Roper Hospital. Southern commanders at the besieged seaports objected to the accu-

P

To forestall Union raids on Andersonville, Winder recruited slaves to build earthworks and surround the enlarged stockade with a second wall.

PAGE 13

mulation of prisoners and moved quickly to rid themselves of them.

These movements of prisoners were decided upon by local commanders rather than by the man who on November 21, 1864, was placed in charge of all prisoners. The Confederate adjutant general issued an order putting General Winder in command of all guard personnel and inmates in prisons east of the Mississippi. Officers were warned not to interfere with his charges. At last the Confederacy had a commissary general of prisoners, but it was too late to do much good. The South's diminishing resources and Sherman's armies made it all but impossible to provide adequately for the prisoners or indeed to move them to places safe from recapture. Nonetheless the elderly general established headquarters at Augusta, Georgia, and set about his job.

The commander at Charleston, Gen. Samuel Jones, had begun in September 1864 to send off prisoners to the interior rail junction at Florence. There thousands were held in an open field while the local military built a stockade surrounded by an earthwork from which guards could keep watch. As at Andersonville and Millen, a stream ran through it, around which developed a swamp occupying six out of twenty-six acres. The men received rations so limited that by late January 1865, the commandant pronounced them near starvation. Of a total of 12,000 men at Florence, 2,802 died. While enlisted men suffered at Florence, their officers were only a little better off at Columbia, South Carolina. There in an open field they were directed to build huts before winter. When syrup was substituted for the meat ration, the prisoners called it "Camp Sorghum." Because so many escaped, the South Carolina state authorities consented to the transfer of the officers to a more secure location on the grounds of a local institution for the insane, which became known as Camp Asylum.

Meanwhile the government at Richmond decided on desperate action to free their capital of imprisoned officers and enlisted men. To eliminate the drain on the food supply of the besieged city before the winter of 1864–1865, they sent the officers to the tobacco warehouses at Danville where 2,400 prisoners of all ranks were crowded. Early in October they emptied the camp of enlisted men on Belle Isle, sending about 7,500 to Salisbury. Given the 800 military and political prisoners already there, the prison was instantly overcrowded. It was rather like someone trying to pour a gallon of water into a quart bottle. General Winder reported in December that conditions at Salisbury were worse than at Florence (indeed, both resembled Andersonville on a smaller scale).

Winder's solution was to build another prison. He sought property on the railroad fourteen miles above Columbia, and there at Killian's Mills began to construct a new stockade, which he hoped would, with Andersonville and Millen, house all his captives. Hence he moved his headquarters to Columbia. But unable either to supply his prisoners or to move them to safety from recapture by Sherman's troops advancing through the Carolinas, he suggested paroling the prisoners and sending them home without exchange. On February 6, 1865, just before the resumption of exchange, Winder died suddenly of a massive heart attack while inspecting the prison at Florence.

The prisoners rejoiced at the death of Winder, whom they viewed as the chief villain responsible for their sufferings. They circulated a rumor that his last words were "Cut off the molasses, boys." On February 14, the Confederates replaced him with Brig. Gen. Gideon Pillow, who had been largely inactive since being discredited by his involvement in the surrender of Fort Donelson. On March 20, he in turn was replaced by the invalided W. M. Gardner, superseded four days later by the more vigorous Gen. Daniel Ruggles. Under the supervision of these men, the prisoners in the Carolinas were moved up to a temporary holding site at Charlotte. Union forces subsequently seized the prisons at Columbia and Salisbury.

Meanwhile exchanges were occurring at Wilmington, North Carolina; City Point, Virginia; Vicksburg; and the mouth of the Red River. The Richmond prisons, including Libby and Castle Thunder, continued to hold mostly transient inmates until the city's fall. Even then, General Ruggles continued construction of the new prison at Killian's Mills and expected to house at Danville prisoners captured by Robert E. Lee.

With Lee's surrender and the collapse of the Confederacy, the prison system was abandoned. The last to close was Camp Ford, evacuated on May 17. Later the Federal authorities arrested a number of the prison officials. Though they were blamed then and later for the terrible conditions, far more responsibility lay with their superiors. They had delayed until too late the systematizing of the prisons and, like their Union counterparts, never gave enough attention to the welfare of the helpless pawns with which they were playing.

[*For further discussion of Confederate prisons, see* Andersonville Prison; Libby Prison; *See also* Enchantress Affair; Prisoners of War; Provost Marshal.]

— FRANK L. BYRNE

PRODUCE LOAN

A series of produce loans contributed to financing the Confederate war effort. The concept had its origin when many people became aware that the Confederacy had to acquire supplies for the military; that it had to secure funds sooner than it could establish a tax system;

and that it had to pay for those supplies when possible with bonds instead of Treasury notes in order to limit the currency and thus forestall inflation. Commodities, still in the hands of their producers, might be exchanged for twenty-year, 8 percent bonds. The produce loan was designed to persuade farmers and planters to lend to the Confederacy a portion of the proceeds from the sale of such staples as cotton, tobacco, and sugar; it might secure military provisions, too. The Confederate Treasury could employ the anticipated receipts as the basis for establishing credit in Europe and across the South.

The Confederate Congress inaugurated the plan in a measure approved May 16, 1861, and expanded its terms to $100 million from $50 million on August 19. Additional acts of April 21, 1862, February 20, 1863, and April 30, 1863, expanded it further. Many planters proved enthusiastic about the plan, though smaller farmers typically had greater need for cash for their crops. In any case, the produce loan had as its premise a sale of commodities, and the Federal blockade rendered the export of cotton problematic. In addition, volunteer personnel failed to canvass some parts of the Deep South, and with much of the upper South the scene of military action, tobacco remained only marginal to the plan's operation. Finally, conditions for many producers had changed mightily between the time in the summer of 1861 when they pledged a loan and the time that fall when the crops came in.

Like so much of Confederate finance, the produce loan was flawed in both conception and implementation. That the 1861 acts generated only $34 million, one-third the stipulated amount (and 1.1 percent of the $3 billion in aggregate Confederate revenue), points to the limited success of the program. To a degree, however, the plan achieved its objectives. The produce loan operated to restrain the issue of Treasury notes and thus postponed destabilization of the currency, and the cotton thus obtained helped secure the Erlanger loan.

[*See also* Erlanger Loan.]

— PETER WALLENSTEIN

PROSLAVERY

The term *proslavery,* as used by antebellum abolitionists and proponents of slavery, and by historians, encompasses two historical phenomena: first, the attitude of favoring slavery (particularly black slavery) and its continuance and of opposing any interference with it, and second, the emergence in the United States from the 1830s through the Civil War of a literature vigorously arguing that the institution of slavery was beneficial for both slaves and society. The term has also been used incorrectly and inconsistently to describe certain writings that denigrate the role of African Americans, Hispanics, Asiatics, and other ethnic groups in the United States.

Once believed to be peculiar to the Old South and the Confederacy, proslavery literature, recent studies have shown, appeared wherever slavery existed; in the United States proslavery books, tracts, and pamphlets were produced prior to the Civil War by a great variety of individuals in both the North and the South. Particularly important in the early articulation of America's proslavery outlook, for example, were individuals who were born or educated in New England and Northern states, well educated (especially at such institutions as Yale and Princeton), professional (clergy, lawyers, journalists), and among the nation's most eminent nonpolitical leaders. As time passed, however, America's proslavery writers more frequently tended to be individuals native to and educated in the South. Many were members of the intellectual and cultural elite of the period.

A number of the more important pieces of proslavery literature appeared in the 1830s and 1840s. Although some historians have cited an 1832 essay by Thomas R. Dew, *Review of the Debate in the Virginia Legislature of 1831 and 1832,* as the launching pad for the aggressive Southern defense of slavery, it was actually an argument against African colonization as a permanent solution to what were seen as the dual problems of slavery and a large African population in the United States. William Harper's *Anniversary Oration* (1836) is often noted as one of the next major articulations of a proslavery perspective. James H. Hammond's *Two Letters on Slavery in the United States, Addressed to Thomas Clarkson, esq.* (1845) expressed the widely held position in the South that not only was slavery not evil; it was a positive benefit to society.

Other studies of the arguments that slavery was a positive good have noted that they also appeared in contexts other than the Old South, including the British West Indies and Great Britain itself. As early as the 1790s, in the course of parliamentary debates on the African slave trade and the future of slavery in the West Indies, numerous British writers held that slavery was not only a benefit to the West Indian plantation economy. They also held that it was a benefit to Africans who were thereby saved from the "savagery" of their native lands to live in peace within the Christian religion under the guidance of enlightened Englishmen. Even at this early period of the Industrial Revolution, these writers argued that the lot of the slave was superior to that of factory workers and their families.

Wherever proslavery literature appeared, virtually identical arguments were used to justify the perpetuation

By 1850 abolitionists from the North were no longer welcome or safe to proclaim their message in the South.

PAGE 18

of the institution. Because most American slaves were African Americans, many arguments related to their African past. Proslavery authors generally maintained that Africans historically had lived in uncivilized, barbaric, and degraded conditions, that many had always been held in slavery, and that therefore they did not find slavery an unusual or irksome condition. Many also held that Africans were racially inferior and were incapable of being civilized or of functioning well in situations where they would have to compete with European Americans. In their view, Africans would always require supervision and control. Indeed, some argued, Africans were happier in an enslaved than in a free condition.

Other proslavery authors maintained that slavery was the most perfect labor and welfare system ever devised: because slaves were property—a capital investment—slaveholders had a direct interest in treating them kindly. To preserve their investment, slaveholders would provide housing, food, and clothing and guard their chattels' health and welfare. No other form of labor—especially "wage slavery"—provided such protection.

The institution, it was argued, also benefited society at large. Because slaves were controlled by laws and occupied a dependent condition, societies with slavery were ensured against radical and revolutionary movements. Whereas capitalism tended to abandon the

indigent and the ill, ran the reasoning, slavery provided a place and a caretaker for every individual.

Its advocates also held that American slavery was qualitatively different from other slave systems in history. Given the enlightened, religious, and freedom-loving character of Americans, they argued that slavery in the United States was the mildest and most benevolent form of slavery that had ever existed. The American system tended to civilize and Christianize barbaric Africans. The writers asserted that slaveholders, guided by the examples of slavery in the Bible, by Christian teachings, and by principles of the American Revolution, looked upon slavery as a "divine trust" practiced as God would have it for all ages.

Slavery, they further argued, was clearly a moral institution. This they supported by reference to the Bible. God had sanctioned slavery by placing his curse on Ham, by issuing laws for the governance of slavery among the patriarchs and the people of Israel, and by countenancing the practice in both the Old and the New Testaments. Not only did Christ and his apostles not condemn the practice of slavery; they admonished slaves to obey their masters and decreed that fugitive slaves should be returned to their owners.

Whereas many in America held with Thomas Jefferson and other framers of the Declaration of Independence that all men have the right to life, liberty, and

PROSLAVERY PUBLISHING

Some of the most widely distributed and frequently cited proslavery publications during and just before the Civil War were the following:

From the North: Nehemiah Adams (Congregational clergyman, Boston), *A South-side View of Slavery* (1854); Charles Hodge (professor, Princeton Theological Seminary), *The Bible Argument on Slavery* (1857); John Henry Hopkins (Episcopal bishop of Vermont), *Bible View of Slavery* (1861) and *Scriptural, Ecclesiastical, and Historical View of Slavery* (1864); Charles Jared Ingersoll (lawyer and congressman, Philadelphia), *African Slavery in America* (1856); Nathan Lord (president of Dartmouth College), *A Letter of Inquiry to Ministers of the Gospel of all Denominations on Slavery* (1860) and *A True Picture of Abolition* (1863); Samuel F. B. Morse (inventor, artist, and manufacturer, New York), *Present Attempt to Dissolve the Ameri-*

can Union (1862); Nathan L. Rice (editor and college professor, Chicago), *Lectures on Slavery* (1860); Stuart Robinson (editor and clergyman, Louisville, Kentucky), *Slavery as Recognized in the Mosaic Civil Law* (1856) (1865); Samuel Seabury (Episcopal clergyman and college professor, New York City), *American Slavery Distinguished from the Slavery of English Theorists and Justified by the Law of Nature* (1861); and Hubbard Winslow (editor and author, Brooklyn), *Elements of Moral Philosophy* (1856).

From the South: E. N. Elliott (lawyer and college president, Mississippi), *Cotton Is King, and Pro-Slavery Arguments* (1860); George Dodd Armstrong (Presbyterian clergyman, Norfolk, Virginia), *The Christian Doctrine of Slavery* (1857); Albert Taylor Bledsoe (college professor at the University of Virginia), *Essay on Liberty and Slavery* (1856); George Fitzhugh (lawyer and author, Virginia),

Sociology for the South (1854) and *Cannibals All!* (1859); James Henry Hammond (planter, governor, and U.S. senator), *Speech at Barnwell Courthouse, Oct. 29, 1858* (1858) and *Speech on the Admission of Kansas* (1858); Josiah Nott (physician, Mobile, Alabama), *Types of Mankind* (1854); Frederick A. Ross (manufacturer, clergyman, Alabama), *Slavery Ordained of God* (1857); Edmund Ruffin (planter, agronomist, Virginia), *The Political Economy of Slavery* (1857); William A. Smith (clergyman, president of Randolph-Macon College), *Lectures on the Philosophy & Practice of Slavery* (1856); Thornton Stringfellow (clergyman, planter), *Scriptural and Statistical Views in Favor of Slavery* (1856); and James H. Thornwell (clergyman, president of South Carolina College), *The Rights and Duties of Masters* (1850).

— LARRY E. TISE

the pursuit of happiness, proslavery writers insisted that such a right did not extend to the enslaved. Since, in these men's minds, slavery was a humane institution that provided for the comfort and care of those enslaved, it followed that it was a reasonable and fair practice, not inconsistent with the laws of nature. Essay after essay contended that the Founding Fathers never intended to argue that the enslavement of a servile race was inconsistent with the laws of nature.

Nor, they argued, was it theologically incorrect. God would not decree sin into existence. Indeed, it seemed to them that God specifically brought slavery into existence as a tool to save the "heathen." The master-slave relationship seemed just as divinely ordained as that of husband and wife or father and child; it would end only with the millennium or the end of time.

Most proslavery writers went beyond the mere justification of slavery as a moral and viable institution. They also held that in the master-slave relationship certain duties and responsibilities fell to the master. Whatever legal authority he had, the master was also morally responsible to provide the comforts of life to slaves, to give them just and fair treatment, to protect their families, and to provide religious instruction. When all was said and done, proslavery writers contended, masters were answerable to God for carrying out their divinely ordained roles.

Within the broad field of proslavery history there developed an American school of ethnology that—through pseudoscientific methods and theories—found the Negro to be a separate species from Caucasian whites. Dr. Samuel George Morton published *Crania Americana* in 1839 documenting his measurements and analyses of human skulls from all parts of the world. George R. Glidden, America's premier Egyptologist; Louis Agassiz, Swiss-born Harvard biologist; and many others added endless data intended to confirm the theory of separate species among humankind.

Although these ethnological treatises suggested separate origins for various races and thereby flew in the face of the biblical account of a single creation, the burgeoning field of scientific studies attracted clergymen who attempted to resolve the disparities among theology, science, and racial theory. Moses Ashley Curtis in North Carolina and John Bachman and Thomas Smyth in Charleston—all Northern-born and educated clergy—wrote profusely on the subject in religious as well as scientific publications.

Others made use of this pseudoscience either to defend slavery or to argue for the expulsion of blacks from America. Dr. Josiah C. Nott, a physician in Mobile, Alabama, and Dr. John H. Van Evrie, a physician in New York City, were among the most prolific popularizers of the theory. But the numbers of disciples were legion and included Sidney George Fisher of Philadelphia, Thomas Ewbank of Washington (U.S. commissioner of patents), and even Boston's Charles Eliot Norton, a conservative intellectual at Harvard.

Despite the abundance of arguments in the proslavery arsenal and the emergence of popular theory about racial disparities, typical proslavery literature wasted little space in recounting arguments that were largely part and parcel of the Western heritage. Most proslavery writers were concerned with other issues relating to the world of slaveholding. Many felt that those who opposed slavery were in actuality "jacobins," "infidels," and revolutionaries who wanted to upend not only slavery but also American society and government. Some were fearful that if slavery were abolished, America would forever harbor an alien population that might rise against whites or descend into "bestiality" and sap the energy and financial resources of the nation. Others looked with disfavor at the effects of laissez-faire capitalism on the nation's work force, wishing to avert what they saw as a system of wage slavery in the United States. Still others argued that slavery and the future of blacks in America were such divisive issues that they would lead to the Union's disruption.

Moreover, most proslavery literature in America not specifically intended to argue issues of race, ethnology, scripture, theology, or the economy contained a specific worldview that was conservative socially and philosophically, that was reformist and positive in purpose, and that promoted order and responsibility in society. It was not allied with any political party or movement; rather, it was an outgrowth of reactions to disruptive and revolutionary forces in the Western world. Fearful of the chaos they associated particularly with the French and Haitian revolutions, most proslavery writers excoriated abolitionists as irresponsible revolutionaries bent on destroying the American republic. To avoid such disruption, they espoused the reform of slavery, urging masters to exercise their proper duties and responsibilities to slaves and to bring their slaves into religious institutions.

Eventually the problems of slavery and Union became so intertwined that they could no longer be avoided. The election of Abraham Lincoln as president in 1860 brought the issues to a head. Immediately following his election, hundreds of orators and clergymen throughout the nation addressed the future of slavery and the Union in furious speeches and sermons. In the South, such men as Benjamin Morgan Palmer of New Orleans called for the Southern states to leave the Union and protect the "divine trust" of slavery. In the North, other voices concurred, including such prominent clergy as Henry J. Van Dyke of the First Presbyterian Church of Brooklyn and Rabbi Morris Jacob Raphall at B'nai Jeshurum in New York City.

"Whenever I hear anyone arguing for slavery, I feel a strong impulse to see it tried on him personally."

ABRAHAM LINCOLN
ADDRESS TO AN INDIANA
REGIMENT, 1865

P

*The Confederate
Constitution
empowered
Congress to
establish rules for
the government of
Confederate
soldiers.*

PAGE 368

As the nation's political institutions faltered, Southerners thought the time at hand when the South could pursue the practice of slavery without interference from outside forces. Proslavery ideas and arguments fused with religious images, as speakers envisioned the Confederacy building the Kingdom of God on earth complete with a perfected form of slavery. The new nation would become a harmonious organic unity with places for masters and slaves, capital and labor, merchants and craftsmen. Some men, such as Leonidas Spratt of Charleston, a proponent for the reopening of the African slave trade, thought that the time was at hand to augment the South's work force with fresh hands from Africa. Others, such as Henry Hughes of Mississippi, called the South's perfected form of slavery "warranteeism"; slaveholders, he said, owned not the person but his productive labor.

Alexander H. Stephens, Confederate vice president, took a contrary point of view in 1861 in what came to be known as the "cornerstone speech." Believing the popular literature classifying whites and blacks as separate species, Stephens asserted that the Confederacy provided an opportunity to enforce the laws of nature: "Our system commits no . . . violation of nature's laws. With us, all the white race, however high or low, rich or poor, are equal in the eyes of the law. Not so with the Negro. Subordination is his place. He, by nature, or by the curse against Canaan, is fitted for that condition which he occupies in our system."

Euphoria surrounding the creation of the Confederacy complete with slavery continued despite the onset of the war. In dozens of fast days and thanksgiving days proclaimed by President Jefferson Davis to celebrate military victories or contemplate the meaning of defeats, the barrage of proslavery pronouncements continued apace. Among the thousands of Confederate imprints still in existence—pamphlets, books, sermons, broadsides, and the like—half or more are reiterations of the centrality of slavery in Southern life and the appropriateness of the institution in the Confederacy.

Nor did the opening of a war for Southern independence halt the publication of proslavery literature throughout the North. After the election of Lincoln, Samuel F. B. Morse gathered like-minded individuals in first the American Society for Promoting National Unity (1861) and later the Society for the Diffusion of Political Knowledge (1863) to issue tracts in support of slavery and the right of the South to secede from the Union. He and his colleagues continued to defend slavery as a moral institution throughout the Civil War period.

And even with the end of the war and the abolition of slavery, some continued to argue the issue. In the South, disgruntled souls such as Robert L. Dubney,

clergyman and former aide to Thomas J. ("Stonewall") Jackson, carried on the debate. His *Defense of Virginia (and through Her of the South) in Recent and Pending Contests* (1867) was an angry digest of virtually every proslavery argument. Dr. John H. Van Evrie of New York presented the racist perspective on slavery as he had for many years in a new book entitled *White Supremacy and Negro Subordination* (1868). Evidence of the tenacity of the issue in America is further indicated by the fact that as late as 1868 Norwegian Lutherans meeting in convention in Chicago attempted—unsuccessfully—to rescind a church tenet originally adopted in 1861 declaring the practice of slavery both moral and consistent with scripture.

[*See also* Cornerstone Speech.]

— LARRY E. TISE

PROVOST MARSHAL

Provost marshals commanded military police in camps or on active service within the Confederacy and in occupied territories. They and their provost guards, collectively called "provost," served as the Confederate version of the Union Provost Marshal General's Department.

Military courts and provost marshals, as authorized by the Articles of War in March 1861, accompanied some armies even before First Manassas. Eventually, to help improve discipline, commanders established provost at every level from brigade to army and at each level within the military departments. Unlike the Union, however, the Confederacy did not immediately appoint a provost marshal general. Brig. Gen. Daniel Ruggles was so appointed in February 1865, and held the appointment until the end of the war in April.

Before that, Brig. Gen. John H. Winder functioned as de facto provost marshal general, in addition to being provost marshal of Richmond in 1861 and 1862 and afterward commissary-general for prisons. Winder, widely regarded as a martinet, was said to have been the most hated man in the Confederacy, a description based, no doubt, on his personal traits—belligerence, irascibility, abrasiveness, and arrogance—and his overzealous, high-handed execution of his duties, which, by their very nature, were difficult, contentious, and thankless. While he was roundly criticized and generally scorned by the public, many of his military contemporaries praised him as energetic, upright, and efficient. His operation of the passport system was commendable, resulting in thorough control of civilian and military movement. It is debatable, however, how effective the system was in achieving another of its chief aims, the apprehension of the spies, subversives, and traitors that were assumed to have infested Richmond. While Winder had some success in coping with crime in Richmond, and his police did reduce, for a time, the level of violence, he was unable to impose consistent or permanent law and order. Overall, Winder deserves credit for his devotion to duty and for his energetic performance as provost marshal. It is difficult to see, in view of the paucity of resources, how another officer could have done better. The task assigned him was probably beyond the capacity and talents of any officer.

A separate provost corps did not exist; rather, officers and men and units were detailed to provost duty, most units only temporarily, although a few served more or less permanently. The Twenty-fifth Georgia Battalion (Atlanta Provost Battalion) was one such unit, as were the First North Carolina, the Fifth Alabama, and the First Virginia Battalions—respectively, the provost guards of the Second Corps, the Third Corps, and the headquarters of the Army of Northern Virginia.

The absence of comprehensive provost strength records and the often ad hoc and transitory nature of such employment prevents definitive compilation of provost strength. The evidence does show that provost duty was manpower-intensive: in 1864 there were 1,200 men on provost duty in Richmond and some 2,200 in the Department of Alabama, Mississippi, and East Louisiana. Two years earlier, provost strength in the Army of Northern Virginia had been about 2,000. Assuming similar manpower allocations in other armies and departments, several thousand or more men experienced provost service.

The primary provost duty—to assist commanders in maintaining good order and discipline—eventually incorporated responsibility for arrest of offenders against military law (and often their custody); apprehension and return to their units of stragglers and deserters (perhaps the most important duty once the armies were in the field); operation on the railroads and throughout the nation of the passport system that was instituted to help the provost identify and capture stragglers, deserters, spies, and subversives; administration of martial law; initial custody of prisoners of war; and enforcement of conscription.

Performance of such intrusive duties, often with excessive zeal, made the provost odious to soldiers and civilians alike. Passports, for example, were seen as an intolerable oppression. Enforcement of martial law, which entailed such unpopular measures as prohibitions on liquor, caused more public outrage. Enforcement of conscription similarly tarnished the provost image. One particularly explosive issue was military arrest of civilians, which, although less common than in the United States, stood condemned as interference with state rights.

Other provost tasks included mobilizing and controlling black laborers; taking custody of captured black soldiers and Union deserters to the Confederacy; guarding hospitals and other vital installations and captured equipment and matériel pending salvage for Confederate use; stopping unauthorized departure from Confederate ports; and preventing valuable commodities like cotton or tobacco reaching the enemy through illicit trade or by seizure.

The provost frequently participated in operations, too, acting as advance and rear guards, reconnoitering the enemy, controlling the activities of scouts and spies, and, when necessary, joining in hard fighting, as they did in the Wilderness in May 1864.

After the Conscription Act of 1862, and more frequently after the 1864 act, many regular soldiers employed as provost returned to the various fronts, leaving disabled men, reserves, and over- and under-age men to fill their place. This posed an insoluble dilemma: using the less able as provost would degrade Confederate ability to keep order and maintain front-line strength; on the other hand, using able-bodied regulars would maintain provost effectiveness at the cost of reducing front-line fighting strength.

Notwithstanding insufficient manpower and the use of incompetent men; sometimes bad or indifferent leadership; abuses of power, which created controversy and dissension; and the inconsistencies of the military judicial system, the provost made a significant contribution to the war effort. Despite their mixed record, they were an important element in the maintenance of Confederate strength.

The enormous vituperation directed at the provost was, in effect, a backhand tribute to them. Although the public often regarded provost as useless, their vigorous execution of their duties also won them a reputation as efficient and ubiquitous. In any case, they became a pervasive feature of life in a beleaguered Confederate States of America.

[*See also* Military Justice.]

— KENNETH RADLEY

PUBLIC FINANCE

The Confederate era involved many innovations in public finance, for the Civil War was not just the end of the slavery era. It was also a transitional period characterized by a partial retrogression to past practices and simultaneously by innovative new procedures that looked forward to the Reconstruction epoch.

By 1862 Robert E. Lee and many other commanders had become convinced that the existing system was not ensuring prompt and certain punishment of offenders.

PAGE 368

The tax system simply failed to absorb a sufficient quantity of the Treasury notes from circulation.

PAGE 603

Money in Circulation

When the U.S. Constitution was debated and written in 1787, James Madison's proposal to allow the Federal government to issue its own currency (then styled "bills of credit") was voted down by a large majority. So too was a section prohibiting such issues. Simultaneously, the states were prohibited from issuing their notes as a currency, and this prohibition was thought to extend to any local government erected under their authority. (Because of these prohibitions, paper currency at this time consisted largely of notes emitted by state-chartered private banks.)

Despite these legal impediments, the United States during the War of 1812 did put out a few circulating notes. From 1837 to 1861, interest-bearing notes, originally intended to be closely held as an investment, were retained after their interest ceased to accumulate in order that they might be used as internal bills of exchange to make remittances to New York.

State governments, from 1789 to 1860, particularly in the South, issued small amounts of currency. North Carolina was the most serious offender, but Alabama, Kentucky, Mississippi, Florida, and Texas also circulated their own notes. Florida, as a territory, did so apparently with Congress's approval. Texas put out quite a few notes, presumably in its capacity as an independent republic. Practically all the other Southern states, except Virginia and Texas, chartered wholly owned state banks. The bills of these institutions were made tax receivable and their payment was guaranteed by the states. Chief Justice John Marshall declared, in *Craig v. Missouri,* that state notes were bills of credit within the meaning of the Constitution. He died, however, before a decision could be reached on state bank notes, and his successors upheld the validity of such issues.

Various counties and municipalities issued due bills in fractional parts of a dollar during the 1814–1821 and 1837–1842 depressions. This action was in part necessitated by the need to provide the public with a currency under the denomination of five dollars. The banks, for the most part, were prohibited from issuing such notes, and the hoarding of gold and silver coins meant that without local government note issues, there would not have been any currency between the copper cent pieces and the bank five-dollar notes. In light of this, they were urgently required for the needs of commerce.

These experiences played an important role in influencing the Southern people's currency policies from 1861 to 1865. Moreover, when it is remembered that John C. Calhoun, the intellectual father of the secession, had advocated a central government currency in 1837 as a cure for a crash and depression, it is not surprising that the Confederate, state, and local governments all issued their own currency.

CONFEDERATE CURRENCY. The Confederate government, in a reprise of events during the American Revolution, proceeded to issue a large quantity of paper currency, which depreciated heavily. To begin with, however, the South copied the antebellum practices of the United States by issuing interest-bearing Treasury notes. But on May 16, 1861, the Confederate Congress, contrary to the recommendations of Secretary of the Treasury Christopher G. Memminger, inaugurated a policy of issuing non-interest-bearing notes in denominations as low as five dollars. Such bills were clearly intended to serve as currency.

Subsequently, in 1862, Congress again took the initiative by ordering the issue of one-dollar and two-dollar notes. Only in 1863 was a fifty-cent note authorized. No lower-denomination note was ever issued because by that time the purchasing power of the Confederate currency had fallen to the point where anything under fifty cents would have been practically worthless.

Congress was encouraged in this policy by three considerations.

- First, it was recognized that taxes were unpopular and that in any case there would be delays before even a well-digested and comprehensive fiscal program could be put into effect. Thus, at a minimum, the issue of Treasury notes was necessary to provide mobilization funds.
- Second, there was also pressure to issue such notes because, unlike those emitted by the state banks, the states, or the local governments, Confederate Treasury notes were receivable throughout the country at their face value without being made subject to bank and note broker collection charges.
- Finally, the popularity of such notes with the financial community and the public differed markedly from the bitter opposition to them in the United States. The Northern banks did not want a more popular rival currency in opposition to their own notes. And in any event, prior to the end of 1861, the Northern banks were still exchanging coin for their notes. The Federal demand notes, by drawing coin from their vaults, threatened them with an ultimate suspension of gold payments on their notes and deposits.

On the other hand, the Southern banks had suspended the payment of gold and silver coin on their obligations (with the notable exception of New Orleans) by the end of 1860. Everyone by mid-1861 was used to an exclusively paper money currency and wanted to have the best available. A currency put out by the central government clearly fell into that category, and so the Confederacy, unlike the United States, never had to pass a legal tender law compelling creditors to receive its notes.

Once started down the slippery path of currency issues, the Congress passed act after act, steadily enlarging the amount authorized. It was hoped that the right of the note holders to purchase bonds paying 8 percent interest in coin would prevent the currency from becoming redundant. But as neither Congress nor Secretary Memminger took any positive steps to assure long-term coin payments, this protective device ceased to function after July 1, 1862, when specie payments on the debt ceased.

Under these circumstances, the prewar circulation, which had had a face value in coin of approximately $150 million, soon underwent a rapid expansion. The Confederate-issued currency amounted to $96 million by February 1862. Act followed act until October 13, 1862, when Congress ceased to put any limits on the amount of currency to be issued. By the act of March 23, 1863, the secretary was allowed to emit $50 million a month. Under these circumstances, it was not surprising that the total amount of such notes in circulation had reached nearly $800 million on April 1, 1864.

Since there was no effective tax legislation passed until April 1863, and few collections were made before the beginning of 1864, efforts to prevent a redundant currency were limited solely to making such notes voluntarily exchangeable for bonds. Despite efforts in 1863 to compel the purchase of bonds with notes by a reduction in interest rates, the currency continued to grow. Then by the act of February 17, 1864, Congress required the note holders to exchange all of their currency for 4 percent registered bonds. Despite the large sums taken in, the issue of a further $460 million of notes dated February 17, 1864, kept the Confederate Treasury notes outstanding in excess of $800 million up to the collapse of the government in April 1865.

It must also be noted that, despite the large sums emitted, the Confederate government as the years passed fell ever further behind in its efforts to meet its obligations. Such arrears were $26 million in early 1862, rising by the war's end to $350 million.

Most of this deficit arose from the Treasury's inability to procure the necessary notes from the Confederate security printers and from the department's inefficiency in distributing its funds to the paymasters. The failure to pay soldiers and contractors in a timely manner promoted supply shortages and massive desertion.

STATE GOVERNMENT CURRENCY ISSUES. The state governments were at first limited in their note emissions because the Confederate Provisional Constitution carried over the Federal prohibition against

LOCAL GOVERNMENT NOTES

Issues by county and municipal governments also flourished during this period. Faced with the same demands as those made on the states, coupled with the widespread suspension of local tax collections, many municipal and county governments felt obliged to emit large quantities of notes, mostly in amounts of less than a dollar.

The prevalence of such notes varied greatly from state to state. South Carolina flatly prohibited them, with a special exemption for fire-devastated Charleston. Others, such as Virginia, Louisiana, and Texas, were marked by state authorizations of such issues and widespread abuses. Virginia was especially notorious in this regard: the capital, Richmond, issued nearly $500,000 worth. Some were used for local defense works and to buy the White House of the Confederacy for the use of Jefferson Davis. Others were issued to cover routine expenses and to help make change.

In addition to the issues in those three states, over one hundred cities and counties in eight other states issued their own money. Such issues, coming to a total of nearly $18 million, of which over $12 million was outstanding at the end of the war, further added to an already redundant currency.

— DOUGLAS A. BALL

such issues. Most states, with the exception of those who styled their issues as "Treasury warrants," contented themselves with selling a few high-denomination interest-bearing notes in 1861. But after February 18, 1862, the states passed act after act authorizing the emission of non-interest-bearing notes. Military mobilization requirements, the demands of the public for small-denomination notes to replace hoarded gold and silver coins, and the necessity of providing aid to the families of soldiers all furnished a plausible pretext or solid grounds to justify such issues.

State notes were issued in denominations of five cents up to $500, with Georgia exchanging some $5,000, $10,000, and $20,000 certificates for smaller bills. Some states, such as Virginia and Arkansas, abstained from issuing notes under the denomination of $1, leaving that function to their local governments.

Most authorizing laws appeared between 1861 and 1863. Thereafter, such legislation became rare because the legislatures feared the inflationary effect of such

The Confederate Treasury Department was created by the Provisional Congress on Feb. 21, 1861, at Montgomery, Alabama.

PAGE 620

The Confederate Treasury Department ceased to exist after the evacuation of Richmond on April 2, 1865.

PAGE 620

acts and were concerned about the public perception that state issues were excessive.

The use of Treasury notes was also to some degree dictated by a state's credit rating and its ability to borrow through the issue of bonds. The absence of state currency issues in Tennessee and South Carolina simply reflected the ability of those states to sell bonds and to order the state-owned Bank of Tennessee and the Bank of the State of South Carolina to issue the desired small notes in denominations from five cents up to two dollars. Georgia authorized the Western and Atlantic Railroad, which it owned, to issue notes in fractional parts of a dollar before undertaking this business directly on its own account.

The financial community, particularly in the East, entertained a higher opinion of the value of the state notes than those put out by the Confederacy. This was particularly true as the tide of battle shifted against the Richmond regime. Consequently, the high-denomination notes of many states, especially those bearing interest, were hoarded by the bankers and were seldom seen in circulation.

Since some states copied the Confederate government by making their notes exchangeable for bonds, a modest quantity of notes was absorbed by this means. Thus by the end of the war, when all such issues were repudiated, the states had issued directly or indirectly over $100 million of treasury notes. With the funding of notes and some tax collections, probably about a total of $65 million was still outstanding in 1865.

Public Debt

The Confederate government, unlike the Union, started the war without a substantial debt. But the rapid expansion of public expenditures for military operations, the payments made for the civil establishment, and the discharge of the interest on the government's bonds led to the creation of a large debt consisting of interest-bearing and circulating Treasury notes, together with interest-bearing bonds and call certificates (an obligation convertible on demand into cash for both principal and interest).

The funded indebtedness commenced on February 28, 1861, with a modest $15 million loan and ended in 1865 with over $825 million outstanding. The interest rates on this debt varied from 8 percent in 1861 down to 4 percent in 1864. Nearly $600 million of this indebtedness was the result of more or less compulsory exchanges of Treasury notes for bonds with a view to reducing the high levels of inflation.

To meet the demands of those who were prepared to make only short-term loans, the Confederacy also authorized various issues of call certificates. Nearly $300 million worth of these were sold between 1861 and 1865, at rates starting at 8 percent and 6 percent in

1861 and dwindling to 5 percent in 1863 and 4 percent thereafter. The total amount outstanding in 1865 was probably less than $75 million.

STATE DEBT. In addition to their prewar debts and their issues of Treasury notes, the states of the Confederacy accumulated substantial funded debts of their own. To begin with, many states copied the Confederate government by providing that holders of their Treasury notes might exchange them for bonds. A few states, such as Georgia, merely allowed such an exchange after the war with a view to diminishing current interest charges. Interest rates, as befitted the public's greater confidence in the states' credit, were typically 6 percent when the Confederacy was paying 8 percent, but less creditworthy western states such as Mississippi and Texas paid up to 10 percent on their bonds. The total amount of these issues came to slightly in excess of $50 million.

COUNTY AND MUNICIPAL DEBTS. Local governments also accumulated debts above and beyond their note issues. Most of these came through the sale of registered bonds whose proceeds were typically employed for recruiting and equipping local military units. Because of the ease with which such governments could issue circulating bills, probably only $3 million or so was raised by these means, primarily for military and other public purposes.

Taxation

An important element in public finance, particularly as it related to the issue of circulating Treasury notes and interest-bearing bonds, could be found in the tax-levying and collecting policies of the Confederate, state, and local governments. The less the public authorities taxed, the more they had to borrow. And the more they borrowed, particularly in the form of circulating notes, the more public expenses were unnecessarily multiplied by price inflation.

CONFEDERATE TAXATION. Confederate fiscal policies directly reflected the South's immediate past experience under the Federal government. No Federal levy on real estate or personal property had been made since 1815, a direct result of the War of 1812. Federal revenues were practically limited to the collection of customs dues and the sale of public lands.

The Confederate government, prior to the outbreak of hostilities, did little to depart from this pattern. There was some tinkering with the tariff rates. In a retrogression to the pattern of the colonial era, allowed by the abolition of the Federal constitutional prohibition against taxes on exports, the Confederate Provisional Congress laid a duty of $1/8$ cent per pound on all cotton shipped out of the Confederacy. Typically, the estimated revenue from this tax was less than that needed for its announced purpose: to pay the interest and principal of the $15 million loan of February 28, 1861.

After the engagement at Fort Sumter, Secretary Memminger asked Congress for a direct tax on real estate, slaves, livestock, securities, and other forms of personal property. After bitter debate, this proposed $25 million levy was reluctantly agreed to. It proved a distinct disappointment in practice since it produced only $15 million in revenue, and 10 percent of the revenue was lost and the benefits of a tax forfeited when the states issued bonds and assumed the tax on behalf of their citizens. This was retrogression to Revolutionary War practices, copied by the Federal government from 1813 to 1815.

Still worse, no provision was made to continue this tax or to get around the prohibition in the Permanent Constitution that blocked similar levies in the absence of a census. Moreover, no serious effort was made by the executive branch to pressure Congress into passing tax legislation of any kind before January 1, 1863. And when Congress did finally pass a tax act on April 23, 1863, it was a complicated grab bag of income and license taxes amalgamated with a tax-in-kind on agricultural produce that was riddled with exemptions.

Nor were matters much improved by the act of February 17, 1864, insofar as it pertained to taxes. Taxes in one area were made dependent upon the complicated calculation of the taxpayer's obligations in regard to some other tax. As a result, the difficulty in administering the internal revenue system was greatly complicated.

The planters, whose property interest in slaves the country was fighting to defend, especially after Abraham Lincoln's Emancipation Proclamation, fought bitterly to exempt themselves from contributing to the cause. Thus the anomalous spectacle was created of those holding roughly 40 percent of the South's property values (slaves) refusing to make any contribution to the cause that was protecting their interests.

Tax revenues by October 1, 1864, were seriously inadequate. Customs and export duties, despite optimistic predictions, came to a paltry $3 million. The war tax produced less than $15 million and the 1863 and 1864 taxes yielded only $123.5 million. In the end, only 8.2 percent of the Confederacy's income was derived from taxes, as compared with 20.1 percent of the Union's.

STATE TAXATION. At the time the Federal Constitution was adopted in 1787, the American states secured most of their income from customs dues. The transfer of this revenue source to the Federal government meant that the states had to find a new way of paying their expenses.

In the years up to 1860, the Southern states had largely depended upon real estate taxes as their primary source of income. State bond sales made for the purpose of providing capital for banks, canals, turnpikes, and railroads, combined with demands for better police protection, aid to public education, and other public expenditures, soon created a growing deficit. Not only did the regular revenues not keep up with the demands on the public Treasury, but many companies in which the states invested went bankrupt or proved less remunerative than had been anticipated. This put pressure on the legislature to increase tax rates or find new sources of revenue.

Tax rates even by 1860 were low, averaging but $1/10$ of 1 percent on the assessed value of property and up $4/10$ of 1 percent in states such as Virginia where the public debt was heavy. Bitter debate revolved around how property should be appraised and how often. Moreover, should rates simply be laid on a flat basis at so much per acre of woodland or agricultural land, or should a real assessment be made? Debates on this point reached such a pitch that South Carolina was unable to conduct a new assessment after 1840.

One of the most contentious points and one that was never satisfactorily handled before the war or during the brief existence of the Confederacy was the question of how slaves should be assessed at the state level and what tax rate was appropriate for a species of property that represented anywhere from 30 to 60 percent of estimated property values in each state. The large slaveholders, anticipating their attitudes during the war, wanted to keep assessment levels low and if possible to avoid assessments altogether. Instead, they argued in favor of a low fixed tax per slave as a means of reducing assessment costs and tax avoidance.

Those who owned only a few slaves or none favored a full assessment of slaves and the same rate of tax on that type of property as on any other. Despite a vigorous rearguard action, the large slaveholders by 1861 had had to compromise. The use of a fixed tax per slave was still largely the rule, but in more and more states the tax began to approximate, as a percentage of value, that levied on land. It should not be thought, however, that state slave tax revenues constituted a small proportion of state revenues. Georgia and Alabama derived nearly half of their tax revenues from slave levies, and South Carolina derived over 60 percent.

The states experimented with other revenue sources. Luxury taxes were laid on "pleasure carriages," gold and silver plate, watches, pistols, pianos, and jewelry. Some states tried taxing the profits and dividends of corporations, then predominantly railroads or banks. Others had a crude income tax for individuals.

In many states the sheriffs were delinquent in their accounts. In some cases, taxes had not been collected but it had not been politically expedient to seize the debtor's property for a tax sale. In other cases, the sheriffs had collected the taxes but had diverted the money for their

At the onset of the Civil War, the South's banking system had emerged virtually unscathed from the panic of 1857 and had seen the culmination of a decade of impressive growth.

PAGE 40

own use. The unreliability of the tax collectors before the war presaged what would happen during the war.

These trends were accentuated during the years of the Confederacy. The states, faced with large military expenses for which the Confederate Treasury did not reimburse them and confronted by the need to pay the interest on the newly issued notes and bonds, had to increase their revenues. And since there was neither time nor the manpower available for property reassessments, this invariably meant tax rate increases.

Yet there were contradictory trends. On the one hand, many state governments authorized tax surcharges on existing rates particularly for the benefit of soldiers' families. On the other hand, while doing this, Mississippi suspended the collection of the levee taxes. Many states in 1864 canceled or suspended their taxes for the duration of the war on the ground that the inadequate Confederate government taxes were so heavy a burden that the states should not add to it. And given the initial popularity of state issues of Treasury notes, the need for heavy taxes was not immediately apparent.

Contradictorily, however, many states did increase their tax rates between 1861 and 1864. Alabama increased its income tax rate from 1 percent to 5 percent. Mississippi ordered a 30 percent surcharge on its real estate taxes. South Carolina increased rates on the assessed value of land from slightly over 1 percent in 1861 to 6 percent in 1865. South Carolina also took the assessment books for the Confederate war tax in 1861 and proceeded to collect the amounts due from its own citizens.

Georgia increased its property levy to 1 percent from its prewar level of $1/10$ of 1 percent. Also, its tax structure became more progressive, with an income tax and an ad valorem tax on other property, particularly cotton held by speculators.

Similar energy was displayed in North Carolina where the tax on land rose from $1/5$ of 1 percent to 1 percent in 1864. Virginia, on the other hand, raised rates from $4/10$ of 1 percent to 1 percent in 1861. It then repealed the increases and lowered rates in 1864. Other states, although prepared to levy heavy but unenforceable taxes against speculators and profiteers, allowed many of their taxes to remain uncollected. This behavior was justified by the incursions of the enemy, the general decline of the economy, and the poverty of the public.

Moreover, it must not be forgotten that though there were rate increases and an apparent increase in nominal total revenues, such proceeds when converted into gold dollars showed an actual decline in real revenue. This anomaly can be attributed to the fact that the state tax rates did not keep pace with inflation. To do even that, by early 1864, taxes would have had to be twenty times what they were in 1861. The states, like the Confederate Congress, were seldom willing to put public sentiment to the test of real tax increases. Nonetheless, higher Confederate-era taxes proved a transition between the low antebellum rates and the comparatively high levies of the Reconstruction period.

LOCAL GOVERNMENT TAXES. Local governments also came under pressure to increase their revenues to cover their expenses in raising military units and looking after the families of soldiers. In many instances, the state governments encouraged this trend. For example, Mississippi permitted the counties to levy a tax up to the amount secured by the prewar state real

estate tax to aid soldiers' families. Virginia required that any local government issuing notes had to retire them in equal installments from 1864 to 1866. Any benefit from this act in the form of a reduction in the bloated currency was dissipated when the redemption date was deferred for up to six years.

Local government tax collections in militarily contested areas practically ceased, particularly when rival pro-Union and pro-Confederate governments competed for the loyalty of the citizenry. Many state and local government functions were abandoned during the war, and these bodies copied the state and the Confederate governments in their reluctance to tax their constituents.

Inflation

Given the fact that the Confederate government alone issued currency in excess of five times the prewar circulation, and taking further into account that state and local governments issued over $112 million of notes and that banks, railroads, other corporations, and private citizens also circulated their due bills, it is not surprising that the Confederacy was afflicted by severe inflation. This inflation was exacerbated by the absence of effective internal revenue systems at any level of government, by the blockade that greatly raised the prices of all imported goods or local goods made with foreign components, and by the breakdown of the

STATE SOCIALISM

The Confederate, state, and local governments did make various efforts to check inflation by exerting their powers over the economy and by taking upon themselves new responsibilities for the welfare of their people.

In the years between 1789 and 1829, in keeping with Alexander Hamilton's view that the government should create an identity of interest between itself and its wealthier citizens, the Federal government chartered two Federal banks, sponsored the construction of canals, built post roads, and took other steps to encourage the economic development of the United States.

After President Andrew Jackson entered the White House in 1829, these activities more or less ceased. The Democrats adopted the doctrine of laissez-faire, which opposed government intervention. This, combined with the South's growing fear of Northern economic power exercised through the Washington regime, and with the popular doctrine of state rights, led many Southerners to adopt the view that economic development or regulation was beyond the proper scope of the central government's powers.

These attitudes found their reflection in both Confederate Constitutions. The general welfare clause present in the Federal Constitution was deleted and provisions inserted against what were then styled "internal improvements." These put a crimp on what the Confederate government might legitimately do either for itself or for its citizens.

Nonetheless, the Davis administration did take a number of actions that had far-reaching effects on the national economy and war efforts. Belatedly, in 1863 and 1864, the government asserted its control over interstate and foreign commerce by prohibiting the import of foreign luxury goods and by commandeering for government use both the incoming and the outgoing cargo space of blockade-running ships. This program, known as the "New Plan," effected a great improvement in governmental supply operations and finances, but it was adopted so late that most ports had been effectively closed before it could be put into operation.

At home, the administration undertook a variety of actions in keeping with the suggestions made by John C. Calhoun in 1816. Without waiting for private enterprise to deal with its various problems, the War Department created powder mills, nitrate beds, and a variety of manufacturing plants to provide the armed forces with weapons, munitions, clothing, shoes, and other equipment. The quantities furnished were never adequate, outside of munitions, but the army could hardly have endured its unequal contest with the Union forces without them.

In another departure from previous practice, the War Department also assumed increasing control over the South's ill-assorted railroad system. Companies were required, where possible, to share equipment, spare parts, and rolling stock. Railroad schedules were regulated. The government also built three important connecting lines. One provided a third route south from Richmond to North Carolina, and another from Georgia tied up with Florida's railroads and cattle supply. The third involved an attempt to complete the line between Montgomery, Alabama, and Jackson, Mississippi.

Despite widespread public clamor for a government advance on the cotton crop, all efforts to enact such a program were opposed by Secretary Memminger. As a result, the so-called 1861 Produce Loan (a scheme whereby the planters lent the government money secured by a pledge of the proceeds of the sale of their crops) produced a paltry $20 million. Only on April 14, 1862, did Congress enact and Jefferson Davis approve a law allowing the government to buy $35 million of produce with bonds. This action was too limited and too late to be of much benefit to either the Confederacy or the planters.

— DOUGLAS A. BALL

transportation system, which made it increasingly difficult to move surplus goods from one part of the Confederacy to another.

Inflation had a devastating effect on the South's public finances. War required that the Confederate and state governments vastly increase their employment of soldiers and sailors, and those civilians needed to pay, clothe, house, equip, and feed them. It also increased the cost of goods purchased by any government, regardless of whether they were made at home or abroad. Inflation, broadly speaking, grew at an accelerating level from year to year. Inflation ran at 20 percent in 1861, 200 percent by the end of 1862, 2,000 percent by the end of 1863, and 5,000 percent in January 1865.

This in turn had a deadly circular effect on the governments' finances. The more that was spent, the more Treasury notes and near-monetary instruments like interest-bearing notes and coupon bonds had to be issued. And with no effective means to curtail the growth of the money supply, each gain in the size of the currency ensured a further expansion of inflation. This process was exacerbated by Confederate defeats that resulted in more desertions and more defeats. These in turn curtailed the area under Confederate control and reduced the number of people and the size of the economy in which Confederate currency could circulate, thus further raising prices.

For the most part, the central government confined its activities to the military sphere and did little for the civilian sector of the economy. The government might have done more and done it earlier, but public suspicion of and state government opposition to any display of activism by the central regime go far to explain its apparent passivity. By 1863, the Richmond regime was seen as a necessitous body, always making demands on the people and giving nothing in exchange.

[*See also* Erlanger Loan; New Plan; Produce Loan; State Socialism; Taxation.]

— DOUGLAS A. BALL

QUANTRILL, WILLIAM CLARKE

Quantrill, William Clarke (1835-1865), pro-Confederate Missouri guerrilla. At age sixteen, following the death of his father, an Ohio school principal, Quantrill drifted west, teaching school in Illinois, Indiana, and finally, in 1857, in Tuscarora Lake, Kansas, a settlement of Ohio migrants. Expelled from Tuscarora Lake as a thief, Quantrill joined an army expedition to Utah as a teamster, from where, late in 1858, he joined a gold party headed for Pikes Peak. Twelve of the nineteen men in the party died of exposure in the Rocky Mountains, and Quantrill's survival led him to believe that he was a man of destiny. Back in Kansas in 1859, Quantrill became something of a double agent, consorting with political bandits of both antislavery Kansans and proslavery Missourians, before finally throwing in his lot with the proslavery camp.

When the war began, the area around Independence, Missouri, went up in flames. Kansas Jayhawkers (antislavery Unionists, some enrolled in the militia, some freebooters) crossed the Missouri River to burn and plunder. In retaliation, many young Missourians took to the bush and spontaneously organized guerrilla bands. Quantrill, a bit older than most of these boys, a fine horseman and dead shot, and with a little military experience and a lot of self-confidence, led one of the most active gangs in attacking Union troops and raiding Kansas border towns. Such bands had the support of many local citizens, a difficult terrain in which to hide, and a cunning ability to attack the enemy at his weak spots, and then to scatter and melt back into the countryside.

In the summer of 1863, Union authorities began expelling or imprisoning suspected guerrilla sympathizers. On August 13, a rickety Kansas City prison collapsed, killing five young female kin of the Quantrill band. In retaliation, Quantrill gathered about 450 guerrillas and, on the morning of August 21, burst into Lawrence, Kansas, burning, looting, and killing about 150 unarmed men and boys, a raid that gained him national notoriety.

When his men sojourned in Texas that winter, Confederate authorities could neither enroll them nor control them. Quantrill's cohort disintegrated into smaller groups, led by younger and even more reckless men, notably George Todd and "Bloody" Bill Anderson, who carried on in 1864 in Missouri as before, while Quantrill sat out the summer in hiding. In October, Todd and Anderson were both killed, and Quantrill reassembled about thirty of his old band for an expedition into Kentucky. On May 10, 1865, Quantrill, surprised while sleeping in a barn, was shot, paralyzed, and captured. He was taken to a military prison hospital in nearby Louisville where, following his conversion to Roman Catholicism, he died on June 6.

Quantrill's fighters had been the James and Younger brothers; as their reputations rose during their postwar careers, so did his. Noble guerrillas had become noble outlaws, fighting those dreaded outsiders—bankers and railroad men—particularly in the historical fiction of the alcoholic newspaperman, John N. Edwards. By 1888, mythically rehabilitated Quantrill veterans were organizing annual reunions,

DEAD SHOT

Former schoolteacher William Clarke Quantrill led a band of guerrillas in attacking Union troops and raiding Kansas border towns.

LIBRARY OF CONGRESS

at which they would have their pictures taken, always holding up a portrait of their fallen captain, Quantrill. In the twentieth century, Hollywood would utilize this romance in films about the Old West. Finally, some of his bones were buried with full Confederate military honors on October 24,

Led by William Clarke Quantrill, a 24-year-old Ohio schoolteacher, Missouri partisans called bushwhackers launched a series of strikes into Kansas that all but paralyzed the state.

PAGE 253

1992, in Higginsville, Missouri, by a rather macabre group of historical romanticists.

— MICHAEL FELLMAN

QUARTERMASTER BUREAU

Established February 26, 1861, the Quartermaster Bureau was responsible for providing the Confederate armies with nonfood and nonordnance items, as well as transportation functions. Thus, the production of uniforms, shoes, shirts, hats, tents, saddles, and wagons and their transportation were quartermaster functions, as was the transportation of the armies themselves. The bureau was headed first by Col. Abraham C. Myers of South Carolina (March 25, 1861–August 10, 1863) and then by Brig. Gen. Alexander R. Lawton of Georgia (August 10, 1863, to the end of the war).

An act establishing the department stipulated that it be manned by a colonel as quartermaster general, six majors as quartermasters, and as many lieutenants (subalterns) as assistant quartermasters as were necessary. All the quartermasters were authorized to act as paymasters.

The department was organized in the same manner as its prewar Federal counterpart. It was to run a simple senior office. The subordinate officers were to oversee functional areas such as shoes or uniforms for the major Confederate armies. Each of the major armies usually had a staff officer assigned to handle quartermaster functions, thus relieving the commanding general of what most officers considered an onerous task. Custom dictated that each division, brigade, and regimental commander assign quartermaster duties to an officer. Those assigned were rarely professional or experienced in supply matters, and those who were often faced the conflict of dual allegiance to their commander in the field and their superior, the quartermaster general, in Richmond. Consequently, supply problems related to the internal functioning of the quartermasters grew as the war progressed. At the company level, quartermaster functions, such as the actual distribution of uniforms to individual soldiers, were handled by a designated sergeant, who was often overseen by an officer.

What appeared to be the simple task of supplying soldiers in the field rapidly became extremely complicated as the number of soldiers and the distance over which they served increased. The quartermasters' problems were exacerbated by a number of factors: declining means of transportation, lack of coordination, spiraling wartime inflation, corruption, divisive politics, shortage of manpower, and the lack of glamour associated with nonbattle staff duties.

Following in the tradition of the Federal army, the Quartermaster Bureau was the senior department and the quartermaster general the ranking staff officer after the adjutant general. Because of seniority, he and his subordinates could and did usurp the assets of other staff departments, particularly in the functional area of transportation. This practice led to friction, rivalry, and an intense competition for limited assets that continued to the war's end. The combat efficiency of the Confederate armies was often affected by departments that rerouted scheduled trains, only to have the rerouted trains rescheduled by a local quartermaster. The lack of clear direction and coordination by the president and secretary of war accentuated this deadly problem.

Wartime inflation was another factor in the failure of the bureau to carry out its mission. The well-known tales of Confederate civilians having to pay incredible prices for goods and services also reflected the situation of the quartermasters, but they had a partial remedy—impressment. Using constitutional powers delegated by the secretary of war, they could commandeer private property, be it cloth for tents and uniforms or leather for shoes and saddles. Necessary goods could be impressed as long as the quartermaster provided just compensation. But given the rapidly spiraling inflation of the Confederacy, quartermasters often paid only half of an item's true market value. Civilians complained vehemently to the Congress, which eventually enacted legislation to curtail and regulate the process. The practice of impressment did nothing to enhance the quartermasters' reputation and stimulated charges of corruption.

Starting in the summer of 1862 and continuing until the end of the war, the Quartermaster Bureau was under almost continual investigation by Congress. Anger about quartermaster practices and in particular corruption led to the introduction of numerous resolutions and acts regarding their activities. One of the most telling was an Act to Protect the Confederate States against Frauds, Etc. The Senate debated the act on December 31, 1864, and the comments of Senator George N. Lester of Georgia reveal the deep-seated anger the Confederacy felt for the quartermasters. Lester admitted that there were some honest men in the bureau but asserted that the rest had been "engaged in plundering the government from the beginning of the war till now."

This sentiment led to legislation that was designed to destroy the department. An act submitted to President Jefferson Davis in March 1865 would have sent all able-bodied quartermasters under the age of forty-five to field positions. Davis vetoed the bill because it would have been a disaster for the already faltering war effort and would have added only two hundred men to the army.

Divisive politics was another factor in the quartermasters' failure. Almost as soon as the war began, state governors withheld vital supplies for their own states' use. Quartermaster General Lawton recognized the problem as soon as he took the job. He wrote two letters in 1864 to the secretary of war complaining that the governors controlled assets, like cotton and woolen factories, that the bureau needed:

We draw not a single yard of any kind of material. . . . It would be better for the State authorities to allow this department to control factory production so far as they may be needed for military purposes. . . . The necessities of the people and the objects of charity must be postponed to the wants of the Army.

In the state rights–oriented Confederacy many governors would continue to control necessary supplies even to the detriment of the war effort.

Another problem for the bureau was manpower. In February 1865, it reported that it needed 2,299 white males, 3,451 blacks full time, and 5,000 women for part-time or piecework. Many important people thought that the department controlled too many skilled white males who in the manpower-short Confederacy were needed on the battlefront. President Davis, however, usually disagreed.

The last factor affecting the performance of the quartermasters was the lack of respect for their specialty. Often not the highest caliber officers, they had a poor reputation. In fact, Lawton, a former brigadier and division commander under Thomas J. ("Stonewall") Jackson, complained at length when he was assigned to his new billet. The comments of Gen. Richard S. Ewell at the Battle of Cedar Mountain reflected the feeling of most Confederate officers regarding quartermasters. When Ewell saw a well-dressed officer on the battlefield, he asked, "I do say, young man with the fine clothes on! Who are you and where do you belong?" Being informed that he was a quartermaster with a Virginia regiment, Ewell exploded: "Great Heavens! A Quartermaster on the battlefield; who ever heard of such a thing before?"

Nevertheless, given the difficulties they faced, it is amazing that the quartermasters accomplished as much as they did. Both Myers and Lawton struggled against impossible odds. Myers did a creditable job and Lawton's work bordered on superb.

— P. NEAL MEIER

Q

QUARTERMASTER BUREAU

The value of the Mississippi River to the Confederacy had been drastically reduced ever since the capture of New Orleans and Memphis.

PAGE 649

RAILROADS

The decade of the 1850s was one of the most important periods in the history of American railroads. What had been at the beginning of the decade a scattering of short lines from Maine to Georgia had become by 1860 an iron network serving all the states east of the Mississippi. New construction in the ten years resulted in a growth from 9,021 to 30,626 miles. The mileage in 1850 was concentrated in a network stretching from Portland, Maine, and Buffalo, New York, south to Richmond, Virginia, and Wilmington, North Carolina. A separate 900-mile system served the major cities in South Carolina and Georgia. West of the mountains the only states with 100 miles or more of line were Michigan, Ohio, Indiana, Illinois, and Alabama.

ANTEBELLUM SECTIONAL DIFFERENCES. In the early 1830s railroad mileage in the Southern states (those south of the Potomac and Ohio rivers) had nearly matched that of the North, but by 1850 the North had 5,612 miles of line and the South only 2,133 miles. Clearly the industrial states in the North felt a greater need for the new mode of transport than did the more agrarian South. But in the 1850s the South did much to catch up. Arkansas and Texas laid their first track and the South (the future Confederate states plus Kentucky) built 7,402 miles of railroad, climbing to a total of 9,535 miles, or an increase of 347 percent.

Probably more significant was the new construction in the West. During the 1850s mileage in the eight Western states (the Old Northwest plus Iowa, Missouri, and California) increased from 1,276 to 11,078 miles. And by the end of the Civil War the network from western Pennsylvania to the Mississippi River seemed complete. Most of the new mileage ran east and west and connected with one or more major trunk lines.

For a generation prior to mid-century steamboats had had a monopoly on commerce and transportation in the Mississippi-Ohio basin, but the major railroad construction in the Old Northwest soon resulted in a

RAILROADS OF THE CONFEDERACY
1861-1865

Compilation: E. M. Coulter   Cartography: H.Q Avera

LEGEND

In Existence
1861

Built
1861-1865

0   100   200
Miles

RAIL NETWORKS

A map of the Confederacy's railroads gives a glimpse of where and to what extent the South was developed and interconnected.

REPRINTED BY PERMISSION OF LOUISIANA STATE UNIVERSITY PRESS

*By the end of
January 1863,
Grant's new
objective was to
isolate Vicksburg
by severing its rail
link to Jackson.*

PAGE 646

new east-west trade axis that replaced the earlier north-south traffic of the Ohio and Mississippi River steamboats. The economic shift is noted by William and Bruce Catton in their *Two Roads to Sumter:* "Southerners who dreamed that the Northwest might be neutral or even an ally in the event of a civil conflict should have looked more closely at the endless parade of freight trains clattering across the mountains between the ocean and the lakes."

Certainly there was no lack of enthusiasm for railroads in the South. On the eve of the Civil War over a hundred companies shared the 9,000 miles of line in the Confederacy. The average length was 85 miles, with a third over 100 miles in length, and nine over 200 miles. Most of the Confederate lines represented a single state, with all their mileage within the state. In 1860 the average investment per mile of road was about $27,000 in the South, $36,000 in the West, and $48,000 in the Northeast. Southern railroads cost less for several reasons: cheaper slave labor, lighter and often inferior rails, easier terrain along the coastal plains of the South, and smaller amounts of rolling stock per mile of road. Financial support for the construction in the decade had come from some cities and counties and a few states, especially Virginia, North Carolina, and Tennessee, but most lines were chiefly financed by the private sector. A Federal land grant pushed through Congress by William R. King, senator from Alabama, and his colleague, Stephen A. Douglas of Illinois, had provided aid for the Mobile and Ohio and the Illinois Central in Illinois.

Construction of the 7,000 miles of new line in the eleven Southern states in the fifties was rather even during the ten years, but more than half of the new track was put down in the four years 1857 through 1860. This was in contrast to the pattern north of the Ohio River where nearly three-quarters was laid between 1852 and 1856. Southern lines, like those in the rest of the nation, were built in a variety of track gauges. The 5-foot gauge was dominant, but three states, with modest mileage, favored the 5-foot 6-inch gauge, and two states favored the 4-foot 8 1/2-inch gauge, which was fairly standard in the North.

The Civil War was the first major conflict in which railroads played an important role. In 1861 the Union and Confederate rail systems were in some ways a study in contrast. The eleven Southern states with their 9,000 miles of line had nearly a third of the nation's rail mileage, but employed less than a fifth of the country's railroad work force. Many workers from the North were employed on Southern lines in 1861, probably because of the Southerners' traditional dislike for mechanical pursuits. When war came, many Northerners returned home, and those who remained were often viewed with suspicion, sometimes rightly so.

The South was also at a disadvantage in motive power, rolling stock, and track materials. The entire Confederacy had hardly as many locomotives as those found on the combined motive power rosters of the New York Central, the Pennsylvania, and the Erie. The states north of the Potomac had a dozen locomotive factories for every one located in the South. The few locomotive factories in the South, such as the Tredegar Iron Works at Richmond, were pressed by the Davis government into the production of ordnance. The states of Virginia, South Carolina, and Tennessee had produced a fair number of railroad cars, but Pennsylvania produced twice as many as the entire Confederacy. Obtaining replacement rail and spikes was also soon a problem. Before the war Southern railroad presidents preferred English to Northern rails, claiming the English to be superior and cheaper. The South produced some rail, but its production of 26,000 tons in 1860 was about a ninth of the Northern output. The Union blockade of Southern ports, plus the Confederate priority given to ordnance production, soon had Southern track maintenance officials hoarding their iron.

While the Confederate railways lagged well behind Northern roads in the quantity and maintenance of equipment, the types of engines and cars used by the rivals varied only slightly. Both North and South relied heavily on the American-type locomotive (a swiveled four-wheel truck in front plus four drivers) with its functional cowcatcher, balloon stack, and large headlight. This kind of engine (4-4-0) had a name rather than a number, weighed from fifteen to twenty-five tons, cost $8,000 to $10,000 new, used wood or coal for fuel, and was the pride and joy of the engine crew to whom it was assigned. Northern lines shifted to coal for fuel far faster than the Southern roads; nearly all Confederate railroads depended on cord wood. A few Northern railroads owned some engines with six rather than four drivers, but such locomotives were rare in the South.

The typical freight car, either Northern or Southern, had two four-wheel trucks, was from twenty-four to thirty-four feet in length, and had a load capacity of eight to twelve tons. First-class boxcars rarely cost more than $400 to $500 per car and often were built in company shops for much less. Passenger cars on the eve of the war normally came equipped with corner toilet, water tank, a wood-burning stove, and inadequate lighting. In 1860 first-class cars were about fifty feet in length, could hold fifty passengers, and were stopped with hand brakes. New cars cost from $1,500 to $3,000 each. Dining cars had not yet been introduced, and sleeping cars were almost unknown on Southern lines.

The principal railroad centers in the Confederacy were Richmond, Chattanooga, and Atlanta. Richmond was served by five roads, whereas the Union capital, a hundred miles to the north, depended upon a single branch line of the Baltimore and Ohio. Chattanooga and Atlanta both were served by three roads, but each was a vital line serving much of the region. At the start of the war, Richmond had two major routes to the south. An eastern coastal line, formed of six railroads, reached Wilmington, Charleston, and Savannah, the major Confederate eastern seaports. A second trans-mountain route via Petersburg, Lynchburg, Bristol, and Knoxville reached Chattanooga in the southeast-ern corner of Tennessee. Late in the war Richmond was served by a third line via Danville and Greensboro, which became a vital supply route for Robert E. Lee. West of Chattanooga the 296-mile Memphis and Charleston ran to Corinth and Memphis with connec-tions serving Tennessee, Alabama, Mississippi, Louisiana, and New Orleans. South of Chattanooga the Georgia state-owned 138-mile Western and Atlantic reached Atlanta and several lines serving the Carolinas, Georgia, and Florida. The Western and Atlantic later would be a bone of contention between Joseph E. Brown, state rights governor of Georgia, and Jefferson Davis. These three junction cities were in states that had the greatest rail mileage in the Confed-eracy.

WAR'S EFFECT ON SOUTHERN LINES. In the spring of 1861 the *American Railroad Journal* predicted that the majority of the railroads would be unaffected by the Civil War, a mistaken prophecy, indeed. South-ern lines leading toward the Virginia and Tennessee fronts soon were overwhelmed with a flood of excited soldiers and ancient ordnance moving north. South of Richmond the Petersburg Railroad doubled its gross revenue by 1862 and in that year had a record low operating ratio under 28 percent. Between 1861 and 1863 the Georgia Railroad lowered its operating ratio from 57 to 42 percent. The Wilmington and Weldon paid a 31 percent dividend in 1863, and between 1860–1861 and 1862–1863 total receipts on the North Carolina Railroad increased nearly fourfold. The oper-ating ratio dropped to 38 percent, and dividends dou-bled. Of course, the lower operating ratios and higher dividends resulted in part from the scarcity of labor and replacement parts.

In these years military personnel made up well over a third of the passenger traffic. But freight traffic was declining on many Confederate lines in the early war months, especially in the cotton-producing states where the rail movement of cotton was reduced by the effective Union blockade of the Southern coastline. Also the early indications of rail prosperity must be discounted because the growing receipts and dividends were expressed in Confederate dollars, which were rapidly declining in real value.

Certainly much of the seeming prosperity was false, given the persistent inflation. The costs of railway operation generally rose faster than did the freight rates and passenger fares. In the first two or three years of war, mechanics' wages climbed from $2.50 to $20.00 a day, nails from 4 cents to $4.00 a pound, shovels from $10.50 to $300.00 per dozen, coal from 12 cents to $2.00 per bushel, and lubricating oil from $1.00 to $50.00 a gallon. Railroad officials found it hard to raise rates fast enough to match these rising costs. John P. King, the president of the 232-mile Georgia Railroad, long a prosperous line, complained in 1864 that because of inflation his road had been losing money for two years. He wrote of his railroad: "The more business it does, the more money it loses, and the greatest favor that could be conferred upon it—if public wants per-mitted—would be the privilege of quitting business until the end of the war!"

Early in the war major problems faced two railroads in border states—the Louisville and Nashville in Ken-tucky and Tennessee, and the Baltimore and Ohio in Maryland and Virginia. Both lines had major mileage in the Confederacy—the L & N in Tennessee on its way to Nashville, and the B & O in northern and west-ern Virginia. As the war came to Kentucky in the spring of 1861, the L & N was enjoying prosperity, with merchants and public officials in Tennessee and points farther south ordering vast amounts of North-ern goods. James Guthrie, its president, found his road so clogged with south-bound freight that he imposed a ten-day embargo late in April to clear his tracks. Through the summer of 1861 the cagey Guthrie tried to serve two masters at once. But by the end of the summer, he was forced to choose, and he broke with the Confederacy. Parts of his lines were in Confederate hands, but before too long northern Tennessee was again under Union control. Guthrie fully supported the Union, and he may have received higher than nor-mal rates for his Federal business.

In a way the first violence of the Civil War had come to the B & O eighteen months before the capture of Fort Sumter, when John Brown made his raid on Harpers Ferry in 1859. In Baltimore John W. Garrett, president of the line, wired the Secretary of War, who sent Col. Robert E. Lee with a detachment of U.S. Marines to subdue Brown. All of Garrett's 379-mile railroad was located in slave states, and the majority of the line was in Virginia, a state soon to secede. Garrett had long considered the B & O to be a Southern rail-road, but he knew that the future of his road lay with the North and the Union rather than the South. West-ern flour and Cumberland coal, both headed north, not the tobacco and cotton from Southern plantations, had made Baltimore and the B & O prosperous. In the troubled days of late April and early May 1861, Garrett

*As plank
roads, river
improvements,
and later railroads
connected the
Southern interior
to northeastern
and midwestern
markets, large
farmers seized the
opportunity
to make ever
greater profits.*

PAGE 213

and the B & O were regarded suspiciously and pressured by both the Union and the Confederacy.

Col. Thomas J. ("Stonewall") Jackson and his Confederate forces started to occupy the Harpers Ferry area in May 1861. Soon he was in effective control of forty-four miles of B & O track west of Harpers Ferry. On May 23, 1861, he captured fifty-six B & O engines and three hundred freight cars. Many of the locomotives were put to the torch, but a few were dragged on wagons behind dozens of horses to other Virginia lines to serve the Confederate war effort. Jackson also destroyed dozens of bridges and other B & O equipment west of Harpers Ferry. The B & O was not able to restore service in the region fully until March 1862. It is not surprising that during the spring months of 1861 Garrett's language describing the Confederacy shifted from "our southern friends" to "misguided friends" and finally to "damned rebels."

CONFEDERATE ADMINISTRATION. During the entire conflict the Confederate government's control of the railroads was far from effective. The widespread belief that the war would be short, the early failure to recognize the importance of the railroads in the war effort, and the reluctance of the Davis administration to override state authority contributed to the lack of effective regulation. Late in April 1861, thirty-three railroad presidents met in Montgomery and agreed to a uniform fare of two cents a mile for troops, and half the normal freight rate for the shipping of war munitions and provisions. They also agreed to accept Confederate bonds at par in payment for military transportation. A second convention of presidents at Chattanooga in October 1861 modified the Montgomery agreement, and the new rate structure was approved by Quartermaster General Abraham C. Myers. As the currency depreciated, steadily higher fares and rates were approved. The government never tried to control railroad charges for the general public.

On the eve of First Manassas, President Jefferson Davis believed rail congestion so severe that he commissioned as a major and assistant quartermaster William S. Ashe, former president of the Wilmington and Weldon. Ashe was placed in charge of military rail transportation in Virginia, especially the lines serving Richmond. Major Ashe quickly set up his Richmond office, but Myers retained real control of railroad traffic, employing Ashe only as a subordinate. Confederate rail traffic problems were little improved, and in December 1862, Secretary of War George Wythe Randolph assigned Col. William M. Wadley to the supervision of "all the railroads in the Confederate States." But Wadley's appointment was never approved, and a third man, Capt. Frederick W. Sims, replaced him in May 1863. Sims had no greater success than his predecessors, however.

Some problems, such as changes of gauge at transfer points, were incapable of solution. At such cities as Richmond, Petersburg, and Lynchburg in Virginia; Wilmington and Charlotte in North Carolina; Columbus in Georgia; and Montgomery in Alabama, the connecting lines were of different gauges: 5 feet or 4 feet 8 ½ inches. At these points the shifting of

RAILROAD CONSTRUCTION IN THE SOUTH DURING THE 1850S					
State	**Mileage in 1850**	**Mileage in 1860**	**Increase in Decade**	**Investment per Mile**	**Dominant Gauge**
Virginia	481	1,731	1,250	$36,679	4'8½"
North Carolina	283	937	654	18,796	4'8½"
South Carolina	289	973	684	22,675	5'0"*
Georgia	643	1,420	777	20,696	5'0"*
Florida	21	402	381	21,356	5'0"*
Tennessee	—	1,253	1,253	24,677	5'0"*
Alabama	183	743	560	25,022	5'0"
Mississippi	75	862	787	27,982	5'0"
Louisiana	80	335	255	35,988	5'6"
Arkansas	—	38	38	30,394	5'6"*
Texas	—	307	307	36,706	5'6"
Total	2,055	9,001	6,946		

*Only gauge in the state

freight from one car to another could not be avoided. Even when connecting lines were in the same gauge, few railroad officials would permit their cars to be used on a foreign road. In many cities, such as Petersburg, Bristol, Knoxville, Chattanooga, Savannah, and Augusta, the terminating lines did not actually connect, and freight had to be hauled by wagon from one station to another. In June 1861, General Lee had urged that connecting track be laid in Petersburg. Many lines had earlier sought such tracks but had been stopped by strong transfer and hotel interests. During the war rail connections were achieved in some cities, but delays in the movement of troops and supplies persisted.

Early in the war both Davis and Lee were aware of several major gaps in the rail system. The 300-mile system in Texas was not tied to the Confederate rail network, and only a weak connecting line on the Georgia border eventually gave service to the 400 miles of railroad in Florida. Far more serious were smaller gaps—one along the Virginia–North Carolina border and a second in Alabama. In November 1861, Davis strongly urged the construction of a 48-mile connecting line between Danville, the southern terminal of the 143-mile Richmond and Danville, and Greensboro, located on the North Carolina Railroad. The building of such a link would give Richmond a third rail route with the states to the south, located between the exposed Weldon-Wilmington coastal line and the mountain route through eastern Tennessee. The Confederate Congress, in February 1862, appropriated $1 million to aid a private company, the Piedmont Railroad, to build such a line. But prominent leaders like Robert Barnwell Rhett, Sr., and Robert Toombs strongly protested the action. North Carolina planters along the route would not permit their slaves to work on the line, and North Carolina Governor Zebulon Vance, a firm advocate of state rights, also opposed it. As a result the project lagged and was finished only in the spring of 1864. The completion was timely since the Weldon-Wilmington coastal route was broken by Union troops later in the year. In the last year of the war a major portion of Lee's supplies moved north over the Piedmont Railroad.

The other major gap closed was between Selma, Alabama, and Meridian, Mississippi, a distance of under a hundred miles. Upon the recommendation of Davis the Confederate Congress on February 15, 1862, provided $150,000 to finish the partially built road between the two cities. The completion of this link late in 1862 provided both a shorter rail route from Vicksburg to Richmond and rail transportation well removed from the vulnerable Gulf coast. But during the war the Confederacy built no more than 200 miles of new line while over 3,000 miles were constructed in the United States.

The most pressing problem facing Confederate railroad officials was simply keeping their lines operating. Proper maintenance grew more difficult with every passing month. Rail, ties, fuel, replacement parts, and labor became more scarce as the war progressed. With all sources for new iron rail exhausted early in the war, managers were desperate to find iron. Though the Southern lines should have had about 4,000 tons of replacement rail each month, not a single new rail was produced in the Confederacy between 1862 and 1865.

The Western and Atlantic stumbled upon 1,100 tons of rail in Savannah and quickly bought it for $50 a ton, giving the line enough for about 15 miles of track. Late in 1861 Stonewall Jackson removed much of the rail from 19 miles of B&O double track between Harpers Ferry and Martinsburg and sent it south for the hard-pressed Confederate roads. In 1862 it was said there were 1,200 broken rails on the line from Nashville to Chattanooga, and many roads were so hard up for replacements they took up rail from side tracks, and later even branch lines, to repair their main stems.

Even the Confederate navy sought railroad iron. In June 1862, the Navy Department, headed by Stephen R. Mallory, impressed 1,100 tons of rail belonging to the 109-mile Atlantic and Gulf Railroad in Georgia to be used for the manufacture of ship's armor. In January 1863, the Iron Commission was created to determine what railroad iron could "best be dispensed with." Soon whole railroads were being taken over so their rail could be used on more important routes. Short lines were seized in North Carolina, Georgia, Florida, and Texas, but this only created new problems: as short or branch lines were dismantled, supplies for the army correspondingly declined.

By the middle years of the war, wood for cross ties and fuel grew scarce because of a shortage of labor to cut the wood. Often train crews made frequent stops on their routes to gather wood. In 1863 the North Carolina Railroad found cordwood so scarce it purchased wooded acres to ensure a steady supply and for a while demanded that half of any wood it hauled had to be sold to it.

The care and repair of locomotives and cars was another problem. Longer trains, the shortage of replacement parts, and the lack of skilled labor combined to make engines deteriorate more rapidly. By 1863 and 1864 a quarter of the locomotives of many lines needed repairs, and at least fifty engines were laid up because of the lack of tires for their drivers. The quality of passenger service also declined. By midwar many passenger cars were operating with broken windows, no water for the passengers, and no firewood for the coach's stove. Army use of passenger cars was often cited as the cause of missing seats, stoves, lamps,

Major rivers carried products from the hinterlands to the sea; roads and railroads supplemented that movement without major redirections of the traffic flow.

PAGE 619

*All but one of the
railroads that
connected
Richmond to
remaining
Confederate
supplies passed
first through
Petersburg.*

PAGE 419

*Transportation
routes in the
antebellum South
developed mainly
to get cash crops
out to the seaports.*

PAGE 619

and water barrels when the coaches were finally returned to the owning road. The vast numbers of soldiers being moved by rail made it frequently necessary to use boxcars fitted with plank seats. In winter weather the troops often built fires on the floors of freight cars and left them burning when they debarked. When Gen. James Longstreet's men rode the rails to Chickamauga in September 1863, the soldiers pried boards from the side walls of the boxcars to improve the ventilation and the view. Passenger trains that had traveled 15 to 20 miles an hour in 1860 had dropped to 6 miles an hour by the end of the war.

The shortage of labor that started in 1861 when Northerners returned home grew worse when wages in munition plants outstripped the pay scales of most railroads. Eventually railroads raised wages but still lagged well behind the growing inflation rate. Several Confederate generals aggravated the shortage of skilled mechanics by keeping such men in uniform when they would have been more useful in railroad work. The Conscription Act of 1862 treated rail workers generously, exempting some six thousand. But the 1864 act was stiffer; it raised the draft age to fifty, and permitted no railroad to have more employees than miles of road.

Though there are no firm figures for the number of railroad employees, it seems probable that the number of employees early in the war was much larger than the number of miles of line (5,500–6,000) in operation in 1864. Of course, slaves made up an important portion of all railroad workers. Usually performing the less skilled jobs, they were either owned by the railroad or rented from slaveholders. Certainly all railroad workers at the end of the war were paid far less in real dollars than they were receiving in 1861. Thomas Webb, president of the North Carolina Railroad, made $6,000 a year in 1864, a figure worth no more at that point than $300 in gold. Before the war locomotive firemen were paid $300 a year, and the president received $2,500 a year.

But even with all their problems, rail lines on several occasions moved large bodies of Confederate troops long distances. When George B. McClellan's Union army threatened Richmond in early June 1862, Lee felt secure enough to send two brigades (nearly 10,000 men) by rail west to Charlottesville to strengthen Stonewall Jackson in the Shenandoah Valley. Later Jackson's enlarged forces returned by rail to face McClellan's left flank and pushed the Union army away from Richmond in the Seven Days' Battles. The entire operation lasted just over three weeks, with the troops moving more than 250 miles over seven or eight railroads.

Two massive troop movements were carried out later near Chattanooga. By the summer of 1862 Corinth and a large portion of the Memphis and Charleston line were in Union hands. In the last days of June, Braxton Bragg decided to move his army of about 25,000 men from northeastern Mississippi to Chattanooga, which was threatened by Union forces under Don Carlos Buell. The distance from Tupelo to Chattanooga is a little over 200 miles as the crow flies. Bragg's route by railroad covered 775 miles via the Mobile and Ohio to Mobile and then northeast over five short Alabama and Georgia lines to Atlanta and Chattanooga. The entire operation took a little more than a week. A year later, in mid-September, Bragg was reinforced during the Battle of Chickamauga when James Longstreet's First Corps of the Army of Virginia arrived from Richmond. The 12,000 Confederate troops had moved south about 900 miles in ten days using a dozen railroads in Virginia, the Carolinas, and Georgia. Confederate railroads were still in reasonable shape in the fall of 1863.

UNION CAPTURE AND DESTRUCTION. During the four years of the war Union forces slowly but steadily encroached upon the northern and western frontiers of the Confederacy. During 1861 the Union armies reclaimed the northwestern counties of Virginia. In 1862 the South lost more of what would become West Virginia, half of Arkansas, the western half of Tennessee, a portion of Mississippi, and the area around New Orleans. The loss of the Mississippi River cut the Confederacy in two, and most of Arkansas and Tennessee plus large portions of Mississippi and Louisiana came under Union control. These Union gains were accompanied by the destruction of hundreds of miles of Confederate railways. The more important of the lines were rebuilt by the U.S. Military Railroad, an agency of the War Department created in 1862, under the supervision of Gen. Daniel C. McCallum.

One of the first railroad raids—colorful but totally ineffective—was the Andrews Raid of April 1862, in which a band of disguised Union soldiers stole the locomotive General and tried to wreck the Western and Atlantic Railroad. Two years later, in spring 1864, William Tecumseh Sherman with a strong Union army left Chattanooga and headed for Atlanta, following the track of the Western and Atlantic. For several months the normal daily flow of supplies to the 100,000 men and 35,000 animals in Sherman's army consisted of sixteen trains, each composed of ten cars (10-ton capacity). This daily total of 1,600 tons was in marked contrast to the pitiful rations reaching Lee's army defending Richmond in 1864 and 1865. In the last months of the war Lee's supply trains were often delayed and his army was frequently reduced to two or three days of rations.

After taking Atlanta late in the summer of 1864 Sherman destroyed the rail line back to Chattanooga and set out for Savannah. On his march to the sea he left the railroads in central Georgia in tatters. He destroyed hundreds of miles of line, especially hitting the 191-mile Central of Georgia and the 102-mile Macon and Western. After leaving Savannah early in 1865, Sherman wreaked equal havoc on the rail system of South Carolina, including the railroads serving Columbia, the state capital.

By 1865 the U.S. Military Railroad controlled 2,100 miles of line, most of it former Confederate railroads. Hundreds of miles of railroads were out of operation by March and April. When Union forces cut the South Side Railroad near Richmond early in April, the end of the long conflict was near. As Lee's exhausted army moved toward Appomattox, the railroads were as crippled and defeated as the Southern armies they had vainly sought to support.

The long war had broken or destroyed the great majority of the Southern railroads, leaving twisted rails, burnt ties, gutted shops and depots, ruined bridges, and dilapidated or lost rolling stock. In May 1865, Chief Justice Salmon P. Chase visited North Carolina. The judge was provided with a train described by the correspondent Whitelaw Reid as "a wheezy little locomotive and an old mail agent's car, with all the windows smashed out and half the seats gone." Some lines were out of operation for many months. But a rehabilitation program aided by the Federal government resulted in both the fast return of the Southern roads General McCallum had rebuilt and the sale of government-owned cars and equipment to private parties. Most Southern roads were offering some kind of service by Christmas, 1865.

The inability of the Southern railways to support the Confederacy adequately resulted from several factors. In 1861 Confederate railroads were generally weak and inferior to Northern lines. Shortages of materials and labor made proper maintenance more difficult with each passing year. But a fundamental factor was the Southern belief in state rights. Since most railroads represented a single state, the individual lines subscribed to this doctrine with the same vigor as the governors and cabinet members who quarreled with Jefferson Davis. As a result the Richmond government was never able to provide a strong centralized supervision of the railroads and failed to support them when they were in peril.

[*See also entries on selected battles and campaigns mentioned herein, particularly* Andrews Raid.]

— JOHN F. STOVER

RAINS, GABRIEL J.

Rains, Gabriel J. (1803–1881), brigadier general. A native of Craven County, North Carolina, Rains graduated from West Point in 1827. He distinguished himself in the Seminole War (1839–1842, 1849–1850) and the Mexican War. Resigning from the U.S. Army with a rank of lieutenant colonel on

LANDMINE PIONEER

Brig. Gen. Gabriel J. Rains killed Union soldiers, sparked controversy, and won a promotion by his use of landmines—weapons whose morality is still disputed.

LIBRARY OF CONGRESS

July 1, 1861, Rains began his Confederate service as a colonel of infantry in the army. On September 23, 1861, he received a brigadier general's commission and a brigade on the Virginia Peninsula. He saw action at Yorktown (April 4–May 3), Williamsburg (May 4–5), and Seven Pines (May 31–June 1). During the retreat from Williamsburg and Yorktown, Rains planted shells with percussion caps in the road, which caused considerable destruction as the Federals advanced. Controversy surrounded his booby traps in the North and the South, and Gen. James Longstreet prohibited him from further engaging in such questionable means of warfare.

Shortly after Seven Pines, George Wythe Randolph, the secretary of war, placed Rains under the War Department so that he could experiment with explosives. Commanding Richmond's Bureau of Conscription during the winter of 1862–1863, Rains convinced Jefferson Davis that mines had military value and were not immoral. Rains reasoned that each new weapon was declared "barbarous" when first introduced, but eventually "each took its place according to its efficacy in human slaughter." On May 25, he began supervising the defense of a number of harbors— namely, Mobile, Charleston, and Savannah. For his efforts, Rains was assigned the superintendency of the Torpedo Bureau on June 17, 1864. His innovative development of an explosive sub terra shell demonstrated the future potential of mines.

Navy Secretary Mallory early recognized the potential of armorclad warships in offsetting the South's numerical disadvantage.

PAGE 651

After the war, Rains worked as a chemist in Augusta, Georgia. He died on August 6, 1881, and was buried in Aiken, South Carolina.

— PETER S. CARMICHAEL

RAMS

The ship-killing ram of the ancient Mediterranean was given new life during the Civil War: steam power replaced the human muscles of the rowed galleys of antiquity, and iron armor protected rams from enemy gunfire. Southern leaders recognized that they would be unable to equal the North in numbers of warships, so they sought to build a fleet that was qualitatively superior. Armored rams provided an equalizing weapon. Existing vessels and power plants (propulsion machineries) were reinforced for ramming and rebuilt with iron armor. In addition, new vessels were built with rams and armored casemates; most had simplified hull forms designed to be built by carpenters unfamiliar with ship construction. Steam propulsion was universal, but rams built for service on the coast used screw propellers; those on the western rivers usually used paddle wheels in armored housings.

The first armored ram to see service was the propeller tugboat *Enoch Train*, which was rebuilt by private parties in New Orleans to become the privateer *Manassas*. It was seized by the Confederate navy and led the Confederate fleet in the Battle of the Mississippi, below New Orleans. *Manassas* rammed two Union warships but ran aground and was destroyed by its crew to prevent capture.

The most famous and influential ram was CSS *Virginia*, rebuilt from the burned steam frigate *Merrimack*. *Virginia* enjoyed a single day of success in Hampton Roads, Virginia, sinking two powerful Union vessels before meeting the Union ironclad *Monitor*, which had been built particularly to counter the threat posed by *Virginia*. *Monitor* and the turreted ironclads that followed it were designed with a projecting knuckle or "raft" to protect against Confederate rams. The two ironclads, the ram and the antiram, stalemated each other for over two months before Norfolk was captured, forcing the destruction of *Virginia*.

Rams were built on the shores of all the major navigable rivers of the Confederacy. They were intended to protect the rivers as interior lines of communication and to prevent the North from dividing the country by taking the rivers. Ironclads were built on the James River; on the North Carolina sounds; at Wilmington, Charleston, Savannah, and Mobile; and on the Mississippi and Red rivers. They were feared by Federal sailors, inducing in many the fearful condition derisively known as "ram fever."

Many vessels on the Western Rivers—the Mississippi, Missouri, Ohio, Red, Yellow, Yazoo, and their tributaries— were heavily reinforced and rebuilt with projecting ram bows. These river rams were usually paddle-wheel river steamers, with fragile hulls and superstructures. Lightly armed because their light hulls could not support the shock of firing heavy guns, they were protected with whatever materials were available: many Southern riverboats were covered with compressed bales of cotton, becoming cottonclads. Both sides also added heavy wood walls (woodclads) or sheets of half- to one-inch iron plates (tinclads). All depended on the ram as their main weapon.

Most Confederate rams were built with a strong armored beak ram on the bow, an armored knuckle protecting the waterline, and a sloping armored casemate to protect a small number of heavy guns. The ram was intended to be the main offensive weapon. The fatal flaw of most Southern rams was their low speed and poor maneuverability. Few foundries were capable of producing marine engines, and those that could were already producing at capacity. Confederate naval engineers adapted engines from other vessels, but few rams could steam over five knots.

Five powerful oceangoing steam rams were built abroad for the Confederate navy. James Dunwoody Bulloch ordered two rams from the shipyards of England and two from France. The first two, to be named *North Carolina* and *Mississippi*, were built by the shipyard of John Laird and Sons, Birkenhead, England. Their destination became known before delivery, however, leading to a lengthy court case and seizure by the British government to prevent the violation of neutrality. Bulloch, at the urging of John Slidell, also ordered a pair of ironclad rams from the shipyard of Lucien Arman of France. The rams were given the cover names *Sphinx* and *Cheops*, but they were prevented from sailing when their destination became known. Through a complicated arrangement, one ram was sold to Denmark, resold to the Confederacy, and delivered at sea. This ram was armed, commissioned CSS *Stonewall*, and taken to Havana, where it was delivered to the Spanish authorities at the end of the war. The fifth and largest ram was ordered by James H. North from the shipyard of James and George Thomson, of Govan, Glasgow, Scotland. It was built using the cover name *No. 61*, but proved too expensive and grand for Confederate needs. The ship was sold and became *Danmark* in the Danish navy. The Thomsons also proposed building a double-turret armored ram that was not ordered.

Only one Confederate ironclad ram was sunk in action by the enemy: *Albemarle*, defending Plymouth,

North Carolina, and much of the interior of the state, was sunk by a small boat expedition using a spar torpedo. Two were captured in action: the rams *Atlanta,* near Savannah, and *Tennessee,* in Mobile Bay, were taken after they were rammed repeatedly and heavily shelled by Union vessels.

Many Confederate rams were destroyed to prevent capture. *Virginia* was blown up when Norfolk was abandoned. The large rams *Louisiana* and *Mississippi* were destroyed near New Orleans after the forts and city surrendered. *Arkansas* was set afire when it lost power and capture appeared imminent. Retreating forces destroyed four ironclad rams of the James River Fleet, two on Mobile Bay, two in Charleston Harbor, and one each on the Chattahoochee, Savannah, and Neuse rivers. Other, incomplete ironclad rams were destroyed across the South before advancing Union ground forces could take possession.

Confederate rams were the capital ships of the navy: fleets were built around the armored juggernauts that could convey naval force anywhere on the rivers. Rams offered the only possible counter to Union seapower and were successful in defending many areas of the South. Despite the small amount of action they saw, the Confederate ironclad rams *Chicora* and *Palmetto State* at Charleston; *Virginia II, Richmond, Fredericksburg,* and *Texas* in the James River Fleet; and *Huntsville, Tuscaloosa, Tennessee, Nashville,* and *Phoenix* in Mobile Bay all protected large seaboard cities for most of the war. Ironclad rams were an integral part of Confederate coastal defense plans. Those defenses allowed the South to retain control of important seaport cities, prevented the enemy from using the easy routes inland along the rivers, and kept seaports open for trade with other areas.

[*See also entry on the ship* Virginia.]

— KEVIN J. FOSTER

RANDOLPH, GEORGE WYTHE

Randolph, George Wythe (1818–1867), brigadier general and secretary of war. Randolph was the most successful of Thomas Jefferson's grandsons. Educated at home, in Boston, and in Washington, he entered the U.S. Navy as a midshipman at the age of thirteen. He became a charismatic leader, toured the ports of the Mediterranean and Caribbean, and attended David Farragut's school at Norfolk. On the USS *Constitution* he contracted tuberculosis, followed by a long period of remission. After qualifying as a passed midshipman, he attended the University of Virginia, where in 1841 he

took one of its first law degrees and studied engineering and science. For a decade he practiced law at Charlottesville before moving to Richmond. Randolph was an officer of the Virginia Historical Society, a founder

ASTUTE ADVISER

Grandson of Thomas Jefferson, George Wythe Randolph drafted Virginia's conscription law, served as secretary of war, and advised Jefferson Davis to devote more attention to the West.

LIBRARY OF CONGRESS

of the Richmond Mechanics Institute, and a leading criminal and admiralty lawyer.

Alarmed by John Brown's raid at Harpers Ferry, Randolph in 1859 organized the Richmond Howitzers, which he took to Charles Town in present-day West Virginia to act as guards until Brown was hanged. In 1860 Randolph served as a Virginia commissioner to contract for armaments in the North. Predicting Abraham Lincoln's election and arguing that neutrality was impossible, he urged that Virginia join in a Southern republic. He was a member of the Virginia convention of 1861, which sent him, William Ballard Preston, and A. H. H. Stuart to confer with President Lincoln. On April 12, Lincoln told them that he would meet force with force. After his call for troops, Virginia seceded.

Colonel Randolph then oversaw the enlargement of the Richmond Howitzers, which he led in winning the Battle of Big Bethel on June 10, 1861. As Gen. John B. Magruder's chief of ordnance, he helped design and arm fortifications at Yorktown. He was promoted to brigadier general and given a command in southeastern Virginia.

Randolph made three major contributions to the Confederacy. The first was his drafting of Virginia's conscription law, based on European models. It, in turn, became the model for Confederate conscription. His second was his work as secretary of war, a post he assumed in March 1862. At the outset of the Peninsular campaign, he and Robert E. Lee advised against Joseph E. Johnston's proposal for a hasty abandonment of Yorktown and retreat toward Richmond.

Randolph's greatest service as War Secretary was in establishing the first military draft in America, in April 1862, with the Conscription Act.

PAGE 658

By mid-1862 Randolph spotted the weak point in the South's defenses, and proposed a strong autonomous Department of the West.

PAGE 658

Randolph resigned in Nov. 1862 after eight months in office.

PAGE 658

Randolph delayed execution of Johnston's order to evacuate Norfolk until war matèriel could be removed.

In organizing the War Office, Randolph named his nephew-in-law Garlick Kean chief of the Bureau of War and Josiah Gorgas chief of the Bureau of Ordnance. To solve problems of procuring war matèriel and foodstuffs, he recruited specialists in foreign trade, agriculture, and railroads, as well as a number of lawyers who were alumni of the University of Virginia and Yale. These technocrats administered centralized planning and control from Richmond. Randolph increased the importation of war goods, including tinned bully-beef and Enfield rifles, by offering foreign suppliers and blockade runners greater profits for essential goods. To encourage manufacturers to convert to war goods, he assigned low priorities on the railroads for shipping civilian goods.

Randolph believed that Confederate armies were under strength not because governors hoarded troops but because lenient officers condoned absenteeism. His proposed remedy was to send missions authorized to investigate and punish offenders. When he became convinced that he could not provide enough food for the Confederate armies, he tried to persuade President Davis to permit the exchange of Confederate cotton for Union bacon. Although Randolph was secretary only nine months, his organization of the War Office endured for the life of the Confederacy.

Randolph's third contribution was his advising Davis to devote more attention to the West. Relying on information from his New Orleans recruits, he devised a scheme to liberate that city in the summer of 1862 through a combination of conventional means and a fifth-column uprising. Military events in Tennessee and Virginia occupied the Southern troops, however. From the outset of his secretaryship, he had declared that, unless there were radical changes in policy, he would be unable to provision adequately the Army of Northern Virginia, much less the other military units or the civilian population. Denying this, Davis procrastinated in authorizing Randolph's plans to recover New Orleans, the South's greatest port, and to import foodstuffs from Europe and the U.S. The secretary and the president did not make a good team. Davis's indecisiveness wore Randolph down, and he finally seized on a procedural pretext to resign in November 1862, leaving no possibility of reconsideration.

No longer in the Confederate army, Randolph assumed command of volunteers to defend Richmond from a threatened Union raid in May 1863. As a member of the city council at the time of the bread riots, he encouraged workers to demand increased wages to meet inflation. In November 1864 his health had so deteriorated that he and his wife ran the blockade and sailed for Europe. He consulted doctors in London, conferred with manufacturers, and wintered in southern France. Randolph delayed his return to the United States until September 1866 when he received a pardon. He died in April 1867 in Albemarle County, Virginia.

— GEORGE GREEN SHACKELFORD

REAGAN, JOHN H.

Reagan, John H. (1818–1905), congressman from Texas and postmaster general. John Henninger Reagan, a native of Tennessee, was born October 8, 1818, and moved to Texas in 1839. He had a farm in Kaufman County and was an attorney, judge, and Democratic politician in the prewar years. He served two terms in the U.S. House of Representatives, 1857 to 1861. Although an advocate of Southern rights, he was not a radical Southerner in Congress and opposed such controversial issues as reopening the African slave trade and the acquisition of territory in Cuba, Mexico, and Central America. His experiences in the Thirty-fifth and Thirty-sixth Congresses convinced him, however, that the Republican majority would not look after the interests of his state or the South.

Reagan returned to the national capital following the election of Abraham Lincoln as president with some hope that the Union could be preserved, but that optimism quickly dissolved as he observed the efforts in Washington to reach a compromise. On December 14, 1860, he and twenty-nine other Southern congressmen composed a joint letter to their constituents. The group concluded that compromise with the Republican majority was impossible and that separation from the Union was necessary. Convinced that he could do nothing more to help achieve a solution to the sectional conflict, Reagan returned to Texas in January 1861.

On the way home Reagan learned that he had been elected to the Texas secession convention. He went directly to Austin but did not arrive there until January 30, two days after the convention began. Reagan nevertheless played a critical role in the proceedings. Believing that Governor Sam Houston, who remained loyal to the Union, might cause trouble for the secessionists, Reagan met with the governor on the day he arrived and tried to persuade him not to obstruct the proceedings of the convention. Houston informed Reagan that he would not oppose the will of the people and that he would meet with a delegation from the convention. Reagan headed the committee sent the next day to confer with the governor. Houston provided a formal announcement that he recognized the results of the election of delegates and the legitimacy of the convention. This paved the way for the passage of an ordinance of secession on February 1.

The convention elected Reagan as a member of the Provisional Congress at Montgomery. Personal business required him to remain in Texas until that March, however; thus he missed the establishment of the Confederacy and the election of Jefferson Davis as provisional president. He arrived in Montgomery on March 1 and took his seat in Congress the next day. There he earned the admiration of President Davis and a reputation for bluntness. Reagan told the newly elected president that he would not have voted for him had he been present. Reagan explained that his decision was not based on any question concerning Davis's fitness for the office; rather, he would have preferred that Davis head the army.

Reagan's encounter with the president may have helped the executive make his decision to appoint the congressman as postmaster general. The cabinet post was a critical one for the new government. Good mail service was essential for the dissemination of information, particularly the distribution of newspapers. The mails were also a potentially important factor in the event of war; letters between soldiers in the field and their families at home could help morale.

The task faced by the postmaster general, however, would be extremely difficult for two reasons: the constitutional provision that the Post Office Department must pay its own expenses out of revenue after March 1, 1863, and the strain a war would place on the system. When the president's first two choices turned the job down, Davis turned to Reagan, who had been a member of the Postal Committee in the U.S. House of Representatives and had been recommended by the Texas delegation. On March 6, Davis asked Reagan to accept the post. Reagan initially turned it down but finally accepted, despite his reluctance to take on such a difficult job. His nomination was immediately confirmed by the Congress.

The new postmaster general began building his system by raiding the Washington offices of the U.S. Post Office for men with knowledge of that system's operations. His department heads brought with them the annual reports of the postmaster general, blank forms, and postal maps and modeled their post office on that of the United States. As much as possible those connected with the Federal post offices in the South were integrated into the Confederate department, although some individuals and contractors refused to remain with it.

From the beginning the constitutional provision requiring the post office to be self-supporting was a major concern for Reagan. Figures showing the cost of mail service in the South during the last full year of peace indicated the extent of his problem. In 1860 the Post Office Department had spent nearly $3 million while producing revenues of less than $1 million. Reagan would not be able to continue that system, but

would have to both cut costs and increase revenues. He kept his own office staff at a minimum, closed some post offices, reduced the number of mail routes, discontinued duplicate service, and cut service on some routes from daily to triweekly delivery. He also negotiated a 50 percent reduction in the rates railroads charged to deliver the mail and cut mail service on the roads. In addition, he raised postage rates with the approval of Congress.

The U.S. postal system continued to operate in the South until Reagan ordered the inauguration of Confederate mail service on June 1, 1861, and provided for a final accounting and the return of all Federal property to the U.S. Post Office Department. From the beginning of its operations Reagan's system elicited complaints. It could not duplicate the service that Southerners had been used to receiving. Inadequate staffing, elimination of routes, reduction of the number of post offices, plus problems associated with creating a new system—contractors could not be found to deliver the mail in Texas and Arkansas, for example—produced a decline in service. Delays in delivery, loss of mail, thefts, lack of stamps and mail supplies, and high postal rates plagued the Confederate post office.

By the autumn of 1861 the press was filled with complaints. Even members of the cabinet expressed concern about the service. Burdened by the illness of his wife and upset by the criticism, Reagan submitted his resignation in 1862. President Davis persuaded him to remain in the cabinet, however, arguing that if he

Navy Secretary Mallory and Postmaster General Reagan were the only two men who remained in their cabinet positions throughout the conflict.

PAGE 343

left, the public might see it as an expression of dissatisfaction with the administration. Reagan continued in office, but though he earned a reputation for hard work and personal integrity, the postmaster general was never able to satisfy the system's numerous critics.

Producing satisfactory service and adhering to the constitutional provision of self-sufficiency became even more difficult as the war progressed. The destruction of railroads and the cutting of communication lines by the movement of the armies inevitably disrupted service. Many materials necessary for postal operations, ranging from stamps to mail bags, were difficult to obtain. Confederate conscription policy, however, proved to be one of the post office's most onerous burdens. This problem developed as the result of a supplemental Confederate conscription law passed in October 1862. The initial law, passed in April 1862, had provided extensive exemptions from conscription, including postal employees, but the October legislation exempted only those postmasters and contractors nominated for their positions by the president and confirmed by the Senate. Reagan reported that the number of individuals available to deliver the mails was thus reduced by some seven-eighths. He lobbied Congress for legislation that ultimately restored many of the exemptions for post office personnel, but as the Confederate army faced growing manpower shortages, conscript officers continued to impress employees. The postmaster general finally became involved in a virtual war with the military, encouraging his men to resist conscription by securing writs of habeas corpus and then suing the conscript officers for false arrest. The fight between Reagan and Secretary of War James A. Seddon over the conscription of post office personnel continued into the autumn of 1864 and ended only when Reagan decided that conditions in the Confederacy were so bad there was no point in pursuing the issue further.

The struggle between the post office and the military did have one favorable result. Reagan was able to obtain staff who would work for low wages and who bid low for mail delivery contracts so long as postal workers were exempt from military service. Mail service may have been inefficient, but the cost was low. This, combined with Reagan's early reduction in the overall size of the system, meant that the postmaster general was able to make the post office self-sustaining in the time allotted to him. By the end of 1863, his report indicated, the department was operating at a surplus.

Despite the criticism leveled at the postal service, many observers from the beginning considered Reagan to be one of the most capable of Davis's cabinet appointees. Even while accusing him of inefficiency, no critic ever considered Reagan to be anything other than of the most upstanding character. Considering the overwhelming problems of creating the new system, Reagan accomplished much, and the Confederacy never experienced within his department the same problems that developed in other government offices.

Reagan's duties as a cabinet officer went beyond his official role as postmaster general. He was one of the men Davis turned to for advice on the general problems facing the Confederacy. Despite his personal loyalty to the president, Reagan was forthright in his opposition to administration policies with which he disagreed. In 1863, the postmaster general found himself consistently in the minority on military matters. In particular, he opposed Robert E. Lee's invasion of Pennsylvania in the summer of that year and argued instead for moving more forces west in order to destroy Ulysses S. Grant's army, which was maneuvering to capture Vicksburg and cut the Confederacy in two. The differences between Reagan and other cabinet officials reached a point where Reagan offered to resign for a second time. But President Davis held his services to be too valuable and dissuaded him from this course.

On April 2, 1865, Postmaster General Reagan abandoned Richmond with President Davis in the hope of establishing the seat of government farther in the Confederate interior—a plan that went awry when Lee surrendered his army in northern Virginia. Another course was taken when Gen. Joseph E. Johnston began negotiating the surrender of his army. Reagan and Secretary of War John C. Breckinridge were sent to assist in the talks, where they offered a total Confederate surrender if the United States preserved the existing state governments, respected the political and property rights of Confederate citizens, and promised to impose no penalties on participants or to persecute them. After presenting this proposal, Reagan rejoined the president at Charlotte, North Carolina. When William Tecumseh Sherman ultimately offered only the terms Grant gave to Lee at Appomattox, the remaining cabinet members and the president resumed their flight, recommending that Johnston simply disband so that the army could reorganize elsewhere. Johnston chose to accept Sherman's terms.

At this point they hoped to reach Texas, where E. Kirby Smith's army remained intact. Other cabinet members resigned and returned home as the South's ultimate fate became obvious, but Reagan remained with the president. He was captured with the president's party on the evening of May 10, 1865, near Irwinville, Georgia.

Reagan was imprisoned until December 1865 at Fort Warren, where he wrote two important letters. The first, on May 28, urged President Andrew Johnson to adopt a lenient policy toward the defeated South, warning that a more radical approach would end in evil. A more controversial letter, on August 11, advised

Texans to accept the results of the war, including the end of slavery and the guarantee of civil rights and suffrage—restricted with educational and property qualifications—for blacks. The second letter was condemned by his constituents, but Reagan believed that such a course was necessary to avoid military rule and unqualified black suffrage.

After his release, Reagan returned to Texas and practiced law. He was also active in Democratic politics. He served in the Texas constitutional convention in 1875 and was a U.S. congressman (1875–1877) and senator (1887–1891). He died at Palestine, Texas, March 6, 1905.

— CARL H. MONEYHON

RED RIVER
CAMPAIGNS

Two ill-fated Union campaigns along central Louisiana's Red River, a natural invasion route into Texas, were fought for political, economic, ideological, and

diplomatic reasons rather than for purely military objectives. The liberation of Texas by the Union would placate Northern antislavery forces who considered Texas's 1845 admission as a slave state the culmination of a conspiracy led by Southern slave owners. Once freed, Texas, it was believed, would provide free-labor-grown cotton, which would simultaneously demonstrate the inferiority of slave labor and keep Northern mills running. This in turn would cement political support for the Republican party. Moreover, the occupation of Texas would eliminate Mexico's role in breaking the blockade and lessen the likelihood of French interference in Mexico. Last, the Red River valley itself contained large supplies of cotton, the capture of which offered huge financial and political incentives to the invading forces.

In the course of the campaigns, the Union lost 5,200 men and the Confederates, 4,200. Most important, these campaigns forced Gen. Ulysses S. Grant to delay his planned attack on Mobile, Alabama, for ten months and denied Gen. William Tecumseh Sherman 10,000 veterans when he marched against Gen. Joseph E. Johnston in Georgia. The campaigns ended in great controversy in both the North and the South.

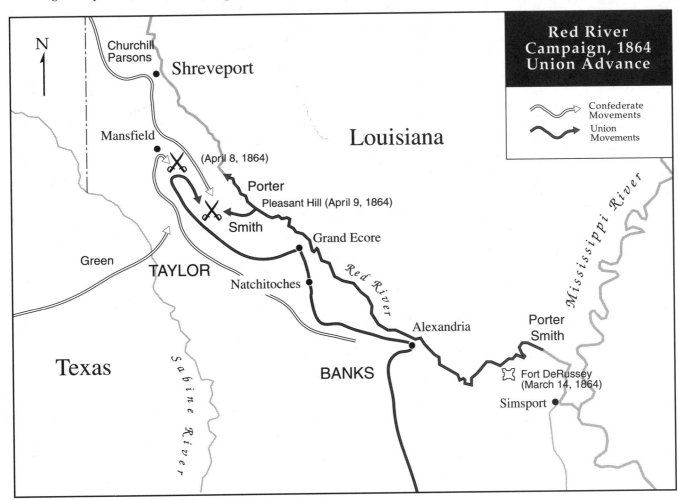

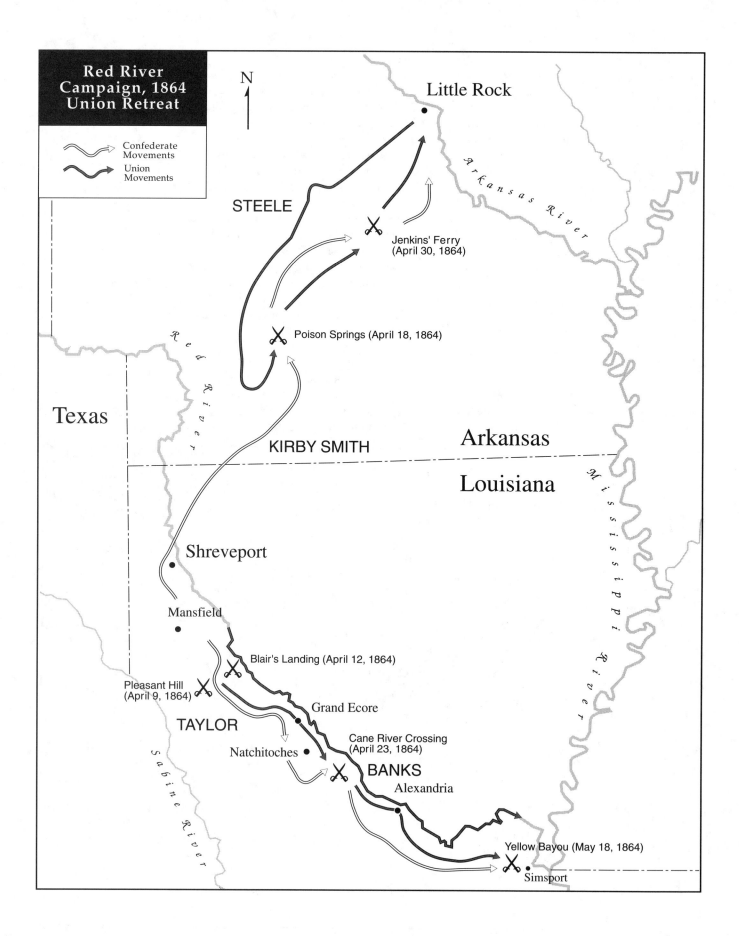

Red River
Campaign, 1864
Union Retreat

N

Confederate
Movements

Union
Movements

Little Rock

Arkansas River

STEELE

Jenkins' Ferry
(April 30, 1864)

Poison Springs (April 18, 1864)

Red River

Texas

KIRBY SMITH

Arkansas

Louisiana

Mississippi River

Shreveport

Mansfield

Blair's Landing (April 12, 1864)

Pleasant Hill
(April 9, 1864)

Grand Ecore

TAYLOR

Cane River Crossing
(April 23, 1864)

Natchitoches

BANKS

Sabine River

Alexandria

Yellow Bayou (May 18, 1864)

Simsport

The 1863 campaign was a sideline to the Union effort to capture Port Hudson, Louisiana, on the Mississippi River. In December 1862 Maj. Gen. Nathaniel P. Banks took command of the Department of the Gulf. He had been sent ostensibly to occupy any part of Texas in order to show the U.S. flag to the French in Mexico. But the more pressing matter of controlling the Mississippi claimed his attention. From April through July 1863 Banks cooperated with army and navy forces under Grant and Rear Adm. David G. Farragut operating against Port Hudson. Determined to clear all Confederate opposition to his west before moving on Port Hudson, Banks advanced up the Atchafalaya River and Bayou Teche as he headed for Alexandria, Louisiana. He defeated a small force under Maj. Gen. Richard Taylor at the Battles of Irish Bend and Fort Bisland on April 12 through 14. Banks then moved unopposed into Alexandria. At this point, Union General in Chief Henry W. Halleck reminded Banks of his orders. As a result Banks's planned move up the Red River to collect cotton and livestock ceased. In late May he left the Red River and moved against Port Hudson, which fell July 9.

With the Mississippi cleared, Banks was free to move against Texas; instead he and Grant wanted to attack Mobile. Halleck, however, now insisted on the campaign against Texas via the Red River, and with President Abraham Lincoln's strong backing, he ordered the campaign. The plan called for Banks with his 17,000 troops to be joined by 10,000 of Sherman's men commanded by Brig. Gen. Andrew Jackson Smith, Brig. Gen. Frederick Steele's force of 15,000 from the Department of Arkansas, and a naval flotilla that included thirteen ironclads under Rear Adm. David D. Porter. Banks was to move north up Bayou Teche, Smith and Porter to steam up the Red River, and Steele to move south from Little Rock. The first two groups were to meet at Alexandria and advance on Shreveport, the ultimate goal of the campaign, where they would join Steele. In opposition, Gen. E. Kirby Smith could concentrate between 25,000 and 30,000 men taken from his commands in Texas, Louisiana, and Arkansas. Smith instructed Taylor, commanding in Louisiana, to decline any offer for a general engagement until all the reinforcements arrived.

The Union plan fell apart from the outset. Banks and A. J. Smith were to meet at Alexandria by March 17, 1864. Timing was crucial for two reasons: first, Porter's vessels required the high water brought by the spring rains to navigate the river; second, Grant released Sherman's men only with the promise that they would be returned no later than April 10. Porter entered the Red River on March 12 and moved upstream. Smith's corps, landed at Simsport by Porter, marched on and captured Fort DeRussy on March 14

after a brief engagement. Porter then steamed unopposed to Alexandria, arriving on the fifteenth, Smith's men joining them the next day. In the meantime, Banks was detained in New Orleans supervising elections to install a new free state government, and he did not arrive until the twenty-fourth; his men were not present until the twenty-sixth.

While the Union forces were assembling in Alexandria, Kirby Smith had ordered all but 2,300 men of Maj. Gen. John B. Magruder's Texas force to join Taylor and also instructed Maj. Gen. Sterling Price's entire Arkansas command of 14,000 to move to Shreveport. Taylor offered only token resistance as he waited for the promised help.

Banks advanced despite the late date. After reaching Grand Encore, he made the key mistake of the campaign. Rather than advancing along the Red River in concert with Porter's powerful fleet, he ordered the bulk of his army to move inland, which gave Porter the opportunity to scour the surrounding countryside for contraband. The two armies skirmished continually through the end of March and into early April as Taylor ordered his forces back, first to Natchitoches, then to Pleasant Hill, and finally to Mansfield.

At Mansfield, Taylor established a strong defensive position with his own men and the recently arrived reinforcements. On the morning of April 8 Banks's advance force encountered Taylor's cavalry under Gen. Tom Green, just in from Texas. Green offered stiff resistance as he fell back to the main defensive line. Banks, thinking his opponent would retreat as he had for the past two weeks, pressed on. Taylor, despite Kirby Smith's orders to avoid a pitched battle, attacked. Gen. Alfred Mouton's division led the Confederate charge that routed Banks's army. Union losses at Mansfield numbered almost 2,900, while Confederate casualties totaled 1,000. During the night Banks fell back to Pleasant Hill. On the afternoon of the ninth, Taylor again attacked, but the Union lines held. Union losses at Pleasant Hill numbered almost 1,400, Confederate losses, nearly 1,500.

Each side considered Pleasant Hill a defeat, and both Banks and Kirby Smith—recently arrived on the battlefield—ordered a withdrawal. When Smith learned that Banks was retreating, he ordered all of Taylor's force except Brig. Gen. Camille J. Polignac's infantry division (formerly under Mouton, who was killed at Mansfield) and Brig. Gen. John Austin Wharton's cavalry to join Price so that he could "dispose of Steele." Taylor pleaded to keep the force together and to pursue Banks, but to no avail.

The Battles of Mansfield and Pleasant Hill marked Banks's farthest advance. The two defeats, the rapidly falling river, the overdue date for A. J. Smith's departure, and the inability to link up with Steele

Jackson was never apologetic about wounding the pride of others. "Through life," he insisted, "let your principal object be the discharge of duty."

PAGE 296

convinced Banks that he had to withdraw. Taylor continued to attack—at Blair's Landing (April 12), and Cane River Crossing (April 23)—but his remaining force was too small to stop Banks. Porter's fleet, meanwhile, faced the dual problems of low water and Confederate attacks. Only the engineering feats of Col. Joseph Bailey, who constructed a series of dams near Alexandria, saved the fleet. Taylor's and Banks's forces skirmished until May 13, the day the fleet finally floated by the rapids in Alexandria. The final engagement of the campaign was at Yellow Bayou on May 18. The next day an improvised bridge of ships allowed Banks's men and wagons to cross the Atchafalaya River. The campaign was over; it was time for the controversy.

In the South, Richard Taylor asked to be and was relieved of his command because of his dispute with Kirby Smith over the latter's deployment of Confederate forces. In the North, Banks, for his failures, was replaced, and the congressional Joint Committee on the Conduct of the War investigated the campaign, infamous for its cotton speculation as well as its military shortcomings.

— THOMAS J. LEGG

REFUGEEING

Beginning with northern Virginia families in the spring of 1861, perhaps as many as 200,000 Southern-

ers became refugees during the Civil War. As the Confederacy shrank, people left Kentucky, Tennessee, New Orleans, the Virginia peninsula, the Shenandoah Valley, and other areas to avoid the Northern invaders. Later on, many more fled from William Tecumseh Sherman's advancing army in Georgia and the Carolinas. Raids, skirmishes, and larger military campaigns all sent Southerners into short-term or long-term exile.

Simple fear of the enemy was the most powerful impetus: newspapers carried frightening tales of depredations and assaults on civilians. But food shortages and widespread suffering also forced families to move, even though some debated, planned, and hesitated for months before finally departing.

Refugees constituted a rough cross section of Southern society, and as the war dragged on, the planter class increasingly joined the exodus. Officers' families, state political leaders, and many professional men added a certain sophistication to this bedraggled group. Cities naturally attracted the most refugees, though yeoman and poor white families generally moved only short distances.

Packing (for those lucky enough to have sufficient warning of approaching Federals) became a major chore and a psychological ordeal as families tried to pile all their worldly possessions onto wagons or boxcars. Sifting through possessions accumulated during a lifetime could add to the distress, but if the refugees tried to take too much with them, they often had to leave surplus baggage along the roads. Given the scarcity and expense of transportation, Southerners

traveled by any available means including train, wagon, horse, or on foot. Hazardous river crossings and washed-out roads made for tortuous journeys. Along the way, filthy rooms and poor food were standard, and the more aristocratic resented hobnobbing with their social inferiors.

Cities, towns, and rural areas lacked the housing and even the food necessary to accommodate the flood of newcomers. "Shew me a safe point and I'll go tomorrow," South Carolinian Jane Pringle wrote, "but no such happy valley exists in the Confederacy." Richmond's population doubled during the war's first year, and displaced persons continued to arrive for the next three years. Other families chose surrounding towns and rural areas, making Virginia the state with the largest refugee population. Those fleeing the Carolina coast flocked to Raleigh, North Carolina, and Columbia, South Carolina. Georgia—especially Atlanta—attracted refugees from Kentucky, Tennessee, and the Deep South. Texas offered a spacious and relatively secure haven for families in the Trans-Mississippi Confederacy.

Refugees who managed to find a new home complained of spartan conditions and extortionate rents. By any standards their housing was uncomfortable, but a simple frame house must have looked magnificent to the poor souls who slept on church pews or in stables, carriage houses, tents, caves and even abandoned boxcars. Landlords seldom provided board and often raised rents, driving families to seek more affordable accommodations. With families often forced to cook in their rooms, speculators soon raised prices for all kinds of provisions. Grits, bacon, and cornbread became staples of the refugee diet, but the more destitute sometimes lived on berries, tomatoes, or fish. Bedding, clothing, and firewood were in equally short supply. The desperately poor finally had to rely on handouts from tight-fisted natives.

Often the social adjustment was even more difficult. Loneliness and despair dogged the lives of normally optimistic people. Families regularly welcomed kinfolk from distant places, but these new living arrangements caused considerable tension. Blood ties were often not strong enough to withstand the strain. Especially for women used to running their own households, living with relatives, much less strangers, could be frustrating. Natives begrudged sharing scarce housing and food with newcomers, particularly those from other states. Newspaper editors sympathized with the refugees' plight but often criticized their behavior. Even churches sometimes shunned them. A social cold war erupted, especially when displaced plantation families tried to lord it over their poorer neighbors. Provincialism and suspicion on both sides reinforced this hostility. So too boredom and home-

REFUGEE REVELRY

Regardless of these problems, refugees did manage to have a social life, notably in the towns and cities. Shared suffering could build a sense of community and even provide opportunity for pleasant diversions. Reading, writing letters, keeping a diary, and going to church filled in the times between special events. Among the fashionable set, parties, dances, and amateur theatricals, including the popular tableaux vivants (staged, motionless representations of famous scenes), helped the lonely and disheartened wile away the hours. Food was scarce and decorations limited, but weddings and holidays offered some relief from the drab lives led by most refugees. Christmas became the occasion for recalling happier times and perhaps momentarily forgetting the war, but makeshift gifts and disappointed children also served as painful reminders of the Confederacy's desperate straits.

— GEORGE C. RABLE

In Virginia in 1862, Federal raiders destroyed crops, confiscated livestock and farm animals, and demoralized the civilian population.

PAGE 539

sickness made some refugees into chronic malcontents. "Everyone speaks of the high spirits and cheerfulness of the refugees," wrote Louisianian Sidney Harding, "They little know of how many sad hours we have."

Refugees who idled away their time sparked resentment, but doctors, lawyers, bankers, and artisans tried to establish their old professions in their new homes. Ministers set up new churches; refugee newspaper editors kept changing their mastheads; in desperation, displaced housewives turned to teaching, though most found their new profession neither profitable nor satisfying. Governors had to move state capitals to more secure locations. Although the Confederate government hired some refugees in the various departments, many had to settle for work as farm or day laborers. Women had few opportunities other than sewing or domestic service but still donated their mite to relief funds and labored long for charitable associations.

Although refugees sometimes became revelers, such pleasures were transitory. Families who thought they had found safety and security were threatened again by the invaders or banished by Federal commanders. Under the best circumstances, crossing enemy lines entailed passes, oaths of allegiance, bureaucratic hassles, and some danger. For both Union and Confederate armies, dealing with refugees created logistical and security headaches.

The Blufftonites were largely younger, inexperienced men drawn to the leadership of Rhett, who was twenty years younger than Calhoun.

PAGE 65

With their property at the Federals' mercy and their lives disrupted, refugees sought public relief. Although indigent soldiers' families received some help, state and local governments discriminated against refugee families. Many disheartened Confederates returned to their homes before the end of the war even if they had to live under military occupation. Others had to wait weeks or even months after Appomattox to begin rebuilding lives that had been shattered by the war.

[*See also* Poor Relief; Poverty.]

— GEORGE C. RABLE

REPUBLICAN PARTY

At its birth, the Republican party was an avowedly sectional party. Arising out of the Northern protest over the Kansas-Nebraska Act (1854), the party opposed the expansion of slavery and called on Congress to exclude the institution from all the territories. Although Republicans denied any intention to interfere with slavery in the Southern states, the party had little strength in the South before 1865.

In the 1856 presidential election, the Republican party polled about one thousand votes in the border states and Virginia, but it had no viable organization below the Mason-Dixon Line. During the next four years, some Republican leaders sought to deflect the issue of sectionalism by building up the party in the South, and the party attracted a few notable Southern adherents, including Francis P. Blair, Jr., in Missouri, his brother Montgomery in Maryland, Cassius Clay in Kentucky, and Archibald Campbell in Virginia. Southern Republicans generally emphasized slavery's adverse effects on Southern whites and disavowed any concern for the welfare of blacks. Yet the party made little headway in the region. In 1860 Abraham Lincoln polled a mere twenty-six thousand votes in the slave states; his Southern support was confined to the border states and the western counties of Virginia.

During the war, the Unionist coalitions that took power in the border states eventually fragmented. Calling for immediate emancipation, the use of black troops, and stringent penalties against Confederates, radical organizations emerged led by such men as Henry Winter Davis in Maryland and Benjamin Gratz Brown in Missouri. Aided by military officials and federal patronage, the radicals won control of Maryland and Missouri and abolished slavery. They provided the nucleus of the full-fledged Republican parties that formed in the border states after the war. In the 1864 presidential election, Lincoln carried Maryland, West Virginia, and Missouri.

In the Confederacy the Republican movement was closely tied to the advance of the Union army. Shadow Republican parties, made up of a handful of die-hard Unionists and propped up by military support, had developed by 1864 in the occupied areas of Virginia, Arkansas, and Tennessee. The most serious attempt to establish the foundation for a postwar Republican party in a Confederate state occurred in Louisiana under the direction of Nathaniel P. Banks, the Union military commander. Wishing to create a white-only party, Banks backed the moderate faction led by Michael Hahn, who was elected governor of the reconstructed government. The moderates wrote a new state constitution that abolished slavery but rejected black suffrage. Prominent state leaders held aloof from the Union party, however, and it attracted support primarily from urban groups in the Union-controlled region around New Orleans.

The Republican party confronted major difficulties in establishing a Southern wing before 1865. Intimidation and violence, Southern whites' hostility to the party's program, the race issue, and factional squabbles all limited the Republican party's strength in the South. When the war ended, the party lacked any organization in most of the former Confederate states, and where it did exist in some guise, it represented only a very small minority of the white population.

[*See also* Kansas-Nebraska Act.]

— WILLIAM E. GIENAPP

RHETT, ROBERT BARNWELL, SR.

Rhett, Robert Barnwell, Sr. (1800–1876), congressman from South Carolina and editor. Born in Beaufort, South Carolina, on December 21, 1800, Robert Barnwell Rhett was a classic Southern fire-eater whose uncompromising devotion to Southern independence earned him the title of "the father of secession." Although Rhett could claim a distinguished Carolina lineage, his father failed as a planter, and the young Rhett had to make his own fortune and carve out his own career. He chose the traditional path of law and politics. He was admitted to the South Carolina bar in 1821 and soon established a thriving legal business, but his real love was politics. As a member of the South Carolina legislature from 1826 to 1832, he quickly stamped himself as a bold and self-assured leader when he championed the cause of nullification. From the very start of his public career, he was identified as a firebrand eager to challenge established authority.

In 1837, the same year that he went along with the wishes of his brothers and changed the family name from Smith to Rhett in recognition of a distinguished ancestor, Rhett entered Congress as a state rights Democrat. Until 1844 he served as John C. Calhoun's lieutenant in Congress and tried to work through the national Democratic organization in an effort to control it in the interests of the South. When Calhoun's bid for the presidency faltered in 1844, and the old issues of the tariff and abolitionism flared up once again, Rhett reverted to the intransigence that had first characterized his political reputation. He led the ultra-radicals of the Carolina low country in the Bluffton movement, a political protest that threatened nullification and even secession if the demands of South Carolina for a lower tariff and an end to abolitionist agitation were not met. The Bluffton movement soon faded, but Rhett's call for separate state action to protect Southern interests became the rallying cry of South Carolina secessionists in the prolonged crisis from 1849 to 1852 that was touched off by Southern demands for equal access to the territories recently won in the Mexican War.

In the midst of this crisis Rhett realized his long cherished goal of reaching the U.S. Senate. In 1851 the South Carolina legislature elected him to fill the seat vacated by Calhoun's death. By this time Rhett was a confirmed secessionist committed to a permanent Southern confederacy. This goal eluded him, however, when his stand on separate state secession in opposition to the Compromise of 1850 was rejected in South Carolina. True to his state rights principles, Rhett then resigned from the Senate in 1852 after his state had repudiated his policies. With his leadership and his party defeated, he retired from politics. When he reemerged in 1857 with all his old radicalism, he worked closely with William Lowndes Yancey of Alabama and Edmund Ruffin of Virginia to fire the Southern imagination in favor of secession. He now owned the *Charleston Mercury* and, with a son as the editor, he used the paper as a pulpit for his secessionist views.

Rhett's unrelenting radicalism finally came to fruition in the fall of 1860. Abraham Lincoln's election triggered a successful secession movement in South Carolina and throughout the lower South, and, as Rhett had long preached that they must, the radicals pursued a strategy of separate state secession. Southern unity in favor of independence, Rhett had concluded as early as the Bluffton movement, could be achieved only if one state took the lead in secession and pulled the others along in its wake.

Rhett played a major role at the South Carolina secession convention. He wrote the *Address to the Slave-Holding States*, a formal statement of South Carolina's justification for secession. Rhett stressed the inalienable right of Southern whites to self-government, a right they must now seize to free themselves from the centralizing despotism of a Federal government dominated by a hostile Northern majority. Slavery, he reasoned, could not long survive a Union controlled by Lincoln's Republican party. On December 26 Rhett also proposed the calling of a Southern convention of the slaveholding states at the earliest possible date. Now that South Carolina had seceded and other states apparently were soon to follow, Rhett's great fear was that an independent South would be stillborn, the victim of scheming politicians who would use secession as leverage to exact concessions from the North with the aim of reconstructing the Union on a basis more favorable to the South. Thus, for Rhett, it was imperative that a new and permanent Southern confederacy be formed as soon as possible. Moreover, such a government had to be irrevocably wedded to the interests of that slave civilization to which Rhett had given his undying devotion.

Rhett headed the South Carolina delegation to the convention that met at Montgomery, Alabama, in early February 1861 to form a provisional government for the Confederate States of America. He went to Montgomery determined to shape the new Confederacy in the image of his beloved Carolina low country. Complete security for the slave society of his Beaufort district required not only separation from the threatening North but the political reshaping of the South into a homogeneous slave society approximating what Rhett knew at home. In pursuit of this goal he pushed a four-pronged program designed to safeguard the revolution of 1860 that he had been so instrumental in fomenting. He wanted a constitutional provision prohibiting the admission of any nonslave state, an opening of the African slave trade when desired by the planters, and full political representation of all slaves as a substitute for the old three-fifths clause in the U.S. Constitution. Since the profits from slave-produced staples were to be the engine of economic growth for the Confederacy, he insisted on a policy of free trade with the outside world so as to maximize the market for Southern exports. Free trade, Rhett believed, would quickly lead to an alliance with Britain, ever eager to guarantee its chief supply of raw cotton. Such an alliance would eliminate any talk of reconstructing the old Union and provide British military protection for Southern independence.

Perhaps more than any other delegate at the Montgomery convention, Rhett had a vision of what he wanted the new Southern republic to be. As he feared, however, his vision was rejected. At the urging of the Mississippi and Georgia delegations, Jefferson Davis of Mississippi, a late convert to secession and a

"After the introduction of the Wilmot Proviso, Rhett favored the immediate secession of South Carolina, believing that other Southern states would follow its example."

FRANCIS BUTLER SIMKINS
A HISTORY OF THE SOUTH
1958

*"The surrender of
life is nothing to
sinking down into
acknowledgment
of inferiority."*

JOHN C. CALHOUN
SPEECH IN U.S. SENATE
1847

reconstructionist in Rhett's view, was chosen as president. When he organized his administration, Davis pointedly did not offer Rhett either of the two posts he most wanted, that of secretary of state or commissioner to England. Rhett distrusted Davis, and the feeling was mutual. Despite serving on the committees for Foreign Affairs, Financial Independence, and a Permanent Constitution, Rhett was unable to implement the fundamental changes he felt were essential for the success of the Confederacy. The U.S. Constitution was adopted virtually without change by the Confederacy. The three-fifths clause for slave representation, the prohibition on the African slave trade, and the Federal tariff of 1857 were all retained. Most galling of all for Rhett was his defeat on the issue of admitting only slave states to the Confederacy. About all that Rhett could claim as victories were constitutional prohibitions against protective tariffs and Confederate expenditures for internal improvements.

Honored in Charleston as a prophet in the heady days of secession, Rhett was spurned in Montgomery as a spokesman for the Confederacy. Unlike Rhett, Davis expected a war with the North, and he rejected Rhett's program at Montgomery in part because he did not want a radically proslavery Confederacy to scare off the states of the upper South that had not yet left the Union. The economic and military resources of the upper South would be essential for any successful defense of the Confederacy against Northern armies. The war came in April 1861 with the firing on Fort Sumter, and five states in the upper South joined the original seven states of the Confederacy. Although heartened by the apparent Southern unity that accompanied the outbreak of war, Rhett remained deeply suspicious of Davis, and he set out as a congressman in the Provisional Congress to shape the policy of the Davis administration.

Rhett first tried to seize the initiative on foreign policy. He introduced resolutions calling for a diplomacy offering favorable and long-term trading ties to Europe in return for Confederate recognition. Unwilling to tie Davis's hands in foreign relations, Congress rejected the resolutions. In June, after Congress had adjourned, Rhett began a campaign through the *Charleston Mercury* to formulate war policy for the Confederacy. The *Mercury* attacked Davis for indecision and delay in waging the war. Frustrated by Union successes in Maryland, Missouri, and Kentucky, and concerned by the ominous signs of extensive war preparations in the North, Rhett called for a rapid and massive Confederate offensive. The war must be carried to the Yankees, proclaimed the *Mercury*. Any delay would favor the North by giving it time to mobilize its superior manpower and industrial resources. Once launched, a Confederate offensive would capitalize on

FOREIGN POLICY RIFT

Foreign policy continued to be a divisive issue between Rhett and Davis. Rhett was both angered and surprised by Britain's refusal to recognize Confederate independence. With his initial policy of diplomatic conciliation rejected by the Davis administration, Rhett switched to a policy of coercion in the summer of 1861. His resolutions in Congress called for an embargo of trade with all nations that did not recognize the Confederacy. Britain, he argued, must be forced to choose sides, and he was confident that the power of King Cotton would force the British to align with the Confederacy. Once again, Rhett met defeat. Most congressmen, as well as the Davis administration, wavered between conciliation and coercion. The result was a voluntary embargo, a withholding of cotton from the seaports by the planters. A compromise that reflected divided sentiment within the South, this policy was favored by the administration because it put economic pressure on Britain without being specifically identified with a hardline policy by the Confederate government.

— WILLIAM L. BARNEY

the enthusiasm and innate fighting skills of Southern troops and smash Northern armies before they were disciplined into effective fighting units.

The Confederate victory at First Manassas on July 12, 1861, confirmed Rhett's belief in an offensive policy. Despite the success of Southern armies in the first major test of the war, Rhett stepped up his criticisms of the administration. The *Mercury* charged that a great opportunity for an advance on Washington after First Manassas had been lost because of Davis's timid generalship and inability to adequately supply Gen. P. G. T. Beauregard's troops. Rhett also returned to his claim that Davis was a reconstructionist at heart. The Northern rout at Manassas led to rumors that Northern commercial interests, especially those in the lower Midwest, were eager for an economic alliance with the Confederacy. Fearful that any commercial reunion would be but the first step toward eventual political reunion, Rhett lashed out at Davis for allegedly restraining Confederate armies in the hopes of a reconciliation with the North. As confirmation of his view, Rhett cited the blockage by the administration in Congress of his July resolutions imposing additional duties on Northern goods and banning trade in any European goods imported through the North.

By the fall of 1861, the time of the elections for the First Congress, Rhett's unrelenting criticism of Davis was beginning to backfire. In the absence of a formal opposition party to serve as an institutional outlet for attacks on the administration's handling of the war, Rhett's opposition came to be seen as a personal vendetta and a drain on Confederate morale. Public opinion in his own state of South Carolina turned against him. Rhett had no interest in running for the Confederate House. His eyes were on the Senate, but he failed to secure either of the two Senate seats chosen by the legislature. On top of this political defeat, his plantation and hometown of Beaufort fell to the Federals in November 1861, when an amphibious invasion occupied much of the Carolina low country.

Chastened but hardly bowed, Rhett returned to Richmond in December for the last session of the Provisional Congress. Consistent with his earlier record, he assailed the administration but was unable to gain passage of the changes he favored. His navigation bill concerning direct trade with Europe, which would have restricted foreign trade to ships built in the Confederacy or by the countries that were supplying imports, was rejected by Congress. He failed to carry a new naturalization bill that would have made it more difficult for Northerners to become Confederate citizens, a measure prompted by Rhett's constant dread of reconstruction. Over Rhett's constitutional objections, the administration won passage of an act permitting the Confederate government to construct connecting lines for railroads in the name of national defense. The constitutional issue of centralization versus state rights involved in the railroad bill also dominated debate over legislation to raise fresh troops for the army now that the enlistments of the original twelve-month volunteers were about to expire. Rhett supported a bill introduced by Robert Toombs of Georgia, which, though requiring the states to raise fresh troops, left the appointment of the new officers for these troops up to the states. The administration blocked the Toombs bill and subsequently pushed through national conscription in April 1862.

The end of the Provisional Congress in the winter of 1861–1862 severed Rhett's only official link with the Confederacy. For all his sharp criticism of Davis, Rhett had never wavered in his commitment to Southern independence. Indeed, on crucial financial and military matters, he was a surprisingly strong supporter of the administration. Despite the obvious challenge to state rights in the Conscription Act of 1862, Rhett backed the measure as essential for military victory. By now he had teamed with his son, Barnwell, Jr., in running the *Charleston Mercury*. For the remainder of the war, the two Rhetts mounted a propaganda offensive in a desperate attempt to effect fundamental changes in the Confederate government and its prosecution of the war.

Their editorials were especially vitriolic in early 1862 after the Confederacy had been staggered by a series of military reverses that opened up Tennessee and the lower Mississippi valley to Union forces. After leading the call for a congressional investigation of the military losses, the Rhetts were bitterly disappointed when Davis vetoed a bill creating the office of commander in chief. The successful defense of Richmond in the Peninsular campaign in the spring of 1862 did little to change their opinion that Davis was utterly unfit to be setting military policy.

As the war reached its midpoint in 1863, Rhett was still confident of Southern victory. Indeed, he worried more about a reconciliation with the North and the subsequent loss of the opportunity to establish a thoroughly slave-based society than he did about the possibility of a vanquished South. When his confidence in victory was badly shaken by the twin Confederate disasters at Gettysburg and Vicksburg in July 1863, he turned on Davis with a renewed vehemence and accused him of criminal incompetence. Rhett now argued that only the South's best men, leaders such as Toombs and himself who had heretofore played but minor roles in the Confederate government, could save the South. Consequently, he ran for Congress in the fall elections of 1863. The result was the most stunning defeat of his political career. Contrary to his expectations, the incumbent in Rhett's Third Congressional District, Lewis M. Ayer, refused to step aside. Ayer won reelection by depicting Rhett as a divisive, if not disloyal, opponent of Davis and the war effort.

Gloom and demoralization permeated South Carolina in the last year and a half of the war. Although he welcomed any actions directed against the administration, Rhett viewed with alarm the peace movements that swelled in neighboring North Carolina and Georgia and gave signs of stirring even in South Carolina. Once Lincoln's reelection in November 1864 apparently ended once and for all the threat of reconciliation, Rhett called on his fellow South Carolinians to rely on their own resources in a last-ditch bid to achieve their independence. Davis and his government, Rhett believed, were now nearly as much to be feared as Lincoln's invading armies. Rhett was aghast when he heard of the plans coming out of Richmond to arm the slaves as Confederate soldiers. In what was to be the last public act of his career, he published a letter in November 1864 damning Davis for destroying the constitutional liberties and institution of slavery that Southerners had gone to war to protect. He hoped against hope that Congress and the states could still bring Davis to his senses and force him to wage the war within the confines of the Confederate Constitution.

A brilliant courtroom lawyer, Robert Toombs was famous for his speeches to juries.

PAGE 611

In Virginia in 1862 a severe drought diminished the years's harvest, followed by excessive rain in 1863.

PAGE 539

At the end of the war all of Rhett's hopes had turned to ashes, but to the end of his life he remained as proud, obstinate, and self-righteous as he had been while fighting for the cause of Southern independence first as an American and then as a Confederate citizen. Many of his last years were spent in writing an unpublished history of the Confederacy, his final testament to the correctness of his views and the failures of Davis. Too proud to seek a pardon from the U.S. government after the war, he retired from public life. He moved to Louisiana in the early 1870s and lived at the plantation of a son-in-law in St. James Parish. He died on September 14, 1876, in the centennial year of the republic whose liberties he had always professed to celebrate.

— WILLIAM L. BARNEY

RICE

Although never king of Southern agricultural staples, rice has been of central importance to the region's economy since the early eighteenth century. Moreover, it has retained its place in the royal retinue long after cotton's departure from the throne. Prior to the Civil War, furthermore, the major rice-producing area in the South—the low country of South Carolina and Georgia—was perhaps the wealthiest and most heavily commercialized plantation district in North America.

Domestication of the cereal *Oryza sativa* began in Southeast Asia seven millennia ago, whence it spread to other parts of Asia, the Middle East, Africa, and, much later, Mediterranean Europe. The cereal was transferred to the Western Hemisphere during the early modern period as part of the so-called Columbian exchange of biogens.

Some rice may have been grown in Spanish Florida in the sixteenth century, and the English experimented with the crop in Virginia in the early seventeenth century. It was not until the last decade of the latter century, however, that rice became firmly established in the American South, and it did so neither in Florida nor in Virginia, but in the youthful English settlement of Carolina.

From the time of initial settlement in 1670, the white colonists in the precociously commercialized Carolina colony searched hard for a viable export commodity. After more than two decades of experiments, failures, and false starts with a variety of minerals, raw materials, and plant and animal products, they began to have some success with rice. The precise origins of rice cultivation in the southern part of the colony (Carolina did not split into two separate entities, North Carolina and South Carolina, until 1729) are controversial, but relatively unimportant. Whether one

believes that rice cultivation initially owed more to Europeans or to Africans ultimately matters little. The cereal was well known throughout the Old World by the late seventeenth century, and small quantities had already been grown successfully in the New. Whichever foundation myth one prefers, it was not until the mid-1690s that the colony possessed sufficient stocks of labor, capital, and local knowledge to begin cultivating, processing, and marketing successfully a staple agricultural commodity such as rice.

For a short period of time, apparently, rice was grown in Carolina without irrigation on dry and relatively high ground in the low country, that is, the easternmost third of what is now South Carolina. By the 1720s, production had shifted almost entirely to freshwater swamps in the area, where rudimentary irrigation works could be employed. Cultivation remained centered in these inland swamps in the low country of South Carolina and, after roughly 1750, Georgia until the last quarter of the eighteenth century, when the locus of activity shifted again, this time to swampland on or adjacent to the area's principal tidal rivers. Indeed, rice production in South Carolina and Georgia, and, to a lesser extent, in the Cape Fear region of North Carolina and parts of northeastern Florida, became increasingly concentrated geographically in the narrow zone on each of this area's major tidal rivers, close enough to the coast to be affected significantly by tidal action, but far enough inland to run with fresh water. It was along such rivers—six major ones in South Carolina and five in Georgia—that American rice production would be concentrated until the late nineteenth century when production shifted increasingly to the Old Southwest.

Rice cultivation in South Carolina and Georgia was arduous in nature—the crop demanded a great deal of hoeing and weeding—and was characterized by tight labor controls and considerable coercion throughout its history. No area in the entire South, in fact, was so thoroughly dominated by the institution of slavery as the low country under the rice regime and in no area were the role of African Americans and the influence of African American culture so profound.

To say this is not to suggest, as some have, that African Americans were alone responsible for the technical evolution of the low-country rice industry. If some slaves were from rice countries in West Africa and some technology—fanner baskets, for example—was clearly of African origin, much of the technology employed was generic in nature, and, thus, familiar to cereal producers throughout the world. The origins of even the task system, the distinguishing feature of labor organization in the low country, are open to question. Under this system, which evolved gradually after the mid-eighteenth century, a slave was responsible for completing a specified amount of work daily, a certain number of specified tasks as it were, upon the completion of which he or she was free to do what he or she so chose. This system most likely grew out of an ongoing process of informal negotiations between laborers bargaining for greater autonomy, and managers hoping to raise productivity and to lessen labor unrest by injecting the incentive of free time into the labor equation. However uncertain the origins of the system, its results are clear: over time, slaves used the relative freedom gained through the task system to work for themselves or to sell their free time to others. In so doing, they were often able to accumulate considerable amounts of personal property, which was, of course, only one of many ironies under slavery.

In any case, with the shift in the early eighteenth century to irrigation, rice production technology became increasingly elaborate and costly. In combination with the geographical limits imposed by nature, such technological considerations helped create an agricultural complex dominated by a relatively small number of capital-intensive plantations, which utilized sizable numbers of dependent laborers to produce rice and, at times, other staples for distant, largely foreign, markets.

The main markets for rice produced in the Southeast were never local. Until the late antebellum period, they usually were not even domestic, for most of the crop produced each year was destined for shipment abroad, particularly to the grain markets of northern Europe. In these markets, rice was viewed as a cheap commodity with numerous uses. It was sold as a dietary supplement or complement, for example, and as an animal feed. It was used in distilling and, by the mid-nineteenth century, in brewing and found employment in the starch, paper, and paste industries. Its most common use, however, was as a source of cheap, bulk calories for the poor and for soldiers, sailors, inmates, and schoolchildren in the absence of, or instead of, more desirable but often more expensive foodstuffs.

Prior to the entrance of American rice in European markets, most of the Continent's supply came from the Italian states of Lombardy and Piedmont, or from the Levant. By the mid-eighteenth century, though, rice from South Carolina and, later, Georgia had supplanted other suppliers in the principal European markets, and American rice maintained this position until the 1830s, when exports from the United States were surpassed by those from India and Southeast Asia.

Given the character of European demand, it is not surprising that Southeast Asia, the lowest-cost supplier in the market, could outcompete other supply sources. As a result of this penetration of its major markets, U.S. producers shifted their attention in the late antebellum period to the domestic market and others in the Western Hemisphere. Despite some success with this strategy, the rice industry of the South Atlantic states was clearly mature well before the Civil War: the rate of growth in output was slowing down, soil fertility was declining, costs (particularly for labor) were rising, and profit possibilities in the industry were diminishing—all of this before the disruption of four years of civil war.

Until recently, historians believed that the problems of the South Atlantic rice industry began in 1861 and that the industry's demise was a direct outgrowth of the Civil War and emancipation. It is now clear, however, that its problems were both structural and long-term in nature, having as much to do with the expansion and elaboration of capitalism and with shifts in international comparative advantage as with Federal occupation, wartime destruction of production facilities, and postwar shortages of capital and changes in labor relations.

To be sure, the latter short-term factors impeded the South Atlantic rice industry. Production in the four South Atlantic states of North Carolina, South Carolina, Georgia, and Florida fell from an all-time high of 179.4 million pounds of clean rice in 1859 (95.9 percent of the U.S. total) to 57 million pounds in 1869. But production in the area rose by nearly 48 percent between 1869 and 1879, and even as late as 1899 almost 69 million pounds of clean rice were produced in the South Atlantic region. By that time, however, Southeast Asian competition had not only knocked U.S. rice out of Europe but had penetrated the domestic market as well. The United States, in fact, was a major importer of rice for a half century after the Civil War.

One important long-term result of such competition was the gradual migration of the U.S. rice industry to Louisiana, Texas, and Arkansas. Here, highly mechanized production technology was employed, particularly after the so-called rice revolution of the mid-1880s, which raised productivity and minimized the problems posed by scarce or restive labor. Although rice *could* still be grown in the South Atlantic region at the turn of the century, highly mechanized production technology was not introduced on the reconstituted plantations, tenant plots, and yeoman freeholdings in the area. Consequently, production no longer meant profits, and the low country of South Carolina and Georgia lapsed into generations of stagnation and decline. In the last analysis, however, the evolution of the U.S. rice industry owed as much to European imperialism and to developments in Calcutta, Batavia, and Rangoon, as to more familiar events closer to home.

— PETER A. COCLANIS

Severe flooding destroyed most of the wheat crop in Virginia and negated any chance of accumulating a reserve for the army.

PAGE 539

RICHMOND, VIRGINIA

In 1860, Richmond was the twenty-fifth largest American city, with a population of 37,910. Its manufactures ranked thirteenth in value, far above those of Charleston, which it soon surpassed in size, and even those of New Orleans, a much larger city. Its industry, and its status since the Revolution as the seat of Virginia's government, impelled the leaders of the infant Confederacy to suggest that Richmond become the permanent capital if the Old Dominion seceded.

The Confederacy's move from Montgomery, the first capital city, in May 1861 was appropriate for a conservative revolution, for Richmond had long been a bastion of Whigs "who knew each other by the instincts of gentlemen." They so dominated antebellum politics that the city's few Democrats were called "the Spartan band." Know-Nothings triumphed in the 1855–1856 elections because of national Whiggery's disintegration and conservative fears of the city's growing ethnic and religious mix, noted by contemporary observer Frederick Law Olmsted. In the 1860 presidential election, the Constitutional Union ticket won 20 percent more of the 6,555 votes cast than the two Democratic slates combined.

Richmond's population was 62 percent white, over a fifth of which was foreign-born, chiefly Irish Catholics, and Germans, many of whom were Lutherans. Catholics had three churches, including a cathedral. Wealthy Methodists, Presbyterians, and Baptists dominated, with Episcopalians at the pinnacle of prestige. There was also a significant Jewish minority with three synagogues.

African Americans, 18 percent of whom were free, had declined from 45 percent of the 1850 population. Corporations owned more slaves and in larger concentrations than did white families, two-thirds of whom owned none. Slaves and free blacks were essential to the city's major industries, where many held skilled jobs. Others worked in the trades and service occupations. There were active charitable and fraternal associations, large churches, and distinct gradations in black society as in white.

Richmond rivaled Baltimore as a milling center, with annual sales of $3 million from its twelve flour and meal mills, including the Gallego, largest in the world. Highly regarded for its quality, city flour was shipped to Australia and South America. Return cargoes of Brazilian coffee made Richmond the leading importer in 1860. In its tobacco market, the world's largest, sixty factories and related firms processed tobacco worth $5 million, making it the city's most profitable sector. Joseph R. Anderson's Tredegar Iron Works, the second largest foundry in the United States, was half of a substantial industry that employed one-fifth of the labor force and included dozens of firms with total sales of over $2 million. Profits from the city's slave trade, described by Charles Dickens and other visitors, probably exceeded those derived from milling or metal working. Only New Orleans was a larger slave mart. To this business and industrial complex, which was already diversifying, the war added powder mills, armories, laboratories, government offices, and huge troop encampments.

Richmond, Virginia's largest port, was a transportation hub. There were overnight steamship connections to Washington and Baltimore down the James River. Ocean and coasting vessels crowded Rocketts, the city's harbor. Five railroads terminated here, bringing passengers and freight from all directions. The Richmond and York River Railroad ran east to West Point, another deep-water port. The Richmond, Fredericksburg, and Potomac went north to Aquia Creek, with steamship connections to Washington and Baltimore via the Potomac. The Virginia Central also ran north to Gordonsville below Manassas Junction, continuing south and west to Charlottesville and Staunton. The Richmond and Petersburg connected to Wilmington via Weldon. The Richmond and Danville was the city's main direct link with the Deep South, although this line also crossed

---

In the spring of 1862 the Shenandoah Valley was the scene of one of the major campaigns of the war—Stonewall Jackson's famous Valley campaign.

PAGE 539

THE CAPITAL

A map from the 1860s shows Richmond and surrounding towns, including Petersburg, Seven Pines, and Washington, D.C.

HARPER'S PICTORIAL HISTORY OF THE GREAT REBELLION

the Virginia and Tennessee, which ran through Bristol. The James River and Kanawha Canal extended west beyond Lynchburg more than two hundred miles from the Richmond docks. As late as 1859 the canal brought more freight tonnage into Richmond than all the railroads combined.

Edgar Allan Poe had lived here and edited the *Southern Literary Messenger,* which continued until 1864. George W. Bagby, George Fitzhugh, Edmund Ruffin, John R. Thompson, and Nathaniel Beverly Tucker all published in Richmond. The city boasted four major dailies, with total circulation of almost 84,000, including the *Whig, Enquirer, Examiner,* and *Dispatch,* and a German daily, *Taglicher Anzeiger.* It added a sixth, the *Sentinel,* during the war, as well as Confederate journals like the *Southern Illustrated News, Magnolia Weekly,* and *Southern Punch.* The city had several theaters and public halls but no library.

Richmond was the social center for Virginia east of the mountains and for much of the Mid-Atlantic seaboard. Genteel antebellum society became rougher in wartime. Entertainment included elegant receptions at the presidential mansion; "starvation parties" for young soldiers and beautiful belles, at which only water was served; and saloons, brothels, and gambling dens or "tigers," all of which ranged from the posh to the squalid. Writers as diverse as Mary Boykin Chesnut, Thomas C. DeLeon, J. B. Jones, and Sallie Brock Putnam described the Confederate citadel.

Schools included the Medical College of Virginia; Richmond College, a Baptist institution; the Richmond Female Institute; and the Virginia Mechanics Institute. All were taken over for military use. There were dozens of private academies, but no true public school system.

The state arsenal, armory, and penitentiary were here, and Richmond became the prison and hospital center of the South. The city held thirteen thousand prisoners in November 1863. Libby Prison, for Union officers, was located in a Maine ship chandler and slave trader's warehouse. Belle Isle, for enlisted men, was on a low island in the middle of the James. There were

smaller prisons like Castle Thunder and Castle Lightning for spies, deserters, rowdies, political prisoners, and women.

Camp Winder, west of the city, was the largest hospital, and Phoebe Yates Pember's Chimborazo, on an eastern hill, was the most famous. There were at least sixty smaller military hospitals, run by the Confederate government, states, private individuals, and churches and other institutions.

The influx of politicians, clerks, office seekers, soldiers, and camp followers from all over the Confederacy, along with Southern refugees from the North, tripled or quadrupled the 1860 population, straining municipal services, including the markets, water and gas works, and police and fire protection. City employees were subject to conscription.

Tension between Richmonders and Confederate officials can be seen in the early furor over Provost Marshal John Winder's enforcement of martial law and resentment of his feared detectives or "plug-uglies," in John M. Daniel's bitter criticism of the Davis administration in his *Examiner,* and in the minutes of the city council.

Rampant inflation caused severe suffering for those on fixed incomes, and even regular increases in government salaries failed to keep pace, resulting in such ironies as a free black cobbler earning more than Confederate congressmen. The April 1863 bread riot was the most serious of the Southern food protests over shortages and high prices.

Organized resistance to the Confederacy by a Union underground included the spy Elizabeth Van Lew and Richmond, Fredericksburg, and Potomac Railroad Superintendent Samuel Ruth, who delayed beef shipments to Robert E. Lee's army. Unionists helped slaves and Federal prisoners to escape, committed arson and other sabotage, and chalked pro-Northern slogans on walls.

More than 7,300 men from the area served in the Confederate army, furnishing over forty companies of infantry, artillery, and cavalry, including two regiments,

The bread riot was organized violence on a large scale conducted openly, a political protest planned and led by women.

PAGE 74

SCENIC RICHMOND

A view from Gamble's Hill, April 1865. From left: St. Paul's, the Second Baptist church, City Hall, the First Baptist church, and the Capitol.

HARPER'S PICTORIAL HISTORY OF THE GREAT REBELLION

WHAT REMAINS

The burnt district of Richmond in April 1865, at war's end.

"[By 1865] a single stick of firewood cost five dollars in Richmond. The price of a barrel of flour had risen to $425—when one could be found."

GEOFFREY WARD
THE CIVIL WAR, 1990

the First and Fifteenth Virginia infantries. Confederate dead filled the city's cemeteries, Shockoe, Oakwood, and Hollywood; the latter, the most famous after the war, is the burial site of J. E. B. Stuart, George E. Pickett and his men, and eventually Jefferson Davis and his family.

Although it may have been a strategic error for Confederate leaders to move their capital so close to the North, a decision still argued by Civil War historians, Richmond's location made it inevitable that Virginia would become the main battleground. Richmond was the goal of the Army of the Potomac for four years. After Irvin McDowell's drive ended at First Manassas in July 1861, George B. McClellan's Peninsular campaign threatened Richmond in 1862. Lee's Army of Northern Virginia pushed the front lines back in 1862 and 1863 in the Seven Days' Battles and at Second Manassas, Fredericksburg, and Chancellorsville. A series of star forts and three concentric lines of trenches encircled Richmond. There were never enough troops to man these earthworks fully, but they were used against major campaigns and raids, notably Stoneman's in May 1863 and Kilpatrick-Dahlgren's in March 1864.

The city was again threatened by Ulysses S. Grant's massive offensive that same spring. He was unable to take Richmond after the Wilderness, Spotsylvania, and Cold Harbor, but his siege of Petersburg eventually cut the city's direct rail link with Wilmington. Forced to evacuate after his lines were finally broken at Five Forks on April 1, 1865, Lee notified Jefferson Davis that Richmond must be abandoned. His army did not survive the loss of its capital for even a week.

The Confederate government evacuated the night of April 2, 1865. The Southerners blew up ironclads in the James and munitions in the city, including its powder magazine. The explosions caused more than a dozen fatalities. Custis Lee's rear guard burned Mayo's Bridge, the only vehicular and pedestrian link, as well as the two railroad viaducts. Fires set to destroy supplies of tobacco and cotton, despite the objections of city officials, were spread by high winds. Hindered by penitentiary inmates who cut their hoses, Richmond's few firemen were unable to control the flames. A mob of thousands of hungry civilians, as well as Confederate stragglers and deserters and Union prisoners, swarmed through the streets ahead of the blaze, looting stores and warehouses.

The evacuation fire consumed much of Richmond's industrial and business district, including all of the banks and most of the food suppliers. Property loss estimates ranged as high as $30 million. Residential neighborhoods were largely spared, but more than eight hundred buildings burned in four dozen blocks, and the downtown area was a smoking wasteland when Union forces entered the city early on April 3, restoring order and putting out fires that were still burning.

Reconstruction in Richmond was moderate, despite legends to the contrary, but the impact of war and defeat was enormous. Rebuilding of the burned district began almost immediately after the Union occupation (largely financed by Northern backers who remain mostly unidentified), although ruins from the evacuation fire could still be seen in the 1870s. Economic recovery was slower and only partially successful. Panics in 1873 and 1893, lack of capital and access to raw materials, failure to adopt new technology, continued reliance on erratic water power from the James, the shift of the wheat belt farther west, and corporate consolidations all had their effect. The Tredegar Iron Works never recovered its antebellum stature. The city's mills declined after 1883, although the last lingered until 1932. Richmond's once-dominant industry was taken over in 1890 by James B. Duke's trust, the American Tobacco Company. Efforts to deepen the river channel failed, and Norfolk had surpassed the port of Richmond by 1881. Canal owners struggled to repair war damage but were stymied by floods, the 1873 depression, and rail competition. The towpath became a railroad right-of-way. The railroads fell under the control of outside interests or built extensions so that the city ceased to be a terminus.

No longer a major industrial center or transport hub, Richmond remained Virginia's capital and became the mausoleum of the Lost Cause, with thousands of Confederate graves, monuments to Southern heroes, and shrines like the White House of the Confederacy, the Lee House, the soldiers' homes, the Southern Historical Society at Battle Abbey (now the Virginia Historical Society), the Home for Confederate Women, and the headquarters of the United Daughters of the Confederacy. Battlefields and other historic sites, most administered by the National Park Service, still ring the capital, and trenches greet the visitor leaving the airport. Richmond's population in the last half of the twentieth century has been roughly one-half black, and African Americans have often controlled the government and elected mayors in Virginia's "Holy City," the capital of a vanished nation.

[*See also* Belle Isle Prison; Bread Riots; Libby Prison.]

— MICHAEL B. CHESSON

RIVER DEFENSE FLEET

To defend the Mississippi south of New Orleans and to the north as far as Memphis, Confederates assembled fourteen river steamers, pilot boats, and tugs under the appellation the River Defense Fleet.

The large, well-armed Union force that threatened the entire Mississippi in 1861 set state legislators in Missouri and Mississippi clamoring for protection. Kentucky boatmen James Edward Montgomery and James H. Townsend originated the idea for the fleet, and Secretary of War Judah P. Benjamin engineered a million-dollar appropriation by late 1861.

In the loosely structured Confederate command system, naval officers assigned to the Mississippi had little or no part in plans or operations for the fleet. In January 1862, orders to purchase the boats went to Maj. Gen. Mansfield Lovell. Gen. M. Jeff Thompson of the Missouri State Guard later added his daring temperament to the enterprise.

The ships were first rechristened for Confederate army leaders. Armed with one 24- or 32-pounder mounted astern, they were not designed to engage the enemy as gunboats. Instead, reinforcing the prow of each boat with iron created a ram that could damage and sink a Union ship in a collision. "Cottonclad" came into the vocabulary of the Civil War when cotton was stuffed inside the hulls; this was done so that a cannonball that pierced the hull would bury itself in the matted fibers.

Six of the boats stood below New Orleans to meet the Union's April 24, 1862, assault on Forts Jackson and St. Philip. Five were run aground and abandoned by their untrained crews: *Defiance, General Breckinridge, General Lovell, Resolute,* and *Warrior. Stonewall Jackson* rammed and sank the Union *Varuna* before being burned by its fleeing crew.

The eight boats upriver saw more action. On May 10, *General Bragg, General Price, General Sumter, General Van Dorn,* and *Little Rebel* engaged the Union fleet at Plum Point, Tennessee, ramming and damaging U.S. ships *Cincinnati* and *Mound City.*

On June 5 and 6, other boats of the fleet joined in the Battle of Memphis. Of the veterans of the May 10 encounter, all were captured except *Van Dorn,* which was later destroyed at its mooring up the Yazoo River. Of the remaining four, *Colonel Lovell* was sunk with great loss of life; *General Thompson* exploded; *General Beauregard* was badly damaged when it and *Price* missed USS *Monarch* and rammed each other.

Thus ended the story of the River Defense Fleet—like so many Confederate naval efforts, better conceived than constructed and operated with a certain raffish optimism in the face of a much superior Union force.

— MAXINE TURNER

RIVES, WILLIAM C.

Rives, William C. (1793–1868), U.S. diplomat, representative to the Washington peace conference, and congressman from Virginia. William Cabell Rives was born May 4, 1793, at Union Hill in Amherst County,

R

RIVES, WILLIAM C.

Johnston arrived in Jackson and learned the full magnitude of the situation: Grant was between Jackson and Vicksburg, and Pemberton had not concentrated his forces.

PAGE 648

Rives studied law under Thomas Jefferson and became an intimate of James Madison.

PAGE 506

Virginia. He was educated at Hampden-Sydney College and the College of William and Mary. After his graduation from the latter in 1809, he studied law under Thomas Jefferson and became an intimate of

James Madison. During the War of 1812 he served as aide-de-camp to John H. Cocke on the Chickahominy River. In 1817 Rives was elected to the first of several terms in Virginia's House of Delegates, where he served on the Courts and Justice, Executive Expenditures, and Finance committees.

Rives married Judith Page Walker on March 24, 1819. As heiress to the Castle Hill estate in Albemarle County, she brought Rives a four-thousand-acre plantation and almost a hundred slaves. After moving to Castle Hill, Rives served an additional year in the House of Delegates as a representative of Albemarle County before being elected to Congress in 1823. During the next six years, he ardently supported the cause of Andrew Jackson. The president rewarded Rives's loyalty by naming him minister to France in 1829.

During his time in Paris, Rives witnessed the deposing of Charles X in favor of Louis Philippe at the head of a new constitutional monarchy, scenes he would replay many times in his mind during the secession winter of 1860–1861. Under the Berlin and Milan decrees, the American minister negotiated a settlement of spoliation claims under which the French agreed to pay a $5 million indemnity and the Americans, in turn, agreed to reduce the duty on French wine imported into the United States.

On his return to America in 1832, Rives was elected to the U.S. Senate. His support for the Force Bill angered a number of members of the state legislature. On January 17, 1834, he rose to support Jackson's removal of Federal deposits from the Second Bank of

the United States. Virginia's General Assembly instructed its congressional delegation to vote for censuring the president for his actions. Refusing to bow to pressure, Rives chose to resign his seat.

In 1835 Rives campaigned behind the scenes to win the vice presidential nomination on the Democratic ticket. Jackson, however, backed Richard M. Johnson of Kentucky for the office. Thwarted in his ambitions, Rives sought to return to the Senate. He lobbied the General Assembly to instruct the state's congressional delegation to vote for Thomas Hart Benton's resolution asking that the censure of Jackson for removing deposits be expunged. Senator John Tyler refused to do as instructed and resigned his seat, to which Rives was then elected.

Soon after his return to Washington in 1836, Rives found himself at loggerheads with President Martin Van Buren over what to do about the country's fiscal situation. Rives favored placing the Federal surplus in state banks and vehemently opposed both Jackson's specie circular and Van Buren's subtreasury system. A group calling itself the Conservative Democrats began to coalesce around Rives's leadership and in the 1838 elections won control of the Virginia General Assembly.

In 1839 Rives came up for reelection and was nominated by the Conservative Democrats. He faced former senator John Tyler, nominated by the Whigs, and John Young Mason, the regular Democratic nominee. Henry Clay, the national leader of the Whigs, wanted the support of the Conservative Democrats in 1840, so he offered Tyler a deal: if Tyler would withdraw from the race in favor of Rives, then Clay would see that Tyler received the Whig vice presidential nomination the next year. Tyler refused. None of the three candidates could win a majority, so the election was postponed until the next session. As a result, Virginia had but one senator until 1841, when Rives finally won reelection after Tyler became vice president.

Once in Washington, Rives consistently supported former rival Tyler against Clay until the question of the annexation of Texas came up. Rives maintained that Texas was a foreign nation and that as such, it was unconstitutional to admit it to the Union. By the end of Tyler's term, Rives had aligned himself with the Whig party, and he gave his support to Clay's candidacy in the presidential election of 1844.

When his senatorial term expired in 1845, Rives retired to Castle Hill and private life. Several works from his pen were published in Richmond, including *Discourse on the Character and Services of John Hampden* (1845) and *Discourse on the Uses and Importance of History* (1847). During this time he served a second stint as a member of the board of visitors of the University of Virginia. His first appointment to the board in 1828 had ended with his departure for France in 1829. His second term, begun in 1834, lasted until 1849, when he again stepped down upon receiving another appointment as minister to France, this one from President Zachary Taylor.

For the second time Rives went to turbulent Paris. Louis Philippe, whose relationship with Rives had been so cordial that his queen had consented to act as godmother to Rives's elder daughter, had been forced to abdicate in February 1848 after a series of revolts. In June a bloody uprising of Parisian workers marred the unstable peace of the newly proclaimed Second Republic. All around him Rives witnessed the aftermath of the bloody nationalist uprisings that erupted in Europe in 1848. He watched as the French moved into Italy to quell Garibaldi's risorgimento. He carried the memories with him when the United States stood on the brink of its own crisis a dozen years later.

Rives returned to Castle Hill in 1853 and again resumed the life of a private citizen. John Brown's raid on Harpers Ferry in October 1859 and Brown's subsequent canonization by radical elements in the North alarmed Rives about the safety of the Union. Fearing what would happen if the Republicans won the White House in 1860, Rives was instrumental in organizing the Constitutional Union party and was mentioned as a possible nominee for president. The party eventually selected as its candidate John Bell, whom Rives supported but did not actively campaign for because of feeble health. After Abraham Lincoln's victory, Rives issued a public *Letter from the Hon. William C. Rives to a Friend, on the Important Questions of the Day* (Richmond, 1860). He condemned the Northern reaction to what he termed "the bloody and revolting tragedy at Harpers Ferry" but believed it was the temporary triumph of a vociferous and radical minority. Calling for "dignity and coolness," he enumerated the legal means of self-protection and defense accorded the states under the Constitution. He called for Virginia to reorganize its militia, form volunteer units, procure arms for its state guard, and encourage domestic manufacture to reduce dependence on the North. He advocated an end to sectionally based parties, both North and South, and the removal of the slavery issue from agitation on the national political level. Finally, he pointed to the lack of feasibility of creating a nation out of the states in which slavery was legal. The differences between the economies of the lower South and the upper South and the ties of the border states to the Old Northwest would, in his opinion, be impossible to overcome.

On December 8 Rives called for a national peace conference to halt the secession crisis in its tracks. In mid-January he traveled to the nation's capital at the urging of several Virginia Unionists, including Winfield Scott, to lobby for such a national convention. During five days of social calls and dinners, Rives capitalized on his position as an elder statesman of the defunct Whig party and as a former intimate of Jefferson and Madison to meet informally with leaders of the Republican party, including Secretary of State-designate William H. Seward. On January 17, Rives advised Unionist Alexander H. H. Stuart to push the resolution calling for a national peace convention through the Virginia General Assembly. Two days later, the state legislature passed the resolution in the wording suggested by Rives and chose the former diplomat and senator as one of the Old Dominion's five delegates. At the same time, however, the General Assembly voted to summon a state convention to consider secession. Rives agreed to stand for election to this convention from Albemarle County and campaigned as well for Unionist Valentine W. Southall. Although Rives was not selected to attend the Richmond convention, he rejoiced at the enormous majority Unionist delegates held.

Rives returned to Washington on February 4 for the opening of the peace conference. He was unhappy with the composition of Virginia's delegation. He and George W. Summers were Unionists; John Tyler and John White Brockenbrough were moderate conditional Unionists but fast moving toward the secessionist position; and James A. Seddon was a fire-eater. To Rives's distress, Tyler was elected president of the convention on February 5, and Tyler, Brockenbrough, and Seddon finagled the selection of Seddon as Virginia's single representative to the Guthrie committee, which was assigned the task of drawing up compromise resolutions to keep the peace and reconcile the sections. To counteract any damage that Seddon might do, Rives began a series of private meetings with members of the Guthrie committee. Although most of the Republicans believed that a second constitutional convention was the only viable solution to the disagreements between the Union and the seceded states, Rives argued that immediate concessions were necessary to halt the spread of secession and to defuse the crisis.

Most of Rives's lobbying was carried on behind the scenes. He made only two major speeches in the course of the peace conference. The first, on February 13, was a eulogy of delegate John C. Wright of Ohio, with whom Rives had served in Congress in the 1820s. The second, on February 19, was a plea for concessions. Secession, he believed, was illegal, but it was a fait accompli. To keep Virginia, the upper South, and the border states in the Union would require only a guarantee of the rights of the slaveholding states. He painted for the conference delegates vivid pictures of what civil war looked like. "I have seen," he reminded them, "the pavements of Paris covered, and her gutters run-

Among the purposes of the Washington Peace Conference was to seek constitutional guarantees that might hold the border slave states in the Union.

PAGE 660

507

The Washington Peace Conference in 1861 was dubbed the "Old Gentlemen's Convention" of "political fossils" by Horace Greeley's New York Tribune.

PAGE 661

ning with fraternal blood: God forbid that I should see this horrid picture repeated in my own country."

With other delegates from the conference, Rives called on Lincoln at the Willard Hotel on February 23. The former senator left the meeting convinced that the president-elect's views had been misrepresented in the Southern press but also that Lincoln did not understand the gravity of the situation facing his administration.

Three days after the delegates' interview with Lincoln, the conference voted on the Guthrie report. Although Rives and Summers supported the resolution calling for a constitutional amendment to extend the Missouri Compromise line to the Pacific Ocean, they were outvoted by the other three members of the Virginia delegation. After the resolution went down in defeat, eight states to eleven, a reconsideration was moved and carried. The conference then adjourned for the day. When the delegates reconvened on February 27, Virginia still voted in the negative, but the resolution passed, nine states to eight. The other proposals of the Guthrie committee also carried, though in most instances the votes of Tyler, Brockenbrough, and Seddon put Virginia in opposition. The convention then rose.

That afternoon Rives received an invitation to call on Lincoln with Alexander Doniphan of Missouri and Charles Morehead and James Guthrie of Kentucky. The president-elect promised he had no intentions to attack slavery in the states in which it already existed and that he would enforce the Fugitive Slave Laws. He would not, however, heed Morehead's pleas for concessions to the border states. Rives warned that if Lincoln did not abandon Fort Sumter, war was inevitable and that if violence broke out, Virginia would secede. Rives stated that if Virginia left the Union, "in that event I go, with all my heart and soul." Lincoln responded that he would withdraw Federal troops from Fort Sumter if Virginia would vote to remain in the Union. Rives said that he could not speak for his state and could make no promises, though he would work to prevent the secession of the Old Dominion.

Worn out by his exertions, Rives slept for twenty hours and then headed not for home but for Richmond, where the secession convention was then sitting. In a two-hour oration at Metropolitan Hall on March 8, he pleaded the cause of Union. He urged the approval of the resolutions of the peace conference as a just and equitable settlement to the sectional crisis. Rives met privately with convention president Robert Young Conrad and other delegates and returned, exhausted, to Albemarle County.

After the attack on Fort Sumter and Virginia's secession, Rives was selected as one of the common-

wealth's delegates to the Provisional Confederate Congress, in which he sat until February 1862. In May 1864 he took a seat in the Second Congress. Because of his experience as minister to France, he served on the Committee on Foreign Relations and succeeded Henry S. Foote of Tennessee as chairman. Rives also sat on the Flag and Seal Committee. His activity was limited by poor health, but he generally supported the policies of the Davis administration.

His only major speech during his second term was a two-hour argument on May 20 opposing Foote's resolution to repeal the suspension of habeas corpus. Rives maintained that the Magna Carta, the Constitution, and the Bill of Rights all allowed the suspension of the writ in wartime. Those who protested the suspension as "a dangerous inroad" on personal liberty and free speech, he declaimed, were ignoring the larger crisis of "an exterminating war of the most tremendous magnitude, waged by a ruthless foe, governed by no rules of humanity, obeying no laws of war." The congressman in fact attributed Richmond's deliverance from the most recent Union assaults at the Wilderness, Spotsylvania, and Yellow Tavern to the suspension of habeas corpus.

On November 21 Rives voted yea on a unanimous resolution reaffirming that the Confederacy would accept no peace terms that did not recognize its independence. The next month, he unsuccessfully opposed a bill to increase the salaries of members of the House by 50 percent. As the year closed, he endorsed a measure for the reduction and redemption of the currency and another for sequestering the property of men fleeing the Confederacy to escape military service. His support was critical in the adoption of a bill authorizing generals commanding departments to consolidate companies, battalions, and regiments; the bill passed by only one vote on January 9, 1865. The next day, he voted to kill the motion to reconsider the measure and return it to the Military Committee. In one of his final official acts, he reported on sundry resolutions on peace negotiations from the Committee on Foreign Relations. Rives was granted a leave of absence on January 28 and resigned his seat on March 2, 1865, citing failing health.

Three days after his resignation, Rives met in Richmond with Robert E. Lee to review a survey of the military situation drawn up by Assistant Secretary of War John A. Campbell. According to Rives, Lee maintained that the only hope for the Confederacy was to come to terms with the United States. The Confederate States could then marshal their resources and await more favorable circumstances to resume the fight for independence. With Lee's assessment in mind, Rives drew up a resolution for the Senate stating that prosecution of the war had become "impracticable" and advising Jefferson Davis to propose, through Lee, "an armistice preliminary to the re-establishment of peace & union." Rives, no longer part of Congress, intended that Senators William A. Graham of North Carolina, James L. Orr of South Carolina, and Robert M. T. Hunter of Virginia should shepherd the resolution through their chamber. The senators considered the resolution but decided in the end that pushing it through Congress would change nothing. Rives returned, for the last time, to Castle Hill and private life.

In the course of his duties as the third president of the Virginia Historical Society (an office he held from 1847 until his death), Rives had been persuaded to undertake a multivolume biography of his old friend James Madison, the Father of the Constitution. The first volume of the *History of the Life and Times of James Madison* had appeared in 1859. The Civil War delayed the composition and publication of volume two until 1866; volume three, which brought Madison up to 1797, made its appearance in 1868. Rives did not live to complete the fourth volume of the work Henry Cabot Lodge called "one of the most solemn, learned and respectable biographies ever penned by the hand of man." He died April 25, 1868, at Castle Hill and was buried in the family cemetery there. His four-volume edition of *Letters and Other Writings of James Madison* was completed by Philip R. Fendall and appeared in 1884.

— SARA B. BEARSS

RUFFIN, EDMUND

Ruffin, Edmund (1794–1865), agricultural reformer, proslavery ideologue, and Southern nationalist. Born into a prominent Tidewater Virginia planter family, Ruffin earned wide acclaim during the first half of the nineteenth century as the preeminent agricultural reformer in the Old South.

When his inherited lands on the James River proved unresponsive to traditional ameliorative practices, Ruffin, in 1818, inaugurated a series of experiments with marl, a shell-like deposit containing calcium carbonate which neutralized soil acidity and enabled sterile soils to become once again productive. When the results proved efficacious, he published his findings, first in *An Essay on Calcareous Manures* (1832) and then in his celebrated agricultural journal, the *Farmers' Register* (1833–1842). After conducting an agricultural survey of South Carolina at the request of Governor James H. Hammond, Ruffin acquired a new tract of land on the Pamunkey River, naming it appropriately Marlbourne, and proceeded to transform it

into a model estate. Subsequently, he was instrumental in reviving the Virginia State Agricultural Society and was four times elected president of that body.

Upon retiring from the management of his agricultural enterprises in the mid-1850s, Ruffin turned his

attention to politics. Strongly opinionated, little disposed to compromise, and sharply critical of democracy, Ruffin had eschewed active participation in politics, serving only an abbreviated term as state senator in the 1820s. By mid-century, however, he, like many others in his class, had become alarmed by the increasingly intemperate attacks upon Southern institutions by the abolitionists and their political allies in the North. Sufficiently moderate in 1831 to have interceded on behalf of a black wrongfully accused of complicity in the Nat Turner revolt, Ruffin later assumed an inflexible proslavery posture. Convinced that slavery was the very cornerstone of Southern society and that its future could not be guaranteed within the existing Union, Ruffin became an outspoken secessionist.

Although he had adopted a secessionist stance at least as early as 1850, it was during the last four years of the antebellum period that Ruffin's crusade for disunion became most intense. Lacking the oratorical skills of fellow fire-eater William Lowndes Yancey or the political influence of Robert Barnwell Rhett, Sr., Ruffin resorted instead to personal conversation and the power of his written prose to influence the course of events. Just as he had earlier propagated the gospel of marl so now he proselytized for his dream of Southern independence. In hotel lobbies from Washington to Charleston, at Virginia summer resorts, at the Southern Commercial Convention in Montgomery, on trains and steamboats—everywhere he traveled—Ruffin was indefatigable in his effort to persuade South-erners that their only salvation lay in separate nation-hood. Even more significant were his voluminous writings. In addition to numerous articles and editori-als prepared for newspapers in Richmond and Charleston, these included three lengthy pamphlets and two major articles, one of them serialized in *De Bow's Review,* as well as a 426-page political novel, *Anticipations of the Future,* which had been inspired by John Brown's raid on Harpers Ferry.

Despite such herculean efforts, Ruffin appears to have had only minimal influence in effecting secession. Certainly he had little in his home state of Virginia, as he later bitterly lamented. His writings, prolific as they were, seem to have attracted little notice from the pub-lic, and his attempt in 1858, in concert with Yancey, to mobilize public opinion behind the secessionist cause through a League of United Southerners proved inef-fectual. Still, he remained active and highly visible. Excited by the events at Harpers Ferry, he enlisted in the Corps of Cadets of the Virginia Military Institute for one day in order to witness the execution of Brown. Subsequently, he dispatched pikes seized from the con-spirators to the governors of all slaveholding states with the injunction that they be displayed as a "sam-ple of the favors designed for us by our Northern Brethren."

It was only after the sectional crisis reached a cli-max in 1860 and 1861 that Ruffin finally received the public adulation so long denied him. Although he began to receive compliments and honors wherever he traveled outside of Virginia, it was in South Carolina that he was most appreciated. When that state became the first to secede he was there to participate in the cel-ebration, and, on the eve of Abraham Lincoln's inau-guration, he again departed for Charleston, vowing never to return to his native state until it joined the Confederacy. With his destiny now bound inextricably to that of his adopted state, it was altogether fitting that the venerable Ruffin was accorded the honor of firing the first artillery shot against Fort Sumter—a distinction that, though still controversial, was recog-nized generally by his contemporaries on both sides.

The notoriety engendered by Ruffin's role in the Sumter engagement elevated him to the status of a popular hero in the South. Rejoining his South Caroli-na unit, the Palmetto Guard, in time for the Manassas campaign, the aging fire-eater once again performed symbolic military service for his beloved Confederacy, firing several artillery rounds at the fleeing Federals as they retreated over the suspension bridge at Cub Run. Plagued, however, by physical infirmities and wartime tribulations, he was soon reduced to the role of a pas-sive observer of the momentous conflict he had helped to instigate. Family properties were pillaged during the successive Federal campaigns against Richmond, and Ruffin was compelled to seek refuge as an exile, settling eventually at Redmoor, a small farm situated about thirty-five miles west of the capital. Despite the deteri-orating military situation, the increasingly embittered Ruffin remained steadfast in his commitment to the cause of Southern independence until that dream was shattered at nearby Appomattox.

With the demise of the Confederacy, Ruffin no longer had any reason to live. Despondent over the deaths of family members and his own declining health, reduced to virtual destitution by enemy depre-dations during the war, and fearful lest he become both a political and a pecuniary burden to his eldest son, Ruffin had long contemplated suicide. After the fall of Richmond his resolve became fixed, and for more than two months he planned methodically for the act of self-destruction, which he carried out shortly after noon on June 17, 1865. Thus did Ruffin, despite numerous reverses and disappointments, once again assume command of his own destiny. Contrary to pop-ular belief, Ruffin did not wrap himself in a Confeder-ate flag before firing the shot that ended his life.

— WILLIAM K. SCARBOROUGH

RULES OF WAR

Even after a full year of fighting, few officers on either side of the Civil War had more than a functional understanding of the customary principles of war and the rights of combatants and noncombatants. In April 1863, Abraham Lincoln approved General Orders No. 100 (the Lieber Code) establishing guidelines for field commanders and soldiers of the Union army, but Confederate Secretary of War James A. Seddon rejected them out of hand in June, saying they encour-aged unrestricted warfare. Thereafter, although both sides continued to stake out severely conflicting theo-retical interpretations of the rules of war, they in fact worked toward the middle and treated each other with a remarkable degree of civility until the summer of 1864.

The war began taking an ugly turn for the South then, but only several months after Ulysses S. Grant had changed his predecessors' strategy from attacking at various weak points to a cordon offensive that attacked along the entire southern perimeter. The Confederates, who had been so good at drawing Union forces into set piece battles at places of their choosing, were now forced onto the defensive because manpower shortages left them unable to respond effectively to broad Northern thrusts. In addition, the extensive use of rifled bores, repeating rifles, machine guns, and even flamethrowers had been exacting especially heavy tolls on Confederate formations, which were still practicing massed assaults. When this change in the North's strategic doctrine and its deployment of increasingly destructive weapons were coupled with the South's own use of land mines and guerrillas, the reasonably humane war conducted up to that point could legitimately be described as having become a total war.

Nowhere was this more evident than during Philip H. Sheridan's Shenandoah campaign in 1864, when John S. Mosby's raids so ravaged Union supply columns that Sheridan destroyed everything in his path on his way out of the valley. A few months later in November, this scorched-earth policy was repeated on the roads to Atlanta, Savannah, and Columbia (which was truly savaged) after William Tecumseh Sherman concluded—correctly, as it turned out—that subjecting Southern civilians to the psychological stresses of military action would break their will. The South had been holding on until then in the vain hope that Lincoln would be upset in November, but with his reelection, based largely on the results of Sheridan's and Sherman's campaigns, vanished what little hope remained in Richmond for reaching some accommodation with peace advocates in the North.

In effect, while total war for the North in late 1864 meant utilizing every offensive means possible, it forced the South into an almost exclusively defensive strategy that came to rely on units like Mosby's—one of the few innovative tools still left at Robert E. Lee's disposal. At this point, Confederate regiments were so depleted that strategic retaliation on a small scale was the only form of offense showing any positive returns. That many professional soldiers on either side looked with great disfavor upon the activities of Confederate and pro-Confederate guerrillas did little to inhibit these scattered, but well-led and highly imaginative groups from holding down tens of thousands of Union troops in guard duty—several thousand in Missouri alone after 1862. Since this form of combat could be so brutal, however, the South felt a certain moral obligation not to employ it in an unrestricted manner, and its generally restrained use of this alternative may well have been one reason it lost the war.

It was also during the summer campaigns of 1864 that the North hardened its view on total war after learning of the treatment of its prisoners. Few had been taken by either side in the first year of conflict, so opposing field commanders often were able to work out paroles and exchanges immediately after skirmishes that included the wounded, their chaplains, and medical personnel; but after 1862, large battles accounted for such enormous numbers of captives that more permanent structures had to be hastily built.

LAWS OF THE SEA

Maritime law was infinitely more formalized than the corpus of agreements dictating military conduct on land. Lincoln announced a blockade of Southern ports a week after the war began, thus ignoring the advice of U.S. Secretary of the Navy Gideon Welles, who insisted that in doing so, the president had inadvertently conferred the status of belligerency upon the Confederacy. A municipal closure of the ports to commerce would have been preferable, Welles felt, because a blockade was legal only in a time of war, and technically, this was nothing more than a domestic insurrection.

Lincoln, though, realized that a policy of port closure—or "paper blockade" in the words of British Foreign Secretary John Russell—was unenforceable and would serve only to antagonize Great Britain by completely destroying its trade with the South, while coincidentally not legally obligating the British, as neutrals, to honor the act.

Neutral crew members serving aboard neutral blockade runners that had been captured by Union ships were seldom even detained, and the penalty was confined solely to the ship and its cargo. Both were sold after a prize court determined the legitimacy of their capture, and the proceeds were divided among Union crew members. Consequently, even Confederate blockade runners were seldom harmed—and then only if they resisted—making this form of war far less risky than what was happening on the fields of Franklin, Cold Harbor, and the Wilderness.

Following the Crimean War, the Declaration of Paris (April 1856) had established four rules that defined a blockade, abolished privateering, protected enemy goods on neutral carriers, and protected neutral goods on enemy carriers. But because it had failed to exempt from capture by privateer the private property of citizens of belligerent nations, Washington withheld its formal acceptance. After all, the United States could (and, of course, would) attain belligerent status sometime in the future and did not want the property of its subjects confiscated at sea. When Confederate privateers began terrorizing Union shipping in 1861, the Federal government debated hanging their crews as pirates, but reconsidered when faced with the certainty of reprisals by the South. Thereafter, the prosecution of privateers as civilian criminals was abandoned and they were afforded prisoner-of-war status with the same rights of parole and exchange as their landlubber colleagues.

— JOHN R. CRONIN

Although conditions at Libby (Richmond, Virginia) were slightly better than average, life in Confederate prisons like Andersonville (Georgia) and Belle Isle (North Carolina) was extremely harsh at best; overcrowding and inadequate supplies of food, water, clothing, medicine, trained guards, and competent administrators led to a 15.5 percent mortality rate. Confederate prisoners, though generally better off than their Union counterparts, still lost about 12 percent of their men in camps like Elvira (New York) and Point Lookout (Maryland).

Unknown to Northern troops, however, the South could barely treat its own wounded by late 1864 because of inadequate hospital facilities. This once led Union Gen. George B. McClellan to offer medical supplies for his wounded being held by Lee. Black Union captives fared the worst, though. Confederate policy in late 1862 denying them and their white officers prisoner-of-war status led initially to their occasional summary execution in the field and to a subsequent suspension of exchanges by the Union in May 1863; but well-publicized retaliations against Confederate prisoners compelled the South, by January 1865, to offer the unrestricted exchange of all prisoners. In fact, the use of cartels for formal exchanges thrived from 1862 until Grant became general in chief in the spring of 1864 and decided that he needed his prisoners back much less than Lee needed his. Ending the cartel was a tough decision to make, but in this attempt to shorten the war, Grant may inadvertently have helped create the very conditions that led to prisons like Andersonville and Fort Delaware.

[*See also* Blockade, *overview article;* Guerrilla Warfare; Prisoners of War.]

— JOHN R. CRONIN

SALT

This mineral was vital to the civilian population as well as the military forces of the Confederacy. In an era with no reliable method of refrigeration, salt was the primary means of preserving meat. In addition, salt was used to pack cheese and eggs and preserve hides during leather making, as well as being employed in numerous chemical processes, various medications, and livestock dietary supplements.

Prior to the war, the Southern states had bought much of their salt from the North or imported it from Europe. Once the war started, the Confederacy had to develop internal sources for its requirements. The primary areas for salt production were Great Kanawha River near Charleston, West Virginia; Goose Creek near Manchester, Kentucky; southwest Alabama; Avery Island, Louisiana; and southwest Virginia. Salt was also produced along the Confederate seacoast. The largest industry to develop in Florida, during the war, was salt making.

Several of these locations (in West Virginia, Kentucky, and Louisiana) were captured early in the war. By 1863, most of the Confederacy's salt, especially for those states east of the Mississippi, was being produced at the Stuart, Buchanan & Co. saltworks in Saltville, Virginia. In 1864, thirty-eight furnaces containing over 2,600 kettles were producing about 4 million bushels of salt per year at just this one saltworks.

There were three methods of producing salt in the 1860s:

- extracting it from brine wells,
- extracting it from seawater or inland salt ponds,
- mining deposits of rock salt.

The process for extracting salt from seawater and brine wells was the same—evaporation. At Saltville, the brine was pumped from a well by steam engine and transported to furnaces through wooden pipes. After the water had evaporated, the crystallized salt was placed in split baskets to dry and then stored in bulk.

Federal forces did not allow salt manufacturing to continue unchallenged. The navy raided coastal salt makers, especially along the Florida coast, and the army made a point of destroying all saltworks in its path.

In the fall of 1864, Federal cavalry made two raids against the Saltville saltworks. In October, the Federals were unsuccessful, and following the battle over one hundred captured black troops were killed by Confederate soldiers. This was one of the war's worst massacres. In December, the Federals were able to capture and temporarily put the saltworks out of operation.

Each Confederate state had its own salt commissioner or agent, who acquired salt from the available sources and then passed it along to local agents for public distribution. Although resources were sufficient to provide all the salt needed, there were shortages throughout the war, especially for civilians. Causes for these shortages included the blockade, speculation and corruption, and inadequate transportation. These shortages, however, were never severe enough to cause serious problems for the army. Lucius B. Northrop, commissary-general, stated on January 25, 1865, that "the supply of salt has always been sufficient and the Virginia works were able to meet the demand for the army."

— MICHAEL E. HOLMES

SALTPETER

Known to the Confederates as niter, this mineral, potassium nitrate (KNO_3), was crucial to the Confederate war effort because it comprised about 75 percent of the gunpowder used. (The other ingredients were about 12.5 percent sulphur and 12.5 percent charcoal.) Although some saltpeter had been mined in the United States for local use since before the War of 1812, most was imported. The Union blockade forced the Confederacy to consider other sources of the mineral, although substantial importation, both by sea and from Mexico, continued throughout the war.

Three possible domestic saltpeter sources were available to the Confederates: limestone caves, residue under old buildings, and artificial niter beds. Caves with appropriate mineral and climatic conditions for the natural production of saltpeter could be found primarily in the foothills of Tennessee, Georgia, Arkansas, Virginia, and Alabama, areas that tended to be occupied by Union troops fairly early in the war. The Sauta Cave in Jackson County, Alabama, and a

In the Confederacy, mining was largely conducted in Virginia where large amounts of iron, coal, and limestone fed the many iron furnaces along the Allegheny frontier and the Shenandoah Valley.

PAGE 369

INGREDIENTS OF GUNPOWDER

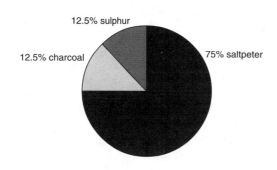

12.5% sulphur

12.5% charcoal

75% saltpeter

cave near Kingston in Bartow County, Georgia, were among the most famous and productive of the sites.

The dirt under old buildings, tobacco barns, stables, outhouses, and manure piles could also bear saltpeter, but mining these sources required the cooperation of private citizens. A potentially more reliable source of the mineral was the artificial manufacture of saltpeter in niter beds. These beds were composed of heaps of earth, manure, rotted vegetable matter, and other waste products, which were carefully tended, moistened with urine, and turned over for a considerable period of time to produce a coating of the mineral. Although the Confederates were able to procure some saltpeter by this method, most of the niter beds, established in "nitriaries" near the major cities, were not mature enough by the time the war ended to produce to their full capacity. In all cases of mining and manufacturing, the raw product was still primarily dirt and had to go through a leaching and refining process before the saltpeter could be used in gunpowder.

The Confederate Niter and Mining Bureau, headed by Isaac M. St. John, supervised the collection and production of saltpeter, sponsoring a number of mining ventures and the thirteen or more nitriaries. But the government also encouraged private citizens to manufacture saltpeter and published pamphlets by George W. Rains and Joseph LeConte to instruct the novice in the proper procedures.

Although complete records for the bureau do not exist, those available indicate that private and government manufacturing had produced 1,735,531.75 pounds of saltpeter and that 1,720,072 pounds had been imported by September 30, 1864.

— GLENNA R. SCHROEDER-LEIN

SAVANNAH SQUADRON

In March 1861 three small wooden gunboats, *Savannah, Sampson,* and *Resolute,* armed with one 32-pounder smoothbore each, were turned over to the Confederate government by the state of Georgia. The vessels had composed the Georgia State Navy created shortly after Georgia seceded. In the Confederate navy they were designated the Savannah Squadron with Capt. Josiah Tattnall as flag officer. The squadron was concentrated on the Savannah River until the fall of 1861 when a powerful Union amphibious force threatened Port Royal, South Carolina. Tattnall shifted his small force, reinforced by the gunboat *Lady Davis* from Charleston, through the sounds and waterways to Port Royal, but his efforts were futile. The small Confederate squadron was forced to retire hastily by the fleet of Flag Officer Samuel DuPont. Port Royal was captured by the Federal force.

The threat to Savannah persuaded the Confederate Navy Department to reinforce the Savannah Squadron. In November 1861 two 150-foot wooden gunboats were laid down on the Savannah River; four months later three additional vessels 112 feet in length were contracted for. Only one of the larger class, *Macon,* and one of the smaller class, *Isondiga,* were completed. The others were unfinished primarily because of the navy's decision to concentrate on building ironclads. In March 1862 the large armored vessel *Georgia* was laid down; the 250-foot warship armed with ten naval guns was completed in the fall of 1862. Because her motive power was incapable of moving the vessel, she was moored in the river to guard the channel approaches to the port.

Shortly after *Georgia* joined the squadron, a second ironclad was completed. *Atlanta* was converted from the iron-hulled blockade runner *Fingal.* In July 1863 *Atlanta* attempted to leave the river and attack Union blockaders in the sounds. Steaming down river, she ran aground, came under fire from two monitors, and surrendered.

In the summer of 1863 a third ironclad, the 150-foot *Savannah,* joined the squadron. Two additional ironclads were laid down in Savannah but never completed.

The Savannah Squadron cooperated with the land fortifications in defending the river approaches to Savannah. In December 1864, however, the city was captured by Gen. William Tecumseh Sherman's army from the west. The ships in the squadron were destroyed by their crews after covering the withdrawal of Confederate troops to South Carolina.

— WILLIAM N. STILL, JR.

SECESSION

The formal withdrawal of individual states from the Federal Union created at the Constitutional Convention of 1787 occurred in two distinct phases of separate state actions. The first took the seven states of the lower South out of the Union by February 1, 1861. This phase, triggered by Abraham Lincoln's election in November 1860, started when South Carolina withdrew on December 20, 1860. When Lincoln responded to the Confederate firing on Fort Sumter in April 1861 by calling upon the states to furnish seventy-five thousand militia to put down the Southern "insurrection," four additional states from the upper South left in the second phase of secession. These states—Virginia, North Carolina, Tennessee, and Arkansas—rounded out the political dimensions of the new Southern Confederacy. The other four slave states of Missouri, Kentucky, Maryland, and Delaware in the border South remained within the Union (the Confederacy claimed Missouri and Kentucky as member states, and both were represented in the Confederate Congress).

Secession rested on the constitutional doctrine of state sovereignty. According to this state rights position, the Union of 1787 was a confederation of sovereign states. The Federal government was simply the agent of the states entrusted with certain specified and limited powers. The individual states retained ultimate sovereign power, and they could leave the Union the same way they had entered it by calling a special state convention. Contrary to this view, most Northerners believed by 1860 that the Union was sovereign and perpetual. The states had surrendered their individual sovereignty when they joined the Union, and the legal right of secession did not exist. Far from residing within the Constitution, secession was a revolutionary act of defiance directed against the Constitution and the Union it had created.

The debate over the legal nature of the Union was as old as the Union itself. Both sides could turn to the Constitution for confirmation of their respective views because of its studied ambiguity over the ultimate locus of sovereign power in the Union. Such ambiguity was necessary in order to provide for a middle constitutional position that could blur the sharp differences between nationalists and state righters at the Philadelphia Convention. The Founding Fathers were able to secure the ratification of the Constitution only by agreeing to set up a Federal system in which power was divided and shared between the central government and the state governments.

Early Sectional Crises

The looseness of the Federal system left plenty of room for Jeffersonian Republicans and Hamiltonian Federalists to jockey for power in the early Republic. Although the Hamiltonians were associated with a broad construction of the Constitution and the Jeffersonians with a strict one, the slaveholding Virginia presidents during the era of Democratic-Republican

dominance from 1802 to 1824 by no means sought to crimp Federal power. Indeed, their control of the Federal government, combined with an aggressive policy of territorial expansion and the imposition of economic sanctions and a declaration of war against Britain in 1812, placed New England in the position of a beleaguered sectional minority chafing under Federal dominance. New Englanders, not Southerners, muttered the first cries of secession.

MISSOURI CRISIS. The Missouri crisis of 1819–1820 marked the first major sectional confrontation in which the South turned to the doctrine of state rights in the defense of slavery. Down to 1819 Congress had routinely admitted new slave states into the Union. Southerners were thus surprised when Representative James Tallmadge of New York, in February 1819, attached a resolution to the Missouri statehood bill banning the future introduction of slaves and providing for the emancipation at the age of twenty-five of all slaves born in Missouri after its admission as a state. Passed in the Northern-dominated House by nearly unanimous Northern votes, the Tallmadge proviso was blocked in the Senate where the slave and free states were in even balance.

Congress finally reached a compromise in March 1820. Missouri, part of the original Louisiana Purchase territory, was admitted as a slave state with no restrictions placed upon slavery, and Maine was admitted as a free state, thereby maintaining sectional parity in the Senate. Slavery was prohibited from the remainder of the Louisiana Purchase territory north of latitude 36° 30′, the southern boundary of Missouri. Only the threat of Southern disunion forced the Northern concessions that made possible the Missouri Compromise. Cries of secession became for the first time a weapon in the Southern arsenal of proslavery defenses. Few Southern whites, however, seriously contemplated secession in 1820. They remained confident of their ability to protect slavery by clinging more tightly to the strict constructionist doctrines of the original Jeffersonians.

NULLIFICATION CRISIS. Despite Southern control of the Jacksonian Democratic party that captured the presidency in 1828, South Carolina planters precipitated another sectional crisis in the early 1830s. These planters insisted that high protective tariffs were sacrificing the export economy of the slave South in the interests of Northern manufacturing capital. Their resistance to Federal authority produced the nullification crisis of 1832 and 1833.

Extending the arguments put forth by James Madison and Thomas Jefferson in the Virginia and Kentucky Resolutions of 1798, John C. Calhoun of South Carolina developed an elaborate constitutional theory by which a state could legally nullify Federal legislation that it determined violated its interests. The

Ever since the founding of the American republic, sectionalism had erupted in a Union-threatening crisis from time to time.

PAGE 141

most delicate of those interests in the South involved slavery. For all the economic opposition to the tariff, the underlying issue ran much deeper. The tariff was only symptomatic of the far greater threat of centralizing Federal power encroaching upon the prerogatives of slave owners and the perceived personal safety of Southern whites.

After the tariff of 1832 failed to reduce duties as much as the nullifiers demanded, a special South Carolina convention met in the fall of 1832 and nullified the tariffs of 1828 and 1832. The result was a major constitutional crisis that produced, for the first time, a firm case in the North for a perpetual Union. Although a compromise tariff in 1833 satisfied the nullifiers, their defiance of Federal authority had sharpened the ideological lines in the sectional conflict. Secessionist doctrines now began to attract a popular following in the South.

The Crisis of Slavery in the Territories

In the midst of the nullification controversy, abolitionism burst upon the national scene. It was a product both of evangelical Christianity and the radical idea in a racist society that equality of opportunity and the right of self-betterment should be color-blind. The abolitionists had an impact far greater than their numbers alone. Never more than a very small minority of Northern whites (Northern blacks, of course, were far more likely to be abolitionists), the abolitionists used every conceivable means to spread their message that slavery was a moral abomination. Most particularly, they targeted slaveholders as moral pariahs who were a disgrace to Christianity and the Republic's ideals of human rights as expressed in the Declaration of Independence.

Slaveholders, many of whom were evangelicals themselves, were stung to the quick. They lashed back at their accusers by using their political power to deny the abolitionists a hearing. Mails were censored in the South to keep out abolitionist literature, and Congress passed a series of gag rules that automatically tabled antislavery petitions. By enacting such measures, Southern politicians unwittingly strengthened the cause of antislavery. The image of the "Slave Power,"

JONES COUNTY, MISSISSIPPI
The Republic of Jones

According to legend, in 1864 the pro-Union populace of Jones County, Mississippi, formed a revolutionary government, adopted a declaration of independence, and formally seceded from Mississippi and the Confederate States of America. This new nation called itself the Republic (or Confederacy, or Kingdom) of Jones. When Mississippi and the Confederacy subsequently attempted to enforce their sovereignties in the county, the Republic of Jones organized its own army and navy and declared war on its parent states. The Republic of Jones, so the story goes, maintained its existence until the defeat of the Confederacy the following year.

The facts behind this legend indicate that the epithet "Republic of Jones" did, indeed, originate in events that occurred in 1864 in Jones County, Mississippi, but the history of the matter differs quite sharply from the legendary accounts. By 1864, Jones County, Mississippi, had been known whimsically for more than a generation as "The Free State of

Jones" because of its geographical remoteness, its lack of formal government and social amenities, and the independent, uninhibited lifestyle of its pastoral citizens. Like other frontier counties, Jones had little share in the cotton and slave economics and politics of the state, and most of its scattered population opposed secession. Nevertheless, when war came, the three thousand white people of Jones County provided two full companies and parts of six others to Southern armies.

Because of its isolation and sparse population, Jones County during the war became a haven for Confederate army deserters, some of whom banded together to plunder the local citizens and resist capture by Southern troops. In early 1864 Sherman's march to Meridian drove the Confederate army briefly from the state. Thinking that Federal troops had come to southeastern Mississippi to stay, some of the deserters sought to justify their robberies, assaults, evictions, and even killings of local citizens by representing such crimes as political

acts. There is little to suggest, however, that the mass of these stragglers were any more ideologically committed to the Union.

In mid-1864 Confederate efforts to quell deserter freebooting in Jones County inspired the newspaper *Courier*, of Natchez, a town long since under Union occupation, to lampoon the idea of secession by claiming that the rustic pineywoodsmen of the Free State of Jones had seceded from Mississippi just as that state had seceded from the Union. A month later, this burlesque was taken up by the New Orleans *Daily Picayune*. The spoof was then taken literally by elements of the Northern press, which portrayed the military policing in Jones County as Confederate attempts to suppress a civilian political revolt. In time, these different versions of the story merged with Jones County oral tradition to produce the modern legend of the Republic of Jones.

— RUDY LEVERETT

a conspiratorial force of tyrannical slaveholders running roughshod over the civil liberties and constitutional rights of Northern whites, began to take root in the popular consciousness of the North.

The demands of Southern Democrats in the early 1840s for the annexation of Texas, an independent slaveholding republic since 1836, fed Northern fears of a Southern plot to spread slavery. The push for Texas ultimately led to the Mexican War of 1846 through 1848. In that war American armies added California and most of the present-day Southwest to the Union and secured American claims to Texas as far south as the Rio Grande. The price of these territorial gains was the nation's worst sectional crisis since the flare-up over the admission of Missouri.

In the early stages of the Mexican War, David Wilmot, a congressman from Pennsylvania, introduced a proviso that prohibited slavery from any territory acquired as a result of the war. A Northern antislavery majority immediately formed in the House in support of the proviso. In response, Southern congressmen, almost to a man, rose up in defense of their right to expand slavery into Federal territories. Although Southern votes in the Senate were sufficient to defeat the Wilmot Proviso, the issues it raised continued to fester until the passage of a series of measures known collectively as the Compromise of 1850.

COMPROMISE OF 1850. Congress, against a backdrop of secessionist activity in the lower South and a call for a Southern convention to meet in Nashville, Tennessee, hammered out a compromise in the late summer of 1850. Concessions by the Northern antislavery majority in the House made possible the compromise. To be sure, California was admitted as a free state, the slave trade in Washington, D.C., was abolished, and the slave state of Texas yielded its claim on New Mexico (the eastern half bordered by the Rio Grande) in return for a Federal buyout of its debt. But the principle of the Wilmot Proviso was abandoned. The remaining lands in the Mexican Cession were organized into the territories of New Mexico and Utah with no mention of slavery. Even more damaging to the cause of antislavery was Northern acquiescence to a strengthened Fugitive Slave Act. This legislation put the full weight of the Federal government behind the efforts of slaveholders to recover their escaped slaves.

The Compromise of 1850 neutralized the Nashville Convention, and the secessionists were checkmated. Their strongholds were in South Carolina and Mississippi, but the refusal of Georgia, politically the bellwether in the lower South, to go along made Unionism respectable and politically profitable once again in the South. Nonetheless, the case for secession was significantly advanced. Even most Southern Unionists were forced to acknowledge that secession

was a legal right. In the lower South the Unionism that triumphed was of a decidedly conditional variety. As the Georgia legislature made explicit, Southern states reserved the right to weigh the value of the Union against the safety of the institution of slavery.

KANSAS-NEBRASKA ACT. Hopes in both sections that the Compromise of 1850 would be the final word on the sectional controversy shattered in 1854 with the passage of the Kansas-Nebraska Act. In order

to gain Southern votes necessary for the passage of his bill organizing the Louisiana Purchase territory north of 36° 30′, Senator Stephen A. Douglas of Illinois had to write into the Kansas-Nebraska Act a repeal of the Missouri Compromise restriction on slavery. Northerners widely interpreted this repeal as confirmation of a plot by the "Slave Power" to monopolize the territories for slavery at the expense of free labor.

The Northern storm of protest over the Kansas-Nebraska Act led to the formation of a sectionalized Republican party committed to preventing the spread of slavery into the territories. By 1856 the Republicans were the strongest party in the North. The Democrats were still a national party, but they were increasingly dominated by their Southern wing. In 1856, and with nearly solid support from the South, James Buchanan of Pennsylvania was elected as the last of the antebellum Democratic presidents.

The Buchanan presidency was a disaster for what remained of national unity. The Supreme Court ruled in the *Dred Scott* case of 1857 that Congress had no constitutional authority to prohibit slavery in the territories. The decision enraged Northerners and lent further credence to the notion of a "Slave Power" controlling the highest councils of government. A year later Democratic unity collapsed when Buchanan attempted to bring Kansas into the Union as a slave state. Convinced that the Free Soil majority in Kansas had been denied a fair opportunity to express its wishes on slavery, Douglas led

SECESSION

The Crisis of Slavery in the Territories

STEPHEN DOUGLAS

Proponent of the Kansas-Nebraska Act, Stephen A. Douglas was the Democratic candidate running against Abraham Lincoln in the election of 1860.

NATIONAL ARCHIVES

"The South seceded in 1861 because it had lost faith in the willingness of the Democratic party to fight for Southern interests."

ROBERT S. COTTERILL
THE OLD SOUTH

a party revolt against Buchanan and his Southern supporters. Although few Southerners felt that slavery could thrive on the plains of Kansas, they were determined to establish the principle that a slave state could still be added to the Union. Largely because of the Douglas-led revolt, a slave Kansas was kept out of the Union. Southern Democrats never again trusted Douglas, and they would wreck the party before they would submit to his presidential nomination in 1860.

ELECTION OF 1860. John Brown's raid against the Harpers Ferry arsenal in October 1859 heightened sectional tensions as the election of 1860 approached. Brown, the epitome of the fiery abolitionist, failed in his attempt to incite a slave uprising and was executed in early December. Most Northerners, including the Republicans, denounced Brown as a wild-eyed fanatic. But, the fact that Brown had mounted a frontal attack upon slavery and then was elevated to martyrdom by a handful of New England reformers sent paroxysms of fear and anger throughout the South. Rumors of conspiracies and slave uprisings were rampant during the winter of 1859–1860, and Southerners were convinced that the Republican party was dominated by abolitionists and was plotting with them to unleash a bloodbath in the slave states.

The presidential election of 1860 was a four-way race. After the Southern Democrats bolted the party's national convention in Charleston, South Carolina, over the refusal of the Douglas Democrats to support a congressional slave code for the protection of slavery in the territories, the separate wings of the party nominated their own candidates for the presidency—Douglas for the North and John C. Breckinridge of Kentucky for the South. The Republicans ran Abraham Lincoln of Illinois, the favorite son of a state in the lower North that was crucial to Republican hopes for victory in 1860. The fourth candidate was John Bell of Tennessee who was backed by members of the now defunct Whig party in the upper South.

As expected, Lincoln was elected on November 6, 1860. With the exception of New Jersey, whose electoral vote was split, he swept the free states and commanded a clear majority in the electoral college though securing only 40 percent of the total popular vote. Breckinridge carried eleven of the fifteen slave states, including the entire lower South. Bell took Virginia, Kentucky, and Tennessee. Douglas, whose popular vote was second to Lincoln's, won only Missouri.

Lincoln's election was the signal the secessionists had been waiting for. Southerners had anticipated with dread the election of 1860, and on November 6 their worst fears were confirmed. Southern political power had shrunk to the point where an antislavery minority party with no pretense of support in the South could capture the presidency. It would be hard to imagine a greater insult to Southern honor than this demonstration of the South's political impotency in the face of a growing Northern majority. Here then was the first great advantage of the secessionists. Regardless of party affiliation or political beliefs, Southerners felt tremendously wronged. For more than a generation they had cast themselves as the aggrieved innocents in an unequal sectional struggle that unleashed more and more Northern aggressions on Southern rights. They believed they had been denied their fair share of the Federal territories and unfairly taxed through high tariffs to subsidize Northern industrial might. They were infuriated by the personal liberty laws passed by many Northern states that made it more difficult to recover fugitive slaves. Above all, they had been branded as moral monsters for upholding the institution of slavery. Their self-respect demanded that a stand be taken against the latest Northern outrage, the election of a Republican president.

Secession Looms

Young, slaveholding lawyers and planters spearheaded secession. They came to political maturity in the 1850s at a time of intensifying sectional hostilities, and they turned to the Breckinridge movement for vindication of their rights and status against the onslaughts of the antislavery North. The Breckinridge demand for Federal protection of slavery in the territories was their answer to the Republican commitment to free soil. Their recently acquired wealth in land and slaves rested on a rickety structure of credit that required rising slave prices to keep from collapsing. Economic self-interest, as well as wounded pride, drove them to secession once Lincoln's election threatened to limit Southern growth by ending the expansion of slavery.

THE FIRE-EATERS. The most prominent secessionists were known as the fire-eaters. In particular, William Lowndes Yancey of Alabama, Edmund Ruffin of Virginia, and Robert Barnwell Rhett, Sr., of South Carolina had earned this label for their long and uncompromising devotion to the cause of Southern independence. Outside the inner circle of Southern political power at the national level, and hence free of the need to fashion a middle position to hold together a bisectional party coalition, the fire-eaters consistently had taken a hard line on Southern rights. They pushed sectional issues to their logical extreme and applauded the breakup of the national Democratic party in 1860. Aided immeasurably by the fears provoked by John Brown's raid, they popularized the right of secession among the Southern masses.

As veterans of sectional agitation, the fire-eaters had learned an invaluable lesson: a united South was a myth. South Carolina had stood alone during the nullification crisis, and Calhoun had called in vain for a monolithic South to rise up and demand its rights from the Yankee aggressors. In the crisis of 1850 and 1851, the secessionists were left isolated in South Carolina and Mississippi. Unity was impossible because of statewide and regional divisions that broke along lines of geography and social development. Virtually every slave state was rife with tensions between the yeoman-dominated backcountry and the planter-dominated black belts and lowcountry. A very broad division ran along a line from South Carolina westward to the Mississippi that differentiated the lower South from the slave states above it. In the upper South slaveholdings and percentages of slave owners were relatively smaller, fears of losing racial control less intense, and integration into the free-labor economies of the North tighter. Following the leadership of Virginia, the states of the upper South counseled moderation in the sectional confrontations of the 1850s.

Now that a Republican victory had fired the Southern resolve to resist, the radicals of the lower South were determined not to repeat their mistakes of the past by waiting for the upper South to act. They rejected any plan of prior cooperation among the slave states and launched secession on their own. They pursued a strategy of separate state action and confidently predicted that wavering states would be forced to join those that had already gone out. Separate state action was indeed the key to secession. It enabled the secessionists to lead from strength and create an irreversible momentum.

"Resistance or submission" was the rallying cry of the secessionists. The former, Southerners were told, was an honorable act of self-defense demanded by a love of liberty and equality. The latter was the slavish servility of a dishonorable coward. Frightened white males, often spurred on by white women, responded by rushing to join vigilance committees, military companies, and associations of "Minute Men." All these paramilitary groups pledged to defend the South against widely feared incursions of abolitionists incited by Lincoln's success. Southern communities were thrown into an emotional frenzy as they mobilized on an emergency footing.

THE REPUBLICAN THREAT. For all the popular hysteria they were instrumental in whipping up, the secessionists quite rationally assessed the nature of the Republican threat. The Republican stand against the expansion of slavery struck at the vital interests of the slave South. Economically, it threatened to choke off the profits of plantation agriculture by denying it access to fresh, arable lands. As a consequence, Southerners told themselves, whites would flee the slave states, and to save themselves, the dwindling numbers of whites would have to wage a preemptive war of extermination against the growing black majority. Politically, as free states were carved out of the territories, Southern power in Congress would be reduced to the point where slavery in the states could be dismantled by the ever larger political majority in the North. Most degrading of all from the Southern perspective was the humiliation implicit in submitting to the rule of an

S

SECESSION

Secession Looms

"The very essence of a free government consists in considering offices as public trusts, bestowed for the good of the country, and not for the benefit of an individual or a party."

JOHN C. CALHOUN

THE PROCESS OF SECESSION

	Secession Ordinance	Popular Ratification	Joined the Confederacy*
South Carolina	Dec. 20, 1860	None	Apr. 3, 1861
Mississippi	Jan. 9, 1860	None	Mar. 29, 1861
Florida	Jan. 10, 1861	None	Feb. 26, 1861
Alabama	Jan. 11, 1861	None	Mar. 13, 1861
Georgia	Jan. 19, 1861	None	Mar. 16, 1861
Louisiana	Jan. 26, 1861	None	Mar. 21, 1861
Texas	Feb. 1, 1861	Feb. 23, 1861	Mar. 23, 1861
Virginia	Apr. 17, 1861	May 23, 1861	Apr. 27, 1861
Arkansas	May 6, 1861	None	May 10, 1861
Tennessee	May 6, 1861	June 8, 1861	May 7, 1861
North Carolina	May 20, 1861	None	May 20, 1861

*With the exceptions of Tennessee and Virginia, these are the dates that the secession conventions ratified the Confederate Constitution. On April 27, the Virginia convention invited the Confederate government to shift its capital to Richmond, and on May 7 Governor Isham Harris of Tennessee committed his state to a military alliance with the Confederacy.

519

S

SECESSION

The South Secedes

By the summer of 1860, with Abraham Lincoln's election a certainty, Lawrence Keitt was in the forefront of those calling for South Carolina's secession.

PAGE 310

antislavery party. To do so would be an admission to Northerners and the outside world that the Southern way of life was morally suspect. Only slaves, the secessionists insisted, acted in such a servile fashion.

The secessionists did not expect the Republicans to make an immediate and direct move against slavery. They were well aware that the Republicans did not control Congress or the Supreme Court. As a new and still untested party, the Republicans would have to cooperate with Southern and Democratic politicians. But, reasoned the secessionists, such a demonstration that the slave South could, in the short run, survive under a Republican administration, would establish the fatal precedent of submitting to Republican rule and blunt the spirit of Southern resistance. In the meantime, the Republicans could use what power they had to begin the slow dismantling of slavery. The whole purpose of the Republican determination to prohibit the expansion of slavery was to put it on the road to extinction in the states where it existed.

In addition to all the perceived horrors of encirclement by a swelling majority of free states, the secessionists warned of changes in the sectional balance that the Republicans could potentially implement. They could move against slavery in Washington, D.C., and in Federal forts and installations. They could force the introduction of antislavery literature into the South by banning censorship of the Federal mails and simultaneously position the Supreme Court to overturn the *Dred Scott* ruling. They could weaken or repeal the Fugitive Slave Act and prohibit the interstate slave trade, a key link in the profitability of slavery to the South as a whole. Most alarming of all from the standpoint of the secessionists was the possibility that the Republicans would use Federal patronage and appointments to build a free labor party in the South. Senator Robert Toombs of Georgia echoed the concerns of many secessionists when he predicted in 1860 that Republican control of Federal jobs would create an "abolition party" within a year in Maryland, within two years in Kentucky, Missouri, and Virginia, and throughout the South by the end of four years.

SOUTHERN DIVISIONS OVER SLAVERY. The Toombs prediction went to the heart of secessionists' fears over the commitment to slavery *within* the South. To be sure, very few Southern whites by 1860 favored an immediate end to slavery. Most such whites had left the South in the preceding generation, either voluntarily or in response to community pressures forcing them out. Nonetheless, deep divisions existed over the future of slavery and the direction of Southern society itself.

The Jeffersonian dream of a gradual withering away of slavery persisted in the upper South. Many whites could contemplate and even accept the eventual end of the institution as long as there was no outside interfer-

ence in the process of disentanglement. In this region, as the proportion of slaves in the total population steadily declined in the late antebellum decades, slavery was increasingly becoming a matter of expediency, not of necessity. The secessionists had every reason to believe that a Republican administration would encourage the emancipationist sentiment that had already emerged among the white working classes in such slave cities as St. Louis, Baltimore, and Richmond.

In the lower South the secessionists doubted the loyalty to slavery of the yeomanry, a class of nonslaveholding farmers who composed the largest single bloc in the electorate. Although tied to the planters by a mutual commitment to white supremacy and often by bonds of kinship, these farmers occupied an ambivalent position in Southern society. They fervently valued their economic independence and political liberties, and hence they resented the spread of the plantation economy and the planters' pretensions to speak for them. But as long as the yeomen were able to practice their subsistence-oriented agriculture and the more ambitious ones saw a reasonable chance of someday buying a few slaves, this resentment fell far short of class conflict. In the 1850s, however, both these safety valves were being closed off. The proportion of families owning slaves fell from 31 to 25 percent. Sharply rising slave prices prevented more and more whites from purchasing slaves. At the same time, railroads spread the reach of a plantation agriculture geared to market production. Rates of farm tenancy rose in the older black belts, and the yeomen's traditional way of life was under increasing pressure.

Distrustful of the upper South as a region and the yeomanry as a class, the secessionists pushed for immediate as well as separate state secession. By moving quickly, they hoped to prevent divisions within the South from coalescing into a paralyzing debate over the best means of resisting Republican rule. Since most of the rabid secessionists were Breckinridge Democrats, the party that controlled nearly all the governorships and state legislatures in the lower South, the secessionists were able to set their own timetable for disunion.

The South Secedes

South Carolina was in the perfect position to launch secession. Its governor, William H. Gist, was on record as favoring a special state convention in the event of a Republican victory, and the legislature, the only one in the Union that still cast its state's electoral votes, was in session when news of Lincoln's election first reached the state. Aware of South Carolina's reputation for rash, precipitate action and leery of the state's being isolated, Gist would have preferred that another state take the lead in secession. But having been rebuffed a month earlier in his attempt to convince other Southern governors to seize the initiative, he was now prepared to take the first overt step. The South Carolina legislature almost immediately approved a bill setting January 8 as the election day for a state convention to meet on January 15.

Secession might well have been stillborn had the original convention dates set by the South Carolina legislature held. A two-month delay, especially in the likely event that no Southern state other than South Carolina would dare to go out alone, would have allowed time for passions to subside and lines of communication to be opened with the incoming Republican administration. But on November 10 a momentous shift occurred in the timing of South Carolina's convention. Reports of large secession meetings in Jackson, Mississippi, and Montgomery, Alabama, and reports that Georgia's governor, Joseph E. Brown, had recommended the calling of a convention in his state emboldened the South Carolina secessionists to accelerate their own timetable. They successfully pressured the South Carolina legislature to move up the dates of the state's convention to December 6 for choosing delegates and December 17 for the meeting.

SECESSION IN THE LOWER SOUTH. The speedy call for an early South Carolina convention triggered similar steps toward secession by governors and legislatures throughout the lower South. On November 14 Governors Andrew B. Moore of Alabama and J. J. Pettus of Mississippi issued calls for state conventions, both of which were to be elected on December 24 and meet on January 7. Moore had prior legislative approval for calling a convention, and Pettus was given his mandate on November 26. Once the Georgia legislature voted its approval on November 18, Governor Brown set January 2 for the election of Georgia's convention and January 16 for its convening. The Florida legislature in late November and the Louisiana legislature in early December likewise authorized their governors to set in motion the electoral machinery for January meetings of their conventions. Texas was a temporary exception to the united front developing in the lower South for secession. Its governor, Sam Houston, was a staunch Unionist who refused to call his legislature into special session. As a result, Texas secessionists resorted to the irregular, if not illegal, expedient of issuing their own call for a January convention.

Within three weeks of Lincoln's election the secessionists had generated a strong momentum for the breakup of the Union by moving quickly and decisively. In contrast, Congress, acting slowly and hesitantly, did nothing to derail the snowballing movement.

Congress convened on December 3, and the House appointed a Committee of Thirty-three (one representative from each state) to consider compromise measures. The committee, however, waited a week before calling its first meeting, and the creation of a similar committee in the Senate was temporarily blocked by bitter debates between Republicans and Southerners. When the House committee did meet on December 14, its Republican members failed (by a vote of eight to eight) to endorse a resolution calling for additional guarantees of Southern rights. Choosing to interpret this Republican stand as proof that Congress could accomplish nothing, thirty congressmen from the lower South then issued an address to their constituents declaring their support for an independent Southern confederacy. A week later, on December 20, South Carolina became the first state to leave the Union when its convention unanimously approved an ordinance of secession.

South Carolina provided the impetus, but the ultimate fate of secession in the lower South rested on the outcome of the convention elections held in late December and early January in the six other cotton states. The opponents of immediate secession in these states were generally known as cooperationists. Arguing that in unity there was strength, the cooperationists wanted to delay secession until a given number of states had agreed to go out as a bloc. Many of the cooperationists were merely cautious secessionists in need of greater assurances before taking their states out. But an indeterminate number of others clung to the hope that the Union could still be saved if the South as a whole forced concessions from the Republicans and created a reconstructed Union embodying safeguards for slavery.

Any delay, however, was anathema to the immediate secessionists. They countered the cooperationists' fears of war by asserting that the North would accept secession rather than risk cutting off its supply of Southern cotton. The secessionists also neutralized the cooperationist call for unanimity of action by appointing secession commissioners to each of the states considering secession. The commissioners acted as the ambassadors of secession by establishing links of communication between the individual states and stressing the need for a speedy withdrawal. In a brilliant tactical move, the South Carolina convention authorized its commissioners on December 31 to issue a call for a Southern convention to launch a provisional government for the Confederate States of America. Even before another state had joined South Carolina in seceding, the call went out on January 3 for a convention to meet in Montgomery, Alabama, on February 4, 1861.

The secessionists won the convention elections in the lower South, but their margins of victory were far

"That the Montgomery statesmen were interested in creating a central government stronger than the logic of secession seemed to justify is further illustrated by the men chosen to lead the new government."

FRANCIS BUTLER
SIMKINS
A HISTORY OF THE SOUTH
1958

THE NORTHERN RESPONSE

Buchanan, the lame-duck president, did nothing to stem the tide of disunion. He officially held the reins of power in the four-month period between the presidential election in early November and Lincoln's inauguration in early March, but he had lost any popular mandate to govern. The secessionists had anticipated his indecision and cited it as confirmation of their argument that secession would be peaceable. Buchanan—reasoning that just as secession was unconstitutional so was any attempt by the Federal government to resist it by force—preferred to leave the problem for the Republicans to settle. He thought they were chiefly responsible for the crisis, and he said as much in his last annual message of December 3, 1860. His policy was a negative one of doing nothing to provoke an armed conflict with the seceding states.

The Republicans initially denied the existence of any real crisis. They were acutely aware of the pattern of Southern bluster and Northern concessions that had characterized former sectional confrontations, and they were not about to surrender their integrity as an antislavery party by yielding to Southern demands. At Lincoln's urging they drew the line at sanctioning the territorial expansion of slavery. Such a sanction was the crucial feature of the Crittenden Compromise, a package of six proposed constitutional amendments that came out of a Senate committee led by John J. Crittenden of Kentucky in mid-December. Under Crittenden's plan, slavery would be recognized south of 36° 30' in all present territories, as well as those "hereafter acquired." To a man, congressional Republicans rejected what they interpreted as a blank check for the future expansion of slavery into Mexico and the Caribbean.

— WILLIAM L. BARNEY

narrower than in South Carolina. The cooperationists polled about 40 percent of the overall vote, and in Alabama, Georgia, and Louisiana they ran in a virtual dead heat with the straight-out secessionists. Somewhat surprisingly, given the issues involved and the high pitch of popular excitement, voter turnout fell by more than one-third from the levels in the November presidential election. The short time allotted for campaigning and the uncontested nature of many of the local races held down the vote. In addition, many conservatives boycotted the elections out of fear of reprisals if they publicly opposed secession. The key to the victory of the secessionists was their strength in the plantation districts. They carried four out of five counties in which the slaves comprised a majority of the population and ran weakest in counties with the fewest slaves. The yeomen, especially in the Alabama and Georgia mountains, were against immediate secession. Characteristically, they opposed a policy they associated with the black belt planters.

Mississippi, Florida, Alabama, Georgia, and Louisiana successively seceded in their January conventions. They were joined by Texas on February 1, 1861. Like falling dominoes, the secession of one state made it easier for the next to follow. In each convention the secessionists fought back efforts for a cooperative approach or last-ditch calls for a Southern conference to make final demands on the Republicans. They also defeated attempts by cooperationists to submit the secession ordinances to a popular referendum. Only in Texas, where the secessionists were sensitive to the dubious legality by which they had forced the calling of a convention, was the decision on secession referred to the voters for their approval. In the end the secession ordinances passed by overwhelming majorities in all the conventions. This apparent unanimity, however, belied the fact that in no state had the immediate secessionists carried enough votes to have made up a majority in the earlier presidential election. Once the decision for secession was inevitable, the cooperationists voted for the ordinances in a conscious attempt to impress the Republicans with Southern resolve and unity.

Delegates from the seven seceded states met in Montgomery, Alabama, in February. Here, on the seventh, they adopted a Provisional Constitution (one closely modeled on the U.S. Constitution) for an independent Southern government and, on the ninth, elected Jefferson Davis of Mississippi as president. Thus, nearly a month before Lincoln's inauguration on March 4, the secessionists had achieved one of their major goals. They had a functioning government in place before the Republicans had even assumed formal control of the Federal government.

SECESSION IN THE UPPER SOUTH. The collapse of the Crittenden Compromise in late December eliminated the already slim possibility that the drive toward secession might end with the withdrawal of South Carolina. Still, when Lincoln took office on March 4, the Republicans had reason to believe that the worst of the crisis was over. February elections in the Upper South had resulted in Unionist victories. In January the legislatures of five states—Arkansas, Virginia, Missouri, Tennessee, and North Carolina—had issued calls for conventions. The

secessionists suffered a sharp setback in all the elections.

On February 4, Virginia voters chose to send moderates of various stripes to their convention by about a three-to-one margin. In yet another defeat for the secessionists, who opposed the measure, they also overwhelmingly approved a popular referendum on any decision reached by the convention. On February 9, Tennessee voted against holding a convention. Had one been approved, the Unionists elected would have composed an 80-percent majority. Arkansas and Missouri voted on February 18, and both elected Unionist majorities. On February 28, North Carolinians repeated the Tennessee pattern. They rejected the calling of a convention, which, in any event, would have been dominated by Unionists.

By the end of February secession apparently had burnt itself out in the upper South. It was defeated either by a popular vote or, as in the case of the slave states of Kentucky, Delaware, and Missouri, by the inability of the secessionists to pressure the legislatures or governors to issue a call for a convention. Despite fiery speeches and persistent lobbying by secession commissioners appointed by the Confederate government, the antisecessionists held their ground. In a region that lacked the passionate commitment of the lower South to defending slavery, they were able to mobilize large Unionist majorities of nonslaveholders. In particular, they succeeded in detaching large numbers of the Democratic yeomanry from the secessionist, slaveholding wing of their party. The yeomanry responded to the fears invoked by the Unionists of being caught in the crossfire of a civil war, and nonslaveholders in general questioned how well their interests would be served in a planter-dominated Confederacy.

A final factor accounting for the Unionist victories in the upper South was the meeting in Washington of the so-called Peace Convention called by the Virginia legislature. The delegates spent most of February debating various proposals for additional guarantees for slave property in an effort to find some basis for a voluntary reconstruction of the Union. Although boycotted by some of the Northern states and all of the states that had already seceded, the convention raised hopes of a national reconciliation and thereby strengthened the hand of the Unionists in the upper South. In the end, however, the convention was an exercise in futility. All it could come up with was a modified version of the Crittenden Compromise. Just before Lincoln's inauguration, Republican votes in the Senate killed the proposal.

PRESSURES FOR ACTION MOUNT. Throughout March and early April the Union remained in a state of quiescence that no one expected to last indefinitely. Both of the new governments, Lincoln's and Davis's, were under tremendous pressure to break the suspense by taking decisive action. Davis was criticized for not moving aggressively enough to bring the upper South into the Confederacy. Without that region and especially Virginia, it was argued, the Confederacy was but a cipher of a nation. It had negligible manufacturing capacity and only one-third of the South's free population. It desperately needed additional slave

THE OTHER PRESIDENT

Abraham Lincoln, Republican winner of the 1860 presidential election. Portrait by Mathew Brady, c. 1863.

NATIONAL ARCHIVES

states to have a viable chance for survival. Just as desperately, Lincoln's government needed to make good on its claim that the Union was indivisible. Buchanan had been mocked for his indecisiveness, and Lincoln knew that he had to take a stand on enforcing Federal authority.

The upper South now became a pawn in a power struggle between Lincoln and Davis. However much moderates in the upper South wanted to avoid a confrontation that would ignite a war, they were publicly committed to coming to the assistance of any Southern state that the Republicans attempted to coerce back into the Union. In short, Unionism in the upper South was always highly conditional in nature. This in turn made the region hostage to events beyond its control and gave the Confederacy the leverage it needed to pull in additional states.

The only major Federal installations in the Confederacy still under Federal control when Lincoln became president were Fort Pickens in Pensacola Harbor and Fort Sumter in Charleston Harbor. The retention of these forts thereby became a test of the credibility of the Republicans as the defenders of the Union. By the same token, the acquisition of these forts was essential if the Confederacy were to lay claim to the full rights of a sovereign nation.

On March 5, Lincoln learned from Maj. Robert Anderson, the commander at Fort Sumter, that dwindling food supplies would force an evacuation of the fort within four to six weeks. Lincoln decided against any immediate attempt to save the fort. On March 12, however, he issued orders for the reinforcement of Fort Pickens. More accessible to the Federal navy because of its location outside Pensacola Harbor beyond the range of Confederate artillery, Fort Pickens had the additional advantage of being overshadowed in the public consciousness by Fort Sumter, a highly charged symbol of Federal resolve in the state that had started secession. Presumably, it could be reinforced with less risk of precipitating a war than could Fort Sumter.

Lincoln's initial decision not to act on Fort Sumter was also a concession to William H. Seward, his secretary of state. Seward was the chief spokesman for what was called the policy of "masterly inactivity." He believed that Unionists in the upper South were on the verge of leading a process of voluntary reunion. If the upper South were not stampeded into joining the Confederacy by a coercive act by the Republicans, Seward argued, an isolated Confederacy would soon have no choice but to bargain to rejoin the Union. Everything depended, of course, on a conciliatory Republican policy.

In pursuing this strategy, Lincoln temporarily considered a withdrawal from Fort Sumter in exchange for a binding commitment from the upper South not to leave the Union. Seward then made the mistake of assuming that evacuation was a foregone conclusion. He was conducting informal negotiations with three Confederate commissioners who were in Washington seeking a transfer of Fort Pickens and Fort Sumter. On March 15 he informed them through an intermediary to expect a speedy evacuation of Fort Sumter. When no such evacuation was forthcoming, Confederate leaders felt betrayed, and they vowed never again to trust the word of the Lincoln administration.

Mounting demands in the North to take a stand at Fort Sumter, combined with Lincoln's growing disillusionment over Southern Unionism, convinced the president that he would have to challenge the Confederacy over the issue of Fort Sumter. On March 29 he told his cabinet that he was preparing a relief expedition. He delayed informing Major Anderson of that decision until after a meeting on April 4 with John Baldwin, a Virginia Unionist. Although no firsthand account of this meeting exists, the discussion apparently confirmed Lincoln's belief that the upper South could not broker a voluntary reunion on terms acceptable to the Republican party. The final orders for the relief expedition were issued on April 6, the day that Lincoln learned that Fort Pickens had not yet been reinforced because of a mix-up in the chain of command.

News of Lincoln's decision to reinforce Fort Sumter "with provisions only" reached Montgomery, the Confederate capital, on April 8. The next day Davis ordered Gen. P. G. T. Beauregard, the Confederate commander at Charleston, to demand an immediate surrender of the fort. If Major Anderson refused, Beauregard was to attack the fort. Davis always felt that war was inevitable, and for months the most radical of the secessionists had been insisting that a military confrontation would be necessary to force the upper South into secession. Davis was convinced that he had no alternative but to counter Lincoln's move with a show of force.

Confederate batteries opened fire on Fort Sumter on April 12, and the fort surrendered two days later. On April 15 Lincoln issued a call for seventy-five thousand state militia to put down what he described as an insurrection against lawful authority. It was this call for troops, and not just the armed clash at Fort Sumter, that specifically triggered secession in the upper South. The Unionist majorities there suddenly dissolved once the choice shifted from supporting the Union or the Confederacy to fighting for or against fellow Southerners.

The Virginia convention, which had remained in session after rejecting immediate secession on April 4, passed a secession ordinance on April 17. Its decision was overwhelmingly ratified on May 23 in a popular referendum. Three other states quickly followed. A reconvened Arkansas convention voted to go out on May 6. The Tennessee legislature, in a move later ratified in a popular referendum, also approved secession on May 6. A hastily called North Carolina convention, elected on May 13, took the Tarheel State out on May 20.

By the late spring of 1861 the stage was set for the bloodiest war in American history. The popular reaction to the firing on Fort Sumter and Lincoln's call for troops unified the North behind a crusade to preserve the Union and solidified, at least temporarily, a divided South behind the cause of Southern independence.

[*See also* Compromise of 1850; Constitutional Union Party; Crittenden Compromise; Declaration of Immediate Causes; Democratic Party; Dred Scott Decision; Election of 1860; Fire-eaters; Fort Sumter, South Carolina; Fugitive Slave Law; Harpers Ferry, West Virginia, *article on* John Brown's Raid; Kansas-Nebraska Act; Missouri Compromise; Nullification Controversy; Republican Party; State Rights; Washington Peace Conference; Wilmot Proviso; *and selected biographies of figures mentioned herein.*]

— WILLIAM L. BARNEY

SEDDON, JAMES A.

Seddon, James A. (1815–1880), Congressman from Virginia and secretary of war. Seddon was descended from English immigrants who arrived in Virginia in the eighteenth century and settled near Fredericksburg. Here they built Snowden, later destroyed by Union soldiers during the Civil War. Seddon was born in the town on July 13, 1815. He graduated from the University of Virginia law school with honors in 1835. Soon afterward, he opened a law office in Richmond and became active in the Calhoun wing of the Democratic party. In 1845 he married Sarah Bruce, daughter of a renowned Virginia family, and settled into the Clay Street mansion that later became the White House of the Confederacy. The couple quickly joined the social elite of the city. Shortly before, he had been elected to the U.S. House of Representatives.

Seddon served in Congress from 1845 to 1847, and again from 1849 to 1851. An ardent disciple of Calhoun, he adopted the state rights stance on most national issues in his first term. He supported the admission of Texas, the acquisition of Oregon, free trade over protectionism, and the necessity and value of slavery to the Southern way of life. He declined reelection in 1847 because of poor health. By 1849, when he returned to Congress, he had become a Southern

Lincoln approved the Lieber Code establishing guidelines for Union field commanders and soldiers, but James A. Seddon rejected them out of hand, saying they encouraged unrestricted warfare.

PAGE 510

WAR SECRETARY

James A. Seddon of Virginia was an able legislator, and as secretary of war he became Jefferson Davis's most influential military adviser next to Robert E. Lee.

James A. Seddon was a vigorous man, a clear thinker, and a tough-minded, dedicated worker.

PAGE 658

expansionist, sharing the dream of a large slave-based empire embracing the Caribbean. He had despaired of securing Southern rights in the Union and secretly favored secession and the formation of a Southern republic. In all measures of the Compromise of 1850, he affirmed ultra-Southern demands, siding with such extremist leaders as Robert Barnwell Rhett, Sr., and Jefferson Davis (with whom he had earlier become acquainted).

After leaving Congress in 1851, Seddon led the life of a planter in outlying Goochland County, where he acquired land, slaves, and a new twenty-six room home, Sabot Hill. He was infrequently in the public eye in the 1850s. Yet behind the scenes he corresponded, politicked, and championed the ambitions of friends, notably Robert M. T. Hunter (his closest political associate); gave strong support to opponents in the state against the Know-Nothings; and continued to be a power in the politics of the South. In 1856 he was a delegate to the Democratic National Convention at Cincinnati and was nominated for vice president on the Buchanan ticket, which he refused. In 1858 he spoke at a dinner in Richmond honoring Nicaragua filibusterer William Walker, whom Seddon praised as an evangel of progress and civilization. His own views on slavery and Southern nationalism deepened as he read the latest Southern theorists and promoted the distribution of their proslavery literature throughout the South.

He saw the election of Abraham Lincoln in 1860 as the death knell of the territorial ambitions of the South. Immediately he counseled resistance to expected Northern aggression and advised friends to prepare for the disruption of the Union. In January 1861 he was chosen as a delegate to the Washington peace conference. As a member of its committee on resolutions, he defended the right of secession (and the legitimacy of the new Southern Confederacy) and submitted a minority report seeking a constitutional amendment protecting the permanence of slavery in the Union. In the end, together with the majority of the Virginia delegation, he voted against the compromise proposals of the body. Throughout the debates he was a vigorous defender of Southern interests. To some he recalled one of his own heroes, John Randolph of Roanoke, while to others he was a firebrand secessionist. Two days before adjournment, a reception was given for the newly arrived President-elect Lincoln. Seddon was among those with questions for the Republican leader, and a heated exchange of views followed, especially regarding abolitionists, their objectives, and the "incendiary" press of the Northern states. Lincoln's response and humorous wit defused the debate.

Seddon returned to Richmond with ex-President John Tyler, also a delegate and old acquaintance, to urge their state to secede and join the Southern Confederacy. Nothing, they felt, of compromise or guarantees would be granted by the Republican-controlled Union. The Seddon-Tyler report to Governor John Letcher concluded that the conference had been a failure and "independent state action" was the only alternative to certain Northern coercion. In several speeches, Seddon urged crowds of frenzied Richmonders to prepare for the worst. He also implored the Virginia state convention, then sitting in the city, to act. On April 16, 1861, following the firing on Fort Sumter and Lincoln's call for troops, Seddon spoke before the "Spontaneous Peoples' Convention," demanding immediate secession. The following day, Virginia responded and left the Union. As Seddon observed to Charles Bruce, his brother-in-law, "The whole State is [now] in movement and the difficulty is rather to restrain any men at home than to fire them to the War." He was elated—the South had at long last been delivered from "Yankee Thralldom," and his dreams for an independent nation had finally been realized.

From April to early summer of 1861, the peace of the Virginia countryside was shattered by the bustle of military preparations. Many of Seddon's relatives responded to the call, and Seddon himself would have donned a uniform but for his health and feeble constitution. Soon after President Davis's arrival in Richmond and transfer of the Confederate capital to Virginia, he met several times with his old friend, perhaps to discuss Hunter's or Seddon's availability for the post of secretary of state. The question was on the lips of many of his friends. In June, he was chosen by Virginia for the Provisional Confederate Congress.

Seddon's eight months in Congress proved helpful to the new Davis administration and to his own political fortunes. In this critical time the unicameral body was setting up the government, recruiting and provisioning armies, and financing the war. Seddon gave special attention to the latter—the revision of the Produce Loan of 1861 to double its bond and currency issue to $100 million; passage of a law to make Treasury notes legal tender for all debts; and issuance of bonds to underwrite the currency and overall deficit spending. He also helped shape the Sequestration Act, in reprisal for similar Federal legislation; a strict embargo on cotton export; subsidies to arms manufacturers; impressment laws for military needs; railroad legislation to consolidate the lines and close major gaps in their routes; prisoner of war exchange and establishment of prison camps; and numerous military bills. As congressman, he had introduced ten bills, most enacted into law. He met not infrequently with the president and lobbied with colleagues to support the administration and a vigorous prosecution of the war. He saw the conflict in large terms and tried to imbue others with his own perception. He thus emerged as a strong Confederate nationalist rather than a narrow state rights advocate on most major issues.

In the summer of 1862, Seddon was approached through a lengthy correspondence by oceanographer Capt. Matthew Fontaine Maury with various schemes for promoting innovations in naval warfare, use of metal ships and torpedo weaponry, and government use, if not control, of blockade runners for the strategic needs of the South. Some of these ideas would later be enacted once Seddon was in charge of the War Department.

In mid-November, when Secretary of War George Wythe Randolph resigned, Davis prevailed upon Seddon to fill the office. The choice was a personal one for Davis: he wanted a solid friend in this difficult post and also another Virginian in his cabinet. Others did as well, including critically outspoken foes of the president. They applauded Seddon's appointment on November 20. He would hold his post almost to the end of the war, longer than the combined tenure of the three previous occupants. The choice proved an excellent one. Seddon brought to his task not only dedication and intelligence but also independence of thought and tact. A good judge of men, he impressed diarist Mary Boykin Chesnut as a warm and caring man and a fascinating conversationalist. Usually diplomatic, he was best as a sympathetic listener and convincing advocate. Seddon's cadaverous appearance was deceptive, for he was a tireless worker. Save for Robert E.

Lee, he became Davis's most influential military adviser and devised much of the South's offensive strategy of concentration and total war. Together with Stephen R. Mallory and Judah P. Benjamin, he was one of the ablest of Davis's cabinet heads.

Unlike his predecessor, Seddon lacked military experience and at first relied heavily on the president, Assistant Secretary of War John A. Campbell, and Inspector General Samuel Cooper. Later he took upon himself the burdens of responsibility. One month after his appointment, he observed to Charles Bruce:

> The life is one rather of close confinement and incessant worry than of severe labor, and so far I have not suffered tho' giving daily from 9 a m to 9 or 10 p m to my duties. Indeed few persons are so well prepared by previous habits for [such] a sedatory life. . . . I trust to do reasonably well, as soon as I get a little more trained to the routine and versed in the military knowledge of the place.

Davis gave most of his cabinet members wide latitude in running their offices. He sought their advice and tolerated opinions contrary to his own. But having been a secretary of war himself and as an experienced military man, Davis naturally took a strong personal interest in the War Department and to a degree regarded it as his own domain. He carefully scrutinized the activities of this office and kept a tighter rein on its head than on other cabinet officers. As armies, strategy, and war itself were the chief concern of the Confederacy's leaders, the secretary and president had to work closely together.

Seddon found Davis not an impossible taskmaster at first, though often a difficult one. In working with him, he had to act by suggestion rather than command, relying on tact in his relations with the egocentric president. In lesser matters Seddon was seldom overruled, but when he was, he bowed to the will of his chief. An unselfish man without political ambition, Seddon did not seek power; rather, he was simply devoted to the Southern cause. He was in no way obsequious; he was much too proud to serve as a mere figurehead. He valued his appointment as an expression of Davis's respect and remained in the cabinet only as long as he shared the esteem of the president and the confidence of the people.

By November 1862 the enemy was again on the move in Virginia. Ambrose Burnside was advancing on the capital by way of Fredericksburg. Lee maneuvered to counter him. At the same time Charleston and Wilmington to the south feared imminent assault; but in the West there were even graver fears that the Union would soon seize the Mississippi and sever the Confederacy in two. Seddon was not long in respond-

Seddon was above all a man possessed of tact and diplomacy, and a close friend of the hypersensitive president.

PAGE 658

The extensive use of rifled bores, repeating rifles, machine guns, and even flamethrowers exacted heavy tolls on Confederate formations.

PAGE 510

Seddon kept a close eye on unfolding developments, down to the double crisis of Gettysburg and Vicksburg in midsummer 1863.

PAGE 659

ing to this impending crisis. With confidence in Lee in Virginia and while giving assurances of support to P. G. T. Beauregard and the Atlantic defenses, he focused major attention on the western theater. He believed that the decisive contest in the war at this time was to be waged there. His deep concern for this theater and the planning he put forth serve as a good index of the kind of strategist he could have been, had Davis given him greater latitude. His fears of a major debacle in the Trans-Mississippi and his recognition of the need for a reorientation of Confederate strategy there had in large measure been shared by his predecessor. But where Randolph had failed, Seddon succeeded. He not only won Davis's support for a newly organized Department of the West and persuaded him to visit the region (the following month) but got him to name Joseph E. Johnston to its command. It was a good solution to a large dilemma but depended for success upon the audacity and imagination of the chosen commander. Johnston failed to rise to the occasion. Seddon repeatedly pleaded with him to assert his authority over the entire area and to assume command of the scattered forces of Braxton Bragg, John C. Pemberton, and lesser units, but to no avail. Disappointment followed disappointment until Pemberton's large army was pent up in Vicksburg by the summer of 1863.

December 1862 had seen Lee again victorious, at Fredericksburg. It was a costly but timely victory. Virginia was freed of the invader until spring, and the capital yet secure. Another lesser triumph came on January 1, 1863, when John B. Magruder retook the vital Gulf port of Galveston. Seddon, in the meantime, "borrowed" troops and taxed the resources of lesser points to brace Beauregard's command at Charleston. On April 7 an ironclad fleet appeared before the city and, after a brisk battle, was turned back.

The year 1863 started out as the high watermark in the life of the Confederacy, but with the loss of Vicksburg and the Mississippi River and the simultaneous repulse at Gettysburg, the Confederates were thereafter on the defensive. Seddon had favored sending a part of Lee's army to the West, but after lengthy debate in the cabinet and with Lee, he abandoned his plan and gave support to a second invasion of the North. Years later he would declare in a letter that the "disaster of Vicksburg . . . was the fatal turning point of the war."

Seddon once again sought to snatch victory in the West. In the fall of 1863 he persuaded Davis and Lee to send James Longstreet from Virginia to Tennessee, where his timely arrival and generalship helped win the Battle of Chickamauga. But no one could singlehandedly win the war, least of all the secretary. Only by mustering its resources could the South hope to drive off the invaders, and only through teamwork, which he sought to promote, was victory possible. Incompetents and malcontents had to be removed, and those with ability, experience, and a will to win be empowered to lead the fight. Pemberton, for instance, found no admirer in the secretary; numerous complaints had poured into Richmond questioning his competency and retention in command. Most tragic to Seddon was the prolonged retention of Bragg in the West. He tried repeatedly for Bragg's recall, but Johnston and later Davis himself blocked him. Only after the disastrous defeat at Chattanooga in November 1863 was Bragg finally removed. William J. Hardee, his most promising subordinate, refused his place. Seddon and a majority of the cabinet favored a second chance for Johnston, and he was returned to the Army of Tennessee. Barely a year later, he would be removed, this time before the defenses of Atlanta. Seddon, in general, supported the "fighting" generals—Lee, Longstreet, later John Bell Hood, and, despite Davis's disdain, Beauregard. One prime fighter that all overlooked was Nathan Bedford Forrest, whose recognition came too late for the West.

By 1864 the South was fighting a holding action. Two-thirds of its territory was gone, and a third of its armies was absent without leave (as Seddon admitted to the president in his annual report). The day for offensives was over. Seddon was now preoccupied with keeping the two major armies alive despite eroding morale, mass desertions, and widespread disaffection and starvation on the home front. He fought with Governors Joseph E. Brown of Georgia and Zebulon Vance of North Carolina over conscription, impressment, and martial law. He struggled to save worn-out railroads, which he commandeered for the government. He sequestered space on blockade runners and sent forth the department's own vessels to bring in vital supplies. He broke the rules and allowed cotton to be traded with the enemy for meat and other food for the army. And he assisted secret service and espionage ventures behind Northern lines to promote disaffection, peace movements, and the defeat of Lincoln's reelection—all this, and much more, during the last months of the war.

The cause was crumbling, yet Seddon could not admit it. There was talk of resignation, but friends urged him to hold on. He did, as he continued to live with only a single body servant, bearing alone the anguish of a lost child and the death from combat wounds of his brother, Maj. John Seddon. Even the threat to his own life, implicit with the Dahlgren raid on Richmond and its plot to kill Davis and his cabinet, he discounted. In February 1865, he saw his old Democrat friend Francis P. Blair, who came to the Confederate capital to promote peace. This and the subsequent Hampton Roads conference were the latest expressions of the reality of ultimate defeat. Nor was he able at this late date to think his way beyond Hunter and Cobb on the issue of black soldiers. (Earlier, in 1863, he had agreed with Davis to suppress Patrick Cleburne's proposal to arm the slaves.) Only when Lee urged the measure because of his desperate need for more men did Seddon reconsider—but it was too late.

Finally, when the Virginia congressional delegation, in anger over conditions generally and in hopes of restoring public confidence, requested the president to reorganize his cabinet, Seddon was piqued and immediately resigned. He had mistaken the motives of this body, who did not seek his ouster. But perhaps it was time for him to step aside and return to his family. Despite Davis's reassurances (and the lengthy correspondence that ensued), his resignation became final. On February 5, 1865, he quit his office and returned to Sabot Hill.

With his retirement, some now realized the breadth of the services he had rendered. Although his name had become a household word throughout the South, his popularity, like that of other politicians in this military-conscious society, never approached that of the fighting generals. But many recognized him as a man of dedication, will, and strength. Perhaps he was not the ideal man for the position, in view of his lack of military background and inexperience as an administrator, but he was the best the South had to offer. "His critics were numerous," wrote Douglas S. Freeman, "but a student will search the list vainly to find the name of one who could have done better than Seddon."

Out of office, he could do little more than witness the last acts of the struggle. He had little hope that Richmond would not fall, he told his sister in March. A week later, in a letter to Davis, he thought better of the cause, which he now believed would prevail; "the Liberties and Independence of your Country" will be achieved, he asserted. When the end finally came, he "was completely crushed . . . and considered his life to have been a complete failure" (as he told his son).

On May 20, Seddon took the oath of amnesty, but three days later he was suddenly arrested and confined in Libby Prison with Hunter and Campbell. On June 5, the three arrived at Fort Pulaski, Georgia, where they were joined by eight other former leaders. After Seddon's release in December, he returned to Sabot Hill. He was able largely to restore his fortunes through his law practice and his plantations in Virginia and Louisiana. He never wrote his memoirs, having destroyed most of his papers out of fear of their seizure by the Radical Republicans. Seddon died on August 19, 1880, and was buried in Hollywood Cemetery, Richmond.

— JOHN O'BRIEN

SEMMES, RAPHAEL

Semmes, Raphael (1809–1877), rear admiral. Semmes was captain of CSS *Sumter* and CSS *Alabama* and admiral of the James River Squadron. His duty on the two ships was to prey upon enemy merchant vessels, and he did that job better than any other naval captain in naval history, burning sixty-four U.S. registered merchant vessels and bonding thirteen others. On *Sumter* he was the first to show the Confederate flag on the high seas and in neutral ports; on *Alabama* he sank USS *Hatteras,* a new U.S. Navy ironclad side-wheeler.

The experiences of his youth foreshadowed the introspective and self-reliant captain of *Sumter* and *Alabama.* Born in Maryland and orphaned at age nine, Raphael and his younger brother moved to Georgetown, D.C., to live with two of their uncles. Raphael, influenced by a merchant shipping uncle, was drawn first to sea life and second to law. A third uncle, a Maryland politician and future congressman, secured an appointment for him as a midshipman in the U.S. Navy, dated April 1, 1826. Raphael was sixteen.

A second career was necessary in the old navy because officers frequently received long enforced leaves without pay. Thus, after Semmes spent five years as a trainee officer, he was promoted to passed midshipman and placed on extended leave. He seized the opportunity to read law, passed the bar exam in 1833, and established a law office in Cincinnati, Ohio.

When recalled to duty, now Lieutenant Semmes was assigned to the Pensacola, Florida, Navy Yard. He moved his family to nearby Alabama and from that moment considered himself a citizen of that state. To help his wife with their growing family, he purchased three household slaves. His conversion to the Southern way of life was complete.

Semmes's experiences in the U.S. Navy prepared him for his role in the Civil War. On various ships he

Under the command of Raphael Semmes, Enrica was rechristened CSS Alabama.

PAGE 6

DAMN THE BLOCKADE

Rear Admiral Raphael Semmes's success in sinking U.S. merchant ships led merchants worldwide to refuse to sail under the U.S. flag.

NAVAL HISTORICAL CENTER, WASHINGTON, D.C.

S

On Feb. 18, 1865,
Rear Adm.
Raphael Semmes,
former captain of
Alabama, *took
command of the
James River
Squadron.*

PAGE 299

*The fall of New
Orleans in April
1862 sparked
numerous
investigations
within the
Confederate
government.*

PAGE 394

sailed the Gulf coasts on survey duty, was lighthouse inspector on the Gulf and Atlantic coasts, and performed blockade duty off Vera Cruz during the Mexican War. He commanded four U.S. Navy vessels.

From the end of the Mexican War until 1855 he remained on leave, practicing law in Mobile and writing *Service Afloat and Ashore during the War with Mexico,* a best-seller in the early 1850s. He was promoted to the rank of commander (1855), assigned as inspector of the Eighth Lighthouse District, and then transferred to Washington as secretary of the Lighthouse Board (1858) and later as member of the board (February 1861). By then his survey and lighthouse assignments had provided him with a thorough knowledge of Gulf, Caribbean, and North Atlantic shorelines, tides, and winds.

When Alabama seceded from the Union, Semmes resigned from the U.S. Navy to offer his services to the Confederacy. In 1861 his appearance commanded respect. Slightly below medium height with an erect bearing, he wore his hair long over his ears, had a large waxed mustache and small goatee, and had piercing black eyes. Highly intelligent and a voracious reader, he based the decision to follow his adopted state out of the Union on the constitutional ground that the Federal government had no right to impose its will on the several Southern states.

While traveling by train to Montgomery, Alabama, where Jefferson Davis had established the Provisional Government, he rode through a pine-forest fire. The flames prompted him to muse that "civil war is a terrible crucible through which to pass character."

He arrived in Montgomery in February 1861, met with President Davis, and left a day later to shop for arms and munitions in Northern states. In Montgomery, on April 4, Secretary of the Navy Stephen R. Mallory appointed Semmes commander in the Confederate navy and chief of the Lighthouse Bureau.

The firing on Fort Sumter led Semmes to realize that "it was time to leave the things of peace to the future." He asked Mallory for a ship suitable for commerce raiding, and Mallory showed him a file on a ship in New Orleans, already examined and condemned. "Give me that ship," Semmes said. On the newly converted *Sumter,* Semmes cleverly eluded USS *Brooklyn* and sailed into the Gulf of Mexico on June 30, 1861.

President Abraham Lincoln's proclamation of a blockade of Southern ports and Davis's statement of intent to issue letters of marque forced Great Britain and France to proclaim their neutrality, which effectively recognized the Confederacy as de facto belligerent with the same international rights and limitations as held by the United States.

Semmes's objective was to draw U.S. warships from blockade duty by sinking U.S. merchant ships. His success against merchantmen led merchants worldwide to refuse to ship under the U.S. flag. (In Singapore, Semmes found seventeen U.S. merchantmen lying without cargoes for over three months.) Still, the United States would not weaken the blockade, and its merchant fleet has never recovered its prewar second position in world commercial shipping.

The *Sumter* cruise was a learning experience for Semmes. The blockade of Southern ports and limitations imposed by neutral countries prevented him from taking a prize into any port for adjudication. He regretfully burned his first victim, *Golden Rocket,* and then vainly attempted to force the weak Caribbean neutrals to accept his captures for adjudication. Afterward, constituting himself a maritime court and carefully following international law, he condemned, bonded, or released his prizes (except for two) according to their flag or registration and ownership of their cargo (neutral ownership protected the ship). On *Alabama* he converted one prize into CSS *Tuscaloosa* (June 1863) and sold another in August 1863.

Sumter was small, slowed when under sail by the drag of her propeller, and could ship only an eight-day supply of coal. Yet in six months Semmes captured eighteen ships, seven of which he destroyed. He hunted along the currents and winds that merchant ships traveled. Only the vessel's limitations hampered his success. He was blockaded at St. Pierre, Martinique, by USS *Iroquois,* but drawing upon his experiences as a blockader he eluded the more powerful ship. Semmes then headed for Cadiz, Spain, to effect needed repairs. Frustrated by Spanish delays, he sailed to Gibraltar, making his last capture within sight of the rock. Unable to repair *Sumter's* boilers and blockaded by three Union vessels, he abandoned the ship and with 1st Lt. John McIntosh Kell went to London.

In England he met Commdr. James Dunwoody Bulloch who had designed a ship (*#290*) being built in the Laird Shipyards on the Mersey River, Liverpool. Semmes admired the ship as being perfect for a commerce cruiser. Assuming Bulloch would command her, Semmes sailed for home. In Nassau on June 8, 1862, he learned of his promotion to captain and assignment to command (*#290*). He returned to England.

Bulloch meanwhile had sent (*#290*), unarmed, to the Azores Islands. Semmes and Bulloch with supplies, arms, officers, and sailors rendezvoused just off the islands in international waters. Semmes's first glimpse of (*#290*) afloat with her "perfect symmetry" and "lifting device to prevent drag when under sail" excited him. From then on, Semmes referred to the ship as if she were his living partner in a great endeavor. The partnership would last for twenty-three months. Together they would set a record of merchant ship captures that still stands. On August 24, 1862, in neutral waters, Semmes commissioned *Alabama* as a regular warship of the Confederate navy.

Alabama's crew, an international mix, required a firm discipline tempered with mercy. Semmes rarely appeared on deck except to take readings of the ship's position and give orders of the day to 1st Lieutenant Kell, who controlled the crew. Most of the officers had served on *Sumter*.

Semmes began the cruise on nearby waters where Northern whalers were at work. His first victim, heavy with whale oil, was the first of 54 ships he would capture and of 447 he would speak or board. When hailing a ship he would fly the U.S. flag and, if answered by the same, raise the Confederate standard and command the ship to halt. Should she attempt to flee, he would fire a shot and send aboard an armed party whose officer would escort the victim's captain and papers to Semmes's cabin. Should the papers show the cargo to be neutral-owned, Semmes would bond the ship and allow it to continue its voyage; if enemy-owned, the boarding party would take off the victim's crew and passengers, if any, plus whatever *Alabama* could use—food, clothing, rigging, coal—and then set the ship afire. Semmes would cruise one area until he felt Northern warships might learn of his location and then seek other hunting grounds.

Semmes moved southward to the Caribbean Sea and the Gulf of Mexico. He resented the reputation Northern newspapers bestowed upon him: "He never fights, just plunders." Learning of a Union fleet off the Texas coast, he decided to disrupt it. Approaching it, he lured USS *Hatteras* from the fleet and sank her in a close exchange.

Later, Semmes, heading for the East Indies, crossed the South Atlantic for South Africa and in Simon's Town refurbished the ship and refreshed the men. En route he noted in his ship's journal that his time afloat "had produced a constant tension of the nervous system and a wear and tear of body . . . . I am supremely disgusted with the sea and all its belongings." After a stormy voyage to the East Indies, he sank three merchant ships, futilely sought combat with USS *Wyoming*, and sailed to Singapore for rest.

Despite disheartening news from America, on the return voyage his spirits were momentarily raised by his last capture. In the eastern Atlantic Ocean, *Alabama* chased a victim all night. "When the day dawned we were within a couple of miles of him. It was the old spectacle of the panting breathless fawn, and the inexorable staghound." But as Semmes read the latest newspapers taken from the victim and learned of the Northern victories—it was late May 1864—he saw himself, in the third person, as one on whose shoulders the stress and strain of three years

had laid "a load of a dozen years." Now *Alabama* was only a "wearied foxhound." And above his visions of man and ship, he saw "shadows of a sorrowful future."

On June 11, 1864, Semmes and *Alabama* limped into the harbor of Cherbourg, France, seeking refuge in the imperial docks. Immediately, Semmes wrote to Comm. Samuel Barron in Paris: "My health has suffered so much from a constant and harassing service of three years almost continuously at sea, that I shall have to ask for relief [from command of *Alabama*]." But fate in the form of Capt. John A. Winslow and USS *Kearsarge* intervened. *Alabama* now faced a possible blockade. Semmes decided that the ship should fight rather than rot in a French port. So he sent a message to Winslow, a former shipmate: "If you will give me time to recoal, I will come out and give you battle."

On June 19, 1864, *Alabama*, her sailors and officers in full dress uniform, sailed out of the harbor before cheering crowds. About seven miles into the English Channel, the two ships began firing; after sixty-five minutes *Alabama* was foundering. As she sank stern first, Semmes threw his sword into the sea, and then he and Kell jumped from the ship and swam to a boat from the English yacht *Deerhound*. "We fought her until she could no longer swim," Semmes later wrote, "and then gave her to the waves."

In Southampton, Semmes wrote his report to Mallory. Devastated by defeat and slightly wounded, he tried to explain the loss of his ship. Noting that *Alabama*'s shells did little damage to the side of the *Kearsarge*, he later blamed the loss on *Kearsarge*'s chain-covered sides. He was entertained by pro-Confederate groups, presented with a new sword, and traveled on the Continent. Refreshed, he began a strenuous seven-and-one-half-week trip to his home in Mobile, arriving on December 19, 1864.

He left Mobile on January 2, 1865, for Richmond, where President Davis and Congress honored him, promoted him to rear admiral, and assigned him to command the James River Squadron. When Ulysses S. Grant turned Robert E. Lee's right flank, Semmes was ordered to destroy his fleet and join Davis in Danville, Virginia. There the president appointed him a brigadier general of artillery. Ordered to join Joseph E. Johnston's forces in North Carolina, Semmes received the generous pardon granted by William Tecumseh Sherman to Johnston at Guilford Courthouse.

Semmes returned to his home in Mobile, but on December 15, 1865, he was arrested and imprisoned in Washington, D.C., charged by Secretary of the Navy Gideon Welles with having fled from the *Kearsarge-Alabama* battle after having surrendered by showing a white flag and, later, "without having been exchanged as a prisoner engaged in hostilities against the United

Semmes and the squadron were powerless to prevent the fall of Richmond.

PAGE 299

States." After four months of imprisonment, he was released for lack of proper evidence.

Semmes returned to Mobile and, forbidden to hold public office, attempted to make a living by teaching in the Louisiana Military Institute, editing a newspaper in Memphis, Tennessee, and lecturing for small fees. Finally, he practiced law in Mobile, specializing in maritime law. In 1869 he published the 833-page *Memoirs of Service Afloat during the War between the States*. He died in 1877 at his summer cottage on Point Clear, across the bay from Mobile, from food poisoning.

—WARREN F. SPENCER

SEVEN DAYS' BATTLES

The battles that took place from June 25 to July 1, 1862, on the Virginia Peninsula were the culmination of Union Maj. Gen. George B. McClellan's Peninsular campaign, which had carried his Army of the Potomac to within seven miles of Richmond.

While McClellan positioned his 100,000-man army just outside the Confederate capital, Gen. Robert E. Lee, who had replaced wounded Gen. Joseph E. Johnston as commander of the newly designated Army of Northern Virginia, shored up the city's defenses and sought an opportunity to seize the initiative. That

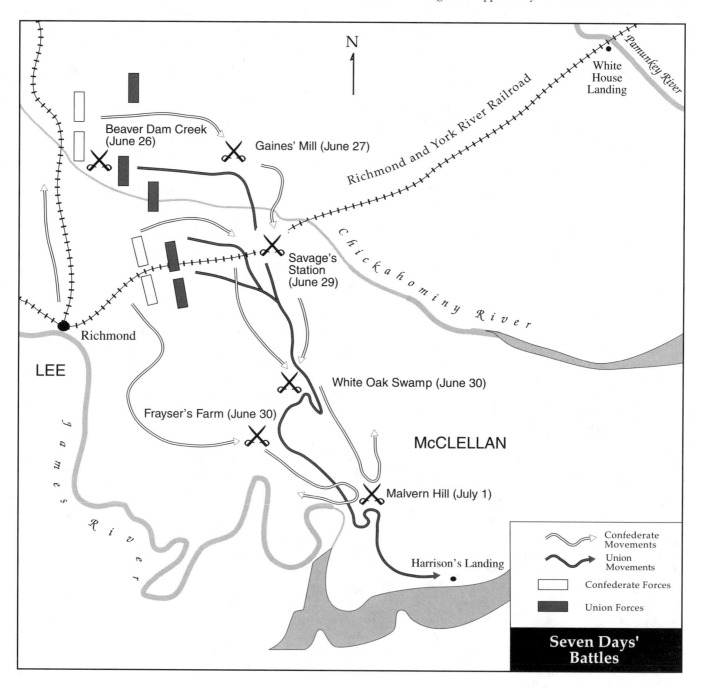

Seven Days' Battles

opportunity came when Brig. Gen. J. E. B. Stuart, following a cavalry reconnaissance that took him completely around McClellan's forces, reported that the Union right flank was unsecured and vulnerable to attack. The Chickahominy River separated Maj. Gen. Fitz John Porter's 30,000 men from the remainder of the Union army.

Lee decided to launch his attack before McClellan realized the flaw in his troop dispositions. Lee divided his smaller army in the face of the enemy, leaving a fraction of his forces to confront McClellan while sending the bulk of his troops to attack Porter. In addition to his own men, Lee would have the services of Maj. Gen. Thomas J. ("Stonewall") Jackson's veterans from the Shenandoah Valley.

The opposing forces clashed briefly at Oak Grove on June 25, the day before Lee planned to open his offensive. Despite this action, he still hoped to surprise Porter with attacks from three divisions under Maj. Gens. A. P. Hill, James Longstreet, and D. H. Hill, in cooperation with Jackson's troops. Uncharacteristically, Jackson failed to arrive, and an impatient A. P. Hill started the attack prematurely. Porter's men, well entrenched in prepared positions along Beaver Dam Creek, near Mechanicsville, easily repulsed the repeated Confederate assaults. The bold but bloody attacks cost the Southerners 1,484 casualties to the Federals' 361.

On the following day, June 27, Lee's Confederates attacked the Federals in their new positions near Gaines' Mill. Again the Southerners suffered heavy losses in brutal assaults on the Union lines. Lee continued to press McClellan, hoping to annihilate his army in one battle. McClellan, now anxious about his army's survival, ordered a change of base from the York River to the James and steadily retreated.

The opposing forces clashed again at Savage's Station on June 29, Frayser's Farm on June 30, and finally at Malvern Hill on July 1. Although Lee had failed to execute his complicated plans to destroy McClellan's army, he had forced the Federals farther from the gates of Richmond. By the time the Seven Days' Battles ended, the Army of the Potomac was thirty miles from the city. Lee had driven his enemy from position to position, but at a tremendous cost to the Southerners:

CASUALTIES OF THE SEVEN DAYS' BATTLES

	South	North
Killed	3,286	1,734
Wounded	15,909	8,062
Missing	946	6,053
Total	20,141	15,849

Robert E. Lee had saved Richmond from capture in 1862. In the process, he established a reputation for boldness and innovation and shook off the derogatory references to "Granny Lee" and the "King of Spades" (the latter for his use of defensive earthworks). McClellan remained at his base on the James River, assessing the campaign and placing blame on anyone other than himself.

— BRIAN S. WILLS

SHARPSBURG CAMPAIGN

Robert E. Lee's withdrawal from the passes of South Mountain on the night of September 14–15, 1862, signaled the end of a frustrating week of campaigning in Maryland. Following his day-long engagement with George B. McClellan at Fox's and Turner's gaps, Lee informed his subordinates, "The day has gone against us, and this army will go by way of Sharpsburg and cross the [Potomac] river." Lee thus canceled further continuation of his first invasion of the North.

Nothing had gone well for the Confederate army since it had entered the Old Line State during the first week of September. Western Marylanders greeted Lee with a cool reception rather than shouts of liberation. The Federals had not abandoned Harpers Ferry as expected, thus blocking critical supply and communication lines into the Shenandoah Valley. Thomas J. ("Stonewall") Jackson's subsequent operations against the Ferry had fallen behind schedule, and Lee's army remained dangerously divided into five parts as McClellan moved toward Frederick. McClellan's fortunate discovery of Special Order 191 on September 13 provided him with "all the plans of the Rebels," and his drive toward South Mountain on the fourteenth was intended to "cut the enemy in two and beat him in detail." Stubborn Confederate resistance at the mountain passes foiled McClellan's plans, but Lee realized that further resistance on the fifteenth would prove futile. No choice remained but retreat from Maryland.

Yet during the withdrawal from South Mountain toward Sharpsburg, Lee received a message from Jackson. "I believe Harpers Ferry and its garrison will be surrendered on the morrow," Jackson reported. The commanding general, boosted by this possible good fortune, halted the retreat at Sharpsburg; and when word arrived of Stonewall's success late on the morning of the fifteenth, Lee gazed over the Antietam Creek and announced, "We will make our stand on these hills."

"I am truly grateful to the Giver of Victory for having blessed us in our terrible struggle. I pray He may continue."

ROBERT E. LEE
TO STONEWALL JACKSON
1862

*The armies met
at Sharpsburg,
Maryland, across
Antietam Creek,
and the battle
became the bloodiest
single day of
the war.*

PAGE 323

Lee's decision to stand at Sharpsburg was influenced by several factors. To begin with, the Southerners needed time to remove the large booty captured at Harpers Ferry. In addition, Boteler's (also known as Blackford's) Ford provided good access across the Potomac for Jackson's force of 23,000 marching seventeen miles north from Harpers Ferry. Lee also realized a stand in Maryland would gain time for the gathering of the fall harvest in the Shenandoah Valley. Foremost, however, was the opportunity to engage McClellan on Northern soil. A Confederate victory would embarrass the Republicans in an election year and perhaps provide the peace Democrats with an upper hand in Congress. The possibility of European diplomatic recognition for the South also loomed on the horizon.

Lee's determination to stand at Sharpsburg also carried great risks. If McClellan attacked before Lee's Harpers Ferry contingent arrived, the Federals would outnumber the Confederate commander five to one. In addition, with the Potomac River to his back and only one practicable crossing available at Boteler's Ford, Lee could be trapped along the Antietam if McClellan turned either flank. Lee's experience with and intuitive understanding of McClellan compelled him to gamble. Lee felt the Union general would not attack until the Confederates had reunited, and McClellan's cautious tendencies would forestall aggressive challenges to the Southern flanks.

Lee's belief that McClellan would not immediately attack proved correct. Although the Union commander pursued the Confederates to the east bank of the Antietam on the fifteenth, McClellan spent the sixteenth reconnoitering the terrain and deploying his 87,000 men. In the meantime, Jackson arrived on the afternoon of the sixteenth with his own division, and the divisions of Richard S. Ewell, and John G. Walker soon followed. The 8,000 men of Lafayette McLaws and Richard Heron Anderson were expected early on the morning of the seventeenth, and A. P. Hill's division, left behind at Harpers Ferry to arrange for the disposition of prisoners and booty, was half a day's march from Sharpsburg.

By the morning of September 17, with the exception of Hill's division, Lee's army of 35,000 sprawled over a four-mile line, anchored two miles north of Sharpsburg on the Potomac and stretching two miles south of the town to the lower bridge crossing of the Antietam. J. E. B. Stuart's horse artillery guarded the extreme left, while the infantry of Jackson's, Ewell's, and Hood's divisions covered the Confederate left in the cornfield and pastures of D. R. Miller and in the West Woods around a small Dunker church. D. H. Hill's division protected the middle, manning a sunken farm lane between the Roulette and Piper farms. D. R.

Jones's and Walker's divisions initially defended the Confederate right on the high bluffs overlooking the Antietam. The Hagerstown Pike provided Lee with interior communications north of Sharpsburg, and the road leading west to Boteler's Ford, four miles from Lee's position, gave the Confederates their only avenue of escape.

McClellan, recognizing Lee's vulnerability with his back to the Potomac and with only one option for escape, devised an initial battle plan that primarily focused on the destruction of Lee's left flank. On the sixteenth, McClellan instructed Joseph Hooker's First Corps and the Twelfth Corps of Joseph Mansfield to cross the Antietam at the upper bridge and to swing north of Lee's line, and then return south at dawn on the seventeenth to smash Jackson and the left flank. Although the column of 20,000 made the flank march without detection, Hooker telegraphed the punch on the evening of the sixteenth when he pushed his advance too far south. Warned by this unexpected appearance of Federals on his left, Lee shifted Walker from his right to his left, and he poised the divisions of McLaws and Anderson, arriving on the seventeenth from Harpers Ferry at 3:00 A.M., toward the left.

At 5:30 A.M., Hooker's advance began. Although the Confederate left was outnumbered three to one, Hooker directed his three divisions badly, sending them forward piecemeal, thus negating his numerical superiority. The brigades of Hays, Laws, and Trimble smashed Hooker's first attack by James Ricketts's division in D. R. Miller's cornfield. Jackson's division crushed the assault by Abner Doubleday's division along the Hagerstown Pike. Hood's Texans drove the Pennsylvanians of George Meade's division backward through the cornfield and into the East Woods. With Hooker's corps demolished, Mansfield's Twelfth Corps began its advance. Piecemeal attacks by its two divisions again enabled the Confederates to stand their ground. To stop the attack of Alpheus Williams's division, Lee transferred three brigades from D. H. Hill's division north from the Confederate center. Then the Federal assault of George Greene's division stalled before the Dunker church.

Five Union divisions had failed to break Lee's left, but the Confederate carnage had been terrible. Almost half of Ewell's division had been slaughtered, and all but two of its regimental commanders had fallen. Brig. Gen. William E. Starke had been killed. Jackson's division suffered such extreme losses that a colonel now commanded a division. Hood's First Texas incurred 82 percent casualties during its assault. All totaled, 5,500 dead and wounded Union and Confederate soldiers lay in the cornfield and its environs after three hours of ferocious fighting.

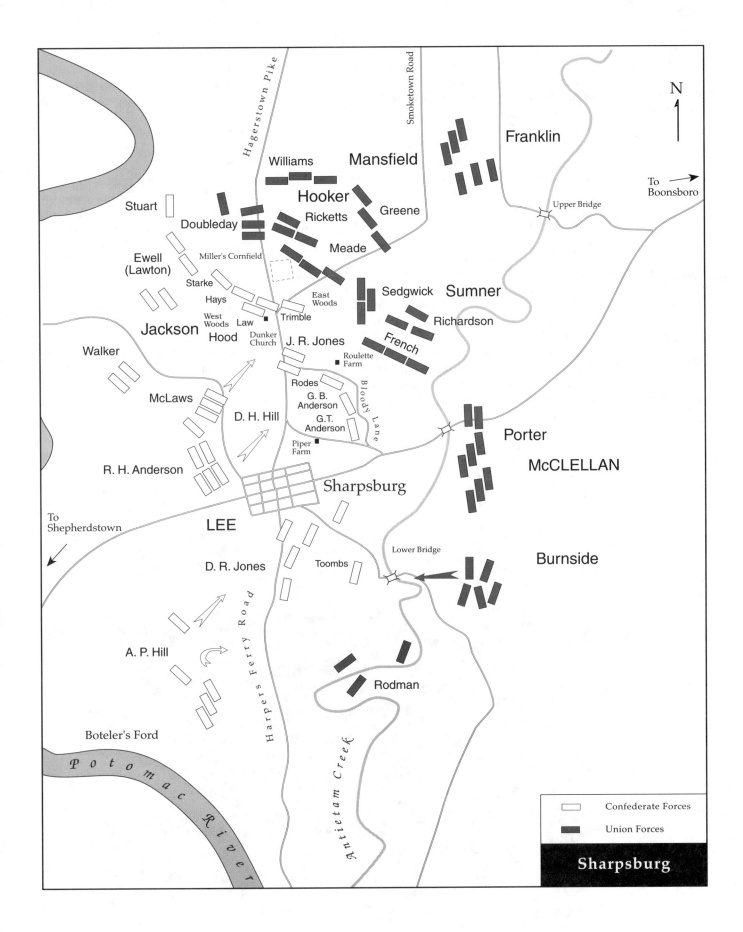

N

Stuart

Hagerstown Pike

Williams

Mansfield

Hooker

Doubleday

Ricketts

Greene

Smoketown Road

Franklin

To Boonsboro

Upper Bridge

Meade

Ewell
(Lawton)

Miller's Cornfield

Starke

Hays

East
Woods

Sedgwick

Sumner

West
Woods

Law

Trimble

Richardson

Jackson

Hood

Dunker
Church

J. R. Jones

French

Walker

Rodes

Roulette
Farm

McLaws

G. B.
Anderson

D. H. Hill

G.T.
Anderson

Bloody Lane

Piper
Farm

Porter

McCLELLAN

R. H. Anderson

Sharpsburg

To
Shepherdstown

LEE

Burnside

Lower Bridge

D. R. Jones

Toombs

A. P. Hill

Harpers Ferry Road

Rodman

Boteler's Ford

Potomac River

Antietam Creek

| | Confederate Forces |
| | Union Forces |

Sharpsburg

535

*"He hath loosed
the fateful
lightning of His
terrible, swift
sword;
His truth is
marching on."*

JULIA WARD HOWE
BATTLE HYMN OF THE
REPUBLIC, 1862

Yet McClellan had not finished with the Confederate left. About 9:20 A.M., marching from the east toward the West Woods, came the three divisions of the Union Second Corps. At first, Southern resistance proved sporadic and light; but as John Sedgwick's division entered the West Woods in line formation, suddenly from its left and center was unleashed the fury of Lafayette McLaws's 4,000 Confederates. Lee had ordered McLaws up from the rear just in time to rout Sedgwick's advance, and the Confederate fire proved deadly—Sedgwick suffered 2,200 casualties in twenty minutes in the West Woods.

The morning phase of the Battle of Sharpsburg had ended. Lee's left remained intact, although tenuous, and attention now shifted south from the cornfield and the West Woods toward the sunken road defining the Confederate center. The 2,000 men in the brigades of George B. Anderson and Robert Rodes, reinforced by Richard Anderson's 4,000, defended the road against 8,000 men in two divisions of the Second Corps. William French's Union division struck first at 10:00 A.M. but, after repeated

assaults, failed to dent the Confederate line. Israel Richardson's division followed and also failed to dislodge the stubborn Southerners. Finally at 1:00 P.M., after the death of G. B. Anderson and the wounding of Rodes, confusion developed in the Southern command, and the Confederates abandoned the lane owing to a misinterpreted order. The Federals quickly occupied the center of General Lee's line, and as one Southerner noted, "the end of the Confederacy was in sight." But McClellan refused to follow up on this breakthrough, and the battle for the Bloody Lane ended.

Attention now focused on the Confederate right. Defending the high bluffs overlooking the lower bridge across the Antietam were 500 Georgians of Robert Toombs's brigade. Facing Toombs were 12,000 men in the Ninth Corps, commanded by Ambrose Burnside. Fortunately for the Georgians, the bridge they defended was located in a narrow defile, making it impossible for Burnside to launch a large-scale frontal assault. For three hours, Toombs's men held off brigade-level attacks ordered by Burnside. At 1:00 P.M., however, a concerted charge by the Fifty-first

BATTLE'S END

Fallen soldiers along the Hagerstown Pike on Sept. 17, 1862. The battle at Sharpsburg, Maryland, was the single bloodiest day in the war.

NATIONAL ARCHIVES

New York and Fifty-first Pennsylvania finally established a bridgehead on the west bank of the Antietam. When Toombs discovered his right flank had been turned as well by I. P. Rodman's division, he abandoned his position, and the lower bridge belonged to Burnside.

For the next two hours, Burnside shuttled men, supplies, and food across the Antietam in preparation for a final assault against the Confederate right, now positioned along the Harpers Ferry Road just south of Sharpsburg. About 3:00 P.M., Burnside's corps began its advance, soon engaging D. R. Jones's thin division. The situation was desperate for General Lee. He could not maneuver Confederates from other parts of his line, and he had no reserves north of the Potomac. Suddenly, from the south, as Burnside methodically pressed forward, A. P. Hill and his Light Division arrived from Harpers Ferry, following a seventeen-mile forced march in seven hours. Lee ordered Hill to attack, and when his brigades smashed into Burnside's left flank, the stunned Federals retired toward the Antietam, ending the battle about dusk. Confederate Brig. Gen. Lawrence O'Bryan Branch was mortally wounded during Hill's assault.

It was the twelve bloodiest hours in American military history. In one day, almost 23,000 Union and Confederate casualties had fallen along the Antietam Creek. More than twice as many Americans lost their lives in one day at Sharpsburg as fell in the War of 1812, the Mexican War, and the Spanish-American War *combined*.

CASUALTIES AT SHARPSBURG

	South	North
Killed	1,546	2,108
Wounded	7,754	9,549
Missing	1,018	753
Total	10,318	12,410

Despite the dangerous weakening of his army, Lee remained on the battlefield on the eighteenth, challenging McClellan to attack. The Union commander refused to reinitiate battle, however, and that night, the Army of Northern Virginia retired across Boteler's Ford and returned to Virginia.

Sharpsburg often is considered a turning point of the war. The Confederate military wave was at its peak in the fall of 1862, but with Braxton Bragg's failure in Kentucky and Lee's disappointing campaign in Maryland, hopes for diplomatic recognition and gains by the peace Democrats soon faded. In addition, Abraham Lincoln used McClellan's victory at Sharpsburg to announce his preliminary Emancipation Proclamation.

[*See also* Harpers Ferry, West Virginia.]

— DENNIS E. FRYE

SHELBY IRON COMPANY

Among the oldest and most prominent of the pioneer iron enterprises in Alabama, the Shelby Iron Company was located near the geographical center of the state some thirty miles southeast of present-day Birmingham. Founded in 1846 by Horace Ware, who soon took on a partner, it was incorporated by the state of Alabama in 1858. With the onset of the Civil War, Ware sold six-sevenths of his interest to local investors to raise capital for expansion.

The improved furnaces had a capacity of approximately 250 tons per week. The firm provided iron to both army and navy facilities in Selma, Mobile, Griswoldville (Georgia), Yazoo City (Mississippi), and Atlanta. Until January 1865, when a spur railroad was completed, all manufactured iron had to be shipped by wagon to the Alabama and Tennessee Rivers Railroad at Columbiana for reshipment.

Shelby experienced difficulty in getting a rolling mill in operation to produce two-inch armor plate for the navy and did not begin production for that purpose until March 1863. Shelby's iron, however, was in demand for producing guns, and most was used for that purpose.

Shelby employed 450 to 550 workers. Skilled white labor was recruited from throughout the South, and details from the army produced 40 to 75 men. Approximately three-fourths of the work force were hired slaves. One hundred or so skilled slave laborers were rented from industrial sites in Virginia, North Carolina, Tennessee, Georgia, and Mississippi, and unskilled slaves came from nearby sources.

The works were raided by forces of Maj. Gen. James H. Wilson's cavalry brigade on March 31, 1865.

— ROBERT H. MCKENZIE

SHENANDOAH

The steam-auxiliary cruiser *Shenandoah* was built as the china clipper *Sea King* in 1863. It was designed by noted London naval architect William Rennie and

"My enemy is dead, a man divine as myself is dead."

WALT WHITMAN
RECONCILIATION

537

> *Geographically the Shenandoah Valley was a natural avenue into the heart of the North and the center of the Deep South.*
>
> PAGE 540

built by Alexander Stephen and Sons, Linthouse, Glasgow, Scotland, for Robertson & Company, London. It measured 2,190 tons, 220 feet long, 32.5 feet in breadth, and 20.5 feet in depth. *Sea King* made one trip to New Zealand before Confederate naval agent James Dunwoody Bulloch bought it for the Confederacy. The steamer *Laurel,* at Funchal, Madeira, provided crew, supplies, and armament (four 8-inch cannon, two Whitworth 32-pounder rifles, and two 12-pounders).

James Waddell commissioned CSS *Shenandoah* on October 20, 1864. The ship captured eleven prizes on the way to Melbourne, Australia. Refitted, it sailed for northern Pacific whaling grounds on February 19, 1865. The ship bonded four vessels and burned twenty-two, mostly whalers, on a continued voyage through the Caroline Islands, the seas of Japan and Okhotsk, and into the Bering Sea. There, on August 2, 1865, Waddell learned that the war had ended. He struck the armament down into the hold, dismantled *Shenandoah* as a warship, and sailed for England.

The cruiser arrived in Liverpool on November 6, 1865, flying the Confederate flag, the last Southern military unit in service. Waddell paid the crew and turned the ship over to the British government. The U.S. consul in Liverpool brought suit, won ownership

of the vessel, and sold it at auction to the sultan of Zanzibar. The ship led an adventurous life before its bottom was torn out on a reef near the island of Socotra in the northern Indian Ocean in 1879.

— KEVIN J. FOSTER

SHENANDOAH VALLEY

[*This entry includes three articles:* An Overview; Shenandoah Valley Campaign of Jackson, *which discusses the campaign of 1862; and* Shenandoah Valley Campaign of Sheridan, *which discusses the campaign of 1864. For further discussion of military action in the Shenandoah Valley, see* Cedar Creek, Virginia; Early, Jubal, *sidebar* Early's Washington Raid; New Market, Virginia; Winchester, Virginia.]

AN OVERVIEW

During the Civil War the Shenandoah Valley of Virginia was vital to the Confederacy for both military and economic reasons. Militarily, the region had a considerable influence on the campaigns in Virginia. The Shenandoah Valley was like a shield, protecting the Confederate capital. A Federal army could not advance against Richmond by the way of the valley because as it marched south it would be moving farther and farther away from its objective. Conversely, the valley was an asset for any Confederate army marching through it, for the army became an immediate threat to Washington, D.C., Baltimore, and other Northern cities. Nor did the Confederates have to maintain possession of the area to retain its advantages. In order to deny the Confederates the use of the valley, the Federals had to gain control of the entire region, which was beyond their capabilities.

Economically, the Shenandoah Valley was a major source of subsistence for the Confederacy. In the early stages of the war the farmers of the valley were called upon for large quantities of supplies, which they gave heartily. But as the war dragged on, their support faltered for several reasons, including adverse weather conditions and the valley's strategic location. It was the scene of continuous military operations; from the start of the war until October 1864, major portions were repeatedly fought over, marched through, or occupied.

Once the war started, the Confederate Subsistence Department began to accumulate the vast quantities of foodstuffs that would be required to sustain the armies in the field. In Virginia, the valley was one of the first regions they turned to for supplies. Its railroad lines were in constant use, so much so that the Virginia Central Railroad was limited at times exclusively to the transportation of supplies.

In the spring of 1862 the Shenandoah Valley was the scene of one of the major campaigns of the war—Confederate Maj. Gen. Thomas J. ("Stonewall") Jackson's famous Valley campaign. In a series of brilliant maneuvers from March 23 to June 9, Jackson's forces defeated three Federal armies in five battles. Jackson's exploits electrified the Southern populace and, more important, completely dismantled the Federal plan of operation in Virginia. Owing to the perceived threat to Washington, D.C., troops scheduled to be sent to Maj. Gen. George B. McClellan on the peninsula were diverted to the valley in an attempt to defeat Jackson. In the end, Jackson eluded his potential captors, united with Gen. Robert E. Lee outside of Richmond, and helped drive the Union forces back from the Confederate capital, while the troops slated to reinforce McClellan floundered in northern Virginia.

Although the valley was one of the major theaters of the war in Virginia in 1862, no major fighting occurred in the region the next year. For the most part, military operations were limited to Federal cavalry raids and scouting expeditions. The only time large bodies of troops were in the valley was during the Gettysburg campaign, when Lee used it as an avenue to invade Pennsylvania. Although the military opera-

tions in the valley had no major effect on the direction of the war in Virginia, they did have an adverse impact on agricultural production. Federal raiders destroyed crops, confiscated livestock and farm animals, and demoralized the civilian population.

Several other factors intervened now to reduce the valley's importance as a primary source of subsistence for the Confederacy. One was the weather. In 1862 a severe drought had diminished the year's harvest, and in 1863 there was excessive rain. Severe flooding destroyed most of the wheat crop in Virginia and negated any chance of accumulating a reserve for the army. Virginia experienced a 50- to 75-percent decline in crop production between 1862 and 1864. A second factor was the war's drain on manpower, as men of military age either joined the army or were later drafted. In many instances women and young children were the only ones left to work the farms. Yet another factor was the military situation. By 1863 a major portion of the valley was under the control of the Federal army. Military exigencies had compelled the Confederacy to abandon the entire lower valley to the enemy. And this loss was not temporary—throughout the rest of the war the lower valley remained in the hands of the Federals. As a result the resources of Berkeley, Clarke, Frederick, and Jefferson counties were lost to the Confederates.

With the commencement of active military operations in May 1864, the Shenandoah Valley once again became one of the major battlegrounds of the war. From May through October the valley was the scene of continuous military action. The Federal strategic plan called for simultaneous attacks against Confederate forces in Virginia from three directions. In one part of the operation, an army under the command of Maj. Gen. Franz Sigel was to march up the valley and destroy the Virginia Central Railroad. Sigel's march went smoothly until he reached the town of New Market on May 15, 1864. There outnumbered Confederate troops routed his army, forcing it to retreat back down the valley.

Lt. Gen. Ulysses S. Grant then replaced Sigel with Maj. Gen. David Hunter and directed him to carry out the previous orders. At first Hunter was successful in his advance. He had reached the outskirts of Lynchburg by June 15, destroying homes and crops as he went. His campaign, however, ended up even more of a disaster than Sigel's. To prevent Lynchburg from being captured and to reclaim the valley, Lee, on June 12, 1864, pulled the Second Corps of his army out of the trenches at Petersburg and sent it west under the command of Maj. Gen. Jubal Early. The reinforcements arrived at Lynchburg five days later. After making several attacks against the Confederate defenses on June 18, Hunter realized he was outnumbered and

"Old Jack" felt that deception, rapid marches, and unexpected attacks would accomplish his goals.

PAGE 542

As for the numerical superiority of the enemy, Jackson would trust God to handle that problem.

PAGE 542

"Such an executive officer the sun never shone on. I have but to show him my design, and I know that it can be done, it will be done."

ROBERT E. LEE
ON STONEWALL JACKSON

The Confederates covered forty-one miles in two days. A third of Jackson's men fell out along the way from exhaustion and sickness.

PAGE 542

made a hasty retreat. But instead of retiring back down the valley, he retreated into West Virginia. This action took his command out of the war for several weeks and left the valley to the Confederates.

Early wasted no time in capitalizing on Hunter's error. After giving his army a day's rest he proceeded to advance down the valley. By the end of the first week in July, Early had traversed the entire valley, crossed over the Potomac River into Maryland, and begun to march on Washington, D.C. The Confederate army reached the outskirts of the city on July 11, but the Confederate commander knew he did not have the strength to capture it. So he began an orderly withdrawal back to Virginia and the valley the next day. By threatening Washington once more, Lee was hoping the Federals would be forced to lessen their hold on the Confederate capital. This time, however, the Confederate tactics were not successful, for Grant never relinquished his grip on Richmond.

Still, Early's continued presence in the valley had become a considerable annoyance to Grant in his efforts to defeat the Army of Northern Virginia. The Confederate advance on Washington had forced him to transfer two full army corps from the Petersburg front to quell the fears of the Lincoln administration. Determined to remove Early as a threat to the Northern capital and to close off the valley as an avenue of invasion and a source of supply, Grant placed Maj. Gen. Philip H. Sheridan in command of all military forces in northern Virginia.

Sheridan assumed command of the Army of the Shenandoah on the night of August 6, 1864, and began to make preparations to engage the enemy. In a series of battles between September 19 and October 19, 1864, the Federal army totally defeated the Confederate forces, routing them so completely that they were never again an effective fighting force. But the most dramatic aspect of Sheridan's campaign was the destruction of the valley's resources. Federal troops burned everything of value between Staunton and Winchester, leaving the valley a barren wasteland. This devastation, however, was not the loss it once would have been. For the last two years of the war the Confederacy had supported its military forces in Virginia with subsistence transported from the Deep South, not the valley.

By 1865 the Shenandoah Valley had become a reflection of the Confederacy itself. Before the war the valley had been one of the most fertile regions in Virginia, but in the course of the conflict its productivity vanished under the onslaught of modern armies. Four years of warfare had converted a fruitful countryside into one of charred homes and desolate farms.

— MICHAEL G. MAHON

SHENANDOAH VALLEY CAMPAIGN OF JACKSON

Few areas in the Civil War had more strategic value for both sides than did the Shenandoah Valley of Virginia. The valley lies between the two most eastern ranges of the Allegheny Mountains. The eastern boundary of the valley is marked by the famed Blue Ridge Mountains, with the Alleghenies proper to the west. The valley stretches 165 miles from Lexington to Harpers Ferry and averages 30 miles in width. At the southern terminus the mountains on both sides press close upon Lexington. The ranges diverge at the other end around Harpers Ferry. There the Shenandoah River merges with the Potomac; there too the Baltimore and Ohio Railroad—then the main line of transportation between Washington and the West—crossed the Potomac. The Shenandoah loses altitude running south to north. Hence, and contrary to usual terminology, one travels northward down and southward up the valley.

Two factors gave the region important military value. The Shenandoah was a veritable breadbasket for the Confederacy. Grain, orchards, and livestock were in great abundance. The Army of Northern Virginia came to be all but totally dependent upon the produce of the area. Geographically the valley was a natural avenue into the heart of the North and the center of the Deep South. Any army that advanced into either Virginia or Maryland had to have control of the valley to protect its western flank against attack. With only eleven passes through the Blue Ridge, the Shenandoah was a long, natural fortress. It became the key to military movements, and military supremacy, in the eastern theater.

In the spring of 1862 the valley was the scene of one of the most brilliant campaigns in history. It was a campaign that made Confederate Gen. Thomas J. ("Stonewall") Jackson the hero of the South and a legend in his own time.

Jackson had returned to the Shenandoah in November 1861 to take charge of its defenses. His headquarters were at Winchester, twenty-six miles southwest of Harpers Ferry. Winchester guarded all the mountain passes in the lower Shenandoah and was a commercial center as well. Jackson's force at that time consisted of 3,600 infantry, 600 cavalry, and twenty-seven guns. Most of his soldiers were Virginians and familiar with the valley.

Late in February 1862, a Federal army slowly moved into the Shenandoah. It numbered 38,000 men, mostly hardy farmboys from the Midwest. Commanding the army was Maj. Gen. Nathaniel P. Banks, a Massachusetts political general with limited military capacities.

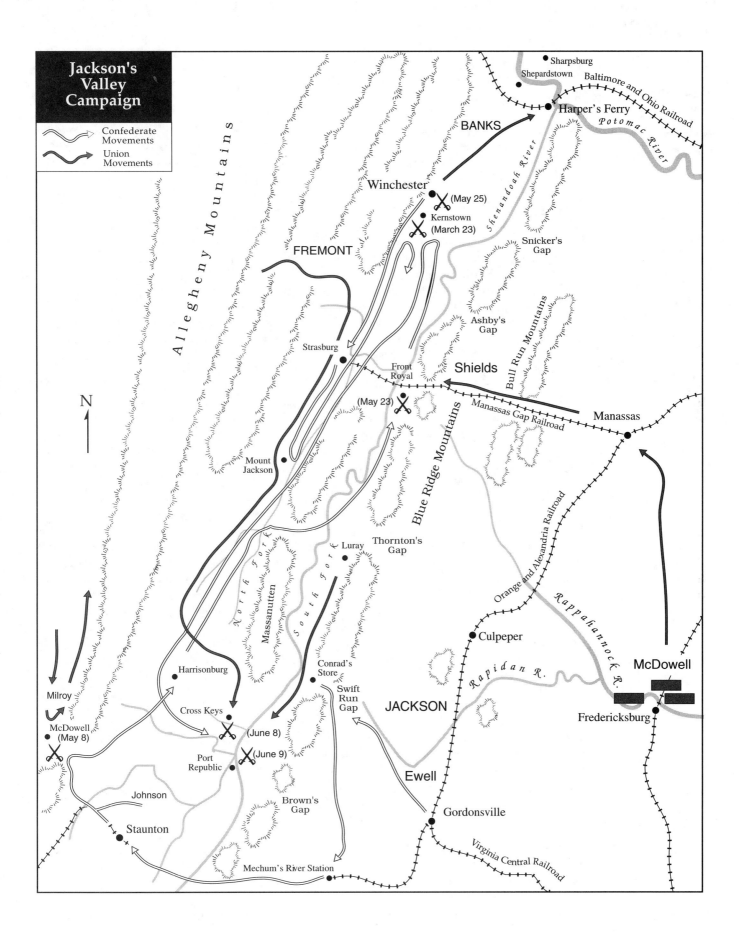

*Jackson's exploits
electrified
the Southern
populace and,
more important,
completely
dismantled the
Federal plan of
operation in
Virginia.*

PAGE 539

The small Confederate force in the valley seemed no threat to Banks's invaders. Yet Jackson was always a man who took responsibility very seriously. His instructions from the beginning had been to protect the left flank of the main Confederate force at Manassas, to guard the valley against all Federal intrusions, and to expect no reinforcements in the process. Determination outweighed concern by Jackson that he was outnumbered by ten-to-one odds. "If this valley is lost," he stated to a friend, "Virginia is lost."

With the Federal army slowly forming an arc around his small force, Jackson on March 11 abandoned Winchester. He retired slowly up the valley to Mount Jackson and encamped. Four Federal regiments of Gen. James Shields's division pursued cautiously at a distance. On a sleety March 21, those Federal units started back to Winchester. Jackson deduced that Shields was consolidating his troops with Banks's main command preparatory to uniting with Gen. George B. McClellan's massive army for a grand offensive against Richmond. He promptly put his brigades into motion heading north.

The Confederates covered forty-one miles in two days. A third of Jackson's men fell out along the way from exhaustion and sickness. On the afternoon of March 23, Jackson and barely two thousand soldiers reached the hamlet of Kernstown, two miles from Winchester. A crushing blow on Shields would stop Banks's withdrawal from the valley and possibly blunt McClellan's offensive as well.

Jackson quickly deployed his fatigued troops and attacked what he thought was only a segment of Shields's command. All too soon, owing to faulty intelligence reports, Jackson found himself locked in combat with a full Union division. Three hours of fighting brought his advance to a halt. After nightfall the Confederates retired up the valley. Yet Jackson's tactical failure proved a strategic success. Even though Shields's men moved on to Fredericksburg, Banks received orders to remain in the valley. This heretofore buffer zone now became a major theater of operations.

Grim resolution marked every step of Jackson's march as he led his forces to Conrad's Store, seventeen miles east of Harrisonburg. That point, at the base of Swift Run Gap, offered the Southern general a number of options. He could attack Banks's army if it sought to pass up the Valley Turnpike to the railroad town of Staunton; he could wage a strong defense if assailed at Conrad's Store; the mountain pass afforded a safe escape if needed. Banks halted at Harrisonburg and then backtracked forty-five miles to Strasburg so as to shorten his line of communication. The Federal general was convinced that Jackson was now a mere nuisance.

For most of April, as Confederate ranks filled and hardened into a tight military force, Jackson developed a master plan. He knew that a second Federal force of 15,000 soldiers under Gen. John C. Frémont was two ranges over in the Alleghenies. Another 40,000 bluecoats of Gen. Irvin McDowell's command were at Fredericksburg and poised to move easily toward Richmond or the valley. What Jackson first hoped to accomplish was to keep Banks and Frémont west of the Blue Ridge and isolated one from the other. At the same time, Jackson did not want McDowell leaving Fredericksburg. If Confederates in the valley could pin down Frémont, Banks, and McDowell, attack and defeat each, one by one, all other Southern defenders in Virginia could concentrate at Richmond and confront McClellan's 120,000 Federals.

The chances of this plan succeeding were slim. Yet "Old Jack" felt that deception, rapid marches, and unexpected attacks would accomplish his goals. As for the overwhelming numerical superiority of the enemy, Jackson would trust God to handle that problem.

Gen. Robert E. Lee, President Jefferson Davis's chief military adviser, was himself a gambler. He not only endorsed Jackson's proposal but sent badly needed reinforcements: 8,000 troops under eccentric, crusty, but highly dependable Gen. Richard S. Ewell. Another 2,000 Southerners, with gruff and profane Gen. Edward Johnson at their head, were in the mountains guarding the western approaches to Staunton. They were added to Jackson's command. By the end of April, Jackson was ready to go into action.

He ordered Ewell's division into the Conrad's Store encampment to keep an eye on Banks's movements. "Old Jack" then disappeared to the south with his own 6,000-man force. The men trudged three days through pouring rain and heavy mud. They finally reached Mechum's River Station on the Virginia Central Railroad and boarded trains with the belief that they were heading east to Richmond. Instead, the trains lumbered west. Confederates disembarked at Staunton to the surprise of townspeople answering the bells for Sunday church services. Jackson sealed the town to mask his presence. Meanwhile, Banks was reassuring officials in Washington that Jackson's "greatly demoralized and broken" army was fleeing toward the safety of Richmond.

On May 6, Jackson led his still-jaded troops in a hard thirty-five-mile march over rugged mountains to McDowell. His objective was Gen. Robert H. Milroy's 4,000 Federals comprising the vanguard of Frémont's army. At 4:00 P. M. on the eighth, from a commanding hilltop, the Confederates fired point-blank volleys of musketry into the advancing columns. The battle lasted until sundown. Though Federals inflicted twice their own losses, they could not pierce Jackson's lines. Milroy retreated. Jackson pursued for a distance.

Confederate engineers closed the mountain passes, thus protecting Jackson's left flank in the upper valley. Now the stern and taciturn Southern commander was ready to clear the valley of Federal intruders.

Thanks in great part to his mapmaker, Maj. Jedediah Hotchkiss, Jackson could discuss valley terrain as easily as he could quote Scripture. He knew that it was eighty miles on the macadamized Valley Turnpike from Staunton to Winchester. East of that main thoroughfare, inside the valley from Harrisonburg to Strasburg, lay a dark ridge called Massanutten Mountain. To the east of it was a parallel and almost hidden road. It snaked through the narrow Luray Valley to Front Royal and beyond. More important, in that forty-mile stretch was only one point where the Massanutten could be crossed: the pass connecting the towns of New Market and Luray.

The next stage of Jackson's strategy was to unite his forces, sneak through and secure that pass, use the Massanutten as a screen, and head north. By hard marching he intended to strike unsuspecting advance positions at Front Royal and Strasburg; then he hoped to shatter Banks's army as he drove to the main Federal supply base at Winchester. Jackson swiftly merged the units of Ewell's and Johnson's forces into an army of 17,000 soldiers. That gave him an almost two-to-one superiority over Banks. Jackson drove his troops down the valley and disappeared across the Massanutten. The first Federal inkling that anything was amiss came on May 23, when a Confederate tidal wave appeared from nowhere and crushed the Union garrison at Front Royal.

Jackson spent the following day urging his near-exhausted soldiers to get between rapidly retreating Federals and Winchester. Confederates struck several times at the long and disjointed Union column but could not break it. Abandoned wagons loaded with goods littered the road for miles. Large numbers of the half-starved Southerners could not resist the temptation to pause for food.

On the morning of May 25, Jackson launched a full-scale assault at Winchester and by noon had Banks's entire army fleeing for the safety of the Potomac River. The three days of fighting had cost Jackson but 400 men. His army had seized 3,030 prisoners, 9,300 small arms, 2 rifled cannon, and such a wealth of quartermaster stores that Confederates scornfully referred thereafter to their Union opponent as "Commissary Banks."

Smashing victories by Jackson had now disrupted the entire Federal offensive in Virginia. With Banks cowering on the north bank of the Potomac and Jackson's army poised like a dagger at the north end of the Shenandoah, Union officials in Washington reacted sharply. McDowell's huge force at Fredericksburg,

about to join McClellan, was to remain there as protection for the Northern capital. Shields's 20,000-man division, which had just reached Fredericksburg, was ordered to return to the valley. Frémont received instructions to advance with all haste into the Shenandoah. With Shields moving west and Frémont advancing east, both toward Strasburg, Jackson seemingly would be caught in the jaws of a massive vise.

The counterstrategy failed because of a combination of Federal vacillation and incredible marching by Jackson's "foot cavalry." In less than a day, Confederate units covered thirty-five to fifty miles and escaped the trap. Jackson retired to Harrisonburg and then to a point southeast of town where the North and South rivers came together to form the South Fork of the Shenandoah. Frémont was giving chase on the Valley Turnpike; Shields was advancing up the Luray Valley road.

On June 8, Ewell's division easily beat back feeble stabs by Frémont at Cross Keys. Jackson waited patiently three miles away at Port Republic. The next day he assailed Shields's force. Severe fighting occurred before the Federals broke off the engagement and headed northward. The great campaign was over; the Shenandoah Valley was still in Confederate hands.

Jackson and 17,000 men had totally thwarted the plans of 64,000 Federals in three different forces sent to destroy him. In forty-eight days his soldiers had marched 676 miles and fought four battles, six skirmishes, and a dozen delaying actions. Confederates had inflicted seven thousand casualties at a loss of half that number. Immense quantities of Union weapons and stores were in Confederate hands. The Federal military machine in Virginia was sputtering badly. Southerners everywhere took new faith in the success of the Confederate cause. Jackson would accept no accolades for his strategic masterpiece. He summarized the Valley campaign in a short note to his wife: "God has been our shield, and to His name be all the glory."

— JAMES I. ROBERTSON, JR.

SHENANDOAH VALLEY CAMPAIGN OF SHERIDAN

This Federal campaign, which took place from August to October 1864, effectively ended the Confederate presence in the Shenandoah Valley.

Following the near capture of Washington, D.C., by Lt. Gen. Jubal Early in mid-July 1864, and Early's subsequent burning of Chambersburg, Pennsylvania, on July 30, Gen. Ulysses S. Grant assigned Maj. Gen. Philip H. Sheridan to the Shenandoah Valley with instructions to "put himself south of the enemy and follow him to the death."

"My duty is to obey orders."

STONEWALL JACKSON

When he died at Guiney Station on May 10, 1863, Jackson took with him much of the army's and the Confederacy's best hope for success.

PAGE 27

Determination outweighed Jackson's concern that he was outnumbered by ten-to-one odds. "If this valley is lost," he said to a friend, "Virginia is lost."

PAGE 542

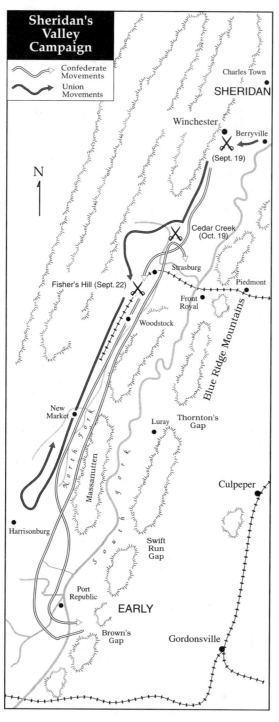

Sheridan's Valley Campaign

Confederate Movements

Union Movements

N

Charles Town

SHERIDAN

Winchester

Berryville

(Sept. 19)

Cedar Creek (Oct. 19)

Strasburg

Fisher's Hill (Sept. 22)

Piedmont

Front Royal

Woodstock

Blue Ridge Mountains

New Market

Luray

Thornton's Gap

Massanutten

North Fork

South Fork

Culpeper

Harrisonburg

Swift Run Gap

Port Republic

EARLY

Brown's Gap

Gordonsville

The thirty-three-year-old Irish-born Sheridan had been commanding Grant's cavalry, and although President Abraham Lincoln, Secretary of War Edwin M. Stanton, and Chief of Staff Henry W. Halleck all considered Sheridan too young and inexperienced for the Shenandoah position, Grant's opinion prevailed. Sheridan subsequently arrived at Harpers Ferry on August 6 to take command of the Army of the Shenandoah, composed of 35,000 infantry and artillery and 8,000 cavalry. The army's infantry consist-

ed of three corps under Maj. Gen. Horatio G. Wright (Sixth Corps), Maj. Gen. George Crook (Eighth Corps), and Maj. Gen. William H. Emory (Nineteenth Corps). Brig. Gen. Alfred T. A. Torbert commanded the three divisions of cavalry.

Sheridan outnumbered Early three to one. Old Jube's Army of the Valley included 10,000 veterans from the Second Corps and 4,000 poorly equipped and ill-disciplined cavalrymen. Recognizing this disparity, Robert E. Lee on August 6 dispatched from the Richmond-Petersburg line the 3,500-man division of Maj. Gen. Joseph B. Kershaw, the artillery battalion of Maj. Wilfred E. Cutshaw, and the cavalry division of Maj. Gen. Fitzhugh Lee. When this additional force arrived at Front Royal on August 14, Sheridan, who had advanced fifty miles from Harpers Ferry to Cedar Creek, ordered a withdrawal north to Halltown, where he entrenched on a commanding ridge four miles west of Harpers Ferry.

From August 22 to September 18, Sheridan and Early marched and countermarched across the lower valley, conducting a "mimic war" that avoided major confrontation. Politics tempered Sheridan's usual aggressiveness; Secretary of War Stanton had informed him that the administration could not withstand one battlefield defeat. "I deemed it necessary to be very cautious," Sheridan wrote in his memoirs. "The fact that the Presidential election was impending made me doubly so . . . .[since] the defeat of my army might be followed by the overthrow of the party in power." Sheridan's political sensitivity led Jubal Early to underestimate badly his dangerous opponent. Concluding that Sheridan "possessed an excessive caution which amounted to timidity," Early agreed to return to Petersburg the reinforcements he had received from Lee in mid-August.

When Sheridan on September 15 learned of this departure, he planned his strike. With Early's army scattered toward the Potomac on a raid to destroy the Baltimore and Ohio Railroad, Sheridan intended to smash Early's rear guard at Winchester and cut off the Confederate line of retreat south via the Valley Pike. Sheridan outlined this plan to Grant at Charles Town on September 17, and the commanding general responded, "Go in."

At 1:00 A.M. on September 19, Sheridan's army roused from its bivouac near Berryville and began marching west toward Winchester. Union cavalry seized the Opequon Creek crossing with little opposition, and Federal infantry soon splashed across the Opequon into the two-mile Berryville Canyon—a narrow defile through which passed the turnpike connecting Winchester and Berryville. Fortunately for Early, Sheridan's army became entangled in the canyon by the slow-moving wagons of the Sixth Corps. This delay robbed Sheridan of his tactical surprise and enabled Early to reconcentrate his army at Winchester.

Sheridan's infantry assault finally commenced at 11:40 A.M. with a blow against Maj. Gen. Dodson Ramseur's division on the Confederate right. A spirited Southern counterattack by Maj. Gen. Robert Rodes's division drove a wedge between the Sixth and Nineteenth Corps and nearly cost Sheridan the battle, but a stand by Maj. Gen. David Russell's division stalled the Confederate offensive. During this bloody action, Rodes lost his life, and General Russell died conducting the Union defense. Meeting failure on the Confederate right and center, Sheridan deployed Crook's Eighth Corps and two divisions of cavalry against the Confederate left flank. When the 10,000-man charge commenced at 4:00 P.M., Early's outnumbered and outflanked army cracked and went "whirling through Winchester" in headlong flight south on the Valley Pike. Early's defeat at the Third Battle of Winchester (known as the Battle of Opequon in the North) cost him 199 killed, 1,508 wounded, and 1,818 missing. Sheridan suffered 697 killed, 3,983 wounded, and 338 missing. For the first time in its history, the Second Corps, formerly commanded by Stonewall Jackson, had been driven from a field it defended.

During the night of September 19, Early retreated twenty miles south from Winchester to Fisher's Hill, a line of dominating ridges running perpendicular to the valley and anchored on the east by the North Fork of the Shenandoah River and to the west by North Mountain. Some considered it a Confederate "Gibraltar," but Early did not have enough men to hold the four-mile line. On September 21 and 22, while Sheridan feinted attack against the Confederate front, the 5,500 men of the Union's Eighth Corps under Crook secretly marched to North Mountain to attain a position behind Early's left flank. At 4:00 P.M. on the twenty-second, Crook's men smashed into the Confederate left held by Lunsford Lindsay Lomax's cavalry division. The panicked horsemen scattered in disarray, and with its left now exposed, Early's army fled from Fisher's Hill in a rout. Although Early's casualties were relatively light (30 killed, 210 wounded, 995 missing), he lost 14 guns to the Federals. He also lost his chief of staff, Lt. Col. William N. Pendleton, who was killed while attempting to rally his routed comrades. Sheridan accomplished his second victory in three days at a cost of 36 killed, 414 wounded, and 6 missing.

Following his September 22 defeat at Fisher's Hill, Early retreated 60 miles south and east to Brown's Gap in the Blue Ridge, where he awaited reinforcement from Kershaw's division and Cutshaw's battalion of artillery. Sheridan followed to Harrisonburg, arriving there on September 25. Concluding that Early's army

was finished, Sheridan commenced burning the upper valley in accordance with Grant's orders to make the Shenandoah Valley a "barren waste." By October 7, as Sheridan's army moved north to Woodstock, his cavalry had systematically destroyed 2,000 barns filled with wheat, hay, and farming implements and over 70 mills filled with flour and wheat. In addition, 3,000 sheep had been slaughtered and 4,000 cattle driven north. Sheridan notified Grant that the destruction was so thorough that the 92 miles from Winchester to Staunton "will have but little in it for man or beast."

As Sheridan retired north, Confederate Brig. Gen. Thomas Lafayette Rosser and his Laurel Brigade arrived in the valley and began menacing Sheridan's rear guard. At Tom's Brook, Sheridan tired of the harassment and ordered his cavalry to "whip the Rebel cavalry or get whipped." Subsequently, on October 9, Maj. Gen. George Armstrong Custer, in his first fight as a division commander, flanked Rosser's left while Maj. Gen. Wesley Merritt smashed Rosser's right, sending the Confederates reeling in a 26-mile chase known as the "Woodstock Races." Sheridan's horsemen captured 330 prisoners, 11 guns, and the headquarters wagons of four Confederate cavalry generals. The Federals lost 9 killed and 48 wounded.

Following the victory at Tom's Brook, Sheridan encamped north of Cedar Creek on October 10. Since he considered Early "disposed of," Sheridan began making plans to transfer his army back to Grant. To confer on future operations, Sheridan started for Washington on October 15, leaving the army in temporary command of General Wright. Meanwhile, Early had advanced north following his reinforcement at Brown's Gap. On October 17, Maj. Gen. John B. Gordon surveyed the Union army from Three Top Mountain and convinced Early that a surprise attack against the Union left flank at Cedar Creek was possible. Following an all-night march by the Second Corps along the base of Massanutten Mountain, Gordon's and Kershaw's 8,000 Confederates routed Crook's unsuspecting Eighth Corps at dawn on the nineteenth and then drove the Nineteenth Corps and Sixth Corps three miles north of their Cedar Creek camps. Early had seized twenty enemy cannon and 1,500 prisoners in the morning victory, but fatigue and rampant plundering stalled the Confederate offensive at about 11:00 A.M.

Meanwhile, Sheridan, who had returned by late morning, rallied his army and redeployed the cavalry on his flanks. At 4:00 P.M., the rejuvenated Federal army advanced. When Custer's cavalry division overran the Confederate left, Early's panicked line broke and a rout began. In one of the most remarkable one-day turnarounds in military history, Sheridan had snatched victory from defeat. As Early lamented, "The Yankees got whipped and we got scared."

All too soon, owing to faulty intelligence reports, Jackson found himself locked in combat with a full Union division. Yet Jackson's tactical failure proved a strategic success.

PAGE 542

Shiloh, April 6, 1862: With Johnston's death, Beauregard assumed full command and at day's end had almost forced Grant's army into the river.

PAGE 46

Confederate losses in the Cedar Creek disaster included 320 killed, 1,540 wounded, and 1,050 missing; General Ramseur was mortally wounded. In addition, Early lost 43 cannon and at least 300 wagons and ambulances. Union casualties were 644 killed, 3,430 wounded, and 1,591 missing.

Early had faced Sheridan's overwhelming numbers and suffered four defeats in thirty days. With the Confederates routed and the valley breadbasket burned, Sheridan transferred much of his army to Grant, while Lee ordered all of Early's remaining infantry, with the exception of one division, to return to Petersburg.

— DENNIS E. FRYE

SHILOH CAMPAIGN

A small Methodist church gave its name to the first major land battle in the West on April 6 and 7, 1862. In February 1862, Gen. Ulysses S. Grant moved south against Confederate Forts Henry and Donelson guarding the Tennessee and Cumberland rivers. He had captured them by the sixteenth. Their loss forced the evacuation of parts of middle and western Tennessee by the Confederate army commanded by Gen. Albert Sidney Johnston. When Johnston abandoned Nashville, Gen. Don Carlos Buell's Army of the Ohio occupied the city. West of the Tennessee River, Gen. P. G. T. Beauregard, Johnston's deputy commander, withdrew the Southern forces from Columbus, Kentucky. He established a new line stretching from Island Number 10 on the Mississippi River to Corinth, Mississippi, and concentrated the bulk of his forces there.

After the surrender of the forts, the gunboats of the Union navy effectively controlled the Tennessee from its mouth to Muscle Shoals, Alabama. The Federals massed at Pittsburg Landing, the closest all-weather landing to Corinth, which, as a major rail junction, was the next Union target. Gen. Henry W. Halleck, now in command of Union forces west of the Appalachian Mountains, ordered Buell to march the Army of the Ohio west from Nashville and join the forces at Pittsburg Landing.

Johnston and Beauregard, to regain the initiative, decided to concentrate a large force at Corinth and attack Grant. Johnston ordered over 44,000 men to the town. These troops, however, were insufficiently trained on the division level. Johnston divided his army into four corps under the command of Gens. Leonidas Polk, Braxton Bragg, William J. Hardee, and John C. Breckinridge. The Reserve Corps, Breckinridge's unit, was no more than a large division.

While the Confederates concentrated at Corinth, four Union divisions were training at Pittsburg Landing. Another division, the Third, commanded by Gen. Lew Wallace, was stationed at Crump Landing seven miles to the north, and the Sixth Division under Gen. Joseph Prentiss was being assembled as new units arrived. Grant, confident that the battle at Corinth would be the last in the West and that he would win it, did not take the necessary steps to keep informed of what was going on in his front.

On the evening of April 2, Beauregard received word from Bethel Springs that a portion of the Union army was moving out of its camps around Shiloh Church. He sent his chief of staff, Col. Thomas Jordan, to Johnston to recommend immediate attack. Johnston conferred with Bragg, who also advised attack, and sent Jordan back to Beauregard's headquarters, where he drafted Special Orders No. 8, the Confederate order of battle. On the morning of the third, Jordan presented this order to all corps commanders except Breckinridge. It called for marching that day and attacking on the fourth. Hardee's corps was to form one long line of battle and then press forward. A thousand yards behind it would be Bragg's corps also in the line of battle. Polk's and Breckinridge's corps would serve as reserves.

Owing to muddy roads and poor discipline during their march, the Confederates were not ready to attack on the fourth or on the fifth. That evening, Beauregard recommended calling the attack off, but Johnston refused. The attack would go on.

In the Union camps, Col. Everett Peabody, commander of the First Brigade, Sixth Division, was not happy with the developments in his front. He sent out a patrol before dawn on the sixth to learn the true strength of the Southerners. These men, at 5:45 A.M., collided with the Third Mississippi Battalion serving as pickets under the command of Maj. Aaron Hardcastle. The patrol sent back word that it had met a major Confederate force and asked for reinforcements. Peabody sent out the Twenty-first Missouri, but before they arrived, the Southerners advanced, pushing the patrol back. Col. David Moore, commander of the Twenty-first, ordered the patrol to stand and fight. Further reinforced by elements of the Sixteenth Wisconsin, the patrol delayed the Confederates for about thirty minutes.

Meanwhile, Prentiss called his Sixth Division into the line of battle and prepared to meet the Confederates. The two forces met just south of the division camps. This was the first battle for most of these men, Northern or Southern. Prentiss's men held for a short while, but then Confederate brigades under John K. Jackson and James R. Chalmers got around their left flank. S. A. M. Woods's brigade found a hole to the left of their Fifth Division, forcing Prentiss to fall back. The Sixth held for a short time in their camps and then fell back again. Prentiss and about 3,000 men dug in at what came to be called the Hornet's Nest.

While the North's Sixth Division was under attack, its Fifth Division, to the right, was also meeting the enemy. First, Patrick Cleburne's brigade slammed into the brigades of Jessie Hildebrand and Ralph Buckland. Cleburne's right pushed back the Fifty-third Ohio, but was stopped cold by Buckland on the Southern left. S. A. M. Woods supported Cleburne on the right. Units from Bragg's and Polk's corps coming up to continue the drive forced Buckland and Hildebrand back.

By late morning, Confederate attacks had pushed the Union right back almost a mile to the Hamburg-Purdy Road. Here the North's First Division joined the line to protect the left of the Fifth. One brigade of the Fourth Division joined the left of the First. This concentration, however, had drawn the bulk of the Confederate troops. By 11:00 A.M., all but two brigades of the Southerners were massed against this line. It broke and was forced back about a half mile. John McDowell's brigade of the Fifth Division was cut off and had to fight its way back to the main force. Due to the shock of the Southern attack, the regiments of Hildebrand's and Buckland's brigades were scattered and ceased to exist as organized units.

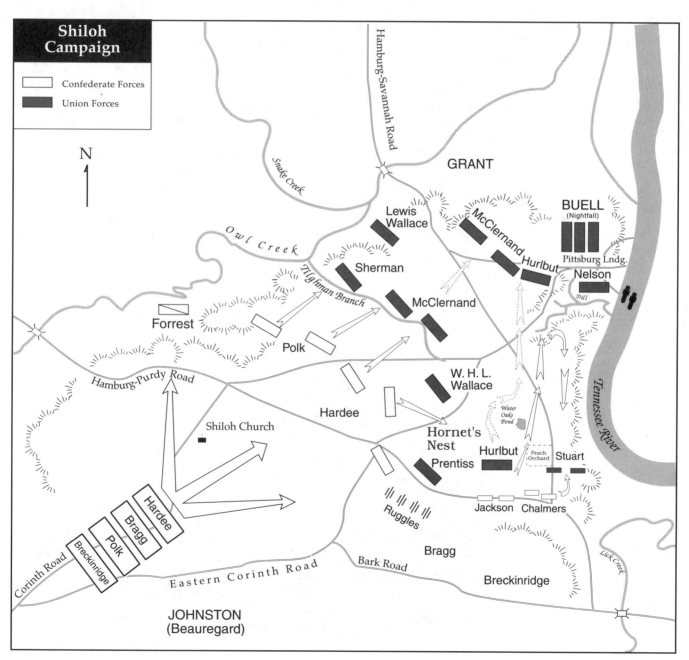

Shiloh Campaign

☐ Confederate Forces
■ Union Forces

N

Snake Creek

Owl Creek

Highman Branch

Hamburg-Savannah Road

GRANT

Lewis Wallace

McClernand

BUELL (Nightfall)

Pittsburg Lndg.

Sherman

Hurlbut

Nelson

McClernand

Dill

Forrest

Polk

Tennessee River

Hamburg-Purdy Road

Hardee

W. H. L. Wallace

Water Oaks Pond

Shiloh Church

Hornet's Nest

Hurlbut

Peach Orchard

Stuart

Prentiss

Ruggles

Jackson   Chalmers

Lick Creek

Breckinridge / Polk / Bragg / Hardee

Bragg

Corinth Road

Bark Road

Breckinridge

Eastern Corinth Road

JOHNSTON
(Beauregard)

Johnston redeemed himself for the loss of Forts Henry and Donelson by surprising Grant in the Battle of Shiloh, April 6–7, 1862.

PAGE 302

On the Union left, Col. David Stuart's brigade of the Fifth Division guarded the eastern approaches to the battlefield. Stuart saw Confederate flags moving in Prentiss's camps and deployed his brigade to meet the expected attacks. Gen. Stephen D. Hurlbut brought his Fourth Division up to support Stuart. Gen. John McArthur's Brigade of the Second Division filled the gap between Stuart and Hurlbut. Behind Hurlbut, Prentiss was rallying the remains of his division, and at 11:00 A.M. they took up a position on Hurlbut's right. Gen. W. H. L. Wallace brought up the Second Division to extend the Union right toward the First Division's left. The First was commanded by Gen. John McClernand.

The first Confederate attacks against the Union left were made by Chalmers's and Jackson's brigades. Stuart's line stopped them at about 10:00 A.M. By using a heavy skirmish line and detaching troops to cover his left, Stuart led the Confederates to believe they were attacking a division. Johnston moved to the Southern right with Jackson's and Chalmers's brigades. There he took personal command of the eastern sector. All along the Confederate line, the various corps became hopelessly intermingled. As a result, the corps commanders split the line into sectors. Polk took the left, Hardee the center left, and Bragg the center right. Breckinridge assisted Johnston on the right.

Johnston began a series of probing attacks looking for the Union left flank. His intention was to turn this flank and force the Northerners to the west and away from Pittsburg Landing. But he was not able to bring enough strength to bear until about 2:00 P.M. Then he advanced five brigades. Aided by Stuart's running out of ammunition, Johnston forced the Union troops out of the Peach Orchard area, and they withdrew toward Pittsburg Landing. Unfortunately, Johnston was hit in the leg by a stray round and bled to death before his aides were able to find the wound.

On the Union right, McClernand and Gen. William Tecumseh Sherman (commanding the Union's Fifth Division) had fallen back to Jones Field. Here they organized a counterattack that forced the Southerners back, but they were unable to sustain the drive and had to withdraw. With Stuart withdrawing, McArthur was forced to fall back. This exposed Hurlbut's left to the attacks of Jackson's and Chalmers's brigades, as well as three other Confederate brigades. Hurlbut sent word to Prentiss that he would have to fall straight back for Pittsburg Landing. Prentiss realized this would leave his left in the air, but his orders from Grant were to hold the Hornet's Nest area at all costs.

Grant arrived on the battlefield in the middle of the morning. Earlier he had sent orders to Buell to march his lead division up the east bank of the river. He planned to ferry the men across to Pittsburg Landing. Grant also stopped at Crump Landing long enough to tell Lew Wallace to prepare his division for a quick move and then await orders. Once he arrived, Grant made a tour of the field and then sent orders to Wallace to move to Shiloh.

Polk and Hardee kept up the pressure against Sherman and McClernand, forcing them to fall back. Their left connected with Wallace's division in the Hornet's Nest. Their right guarded the River Road by which they expected Lew Wallace to arrive. As the pressure mounted, Sherman and McClernand fell back, breaking contact with Wallace on their left, which opened up a hole in the Union line. The Confederates poured through it and met their right

flank brigades. The movement surrounded the Hornet's Nest.

In the Confederate center, Bragg threw attack after attack against Prentiss's and Wallace's divisions. They were all forced back until Gen. Daniel Ruggles took over the sector. A gun line established under his command pinned the Union troops down. This prevented many of them from withdrawing while the Confederates closed the purse on the Hornet's Nest.

With Prentiss's surrender, the Southerners regrouped for a final attack on Pittsburg Landing. Grant, however, had managed to establish a gun line of fifty-four cannons. This line, supported by those soldiers who were able to fall back, stopped the final Confederate attacks of the day. At dusk, Beauregard, who did not realize that Buell was arriving, called off the fighting. With Buell's arrival, along with that of Wallace, the Union losses of the day were more than made good.

On April 7 Grant went over to the offensive. Buell's fresh troops were on the left; the elements of the army that fought on the sixth were in the center; and Lew Wallace's Third Division was on the right. Beauregard tried to stop their advance, but with no fresh troops at hand, he didn't have a chance. Local counterattacks were successful (the most notable one was at Water Oaks Pond), but they did not stop the Union drive. At 2:30 Beauregard realized that the Confederates could not regain the offensive, and he ordered a withdrawal back to Corinth. Breckinridge took command of the rear guard. The Battle of Shiloh ended.

On the morning of the eighth, Grant sent out Sherman with some of his troops to discover how far the Confederates had withdrawn. At Fallen Timbers, just west of the battlefield, he ran into the rear guard under Col. Nathan Bedford Forrest. Forrest forced Sherman back. There was no further pursuit because Grant had lost the bulk of his ammunition and equipment. Buell's reserves were still downriver in Savannah awaiting shipment to Pittsburg Landing.

As a result of the battle, the losses were

CASUALTIES AT SHILOH

	South	North
Killed	1,727	1,254
Wounded	8,012	8,408
Missing	959	2,885
Total	10,698	12,547

The Union did not relax its pressure on Corinth and on June 1, took the city. As a result, the Confederates lost Memphis and the rest of western Tennessee.

— GEORGE A. REAVES III

SHIPYARDS

At war's outbreak the Confederacy seized two U.S. Navy shipyards, Gosport Navy Yard at Norfolk, Virginia, and Pensacola Navy Yard on Florida's Gulf coast.

The Gosport yard converted the frigate *Merrimack* to the ironclad *Virginia*, which battled *Monitor* in Hampton Roads (March 9, 1862). Then advancing Union troops forced Norfolk's abandonment. A similar fate befell Pensacola, and both government yards were lost. The navy established a new yard at Rocketts in Richmond, a site described by one officer as "a shed with 200 or 300 carpenters." Rocketts was active throughout the war, building three ironclads—*Richmond, Fredericksburg,* and *Virginia II*—and maintaining the other ships of the James River Squadron.

Whenever possible, the Navy Department sought to use private industry for wartime manufacturing, including shipbuilding. In the first months of the war both the Confederate and state governments bought commercial steamers and had them converted to warships by private shipyards in Nashville, Savannah, Mobile, and New Orleans. Gunboat contracts were signed with individuals in Mars Bluff and Charleston, South Carolina; Washington and Elizabeth City, North Carolina; Jacksonville and Pensacola, Florida; and Savannah, Saffold, and Early County, Georgia.

When the Navy Department's focus shifted to ironclads, the government continued to rely on independent contractors to build most of the new-style fighting ships. Usually, contractors were forced to create a building site for their project, in effect building their shipyard and then building their ship. Charleston foundry owner James Eason built *Chicora* in a vacant lot behind the post office. To build *Mississippi* at New Orleans, contractors Nelson and Asa Tift first tried to rent the Hughes shipyard at Algiers and then to subcontract the hull to the Harrem and Company or Hyde and Mackey yards. Failing in these efforts, they acquired four acres on the river, installed a sawmill, and opened their own yard. Contractor E. C. Murray rented a lot adjoining that of the Tifts and, in the same way, began building the ironclad *Louisiana.*

Neither New Orleans ironclad survived the capture of the city. Nelson Tift went to Savannah and contracted to convert a blockade runner to the armored *Atlanta* at Henry F. Willink's shipyard. Willink's, one of the few professional shipbuilding facilities left in Confederate control after the spring of 1862, also turned out the ironclads *Savannah* and *Milledgeville* and serviced the rest of the Savannah River Squadron.

By the summer of 1862, with most of the coast and both ends of the Mississippi lost to the South, most Confederate shipbuilding had moved to locations on

Beauregard's attempts to portray Shiloh as a misrepresented success only further diminished his reputation.

PAGE 46

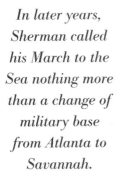

In later years, Sherman called his March to the Sea nothing more than a change of military base from Atlanta to Savannah.

PAGE 354

inland rivers. John Shirley began two ironclads at a steamboat landing below Memphis. When Memphis fell, he burned one and had the other—*Arkansas*—towed up the Yazoo River, where a shipyard was created at the Yazoo City cotton wharf. Gilbert Elliott built the ironclad *Albemarle* in a cornfield at Edwards Ferry, North Carolina. Swampy land at Oven Bluff, Alabama, on the Tombigbee River served as the construction site for three hulls (which were towed to Mobile and never completed).

That contractors had to create their building sites was not a peculiarity of the war. Of the 145 Southern shipyards listed in the 1850 census, the great majority were created for the construction of a single river-going commercial steamer. The wartime experience of shipyards springing up along river banks was just the peacetime practice of Southern shipbuilding gone to war.

Once a yard like Yazoo City or Edwards Ferry was established, other ships were often laid down but rarely completed. Initial construction usually went quickly, as timber was plentiful. But when armor plate and machinery were needed, the work would halt for lack of materials. The ships sat incomplete until advancing Union troops forced the destruction of the vessels and the abandonment of the yard. The Confederate navy contracted for—and saw begun—nearly four times as many ships as were commissioned.

[*See also* Charlotte Navy Yard; Gosport Navy Yard.]
— MAURICE K. MELTON

SIGNAL CORPS

The Confederate Signal Corps was, in effect, the creation of a single officer, Edward Porter Alexander, who, while an instructor at West Point, had assisted army surgeon Albert J. Myer in the perfection of his "wig-wag" system of military signaling. After going South in 1861, Alexander was at once put to work organizing, training, and equipping a Signal Corps. Thanks to his skill and energy, the Confederates had a functioning signal service with their forces at First Manassas (July 21, 1861), several months before the confused U.S. War Department could put an effective organization into the field with the Federal armies.

Alexander formed his first signal unit by requesting the detail of some twenty intelligent young privates who could be commissioned if they proved competent. In April 1862 the Confederate government officially established the Signal Service as a branch of its Adjutant General's Department, to consist of one major, ten captains, ten first lieutenants, ten second lieutenants, and twenty sergeants. These men were assigned in small teams to the headquarters of the Confederacy's various field armies, which furnished any needed additional personnel. In 1865 its total strength was approximately 1,500. Its missions were to include signaling, telegraphy, and secret service work.

The Confederate Signal Corps had no distinctive uniform or insignia. Signaling equipment was the same as that used by the Federal Signal Corps, though probably not as complete. The basic items were the signal flags (in the Federal signal service, these were in three sizes—six feet, four feet, and two feet square) and a sixteen-foot staff, made up of four 4-foot sections. The flag commonly used was white, with a red central square, but under some conditions a red flag with a white central square might have greater visibility. A black flag with a white center was used when the ground was snow-covered.

WAITING
FOR WORD

*A signal station near
Beverley Ford, Virginia.*

FRANK LESLIE'S
ILLUSTRATED FAMOUS
LEADERS AND BATTLE
SCENES OF THE CIVIL WAR

For night signaling, flags were replaced by torches—hollow copper cylinders filled with turpentine or other liquid fuel. Members of the signal detail would carry extra fuel in large round canteens. Torches could be supplemented by a variety of pyrotechnics, such as rockets, flares, and star shells. There were also a variety of improvised methods of communication—fires, signal cannon, and contraptions like the four black-cloth balls that Alexander used for signaling from the Confederacy's one short-lived observation balloon. A Signal Corps officer's most important item of equipment was a powerful telescope or field glasses, essential for reading signals from other stations and observing enemy movements.

The Signal Corps established chains of signal stations, each manned by one or two officers and several enlisted men, from their army's outposts back to its headquarters. These were placed on commanding heights so that each station had a clear line of sight to the stations on either side of it. Where such hills were lacking, tall buildings or specially built signal towers (shaped much like oil derricks) were utilized. The distance between stations depended on the terrain.

Since these stations frequently provided excellent views of the opposing army, the Signal Corps detachments manning them thus had the dual mission of transmitting messages and observing and reporting enemy activities. They also could often observe and copy the messages from the enemy's signal stations. Though all important messages were sent in some type of code, Confederate skills in this art were decidedly inferior to the Federals', who periodically broke Confederate codes and so gained valuable military intelligence. In contrast, the Confederates never were able to read Federal messages, though they occasionally deceived their opponents by sending false information they knew would be intercepted.

One unusual communications function of the Confederate Signal Corps was service aboard blockade runners. Exchanging signals with the Confederate shore defenses, they could obtain the location of close-in Federal warships blockading the seaport and of the safest channels for their ship to use. In 1864 numerous blockade runners reportedly were forced to wait idly in the Bahamas until signal officers could be run out through the blockade to help pilot them in.

The Signal Corps' role in telegraphic communications is not too well recorded. The Confederacy had only limited commercial telegraph service in 1861; there was no unified network to connect Richmond with the various battle fronts and armies. Also, there were relatively few skilled telegraph operators, and telegraph wire was in short supply. The weaknesses of the existing system were aggravated by the damage done to it by Federal raiders—damage that was increasingly difficult to repair as supplies of materials dwindled. (On at least one occasion in 1864 considerable quantities of telegraph wire were stolen by Southern planters for use in baling their cotton.) Though the Signal Corps utilized the existing Southern telegraph systems with their civilian employees and may have somewhat improved and extended them, they never achieved either a nationwide system (such as the North possessed) or a military telegraph service (such as the North had from 1864) to accompany Confederate armies into the field.

The Signal Corps' involvement in "secret service" (a phrase covering what now would be called military intelligence operations) probably grew out of its efforts during the period after First Manassas, when the Confederate outposts were within sight of Washington, D.C., to set up a signal station within that city itself. It was to be managed by a daring spy to whom Confederate sympathizers (including the famous Rose O'Neal Greenhow) would furnish information on

Once the Signal Corps was involved in clandestine operations, it was a small step to have both the Corps and the War Department espionage apparatus managed by the same people.

PAGE 192

Federal forces in the Washington area. This effort failed because the outposts had to be withdrawn, but the Signal Corps continued to be involved in espionage of one sort or another for the duration of the war. It did not have a monopoly on this activity; the Confederate State Department maintained its own intelligence network and practically every Confederate commander utilized his personal contingent of scouts, agents, and spies. (Also there was practically a surplus of enthusiastic amateur spies of both sexes.) This whole business was under no sort of central coordination and control; records of its workings are very incomplete and those available generally exaggerated.

The Signal Corps' one special function in all this seems to have been wire tapping—cutting into Federal telegraph lines and reading the messages being transmitted or inserting their own messages containing false information. Skilled telegraph operators rode with J. E. B. Stuart and John Hunt Morgan on their famous raids; on one occasion Stuart had his operator, a soldier named Sheppard, send the quartermaster general of the U.S. Army a taunting dispatch concerning the poor quality of the mules he had just captured. Other operators infiltrated Federal-occupied territory, tapped wires in some secluded area, and remained there quietly for days recording all messages, as did C. A. Gaston, who was Gen. Robert E. Lee's confidential operator in 1864. Since all important Federal messages were encoded, the amount of valuable information gained

from such exploits was minor. But a good many operational messages—such as those directing forces attempting to trap Confederate raiders—were sent "in the clear," and their interception could be highly valuable to the raiders.

Organized hurriedly from scratch, always hampered by shortages of equipment, the Confederate Signal Corps nevertheless rapidly became an effective force. Unfortunately, its services have received little recognition.

[*See also* Alexander, Edward Porter; Balloon; Espionage; Telegraph.]

— JOHN R. ELTING

SLAVERY

[*This entry is composed of three articles:* Antebellum Slavery *and* Slavery during the Civil War, *which discuss the institution of slavery before and during the war, and* Slave Life, *which discusses the daily lives of slaves and their society and culture. See also* African Americans in the Confederacy; Antislavery; Cotton; Plantation; Proslavery; Slave Traders; Sugar; Tobacco.]

ANTEBELLUM SLAVERY

The enslavement of African Americans in what became the United States formally began during the 1630s and 1640s. At that time colonial courts and legislatures made clear that Africans—unlike white indentured servants—served their masters for life and that their slave status would be inherited by their children. Slavery in the United States ended in the mid-1860s. Abraham Lincoln's Emancipation Proclamation of January 1863 was a masterful propaganda tactic, but in truth, it proclaimed free only those slaves outside the control of the Federal government—that is, only those in areas still controlled by the Confederacy. The legal end to slavery in the nation came in December 1865 when the Thirteenth Amendment was ratified. It declared: "Neither slavery nor involuntary servitude, except as a punishment for crime whereof the party shall have been duly convicted, shall exist within the United States, or any place subject to their jurisdiction."

Development of American Slavery

The history of African American slavery in the United States can be divided into two periods: the first coincided with the colonial years, about 1650 to 1790; the second lasted from American independence through the Civil War, 1790 to 1865. Prior to independence, slavery existed in all the American colonies and therefore was not an issue of sectional debate. With the arrival of independence, however, the new Northern states—those of New England along with New York, Pennsylvania, and New Jersey—came to see slavery as contradictory to the ideals of the Revolution and instituted programs of gradual emancipation. By 1820 there were only about 3,000 slaves in the North, almost all of them working on large farms in New Jersey. Slavery could be abolished more easily in the North because there were far fewer slaves in those states, and they were not a vital part of Northern economies. There were plenty of free white men to do the sort of labor slaves performed. In fact, the main demand for abolition of slavery came not from those who found it morally wrong but from white working-class men who did not want slaves as rivals for their jobs.

Circumstances in the newly formed Southern states were quite different. The African American population, both slave and free, was much larger. In Virginia and South Carolina in 1790 nearly half of the population was of African descent. (Historians have traditionally assumed that South Carolina had a black majority population throughout its pre–Civil War history. But census figures for 1790 to 1810 show that the state possessed a majority of whites.) Other Southern states also had large black minorities.

Because of their ingrained racial prejudice and ignorance about the sophisticated cultures in Africa from which many of their slaves came, Southern whites were convinced that free blacks would be savages—a threat to white survival. So Southerners believed that slavery was necessary as a means of race control.

Of equal importance in the Southern states was the economic role that slaves played. These states were much more dependent on the agricultural sector of their economies than were Northern ones. Much of the wealth of Delaware, Maryland, Virginia, the Carolinas, and Georgia came from the cash crops that slaves grew. Indeed, many white Southerners did not believe white men could (or should) do the backbreaking labor required to produce tobacco, cotton, rice, and indigo, which were the region's chief cash crops.

As a consequence of these factors, the Southern states were determined to retain slavery after the Revolution. Thus began the fatal division between "free states" and "slave states" that led to sectionalism and, ultimately, to civil war.

Some historians have proposed that the evolution of slavery in most New World societies can be divided (roughly, and with some risk of overgeneralization) into three stages: developmental, high-profit, and decadent. In the developmental stage, slaves cleared virgin forests for planting and built the dikes, dams, roads, and buildings necessary for plantations. In the second, high-profit stage, slave owners earned enormous income from the cash crop they grew for export. In these first two phases, slavery was always very brutal.

During the developmental phase, slaves worked in unknown, often dangerous territory, beset by disease and sometimes hostile inhabitants. Clearing land and performing heavy construction jobs without modern machinery was extremely hard labor, especially in the hot, humid climate of the South.

During the high-profit phase, slaves were driven mercilessly to plant, cultivate, and harvest the crops for market. A failed crop meant the planter could lose his initial investment in land and slaves and possibly suffer bankruptcy. A successful crop could earn such high returns that the slaves were often worked beyond human endurance. Plantation masters argued callously that it was "cheaper to buy than to breed"—it was cheaper to work the slaves to death and then buy new ones than it was to allow them to live long enough and under sufficiently healthy conditions that they could bear children to increase their numbers. During this phase, on some of the sugar plantations in Louisiana and the Caribbean, the life span of a slave from initial purchase to death was only seven years.

The final, decadent phase of slavery was reached when the land upon which the cash crops were grown had become exhausted—the nutrients in the soil needed to produce large harvests were depleted. When that happened, the slave regime typically became more relaxed and less labor-intensive. Plantation owners turned to growing grain crops like wheat, barley, corn, and vegetables. Masters needed fewer slaves, and those slaves were not forced to work as hard because the cultivation of these crops required less labor.

This model is useful in analyzing the evolution of Southern slavery between independence and the Civil War. The process, however, varied considerably from state to state. Those of the upper South—Delaware, Maryland, and Virginia—essentially passed through the developmental and high-profit stages *before* American independence. By 1790, Maryland and Virginia planters could no longer produce the bumper harvests of tobacco that had made them rich in the earlier eighteenth century, because their soil was depleted. So they turned to less labor-intensive and less profitable crops such as grains, fruits, and vegetables. This in turn meant they had a surplus of slaves.

One result was that Virginia planters began to free many of their slaves in the decade after the Revolution. Some did so because they believed in the principles of human liberty. (After all, Virginian slave owners wrote some of the chief documents defining American freedom like the Declaration of Independence, the Constitution, and much of the Bill of Rights.) Others, however, did so for a much more cynical reason. Their surplus slaves had become a burden to house and feed. In response, they emancipated those who were too old or feeble to be of much use on the plantation.

SLAVERY

Antebellum Slavery

South Carolina had a larger percentage of slaves than any other state.

PAGE 151

"I have borne thirteen children and seen them most all sold off into slavery, and when I cried out with a mother's grief, none but Jesus heard—and aren't I a woman?"

SOJOURNER TRUTH
1851

553

Ironically, one of the first laws in Virginia restricting the rights of masters to free their slaves was passed for the protection of the slaves. It denied slave owners the right to free valueless slaves, thus throwing them on public charity for survival. Many upper South slave owners around 1800 believed that slavery would gradually die out because there was no longer enough work for the slaves to do, and without masters to care for them, the ex-slaves would die out as well.

Two initially unrelated events solved the upper South's problem of a surplus slave population, caused slavery to become entrenched in the Southern states, and created what we know as the antebellum South. They were the invention of the cotton gin by Eli Whitney of Connecticut in 1793 and the closing of the international slave trade in 1808.

The cotton gin is a relatively simple machine. Its horizontally crossing combs extract tightly entwined seeds from the bolls of short-staple cotton. Prior to the invention of the gin, only long-staple cotton, which has long soft strands, could be grown for profit. Its soft fibers allowed easy removal of its seeds. But this strain of cotton grew in America only along the coast and Sea Islands of South Carolina and Georgia. In contrast, short-staple cotton could grow in almost any non-mountainous region of the South below Virginia. Before the invention of the cotton gin, it took a slave many hours to de-seed a single pound of "lint," or short-staple cotton. With the gin, as many as one hundred pounds of cotton could be de-seeded per hour.

The invention of the cotton gin permitted short-staple cotton to be grown profitably throughout the lower South. Vast new plantations were created from the virgin lands of the territories that became the states of Kentucky, Tennessee, Alabama, Mississippi, and Arkansas. (Louisiana experienced similar growth in both cotton and sugar agriculture.) In 1810, the South produced 85,000 pounds of cotton; by 1860, it was producing well over 2 billion pounds a year.

There was an equally enormous demand for the cotton these plantations produced. It was so profitable that by 1860 ten of the richest men in America lived not just in the South but in the Natchez district of Mississippi alone. In 1810, the cotton crop had been worth $12,495,000; by 1860, it was valued at $248,757,000.

Along with this expansion in cotton growing came a restriction on the supply of slaves needed to grow it. The transatlantic slave trade was one of the most savage and inhumane practices in which people of

COMPARISON OF BLACK AND WHITE POPULATIONS IN THE SOUTHERN AND BORDER STATES, 1790–1860

(Black population, in thousands, to left of asterisk; white population, in thousands, to right of asterisk.) [1]

	1790	1800	1810	1820	1830	1840	1850	1860
Ala.				42*85	119*190	256*335	345*427	438*526
Ark.				2*13	5*26	20*77	48*162	111*324
Del.	13*46	14*50	17*55	17*55	19*58	20*59	20*71	22*91
Fla.					16*18	27*28	40*47	63*78
Ga.	30*53	60*102	107*145	151*190	220*297	284*408	385*522	466*592
Ky.	13*61	41*180	82*324	129*435	170*519	190*590	221*761	236*919
La.			42*34	80*74	126*89	194*158	262*255	350*357
Md.	111*209	125*216	145*235	147*260	156*291	152*318	165*418	171*516
Miss.			17*23	33*42	66*70	197*179	311*296	437*354
Mo.			4*16	11*56	26*115	60*324	90*592	119*1,063
N.C.	106*288	140*388	179*376	220*419	265*473	269*485	316*553	362*630
S.C.	109*140	149*196	201*214	265*257	323*258	335*259	394*275	412*291
Tenn.	4*32	14*92	46*216	83*340	146*536	189*641	246*757	283IT1*
Tex.							59*154	183*421
Va.	306*442	367*518	426*557	465*610	520*710	502*748	527*895	549*1,047

[1] No population figures are given for years prior to a state's admission to the Union.

Source: Computed from figures in U.S. Census Office, First through Eighth Census [1790–1860], *Population*, Washington, D.C. 1790–1864.

Year	Crop (In Thousands of Lbs.)	Value (In Thousands)	Crop Value (Per Slave)	Price of Prime Field Hand
1810	85,000	$12,495	$17.94	$900
1820	160,000	$24,320	$26.88	$970
1830	331,150	$27,817	$23.03	$810
1840	834,111	$75,904	$50.34	$1,020
1850	1,001,165	$117,136	$59.19	$1,100
1860	2,241,056	$248,757	$101.09	$1,800

VALUE OF COTTON PRODUCTION AND SLAVE POPULATION, 1810–1860, NEW ORLEANS PRICES

"I believe this government cannot endure permanently half slave and half free."

ABRAHAM LINCOLN
1858

European descent have ever engaged. The writers of the Constitution had recognized its evil, but to accommodate the demands of slave owners in the lower South, they had agreed to permit the transatlantic slave trade to continue for twenty years after the Constitution was ratified. Thus, it was not until 1808 that Congress passed legislation ending the transatlantic trade.

These two circumstances—the discovery of a means of making the cultivation of short-staple cotton profitable throughout the lower South and territories and the restriction on the supply of slaves needed to produce it—created the unique antebellum slave system of the South. It made at least some Southerners very rich and it also made slaves much more valuable. One consequence was that some American slaves were perhaps better treated than those elsewhere in the New World, not because American slave owners were kinder, but because American slaves were in short supply and expensive to replace. The price of slaves increased steadily from 1802 to 1860. In 1810, the price of a "prime field hand" was $900; by 1860, that price had doubled to $1,800.

The Slave System in the Nineteenth Century

Slavery in the antebellum South was not a monolithic system; its nature varied widely across the region. At one extreme one white family in thirty owned slaves in Delaware; in contrast, half of all white families in South Carolina did so. Overall, 26 percent of Southern white families owned slaves.

In 1860, families owning more than fifty slaves numbered less than 10,000; those owning more than a hundred numbered less than 3,000 in the whole South. The typical Southern slave owner possessed one or two slaves, and the typical white Southern male owned none. He was an artisan, mechanic, or more frequently, a small farmer. This reality is vital in understanding why white Southerners went to war to defend slavery in 1861. Most of them did not have a direct financial investment in the system. Their willingness to fight in its defense was more complicated and subtle than simple fear of monetary loss. They deeply believed in the Southern way of life, of which slavery was an inextricable part. They also were convinced that Northern threats to undermine slavery would unleash the pent-up hostilities of 4 million African American slaves who had been subjugated for centuries.

REGULATING SLAVERY. One half of all Southerners in 1860 were either slaves themselves or members of slaveholding families. These elite families shaped the mores and political stance of the South, which reflected their common concerns. Foremost among these were controlling slaves and assuring an adequate supply of slave labor. The legislatures of the Southern states passed laws designed to protect the masters' right to their human chattel. Central to these laws were "slave codes," which in their way were grudging admissions that slaves were, in fact, human beings, not simply property like so many cattle or pigs. They attempted to regulate the system so as to minimize the possibility of slave resistance or rebellion. In all states the codes made it illegal for slaves to read and write, to attend church services without the presence of a white person, or to testify in court against a white person. Slaves were forbidden to leave their home plantation without a written pass from their masters. Additional laws tried to secure slavery by restricting the possibility of manumission (the freeing of one's slaves). Between 1810 and 1860, all Southern states passed laws severely restricting the right of slave owners to free their slaves, even in a will. Free blacks were dangerous, for they might inspire slaves to rebel. As a consequence, most Southern states required that any slaves who were freed by their masters leave the state within thirty days.

To enforce the slave codes, authorities established "slave patrols." These were usually locally organized

bands of young white men, both slave owners and yeomen farmers, who rode about at night checking that slaves were securely in their quarters. Although some planters felt that the slave patrolmen abused slaves who had been given permission to travel, the slave patrols nevertheless reinforced the sense of white solidarity between slave owners and those who owned none. They shared a desire to keep the nonwhite population in check. (These antebellum slave patrols are seen by many historians as antecedents of the Reconstruction era Ku Klux Klan, which similarly tried to discipline the freed blacks. The Klan helped reinforce white solidarity in a time when the class lines between ex–slave owners and white yeomen were collapsing because of slavery's end.)

SLAVE LABOR IN THE UPPER SOUTH. If there was a "least bad" place to be a slave in the antebellum South, it was in the towns and on the smaller farms of Virginia and Maryland. When those states turned from growing high-yield crops like tobacco to cultivating crops like grains and vegetables, the change carried some benefits for slaves. The new crops required less intensive labor and permitted some slaves to work under the "task system." Slaves were assigned chores individually or in small groups. They were permitted to work at their own pace, often without direct white supervision. They would be assigned another task upon completion of the first.

The decline in the profitability of slavery appears to have led to a more relaxed and open regime for some slaves in the upper South. Since fewer slaves were needed on plantations, many were allowed by their master to live in town and "hire their own time"—find their own work—paying their masters a portion of their wages, usually two-thirds to three-quarters. This benefited the masters by enabling them to make a profit on an otherwise surplus slave. It was attractive to the slaves because it gave them more independence. Many hoped to save enough from their wages to buy their freedom from their owners.

This more relaxed system extended to other aspects of slave life in the upper South. It appears that most slaves in Virginia and Maryland were allowed to marry and have families, although these families had no legal standing. They existed only through permission of the master. In addition, laws against literacy and holding church services without a white person present were widely ignored or unenforced.

Of course, Virginia slaves were still the property of white masters, to be used as the masters saw fit. To put it bluntly, the chief cash crop of Virginia slave owners after 1807 was the slaves themselves. Historians have been unable to find plantations that openly "bred" slaves for sale, but this does not change the central appalling fact—the number of slaves born in Virginia between 1807 and 1860 was the same number as those

THE INTERNAL SLAVE TRADE

The factor that made the antebellum system viable was the internal slave trade. White Southerners were embarrassed by the trade, and there is little documentation about how it operated. Slave traders were considered the least reputable of white men. Nevertheless, the genteel aristocrats of the upper South and the aggressive new planters of the lower South both needed slave traders to keep their economic system working. The economy could prosper only because of the transfer of surplus slaves from the upper South to the labor-short, high-profit plantations of the cotton-growing lower South.

The slave trade operated in two forms. The first form of transfer occurred through endowment of heirs. Because states of the upper South still had laws of primogeniture (the eldest son inherited all his father's property), fathers often purchased land for their younger sons in the developing lower South and gave them a number of slaves to work the new land. This meant that some of the caravans of slaves seen by Northern observers traveling southward were, in fact, plantation units composed of intact families being transferred to new locations.

Most historians agree, however, that the second form of slave trade—commercial sale—was by far the most dominant means of transferring slave property from the upper to the lower South. Hundreds of thousands of slaves were sold as individuals, separated from their loved ones through the internal slave trade. Husbands were separated from their wives; children, from their parents. Two million slaves were transferred from one region to the other between 1790 and 1860.

The extent of the interstate slave trade is revealed by figures showing the distribution of the black population between 1790 and 1860. The number of slaves in the upper South grew by 175,000, whereas the number in the lower South increased from 237,000 in 1790 to over 3 million in 1860. Basically, the entire natural increase in the slave population of the upper South was exported to the lower South cotton plantations between 1820 and 1860. Very few slaves born in the upper South grew up there. The antebellum Southern slave economy survived because the upper South—in which fewer slaves were needed because the soil was exhausted—sold its excess slaves to the burgeoning cotton plantations of the lower South.

— ROBERT FRANCIS ENG

sold farther South. So if conditions for slaves *were* better in Virginia, few of those born there grew up to enjoy them there. Indeed, the standard and most effective way to discipline a slave was to threaten to sell him or a loved one to the Deep South.

SLAVE LABOR IN THE LOWER SOUTH. The possibility of being "sold south" was no empty threat. Slaves in the lower South were often ill housed, ill fed, and ill cared for. It was more profitable to keep them at work on cotton than allow them time to build decent shelter. It was more profitable to plant every inch of land in cotton than to allot space for growing food-

stuffs. Even the little garden plots allowed slaves in the upper South were usually absent in Mississippi. That state, with some of the richest soil in America, was actually a net importer of foodstuffs before the Civil War.

Life on the Deep South plantations was also characterized by the impersonality of master-slave relationships. Owners were often absent, and overseers were paid by how much cotton they produced, not by the condition of the slaves they supervised.

On lower South plantations, like those of the upper South, both men and women slaves were expected to

---

SLAVE DRIVERS
Ruling with an Iron Will and a Whip Hand

Drivers were slaves responsible for plantation field production and labor discipline. By the 1830s they were widely employed in the Tidewater rice- and Sea Island cotton-growing areas, the Delta region, and Louisiana sugar parishes, where large agricultural units required close management; many small cotton planters also relied on drivers. On large plantations drivers worked directly under white (and sometimes black) overseers meting out daily work tasks, leading and disciplining work gangs, and managing crop production. On small plantations drivers served as foremen-overseers who reported directly to the master. The staple-crop economy of the plantation South, with its emphasis on regimentation and discipline, meant that the drivers' principal role was to "drive" the slaves by coaxing or coercion. But masters also expected drivers to maintain order in the quarters and to relate the masters' interests to the slaves. Masters rewarded drivers with extra rations, money, access to the local market, and other privileges. Slaves, in turn, suffered drivers so long as they did not abuse their power, kept the masters out of their lives in the quarters, and respected the slaves' community norms. Drivers thus occupied a precarious middle ground between master and slave.

The Civil War fundamentally altered the master-slave relationship, even before emancipation. With the menfolk

away, plantation management often was left to planters' wives and "trustworthy" slave drivers. The situation expanded the driver's responsibilities, while paradoxically eroding the structure of bondage on which his power rested. Where drivers had ruled by undue force, embittered slaves retaliated for past abuses by beating and even murdering overseers and drivers, violent acts that were especially widespread in the sugar parishes in 1863 during the Union army advance. Mostly, the unraveling of planter authority forced drivers increasingly to accommodate the slaves' interests to maintain their own authority. Meanwhile, whites at home complained of driver complicity in raiding plantation storehouses (to which drivers often held the keys), aiding runaways, and slowing work, yet planters continued to entrust daily farm management to black drivers and overseers. The trust was not wholly misplaced, for even as drivers lightened slavery's burdens, they tried to maintain minimum levels of production and upkeep. Perhaps more than any other slave, the driver understood that the slaves' physical well-being, and even avoidance of sale, depended on their producing enough foodstuffs and cash crops to keep slaves fed and masters solvent.

Southern whites' postwar accounts of faithful slaves, especially drivers and house servants, protecting the farms and hiding the master's silver from Northern

bummers exaggerated the loyalty of slaves but revealed what had bound such "privileged bondmen" as drivers to the plantations—namely, that they claimed a vested, proprietary interest in the goods and farmsteads they had planted and built. This was most graphically demonstrated on the South Carolina Sea Islands in 1861 when the masters fled their plantations during the Union landing at Port Royal. Before the abolitionists arrived to begin their famous "Port Royal experiment," the drivers already had kept the slaves growing food crops and prevented destruction of farm equipment and buildings.

Immediately after the war some drivers functioned as straw bosses on plantations where owners sought to bind former slaves to long-term contracts in gang-labor systems, but virtually everywhere by the late 1860s sharecropping and tenancy arrangements left no place for drivers. Many former drivers, especially in the Sea Island and Delta areas, parlayed their planting and marketing experience and personal relationships with former masters into access to credit and local markets few other freedmen could command. Their conservative mediating behavior during slavery inclined former drivers toward personal profit and away from politics. Few former drivers held office during Reconstruction. Their public lives had ended with slavery.

— RANDALL M. MILLER

OWN A MAN

A receipt for the sale of "one Negro Slave," named Caleb (or Philip), "about eighteen years old," in Charleston, 1859. Caleb was S. I. Morgan's for $1,100.

GORDON BLEULER

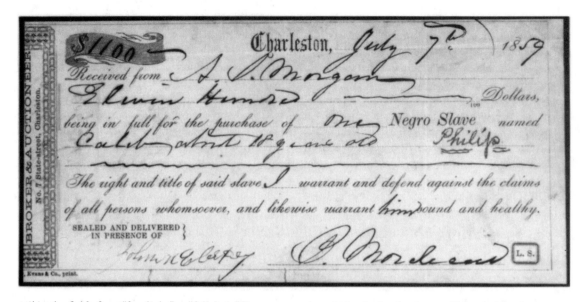

> *"I speak for the slave when I say that I prefer the philanthropy of Captain Brown to that philanthropy which neither shoots me nor liberates me."*
>
> HENRY DAVID THOREAU
>
> A PLEA FOR CAPTAIN JOHN BROWN, 1859

toil in the fields from "first light" to "full dark." Because men were stronger and able to work harder, the plantations often had a much larger number of male slaves than female. This made the possibility of marriage problematic for the slave men. Moreover, women were sometimes seen as liabilities because "female problems" such as the menstrual cycle and pregnancy periodically incapacitated them for hard labor. In the cotton and sugar South, slaves were usually worked in gangs supervised by black drivers and white overseers with whips. The pace for plowing, hoeing, weeding, or picking was set by the overseers, and if a worker fell behind, he or she felt the sting of the lash.

Impact of Slavery on the Southern Economy

As the preceding discussion makes clear, slavery in the antebellum South was overwhelmingly a rural phenomenon. This was, in part, because most slave owners believed that slavery would not work well in an urban industrialized environment. Slaves were thought to be too stupid to understand machinery and too careless to be trusted with complex tools.

In fact, however, slaves *were* used successfully in factories such as the Tredegar Iron Works in Richmond. They also labored in the salt mines and turpentine plants of North Carolina, the coal mines of western Virginia, and the sugar mills of Louisiana. Moreover, when, during the Civil War, Southerners confronted a manpower shortage and the need for rapid industrialization, they quickly overcame their prejudices against using slaves in factories.

OBJECTIONS TO URBAN SLAVERY. A major reason for slavery being confined mostly to rural areas in the South concerned its dual purpose for the white population. It was both a means of labor exploitation and a means of race control. It was this second aspect

that made the institution problematic in urban areas. Simply put, slaves in cities were much more difficult to supervise.

It was the custom of factory owners to hire slaves from masters rather than purchase them outright. In the upper South, where urban slaves were more common, this allowed slave owners to profit from their excess slaves without having to sell them South. The problem was that industrialists preferred to avoid the burden of overseeing their slave employees outside of the factory, and they tended to give them stipends to pay for their own housing and board. This enabled urban slaves to live in a varied community that included free blacks, slaves who hired their own time, and white people—some of whom might oppose slavery.

As white Southerners saw it, the urban environment exposed slaves to dangerous ideas about freedom. Most Southern cities were ports that provided access to the outside world where slavery was generally outlawed. Free black sailors and sympathetic white ship captains were known to help slaves escape aboard their vessels.

Cities, therefore, were considered antithetical to effective slave control. White Southerners well remembered that the two largest slave conspiracies (those of Gabriel Prosser in Richmond in 1800 and Denmark Vesey in Charleston in 1822) were urban phenomena. Moreover, both men were free blacks who had persuaded urban slaves to join them in their plots.

Yet another factor militating against urban slavery was the attitudes of workers in antebellum America. Southern white men felt demeaned if they were required to perform the same sort of job as a slave. Moreover, slaves, who received no wages, could do the same labor more cheaply than free white men. White workers—like the caulkers in Baltimore who beat up Frederick Douglass when his master sent him to work in the dockyards—often refused to labor alongside slaves.

So, to maintain better supervision of slaves and assure white solidarity and the status of white laborers, urban slavery in the antebellum South was minimal. The numbers of urban slaves actually declined between 1830 and 1860.

NEGATIVE EFFECTS OF RURAL SLAVERY. The rural nature of antebellum slavery had unintended negative effects on the Southern economy. The investment of so much capital in land and slaves discouraged the growth of cities and diverted funds from factories. This meant that the South lacked the industrial base it needed to counter the North when the Civil War began. Indeed, in 1860, the South had approximately the same number of industrial *workers* (110,000), as the North had industrial *plants*.

Other detrimental effects arose from the South's devotion to rural slavery. Wealthy planters liked to claim they were living out the Jeffersonian ideal of an agrarian democracy. In truth, the South was agrarian because slave owners found that the best way to maintain their wealth and contain their slaves. Moreover, its "democracy" was very limited because the planters had enormous influence over how white yeomen cast their votes. Except in remote areas of the South with few slaves or plantations, it was the needs and beliefs of the planter class that shaped Southern politics on the local, state, and national levels.

The consequences of this planter dominance was seen in many aspects of the society. The South failed to develop a varied economy even within the agricultural realm. All the most fertile land in the South was owned by slaveholders who chose to grow high-profit staple crops—cotton, tobacco, sugar. That left only marginal land for the vast majority of white farmers. This problem was compounded by the dominance of the planter's image as the social ideal. Alternative means of advancement were unavailable, so yeomen farmers aspired to become planters themselves. They used some of their land to grow food for their family's consumption and devoted the rest to cash crops like cotton. Their hope was to produce enough to save, buy a few slaves, produce yet more, and, ultimately, accumulate the wealth that would elevate them to planter status. For most, this was a futile dream, but they remained committed to it, thereby neglecting other possible avenues for economic advancement.

One reason for the yeomen farmers' lack of aspirations was ignorance. The antebellum South neglected to provide for the education of its people. Planters controlled the governmental revenues that could have financed public education, but they saw no need to do so. Their slaves were forbidden to learn; their own children were educated by private tutors or in exclu-

Ten Dollars Reward.

RAN AWAY from the Subscriber, on the night of the 15th instant, two apprentice boys, legally bound, named WILLIAM and ANDREW JOHNSON The former is of a dark complexion, black hair, eyes, and habits. They are much of a height, about 5 feet 4 or 5 inches The latter is very fleshy freckled face, light hair, and fair complexion. They went off with two other apprentices, advertised by Messrs Wm. & Chas. Fowler When they went away, they were well clad—blue cloth coats, light colored homespun coats, and new hats, the maker's name in the crown of the hats, is Theodore Clark. I will pay the above Reward to any person who will deliver said apprentices to me in Raleigh, or I will give the above Reward for Andrew Johnson alone.

All persons are cautioned against harboring or employing said apprentices, on pain of being prosecuted.

JAMES J. SELBY, Tailor.
Raleigh, N. C. June 24, 1824   26 3t

REWARD OFFERED

A tailor in Raleigh, North Carolina, advertises a reward for the return of his property, "two apprentice boys," William and Andrew Johnson.

NATIONAL ARCHIVES

sive and expensive private academies. As a result, most white yeomen were left without access to education. A few lucky ones near towns or cities could sometimes send their children to fee schools or charity schools, but many were too poor or too proud to use either option.

In a similar vein, the dominating slaveholding class saw no need to create the means to produce inexpensive consumer goods for ordinary whites or to build an infrastructure by which such goods could be moved from production sites to markets in the countryside. Wealthy planters acquired what they wanted by importing expensive European or Northern goods. Thus poor whites were left to their own minimal resources and were deprived of goods they might have bought, had they been available.

This lack of consumer production and markets also retarded the growth of Southern transportation. Highways, canals, and railroads were constructed to move crops to ports and bring in luxury items for the planter class. The need of yeomen farmers to transport their crops to local markets was ignored. As a consequence, it was usually cheaper for plantation owners to import food from the North or upper South than to purchase it from white farmers in the same region. This deficiency in the Southern transportation system proved a serious liability for the Confederacy during the Civil War.

Slavery in the antebellum South, then, made a minority of white Southerners—owners of large slaveholdings—enormously wealthy. At the same time, it demeaned and exploited Southerners of African descent, left the majority of white Southerners impoverished and uneducated, and retarded the overall economic, cultural, and social growth of the region. Slavery was the institution by which the South defined

"So we defend ourselves and our henroosts, and maintain slavery."

HENRY DAVID THOREAU
A PLEA FOR CAPTAIN JOHN BROWN, 1859

WHIPPED BAD

"I was two months in bed sore from the whipping" by an overseer, said Peter, a slave photographed on April 2, 1863, in Baton Rouge, Louisiana.

NATIONAL ARCHIVES

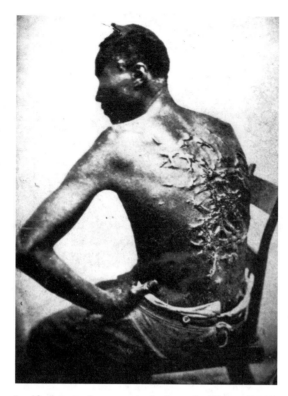

"What, to the American slave, is your Fourth of July? . . . To him your celebration is a sham."

FREDERICK
DOUGLASS
1852

itself when it chose to secede from the Union. But it was the existence of slavery, with its negative impact on politics, economics, and social relations, that fatally crippled the South in its bid for independence.

[*See also* Expansionism in the Antebellum South; Urbanization.]

— ROBERT FRANCIS ENGS

SLAVERY DURING THE CIVIL WAR

Although slavery was at the heart of the sectional impasse between North and South in 1860, it was not the *singular* cause of the Civil War. Rather, it was the multitude of differences arising from the slavery issue that impelled the Southern states to secede.

The presidential election of 1860 had resulted in the selection of a Republican, Abraham Lincoln of Illinois, as president of the United States. Lincoln won because of an overwhelming electoral college vote from the Northern states. Not a single Southern slave state voted for him. Lincoln and his Republican party were pledged only to stop the expansion of slavery. Although they promised to protect slavery where it existed, white Southerners were not persuaded. The election results demonstrated that the South was increasingly a minority region within the nation. Soon Northerners and slavery's opponents might accumulate the voting power to overturn the institution, no matter what white Southerners might desire.

Indeed, many Southern radicals, or fire-eaters, openly hoped for a Republican victory as the only way

to force Southern independence. South Carolina had declared it would secede from the Union if Lincoln was elected, and it did so in December 1861. It was followed shortly by the other lower South states of Alabama, Mississippi, Louisiana, Georgia, Florida, and Texas. In February 1861, a month before Lincoln was inaugurated, these states formed a new nation, the Confederate States of America. After the firing on Fort Sumter and Lincoln's call for volunteers to suppress the rebellion, the other slave states of Virginia, North Carolina, Tennessee, and Arkansas joined the Confederacy. The border slave states of Delaware, Maryland, Kentucky, and Missouri remained—not entirely voluntarily—in the Union.

The new republic claimed its justification to be the protection of state rights. In truth, close reading of the states' secession proclamations and of the new Confederate Constitution reveals that it was primarily *one* state right that impelled their separation: the right to preserve African American slavery within their borders. But the white South's decision to secede proved to be the worst possible choice it could have made in order to preserve that right.

There was enormous antislavery sentiment in the North, but such sentiment was also strongly anti-Negro. White Northerners did not wish slavery to expand into new areas of the nation, which they believed should be preserved for white nonslaveholding settlers. This was, in part, why Republicans pledged to protect slavery where it existed. They and their constituencies did not want an influx of ex-slaves into their exclusively white territories, should slavery end abruptly.

Some historians argue that, had the South remained within the Union, its representatives could have prevented any radical Northern plan for emancipation. By leaving the Union, white Southerners gave up their voice in national councils. Moreover, by seceding, the South compelled the North to realize the extent of its allegiance to a united American nation. Thus, the North went to war to preserve the Union, and the white South went to war for independence so that it might protect slavery. Most participants on both sides did not initially realize that the African American slaves might view the conflict as an occasion that they could turn to their own advantage.

SLAVES' EFFORTS TO UNDERMINE THE SOUTH. In 1861, as the Civil War began, there were four open questions among Northerners and Southerners with regard to the slaves: First, would they rebel? Second, did they want their freedom? Third, would they fight for their freedom? And, finally, would they know what to do with their freedom if they got it? The answer to each question was yes, but in a manner that reflected the peculiar experience of blacks in white America.

First was the question of whether bondsmen would rebel or remain passive. The fear of slave rebellion pre-occupied both the Southern slaveholder and the Northern invader. Strikingly, Northerners were as uneasy about the possibility as were Southerners. Initially the Northern goal in the war was the speedy restoration of the Union under the Constitution and the laws of 1861, all of which recognized the legitimacy of slavery. Interfering with slavery would make reunion more difficult. Thus, Union generals like George B. McClellan in Virginia and Henry W. Halleck in the West were ordered not only to defeat the Southern armies but also to prevent slave insurrections. In the first months of the war, slaves who escaped to Union lines were returned to their masters in conformity with the Fugitive Slave Act of 1850.

Concern about outright slave insurrections proved unfounded, however. Slaves were not fools, nor were they suicidal. Mary Boykin Chesnut, the famed Southern diarist and one of the South's most perceptive observers of slavery, understood the slaves' strategy. She wrote from her plantation: "Dick, the butler here, reminds me that when we were children, I taught him to read as soon as I could read myself. . . . But he won't look at me now. He looks over my head. He scents freedom in the air."

Slaves like Dick knew the war was about their freedom, but they were both shrewd and cautious. To rebel on their own was hopeless; the whites were too powerful. But now the Southern whites had an equally powerful outside enemy, and the odds had changed. The slaves, like successful rebels everywhere, bided their time until a revolt could succeed.

Meanwhile, through desertion and noncooperation, they did much to undermine the South long before Union armies triumphed. When the war began, some Confederates claimed that the disparity in white manpower between North and South (6 million potential soldiers for the North versus only 2 million for the South) was irrelevant. The South, Confederates claimed, could put a far higher proportion of their men in the field because they had slaves to do the labor at home.

The South, however, quickly learned that it had what would now be called a "fifth column" in its midst, providing aid and comfort to the enemy. At the beginning of the war, Southern officers took their body servants with them to the front to do their cooking and laundry. A unit of two thousand white soldiers would sometimes depart with as many as a thousand slaves in tow. The custom did not last beyond the first summer of the conflict. The servants deserted at the first opportunity and provided excellent intelligence to Union forces about Southern troop deployments.

In one incident during the early months of the war, Union soldiers on the Virginia Peninsula, stationed at Fort Monroe, repeatedly set out to capture the nearby city of Newport News, but without success. Their inaccurate maps showed the town to be *southwest* of Fort Monroe. Each would-be attack concluded with the troops mired in the swampy land bordering Hampton Roads (the bay between the Virginia Peninsula and Norfolk on the "Southside"). In fact, Newport News was slightly *northwest* of Fort Monroe, and Union forces were unable to find it until an escaped body servant led them there.

SLAVE LABOR WITH THE CONFEDERATE MILITARY. Despite such subversion by the slaves, the Confederacy nevertheless successfully used them to advance its war effort. White Southerners, though convinced of the African Americans' inherent inferiority, were far less reluctant about putting the slaves to work militarily than were white Northerners. The Confederate government never used them as soldiers, but it did press them into labor brigades to build fortifications, dig latrines, and haul supplies. Tens of thousands of slaves toiled for the Confederacy in a service both the bondsmen and their owners disliked. For the slave impressed into labor on the frontline, the work frequently was not only harder than that on the plantation but also dangerous. Because of the possibility of escape through Union lines, slaves at the front were much more closely supervised than on their home farms. Moreover, those sent to work with the Confederate army were usually men in their prime, between eighteen and forty. Service with the army denied them their accustomed time with their wife and family.

The slave owners, for their part, were reluctant to send their bondsmen to the front for two reasons. First, they risked the loss of their most valuable property, and, second, because the men were usually overworked and mistreated, they frequently returned to their homes in very poor physical condition. Thus, the owners often contrived to send only their most unmanageable and therefore least marketable slaves to the army. During the war, threatening to send a slave to the front became the disciplinary equivalent of threatening to sell a slave farther South in antebellum days. Ironically, as the South's cause became more desperate, masters were increasingly reluctant to send their slaves to the military. Slavery was dying, yet those with the most to lose hung on tenaciously to their human property, thereby withholding the one remaining resource that might have saved their nation—and them.

The exigencies of war also finally settled the decades-old debate as to whether slaves could be used safely and efficiently in industry. The shortage of white manpower left the South with no other choice than to put slaves to work in its factories and mines. In the

The impressment of slaves for building coastal fortifications began early in the war.

PAGE 66

As more slaves were taken for varying lengths of time by both state and Confederate authorities, the mood of the planters changed.

PAGE 66

Tredegar Iron Works of Richmond alone, thousands of slaves were employed. The Augusta munitions plants of Georgia likewise were primarily staffed by bondsmen. Thousands of others labored in the ultimately futile effort to keep Southern rail lines operating. As with service on the front lines, this labor—especially in extractive industries like the coal mines and salt factories—was harsher than life on the plantation, and slaves resisted it if they could. Many made the long-delayed decision to run away when faced with such dire prospects.

Although their service was extracted involuntarily, slaves in industry and on the battlefield enabled the South to fight on longer than would have been possible otherwise. In the final desperate days of the war, the Confederacy even considered using blacks as soldiers, offering emancipation as a reward. The Union had struck that bargain two years earlier. The Southern proposal was made in February 1865 and approved, in part, on March 13 of that year. By then Southerners of both races knew the Confederacy was doomed. Richmond fell less than thirty days later. The provision was never implemented and no slaves officially served as soldiers in the Confederate military.

SLAVE RESISTANCE ON THE PLANTATIONS. When given the option, slaves made it very clear that they wanted *freedom*. The vast majority of slaves, however, remained on their plantations in the countryside. Nevertheless, even these slaves in the Southern interior found ways to demonstrate their desire for freedom. Their behavior could be described as the first massive labor slowdown in American history. They did not cease to work, but they contrived to do considerably less than they had before the war.

Part of the reason for the drop in their industriousness was the South's ill-advised self-imposed cotton embargo. Although this was never official policy, many Southerners believed they could provoke European intervention in the war by refusing to grow or export cotton. This decision changed the nature of Southern agriculture. The region began to emphasize food production, a less intensive form of agricultural labor. But this change did not necessarily reduce the burden on slave laborers. The war cut off many of the South's

THE WARTIME SLAVE ECONOMY

Just as it did all other aspects of Southern life, the war severely disrupted the slave economy and the market for slaves. The chaos of the period makes an accurate account of change very difficult. Three conclusions, however, can be made about the war years. First, masters tried desperately to protect their investment in slave property to the very end of the war. Second, the slave trade and the antebellum trend of a slave population movement toward the Southwest continued during the war. Third, the prices of slaves rose astronomically (although in inflated currency) during the war even as the security of that form of property became increasingly doubtful.

Slaveholders had seceded and gone to war in the first place to protect their property in human beings, and they adopted various protective measures in the course of that war. Besides resisting the use of their slaves in the Confederate military, they developed another strategy: they transferred their slaves to more secure regions of the Thus, early in the war, thousands of slaves were moved from areas of active conflict or potential invasion—such as Tidewater Virginia and coastal areas along the Atlantic seaboard—to seemingly more secure inland regions. As the war continued to go badly and Northern armies penetrated more deeply into the Confederacy, slave owners moved their bondsmen across the Mississippi to areas in the West, especially Texas.

Their attempt to secure their investment in slave property also resulted in a continuation of the internal slave trade during the war. Owners of healthy young males or of females who were potentially "good breeders" tried to sell them to buyers from more secure regions of the South or simply to those willing to risk their money on Confederate victory. As Union forces triumphed, however, the trade was much disrupted, and it became impossible to move large bands of slaves through areas of possible conflict. The largest slave-trading city, New Orleans, was captured by the North in April 1862. By war's end, only Charleston in the East had an active slave market, although slaves were reportedly still being traded in Richmond on the eve of its fall.

Prices of slaves increased exponentially during the war. A "prime field hand" valued at a thousand dollars in 1860 could fetch ten thousand dollars in 1865. The increased price, however, reflected the inflated Confederate currency. It is impossible to estimate the volume of the slave trade during the war. The corresponding value of these prices in gold—from one thousand dollars in 1861 to one hundred dollars in 1865—is evidence of a dramatic price collapse. The inflation of slave prices and the growing insecurity of slave property both grew out of and reinforced the general disintegration of the Southern economy. In the end, it appears that many masters had more faith in the survival of slavery than in Confederate money or bonds. They tried to hold onto their human property until forced to surrender it because of Union victory.

— ROBERT FRANCIS ENGS

antebellum sources of food and other goods in the North and abroad. These shortages had to be replaced by what the slaves could produce at home. Their inability to make up the shortfall meant that they, their masters, the soldiers in the field, and the general population all suffered from increasing deprivation as the war went on. Especially problematic were shortages of wool, leather, and salt for the curing of meat, since most of these were diverted for military use. One consequence was the rapid escalation of prices for such necessities. Frugal planters cut back on these supplies for their slaves. Bondsmen did not receive their prewar rations of clothes and shoes, and they had less meat and vegetables in their diet. Even those slaves well removed from the front lines throughout the war recalled it later as a time of great privation.

In addition to the change in the kinds of crops grown and the increasing scarcity of necessities, the quality of management on the plantations changed. Once the war intensified in 1862, there were not enough white men left on the farms and plantations to provide adequate supervision of slave laborers. The Confederacy had attempted to defuse this potential problem through the Ten-Slave Law (later, the Twenty-Slave Law), whereby a percentage of white men were exempted from military service in proportion to the number of slaves in a county or on a plantation. The law clearly favored slaveholders and drew a storm of protest from white yeomen who owned no slaves yet were called upon to defend the Southern cause.

As the war progressed, Southern manpower shortages became acute. In some parts of Georgia, it was reported that there was only one able-bodied white man in a ten-square-mile area. As a result, management of agriculture increasingly fell to white women and their youngest children, elderly fathers, and black slave drivers. All proved less effective taskmasters than the earlier overseers, and the efficiency of Southern farm production declined markedly.

Slaves quickly took advantage of the situation, reducing the pace of their labor, disobeying orders, leaving their farms to visit with friends and relatives. Their perceived "impudence" and "laziness" caused enormous frustration for the white women left to oversee them. Although these women had often been most resourceful managers of household economies in the prewar South, they had never been trained or given experience in day-to-day supervision of farming operations. Many were unequal to the burden and resentful that they were being forced to shoulder it.

One important consequence of this management crisis was the disappearance of even the veneer of paternalism in the master-slave relationship. White women and the few white men left in the countryside viewed the increasingly recalcitrant slaves as a threat, especially the young males. Slave patrols composed of the remaining white men became more energetic and violent in "disciplining" slaves. Those accused or suspected of "misconduct" were brutally punished and sometimes murdered.

Despite these draconian efforts, slaves in the South's interior stepped up their resistance and increasingly worked at a much slower pace. More disturbing yet to the whites around them was their outright refusal to obey orders when they could get away with it.

*"When I found I
had crossed that
line, I looked at
my hands to see if
I was the same
person. There was
such a glory over
everything."*

HARRIET TUBMAN
ON HER FIRST ESCAPE
FROM SLAVERY

Slaves ran off with greater frequency; they stole food and violated curfew with impunity. They began to hold religious services more openly and even created schools for their children in violation of state laws.

ESCAPING FROM SLAVERY. The second of the four questions preoccupying European Americans, North and South, was: Did the slaves want freedom? Of course they did, as long as they could attain it without losing their lives in the process. The unrest on the plantations clearly indicated their longing for freedom. Even more demonstrable evidence was offered by slaves living on the borders of the Confederacy. Beginning in 1861, and continuing throughout the war, whenever the proximity of Union troops made successful escape likely, slaves abandoned their plantations by the hundreds, even the thousands.

The process of successful slave escapes began in Virginia, in Union-held territory across the Potomac from Washington and around Fort Monroe at the tip of the Virginia Peninsula in Hampton Roads. In May 1861, three slaves fled to the fort and claimed sanctuary because their masters were about to take them South to work on Confederate fortifications. The Union commander there was Gen. Benjamin Butler, a War Democrat from Massachusetts and a perennial thorn in Lincoln's side. Thinking more about the political advantage to be gained among Northern antislavery advocates than about the needs of the fugitives, Butler declared the blacks to be "contraband of war"—enemy property that could be used against the Union. This designation neatly avoided the question of whether or not the escapees were free and turned the Southerners' argument that slaves were property against them. Lincoln reluctantly approved the ruling, and as a consequence, escaped slaves throughout the war were referred to by Northerners as "contrabands."

This legal hairsplitting was of no concern to Virginia slaves. All they knew was that fugitives had gone to Fort Monroe and found sanctuary. Within a month, over 900 had joined those first three. By war's end, there were over 25,000 escaped slaves in and around Fort Monroe. Many of them served in the Union army.

A more massive instance of slaves' defecting occurred the following spring in the Sea Islands off South Carolina. The Union navy landed troops on the islands and the whites fled. Despite efforts by masters—some told the slaves that the Yankees were cannibals—the slaves refused to join their owners and fled to the woods until the Southern whites had left. As a consequence, the Union army suddenly had several thousand contrabands to care for. Interestingly, the first task of the Union commanders on the Sea Islands was to stop the ex-slaves from looting and burning their masters' mansions.

With the fall of New Orleans, also in the spring of 1862, the informal emancipation process expanded into the lower Mississippi valley. It never reached much of the Trans-Mississippi South until war's end because Union forces did not penetrate deeply there.

Throughout the South, the first slaves to escape were typically house servants and skilled craftsmen. They were the people who had the most access to information about Union troop movements (acquired primarily by overhearing their masters' indiscreet conversations around them) and those who had the greatest knowledge of the outside world. Usually the first ones to escape were men. Once they found they would be protected behind Union lines, they returned for their friends and relatives.

The North had not anticipated massive slave escapes. It had no plans about how to care for these black refugees. As a consequence, many escapees found themselves in worse physical conditions than they had known on the plantations. They were herded into camps and given tents and rations in exchange for work. The blacks were put to work in much the way Southern troops were using them, building fortifications, digging latrines, and cleaning the camps. Blacks frequently complained that their Union supervisors treated them worse than their former masters and overseers. In truth, many Union soldiers resented having to serve in the war, especially those who were draftees, and they blamed the blacks for their predicament.

The black refugees in the Union camps usually received no actual income. Most of the money they earned was withheld to pay for their food and clothing, and any remainder was reserved to pay for indigent or crippled escapees who could not work. This was administered by the Quartermaster's Department, a notoriously unreliable branch of any army throughout history. Blacks were defrauded at every turn. Often their rations and clothing were sold on the black market—sometimes to the Southerners—by greedy supply officers.

Hearing of the plight of the contrabands in the camps, Northern benevolent organizations, such as the Freedmen's Aid Societies, and religious groups, such as the American Missionary Association, sent hundreds of missionaries and teachers to the South to aid the blacks. They provided much of the food and clothing that enabled the refugees to survive. They also created the first schools and churches most blacks had ever attended.

It was the blacks themselves, however, who were primarily responsible for their survival in these harsh circumstances. The more enterprising of them earned cash through private work with officers of the camps. Those who fared best struck out from the encampments and squatted on lands abandoned by fleeing Confederates. Frequently they were able to make the land far more productive than it had ever been during slavery.

LINCOLN AND THE EMANCIPATION PROCLAMATION. The extent of slave escapes in the South and the burden it placed upon the Union presented a major dilemma for President Lincoln. From the moment the conflict began at Fort Sumter, Lincoln's foremost goals had been to preserve the Union, to bring the war to an end with a minimum of bloodshed, and to avoid lingering animosity between Northern and Southern whites. If that could best be achieved by preserving slavery, he said, he would do so; if it could be achieved by freeing every slave, he would do that instead. Lincoln despised slavery, but he, like Thomas Jefferson and many others before him, doubted that blacks and whites could ever live in America in a condition of equality.

The spring and summer of 1862 aggravated Lincoln's problem. The slaves, by running away in massive numbers, were freeing themselves. The border slave states of Delaware, Maryland, Kentucky, and Missouri were resisting all of Lincoln's proposals for gradual compensated emancipation. His own schemes to find somewhere outside of the United States where the freed black population could be colonized failed completely.

At the same time, Lincoln was confronted at home by abolitionists who insisted that the war should be one for emancipation. Abroad, he was faced with growing skepticism about Northern war aims. If the Union goal was simply to reunite the country and preserve slavery, then the North was undertaking a war of aggression. The South's claim that it was fighting for its independence, just as the United States had done during the Revolution, was therefore valid, and foreign powers had the right to intervene as the French had done in 1778. All these pressures forced Lincoln to conclude that emancipation would have to become a Union war goal.

The critics of Lincoln and the Emancipation Proclamation are technically correct in observing that the proclamation in January 1863 did not *legally* free a single slave. Slavery's end required a constitutional amendment, which Lincoln advocated and which was ratified as the Thirteenth Amendment in 1865. The *symbolic* importance of the Emancipation Proclamation should not, however, be underestimated. Lincoln thereby silenced his abolitionist critics in the North, defused interventionist sentiment abroad, and energized black slave resisters to continue their efforts in the South.

Lincoln advised his cabinet of his plan in the early summer of 1862. Because the Union cause was not faring well on the battlefield, he delayed its issuance until a Union victory could be attained. He claimed the bloody Battle of Sharpsburg (Antietam), during which Robert E. Lee's first invasion of the North was repulsed, as an appropriate occasion. Slaves in states or territories still in rebellion against the United States on January 1, 1863, would be freed. He hoped, probably only halfheartedly, that this threat would energize Southern moderates and influence them to persuade their leaders to lay down their arms. That was not to be the case.

On January 1, 1863, throughout the Union-occupied areas of the South, contrabands, their Northern white allies, and some Union soldiers gathered to pray, to sing hymns, and to celebrate slavery's demise. (The fact that none of those contrabands had been *legally* freed was irrelevant.) Moreover, the proclamation welcomed all escaping slaves into Union lines and held out the prospect that ex-slaves could volunteer for service in the Union military. African American slaves had tried to make the Civil War one of black liberation. In the Emancipation Proclamation, Abraham Lincoln and the Union appeared to have embraced their cause.

Certainly this was the belief of Southern slave owners. They wrote that both "misbehavior" on the plantations and escape attempts increased significantly after the issuance of the proclamation. Only in the Trans-Mississippi regions of Arkansas, Louisiana, and Texas was the impact of the proclamation minimal. One reminder of that difference is that blacks in that area and their descendants in the Midwest celebrate emancipation not on January 1 but on "Juneteenth," that period in mid-June after the surrender of the last Confederate armies in the West under E. Kirby Smith. Union officers, many now also superintendents of the newly formed Freedmen's Bureau, rode around those western states announcing Lincoln's Emancipation Proclamation to slaves and their masters.

In the eastern half of the Confederacy, slavery had collapsed long before those final western Union victories, in part because of the efforts of former slaves as Union soldiers.

EX-SLAVES IN THE UNION ARMY. The third of the four questions preoccupying white Americans during the Civil War was whether blacks would be willing to fight for their freedom. Once again the answer was yes. The fury of the white South when the North decided to make escaped slaves into soldiers is not surprising. What may be more so is the horror with which much of the white North regarded the idea.

Some Northerners, including the editorial board of the *New York Times,* claimed that using black troops

"*The black man occupied the position of a mere domestic animal, without will or right of his own. The lash lurked always in the background.*"

W. J. CASH
THE MIND OF THE SOUTH
1941

SLAVE PEN

*Interior of a holding pen at
Price, Birch & Co., where
slaves were kept pending
their sale in the markets of
New Orleans and elsewhere
in the lower South.*

NATIONAL ARCHIVES

would sully the purity of the North's cause. "Better lose the War," it cried, "than use the Negro to win it." A more representative statement was made by a Northern soldier who reflected, "I reckon if I have to fight and die for the nigger's freedom, he can fight and die for it along with me." That was really the point. The Union needed more men, and its efforts to enlist them were encountering increasing resistance among Northern white men. Why not let the black man fight for his own freedom?

In the fall of 1862, with Union victory still doubtful and the Preliminary Emancipation Proclamation already announced, Lincoln yielded to pressure and authorized the formation of the first black army units. African Americans were offered a step toward freedom not because the white North especially wanted them but because the North needed them so much.

The fashion in which black troops were treated was illustrative of Northern white attitudes toward the whole enterprise. At first, black soldiers were confined to service units and not allowed to fight—until white Union casualties became so high that blacks, though often untrained for combat, were simply thrown into the battle. Moreover, until just before the war's end, African American soldiers received unequal pay for the same duty and were denied the enlistment bonuses given to white troops.

The record of one of the most famous black Union regiments illustrates the contributions of ex-slave soldiers in the Confederacy's defeat. The First South Carolina Volunteers was the darling of Northern imagination. It was the first regiment composed entirely of fugitive slaves, organized, as Northerners loved to say, "in the birthplace of treason."

It was at first unclear that the North was entirely serious about this regiment. The unit was supposed to be made up of volunteers, but the first soldiers were acquired by sending white troops on raiding parties into the refugee camps and hauling back any able-bodied

DEALERSHIP

*Exterior of Price,
Birch & Co.,
Dealers in Slaves,
Alexandria, Virginia.*

NATIONAL ARCHIVES

black men they could find. Their uniforms were made up of a bright blue jacket, brighter red pantaloons, and a red fez, making them ideal targets for sharpshooters. Nevertheless, the First South Carolina ran up a credible record in Union service. They were, for example, the first known military unit to consistently return from battle with more soldiers than those which with they entered. Slaves on outlying plantations, seeing them in uniform, simply laid down their hoes, picked up discarded guns, and followed the troops back to their camp.

The soldiers of the First South Carolina were only the first of tens of thousands of former slaves who fought for the Union cause. Despite discrimination throughout the war, African American troops distinguished themselves and were instrumental in the North's victory. Overall, about 180,000 blacks served in the Union army, and another 20,000 in the Union navy. Together, they made up about 15 percent of all Northern forces in the war. Of all the Union troops, the African American soldier was fighting for the most tangible of causes—freedom for himself and his people.

THE FINAL QUESTION. The determination with which blacks seized freedom shocked whites, both North and South. In an unanticipated and unplanned war, the African Americans' behavior may have been the element for which both sides were least prepared. In the end, black slaves played a major role in bringing down the Confederacy. They had demonstrated that they wanted freedom and were prepared to fight for its realization.

The fourth question that whites had posed about the slaves—"Would they know what to do with their freedom if they got it?"—would be more candidly phrased—"Would white America let blacks truly exercise their freedom?" That question remains unresolved at the end of the twentieth century. But the limitations that crippled black freedom after Reconstruction did not discourage many African Americans who had been slaves. As one black Union veteran said after the war, "In slavery, I had no worriment. . . . In freedom I'se got a family and a little farm. All that causes me worriment. . . . But I takes the FREEDOM!"

[*See also* African Americans in the Confederacy; Antislavery; Contraband; Cotton; Emancipation Proclamation; Navy, *article on* African Americans in the Confederate Navy; Thirteenth Amendment.]

— ROBERT FRANCIS ENGS

SLAVE LIFE

The African American slave society in the antebellum South (1807–1860) was unique among New World slave systems. In the United States, the slave popula-

tion not only sustained itself; it expanded exponentially. In other New World nations, slave populations were maintained by continuous importation from Africa. In the American South, however, the slave population grew through natural increase—that is, slave mothers had children who also became slaves. As a result, the vast majority of African Americans in slavery in the United States after 1810 were not African captives but native-born Americans, some of whose ancestors had been in this country nearly as long as the oldest white families.

This longevity of residence in America did not mean that slaves lost all their rich heritage from their African origins. White slave owners, however, were frightened by African customs and behaviors they could not understand. They forced their slaves to give up African means of communication such as their own languages and their drums (a widely used means of "talking" across great distances in West Africa). Indeed, slaves were denied even their original African names and made to accept whatever names their master imposed upon them.

In these circumstances, Southern slaves were forced into syncretism—the process of mixing divergent cultural elements together to create an entirely new culture. They had to combine what they could retain of their African culture with the new European and Native American cultures imposed upon them by their masters. The result was the first genuinely United States culture. It was part African, part European, and part Native American, but refined and developed in a land new to all but one of these groups.

American slaves were able to carve out a unique culture of their own because of the way in which Southern slavery was structured. Most white Southerners did not own slaves. In 1860 only ten thousand Southern white families owned more than twenty slaves, and only three thousand owned more than fifty slaves. Nevertheless, most slaves lived in units of twenty or more. This meant that, on most plantations, blacks far outnumbered whites. They could not all be kept under constant white supervision.

Masters had to evolve a system of rewards and punishments to maintain control over their more numerous slaves. As in any brutal system of unpaid labor, punishment was used more often than reward. As historian Kenneth Stampp has written, the slave owners' strategy in handling their slaves was "to make them stand in fear!" A plantation, however, was not an extermination camp; it was a profit-making enterprise, and blacks had to be given certain rights and privileges to maximize their productivity. They were also valuable pieces of "property." To abuse them too harshly would diminish their value. Slaves seized upon this necessity to create a culture of their own possessing

In 1850 a St. Louis court found that Dred Scott had become free while living outside Missouri, a slave state, and once free, he remained free despite his return to Missouri.

PAGE 176

"This is a world of compensations; and he who would be no slave must consent to have no slave."

ABRAHAM LINCOLN
1859

the values that shaped family life, religion, education, and attitudes toward work.

RELIGION. Religion was one of the main buttresses that supported the slave family. African American slaves were denied the right to practice the religion of their ancestors. Some African slaves were Muslims; most believed in a variety of forms of ancestor worship that was more similar to Christianity than Europeans understood. Slave owners viewed African religion as a combination of witchcraft and superstition, and they banned its practice, in part, for fear that slaves might use it to put spells or curses on them.

Most slave owners believed that Christianizing their slaves would make them more passive. They also pointed to Christianization as a justification for slavery; they claimed to be uplifting the slaves from their barbarous past. Although the slave owner extracted unpaid labor from his slaves in this life, he ensured their salvation in the next by making them Christians.

Of course, the Christianity taught to slaves by their masters was very different from that which the masters practiced themselves. Omitted were the implicit and explicit messages in the New Testament about individual freedom and responsibility. Instead, slave owners

used the Bible selectively. They argued that Africans were the descendants of Ham, who, in the Old Testament, were cursed by Noah to be "servants of servants." From the New Testament, slave owners cited Christ's admonition to "render unto Caesar that which is Caesar's" to justify their right to demand obedience from their slaves. In part to ensure that slaves could not learn all of the other, contrary messages about freedom to be found in the Bible, slavemasters outlawed the teaching of reading and writing to slaves.

Slaves, however, once again combined what they could remember from their old religions with what their masters told them about Christianity and what they learned about Christianity from literate blacks and antislavery whites. From this information they evolved their own form of Christianity, which was a religion of hope and liberation.

In the slaves' version of Christianity, Christ and Moses played almost equal roles as heroes who had led their people to freedom. Black religion was very much anchored in the real world rather than in life after death. Slaves learned to phrase the words of their prayers and spirituals to speak of salvation and freedom in heaven, but, in truth, they were praying and singing

SLAVE FAMILY LIFE

The black family in slavery had no legal standing. Slaves and their children were the property of their masters. Slavery was hereditary through the status of the mother; therefore, even children conceived through the rape of a slave woman by a white man (sometimes the woman's master) were still legally slaves. Husbands and wives and their children could be sold apart from one another whenever the desires or economic needs of the master required such sales. Indeed, probably 2 million slaves were sold from the upper South (Virginia, Maryland, and Delaware) to the Deep South between 1800 and 1860. Many of these sales involved the breakup of families.

In the face of the constant threat of separation from loved ones, a strong family system developed. Most slave families in the South were structured like other American families. They were nuclear—that is, they consisted of a father, mother, and their children. The realities of slavery, however, forced the

additional creation of an extended family that incorporated all the other slaves on a plantation. This informal family helped protect children (and adults) when a family member was sold away. Thus, every slave child had many honorary aunts, uncles, and cousins who were not biologically related, but who were prepared to assume family roles, should a child be orphaned by the workings of the slave trade.

In the upper South, it was the custom among many slave owners to encourage slave families. The offspring of such unions brought high prices in the lower South's slave markets. In addition, it was an excellent means of slave control. Those slaves most likely to run away were young males between sixteen and thirty. A wife and family might make them more content. Moreover, since successful escape in groups, especially ones including children, was almost impossible, a husband and father was less likely to run away and leave his family behind.

In the lower South, however, cotton profits were so high that some slavemasters had no regard for slave family life. Pregnant women could not pick as much cotton as other field hands. Birth incapacitated mothers for days, and infants or little children were of no use in the fields. Some planters of the lower South thought it cheaper to work their slaves to death and buy more slaves rather than encourage families.

For the slaves, like all other Americans, their families were central to the definition of who they were. Evidence of this truth was demonstrated when the Civil War started and slaves began to desert their plantations in the upper South. To the surprise of whites, both North and South, these escapees often fled south rather than to the so-called Freedom Land in the North. They were going in search of loved ones sold through the interstate slave trade.

— ROBERT FRANCIS ENGS

about deliverance from slavery in this world, not the next. Thus, a black woman like Harriet Tubman who led dozens of slaves to freedom, used spirituals like "Steal Away to Jesus" to signal plans for escape. She became known, as a result, as "The Moses of Her People."

The burdens of slavery led African Americans to different definitions of God, sin, and even the devil. Slaves did not conceive of God as the stern taskmaster envisioned by their white owners. Rather, they thought of God as an all-forgiving Father who understood the tribulations that his people were suffering and who was planning a better world for them. This vision of the Almighty led, among other things, to a very different style of worship among slaves. As one ex-bondsman tried to explain: "White folks pray powerful *sad*. Black folks pray powerful *glad*!"

Slave religion even resulted in a different understanding of sin. It was, for example, a sin to steal from a fellow slave who, like yourself, had nothing. But it was not necessarily a sin to steal food or clothing from the master. He had "aplenty," as the slaves would say, while their children were hungry and naked. God would understand your necessity and forgive you your small transgression.

It was in their conception of the devil that the slaves' remembrance of their African religion was most evident. To white Protestant slave owners, the devil was the Antichrist, the embodiment of evil. To the slaves, however, the devil was just another powerful spirit, albeit a malevolent one. African religions often contained such entities. They were spirits one tried to avoid, but if one was trapped by a devil, African faiths taught that through wit and guile, the spirit could be overcome. Thus, white slave owners were befuddled when a slave, threatened with a whipping or worse, would joke and lie. In the slave's eyes, the man about to punish him was simply possessed by a devil with whom he might be able to negotiate. Sometimes this strategy actually worked. A master would become so exasperated, yet amused, by his slave's excuses and self-deprecation that he would withdraw his threat of punishment. This is only one example of how slaves' African heritage prevented them from making the European distinction between secular and religious behavior. They used their religious vision of the world to help them cope with everyday crises between themselves and their masters.

EDUCATION. A scholar once defined education as "all the ways a culture tries to perpetuate itself from one generation to another." Slave owners, in their defense of their peculiar institution, often claimed that slavery was a "school" that helped "civilize" the "savage African." White Southerners proved to be right about slavery being a school, but, much to their surprise and dismay, not the sort they had intended. When emancipation came, they discovered that slavery had taught blacks how to be *Americans* and to demand all the attributes of freedom enjoyed by other Americans.

Slaves were legally denied the foundation of European education—the knowledge to read and write. Nonetheless, thousands of slaves acquired those skills, usually through voluntary or unintentional help from their young masters and mistresses as they were learning their lessons. (Urban slaves like Frederick Douglass sometimes bribed their white playmates or coworkers to teach them.) Literate slaves then tried to pass on their knowledge to others. It was a special goal of older slaves to learn enough to read the Bible before they died.

Because of the peculiar nature of slavery, forms of education within it were frequently unorthodox. One method of education within the slave community clearly had African roots. This was the teaching of survival strategies through folktales, usually ones involving animals. Many of these stories have come down to us as "Br'er Rabbit" tales. Too often, these have been dismissed as merely charming stories to entertain children. They were that, but—in the complex society of slavery—they served other purposes as well. Western African folklore is full of tales about the hare, who is usually a trickster. In the African American stories, Br'er Rabbit is the hero; he is a weak animal in a forest full of larger, more powerful animals that could not be overcome through direct confrontation. The big animals, however, tended to be clumsy and stupid because they never had to work hard to get what they wanted; they also tended to be very greedy. As a result, the smaller animals could sometimes triumph over the larger ones through wit and guile, through tricking the big animals into using their greater strength against themselves.

Slave owners tended to see these tales as harmless. In fact, slave elders were using them to teach their young the all-important skills of "handling master." They should never confront whites directly. But whites were not very bright, as was best proven by their belief that blacks were stupid. It was important never to disabuse the master of that belief. You would thereby be able to get away with things that were otherwise forbidden. For example, if you could convince the master that you were so terrified of the dark that he did not try to make you work late at night, you then had the opportunity to sneak away for a secret prayer meeting or to visit a loved one on another plantation.

ATTITUDES TOWARD WORK. Nowhere were the consequences of this secret education more apparent than in slave work habits on the plantations. There is no doubt that slavery was enormously profitable for large plantation owners. This did not mean, however, that slave labor was efficient. Slaves worked from sunup to sundown in awful conditions. They were usually ill-housed, ill-clothed, and ill-fed. For most slaves, their primary motivation for labor was fear of physical punishment. So, without real incentives to be productive, to take pride in their work, slaves did everything they could to minimize their labor and to do it as poorly as they could without being punished.

Slaves were shrewd in their avoidance of work. They feigned ignorance so that the master could not trust them with livestock or complex machinery. They would claim that illness prevented them from working. They pretended to be superstitious to avoid unpleasant tasks. For example, they might claim a swamp that needed draining was inhabited by "haunts" that would attack them.

All of these tactics were known to slaveowners. They knew that slaves often deliberately lost livestock and sabotaged machinery, but they could seldom prove it. Moreover, they themselves claimed that the slaves were stupid. To acknowledge that the slaves were outwitting them would undermine their authority. Slave owners tried to dismiss the slaves' superstitions, but secretly they shared some of them. They risked even more inefficiency if they tried to force slaves to work when the majority claimed that they were too terrified to do so. Finally, slave owners were completely confounded by slaves' claims of illness. They knew their bondsmen were skilled at faking all kinds of symptoms. They also knew that an unchecked epidemic could sweep through the usually overcrowded and unsanitary slave quarters, incapacitating the entire work force. This could result not only in the loss of the precious cash crop but also in the deaths of equally valuable property: enslaved human beings.

African American slaves, through their commitment to family, their devotion to their religion, their acquisition of education, and their rationing of their labor, forced compromises from their owners. The master unquestionably remained the more powerful force in the relationship. Nevertheless, within the small space that compromises created in the brutal system of bondage, slaves were able to carve out lives that allowed many of them to retain their humanity and courage. When freedom came, they were ready. It was their former masters who were not.

— ROBERT FRANCIS ENGS

SMITH, E. KIRBY

Smith, E. Kirby (1824–1893), general. Edmund Kirby Smith was born at St. Augustine, Florida, on May 16,

1824. Two years before his birth his New England parents moved to the Florida Territory where his father served as a Federal judge. As a young man Smith attended school in Alexandria, Virginia, before entering West Point where he graduated in 1845, twenty-fifth in a class of forty-one. He fought in the Mexican War under both Zachary Taylor and Winfield Scott and then went on to a career in the U.S. Army. When Abraham Lincoln was elected, Smith was on duty in Texas as part of the Second U.S. Cavalry—the regiment known as Jeff Davis's own, which produced half of the full generals for the Confederate States.

As a young man Smith had gone by the name Ted or Ned, and his elder brother Ephraim Kirby Smith had used E. Kirby Smith. But sometime after the elder Smith died in the Mexican War, the younger brother began signing his name as E. Kirby Smith, and in 1861 this was how he endorsed all official correspondence.

When Texas seceded, Smith was in charge of Camp Colorado in West Texas but evacuated his command on February 26 after surrendering the post to Col. Henry Eustace McCulloch. Smith was in line for promotion when he resigned his commission to join the Confederacy. Upon hearing this Earl Van Dorn wrote the Confederate secretary of war: "Major Smith has always been considered by the Army as one of its leading spirits . . . .He is so well known to the President, however, that it would be superfluous to say anything to call his attention to his merits as an officer."

Although Van Dorn requested that his friend be assigned to him in Texas, Smith was placed in command at Lynchburg, Virginia. But he was soon assigned to Joseph E. Johnston at Harpers Ferry and became the general's adjutant. On June 17, 1861, while at Winchester, Smith was promoted to brigadier general and accompanied Johnston to Manassas. He was slightly wounded in the battle, a bullet striking him near his collarbone, and while recovering from his wound at Lynchburg, he married Cassie Selden. Smith was promoted to major general on October 11 and assigned a division in P. G. T. Beauregard's Potomac District. During the winter Smith was ordered to report to Richmond, and in March he took command of the Department of East Tennessee at Knoxville.

In the summer of 1862 Smith was part of the Confederate plan for a far-reaching offensive in the West. One army under Braxton Bragg would move north toward Kentucky while Smith marched from Knoxville. By September both armies had reached Kentucky where they had a chance to cut the supply line for Don Carlos Buell's army in Tennessee. Over Smith's objections, the two armies met at Frankfort to inaugurate a Confederate governor, but the approach of Federal troops broke up the ceremony. Although the

"KIRBY SMITHDOM"

Described by Robert E. Lee as "one of our best officers," Gen. E. Kirby Smith fought in Virginia before taking command of the Trans-Mississippi Department.

CIVIL WAR LIBRARY AND MUSEUM, PHILADELPHIA

early offenses were successful, the campaign failed because of a lack of cooperation between the two armies. After the Battle of Perryville on October 8 the Southern armies withdrew to Tennessee, and Smith returned to Knoxville on October 24. Depressed over the recent failures, Smith thought about resigning and entering the ministry, a move he had contemplated before, but on October 26 he learned of his promotion to lieutenant general.

Although still at his post in Knoxville in late December, Smith, early in January 1863, was called to Richmond where he was reassigned to duty west of the Mississippi River. This apparently came as a result of a combination of reasons; the relationship between Smith and Bragg was strained, and President Jefferson Davis needed to appoint a competent commander west of the Mississippi. Robert E. Lee had recently written Davis: "I need not remind you of the merits of General E. K. Smith whom I consider one of our best officers." On January 14, 1863, Smith was ordered to take command of the Southwestern Army, but on February 9, while on his way to Alexandria, Louisiana, he received a second communication that read "The command of Lieut. Gen. E. Kirby Smith is extended so as to embrace the Trans-Mississippi Department." He replaced the unpopular Theophilus H. Holmes and thus entered a new phase of his career.

After the surrender of Vicksburg and Port Hudson in the summer of 1863 the Trans-Mississippi region was virtually isolated from the rest of the Confederacy; operating independently, the area became known as

"Kirby Smithdom." Not all the commanders in the region were pleased with Smith's measures. Most important, he had several disagreements about strategy with the influential Maj. Gen. Richard Taylor, who commanded in Louisiana. But President Davis gave Smith a wide range of powers and backed them up by promoting him to the permanent rank of general in the Provisional Army on February 19, 1864.

The greatest threat to Smith's department came in the spring of 1864 when two Federal armies moved toward Shreveport, Louisiana. Nathaniel P. Banks pushed his army up the Red River, being stopped at Mansfield and Pleasant Hill in April, while Frederick Steele marched his army south out of Little Rock toward the same objective. Neither succeeded, but the results of the campaign magnified the differences between Smith and Taylor, and the outcome of this was Taylor's transfer out of the department. Another controversial act was Smith's independent appointment of several Confederate generals, many of whom were later rejected by Richmond.

As the war drew to an end, Smith moved his headquarters from Shreveport to Houston. On June 2 he officially signed a surrender agreement aboard a Federal steamer in Galveston Harbor, but fearing that he might be arrested, he fled to Mexico. He returned to the United States several months later and signed an amnesty oath on November 14 at Lynchburg.

After the war Smith held various positions. Two companies he was associated with, the Accident Insurance Company and the Atlantic and Pacific Telegraph Company, failed. He also served as president of the University of Nashville before moving to Sewanee, Tennessee, in 1875 where he taught at the University of the South. He was the last survivor of the eight full Confederate generals, dying on March 28, 1893. Smith was buried in Sewanee Cemetery.

— ANNE J. BAILEY

SMITH, WILLIAM "EXTRA BILLY"

Smith, William "Extra Billy" (1797–1887), major general, Virginia congressman and governor. Smith grew up in a well-to-do, middle-class plantation family near Fredericksburg. He received a sound education at private academies, clerked in several law offices, and in 1818 became a practicing attorney in the upper Piedmont, first at Culpeper and then at Warrenton. He married and started a large family. He did some farming with slave labor and ran a successful mail and coach service that wangled so many extra fees from the post

office that he won the enduring nickname "Extra Billy."

An ardent Jacksonian Democrat, he soon became primarily a politician. From 1836 to 1841 he served in the state senate and from 1841 to 1843 in the U.S. House of Representatives. Then the state legislature elected him governor. He served from January 1, 1846, to December 31, 1848, enthusiastically and effectively supporting the war against Mexico. He was especially successful in mobilizing Virginia troops for combat. As soon as his term was over, Smith moved alone to California to recoup his finances, and he prospered by practicing law and speculating in land. In 1853 he returned to his family in Virginia and almost immediately won election again to the U.S. House of Representatives where he served until 1861.

When war erupted the sixty-three-year-old Smith volunteered to serve his state in combat, and Governor John Letcher appointed him colonel of the Forty-ninth Virginia Infantry Regiment. Brave but inexperienced, Colonel Smith was a barely adequate military leader, though he saw much action and was wounded in the Peninsular campaign and more seriously at Sharpsburg in September 1862. Eight months later Brigadier General Smith returned to active duty in time for the Battle of Chancellorsville, but a poor performance at Gettysburg led to his removal from combat command and reassignment to recruiting duties where his gubernatorial experience during the Mexican War proved useful.

During the first two years of the war Smith had also been a member of the Confederate Congress. Since he participated only while on leave from the army, he played a minor role, concentrating on financial and military affairs and generally supporting President Jefferson Davis and the Confederate central government. Then Smith returned to full-time politics by winning a second term as governor of the state. Virginians were distracted by the war, but Major General Smith won a large majority of the army vote, and on January 1, 1864, he began his new administration.

The new governor was elected to serve four years, but the massive Union war machine had already gained a clear advantage over the battered Southern armies. In reality Smith would hold office only a little over fifteen months within the doomed Confederacy.

At first he occasionally bogged down in routine matters, but generally he performed efficiently. Like his predecessor, John Letcher, he followed the practical policy of broadly cooperating with the Confederate government, and, again like Letcher, he urged Virginians to put away for the duration of the war their traditional devotion to state rights, individual freedoms, and strict legalism and to strive even harder for victory. And just like Letcher, he clashed frequently with the increasingly disaffected legislature.

Concerned about Virginia's growing vulnerability, Governor Smith tried to marshal new home defense forces, but the steadily expanding Confederate draft soon drained away manpower from this program. Smith yielded to the draft and called out his few remaining state troops whenever the Confederates made such a request. He also supported Confederate efforts to reduce the number of draft-exempt state and local officials, a scam all over the South, and he especially opposed exempting such officials who had refugeed from enemy-held parts of Virginia, though he did occasionally yield to local protests. He cooperated, too, with Confederate impressment, including the seizure of slave laborers, always an especially sensitive issue. He even ordered state officials to seize uncooperative saltworks in southwestern Virginia, something his predecessor could never quite bring himself to do. And finally Governor Smith acceded to rapidly expanding Confederate control of Virginia's manufacturing facilities and transportation systems. Inevitably these emergency wartime policies led to rising protests that were soon concentrated in the restive legislature, but the pragmatic governor knew that extraordinary, even desperate measures had to be taken if the South was to have any real hope of victory.

A combat veteran, Smith was fully aware of the desperate manpower shortage in the Confederate armed forces. The South still had one great untapped manpower pool—slaves, black Southerners by the hundreds of thousands. Early in 1862 invading Union armies had begun to recruit Southern blacks, and after the Emancipation Proclamation this policy accelerated, so that by the end of the war the Union armed forces had enlisted almost 200,000 blacks, mostly Southerners. Yet even as the war dragged on and Southern casualties soared, the Confederates hesitated to take this final step.

Then in September 1864 Louisiana governor Henry W. Allen's secret call for the use of black troops surfaced. The next month the governors of Virginia, Alabama, Georgia, Mississippi, and the Carolinas met in Augusta, Georgia, and Smith prodded them into issuing a resolution obliquely calling for the use of black troops. Finally, very late in the war, the Davis administration itself moved toward this position.

With Atlanta lost and Abraham Lincoln reelected, Governor Smith in December appealed to the hostile legislature to begin recruiting slaves as soldiers. Conservative Virginia wavered, but when Robert E. Lee called for black troops in January 1865, Smith renewed his appeals, and finally early in March the legislators approved furnishing black Virginians to the Confederate army. In the middle of March the Confederate Congress passed similar legislation, and, thanks in part to continued agitation by Governor Smith, the War Department's new regulations for slave soldiers promised freedom for honorable service. Never in his career had Smith challenged slavery or the assumption of black inferiority upon which it was based, but he saw the desperate need for new manpower and placed contemporary crisis ahead of old dogma. A dramatic, indeed radical change in recruitment finally came, but Virginia and the Confederacy had waited far too long; the war was already lost.

The governor also pushed other sweeping changes during his administration. He early advocated action to control inflation, but the legislature delayed, and the Confederates also failed to restrain the soaring prices that were undermining the Southern economy. After the legislature rejected one of his specific appropriations, the governor tapped his own contingency funds and borrowed more money from a Richmond bank to finance the operation of his state supply system to ease some extreme shortages. A few scarce items began to come in from abroad and from the Deep South, but again it was too little too late as the economy continued to disintegrate.

Early in his administration Governor Smith did gain one large appropriation from the legislature to combat the clothing shortage. He set up a new bureaucracy to obtain cotton and cotton cards to sell to the people at reasonable prices, and he even talked the Confederates into handing over a mill where cotton cloth could be cheaply manufactured. But such stopgap measures could not halt the accelerating decline of Virginia and the Confederacy.

Throughout his administration of slightly more than fifteen months, Governor Smith's best efforts made much sense. He selflessly cooperated with the Confederate central government, convinced that this was the only possible way to win the war against the huge Federal military forces that threatened Virginia on several fronts. But the tide had turned too powerfully against the South. Like Davis and Lee, Smith might delay defeat, but he could not gain victory.

In the last year of the war Union armies knifed deeper and deeper into Virginia's vitals, and finally on April 1, 1865, troops under Ulysses S. Grant overran Lee's massive defenses at Petersburg. On April 3 Smith fled from Richmond just one step ahead of Federal troops. He and a pathetic remnant of the state government fled to Lynchburg and then farther west to Danville. Smith thought about fighting on after Lee surrendered on April 9. He unsuccessfully tried to take command of all remaining Confederate forces in the state and even considered guerrilla warfare. But he soon saw that his people had had enough, and on June 8 he surrendered to Federal officials in Richmond. Five

SMITH, WILLIAM "EXTRA BILLY"

"Yes, we'll rally round the flag, boys, we'll rally once again, Shouting the battle cry of Freedom."

GEORGE FREDERICK ROOT
THE BATTLE CRY OF FREEDOM, 1863

days later he went home to Warrenton and the following month received a pardon from President Andrew Johnson.

Still healthy at sixty-seven, Smith farmed for a living. He remained active in politics and in the mid-1870s served again in the state legislature. On May 18, 1887, he died at home just short of his ninetieth birthday.

— F. N. BONEY

Early in the war speculators hoarded salt, bacon, and leather, and six men gained control of the Confederacy's two nail factories.

PAGE 444

SPECIAL UNITS

Confederate elite units were many in number, spanning both the western and eastern theaters of operations, as well as the inland water navy, the high seas navy, and coastal defense units.

In the western theater of operations the infantry division of Maj. Gen. Patrick Cleburne stands out as such a unit, as do the First Missouri Brigade and the Kentucky Orphan Brigade. Nathan Bedford Forrest's cavalry and his artillery under the command of Capt. John Morton were outstanding in every respect. An elite Confederate western artillery unit was the Fifth Company, Washington Artillery of New Orleans, also known as Slocum's Battery. Other units included John Hunt Morgan's cavalry, and Capt. John Dickinson's guerrillas who operated in Florida. Another special unit, the Davis Guards, received medals (the only ones awarded by the Confederacy) for their heroic stand at Sabine Pass, Texas, in 1863.

The eastern theater of operations saw an abundance of elite ground forces. Foremost were the Stonewall Brigade and John Bell Hood's Texas Brigade, both of which were models of courage, discipline, and esprit de corps. In addition, A. P. Hill's Light Division and the Louisiana Tiger Brigade were exceptionally fine units, as was Wade Hampton's Legion, formed early in the war. The First Virginia Infantry Regiment, which traced its origin to George Washington in the French and Indian War, spearheaded George E. Pickett's charge at Gettysburg. Composing an elite unit that was not a regular part of the Army of Northern Virginia were the Virginia Military Institute cadets who gained immortality at the Battle of New Market in 1864. The Army of Northern Virginia included the famed Washington Artillery of New Orleans, the Rockbridge Artillery of the Stonewall Brigade, the Richmond Howitzers, and John Pegram's and William T. Pougue's Artillery Battalions.

Like the western theater, the Confederate cavalry in the eastern theater contained many elite units. Their names ring across the years: Turner Ashby's cavalry, John S. Mosby's Rangers, the Laurel Brigade, and J. E. B. Stuart's Cavalry Corps. Accompanying the latter was the elite Stuart Horse Artillery under John Pelham.

On the high seas the Confederacy was equally well served. Such vessels as *Alabama* and *Shenandoah* were renowned. In the inland water navy, elite units manned *Virginia* and *Tennessee*. The volunteer crew of *Hunley*, the first submarine that sank a warship, manned an experimental vessel whose previous crews had drowned during test voyages. Such courage could be found only among the finest of fighting units.

— KIM BERNARD HOLIEN

SPECULATION

Both real and imagined, speculation hit all Southerners at one point or another during the war and created bitterness and anger toward the perpetrators. Moreover, it precipitated a decline in living standards and thus affected morale.

From the beginning of its existence, the Confederacy faced the problem of how to pay for the war effort. Secretary of the Treasury Christopher G. Memminger tried a number of plans, but by the midpoint of the war, his office was forced to rely upon the printing press and loans to pay for the war. The increased circulation of paper currency produced inflation. At first, the general commodity price index stood at antebellum levels, but by 1863 it had skyrocketed to levels twenty-eight times higher than those of 1861.

The increased cost of manufactured goods and agricultural products hit people hard, especially those living in the urban centers. Residents of Richmond and Atlanta, for example, saw the cost of foodstuffs grow prohibitive: in 1864, flour was sold for $250 a barrel—when it could be had; sweet potatoes garnered $16 a bushel; and meat commanded over $2 a pound. Discontent increased in proportion to the rise in prices, and most Southerners began to seek a cause for the exorbitant cost of necessities. Initially, they blamed the Commissary Department for buying up goods for the army and thus creating shortages on the home front which led to higher prices. Soon, manufacturers were also targeted: editorials and diarists argued that the factories charged higher prices on goods for the public in order to compensate for the loss they took producing for the government at lower fixed prices. Before long, merchants and traders were also pilloried in the press and in private. Such accusations often became anti-Semitic in tone, as Confederates began equating all traders with Jews and all Jews with Shylock-like practices.

Some Southerners, mostly women, refused to accept inflation and speculators without protest. The year 1863 witnessed a number of food riots throughout the urban Confederacy. Women, beaten down by high prices, took matters into their own hands in Richmond, Atlanta, Salisbury and High Point, North Carolina, and other places and demanded relief. These outbursts of violence can be interpreted as manifestations of unrest motivated by the perception and reality that speculation and speculators caused inflation and shortages, and hence deprivation.

The extent of real speculation in the Confederate South is difficult to assess. Basically, anyone who bought food, clothing, or other goods and held them for a period of time could expect to make a profit as money became increasingly cheaper. Still, some did not realize as great a profit as critics alleged. Though a merchant or manufacturer might hold an item off the shelves for a while to realize a profit, that profit was gained in inflated currency and was probably less than the original price of the good.

Speculators did exist in the Confederacy from the very beginning. Their practices were time-honored: buy a commodity in bulk to corner the market, float rumors of shortages, and then raise prices and sell at a profit. Most speculators dealt in such goods as cotton, salt, and meat; others dealt in necessities like shoes and clothing.

Confederate state governments could not ignore the problem of speculation—public outrage as inflation grew made some type of action imperative. Governors Andrew B. Moore of Alabama and Zebulon Vance of North Carolina published denunciations of speculators and extortioners (the words were usually used synonymously) and threatened to take drastic action. But Governor Joseph E. Brown of Georgia admitted laws against speculation were largely meaningless because speculators would find a way to evade them by continuing to withhold goods from the market or by refusing to sell goods to military authorities. Brown's comments to the General Assembly of Georgia in April 1863 epitomize the kind of language used to describe speculators: They are "a class . . . who remain at home preying upon the vitals of society, determined to make money at every hazard, who turn a deaf ear to the cries of the soldiers' families and are prepared to immolate even our armies and sacrifice our liberties upon the altar of mammon." Brown saw to it that Georgia taxed those speculating in needed commodities, but like other legislation aimed at speculators, it had little effect.

Although it is true that many did seek private gain at public expense, the real reasons for inflated prices and shortages of goods lay elsewhere. Many farmers found that government policies of impressment and the tax-in-kind hurt them; consequently, they withheld food from the market or planted less, which added to the inflationary spiral. Other farmers who did produce for both the people and the army had to cope with a transportation system that was woefully inadequate: often food would rot at depots awaiting transportation to markets or the front. Finally, the Union blockade stopped the flow of European goods, adding to the shortages and inflated prices. The net effect of all these factors—poor transportation facilities, the blockade, government policies, and the unscrupulous efforts of some who sought to reap profits during wartime—created inflated prices and led to charges of speculation and extortion.

There is no doubt that speculation—real and imagined—had a tremendous impact on the Confederate nation. Diaries, newspaper editorials, and public pronouncements against speculation demonstrate that Southerners detested the problem and the culprits. Disgust with unsavory practices and the inability to obtain needed goods for survival caused many Confederates to lose faith in a government that seemed ill equipped and unprepared to deal with the problem. The net result of inflation and speculation was a noticeable decline in support for the Confederate cause.

[*See also* Bread Riots; Extortion; Inflation.]

— MARY A. DECREDICO

SPOTSYLVANIA CAMPAIGN

Spotsylvania Court House, Virginia, a county seat approximately nine miles southwest of Fredericksburg, became for a two-week period in May 1864 the focus of a series of engagements between the Army of Northern Virginia and the Army of the Potomac commanded respectively by Gens. Robert E. Lee and George G. Meade. When the opposing armies began to depart the area on the evening of May 20, the Confederates had sustained between 9,000 and 10,000 casualties here and the Federals more than 18,000.

Following two days of fighting in the Wilderness on May 5 and 6, Union General in Chief Ulysses S. Grant, who accompanied Meade's army in this summer campaign, ordered the army commander to move his force southeast twelve miles to the vicinity of Spotsylvania Court House. The movement began after dark on May 7. Lee also decided to move his First Corps to the same location during the night. The Confederates arrived just before the Federals, and the opposing advanced forces collided one and a half miles northwest of the village on the morning of May 8. Throughout the remainder of the day additional units from each army arrived and became engaged, with the Confederates maintaining their original position.

"General Grant is not going to retreat. He will move his army to Spotsylvania. I am so sure of his next move that I have already made arrangements . . . so that we may meet him there."

ROBERT E. LEE

During the campaign Lee was operating at a disadvantage concerning two of his key subordinates. His ablest corps commander, Lt. Gen. James Longstreet, had been seriously wounded by friendly troops in the Wilderness fighting. Lee selected Maj. Gen. Richard Heron Anderson to command his First Corps until "Old Pete" returned. On the morning of May 8 Third Corps commander Maj. Gen. A. P. Hill was too ill to mount his horse. Maj. Gen. Jubal Early, a division commander in Maj. Gen. Richard S. Ewell's Second Corps, was chosen to replace Hill.

On May 9 the Union Ninth Corps, commanded by Maj. Gen. Ambrose E. Burnside, advanced south from the area of Chancellorsville and assumed position east of the courthouse with its left lying on the Fredericksburg-Spotsylvania Court House Road. As a result, when Early's Third Corps arrived, Lee placed it opposite Burnside's troops immediately east of the village. In the morning a Confederate sharpshooter killed the commander of the Union Sixth Corps, Maj. Gen. John Sedgwick. On this day, the Union's chief of cavalry, Maj. Gen. Philip Sheridan, led most of the Federal cavalry corps from the area on a raid south toward Richmond. Lee dispatched his chief of cavalry, Maj. Gen. J. E. B. Stuart, with Maj. Gen. Fitzhugh Lee's division to pursue the Federal horsemen. Two days later Stuart was mortally wounded in an engagement at Yellow Tavern, immediately north of Richmond. This was a crippling loss to the Confederacy.

At Spotsylvania the Confederate battle line consisted of Anderson's First Corps on the left and Ewell's Second in the center; both of these units faced north. Early's Third Corps manned the right of the line facing east. The center of the line occupied by Ewell's troops bulged forward to the north in the form of a salient, or "mule-shoe."

On May 10 the Federals executed attacks all along the line but were unable to coordinate them. Union Maj. Gen. Winfield S. Hancock's Second Corps advanced beyond Anderson's left flank, but darkness fell before the Northerners were prepared to assault that vulnerable flank. Late in the afternoon twelve Union regiments commanded by Col. Emory Upton succeeded in penetrating a segment of Ewell's line along the western face of the salient and captured nearly a thousand Confederates. The Unionists were not supported, however, and were pushed back by Confederate reserve forces. Upton's temporary success gave Grant an idea. The twelve regiments had been massed compactly and had penetrated the Southern position with relative ease. Grant ordered Meade to move Hancock's entire Second Corps from the right of the Union line to the center opposite Ewell and with it attack the tip or apex of the Confederate salient at first light on May 12.

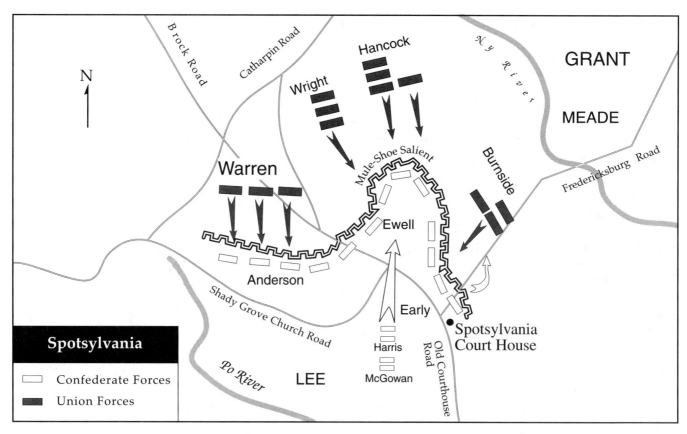

Spotsylvania

▭ Confederate Forces
■ Union Forces

On May 11 General Lee, evaluating certain Union activities behind their lines such as reconnaissance missions and the repositioning of supply wagons, erroneously concluded that the Federals were preparing to break contact that night and move east to Fredericksburg and thence south toward Richmond. If this occurred, the Southern commander was determined to attack the Federals in transit. He ordered his artillery corps commanders to move rearward after dark any batteries that would be difficult to relocate rapidly once a movement by the army had been determined. Thus, many of the guns positioned along the apex of the salient were withdrawn.

As Hancock's troops moved into position for the attack, they were heard by Ewell's pickets who immediately reported these sounds. Ewell was eventually persuaded by one of his division commanders, Maj. Gen. Edward ("Allegheny") Johnson, whose division was positioned along the apex of the salient, to recall the artillery pieces that had been withdrawn. The recall order did not reach the artillerymen in the rear until 3:40 A.M.

Visibility on the morning of May 12 was reduced to fifty yards by ground fog. Hancock's troops began their advance at 4:35 A.M. Their number totaled 19,000 with the two leading divisions consisting of 11,000. "Allegheny" Johnson's division of 4,000 infantrymen would bear the brunt of this onslaught with little artillery support. Some Confederate pickets were captured. Others fired a hasty round and took to their heels. They warned their comrades manning the main line of the mass of Federals approaching, but the troops could only wait until the Bluecoats became visible about a hundred yards in front. At this time the orders to fire were given. Rain had fallen intermittently during the night, and much of the Southern powder was damp and did not ignite. The Northerners poured over the works in overwhelming numbers. The returning artillery pieces arrived at this time and were overrun and captured. A few gun crews were able to fire a round or two before surrendering.

Many of the Federals continued to advance southward inside of the salient in disorganized groups. These were stopped and driven back to the outside of the works by Confederate reserves. Approximately 3,000 Southerners including "Allegheny" Johnson were captured in the attack along with twenty pieces of artillery.

With most of Johnson's division gone, a considerable segment of the line was unoccupied on the inside by any Confederate troops. To correct this, Lee forwarded two brigades from the Third Corps during the morning. These were Brig. Gen. Nathaniel H. Harris's Mississippi Brigade and the South Carolinians of Brig. Gen. Samuel McGowan's brigade who arrived on the scene at 7:30 A.M. and 9:30 A.M., respectively. These troops upon arrival drove the Federals away from the outside of the works and reoccupied a portion of the trench line formerly held by Johnson's troops. McGowan was wounded in the advance to the front line and was superseded in command by Col. Joseph N. Brown. By noon the entire Federal Sixth Corps, now commanded by Brig. Gen. Horatio G. Wright, had been moved opposite Harris's and McGowan's positions.

These opposing forces—Harris's and Brown's brigades inside the works, and the Union Sixth Corps and portions of Hancock's Second outside—retained their relative positions along the northern face of the salient front and maintained continuous fire of varying intensity until 4:00 the following morning. At times the antagonists were only twenty yards apart. Occasionally an impulsive surge forward by a hundred or so Northerners would carry over the works and be immediately hurled back in bloody hand-to-hand fighting. Rain fell intermittently during the afternoon.

While this desperate fighting occurred, other Confederates were constructing a new defensive line of works across the base of the salient nearly one mile to the rear. Finally, at 4:00 A.M., Harris's, Brown's, and the remaining Confederate troops in position along the sides of the salient were permitted to retire to the new line. Thus ended what was probably the most intense twenty-three-hour period of land warfare in a confined area up to that time.

The operations conducted during the remaining ten days of the campaign were anticlimactic. The Army of the Potomac joined the Ninth Corps east of the village where its line lay in a north-south direction facing west. The Confederates changed their relative alignment accordingly. The opposing forces departed the vicinity of Spotsylvania Court House on May 21 and May 22. They would meet again at the North Anna River.

Assuming that Lee's objective in the campaign was to keep the enemy out of central Virginia by holding the line of the Rapidan River, the Battle of Spotsylvania can be considered a strategic defeat. After the Wilderness fighting on May 7 and again on May 21, Lee was unable to prevent the Federals from moving their forces in the direction they desired. This had not happened before in northern Virginia during the war.

The Army of Northern Virginia had once again inflicted severe casualties upon its old antagonist, but its own losses were in some respects more damaging. On May 12 alone Lee lost the services of one major general and seven brigadier generals. During the two weeks of Spotsylvania, 4,600 troops from Ewell's Second Corps became prisoners. Lee could not readily replace these losses.

For fourteen days near the Spotsylvania Court House the armies locked in incessant combat, often fighting over imposing lines of breastworks in a first precursor of the trench warfare of later conflicts.

PAGE 30

"Death, in its silent, sure march is fast gathering those whom I have longest loved, so that when he shall knock at my door, I will more willingly follow."

ROBERT E. LEE
1869

Spotsylvania was only one of the many series of battles that swept across Virginia in May and early June of 1864. It took a heavy toll of experienced officers and invaluable enlisted men from the Army of Northern Virginia. These losses contributed significantly to the weakening of the Confederacy's military capabilities.

[*See also* Yellow Tavern, Virginia.]

— WILLIAM D. MATTER

STATE DEPARTMENT

Diplomacy could not ensure the Confederacy's independence, but it could open channels of communication to the major powers of Europe and encourage the assertion of foreign interests that favored the Southern cause. With the formation of the Confederate State Department on February 21, 1861, Jefferson Davis selected Robert Toombs, a leading Georgia Whig and recent member of the U.S. Senate, as secretary. Toombs's detailed instructions of March 16, 1861, to the Confederate commissioners—William Lowndes Yancey, Pierre A. Rost, and A. Dudley Mann—inaugurated the Confederate quest for European recognition. To aid the commissioners Toombs provided a full rationale for Southern secession and delineated all the political and moral reasons why the Confederacy merited membership in the family of nations.

While the commissioners made their way to London, Toombs lost interest in the department. His staff was small, and except for writing occasional instructions, he found little to occupy his time. He once refused to accept additional assistants, explaining, in the words of the *Daily Richmond Examiner,* that he "carried the business of the State Department around in his hat." In May 1861 the Confederate government moved from Montgomery to Richmond. There the State Department acquired offices, as did the president, on the upper floor of a spacious granite building known as the Federal Customs House. In July, Toombs, long preferring a military career, sought and obtained an appointment as brigadier general. He fought at Manassas and Sharpsburg in 1862, resigned, and returned to Georgia in 1863.

President Davis named Robert M. T. Hunter of Virginia as Toombs's successor. During his long political career Hunter had remained a Democrat and a strong defender of slavery and its expansion. In 1861 he was, like Toombs, a member of the U.S. Senate. Hunter was far more learned and methodical than Toombs, however, and had a better grasp of public affairs. His elaborate instructions to James M. Mason and John Slidell, commissioned to London and Paris,

respectively, in September 1861, embodied the grand policy of the Confederacy toward the European powers. Hunter argued again that the Confederacy was not a coalition of rebellious states but a country presenting itself to the world "through a Government competent to discharge its civil functions, and strong enough to be responsible for its actions to the other nations of the earth." He emphasized the ineffectiveness of the Federal blockade and its contravention of the Treaty of Paris (1856), which declared that blockades, to be legal, had also to be effective.

Hunter saw the immense danger to Confederate interests in Europe's refusal to challenge the blockade; it permitted the North, with a minimum of naval power, to seriously curtail the Southern war effort. Despite his determination to enlist European support, Hunter was powerless to capitalize on the South's victory at Manassas in July 1861 and the *Trent* affair of November and December. The decision of Union naval captain Charles Wilkes to remove two Confederate leaders from the British mail-steamer *Trent* unleashed a seething anger in Britain and, for expectant Southerners, the specter of war and a British-Confederate alliance. But Lincoln and Secretary of State William H. Seward acknowledged Wilkes's error, freed the Confederates, and quickly terminated the crisis. Hunter left the State Department in March 1862 to become a senator from Virginia, a position he held until the end of the war. Beyond Europe's acknowledgment of Confederate belligerency in May 1861, Confederate diplomacy had achieved nothing.

During March, as the Confederacy's permanent government went into effect, President Davis faced the task of reconstituting his generally unpopular cabinet. Among its least popular members was Judah P. Benjamin, then temporary secretary of war. Benjamin, who had the appearance of a stocky, prosperous shopkeeper, was renowned for his wit and intelligence, his strong yet ingratiating personality, and a fatalism that attributed importance only to the present. A New Orleans lawyer of major repute, he had won election to the U.S. Senate in 1852 and, like Toombs and Hunter, was a member of that body in 1861. Benjamin had entered the cabinet in February 1861 as attorney general, a position too confining for his energy and ambition. His open criticism of the Southern war effort led him to the War Department, where Secretary Leroy P. Walker had found the challenge of organizing and directing the Confederate army beyond his capabilities. Upon Walker's resignation in September, the president appointed Benjamin acting secretary of war. Benjamin brought order to the department, but made mistakes and carried the blame for the army's reverses after Manassas. Nevertheless

Davis appointed him secretary of state in the permanent cabinet.

Benjamin inherited from Hunter his assistant secretary, William M. Browne, a former Washington newspaperman. Browne, a man of considerable talent and totally acceptable to Benjamin, resigned in April to become a member of President Davis's personal staff. Benjamin did not fill Browne's position but relied rather on the department's chief clerk, Lucius Quinton Washington, formerly an editorial writer for the *Richmond Examiner*. Washington, who had entered the department in November 1861, remained at his post until April 1865. The other members of the State Department staff consisted of three clerks, a messenger, and a laborer—Philip Green, a hired slave. A Northern visitor described Benjamin's office in 1864 as unattractive, with maps and battle plans on the walls, a tier of shelves loaded with books in one corner, and a green-baize-covered desk, littered with papers, in the middle of the room.

Years later Washington recalled Benjamin's high competence as secretary of state:

> He was a man of wonderful and varied gifts, rare eloquence and accomplishments, a great lawyer, senator, and man of affairs. He could despatch readily and speedily a very large amount of business. I have known him to compose a most important State paper of twenty pages or more at a single sitting in a clear, neat chirography, and hardly a single word interlined or erased. His style was a model of ease and perspicuity.

President Davis set great value on Benjamin's services and friendship. Their offices were separated by only a hundred feet, permitting Benjamin to visit the president almost every day to discuss the problems confronting the Confederacy.

Benjamin was determined to succeed where his predecessors had failed. In letters to Mason and Slidell on April 8, 1862, he launched an attack on the legitimacy of the blockade by listing over a hundred vessels that had passed between Southern and foreign ports during November, December, and January. Seven European nations including the five great powers had, in the Treaty of Paris, adopted the principle that blockades "to be binding, must be effective—that is to say, maintained by a force sufficient really to prevent access to the coast of the enemy." The Confederation had accepted that principle.

Then on February 11, 1862, British foreign minister Earl Russell explained to Lord Lyons in Washington:

> Her Majesty's government . . . are of opinion that, assuming that the blockade was duly notified and also that a number of ships is stationed and remains at the entrance of a port sufficient really to prevent access to it, or to create an evident danger of entering it or leaving it, *and that these ships do not voluntarily permit ingress or egress, the fact that various ships may have successfully escaped through it . . . will not of itself prevent the blockade from being an effectual one by international law.*

Benjamin observed that the underscored words in Russell's statement did not appear in the Treaty of Paris and seemed to be an abandonment of its principles. He noted additionally that Russell's defense of the British decision hinged on the premise that the ships stationed at the entrance of a port were sufficient to prevent access or at least to render it dangerous. The fact that vessels moved freely through the blockade challenged the validity of the British assumption. "The absurdity of pretending that 2,500 miles of seacoast are guarded by the United States 'by a force sufficient really to prevent access,'" he wrote, "is too glaring to require comment; yet it is for this extravagant assumption that the United States claim and neutral powers accord respect." By Russell's definition, Benjamin added, any blockade could be rendered effective if, by common consent, no nation chose to challenge it.

Benjamin simultaneously assaulted Europe's refusal to recognize the Confederacy as a separate nation. Nonrecognition, he reminded Mason, merely sustained an unnecessary war by perpetuating the notion that conquest of the South was possible. But recognition, as the verdict of an impartial jury, Benjamin predicted, would lead to "the immediate organization of a large and influential party in the Northern States favorable to putting an end to the war." Thus Britain, with little effort or detriment to its interests, could end the desolating struggle in America.

Benjamin's special appeal for French recognition focused on material considerations. He offered that country a Southern commercial dependency by instructing Slidell to propose a treaty under which the South would accept French products free of duty for a specified period of time in exchange for France's abandonment of its policies regarding recognition and the blockade. Benjamin suggested that the Confederacy supply French merchant vessels in designated ports 100,000 bales of cotton, worth enough to "maintain afloat a considerable fleet for a length of time quite sufficient to open the Atlantic and Gulf ports to the commerce of France." Benjamin wanted the French, like the British, to understand that the continuance of the war was "attributable in no small degree to the attitude of the European powers in abstaining from the acknowledgement of our independent existence as a nation of the earth."

When pressed by a would-be bureaucrat for a job in the State Department, Toombs removed his hat and informed the supplicant that his entire department was inside.

PAGE 612

When Judah Benjamin resigned as war secretary, Davis, as a reward for loyalty, promptly named him secretary of state.

PAGE 51

Emboldened by the Confederate military successes of June and July 1862, especially in Virginia, Benjamin framed a new approach to break Europe's neutrality. During July Mason and Slidell, on their own, agreed to demand recognition as a matter of right, but concluded that such a course, without the leverage of additional Confederate victories, would produce only further European alienation. On August 14, however, Benjamin advised A. Dudley Mann, assigned to Brussels in September 1861 with the appointments of Mason and Slidell, that further communications with foreign governments would presume the unquestioned justice of the Confederate cause. Earlier Confederate efforts to explain the South's right to secede may have been proper, Benjamin conceded, but when common sense had failed to elicit any response but a timid neutrality, he concluded, "we prefer speaking in other tones and insisting that an admission into the family of nations is a right which we have conquered by the sword." In November Benjamin instructed L. Q. C. Lamar, commissioner to Russia, that he should not maintain the Southern right of secession unless the czar's government should inquire about it, but rather insist that the Confederacy had won its right to recognition in war.

In August 1863, convinced that Britain would never grant recognition or modify its attitude toward the blockade, Benjamin ordered Mason to conclude his mission and withdraw from London unless the British cabinet revealed a changed attitude. After receiving Benjamin's instructions on September 21 and conferring with Slidell, Mason departed for Paris. For more than a year Benjamin had argued that breaking the blockade would enhance British commerce and that recognition would bring peace, but he failed to convince the British ministry.

In September 1863 Benjamin turned to France, reminding the emperor of the damage that Europe's recognition of the Federal blockade had imposed on the South. He instructed Slidell to urge the French government to stop giving countenance "either to the validity of the pretended blockade, . . . or to the innovations and modifications which the Government of Great Britain has attempted to engraft on the declaration of Paris in derogation . . . of the rights of all other parties." In November the French minister, Édouard Drouyn de Lhuys, declared that France was not responsible for Europe's decision on the blockade and that the vulnerability of French interests in Europe and Mexico ruled out any policy that might antagonize the governments in London and Washington. In the end Benjamin revealed only contempt for French behavior, troubled by the contrast between the emperor's perennial professions of sympathy for the Southern cause and his persistent subservience to the anti-Confederate policies of Britain and the United States.

In a dispatch to Slidell on December 27, 1864, Benjamin lamented the contribution that the neutral powers had made to the Union cause. Why, he wondered, had the Europeans refused to recognize the Confederacy? He concluded that the elusive element had been the South's failure to offer a program of emancipation. He dispatched Duncan F. Kenner, congressman from Louisiana, to convey such a proposal to Mason and Slidell in Paris. In March 1865 the French emperor assured Slidell that the offer of emancipation would not have influenced his decision regarding recognition; in London Prime Minister Lord Palmerston offered the same response to Mason.

Before Benjamin could receive the assurance that slavery had not damaged the Southern cause in Europe, the Confederacy no longer existed. The secretary had acknowledged often enough that the experience on the battlefield would determine the success of Southern diplomacy no less than the future of the Confederacy itself. His quest for recognition and foreign cooperation failed because he could never convince Europe's leaders that Confederate arms would triumph. With the fall of Richmond, Benjamin, in a variety of disguises, fled to the Florida coast and made his way to Europe. Throughout the war his wife and family had resided in Paris. Benjamin chose, however, to move to England where he became a distinguished member of the English bar, leaving behind the trials of his Confederate years as if they had never occurred.

[*See also* Blockade, *overview article;* Great Britain; Mexico; Trent Affair; *and selected biographies of figures mentioned herein.*]

— NORMAN A. GRAEBNER

STATE NAVIES

Seven Southern states—South Carolina, Georgia, Florida, North Carolina, Louisiana, Alabama, and Texas—established state navies following secession and prior to joining the Confederacy. Each state had a different conception of its navy's function. Georgia floated the Naval Coast Guard; Florida called its service the Marine Police; and North Carolina operated a force of small steamers dubbed the Mosquito Fleet.

Although each state gave its navy a different name, all had similar characteristics. They were makeshift forces comprising former Federal vessels and merchant steamers. The ships flew the state flag, performing coastal patrols. They served as much for peace of mind as for action against the enemy. Officers were commissioned in state service at the rank held in the U.S. Navy or Revenue Cutter Service.

South Carolina was the first state to create a navy; it also commissioned the largest fleet. It seized vessels and armed them, making them serviceable. On December 30, 1860, ten days after declaring secession, South Carolina took over the revenue schooner *William Aiken* at Charleston. In the following weeks a lighthouse tender schooner, a coastal passenger side-wheeler, and two coast survey schooners were added to the South Carolina State Navy. The state purchased the iron propeller tug *James Gray* at Charleston, armed it, and renamed it *Lady Davis*. The large coastal passenger side-wheeler *Marion* was seized and armed.

The Georgia State Navy arose from a resolution of the Georgia state convention on January 25, 1861, six days after secession, authorizing the navy to procure three steamers to defend the state. The first officer appointed was Lt. John McIntosh Kell of Darien. On February 25, Kell purchased the side-wheel steamer *Everglade*, which was armed and renamed *Savannah*. Three days later, Capt. Josiah Tattnall became senior flag officer. *Savannah* reported ready for service March 7. The 500-ton sidewheel steamer *Huntress* was bought at New York by a "Mr. Hall" and armed. The U.S. steamer *Ida* was seized by the state. The Georgia navy was absorbed into the Confederate States Navy in mid-April 1861. *Savannah* and *Ida* were both taken into the navy under the same names. They operated in the Naval Coast Guard squadron primarily on the Georgia coast. *Huntress* later became the blockade runner *Tropic*.

Florida seized the coast survey schooner *F. W. Dana*, used it briefly, and released it. The state also seized the U.S. war steamer *Fulton* under repair at the Pensacola Navy Yard. The state employed the schooner *Judah* as a vessel of the Florida Marine Police.

North Carolina's Mosquito Fleet acquired the 207-ton passenger steamer *J. E. Coffee*, armed it, and renamed it *Winslow*. Four river tugs rounded out the fleet. *Winslow* captured sixteen prizes while operating out of Hatteras Inlet. It was lost while attempting to rescue a shipwrecked crew. When North Carolina joined the Confederacy, the entire flotilla entered the navy. It fought in several battles in the sounds of North Carolina.

The state of Louisiana likewise seized revenue service vessels: the schooner *Robert McClelland* and the brig *Washington* at New Orleans on January 26. The state also seized the armament of the cutter *Lewis Cass*, using it to arm other vessels.

Alabama seized two Federal vessels for the state. The revenue cutter service schooner *Lewis Cass*, and the lighthouse tender schooner *Alert* were taken on January 30, 1861, at Mobile. *Lewis Cass* was later transferred to the Confederate States Navy.

The commander of the decrepit revenue service schooner *Henry Dodge*, armed with one pivot gun,

turned it over to the state of Texas on March 2, 1862, at Galveston. Texas operated a Marine Department throughout the war as an adjunct of the Confederate forces. The department was instrumental in the recapture of Galveston in 1864, seizing seven vessels in the process.

State leaders appear to have expected that the state navies would be subsumed into the national service. As anticipated, all were taken into the Confederate States Navy and served as regional coastal forces. The state navies served a valuable purpose—as an interim force until a Confederate navy could be created.

— KEVIN J. FOSTER

STATE RIGHTS

Secession was based on the idea of state rights (or "states' rights," a variant that came into use after the Civil War). This exalted the powers of the individual states as opposed to those of the Federal government. It generally rested on the theory of state sovereignty—that in the United States the ultimate source of political authority lay in the separate states. Associated with the principle of state rights was a sense of state loyalty that could prevail over a feeling of national patriotism. Before the war, the principle found expression in different ways at different times, in the North as well as in the South. During the war it reappeared in the Confederacy.

HAMILTONIANS AND JEFFERSONIANS. The Constitution could be interpreted in opposite ways. In its clause giving Congress all powers "necessary and proper" for carrying the specified powers into effect, Alexander Hamilton as secretary of the treasury found ample authorization for his financial program, including a national bank. In the Tenth Amendment, however, Thomas Jefferson as secretary of state discovered a bar to congressional legislation of that kind: no power to establish a bank having been delegated to Congress, that power must have been reserved to the states. As president, George Washington sided with Hamilton and signed the bills that Congress passed to enact Hamilton's plan. Eventually Jefferson withdrew from the Washington administration and, with Madison, organized an opposition to it. Thus, in the 1790s, originated the two parties, Federalist and Republican, the one willing to exploit the "implied powers" of the Constitution, the other demanding a "strict construction" of the document.

The Republicans, already convinced that much of the Federalist legislation was unconstitutional, were further outraged when, in 1798, Congress passed the Alien and Sedition Acts. The Sedition Act—providing

The state rights tone was set in the preamble to the Confederate Constitution in the significant phrase, "each State acting in its sovereign and independent character."

PAGE 151

In March 1861, state rights radicals succeeded in eliminating the jurisdiction of Confederate courts over disputes between citizens of different states.

PAGE 306

for the fining and imprisoning of those who uttered anything "false, scandalous, and malicious" against the government, the Congress, or the president—seemed flagrantly to violate the First Amendment, which stated that Congress should pass no law abridging freedom of speech or of the press.

What agency should decide the question of constitutionality? The Constitution did not, in so many words, give the Supreme Court the power to decide, and the Republicans denied that the Court could rightfully assume the power. Their leaders, Jefferson and Madison, arguing that the state legislatures should decide, ably expounded their views in two sets of resolutions, one written (anonymously) by Jefferson and adopted by the Kentucky legislature (1798–1799) and the other drafted by Madison and approved by the Virginia legislature (1798).

These Kentucky and Virginia Resolutions asserted the following propositions: The Federal government had been formed by a "compact" or contract among the states. It was a limited government, possessing only specific delegated powers. Whenever it attempted to exercise any additional, undelegated powers, its acts were "unauthoritative, void, and of no force." The parties to the contract, the states, must decide for themselves when and whether the central government exceeded its powers. The state legislatures must serve as "sentinels" to watch out for unconstitutional acts. And "nullification" by the states was the "rightful remedy" whenever the general government went too far. The resolutions urged all the states to join in declaring the Alien and Sedition Acts null and void and in demanding their repeal at the next session of Congress, but none of the other states went along with Virginia and Kentucky.

FROM COLONIES TO CONSTITUTION

The idea of state rights antedated the U.S. Constitution. During the colonial period the people of each colony showed an attachment to their own and often an antagonism toward other colonies. Intercolonial jealousies prevented union when, in 1754, Benjamin Franklin proposed the Albany Plan for combining to meet a threat from the French and their Indian allies. The same sentiments hampered intercolonial cooperation during the ensuing French and Indian War. Traveling through the middle settlements in 1759 and 1760, the Englishman Andrew Burnaby was struck by the disparities he observed: "Fire and water are not more heterogeneous than the different colonies in North America. Nothing can exceed the jealousy and emulation which they possess in regard to each other." Burnaby thought the colonies differed so much in culture and in economic interests that "were they left to themselves, there would even be a civil war."

Their shared hostility to the British government enabled the colonies to join in the Continental Congress and, as states from 1776 on, to win the Revolutionary War. Their rivalries continued, however, and delayed the adoption of the Articles of Confederation until 1781. The second of the Articles affirmed: "Each state retains its sovereignty, freedom and independence, and every Power, Jurisdiction and right, which is not by this confederation expressly delegated to the United States, in Congress assembled." The separate states retained, among other powers, the exclusive power to tax. All had to approve before the Articles could be amended. When New York refused to approve an amendment giving Congress the power to levy customs duties, it failed to be adopted.

Alexander Hamilton and other "nationalists" desired a stronger government, and since they could not amend the Articles, they undertook to replace them. At the Philadelphia Convention of 1787, delegates from the various states drew up a new plan of government, which its "father" James Madison said was "in structure, neither a national nor a federal Constitution, but a composition of both." Indeed, it was the result of compromises between nationalists and state-rightists, and it evaded a number of issues that might have prevented any agreement. Still, the new Constitution gave much greater power to the central government than the Articles of Confederation had given.

The Constitution was to be ratified by separate state conventions and was to go into effect among the ratifying states when nine of them had acted. Antinationalists, who called themselves "Antifederalists," opposed ratification. To reassure them, Madison wrote in one of the Federalist Papers (later gathered in The Federalist) that the document was to be ratified "by the people, not as individuals composing one nation; but as composing the distinct and independent States to which they respectively belong." Before the end of 1788 eleven states had ratified, but some had done so only on the understanding that certain amendments would soon be added. Two others (North Carolina and Rhode Island) still held out, waiting to see what would happen.

All were satisfied by the ten amendments proposed by the new Congress at its first session. These amendments further limited the powers of the central government, and the tenth provided: "The powers not delegated to the United States by the Constitution, nor prohibited by it to the States, are reserved to the States respectively, or to the people." Thus amended, the Constitution was more nearly balanced between national and state rights tendencies—and was more ambiguous.

— RICHARD N. CURRENT

State rights and strict construction were usually the arguments of the party out of power (and so they were to be throughout American history). As long as the Republicans were outsiders, they remained strict constructionists, but once they had become insiders, with Jefferson as president, they used the full powers of the Federal government to further the agrarian interests they represented. Indeed, they used much more than the rightful and constitutional powers, according to the Federalists, who now adopted the state rights point of view.

The Jefferson administration bought Louisiana from France in 1803 even though the Constitution gave Congress no explicit power to acquire new territory. On the constitutionality of the purchase Jefferson himself had serious doubts but managed to overcome them. The administration also imposed an embargo in 1807 forbidding American ships to leave American ports, though the Constitution allowed Congress only to regulate interstate and foreign commerce, not to prohibit it. In anger against the Louisiana Purchase, a few extreme Federalists, the Essex Junto, conspired to bring about the secession of New England. In condemning the embargo, a much larger number resorted to the doctrine of state rights. The young New Hampshire Federalist Daniel Webster, for one, paraphrased the Virginia and Kentucky Resolutions: "The Government of the United States is a delegated, *limited* Government."

During the presidency of Jefferson's friend and successor James Madison, the New England state rights men gained their largest following in opposition to the War of 1812. In Congress, Webster attacked and helped defeat a conscription bill. "The operation of measures thus unconstitutional and illegal ought to be prevented by a resort to other measures which are both constitutional and legal," he declared, hinting at nullification by New Hampshire. "It will be the solemn duty of the state governments to protect their own authority over their own militia and to interpose between their citizens and arbitrary power." In fact, some of the New England states, by refusing to support the war, virtually nullified the war effort of the Federal government. New England state-rightism and sectionalism reached a climax in the Hartford Convention (1814–1815), which demanded changes in the Constitution and threatened secession if they were not made.

Some of Jefferson's followers had turned against him when, as they saw it, he departed from his own principles. His distant cousin and (before 1804) House leader John Randolph of Roanoke organized within the Republican party a state rights faction known as the Quids. Randolph remained a fanatical defender of Virginia rights. John Taylor of Caroline, an equally consistent but more original thinker than Randolph,

led the Virginia School, which included St. George Tucker and Spencer Roane. These men rationalized resistance to the centralizing trend, especially to the work of the Supreme Court under Virginian John Marshall. Jefferson, after his retirement from the presidency, joined in opposing the Federalist-minded judges as "sappers and miners" who were undermining the Constitution. The Georgia state rights men, whose leader was William H. Crawford, had their own quarrel with Marshall, who ruled against them when the state undertook to evict its Indians from their tribal lands.

CALHOUN'S CONTRIBUTION. John C. Calhoun was a latecomer to the state rights cause, but he developed the theory more fully than anyone else. In Congress he had favored the War of 1812 and had advocated protective tariffs, internal improvements at Federal expense, and a national bank. By 1828 he was convinced that a protective tariff was not only harmful to his state, South Carolina, but was also contrary to the Constitution. He then began to work out his system for state resistance to unconstitutional laws.

Calhoun refined and elaborated the doctrine of sentinelship that Madison and Jefferson had presented in the Virginia and Kentucky Resolutions. He based his theory on the assumption that the people (not the government) in each state were sovereign and, in their sovereign capacity, had ratified and thus given validity to both the state constitution and the U.S. Constitution. They had done so, he argued, through their delegates in specially elected conventions. In this ratification process he discovered the procedure for dealing with questions of constitutionality. A state convention—not the state legislature as in Madison's and Jefferson's proposal—could nullify a Federal law. That law would remain null and void within the state until three-fourths of all the states had ratified a constitutional amendment specifi-

STATES' CHAMPION

South Carolina's John C. Calhoun developed a theory of state rights based on the view that the people (not the government) in each state were sovereign—and could secede.

NATIONAL ARCHIVES

"How far shall the South surrender its moral, social, and economic autonomy to the victorious principle of Union? That question remains open."

TWELVE SOUTHERNERS
INTRODUCTION, I'LL TAKE MY STAND, 1930

cally giving Congress the power in question. If they should ever do so, the nullifying state would still have a recourse—secession. Just as a state could "*ac*cede" to the Union by ratifying the Constitution, it could "*se*cede" by repealing its ordinance of ratification.

South Carolina put nullification to the test in 1832, when a state convention declared all protective tariffs, particularly those of 1828 and 1832, to be null and void within the state. Calhoun having resigned the vice presidency, the nullifiers sent him to the Senate to present their case. Debating him was Daniel Webster, now a senator from Massachusetts, who had switched from a state rights position to a nationalist one while Calhoun was doing the reverse. "The truth is," Webster contended, "and no ingenuity of argument, no subtlety of distinction, can evade it, that, as to certain purposes, the people of the United States are one people." According to the new Webster, a state might secede from the Union, but only on the basis of the right of revolution, not on the basis of any constitutional right. While remaining in the Union, however, a state could not nullify congressional acts, for nullification was no right at all, he maintained.

President Andrew Jackson, agreeing with Webster, denounced nullification as treason and asked Congress for authority to use the army and the navy to enforce the laws. Though the nullificationists had sympathizers in other Southern states, not one of those states officially endorsed the South Carolina stand. Calhoun claimed a victory for nullification when Congress passed and Jackson signed a compromise bill for gradually lowering the tariff. But nullification had not really worked the way Calhoun had intended. It had not been generally accepted as a legitimate and constitutional procedure. Calhoun came to realize that a single state, unaided, was powerless to interpose against Federal authority. So he set about cultivating a spirit of unity among all the slave states.

Slavery, according to Calhoun, occupied a special place in the Constitution, and certainly it occupied a special place in his theory of state rights. It was, he insisted, the only kind of property that the Constitution specifically recognized (though, in fact, the document did not mention slaves or slavery by name; it referred only to "free Persons" and "all other Persons" and to a "Person held to Service or Labour"). Therefore, nullification could be used to defend or strengthen slavery but not to attack or weaken it. Calhoun strenuously objected when, after 1842, several free states tried their own brand of nullification by adopting "personal liberty" laws that forbade state authorities to assist in the enforcement of the Federal Fugitive Slave Act of 1793.

Calhoun was further outraged when the House, though not the Senate, passed the Wilmot Proviso in

1848, which aimed to exclude slavery from all territories to be acquired in consequence of the Mexican War. Then, when the Compromise of 1850 proposed to admit California as a free state and thus to upset the balance of free and slave states, he thought the time had come for the slave states to resort to their ultimate redress, secession.

TANEY AND THE TERRITORIES. During the 1850s the doctrine of state rights became a dogma of state powers—powers that extended beyond the boundaries of the states themselves. The development of this dogma was occasioned by the question of slavery in the territories.

Many Northerners held that Congress could exclude slavery, as it had done with respect to the Northwest Territory in the Northwest Ordinance (1787, 1789) and with respect to part of the Louisiana Purchase in the Missouri Compromise (1820–1821). Some advocated "popular sovereignty," or "squatter sovereignty," which would allow the settlers themselves to decide whether to permit slavery in a particular territory, and this principle was embodied in the Kansas-Nebraska Act of 1854. But proslavery Southerners insisted that any prohibition of slavery in a territory, whether by Congress or by the local people, was unconstitutional.

From the proslavery point of view, the sovereign states had delegated to Congress only the power to make routine "rules and regulations" for the territories, not the power to make basic policies for them. When dealing with the subject, the Federal government must act merely as a trustee for the states and must give effect to their laws, particularly the laws respecting slavery. State rights was no longer just a defense of local self-determination; it had become a means of imposing a state's laws on people outside the state.

The theory now called for an enlargement rather than a reduction of Federal authority, at least in regard to the territories, though this authority could be exercised only to protect slavery. As President Franklin Pierce said in 1855, the Federal government was "forbidden to touch this matter in the sense of attack or offense" and could do so only "in the sense of defense." Proslavery advocates looked to the Supreme Court for an endorsement of their new theory of state sovereignty. The Court obliged in the *Dred Scott* case (1857) with an obiter dictum declaring unconstitutional the Missouri Compromise prohibition of slavery in part of the Louisiana Purchase. Chief Justice Roger B. Taney said: "The Government of the United States had no right to interfere for any other purpose but that of protecting the rights of the [slave] owner."

For the time being, the strongest assertion of state rights in defiance of Federal authority came not from any Southern state but from Wisconsin, which invoked the doctrine to oppose slavery rather than to support it. When a Federal court convicted Sherman Booth of violating the Fugitive Slave Act of 1850, the Wisconsin Supreme Court repeatedly (1854–1855) issued writs of habeas corpus to release him on the ground that the act was unconstitutional. Booth and fellow antislavery radicals made state rights a test of orthodoxy in the newly formed Republican party; they demanded that the party's candidates endorse the principles of the Virginia and Kentucky Resolutions of 1798 and 1799. In the case of *Ableman* v. *Booth* (1859) Taney and the Supreme Court again upheld the Southern as opposed to the Northern state rights position. They overruled the supreme court of Wisconsin.

The Wisconsin governor then reasserted the sovereignty of his state. As commander in chief of the state militia, he challenged the president as commander in chief of the U.S. Army and Navy. "It is reported," a Wisconsin official notified the captain of one of the militia companies, ". . . that you have stated that, in the possible contingency of a conflict between the U.S. authorities and those of this State, you . . . would obey a call for your company to turn out, made by the U.S. authorities, but would *not* obey a call by your superior officials under the State laws." When the captain replied that he would consider it treason to disobey a presidential order, the governor dismissed him and disbanded his company. That was in 1860, only months before South Carolina began the secession of the Southern states.

SECESSION AND THE CONFEDERATE CONSTITUTION. Some advocates of secession justified it as a revolutionary right, but most of them based it on constitutional grounds. The 1860 South Carolina Declaration of the Causes of Secession quoted the state's 1852 declaration, which said that "the frequent violations of the Constitution of the United States by the Federal Government, and its encroachments upon the reserved rights of the States," would justify the state in withdrawing from the Union. The South Carolina secession ordinance, following the procedure that Calhoun had prescribed, simply repealed the state's ratification of the Constitution and subsequent amendments. The secession ordinances of other states did the same.

The Confederate Constitution proved to be somewhat inconsistent in regard to state rights. It contained no provision for secession, though its preamble averred that each Confederate state was "acting in its sovereign and independent character." One article (like the Tenth Amendment of the U.S. Constitution) affirmed that the "powers not delegated" were "reserved to the States." The states, however, were limited in important ways. For example, they could not (just as the states of the Union could not) pass any law

"impairing the obligation of contracts." They could not get rid of slavery, for the citizens of each state were to "have the right of transit and sojourn in any State . . . with their slaves."

Congress was forbidden to impose duties or taxes "to promote or foster any branch of industry" but in some ways was given even greater powers than the U.S. Congress. The ambiguity regarding territories and slavery was removed. The Confederacy could "acquire new territory," and Congress could "legislate" (not merely make "rules and regulations") for the territories. In all of them "the institution of negro slavery" was to be "recognized and protected by Congress and by the territorial government." Congress could make all laws "necessary and proper" for carrying out its specified powers. If this or any other clause should lead to a dispute over the constitutionality of a law, the Confederate courts (rather than state legislatures or conventions) would presumably decide the issue. This was implied by the following provision: "The judicial power shall extend to all cases arising under the Constitution."

In sum, the new Constitution was more *national* than the old one with regard to slavery, which it guaranteed as a nationwide institution. The document provided no more basis for nullification or secession than its predecessor had done—despite the preamble's reference to the member states as "sovereign" and "independent." Nevertheless, there remained room for the reassertion of state rights in the Confederacy.

STATE RIGHTS IN THE CONFEDERACY. To win its independence, the Confederacy needed a government strong enough to make the most of all the available human and material resources, but some of the state leaders were no more willing to concede power to the Confederate government than they had been to the Federal government. Appealing to the principle of state rights, they resisted the efforts of the Jefferson Davis administration to control blockade running and manufacturing, to impress slaves and other property, and even to raise troops. Georgia was the locus of the greatest recalcitrance, Joseph E. Brown the most obstreperous of the governors, and Vice President Alexander H. Stephens the busiest fomenter and philosopher of resistance. North Carolina, under Governor Zebulon Vance, was the next most important center of obstructionism, but practically all the states had some occasion for expressing opposition to Confederate measures.

The most serious question was the constitutionality of the conscription acts (April/September 1862, and February 1864). Davis justified the legislation on the basis of the constitutional clause giving Congress the power to raise and support armies. But Brown and Stephens argued that the Confederate government

Governor Milledge L. Bonham was determined that South Carolina "in every legitimate way should sustain the Confederate authorities."

PAGE 66

could raise troops only by making requisitions upon the states, which alone, they said, had the constitutional power to impose a draft. Stephens declared: "The citizen of the State owes no allegiance to the Confederate States Government . . . and can owe no 'military service' to it except as required by his own State." Brown protested to Davis that conscription was a "bold and dangerous usurpation by Congress of the reserved rights of the States."

To enforce conscription, Congress authorized the president to suspend the privilege of the writ of habeas corpus. To Stephens, this seemed as bad as conscription itself. He denounced the suspension in resolutions which the Georgia legislature passed and which, along with speeches by Brown and Stephens's half-brother Linton Stephens, were printed and widely circulated. The legislatures of North Carolina and Mississippi adopted similar resolutions.

The question of constitutionality could not be referred to a Confederate supreme court, for there was none. In 1861 the Provisional Congress provided for such a court, with the power of judicial review, but the permanent Congress established only a system of lower tribunals. When Congress considered adding a supreme court in 1863, opponents objected to the potential subordination of the state supreme courts. These consequently were left to go on deciding the constitutionality of both state and Confederate laws. The supreme court in Georgia and in every other state

except North Carolina upheld the Confederate conscription acts. "When Congress calls for the military service of the citizen," the Texas judges ruled, " . . . the right of the State government must cease or yield to the paramount demand of Congress."

Despite the pro-Confederate decisions of state courts, conflicts between the Confederate government and the state governments persisted. Texas objected to giving up control of state troops, as did Alabama, Mississippi, and all the Gulf states except Florida. A Florida judge, however, issued an injunction against Confederate officers who were ordered to take up some of the track of the Florida Railroad—and who disregarded the injunction.

More serious obstruction came from North Carolina, where Governor Vance took pains to "preserve the rights and honor of the State." He said it was "mortifying" to see North Carolinians "commanded by strangers"—that is, by men from other states—and he demanded that their officers be North Carolinians. Operating a state-owned blockade runner, *Advance,* he objected to the Confederacy's claim to half of the cargo space. He warehoused uniforms, shoes, and blankets for the exclusive use of North Carolina troops at a time when Robert E. Lee's army in Virginia was suffering from the want of such supplies. State officials being exempt from the draft, he appointed thousands of men to state jobs to keep them out of the Confederate army.

Governor Brown of Georgia went even further in making unnecessary state appointments. Then, after enrolling ten thousand militiamen, he refused to allow them to enter the Confederate service even when in 1864 Davis attempted to requisition them—as Brown had previously said the president had a right to do. Brown now insisted he was protecting his state against both "external assaults and internal usurpations." The Confederate secretary of war compared him to the New England governors who had resisted the war effort during the War of 1812. Brown rejected the Richmond authorities' references to "refractory Governors" and "loyal States." Such remarks were "utterly at variance with the principles upon which we entered into this contest in 1861," he said. The Confederate government was "the agent or creature of the States," and its officers had no business "discussing the loyalty and disloyalty of the sovereign States to their central agent—the loyalty of the creator to the creature."

The right of secession followed logically from such Calhounian doctrine. Vance, however, would not hear of it when disaffected North Carolinians talked of calling a secession convention in 1863. Brown and Stephens declined when, after taking Atlanta, Gen. William Tecumseh Sherman proposed a meeting to discuss Georgia's leaving the Confederacy and making a separate peace. But Stephens wrote privately:

DRAFT RESISTER

Vice President Alexander H. Stephens confounded Jefferson Davis with his opposition to conscription and his statement that "the citizen of each State owes no allegiance to the Confederate States Government."

HARPER'S PICTORIAL HISTORY OF THE GREAT REBELLION

"Should any State at any time become satisfied that the war is not waged for purposes securing her best interests . . . she has a perfect right to withdraw." By early 1865, at least one Georgia planter had come to suspect that Stephens and his associates were plotting to "withdraw if possible this and two other States from the Confed. and set up for themselves."

In fact, none of the states ever came close to seceding from the Confederacy, and most of them avoided an extreme state rights position all along. Nevertheless, Davis had ample cause for complaint. In a private letter of December 15, 1864, he wrote that his difficulties had been "materially increased by the persistent interference of some of the State Authorities, Legislative, Executive, and Judicial, hindering the action of the Government, obstructing the execution of its laws, denouncing its necessary policy, impairing its hold upon the confidence of the people, and dealing with it rather as if it were the public enemy than the Government which they themselves had established for the common defense, and which was the only hope of safety from the untold horrors of Yankee despotism."

Historians have differed about the importance of state rights as a cause of Confederate defeat. One writer has gone so far as to suggest that the following words should be engraved on the Confederacy's tombstone: "Died of State Rights." Others minimize its effects, pointing out that it was a symbol of more fundamental grievances (as, indeed, it had been throughout American history). Some have even argued that it was an asset rather than a liability to the Confederate cause, since, they say, it served as a safety valve for possibly disruptive discontent.

The doctrine may have influenced the outcome through its effect on Davis personally and directly. He prided himself on being a state-rightist and a strict constructionist, and though his state rights opponents accused him of dictatorship, he was generally careful to confine himself to the letter of the Confederate Constitution. The *Times* of London said in 1865 that one reason for the defeat of the Confederacy was his reluctance to "assume at any risk the dictatorial powers" that were "alone adapted to the successful management of revolutions."

Afterward Davis agreed with Stephens about the basic issue of the war. In *A Constitutional View of the Late War between the States* (1868–1870) Stephens maintained: "It was a strife between the principles of Federation, on the one side, and Centralism, or Consolidation, on the other." In *The Rise and Fall of the Confederate Government* (1881) Davis held that the Confederates had "fought for the maintenance of their State governments in all their reserved rights and powers." Both men forgot that the preservation of slavery

had been the object of state sovereignty, state rights, secession, and the formation of the Confederacy.

[*See also* Civil War, *article on* Causes of the War; Compromise of 1850; Conscription; Constitution; Dred Scott Decision; Fugitive Slave Law; Habeas Corpus; Judiciary; Kansas-Nebraska Act; Nullification Controversy; Secession; Wilmot Proviso; *and entries on selected states and biographies of figures mentioned herein.*]
— RICHARD N. CURRENT

STEPHENS, ALEXANDER H.

Stephens, Alexander H. (1812–1883), vice president, and postwar Georgia congressman and governor. The son of a yeoman farmer of modest fortune, Alexander Stephens, sickly from birth to death and cursed with a freakish, spectral appearance, never weighed more than ninety pounds. His myriad physical ailments and the early death of his father doubtless contributed to a crippling melancholy that plagued Stephens for most of his life. Despite these handicaps in a society that put a premium on physical prowess, he parlayed driving ambition, substantial intelligence, spellbinding oratorical talents, and prodigious capacity for work into one of the antebellum South's most illustrious political careers.

After a short, unhappy stint as a teacher upon graduation from Franklin College at Athens, Georgia, in 1832, Stephens took up the practice of law in his hometown of Crawfordville, Georgia. His success as a lawyer led him, in 1836, into politics, his first and last love. He never married, but throughout his life he maintained an extraordinarily close relationship with his half-brother Linton.

Elected to the U.S. Congress in 1843 as a Whig, he soon assumed a position of leadership in the party. When the Whigs foundered on the shoals of the Compromise of 1850—which he vigorously supported—Stephens pursued an independent course until 1855, when he became a Democrat rather than espouse Know-Nothingism. The year before, he had played a pivotal role in the passage of the Kansas-Nebraska Act in the House. Although he served as a key administration operative in the unsuccessful attempt to gain acceptance of the proslavery Lecompton constitution for the admission of Kansas, he did not break with Stephen A. Douglas and the Northern Democrats on the issue. Worn out and disgusted, he retired from the House in 1859. Deploring the split of the Democratic party in 1860, he supported Douglas in the election. After Abraham Lincoln's election, he opposed seces-

Thoughtful Southerners, including Jefferson Davis, deplored Stephens's emphasis on slavery rather than the politically advantageous theme of state versus national sovereignty.

PAGE 156

"Now I am beginning to doubt his good intentions. . . . His whole policy on the organization and discipline of the army is perfectly consistent with the hypothesis that he is aiming at absolute power."

ALEXANDER H. STEPHENS
ON JEFFERSON DAVIS, 1864

sion as a hasty and ill-advised movement undertaken without sufficient provocation. Nonetheless, he bowed to the wishes of his state when it seceded.

The Georgia secession convention then selected him as a delegate to the Montgomery convention.

There he played a leading role in the shaping of the Confederate Constitution, especially the provision allowing the future admission of free states. As the most prominent opponent of secession in the South, Stephens was a logical choice for executive office in the new Confederate government. Impelled by a desire to balance competing factions in the South, to appeal to the border states, and to present a united front to the world, the convention elected Jefferson Davis, a moderate secessionist and old Democrat, provisional president and Stephens, cooperationist and old Whig, as provisional vice president of the Confederacy on February 9, 1861. (They were elected, without opposition, to their permanent positions in national elections on November 6, 1861.)

Although the working relations between these two proud men began amicably enough, they were deteriorating even before the war started. Davis regarded Stephens's extolling of slavery as the "cornerstone" of the Confederacy in a widely reported speech at Savannah as heedless of the paramount issue at stake between the Federal and Confederate governments: state versus national sovereignty. Ironically, the future split between Davis and Stephens turned on this issue within the Confederacy itself.

Stephens grew increasingly disenchanted with his office. In Montgomery, the president had consulted with him frequently, had dispatched him as commissioner to Virginia before that state seceded, and had offered other important assignments. In early summer, the vice president diligently undertook an extensive

speaking tour on behalf of the produce loan to raise money for the government, and he faithfully attended to his official duties. But things had changed by early 1862. For months Stephens had been systematically ignored by Davis and the cabinet. For a man of ability once secure in his power and influence, this inactivity was a bitter pill. With little to do but preside over the Senate where he could neither speak nor vote, Stephens saw no point in spending much time in the capital. He began staying at home for long periods of time.

After months of frustration, Stephens moved to more overt opposition against the government with passage of the first Confederate Conscription Act in April 1862. He regarded conscription as a dangerous and unconstitutional centralization of power, counter to the whole reason the Confederacy existed: to be a bastion of both state sovereignty and personal liberty. Accordingly, he approved of Georgia Governor Joseph E. Brown's long public argument with Davis on the subject and under a pseudonym in September 1862 denounced the draft himself in a public letter. Shortly thereafter, in another public letter, he denied that martial law even existed under the Constitution.

Contrary to his detractors, who contended that he was at heart a Unionist, Stephens remained devoted to the cause of Southern independence. But he differed sharply with the administration over the means to achieve the end. For example, from the beginning and throughout the war he was one of the few to espouse stiff taxation in lieu of issuance of Treasury notes to finance the war. For this reason, Confederate financial policy, which rested on the highly inflationary expedient of printing money to finance its debts, never met his approval. He had similarly urged, to no avail, that the government use cotton as credit to back its bonds and finance the purchase of war matèriel abroad. And although not theoretically averse to impressment—indeed, he sanctioned a broad reading of the Constitution to reach the taxable property of the wealthy—he deplored the capricious way in which the law operated.

Far more than Davis, Stephens heeded political currents in the North and was willing to court them to achieve independence. The best time to extend peace feelers, he thought, was during times of relative quiescence on the battlefields. Accordingly, in June 1863, following Robert E. Lee's great victory at Chancellorsville and with the North discontented over the passage of conscription there, he placed a proposal before Davis. He would undertake a mission to the North to reestablish the cartel for the exchange of prisoners that had broken down amid bitter threats of mutual retaliation on innocent prisoners after the Emancipation Proclamation in January. Such a conference, Stephens hinted, might afford him the opportunity to address the larger issue of a general settlement. Davis, who knew as Stephens did not that Lee was invading the North, accepted the offer.

Upon his arrival in Richmond, Stephens discovered to his horror that the president wanted him to accompany Lee's army north. The president thought this would improve Stephens's chances of being received. Stephens emphatically disagreed, but at the urging of cabinet and president, he consented to undertake the mission. According to his instructions, its purpose was "humanitarian" with "no political aspect." Rainy weather, which made roads impassable, dictated that Stephens travel to Washington by steamer. As he had anticipated, the venture came to naught. Stephens arrived at Newport News, Virginia, at noon on July 4, 1863. After keeping the Confederate envoy waiting for two days, the Lincoln government, buoyed by the victories at Gettysburg and the fall of Vicksburg, refused to let him proceed. Disgusted that his advice had once again been disregarded, Stephens returned to Georgia.

Except for a few speeches trying to encourage his countrymen in the wake of the midsummer disasters, Stephens kept his peace for the balance of 1863. But he had not retreated an inch from his convictions about the course the Confederacy should take. He could barely find words to express his abhorrence of the notion in some quarters that the South appoint a dictator to rule the country during the war. The only way to preserve "constitutional liberty," his umbrella term for individual and state rights, was to preserve constitutional limits on authority. Preserving the purity of that document was the war's chief object; even independence was secondary. "Nothing could be more unwise than for a free people," he told Howell Cobb, "at any time, under any circumstances, to give up their rights under the vain hope and miserable delusion that they might thereby be enabled to defend them."

Stephens dallied over returning to Richmond for the opening of the congressional session in November 1863; first one thing and then another delayed his leaving Georgia. Meanwhile, Governor Brown was seriously considering calling the Georgia legislature into special session to formally protest government policies as well as broach the subject of peace negotiations with the Federal government. Stephens dissuaded Brown from doing so until Congress had acted on some of the vexatious issues. And from his sickbed, he penned a long letter to the president warning that it would be impolitic to suspend again the writ of habeas corpus and to extend conscription; he also reasserted the evils of the present impressment machinery, to no avail. In mid-February, the Congress authorized another six-month suspension of the writ and extended conscription.

The events in Richmond spurred Brown to go ahead with his plans: he called the Georgia Assembly into special session on March 10, 1864. The vice president and his brother Linton, a member of the legislature, both advised Brown about how the protest should be handled. In accordance with these plans, Brown delivered a scalding message on Confederate policy on the heels of which Linton Stephens offered two sets of resolutions. The first condemned the suspension of the writ; the second proposed that the South proffer peace negotiations to the North after every victory it won in the field. Although he had not intended to become publicly identified with the protest for obvious reasons of propriety, the vice president yielded to the entreaties of his brother to come to Milledgeville, the capital, when it appeared that the resolutions might fail.

There, on the night of March 16, Stephens delivered an impassioned address in support of the resolutions. He branded both conscription and suspension of the writ as unconstitutional and unwise. The latter act also presented a grave danger to public liberty: the legislature should request its immediate repeal and its constitutionality should be tested in the courts. Stephens dismissed the notion that Davis would be circumspect about using the power. Abuses would inevitably arise from the military authorities who would enforce the law. Stephens took pains to deny that he desired a counterrevolution. What he wanted was to keep the present revolution on the right track. The best way to prevent a counterrevolution was for the state to speak out. The truest supporters of the government and the troops in the field upheld the fundamental law.

After a fierce struggle, the Georgia Assembly passed the resolutions two days later but accompanied them with another expressing undiminished confidence in Davis. Stephens had long since lost such confidence, but with palpable self-delusion, he also denied any personal antipathy to the president. In fact, he had always considered Davis unfit for the presidency, and although he professed in March 1864 to believe Davis "a man of good intentions," their ensuing relations would prove just how corrosive Stephens's suspicions of him had become.

As the war dragged on into the summer of 1864, an increasing number of prominent Confederates both in and outside of Congress began broaching various plans for peace. Stephens, too, was vitally interested in the subject. One of his enduring beliefs from the beginning of the war was that the political, economic, and cultural ties between the South and the Old Northwest could be used to further the cause of the Confederacy. Consequently, he believed that the Confederacy should do all it could to influence Northern elections, should offer to negotiate on the basis of state sovereignty, and, if need be, should accept an offer to negotiate on the basis of reunion. With a friendly government in place,

STEPHENS,
ALEXANDER H.

By the end of the war, Stephens and other leading politicians no longer supported the administration, in part because of Davis's "betrayal" of Southern Constitutional principles.

PAGE 150

589

the South could obtain an armistice through negotiation, which, in Stephens's opinion, would inevitably lead to its independence.

Davis, though he sanctioned covert aid to anti-Lincoln elements in the North, did not believe the Confederacy should be involved with foreign elections. Nor should it court negotiation with the enemy save only on one unalterable basis: Confederate independence. The surest way of securing independence in his view was to demonstrate the futility of subduing the South by force. This fundamental difference of opinion led to the final breach between the Confederacy's two top executives.

Davis had already publicly misrepresented Stephens's futile 1863 mission as an illustration of the North's intractability on the peace issue. This enraged the vice president, who was even more upset when in a speech at Columbia, South Carolina, in October 1864 the president repeated the charge and barely alluded to the Northern elections. Stephens found it incomprehensible that the Confederate government did not respond favorably to the peace plank in the platform of the Northern Democrats in 1864, which demanded a cessation of hostilities so that "at the earliest moment peace may be restored on the basis of the Federal Union." Contrary to what many thought, the vice president did not favor any scheme for separate state action for peace—indeed, for any course of action that bypassed the Richmond government. As the fortunes of

the Confederacy became increasingly desperate, many in the South, including Governor Brown and Linton Stephens, came to favor this course. Stephens opposed them all, arguing that under the Constitution only the central government was empowered to conclude treaties. Even a general convention of the states would have to be acceded to by Richmond and Washington.

Partly to further legitimate peace initiatives and partly to oppose additional draconian war measures being proposed by the government, Stephens returned to Richmond in December 1864. Almost immediately he engaged in an acrimonious exchange of letters with Davis over the latter's remarks in Columbia. Shortly thereafter, his considerable dignity wounded when the Senate refused to allow him to speak on the habeas corpus issue, Stephens decided to resign his office. Only the importuning of the president pro tem of the Senate, Robert M. T. Hunter, dissuaded him.

To Stephens's surprise, however, on January 6, 1865, the Senate invited him to address it after adjournment. He spoke for two hours, urging a complete revision of policy to reanimate the people: an end to conscription and impressment, friendship toward the Northern Democrats (i.e., agreement to a general convention of the states), and a revamped military policy. Although typically unrealistic, it had not been a gloomy speech. Stephens gave up his idea of returning home for the moment and continued to aid those in Congress who were trying to force the president's hand on peace nego-

STEPHENS IN THE POSTWAR PERIOD

Elected to the U.S. Senate by the Georgia legislature in 1866, Stephens, like many other ex-Confederates, was prevented from taking his seat. Thus barred by the provisions of Reconstruction and extremely poor health from participation in public life in the immediate postwar period, Stephens devoted his time to writing. His ponderous two-volume work, *A Constitutional View of the Late War between the States,* published from 1868 through 1870, presented a detailed justification of secession and the antebellum Southern interpretation of the Union. It has been judged the ablest defense of the Southern position ever made.

With his political disabilities removed, Stephens in 1873 assumed his familiar position as representative of Georgia's Eighth District in the U.S. House. He

remained there until 1882 when he was elected governor of Georgia. Stephens died in office the next year, barely one hundred days into his term.

Less understood than labeled, Alexander Stephens has not been treated kindly by most historians. Although guilty of many of the sins they have accused him of—naiveté, pettiness, narrowness, rashness—Stephens does not deserve the reputation of either a closet Unionist or traitor to the Confederate cause. His critics often overlook or excuse the obstinate refusal of Davis to countenance criticism from any source and his political ineptness in dealing with a host of other antagonists. Stephens represented a widespread segment of Southern opinion. He was hardly alone in his passionate concern for individual liberties and state

rights against what was widely perceived as encroachments by a powerful central government. But at no time during the conflict did Stephens ever counsel resistance to government authority except through lawful, constitutional means: the courts and Congress.

Stephens's critics also ignore clear evidence of the vice president's commitment to Confederate independence. It never wavered throughout the war. Whether the remedies to the Confederacy's ills that Stephens proposed would have worked is not the question. A better question might be whether anyone who opposes a government's policy in the midst of war is likely to get a fair hearing—then or later.

— THOMAS E. SCHOTT

tiations. Several resolutions to do this (a couple framed by Stephens) had been introduced in the Congress.

It was largely to forestall these plans that Jefferson Davis entertained a proposal that had been carried down from Washington, with Lincoln's blessing, by Francis P. Blair. Blair suggested that the two sides cease fighting and join forces against the French in Mexico. Lincoln did not subscribe to this idea, but he was willing to talk "informally" to secure peace "to the people of our common country." Davis, for political reasons of his own, seized the opportunity. Not only was peace sentiment strong and increasing among congressmen, press, and people, but several states, including Georgia, threatened separate state action for peace. By responding favorably to Blair's initiative, Davis, who knew Lincoln's terms but felt fairly sure that a Confederate delegation would be received and fail, saw the chance to silence his critics and rally the populace to the government again.

At the urging of Georgia Senator Benjamin H. Hill, Davis appointed Stephens (along with Hunter and John A. Campbell) to the Confederate delegation. Unknown to Davis, Hill had struck a deal with Stephens: the support of Georgia's delegation for peace resolutions in Congress in exchange for the vice president's help in restraining Brown from initiating separate state action for peace in Georgia. Fearful of being hamstrung by his instructions, Stephens tried to avoid serving on the commission, but he could not. As he had feared, the object of the mission spelled out in the official commission was "an informal conference . . . for . . . securing peace to the two countries."

The three Confederate commissioners met with Lincoln and U.S. Secretary of State William Seward on board a steamer at Hampton Roads, Virginia, on February 3, 1865. Although Stephens tried to steer discussion to the Blair proposal, Lincoln would have none of it and insisted on reunion and an end to the rebellion. After four hours, the conference ended. All that had been decided was that the war would continue, although Stephens did secure Lincoln's promise to release his nephew from a Federal prisoner of war camp.

Stephens returned to the capital and stayed only long enough to write his report of the conference. The result at Hampton Roads, besides engendering a final upsurge of warlike resistance in the South, had effectively silenced Davis's congressional critics. In his last interview with Davis, Stephens said he would return home and say nothing further. On May 11, 1865, Stephens was arrested by Union troops and two weeks later was incarcerated at Fort Warren in Boston Harbor. He was released on parole in early October.

[*See also* Cornerstone Speech; Hampton Roads Conference.]

— THOMAS E. SCHOTT

STONEWALL BRIGADE

One of the most famous battle units in American history, the Stonewall Brigade achieved a record for marching, fighting, and sacrifice rarely equaled in the annals of war. Writers over the years have likened it to Caesar's Tenth Legion, Charlemagne's Paladins, and Napoleon's Old Guard. The brigade's original members were in the initial wave of volunteers who answered Virginia's call to arms. All the soldiers in the unit were from the Shenandoah Valley and adjacent areas.

In the spring of 1861, the Second, Fourth, Fifth, Twenty-seventh, and Thirty-third Virginia Infantry Regiments, plus the Rockbridge Artillery Battery, were organized into a brigade. Their commander was Gen. Thomas J. Jackson. The unit was Virginia's First Brigade until July 21, 1861, when, at the Battle of First Manassas, it and its general received the nickname "Stonewall." Jackson left his regiments in the autumn for higher command, but the Stonewall Brigade remained under him, was always his favorite unit, and became the brigade on whom he called as a pacesetter both on the march and in combat.

The brigade's mobility in the 1862 Shenandoah Valley campaign (particularly a fifty-seven-mile march in fifty-one hours) earned it the title "Jackson's foot cavalry." It, along with Jackson's forces, joined the Army of Northern Virginia on the eve of the Seven Days' Battles. Thereafter, from Mechanicsville to Appomattox, the brigade participated in every major battle in the East. It took especially heavy losses at First Manassas, Kernstown, Cedar Mountain, Groveton, Second Manassas, Chancellorsville, Gettysburg, and Spotsylvania. On May 30, 1863, following Jackson's death, the Confederate War Department officially designated the unit as the Stonewall Brigade. It was the only large command in the Southern armies to have a sanctioned nickname.

After vicious 1864 combat at Spotsylvania's Bloody Angle, so few troops remained in the brigade that it ceased to exist as a separate command. Its survivors, along with those of other equally decimated units, were reorganized into a loose brigade. Over 6,000 men served in the Stonewall Brigade during the course of the Civil War. At Appomattox, after thirty-nine engagements, only 210 ragged and footsore soldiers were left—none above the rank of captain.

Jackson's successors as brigade commander were Gens. Richard B. Garnett and Charles S. Winder, Col. William S. H. Baylor, Gens. Elisha Franklin Paxton, James Alexander Walker, and William Terry. Not one of those six officers lived, or escaped serious wounds long enough to be promoted to higher command.

The original Stonewall Brigade had a makeup and personality unique among Confederate units.

"Old Jack" disappeared to the south with his own 6,000-man force, mostly Virginians familiar with the Shenandoah Valley. The men trudged three days through pouring rain and heavy mud.

PAGE 542

Two of every three of its members were farmers, blacksmiths, masons, or machinists. An unusually high percentage of non-English, foreign-born men were in the ranks; Irish and Scotch-Irish were the largest ethnic groups. Few slaveholders were members of the brigade. In addition, the five regiments were typically a family affair, with numerous companies consisting of fathers, sons, brothers, uncles, and cousins.

The brigade came to possess a combination of Jackson's iron discipline and a feeling of confidence gained from repeated successes. It was always an independent-minded unit: a brigade that was outstanding and knew it.

— JAMES I. ROBERTSON, JR.

STUART, J. E. B.

Stuart, J. E. B. (1833–1864), major general. Born February 6, 1833, at Laurel Hill in Patrick County, Virginia, James Ewell Brown ("Jeb") Stuart spent his youth in a large family possessed of political and social influence, but lacking comfortable wealth. At age twelve Stuart took an oath at his mother's knee that he would never drink alcohol—very likely a commentary upon Elizabeth Letcher Pannill Stuart's rectitude and Archibald Stuart's fondness for creature comforts.

Young Stuart attended Emory and Henry College and then secured an appointment to West Point, where he became "Beauty" Stuart because his classmates considered him anything but.

Despite a penchant for fistfights, Stuart enjoyed success at West Point. His pattern of attaching himself to successful people began now, and he counted such disparate cadets as Custis Lee, son of academy Superintendent Robert E. Lee, and Oliver Otis Howard, at the time a stereotypical Yankee prig, among his friends. In 1854 Stuart graduated thirteenth in his class of forty-six and secured a commission in the cavalry. By this time he was committed to a career as a "bold dragoon."

Following a short tour of duty in western Texas, Stuart joined the First Cavalry at Fort Leavenworth, Kansas. There he met and married (November 14, 1855) Flora Cooke, daughter of the post commander, Phillip St. George Cooke. The couple named their firstborn son Phillip St. George Cooke Stuart.

Stuart saw action against Cheyenne warriors in Kansas and once survived a pistol ball fired at him at point-blank range. Fortunately for Stuart, the powder charge was too small, and he suffered only a flesh wound. While on the frontier Stuart served at Forts Leavenworth and Riley in Kansas and at Fort Wise, Colorado. In 1856, while involved in a peacekeeping force attempting to staunch civil unrest in Bleeding Kansas, Stuart encountered radical abolitionist John Brown, an incident that later rendered Stuart the only person at Harpers Ferry able to identify the insurgent "Mr. Smith" as Brown.

Alert to ways of improving his fortune, Stuart spent time during the winter months on the plains tinkering with inventions. He developed something he called "Stuart's Lightening Horse Hitcher" and in the fall of 1859 secured leave to go to Washington to try to sell the War Department a device designed to assist cavalrymen to mount and dismount while armed with sabers.

By coincidence Stuart was at the War Office when the first reports of trouble at Harpers Ferry arrived. He volunteered to help quell the disturbance and served as aide to Robert E. Lee, who commanded the marines sent to Harpers Ferry. Very early on the morning of October 18, 1859, Stuart delivered Lee's demand for surrender to the raiders, who were barricaded in a fire engine house with thirteen hostages. When the engine house door opened a crack, Stuart recognized John Brown pointing a carbine at him. Brown tried to bargain—hostages for freedom—but Stuart in accord with Lee's orders gave a signal to the storming party of marines, and they soon overwhelmed Brown and his followers. Stuart acquired Brown's Bowie knife and some local notice from the event.

As the secession crisis deepened during 1860 and 1861, Stuart vowed to "go with Virginia" but otherwise remained essentially apolitical. When Virginia seceded, Stuart resigned his U.S. commission and secured first a Virginia, later a Confederate, commission as colonel of cavalry. He commanded the First Virginia Cavalry at Harpers Ferry initially under the command of Thomas J. ("Stonewall") Jackson and then in the army of Joseph E. Johnston.

Soon Stuart emerged as a master teacher of cavalry tactics, and he trained his regiment by toying with the then less competent Union horsemen. Stuart grasped the essentials of the mission of mounted troops in the mid-nineteenth century. He had intuited that cavalry charges against massed infantry were doomed relics of Napoleon's day, and although he once said that he wanted to die at the head of a cavalry charge, he never led a charge against an enemy prepared to receive such an assault. Cavalry, Stuart realized, had to dominate the ground between major armies, discern the enemy strength, disposition, and intentions, and deny such information about friendly forces to the enemy. Cavalry could raid, wreck, and disrupt enemy supply and communications; but the first function of horsemen in this conflict was reconnaissance, and to this purpose Stuart schooled his soldiers.

In the campaign that produced the first major battle of the war, Stuart and his three hundred men were appropriately active. He screened the movement of Johnston's army from the Shenandoah Valley to Manassas Junction and then rejoined Johnston for the battle on Bull Run. The First Virginia did charge some disorganized New Yorkers during fighting on July 21, 1861, but for the most part Stuart directed artillery and guided troop units during the conflict. It was Stuart who led Jubal Early and his brigade to the position on the Federal flank at the critical moment in the battle. Early's appearance provoked the Federal withdrawal and the Confederate rush that won the day for the Southerners.

Promoted to brigadier general on September 24, 1861, Stuart commanded the cavalry attached to the Confederacy's primary eastern army. A massed mounted command gave Stuart the advantage over Federal cavalry, which then operated in smaller units dispersed throughout the Union army. Stuart rode in strength, confident of his capacity to overwhelm his adversaries, and so he continued his control of the space between field armies in Virginia. He cultivated his reputation as a "jolly centaur," recruited musicians for his retinue, and seemed to have wonderful fun playing at war.

In June of 1862 Stuart expanded his fame and became known throughout the United States and the Confederacy. Union Gen. George B. McClellan and his huge army threatened Richmond from the suburbs of the Confederate capital. Stuart's West Point superintendent and Harpers Ferry superior Robert E. Lee assumed command of the Army of Northern Virginia and, intending to attack the Federal right flank and rear, dispatched Stuart upon the crucial mission of reconnaissance beyond the Confederate left. On June 12, 1862, Stuart roused his staff at 2:00 A.M. with the proclamation, "Gentlemen, in ten minutes every man must be in his saddle!" and led 1,200 troopers behind the Federal right flank to discover what Lee needed to know. Then he continued his ride completely around the Union army, covering one hundred miles in three days and causing considerable destruction of enemy property and frustrated embarrassment for the Federals—all at the cost of only one Confederate casualty.

Stuart's only regret regarding his Ride around McClellan, or Pamunkey raid, was not encountering his father-in-law in combat. Most of Stuart's in-laws in some way served the Confederacy; Flora Cooke Stuart's cousin John Esten Cooke, for example, served periodically on Stuart's staff. But Phillip St. George Cooke remained with the U.S. Army. "He will regret it [his decision] but once," Stuart remarked, "and that will be continuously." Stuart also directed that his son no longer bear the name of this loyal traitor; Phillip St. George Cooke Stuart became James Ewell Brown Stuart, Jr. During the Ride around McClellan, Cooke commanded the Union cavalry reserve, but he was too slow and cautious to intercept Stuart's horsemen.

Stuart's success enhanced his legendary fame. But the jingling spurs, plumed hat, and fiddle music were in a sense a façade concealing hard work and meticulous planning. Stuart had dispatched John S. Mosby to scout this region days before his ride, and Stuart had consulted with his spies before he ever left camp. He knew what he would find on his reconnaissance before he made his scout. And he carefully placed in his ranks men familiar with the ground over which he would ride and brought them forward as guides at the appropriate times. Stuart was indeed a calculating cavalier.

Lee's army made good use of Stuart's intelligence in the Seven Days' campaign and drove McClellan from Richmond. In the aftermath of victory Stuart became a major general (July 25, 1862), and his cavalry played important roles in the series of victories subsequently achieved by the Army of Northern Virginia. In addition Stuart led a raid on Catlett's Station (August 22, 1862), purloining Union Gen. John Pope's uniform and dispatch book, and he seized 1,200 horses during the Chambersburg raid (October 10–12, 1862). With each new adventure Stuart's fame expanded, giving rise to stories, songs, and poems about him.

In the spring of 1863 Stuart discovered the exposed flank of Joseph Hooker's Union army near Chancellorsville and guided Stonewall Jackson's corps on the flank march to launch the Southern assault. Stuart was at hand when Jackson suffered his mortal wound, and thereafter Stuart took command of Jackson's infantry corps. Stuart handled his sudden assignment quite well

"Form platoons! Draw saber! Charge!"

J.E.B. STUART
STUART'S STANDARD
CAVALRY ORDER

"It is called the Army of the Potomac but it is only McClellan's bodyguard. . . . If McClellan is not using the army, I should like to borrow it for a while."

ABRAHAM LINCOLN
APRIL 9, 1862

and managed the crucial reconnecting with Lee's lines at the same time that he pounded Hooker's with massed artillery. Once more Lee won a significant victory, with Stuart playing an important part.

By June 1863, Stuart commanded almost 10,000 horsemen as Lee's army concentrated for a thrust into Pennsylvania. On June 9, however, Union Gen. Alfred Pleasonton sent an equal number of Federal troopers, plus infantry, against the unsuspecting Stuart at Brandy Station. The Federals achieved surprise and compelled the Confederates to fight for their lives. Brandy Station was the largest, exclusively cavalry battle of the war—indeed, the largest ever in North America—and Stuart held his own only with immense difficulty. His enemies had served notice that they could fight him on equal terms. Still, Stuart claimed victory, although most Southerners knew otherwise.

As Lee persisted with his campaign into Pennsylvania, Stuart dutifully screened the army's march. Then, however, he determined again to ride around another Union army and began his own march north by circling east of the Federal force. En route Stuart captured 150 supply wagons, and this baggage impeded his capacity to move and scout. Thus, on the eve of the Gettysburg campaign, Stuart somehow lost contact with two huge armies, friend and foe, and failed in his vital obligation of reconnaissance.

"Well, General Stuart, you are here at last," were Lee's reported words when Stuart finally joined the army at Gettysburg on the second day of the battle. Stuart's tardiness left Lee uninformed about the strength of his enemy, but he knew the location of George G. Meade's Federals by this time; on the third and climactic day of Gettysburg he sent a massive infantry charge at the center of Union lines on Cemetery Ridge. As George Pickett led the assault that bears his name, Stuart mounted his own charge against Federal cavalry a mile or two from the infantry action. Both Stuart's and Pickett's charges failed; had they succeeded, Stuart would certainly have shared the glory of having slashed Meade's army into fragments. As he had done after Brandy Station, Stuart attempted to compensate for his errors in the field with a bombastic report of his actions. Unfortunately, he confused fantasy and reality, in much the same way he confused fame with greatness, because he lacked the depth and maturity to know the difference.

Stuart nevertheless was a great cavalry commander, arguably the best in the war. He had proved capable of leading a large mounted force, of cooperating and contributing within a major field army, and of carrying out raids and reconnaissance with equal facility.

By 1864, though, his horsemen were outnumbered and outmounted. He served Lee well in the Wilderness campaign, but then had to confront a thrust against Richmond by Union Gen. Philip Sheridan. The Federal commander planned to lure Stuart away from Lee's army and destroy him. On May 11, at Yellow Tavern, only six miles from Richmond, Stuart confronted Sheridan's 10,000 men with a force less than a third its size. In the battle Stuart suffered a wound that proved mortal. Carried to Richmond, he lay in pain as well-wishers, including Jefferson Davis, visited him. At 7:38 P.M. on May 12 Stuart died; his legend, though, still lives.

[*See also* Stuart's Raids.]

— EMORY M. THOMAS

STUART'S RAIDS

James Ewell Brown ("Jeb") Stuart and his cavalry disrupted Union supply lines and gathered significant intelligence for Robert E. Lee in support of operations of the Army of Northern Virginia throughout 1862.

Stuart's most spectacular expedition occurred on June 12 through 15 in the Peninsular campaign. As a prelude to his plan to relieve Northern pressure upon Richmond, Lee instructed the twenty-nine-year-old Stuart to "make a secret movement to the rear of the enemy" to determine the practicability of striking the Federal army's right wing north of the Chickahominy River. Subsequently at 2:00 A.M. on the twelfth, Stuart ordered 1,200 troopers from four Virginia regiments into the saddle, and the half-mile-long column began moving northwest toward Hanover Court House.

Breaking bivouac early on the thirteenth, Stuart shifted his direction from north to east, heading for Old Church Crossroads. With the exception of a brief encounter with a Fifth U.S. Cavalry detachment, in which Capt. William Latané of the Ninth Virginia Cavalry was killed, Stuart met with no opposition. (The *Burial of Latané*, an 1864 oil painting by William Washington, idealized Southern womanhood and soldierly valor and became a central icon of the postwar Lost Cause movement.)

Arriving at Old Church on the afternoon of the thirteenth, Stuart's semicircular route had carried him thirty-five miles from Richmond and behind George B. McClellan's army. He had discovered McClellan's right was vulnerable, but the Confederate cavalier now became concerned about his own rear. Reasoning that the Federals would intercept his return, Stuart decided upon "the quintessence of prudence," turning his mounts south in an attempt to ride completely around McClellan's army. "There was something of the sublime in the implicit confidence and unquestioning trust of the rank and file," Stuart later informed Lee, "in a leader guiding them straight . . . into the very jaws of the enemy."

Nine miles south at Tunstall's Station, on the York River Railroad, Stuart seized and burned supply wagons and nearly captured a train. By midnight of the fourteenth, the column reached the Chickahominy, but its rain-swollen swamps prevented easy passage. Stuart ordered a bridge constructed, and his troopers crossed the river just ahead of pursuing Federals, commanded by Stuart's father-in-law, Brig. Gen. Philip St. George Cooke. Stuart then headed for the James River, returning to Richmond on June 15 after nearly a hundred miles of riding. He had captured 165 prisoners and 260 mules and horses during his journey around 105,000 Union soldiers, and he had learned that McClellan's right flank was "in the air." McClellan likewise observed this vulnerability, and he

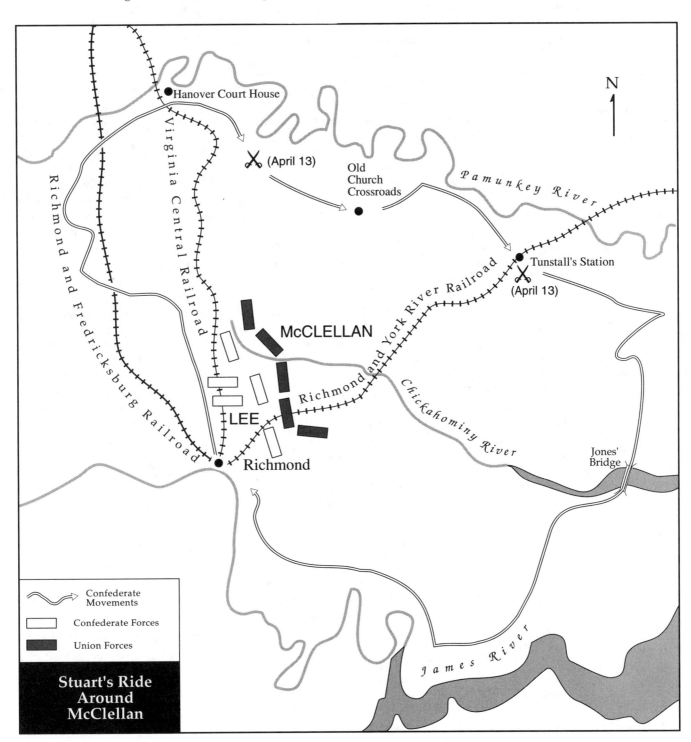

Stuart's Ride Around McClellan

On June 12, 1862, Lee sent J.E.B. Stuart on a reconnaissance mission into Union lines to determine enemy strength.

PAGE 417

began moving his base of supplies and his army south toward the James.

Following the Seven Days' campaign and the Union decision to withdraw McClellan from the Virginia Peninsula, Lee turned north to encounter John Pope. On August 22, while sparring with Pope along the Rappahannock, Stuart received approval to strike the enemy's rear. With 1,500 men and two guns, Stuart crossed the Rappahannock at Waterloo Bridge and proceeded toward Catlett's Station on the Orange and Alexandria Railroad. Reaching Catlett's after dark on the twenty-second, Stuart surprised Pope's headquarters camp and seized Pope's uniform and dispatch book. The Confederates failed to sever Pope's supply line, however, as the railroad bridge across Cedar Run had become saturated during a terrific thunderstorm. In addition to Pope's personal baggage, Stuart captured over three hundred prisoners during this one-day raid.

Three weeks after the conclusion of the Sharpsburg campaign, Lee and McClellan remained stationary about sixty miles northwest of Washington. On October 8, in an effort to determine the Federals' "position, force, and probable intention," Lee ordered Stuart to embark on an expedition into western Maryland and southern Pennsylvania. Lee specifically instructed Stuart to slice McClellan's main supply line by destroying the Conococheague bridge of the Cumberland Valley Railroad near Chambersburg. Lee also asked Stuart to arrest "citizens of Pennsylvania holding State or government office . . . [so] that they may be used as hostages, or the means of exchange." Lee also granted Stuart permission to round up horses from Maryland and Pennsylvania farmers.

Execution of Stuart's Pennsylvania raid commenced during the night of October 9–10 when a force of 1,800 cavalry and four guns left Darkesville near Opequon Creek. When the Confederate crossing of the Potomac began about 3:00 A.M. at McCoy's Ferry, Union cavalry detected the movement and quickly spread the word. Meanwhile, Stuart rode swiftly north, arriving at Chambersburg at dark. The Confederates had ridden forty miles without opposition.

While at Chambersburg, Stuart's men failed to destroy the iron trestle of the Conococheague bridge, but the Southerners did torch the railroad's extensive machine shops and depot buildings. In addition, about five thousand muskets were destroyed, and 280 wounded Federals paroled.

As Stuart headed east toward Gettysburg on the eleventh, Union authorities plotted to seal off his escape routes. "Not a man should be permitted to return to Virginia," insisted General in Chief H. W. Halleck. McClellan responded by sending infantry divisions north and west of the Potomac and cavalry to the east. As McClellan declared, "I hope we may be able to teach them a lesson they will not soon forget."

Stuart, anticipating the Union clamp, kept the Federal chasers off guard with deceptive cross-country maneuvers. Finally he recrossed the Potomac at White's Ford near Poolesville late in the morning on the twelfth.

In three days, Stuart's command had traveled 180 miles, 80 in the last twenty-four hours of the raid. The Confederates captured over 1,200 horses and suffered no men killed and only one wounded. In addition to detecting the position of the enemy and causing a political fallout for the Lincoln administration, Stuart concluded that "the consternation among property holders in Pennsylvania beggars description."

Stuart's final behind-the-enemy raid of 1862 occurred following the Confederate victory at Fredericksburg in mid-December. On Christmas Day, Stuart led 1,800 men and four guns across the Rappahannock at Kelly's Ford and then in the direction of Dumfries and the Occoquan River. His purpose was to seize the Telegraph Road and destroy any trains supplying Ambrose Burnside's Army of the Potomac.

Stuart discovered Dumfries too well defended by Federal infantry and little traffic on the Telegraph Road. His command did capture nearly a hundred prisoners at Greenwood Church near the Occoquan before moving northwest toward the Orange and Alexandria Railroad. At Burke's Station, Stuart seized the telegraph and wired the quartermaster general of the United States to complain about the poor quality of the Federal mules he had lately captured. His command then destroyed the railroad bridge over the Accotink River before proceeding north and west toward Fairfax Court House and Loudoun County. Stuart returned to Fredericksburg on New Year's Day with more than two hundred prisoners and twenty-five wagons, with a loss of only one killed and six wounded.

[*See also* Brandy Station; Gettysburg Campaign.]

— DENNIS E. FRYE

SUBMARINES

The Union blockade of Southern ports forced Confederates to develop a variety of weapons to counter it: the ironclad, the rifled cannon, the torpedo, the semi-submersible torpedo boat, and, most remarkably innovative, the submarine.

Experiments with submarines had been made as early as the American Revolution; Robert Fulton was among the first inventors. The Civil War concentrated and accelerated efforts that had previously been merely speculative.

By the late summer of 1861, submarine development got underway at Tredegar Iron Works in Richmond and along the James River. The major effect was psychological, for the Union fleet at Hampton Roads was unnerved by rumors and false sightings of what later came to be known as an "infernal machine." A strong possibility exists that the Confederacy also built other submarines for which no conclusive evidence exists. Federal reports placed submarines in the James River, Virginia, at Houston, Texas, and Shreveport, Louisiana.

The dreaded threat of a submarine strike did not become reality until February 17, 1864, when USS *Housatonic* became the first ship sunk in battle by a submarine—*H. L. Hunley* in Charleston Harbor. That single triumph had been hard bought by a New Orleans group composed of inventor J. R. McClintock and investors H. L. Hunley, R. F. Barrow, Henry L. Leovy, Baxter Watson, and J. K. Scott.

The men first constructed *Pioneer* at Leeds Foundry in a civilian for-profit operation. *Pioneer* was commissioned as a privateer, and the group applied for a letter of marque to attack Union shipping. The risks were great, but so were the potential returns on their investment.

Pioneer served as a prototype for the more famous *Hunley*. The cigar-shaped craft was thirty-four feet long, with a cabin four feet by four feet by ten feet. The crew could sight through circular windows on the sides, and a manhole on the conning tower above provided access to the vessel. This earliest design of a submarine carried a crew of two, one to man a hand crank that turned the propeller and the other to steer the sub beneath a ship and screw a clock torpedo (mine) to the hull. Tests conducted in Lake Pontchartrain were successful, but New Orleans fell to Adm. David Farragut's fleet before *Pioneer* could inflict any damage on Union vessels. It was destroyed to avoid capture. (The submarine currently preserved at the Louisiana State Museum in New Orleans is believed not to be *Pioneer*, but some other, unknown vessel.)

Hunley, Watson, and McClintock moved their operation to Parks and Lyon's Foundry in Mobile, where they constructed *American Diver,* with dimensions thirty-six feet long by three feet wide by four feet deep. Because the cylindrical ends of *Pioneer* had created steering problems, twelve feet of hull on each end were tapered. An expensive effort to develop an electromagnetic engine was abandoned in favor of four crewmen cranking the propeller shaft. Foul weather prevented *American Diver* from attacking the Mobile blockaders, but Hunley's group, now joined by army engineers Lts. W. A. Alexander and G. E.

The H. L. Hunley was the last in a series of privateer submarines built by a consortium of investors and engineers in Mobile and New Orleans.

PAGE 276

Dixon, was determined to launch a fully operational submarine.

H. L. Hunley was a larger, nine-man version of previous ships at 40 feet long by 3½ feet wide by 4 feet deep. Ballast tanks at either end of the hull could be flooded for submersion and pumped out to ascend. A heavy iron keel plate supplied ballast, but could be released by loosening bolts inside the hull should an emergency ascent be necessary. Eight men cranked the propeller. In addition to the manhole in the conning tower and the round windows, this sub had more sophisticated equipment: two hollow pipes with stop cocks that extended above the surface as a kind of snorkle, a mercury depth gauge, and a compass. A candle served the dual purpose of providing light and warning of dangerously low oxygen.

The original design called for *Hunley* to pass under a ship with a cylinder torpedo in tow. Once the sub had cleared the hull, the torpedo would detonate on contact. Because this tactic would not work against a ship in shallow water, this design was replaced by a spar torpedo.

Reports of *Hunley* distressed the Union blockaders but so impressed Gen. P. G. T. Beauregard that he ordered it transferred from Mobile Harbor to Charleston, where the need for such a weapon was more critical. In August 1863, the submarine was raised and sent with priority scheduling through the rail system to Charleston. Test runs immediately got underway with the help of veteran pilots who knew the slightest variations of wind and tide in the harbor. Even so, a navy crew promptly sank the "New Fangled boat," which was beginning to earn another name: "peripatetic coffin."

Hunley was summoned from Mobile, with Dixon, Alexander, and Thomas Parks, to train a crew and manage the sub. On October 15, Hunley, Parks, and six crewmen were lost when they were unable to raise the ship in an emergency. Partially turned bolts on the keel plate, a cock inadvertently left open, and the death agonies apparent in the bodies of the crew were painful evidence of the risks of the new technology.

Despite Beauregard's refusal to allow further risk of life, Dixon assembled a crew and soon was conducting further training, including submersion for increasingly longer periods. Once, when they remained submerged for more than an hour, anxious observers mistakenly gave them up for dead and left the wharf.

Sinking *Housatonic* after more than two years of labor became, then, an immense achievement for the Confederacy. The event was all *Hunley's* inventors and crew might have imagined. Just after 8:00 P.M., the officer of the deck glimpsed what appeared to be a log floating toward his ship; he shouted a warning, the drummer beat to quarters, and in another moment the giant ship was lifted out of the water by an exploding torpedo.

At dawn, Union rescue boats found many crewmen perched in the ship's rigging, for it had settled into the relatively shallow harbor. *Hunley*, however, was nowhere to be found. The effect of the threat remained, for Union blockaders thought it had been concealed or even returned to Mobile. Alexander, Beauregard, and the rest knew better. Dixon, his crew, and *Hunley* had vanished. Years later, a diver found the little craft, which apparently had been trapped beneath the hull of the sinking *Housatonic*.

The Confederacy had repeated a familiar chapter in its naval history: inventive, persistent, heroic, and ultimately futile—except in this sense: future navies would successfully adapt the technology that claimed the lives and fortunes of history's first submariners.

— MAXINE TURNER

SUBSTITUTES

[This entry discusses the use by Confederate citizens and soldiers of substitutes for previously available goods that became unavailable as the Civil War progressed. For discussion of the hiring of military substitutes to avoid conscription into the Confederate army, see Conscription.*]*

The establishment of the Confederate nation produced many changes in the daily life of the average Southerner. Very early in the conflict Southerners discovered that the common things they had taken for granted in the past had become scarce or nonexistent. The increased effectiveness of the Union blockade and the South's shortage of essential—and nonessential—raw materials and finished goods forced Southerners to develop substitutes. In this realm, they proved to be resourceful and ingenious.

One of the most common complaints was the lack of certain foods and beverages, especially coffee. Southerners became adept at creating substitutes for that favorite drink. Many women submitted recipes to local newspapers calling for such ingredients as chicory, okra, crushed acorns, or rye. Confederate soldiers, too, argued the merits of various nut and fruit concoctions that produced a dark liquid reminiscent of coffee—at least in color. Sugar for that coffee or for baking was also in short supply. Southerners turned to sorghum or honey or boiled down fresh fruits to make a thick, sweet syrup.

Clothing shortages affected everyone. The South's textile base was virtually monopolized by the demands of the Quartermaster Bureau. Consequently, civilians were often forced to make do with old clothes. People recycled old material to create everyday clothing. Many women pulled spinning wheels out of the attic and began to manufacture homespun, or they utilized their sewing skills to convert draperies, carpets, and bed sheets into usable clothing for their families. The loss of wool supplies from areas overrun by Federal troops produced severe shortages of that commodity. In its place, Southerners combined cotton with rabbit or raccoon fur to make warmer garments. In order to render these homemade pieces more attractive, people turned to nature for dyes: berries, bark, and the like produced colors that helped hide the makeshift nature or origin of the piece. Shoes, however, were the scarcest item, and it took every bit of ingenuity to devise usable substitutes. Generally, families recycled old bits of leather, but some used wood and heavy canvas duck to create shoes.

On both the battle front and the home front the shortage of medicine had potentially dire consequences. In this realm, the blockade had a far-reaching effect, as did the cessation of trade with the Northern states. Shortages of quinine, morphine, and other necessary drugs were common. Home remedies enjoyed some popularity, but for many ailments, there was no adequate substitution. Substitutes for quinine were tried and found to be effective—cottonseed tea and dog fennel, for example. But for other drugs, such as chloroform or morphine, no makeshift sufficed, so Southerners were forced to rely upon the contraband trade in drugs.

Although most shortages affected mainly the civilian population behind the lines, other people, more directly related to the war effort, also encountered difficulties. For example, many war contractors found that shortages of raw materials hampered their production for the government. These entrepreneurs tried myriad experiments with substitute items. When supplies of oil for engines and lubrication ran short, railroad engineers discovered that lard oil, peanut oil, and castor oil worked just as well. Those manufacturing artillery or cavalry harnesses substituted oak or hickory wood splints for leather. People made ropes for battlefield or farm use by weaving moss, grasses, cotton, or okra stalks into twine.

It is safe to say that shortages of goods affected all Confederates at one time or another, and the dearth of everyday items probably took a toll after a while. Wax for good-quality candles was lacking; paper and ink for letters and newspapers disappeared; lost buttons became irreplaceable. Through it all, Southerners adapted. But as ingenious as they were, they never fully solved the problem. Shortages, and the adoption of substitutes, testifies to how dependent the region was upon foreign and domestic importations for the most common goods.

[*See also* Sugar; Uniforms.]

— MARY A. DECREDICO

SUGAR

The sugar industry of the antebellum South was largely concentrated in south Louisiana (95 percent) with some small production in Texas, coastal South Carolina and Georgia, and south Florida. In the 1850s the annual crop averaged about 150,000 tons (300,000 hogsheads of 1,000 pounds). Sugar planters shipped their product to the southern Mississippi valley and to eastern cities where it was consumed largely as raw sugar rather than refined. Southern sugar production supplied one-third to one-half of total U.S. consumption. The remainder was imported from the West Indies.

Ideal conditions for the growth of sugar cane include a temperature averaging 75°F year-round with no freezes, an annual rainfall of sixty inches well distributed, and a fertile soil that drains rapidly and thoroughly. The Southern sugar region possessed most of these characteristics, but it was subject to cold weather and freezes, which threatened the crops.

Sugar cane is planted from seed cane taken from the preceding year's crop. Southern cane planters took only three crops from a field before replanting, in contrast to the many years cane was allowed to ratoon (sprout from the roots) in tropical areas. Cane, planted in rows of five to seven feet in width, was cultivated mainly by mule-driven plows by the 1850s, although hoe cultivation was still used from time to time.

The large farm or plantation was the dominant agricultural unit in the Southern cane region; farms of fewer than a hundred acres were neither numerous nor important in the output of sugar. The working force included planter-owners, overseers, sugar makers, and from time to time hired skilled laborers. But the major part of the labor force was made up of slaves, who by 1860 composed 60 percent of the population of the Louisiana sugar region.

The harvesting season began in mid- or late October when the slaves, working with huge knives, began the cutting, which was completed in late December or early January. Once the juice was crushed from the cane with steam-driven rollers, the process of making sugar began. Most common was the open-kettle process utilizing a set of six cast iron kettles. The heated juice was ladled from one to another as impurities were removed, water evaporated, and the juice clarified. When the juice reached the last kettle, the temperature was extremely hot and the syrup was ready for granulation; after the crystals had formed, the sugar was packed into hogsheads and the remaining syrup allowed to drain.

Southern sugar houses produced raw sugar of varying quality that was usually consumed in that form. By the 1850s, greatly improved apparatus for sugar mak-

A slogan that appeared in the press captured Confederate philosophy: "*Plant Corn and Be Free, or plant cotton and be whipped.*"

PAGE 430

ing had been developed by Norbert Rillieux, a distinguished black creole of Louisiana who had studied physics and mechanics in France and was familiar with developments in the manufacture of beet sugar. The advanced equipment utilized vacuum pan evaporators, which produced a sugar that was of more uniform consistency and whiter and dryer than open-kettle sugar.

The Texas and Florida sugar areas escaped the ravages of war, but the Louisiana area was not so fortunate. Life in that region experienced abrupt changes when Federal troops arrived in 1862. As the troops extended their control, great numbers of blacks left the plantations in order to join the Northerners. Both planters and newly freed blacks attempted to adjust to the altered situation in 1862 and 1863, but neither group was satisfied with the new relationship. In order to ensure an adequately disciplined labor force, especially during the harvesting season, planters sought to regulate both the working and nonworking hours of the cane cutters. Many of the blacks viewed their efforts as tantamount to a reimposition of slavery.

In January 1863 Gen. Nathaniel P. Banks, commander of the Department of the Gulf, issued orders dealing with the operation of plantations. Planters were to provide "food, clothes, proper treatment, and just compensation" for the blacks. Workers were to receive one-twentieth of the proceeds of the crop at the end of the year or a fixed monthly compensation of two dollars for field hands and three dollars for mechanics and sugar hands.

Early in 1864 General Banks, attempting to respond to dissatisfaction by both planters and sugar cane workers, issued new orders, which increased wages, regulated the workday, and guaranteed just treatment, healthy rations, clothing, quarters, medical attention, and education for children. Workers could choose their employers, but contracts were to remain in force for one year. In order to ensure completion of the year, one-half of a worker's wages could be withheld until the end of the year. Contracts based on these stipulations were entered into throughout the sugar region in 1864 and 1865.

After the Confederates lost control of the Mississippi River and the sugar region of south Louisiana in 1862, the sugar supply almost entirely disappeared from Mississippi to Virginia. Only the small amounts arriving by blockade-runners and that cultivated in Florida and Georgia were available. Substitute sweeteners such as honey, maple syrup, and especially sorghum cane syrup were used instead.

Under the disordered conditions of the war years, it was impossible to grow, harvest, manufacture, and market the sugar crop successfully. From a record 460,000 hogsheads (230,000 tons) of sugar valued at $25 million, the crop declined steadily until the cumulative effect of an inadequate labor force and widespread destruction of capital equipment resulted in an 1864 crop of only 10,000 hogsheads valued at less than $2 million. Although more than 1,200 plantations in twenty-four parishes had produced sugar in 1861, in 1864 only 175 plantations in sixteen parishes were still making sugar.

The collapse of the industry can be seen in its capital losses. In 1861 the total capital invested in the industry was estimated at $194 million of which $100 million was in slave property, $25 million in land, and $69 million in capital equipment and rolling stock. With the investment in slave property wiped out, capital equipment largely destroyed, and a drastic decline in the value of sugar lands, the industry was worth only $25 million in 1865.

With the end of the Civil War, sugar planters and workers alike had to adjust to a new order of society, which demanded abandonment of old habits, convictions, and prejudices.

— J. CARLYLE SITTERSON

SUMNER, CANING OF

On May 22, 1856, Preston Brooks, a congressman from South Carolina, entered the chambers of the upper house and beat Senator Charles Sumner of Massachusetts senseless with a cane. This event, which came at a time when the struggle over slavery in Kansas was creating powerful tensions between the North and the South, further polarized the sections, contributed to the rapid rise of the Republican party, and was an important landmark on the road to the Civil War.

Sumner had been elected to the Senate in 1851; by that date he was already well known in Massachusetts as a leading critic of slavery. In 1855 he had helped organize the Republican party, which was pledged to stop the expansion of slavery into the western territories. On May 19 and 20, 1856, he delivered a carefully prepared speech in the Senate on "The Crime against Kansas" in which he lashed out at slavery and the South. Sumner launched scathing attacks on individual Southerners, including his fellow senator Andrew P. Butler of South Carolina, who was absent at the time Sumner spoke. Butler, Sumner charged, had taken "the harlot, Slavery" as "his mistress to whom he has made his vows," and Sumner contended that if the whole history of South Carolina were blotted out of existence "civilization might lose . . . little." Most who heard the speech were appalled at Sumner's language, and Congressman Brooks, who was a cousin of Butler's, was outraged. Two days after Sumner had concluded his remarks, Brooks assaulted him.

"THE SYMBOL OF THE NORTH IS THE PEN; THE SYMBOL OF THE SOUTH IS THE BLUDGEON.—"

RAISIN' CANE

A lithograph by Winslow Homer depicts South Carolina Sen. Preston Brooks's version of chivalry as he prepares to beat Massachusetts Sen. Charles Sumner senseless.

LIBRARY OF CONGRESS

News of Sumner's caning rapidly swept the nation. In the North, even conservatives who were critical of Sumner's antislavery views and vituperative speeches were infuriated by Brooks's assault. Their anger mounted as it became evident that Southerners, rather than condemning Brooks, revered him for defending the honor not only of his relative but of the whole section. Constituents showered him with new canes; merchants of South Carolina sent him one inscribed with the words "hit him again." Southern votes prevented the House from expelling Brooks, who resigned anyway but was triumphantly reelected by his constituents. A fine of three hundred dollars levied by a Washington court proved to be his only punishment.

At the very time news of Sumner's caning reached the North, word came from Kansas that a proslavery mob had attacked the homes, shops, and newspapers of free-state advocates in Lawrence. Republicans, whose party had just been formed and whose future seemed uncertain, were quick to exploit Northern anger at both these actions, characterizing them as proof of Southern willingness to assault free institutions in order to defend slavery. This contention proved popular with many Northerners who were not particularly concerned about the issue of slavery but were worried about defending freedom of speech and press from Southern attack.

Sumner's caning, rather than the sack of Lawrence, provided the Republicans with their most effective image of Southern arrogance. Widespread indignation at the deed led many moderates and conservatives who had previously joined the newly formed American, or Know-Nothing, party to join them instead, and in the 1856 presidential election the Republicans almost defeated the Democratic candidate.

Sumner did not return to the Senate until December 1859, and his empty seat was a constant reminder to the North of Brooks's deed. His critics argued that the senator was feigning illness, but his injuries, complicated by posttraumatic syndrome, had truly disabled him. In 1860 the Republicans took the White House, thereby precipitating the secession of the lower South. Sumner's caning, by arousing the North and helping to make the Republican party a major political force, had proved to be a long step toward war.

[*See also* Bleeding Kansas.]

— RICHARD H. ABBOTT

T

TAXATION

Taxation supplied only a fraction of all government revenues, state and Confederate, in the Civil War South. Throughout the war, the Confederate government issued Treasury notes, from which it derived half of all its revenue (in current dollars), and sold bonds, which generated another one-fourth of the total. In addition, it impressed, or seized, vast quantities of supplies and thus obtained 17 percent of its aggregate purchasing power. That left only 7 percent of all Confederate national revenue secured through taxation. That increment of taxation permitted the Confederacy to purchase some supplies on the open market, while also offering a means of absorbing a minor portion of the Confederacy's redundant currency.

Only gradually did the Confederacy adopt direct taxes. At first, members of the new national government anticipated either no war or only a short one. Moreover, given the pervasive unpopularity of direct taxes, the Provisional Congress enacted only import and export duties. But the war came, expenditures grew, and the Federal blockade curtailed revenues from duties. Therefore, in August 1861, the Congress imposed direct taxes payable in Treasury notes. The new tax, at one-half of 1 percent of assessed property valuation, relied on the fiscal machinery of the state governments and ultimately generated $17.4 million. Reflecting the structure of the tax base across the South, the new tax derived 35 percent of that amount from slaves and another 33 percent from real estate. Most states took advantage of a provision that permitted a state to pay its citizens' share of the tax by April 1, 1862, at a 10 percent discount. Similarly, most states borrowed to obtain that money and then failed to tax their citizens to retrieve the amount paid over to the Confederacy. Thus the national tax took the form of state debt.

Only in April 1863 did the Confederacy enact a comprehensive tax law. It levied taxes on occupations, income, and produce as well as on property. Like the 1861 act, which had exempted any head of family whose taxable property was valued at less than $500, the new law was designed to secure purchasing power, on a graduated (or at least proportional) basis, only from those families who likely had some surplus to contribute. The statute placed license taxes ranging from $50 to $500 on many occupations, levied a grad-

uated tax on annual incomes of more than $500, taxed at 8 percent all naval stores, money, and agricultural products "not necessary for family consumption," and imposed a tax-in-kind of 10 percent of annual agricultural productions beyond an allowance for subsistence. Subsequent measures in February 1864, June 1864, and March 1865 raised these rates.

The Confederate system of direct taxes, such as it was, carried several unmanageable burdens. For one, though reliance on taxation became greater in the second half of the war, the aggregate value of supplies seized through impressment dwarfed the revenue achieved through taxation, and nothing guaranteed anything remotely resembling fiscal fairness in the activities of the impressment agents. Heedless of local needs or of producers' ability to pay, those agents gathered supplies, instead, according to local availability and government need. For another, the issue of Treasury notes generated seven times the purchasing power that taxation did, three times the amount raised through impressment, and twice the combined total of impressment and taxation. The tax system simply failed to absorb a sufficient quantity of the Treasury notes from circulation. Inflation raced ahead of revenues.

With four years of war, state and local governments, too, faced huge demands. Their revenue systems, however, were already in place and fully functional in 1861, though the war forced major adjustments in their operations. The states varied widely in particulars of their wartime fiscal behavior, yet they tended to share a number of general features. They typically resorted at first to huge bond issues and then moved primarily to the issue of Treasury notes. They maintained the core of their prewar tax systems throughout the war, but rates on traditional objects of taxation climbed, and new measures tapped new objects.

Though taxation supplied only a small fraction of each state's wartime revenue, taxation provided an even smaller share of the Confederate government's total income. In contrast to both Confederate and state governments, counties generated little long-term debt, as they typically paid for large portions of their expenditures by issuing certificates of indebtedness, which they then called back in by means of taxes payable in those certificates. The larger political units mostly ignored calls that they do likewise. Nobody thought that wartime taxes

The Confederacy hoped to raise tax revenue on the sale of cotton abroad.
PAGE 158

The Confederacy was convinced that it could become self-sufficient.
PAGE 158

The Confederacy never took a census of its own and refused to use the Federal census of 1860.

PAGE 175

should fully match public expenditures, whether by the states or the Confederate governments, but, though bonds offered a means of making long-term loans, many Southerners argued that a larger fraction of Treasury notes should be called in for taxes than was the case.

Georgia offers one model of fiscal change in the Confederate South. On the eve of the war, its state tax system relied on a general property tax that, with low (and even declining) rates, supplied all the tax revenue that expenditures required. A poll tax more or less off-set a standard deduction against the property tax. The state poll tax stayed unchanged through the war, while state property taxes multiplied by almost sixteen between 1860 and 1864. That increase was greater than any other state displayed, but virtually every state substantially hiked its rates on property.

Georgia also illustrates another major facet of the Confederate South's fiscal experience. On the tax side of the state budget, Georgia favored its less wealthy citizens. Across the South, public authorities sought to cushion the smaller farmers and other less wealthy white families from the full force of the tax rate increases. Exemptions from the property tax grew for Confederate soldiers' families who held property of only modest valuation. Thus new exemptions characterized Southern tax systems at the same time that much higher general property tax rates did. Moreover, Georgia left its poll tax rates unchanged throughout the war, and by 1863 it suspended even those rates for all soldiers with only small holdings.

On the spending side, too, Georgia proved a representative state in offering benefits to small farmers that it denied the more wealthy. State and local authorities recognized early on that winning the war depended on retaining in the army the tens of thousands of soldiers from farm families who had little economic cushion. As one Mississippi soldier wrote his governor, "we are poor men and are willing to defend our country but our families first and then our count[r]y." Soldiers would, and did, desert the battlefront to head back home when they believed their loved ones to be suffering from inadequate supplies of food and other necessities.

Authorities therefore made commitments to allocate enormous sums for the support of soldiers' families. At first, the counties acted, particularly when it became clear that calls for voluntary contributions drew uneven—and thus unequal and insufficient—amounts of aid. Counties responded by resorting to the coercion of the tax system to obtain the funds (or the provisions) that they needed. But then it became clear that the counties most in need often had the least resources, and thus the state stepped in. Georgia's state government, matching its own direct military expenditures almost dollar for dollar through the war, supplied huge sums for the support of soldiers' families. Throughout much of the South, state and local authorities alike allocated large, even major, portions of their budgets to the distribution of cash or such commodities as salt, corn, and bacon.

In these ways, the Georgia experience demonstrates how Southern state and local governments became more progressive during the war, and how authority and responsibility grew more centralized. The tax system became more progressive as rates on the wealthy rose at the same time that the less wealthy gained exemptions. And, on the spending side, the state government taxed planters in the black belt to generate funds with which to acquire food to supply soldiers' families in the nonplantation counties. The huge

WAR BOND

A Confederate $10,000 bond. The Confederate States of America sold $577 million of bonds and $291 million of call certificates to finance the war.

GORDON BLEULER

increases in state tax rates midway through the war reflected, in part, an assumption by the state of responsibilities that the counties had undertaken in the first two years of the war.

In these various ways, state and local authorities demonstrated that they acted with one eye on the home front and one eye on the battlefront. And they supplied tangible benefits to constituents whose support was essential if the war was to be prosecuted with much chance of success. As part of a wartime agenda, the higher taxes—first at the county level, then at the state—could be seen to be purchasing real goods for real constituents. Governments at the state and local levels revealed themselves as in the business of caring for civilians as much as they were covering the costs of rifles, tents, and boots for the troops. Such could not be said for Confederate national spending policies. These facets of state and local operations may help explain why the men who set state and local taxes felt that they could demand escalating taxes—why they may have detected less resistance to higher and higher taxes than their national counterparts seemed to perceive.

Yet all such considerations highlight, too, the differences, by class and by region within each state, that separated the larger slaveholders from their less prosperous fellow citizens. The differences were real, and they emerged in struggles over tax policy. Indeed, a central issue in parts of the South related to the taxes on planters' slaves. In North Carolina, for example, perhaps the leading issue in state politics in the 1850s had been whether slave property should carry a larger share of the state tax burden. On the eve of the war, small farmers had finally achieved success, they thought, in demanding that planters carry a larger share, but their victory proved illusory, even in the crucible of war. In Virginia in 1861, by contrast, planters from the eastern half of the state offered the small farmers of the west a major concession—higher taxes on slaves—in hopes of cementing their support for the Confederacy. Though the concession was real, much of that support evaporated, as West Virginia went its separate political, military, and fiscal way.

By late 1864 and early 1865, the Confederacy's war effort was winding down, and for more reasons than a

TAX-IN-KIND

The Confederate States of America tried from its inception to develop a system to provide revenue for its treasury. Resistant to enacting an income tax, Confederate Treasury Secretary Christopher G. Memminger and the Congress proposed and passed into law other initiatives. One of the most unpopular was the tax-in-kind, enacted in April 1863.

Secretary Memminger designed the tax-in-kind to serve as an alternative to the impressment of agricultural products. The Treasury and War departments, the chief administrators of the tax-in-kind, enumerated items that agents, or "T.I.K. men," would collect in each locality. The list of goods included wheat, oats, corn, rice, potatoes, fodder, sugar, cotton, wool, tobacco, and rye. Each farmer was to retain for his or her own use fifty bushels of sweet potatoes, either one hundred bushels of corn or fifty bushels of wheat, and twenty bushels of peas or beans; from what remained, the farmer was required to donate 10 percent to government agents. Southern agriculturalists were

also required to pay in kind on bacon and pork, based upon a 10 percent tax on all hogs slaughtered during 1863. The agents would assess the value of the farms' products and notify the farmers of the amount they were required to tithe. If the assessor's estimate varied greatly from the farmer's, a mediator would make the final determination of the value of the goods. Farmers who failed to pay their tithe were subject to a stiff penalty. The agents collected the goods and funneled them to local and district-level quartermasters who were supposed to ensure that the items reached the armies in the field.

The tax-in-kind proved to be one of the most, if not the most, unpopular acts the Confederate Congress ever passed. Farmers resisted the quotas, especially since they were based on the gross value of crops, not on profits, and they loathed the T.I.K. men who pressed them for payment. A serious problem with the tax lay in its collection and distribution: often crops would rot at depots before quartermasters could transport them to the army. The program

was also plagued by phony agents who swindled farmers out of their produce.

It is difficult to determine how much the Treasury gained from the tax-in-kind. Confederate agents estimated that about $6 million in produce was collected by the end of 1863; by late winter of 1864, the figure stood at $40 million. Public outcry against the tax led to its amendment. In December 1863, Congress allowed the tax on sweet potatoes to be paid in cash. By February 1864, Congress was extending exemptions on the collection of the tax-in-kind for soldiers' families and small farmers; by 1865, the act barely resembled its 1863 version: individuals could substitute cash payments for payments in farm produce.

The criticisms of and alterations to the tax-in-kind indicate that Congress was not oblivious to the flaws of the original act. Despite the chorus of protest, however, the tax-in-kind did help supply and feed the Confederate armies during the final two years of the war.

— MARY A. DECREDICO

Georgia and Alabama derived nearly half of their tax revenues from slave levies, and South Carolina derived over 60 percent.

PAGE 471

On at least one occasion in 1864 considerable quantities of telegraph wire were stolen by Southern planters for use in baling their cotton.

PAGE 551

shortage of military manpower in a war of attrition. Real shortages and runaway inflation each help explain why the Confederacy lost. Tax rates climbed much higher than ever before, yet they played only a minor role in the Confederate government's efforts to finance its operations, and they proved too low to absorb enough of the endless supply of state and Confederate Treasury notes. Though state and local governments clearly treated their citizens on the bases of ability to pay and nature of need, the Confederacy's heavy reliance on impressment could operate to vitiate those policies. In any case, the logistical problems of distributing aid to civilians proved as great as the logistical problems of moving battalions of troops. The Confederacy ran too low on food and clothing, on the means of purchasing them, and on the means of distributing them. The fiscal system failed. And the war ended.

[*See also* Impressment]

— PETER WALLENSTEIN

TELEGRAPH

The Civil War was the first war in which the electric telegraph played a major role. It was used by both sides at both the tactical and strategic levels, though much more effectively by the Union. Indeed, it can be said with some justification that the way that Union forces used telegraph communications was a major factor in determining the outcome of the war.

The simple and rugged American telegraph design was well suited to battlefield use. For transmitting, the operator used a "key" to make and break electrical contact and to send short and long pulses of current from a battery over the wire (only a single wire was needed; connections were made to the ground at each end, and the ground performed the function of a second wire to complete the circuit.) At the receiver the current activated an electromagnet, which pulled against a lever to make short and long clicking noises—"dots" and "dashes" that in combinations represented letters and numbers.

Samuel F. B. Morse, a portrait painter, had invented this form of telegraphy in the 1830s. With money from Congress and practical assistance from Alfred Vail, he constructed a successful demonstration line between Baltimore and Washington in 1844. When no further interest was shown by the government, he licensed private individuals to develop the system. The result was a rapid expansion over the next decade and a half (including competition from non-Morse systems),

culminating in a transcontinental line that was completed in the fall of 1861. A transatlantic cable was momentarily successful in 1858, but it failed before it could be placed in commercial operation and was not replaced until 1866.

On the eve of the war there thus existed an infrastructure of tens of thousands of miles of wire, about 10 percent of it in the states of the Confederacy. These latter lines lay along two major routes reaching to New Orleans: in the east, from Washington through Richmond, Petersburg, Raleigh, Columbia, Augusta, Macon, Montgomery, and Mobile (with side links to Charleston, Savannah, and Atlanta); in the west, along two competing lines from Nashville, one by way of Vicksburg and Natchez, the other through Florence and Jackson. Along with the advantage in miles of wire, the Union had a comparable advantage in numbers of trained operators. The North also, apparently, had a better sense of the value of this form of communications. The Union established a military telegraph service, which constructed and operated fifteen thousand miles of lines during the war; individual Confederate forces established a total of one thousand miles. Furthermore, Union forces used codes to protect their messages; the Confederates, in general, did not.

The significance of these communications systems had thus far been told only in anecdotal form. At the Battle of First Manassas, for instance, P. G. T. Beauregard used the telegraph to call for reinforcements; Theophilus H. Holmes arrived in time to be a decisive factor in the outcome. Another account tells that C. A. Gaston, Robert E. Lee's confidential operator, was able to wiretap Ulysses S. Grant's line for six weeks during the siege of Richmond and Petersburg. Among the unciphered messages was one telling of the impending arrival of 2,536 head of beef at Coggins' Point. A timely raid captured the entire herd. On another front, John H. Morgan's success has been attributed in considerable part to the skill of his operator in intercepting messages and in sending false and misleading messages. Similar stories have been told about virtually every major battle of the war.

Use of the telegraph dramatically altered the manner in which commanders exercised their authority. No longer did they have to be close to the battlefield, and they could be aware of all aspects of a conflict, no matter how large. Thus, during the Wilderness and Atlanta campaigns both Grant and Lee were in almost hourly contact with the various elements of their troops. During the period before and during the battle at Gettysburg, Abraham Lincoln followed the action closely from the War Department office in Washington, where he spent much of his time. By telegraph before the conflict he relieved Joseph Hooker of command and replaced him with George G. Meade. In the aftermath he unsuccessfully urged Meade to pursue Lee to prevent him from escaping across the Potomac River.

The significance of the telegraph in the American Civil War (during which 6.5 million messages are estimated to have been sent by the Union side alone) was not lost on military planners elsewhere. Every regular army in Europe soon had its telegraph corps, and every war fought since then has depended on electrical communications for command and control systems.

— BERNARD S. FINN

THIRTEENTH AMENDMENT

Drawing on the antislavery belief that slavery destroyed an inherent right to self-ownership, Republican members of Congress, in late 1863 and early 1864, introduced several bills to abolish slavery by constitutional amendment. The precise wording of those bills elicited an intense and protracted debate. Some argued that the amendment should specify only that slaves be freed from physical restraint; others said it should vest blacks with certain rights, including the right to own property, testify in court, and sign marriage contracts. Charles Sumner declared that the amendment should state that "all persons are equal before the law." In the end, after intense lobbying by President Abraham Lincoln, a final version passed the House of Representatives on January 31, 1865, by a vote of 119 to 56, two votes more than the necessary two-thirds. The proposed amendment read simply: "Neither slavery nor involuntary servitude, except as a punishment for crime whereof the party shall have been duly convicted, shall exist within the United States, or any place subject to their jurisdiction." Section 2 said that "Congress shall have power to enforce this article by appropriate legislation."

During the final months of the Civil War, most white Southerners recognized that slavery was doomed. Nevertheless, after the war, when the amendment was submitted for ratification to Southern states now under President Andrew Johnson's newly formed governments, some former Confederates worked to defeat the article. The question, they argued, was not whether chattel slavery was dead but whether Congress should be granted the power to intrude into the "domestic affairs" of a state. When the Mississippi legislature rejected the amendment by a vote of 45–25 in the fall of 1865, a writer for the *Jackson Clarion*, reflecting the views of other whites in the lower South, proclaimed that to adopt the amendment would be

tantamount to surrendering "all of our rights as a State to the Federal Congress." He and others refused "to sharpen the sword" that would "sever the arteries of our political life." The Alabama legislature ratified the amendment, but only after declaring that its approval did not extend to the second section.

President Johnson, however, pressed the former Confederate states to ratify the amendment as one precondition for restoration to the Union, assuring them that an end to slavery meant essentially that freedmen and women should be at liberty to work and enjoy the fruits of their labor. With such assurances and the backing of the president, the amendment was ratified by three-fourths of the states on December 18, 1865.

In proposing the amendment, neither Congress nor the framers envisioned a radical change in the relationship between the states and the Federal government; nor did they seek to endow newly freed slaves with citizenship rights. Nevertheless, Article 13 was the first amendment designed to accomplish a national reform, the first to grant Congress power of execution, and the first of the Reconstruction era. During the next few years Congress passed several civil rights laws and the nation ratified two additional constitutional amendments—the Fourteenth Amendment (1868) granting citizenship rights to former slaves, and the Fifteenth Amendment (1870) extending the franchise to freedmen. Thus, the passage of the amendment ending slavery began a process that would fundamentally alter the legal position of blacks in the United States and increasingly shift the responsibility for the protection of former slaves to the Federal government.

— LOREN SCHWENINGER

THOMPSON, JACOB

Thompson, Jacob (1810–1885), U.S. congressman, U.S. secretary of the interior, Confederate colonel, and agent for the Confederacy. Born and raised in North Carolina, Jacob Thompson graduated from the University of North Carolina in 1831 and was admitted to the bar in 1835. He moved to Mississippi where he married well, practiced law, became a planter, and was politically active. A Democrat, he served six terms (1839–1851) in the U.S. House of Representatives but lost a bid to become U.S. senator from Mississippi in 1855. Active in national party politics, Thompson supported Franklin Pierce in 1852 and worked for the nomination and election of James Buchanan in 1856. Buchanan made Thompson secretary of the interior, and he was an energetic department head.

With regard to the intensifying sectional controversy, Thompson insisted that Southern grievances were

"Neither slavery nor involuntary servitude, except as a punishment for crime whereof the party shall have been duly convicted, shall exist within the United States.'

FROM AMENDMENT XIII
TO THE CONSTITUTION OF THE UNITED STATES, 1865

T

NORTHWESTERN CONSPIRACY

Even before the Civil War reached the halfway mark, Governor Oliver P. Morton of Indiana expressed fears that Democrats dissenting from the war effort were planning to revolutionize the upper Midwest. He claimed that certain groups intended to free Confederate prisoners held in Camp Morton near Indianapolis and establish a Northwest confederacy allied with the South. In the fall of 1864 a Morton protégé raided the quarters of Harrison H. Dodd and seized papers that enabled him to concoct an exposé of the Sons of Liberty and publicize Morton's conspiracy theory. Dodd, a printer and Democratic activist, had founded the Sons of Liberty as a secret order to promote conservative measures and win elections.

Just prior to the November 1864 elections soldiers seized some revolvers shipped to Dodd's printing plant from New York and made a round of arrests, including Dodd and Joseph J. Bingham, editor of the Democratic-oriented Indianapolis State Sentinel. Governor Morton parlayed the arrests into "a gigantic Northwestern conspiracy." Later Dodd and four others were tried by a military commission in the Indianapolis treason trials. Actually, Morton's molehill-to-mountain plot consisted of a few facts and much conjecture—there was no overt act.

In Illinois, too, on the eve of the 1864 elections, an editor of the Chicago Tribune and the commandant at Camp Douglas (a compound holding eleven thousand Confederate prisoners) claimed that secret society members and Copperheads intended to free the prisoners, burn Chicago, take over the polls, and establish a Northwestern confederacy. Authorities made a number of arrests and the "Camp Douglas conspiracy," or "Chicago conspiracy," received national publicity. A military commission conducted a treason trial in Cincinnati the next year.

A few Confederate officials at the time convinced themselves that there was a possibility of dissenters establishing a separate confederacy in the upper Midwest. But some present-day historians have debunked the Chicago and Indianapolis conspiracies, contending they were little more than fantasies devised to discredit Democrats and influence the 1864 elections. [See also Copperheads.]
— FRANK L. KLEMENT

legitimate. The central issue in his view was Northern unwillingness to vouchsafe "the rights of Southern men in their slave property." Although defending secession as an inherent right of the states, he was not eager to see the South withdraw from the Union and took a cooperationist stance on the matter. Following Abraham Lincoln's election in November 1860, Thompson hoped that the Buchanan administration could preserve the peace in the crucial months before Lincoln's inauguration and thereby provide an opportunity for the success of compromise efforts that were underway within and without Congress. During cabinet sessions, Thompson counseled restraint in dealing with the secessionists and, if necessary, acceptance of disunion. While still a member of the cabinet and with the acquiescence of the president, Thompson visited the legislature of North Carolina as a formal representative of Mississippi to discuss a cooperationist strategy in the event of drastic provocation on the part of the Federal government. Upon learning of the presidential decision that dispatched *Star of the West* with reinforcements and supplies for Fort Sumter, Thompson resigned his cabinet post.

During the early years of the war, Thompson served with the Confederate army in Tennessee and Mississippi and was also a member of the Mississippi legislature. He accepted an assignment from Jefferson Davis in the spring of 1864 to head a mission to Canada for the purpose of exploiting and encouraging discontent and peace sentiment throughout the North. To finance the undertaking, Davis authorized Thompson to spend as much as $1 million at his own discretion. Clement C. Clay of Alabama agreed to serve with Thompson, and they traveled to Wilmington, North Carolina, where they slipped through the blockade to Bermuda and took passage to Halifax, Nova Scotia. Thompson's usual base of operations while in Canada was Toronto, and Clay operated from St. Catharines, Ontario. Thompson coordinated activities with Clay and had the services of agents sent from the Confederacy. Thompson also enlisted the cooperation of Confederate soldiers who had escaped from Northern prisons, Southerners residing in Canada, and sympathetic Northerners.

He invested considerable time and money in efforts to wreak havoc in the North. He joined with leaders of the Order of the Sons of Liberty during the summer of 1864 in plotting armed uprisings timed to coincide with the return of Clement L. Vallandigham to Ohio from exile and with the Democratic National Convention at Chicago. These plots collapsed amid the hesitation, indecision, and disorganization of the Sons of Liberty. In another scheme, Thompson helped lay plans for armed insurrections in Chicago and New York City on election day, November 8, 1864. The work of spies brought the arrest of key leaders in Chicago, and rumors of trouble in New York prompted the Federal government to send ten thousand soldiers to patrol the city during the canvass. After the troops withdrew, the conspirators, with Thompson's sanction, undertook a plan to burn the city by simultaneously setting fires in several buildings. The resulting blazes created panic but produced little property damage. Various schemes forcibly to release Confederate soldiers held as prisoners of war at Camp Douglas and Johnson's Island also came to naught.

Not all the plans Thompson laid involved violence. He contributed money to the political campaign of the Democratic candidate for governor of Illinois. He gave financial backing to a feeble effort to undermine the Federal currency by converting greenbacks to gold and shipping the gold to England where it was converted to sterling bills of exchange with which to purchase more U.S. gold for export to England. Through repeating the process, the conspirators managed to send $2 million in gold out of the country before ending the operation out of fear of detection and arrest. Thompson also worked to obtain the release of fellow conspirators in the custody of either Canadian or U.S. authorities.

As the mission to Canada drew to a close, Thompson recognized that his efforts had been largely unsuccessful. He attributed his failures to the frustration of his plans by Federal spies who managed to obtain crucial information and to arrest important leaders. He also cited the presence of large numbers of Federal troops who made organization of disaffected citizens impossible. Thompson did not realize that his failures were also due to a misreading of Northern public opinion. Contrary to his assumptions, Northerners who were weary of the war and unhappy with the Lincoln administration were not necessarily Confederate sympathizers or willing to aid in the dismemberment of the Union. On the other hand, Thompson rightly contended that his mission successfully brought consternation and fear in the North.

The assignment ended when Edwin Gray Lee reached Canada early in 1865 at the behest of the Confederate government to relieve Thompson. As instructed, Thompson gave some of the funds entrusted to him to Lee and deposited about $400,000 to the credit of the Confederacy in a British financial institution. Prior to departing Canada for Europe, he learned of President Andrew Johnson's proclamation of May 2, 1865, naming Thompson as one of the conspirators in the assassination of Lincoln. The charge was utterly false, as Thompson declared in a public letter sent to a New York newspaper. He remained out of the United States until 1869 when he returned only to find his property in northern Mississippi devastated. Shunning

politics, he went into business in Memphis, Tennessee, and was residing there at the time of his death.

— LARRY E. NELSON

TOBACCO

Native Americans cultivated tobacco in North America before the first English settlers arrived in Jamestown in 1607. The Indians believed that native tobacco had both religious and medicinal importance. Its use, for example, had great ritual significance for the Indians in the Chesapeake region. Native Americans often smoked tobacco in a pipe to cement a peace accord.

Colonists at Jamestown were the first Europeans on the North American mainland to cultivate tobacco. As early as 1610 John Rolfe shipped a cargo to England for sale. But the naturally occurring tobacco plant in the Chesapeake region *(Nicotiana rustica)* was considered too bitter and harsh, and in 1611 Rolfe obtained seeds of the milder *Nicotiana tabacum* from the Spanish West Indies, Venezuela, and Trinidad for the Jamestown colonists. Thereafter, tobacco production increased rapidly in the Chesapeake Bay area, soon spreading to Maryland. Production continued to increase throughout the colonial period and by the middle of the eighteenth century, Maryland and Virginia were shipping nearly 70 million pounds of tobacco a year to Britain.

Some colonial aristocrats in both Britain and the American colonies believed that tobacco smoking was evil and hazardous to the health. This had little effect in halting the spread of the practice. By the eve of the Revolutionary War, tobacco had become the leading cash crop produced by all the colonies, North and South. Exports rose to over 100 million pounds a year, constituting half of all colonial export trade with Britain.

The methods used for cultivating and curing tobacco have changed over time and varied from region to region. Initially, planters in the Chesapeake region cured tobacco by gathering the plant on the ground and letting the sun dry the leaves, but sun-curing was soon given up in favor of a technique known as air-curing. Tobacco workers gathered leaves in parcels called "hands" and placed them over polls five feet in length. Then the hands were hung inside an open barn to complete the curing process. When fully dried, the tobacco was packed into large containers called hogsheads for shipping. Air-curing, popular in the Piedmont and tidewater regions until the early nineteenth century, resulted in a milder-tasting leaf.

The most important Secret Service operation of the entire Confederate effort was the attempt to turn widespread disaffection with the war and the Lincoln administration into an effective peace movement.

PAGE 192

609

*Those farmers
who had most
thoroughly
committed
themselves to
supplying markets
outside the South
took the first blow
in the conflict.*

PAGE 213

Methods of curing tobacco by heat were known in the 1700s, but the process did not become popular until the early nineteenth century. In the 1820s the bright tobacco leaves of North Carolina and eastern Virginia, and later Kentucky and middle Tennessee, were cured by using enclosed smoking-sawdust fires to dry the tobacco hung in small barns. Although the modern method of flu-curing tobacco using charcoal heat was invented in 1839 in North Carolina, this method was not widely used until after the Civil War.

Both tobacco cultivation and manufacturing are labor-intensive activities. Initially, the Virginia Company of London used white indentured servants to harvest the crop, but they were soon replaced by African slaves. The presence of a large slave population engaged in the cultivation and curing of tobacco tied the growth of slavery to the rise of the plantation system. By 1860, 350,000 slaves were cultivating tobacco. It was, however, an exploitive crop that quickly exhausted the soil, requiring constant clearing of new land. The system also worked against the establishment of urban industrial centers in the colonial and antebellum South.

Throughout the colonial period commercial production of tobacco had centered in Northern port cities, but by the antebellum period, as a result of a surplus of slave labor and the great supply of raw material, commercial manufacturing shifted to the tobacco-growing regions in the South. Virginia dominated the industry with factories located at Richmond, Petersburg, Lynchburg, and Danville, and the border states of Kentucky, Tennessee, and Missouri also became tobacco-manufacturing centers.

The differing ways of consuming tobacco have often mirrored larger cultural trends. Tobacco has been smoked in pipes, cigars, and cigarettes, and also chewed and taken as snuff. Pipe smoking was the most prevalent form of tobacco consumption in the colonial period, although in the late 1700s taking snuff became popular among the elite who were emulating the European aristocracies. Chewing was distinctly American and became popular on the expanding frontier. After the Mexican War cigar smoking became the fad, but during the Civil War people returned to pipes and began rolling cigarettes for the first time.

As in so many other areas of Southern life, the Civil War seriously disrupted the South's tobacco growing and manufacturing. The tobacco-rich states of Virginia, North Carolina, and Tennessee sided with the Confederacy; the success of their crop rose and fell with that of the rebel nation. The tobacco-producing border states of Missouri, Kentucky, and Maryland fell early to Union control. Under the pressure of war, tobacco manufacturing, located in the South throughout the antebellum period, shifted quickly to the

North. New York City became the North's tobacco-manufacturing center, servicing the area once dominated by Virginia tobacco planters. Like New York, Louisville also profited by the war's disruption of Southern market towns, becoming the center of tobacco trade in the West.

Confederate policy and military campaigns in the heartland of the South's tobacco regions devastated Southern tobacco planting and manufacturing. In an attempt to encourage the planting of foodstuffs, the Confederate Congress in March 1862 passed a joint resolution recommending that Confederate states refrain from planting tobacco. Planters often ignored Congress's suggestions, however. The Virginia Assembly also attempted to limit tobacco growing with a law passed in March 1863, and renewed planting restrictions again in February 1864. Other tobacco-growing states passed similar legislation during the war. In addition, local newspapers such as the *Edgefield Advertiser* of South Carolina also exhorted their readers to switch from the planting of tobacco to desperately needed foodstuffs.

Union control of the Mississippi from mid-1863, combined with the naval blockade, restricted the export and manufacturing of tobacco products, as did the shift of factories to manufacturing war matériel. In Richmond, after the First Battle of Manassas, several tobacco warehouses were converted into prisons for Union soldiers. The tobacco-rich county of Louisa, Virginia, saw the kind of physical destruction typical of regions exposed to intense military activity. Intermittent Union raids into the county and one of the war's largest cavalry battles at Trevillian's Depot destroyed not only the crops and livestock but also the county's infrastructure. Every Confederate and border state saw a decline in tobacco production in the 1860s.

The tobacco town of Danville, Virginia, however, took advantage of the vicissitudes of war. In the late 1850s its tobacco industry was in decline, and the community was reluctant to answer the call to arms in 1861. Nevertheless, Danville prospered during the war. Located safely behind enemy lines along a major railroad to Richmond, Danville became a lucrative place for the activities of merchants and manufacturers. Through their investments, the town and the surrounding county saw a revival in the tobacco industry. As a result of its returning prosperity, Danville citizens opposed attempts by Confederate soldiers to destroy the rail connection with Richmond in order to stop the Union advance. Local businessmen also looked favorably upon the Union takeover on the ground that it would bring peace and stability to the region.

While the war made it difficult for the public to obtain tobacco, both Confederate and Union soldiers found it plentiful. Since much of the fighting took place in the tobacco-rich regions of the South, soldiers often helped themselves. For years the U.S. Navy had supplied its sailors with tobacco rations. In February 1864 the Confederate government followed suit and included tobacco as part of the army's rations. Often, in the quiet moments between battle, Confederate and Union soldiers would exchange goods. The traditional swap was Northern coffee for Southern tobacco. Tobacco habits also revealed class distinctions in the South. Confederate officers did not receive the tobacco rations granted to soldiers. Nevertheless, Confederate officers favored the more fashionable smoking of cigars.

Tobacco had a profound influence on the history of the South. Early cultivation brought prosperity and helped ensure the economic survival of the colonies. The development of the tobacco plantation system, however, helped establish slavery in the South to a degree not found in the North. Because tobacco cultivation quickly wore out the soil, planters were constantly clearing new land, leading to the expansion of slavery and tobacco growing. The slave plantation system also worked to slow urban industrial development in the South. Moreover, the early opponents of tobacco use have been proven correct in their argument that it is hazardous to one's health. Thus, at best, tobacco has been a mixed blessing for the South.

— ORVILLE VERNON BURTON
HENRY KAMERLING

TOMPKINS, SALLY L.

Tompkins, Sally L. (1833–1916), captain and nurse. On November 9, 1833, Sally Tompkins was born at Poplar Grove in Matthews County, Virginia, and lived in Richmond from the age of five. When troops from the Battle of First Manassas overwhelmed the city's medical facilities, President Jefferson Davis appealed to the citizens to establish private hospitals.

Responding to his call, Tompkins received permission from Judge John Robertson to utilize his home on Third and Main streets as a hospital. Established on July 31, 1861, the Robertson Hospital opened under her supervision. Within weeks, it was evident that too many patients lingered in Richmond well past their recovery, and Davis ordered all private hospitals to be placed under military personnel. With the help of Judge W. W. Crump, assistant secretary of the treasury, Tompkins met with Davis in an attempt to retain control of Robertson Hospital. To circumvent the military order rule, the president commissioned Tompkins a captain of cavalry (unassigned) in charge of her hospital. When signing her commission, Tompkins noted underneath her name that she

"would not allow my name to be placed upon the pay roll of the army."

Tompkins operated Robertson Hospital until June 13, 1865, using her family's money and government rations. Among the 1,333 patients who passed through her hospital, only 73 died. It primarily served the most seriously wounded and earned the distinction of having the highest rate of soldiers returning to action.

In postwar Richmond, the woman described by her contemporaries as "not over 5 feet, hardly a Southern beauty, with a splendid face, her dark eyes [shining] out under smooth hair parted squarely in the middle," continued to be active in charity work and religious activities. Affectionately referred to as "Captain Sally," she regularly attended Daughters of the Confederacy and veterans' meetings. In 1905, she retired to the Confederate Women's Home in Richmond, where having exhausted her resources, she remained as a guest until her death on July 25, 1916.

As an honorary member of the R. E. Lee Camp of the Confederate Veterans, she was buried with full military honors in Matthews County. In the Confederate Women's Home, her room became a hospital ward. Four chapters of the United Daughters of the Confederacy are named in her honor. On September 10, 1961, a stained glass window depicting her many works was dedicated at the church she attended, St. James's Episcopal in Richmond.

— SANDRA V. PARKER

TOOMBS, ROBERT

Toombs, Robert (1810–1885), U.S. congressman, Confederate secretary of state, and brigadier general. Wilkes County, Georgia, was the first and last home of Robert Toombs, who was born there in comfortable economic circumstances on July 2, 1810. Toombs seemed to enjoy a tempestuous youth that presaged his mercurial life and career. He attended Franklin College (which became the University of Georgia) but suffered expulsion on the eve of his graduation in 1828. Legend has it that Toombs appeared at the ceremony anyway, stood beside an oak tree outside of the college chapel, and delivered his own graduation oration. He did graduate from Union College in Schenectady, New York, and then studied law for a year at the University of Virginia. He returned to Georgia in 1830, married Julia Ann Dubose, and gained admittance to the Georgia bar.

Toombs, a large man, lived on an equally large scale. He was six feet tall and weighed over two hundred pounds. A brilliant courtroom lawyer, he was famous for his speeches to juries. He possessed inherit-

Toombs provided a full rationale for Southern secession and delineated all the political and moral reasons why the Confederacy merited membership in the family of nations.

PAGE 578

T

In July 1863 Rhett argued that only South's best men, leaders such as Toombs and himself, could save the South.

PAGE 499

ed wealth and augmented his inheritance with the profits from his law practice and speculations in land and slaves. Toombs lived in a Greek Revival mansion in Washington, Georgia, and at various times owned

plantations in Stewart County, Georgia; Desha County, Arkansas; and Tarrant County, Texas.

Elected to the Georgia House of Representatives six times (1837–1843), Toombs then won election to the U.S. Congress for four consecutive terms (1844–1851). He became a Whig in Georgia and national politics and voted for the tariff and against war with Mexico. Agitation over slavery alarmed Toombs, however, and in the course of supporting the Compromise of 1850, he helped form the Constitutional Union party as a haven for dissident Whigs. In 1855 Toombs became a Democrat and thereafter counted himself a strong Southern rights advocate, if not a fire-eater. By this time Toombs was in the Senate (1852–1861), where he was one of the leading Southern radicals.

Although he had serious second thoughts about secession following the election of Abraham Lincoln to the presidency, Republican rejection of the Crittenden Compromise drove Toombs into the front ranks of the immediate secessionists. And when delegates from seceded states convened in Montgomery to form the Confederacy, Toombs was a serious candidate for president of the new republic.

Toombs, however, seemed too radical to many of the delegates, and according to fellow Georgian Alexander H. Stephens, he sealed his fate with his fondness for the grape in Montgomery. Stephens wrote that Toombs was "tight every day at dinner" and on one evening shortly before the election became *"tighter than I ever saw him."* Whatever the reason, Toombs lost to Jefferson Davis and did not much like it. He did accept Davis's offer to name him secretary of state, though, and began his Confederate career in what was supposed to be an exalted post.

Toombs wrote out the instructions for the Confederacy's unofficial foreign ministers before they left to try to secure recognition in Europe. But then he had nothing left to do. He was secretary of state in a nation with no foreign relations, and he chafed at his inactivity and at what he perceived to be a lack of influence in the Davis administration. When pressed by a would-be bureaucrat for a job in his department, Toombs removed his hat and informed the supplicant that his entire department was inside. He resigned his position in July 1861, used his influence to secure an appointment as a brigadier general, and tried to contribute to the war effort.

General Toombs was a poor soldier made worse because he was entirely unaware of how unsuited he was for the military. He resented professional officers and carried on his own campaign against "West Pointers" in the Southern army. He derided the defensive strategy to which the Davis government resorted out of necessity. After the Seven Days' campaign (June 25–July 1, 1862), Toombs challenged D. H. Hill, his immediate superior, to a duel; Hill declined and pointed out that they might better spend their energy killing the enemy. At Sharpsburg on September 17, Toombs and his brigade fought well and Toombs himself was wounded. For this service he demanded a promotion; when it was not forthcoming, he resigned his commission.

Back home in Georgia, Toombs devoted most of the remainder of his Confederate career to criticizing Davis and the Richmond government. In this enterprise he joined Georgia Governor Joseph E. Brown and Vice President Alexander H. Stephens. Brown in 1864 made Toombs a colonel of Georgia troops and gave him a cavalry regiment in the effort to thwart Gen. William Tecumseh Sherman's invasion. Like everyone else, Toombs was ineffective.

When the Confederacy collapsed, Toombs fled to Europe and lived in Paris until 1867. He then returned home, resumed his practice of law in Washington, Georgia, and regained much of his antebellum influence in state politics. He never asked for a pardon— "Pardon for what? I haven't pardoned you all yet!" he supposedly said—and so was never able to hold national office again. Nevertheless he furthered the efforts of white conservatives for "home rule" and also supported some protopopulist causes such as state regulation of railroads and other corporations.

Toombs's health declined rapidly during the 1880s, and he died December 15, 1885. He remained very much unreconstructed to the end. Local lore in Wilkes County has Toombs at the telegraph office in town during the Great Chicago Fire of 1870. When he emerged, a crowd gathered to hear the news, and Toombs described the heroic efforts of the many fire companies to stem the spread of the flames. Firemen and volunteers from miles around Chicago were doing their best. "But the wind," Toombs added, "is in our favor."

— EMORY M. THOMAS

TRANS-MISSISSIPPI DEPARTMENT

The Trans-Mississippi region included Texas, Arkansas, Missouri, Indian Territory, that part of Louisiana west of the Mississippi River, and the Arizona Territory (about two-fifths of the modern states of New Mexico and Arizona). Although there were numerous minor campaigns and battles in this area, none affected the war's outcome. The Trans-Mississippi was made a separate department in May 1862, but because President Jefferson Davis's primary concern was Virginia and Tennessee, he relegated the region to secondary importance. The surrender of Vicksburg assured the area's virtual isolation, and for all practical purposes the department was out of the war after 1863. Nevertheless, the Trans-Mississippi contributed significant numbers of men to the armies serving east of the river, and provided the Confederacy with a considerable quantity of food and supplies. Moreover, the small Army of the Trans-Mississippi forced the Union to retain a military presence in the region, thus tying up Federal soldiers that could have been used elsewhere.

Although the Trans-Mississippi was not part of the main war effort, the area west of the river comprised a notable portion of the total land mass of the Confederate states. From the Mississippi River to the California border and from Iowa to the Gulf of Mexico, the region covered around 600,000 square miles, but realistically Texas, Arkansas, and West Louisiana (thirty-one complete parishes and parts of six others) became the nucleus of the western limits of the Confederate nation. In 1860 the population of these three states included about 908,000 whites, around 5,500 free blacks, about 543,000 slaves, and 600 Indians. In addition, the Indian Territory reported about 58,000 Indians, whites, and free blacks and over 7,000 slaves. That Missouri did not secede and join the Confederacy was significant because, with 1 million white citizens, it was the second-largest slave state, ranking only behind Virginia.

The area was the fastest growing in the South and rich in many commodities. The inhabitants raised a variety of agricultural products, including cotton in the river valleys of Louisiana and Texas. Missourians produced more corn than in any other Southern state and harvested impressive quantities of wheat and oats. Missouri also counted more swine than any other slave state and ranked only behind Kentucky in the number of horses. Texas led the nation in the production of beef: the census reported over 3.5 million cattle in the state. The Trans-Mississippi's geographic location, too, offered advantages. Texas was the only Confederate state to border on a neutral foreign nation, Mexico, and an international waterway, the Rio Grande; thus it gave the South a link to the outside after the Union blockade became effective along the coastline. The region was also the gateway to any dreams of a Confederate empire in the Far West.

The states that composed the Trans-Mississippi had the same problems that plagued other agrarian areas in wartime. The population was widely scattered; there were few towns of any size, and even these were very small. Some of the largest population centers were San Antonio with 8,235, Galveston with 7,307, Little Rock with 3,727, and Shreveport with 2,190. The department had few railroads, almost no industrial facilities, and inadequate telegraph lines. Moreover, it was the only part of the Confederacy that had an Indian problem; the region had some 50,000 to 60,000 "hostile" Indians. The frontier in Texas retreated east after the able-bodied men joined the army, and the dangerous situation in West Texas added to the troubles facing the state authorities.

Early Military Operations

When the war began there was neither an overall military plan for the area nor an intention to make it into one department. In 1861 Louisiana belonged to Department No. 1 and parts of Arkansas belonged to Department No. 2. A separate Department of Texas was created on April 21 and placed under Col. Earl Van Dorn, who soon after capturing *Star of the West* at Galveston was promoted to brigadier general. Van Dorn left the state in September, briefly transferring command to Col. Henry Eustace McCulloch, but on September 18 Brig. Gen. Paul O. Hèbert assumed command. In theory, Confederate commanders worked with state officials to organize and equip the army. Each state raised troops, and each seized Federal arsenals and forts within its boundaries. This arrange-

After April 1863, steamboats could no longer safely reach the railhead at Vicksburg, thus severing the Trans-Mississippi supply line.

PAGE 649

Little help would be coming from the Trans-Mississippi, either; Johnston informed the War Department that saving Vicksburg was "hopeless."

PAGE 649

ment obviously led to difficulties between state and Confederate authorities, and in Missouri it provoked armed conflict.

Missouri was the only state in the department that never officially seceded, and throughout the war it had two rival governments. In May 1861 pro-Confederate Governor Claiborne F. Jackson tried to lead the state out of the Union, but in St. Louis this effort had been thwarted by Union Capt. Nathaniel Lyon, who organized a force and seized the state militia at Camp Jackson. The ensuing riot had left many civilians dead and persuaded the popular Unionist Sterling Price to throw his support to the South. This led to an armed conflict between the pro-Southern forces of Jackson and Price, on one hand, and the pro-Union army of Lyon, on the other. When the two sides met at Wilson's Creek, Missouri, on August 10, 1861, Lyon was killed. Price tried to take advantage of the victory by moving into Missouri, but Union soldiers forced him back into southwestern Missouri and finally into northwestern Arkansas. Missouri, in effect, had two governors. The pro-Union legislature replaced Jackson with Hamilton R. Gamble and voted to remain within the Union. Jackson, ignoring this, joined the Confederacy and moved his headquarters south.

There were also plans to establish a Confederate empire in the West. In June 1861 Col. John R. Baylor led Confederate troops up the Rio Grande into the New Mexico Territory. In August he claimed Arizona and made himself governor of the territory. Brig. Gen. Henry Hopkins Sibley also moved into the region and early in 1862 defeated Federal forces at Valverde before taking Albuquerque and Santa Fe. After a loss at Glorieta Pass in March, however, Sibley retreated to San Antonio, and the dreams of a Confederate empire in the West vanished.

The first major clash in the Trans-Mississippi came along the Missouri-Arkansas border. In December 1861 Brig. Gen. Samuel R. Curtis took command of the Union Army of the Southwest and early in 1862 advanced toward Springfield, Missouri. The friction between Sterling Price, commanding the Missouri State Guard, and Brig. Gen. Ben McCulloch, commanding Confederate troops, was rectified on January 10, 1862, with the creation of the Trans-Mississippi District of Department No. 2. This district contained the Indian Territory, that portion of Louisiana north of the Red River, and all of the counties of Missouri and Arkansas except those located between the St. Francis and Mississippi rivers. Maj. Gen. Earl Van Dorn was placed in command; he arrived late in January and led the Confederate Army of the West at Elkhorn Tavern, Arkansas, in March. Van Dorn planned to stop Curtis's move south, and the two armies met in the Boston Mountains near Fayetteville. Although the Federals

were outnumbered, around 11,000 to Van Dorn's almost 17,000, Van Dorn's plan to split his army and attack from two directions failed. During the fighting on March 7 McCulloch and Brig. Gen. James McIntosh were killed, leaving no one in charge of one wing of the assault. On the second day of the battle, Curtis's men were able to drive the Confederates from the field. Van Dorn moved south toward the Arkansas River and then received orders to join the Confederate army under Gen. Albert Sidney Johnston in Mississippi. Although he did not reach his destination in time to take part in the Battle of Shiloh, he left Arkansas virtually defenseless.

Elkhorn Tavern was the first major battle in which Indians from the Five Civilized Tribes participated. The early fighting in the Indian Territory had consisted mainly of skirmishes between pro-Confederate and pro-Union Indians. When the war began Confederate representatives had negotiated alliances with the five tribes—the Chickasaws, Creeks, Cherokees, Choctaws, and Seminoles. Eventually, the pro-Union Indians retreated to Kansas and left the region briefly under Confederate control. The Indians who fought at Elkhorn Tavern returned to the Indian Territory when Van Dorn crossed the Mississippi River, and by 1863 many had become disillusioned with the Confederacy; both Creeks and Choctaws talked of resuming relations with the United States. Cherokee Stand Watie, who commanded an Indian cavalry brigade in the Army of the Trans-Mississippi, was the only Indian to attain the rank of brigadier general in the Confederate army, and the last general officer to surrender at the end of the war, June 23, 1865.

The Trans-Mississippi under E. Kirby Smith

On January 14, 1863, Lt. Gen. E. Kirby Smith was assigned to the command of the Southwestern Army, "embracing the Departments of West Louisiana and Texas." The order made it clear that the geographical limits of this "new department" would be separate and distinct from the Trans-Mississippi Department. But Holmes wanted out and urged his friend Davis to find a replacement for him. On February 9 Smith took command of all Confederate forces west of the Mississippi River and made Alexandria, Louisiana, headquarters of the Trans-Mississippi Department. On March 18, Holmes was officially relieved, although he remained in charge at Little Rock.

At the time of Smith's arrival the department still comprised several districts, although some of the commanders had changed since the summer. Holmes took over the District of Arkansas and held this position until he resigned on March 16, 1864. Taylor continued in the District of Western Louisiana and, though he and Smith frequently disagreed, remained in command until late 1864. Brig. Gen. William Steele headed the District of the Indian Territory until replaced by Brig. Gen. Samuel Bell Maxey; and Maj. Gen. John B. Magruder commanded Texas, New Mexico, and Arizona. Magruder had arrived in Texas in October 1862 and promptly recaptured Galveston from the Union forces on January 1, 1863. Magruder, known as "Prince John," would remain in this position until transferred to Arkansas near the war's end. Texas was divided into three subdistricts: Brig. Gen. James E. Slaughter headed the Eastern Sub-District; Brig. Gen. Hamilton P. Bee, the Western Sub-District; and Brig. Gen. Henry McCulloch, the Northern Sub-District. Upon his arrival, Smith complained, "There was no general system, no common head; each district was acting independently."

The department also encountered problems keeping its men fit and in camp. Sickness took a heavy toll, and it was difficult to procure medicine. Desertion was another serious problem, with men going home and returning to the army at will. The extent of the problem is indicated by the figures reported after an inspection of the department in February 1864. In the District of Arkansas there were 10,354 troops present for duty, 25,623 aggregate present and absent; in the District of Western Louisiana, 10,657 troops present, 21,808 aggregate present and absent; in the District of Texas, 7,574 troops present, 12,992 aggregate present and absent; among state troops, 1,529 present, 3,960 aggregate present and absent; and in the District of the Indian Territory, 1,666 troops present, 8,885 aggregate present and absent. Overall, counting various other commands, it was reported the total present for duty in the department was 31,780, aggregate present and absent, 73,268.

Supplying these troops was a formidable task. It was imperative, Smith thought, to begin "general systematizing and development of the departmental resources." When Smith arrived, the Quartermaster's Bureau, recently established, reported on hand almost $17 million, but only $12,350 was in money. The

CREATION OF THE TRANS-MISSISSIPPI DEPARTMENT

After the disaster at Elkhorn Tavern the Confederate government recognized that something drastic had to be done. Faced with the serious situation of having Curtis's army positioned in northwestern Arkansas and with no way to defend the region, the Confederate government finally created a separate territorial organization, the Trans-Mississippi Department on May 26, 1862. General Order No. 39 stated that the department would embrace the states of Missouri and Arkansas, including the Indian Territory, that part of Louisiana west of the Mississippi River, and the state of Texas. On May 31 Maj. Gen. Thomas C. Hindman was appointed commander, and he did an excellent job of organizing an army and defending Little Rock. Hindman, however, argued with Albert Pike in the Indian Territory. Partly because of this argument (Pike was a friend of Jefferson Davis) and partly because Hindman's draconian measures to instill discipline and order in the army were unpopular, Hindman was replaced by Maj. Gen. Theophilus H. Holmes,

another of Davis's personal friends. On July 16, 1862, Holmes was ordered to Little Rock, and he assumed command on July 30. On August 20 the department was divided into districts: the District of Texas was composed of the state of Texas and the territory of Arizona and remained under Hébert; the District of West Louisiana was under the command of Maj. Gen. Richard Taylor; and the District of Arkansas, which included the states of Arkansas and Missouri and the Indian Territory, was under Hindman.

But as overall department commander Holmes was a poor choice; he was difficult to get along with and was sometimes excessively rude. Holmes thought in terms of what best served his own department rather than what might be best for the Confederate nation. When asked to send reinforcements to Vicksburg, he delayed and used his personal friendship with Davis to frustrate the movement of troops out of his department. Not only did he keep his soldiers in the Trans-Mississippi, never providing any real assistance to Vicksburg, but he never satisfactorily

defended his own borders. In December, Hindman in northwestern Arkansas was defeated by Federal Brig. Gens. James Blunt and Francis Herron at Prairie Grove, and in early January 1863 Arkansas Post in the southeast surrendered to a superior Union force.

Certainly there were serious problems in the Trans-Mississippi when Holmes took over, but his actions did nothing to improve the situation. Citizens living in the Trans-Mississippi felt abandoned, which created perilous morale problems throughout the department. Holmes, as early as October 1862, had asked Richmond to relieve him. In January 1863 the government was ready to agree. Secretary of War James A. Seddon reported in March that "the most deplorable accounts reached Richmond of the disorder, confusion, and demoralization everywhere prevalent, both with the armies and people of that State." Holmes, he claimed, had "lost the confidence and attachment of all," and the result was "fearful."

— ANNE J. BAILEY

*After the surrender
of Vicksburg and
Port Hudson in
the summer of
1863 the Trans-
Mississippi region
was virtually
isolated from
the rest of the
Confederacy.*

PAGE 571

T

remainder was in drafts, which the chief quartermaster complained he could not cash. "The want of funds to meet the necessities of the army embarrasses to a great degree the efficiency of my department," he noted. Moreover, the head of the Clothing Bureau clamored for funds to outfit his men. Hats and shoes were manufactured at several locations, and the Huntsville penitentiary turned out cloth, cotton jeans, woolen plaids, and woolen jeans. But money was needed to meet other pressing demands: many soldiers had not been paid for months.

KIRBY SMITHDOM. The Trans-Mississippi was isolated, with the U.S. Navy making it difficult for troops and supplies to cross the Mississippi River. With Smith in charge, the region became known as "Kirby Smithdom." Powerful Texans believed the Confederate government had abandoned their state by surrendering it to Smith's control. Even Richard Taylor complained that Smith worried too much about "the recovery of his lost empire, to the detriment of the portion yet in his possession," and Taylor believed that "the substance of Louisiana and Texas was staked against the shadow of Missouri and Northern Arkansas." Smith, in fact, assumed exceptional power, but Jefferson Davis supported him, declaring that his "confidence in the discretion and ability of General Smith assures me that I shall have no difficulty in sustaining any assumption of authority which may be necessary."

Governors and state officials met in the late summer of 1863 and agreed that the department must become self-sustaining. They called for public support and closed with a vote of confidence in Smith. Soon after, Smith organized the Cotton Bureau for the purchase, collection, and disposition of government-owned cotton. Bureaucrats hoped that cotton taken to Mexico could be exchanged for weapons and supplies desperately needed by the South. Although the plan did supply many essential goods, the work of the bureau was hampered by private speculators, currency problems, and an inability to convince Texans of the need to cooperate. Illicit commerce flourished, particularly along the Red River, as Southern cotton made its way to New England factories with the knowledge and support of government officials on both sides. But by mid-1864 most of the available cotton was gone, and Smith, who had come to depend upon this source of revenue, realized his department was in danger of financial collapse. Therefore, without official sanction from Richmond, he ordered the bureau to buy or impress one-half of all cotton grown, thus keeping the trade going until the war's end.

The Trans-Mississippi was unique in the Confederacy in that a Union attack was not the only danger it faced. In the summer of 1863 a serious threat to the region came from the Indians. Comanches and Kiowas

began to raid closer to large settlements—at one point just west of Fort Worth. Many families left their homes, moved in together, and built small forts. Confederate soldiers, receiving letters from home, became alarmed; many deserted to check on their families, although most returned when assured that their homes were safe. Texas's governors, first Francis R. Lubbock and then Pendleton Murrah, did their best to control the situation. Henry McCulloch, in command of the Northern Sub-District with headquarters at Bonham, had to deal with Indian war parties roaming along the frontier.

In addition, the frontier was alive with deserters, outlaws, and Unionists. Even the notorious Confederate William Quantrill plagued Texans when he moved south out of Missouri. McCulloch never had enough men to deal with all the problems, and in 1864 the authorities finally closed the frontier in an effort to protect the citizens.

Yet another burden was the sizable number of refugees that flooded Texas. Many Southerners with friends or relatives in the Trans-Mississippi fled other states to escape Federal armies. It is impossible to estimate accurately the number of people who relocated in Confederate-held regions. Women and children often brought slaves with them in order to avoid confiscation of their property, and as many as 200,000 blacks may have entered Texas during the last years of the war. The drain on the department created by these exiles placed a severe strain on Smith's resources, and contributed to the war-weariness that pervaded the region after 1863.

MILITARY OPERATIONS OF 1863. While Smith wrestled with domestic matters, he had also to cope with the military situation. Davis and the War Department had directed him to give top priority to defending Confederate-held territory along the Mississippi River. Throughout the spring and early summer of 1863, he tried to furnish aid to both Port Hudson and Vicksburg. In an attempt to draw Federal troops away from Vicksburg, Smith authorized an invasion of Missouri in April. Confederates under Brig. Gen. John Sappington Marmaduke tried unsuccessfully to take Cape Girardeau on the Mississippi River and quickly retreated into Arkansas. This strategy to assist Vicksburg failed, and Ulysses S. Grant continued his movement south. Although Holmes had resisted any efforts to send troops from the Trans-Mississippi to Vicksburg while he was department commander, Smith did order Confederates from Arkansas to reinforce Richard Taylor in Louisiana. Also as a diversion to help the Vicksburg defenders, Holmes authorized an attack on the Federal stronghold of Helena, Arkansas, on July 4. But in a mismanaged affair the Confederates were quickly repulsed with heavy losses on their side. Moreover, all attempts to aid Vicksburg from the west side of the river failed, and the town surrendered on July 4, 1863. Port Hudson fell five days later, and with the Union taking control of the river, the Confederacy was split in two.

On July 17, Federal troops decisively defeated the Confederates at the Battle of Honey Springs (or Elk Creek), the largest single engagement of the Civil War in the Indian Territory. Late in August Federal forces headed toward Little Rock, and in southern Louisiana Taylor made preparations for an attack. Texans, especially in the Rio Grande valley, feared an invasion. The situation in Mexico provided diplomatic reasons to control Texas; Napoleon III, the French ruler who was openly pro-Southern, had taken advantage of the weakened U.S. government and backed a puppet monarchy in Mexico. Moreover, Abraham Lincoln was not unaware of the interest that New Englanders had in Texas cotton. And yet the important decision of where the assault should be made along the Texas coast was left to the incompetent political general Nathaniel P. Banks.

Banks decided to strike at the mouth of the Sabine River, the boundary between Louisiana and Texas. A surprise assault at Sabine Pass would give access to the port of Beaumont. Moreover, the Confederates manning the pass were not adequately armed and made an easy target for the Union fleet. A combined force under Banks and Adm. David Farragut left New Orleans and sailed for Sabine Pass. On September 8, 1863, they faced the guns of Lt. Dick Dowling and forty-two men of the Davis Guard, a rowdy group composed primarily of Irishmen from Houston. The determined Confederates, members of the First Texas Heavy Artillery Regiment, turned their cannons on the naval force under Maj. Gen. William B. Franklin. About 4:00 P.M. *Sachem* was struck in the boilers and *Clifton* was grounded; both ships soon surrendered. The attack lasted less than an hour, and Federal losses were substantial, including the two gunboats. Dowling and his men, who fired their artillery over a hundred times, were unscathed. As a result of this impressive Confederate victory, Lincoln watched Northern morale fall and the stock market temporarily drop. Davis called it "the greatest military victory in the world," and Franklin took his place in American military history as the first general to lose part of his fleet to land batteries alone.

While Banks unsuccessfully struck at Texas, the Federals were victorious in Arkansas. On September 10, 1863, Little Rock fell to Union forces under Maj. Gen. Frederick Steele, and the Confederates fled the city. As Little Rock became the headquarters of the Union Department of Arkansas, another Union expedition under Brig. Gen. James G. Blunt drove Brig. Gen. William Steele from Fort Smith into the Indian Territory. On September 1, the Federals moved into Fort Smith, and Arkansas was divided in half on an east-west line that ran from Helena on the Mississippi to Little Rock and across to Fort Smith. Even Pine Bluff fell to the Union advance, and the Confederates controlled only a strip of land in the southern part of Arkansas. Moreover, except for scattered skirmishes, the Indian Territory was virtually out of the war.

Lincoln, however, still wanted to capture locations on the Texas coast. A new force invaded the Rio Grande valley in November and occupied Brownsville, forcing the Confederates to reroute the cotton crop heading for Mexico. The Union troops continued to move up the coast, and Magruder had to work hard to quell rumors that he had abandoned South Texas. In December, when a threat to Galveston developed, he asked that the Texas cavalry in Louisiana under Brig. Gens. Thomas Green and James Patrick Major be returned to the coast. But the Union released its grip, except at the Rio Grande, when the authorities realized it was impossible to hold the entire shoreline. Washington now turned to strategy for the 1864 spring campaign.

UNION OFFENSIVE OF 1864. As the new year opened, Union authorities plotted a major offensive in the Trans-Mississippi. As spring approached Lincoln's government planned to invade Arkansas and Louisiana in an effort to move into the rich cotton land of East Texas. Banks was to march up the Red River from Alexandria and meet Steele's advance from Little Rock at Shreveport. Neither army would have to march very far to reach Smith's headquarters. Once they had taken this Red River port, it would be easy to move into Texas. Moreover, victories in this part of the Confederacy could eliminate Arkansas and Louisiana from the war. Perhaps more important, Lincoln needed a meaningful military victory, for the fall election was only months away.

The two-pronged invasion began in March. Banks's force, increased by 10,000 men on loan from William Tecumseh Sherman's army and assisted by Porter's fleet, numbered around 22,000. He easily took Fort DeRussy on the Red River and headed for Shreveport. Smith and Taylor disagreed on how to respond to the columns moving north. Taylor started the campaign with around 6,000 men, and reinforcements from Texas and Arkansas increased the number to about 12,000. With this disparity in numbers, Smith urged caution, but Taylor was eager to strike quickly. On April 8 Taylor hit the strung-out Federal army near the little town of Mansfield. Banks's advance force fell back on their long wagon train, and a complete rout would have occurred if reinforcements had not arrived in time. The next day the Confederates hit Banks's army at Pleasant Hill. Although Taylor did not defeat Banks, the Federal army pulled back to Grand Ecore.

Jefferson Davis needed a competent commander west of the Mississippi; he chose E. Kirby Smith, who was recommended by Robert E. Lee.

PAGE 571

GOING HOME

*E. Kirby Smith's troops of
the Army of the Trans-
Mississippi are depicted at
Shreveport, Louisiana, in
May 1865.*

FRANK LESLIE'S
ILLUSTRATED FAMOUS
LEADERS AND BATTLE
SCENES OF THE CIVIL WAR

Taylor then asked Smith for permission to pursue the disorganized Union army, but Smith refused; he had to shift some of Taylor's troops north to prevent the Federals from succeeding in Arkansas.

The second prong of the Federal advance started in a more promising fashion. Sterling Price had around 8,000 men in Arkansas, along with some recently arrived cavalry from the Indian Territory, to oppose Frederick Steele's 10,000 to 12,000 troops. While Banks pushed up the Red River, Steele advanced south toward Washington, Arkansas. He occupied the town of Camden by the time that Smith had shifted troops back to Arkansas. In late April Confederate forces captured a supply train coming from Pine Bluff. The Battle of Poison Spring was notable because the loss of the supply train was a major factor in Steele's decision to retreat, but it was also a controversial battle in which many black soldiers died. Both sides claimed victory, but Steele withdrew to Little Rock.

The Confederate Trans-Mississippi Department had survived. As Steele fell back to Little Rock, Banks retreated to Alexandria. The politician-turned-general had to use all of his ingenuity to save the army, and Porter was fortunate to maneuver his fleet down the falling river. A Wisconsin soldier suggested that the navy build a dam to raise the water level; the river, having fallen to three feet in some places, was too shallow for the passage of the gunboats. When Banks escaped, Smith and Taylor had another serious disagreement, and Taylor was replaced in Louisiana by Maj. Gen. John G. Walker.

FINAL CONFEDERATE OPERATIONS. In August Taylor took command of the Department of East Louisiana, Mississippi, and Alabama, and crossed the river. In fact, Jefferson Davis told Kirby Smith to send any units he could spare to help at Mobile, and Smith received specific orders to have several Trans-Mississippi brigades join the campaigns in the East. He protested that the loss of troops would seriously damage the morale of the department, and when the men learned of the proposed plans they threatened to mutiny rather than fight. As the plan bogged down in controversy, it was dropped. Taylor maintained this was because too many gunboats had arrived at the crossing point to allow such an operation to succeed, but Davis later claimed he had never really planned to cross huge numbers. In fact, Taylor revealed that many men had decided to desert rather than comply. Smith hotly denied this, charging that because of his disagreements with Taylor, the Louisiana general was trying to discredit him. For whatever reason, the scheme to shift Trans-Mississippi troops across the Mississippi failed.

While all of this was occurring in Louisiana, Kirby Smith and Sterling Price were planning a raid into Missouri—the last major campaign in the Trans-Mississippi. Price, who had succeeded Holmes in command of the District of Arkansas, had been a politician before the war, and he was aware of the advantage to be gained by successfully invading his home state before the November presidential election. He personally hoped to take control of regions of the state long enough to elect a new governor and legislature. By taking command of the expedition, however, Price was forced to relinquish command of the District of Arkansas, and he was replaced by Maj. Gen. John B. Magruder. Price headed for Missouri with only cavalry from Arkansas organized into three divisions under Maj. Gen. James Fleming Fagan and Brig. Gens. Joseph O. Shelby and John S. Marmaduke. Price and his 12,000 men entered Missouri in September; he hoped to gain recruits and supplies as he went along. The raid, which covered over 1,500 miles and took three months, turned into a disaster; Price and his badly beaten army returned to Arkansas in early December.

In the winter of 1864–1865 morale plummeted throughout the department. Smith was always fearful that Richmond might order his troops to fight in the East, and he could ill-afford a drain on his manpower; the army was already badly depleted by desertion as many men on leave failed to return. Trade with Mexico was at a wartime low, and much of the gunpowder coming in from that country was of such poor quality it would not fire. Although the states in the department suffered less from shortages than other Southern states, inflation hit hard by winter. Moreover, the Texas frontier was rife with rumors of Indian raids, and large bands of deserters and bushwhackers tried to take over areas where the military had little control.

When Lee surrendered in April 1865, Kirby Smith, along with military and civil authorities, issued calls for the people of the Southwest to continue the fight. The last battle of the war occurred in the Trans-Mississippi deep in South Texas where Col. John S. ("Rip") Ford and the Second Texas had not learned that the end was near. Three hundred Federal troops from the island of Brazos Santiago under Col. T. H. Barrett landed on the mainland and headed toward Confederate-held Fort Brown. Barrett, whose command was mostly black soldiers, met a detachment of Ford's regiment at Palmito Ranch near Brownsville, but after a brief skirmish both sides withdrew. The following day, May 13, Ford struck at the Union soldiers; 113 surrendered and 30 were killed or wounded. The Texans learned from their prisoners that Lee and Johnston had surrendered in April.

In May military units in the department began to disband, and by the end of the month Smith had only a few scattered troops left in Texas and Louisiana. Lt. Gen. Simon Bolivar Buckner, acting Brig. Gen. Joseph L. Brent, and Maj. Gen. Sterling Price headed for New Orleans to negotiate terms, and on May 25 the military and naval forces of the Trans-Mississippi surrendered to Maj. Gen. E. R. S. Canby. The next day Buckner signed the official terms of surrender, which paroled the Trans-Mississippi soldiers and allowed them to return home unmolested. Kirby Smith, who decided to transfer his headquarters from Shreveport to Houston, arrived there on May 27 only to find he was a general without an army. On June 2 he boarded a Federal steamer in Galveston Harbor and placed his signature on the completed agreement, officially surrendering the Trans-Mississippi Department.

[*See also* Price's Missouri Raid; Red River Campaigns; Wilson's Creek Campaign; *and selected biographies of figures mentioned herein.*]

— ANNE J. BAILEY

TRANSPORTATION

Transportation routes in the antebellum South developed mainly to get cash crops out to the seaports, to bring in manufactured goods from the Northeast, and to bring in grain from the Middle West. Transportation was geared more toward providing access to local markets than toward binding sections of the country together or facilitating rapid transport of military forces, as the great highways of the Roman Empire had done.

In the early days drovers would move herds of cattle and hogs along trails and primitive roads over the mountains to eastern markets, negotiating with farmers along the way to allow the animals to feed in their cornfields. Later the railroads took over most of this business. But the greatest stimulus to railroad building in the South came from the competition of seaport cities whose merchants were anxious to improve their trade.

Major rivers carried products from the hinterlands to the sea, and roads and railroads tended to supplement that movement without major redirections of the flow of traffic. Few major interstate highways were to be found. The South for the most part resisted the canal-building craze that spread across the North. It participated to an extent in the great railroad building of the 1850s, but only on a small fraction of the scale and still with few long-distance lines.

In 1850 if a man wanted to travel from Richmond to New Orleans, for instance, he could go by a series of railroads from Richmond to Wilmington, North Carolina, in twenty-one hours for $8.40. From Wilmington he would take a steamboat for a sixteen-hour voyage to Charleston at a fare of $6.00. Thence he would take a railroad train to Atlanta, with a change in Augusta. There he would have to take a stagecoach for twenty-four hours to the town of Chehaw on the Alabama border and then a railroad again to Montgomery. Now came a long leg of 200 miles that took thirty-six hours by stagecoach to reach Mobile. He would make the final leg of 175 miles to New Orleans by steamboat. The whole trip of about 1,460 miles would take seven days at a cost of about $56.00.

In 1861 it was possible to go by rail all the way from Richmond to New Orleans by way of Abingdon,

The entire Confederacy had hardly as many locomotives as those found on the New York Central, the Pennsylvania, and the Erie lines combined.

PAGE 480

Knoxville, Chattanooga, Decatur, Alabama, and Corinth and Jackson, Mississippi. But there still was no rail connection between Texas and the Mississippi, and none for Arkansas except a short line from Madison.

Similar obstacles blocked travel by highways and waterways, although in 1850 one could travel by main roads and turnpikes from Washington to New Orleans or from Nashville to Augusta. Improvements of the waterways went little beyond clearing snags from the rivers.

The attitude in the South was one of hostility toward internal improvements at the expense of the general government. In 1856, when Congress passed an internal improvements bill that included $100,000 for clearing impediments to navigation on the Mississippi, and another $50,000 for the Tennessee, it was over the strong opposition of Southern leaders who insisted that the locales and the users should pay for their own improvements.

Indeed the Confederate Constitution forbade appropriations for internal improvements. It stated: "Neither this, nor any other clause contained in the Constitution, shall ever be construed to delegate the power to Congress to appropriate money for any internal improvement intended to facilitate commerce." The only exceptions were for lights and buoys on the coasts, the improvement of harbors, and the removal of obstructions in the rivers, but in all cases the users were to be taxed to pay the costs.

When war came in 1861, the whole Southern transportation system suffered and then broke under the strain. The advance of Federal armies and river flotillas gained control of the Cumberland and Tennessee rivers and then of the Mississippi for its entire length. In his campaign to Atlanta and then the marches to Savannah and to Goldsboro, William Tecumseh Sherman wrought havoc with the railroads in his path. Cotton could not be moved out to market, and many farmers planted corn instead. But much of what did not fall to the enemy remained in the granaries for want of horses and wagons and railroads and boats. Local roads fell into such disrepair as to be almost impassable for wagons, but most of the wagons and horses were with the armies anyway.

Railroads deteriorated further with each month of war. There was no iron to repair the tracks. There were no new cars or locomotives to replace worn rolling stock. The army itself was hard pressed to keep up supplies of food, ammunition, and replacement weapons with the altogether insufficient means of transportation in the country to support it.

The U.S. Congress in 1862 passed an act that authorized the president to take possession of the railroads whenever he considered that the situation demanded it. The Confederates were reluctant to do this. Not until February 28, 1865, did the Confederate Congress approve such a measure, and then it was a broad one. Although coming at a time when it could have little practical effect, it gave the secretary of war power to put navigation and railroad companies under military officers and to provide assistance to secure their efficiency.

[*See also* Railroads.]

— JAMES A. HUSTON

TREASURY DEPARTMENT

The Confederate Treasury Department was created by the Provisional Congress on February 21, 1861, at Montgomery, Alabama. The department then moved to Richmond, Virginia. Its operations in Richmond were hindered because, from 1863 on, all the able-bodied men were frequently called out for military duty. At such times, the dispatch of business slowed to a crawl. The department ceased to exist after the evacuation of Richmond on April 2, 1865.

Next to the War Department, the Treasury was the most important arm of the government. It not only collected and dispersed all the government's funds, but its payment or nonpayment of the War Department's bills meant the difference between success and defeat.

The department was a copy of that existing in Washington. It comprised the secretary, the assistant secretary, the chief clerk, the treasurer, the register, the comptroller, an auditor, and their staffs. This force totaled roughly one hundred persons at the seat of government and seven hundred more at the ports and mints. Many of these persons had Washington experience, and some brought with them sets of the Federal Treasury forms. Thus, within a few weeks, the Confederate Treasury was organized with an invaluable continuity of bureaucratic procedure and experience. By 1864, the Treasury had one thousand employees in Richmond and two thousand in the field offices.

The key figure in the department was the secretary, an office occupied by Christopher G. Memminger from February 21, 1861, until June 15, 1864, when he was succeeded by George Trenholm. The secretary was responsible for his department's efficient operation, and he had to prepare for Congress the government's recommendations for financial legislation.

The assistant secretary was the department's special projects officer and the acting secretary in the absence of his chief. This post was filled in February 1861 by

Philip Clayton, who had been Howell Cobb's assistant secretary. His unbusinesslike practices forfeited the confidence of his chief, and he was dismissed in 1863. He was replaced by William W. Crump, who served until 1865.

The Office of the Treasurer was headed by Edward C. Ellmore from March 1861 until October 1, 1864, when he was succeeded by John N. Hendren. The treasurer received, held, and dispersed Confederate government funds, signed all but the post office warrants, and kept records of all receipts and disbursements. He signed, together with the register, the first Confederate notes.

The treasurer also supervised the Treasury Note Bureau. This bureau was headed by Thompson Allen until it was split into two parts in May 1862; one division, which printed the notes, moved to Columbia, South Carolina. The other, which signed, numbered, clipped, packed, and shipped the notes, remained in Richmond. The Columbia bureau was headed by Joseph Daniel Pope until April 1863, when he was succeeded by Charles F. Hanckel. The Richmond bureau was headed by Sanders G. Jamison until September 1864, when the two parts were reunited in Columbia and Jamison resumed sole control. The bureau broke up with the fall of Columbia in February 1865.

The printers required close supervision because they were short of men and supplies and were far more interested in their profits than in the proper execution of their contracts. In addition, there were obstructions to getting treasury notes and securities to Richmond because of a shortage of trains and couriers. This delayed the preparation and distribution of the treasury notes, which in turn prevented the government from making urgently needed military payments.

The Treasury Note Bureau in Richmond had to number and sign twice over eighty million notes, requiring a staff of nearly three hundred clerks. Because of the manpower shortage, Secretary Memminger hired women to perform these tasks.

A related bureau was the Office of the Register, headed by Alexander B. Clitherall in early 1861 and subsequently by Robert Charles Tyler, from August 13, 1861, on. The register was responsible for appointing individuals to countersign the treasury notes and to keep registers of those emitted and canceled. The register's staff had to number every Confederate bond and to sign the coupons on each of over 800,000 bonds. In 1864 the register's signature was printed on each coupon. The register was also required to sign all warrants, transfer drafts, coupon bonds, registered bonds, and call certificates. This paperwork load resulted in the designation of Charles T. Jones, Tyler's chief clerk

(another Washington veteran), as acting register and the appointment of two assistant registers in early 1863.

The duty to audit claims and accounts devolved upon the comptroller. This office was occupied throughout the war by Louis Cruger, who had held a similar position in Washington. In performing his duties, Cruger was required to adjust and preserve the public accounts, to examine all accounts and certify the balances to the register, to countersign all the warrants drawn by the secretary, to report the collection of the customs and export duties to the secretary, and to provide for the payment of all moneys collected. Finally, he was to sue delinquent officers or debtors and to rule on all claims made against the Confederacy. To perform these tasks, Cruger was furnished with twenty clerks and one messenger. His work force had increased to thirty-two clerks by 1864, in five sections: those covering civil expenses, the War Department, canceled treasury notes, deceased soldiers' claims, and the bookkeepers.

The first auditor of the treasury, Bolling Baker, who had held that post in Washington, was initially responsible for auditing all the government's accounts. By 1864 he had fifty-three employees who were assigned to six divisions covering the customs service, the navy, the interest on the public debt, taxes, funding, and a miscellaneous section.

To reduce Baker's work load, the office of second auditor was created on March 16, 1861, and Walter H. S. Taylor, a former U.S. Treasury clerk, was appointed to the post. He was responsible solely for the War Department's accounts. To perform this duty, he was assigned 40 clerks, which by 1864 had become 158 persons working in seven divisions—bookkeeping, claims, pay, ordnance, engineer and medical, quartermaster, and subsistence expenses.

In 1864, the position of third auditor was created. That officer dealt exclusively with the voluminous post office accounts.

The Lighthouse Bureau was a small office carried over from the Federal government. It supervised the operation of lighthouses in twenty-nine districts from Tappahannock, Virginia, to Padre Island, Texas. The outbreak of hostilities and the suppression of most of the lighthouses left this bureau largely dormant.

There were two bureaus created after the war began. The first of these was the Produce Loan Bureau. The Produce Loan Bureau was supervised during the provisional government by James D. B. De Bow. The register then took over until May 1, 1863, when Archibald Roane became Produce Loan Bureau manager. He supervised produce loan agents in each state and insured that all government cotton was safeguarded and all food products were handed over to the army commissary department.

Before secession, several Southern states had developed branch banking, which the North ignored.

PAGE 40

Branch banking allowed rapid transfer of resources among branches, treating the resources of each individual as part of the whole.

PAGE 40

*Deposits in
Louisiana and
North Carolina
remained high,
and there's little
evidence that
Southern bankers
gave much thought
to the practical
problems of a war.*

PAGE 40

*By Dec. 1864,
Secretary of War
James Seddon
reported that over
27,299 bales of
cotton had been
exported, for $5.3
million of sales.*

PAGE 403

The office of the commissioner of taxes was created in 1863. This position was filled by Thompson Allen, another man with Washington experience. In addition to supervising his staff both in Richmond and the field offices, he issued regulations, advised the secretary in tax matters and furnished the Congress with reports and recommendations.

In addition to the officials located at Richmond, there were officials located throughout the Confederacy. The Treasury was fortunate that the personnel at the mints and customs houses stayed at their posts after secession. The secretary therefore did not have to train employees to perform routine government functions. The field offices were located at three sites: the lighthouses, the customs houses, and the mints.

The customs houses were mostly located along the coast and the Mexican border. This service was divided into twenty-five districts, employing approximately six hundred officials. With the proclamation of the blockade and the loss of several ports, there were considerable reductions in this work force. At the same time, because of the increase of trade with Mexico, more officials were posted to that frontier. The remaining officials found it difficult to regulate trade or collect a revenue from it. For example, the export duty on cotton was collected on only a fifth of the bales that left the ports or went overland to Mexico.

A large prewar force was employed by the mints at New Orleans, Dahlonega, and Charlotte. The Confederacy did not have a Bureau of the Mint to coordinate mint activities, and the shortage of supplies needed for minting operations resulted in Charlotte and Dahlonega being reduced to the status of assay offices. The mint in New Orleans was captured on April 25, 1862.

If the previously existing field offices atrophied, new branches burgeoned. The receipt and payment of vast sums for taxes, loans, and government expenses necessitated an expansion of the treasurer's offices. Anthony J. Guirot, formerly the treasurer of the New Orleans mint, was made assistant treasurer on May 11, 1861. Forced to flee from New Orleans in 1862, he was driven from one city to another, ending up at Mobile.

A second assistant treasurer's office was created in Charleston. Later, because of the siege, it relocated to Columbia.

In addition to the two assistant treasurers, there were depositories located throughout the Confederacy. Although there was usually only one office per city, multiple offices existed in Richmond, Wilmington, Charleston, Mobile, and Jackson. There were two kinds of depositories: those that paid out funds ("pay depositories" of which there were usually only two or three per state), and those used only to fund notes ("funding depositories").

Secretary Memminger was slow to establish depositories prior to 1863. The 1864 funding records suggest that had a comprehensive system of depositories been set up in 1861, a considerably larger amount of currency would have been funded at an earlier date.

Most of the depositaries were bank officers, but in Florida, Arkansas, Mississippi, and Texas, the Treasury hired local financiers. There were approximately two hundred depositories, and the Confederate government's ability to supervise their operations or furnish them with standardized forms was limited. For example, after the loss of the Mississippi Valley, the secretary of the treasury was cut off from the Trans-Mississippi Department. As a result, in November 1864, the Treasury was largely ignorant of the names and locations of its agents in that area.

In 1861, when the produce loan idea was first broached, large numbers of citizens volunteered to serve as agents. But there were no agents west of the Mississippi River, and the government put this volunteer effort on a more professional basis in early 1862. Agents were given formal appointments and commissions on subscriptions allowed.

When the Confederate Congress authorized the secretary to purchase cotton with bonds under the act of April 14, 1862, the government created the Produce Loan Bureau, appointing one full-time agent with a staff for each state. These agents collected and safeguarded the produce subscribed, donated, or later collected as part of the tithe tax. These duties proved increasingly onerous as Federal armies captured or compelled the destruction of the government's cotton. The absence of proper bagging and the collapse of the transportation system resulted in much waste.

The last group of field offices were those of the Confederate tax collectors. Under the war tax of August 19, 1861, the secretary was authorized to appoint a chief collector for each state, who in turn appointed a collector and one or more assessors for each county. These persons were to secure appraisals or declarations on all property and then forward a consolidated local report to the chief collector, who furnished a statewide valuation to the Treasury.

The tax machinery created in 1861–1862 then lapsed, and a new tax collection system had to be created for the act of April 24, 1863. Under that law, collectors were appointed for each congressional district, with a collector having one or more assistants. This tax force came to less than five hundred persons.

Taken as a whole, the Treasury Department proved reasonably efficient. The deficiencies of Secretary Memminger, however, particularly in fiscal policy formulation, his governance of the Treasury printers, his mismanagement of the Produce Loan Bureau, and his refusal to collect a specie reserve, reduced the department's effectiveness.

[*See also* Produce Loan; Taxation; *and* Memminger, Christopher G.]

— DOUGLAS B. BALL

TREDEGAR IRON WORKS

The Tredegar Iron Works in Richmond, Virginia, the largest industrial base in the South at the beginning of the Civil War, was the only facility capable of producing major ordnance, iron plate, and iron products in 1861. During the war, other ironworks were developed in the lower South, but Tredegar remained the leading ordnance producer and served as a model for further Southern industrialization.

Francis B. Deane, a Richmond businessman, with a group of partners combined a forge, rolling mill, and foundry in the mid-1830s, initiating the Tredegar operations. The company was officially incorporated by the Virginia legislature on February 27, 1837. (Its name derives from ironworks in Tredegar, Wales.) In 1841, sluggish sales and indebtedness induced company directors to accept a proposal by Joseph Reid Anderson that he become the company's commercial agent. Anderson, a West Point graduate and a state engineer for turnpike construction, brought in new investments and provided favorable sales management. He became a leaseholder of the entire company in 1843, and after five years he purchased the company outright from stockholders for $125,000.

In the 1850s the Tredegar Iron Works increased in capacity, and Anderson maintained high quality in order to secure U.S. government contracts for its products. The company diversified its output and used varied partnerships for its different operations in an attempt to promote good management and increase expertise. By 1859, Anderson had merged with an adjacent munitions works run by his in-laws, bought off some old partners, and consolidated remaining ones as Joseph R. Anderson and Company. By this time also, the Tredegar Works was attracting wider markets in the South and was recognized as the largest industrial complex south of the Potomac River.

When the Confederacy was established, Anderson and his partners supported it wholeheartedly. The company severed all trade and sales in the North and concentrated on supplying orders from seceding states for ordnance and munitions. By the end of 1861 Tredegar's work force had grown from 350 free and slave laborers in 1853 to nearly 1,000 men, of whom 10 percent were slaves.

Labor problems in the company had existed since its early days. Anderson in the 1840s increased the firm's use of slave labor, which in 1847 precipitated a strike of white workers who sought to eliminate their black competition. Their demands were overridden by Anderson, and the black labor force—some free, some slave—continued to increase with Tredegar's expansion. But since slaves had to be fed, clothed, and housed on the premises, their use failed to reduce production costs significantly. Nevertheless, black labor proved more and more essential as some Northern and foreign workers departed the company at war's start, and by early 1863, with more skilled labor drawn away for military duty, blacks constituted one-half of Tredegar's 2,000 workers.

As the war got underway, longer-term contracts between the Tredegar Iron Works and the Confederacy's War and Navy departments took the place of orders from individual states, although those from the private railroad system continued. The Confederacy never took over railroads, but very early it moved to centralize and coordinate the securing of war supplies. Steady orders from the government prompted the expansion of Tredegar's rolling mill and ordnance facilities and was further encouraged by the Confederacy's promise of annual financial backing. What the government could not do was live up to its promise to supply all the pig iron and coal that Tredegar's operations needed. In April 1862 the Confederate Congress allowed the War and Navy departments to provide loans to Tredegar to expand the company's pig iron and fuel sources, and new blast furnaces were opened up. Further assistance proved to be very limited, however, and despite Tredegar's wartime growth, its operations remained at only one-third its full capacity throughout the war.

By the years 1863 and 1864 new ironworks at Selma, Alabama, and elsewhere in the lower South, as well as facilities set up by Confederate bureaus, created further difficulties for Tredegar by competing for scarce resources. The Confederacy's industrial thrust, as expansive as it seemed, was slowed by the lack of raw materials. This disadvantage, coupled with the poor distribution service of its rail system, was an ominous portent for the government's survival.

At the outset of the war Joseph Anderson had offered to turn the Tredegar Works over to the Confederate government for lease or purchase, which was rejected in favor of sustaining private business. Increasingly, Anderson and his partners, whose commitment to Southern independence never faltered, complained that the government's control over the prices it would pay for war supplies left Tredegar with

The Tredegar Iron Works at Richmond cast over a thousand cannons, in addition to armor plate, shells, shot, and components for arms.

PAGE 370

*Union campaigns
through Tennessee,
Georgia, and
down the
Shenandoah
Valley left only
Richmond as
the source of iron
and coal.*

PAGES 369–70

*George Trenholm
succeeded his
friend Christopher
G. Memminger as
Treasury secretary
on June 15, 1864.*

PAGE 620

no profit margin. The situation worsened in the last year of the war as government payments fell short. In April 1865, the government still owed almost $1 million to the Tredegar Iron Works.

The company had in the early years fulfilled much of its industrial potential, supplying the big guns for the Confederacy before 1863, as well as iron plate for ironclads (e.g., *Merrimac*'s conversion to *Virginia*), munitions, and other war products. It had even participated in experimental developments of submarines and torpedoes and the modernization of naval weapons and machine guns. But by war's end, the insurmountable problems of skilled labor shortages, the depletion of basic raw materials, and the failure to obtain adequate provisions for Tredegar workers had drastically hampered the firm's high-quality productivity.

Near the end of the war Anderson once again offered the Tredegar Works for lease to the government, but it was too late. The Tredegar Battalion, a militia of employees established in 1861, guarded the company's physical plant against rampage when the Confederacy collapsed in April 1865. With the fall of Richmond the Tredegar Iron Works remained intact, though occupied by Union troops for a short while. The company partners feared confiscation of the firm's property under Federal law, and Anderson immediately sought a way to resume operations, underscoring Tredegar's readiness for production and employment. Private meetings with President Andrew Johnson resulted in personal pardons for Anderson and his partners in September 1865. The company reorganized in 1867 with Anderson continuing as president.

Anderson earlier had hedged against future loss or collapse by engaging in blockade running for consumer goods from Europe. Profit from those sales had provided him with the means to maintain a separate London bank account. The London sterling deposits plus additional investments, including some from Northern financiers, enabled the Tredegar Works to move from the leading wartime producer of ordnance for the Confederacy to peacetime operations assisting in the renewal of the South's commerce and industry.

But Tredegar's heyday as the South's major industrial complex was over. Financial ties with a failing New York railroad operation during the panic of 1873 forced the company into receivership, with Joseph Anderson serving as receiver until 1879. Moreover, iron production was rapidly giving way to steel production, and Tredegar could not afford to shift operations to steel. What had once been a great model for Southern industrialization had receded to a more modest operation, which was carried on at the site until 1958.

— FREDERICK SCHULT

TRENHOLM, GEORGE

Trenholm, George 1807–1876), merchant and secretary of the treasury. George Alfred Trenholm was born on February 25, 1807, at Charleston, South Carolina. After his father's death in 1822, he went to work for John Fraser and Company, a firm engaged in shipping and factoring Sea Island cotton. Trenholm's progress was rapid. In 1836, he succeeded his employer as a director of the Bank of Charleston, the largest bank in South Carolina. He was elected to the legislature (1852–1856), and by 1860 he was a rich man. His personal assets, and those of his firm, consisted of plantations, slaves, warehouses, wharves, ships, and substantial investments. The company had branches in New York (Trenholm Brothers) and Liverpool (Fraser, Trenholm). Trenholm's reputation for integrity assured him of almost unlimited credit.

In a private capacity, Trenholm faithfully served the Confederacy. He built and donated to South Carolina the gunboat *Chicora*. In addition, he worked on the Board of Commissioners fortifying Charleston. He also expanded his fleet until by 1864, his firm either owned or held under charter fifty ships. He used these not to import high-priced luxury goods for profit but to bring in urgently needed military supplies and items for the Confederate civilian market. When James M. Mason and John Slidell, the Confederate commissioners, were unable to get out of Charleston because of the blockade, Trenholm personally leased a ship at half price to convey the two diplomats to Havana.

Nor did his services end there. A personal friend of Secretary of the Treasury Christopher G. Memminger, he provided both practical aid and sound advice in the management of the Confederacy's financial affairs. Starting in April 1861, the firm of Fraser, Trenholm became the government's financial agent in Europe. That office furnished cash advances to the Confederate procurement agents, who otherwise would have been seriously delayed in securing supplies for the army. This relationship was formalized by an act dated November 26, 1861.

Recognizing the importance of furnishing the government with the means for exporting its own produce and importing urgently needed supplies, Trenholm sent his son William to Montgomery in May 1861 to propose the purchase by the government of one or both of two available British shipping lines. The cabinet and President Jefferson Davis rejected this idea, thereby doing serious injury to the Confederate cause.

Trenholm was frustrated on other blockade-related issues. He strongly urged the government to stop the Committees of Safety from inhibiting cotton exports. The government, however, refused to confront the committees, preferring instead to deal with the situation one problem at a time. Trenholm also tried to lease ships on the government's behalf, but his efforts to promote exports of Treasury-owned cotton failed because Memminger blocked the procurement of the requisite cotton.

Trenholm also advised Memminger that it was vital to make treasury notes the South's currency. With that aim in view, Trenholm organized and attended a bankers' convention in June 1861. The meeting was adjourned to Richmond from July 24 to 26, 1861, when the banks agreed to receive and pay out Confederate treasury notes, thereby ensuring a nationwide demand for them.

Moreover, Trenholm was also behind the series of laws passed in February 1864 that provided for stringent controls over imports and exports, the acquisition of government ships, and the preemption of cargo space on the government's account to export cotton and import supplies needed by the army. Had this program been enacted in 1861, as Trenholm had originally proposed, the Treasury would have been strengthened, the army better supplied, and the Confederacy's economic deterioration mitigated.

Disgusted by the uncooperative attitude of the Confederate Congress and its mismanagement of the economy, Trenholm urged Memminger to resign, which he did on June 15, 1864. Much to Trenholm's surprise, President Davis then offered to appoint him secretary of the treasury. Trenholm reluctantly accepted this position on July 18, 1864.

At the time he took office, Trenholm confronted a bankrupt Treasury. He tried to educate the public and win the respect of the congressmen. But he was unable to induce them to pass better legislation, and this soon led to disaster. In November 1864, Trenholm found that the Treasury was over $360 million in arrears in its payments for the army. These arrears undermined the troops' morale and resulted in mass desertions. Trenholm did his best to prevent this by selling off government coin and cotton and even donated $200,000 himself.

Evacuating Richmond on April 2, 1865, Trenholm fled south. By April 27, however, he was so ill he had to resign his post. Accompanied by his son William, Trenholm rejoined his family in Columbia. There he remained under house arrest until June 21, when he was instructed to report to the provost marshal at Charleston.

Arriving with a valise containing the assets of his firm, which he planned to give to its trustees, Trenholm and William were arrested and escorted to jail. There he was told he was to be imprisoned and his assets sequestered. Ordered to leave, William calmly walked out with the bag containing the John Fraser

assets. The elder Trenholm went to Fort Pulaski, from which, on October 11, 1865, he was released on parole.

The remaining eleven years of Trenholm's life were devoted to salvaging his personal affairs. The U.S. government sued Fraser, Trenholm for the former Confederate assets the firm had used to offset its claims against the Confederacy. Defeated in the British courts and assessed costs, the Federal government then filed immense claims against Trenholm and his firm in Charleston, seeking penalties and interest for nonpayment of customs dues. As a result of this and bad cotton crops, Trenholm's firms went bankrupt. Nonetheless, by 1874, he was once more a wealthy man. As a token of respect, Charlestonians lowered their flags to half-mast following his death on December 10, 1876.

— DOUGLAS B. BALL

TRENT AFFAIR

On October 12, 1861, newly appointed Confederate commissioners James Mason and John Slidell boarded the steamer CSS *Theodora* in Charleston, South Carolina. Their mission was to secure recognition for the Confederate States of America in both England and France and find military supplies and negotiate commercial trading agreements that would support the newly declared country. *Theodora* carried Mason and Slidell safely through the Union blockading squadron off Charleston and then to Nassau in the Bahamas. Unable to find immediate passage to Europe from Nassau, the Confederate commissioners were taken on to Cuba aboard *Theodora*. After several weeks of socializing and being entertained by the governor of Cuba, Mason and Slidell booked passage to England on the royal mail steamship *Trent* on November 8, 1861. Both men assumed their voyage on *Trent* would be protected by international laws that guaranteed the sovereignty of every nation's vessels. As a consequence they made no effort to conceal their plans.

When word of their voyage reached Capt. Charles Wilkes aboard USS *San Jacinto* at Cienfuegos, he decided to intervene. After a serious examination of the potential consequences and consultation with the U.S. consul general, Wilkes decided to intercept *Trent* and capture Mason and Slidell. On November 8, Captain Wilkes discovered the British steamer 240 miles east of Havana. Against legal council Wilkes fired a shell across *Trent*'s bow, forcing the ship to stop, and brought *San Jacinto* alongside. Over the protests of Capt. James Moir, an armed crew from *San Jacinto* forcibly removed Mason and Slidell. As *Trent* steamed on to St. Thomas, Captain Wilkes headed for

From London the Confederate commissioners reported a wave of anger and resentment.

PAGE 171

Hampton Roads, Virginia. There he took on coal and telegraphed the secretary of the navy of his intent to sail for Boston. Upon arrival there Wilkes received orders from Secretary of State William H. Seward to take the prisoners to Fort Warren in Boston Harbor for detention.

The incident lasted less than three hours but reverberated across the ocean for weeks to come.

PAGE 358

News of Wilkes's seizure of the Confederate commissioners was greeted with enthusiasm throughout the Union. At a time when the fortunes of war appeared to favor the Confederacy, the event was perceived as something of a military victory over the South if not also Great Britain. Northern newspapers generally reflected the public opinion. With the exception of newspapers in some northeastern cities that would be vulnerable in the event of hostilities with Great Britain, most viewed the incident as Wilkes's victory and glossed over or denied the impact of potential political repercussions. Regardless of international consequences, the press expressed a consensus that the captives should not be surrendered. Many editorialized that Captain Wilkes had not done anything more serious than the British had on numerous occasions. The *Philadelphia Sunday Dispatch* commented that Britain could hardly protest "a good old English practice" of search and seizure. Union leaders, however, were divided in their feelings. Seward was reported to be "elated," but Abraham Lincoln was concerned that the British

reaction would provide political support for the Confederacy. It was clear that the Union was in no position to risk angering the European community. At the same time Lincoln did not want to dampen much-needed enthusiasm in the North. Instead of adopting an antagonistic position, he waited for Britain to officially react to the incident.

In the Confederacy Wilkes's forcible removal of Mason and Slidell was received with both indignation and satisfaction. Southerners were outraged by the United States's blatant disregard for the sovereignty of a British vessel and the seizing of duly appointed commissioners of the Confederate States of America. At the same time they appear to have been as elated about the incident as Northern supporters of Wilkes. Many felt that the affair would advance the South's cause by generating support for British recognition of the Confederacy. Southern newspapers were as vocal on the issue as those of the North. The *Richmond Enquirer* stated that Great Britain would find it impossible to accept the "disgrace," and the *Atlanta Southern Confederacy* called the *Trent* affair "one of the most fortunate things for our cause." Secretary of War Judah P. Benjamin agreed with the *Southern Confederacy*. Many officials felt the crisis would lead Great Britain into a war with the United States and thus assist the Confederate bid for independence.

Relations between Great Britain and the United States had frequently been strained prior to the Civil War. The rebellion in Canada; disputed boundaries between Maine, Oregon, and Canada; the acquisition of Texas and California; competing interests in Central America; and American reaction to British recruiting in the United States during the Crimean War all contributed to the impression that Americans were a disagreeable sort at best. Lincoln's selection of William H. Seward to head the State Department had reinforced British apprehension, as Seward was on occasion highly antagonistic toward Great Britain. The situation did not improve when Queen Victoria issued a proclamation of neutrality in May 1861. The seizure of Mason and Slidell appeared to bring many festering issues to a head. Though British newspapers admitted that "the honor of England" was "tarnished" and the injustice should be resolved, some were willing to admit that the United States had done nothing more than Great Britain had on previous occasions.

Richard B. Pemell, the second Lord Lyons and Her Majesty's minister to the United States, suggested possible courses of action. The first was to clearly establish that Britain would not condone violations of its sovereignty. Lord Lyons also suggested that the threat of war warranted the reinforcement of Canada and the strengthening of naval squadrons in the Atlantic, Pacific, and West Indies. He was of the opinion that

Britain should act in concert with France in responding to the affair and to resist offering aid to the South but not reject their envoys. The French minister of foreign affairs, Antoine Edouard Thouvenel, confirmed that though France was not directly involved, the government viewed the incident as a breach of international law.

The gravity of the *Trent* affair was evident in the creation of a War Committee in the British cabinet. The committee members considered their options and, after determining that Wilkes's act was illegal, contemplated preparing for war with the United States. At the same time they approved a dispatch drafted by Lord John Russell to be delivered in Washington by Lord Lyons. Great Britain was willing to concede that Wilkes may have acted on his own or had misunderstood his orders, but the prisoners had to be released and a public apology issued. For Britain the matter was one of national honor. Lord Lyons was to give Lincoln and his government seven days to respond to the communication. If a satisfactory answer was not received within that time, Lyons was to break off relations with the United States and return with his staff to England.

President Lincoln's initial reaction to the British note was immediate rejection. News of it set off waves of public protest and heated debate in Congress. In spite of intense popular opinion and congressional pressure, Lincoln eventually yielded to Seward's argument that the United States could not risk war with Great Britain at a time when suppression of the rebellion and major financial problems were paramount. After lengthy consideration of the matter, Lincoln and his cabinet agreed that the prisoners must be released and a satisfactory apology issued to Great Britain. Seward drafted a complex and rambling document that affirmed that Wilkes had indeed acted without orders and that by "voluntarily" intercepting *Trent* he had committed an illegal act for which Britain justifiably deserved reparations. On January 1, 1862, amid public protests, Slidell and Mason were released and transported aboard HMS *Rinaldo* to Bermuda, where they boarded the vessel *La Plata* and continued their voyage to Britain. The *Trent* crisis had been resolved after an intense two months of negotiations and compromise. In Great Britain and France, Mason and Slidell served the Confederate States of America until the end of the war, but failed to secure official recognition of the new government.

The *Trent* affair was the most serious crisis of diplomacy faced by the United States during the Civil War. Although resolved to the mutual satisfaction of the United States and Great Britain, the issues associated with the affair complicated diplomacy well into the twentieth century. The problems of neutral and belligerent rights, search and seizure at sea, the nature of contraband and government dispatches, the legal status of mail ships, transport of military and civilian belligerents, and diplomatic privileges and immunities demanded international consideration but defied immediate and concise definition.

— GORDON WATTS

TRIMBLE, ISAAC

Trimble, Isaac (1802–1888), major general. Regarded as the most prominent soldier contributed by Maryland to the Southern cause, Isaac Ridgeway Trimble was born May 15, 1802, in Culpeper, Virginia. He graduated from West Point in 1822 and spent ten years as an artillery officer. Trimble then left the army and devoted almost three decades to railroad construction, much of it in his adopted state of Maryland.

In April 1861, as commander of Baltimore defenses, Trimble burned a number of bridges north of the city to impede passage of Federal troops en route to Washington. The next month he accepted a colonelcy of engineers in Virginia forces and helped in the construction of Norfolk's defensive works. Following his appointment on August 9, 1861, as a Confederate brigadier general, Trimble took command of a brigade in Richard S. Ewell's division. He was, a fellow officer stated, "a veteran in years but with the fire and aggressiveness of youth."

YOUNG ENOUGH

Born in 1802, Maj. Gen. Isaac Ridgeway Trimble was described by a fellow officer as "a veteran in years but with the fire and aggressiveness of youth."

LIBRARY OF CONGRESS

Dependable service in Jackson's Shenandoah Valley and the Seven Days' campaigns ended momentarily at Second Manassas when a Federal bullet shattered Trimble's left knee. On January 17, 1863, while still recuperating from his wound, Trimble received advancement to major general. He returned to duty, but on July 3,

1863, while leading two North Carolina brigades in the Pickett-Pettigrew charge, Trimble again was shot in the left leg. Dr. Hunter McGuire amputated the limb the next day. Unable to travel, Trimble surrendered to Union authorities. He endured imprisonment at Johnson's Island and Fort Warren before his February 1865 release.

After the war, and equipped with an artificial leg, Trimble resumed his engineering work. He resided in Baltimore, where he died January 2, 1888. He is one of five Confederate generals buried in that city's Green Mount Cemetery.

— JAMES I. ROBERTSON, JR.

Former president John Tyler, one of Virginia's five delegates to the Washington Peace Conference, had wanted to invite only the border states.

PAGE 660

TYLER, JOHN

Tyler, John (1790–1862), governor of Virginia, U.S. president, president of the 1861 Washington peace conference, and congressman from Virginia. The only former U.S. president to serve in the Confederate Congress, Tyler was born March 29, 1790, at Greenway, Charles City County, Virginia, the sixth child of John and Mary Marot (Armistead) Tyler. The younger John Tyler entered the College of William and Mary at age twelve and graduated five years later. After reading law with his father, he was admitted to the Virginia bar in 1809. In 1811 he was elected to the Virginia House of Delegates as a representative from Charles City County; he held this seat for five years until his elevation to the Virginia Council. During the War of 1812 he served as a captain of volunteers protecting the state capital. On March 29, 1813, he married Letitia Christian of New Kent County.

In 1816 Tyler was elected to the U.S. House of Representatives, where he showed himself a strict constructionist and opposed the Missouri Compromise. Poor health, which plagued him much of his life, forced him to resign in 1821. Two years later the citizens of Charles City County again sent him to the House of Delegates. In 1825 and 1826 he served one-year terms as governor. Following the completion of Tyler's second term, anti-Jackson forces in the General Assembly elected him to the U.S. Senate, where he remained until he was forced to resign in February 1836 after a dispute over legislative instructions. He retired briefly to Williamsburg to practice law. During the election of 1836 he was nominated for the vice-presidential slot on two of the four regional Whig tickets as the running mate of both William Henry Harrison and Hugh L. White, but he did no campaigning. He returned to the Virginia House of Delegates in the April 1838 election.

An attempt to regain his seat in the U.S. Senate in 1839 was abortive, but Tyler was named as the running mate of William Henry Harrison of Ohio at the Whig National Convention in December. The "log cabin and hard cider" campaign of 1840 swept the Harrison-Tyler ticket into office. When the sixty-eight-year-old Harrison died one month after his inauguration, Tyler settled the question of the status of a vice president who assumes executive duties on the death of the president. Instead of becoming acting president, Tyler became president in his own right and thus established the precedent for future generations.

Tyler's strict constructionism had always made his association with the Whigs an uneasy one, and his accession to the presidency ruptured his alliance with Henry Clay. Tyler's effort to sustain the delicate balance of factions by not immediately introducing a program allowed Clay, who was seeking to secure absolute control of the Whig party and to ensure his own election to the White House in 1844, to seize the initiative. Tyler had made it clear that he would support repeal of Martin Van Buren's Independent Treasury but left it to the special session of Congress that had been called by his predecessor to propose a new banking plan, though he reserved the right of veto.

When it became clear that Clay intended to revive the Bank of the United States, Tyler indicated his preference for a district bank. Clay maneuvered several amendments to the presidential plan that rendered it unacceptable to Tyler, who vetoed it on August 16. Unable to override the presidential veto, Clay tried vainly to introduce an amendment to the Constitution that would allow presidential vetoes to be overturned by a simple majority vote. On September 9 Tyler vetoed a second bank bill. In a move engineered by Clay in hopes of forcing Tyler to step down, the entire cabinet, with the exception of Secretary of State Daniel Webster, resigned on September 11. Two days later, Tyler was publicly read out of the Whig party.

For the next two years of his administration, Tyler faced a hostile Whig Congress that delighted in passing bills that the president routinely vetoed as unconstitutional. Several House committees recommended at various times that he be impeached for impeding the operation of government. Of necessity, low-key domestic policy characterized the last years of the administration. Tyler's most lasting contribution—aside from the precedent set by his accession to power—was the annexation of Texas.

Seeking an issue on which to found a third major political party centered on himself, Tyler settled as early as October 1841 on adding Texas to the Union. Downplaying the issue of the expansion of slavery, a specter that raised its head each time talk of Texas was introduced, Tyler and his secretary of state, Abel P. Upshur of Virginia, entered into secret negotiations with Sam Houston, the president of Texas. Midterm elections in 1842 had returned a Democratic majority to the House and reduced the Whig dominance in the Senate, so by the time the finishing touches were being put on the treaty of annexation in February 1844, Tyler was confident of winning congressional approval.

On February 28, however, Secretary of State Upshur and seven others were killed when a bow cannon called the "Peacemaker" exploded on the frigate *Princeton* while on a pleasure cruise on the Potomac. Tyler intimate Henry A. Wise of Virginia made a public pronouncement that Tyler would name John C. Calhoun to succeed Upshur. Backed into a corner, Tyler turned the delicate negotiations over to Calhoun. When the annexation treaty went to the Senate, Calhoun sent along copies of two official letters he had written to the British minister in Washington, stating that annexation was imperative to protect Southern slaveholders and the national security of the United States from the danger of British abolitionists working to eradicate the peculiar institution in the independent Texas nation. By resurrecting the slavery issue, Calhoun took the treaty down to defeat.

In the meantime, Tyler used his nascent third party to great advantage. On the same day that the Democratic convention met in Baltimore to nominate its presidential candidate for the 1844 election, Tyler followers convened in the same city to nominate their incumbent with the rallying cry "Tyler and Texas." Apprehensive of the potential pulling power of Tyler's state rights, strict constructionist stand and manipulated by Calhoun loyalists, the Democratic convention ignored front-runner Martin Van Buren, who was on record as opposed to annexation, and gave the nod to dark-horse candidate James K. Polk on a platform that included a call for the annexation of Texas. In August Tyler endorsed Polk rather than Clay, the Whig nominee. When Polk won the White House in the November election, Tyler announced that the Democratic victory had been a mandate on the annexation issue. Because a two-thirds majority in the Senate favoring ratification of the treaty was unlikely, Congress passed a joint resolution calling for the annexation of Texas, which Tyler signed into law on March 1, 1845, three days before his term expired.

Tyler retired to Sherwood Forest, a plantation near his birthplace in Charles City County that he had purchased during his presidency, and settled down to the life of a gentleman planter. His wife, Letitia, long partially paralyzed from a stroke, had died on September 10, 1842, while Tyler was in the White House. During his last year in office, on June 26, 1844, the president had married New York belle Julia Gardiner. (He was the first president to marry while in office.) Her father, David, had been one of those killed on board *Princeton;* indeed, both she and Tyler had been present on the fatal Potomac cruise.

Tyler's annexation of Texas exacerbated sectional tensions. Bitter debates over the expansion of slavery into the territories won during the Mexican War seized the national stage. From the peace of Sherwood Forest, Tyler commented on the Compromise of 1850, the Kansas-Nebraska Act, and the *Dred Scott* decision and was even occasionally mentioned as a presidential candidate.

Fearing slave rebellion in Charles City County in the wake of John Brown's raid on Harpers Ferry, Tyler collected firearms at Sherwood Forest and became captain of the Silver Greys, a cavalry unit that would serve as the second line of defense in the event of an uprising.

In the spring of 1859 he supported Henry Wise and his own son, Robert Tyler, for the 1860 Democratic presidential nomination, but by July he was being prodded by moderates such as James D. B. De Bow of *De Bow's Review* to make himself available as a compromise candidate at the upcoming Democratic convention. Tyler believed that the worst mistake the party could make would be to adopt a platform of any sort and criticized the withdrawal of some of the Southern delegates at Charleston as a strategic blunder. During the ensuing campaign he backed Southern Democrat John C. Breckinridge, although he hoped that the election would in fact give none of the candidates a majority in the electoral college and that the election would be thrown to the House of Representatives, where he was sure that Joseph Lane of Oregon would win approval as president.

When sectional tensions mounted after the election of Abraham Lincoln, Tyler called on December 14, four days before South Carolina seceded, for a peace convention of the twelve border states. The Virginia General Assembly responded the next month by proposing a convention of all the states, a move Tyler considered abortive because it would involve both abolitionist and fire-eater extremists. Tyler won appointment as one of the five representatives the Old Dominion sent to the Washington peace conference. Simultaneously, he was also named as Virginia's special commissioner to James Buchanan with instructions to persuade the lame-duck president to take no action against the seceded states until the peace conference had convened on February 4. Three days later, Tyler was elected to represent Charles City, James City, and New Kent counties in the emergency Virginia convention that was to assemble in Richmond on February 13.

The peace conference unanimously chose Tyler president on February 5. As he had feared, because of the secession of the lower South, there were twice as many free states represented at the conference as there were slave states. Tyler divided his time between chair-

John Tyler was the only former U.S. president to serve in the Confederate Congress.

PAGE 142

ing the conference and beseeching Buchanan to abandon Fort Sumter and thus avoid a showdown with the hotheads in South Carolina. During the critical period between the convening of the peace conference and the reporting by the resolutions committee chaired by James Guthrie of Kentucky, Tyler abandoned his moderate Unionist stand. Previously he had been a conditional Unionist—one who supported the preservation of the Union but not at the cost of emancipation, even a compensated one. By February 15, Tyler no longer believed that a political solution to the sectional crisis was possible. Instead, he believed that Virginia should leave the Union. The Old Dominion's secession would force the withdrawal of the border states, Pennsylvania, New York, and New Jersey, thus crippling the North, which would not be able to retaliate militarily. In Tyler's view, Virginia's secession would allow the South to battle to a stalemate without a shot being fired.

Tyler's change in view, and his despondency after he and several other commissioners to the peace conference met with Lincoln on February 23, led him to support James A. Seddon's minority report to the peace conference, which reiterated the right of any state to secede from the Union and which would have guaranteed the South control of executive appointments below the old Missouri Compromise line. He consistently voted against the Guthrie resolutions but passed them along to Congress as instructed after they carried by narrow margins.

On the last day of February, Tyler returned to Richmond, condemned the results of the peace conference, and advocated the immediate secession of Virginia. Taking his seat in the state convention, he rose on March 13 and 14 to deliver a set piece calling for secession if Lincoln did not abandon the Federal forts, recognize the Confederate States of America, and begin treaty negotiations with the new nation. In the roll calls on April 3, 15, and 17, he cast his vote for secession.

After the firing on Fort Sumter and Virginia's decision to leave the Union, Tyler served on the Virginia commission that negotiated joining the Confederacy and drafted the resolution placing the commonwealth's military forces under the command of Jefferson Davis. Citing poor health, he declined nomination to the Provisional Confederate Congress while it met in Montgomery but accepted his unanimous election by the Virginia state convention once the Confederate government relocated to Richmond.

In the Confederate House of Representatives elections of November 1861, Tyler handily defeated William H. Macfarland and James Lyons in Virginia's Third Congressional District but had little opportunity to serve his constituents. He died January 18, 1862, at the Exchange Hotel in Richmond after a brief illness. His express wish that he be buried simply at Sherwood Forest was ignored. Tyler's body lay in state in the Confederate Congress on January 20. After an elaborate service the next day at St. Paul's Episcopal Church, he was interred in Hollywood Cemetery near the grave of former president James Monroe.

On May 7, 1864, black troops under the command of Brig. Gen. Edward A. Wild occupied Sherwood Forest. A month later Wild turned possession of the house over to two of the Tyler family slaves. The plantation was looted and the ground floor turned into a school. Although furniture was destroyed, a death mask of Tyler smashed, and outbuildings and fences burned, the former president's papers and most of the family silver and portraits were saved, all having been removed to Richmond for safekeeping in April (ironically, most of the papers were destroyed during the evacuation fire in 1865). In spite of Tyler's position as the only former U.S. president to have advocated secession and served in the Confederate government, his widow successfully lobbied Congress in 1881 for an annual Federal pension of $1,200, an amount increased to $5,000 in March 1882 after the assassination of President James A. Garfield.

— SARA B. BEARS

U

UNIFORMS

[*This entry is composed of two articles that discuss the design, production, and distribution of uniforms for the Confederate armed services:* Army Uniforms *and* Navy and Marine Uniforms. *For further discussion of the uniforms of particular branches of the Confederate armed services, see* Infantry; Medical Department; *and* Signal Corps. *See also* Medals and Decorations.]

ARMY UNIFORMS

Within the Confederate army, from beginning to end, simply clothing the troops consistently took precedence over achieving uniformity. This fact is central to an understanding of both the variety and the uniformity of Confederate clothing. Also crucial is a grasp of the two main systems the Confederate government employed to get clothing to the troops, the commutation system and the issue system.

The commutation system, decreed by the Confederate Congress at the beginning of the war, was intended to save precious government resources by requiring the 100,000 volunteers of the Provisional Army to clothe themselves. They were to be paid fifty dollars a year per man in commutation money for the use of the clothing. Although the money sometimes was paid to the states, a few of which provided clothing according to state uniform regulations, most went to the captains of companies or the men themselves. With no uniform regulations to follow, the clothing the volunteers obtained was as varied as the hundreds of companies in Confederate service.

The uniform regulations issued by the Confederate government in May 1861 were intended only for the Confederate Regular Army, an organization of about 6,000 men. These regulations were inspired by Austrian Jager and French officers' uniforms and for both officers and enlisted men consisted of cadet gray double-breasted frock coats trimmed in a color indicating the wearer's branch of service, sky blue trousers (dark blue for field and general officers), and branch-color kepis. Only the quality of the uniforms and the insignia distinguished officers from enlisted men. Very few of the enlisted uniforms were actually made, but eventually most officers of both the Regular and Provisional armies adopted versions of the Regular Army uniform.

Confederate insignia was one of the few areas where the Regular Army regulations took a firm hold, in part because it was based on the old U.S. Army system. Branch colors were as follows: infantry, sky blue; artillery, red; cavalry, yellow; medical, black; and staff, buff. These colors were used to trim collars, cuffs, and the fronts of coats and were also the body color of the kepi. Noncommissioned-officer rank insignia was based on chevrons on each sleeve in the branch color,

The standard infantry uniform was a gray forage cap, a short, single-breasted gray jacket, sky-blue trousers, and heavy shoes.

PAGE 289

WELL–SUITED

At left is a jacket typical of those worn by enlisted men. The double-breasted officer's frock coat belonged to Brig. Gen. James Conner, C.S.A.

THE MUSEUM OF
THE CONFEDERACY,
RICHMOND, VIRGINIA

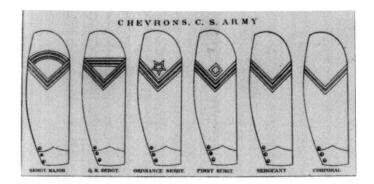

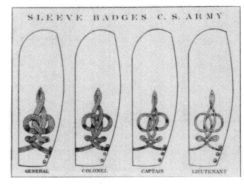

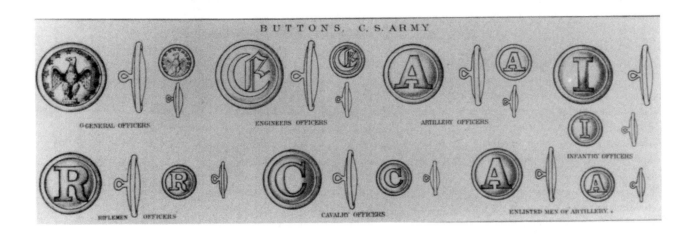

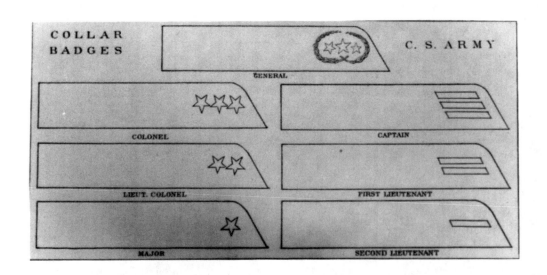

SIGNS OF RANK *Patterns for chevrons, sleeve badges, buttons, and collar badges used in the Confederate army.*
CIVIL WAR LIBRARY AND MUSEUM, PHILADELPHIA

worn points down, two for corporals and three for sergeants. First sergeants wore a lozenge within the angle of the chevrons, ordnance sergeants a star, quartermaster sergeants a tie, and sergeants major an arc. Their trousers were trimmed with branch-color stripes in widths based on rank. Privates wore no insignia, but did wear branch trim on their coats.

Officers' rank insignia was based on the Austrian system of stars or bars worn on the collar, and the French sleeve braid system known as "galons." Line officers—second lieutenants, first lieutenants, and captains—wore one, two, or three bars, respectively, on each side of the collar, with lieutenants wearing one strand of sleeve braid and captains two. Field officers—majors, lieutenant colonels, and colonels—wore one, two, or three stars, respectively, and three strands of sleeve braid. General officers wore three stars surrounded by a wreath and four strands of sleeve braid. The number of sleeve braids was repeated on the kepi. There was also a system of trouser stripes of different widths of gold braid based on rank. Buttons were of brass, sometimes gilt, with a spread eagle for staff officers, a German *E* for engineer officers, and a block *A, I,* or *C* for artillery, infantry, and cavalry.

Waistbelt plates were not specifically uniform items, but rather parts of ordnance-supplied accoutrements. Although regulations specified that the device would be the "Arms of the Confederate States," such arms were never designed. This, plus the fact that officers procured their own sword belts, resulted in a wide variety of plates being worn, some with "CS" or "CSA" on the face, others plain brass, and still others in a buckle form; state seal plates also saw wide use. The most common forms actually used were probably the brass frame buckle, iron roller buckles, or captured U.S. belt plates.

Although the commutation system was intended to avoid both the stockpiling of uniforms and the need for making them, as early as the summer of 1861 there were reports of ragged Confederate troops in the field. The Confederate Quartermaster's Department discovered that much of the clothing the volunteers had purchased was of inferior quality. Far from home, these men now had no way to replenish their supply. As a result, the department sought and obtained congressional sanction to issue clothing. By the fall of 1861 the department had established clothing manufactories in several Southern cities and began to issue clothing to troops in need. This system was considered successful enough by October 1862 that it officially replaced the commutation system, although the changeover took some time to accomplish.

The issue system resulted in large quantities of simple jackets, trousers, shirts, drawers, shoes, and socks being issued, and lesser quantities of hats, caps, overcoats, and blankets. Each depot produced its own patterns and developed its own sources of supply, usually utilizing materials such as gray woolen jeans produced by local mills and supplemented, particularly later in the war, by large quantities of imported English cadet gray cloth. Thus, though each depot's product had some uniformity of its own, there was pattern variation between the depots. The quantity was usually sufficient for overall issue, but the quality of the clothing sometimes left much to be desired. Moreover, baths and the washing of clothing in the field was infrequent or nonexistent, which resulted in an accelerated wearing out of what should have been a sufficient supply. Often the issue clothing was supplemented by contributions from home or by captured Federal items. Occasionally, this captured clothing was dyed to conceal the blue color. When combined with the Confederate soldier's propensity to affect an individual look, these varied sources and styles resulted in a lack of uniformity in the Confederate ranks.

— LES JENSEN

NAVY AND MARINE UNIFORMS

Both the Confederate navy and the Marine Corps were small organizations, and although they faced shortages like the army, their size often allowed them to achieve a degree of uniformity in clothing that the army lacked.

Unlike the army, the Confederate navy issued clothing to its sailors from the beginning of the war. The initial supply came from captured U.S. Navy uniforms obtained from the Gosport Navy Yard in Norfolk, Virginia; soon after, this supply was supplemented by clothing purchased in England. In both cases, the uniforms were largely dark blue, and most of the navy wore this color through at least 1862. Confederate naval officers also wore dark blue uniforms, often old U.S. Navy clothing with the insignia changed.

Sometime in 1862, the Navy Department issued uniform regulations changing the basic color to gray. The change was not universally liked, many officers objecting on the basis that no navy in the world wore gray. By 1863, however, the changeover had largely been accepted.

The regulations seem to have been based mainly on the U.S. Navy's 1852 regulations, with the exceptions that there were no dress uniforms and a considerably different and complicated system of rank insignia was adopted. Officers wore double-breasted frock coats of steel gray cloth with rolling collars, gray trousers, and gray visored caps; enlisted ranks wore gray jackets or gray frocks with white duck collars, gray pants, and black or gray visorless caps in winter and white duck frocks with blue collars and cuffs, white pants, and gray

The Army of Northern Virginia's most ragged period was during the Second Manassas and Sharpsburg campaigns of August-September 1862.

PAGE 289

or white visorless caps in summer. Officers wore rank insignia on the sleeves and shoulder straps; seamen wore it on their sleeves.

The Confederate Marine Corps was never officially allowed more than ten companies, and only six were recruited during the war. These companies never served together as a unit, instead operating as small detachments on board ship or at naval stations. No Marine Corps uniform regulations are known to exist, and it is probable, given the small size of the corps, that none were issued. Marine uniforms were therefore subject to variations based on local supply situations; yet some elements seem to have been common to most, if not all uniforms. Marine officers appear to have worn navy gray frock coats, double-breasted and cut in either the rolling collar navy style or the standing collar army style. Rank insignia was often the army sleeve braid, although distinctive marine shoulder knots were also sometimes worn.

Enlisted uniforms were probably based on the U.S. Marine Corps 1859 regulations. Enlisted men probably wore double-breasted gray frock coats or single-breasted jackets like the army's. At least in 1862, the style was distinctive and different from the Army's. Rank chevrons were probably worn points up rather than down as in the army. But the fact that there are no known photographs of Confederate enlisted marines, no known surviving enlisted uniforms, and no known regulations make specifics very difficult to establish.

— LES JENSEN

UNION OCCUPATION

[*This entry serves only as an introduction to the Union occupation of Confederate territory. For a more detailed examination of selected areas under occupation, see entries on selected states and cities. See also* Contraband.] Large sections of the Confederacy, including a number of important cities, fell under Union control during the Civil War. By mid-1862 the following areas were in Federal hands: northern, southeastern, and western Virginia, including Alexandria and Norfolk; middle and western Tennessee, including Nashville and Memphis; southeastern Louisiana, including New Orleans and Baton Rouge; and several points along the coasts of North and South Carolina and northeastern Florida. By the end of 1863 more territory had been conquered: the remaining cities along the Mississippi River, including Natchez and Vicksburg; the section of Alabama north of the Tennessee River; the northern half of Arkansas; and eastern Tennessee. The final year of the war saw the capture of Atlanta, Savannah, Charleston, and Wilmington.

Military occupation of the South confronted the Union army and government with vast and unprecedented military, political, economic, and social problems. Holding towns and protecting communication lines in the midst of a mostly hostile population required tens of thousands of troops and constant vigilance. Spying, smuggling, guerrilla attacks, and other forms of civilian resistance plagued the occupiers.

Federal commanders imposed martial law in the occupied regions and endeavored not only to subdue resistance but also to assume the functions of municipal government. Moreover, in four states—Tennessee, Louisiana, North Carolina, and Arkansas—President Lincoln appointed military governors to oversee occupation and political reconstruction. Before the war's end, civil governments controlled by native Unionists were established in Tennessee, Louisiana, Arkansas, and Virginia. The military governors and state officials had frequent conflicts of authority with army commanders and with Treasury Department agents who supervised wartime trade.

Foremost among the transformations wrought by Union occupation was the dissolution of slavery. Wherever Federal forces invaded the South, slaves flocked to their lines. Most military commanders initially declined to tamper with the institution of slavery, but eventually they welcomed runaways as laborers. As the Union government's slavery policy moved from conservative to radical, the army became an active agent of emancipation. Military officials established "contraband camps" to shelter black fugitives, oversaw contracts between black laborers and white employers, and enlisted black recruits. Northern humanitarians went south to organize schools for the freedmen.

Federal actions against slavery were just one aspect of the revolutionary upheaval precipitated by Union occupation. To a far greater extent than in the regions held by the Confederacy, society in the occupied South fractured along its fault lines. Slaves by the hundreds of thousands defied their masters, liberated themselves, and took control of their own lives, even where military authorities were conservative or where the Emancipation Proclamation did not apply. Poor whites likewise seized opportunities to challenge the hegemony of the South's ruling elite. Southern Unionists struck back at the secessionist majority who had tyrannized them. This social turmoil was aggravated by widespread devastation, privation, and institutional disruption.

Facing extreme hardship and unchallengeable Federal power, Confederate sympathizers in the occupied regions soon forsook their cause. Well before Appomattox, most resigned themselves to defeat and grudgingly accepted black emancipation.

— STEPHEN V. ASH

URBANIZATION

The role of cities in the antebellum and Confederate South exhibited a paradox. On the one hand, the cities of the future Confederacy were crucial to the existence of the plantation economy, linking it to the international markets that had created it and the flow of capital and supplies that sustained its growth. In the Confederacy, cities became even more vital as administrative centers, supply depots, and manufacturing points. Yet at the same time cities were marginal to the antebellum South, seriously constricted in their range of functions and in their vitality. In an age when American cities outside the region were developing integrated networks of cities and towns and launching on a process of self-sustaining and mutually reinforcing growth, the urban centers of the future Confederacy remained largely tethered to their hinterlands, on the one hand, and to the great centers of international commerce and credit, on the other. Their inadequacies, like those of other components of Southern society, would be glaringly revealed in the harsh light of war.

Urbanization in the Antebellum South

That the process of urbanization in the future Confederate states lagged behind that of the future Union states is apparent from the summary statistics. In 1790 less than 2 percent of Southerners lived in incorporated places of at least 2,500 people, the current census definition of an "urban place." To be sure, the difference from the North was not striking; the young Republic north of the Potomac was at that time only 7 percent urban. By the time of secession, however, nearly a quarter of the Union's population counted as city people; less than 7 percent of the Confederacy's population did. Of the 102 American cities of over 10,000 people in 1860, the Confederacy, with 29 percent of the old Union's total population, contained only 11. If a more sophisticated measure, the index of relative urbanization, is used to trace Southern urbanization over time, it reveals that the region, while generally less than half as urban as the nation as a whole, urbanized at a slightly faster rate than the larger nation until 1840 and then dramatically lost ground in the late antebellum period.

The summary statistics mask enormous variation, for there was no single kind of "Southern city," nor was there a coherent urban hierarchy in the region before secession. Looming large in the summary statistics was New Orleans . Entering the Union through the Louisiana Purchase in 1803, it was immediately the fifth largest American city, maintaining that rank throughout the antebellum period. The development of the western river steamer after

the War of 1812 allowed the city to burgeon as the great entrepôt (intermediary center of trade and transshipment) of the Mississippi valley as well as the leading cotton and sugar port, so that by 1840 it contained nearly 40 percent of the total urban population of the future Confederacy. Its growth slowed dramatically after 1840, though, as the canals and railroads of the later transportation revolution increasingly directed the trade of the Old Northwest toward the Northeast.

Another anomalous case was the state of Virginia. Relatively nonurban in 1790, the Old Dominion (here not including the future West Virginia) by 1840 was, after Louisiana, the South's most urban state, containing eight of the region's twenty-three cities, including the third largest, Richmond, and over a quarter of its urban population. A complex of factors contributed to Virginia's relatively rapid urbanization. The agricultural shift from tobacco to wheat encouraged a vigorous grain trade, increasingly supplemented by the manufacture and export of flour. Changes in tobacco marketing concentrated the trade in Richmond, Petersburg, and Lynchburg and fed their burgeoning tobacco factories. Norfolk and Portsmouth became entrepôts for both Virginia and nearby North Carolina, while Richmond and Petersburg became the South's only true manufacturing cities. After 1840, though, as the pace of urbanization picked up in the North, Virginia lost relative ground, and in 1860 it was less than half as urban as the nation as a whole; except for Richmond, its cities

"[The Civil War] was defined once in an outrageous way by Allen Tate as an attempt on the part of the North to put the South into Arrow collars."

SHELBY FOOTE
IN GEOFFREY WARD,
THE CIVIL WAR, 1990

PERCENTAGE OF URBAN POPULATION, 1790–1860

Year	Future CSA*	Virginia	Non-CSA
1790	1.97	1.78	6.99
1800	2.36	2.62	8.15
1810	3.18	3.63	9.38
1820	3.34	3.78	9.12
1830	3.87	4.82	11.21
1840	5.05	6.92	13.45
1850	5.86	7.97	19.33
1860	6.89	9.50	24.72

*Includes the eleven states of the future Confederate States of America; West Virginia is excluded from the Future CSA and Virginia totals. Future CSA totals for 1790 include the states of Virginia, North Carolina, South Carolina, Georgia, and Tennessee; later additions are Alabama and Mississippi (1800), Louisiana and Arkansas (1810), Florida (1830), and Texas (1850).

SOURCE: Computed from figures in *U.S. Census of Population: 1970.* Vol. 1, pt. 1, sec. 1, tables 8 and 18.

New Orleans was
home to the most
prosperous and
sophisticated free
black community
in the
United States.

PAGE 399

grew slowly, and only one new center, the Shenandoah Valley town of Staunton, appeared in the late antebellum period.

With minor exceptions, notably the western outfitting and provisioning center of Nashville, virtually every other significant Southern city was at least in part the product of the cotton trade, and cotton largely defined the Southern urban character. Dominating the lower South as far north as Tennessee and North Carolina were the cotton ports, which in addition to New Orleans included Charleston, Savannah, Mobile, and Memphis. These cities performed variably during the years before 1860. Charleston, the major city of the South in 1790, stagnated but remained the second city in 1860. As the cotton belt pushed westward, Mobile and, later, Memphis arose, first as outfitting centers for settlers and then as outlets for their staple production. To the interior of these centers there developed a string of much smaller towns, usually on rivers at or near the fall line. In late antebellum times interior points proliferated; the number of incorporated towns in the region tripled between 1840 and 1860. Generally, though, cotton belt urbanization lagged badly; outside of Virginia and Louisiana only 4.4 percent of the region's people lived in cities.

Behind these and other indicators of antebellum urban underdevelopment lay the failure of most Southern cities to transcend their original roles as entrepôts for the plantation staple economies of their hinterlands. All U.S. cities originated as colonial outposts, funneling settlers and supplies to expanding frontiers and exporting primary products abroad. In the nineteenth century, however, cities outside the future Confederacy launched on a path of self-sustaining and mutually reinforcing growth while at the same time drawing strength from relatively densely populated hinterlands generating strong and diverse demand. Southern cities, though, traded little with each other and engaged in little innovative growth; dealing chiefly in one major staple, cotton, these centers did not have much to offer each other. Accordingly, no Southern *system* of cities developed; major centers with their hinterlands developed independently of each other, maintaining their principal trading links with the rising metropolises of western Europe and the American Northeast. Like their colonial forebears they served the undemanding needs of the plantations and the narrowly focused desires of a distant metropolitan core, with profound and deleterious consequences for their development.

The most striking structural feature of Southern urban systems, especially in the cotton belt, was their *primate* character—that is, relative to the North, local centers in the hinterlands of cotton ports were few and underdeveloped, so that the central city largely monopolized both population and urban services. Charleston comprised 83 percent of South Carolina's urban population in 1860, and Mobile 60 percent of Alabama's; New Orleans (with its suburbs) and Memphis together contained 87 percent of the urban dwellers in Louisiana, Mississippi, Arkansas, and western Tennessee. Because cotton and other plantations oriented their production toward outside markets, and because modern means of transportation and communication were slow to develop in the region, planters needed to move their crops to a seaport or one of the larger river towns. Lacking adequate marketing information, they needed the services of agents in those few points enjoying adequate contact with the outside world. Accordingly, the staple trade, and the factors, buyers, and bankers who controlled it, concentrated at very few points, chiefly on the edge of the region, where shipping facilities could be located and where fast, reliable information was most readily available.

The central figures in antebellum Southern urban commerce were commission merchants called *factors*. Specializing in a specific staple, factors served planters as sales agents, offering their strategic locations and specialized knowledge to interior producers seeking advantageous prices. The same advantages encouraged factors to become all-purpose commercial intermediaries for their clients, purchasing and shipping supplies, providing short- and long-term loans, and vouching for credit. Primarily serving the needs of factors, Southern banks were few in number, relatively large in scale, and highly concentrated in location; in 1860 nine of the eighteen banks in South Carolina were located in Charleston. Buyers similarly clustered around factorage centers, as did merchants catering to the planting trade. Because of the slow pace of these urban outposts, and because factors' businesses relied heavily on personal relationships with their clients, the tone of business life was unhurried and social; Charleston, in particular, had a reputation for being almost as much a resort as a business center. Factors typically forged close alliances with their planter clients, and probably a majority were native Southerners. There was a significant non-Southern presence in the trade, however, especially among buyers and agents for northeastern or English houses; Scotch-Irish merchants became powerful in early nineteenth-century Charleston, and in the newer southwestern ports New Yorkers and Englishmen, often part-time residents, played major commercial roles.

Whatever the origins of urban merchants, they worked within a system that left them dependent for markets, capital, and services on cities outside the region. Although Southern banks became increasingly prominent in late antebellum times, many financial services were obtained from the banks, insurance companies, merchants, and shippers of England and the great northeastern ports. Of the latter, New York became increasingly dominant, in large part because of its success in organizing the international cotton trade. Most shipping was controlled by outside interests; moreover, the pattern of shipping that developed enhanced dependence. Southern ports were typically heavy exporters but light importers; accordingly, to minimize backhaul unit costs on the westbound Atlantic voyage, New York shippers established a triangular trade, carrying cotton directly to England, manufactured goods and immigrants to New York, and manufactured goods south. Although Southern urban spokesmen complained loudly of the tribute they thus had to pay the Northerners, no Southern city save New Orleans could sustain direct European trade on its own, and attempts, notably through the commercial convention movement, to foster a cooperative effort at establishing direct Southern ties to Europe ran chronically afoul of urban rivalries within the region.

The low level of imports through Southern cities was, in turn, primarily a product of the low density of demand in their outlying areas. The very lack of a significant urban population with its characteristic abandonment of rural habits of domestic production was part of the problem, as was the large proportion of poor, thinly populated mountain and pine barren land in the region. The most critical inhibitor of demand for goods, though, was the plantation system itself. Its large units helped reduce population density in the Southern countryside relative to that in the North. More important, the economic logic of the slave plantation system led it to minimize outside consumption. Slaves were underutilized in staple crop production, but as "fixed capital" they were available year-round to perform a variety of provisioning and domestic manufacturing operations at little marginal cost. Because they were slaves, it was to the interest of their masters to keep their consumption, especially of high-value goods, to a minimum. Since planters served as purchasing agents for their slaves and dealt chiefly with factors in the nearest major city, plantations provided little stimulus to the development of smaller commercial centers, reinforcing the primate character of the urban system. To be sure, between two-thirds and three-quarters of the white Southern rural population lived in nonslaveholding households, but the plain folk lived plainly. Fearing the risks of commercial agriculture, they involved themselves little in staple production and either produced for themselves or obtained what they needed through local trade. In any case, they lived disproportionately in up-country regions well away from the predomi-

nantly coastal major centers, regions made accessible only near the very end of the antebellum period. Whether planter, slave, or yeoman, then, rural Southerners were generally poor customers for urban importers.

Likewise, they were poor customers for urban manufacturers. Although American cities generally were mercantile in character as late as 1840, manufacturing became increasingly associated with cities over the next twenty years—but not in the South. In 1860, the eleven future Confederate cities with populations of over ten thousand employed proportionately less than half as many workers in manufacturing as did their non-Southern counterparts. Of the 102 American cities for which the statistics were reported, Charleston and Mobile had the lowest proportions, 2.1 percent and 2.3 percent, of the nonsuburban incorporated places; with Norfolk, Savannah, and New Orleans, they composed half of the bottom ten, and Memphis followed three ranks further down.

A yet greater deficiency for the long term was the structure of Southern urban manufacturing. Most Southern industry was designed to process raw materials for shipment (tobacco, lumber), supply commercial services (printing and publishing), or provide cheap slave cloth (cotton textiles). On the other hand, in contrast to the factories and shops of cities in the contemporary West, Southern cities developed few of the varied consumers' and producers' goods industries that would lay the groundwork for the subsequent rise of smokestack America. Not only was consumer demand inhibited, but the crude techniques of plantation agriculture and the ability of planters to extend their operations simply by adding more slaves (contrasting with the limited labor available to family farmers in the free states) smothered the development of a large-scale agricultural implement industry. With thin demand in the countryside and poorly developed trading links between cities within the region, few Southern cities could reach the threshold of demand required to sustain urban industrial production.

Finally, Southern cities were handicapped by a dearth of cheap energy sources; usually neither fossil fuels nor water power was available in the coastal zones where Southern cities arose. Petersburg and Richmond, the major exceptions to this rule among cities of over ten thousand in 1860, were likewise the only ones specializing in manufacturing, 17.0 percent and 19.7 percent of their populations being so employed. The two Virginia cities were at or near tidewater, but were endowed with ample water power by virtue of their location on the fall line and had access to nearby deposits of coal. The two cities became leading centers

Many workers from the North were employed on Southern rail lines in 1861, probably because of the Southerners' traditional dislike for mechanical pursuits.

PAGE 480

*In 1860,
Richmond was the
twenty-fifth largest
American city,
with a population
of 37,910.*

PAGE 502

of tobacco manufacture; Petersburg developed extensive cotton mills, and Richmond milled flour and tapped supplies of pig iron that had been floated down the James River and Kanawha Canal from the Great valley to develop a sizable ironworking industry, epitomized by the famous Tredegar Iron Works. Other manufacturing developed at smaller interior points, chiefly along the fall line; the cities of Fayetteville, North Carolina, and Augusta and Columbus, Georgia, became important textile centers, and Lynchburg, up the James River from Richmond, flourished as a tobacco center. Generally, though, the urban manufacturing sector was poorly developed and poorly balanced, and moreover operated under severe handicaps; Tredegar, the flagship iron maker, suffered from high costs, inadequate supplies of pig iron, and poor markets, depending heavily (and, for the Confederacy, fortunately) on Federal ordnance contracts for much of its prewar sustenance.

Southern cities, then, even in relatively favored Virginia, were handicapped in their development by a host of structural disabilities, most of them imposed by the constricted role assigned them by the plantation slave economy. Although the dynamic impulse in antebellum Southern urbanization was weak by comparison with that further north, it was by no means absent. Cities were almost always dominated by a commercial-civic elite, a core of merchants and their commercial allies that commanded not only the central economic institutions of the city but also its press and its government. As with booster elites elsewhere in the country,

Southern urban leaders identified their own aspirations with those of the town, and vice versa. To facilitate their common business they organized banks and insurance companies and developed port facilities. Through franchised private companies and municipally owned enterprises they worked to extend city services such as water, gas, paved streets, police and fire protection, and public amenities such as markets and parks; undertaken to enhance the city's attractions as a business location and improve the quality of life for the elite, these services were unevenly distributed, being concentrated in the business district and the better residential neighborhoods.

Most important, Southern urban boosters sought to extend and consolidate their trade through transportation projects. Economic and geographic expansion in the nineteenth century sparked increasing rivalry among American cities generally, and Southern cities were no exceptions, ardently seeking ways to exploit new opportunities and protect themselves from their competitors. A brief canal boom in the 1820s brought few lasting benefits outside Virginia, but new opportunities appeared with the advent of the railroad. Worried about the constriction of its hinterland by its rival Savannah, Charleston capitalists completed the South Carolina Railroad to Hamburg, opposite Augusta, in 1833; 136 miles in length, it was at the time the longest railroad in the world. In later years other major cities, notably those of Virginia and Georgia, took up the challenge. But Southern railroads suffered from the same lack of hinterland demand and

RELATIVE URBANIZATION INDEXES, 1790–1860			
Year	**Future CSA**[a]	**Virginia**	**CSA without VA, LA**[b]
1790	.384	.346	.419
1800	.389	.431	.359
1810	.439	.500	.270
1820	.465	.525	.293
1830	.442	.551	.262
1840	.468	.640	.220
1850	.383	.522	.227
1860	.349	.481	.224

[a]"Future CSA" is defined as in Table 1. The "relative index of urbanization" is calculated by dividing the relevant subunit's share of U.S. urban population by its share of total population.

[b]This column is designed to illustrate urbanization in the future Confederacy when the anomalous cases of Virginia and New Orleans (Louisiana) are excluded. Because New Orleans's hinterland was considerably larger than Louisiana alone, excluding Louisiana understates the extent of antebellum Southern urbanization. However, because New Orleans's hinterland included extensive non-Southern territory as well, and because the Crescent City's role as interregional entrepôt made it unique among southern cities, including it in Southern urbanization statistics is equally distorting in the other direction.

SOURCE: Computed from figures in *U.S. Census of Population: 1970*, Washington, D.C., 1970. Vol.1, pt. 1, sec. 1, tables 8 and 18

PRINCIPAL CITIES OF THE FUTURE CONFEDERACY, POPULATIONS AND RANKS

City	1800 Pop.	1800 Rank	1820 Pop.	1820 Rank	1840 Pop.	1840 Rank	1860 Pop.	1860 Rank
New Orleans			27,176	1	105,400[a]	1	179,598[b]	1
Richmond	5,737	3	12,067	3	20,153	3	40,703[c]	2
Charleston	18,924	1	24,780	2	29,261	2	40,522	3
Mobile					12,672	5	29,258	4
Norfolk[d]	6,926	2	8,478	4	17,397	4	24,116	5
Memphis							22,623	6
Savannah	5,166	4	7,523	6	11,214	6	22,292	7
Petersburg	3,521	6	6,690	7	11,136	7	18,266	8
Nashville					6,929	9	16,988	9
Alexandria	4,971	5	8,218	5	8,459	8	12,654	10
Augusta					6,403	10	12,493	11

[a] Includes Lafayette.   [b] Includes Algiers and Jefferson.   [c] Includes Manchester.   [d] Includes Portsmouth in 1840 and 1860.

SOURCE: *U.S. Census of Population*, Washington, D.C., 1800–1860.

NUMBER OF URBAN PLACES, 1790–1860

Year	Future CSA[a]	Virginia	Outside Virginia	U.S.[b]
1790	2	1	1	24
1800	6	4	2	33
1810	7	4	3	46
1820	7	4	3	61
1830	16	6	10	90
1840	22	8	14	131
1850	33	8	25	236
1860	52	9	43	392

[a] Includes all incorporated places, excluding suburbs (Lafayette, Louisiana, in 1840 and 1850; Algiers and Jefferson, Louisiana, in 1860; Manchester, Virginia, in 1860).

[b] Figures include the future Confederacy.

SOURCES: Urban places in future Confederacy compiled from *U.S. Census of Population*, Washington, D.C., 1790–1870. U.S. figures from Allan Pred, *Urban Growth and City-Systems in the United States, 1840–1860 (Cambridge, Mass., 1980), p. 23.*

*Richmond's
manufactures in
1860 ranked
thirteenth in the
nation in value,
far above those of
Charleston, and
even those of New
Orleans, a much
larger city.*

PAGE 502

unbalanced traffic flows afflicting their terminal cities, and expansion was slow until the 1850s, when a major building boom tripled Southern mileage.

Financed by combinations of private, municipal, state, and outside investment, Southern railroads were planned and operated in accordance with what one historian has termed a developmental strategy; each city's system served to define and extend its hinterland, encourage market production, and channel shipments down the line to the primate city. Accordingly, railroad systems long remained isolated from each other, maintaining separate terminals, refusing connections, and using different gauges. Even as late as 1860, interconnections between city systems were rare and roundabout; with numerous unfilled gaps and dead ends, the Southern rail network was far less articulated than its

With a population of 40,522 in 1859, the city of Charleston ranked twenty-second in the nation.

PAGE 96

Northern counterpart (no model of organization itself). Designed to serve the restricted needs of a staple-producing periphery, Southern railroads were thus poorly equipped to support the Confederacy in its struggle for existence.

Some moves toward articulation, though, began to appear late in the antebellum period. Several major cities nursed regional, and even interregional, aspirations; though none successfully met the competition of northeastern ports for the western trade, these larger ambitions began to create embryonic long-haul systems by the 1850s, drawing overland shipments from the Deep South and Southwest into South Atlantic ports. Of major future consequence for Southern urbanization was the resulting rise of a new kind of urban place, the interior railroad city. Most of them were still small in 1860; Atlanta, the future regional rail hub, had fewer than ten thousand inhabitants, despite mushroomlike growth since its incorporation in 1843. But the appearance on the scene of cities such as Atlanta and Chattanooga, and the rail-induced expansion of older centers such as Nashville, portended a revolution in the character and spatial distribution of Southern cities. Improved transportation and telegraphic communication not only encouraged interior economic development but undercut the economic monopoly of the factorage system, on which rested the primacy of the cotton ports, and created new centers with vested interests in breaking free of coastal domination. Interior merchants had long sought to dispense with the factor's expensive services, and direct, ready access to the centers of international markets and finance offered opportunities they were eager to exploit. As a result, the Southern urban landscape would look quite different in 1900 than it did in 1860.

Demographics

However commercial they were, Southern cities were hardly mere nodes of merchants, and the great bulk of their inhabitants were of far humbler status than the commercial-civic elites. Inevitably in a slave society, a large number of city dwellers were slaves; the proportion ranged widely, though only rarely exceeding 50 percent. Some slaves were in town as personal servants of their owners; most worked in the commercial economy, chiefly in unskilled work but in numerous skilled trades as well. Slaves provided the principal work force for the tobacco factories, flour mills, and ironworks of Virginia. In contrast to the countryside, slave hiring was common in the cities, especially in manufacturing centers, where the majority were hired. Despite legal restrictions, many of these hired slaves managed their own employment, paying their owners

for the privilege. A minority, again larger in manufacturing centers and again despite legal prohibitions, were allowed to live apart from either owner or user. As this evidence suggests, slavery could be easily adapted to the needs of an urban society, and city growth does not appear to have been inhibited by the institution's inflexibility. Nonetheless, slavery was less important in cities, where there were alternative sources of labor, than it was on the plantation, where the advantages of forced labor were much clearer. Accordingly, urban slave populations tended to drop proportionately over time and in the cotton boom of the 1850s frequently dropped absolutely. Because it encouraged planters to use their chattels in relatively lucrative rural pursuits, plantation slavery thus imparted a structural anti urban bias to the population distribution of the Old South.

Free blacks constituted a small group in Southern cities (usually less than 10 percent of the population), but they were far more urban in their residence than either native whites or slaves; in the upper South one-third of free blacks, and in the lower South a majority, were urbanites, disproportionately concentrated in larger cities. In Virginia, where they constituted 10 percent of all blacks, urban free blacks engaged largely in unskilled pursuits; farther south, where they were fewer in number, they were more likely to be skilled. Typically, skilled workers tended to be of mixed blood and to be heavily concentrated in personal-service occupations catering to whites, such as barbering. The most successful of these artisans were able to establish themselves as a "colored aristocracy." Other free blacks engaged in petty retailing and other services to fellow blacks, free and slave, and over the course of the antebellum period developed institutions, notably the black church, that would lay the foundation for racial consciousness and solidarity after emancipation.

A majority of residents in most cities, as in the region generally, were white, but white urbanites differed in striking respects from those in the countryside. A great many propertyless white poor congregated in the cities, producing greater extremes of wealth and poverty than existed even in the plantation districts; in particular, single or widowed females sought employment in the factories of cities such as Petersburg. Native white males tended to concentrate in white-collar occupations and in skilled pursuits such as printing. The most unusual characteristic of the Southern white urban population, though, was its large foreign-born component. Although few antebellum immigrants chose to settle in the South, most who did moved to the larger cities; sizable minorities of city populations were foreign-born, and non-natives not uncommonly dominated the white male working class. Many of these immigrants, the Irish in particular, were relegated to unskilled work, often substituting for slaves; many more, though, especially among the Germans, provided a number of essential skills and developed vigorous petty entrepreneurial communities. With immigrant people came immigrant culture; Judaism and (outside Louisiana) Roman Catholicism established their principal beachheads in the major cities, ethnic social and mutual-aid institutions became important to urban life and commerce, and the Irish in places like New Orleans left an enduring imprint on local accents. Finally, it was in cities that class consciousness and class conflict were most likely to arise. These took the usual forms (labor unions and strikes) appearing in other American cities, but the presence of slave and free black workers, along with an official ideology of white supremacy, added peculiar twists and complexities to class relationships among whites, leading in particular to increased pressure on vulnerable free black communities in the 1850s.

In contrast to the countryside, cities were crowded, and social relations were characterized by relative anonymity and fluidity, enhancing the concerns of the elite over their ability to control social turmoil. As was underscored by the abortive slave uprising planned by Denmark Vesey and others in Charleston, urban black populations could not be constrained as easily as rural ones. Accordingly, municipalities assumed much of the task of domination handled on plantations by the individual slave owner, and inevitably in the name of the white race rather than the slaveholding class. Thus many of the institutions associated with postwar segregation appeared in antebellum times, although racial separation was explicitly harsher on both slaves and free blacks. The white working class could not be treated so bluntly; nonetheless, the influx of immigrants, in particular, heightened elite concerns over social control, and the visibility of the white urban poor stirred consciences among an elite wedded both to white supremacy and to Whiggish notions of moral stewardship. Cities thus became centers of social benevolence, creating orphanages, hospitals, public and private relief agencies, and, toward the end of the antebellum period, the first genuine public schools in the South. In many of these endeavors the lead was taken by societies of middle-class women assuming roles as "civic housekeepers," in the process beginning a redefinition of their constricted sphere that would prove of long-term significance.

Cities during Secession and the Confederacy

As the antebellum period progressed, especially into the 1850s, the sectional conflict increasingly brought a variety of pressures on cities, and they in turn played a significant role of their own in the events leading up to secession. Engaged as they were in commerce, the Southern commercial-civic elites valued stability and maintained close business and personal ties with their northeastern correspondents. Moreover, their desires for commercial and industrial development, frequently with government aid, had traditionally clashed with the free-trade proclivities of rural Southerners. They had traditionally been inclined to Whiggery, regretted the rise of radicalism in both North and South, and thus in the 1860 election tended to support Constitutional Union party candidate John Bell. Moreover, immigrant workers, in particular, were questionable loyalists to the cause of Southern rights; in 1860, in large part because of their vote, Democratic Stephen A. Douglas, otherwise scarcely a factor in the South, scored heavily in cities such as Memphis, Mobile, and New Orleans.

On the other hand, Southern cities were intellectual centers for the ideology of Southern rights; the leading fire-eaters tended to be young, ambitious urbanites of the sort that generally take the lead in developing nationalist movements, and cities such as Charleston became hotbeds of secessionist sentiment. Moreover, the close ties binding Southern cities to the northeastern metropolises generated frustration over their continued dependency and fears that a Federal government in the hands of the North would distribute internal improvement aid inequitably. Industrialists such as Tredegar's Joseph R. Anderson dreamed that an independent South would provide them a huge protected market. Finally, white Southern urbanites were, above all, white Southerners; when the stark choice was posed between secession and "submission" to a "tyrannical" Federal government, secession won easily.

For many cities the Confederate period was brief, as their strategic importance made them early targets of Union advances. Alexandria, Virginia, nominally the tenth largest Confederate city, was under Federal control from the beginning; within little more than a year after the firing on Fort Sumter, Memphis, Nashville, Norfolk, Portsmouth, and the major urban prize of New Orleans had passed behind enemy lines, spending the remainder of the war chafing under hostile occupation but prospering from the military supply trade and from illicit commerce between the two sides.

For the remaining cities, however, war brought unprecedented importance. Although the expanding Union blockade effectively shut down some ports, notably Savannah, others, such as Charleston (until the summer of 1863), Wilmington, and to a lesser extent Mobile, became major centers of blockade running, thanks not only to their harbors but to their financial and entrepreneurial communities. Richmond, the Confederate capital, swelled to 128,000, over three times its prewar size, with the burgeoning of the Confederate wartime bureaucracy. Manufacturing and supply opera-

Comprising nearly 40 percent of the 1860 population, New Orleans's foreign-born community was larger than any other Southern city's at the time.

PAGE 399

New Orleans's heterogeneity, plus the city's historic trade ties with the upper Mississippi valley, rendered secession difficult.

PAGE 399

tions doubled the populations of cities in interior Georgia. Industrial demands brought a flood of new entrepreneurs into manufacturing, along with the Confederate government itself, which established important facilities at, among other locations, Augusta, Georgia, and Selma, Alabama. Military authorities developed urban infrastructure, such as sewers, in the interest of preserving the health of their troops; the Confederate government filled in critical gaps in the rail network, notably between Greensboro, North Carolina, and Danville, Virginia, an action that would have a major impact on future Southern urban patterns.

In the end, though, the war lent little enduring impetus to urbanization. The operations of critical manufacturing firms such as Tredegar were hampered by supply bottlenecks, and the monopolization of scarce industrial capacity by military production left little opportunity for city building; indeed, the Southern infrastructure deteriorated in the course of the conflict. War-induced growth was hothouse growth, and enterprises begun to satisfy a single tolerant customer were ill equipped to satisfy many demanding ones. Indeed, all told, the war's significance to Confederate cities lay less in its benefits than in the intense strains it placed on them. Cities became bloated with workers and refugees. The deurbanization of slavery was reversed, as numbers of slaves were impressed for military work, brought to town by refugee owners, or simply abandoned by hard-pressed masters and mistresses. Municipal efforts to counter increased slave independence were largely dead letters, and the institution showed clear signs of decay well before formal emancipation. The swelling numbers of propertyless employees, especially women whose men were in military service, were peculiarly vulnerable to the rampant inflation tearing through the Confederate economic fabric; it has been estimated that real wages dropped by 60 percent in the course of the war. Blockade-running ports such as Charleston and Wilmington enjoyed a diseased prosperity, as runners and merchants profited from trade in military supplies and luxuries that clogged supply lines and sent the cost of living soaring. Despite efforts at expanding poor relief, inflation, impressment, and the inadequacies of the Confederate distribution system left poorer urbanites in an increasingly serious plight and generated enormous social tensions, usually directed against speculators. These tensions culminated in a number of bread riots, frequently led by women, the greatest number of which occurred in the spring of 1863.

Confederate cities generally managed to withstand social tensions, but the powerful Union offensives beginning in the summer of 1864 began to tear the urban system apart. Cities, notably Richmond, had long been important Union objectives; by the end of the summer the capital and nearby Petersburg were under siege, and in early 1865 the last major ports east of Texas, Mobile and Wilmington, were sealed by the Union navy. Moreover, beginning in 1864 the deliberate destruction of cities and the transportation links tying them together became integral to a policy of crippling the Confederate war-making capacity. After capitulating in the summer, Atlanta was burned by Gen. William Tecumseh Sherman in November as he embarked on his March to the Sea and the capture of Savannah; in February 1865 Columbia shared Atlanta's fate, although Sherman's culpability in the burning of the South Carolina capital remains in dispute. Gen. James H. Wilson's cavalry, on its sweep through the Deep South in the spring of 1865, destroyed the war-industry centers of Selma and Columbus, aided in the looting of the Georgia city by slaves and women workers. Other cities, such as Charleston, Richmond, and Petersburg, suffered severe damage incidental to military action in the course of the war.

Above all, the end of the war brought the end of the system of plantation slavery that had shaped the character of Southern cities. To be sure, its legacy would continue to influence Southern urban development in profound ways, some still discernible today. Nonetheless, the destruction of the slave regime would fundamentally alter the course of urbanization in the region. From the ashes of the Confederacy would arise a different and more dynamic Southern urban order.

[*See also* Bread Riots; Poor Relief; Poverty; Railroads.]

— DAVID L. CARLTON

VANCE, ZEBULON

Vance, Zebulon (1830–1894), colonel, governor of North Carolina, and U.S. senator. Zebulon Baird Vance was born on May 13, 1830, in the Reems Creek community of Buncombe County, North Carolina. A comfortable childhood ended in 1844 when his father died and the family farm and slaves had to be sold. This ended Vance's formal education until 1851 when he studied law at the University of North Carolina. In 1852, he passed the bar examination and was elected solicitor of the Buncombe County court.

In 1854, he was elected to the state legislature as a Whig and soon after became an editor of the *Asheville Spectator*. When the Whig party collapsed, Vance joined the Know-Nothings. He won a special election for the U.S. Congress in 1858 and was reelected the next year. Vance's success was largely due to his popular speaking style, which combined skilled partisan rhetoric with bawdy good humor.

Although Vance was a firm advocate of slavery, he was a strong defender of the Union during the secession crisis. He campaigned for the John Bell presidential ticket during the election of 1860, and in Congress he supported many compromise proposals to end the crisis. During February 1861, Vance campaigned as a Union supporter in the secession referendum held in North Carolina. His stand was vindicated when a large majority of the state's voters rejected the call for secession. Because Vance had been assured by William H. Seward that Abraham Lincoln would withdraw the troops from Fort Sumter, he felt betrayed by the attempt to resupply the fort and Lincoln's call for troops.

Vance's career as a Confederate officer was not distinguished. He helped organize the "Rough and Ready Guards" of Buncombe County and was elected company captain. Before the unit saw action, however, he was elected colonel of the Twenty-sixth North Carolina Volunteer Regiment. Vance was poor at organizing a military unit, and only the presence of Henry King Burgwyn, Jr., as second in command ensured that the regiment learned elemental military tactics. During the Battle of New Bern on March 14, 1862, Vance's regiment was placed on the extreme right of a weak Confederate line. An attack by General Ambrose Burnside's much larger army shattered the Confederate line and forced Vance and his men into rapid retreat. The regiment joined the Army of Northern Virginia and took part in the Seven Days' Battles around Richmond. Vance and his regiment participated in the final and unsuccessful assault on Malvern Hill on July 1, 1862.

Vance's military career ended in 1862 when he reentered politics. On June 15, he became the Conservative party's gubernatorial nominee. That party was formed by the Whig party leadership and William W. Holden, a former leader of North Carolina Democrats. Vance's opponent was William Johnston, the candidate of the original secessionists who now called themselves Confederates. Vance won the August election overwhelmingly by gaining the support of those who opposed the war and those who thought that the Confederate party was responsible for the inadequate defense of the state. Since Vance was the candidate of the dissatisfied, many observers expected him to challenge the Confederacy. Starting with his inaugural address in September 1862, however, he proclaimed his allegiance to the Southern nation.

Although Vance never repudiated his support of the Confederacy, he was more than willing to defend his state and challenge Confederate policies. When North Carolina Supreme Court justice Richmond Pearson ruled that the state militia could not enforce conscription and that men who had hired substitutes could not be subsequently conscripted, Vance refused to override these rulings despite frequent requests from Confederate authorities to do so. Vance defended Pearson despite his personal disagreement with Pearson's findings. Vance's commitment to North Carolina's welfare had many other manifestations. He initiated a very successful state blockade-running plan that predated that of the Richmond government. In addition, he pushed a state program to clothe North Carolina troops, a salt procurement program, and a series of measures to provide more food for the poor.

During this same period, Vance frequently clashed with James A. Seddon and Jefferson Davis. Among his most common complaints were that North Carolina officers were not being promoted as rapidly as those from other states, that Confederate troops were abusing North Carolina civilians, and that the Confederate government was trying to conscript state officials. The correspondence was often heated, and at one point,

Zebulon Vance of North Carolina quickly became the paradigm of a state and individual rights fanatic.

PAGE 247

Both Vance and his state actually appeared to be anti-Confederate despite their enormous contributions to the war.

PAGE 247

Davis attempted to break off further communication with Vance. Despite the rather sharp rhetoric in the letters, Vance rarely impeded the war effort and publicly defended conscription and unpopular Confederate tax policies. As late as October 1864, Vance was a moving force in the Confederate governor's conference held in Augusta, Georgia, that reaffirmed the allegiance of the states to the Confederacy.

A significant minority of North Carolinians opposed Vance and the Confederacy. From the beginning of the war, Unionists in all parts of the state resisted Confederate conscription. Despite the use of force in such disparate areas as Washington County, Randolph County, and the Shelton Laurel community, Vance's Home Guards and the Confederate army were unable to eliminate this persistent opposition. By the summer of 1864, there were an estimated ten thousand Unionists enrolled in the Heroes of America. Many other North Carolinians also began to withdraw their commitment to the Confederacy. As early as 1862, yeoman farmers were outraged that those who owned twenty slaves were exempted from conscription. After Confederate defeats at Gettysburg and Vicksburg, Vance's political ally William W. Holden issued a call for peace meetings throughout the state to bring an end to the fighting.

The North Carolina peace movement was the most vocal in the Confederacy. During July and August 1863, about a hundred public meetings were held urging a peaceful end to the war. Vance reluctantly broke with Holden and issued a proclamation on September 7, 1863, that ended the public demonstrations. In the congressional elections of 1863, the peace candidates were successful in a majority of districts. Following up on this victory, Holden urged peace advocates to demand a state convention where delegates could negotiate a truce with Northern political leaders. Vance challenged Holden's program when he opened his reelection campaign in February 1864. After Holden announced his candidacy, Vance stumped the state attacking him and claiming that the peace program would involve North Carolina in a war with the Confederacy. Vance also attacked Davis's use of the writ of habeas corpus. The strategy was successful, and Vance was reelected by an overwhelming majority in August.

Vance tried unsuccessfully to prevent the collapse of the Confederacy in North Carolina after his election. He sought to collect supplies for the Confederate army and to return deserters to Robert E. Lee's army; he rushed the state militia to Wilmington to assist in the defense of Fort Fisher. A month later, Vance refused to take part in an attempted coup against Jefferson Davis engineered by William A. Graham and other members of Congress. When William Tecumseh Sherman's large army entered North Carolina in April 1865,

Vance arranged for the surrender of Raleigh before attending one last meeting with the fleeing Davis. On May 13, 1865, Vance was arrested in Statesville, North Carolina, and transported to Washington where he was placed in the old Capitol prison. On July 6, he was paroled to his home in North Carolina.

During Reconstruction, Vance resumed the practice of law and moved to Charlotte. In 1870, he was elected to the U.S. Senate, but the Republican majority refused to remove his political disabilities and Vance had to relinquish his seat. The Democrats nominated Vance as their gubernatorial candidate in 1876. The outstanding rhetorical abilities of Vance and his Republican opponent, Thomas Settle, and their debates across the state made this the most famous campaign in North Carolina's history. Vance's narrow victory over Settle ended Republican Reconstruction in North Carolina. Vance was elected to the U.S. Senate in January 1879, but his Senate career was frustrating and largely unproductive.

Starting in 1889, Vance suffered from failing health, and he died in Washington on April 14, 1894. His death prompted a massive outpouring of grief in North Carolina where scores of memorial services honored the state's war governor. He is still regarded as the most popular public figure in North Carolina history.

— GORDON B. McKINNEY

VAN LEW, ELIZABETH

Van Lew, Elizabeth (1818–1900), Union spy. An outspoken opponent of slavery, Van Lew ran a Union spy ring in her hometown of Richmond, Virginia, during the war. At Van Lew's behest, Mary Elizabeth Bowser, a former servant of the Van Lews, gained employment as a domestic in the Confederate White House. There Bowser gathered military information and passed it on to Van Lew, who in turn transmitted it to Union forces.

Van Lew frequently visited Federal prisoners in Libby Prison in Richmond to bring them food, books, and clothing; she is rumored to have helped some escape. In April 1864 she arranged for the clandestine reburial of Union hero Col. Ulric Dahlgren, whose body was mutilated and secretly buried by Confederate forces after he was killed leading a surprise raid on Richmond in March.

Although Van Lew was under close surveillance by Confederate agents during the war, she was never caught at espionage work; her bizarre dress and behavior, which earned her the name "Crazy Bet," was her ploy to divert suspicion. During the last year of the war, her intelligence operations included a network of five relay stations from Richmond to Federal headquarters downriver. When Union forces occupied her native city in 1865, Van Lew raised the first American flag to be seen there since 1861.

After the war President Ulysses S. Grant appointed Van Lew postmistress of Richmond, an office she held until 1877. In her last years she became an advocate of women's suffrage, paying her taxes under protest. In 1900, after enduring years of social ostracism from ex-Confederates, she died and was buried in Richmond.

— ELIZABETH R. VARON

VICKSBURG CAMPAIGN

The city of Vicksburg, Mississippi, located on the east bank of the Mississippi River midway between Memphis and New Orleans, was the site of a key Confederate river defense and the focal point of Maj. Gen. Ulysses S. Grant's operations in the West from October 1862 to July 1863. The surrender of its fortifications and a garrison of 29,500 men on July 4, 1863, was a severe psychological blow to the Confederacy and, combined with the simultaneous defeat of the Army of Northern Virginia at Gettysburg, a loss of manpower that the South could ill afford.

In 1861, Vicksburg's population of nearly five thousand was the second largest in the state. Its economy was prospering, thanks to the city's status as a commercial center and transportation hub for Mississippi and Louisiana planters. To the east, the Southern Railroad of Mississippi linked Vicksburg and Jackson and connected the former to other lines including the northward-running Mississippi Central Railroad. To the west, the Vicksburg, Shreveport and Texas Railroad went as far as Monroe, Louisiana, giving planters in the bottomlands access to the river and New Orleans. Riverboats of all shapes and sizes docked at the city's wharves and took cargoes of cotton and passengers south to the Crescent City.

When the war began, Vicksburg took on an even greater significance. It became one of the key links between the eastern Confederacy and the Trans-Mississippi South, serving as a transit point for troops and as a port of entry for Louisiana salt, sugar, and molasses, the latter two frequently exchanged for meat for the armies. Efforts to safeguard the city became crucial in the spring of 1862 when Memphis and New Orleans fell to Federal forces. Vicksburg remained the only railhead on the east bank of the river and as such provided the last direct link between the two "halves" of the Confederacy. Its maintenance also effectively blocked Federal waterborne communications down the river.

In May 1862, three thousand troops, evacuated from New Orleans, arrived in Vicksburg along with their commander, Brig. Gen. Martin Luther Smith. They were joined by companies from Mississippi and Louisiana, turning the city into a garrison. Smith concentrated on fortifying the city's river approaches, where he was aided by the natural features of the area. Vicksburg sat in a cluster of hills two hundred feet above the river opposite De Soto Peninsula—ideal defensive terrain. Seven batteries were erected on the bluffs just in time for the arrival of USS *Oneida*, which on May 20 fired upon the city, commencing the thirteen-month-long campaign for Vicksburg.

EARLY FEDERAL MOVES AGAINST VICKSBURG. Throughout the rest of May and into June, ships from Flag Officer David Farragut's deepwater fleet multiplied in the river south of Vicksburg, reinforced by mortar schooners under Commdr. David D. Porter. On June 27, work began on a plan to bypass the Confederate river defenses by using troops and impressed slaves to dig a canal across the base of the peninsula created by the river's bend. The following day, Farragut's fleet conducted an early morning run past Vicksburg's gauntlet of batteries and linked up with

VICKSBURG CAMPAIGN

Early Federal Moves against Vicksburg

From the Confederate point of view, the Vicksburg campaign was a debacle from start to finish.

PAGE 304

RIVER TOWN

Vicksburg, Mississippi, as seen from the hills to the north of the city, with the Mississippi River on the right.

HARPER'S PICTORIAL HISTORY OF THE GREAT REBELLION

*Pemberton
remembered Lee's
admonishment
and fought to
hold Vicksburg at
all costs.*

PAGE 415

*In the spring of
1863, Grant
confused
Pemberton with
a series of
diversions and
crossed the
Mississippi below
Vicksburg
practically
unnoticed.*

PAGE 415

Flag Officer Charles H. Davis's gunboat flotilla north of the river's bend out of range of Confederate guns. But the Federal navy was unable to develop a plan to force the city's capitulation and reverted to bombarding Vicksburg while continuing construction on the canal.

Farragut's fortunes took a turn for the worse in July when Porter was transferred east, the subsiding waters of the Mississippi threatened to leave his oceangoing fleet stranded upriver for the remainder of the year, and the Confederate ram *Arkansas* created havoc by sailing into the Federal fleet on July 15. Unable to destroy *Arkansas,* Farragut took his ships out to sea on July 25 while Davis steamed north to Helena, Arkansas. It was clear that the U.S. Army would play the predominant role in subduing Vicksburg, and Major General Smith, aware of this, focused on building up the city's fortifications.

On June 28, Maj. Gen. Earl Van Dorn had arrived in the city to assume command. Van Dorn continued to strengthen the defenses of Vicksburg and of the stretch of river south of the city by fortifying Port Hudson. With the departure of the Federal fleet, Van Dorn turned his attention to enemy troops in northern Mississippi and western Tennessee under the command of Grant. The resulting fiasco at Corinth cost Van Dorn five thousand troops and left Vicksburg exposed. Grant now suggested to Maj. Gen. Henry Halleck that he be allowed to conduct "a forward movement against Vicksburg."

While Van Dorn was engaging Federal troops at Corinth, the Confederate War Department appointed Maj. Gen. John C. Pemberton to head a military district comprising the state of Mississippi and that part of Louisiana east of the Mississippi River. Pemberton assumed command on October 14, establishing his headquarters in Jackson. His assignment was part of a large-scale administrative change that placed all Confederate forces west of the Alleghenies and east of the Mississippi River under Gen. Joseph E. Johnston. Johnston, lukewarm about his new assignment, argued that the ambiguities inherent in President Jefferson Davis's new command arrangements made his role purely "nominal" and that he possessed little authority but great responsibility. Although he established his headquarters at Chattanooga, Johnston did not ignore Vicksburg.

GRANT TAKES COMMAND. Grant's campaign to capture the city officially began on November 2 when he assembled an army of thirty thousand at Grand Junction, Tennessee, and began moving in three columns down the line of the Mississippi Central Railroad toward Holly Springs, twenty miles south. Pemberton's initial response was to fortify the south bank of the Tallahatchie River. But turning movements on

both flanks threatened the Confederate rear and forced Pemberton to withdraw to the south bank of the Yalobusha River at Grenada.

Grant, with Halleck's approval, now detached Maj. Gen. William Tecumseh Sherman to lead a waterborne operation. His plan called for simultaneous advances south by his army and Sherman's, forcing Pemberton to divide his resources and fight on two fronts.

Although well conceived, Grant's operation fell victim to Confederate cavalry attacks against the vulnerable Federal lines of communication. Brig. Gen. Nathan Bedford Forrest's destruction of sixty miles of rail lines in western Tennessee caught Grant by surprise. Most damaging of all was a December 20 strike by Van Dorn (now commanding Pemberton's cavalry) against the Federal supply depot at Holly Springs. Grant lost the supplies necessary to continue his half of the two-pronged operation and, thanks to Forrest, could not replace them. By the time Sherman heard of Grant's withdrawal northward he was already committed to proceeding with his own attack. On December 26 and 27, Sherman's expeditionary force of 32,000 men disembarked from transports near Chickasaw Bayou on the Yazoo River and assaulted the city's northernmost defenders under Brig. Gen. Stephen D. Lee. The three-day battle proved to be a Federal disaster, and Sherman withdrew on January 2.

By the end of January, Grant's new objective was to isolate the city by severing its rail link to Jackson. To accomplish this, he planned to execute a turning movement from the north and east. Realizing that movement along the railroad would leave him vulnerable to attack, he chose to forgo land communications and use the Mississippi as his main line of operations. The Mississippi route was secure from enemy attacks thanks to the return of Union gunboats now under the command of Porter, but lacked sufficient dry ground for offensive operations. The ideal terrain for Grant's army was south of the city, but getting vulnerable transport ships south past the batteries would be difficult at best.

Grant's efforts to get his army on dry ground south and east of the city led to several unorthodox maneuvers. Initially, he considered using the transpeninsula canal begun the previous year, but it was turning into a quagmire. He then thought of creating a southerly route to the river south of the city by using a combination of lakes, bayous, and streams west of the Mississippi, including Lake Providence, a six-mile-long body of water that was once part of the river. Grant, however, grew disenchanted with the project after a February 4 inspection trip to the lake and looked for yet another solution.

An alternative was already materializing on the east bank of the river. Grant was notified that by destroying a levee at Yazoo Pass, fifty miles below Memphis, vessels could pass through an old channel to the Coldwater River, enter the Tallahatchie, and steam down the Yazoo River to the rear of Vicksburg. Pemberton quickly caught on to Grant's scheme after the levee was opened on February 2 and responded by sending two thousand troops under Maj. Gen. W. W. Loring to block the movement. Loring constructed a stronghold called Fort Pemberton out of cotton bales and sand, and armed it with thirteen guns, including a 6.5-inch rifled cannon. Between March 11 and 16, a Federal expedition led by Lt. Commdr. Watson Smith and Brig. Gen. Leonard Fulton to reduce the fort was foiled by the ineffectiveness of the gunboats, the accuracy of the Confederate's rifled cannon, and the fort's inaccessibility from land. An operation begun on March 14 by Porter and Sherman up Steele's Bayou in

an effort to enter the Yazoo below Fort Pemberton was transformed by Grant into another would-be solution to his problem. Instead of moving to help Smith and Fulton, Porter was ordered to operate against Vicksburg itself with the goal of deploying Sherman's troops northeast of the city. After battling obstructions and sharpshooters, Porter abandoned the operation on March 20 and returned to the Mississippi. On April 4, Grant recalled the Yazoo Pass expedition and prepared to try something else.

Grant's new plan originated out of his earlier designs for Lake Providence and the success in February of two vessels in running past the Vicksburg batteries. His idea was to move the majority of his army down the west side of the Mississippi River below Vicksburg and then run Porter's gunboats and empty transports southward past the Confederate

VICKSBURG CAMPAIGN

Grant Takes Command

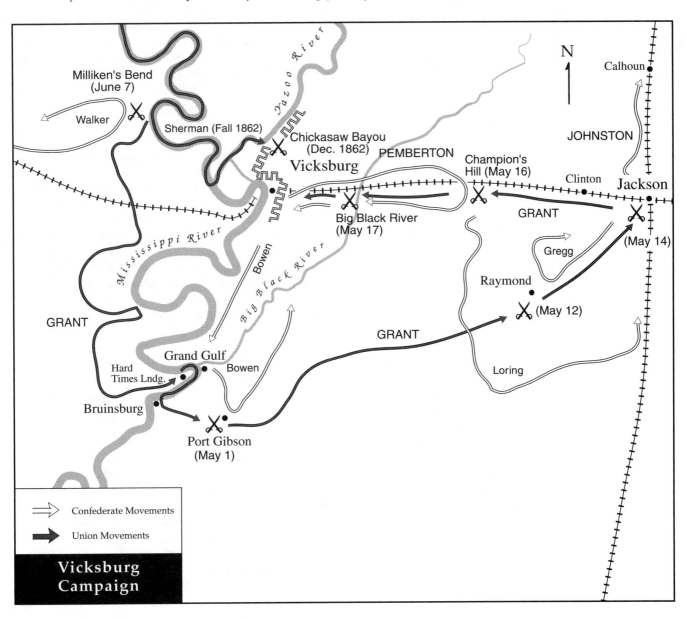

Torn by conflicting orders, Pemberton marked time while Grant swept inland scoring a series of quick victories at Port Gibson, Raymond, and Jackson.

PAGE 415

defenses to Hard Times, where they would rendezvous with the awaiting army. The vessels could then ferry the army across the river, allowing Grant to begin his campaign against the city and the rail line. Sherman's corps would initially stay behind to conduct demonstrations near Vicksburg. Col. Benjamin H. Grierson's 1,700 cavalrymen would undertake an extensive raid into Mississippi to disrupt Confederate communications and draw attention away from Grant's operation.

Federal troops began moving south on March 31, and twenty-eight days later two corps had reached Hard Times. On April 16, eleven out of the twelve boats (including two transports) assigned by Porter completed a midnight run past the Vicksburg batteries and proceeded south to join Grant. The next day, Grierson's troopers left their camp in southwest Tennessee and headed south toward the railroads, supply depots, and plantations of eastern Mississippi. On April 22, five more transports and six barges successfully ran the gauntlet. By April 29, Grant was prepared to ferry his army across the river. From April 30 through May 1, while Sherman conducted his diversion north of Vicksburg, 23,000 Federal troops disembarked at Bruinsburg on the east bank of the Mississippi. Grant was now on dry soil, and the final phase of the campaign for Vicksburg was about to begin.

For Pemberton, the flurry of Federal activity across the river in early April was indicative of a withdrawal. After assuring Davis and Johnston that Grant was abandoning his operations against Vicksburg, Pemberton went so far as to prepare to send reinforcements to Gen. Braxton Bragg's Army of Tennessee, the next logical target of a Federal western offensive. But on April 17, Johnston and Adj. Gen. Samuel Cooper learned from Pemberton that Grant's army was not leaving after all. Nevertheless, Pemberton chose to focus his attention upon Grierson's raid rather than on determining Grant's intentions, deploying an infantry division to try and trap Grierson's cavalry. Johnston, a proponent of maneuverability, informed Pemberton from Tennessee that he should unite his whole force to beat Grant, remarking "Success will give back what was abandoned to win it." Davis, on the other hand, sent Pemberton instructions to hold both Vicksburg and Port Hudson—evacuation ran counter to the president's strategic principles. Thus Pemberton, who had never commanded an army in combat, received conflicting instructions and chose to comply with the president's and his own preference for holding fortifications.

The Confederate indecision and confusion allowed Grant to pursue his strategy at will. After landing at Bruinsburg, he moved quickly against Brig. Gen. John Stevens Bowen's small and divided force at Port Gibson and Grand Gulf, forcing the latter's evacuation on May 3. The line of march chosen by Grant out of now Federally controlled Grand Gulf was in part dictated by the general's original plan to move on Vicksburg from the east after first securing the Southern Railroad of Mississippi. A second factor was the 100-mile-long Big Black River that ran from the center of the state above Jackson southwestwardly to Grand Gulf. Crossing the river and moving directly north toward Vicksburg could be risky if his force was challenged, and the broken terrain between the Big Black and the city favored Pemberton. Therefore, Grant chose to move north and east, threatening both Vicksburg and Jackson. His army advanced in three columns: Maj. Gen. John McClernand's corps on the left, with instructions to "hug the river [the Big Black]," the recently arrived Sherman in the center, and Maj. Gen. James McPherson on the right.

The first major Confederate resistance to the march occurred on May 12 near Raymond, fourteen miles southwest of Jackson. Brig. Gen. John Gregg brought his brigade out of the capital and struck the vanguard of McPherson's corps, led by Maj. Gen. John A. Logan. The Confederates held for six hours before being forced to retire. Grant now knew that Southern troops might be concentrating in Jackson. He decided therefore to take advantage of his central position between two Confederate forces, sending McPherson northeast to Clinton where he was to destroy the railroad and move east to the capital. Sherman was to move his corps through Raymond toward Jackson. McClernand was ordered to be in position to reinforce either of the other two corps and to watch for an advance by Pemberton from the west.

On the same day that Grant issued these orders, Johnston arrived in Jackson to assume command of Confederate forces in Mississippi and learned the full magnitude of the situation: Grant was between Jackson and Vicksburg and Pemberton had not concentrated his forces. Johnston was too late to execute the speedy concentration of force that he had hoped to use against Grant. The railroad and telegraph lines were cut and any union of Pemberton's army and Johnston's gathering reinforcements would have to be coordinated from a distance using unreliable communications. For his part, Pemberton and 17,500 troops ventured out of the Vicksburg defenses on May 12 and advanced as far as Edwards Station, a railroad town east of the Big Black and halfway to Jackson. Aware of Pemberton's general location and seeing an opportunity to strike Grant while his army was divided, Johnston sent word via three couriers for Pemberton to strike the rear of the Federal force on the railroad at Clinton.

On May 14, with only 6,000 troops available in Jackson and inadequate earthworks to use as protection, Johnston evacuated the capital and moved north toward Calhoun. Dispatches were sent east and south to inform incoming reinforcements of the situation. By midafternoon, Federal troops had successfully fought their way through the Confederate rear guard and entered Jackson where they remained until May 16. Pemberton meanwhile pondered Johnston's instructions and held a council of war with his subordinates. Although the majority of his officers favored compliance with Johnston's directive, the council nevertheless decided to move southeast to cut Grant's supply line to the Mississippi. Thus Pemberton decided essentially to send his army away from rather than toward a unification with Johnston's. When the latter was informed of this development, he quickly sent another message urging conformity to his original instructions. By that time it was too late. Grant, learning Johnston's intentions from a Northern sympathizer who happened to be one of the Confederate general's original three couriers, was rapidly moving westward to confront Pemberton.

The two forces clashed on May 16 at Champion's Hill, eighteen miles east of Vicksburg. In an all-day fight, Pemberton displayed little tactical skill and was eventually defeated. In his report to Johnston, Pemberton stated that his current position was too vulnerable, and he felt compelled to withdraw back to the safety of Vicksburg. Consequently, after attempting to slow the Federal advance across the Big Black River on May 17 and losing Loring's division when it was separated from the main body of the army, the majority of Pemberton's troops returned to the city with Grant's entire army in pursuit.

Johnston sent word to Pemberton instructing him to evacuate Vicksburg and march to the northeast. For the commanding general, the object of the campaign was the defeat of Grant's army, not the retention of a geographic point. By now, the strategic significance of Vicksburg was at best questionable. The value of the Mississippi River to the Confederacy had been drastically reduced ever since the capture of New Orleans and Memphis and the resulting loss of two of the three most important rail termini on the river. After Porter's gunboats successfully ran past the batteries in April, steamboats could no longer safely reach the railhead at Vicksburg, thus severing the Trans-Mississippi supply line. The only remaining significance of Vicksburg was political and psychological. Davis had promised his fellow Mississippians that Vicksburg would not fall. Moreover, from his point of view, he could ill afford to lose this symbol of Confederate control on the Mississippi.

In response to Johnston's request for an evacuation, Pemberton held a second council of war and this time

received, according to his own account, unanimous support for remaining in the city. He wrote Johnston that "I still conceive it to be the most important point in the Confederacy." The decision made, he prepared to turn away the approaching Federals.

THE SIEGE OF VICKSBURG. Grant, eager to take Vicksburg and avoid a protracted siege, attacked the city's defenses on May 19 and again three days later. Both assaults were repulsed with heavy casualties. He was now forced to resort to a siege and instructed his engineers to begin encircling the nine miles of Confederate entrenchments. Once completed, the twelve-mile-long Federal line paralleled the Confederate earthworks at an average distance of six hundred yards and was anchored at both ends on the Mississippi River. By the end of May, 50,000 men surrounded the city; two weeks later 27,000 more were on hand.

Through May and into June, Johnston, focusing on raising an army sufficient to lift the siege or at least open a hole long enough for Pemberton to escape, wrote repeatedly to the War Department requesting troops from all available sources. On June 1, Johnston reported he had 24,053 effectives and needed more. He, along with Lt. Gen. James Longstreet and Gen. P. G. T. Beauregard, suggested to the War Department that an operation in middle Tennessee might draw Federal troops away from Pemberton. Longstreet and Beauregard also suggested that reinforcements from Virginia be used to aid Bragg in a strike against Maj. Gen. William Rosecrans, followed by an advance to the Ohio valley, but Gen. Robert E. Lee's aversion to reinforcing the West undermined the plan. Little help would be coming from the Trans-Mississippi either, as Maj. Gen. John G. Walker's division attempted too late to destroy Grant's supply base at Milliken's Bend. Consequently, on June 15, Johnston informed the War Department that saving Vicksburg was "hopeless."

Grant, however, was conscious of Johnston's potential ability to disrupt Federal operations if allowed to go unchecked, so he took measures to ensure his army's safety. He had already destroyed the railroads around Jackson, so that Johnston would have to rely upon an insufficient number of wagons to move his army. Likewise, the Federal army thoroughly foraged the countryside, making it difficult for Johnston's troops to sustain themselves within striking distance of Grant's army without an adequate supply line. Most important, Grant was concerned about his central position between two Confederate forces and posted Sherman and 34,000 men on a defensive line fifteen miles east of Vicksburg to protect his rear.

Although often the subject of historical debate, Johnston's military options were very limited. Ideally, he

Johnston offered the impracticable proposal of shifting troops from west of the Mississippi to help defend Vicksburg.

PAGE 303

A few months after Vicksburg, Pemberton showed his loyalty to the Confederate cause by requesting a reduction in rank.

PAGE 416

Rams were feared by Federal sailors, inducing in many the fearful condition derisively known as "ram fever."

PAGE 486

could cooperate with Pemberton in a simultaneous assault against Grant and Sherman. In this scenario, neither Federal army would easily be able to reinforce the other, and the Confederates could hope for a blunder that might open a window of opportunity for success. In order for this plan to work, however, timing, organization, and numerical superiority were critical. With the uncertainty and delays necessarily associated with the courier system, neither general could depend upon timing or be certain about organization. Moreover, both Pemberton and Johnston would have to launch assaults against a numerically superior, entrenched army. Johnston therefore chose another option. By June 28, he had pieced together over 31,000 troops and sent a courier to Pemberton informing him of one last hope—he would make a diversionary attack on July 7 designed to allow the Vicksburg garrison to cut its way out. (Pemberton had earlier informed him that he could hold the city until July 10.) Johnston's message never arrived.

The situation within the city was rapidly deteriorating. Citizens sought shelter from daily bombardments by hiding in basements or digging caves into the hillsides. Water became scarce and the meat supply dwindled. By the end of June mule meat was substituted for bacon and bread rations were reduced. After questioning his senior officers on the status of their men, Pemberton decided that his garrison was too weakened by the forty-six-day siege to undertake the rigors of the field. Accordingly, on July 3, Pemberton met Grant between the lines and arranged to surrender the following day. All told, he surrendered 2,166 officers, 27,230 enlisted men, 115 civilian employees, 172 cannons, and

60,000 long arms. The symbolic bastion on the Mississippi was now in Federal hands. Port Hudson surrendered five days later, freeing the river of all major Confederate resistance. "The Father of Waters," President Abraham Lincoln observed, "again goes unvexed to the sea."

Johnston heard the news of Vicksburg's surrender on July 5 and, after a brief skirmish with Sherman, fell back from his position on the east bank of the Big Black to Jackson. Eleven days later, the general evacuated the capital city and headed east, first to Brandon and then to Morton, Mississippi. For Grant, the capture of the river fortress vaulted him into national prominence; his martial abilities were confirmed five months later at Chattanooga. For the Confederacy, the first week of July 1863 proved to be a major turning point in the war. The defeats at Gettysburg and Vicksburg did not guarantee ultimate Federal victory, but many Southerners now realized that the Confederacy was running out of manpower and time.

— ALAN C. DOWNS

VIRGINIA

Built on the hull of the ex-Union steam frigate *Merrimack,* the ironclad ram *Virginia* measured 262 feet in length, 51 feet in width, and 22 feet in draft of water. Its 195-foot-long casemate, angled on sides and ends at thirty-five degrees to better deflect projectiles, carried four inches of iron plate backed with two feet of wood.

IRON STALEMATE

At Hampton Roads on March 9, 1862, the USS Monitor *(in foreground) fought the CSS* Virginia *for four hours, but neither seriously damaged the other.*

NAVAL HISTORICAL CENTER, WASHINGTON, D.C.

Within the casemate were ten guns: six 9-inch Dahlgren smoothbores and two 6.4-inch Brooke rifles in broadside, and a 7-inch Brooke rifle pivot-mounted at each end. A crew of 320 was required to operate *Virginia.*

Faced with insurmountable odds in the form of an established and rapidly expanding U.S. Navy, Confederate Navy Secretary Stephen R. Mallory early recognized the potential of armorclad warships in offsetting the numerical disadvantage under which the South labored.

After first attempting to purchase an ironclad in Europe, Mallory decided to construct an armored vessel in the Confederacy. On June 22, 1861, following consultations with Lt. John M. Brooke, Naval Constructor John L. Porter, and Chief Engineer William P. Williamson, the secretary accepted a plan submitted by Brooke and directed that suitable machinery be found with which to power it. Three days later, finding no acceptable engines and boilers and determining that the time entailed in constructing them would be too great, the three officers, on the recommendation of Williamson, suggested that instead the remains of USS *Merrimack* be altered into the desired armor-plated warship.

Mallory agreed and immediately ordered Porter to produce plans based on the previously accepted design and supervise the conversion. Williamson was to refurbish the steam machinery, and Brooke was to arrange the armor and ordnance. Accordingly, *Merrimack,* which had been burned at Gosport Navy Yard in Norfolk, Virginia, the previous April by retreating Union sailors, was raised and placed into dry dock, and on July 11, Mallory ordered the conversion to proceed with all possible dispatch. These orders not only produced one of the most celebrated warships in naval history but launched an acrimonious debate among the officers involved, particularly Brooke and Porter, over who should receive credit for *Virginia*'s design. Although this controversy has been carried over into modern times by devotees of each, the evidence indicates that Brooke, Porter, and Williamson each made significant contributions to the vessel's plan.

In a race to finish the conversion of *Merrimack* before the completion of the Union turreted ironclad *Monitor,* known by the Confederates to be under construction at New York, the huge ironclad was floated in dry dock February 17, 1862, and commissioned *Virginia.* Under the command of Commo. Franklin Buchanan, with Lt. Catesby Jones as ordnance and executive officer, *Virginia* sortied March 8, 1862, from the navy yard into Hampton Roads to assault the Union fleet. Fearing its rifled cannon, Buchanan first attacked the sloop-of-war *Cumberland.* After exchanging broadsides, *Virginia* rammed and sank the Union warship but lost its cast-iron prow in the process. Turning to *Congress, Virginia* pounded the helpless frigate into submission with gunfire and then set it afire with hot shot. During the course of this

action Buchanan was wounded by musket fire from shore, and command of *Virginia* passed to Jones. Darkness brought an end to the first day's fighting with the steam frigate *Minnesota* aground in shallow water just out of reach of the Confederates' guns.

Intending to renew combat with *Minnesota* and other Federal warships the following morning, Jones

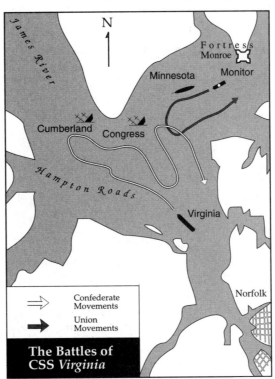

The Battles of CSS *Virginia*

Confederate Movements
Union Movements

was confronted instead by *Monitor,* which had arrived dramatically the night before by the glow of the burning *Congress.* The ensuing four-hour combat between the two armor-plated antagonists was furious but inconclusive. Finally, a well-placed shot by *Virginia*'s stern rifle hit *Monitor*'s pilot house, temporarily blinding its captain and causing the ironclad to veer off. Low on ammunition and faced with a falling tide, *Virginia* returned to the navy yard. Although neither vessel inflicted serious damage on the other, the remainder of the Federal fleet in Hampton Roads was saved and the blockade was preserved.

Placed under the command of Capt. Josiah Tattnall, *Virginia* was repaired and continued to operate as a threat to Union forces in the area. The Confederate evacuation of Norfolk resulted in the destruction of *Virginia* by its crew on May 11, 1862, when its excessive draft prevented removal up the James River. In 1867 and again from 1874 through 1876, portions of the shattered *Virginia* were recovered and scrapped. A drive shaft and an anchor with chain, currently at the Museum of the Confederacy in Richmond, and a few other relics scattered in museums around the country are all that remain of the once-mighty ironclad.

Buchanan turned Virginia *toward the frigate* Congress, *whose captain ran the ship aground to avoid being rammed.*

PAGE 78

Jackson was personally responsible for the expulsion of a half-dozen cadets from VMI. At least two of them challenged him to duels; one threatened to kill him on sight.

PAGE 294

Virginia's actions in Hampton Roads had worldwide implications. The destruction of *Cumberland* and *Congress* symbolically ended the centuries-long reign of the wooden, sail-powered warship, and its battle with *Monitor* presaged the modern era, adding impetus to a technological revolution in naval warfare already underway.

— A. ROBERT HOLCOMBE, JR.

VIRGINIA MILITARY INSTITUTE

After the War of 1812, the Commonwealth of Virginia had a quantity of arms and munitions that needed to be protected and maintained. As a result, the legislature authorized in 1816 the creation of three arsenals, one of which was to be located west of the Blue Ridge Mountains. The site chosen, originally a tract of slightly less than eight acres, was located in Lexington, Virginia, a beautifully situated village in the upper end of Virginia's famed Shenandoah Valley. The arsenal property was to be garrisoned by twenty militiamen and a captain. Because of disturbances and several incidents created by the soldiers at the arsenal, the Virginia state government created the Virginia Military Institute to replace the soldiers with young men whose education was to be combined with military training and guard duty at the arsenal.

Patterned after the Ecole Polytechnique of France and the U.S. Military Academy at West Point, VMI was organized several months before it officially opened on November 11, 1839, when the first cadet sentinel, John B. Strange, mounted the guard at the old arsenal. Largely the brainchild of John Thomas Lewis Preston, a Lexington lawyer and graduate of neighboring Washington College (later Washington and Lee), VMI was brought into being by an organizing board but governed by a board of visitors with a superintendent to oversee the daily operations. The first president of the board was Col. Claudius Crozet, a graduate of the Ecole Polytechnique, former artillery officer under Napoleon and professor of engineering at West Point, and state engineer of Virginia. Professor (later Maj. Gen.) Francis Henney Smith, distinguished graduate of West Point, was named the first superintendent.

Smith found the arsenal to be thoroughly inadequate for the new institute. He worked for nearly a decade formulating plans for a new barracks, parade ground, mess hall, and residences. New York architect Alexander Jackson Davis was employed to carry out Smith's plans. Davis, who was to become one of the foremost American architects of the nineteenth century, designed the first of the institute's buildings in the Gothic revival style, a style which influenced every other building on the VMI Post. The first of the new buildings was opened in September 1851. The other buildings of the pre-Civil War period were completed during the 1850s.

Unlike West Point, which had as its educational goal the training of cadets to be professional officers in the American military, VMI focused first on leadership in civil life, but also trained its cadets for service as citizen-soldiers in time of war or national emergency. VMI, from the beginning, has maintained that the best way to achieve its educational goal is within a military framework and a system of individual discipline and guidance based on an honor system.

At the outbreak of the Civil War nearly 300 of the 348-man Corps of Cadets were sent to Richmond to help drill and instruct the thousands of recruits who were daily pouring into the Confederate capital. Estimates vary, but it has been suggested that the recruits drilled by the cadets ranged in number from 25,000 to 50,000. At the beginning of the war there had been 1,217 matriculates at the institute, and another 813 enrolled during the war, bringing the total to 2,030. Of these, 1,902 were living at the commencement of hostilities, and 1,796 (94 percent) went into Confederate service. Of this total, 259 (14.5 percent) died, either killed outright or by wounds or disease. Small wonder, then, that VMI has been referred to as the "West Point of the South" or that Superintendent Francis H. Smith was prompted to say in 1877 that the Institute "left more of its alumni on the battle-field among the slain in the civil war of 1861–65 than West Point in all the wars of the United States since 1802, when the United States Military Academy was established."

The institute gave to the Confederacy 3 major generals, 17 brigadier generals, 92 colonels, 64 lieutenant colonels, 107 majors, 306 captains, and 221 lieutenants. Nor were the casualties or volunteers confined to the ranks filled by cadets or former cadets. The VMI faculty contributed its share. Among these were Lt. Gen. Thomas J. ("Stonewall") Jackson, Maj. Gen. Robert Rodes, Col. Stapleton Crutchfield, Brig. Gen. John McCausland, Lt. Scott Shipp, and more than a dozen others.

Probably the most dramatic moment in VMI history came in May of 1864 when the Corps of Cadets was called out to help repel the invasion of the Shenandoah Valley by Federal Gen. Franz Sigel. The cadets, some 241 in number under the command of Scott Shipp, joined Confederate Gen. John C. Breckinridge's command near New Market, Virginia, in time to participate in the rout of the Union army. The charge of the cadets across a muddy field in the face of determined musketry and artillery fire brought undying fame to the institute; in the course of that brief action ten cadets

were killed or mortally wounded and another forty-five wounded. Today, six of the slain, known as New Market Cadets, lie buried on the VMI grounds beside Moses Ezekiel's statue "Virginia Mourning Her Dead." (Ezekiel himself was a New Market Cadet, class of 1866.)

VMI was shelled, needlessly sacked, and burned on June 12, 1864, by Federal Gen. David Hunter. The library was scattered across the grounds and put to the torch along with other property, and many items that belonged to cadets or townspeople, including a replica of Houdon's statue of Washington, were carted off as souvenirs. Had it not been for the tireless efforts of Gen. Francis H. Smith and other members of the faculty, the VMI might never have reopened its doors as it did on October 17, 1865. In 1916 the U.S. government awarded it $100,000 for damages sustained during the war, part of the claim VMI had pressed as a result of property loss during Hunter's raid.

Superintendent Smith continued to lead the institute during the postwar years until his resignation and death in 1890, whereupon Scott Shipp became VMI's second superintendent. Counted among its faculty or the Corps of Cadets during the latter part of the nineteenth century were Matthew Fontaine Maury, Gen. George C. Marshall, Gen. John A. Lejeune, Richard Evelyn Byrd, Jr., and Charles E. Kilbourne. Two national fraternities were founded by or at VMI—Alpha Tau Omega (1865) and Sigma Nu (1869). In the time-honored tradition, VMI continues to educate citizen-soldiers who serve their state and country.

— TERRENCE V. MURPHY

VOLCK, ADALBERT

Volck, Adalbert (1828–1912), artist. His only biographer claimed that "what Thomas Nast . . . was to do for the North, Volck . . . did for the South." In truth, this gifted artist was all but unknown to Confederate audiences because during the war his works could not be shipped through the lines into the South. After peace was restored, however, Volck had an enormous impact on the culture of the Lost Cause through the circulation of his brilliantly conceived and crafted etchings.

Born in Bavaria, Volck learned to draw at artists' colonies near Nuremberg. After the Revolutions of 1848 he fled to America, settling in Baltimore and there earning a degree in dental surgery in 1852. Six years later he joined the Allston Association, a devoutly pro-Southern art league.

When war broke out and Baltimore was occupied, Volck was inspired to produce a series of incisive etchings variously vilifying the North and lauding Southern virtues. His first collection, *Ye Exploits of Ye Distinguished Attorney and General B. F. B. (Bombastes Furioso Buncombe)* assailed Union Gen. Benjamin F. Butler. His *Comedians and Tragedians of the North* viciously lampooned such Union leaders as Henry Ward Beecher, whom Volck portrayed as a black man.

Volck's greatest work was his *Sketches from the Civil War in North America*, first published in 1863 under the thinly veiled pseudonym "V. Blada" (the first five letters of his given name spelled backward). Although it bore a London imprint, like his previous works it was published secretly in Baltimore and distributed to only two hundred fellow Confederate sympathizers there.

In several editions of the portfolio, Volck expanded his vitriolic pictorial assault on Northern policies and leaders, particularly Abraham Lincoln, and portrayed Union generals as Hun-like plunderers. By contrast, the artist celebrated Southern life by depicting bathetic but inspiring scenes, which fellow artists overlooked. His *Making Clothes for the Boys in the Army* and *Cave Life in Vicksburg,* for example, poignantly celebrated brave and selfless Southern women. *Slaves Concealing Their Master from a Searching Party* illumined the myth of the eternally loyal slave. And both *Offering of Church Bells to be Cast into Cannon* and *[Prayer] Scene in Stonewall Jackson's Camp* suggested a holy aspect to the Confederate struggle.

After the war, Volck's etchings at last were circulated in the South, where they became immensely popular and helped define the myth of the Lost Cause. Volck himself stayed active, producing several canvases of Robert E. Lee for adaptation into chromolithographs, but he never again approached the brilliance he displayed as an underground artist in wartime.

Although Volck never recanted his pro-Confederate sympathies, he did confess regret at directing "ridicule at that great and good Lincoln." Otherwise, he insisted that his works had shown Civil War events "as truthfully as my close connections with the South enabled me to get at them."

— HAROLD HOLZER

WALKER, LEROY P.

Walker, Leroy P. (1817–1884), secretary of war and brigadier general. Leroy Pope Walker was born in Huntsville, Alabama, the son of U.S. Senator John Williams Walker. He attended the universities of Alabama and Virginia in preparation for a career in law. After his admission to the bar in 1837, he practiced law in several Alabama towns before settling in Huntsville in 1850. In 1843 Walker was elected to the Alabama House of Representatives where, as a Democrat, he subsequently played an important role in the formulation of the extremely proslavery Alabama Platform protesting the Wilmot Proviso and threatening secession. His efforts in defense of Southern rights and slavery led to his election in 1847 as Speaker of the Alabama House of Representatives and his reelection in 1849. During the 1850s he became one of the leading attorneys in the state.

In 1860 Walker served as William Lowndes Yancey's chief lieutenant in the Alabama legislature in reaffirming the state's commitment to a strong Southern rights position. He chaired the state's Democratic delegation that bolted the national convention at Charleston, and during the campaign he canvassed northern Alabama for Southern Democratic candidate John C. Breckinridge. When Abraham Lincoln won the election, he called for the immediate secession of the state. During the winter of 1860–1861 Walker served as a state commissioner to secure Tennessee's support for secession.

After the Confederacy was formed, President Jefferson Davis, desiring to have every state represented in his cabinet, looked to Alabama for his secretary of war. Both Clement C. Clay and Yancey, the state's most prominent political leaders, declined the appointment and instead recommended Walker for the position. Although Davis did not know Walker personally, he selected him for the War Department. Despite the fact that the new secretary had no military or even administrative experience, the Southern press, which, like Davis, actually knew little about Walker, applauded the appointment. Astute observers, however, privately predicted that Walker would be only a man of straw for President Davis who would exercise his well-known love for military affairs and control the War Department. They were largely correct.

Walker's term as Confederate secretary of war, extending from February 21 to September 16, 1861, was a brief and troubled one. Beginning with the Fort Sumter crisis, it was clear that Walker would not have an important role in the formulation of policy. Although he participated in the cabinet meetings on Fort Sumter, he did little more than dispatch Davis's messages to Gen. P. G. T. Beauregard at Charleston. It was Walker who wired the fateful order of April 10 for Beauregard to demand the evacuation of Fort Sumter, "and if this is refused proceed, in such manner as you may determine, to reduce it." After the bombardment and surrender of the Federal garrison, Walker gained notoriety in the North when he predicted that "in a few months more the flag of the Confederate States would wave over the capitol at Washington." This rash statement outraged Northerners and helped rally Union support for the war.

Although Davis gave Walker little authority over the planning and conduct of military operations, he did delegate to his secretary the main responsibility for raising the armies and providing the means for them to fight. This task would have taxed the ingenuity and energy of the ablest administrator. Nevertheless, Walk-

Leroy P. Walker, writes Thomas Cooper DeLeon, was a "pure civilian, a shrewd lawyer, of great quickness of perception, high cultivation, and grasp of mind."

PAGE 658

WAR SECRETARY

Jefferson Davis appointed Leroy P. Walker as his first of six war secretaries, but gave Walker little voice in formulating policy.

LIBRARY OF CONGRESS

*Jefferson Davis
naturally took a
strong personal
interest in the War
Department and to
a degree regarded
it as his own
domain.*

PAGE 527

er and his subordinates in the War Department managed by September to raise a force of 200,000 men. Although one of the Confederate armies won a stunning victory at Manassas in July, Walker's inability to provide sufficient arms, ammunition, and equipment for Southern forces made him a convenient target for critics.

Walker also received more than his share of blame for the continued vulnerability of coastal defenses. When Fort Hatteras fell to a Federal assault in August, shocking Confederates everywhere, he was severely criticized. His lack of a military background increasingly hurt him among those who wanted a professional army officer in charge of the War Department. Jealous of his prerogative and realizing the necessity for a unified command, Walker became embroiled with state rights–obsessed governors like Joseph E. Brown of Georgia in a conflict over the recruitment and control of troops. His failure to grant commissions to friends of governors created further opposition from powerful politicians.

For a variety of reasons, Davis by the late summer of 1861 had lost confidence in Walker. The president, who had a fetish for administrative detail, became upset when Walker did not maintain a similarly high standard of administration. Walker's periodic absences from the War Office contributed to Davis's concern that the secretary was not doing his job. In early September a conflict over military policy occurred between the two men. The president became irritated when Walker directed Gen. Leonidas Polk to withdraw from Columbus, Kentucky. Although the occupation of Columbus violated Kentucky's neutrality, Davis countermanded the order and indicated his general displeasure with Walker. On September 10, Walker submitted his resignation and asked the president for a military command in Alabama. Davis appointed him a brigadier general and placed him in charge of three regiments of Alabama troops, none of which was properly armed or equipped. Failure was certain, and on January 27, 1862, Gen. Braxton Bragg, an old nemesis, removed Walker from command.

Returning to his law practice in Huntsville, Walker defended Unionists accused of treason against the Confederate government. Although he had reached the conclusion by 1863 that the Confederate cause was hopeless, he accepted an appointment as presiding judge of the Military Court of North Alabama, a position he held until the surrender.

During Reconstruction Walker was one of the Democratic leaders in the overthrow of Republican rule in Alabama, and in 1875 he served as president of the state convention that reversed important and, on the whole, progressive provisions of the so-called Rad-

ical Constitution of 1867. He died in Huntsville on August 23, 1884.

— WILLIAM C. HARRIS

WAR DEPARTMENT

The largest and most important department of the Confederate government, the War Department, was founded with the creation of the Confederacy. Established by an act of Congress on February 21, 1861, it was given charge of all matters pertaining to the army (and Indian tribes), subject to the general direction of the president. Its offices were located in an abandoned warehouse, known as Government House, which shared space with other departments in Montgomery, Alabama, then the capital. Here the military establishment of the South was born, as hundreds of officeseekers appeared and thousands of army commissions and officers' assignments were issued. After Virginia joined the Confederacy in late May, the capital was moved to Richmond, a city of forty thousand people.

The War Department was served by five secretaries and one ad interim appointee during the life of the Confederacy: Leroy Pope Walker (February 21 to September 16, 1861); Judah P. Benjamin (acting secretary starting September 17, official secretary from November 21, 1861, to March 17, 1862); George Wythe Randolph (March 18 to November 15, 1862); Gustavus Woodson Smith (ad interim secretary, November 17 to 20, 1862); James A. Seddon (November 21, 1862, to February 5, 1865); John C. Breckinridge (February 6 to May 3, 1865).

Organization of the War Department

The mission of the department was to raise and arm men for the defense of the South. On March 6, Congress authorized recruitment of 100,000 men, twelve-month volunteers, for a provisional army. State militia and volunteers were mustered into national service, despite a critical deficiency in weapons, uniforms, and equipment. In April, following the opening of hostilities at Fort Sumter, tens of thousands of enthusiastic volunteers thronged Southern towns and cities, only to find the government unable to equip them. Early efforts to purchase war matériel in the North (the Raphael Semmes mission) were terminated with the outbreak of war; similar missions to Europe (those of Maj. Caleb Huse and Capt. James D. Bulloch) were not productive until November 1861 when the blockade runner *Fingal* arrived, carrying ten thousand Enfield rifles from England. Seizure of Federal arms stored in the South, plus the limited resources of state authorities and privately held weapons, provided most of the means for the first battles.

Walker, the new secretary of war, undaunted, requested authorization from Congress in July of 560 regiments, and the following month was granted power to enlist up to 400,000 men, again for only twelve months' service. By September, the department had armies in the field totaling 200,000 men.

The War Department in Richmond was located in an old brick building at Ninth and Franklin streets, which once had housed the Mechanics Institute. All other government departments also occupied this building except the Treasury and State departments. To reach the secretary's office, a visitor had to climb a gas-lighted stairway and traverse a long, gloomy corridor. In the outer room one found clericals pouring over the details of administration (among these, the *Rebel War Clerk* diarist J. B. Jones). Off in one corner (by October 1862) was the assistant secretary, former U.S. Supreme Court justice John A. Campbell, conferring with war leaders. At other desks, paymasters explained arrears in pay to some field officer, while soldiers plied officials for furloughs, and couriers, often mud-splattered, occasionally rushed in and were immediately brought before the secretary. Other callers waited, talking, chewing, speculating (as a foreign visitor noted in mid-1862). The appointments blackboard seldom seemed empty, owing to the department's genial, personal way of doing business. When finally shown into the secretary's presence, a visitor would find a room that breathed austerity. The walls bore no paint or decoration; the floor was without covering. Here, six hours daily, and often late into the night, the secretary waded through the routine of appointments, correspondence, consultation, planning, forwarding telegrams, signing commissions, and advising on the myriad details of running a war.

By the time of the first secretary's resignation in the fall of 1861, the department had become a going concern. Although the leaders of the Confederacy had originally contemplated a small military organization, by the fall of 1862 a comprehensive system of bureaus staffed by military officers had come into being. In addition to an assistant secretary there was an adjutant and inspector general, the Confederacy's ranking officer Samuel Cooper. A professional soldier and intimate of Jefferson Davis, Cooper was responsible for departmental orders, army records, and the inspection of army personnel. But his purview of power broadened as he became the essential tie between commanders in the field and the civilian administration. His name routinely appeared on all general orders emanating from the department to the armies throughout the South and often on many specific orders to key generals at the front.

Within the War Department were nine bureaus, including Cooper's office. These were staffed by some of the ablest and one or two of the most mediocre officers in the South. Col. Abraham C. Myers was quartermaster general and Col. Lucius B. Northrop, commissary general of subsistence. These two were responsible for furnishing the armies with food, clothing, and all other supplies except munitions. In time, perhaps more from the nature of their task than their personal conduct, they were subjected to increasingly harsh criticism. Myers, victimized by a personal quarrel with the president, was replaced by Gen. Alexander R. Lawton in August 1863. Northrop, because he was a personal friend of Davis's, remained in office until almost the end of the war. To most he seemed hopelessly incompetent and, in the estimation of most historians, the least qualified man for the critical position he held.

Munitions was the responsibility of the Confederacy's ordnance genius, Col. Josiah Gorgas, who at first headed both the Engineer and the Ordnance bureaus. Later, Capt. Alfred L. Rives and Col. Jeremy P. Gilmer alternately served as chief engineer. Gorgas was the outstanding bureau chief of the department. Thanks to his singular drive and pertinacity, by 1862 the armies of the agricultural South were never without arms or powder.

Related to the Ordnance Bureau was the Niter and Mining Bureau, headed by Isaac M. St. John. Its chief was one of the minor figures in the Confederate hierarchy whose invaluable services made possible its well-equipped armies. In February 1865 his talents were recognized when he was promoted to brigadier and commissary general, to succeed the hapless Northrop.

The Medical Department was first headed by Surgeon General David Camden De Leon, previously a surgeon in the U.S. Army. He served briefly from May 6 to July 12, 1861, then resigned to serve in the field for the remainder of the conflict. On July 30 Samuel Preston Moore, a surgeon before the war, was appointed in De Leon's place. Described as a "venerable, dandyish old fellow," Moore was competent and resolute, with the harrying task of providing medical supplies and overseeing maintenance of military hospitals. His whole medical corps had 3,237 medical officers (23 of whom served with the navy), or less than 4 doctors for every thousand men. There were 6 medical officers on duty in the surgeon general's office.

Two other bureaus completed the original organization of the department, that of Indian Affairs and the Bureau of War, which was the coordinating office of the department. After Seddon's appointment, two additional bureaus were created—the Signal Corps and the Conscription Bureau. The latter was headed successively by two generals, Gabriel J. Raines (until May

The Ordnance Bureau of the Confederate army functioned as a subsection of the Artillery Corps.

PAGE 406

Brig. Gen. Josiah Gorgas knew many of the arsenals in the South well, and he worked quickly to revamp and modernize several.

PAGE 406

Walker and his subordinates in the War Department managed by Sept. 1861 to raise a force of 200,000 men.

PAGE 656

Walker's inability to provide sufficient arms, ammunition, and equipment made him a convenient target for critics.

PAGE 656

1863) and John S. Preston. The secretary worked diligently with them, and with the many conscript officers stationed throughout the South, on the problems of manpower procurement. The Signal Corps, headed by Maj. William Norris, was given authority to supervise the operations of the Confederacy's military communications and the Southern Telegraph Company, a privately owned system. In 1864 this resourceful officer worked intimately with the secretary in the shadowy realm of espionage and secret service activities behind Northern lines.

The War Department bureaus were organized in such a way that each was independent in its own sphere, and the secretary gave the respective heads a wide latitude of authority. Requisitions for special services or for ordnance or quartermaster supplies passed directly from the field commanders to the bureau concerned, and only when the system broke down or specific criticisms were raised did the secretary of war intervene. With the exceptions of criticisms of Northrop and conscription and impressment officers in the field, few complaints were lodged against War Department officials by Confederate commanders or the press. The most important bureaus were, of course, those directly concerned with the maintenance of the armies—the Commissary, Quartermaster, Ordnance, and Conscription bureaus. Each was subjected to excessive demands and responsibilities, which only Gorgas was able to fulfill completely in his own sphere.

Subordinate to the secretary in the daily routine was the collection of clerks and messengers who constituted the Bureau of War. It was headed by a young Virginia captain, Robert Garlick Hill Kean. Although a strong Randolph partisan who disliked Davis, Kean came to view Seddon and Assistant Secretary Campbell with admiration and respect. He worked closely with the latter in coordinating the administrative functions of the department and was directly concerned with keeping the overall operations of his office functioning smoothly. As supervisor of a large clerical staff, Kean was responsible for directing the vast flow of correspondence in the bureaucratic empire. He observed much policy-making at first hand and was a good judge of his superiors and colleagues. He was in a key position to sympathize with the plight of the grossly overworked department and its chiefs, much of which he recorded in his valuable diary (which is often more reliable and perceptive than the more quoted diary of J. B. Jones).

The Department in Action

The first secretary of war, Leroy P. Walker, an Alabama aristocrat, planter, and politician, was selected by Davis to represent his state in the seven-member cabinet. He was "a pure civilian," as Thomas Cooper

DeLeon characterized him, "a shrewd lawyer, of great quickness of perception, high cultivation, and grasp of mind." In his initial months, he worked successfully with military and civilian leaders (despite state rights problems with several governors), although he was slow to perceive the dimensions and length of the war. His relations with Davis were harmonious. When Walker left office to seek service in the field, the military establishment of the Confederacy was a fait accompli, even if on delicate foundations. Its armies had won victories east and west, and some part of the credit for these achievements must rest with this civilian leader.

The second secretary of war, Judah P. Benjamin, held office for a brief stormy period. A brilliant lawyer and solid friend of Davis and his wife, he possessed a keen intellect and qualities of statesmanship that earned him the soubriquet "the brains of the Confederacy." But he was often lacking in patience with stiff military protocol and at times was insensitive of the egos and ambitions of army men. Too often he sided, uncritically, with Davis. His efforts to obtain from the Congress long-term enlistment laws for the armies failed, though his measures to encourage manufacturing in the South were fruitful. Much of his usefulness was overshadowed by public clashes with several generals. Blame for military reverses (Forts Henry and Donelson, Roanoke Island) he took upon his own shoulders, thus shielding Davis from his critics and, more important, concealing the internal military weakness of the Confederacy. Benjamin was a dedicated public servant but a failure as war secretary.

His successor, George Wythe Randolph, was popular with military leaders, and they expected much of him. But his term was too brief for him to accomplish much. His greatest service was the achievement of the first military draft in America, in April 1862, when the Conscription Act was adopted to meet the Confederacy's manpower needs. Randolph also had a try at grand strategy. By mid-1862 he saw that the weak point in the South's defenses was in the West, and he proposed a strong autonomous Department of the West, with a commander who could coordinate the disparate forces within the region. Differences with Davis over implementation of the plan worsened relations between the two, and Randolph resigned in November after eight months in office.

His successor, James A. Seddon, was a vigorous man, a clear thinker, and a tough-minded, dedicated worker. He was also a Southern zealot respected by similar men and much of the press of the South, yet above all a man possessed of tact and diplomacy, and a close friend of the hypersensitive president.

The new secretary's initial months in office saw his efforts to invigorate the Confederate cause by an active prosecution of the war in Virginia, increased support for the Atlantic coastal defenses, and new strategic considerations for the western theater (with the appointment of Joseph E. Johnston to its supreme command). He persuaded Davis to travel to the West, conciliate the commanders there, and rally the people and soldiers against the invaders. He urged the use of internal lines for supply and troop reinforcement, favoring the shifting of men from one theater to another as needs or opportunity suggested. He kept a close eye on unfolding developments, down to the double crisis of Gettysburg and Vicksburg in midsummer 1863. While his concern centered on the two major fronts, the daily activities of the department were focused upon food needs of the armies, the shortage of horses for the cavalry, the deteriorating railroads, the need for regulation of the overall transport system, and better use of blockade runners for supplies from abroad (a small fleet of ships was soon hired by the department, at Seddon's insistence). Another problem was financial. Desperate measures were necessary to replace depreciated currency, and the department began to use cotton as a medium of exchange. The staple was shipped through the blockade almost daily, and a steady stream of war matériel, uniforms, and rations soon poured into the Confederacy. In 1864 authorization was granted to exchange cotton for meat and other foodstuffs with the Federals in the Trans-Mississippi theater. The starvation that had stalked areas of the South since the second year of the war—the armies were on half-rations—justified such measures.

Manpower needs were reaching a crisis by 1863. In the remaining months of that year, the department had to deal with declining manpower resources, large-scale desertions, and obstructions from the governors of Georgia and North Carolina in matters of conscription and impressment. Defeatism, by early 1864, was rampant in many parts of the South.

Deficiency in military strength was matched by the lack of workers in industry and government bureaus. The low salary scale did not attract employees unless they also received exemption from military duty. After passage of the Third Conscription Act, a system of detail from field duty was put into effect by which soldiers were assigned to service in offices or as industrial or railroad workers. This system succeeded in obtaining laborers at low costs, but military leaders complained that it stripped their commands of fighting men.

The War Department was directly involved in the development and operation of munitions and arms works, mining establishments, and clothing factories. Instead of turning to private industries for most of its needs, the government had created its own war enterprise. During Seddon's tenure, attempts were made to expand almost every segment of the military-industrial

organization. It was in the scope and magnitude of these government-owned industries that the civil administration of the South differed most from that of the North. Almost all industries in the Union remained in private hands.

Of 70,000 civil employees in the service of the Confederate government, 57,124 were employed by the War Department. The Engineer Bureau and Niter and Mining Bureau alone employed 17,000 persons, which included many blacks (both free and impressed slaves), women, and some children. At the close of 1863, Gorgas reported that the Ordnance Bureau was operating seventeen arsenals, armories, foundries, depots, and powder mills. In Richmond, the department controlled and supervised ordnance shops, munitions plants, foundries, medical laboratories, and uniform and shoe factories.

The department's staff continued to grow as the war progressed. There were, in 1864, twelve major officials (four of them civilians) and 265 clerks and messengers. But unlike the U.S. government, there was no chief of staff, only a military adviser to the president, Gen. Braxton Bragg, and instead of three assistant secretaries such as Edwin M. Stanton had at his service, Seddon had only one, the invaluable Campbell. Lacking these important posts, the War Department suffered much unnecessary inefficiency. The most unsuccessful bureau, Conscription, was dissolved in February 1865 and its duties delegated to the generals of reserve forces in the individual states. The overall governmental machinery at Richmond was frequently inadequate, yet somehow many of the needs of the fighting South were provided by this overworked and pathetically small bureaucracy.

Foreign imports continued to provide the mainstay needs of the department from 1864 until the end of the war. A special agent, Colin J. McRae, sent by Seddon to England to supervise purchasing operations there, was working near-miracles. A thoroughgoing businessman, he is to be credited with the astute use of funds (especially from the Erlanger cotton loan). In March, Col. Thomas L. Bayne of the Ordnance Bureau was made head of the newly created Bureau of Foreign Supplies and was granted control of the importation of all war matériel that was to be paid for with exported cotton. All vessels operated by the department were now transferred to his control. Working both sides of the Atlantic, McRae and Bayne supervised the blockade traffic for the remainder of the war. The reports of the secretary and of various bureau heads, as well as letters and dispatches from Fraser, Trenholm, and Company of Liverpool and foreign service correspondence in the Library of Congress, testify to large returns from the department's system. Millions of pounds of meat, coffee, lead, and saltpeter, more

WAR DEPARTMENT

The Department in Action

An unselfish man without political ambition, Seddon did not seek power; rather, he was simply devoted to the Southern cause.

PAGE 527

*The year 1863
started out as the
high-water mark in
the life of the
Confederacy, but
with the loss of
Vicksburg and
the Mississippi
River and the
simultaneous
repulse at
Gettysburg, the
Confederates were
thereafter on
the defensive.*

PAGE 528

than 500,000 pairs of shoes, 316,000 blankets, 2,600 packages of medicines, 69,000 rifles, 43 cannons, and large amounts of other articles came into the Confederacy between October 26, 1864, and January 2, 1865. Vast quantities of cotton shipped out of Southern ports, together with funds on deposit or being created in Europe, completed this bold enterprise.

The last great issue before the department and its leaders and the Southern people in late 1864 was the question of arming the slaves. As the number of troops was drastically reduced by deaths and desertions (Seddon had admitted earlier that one-third of Confederate armies were AWOL in November 1863), it was clear to many that the last great untapped manpower resource of the South must be used. Some military and civil leaders had advocated such a radical policy at different turns in the war, and in November 1864 a conference of Southern governors went on record favoring it.

The War Department had long used blacks (free and slave) in menial roles, especially as workmen on coastal defenses; in earthworks about Charleston, Atlanta, and Richmond; and in various parts of the western theater. Blacks had also been in service in all Confederate armies since the beginning of the war as teamsters, cooks, and body servants to officers. Seddon, strongly influenced by his friend Robert M. T. Hunter, held back. Gorgas, Campbell, and others in the war office, however, were in support. Finally when Robert E. Lee, Benjamin, and Davis came out publicly in favor, Congress acted early in February 1865. The department's mission was to implement the policy. Orders quickly were passed down the line, as recruiting officers began to receive volunteers. Two companies of Confederate blacks soon appeared in Richmond—too late to effect the outcome of the struggle.

Early in 1865, as a sense of gloom overshadowed much of the Confederacy, Congress recommended that Davis restructure his cabinet in the hope of restoring public confidence in the cause. Seddon took personal umbrage at this motion and abruptly resigned. The president failed to persuade him to withdraw his resignation, and a popular successor was sought. In John C. Breckinridge, former U.S. vice president and Confederate general, the fifth secretary of war was found. He presided over the department for less than four months—largely, it seems, to terminate its life preparatory to ending the war. He immediately took stock of its health (results mostly negative) and urged the president to seek peace. In this he was strongly supported by Campbell. Both men felt that the only course was an honorable surrender.

Breckinridge organized the government's evacuation of the capital on April 2 and accompanied the president and cabinet on its flight to Danville, Virginia. Here efforts were made *not* to surrender but to restructure the administration. Two weeks later, the "government on wheels" was in further flight south—to Charlotte, North Carolina, and finally Washington, Georgia, where the last official cabinet meeting was held. Here the final disintegration occurred. The War Department ceased to exist as the secretary and other cabinet heads fled. Cooper, who had taken charge of its physical remains, namely its archives, surrendered these valued records to the Federal authorities.

The history of the Confederate War Department is yet to be written. It is contained in the tens of thousands of documents in the "Rebel War Archives" of the National Archives and in related papers in the Library of Congress. Mastery of these materials may reveal the unromantic, yet herculean labors of this body of bureaucrats who helped form the backbone and substance of the Confederate army. When these records are searched, and the odds against which its employees struggled are weighed, the resulting annals will show that the Confederate War Department worked marvels with meager means.

[*See also* Army; Espionage, *article on* Confederate Secret Service; Impressment; Medical Department; New Plan; Ordnance Bureau; Quartermaster Bureau; Signal Corps; *and selected biographies of figures mentioned herein.*]

— JOHN O'BRIEN

WASHINGTON PEACE CONFERENCE

In response to a call of the Virginia General Assembly, the Washington Peace Conference met February 4–27, 1861, in the Willard Hotel's Dancing Hall in Washington, D.C. The purpose of the meeting was to seek constitutional guarantees that might hold the border slave states in the Union and ease tensions between the states that had seceded and those dominated by the Republican party whose candidate was soon to occupy the presidential office. Virginia had suggested that the proposals introduced in the Senate by John J. Crittenden of Kentucky in December 1860, though they had been rejected in committee, could be the basis for a resolution of the controversy between slave and free states.

Former president John Tyler, one of Virginia's five commissioners to the conference, had wanted to invite only the border states. Knowing that the Deep South states would not attend, he feared that Northerners would control the meeting. But the General Assembly opted to invite all the states. Eventually 133 commissioners from twenty-one of the existing thirty-four states attended, though only 60 men from eleven states had arrived by the opening day.

In spite of Virginia's plea to all concerned to avoid acts that might lead to war, representatives of six Deep South states met in Montgomery, Alabama, to organize a Southern government on the same day the Peace Conference convened. Those states, as well as one other that had seceded, sent no delegates, nor did Arkansas, Minnesota, Michigan, Wisconsin, California, or Oregon.

Dubbed the "Old Gentlemen's Convention" of "political fossils" by Horace Greeley's *New York Tribune*, the assemblage nevertheless included the "best and the brightest" their states could offer. The delegates selected John Tyler as president of the conference and decided that each state would have one vote and that the proceedings would be kept secret.

Moderates had high hopes of resolving the issue, but the opposing sides made success seem unlikely. Most Republicans had no intention of budging from the Chicago platform that called for a ban on any further extension of slavery in the territories. Southern radicals, for their part, sought extreme measures that had no chance of acceptance. The legislatures of Ohio and Indiana had instructed their commissioners to seek adjournment of the conference at least until after the inauguration of the new president. Ohio had also instructed its delegates that no concessions to the South were necessary. Indiana's governor appointed as delegates only those persons who had convinced him by their answers to a written questionnaire that they likewise would make no concessions.

The Resolutions Committee submitted its report on February 15 after several postponements because of the late arrival of many delegations. Confused debate then ensued over the committee's report and several minority reports. Some delegates defended slavery; others attacked it. All impugned each other's motives. On February 22 the conference agreed to limit debate to ten minutes for each person and got down to business.

The Resolutions Committee had reported seven provisions as a proposed amendment to the Constitution. The first would extend the Crittenden Compromise line of 36° 30` to the Pacific, with involuntary servitude permitted below the line and prohibited above it during territorial status. States subsequently would be admitted on either side of the line as their constitutions directed. The chief argument concerned Virginia's demand that slavery in any territories acquired in the future should be protected, but the conference adopted a substitute resolution that limited the protection of slavery to present territory.

Other sections of the final report provided that major acquisitions of new territory would have to be approved by a majority of all senators from both the free and the slave states and that Congress would have no control over slavery in the District of Columbia without the owners' and Maryland's (but not Virginia's) consent. The slave trade would continue to be prohibited in the District of Columbia and the interstate slave trade protected, at least to a degree. Congress was to prohibit the importation of slaves and of Chinese laborers forever. Congress would compensate an owner when authorities were prevented from recovering a fugitive slave, but the person would lose ownership of the slave by accepting compensation. Key provisions of the proposals and of the existing U.S. Constitution could never be amended or abolished in the future without the agreement of all the states.

Virginia delegates had sought to prohibit blacks from voting and to gain the right to acquire territory for colonization of blacks. They had also hoped to secure condemnation of personal liberty laws, the strengthening of the Fugitive Slave Law, and a declaration of the constitutionality of secession.

The final package, which was not voted on as a whole, satisfied almost no one. William C. Rives had declared that "Virginia steps in to arrest the country on its road to ruin"—but Virginia voted against the key section (which carried by only one vote) and three others. Two states opposed all seven propositions adopted by the conference, one state opposed six, and four states opposed five. New York deadlocked on every vote and Kansas on all but one, though four Northern states and four border states were on the winning side every time. Had Michigan, Wisconsin, and Minnesota participated, the Peace Conference would have no doubt been totally paralyzed.

Tyler submitted the report as a proposed thirteenth amendment to the Constitution, but with a lukewarm endorsement, and departed for Virginia, where he soon urged his state's secession. It was February 27, less than a week before Lincoln's inauguration and the scheduled adjournment of Congress. Many Southern congressmen had returned to their states, and the remaining representatives were probably less interested in compromise than they had been two months before. The Senate voted against the proposals, 28–7. The House refused to suspend its rules to receive them. The Peace Conference had failed. Once South Carolina had seceded, it was probably too late to arrest the march to war, for Southern secessionists and Northern Republicans had fixed on a collision course.

— LYON G. TYLER

WASHINGTON PEACE CONFERENCE

Approximately 100,000 weapons were stored at the Harpers Ferry arsenal in 1859— weapons Brown intended to seize and distribute throughout the South in an attempt to end slavery.

PAGE 264

"Virginia steps in," said an optimistic citizen of the state [William C. Rives], "to arrest the progress of the country on its road to ruin."

FRANCIS BUTLER SIMKINS
A HISTORY OF THE SOUTH
1958

WATERWAYS

The Southern states were surrounded by navigable waterways, indeed by protected waterways where small craft could carry the commerce and the forces of the Confederacy. On the northeast was the Chesapeake Bay and the Potomac River; then on the north the great Ohio, and on the west the mighty Mississippi with its tributaries, the Arkansas and the Red River, connecting it with Arkansas and Texas. All along the Atlantic coast, from Virginia to Florida, with some interruptions, a protected waterway, hospitable to shallow-draft steamboats and smaller vessels, ran between the mainland and strings of offshore islands; it continued for most of the way along the Gulf coast, around Florida to Pensacola and on to New Orleans, and then for much of the way along the Texas coast.

The South for the most part resisted the canal-building craze that spread across the North.

PAGE 619

There were no great rivers flowing in an east-west direction that could have connected the Confederacy at its heart. But in all the states major rivers drained a rich hinterland to the sea and provided a means of getting crops to seacoast markets and of getting manufactured goods into the interior:

- the James River from Lynchburg and Richmond to Hampton Roads and Norfolk;

- the Roanoke from central Virginia to the Carolina coast;

- the Cape Fear from Fayetteville to Wilmington, North Carolina;

- the Pee Dee River and the Santee from central South Carolina to Charleston;

- the Savannah from Augusta to Savannah;

- the Chattahoochee and the Flint from Atlanta to the Gulf of Mexico;

- the Alabama from Montgomery to Mobile;

- in Mississippi the Pearl River from Jackson to the approaches to New Orleans;

- in the north, the New River connecting the Great Appalachian Valley from western Virginia to the Ohio;

- the Tennessee connecting the Great Valley, around Knoxville, with Chattanooga and northern Alabama thence across western Tennessee and Kentucky to the Ohio;

- and the Cumberland connecting northern Tennessee with the Ohio.

And the beltway of coastal waterways and major rivers connected them all. It was like a great geopolitical wheel, with the spokes, radiating from the interior, joined by the rim of coastal waterways and peripheral rivers.

Control of this water beltway surely was a key to the solvency of the Southern states and even to the Confederacy's success in the war. But from the outset Federal forces began slowly but inexorably to constrict it. Seizure of Harpers Ferry by Federal forces assured Northern control of the upper Potomac, and George B. McClellan's first action, a relatively minor campaign in western Virginia in July 1861, assured Northern control of the upper Ohio. Before the year was out U.S. forces captured Hatteras Inlet, North Carolina; Port Royal Sound, commanding the waterway between Charleston and Savannah; Tybee Island on the Georgia coast; and Biloxi, Mississippi, on the Gulf of Mexico.

In February 1862, Ulysses S. Grant, with the support of a flotilla of river gunboats under David Farragut, captured Fort Henry on the Tennessee and Fort Donelson on the Cumberland River, and other U.S. forces captured Roanoke Island, North Carolina. Succeeding weeks saw the occupation of Jacksonville, Florida; the neutralization of the ironclad *Virginia* by the *Monitor* in Hampton Roads; the fall of New Orleans on April 25; the loss of Norfolk, Virginia, and Pensacola, Florida, and, on June 6, the loss of Memphis on the Mississippi. The great belt waterway, the rim of the wheel, was being broken all along its course. Surely the fall of Vicksburg on the Mississippi in July 1863 was as much a turning point of the war as was the Battle of Gettysburg going on at the same time in Pennsylvania.

The waterways could have been of utmost advantage to the South in carrying commerce and supporting military forces if all or most of its segments could have been controlled. Commerce-raiding cruisers, such as *Alabama, Shenandoah,* and *Georgia,* were a nuisance and a menace to Northern shipping, but they could have no influence on the outcome of the war. On the other hand, if the Confederate States somehow could have gained and maintained command of the rivers, particularly the Ohio and Mississippi, and the adjacent seas of the Atlantic and the Gulf of Mexico, their success at arms scarcely could have been denied. Great flotillas of gunboats would have been more valuable than great armies without adequate means of support, and a high-seas fleet plus shallow-draft gunboats capable of breaking the Northern blockade would have been more valuable than scores of commerce raiders. It may not be without symbolic significance that the Federals named their armies (with some exceptions) for the rivers—the Army of the Potomac, the Army of the James, the Army of the Ohio, the Army of the Cumberland, the Army of the Tennessee—whereas the Confederates (with a few exceptions) named theirs for states or regions—the Army of Northern Virginia, the Army of Tennessee.

During the first half of the nineteenth century watercraft of many kinds had appeared on the interior rivers. A common one for downstream trips was the flatboat, about twenty feet long and ten feet wide, with a hull rising three feet or so above the water, a little house or shelter in the middle, and a sweep or long oar at the stern to guide it. Rivermen would transport cargoes of grain, salted meat, or other products, then sell the boat as well as the cargo and walk or find wagons or stages back for another boat. Families sometimes would move with all their belongings downstream on a flatboat and then use the boat for lumber at their destination. Pirogues were large, flat-bottom boats with oars and poles to enable them to move upstream. Scows were large flatboats, sometimes referred to as arks. Broadhorns were like scows, but with sweeps both on bow and stern for steering downstream. Similar to the scows were the batteaux, especially significant on the James River. The skiff was a small flat-bottom boat used for local traffic and sometimes carried in tow by larger boats for side trips to the shore. Keel boats were built with heavy timber keels down the center; these had the advantage of being able to absorb the shock of collisions with obstacles in the rivers. Barges were bigger boats, thirty to seventy feet long, equipped with a passenger cabin and oars and sails to move upstream as well as down on the big rivers. Packet boats were larger barges.

A canal-building boom in the Northern states between 1820 and 1850 did not extend into the South. The major exceptions were in Virginia. The Chesapeake and Ohio Canal, a cooperative effort of Virginia, Maryland, and the Federal government, after many years of effort was completed in 1850 between Alexandria, Virginia, and Cumberland, Maryland. When war came this was beyond the reach of the Confederacy, however. More important for its purposes was the James River canal that was completed from the fall line at Richmond 146 miles to Lynchburg in 1840 and to Buchanan in 1856. Plans to extend it to Covington were interrupted by the war. A canal of twenty-three miles connected Deep Creek and Joyce's Creek and the Dismal Swamp area.

Except for one major obstacle the Tennessee River was navigable for large boats for the full 650 miles from Knoxville to Paducah, Kentucky. The obstacle was a series of rapids known as Muscle Shoals in northern Alabama. Attempts to bypass the shoals by a canal ended in failure. Connection of the upper and lower Tennessee valley had to depend on the Tuscumbia and Decatur Railroad, completed in 1834. There were some short connecting canals in Georgia and the Carolinas, but they were in large part abandoned before the war.

In 1845 there were 332 steamboat arrivals and departures at Nashville and 580 in 1860. Steamboat arrivals at New Orleans numbered 3,024 in 1847 and 3,566 in 1860. The 1,600 steamboats that plied the

RIVER STEAMBOATS

The decade preceding the Civil War saw the apogee of the steamboat on the rivers. That also was the decade of great expansion of the railroads that would lead to the steamboat's decline. The first steamboat on the western rivers was *New Orleans,* built at Pittsburgh in 1811. It descended to New Orleans, but never made it back from that city. Others, appearing in subsequent years, were bigger and more powerful; *Eclipse,* built in 1852, reached a length of 363 feet, a width of 76 feet, and carried a crew of 121 men (the smallest steamers might have a crew of only 4 or 5). Most of the early steamboats were driven by sidewheels, but later sternwheelers came to be favored. Many carried passengers above and freight below, although sometimes bales of cotton were piled so high on the deck that it was necessary to light candles or lamps in the cabins. Most of the boat building for the Mississippi valley was on the upper Ohio; the one boat-building center within the South was at Nashville on the Cumberland.

— JAMES A. HUSTON

Mississippi before the war represented an investment of perhaps $60 million.

Coastal shipping still depended to a considerable extent on wooden sailing vessels, although paddlewheel steamers were coming into use. River-type boats could be used on the inner coastal waterways.

During the war rivers were not subject to sabotage and destruction to the extent that railroads were. The Federal forces, however, gained control of key points or entire segments of the peripheral waterways, and without the rim, the spokes were of little use—and beyond that, in many places, the spokes too were broken. The waterways could have been critical for Confederate success; the foresight and resources were not there to take advantage of them.

— JAMES A. HUSTON

WATIE, STAND

Watie, Stand (1806–1871), brigadier general and principal chief of the Confederate Cherokees. Born at Oothcaloga in the Cherokee Nation, Georgia, on December 12, 1806, Stand Watie's Cherokee name was De-ga-ta-ga, or "he stands." He also was known as

Improvements of the waterways went little beyond clearing snags from the rivers.

PAGE 620

Isaac S. Watie. He attended Moravian Mission School at Springplace, Georgia, and served as a clerk of the Cherokee Supreme Court and Speaker of the Cherokee National Council prior to removal.

CHEROKEE REBEL

Stand Watie, brigadier general and principal chief of the Confederate Cherokees, raised a regiment of his tribesmen, the Cherokee Regiment of Mounted Rifles.

LIBRARY OF CONGRESS

As a member of the Ridge-Watie-Boudinot faction of the Cherokee Nation, Watie supported removal to the Cherokee Nation, West, and signed the Treaty of New Echota in 1835, in defiance of Principal Chief John Ross and the majority of the Cherokees. Watie moved to the Cherokee Nation, West (present-day Oklahoma), in 1837 and settled at Honey Creek. Following the murders of his uncle Major Ridge, cousin John Ridge, and brother Elias Boudinot (Buck Watie) in 1839, and his brother Thomas Watie in 1845, Stand Watie assumed the leadership of the Ridge-Watie-Boudinot faction and was involved in a long-running blood feud with the followers of John Ross. He also was a leader of the Knights of the Golden Circle, which bitterly opposed abolitionism.

At the outbreak of the Civil War, Watie quickly joined the Southern cause. He was commissioned a colonel on July 12, 1861, and raised a regiment of Cherokees for service with the Confederate army. Later, when Chief John Ross signed an alliance with the South, Watie's men were organized as the Cherokee Regiment of Mounted Rifles. After Ross fled Indian Territory, Watie was elected principal chief of the Confederate Cherokees in August 1862.

A portion of Watie's command saw action at Oak Hills (August 10, 1861) in a battle that assured the South's hold on Indian Territory and made Watie a Confederate military hero. Afterward, Watie helped drive the pro-Northern Indians out of Indian Territory, and following the Battle of Chustenahlah (December 26, 1861) he commanded the pursuit of the fleeing Federals, led by Opothleyahola, and drove them into exile in Kansas. Although Watie's men were exempt from service outside Indian Territory, he led his troops into Arkansas in the spring of 1861 to stem a Federal invasion of the region. Joining with Maj. Gen. Earl Van Dorn's command, Watie took part in the Battle of Elkhorn Tavern (March 5–6, 1861). On the first day of fighting, the Southern Cherokees, which were on the left flank of the Confederate line, captured a battery of Union artillery before being forced to abandon it. Following the Federal victory, Watie's command screened the Southern withdrawal.

Watie, or troops in his command, participated in eighteen battles and major skirmishes with Federal troops during the Civil War, including Cowskin Prairie (April 1862), Old Fort Wayne (October 1862), Webbers Falls (April 1863), Fort Gibson (May 1863), Cabin Creek (July 1863), and Gunter's Prairie (August 1864). In addition, his men were engaged in a multitude of smaller skirmishes and meeting engagements in Indian Territory and neighboring states. Because of his wide-ranging raids behind Union lines, Watie tied down thousands of Federal troops that were badly needed in the East.

Watie's two greatest victories were the capture of the federal steamboat *J. R. Williams* on June 15, 1864, and the seizure of $1.5 million worth of supplies in a Federal wagon supply train at the Second Battle of Cabin Creek on September 19, 1864. Watie was promoted to brigadier general on May 6, 1864, and given command of the First Indian Brigade. He was the only Indian to achieve the rank of general in the Civil War. Watie surrendered on June 23, 1865, the last Confederate general to lay down his arms.

After the war, Watie served as a member of the Southern Cherokee delegation during the negotiation of the Cherokee Reconstruction Treaty of 1866. He then abandoned public life and returned to his old home along Honey Creek. He died on September 9, 1871.

— KENNY A. FRANKS

WEST VIRGINIA

For Virginians who lived in what became West Virginia the Civil War was a painful experience. Many of them had strong ties to Virginia, but most of the 357,678 white residents, who were chiefly of English, Scotch-Irish, and German extraction, had an even deeper attachment to the Union. In 1860 the 16,401 slaves made up slightly more than 4 percent of the population, and the 2,742 free blacks constituted less than 1 percent. For political, economic, and psychological reasons, both the Union and the Confederacy strove to control this borderland, where communities and even families were divided and brother often fought against brother.

On the eve of the Civil War a spirit of moderation prevailed in western Virginia. In 1860 Virginia gave its electoral vote to John Bell, the Constitutional Unionist, and Southern Democrat John C. Breckinridge was second in popular votes. But in the western part of the state Breckinridge led with 21,961 votes, followed by Bell with 21,175. Stephen A. Douglas, the Northern Democrat, trailed with 5,112, and Abraham Lincoln won about 1,200. With the support of the party organization, press, and leaders, Breckinridge carried the normally Democratic counties of Virginia, including present-day West Virginia, where party loyalty apparently remained intact. Moreover, many voters evidently believed that neither Douglas nor Bell could win the election and that Breckinridge offered the best assurance of defeating Lincoln and preserving the Union.

During the crisis that followed the secession of South Carolina and other states, most western Virginians opposed any hasty action by their state. A large gathering at Parkersburg declared that national well-being and prosperity depended upon preservation of the Union and that the election of Lincoln was no reason to abandon "the best Government ever yet devised by the wisdom and patriotism of men." A Union meeting at Lick Creek, in Greenbrier County, considered it "unwise, impolitic, and unpatriotic not to give Mr. Lincoln a fair trial before we either secede from the Union or condemn his administration."

Following the firing upon Fort Sumter and Lincoln's call for troops, forces of moderation lost ground. On April 17, 1861, the Virginia convention adopted an ordinance of secession by a vote of eighty-eight to fifty-five. Of the forty-seven delegates from present-day West Virginia, thirty-two voted against secession, eleven voted for it, and four did not vote. (Two of those opposing secession and two who did not vote later signed the ordinance.) A popular referendum on the matter was set for May 13.

Western delegates opposed to secession hastened home to organize resistance movements. A mass meeting at Clarksburg, assembled on April 22 by John S. Carlile, initiated steps that led to the First Wheeling Convention on May 13 through 15. The Wheeling gathering, also essentially a mass meeting, had 436 irregularly chosen or self-appointed participants from twenty-seven counties. All but one county became part of West Virginia, and all but four were located west of the Alleghenies and north of the Kanawha River. Carlile favored an immediate proclamation of separate statehood. Waitman T. Willey, John J. Jackson, and others urged another convention, to meet in June after the results of the referendum were known. In the referendum, popular support for secession in eastern Virginia was strong, but almost 65 percent of the voters in present-day West Virginia opposed it.

The Second Wheeling Convention, which met in regular session on June 11, 1861, had 105 delegates from thirty-eight counties, two of which never became part of West Virginia. Fifteen trans-Allegheny counties, later included in the state, sent no delegates. The convention declared all state offices vacant and set up a Reorganized Government of Virginia at Wheeling, on the basis of loyalty to the Union. It chose Francis H. Peirpoint governor, arranged for a complement of state officials, and filled the U.S. Senate and congressional seats vacated by Virginia Confederates. The Senate seats of Robert M. T. Hunter and James M. Mason went to Willey and Carlile.

Meanwhile, twenty-one men represented West Virginia counties or delegate districts in the Richmond legislature, and eight represented senatorial districts embracing forty-six West Virginia counties. Allen T. Caperton of Monroe County became a member of the Confederate Senate. Alexander R. Boteler of Shepherdstown, Albert Gallatin Jenkins of Cabell County, Robert Johnston of Clarksburg, Samuel Augustine Miller of Charleston, and Charles Wells Russell of Wheeling served in the Confederate House of Representatives.

The number of West Virginians who fought for the Confederacy and the Union has not been ascertained. Older histories give figures ranging from 28,000 to 36,000 Union troops and 9,000 to 12,000 Confederate troops. But a recent challenge to these statistics substantially reduces the number of Union troops and increases that of Confederates.

MILITARY ACTIONS IN THE REGION. At the outset of the war the military picture in western Virginia was confused, with Union and Confederate volunteers drilling in many of the same towns. The U.S. secretary of war added the part of the region north of the Kanawha to the Department of Ohio, under Gen. George B. McClellan. Col. George A. Porterfield, the Confederate commander in the Monongahela valley, occupied Grafton, a key junction on the Baltimore and Ohio Railroad, and ordered bridges destroyed between that point and Wheeling. At McClellan's direction, Col. Benjamin F. Kelley occupied Fairmont, forced Porterfield to withdraw from Grafton to Philippi, and on June 3, 1861, routed the Confederates from Philippi in what has sometimes been called the first land battle of the Civil War. McClellan then forced Brig. Gen. Robert S. Garnett, who replaced Porterfield, from defensive positions at Rich Mountain Pass near Beverly and Laurel Hill near Belington, which were within striking distance of the Baltimore and Ohio, and into battle at Corricks Ford, where Garnett lost his life. The Confederates were

WEST VIRGINIA

Military Actions in the Region

The Commonwealth of Virginia seceded on April 17, 1861, but in the trans-Allegheny region, the majority of the mostly non-slaveholding, small-farm Virginians were extremely pro-Union.

PAGE 668

HARPERS FERRY   *Erected on the heights overlooking the town of Harpers Ferry, the Confederate battery commanded the railroad bridge and the canal.*   THE SOLDIER IN OUR CIVIL WAR

left with no important positions in the Monongahela valley.

The Confederate hold upon the Kanawha valley, where Gen. Henry A. Wise had 2,700 men, seemed more secure. In July 1861, however, Gen. Jacob D. Cox, with Federal troops from Ohio, advanced up the Kanawha and engaged the Confederates in an indecisive battle at Scary Creek, about fifteen miles west of Charleston. Believing that Cox was receiving reinforcements, Wise abandoned Tyler Mountain and Charleston and withdrew by way of the James River and Kanawha Turnpike to White Sulphur Springs. Cox pursued the Confederates and occupied Gauley Bridge at the junction of the New and Gauley rivers.

Confederate authorities directed Gen. John B. Floyd to reoccupy the Kanawha valley, a plan that threatened Cox at Gauley Bridge and Gen. William S. Rosecrans, who had succeeded McClellan in the Monongahela Valley. Failure of Floyd and Wise to cooperate, however, wrecked the plan, and Federal forces defeated the Confederates in the Battle of Carnifex Ferry. With northwestern Virginia under Federal control, the Reorganized Government at Wheeling could continue its work unmolested and the West Virginia statehood movement could proceed.

Keenly aware of the importance of his crumbling mountain front, Gen. Robert E. Lee undertook "a tour of inspection and consultation." He found the Confederates "too wet and too hungry" to dislodge Union forces from Cheat Mountain and their camp at Elkwater, but on December 13 they beat back an attack on their own position at Allegheny Mountain. Meanwhile, angered by the feud between Floyd and Wise, President Jefferson Davis ordered Wise to turn over his command to Floyd, who was instructed to move via the Coal River to the Kanawha and cut Cox's communications with Ohio. Gen. W. W. Loring was directed to push Rosecrans back toward Clarksburg. Wise's men proved too demoralized to provide assistance, and the initiative passed to Rosecrans.

In the eastern panhandle much of the military activity centered around the Baltimore and Ohio Railroad, with Romney as its focal point. In 1861 Thomas J. ("Stonewall") Jackson, West Virginia's most distinguished Confederate officer, harassed Federal troops and destroyed tracks between Harpers Ferry and Martinsburg, appropriating the rails to Southern use. Jackson also urged a vigorous defense of Harpers Ferry, with its armory and arsenal, but Gen. Joseph E. Johnston regarded it as indefensible.

Jackson then proposed to sweep across the Alleghenies, complete the destruction of the Baltimore and Ohio, and recover northwestern Virginia. He forced Kelley out of Romney, which he placed under Loring before going into winter quarters at Winchester. Chaf-

ing under his assignment, Loring engaged in machinations that induced Secretary of War Judah P. Benjamin to direct Jackson to give up Romney and move Loring to Winchester. The distraught Jackson sent a letter of resignation to Governor John Letcher but was persuaded, with great reluctance, to withdraw it.

In order to stop Jackson's devastations in the valley of Virginia and the Potomac valley, Lincoln in 1862 placed John C. Frémont in charge of the newly created Mountain Department, with headquarters at Wheeling. Frémont's plans failed, and Jackson dealt him such a defeat that he resigned his command. Meanwhile, Confederate Gen. Henry Heth, in expectation of an attack upon the Virginia and Tennessee Railroad, dispatched troops to Flat Top Mountain and to Muddy Creek, near Lewisburg, on the James River and Kanawha Turnpike. After indecisive action around Princeton, the Confederates fell back toward Lewisburg, which Gen. George Crook attacked on May 12. Fearing that he himself might be cut off, Crook withdrew to Meadow Bluff, and Cox declined to attack the Virginia and Tennessee line. By then, it was said, "the long shadow of Stonewall Jackson reached even to the banks of the New and Greenbrier rivers."

The Confederates achieved other successes in 1862. Preparatory to an invasion of the Kanawha valley, Brig. Gen. Albert Gallatin Jenkins made a sweeping raid with about six hundred cavalry through the southeastern and central parts of West Virginia. Loring then moved from Fayetteville into the Kanawha valley, forcing Gen. Joseph A. J. Lightburn to give up Gauley Bridge and Charleston and to withdraw toward the Ohio River. Loring, however, disobeyed orders to use the Kanawha valley as a base and attack the Cheat Bridge with part of his troops. In doing so, he threw away Confederate gains, allowing the Federals under Cox to regain control of the Kanawha valley.

The most spectacular Confederate actions in West Virginia in 1863 were daring raids. The Jones-Imboden raid, which covered much of north-central West Virginia, resulted in the destruction of twenty-one railroad bridges and a tunnel, turnpike bridges, oil and oil field equipment, and military installations and supplies; the taking of about five thousand cattle and two thousand horses; and recruitment of about four hundred men for Confederate service. Federal forces under Gen. William W. Averill, however, defeated the Confederates under Gen. John Echols at Droop Mountain and extended the area under Federal control to roughly the eastern boundaries of West Virginia.

Confederate raids also punctuated the fighting in 1864. Gen. John McCausland, a West Virginian, dashed into Pennsylvania and burned the town of Chambersburg. Federal counterstrikes included a raid

*For Washington,
the western part
of Virginia was of
vital strategic
importance because
of the long stretch
of the Ohio River
on its border and
the Baltimore and
Ohio Railroad.*

PAGE 669

on Dublin and the Battle of Cloyds Mountain in Virginia. In February 1865 Capt. John McNeill of Hardy County and his son Jesse struck into Maryland and captured Union generals Crook and Kelley in their hotel rooms in Cumberland.

THE CREATION OF WEST VIRGINIA. Federal military dominance of the trans-Allegheny region allowed the creation of West Virginia, toward which the first steps had been taken at the adjourned session of the Second Wheeling Convention in August 1861, to proceed without serious interruption. A constitutional convention, which met from November 26, 1861, until February 18, 1862, drew up a framework of government and defined boundaries approximating those of the present state. Slavery hung like a shadow over the convention. Gordon Battelle, a Methodist minister and educator, introduced resolutions forbidding the entry of additional slaves into the proposed state and providing for gradual emancipation of those already there. Failing in that, he introduced other resolutions, one of which, calling for a popular referendum on gradual emancipation, failed by a single vote. A compromise provided that no free person of color should be brought into the state for permanent residence.

To comply with a requirement of the U.S. Constitution that a new state must have the approval of the state from which it is carved, the makers of West Virginia turned to the Reorganized Government of Virginia at Wheeling, already known to be friendly to the idea. Since a popular referendum on the question had already resulted in 18,862 votes in favor of statehood and only 514 votes against it, the Virginia General Assembly readily gave its approval on May 13, 1863, and Governor Peirpoint signed the measure.

The West Virginia statehood bill encountered unexpected opposition in the U.S. Senate when Carlile, an original champion of statehood and a member of the Senate Committee on Territories to which the statehood question was referred, drafted a bill calling for the addition of fifteen counties, a new constitutional convention of sixty-three counties (many of them known to be opposed to statehood), and the gradual abolition of slavery. With statehood teetering on the brink of failure, Senator Willey, with help from Senator Benjamin F. Wade of Ohio, saved the bill with an amendment whereby slaves under twenty-one years of age on July 4, 1863, would become free upon attaining that age. Carlile made yet another vain effort to kill the statehood bill by requiring popular ratification of gradual emancipation by a majority of the registered voters in the proposed state; in the end he refused to vote in favor of the new state. President Lincoln, after much consideration, signed the statehood bill, and on June 20, 1863, West Virginia entered the Union as the thirty-fifth

state. The Reorganized Government of Virginia, which was still recognized by Lincoln and the U.S. Congress as the government of Virginia, thereupon moved to Alexandria. At the close of the war, when the Confederate government of the state fell, it moved to Richmond. Wartime animosities gradually receded, and questions regarding the constitutionality of the methods by which West Virginia achieved statehood became academic. For its people, the new state, won at such a frightful cost in human and material resources, stood as the central achievement of the war and as an assurance that they would share in the new economic and social order presaged by the victorious Union.

[*For further discussion of battles and campaigns fought in West Virginia, see* Early, Jubal, *sidebar* Early's Washington Raid; Gettysburg Campaign; Sharpsburg Campaign; Shenandoah Valley, *articles on the campaigns of Jackson and Sheridan;* West Virginia Operations. *See also* Harpers Ferry, West Virginia; Loring-Jackson Incident; *and selected biographies of figures mentioned herein.*]

— OTIS K. RICE

WEST VIRGINIA OPERATIONS

[*This entry is composed of two articles,* Operations of 1861 *and* Operations of 1862 and 1863.]

OPERATIONS OF 1861

When the Civil War began on April 12, 1861, after the Confederate bombardment of Fort Sumter in Charleston, South Carolina, many Southerners loyal to the U.S. government were unwilling to side with the secessionist cause. This was particularly true in border states, as well as areas such as eastern Tennessee and western Virginia.

The Commonwealth of Virginia seceded from the Union on April 17, 1861, but the citizens of the state were radically divided on the issue. In the trans-Allegheny region, the majority of the mostly non-slaveholding, small-farm Virginians were extremely pro-Union, their culture and economy long tied more to that of Ohio and Pennsylvania to their north, while the generally politically powerful landed slaveholding class in the Tidewater and Piedmont sections of the state was, by and large, vehemently pro-Confederacy. Western Virginians felt they were very much underrepresented in the legislature and severely overtaxed, receiving little public assistance from the state; to add insult to injury, they felt looked upon as inferior mountain dirt farmers by the well-heeled eastern planter elite. With the state split in two and the population of one section adamantly opposed to the politics of the other, it is not surprising that the outcome was the formal parting of western Virginia from the eastern region of the state.

Upon learning of Virginia's ordinance of secession, the citizenry of the trans-Alleghenies began holding mass pro-Union meetings stating their refusal to secede from the Federal government and, in some cases, raising armed militia for the Union. And with Virginia's separation from the Federal government, the people of the western counties of the state reacted violently and bitterly against any of their fellow citizens—and there were a sizable number of them—who advocated Confederate secession. (This rancor and viciousness would last throughout the war and, in some cases, for generations to come.)

For Washington, the western part of Virginia was of vital strategic importance because of the long stretch of the Ohio River on its border and the Baltimore and Ohio Railroad. The latter tied East Coast cities to western destinations such as Louisville, Indianapolis, and St. Louis, enabling Federal troops and supplies to be shuffled quickly to where they were most needed. The Alleghenies protected Ohio and Pennsylvania, as well as western approaches to the Shenandoah Valley. The mountains also covered eastern Tennessee. One other advantage in holding this area for the Union lay in the fact that many men who might enter the Confederate army would now be available to fight for the North.

Twenty thousand Northern troops from the Department of the Ohio under the command of Gen. George B. McClellan soon came to the aid of the western Virginians, routing a small party of Confederate bridge burners at Philippi on June 3, one of the first actual field combats of the Civil War. Meanwhile, Southern troops from eastern Virginia and Georgia were moving into the mountains. These men were under the command of Gen. Robert S. Garnett, and Garnett had entrenched his troops on Laurel Hill and

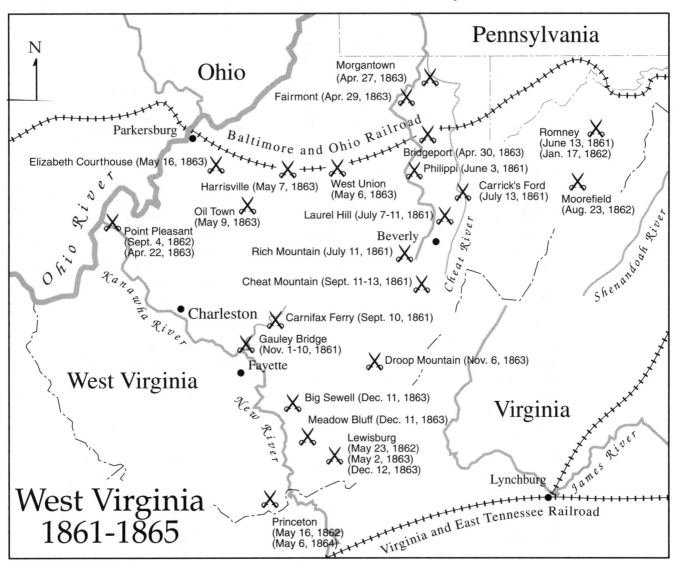

*"This army stays
here until the last
wounded man is
removed. Before I
will leave them
to the enemy, I
will lose many
more men."*

STONEWALL JACKSON
WINCHESTER, 1862

nearby Rich Mountain in June. On July 6, 1861, McClellan advanced his soldiers, who began skirmishing with Garnett's Confederates on July 7. Then on July 11, after four days of parrying, McClellan's Ohio troops assaulted and defeated the Confederate forces on Laurel Hill.

Meanwhile, on the same day, a Federal brigade commanded by Gen. William Rosecrans attacked up the steep slopes of Rich Mountain in a rainstorm, swiftly overpowering the weak 1,300-man force and four field-pieces—under the command of Lt. Col. John Pegram—left there by Garnett to defend that mountain. These victories secured for the Union an important crossroads of the Parkersburg-Staunton Turnpike at Beverly in the Tygart River valley, fifty miles west of the Shenandoah Valley. Holding this road and these two mountains assured the Union victors of the ability to control access to northwestern Virginia. At his disposal for these two relatively minor actions, McClellan had about 15,000 soldiers—not all of whom actually fought—while Garnett could field only some 4,500 men.

After the small battles at Laurel Hill and Rich Mountain, Garnett retreated across Cheat Mountain into the Cheat River valley, while Indiana and Ohio troops in Gen. Thomas A. Morris's brigade pursued over difficult roads and in a driving rain. On July 13, at midday, Morris's men overtook Garnett's Confederates at Carrick's Ford and opened fire, chasing them back to another ford a couple of miles distant. There, fighting resumed until the Confederates were defeated and routed. During this action, while directing his skirmishers, Garnett was killed by Federal gunfire. Total casualties were very light on both sides, however.

With such decisive—but greatly exaggerated—victories in quick succession, George McClellan became a national hero in the North and was called to Washington to assume greater responsibilities. Two weeks later, Gen. Robert E. Lee would come to the Alleghenies in a futile bid to control these western counties.

Politically, meanwhile, the people of the area had been taking every step to become independent from eastern Virginia. On June 11, 1861, delegates from thirty-four northwestern counties—representing four-fifths of the population in the mountainous area—convened in Wheeling and demanded to remain in the Union. The intention of the convention was not to secede from the state of Virginia, but rather to proclaim itself the legitimate government of the commonwealth and to declare the secession of the state illegal.

The plans espoused by this convention were hardly practical, however, and two months later ordinances were adopted by the delegates that effectively made West Virginia—initially called Kanawha—a separate state, with Francis H. Peirpoint its governor. In November, a convention was held to draft a new state

constitution, and it was ratified by citizens loyal to the Union on April 2, 1862. On May 13, the West Virginia legislature petitioned the U.S. government for admission to the Union, and after much political wrangling, and an agreement by Wheeling for the eventual abolition of what little slavery existed there, West Virginia became a state on June 20, 1863.

— WARREN WILKINSON

OPERATIONS OF 1862 AND 1863

Military activity in West Virginia in 1862 and 1863 centered in the upper Potomac valley and along the Allegheny front, which extended from Flat Top Mountain northward to Cheat Mountain. The upper Potomac front was one of great fluidity. Confederate objectives there included control of its section of the Baltimore and Ohio Railroad and of the lower part of the Shenandoah Valley, which was commonly regarded as the gateway into Virginia and the Confederacy. Towns along the railroad changed hands frequently. Romney, for instance, passed back and forth fifty-six times during the war.

In order to achieve its goals, the Confederacy created its Shenandoah District and placed Thomas J. ("Stonewall") Jackson in command of the 8,500 troops in the region. Jackson immediately undertook to drive Union forces out of his district and to destroy the Baltimore and Ohio Railroad between Harpers Ferry and Martinsburg. Later he organized his winter march against Romney, which he considered one of the most important towns on the railroad. He also believed that if the Confederacy were to move against northwestern Virginia, it must do so in the winter of 1861–1862.

Although he was confident that Federal officers in Romney would not expect an attack in midwinter, Jackson did not march directly from his Winchester headquarters to Romney. Instead, he made use of a feint by marching north to Berkeley Springs and from there into Maryland. Jackson encountered some resistance, but on January 17, 1862, he captured Romney with only minimal difficulty.

Jackson's success in the Shenandoah Valley, especially his deftness in striking and then eluding forces under Nathaniel Banks, influenced Abraham Lincoln's decision to create the overarching Mountain Department in March 1862. He ordered Gen. John C. Frémont, the commander, who had 35,000 troops at Wheeling, to destroy the Virginia and Tennessee Railroad, but before Frémont could do so, Lincoln sent him to assist in efforts to trap Jackson in the Shenandoah Valley.

Union strength in the Kanawha valley was also reduced when Brig. Gen. Jacob D. Cox, with headquarters at Gauley Bridge, was ordered to the defense of Washington, D.C. The defense of the Kanawha valley then fell to Brig. Gen. Joseph A. J. Lightburn, who was at Gauley Bridge with six regiments of infantry, one of cavalry, and some local organizations left him by Cox. Aware of Union vulnerability in the Kanawha valley, Confederates believed that the time was propitious for an offensive against northwestern Virginia. They hoped to destroy western sections of the Baltimore and Ohio Railroad, harass the Unionist government of Restored Virginia, obstruct the West Virginia statehood movement, and recruit for the Confederate army.

Fearing that any escape down the Kanawha might be cut off, Lightburn moved his headquarters to Charleston and later to Ohio. W. W. Loring followed him down the Kanawha, but he prepared for any confrontation by sending Gen. Albert Gallatin Jenkins on a wide-ranging raid into territory north and south of the Kanawha River. Their movements dealt Union forces their most severe setback in West Virginia up to that time.

By 1863 the Confederates, as well as the Federals, had reassessed their military objectives and strategies. Confederates thereafter placed less emphasis on moving armies across mountains than in well-executed raids and strikes, as well as moves against Unionist Restored Virginia. The most spectacular and effective military move in 1863 was the William E. Jones–John D. Imboden raids, which covered a vast area of north-central West Virginia. They destroyed large segments of the Baltimore and Ohio Railroad, netted the Confederacy large numbers of cattle and horses, resulted in recruitment of men for the Confederate service, wrecked oil production on the Little Kanawha, and spread panic across the state. Such successes helped to mitigate disasters on other fronts.

By the end of 1863 Confederate military and political objectives in West Virginia were no longer attainable. West Virginia had become a state, and Union armies occupied most of the territory within its boundaries. Confederate forces were decimated by deserters, large numbers of whom joined guerrilla bands or became bushwhackers. Although many of these irregulars continued to profess Confederate sympathies, they were no longer a reliable fighting force and constituted no threat to Union supremacy. Prospects for Confederate success had, in fact, vanished forever.

— OTIS K. RICE

WHEELER, JOSEPH

Wheeler, Joseph (1836–1906), major general and U.S. congressman. Born September 10, 1836, in Augusta, Georgia, Wheeler spent much of his childhood in Connecticut. In 1859, he graduated from West Point and received the rank of second lieutenant in the regiment of mounted rifles stationed at Fort Craig, New Mexico Territory. On April 22, 1861, Wheeler resigned his commission to join the Confederate army as a first lieutenant of artillery.

By 1862, West Point officers were in great demand in the South, and Wheeler received a quick promotion to colonel, leading the Nineteenth Alabama Infantry into combat at Shiloh. Afterward, he transferred to the cavalry. Gen. Braxton Bragg, now in command of the Army of Mississippi, named Wheeler his cavalry chief. In this capacity he led the mounted arm of the Confederate armies of Mississippi and later Tennessee throughout the rest of the war.

During Bragg's invasion of Kentucky, Wheeler was notable for his daring leadership of the Southern horsemen, earning promotion to brigadier general on October 30, 1862. He received the rank of major general on January 30, 1863, and later was recommended for, but not confirmed as lieutenant general. Wheeler ably commanded Bragg's cavalry in the Murfreesboro, Tullahoma, and Chattanooga campaigns. By May 1864, he was the ranking Confederate cavalry leader.

During the Atlanta campaign, Wheeler gained additional notoriety by raiding Union Gen. William Tecumseh Sherman's supply and communications lines. After the fall of Atlanta, Wheeler's troopers were the only organized opposition to Sherman's march through Georgia, and the Confederate cavalrymen fared badly. By the end of the year, the corps had earned a reputation for lack of discipline. Wheeler continued to lead the cavalry in the Carolina campaigns until superseded by Lt. Gen. Wade Hampton.

During the course of the war, Wheeler fought in 127 battles; he was wounded three times, had sixteen horses shot out from under him, and had thirty-six staff officers fall by his side. His active style of fighting led to his sobriquet "Fighting Joe." Though he was somewhat disappointing as an independent commander, his true genius was displayed when his cavalry covered the movements of the main army. In 1863, he published *Cavalry Tactics,* a manual for use by the mounted arm.

Wheeler was captured by Federal troops in May 1865 and imprisoned temporarily at Fort Delaware. After his release, he moved first to New Orleans and then in 1868 to Wheeler Station, Alabama, where he started a law practice and a plantation. In 1881, he entered politics, serving eight terms in the U.S. House of Representatives. During the Spanish-American War, Wheeler joined the U.S. Army, serving with the rank of major general of volunteers. He led a division of troops at the Battles of El Caney and Kettle Hill, Cuba, and later served in the Philip-

The Shenandoah Valley of Virginia stretches 165 miles from Lexington to Harpers Ferry and averages 30 miles in width.

PAGE 540

pines. He retired from the service on September 10, 1900, with the rank of brigadier general of regulars. Wheeler died on January 25, 1906, in Brooklyn, New York.

— DONALD S. FRAZIER

WHIG PARTY

Disturbed by Andrew Jackson's increasing executive power and his opposition to governmental economic activism, opponents organized a coalition of National Republicans, conservative Democrats, and Anti-Masons. Jackson's opponents eventually adopted the name "Whig" as a symbol of resistance to tyranny, since they believed Old Hickory far too powerful an executive who consulted too frequently with personal friends rather than with cabinet members confirmed by

Congress. Originally derived from Whiggamore, a Scot who marched on Edinburgh in 1648 to oppose the court party, and applied by extension to those who opposed the royal prerogative in Britain, the name Whig had been adopted by American revolutionaries during the war for independence before its use in the 1830s.

Until the controversy over the expansion of slavery into the territories tore the Whig party apart in the 1850s, the Democratic and Whig parties remained quite evenly balanced in the South. The Whigs dominated in North Carolina, Kentucky, and Tennessee, holding at the same time competitive strength in Virginia and Georgia. The competition offered by the Whigs promoted voter participation and broadened the scope of politics.

Strong party leadership developed in the Southern states. Notable among the Whig luminaries were Alexander H. Stephens and John M. Barrien of Geor-

WHEELER'S RAIDS

As commander of the cavalry corps of the Army of Tennessee, Joseph Wheeler, Jr., enjoyed only limited success as a raider. His first expedition, reminiscent of J. E. B. Stuart's famous ride around McClellan, came during the Battle of Murfreesboro, December 31, 1862 to January 2, 1863. With 1,100 men, Wheeler rode around the opposing Army of the Cumberland, not once, but two and a half times, destroying a thousand wagons and capturing hundreds of horses, mules, and prisoners.

A week later, he captured five transports and a gunboat on the Cumberland River, northwest of Nashville. Some of his men also swam the icy river and burned an enormous supply depot at Ashland, Tennessee, on January 12, 1863, which, combined with the losses at Murfreesboro, virtually immobilized the Army of the Cumberland for the next six months.

The exploit earned Wheeler a promotion to major general and a vote of thanks from the Confederate Congress. It also roused the ire of older, more experienced subordinates, such as Nathan Bedford Forrest, John Hunt Morgan, and John Austin Wharton, who resented taking orders from "that boy."

After the Confederate victory at the Battle of Chickamauga left the Army of the Cumberland besieged in Chattanooga, Wheeler led 3,700 men across the Tennessee River forty miles east of the city on September 29, 1863. Sweeping over Walden's Ridge, he intercepted a heavily laden supply train in the Sequatchie Valley on October 2, destroying an estimated eight hundred to one thousand wagons, but Federal horsemen hounded him so closely he was unable to inflict any lasting damage on the vital railroad linking Chattanooga and Nashville. Blue-coated cavalry overtook him near Farmington, Tennessee, and drove him across the Tennessee River at Muscle Shoals, Alabama, on October 9 with the loss of 2,000 men.

During the Atlanta campaign, Confederate newspapers and politicians were sharply critical of Wheeler for failing to cut the Western and Atlantic Railroad, the sole source of supply for Union Maj. Gen. William Tecumseh Sherman's advancing armies. Wheeler was eager to try, but the Army of Tennessee was so badly outnumbered his cavalry was compelled to fight on foot alongside the infantry.

Not until the army reached Atlanta and withdrew inside the city's formidable

defenses was Wheeler given free rein. Between July 27 and 31, 1864, he pursued, caught, and defeated three raiding columns bent on wrecking the Macon and Western Railroad, putting Sherman's cavalry corps out of action for almost a month.

This enabled Wheeler to leave Covington, Georgia on August 10, 1864, with 4,000 men and the long-awaited orders to cut Sherman's supply line. He tore up a few sections of track between Atlanta and Chattanooga and captured a herd of beefs, but when high water kept him from crossing the rain-swollen Tennessee River near Chattanooga, he wandered into the strategically barren highlands of eastern Tennessee. Eventually he swung west, cutting the railroads south of Nashville before being chased across the Tennessee River at Florence, Alabama, on September 9. The damage was quickly repaired, and despite his glowing reports, Wheeler's last raid did little more than deprive the Army of Tennessee of half its cavalry during a critical stage of the Atlanta campaign.

—DAVID EVANS

gia, John Bell and Ephraim Foster of Tennessee, and Henry Clay and John J. Crittenden of Kentucky.

Countering Jackson's general opposition to Federal promotion of economic development, Clay proposed the American System. The Kentuckian offered a protective tariff, distribution of money from sale of Federal lands, construction of roads and canals, and the rechartering of the Second Bank of the United States. As conservatives, the Whigs expected to avoid economic leveling through growth and increased opportunity.

Clay's program did not prove uniformly attractive to Southerners. Proposals for public roads and canals attracted certain well-placed commercial interests. Some, however, opposed internal improvements because they feared the Federal government would fund such projects through revenue from the protective tariff, which bore most heavily on the South. The southeastern Whigs generally opposed the construction of a national road, but many in the Southwest supported it.

At the same time, Whig principles appealed to many evangelical Protestants. Profoundly influenced by the Second Great Awakening, the Southern Whigs proudly stood for religion, morality, paternalism, and duty. Accusations of adultery against Jackson and Secretary of War John Eaton drew denunciations of the two men from moralistic Whigs. Whigs promoted public education, prison and mental hospital reform, and social justice. Even Southern frontiersman Davy Crockett opposed the theft of Cherokee lands.

In practice, the Whigs remained viable competitors until the 1850s. They did well in congressional elections during the 1840s, controlling the House from 1841 through 1842 and from 1847 through 1850. They lost the presidential elections of 1832 and 1836, but succeeded in electing two Virginia-born war heroes—William Henry Harrison (then of Ohio) in 1840 and Zachary Taylor (who grew up in Kentucky but lived in Louisiana) in 1848.

After Whig presidential candidate Winfield Scott's decisive 1852 defeat, the demoralized party failed to mend the growing rift over slavery between its two great sectional wings. Northern Whigs generally opposed slavery and its expansion into the territories, whereas Southerners defended it as a positive good. As the division over slavery deepened, many Southern Whigs like Stephens swallowed their pride and moved into the Democratic party.

When Southern states began to secede, many old Whigs like Stephens opposed the breakup of the Union. As businessmen, professionals, and planters tied to a national market, they had little to gain from disruption or war. Nevertheless, loyal to their section, they went along when their states seceded.

As a ticket-balancing measure, Stephens was elected vice president of the Confederacy to complement Mississippi Democrat Jefferson Davis. The Confederacy repudiated some Whig principles by prohibiting protective tariffs and appropriations for internal improvements. The Confederate Constitution offered a sop by proposing congressional seats for cabinet members, but the Congress failed to approve implementing legislation. Although organized political parties failed to emerge in the Confederacy, ex-Whigs tended to show less enthusiasm for military and executive power than did ex-Democrats. Whigs enjoyed a resurgence in some Southern states during the war because of their defense of constitutionalism and compromise. In the Georgia legislature, for instance, Stephens's brother Linton secured the passage of resolutions calling for an armistice followed by plebiscites on joining the Union or Confederacy. The party did not reemerge after the Civil War, and though some former Southern Whigs joined the Republican party, most became Democrats.

— G. ALEXANDER
TRACY L. ALEXANDER

"If we could cross the Potomac with one hundred and fifty thousand men, I think we could demand Lincoln to declare his purpose."

JAMES LONGSTREET
LETTER TO SEN. LOUIS
WIGFALL, MAY 1863

WIGFALL, LOUIS T.

Wigfall, Louis T. (1816–1874), brigadier general and congressman from Texas. Louis Trezevant Wigfall was born April 21, 1816, to Levi Durand and Eliza (Thomson) Wigfall, in Edgefield, a frontier district of South Carolina. Both his parents' families had been among the first to arrive in South Carolina and were socially prominent. As a boy and a student at a private military academy, the University of Virginia, and South Carolina College, Wigfall came to believe in a society led by the planter class and based on black slavery and the chivalric code. Politically, he became an avid spokesman for state rights and secession, drawing on his classical education in oratory, history, literature, and Latin.

Wigfall's brief experiences in military school and in the Seminole War helped him get an appointment as a South Carolina militia colonel. He became known for pistol marksmanship, reckless courage, and a thin-skinned sense of honor. He also earned a reputation for drinking, gambling, and financial carelessness while neglecting the law practice his brother had left to him.

In the 1840 South Carolina gubernatorial campaign that pitted two aristocratic cliques against each other, Wigfall supported John P. Richardson out of dislike for the Brooks family, who supported James H.

*Johnston made
available to Davis's
critics, such as Sen.
Louis T. Wigfall,
information about
the Vicksburg
campaign that they
were able to use in
attacking the
president.*

PAGE 304

Hammond, Richardson's principal rival. Wigfall's contribution to the campaign was to take over covert editorship of the *Edgefield Advertiser,* turning the newspaper's support from Hammond to Richardson.

TEXAS RADICAL
*Brig. Gen. Louis T. Wigfall
helped discredit Stephen A.
Douglas and split the
Democratic party in 1860,
then contributed to
thwarting compromises
to save the Union.*

LIBRARY OF CONGRESS

In well-reasoned editorials, Wigfall helped win the state for Richardson.

When it became known that Wigfall had written the editorials, some of the Brooks family attacked him personally. Over the next five months, Wigfall was involved in a fistfight, three near-duels, two actual duels, and a shooting with the Brooks family—all of which left one man dead and two, including Wigfall, wounded. In the shooting incident, Wigfall fired upon and killed a young man who had shot at him first. In one of the duels, Wigfall and another Brooks family member missed on their first shots and were persuaded to accept an arbitrated settlement favorable to Wigfall. In the last duel, both men were wounded, Wigfall in the thigh and Preston Brooks in the hip. (This wound may have been the reason Brooks carried the cane he later used to beat Senator Charles Sumner of Massachusetts on the floor of the Senate.)

Although Wigfall remained a firm believer in the dueling, this was his last duel. His reputation for violence persisted, however, and he did nothing to discourage false stories about his dueling exploits. Rather, he capitalized on his purported willingness to shoot people who disagreed with him, intimidating political opponents who were fearful of triggering his temper.

Governor Richardson appointed Wigfall aide-decamp for his services in the 1840 election campaign, but his first foray into politics and newspaper editing had been costly. Although a grand jury failed to bring in an indictment for the killing of the young man and

murder charges were dropped, many people in the community still blamed Wigfall. His neglected law practice dwindled further, and despite his marriage to his respected second cousin, Charlotte Cross, Wigfall was nearly ruined socially, professionally, and financially. Their first son's serious illness became an additional drain on their finances.

But even as his son lay dying and his debts mounted, Wigfall became more interested than ever in politics. As a delegate to the state Democratic convention, he helped draw up resolutions for the 1844 campaign. At the convention, Wigfall spoke in favor of the annexation of Texas in order to maintain the right of slavery, and against protective tarriffs, seeing them as a threat to Southern civilization. John C. Calhoun argued only for nullification to oppose the tariffs, but Wigfall, sixteen years ahead of most South Carolinians, said the state should secede, alone if necessary.

Unable to rebuild his standing in South Carolina, Wigfall moved Charlotte and their three children to Texas in 1846, a year after it joined the Union. He opened a law office in Marshall, Texas, building a practice and a reputation as a lawyer. Nevertheless, his first concern was still politics, and he was never financially solvent for more than a few weeks at a time.

Wigfall headed a committee that formulated resolutions reiterating the state rights argument and condemning the Wilmot Proviso and the concept of "squatter sovereignty" to prevent expansion of slavery into territories. Speaking for the resolutions, Wigfall asserted that the Federal government was a creation of the states, not of the people, and that each state had the right to leave the Union if it acted "unconstitutionally." Although the resolutions passed, Wigfall expressed sorrow that Texas would not take the lead in seceding.

Named in 1850 to the Texas House of Representatives, Wigfall attacked Sam Houston, then a U.S. senator and strongly pro-Union, as a recreant to Texas and the South and denounced him for voting for the Compromise of 1850. Wigfall played a major role in organizing Texas Democrats to oppose Houston and the Know-Nothings in 1855 and 1856. He led a successful fight in the Texas legislature to pass a resolution censuring Houston for his opposition to the Kansas-Nebraska Act and was widely credited with Houston's defeat for the governorship in 1857, which put an end to Houston's influence in the U.S. Senate. Now recognized in Texas as the leader of the radical state rights Democrats, Wigfall was elected to the Texas Senate in 1857 and had a strong voice in the 1858 state Democratic convention, which adopted a state rights platform.

With the breakup of the Know-Nothings, however, many moderates moved back into the Democratic party, and it appeared that Wigfall's radicalism was repudiated. He chose this time, however, to push two of his ultraradical proposals: the revival of the foreign slave trade and filibustering in Cuba, Mexico, and farther south for more slave territory. When these proposals split Texas Democrats, Wigfall had to abandon them. Nevertheless, he was elected to the U.S. Senate in 1859, with the inadvertent help of John Brown. By capitalizing on the fear engendered by Brown's Harpers Ferry raid, Wigfall defeated more moderate candidates.

Wigfall was the most pugnacious of the radical members of the Thirty-sixth Congress, who were intensifying the sectionalism that was leading to war. As a freshman senator, Wigfall was in the forefront of the Southern fire-eaters, earning a reputation for eloquence, witty but bitter debate, acerbic taunts, and a readiness for personal encounters. And his debates did not end on the Senate floor; he frequented bars and gaming rooms, always seeking out adversaries. In opposing the Homestead Act, partly on the ground that 160 acres was too small for a plantation with slaves, Wigfall lampooned it as a bill that would provide land for the landless and homes for the homeless, but not "niggers for the niggerless," as he put it. It is not surprising that he failed to obtain Federal funds for Texas to defend its frontiers against Indian attacks and to build the Southern Pacific Railroad into the state. He assured his fellow senators that the South would never accept a Black Republican as president. Let war come, he declared, "and if we do not get into Boston . . . . before you get into Texas, you may shoot me."

In the campaign of 1860, Wigfall helped discredit Stephen A. Douglas and split the Democratic party. After Abraham Lincoln was elected president, Wigfall coauthored the Southern Manifesto, declaring that any hope for relief within the Union was gone and that the honor, safety, and independence of the Southern people required the organization of a Southern confederacy. The manifesto was widely quoted in the Deep South, and even Southern moderates seemed to give up any idea of remaining in the Union.

Wigfall contributed greatly to thwarting compromises to save the Union. Although he occasionally expressed hope that separation would be peaceful, most of the time he equated it with war, avowing that the concluding treaty would be signed in Boston's Faneuil Hall. Wigfall stayed in the U.S. Senate even after Texas left the Union. He spied for the South, baited Northern senators, raised and trained troops in Maryland and sent them to South Carolina, and bought revolvers and rifles for Texas Confederates through July 1861, when he was finally expelled from the Senate well after the war started.

Typically, Wigfall had made his presence felt when the Civil War began at Fort Sumter in April, rowing under fire to the fort and dictating unauthorized surrender terms to the Federal commander. Many Southern newspapers hailed the recklessness and gallantry of Senator Wigfall, calling him the Confederate man of the hour. He refused an offer of the Texas governorship and became instead an aide to President Jefferson Davis, a Texas colonel, a Confederate colonel, and a member of the Confederate Provisional Congress, for a time concurrently while he was still a U.S. senator.

Wigfall initially was a friend and supporter of Davis and helped him become president. Most fire-eaters had wanted Barnwell Rhett, but Wigfall helped persuade Rhett to support Davis. Wigfall was influential with Davis, prevailing upon him to select Leroy P. Walker as the Confederacy's first secretary of war. The Davises and Wigfalls were together a great deal during May and June 1861. And in early July, Gen. P. G. T. Beauregard, in command of the Confederate troops at Manassas, wrote to Wigfall, seeking his assistance in presenting his grievances to Davis.

In early July, Wigfall became commander of the Texas troops, now a battalion, near Richmond. Since the command was not a large one, his appointment carried only a lieutenant colonelcy. Wigfall had hoped to be named a general, but the battalion was being mustered into Confederate service, and more troops from Texas were slow in coming.

Because Wigfall's battalion was in a train wreck on the way to the First Battle of Manassas, it did not arrive until the morning after the fighting. Nevertheless, Wigfall criticized the Confederates' failure to march on to Washington after the victory. Gen. Joseph E. Johnston said his army had been unable to press the attack because of a shortage of food supplies—a shortage he attributed to the failure of Davis's commissary general, Lucius B. Northrop, to deliver them. Wigfall sided with his friend Johnston, and apparently Davis considered criticism of Northrop to be criticism of himself.

Wigfall also took Johnston's side in the controversy over his rank, agreeing with his friend that he should be the highest ranking Confederate general because he was the highest to leave the U.S. Army. The controversy began when Robert E. Lee, then Davis's military adviser, ordered a new adjutant general into Johnston's headquarters. Johnston, certain he outranked Lee, protested repeatedly to the War Department. Even Lee was uncertain of his rank and position. But instead of clarifying their positions, Davis simply marked Johnston's letters "Insubordinate."

Wigfall soon had his own disagreement with Davis over rank. Prominent Texas friends recommended that Wigfall be moved up two steps to brigadier general. But Davis in August nominated him to move up only one step, to colonel, and Congress confirmed it imme-

WIGFALL, LOUIS T.

James Orr complained that he and another senator were almost ejected from a train carrying soldiers; Wigfall said the incident was not abuse of military power but an oversight.

PAGE 410

675

diately. The number of Texas troops was increasing to brigade level, however, and Davis nominated Wigfall for a brigadier generalcy in November. Wigfall was then still devoting part of his time to serving as Texas senator in the Permanent Congress. About the time Congress confirmed his generalcy in December, Wigfall resigned it to devote full time to Congress in order to press for military legislation.

During the optimistic period of February 1862 until May 1863, Congress debated many important military topics but took little action on them. During these months, Wigfall was a pro-administration militarist if not a nationalist. He backed almost all legislation that Davis favored and introduced several administration bills, including a proposal for the first conscription system in American history. One of the few staunch state rights advocates to support the measure, Wigfall argued that there should be only Confederate armies under Confederate generals, a stance that put him at loggerheads with other Texas delegates, who wanted to retain soldiers in their own state to protect its borders. Texas colleague W. P. Ballinger said that some of his friends thought Wigfall was a ruthless man.

During the Peninsular campaign, Wigfall blamed Gen. George B. McClellan's threat to Richmond on Davis's failure to order an invasion of Maryland. To a friend, Wigfall confided that he regretted ever having tried to move such a "dish of skimmed milk" to honorable action. Davis for his part said he lost confidence in Wigfall because of his drunkenness and his antipresident speeches in hotels. In the Peninsular campaign's Battle of Seven Pines, Wigfall cared for the wounded and became an aide to Gen. James Longstreet and a good friend of his and Lee's. They and other Confederate generals considered him their champion in pleading their needs to Congress and Davis.

Both Davis and Wigfall considered themselves expert military strategists, and this was the focus of many of their quarrels. Nevertheless, they agreed on the need for widespread conscription to defend the Confederacy. This issue brought Wigfall into conflict with many of his colleagues in Congress. By 1863 when others were coming to agree with him, Wigfall was still ahead of them, proposing extending the original age limits of eighteen through thirty-five to sixteen through sixty. Both houses accepted his basic bill, though lowering the upper age to fifty. And yet Wigfall seemed surprised when his own sixteen-year-old son Halsey ignored advice to stick to his schoolbooks and instead volunteered and saw extensive action as a member of J. E. B. Stuart's cavalry.

Wigfall used the argument of military necessity to pass a bill he had tried to get through the U.S. Senate, calling for the construction of a railroad through Texas. This would connect Richmond with key positions in the West and South. Texas would have played a greater role in the war effort had it not been so remote and cut off by the Federal sea blockade. Ten days after the bill was enacted, however, New Orleans fell to Union troops and Texas was effectively separated from the rest of the Confederacy. Wigfall led the legislative struggle that established the government's power to impress private railroads and finally, in February 1865, to take control of all railroads in the Confederacy.

Although Wigfall was consistent with his earlier state rights arguments in insisting that Confederate courts had no right to override the decisions of state courts, he generally worked to provide the central government with enough powers to sustain itself. Concerned that state rights were hampering the military, Wigfall introduced a resolution in May 1864, seeking to define Confederate and state jurisdiction over civil rights. Wigfall defined a federal rather than a confederate system of government and even introduced a successful bill providing for military impressment of private property as needed to sustain the army.

When many conscripts defied the draft law and were protected by state judges who readily released them by issuing writs of habeas corpus, Wigfall responded to another Davis plea. He introduced and helped pass a bill in Congress to authorize the president to suspend the writ when necessary to ensure viable Confederate armies.

In arguing for suspension of the writ of habeas corpus, Wigfall assured his colleagues that Davis could be trusted to use the power wisely. Nevertheless, Wigfall did not trust the president to appoint army staff. In October 1862, he persuaded both houses to pass a bill limiting Davis's power of appointment and providing generals with staffs of their own choosing. The president vetoed the bill. Nor did Wigfall trust the president to appoint heads of armies. Wigfall's covert efforts forced Davis to replace Gen. Braxton Bragg with Joseph Johnston as head of the Army of Tennessee, but Wigfall could not induce Davis to provide Johnston with adequate support. Announcing his loss of trust in Johnston, the president replaced him with John Bell Hood, with ruinous results. Wigfall admired Hood's bravery and probably encouraged the close relationship that developed in his home between his fifteen-year-old daughter and the Texas general while he recuperated there from serious battle wounds. But the senator predicted Hood's fiasco at Atlanta.

Having lost all faith in Davis, Wigfall decided that the Confederacy's only hope lay in leadership by Senate hegemony. During the last two years of the war, Wigfall waged a four-pronged public and conspiratorial campaign against the president's power and popu-

larity in an effort to bend him to the Senate's will: the Senate rejected his unwise appointments; Wigfall fixed responsibility for military losses on Davis, where he thought they belonged; Congress tried to force the president to observe the Constitution and hemmed him in with restrictions; and Wigfall and others belittled Davis in public to destroy the people's confidence in him. A positive relationship between Wigfall and Davis might have made it possible for the executive and legislative branches to collaborate, extending the life of the Confederacy. But neither the president nor the senator was willing to compromise, even as the Confederacy was facing destruction.

Probably Wigfall's policies were more sound than Davis's, and it is not surprising that several of the best generals looked to Wigfall for legislation and to plead their cases. But he rejected their pleas to strengthen their armies by arming slaves. Wigfall was willing to lose the war rather than admit that African Americans were worthy of being soldiers.

After the fall of the Confederacy, Wigfall fled to England where he tried to foment war between Britain and the United States, hoping to give the South an opportunity to rise again. He returned to Texas in 1872, died in Galveston in 1874, and was buried there in the Episcopal Cemetery.

— ALVY L. KING

WILDERNESS CAMPAIGN

The Wilderness, a region in Orange and Spotsylvania counties in northern Virginia, gave its name to a major battle fought in its tangled thickets on May 5 and 6, 1864. The battle pitted Robert E. Lee against Ulysses S. Grant in the opening stage of the overland campaign that eventually led to the siege of Richmond and Petersburg. Lee had wintered his Army of Northern Virginia in Orange County, west of the Wilderness, while the Federal Army of the Potomac camped across the Rapidan River in Culpeper County. Grant, newly appointed commander in chief of all Federal armies, took his headquarters into the field with the Army of the Potomac in March. Gen. George G. Meade remained in nominal command of that army for the rest of the war, but Grant exerted his authority over all substantive decisions. During the Wilderness, for instance, Meade had no control over one of the army's four corps, Burnside's Ninth.

The Army of the Potomac began its move south over the Rapidan early on May 4, crossing primarily at Germanna Ford, with nearly 120,000 men in the ranks.

That number seemed to Grant to be operationally appropriate to begin the campaign. He also could draw on virtually limitless replacements. Lee's army counted about 65,000 troops, with only limited reserves in prospect, and those available only at the cost of stripping other threatened points. Grant and Meade hoped to march straight through the Wilderness in the direction of Spotsylvania Court House without hindrance, moving past Lee's right flank before he could respond effectively and thus interposing between the Confederate army and Richmond.

Lee responded to the threat by moving swiftly eastward toward the Wilderness, camping on the night of May 4 within easy striking distance of the roads Grant had to use on his projected southward march. The Confederate army moved on two roads that ran through the Wilderness on roughly parallel courses and that eventually joined east of the ground that became the battlefield. The old Orange Turnpike was about two miles north of the newer Orange Plank Road at the longitude of the heaviest fighting. No means of ready communication between the two roads existed. As a result the Battle of the Wilderness was fought in two discrete halves that remained remarkably isolated from each other. Richard S. Ewell's Second Corps marched east on the turnpike while A. P. Hill's Third Corps paralleled it on the Plank Road. The other corps of Lee's army, the First under James Longstreet, began its march unfortunately far to the southwest in the vicinity of Boswell's Tavern in Louisa County. Lee's incaution in leaving so large a force so far from his other units, combined with a slow and confused march to action by the First Corps, would have a major impact on the conduct of the battle.

Fighting broke out first on the turnpike on the morning of May 5. The advance brigades of Ewell's force clashed with Federals marching south past the vicinity of Wilderness Tavern. Union Gen. G. K. Warren's Fifth Corps turned west onto the turnpike to face Ewell's men. Northern troops rolled over the first opposition they met and Confederate Brig. Gen. John M. Jones was shot from his horse. Elements of the division commanded by Robert Rodes restored order for the Confederates, who took up a line perpendicular to the turnpike in woods at the western edge of a large clearing straddling the pike known as Saunders Field. Fighting in this northern sector of the Wilderness on both days of the battle centered on the turnpike and especially on Saunders Field. Grant and Meade established their headquarters on a knoll just north of the pike and a mile east of the field. Warren made his headquarters just across the road from his two superiors at the Lacy house, Ellwood, which is the only building on the battlefield that survives today. Fighting ebbed and flowed around Saunders Field during May 5 as the rest of Ewell's Second Corps arrived and the Federal Fifth

The Battle of the Wilderness was the first in which the Confederate cavalry fought almost exclusively as infantry.

PAGE 90

Lee and Jackson blunted Hooker's drive near the edge of a seventy-square-mile body of dense woodland known as the Wilderness of Spotsylvania.

PAGE 27

Corps, supported by most of the Sixth, deployed to face it. The Confederates lost Brig. Gen. Leroy A. Stafford, who was mortally wounded in one fierce localized attack by the Sixth Corps.

Meanwhile the Confederate column on the Plank Road had approached its intersection with the north-south Brock Road, on which Grant was moving south, and fighting broke out in that zone. Confederate control of the intersection would break Grant's attenuated

army into two pieces and leave it susceptible to destruction in detail. During May 5 Hill came up against stout resistance from Union Gen. W. S. Hancock's Second Corps, supported by one division of the Sixth Corps under George W. Getty. Most of the fighting raged in the thickly overgrown woodland on either shoulder of the Plank Road not far west of the intersection. The only clearing of note along the road in the battle area was the meager subsistence farm of a

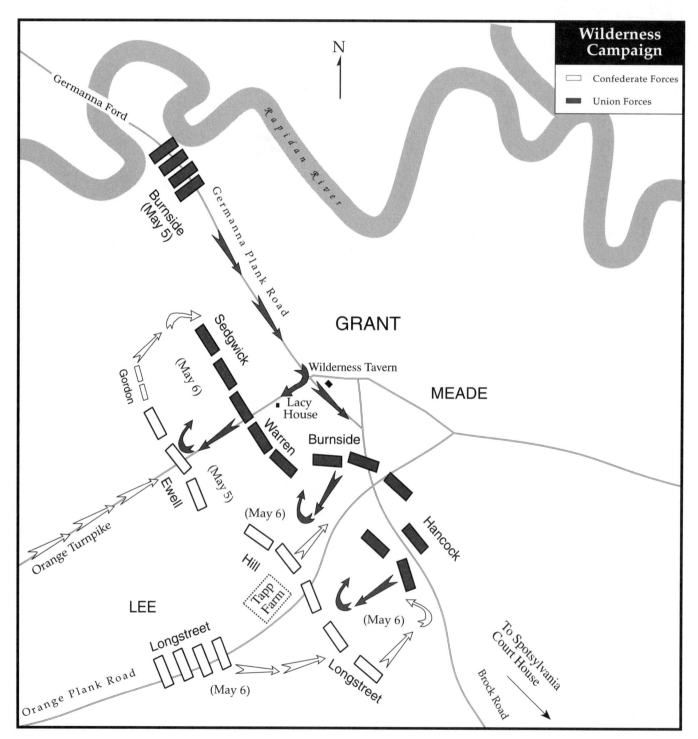

widow named Catharine Tapp, and that lay west of the front lines during the first day of the battle.

As darkness closed the fighting on May 5, the Southern position near the turnpike remained along the western edge of Saunders Field and extended beyond the field on both sides in a straight line, particularly northward, to counter Federal threats. All over the battlefield the soldiers of both sides energetically threw up earthworks reinforced with logs; the era of major entrenchments had arrived to stay and would reach unprecedented levels during the next two weeks. On the Plank Road front, Hill's brigades maintained a tenuous grip on ground fairly close to the crucial intersection with the Brock Road. They had been fought to a frazzle, however, and lay haphazardly in the thickets without adequate connection between units. Hill's subordinates desperately petitioned the corps commander to fall back and regroup. He refused on the premise that Longstreet's men would be on hand by morning as reinforcements and insisted that the weary soldiers be allowed to rest.

Early on May 6 a massive assault arranged by the capable Hancock rolled irresistibly over Hill's tattered remnants and threatened to destroy the Army of Northern Virginia. According to Edward Porter Alexander and James Fitz Caldwell, Lee rode among his fleeing troops, asking one veteran brigade why it was "fleeing like wild geese" and atypically expressing himself "rather roughly." At this critical moment, probably the most desperate in the army's career to date, the first units of Longstreet's First Corps finally began arriving on the field. Hancock had smashed through the woods to the Widow Tapp's clearing, where a battalion of Confederate artillery had been parked. The artillery of both armies accomplished little during the battle because of dense ground cover that rendered cannon less important here than in any other major action in the Virginia theater. These reserve guns suddenly became Lee's last line of defense, however, while Longstreet's men deployed. When the veteran Texas Brigade (three Texas and one Arkansas regiments) moved past the guns and into the breach, Lee attempted to lead them forward in an episode that became instantly famous and eventually grew larger than life in later years. Fearing for Lee's safety, the men of the brigade turned him back and then rushed forward in an attack that left half of them casualties.

Longstreet's reinforcements gradually stabilized the front along the Plank Road. The tide turned when a broadly mixed Confederate task force—four brigades from four divisions—moved secretly through the woods south of the road to an unfinished railroad bed that provided them with a corridor to use in creeping past the far left Federal flank. When the flanking column spread out into line and then dashed north, it routed the Union troops who had been flushed with success, rolling up the line "like a wet blanket," in Hancock's phrase. As the victorious Confederate attackers dashed northward toward the Plank Road, Longstreet and his subordinates led their men east on that road to exploit Hancock's collapse. But some of the Confederates in the woods, apparently of William Mahone's Virginia Brigade, fired at the group of horsemen along the road and with that volley ruined their army's chance for a great success. The volley killed Gen. Micah Jenkins and severely wounded Longstreet. In the shocked aftermath, the movement lost its momentum. Later in the day, Lee directed a renewal of the attack toward the intersection, but it resulted in a costly repulse after surging close to its goal.

May 6 on the Orange Turnpike front featured more fighting over and around Saunders Field. The exposed Federal right north of the field offered a tempting target, but corps commander Ewell timidly refused suggestions to exploit the opening. Finally, near dusk, Georgian John B. Gordon led a column that smashed the Federal right, just as Longstreet had destroyed the Federal left earlier in the day. Gordon captured hundreds of prisoners, including two brigadier generals, and pushed the Union right back through an arc of nearly ninety degrees in the gathering darkness.

The two armies faced each other from behind steadily deepening earthworks on May 7. Then Grant moved south in a race for the next crucial crossroads, a race that resulted in a two-week battle around Spotsylvania Court House. The Wilderness battlefield meeting between Lee and Grant had cost the Federal army about eighteen thousand casualties. Lee's losses, which cannot be computed precisely for this stage of the war, totaled at least eight thousand and probably reached near ten thousand. Lee's tactical skill had thwarted the intentions of an army twice the size of his own. Grant had quickly discovered the difference between fighting Lee and toying with Braxton Bragg. At the Wilderness Grant's army earned the distinction of having both of its exposed flanks abruptly turned and crumpled, the only such result in any of the war's battles in the Virginia theater. Nonetheless he pushed steadily on from the Wilderness toward Richmond. The war had turned its final corner in the Wilderness, and now it would grind inexorably by means of attrition through eleven months of steady fighting to Appomattox.

— ROBERT K. KRICK

WILMOT PROVISO

During an 1846 debate over a $2 million appropriation for the acquisition of California and New

"Alabama soldiers, all I ask of you is to keep up with the Texans!"

ROBERT E. LEE
PREPARING TO ADVANCE,
THE WILDERNESS, 1864

Patronage and pressure induced just enough Northern Democrats to vote for the Kansas-Nebraska Act in 1854 to obtain its passage.

PAGE 110

**WILSON'S CREEK
CAMPAIGN**

PAGE 109

In 1846 David
Wilmot of
Pennsylvania
introduced a
resolution banning
slavery in all
territory that
might be
conquered from
Mexico.

PAGE IO9

*Running on the
Wilmot Proviso
platform of
excluding slavery
from the
territories, the
Republicans
carried most
Northern states in
the presidential
election of 1856.*

PAGE IIO

Mexico, Pennsylvania Congressman David Wilmot proposed a prohibition on slavery in any territory acquired in the Mexican-American War that was then underway. Wilmot's motivations for offering the proposal were mixed. As a Northern Democrat he supported the war effort and Manifest Destiny but opposed the expansion of slavery and the settlement of free blacks in the territories. He told the Congress that the proviso would create territories where "my own race and own color can live without the disgrace" of "association with negro slavery." By offering the proviso, Wilmot hoped to finesse the issue—coming out both for the war and against the expansion of slavery. This would allow Northern Democrats to resist Whig attacks on them as doughfaces who always appeased the South.

The House adopted Wilmot's proviso by a vote of 83 to 64 in the face of almost unanimous Southern opposition, but the Senate adjourned before taking action on the appropriations bill to which it was attached. In 1847 the House attached the proviso to a $3 million appropriation despite unanimous Southern opposition in that body. In the Senate a few Northerners joined their unanimous Southern colleagues to defeat the proviso. Southern members of Congress unanimously rejected both the goal of the proviso—to prohibit slavery in the new territories—and its implication that Southern institutions (and thus Southerners) were too immoral to enter the new territories. The debate over the proviso revealed the danger to the South posed by a Congress increasingly polarized over slavery. The change of one vote in the Senate could prevent slaveholders from taking their slaves into Mexican Cession territory.

The proviso was a radical departure from American politics before the Mexican War. From the Northwest Ordinance (1787) until 1846, American politics had institutionalized the notion that the Southern territories were open to slavery and the Northern ones were not. The proviso threatened this balance, and in the process put the South on the defense in a new and dramatic way. A resolution of the Virginia legislature, adopted in February 1850, illustrates how the proposal of the proviso helped shape Southern thought and served as a prelude to secession. After asserting that Virginia's "loyalty to the Union . . . is stamped upon every page of her history," the legislature declared, "in the event of the passage of the Wilmot proviso . . . Virginia will be prepared to unite with her sister slaveholding states, in convention or otherwise" to consider "measures . . . for their mutual defence."

While the proviso inspired Southern fears and secessionist stirrings, it inspired an entire political party in the North, the Free-Soil party. The new party was a coalition of forces, including political abolitionists and former Liberty Party members, antislavery (conscience) Whigs, and antislavery Democratic negrophobes who were fed up with Southern domination of their party. The main platform of the party was the proviso and a demand for keeping slavery (and blacks) out of the territories. Although the party did poorly in 1848, the idea behind the proviso remained strong and reemerged as part of the main slogan of the Republican party in 1856, "Free Soil, Free Labor, Free Speech, Free Men."

[*See also* Compromise of 1850; Kansas-Nebraska Act; Missouri Compromise; Republican Party.]

— PAUL FINKELMAN

WILSON'S CREEK CAMPAIGN

The Planter's House conference had failed. The meeting between Unionists Brig. Gen. Nathaniel Lyon and Congressman Frank Blair and secessionists Governor Claiborne F. Jackson and Maj. Gen. Sterling Price had represented the last chance to quell the unrest growing in Missouri. On June 11, 1861, after hours of fruitless discussion, Lyon terminated the meeting by declaring war on the state of Missouri. The campaign that culminated in the Battle of Oak Hills (or Wilson's Creek) began two days later.

Lyon left St. Louis, marching with one column of Union troops up the Missouri River to capture Jefferson City, the state capital. Aware that Confederate troops were organizing in northern Arkansas, a logical rendezvous point for the pro-Confederate Missouri State Guard and Confederate troops, he directed Brig. Gen. of Missouri Volunteers Thomas Sweeny to lead a column to southwestern Missouri.

On June 15, as Lyon neared Jefferson City, Jackson abandoned the capital and moved up river to Boonville. The Federals secured the capital, pursued Jackson, and defeated him in a skirmish on the seventeenth. Jackson and his troops retreated southwest, while Lyon concentrated his efforts on establishing Union control of the vital Missouri River. Meanwhile, Sweeny's column easily secured the route from St. Louis to Springfield.

While Jackson marched south with elements of the state guard, Price moved to the southwestern corner of the state and selected Cowskin Prairie as the rendezvous point for the state guard. Camped just across the state line, in Arkansas, were the troops of Gens. Ben McCulloch and N. Bart Pearce. On July 1, a portion of Sweeny's column led by Col. Franz Sigel marched west from Springfield in an attempt to block Jackson and Price from joining forces. As Jackson's column moved south, however, thousands of Missourians joined him. Sigel was outnumbered four to one, and his command of a thousand men was defeated in the Bat-

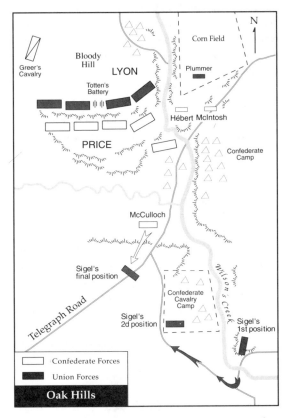

Oak Hills

tle of Carthage on July 5. The Federals retreated to Springfield, while Jackson continued south and joined forces with Price.

Lyon, having secured the Missouri River, began marching south. On July 7, his command was reinforced by Maj. Samuel Sturgis's troops from Fort Leavenworth, Kansas. Two days later, Lyon received word of Sigel's defeat at Carthage, and he ordered an immediate forced march to Springfield. After four grueling days during which the Federals marched over a hundred miles and crossed three major rivers and numerous streams, they arrived in Springfield on the thirteenth.

Although Lyon's force now numbered about seven thousand effectives, the Army of the West faced numerous problems. The men were in need of food and supplies, and still more worrisome were three Southern forces camped to the southwest. If they united and moved against Lyon, he would be outnumbered almost two to one. Nevertheless, Gen. John C. Frémont in St. Louis repeatedly denied Lyon's requests for reinforcements. In addition, most of Lyon's army was composed of ninety-day enlistees whose terms of service were coming to an end. By

mid-August, the army would be reduced to a skeleton force facing a growing Southern army.

On July 31, Lyon's fears became a reality. At the town of Cassville, about fifty miles southwest of Springfield, McCulloch, Price, and Pearce rendezvoused. Their twelve-thousand-man force began its march up Telegraph Road toward the enemy on the first of August. Lyon learned of the advance, but mistakenly thought the Southerners were moving in three separate columns and would unite near Springfield. He knew that once united, the larger Southern army could defeat his command and force him to abandon the region's pro-Union population. To avert this, Lyon led a column of more than 5,800 down Telegraph Road, planning to engage each column separately.

The next day, when advance elements of both armies fought a brief skirmish at Dug Springs, the victorious Federals learned that the Confederates were now united. Lyon ordered his men back to Springfield. The Southern army followed and went into camp where Telegraph Road crossed Wilson's Creek, only ten miles from the city.

By August 9, both armies had decided on similar plans of action. The Confederates planned to advance up Telegraph Road and strike the Federals at dawn on the tenth. But a light rainfall and the threat of a downpour canceled the operation. The majority of Southerners were without cartridge boxes, and heavy rain would disarm them. Lyon planned to leave a small force in Springfield, while he led 4,200 men out to attack the Confederate encampment from the north. At the same time Sigel, with 1,200 soldiers, would attack from the south. The element of surprise would be critical to the success of the operation.

To Lyon's great fortune, the Southern pickets had not returned to their posts after the night march was canceled, and the dawn attack was a success. The Federals overran several camps and drove the enemy south. The Union column advanced about one mile, reaching a ridge crest later called "Bloody Hill." From the east and across Wilson's Creek, a Confederate battery opened fire and stalled the advance. Price seized the opportunity to organize elements of the state guard into line of battle and ordered them up the hill's south slope to repulse the Federals.

As the Federals advanced down the west side of Wilson's Creek, Lyon, realizing his left flank was vulnerable to any force on the east side of the stream, ordered Capt. Joseph Plummer across the creek with a small force to advance in conjunction with the main column and guard the flank. After crossing the creek, Plummer observed the Confederate artillery's effect on the Federals on Bloody Hill and immediately moved against the battery. But two Confederate regiments blocked Plummer in John Ray's cornfield. In a brief,

"The war is over—the rebels are our countrymen again."

ULYSSES S. GRANT
STOPPING HIS MEN FROM CHEERING AFTER LEE'S SURRENDER, APRIL 9, 1865

violent fight the Federals were routed and retreated across the stream. Plummer's defeat secured this section of the battlefield for the Southerners.

About a mile and a half south of Bloody Hill, Sigel had heard Lyon's attack and ordered his artillery to open fire on the main Southern cavalry camp. The Confederates abandoned their camp and retreated to the protection of nearby woods, leaving the way unopposed for Sigel's Federals to cross to the west side of Wilson's Creek, advance north, and take a position on a hill where they overlooked the cavalry camp and blocked Telegraph Road. Despite the strength of this position, Sigel was attacked and routed by Southern infantry led by McCulloch. The rear of the Confederate army was now secure, and all its efforts could be concentrated on Bloody Hill.

By 6:30 A.M. the battle lines had been drawn on Bloody Hill. The Federals held the crest and Price's Missourians the south slope. Between 7:30 and 10:00 A.M., the state guard assaulted the Union line twice, failing in each attempt. During the second attack Lyon was wounded but continued to direct his command. Around 9:30 Lyon ordered the Second Kansas and First Iowa Infantry regiments forward to reinforce the line, and the Southern attack stalled. But while leading the Second Kansas into position Lyon was killed by a musket ball.

As Price's attack lost its momentum, Confederate cavalry launched an assault on the Union right and rear. This diversion of the Federals' attention permitted Price to disengage his troops and fall back down the hill. As the cavalry closed on the enemy's line, musket volleys and artillery broke the charge, turning it back.

After Lyon's death, Sturgis, as senior officer, assumed command of the Union forces. Realizing that Price was organizing for a third assault, Sturgis reinforced his line to meet the attack. Around 10:30, some five to six thousand Confederates surged up the hill, and the fighting raged unabated for thirty minutes. At one point Southern infantry closed to within twenty paces of the Union-held crest, and battle smoke from both lines formed one huge cloud on the south slope. The Federal line was hammered along its entire length, but it did not break. By 11:00 Price realized the attack had failed and withdrew to the base of the hill.

During this lull Sturgis learned that Sigel had been routed and that the troops on Bloody Hill were dangerously low on ammunition. Deciding he could not withstand a fourth assault, Sturgis began withdrawing his forces, and by 11:30 the Federals had abandoned Bloody Hill. Unaware of Sturgis's move, the Southerners launched a fourth assault. Upon reaching the crest, they observed the Union rear guard and main column retreating to Springfield. Exhausted by almost five hours of combat, low on ammunition, lacking in experience, and misled by rumors of Federal reinforcements approaching Springfield, the Confederates chose not to pursue their adversaries.

The Battle of Oak Hills was over. Of the 5,400 Federals on the field, 1,317 were casualties with 258 killed, 873 wounded, and 186 missing. The Southerners suffered 1,222 losses, with 277 dead and 945 wounded out of 10,125 effectives. Losses totaled 24.5 percent for the Federals and 12 percent for the Confederates.

The campaign marked the beginning of the war in Missouri and the Trans-Mississippi. Afterward the Federal army withdrew to Rolla, Missouri, leaving the Southerners in possession of most of the southwestern region of the state. McCulloch and Pearce returned to Arkansas, and Price and the Missouri State Guard advanced north toward Lexington, where, on September 20, they captured the Union garrison. With victories at Wilson's Creek and Lexington, Confederate hopes in the state reached new heights. In October, Governor Jackson led his exiled state government out of the Union, and Missouri became the twelfth Confederate state. Meanwhile, pro-Union Missourians organized a loyal government in Jefferson City. Throughout the remainder of the war, Missouri never politically reunited.

— RICHARD W. HATCHER III

WISE, HENRY A.

Wise, Henry A. (1806–1876), U.S. diplomat, governor of Virginia, and brigadier general. Born on December 3, 1806, and reared in Drummondtown, Virginia, Henry Alexander Wise was graduated with honors in 1825 from Washington and Jefferson College in Washington, Pennsylvania. Admitted to the bar after studying law for two additional years, Wise practiced the legal profession in Virginia and Tennessee. A successful farmer, Jacksonian Democrat, and outspoken champion of slavery and state rights, he was elected to the U.S. House of Representatives in 1835, serving in that body and vehemently espousing the Southern way of life until 1843. In 1844, Wise was named U.S. minister to Brazil. Wise was too candid with his views to ever succeed as a diplomat, however, and in 1847 he resigned his post and returned to Virginia. Elected governor of Virginia in 1855 by the Democrats, he served as chief executive of that state from 1856 until 1860. After John Brown was convicted for his 1859 attempt to seize the U.S. Arsenal at Harpers Ferry, Wise oversaw Brown's hanging, even visiting him before his execution.

After the start of the Civil War, Wise helped engineer the capture of Harpers Ferry in the spring of

1861. On June 5, 1861, Henry Wise, with much political clout but absolutely no military experience, was commissioned a brigadier general in the Confederate army. His first assignment was commanding the Confederate Army of the Kanawha in present-day West Virginia. A failure in all respects, Wise was soon replaced by Gen. John B. Floyd, an equally inept political soldier with whom Wise could not and would not get along. After an unqualified defeat at Carnifix Ferry in September and a disastrous November campaign, Wise and his brigade, known as Wise's Legion, were ordered to North Carolina.

On February 7, Union Gen. Ambrose Burnside made a successful amphibious assault on Roanoke Island, North Carolina, and the following day his troops defeated the Confederate forces there. Wise was in overall command of the island, and his son was killed during the battle. Posted next with Gen. Robert E. Lee's Army of Northern Virginia, he and his men saw action during the Seven Days' fighting as Union Gen. George B. McClellan battled up the Virginia Peninsula in a disastrous attempt to capture Rich-

mond. Remaining in the Richmond defenses for about a year following the Peninsular campaign, Wise was sent to command the Sixth Military District of South Carolina from October 1863 until returning to the Army of Northern Virginia to take part in the Battle of Drewry's Bluff on May 16, 1864. There, the Confederate forces under Gen. P. G. T. Beauregard effectively sealed up the Union army of Gen. Benjamin Butler at Bermuda Hundred.

Commanding a district at Petersburg, Virginia, Wise served with Lee's army during the ten-month-long siege there. When Petersburg fell to the Union forces on April 2, 1865, Wise joined the Confederate retreat to Appomattox, fighting with his troops at the Battle of Sayler's Creek on April 6. Present at Lee's surrender at Appomattox Courthouse three days later, Wise took his parole, but never applied for amnesty for his role in the Confederate service.

Following the war, he resumed his career in law until he died in Richmond on September 12, 1876.

— WARREN WILKINSON

Y

YANCEY, WILLIAM LOWNDES

Yancey, William Lowndes (1814–1863), diplomat and congressman from Alabama. Renowned in his lifetime as the most fiery and eloquent orator for Southern independence, Yancey was born in Warren County, Georgia, in 1814. His father died of yellow fever a year later, and in 1821 his mother married the Reverend Nathan Beman, the headmaster of a Presbyterian academy in Georgia, which the young Yancey attended. After selling his wife's slaves, Beman, a native New Englander, moved his family to Troy, New York, in 1823 and soon took up the cause of abolitionism. Beman's relations with Carolina, Yancey's mother, were stormy, and the adolescent Yancey bitterly resented what he saw as the hypocritical and cruel self-righteousness of his abolitionist stepfather. Indeed, throughout his public career Yancey would attack the abolitionists in much the same terms as he had denounced the values of his stepfather.

In 1833 Yancey returned to the society and culture his stepfather had rejected. He left Williams College in Massachusetts before graduating and moved to South Carolina. He read law in Greenville under Benjamin Perry, the leader of the up-country Unionists during the nullification crisis, and, like his mentor, defended the Union against the Calhounite state rights enthusiasts. Marriage in 1835 to Sarah Caroline Earle, the daughter of a wealthy slave owner, brought with it thirty-five slaves and instant elevation to planter status. Yancey abandoned his law practice and moved in 1836 to Dallas County in the Alabama black belt where he rented a plantation. In 1838, while on a return trip to Greenville, Yancey killed his wife's uncle, Dr. Robinson Earle, in a brawl that stemmed from an exchange of personal insults. Although convicted of manslaughter, Yancey exulted in the affair as a vindication of his honor. Far more damaging to his career than any notoriety in the wake of the killing of Earle, however, was the economic loss occasioned by accidental poisoning of his slaves in 1839. Already suffering financially from low cotton prices after the panic of 1837, Yancey was now forced to return to law for the funds needed to rebuild his estate.

Yancey entered politics for a second time in 1840, and, in a marked reversal of his earlier attitudes, he returned as a committed state righter. He edited a newspaper and backed Martin Van Buren for the presidency in 1840. After serving in the Alabama house in 1841 and 1843, he was elected to fill a vacant seat in Congress in 1844 and was reelected in 1845. But Yancey had neither the taste nor the talent for the compromising posture that was necessary for effective party politics at the congressional level, and he resigned his seat in 1846. Before he did so, he fought a duel (ending in a harmless exchange of shots) with Congressman Thomas Lanier Clingman of North Carolina, a future Confederate general. Clingman challenged Yancey in response to a congressional speech that Clingman believed had sullied his honor.

Yancey held no other political office before the outbreak of the Civil War. His fame and influence rested on his oratory. He had a beautifully clear speaking voice that could hold an audience enraptured while he espoused the cause of Southern rights. Yancey first became identified in the public mind as the champion of the South against the antislavery North as the result of the Alabama Platform of 1848, a set of resolutions passed by the Alabama legislature denying the right of

FIERY ORATOR

William Lowndes Yancey, renowned in his time as the most eloquent speaker for Southern independence, was ineffective in seeking Britain's recognition of the Confederacy.

LIBRARY OF CONGRESS

Congress to prevent slavery from expanding into the Federal territories. Reveling in the role of a sectional agitator in the 1850s, he spread the message of secession as a legal right of individual Southern states in hundreds of speeches. He helped make secession possi-

> *Yancey's quick temper, impatience with temporizing, and rhetorical outbursts were precisely those personality traits most ill-suited to effective diplomacy.*
>
> PAGE 686

*By the summer of
1864, the
Confederacy's fate
in the courts of
Europe hinged
on the success
or failure of
Ulysses S. Grant.*

PAGE 175

ble by first making it conceivable. In a famous publicized letter of 1858 to James S. Slaughter, a letter that Yancey insisted was meant to be private, he called for committees of safety to "fire the Southern heart" in defense of liberties allegedly being trampled by a hostile North.

His oratory won him a reputation as the "prince of the fire-eaters," and it was only fitting that he led the Southern delegates who bolted the National Democratic Convention at Charleston in 1860 over the party's refusal to endorse the old Alabama Platform of 1848 with its demand for the right of slavery to expand into the territories. Yancey went on a Northern speaking tour in support of John C. Breckinridge, the nominee of the Southern state rights Democrats in 1860. When the election resulted in Abraham Lincoln's victory, Yancey capped his career as a fire-eater by leading the secessionist forces in the state convention of January 1861 that took Alabama out of the Union.

Yancey's reputation and career peaked in the flush of enthusiasm over the success of secession. Yet neither he nor the other leading fire-eaters were to be entrusted with positions of power in the new Confederate government. He received scant support for the presidency of the Confederacy from the delegates assembled at Montgomery, Alabama, in February 1861. Indeed, Yancey himself was not even chosen as a delegate. The founders of the Confederacy wanted to project an image of careful moderation, and Yancey was considered far too radical and headstrong for such politically delicate tasks as persuading the upper South, especially Virginia, to join the lower South in leaving the Union.

Yancey's oratorical skills as an agitator and his influence in Alabama politics, however, made him a potential disruptive threat to the fledgling Davis administration, were he denied any position or office. Jefferson Davis moved to counteract the threat by offering Yancey his choice of either the relatively minor cabinet post of attorney general or leadership of a three-man diplomatic mission to Europe. Against the advice of his fellow radical, Robert Barnwell Rhett, Sr., of South Carolina, Yancey accepted the diplomatic assignment in March 1861 and sailed for England in early April with the other commissioners, Pierre A. Rost of Louisiana and A. Dudley Mann of Georgia.

Yancey's diplomatic mission was a failure, but it is hard to see how it could have succeeded in its goal of securing official recognition of the Confederacy. One problem was Yancey himself. His quick temper, impatience with temporizing, and rhetorical outbursts were precisely those personality traits most ill-suited to effective diplomacy. Moreover, and as Rhett had forewarned him, he brought very little leverage to his discussions with the British and French. Contrary to Rhett's urgings, Davis did not empower Yancey to offer long-term commercial treaties in exchange for diplomatic recognition. Without this power, Yancey could not make any direct appeal to the economic self-interest of his European adversaries. All he could do was argue for the legitimacy of the Confederate cause and hint at a cotton embargo in the event of European nonrecognition.

Lord John Russell, the British foreign secretary, coldly distanced himself from Yancey's diplomatic team. He did grant a brief interview on May 3 and an even shorter one on May 9, but he refused to commit himself. In response to Lincoln's proclamation of a Union blockade of the Southern coast, the British issued a proclamation of neutrality in mid-May conferring on the Confederacy the rights of a belligerent, but they withheld official diplomatic recognition. Meanwhile, Napoleon III of France, although professing sympathy for the Confederate cause, made it clear that he would not move unless Britain took the first step toward recognition. By the late summer, after Lord Russell had cut off personal interviews with the Confederate commissioners and limited contact with them to formal, written statements, Yancey was ready to leave for home. Requested to stay until the arrival of James Mason of Virginia, the newly appointed Confederate commissioner to England, Yancey was still in London when news of the *Trent* affair reached England in late November. This Union seizure of two Confederate diplomats from a British mail packet ignited a crisis in Anglo-American affairs that gave Yancey one last chance to make his case for British assistance to the Confederacy.

In a letter of November 30 Yancey repeated his argument that the British were not bound by international law to recognize a Union blockade that was both ineffective and harmful to European commercial interests. He declared that the Confederacy would never be subdued by the blockade and urged the British to reopen their access to the cheap, abundant cotton supplies of the South. Lord Russell was unmoved and on December 7 informed Yancey, Rost, and Mann that "he must decline to enter into official communication with them." This was the final insult for Yancey, and he sailed for home once Mason arrived in January.

Yancey was chastened and angry when he returned to the South in February 1862. Shortly after disembarking in New Orleans, he told a crowd of well-wishers that the Confederacy could count on no friends abroad. He blamed the prevalence of antislavery public opinion in England for the failure of his diplomatic mission and confessed that it was naive to believe that the power of King Cotton could force European recognition of the Confederacy. The South's salvation, he concluded, could be achieved only through military victories that subjugated the Northern enemy.

Yancey had passed on word from England that he would gladly consent to serve as a senator in the First Regular Confederate Congress. So elected in his absence by the Alabama legislature, Yancey took his seat in Congress in April 1862. He soon became entangled in a contest of wills with Davis. Now believing, as Rhett had from the very beginning, that Davis had played him for the fool on the abortive European mission, Yancey was quick to find fault with Davis's handling of the war effort.

Having been forced to borrow funds in London to pay for his passage home, Yancey knew from personal experience that Confederate diplomats and foreign agents suffered from a lack of timely financial assistance. In a thinly veiled criticism of the administration's conduct of its foreign affairs, he wrote Davis in early April outlining missed opportunities for arms purchases by Confederate agents in Europe. Davis's reply was cool but tactful. He was stung more deeply by a letter of April 21 written by Yancey and his Alabama colleague in the Senate, Clement C. Clay. The senators lodged an official protest over Davis's appointment policy for generals. They cited figures showing that Alabama had forty regiments in the field but only five brigadier generals. After hinting that Davis was guilty of political favoritism in his appointments, they submitted the names of five regimental commanders of Alabama troops for promotion to brigadier general. Offended by what he viewed as a blatant challenge to his constitutional prerogatives, Davis indignantly responded that the charges were unfair and unworthy of any further consideration.

Yancey's early clashes with Davis were symptomatic of the ideological rift that soon developed in the Confederacy between the Davis administration and the more radical secessionists, men such as Yancey, Rhett, and Louis T. Wigfall of Texas. Yancey, like his fellow fire-eaters, was willing enough to support essential war measures. For example, he voted for the first Conscription Act in April 1862. He set aside his constitutional misgivings over granting such a power to the national government in consideration of the overriding military necessity of retaining in the field the original twelve-month volunteers raised through the action of the individual states. By the same token, he generally backed the economic measures of the increasingly unpopular Treasury Department. For Yancey and other radicals, however, the Confederate bid for independence rested above all else on the individual rights and liberties of the Southern (white) people. He was thus quick to see in the broadening powers of Davis and Confederate officials a pattern of executive tyranny that endangered the very liberties he believed the Confederacy had been created to protect.

Consistent with the prewar stand that had won him fame as a fire-eater, Yancey the senator repudiated party ties and institutional loyalties for the role of agitator. He used his position in the Senate as a forum to warn fellow Confederates of the despotic threats of a distant, centralizing government controlled by President Davis. He granted the military need for such government programs as the impressment of private goods to supply Confederate armies but argued in vain that such seizures should be pegged to the market value of the impressed property in order to be fair and equitable. Despite his early rebuff by Davis on the issue of appointing generals, Yancey continued to accuse Davis of damaging army morale through a policy that slighted the pride and valor of state troops in its selection of brigadier generals. In particular, Yancey still believed that Davis was ignoring the rightful claims of Alabamians to top commands. In September 1862, at a time when Virginia had twenty-four brigadier generals and Alabama but four, he introduced a bill setting up a quota system for the nomination and appointment of brigadier generals based upon the number of troops furnished by each state. The bill was defeated, in part because many senators felt that Yancey was engaging in a personal vendetta against Davis.

One of the clearest expressions of Yancey's conceptions of the Confederate experience came during a debate over an amendment offered by Senator William T. Dortch of North Carolina to the Conscription Act in the late summer of 1862. Dortch proposed that the Confederate government be authorized to draft justices of the peace. Benjamin H. Hill of Georgia, a leading spokesman for the Davis administration in the Senate, supported Dortch's amendment by claiming that the war-making powers of Congress extended to the conscription of civil officials. For Yancey, this claim smacked of the heretical nationalism of the hated Lincoln government. He feared that such a nationalist belief, what he called the fallacy of a "national life," would supersede and submerge individual and state liberties and thus negate the constitutional freedoms Southern armies were fighting to uphold. "The province of this government, its sole province," he insisted, "is to defend Constitutional government—the Constitutional liberties of States and of the people of States. There is no National life to defend." The unwarranted power of the national government to draft civil officials, he warned, was the power to destroy state governments, and it was a form of despotism that he feared "more than a million Yankee bayonets."

In his unsuccessful attempts to liberalize the access of the press to Senate debates and to loosen the rules by which the Senate often sat in secret sessions, Yancey

YANCEY, WILLIAM LOWNDES

Yancey had a beautifully clear speaking voice that could hold an audience enraptured while he espoused the cause of Southern rights.

PAGE 685

*Contrary to Rhett's
urgings, Davis did
not empower
Yancey to offer
long-term
commercial treaties
in exchange for
diplomatic
recognition.*

PAGE 686

continued to portray himself as the champion of the Southern people against a national government that shrank from full public accountability for its actions. His last major battle for what he construed as endangered Southern liberties culminated in the most celebrated episode of his Senate career when Benjamin Hill hurled two glass inkstands at him on February 4, 1863. Hill hit Yancey flush on the right cheekbone with the first inkstand. The two men had been exchanging personal insults for days. Before a bleeding Yancey could attack the Georgian, fellow senators restrained the combatants. Yancey, but not Hill, was officially censured by the Senate for his part in the affair.

The Yancey-Hill clash erupted in the context of a debate over Hill's bill to establish a Confederate supreme court with appellate jurisdiction over state supreme courts. Yancey led the floor fight against the bill, and his state rights arguments were by now familiar to his colleagues: "When we decide that the state courts are of inferior dignity to this Court, we have sapped the main pillar of this Confederacy." He conceded to supporters of the bill that the First Congress of the United States under the venerable George Washington had established a supreme court in 1789, but, in a remarkable statement, given the near deification of Washington's generation in Southern political rhetoric, he claimed that "we are wiser than the men of those days." The Founding Fathers, he noted, could only speculate as to the impact of their legislation. The founders of the new Southern republic, however, should have known from bitter experience how the implied centralizing powers of a federal government could be used to sap individual liberties.

Yancey may have been bloodied by Hill, but he won the court battle. The Confederacy never did have a supreme court. In addition to Yancey's success in arousing fears of centralization, the Davis administration decided there was no pressing need for such a court in light of the generally favorable treatment of Confederate legislation by the existing state courts.

Yancey did not live to see the death of the Confederacy that his oratory had been so instrumental in bringing to life. Already plagued by the late 1850s with a severe case of neuralgia, he suffered through increasingly poor health during his years of Confederate service. Bladder and kidney ailments reduced him to a bedridden invalid by the summer of 1863, and he died at his farmhouse near Montgomery on July 27. In a final tribute to the prince of the fire-eaters, a magnificent funeral procession accompanied the body from the Presbyterian church to its interment in the city cemetery.

— WILLIAM L. BARNEY

YELLOW TAVERN, VIRGINIA

Six miles outside Richmond, J. E. B. Stuart's Confederate cavalry corps met Philip Sheridan's force on May 11, 1864. The fierce battle took its toll on both armies, but the Southerners suffered an irreplaceable loss—the death of J. E. B. Stuart.

At the beginning of May, the Army of the Potomac crossed the Rapidan and began thrusting southward. From the densely covered terrain of the Wilderness to the crossroads at Spotsylvania Court House, the Federals engaged the Army of Northern Virginia in desperate and bitter fighting while inching ever closer to the Confederate capital.

Philip Sheridan, the commander of the Federal cavalry corps, had brashly told Gen. George Meade that, given the chance, he could beat J. E. B. Stuart. Meade conferred with Ulysses S. Grant, and on May 8 Sheridan received orders to move southward, "engage Stuart, and clean him out." Sheridan hoped to find Stuart in an isolated position, cut off from Robert E. Lee's infantry.

Early on the morning of May 9, Sheridan set out with seven brigades, totaling nearly ten thousand troopers, to meet Stuart. That same day, Stuart received the news that Sheridan and his force were moving down Telegraph Road in the direction of Richmond. The Confederate general mobilized his three brigades to pursue the Union cavalry.

Sheridan veered his men southwest from Telegraph Road until they reached Beaver Dam, a Confederate supply base. There the Union troops destroyed precious rations and medical supplies and liberated over three hundred prisoners before continuing toward Richmond.

Arriving at Beaver Dam the next morning, Stuart surveyed the damage and tried to anticipate Sheridan's next move. He had information that Sheridan was traveling with an enormous number of soldiers; hence Stuart supposed that he planned to take Richmond. Yet Sheridan also might strike the Richmond, Fredericksburg, and Potomac Railroad. To ascertain Sheridan's real objective, Stuart sent one brigade to follow the Union troops while he took his remaining two brigades to rush toward Richmond in an attempt to place himself between the Confederate capital and the enemy.

That night, following on the heels of the Federal troops, Stuart and his men reached Hanover Junction where they briefly stopped to rest. At 1:00 A.M., they began moving again in the direction of Ashland, which they found in a shambles. During the night Sheridan's cavalry had torn up six miles of the railroad, destroyed several railroad cars, and burned Confederate store-houses.

Stuart forged ahead, and at 8:00 A.M. on May 11 he reached Yellow Tavern ahead of the Federal troops. Yellow Tavern sat at the junction of Mountain Brook Road from Louisa, Telegraph Road from Fredericksburg, and Brook Turnpike, which led into Richmond. There Stuart chose to wait for the Federals.

In the hours before Sheridan arrived, Stuart planned his strategy. He pondered whether to confront Sheridan's corps outright or rely on help from Braxton Bragg, the commanding officer in Richmond, and attempt to flank the Federals. Stuart sent a messenger to Bragg to ask him if he could hold Richmond, manned only by local troops.

At 11:00, before Bragg had time to answer Stuart's inquiry, Sheridan's troops began positioning themselves in front of the Confederate lines. Stuart chose to place his men, unmounted, along Mountain Road and hope for the best from Richmond. The Confederates held off the waves of Federal attacks through the afternoon. At 2:00 P.M. the messenger returned with Bragg's answer; he felt he could defend the capital with his four thousand local men. Stuart breathed easier.

After a lull in the fighting in the late afternoon, the Federals launched a coordinated attack at 4:00. They simultaneously struck both the center and the left of Stuart's line. On the extreme left, George Armstrong Custer's troops hit Lunsford Lindsay Lomax's brigade particularly hard. Stuart rode to the left to lend encouragement to Lomax's men. Another wave of Federals advanced on the Confederates. In the ensuing melee the Southerners rallied and beat Custer's men back behind the Union lines.

Though the Confederates had managed to repel the latest Northern attack, a retreating Federal shot Stuart in his right side; the ball pierced his abdomen and lodged in his body. Stuart's corps continued to repulse Sheridan's division until dark as an ambulance carried Stuart to his brother-in-law's home in Richmond. He died the next day.

At Yellow Tavern, Stuart's cavalry succeeded in resisting the Federal move on the Confederate capital. Sheridan abandoned his position around Richmond and then moved east and down the Chickahominy River. He later stated that he chose not to enter Richmond because he would have lost five hundred to six hundred soldiers in the process, and he did not have sufficient strength to hold the city. Besides, he had already accomplished what he set out to do—beat J. E. B. Stuart.

— JENNIFER LUND

YORK, ZEBULON

York, Zebulon (1819–1890), brigadier general. Born on October 10, 1819, in Avon, Maine, York moved to Louisiana and became one of the state's wealthiest planters. When the war began he raised a company of infantry and was elected major of the Fourteenth Louisiana Volunteers. He later was promoted to lieutenant colonel and fought well at the Battle of Winchester, Virginia, where he was wounded.

Widely known as a very brave but profane officer, York became colonel of the regiment in August 1862 and was wounded again at Second Manassas. After serving at Sharpsburg and Fredericksburg, he spent much of 1863 in Louisiana recruiting and drilling conscripts. During the Wilderness campaign the First and Second Louisiana Brigades were consolidated under the overall command of Gen. Harry Thompson Hays. York was given command of the Second Brigade but apparently was absent at the Battle of Spotsylvania. When Hays was wounded at Spotsylvania, York was promoted to brigadier general on June 2, 1864, (to date from May 31) and given command of the consolidated brigade. He was the only Polish-American to become a Confederate general.

York's brigade participated in Jubal Early's raid on Washington and played a major role in his victory at Monocacy, where York's casualties ran at almost 50 percent. At the Third Battle of Winchester, York again was in the thick of the fighting and received a wound that led to the amputation of his arm. He ended his military career in Salisbury, North Carolina, trying unsuccessfully to gather recruits from the disillusioned German and Irish Union prisoners held there.

After the war, York moved to Natchez, Mississippi. Financially ruined by the war, he operated the York House until his death on August 5, 1890.

— TERRY L. JONES

In July, 1864, Jubal Early and his men raided Maryland, threatened to enter Washington, D.C and forced the Union to divert two corps that would have been pitted against the Army of Northern Virginia.

PAGE 689

Appendixes

SOUTH CAROLINA'S ORDINANCE OF SECESSION

Charleston, South Carolina, December 20, 1860

[Reprinted from Frank Moore, ed., *The Rebellion Record*, vol. 1, New York, 1862, p. 2.]

An Ordinance to Dissolve the Union between the State of South Carolina and other States united with her under the compact entitled the Constitution of the United States of America.

We, the people of the State of South Carolina, in Convention assembled, do declare and ordain, and it is hereby declared and ordained, that the ordinance adopted by us in Convention, on the 23d day of May, in the year of our Lord 1788, whereby the Constitution of the United States of America was ratified, and also all Acts and parts of Acts of the General Assembly of this State ratifying the amendments of the said Constitution, are hereby repealed, and that the union now subsisting between South Carolina and other States under the name of the United States of America is hereby dissolved.

DECLARATION OF THE IMMEDIATE CAUSES OF SECESSION

Charleston, South Carolina, December 24, 1860

Adopted by the South Carolina secession convention as the official explanation for the state's withdrawal from the Union, the declaration was drafted by a special committee chaired by Christopher G. Memminger. Reprinted from Frank Moore, ed., *The Rebellion Record*, vol. 1, New York, 1862, pp. 3–4.

The people of the State of South Carolina in Convention assembled, on the 2d day of April, A.D. 1852, declared that the frequent violations of the Constitution of the United States by the Federal Government, and its encroachments upon the reserved rights of the States, fully justified this State in their withdrawal from the Federal Union; but in deference to the opinions and wishes of the other Slaveholding States, she forbore at that time to exercise this right. Since that time these encroachments have continued to increase, and further forbearance ceases to be a virtue.

And now the State of South Carolina having resumed her separate and equal place among nations, deems it due to herself, to the remaining United States of America, and to the nations of the world, that she should declare the immediate causes which have led to this act.

In the year 1765, that portion of the British Empire embracing Great Britain undertook to make laws for the Government of that portion composed of the thirteen American Colonies. A struggle for the right of self-government ensued, which resulted, on the 4th of July, 1776, in a Declaration, by the Colonies, "that they are, and of right ought to be, FREE AND INDEPENDENT STATES; and that, as free and independent States, they have full power to levy war, conclude peace, contract alliances, establish commerce, and to do all other acts and things which independent States may of right do."

They further solemnly declared that whenever any "form of government becomes destructive of the ends for which it was established, it is the right of the people to alter or abolish it, and to institute a new government." Deeming the Government of Great Britain to have become destructive of these ends, they declared that the Colonies "are absolved from all allegiance to the British Crown, and that all political connection between them and the State of Great Britain is, and ought to be, totally dissolved."

In pursuance of this Declaration of Independence, each of the thirteen States proceeded to exercise its separate sovereignty; adopted for itself a Constitution, and appointed officers for the administration of government in all its departments—Legislative, Executive and Judicial. For purposes of defence they united their arms and their counsels; and, in 1778, they entered into a League known as the Articles of Confederation, whereby they agreed to intrust the administration of their external relations to a common agent, known as the Congress of the United States, expressly declaring, in the first article, "that each State retains its sovereignty, freedom and independence, and every power, jurisdiction and right which is not, by this Confederation, expressly delegated to the United States in Congress assembled."

Under this Confederation the War of the Revolution was carried on; and on the 3d of September, 1783, the contest ended, and a definite Treaty was signed by Great Britain, in which she acknowledged the Independence of the Colonies in the following terms:

"ARTICLE 1. His Britannic Majesty acknowledges the said United States, viz.: New Hampshire, Massachusetts Bay, Rhode Island and Providence Plantations, Connecticut, New York, New Jersey, Pennsylvania, Delaware, Maryland, Virginia, North Carolina, South Carolina and Georgia, to be FREE, SOVEREIGN, AND INDEPENDENT STATES; that he treats with them as such; and, for himself, his heirs and successors, relinquishes all claims to the government, propriety, and territorial rights of the same and every part thereof."

Thus were established the two great principles asserted by the Colonies, namely, the right of a State to govern itself; and the right of a people to abolish a Government when it becomes destructive of the ends for which it was instituted. And concurrent with the establishment of these principles, was the fact, that each Colony became and was recognized by the mother country as a FREE, SOVEREIGN AND INDEPENDENT STATE.

In 1787, Deputies were appointed by the States to revise the articles of Confederation; and on 17th September, 1787, these Deputies recommended, for the adoption of the States, the Articles of Union, known as the Constitution of the United States.

The parties to whom this constitution was submitted were the several sovereign States; they were to agree or disagree, and when nine of them agreed, the compact was to take effect among those concurring; and the General Government, as the common agent, was then to be invested with their authority.

If only nine of the thirteen States had concurred, the other four would have remained as they then were—separate, sovereign States, independent of any of the provisions of the Constitution. In fact, two of the States did not accede to the Constitution until long after it had gone into operation among the other eleven; and during that interval, they each exercised the functions of an independent nation.

By this Constitution, certain duties were imposed upon the several States, and the exercise of certain of their powers was restrained, which necessarily impelled their continued existence as sovereign states. But, to remove all doubt, an amendment was added, which declared that the powers not delegated to the United States by the Constitution, nor prohibited by it to the States, are reserved to the States respectively, or to the people. On the 23d May, 1788, South Carolina, by a Convention of her people, passed an ordinance assenting to this Constitution, and afterwards altered her own Constitution to conform herself to the obligations she had undertaken.

Thus was established, by compact between the States, a Government with defined objects and powers, limited to the express words of the grant. This limitation left the whole remaining mass of power subject to the clause reserving it to the States or the people, and rendered unnecessary any specification of reserved rights. We hold that the Government thus established is subject to the two great principles asserted in the Declaration of Independence; and we hold further, that the mode of its formation subjects it to a third fundamental principle, namely, the law of compact. We maintain that in every compact between two or more parties, the obligation is mutual; that the failure of one of the contracting parties to perform a material part of the agreement, entirely releases the obligation of the other; and that, where no arbiter is provided, each party is remitted to his own judgment to determine the fact of failure, with all its consequences.

In the present case, that fact is established with certainty. We assert that fourteen of the States have deliberately refused for years past to fulfil their constitutional obligations, and we refer to their own statutes for the proof.

The Constitution of the United States, in its fourth Article, provides as follows:

"No person held to service or labor in one State under the laws thereof, escaping into another, shall, in consequence of any law or regulation therein, be discharged from such service or labor, but shall be delivered up, on claim of the party to whom such service or labor may be due."

This stipulation was so material to the compact that without it that compact would not have been made. The greater number of the contracting parties held slaves, and they had previously evinced their estimate of the value of such a stipulation by making it a condition in the Ordinance for the government of the territory ceded by Virginia, which obligations, and the laws of the General Government, have ceased to effect the objects of the Constitution. The States of Maine, New Hampshire, Vermont, Massachusetts, Connecticut, Rhode Island, New York, Pennsylvania, Illinois, Indiana, Michigan, Wisconsin, and Iowa, have enacted laws which either nullify the acts of Congress, or render useless any attempt to execute them. In many of these States the fugitive is discharged from the service of labor claimed, and in none of them has the State Government complied with the stipulation made in the Constitution. The State of New Jersey, at an early day, passed a law in conformity with her constitutional obligation; but the current of Anti-Slavery feeling has led her more recently to enact laws which render inoperative the remedies provided by her own laws and by the laws of Congress. In the State of New York even the right of transit for a slave has been denied by her tribunals; and the States of Ohio and Iowa have refused to surrender to justice fugitives charged with murder, and with inciting servile insurrection in the State of Virginia. Thus the constitutional compact has been deliberately broken and disregarded by the non-slaveholding States; and the consequence follows that South Carolina is released from her obligation.

The ends for which this Constitution was framed are declared by itself to be "to form a more perfect union, to establish justice, insure domestic tranquility, provide for the common defence, promote the general welfare, and secure the blessings of liberty to ourselves and our posterity."

These ends it endeavored to accomplish by a Federal Government, in which each State was recognized as an equal, and had separate control over its own institutions. The right of property in slaves was recognized by giv-ing to free persons distinct political rights; by giving them the right to represent, and burdening them with direct taxes for, three-fifths of their slaves; by authorizing the importation of slaves for twenty years; and by stipulating for the rendition of fugitives from labor.

We affirm that these ends for which this Government was instituted have been defeated, and the Government itself has been destructive of them by the action of the non-slaveholding States. Those States have assumed the right of deciding upon the propriety of our domestic institutions; and have denied the rights of property established in fifteen of the States and recognized by the Constitution; they have denounced as sinful the institution of Slavery; they have permitted the open establishment among them of societies, whose avowed object is to disturb the peace of and claim the property of the citizens of other States. They have encouraged and assisted thousands of our slaves to leave their homes; and those who remain, have been incited by emissaries, books, and pictures, to servile insurrection.

For twenty-five years this agitation has been steadily increasing, until it has now secured to its aid the power of the common Government. Observing the *forms* of the Constitution, a sectional party has found within that article establishing the Executive Department, the means of subverting the Constitution itself. A geographical line has been drawn across the Union, and all the States north of that line have united in the election of a man to the high office of President of the United States whose opinions and purposes are hostile to Slavery. He is to be intrusted with the administration of the common Government, because he has declared that that "Government cannot endure permanently half slave, half free," and that the public mind must rest in the belief that Slavery is in the course of ultimate extinction.

This sectional combination for the subversion of the Constitution has been aided, in some of the States, by elevating to citizenship persons who, by the supreme law of the land, are incapable of becoming citizens; and their votes have been used to inaugurate a new policy, hostile to the South, and destructive of its peace and safety.

On the 4th of March next this party will take possession of the Government. It has announced that the South shall be excluded from the common territory, that the Judicial tribunal shall be made sectional, and that a war must be waged against Slavery until it shall cease throughout the United States.

The guarantees of the Constitution will then no longer exist; the equal rights of the States will be lost. The Slaveholding States will no longer have the power of self-government, or self-protection, and the Federal Government will have become their enemy.

Sectional interest and animosity will deepen the irritation; and all hope of remedy is rendered vain, by the fact that the public opinion at the North has invested a great political error with the sanctions of a more erroneous religious belief.

We, therefore, the people of South Carolina, by our delegates in Convention assembled, appealing to the Supreme Judge of the world for the rectitude of our intentions, have solemnly declared that the Union heretofore existing between this State and the other States of North America is dissolved, and that the State of South Carolina has resumed her position among the nations of the world, as separate and independent state, with full power to levy war, conclude peace, contract alliances, establish commerce, and to do all other acts and things which independent States may of right do.

CONSTITUTION OF THE CONFEDERATE STATES OF AMERICA

Montgomery, Alabama, March 11, 1861

Reprinted from Emory M. Thomas, *The Confederate Nation: 1861–1865.* New York, 1979, pp. 307–322.

We, the people of the Confederate States, each State acting in its sovereign and independent character, in order to form a permanent government, establish justice, insure domestic tranquillity, and secure the blessings of liberty to ourselves and our posterity—invoking the favor and guidance of Almighty God—do ordain and establish this Constitution for the Confederate States of America.

Art. I

SEC. 1.—All legislative powers herein delegated shall be vested in a Congress of the Confederate States, which shall consist of a Senate and House of Representatives.

SEC. 2. (1) The House of Representatives shall be . . . chosen every second year by the people of the several States; and the electors in each State shall be citizens of the Confederate States, and have the qualifications requisite for electors of the most numerous branch of the State Legislature; but no person of foreign birth, not a citizen of the Confederate States, shall be allowed to vote for any officer, civil or political, State or Federal.

(2) No person shall be a Representative who shall not have attained the age of twenty-five years, and be a citizen of the Confederate States, and who shall not, when selected, be an inhabitant of that State in which he shall be chosen.

(3) Representatives and direct taxes shall be apportioned among the several States which may be included within this Confederacy, according to their respective numbers, which shall be determined by adding to the whole number of free persons, including those bound to service for a term of years, and excluding Indians not taxed, three-fifths of all slaves. The actual enumeration shall be made within three years after the first meeting of the Congress of the Confederate States, and within every subsequent term of ten years, in such manner as they shall by law direct. The number of Representatives shall not exceed one for every fifty thousand, but each State shall have at least one Representative; and until such enumeration shall be made the State of South Carolina shall be entitled to choose six; the State of Georgia ten; the State of Alabama nine; the State of Florida two; the State of Mississippi seven; the State of Louisiana six; and the State of Texas six.

(4) When vacancies happen in the representation of any State, the Executive authority thereof shall issue writs of election to fill such vacancies.

(5) The House of Representatives shall choose their Speaker and other officers; and shall have the sole power of impeachment; except that any judicial or other federal officer resident and acting solely within the limits of any State, may be impeached by a vote of two-thirds of both branches of the Legislature thereof.

SEC. 3. (1) The Senate of the Confederate States shall be composed of two Senators from each State, chosen for six years by the Legislature thereof, at the regular session next immediately preceding the commencement of the term of service; and each Senator shall have one vote.

(2) Immediately after they shall be assembled, in consequence of the first election, they shall be divided as equally as may be into three classes. The seats of the Senators of the first class shall be vacated at the expiration of the second year; of the second class at the expiration of the fourth year; and of the third class at the expiration of the sixth year; so that one-third may be chosen every second year; and if vacancies happen by resignation or otherwise during the recess of the Legislature of any State, the Executive thereof may make temporary appointments until the next meeting of the Legislature, which shall then fill such vacancies.

(3) No person shall be a Senator, who shall not have attained the age of thirty years, and be a citizen of the Confederate States; and who shall not, when elected, be an inhabitant of the State for which he shall be chosen.

(4) The Vice-President of the Confederate States shall be President of the Senate, but shall have no vote, unless they be equally divided.

(5) The Senate shall choose their other officers, and also a President pro tempore in the absence of the Vice-President, or when he shall exercise the office of President of the Confederate States.

(6) The Senate shall have sole power to try all impeachments. When sitting for that purpose they shall be on oath or affirmation. When the President of the Confederate States is tried, the Chief Justice shall preside; and no person shall be convicted without the concurrence of two-thirds of the members present.

(7) Judgment in cases of impeachment shall not extend further than removal from office, and disqualification to hold and enjoy any office of honor, trust, or profit, under the Confederate States; but the party convicted shall, nevertheless, be liable and subject to indictment, trial, judgment, and punishment according to law.

SEC. 4. (1) The times, places, and manner of holding elections for Senators and Representatives, shall be prescribed in each State by the Legislature thereof, subject to the provisions of this Constitution; but the Congress may, at any time, by law, make or alter such regulations, except as to the times and places of choosing Senators.

(2) The Congress shall assemble at least once in every year; and such meeting shall be on the first Monday in December, unless they shall, by law, appoint a different day.

SEC. 5. (1) Each House shall be the judge of the elections, returns, and qualifications of its own members, and a majority of each shall constitute a quorum to do business; but a smaller number may adjourn from day to day, and may be authorized to compel the attendance of absent members, in such manner and under such penalties as each House may provide.

(2) Each House may determine the rules of its proceedings, punish its members for disorderly behavior, and, with the concurrence of two-thirds of the whole number, expel a member.

(3) Each House shall keep a journal of its proceedings, and from time to time publish the same, excepting such parts as may in their judgment require secrecy, and the ayes and nays of the members of either House, on any question, shall, at the desire of one-fifth of those present, be entered on the journal.

(4) Neither House, during the session of Congress, shall, without the consent of the other, adjourn for more than three days, nor to any other place than that in which the two Houses shall be sitting.

SEC. 6. (1) The Senators and Representatives shall receive a compensation for their services, to be ascertained by law, and paid out of the Treasury of the Confederate States. They shall, in all cases except treason and breach of the peace, be privileged from arrest during their attendance at the session of their respective Houses, and in going to and returning from the same; and for any speech or debate in either House, they shall not be questioned in any other place.

(2) No Senator or Representative shall, during the time for which he was elected, be appointed to any civil office under the authority of the Confederate States, which shall have been created, or the emoluments whereof shall have been increased during such time; and no person holding any office under the Confederate States shall be a member of either House during his continuance in office. But Congress may, by law, grant to the principal officer in each of the Executive Departments a seat upon the floor of either House, with the privilege of discussing any measure appertaining to his department.

SEC. 7. (1) All bills for raising revenue shall originate in the House of Representatives; but the Senate may propose or concur with amendments as on other bills.

(2) Every bill which shall have passed both Houses shall, before it becomes a law, be presented to the President of the Confederate States; if he approve he shall sign it; but if not, he shall return it with his objections to that House in which it shall have originated, who shall enter the objections at large on their journal, and proceed to reconsider it. If, after such reconsideration, two-thirds of that House shall agree to pass the bill, it shall be sent, together with the objections, to the other House, by which it shall likewise be reconsidered, and if approved by two-thirds of that House, it shall become a law. But in all such cases, the votes of both Houses shall be determined by yeas and nays, and the names of the persons voting for and against the bill shall be entered on the journal of each House respectively. If any bill shall not be returned by the President within ten days (Sundays excepted) after it shall have been presented to him, the same shall be a law,

in like manner as if he had signed it, unless the Congress, by their adjournment, prevent its return; in which case it shall not be a law. The President may approve any appropriation and disapprove any other appropriation in the same bill. In such case he shall, in signing the bill, designate the appropriations disapproved; and shall return a copy of such appropriations, with his objections, to the House in which the bill shall have originated; and the same proceedings shall then be had as in case of other bills disapproved by the President.

(3) Every order, resolution, or vote, to which the concurrence of both Houses may be necessary (except on a question of adjournment) shall be presented to the President of the Confederate States; and before the same shall take effect shall be approved by him; or being disapproved by him, shall be repassed by two-thirds of both Houses, according to the rules and limitations prescribed in case of a bill.

SEC. 8.—The Congress shall have power—(1) To lay and collect taxes, duties, imposts, and excises, for revenue necessary to pay the debts, provide for the common defence, and carry on the Government of the Confederate States; but no bounties shall be granted from the treasury; nor shall any duties or taxes on importations from foreign nations be laid to promote or foster any branch of industry; and all duties, imposts, and excises shall be uniform throughout the Confederate States.

(2) To borrow money on the credit of the Confederate States.

(3) To regulate commerce with foreign nations, and among the several States, and with the Indian tribes; but neither this nor any other clause contained in the Constitution shall be construed to delegate the power to Congress to appropriate money for any internal improvement intended to facilitate commerce; except for the purpose of furnishing lights, beacons, and buoys, and other aids to navigation upon the coasts, and the improvement of harbors, and the removing of obstructions in river navigation, in all which cases, such duties shall be laid on the navigation facilitated thereby, as may be necessary to pay the costs and expenses thereof.

(4) To establish uniform laws of naturalization, and uniform laws on the subject of bankruptcies throughout the Confederate States, but no law of Congress shall discharge any debt contracted before the passage of the same.

(5) To coin money, regulate the value thereof, and of foreign coin, and fix the standard of weights and measures.

(6) To provide for the punishment of counterfeiting the securities and current coin of the Confederate States.

(7) To establish post-offices and post-routes; but the expenses of the Post-office Department, after the first day of March, in the year of our Lord eighteen hundred and sixty-three, shall be paid out of its own revenues.

(8) To promote the progress of science and useful arts, by securing for limited times to authors and inventors the exclusive right to their respective writings and discoveries.

(9) To constitute tribunals inferior to the Supreme Court.

(10) To define and punish piracies and felonies committed on the high seas, and offences against the law of nations.

(11) To declare war, grant letters of marque and reprisal, and make rules concerning captures on land and water.

(12) To raise and support armies; but no appropriation of money to that use shall be for a longer term than two years.

(13) To provide and maintain a navy.

(14) To make rules for government and regulation of the land and naval forces.

(15) To provide for calling forth the militia to execute the laws of the Confederate States; suppress insurrections, and repel invasions.

(16) To provide for organizing, arming, and disciplining the militia, and for governing such part of them as may be employed in the service of the Confederate States; reserving to the States, respectively, the appointment of the officers, and the authority of training the militia according to the discipline prescribed by Congress.

(17) To exercise exclusive legislation, in all cases whatsoever, over such district (not exceeding ten miles square) as may, by cession of one or more States, and the acceptance of Congress, become the seat of the Government of the Confederate States; and to exercise a like authority over all places purchased by the consent of the Legislature of the State in which the same shall be, for the erection of forts, magazines, arsenals, dock-yards, and other needful buildings, and

(18) To make all laws which shall be necessary and proper for carrying into execution the foregoing powers, and all other powers vested by this Constitution in the Government of the Confederate States, or in any department or officer thereof.

SEC. 9. (1) The importation of negroes of the African race, from any foreign country, other than the slaveholding States or Territories of the United States of America, is hereby forbidden; and Congress is required to pass such laws as shall effectually prevent the same.

(2) Congress shall also have power to prohibit the introduction of slaves from any State not a member of, or Territory not belonging to, this Confederacy.

(3) The privilege of the writ of habeas corpus shall not be suspended, unless when in cases of rebellion or invasion the public safety may require it.

(4) No bill of attainder, ex post facto law, or law denying or impairing the right of property in negro slaves shall be passed.

(5) No capitation or other direct tax shall be laid unless in proportion to the census or enumeration hereinbefore directed to be taken.

(6) No tax or duty shall be laid on articles exported from any State, except by a vote of two-thirds of both Houses.

(7) No preference shall be given by any regulation of commerce or revenue to the ports of one State over those of another.

(8) No money shall be drawn from the treasury but in consequence of appropriations made by law; and a regular statement and account of the receipts and expenditures of all public money shall be published from time to time.

(9) Congress shall appropriate no money from the treasury except by a vote of two-thirds of both Houses, taken by yeas and nays, unless it be asked and estimated for by some one of the heads of departments, and submitted to Congress by the President; or for the purpose of paying its own expenses and contingencies; or for the payment of claims against the Confederate States, the justice of which shall have been judicially declared by a tribunal for the investigation of claims against the Government, which it is hereby made the duty of Congress to establish.

(10) All bills appropriating money shall specify in federal currency the exact amount of each appropriation and the purposes for which it is made; and Congress shall grant no extra compensation to any public contractor, officer, agent, or servant, after such contract shall have been made or such service rendered.

(11) No title of nobility shall be granted by the Confederate States; and no person holding any office of profit or trust under them shall, without the consent of the Congress, accept of any present, emolument, office, or title of any kind whatever, from any king, prince, or foreign state.

(12) Congress shall make no law respecting an establishment of religion, or prohibiting the free exercise thereof; or abridging the freedom of speech or of the press; or the right of the people peaceably to assemble and petition the Government for a redress of grievances.

(13) A well-regulated militia being necessary to the security of a free State, the right of the people to keep and bear arms shall not be infringed.

(14) No soldier shall, in time of peace, be quartered in any house without the consent of the owner; nor in time of war, but in a manner to be prescribed by law.

(15) The right of the people to be secure in their persons, houses, papers, and effects, against unreasonable searches and seizures, shall not be violated; and no warrant shall issue but upon probable cause, supported by oath or affirmation, and particularly describing the place to be searched, and the person or things to be seized.

(16) No person shall be held to answer for a capital or otherwise infamous crime, unless on a presentment or indictment of a grand jury, except in cases arising in the land or naval forces, or in the militia, when in actual service, in time of war, or public danger; nor shall any person be subject for the same offence to be twice put in jeopardy of life or limb; nor be compelled in any criminal case to be a witness against himself; nor be deprived of life, liberty, or property, without due process of law; nor shall private property be taken for public use without just compensation.

(17) In all criminal prosecutions the accused shall enjoy the right to a speedy and public trial, by an impartial jury of the State and district wherein the crime shall have been committed, which district shall have been previously ascertained by law, and to be informed of the nature and cause of the accusation; to be confronted with the witnesses against him; to have compulsory process for obtaining witnesses in his favor; and to have the assistance of counsel for his defence.

(18) In suits at common law, where the value in controversy shall exceed twenty dollars, the right of trial by jury shall be preserved; and no fact so tried by a jury shall be otherwise reexamined in any court of the Confederacy, than according to the rules of common law.

(19) Excessive bail shall not be required, nor excessive fines imposed, nor cruel and unusual punishment inflicted.

(20) Every law, or resolution having the force of law, shall relate to but one subject, and that be expressed in the title.

SEC. 10. (1) No State shall enter into any treaty, alliance, or confederation; grant letters of marque and reprisal; coin money; make any thing but gold and silver coin a tender in payment of debts; pass any bill of attainder, or ex post facto law, or law impairing the obligation of contracts; or grant any title of nobility.

(2) No State shall, without the consent of Congress, lay any imposts or duties on imports or exports, except what may be absolutely necessary for executing its inspection laws; and the net produce of all duties and imposts, laid by any State on imports or exports, shall be for the use of the Treasury of the Confederate States; and all such laws shall be subject to the revision and control of Congress.

(3) No State shall, without the consent of Congress, lay any duty on tonnage, except on sea-going vessels, for the improvement of its rivers and harbors navigated by the said vessels; but such duties shall not conflict with any treaties of the Confederate States with foreign nations; and any surplus revenue, thus derived, shall, after making such improvement, be paid into the common treasury; nor shall any State keep troops or ships of war in time of peace, enter into any agreement or compact with another State, or with a foreign power, or engage in war, unless actually invaded, or in such imminent danger as will not admit of delay. But when any river divides or flows through two or more States, they may enter into compacts with each other to improve the navigation thereof.

Art. II

SEC. 1. (1) The Executive power shall be vested in a President of the Confederate States of America. He and the Vice-President shall hold their offices for the term of six years; but the President shall not be reeligible. The President and Vice-President shall be elected as follows:

(2) Each State shall appoint, in such manner as the Legislature thereof may direct, a number of electors equal to the whole number of Senators and Representatives to which the State may be entitled in the Congress; but no Senator or Representative, or person holding an office of trust or profit under the Confederate States, shall be appointed an elector.

(3) The electors shall meet in their respective States and vote by ballot for President and Vice-President, one of whom, at least shall not be an inhabitant of the same State with themselves; they shall name in their ballots the person voted for as President, and in distinct ballots the person voted for as Vice-President, and they shall make distinct lists of all persons voted for as President, and of all persons voted for as Vice-President, and of the number of votes for each; which list they shall sign, and certify, and transmit, sealed, to the . . . government of the Confederate States, directed to the President of the Senate. The President of the Senate shall, in the presence of the Senate and House of Representatives, open all the certificates, and the votes shall then be counted; the person having the greatest number of votes for President shall be the President, if such number be a majority of the whole number of electors appointed; and if no person shall have such a majority, then, from the persons having the highest numbers, not exceeding three, on the list of those voted for as President, the House of Representatives shall choose immediately, by ballot, the President. But, in choosing the President, the votes shall be taken by States, the representation from each State having one vote; a quorum for this purpose shall consist of a member or members from two-thirds of the States, and a majority of all the States shall be necessary to a choice. And if the House of Representatives shall not choose a President, whenever the right of choice shall devolve upon them, before the fourth day of March next following, then the Vice-President shall act as President, as in case of the death, or other constitutional disability of the President.

(4) The person having the greatest number of votes as Vice-President shall be the Vice-President, if such number be a majority of the whole number of electors appointed; and if no person have a majority, then from the two highest numbers on the list, the Senate shall choose the Vice-President; a quorum for the purpose shall consist of two-thirds of the whole number of Senators, and a majority of the whole number shall be necessary for a choice.

(5) But no person constitutionally ineligible to the office of President shall be eligible to that of Vice-President of the Confederate States.

(6) The Congress may determine the time of choosing the electors, and the day on which they shall give their votes; which day shall be the same throughout the Confederate States.

(7) No person except a natural born citizen of the Confederate States, or a citizen thereof, at the time of the adoption of this Constitution, or a citizen thereof born in the United States prior to the 20th of December, 1860, shall be eligible to the office of President; neither shall any person be eligible to that office who shall not have attained the age of thirty-five years, and been fourteen years a resident within the limits of the Confederate States, as they may exist at the time of his election.

(8) In case of the removal of the President from office, or of his death, resignation, or inability to discharge the powers and duties of the said office, the same shall devolve on the Vice-President; and the Congress may, by law, provide for the case of the removal, death, resignation, or inability both of the President and the Vice-President, declaring what officer shall then act as President, and such officer shall then act accordingly until the disability be removed or a President shall be elected.

(9) The President shall, at stated times, receive for his services a compensation, which shall neither be increased nor diminished during the period for which he shall have been elected; and he shall not receive within that period any other emolument from the Confederate States, or any of them.

(10) Before he enters on the execution [of the duties] of his office, he shall take the following oath or affirmation:

"I do solemnly swear (or affirm) that I will faithfully execute the office of President of the Confederate States, and will, to the best of my ability, preserve, protect, and defend the Constitution thereof."

SEC. 2. (1) The President shall be commander-in-chief of the army and navy of the Confederate States, and of the militia of the several States, when called into the actual service of the Confederate States; he may require the opinion, in writing, of the principal officer in each of the Executive Departments, upon any subject relating to the duties of their respective offices; and he shall have power to grant reprieves and pardons for offences against the Confederate States, except in cases of impeachment.

(2) He shall have power, by and with the advice and consent of the Senate, to make treaties, provided two-thirds of the Senators present concur; and he shall nominate, and, by and with the advice and consent of the Senate, shall appoint ambassadors, other public ministers, and consuls, Judges of the Supreme Court, and all other officers of the Confederate States,

whose appointments are not herein otherwise provided for, and which shall be established by law; but the Congress may by law vest the appointment of such inferior officers, as they think proper, in the President alone, in the courts of law, or in the heads of departments.

(3) The principal officer in each of the Executive Departments, and all persons connected with the diplomatic service, may be removed from office at the pleasure of the President. All other civil officers of the Executive Departments may be removed at any time by the President, or other appointing power, when their services are unnecessary, or for dishonesty, incapacity, inefficiency, misconduct, or neglect of duty; and when so removed, the removal shall be reported to the Senate, together with the reasons therefor.

(4) The President shall have power to fill all vacancies that may happen during the recess of the Senate, by granting commissions which shall expire at the end of the next session; but no person rejected by the Senate shall be reappointed to the same office during their ensuing recess.

SEC. 3. (1) The President shall, from time to time, give to the Congress information of the state of the Confederacy, and recommend to their consideration such measures as he shall judge necessary and expedient; he may, on extraordinary occasions, convene both Houses, or either of them; and, in case of disagreement between them, with respect to the time of adjournment he may adjourn them to such time as he shall think proper; he shall receive ambassadors and other public ministers; he shall take care that the laws be faithfully executed, and shall commission all the officers of the Confederate States.

SEC. 4. (1) The President and Vice-President, and all Civil officers of the Confederate States, shall be removed from office on impeachment for, or conviction of, treason, bribery, or other high crimes and misdemeanors.

Art. III

SEC. 1. (1) The judicial power of the Confederate States shall be vested in one Supreme Court, and in such inferior courts as the Congress may from time to time ordain and establish. The judges, both of the Supreme and inferior courts, shall hold their offices during good behavior, and shall, at stated times, receive for their services a compensation, which shall not be diminished during their continuance in office. . . .

Art. IV

SEC. 1. (1) Full faith and credit shall be given in each State to the public acts, records, and judicial proceedings of every other State. And the Congress may, by general laws, prescribe the manner in which such acts, records, and proceedings shall be proved, and the effect thereof.

SEC. 2. (1) The citizens of each State shall be entitled to all the privileges and immunities of citizens of the several States, and shall have the right of transit and sojourn in any State of this Confederacy, with their slaves and other property; and the right of property in said slaves shall not be thereby impaired.

(2) A person charged in any State with treason, felony, or other crime against the laws of such State, who shall flee from justice, and be found in another State, shall, on demand of the executive authority of the State from which he fled, be delivered up to be removed to the State having jurisdiction of the crime.

(3) No slave or other person held to service or labor in any State or Territory of the Confederate States, under the laws thereof, escaping or [un]lawfully carried into another, shall, in consequence of any law or regulation therein, be discharged from such service or labor; but shall be delivered up on claim of the party to whom such slave belongs, or to whom such service or labor may be due.

SEC. 3. (1) Other States may be admitted into this Confederacy by a vote of two-thirds of the whole House of Representatives, and two-thirds of the Senate, the Senate voting by States; but no new State shall be formed or erected within the jurisdiction of any other State; nor any State be formed by the junction of two or more States, or parts of States, without the consent of the Legislatures of the States concerned as well as of the Congress.

(2) The Congress shall have power to dispose of and make all needful rules and regulations concerning the property of the Confederate States, including the lands thereof.

(3) The Confederate States may acquire new territory; and Congress shall have power to legislate and provide governments for the inhabitants of all territory belonging to the Confederate States, lying without the limits of the several States, and may permit them at such times, and in such manner as it may by law provide, to form States to be admitted into the Confederacy. In all such territory, the institution of negro slavery, as it now exists in the Confederate States, shall be recognized and protected by Congress and by the territorial government; and the inhabitants of the several Confederate States and Territories shall have the right to take to such territory any slaves lawfully held by them in any of the States or Territories of the Confederate States.

(4) The Confederate States shall guarantee to every State that now is or hereafter may become a member of this Confederacy, a Republican form of Government, and shall protect each of them against invasion; and on application of the Legislature, (or of the Executive when the Legislature is not in session,) against domestic violence.

Art. V

SEC. 1. (1) Upon the demand of any three States, legally assembled in their several Conventions, the Congress shall summon a Convention of all the States, to take into consideration such amendments to the Constitution as the said States shall concur in suggesting at the time when the said demand is made; and should any of the proposed amendments to the Constitution be agreed on by the said Convention—voting by States—and the same be ratified by the Legislatures of two-thirds thereof—as the one or the other mode of ratification may be proposed by the general convention—they shall thenceforward form a part of this Constitution. But no State shall, without its consent, be deprived of its equal representation in the Senate.

Art. VI

1.—The Government established by this Constitution is the successor of the Provisional Government of the Confederate States of America, and all the laws passed by the latter shall continue in force until the same shall be repealed or modified; and all the officers appointed by the same shall remain in office until their successors are appointed and qualified, or the offices abolished.

2. All debts contracted and engagements entered into before the adoption of this Constitution, shall be as valid against the Confederate States under this Constitution as under the Provisional Government.

3. This Constitution, and the laws of the Confederate States, made in pursuance thereof, and all treaties made, or which shall be made, under the authority of the Confederate States, shall be the supreme law of the land; and the judges in every State shall be bound thereby, any thing in the Constitution or laws of any State to the contrary notwithstanding.

4. The Senators and Representatives before mentioned, and the members of the several State Legislatures, and all executive and judicial officers, both of the Confederate States and of the several States, shall be bound, by oath or affirmation, to support this Constitution; but no religious test shall ever be required as a qualification to any office or public trust under the Confederate States.

5. The enumeration, in the Constitution, of certain rights, shall not be construed to deny or disparage others retained by the people of the several States.

6. The powers not delegated to the Confederate States by the Constitution, nor prohibited by it to the States, are reserved to the States, respectively, or to the people thereof.

Art. VII

1.—The ratification of the conventions of five States shall be sufficient for the establishment of this Constitution between the States so ratifying the same.

2. When five States shall have ratified this Constitution in the manner before specified, the Congress, under the provisional Constitution, shall

prescribe the time for holding the election of President and Vice-President, and for the meeting of the electoral college, and for counting the votes and inaugurating the President. They shall also prescribe the time for holding the first election of members of Congress under this Constitution, and the time for assembling the same. Until the assembling of such Congress, the Congress under the provisional Constitution shall continue to exercise the legislative powers granted them; not extending beyond the time limited by the Constitution of the Provisional Government.

Adopted unanimously by the Congress of the Confederate States of South Carolina, Georgia, Florida, Alabama, Mississippi, Louisiana, and Texas, sitting in convention at the capitol, in the city of Montgomery, Alabama, on the Eleventh day of March, in the year Eighteen Hundred and Sixty-One.

HOWELL COBB
President of the Congress
(Signatures)

CORNERSTONE SPEECH

Savannah, Georgia, March 21, 1861

The Cornerstone Speech was delivered extemporaneously by Vice President Alexander H. Stephens, and no official printed version exists. The text below was taken from a newspaper article in the *Savannah Republican*, as reprinted in Henry Cleveland, *Alexander H. Stephens, in Public and Private With Letters and Speeches, before, during, and since the War*, Philadelphia, 1886, pp. 717–729.

At half past seven o'clock on Thursday evening, the largest audience ever assembled at the Athenæum was in the house, waiting most impatiently for the appearance of the orator of the evening, Hon. A. H. Stephens, Vice-President of the Confederate States of America. The committee, with invited guests, were seated on the stage, when, at the appointed hour, the Hon. C. C. Jones, Mayor, and the speaker, entered, and were greeted by the immense assemblage with deafening rounds of applause.

The Mayor then, in a few pertinent remarks, introduced Mr. Stephens, stating that at the request of a number of the members of the convention, and citizens of Savannah and the State, now here, he had consented to address them upon the present state of public affairs.

MR. STEPHENS rose and spoke as follows:

Mr. Mayor, and Gentlemen of the Committee, and Fellow-Citizens:— For this reception you will please accept my most profound and sincere thanks. The compliment is doubtless intended as much, or more, perhaps, in honor of the occasion, and my public position, in connection with the great events now crowding upon us, than to me personally and individually. It is however none the less appreciated by me on that account. We are in the midst of one of the greatest epochs in our history. The last ninety days will mark one of the most memorable eras in the history of modern civilization.

[There was a general call from the outside of the building for the speaker to go out, that there were more outside than in.]

The Mayor rose and requested silence at the doors, that Mr. Stephens' health would not permit him to speak in the open air.

MR. STEPHENS said he would leave it to the audience whether he should proceed indoors or out. There was a general cry indoors, as the ladies, a large number of whom were present, could not hear outside.

MR. STEPHENS said that the accommodation of the ladies would determine the question, and he would proceed where he was.

[At this point the uproar and clamor outside was greater still for the speaker to go out on the steps. This was quieted by Col. Lawton, Col. Freeman, Judge Jackson, and Mr. J. W. Owens going out and stating the facts of the case to the dense mass of men, women, and children who were outside,

and entertaining them in brief speeches—Mr. Stephens all this while quietly sitting down until the furor subsided.]

MR. STEPHENS rose and said: When perfect quiet is restored, I shall proceed. I cannot speak so long as there is any noise or confusion. I shall take my time—I feel quite prepared to spend the night with you if necessary. [Loud applause.] I very much regret that every one who desires cannot hear what I have to say. Not that I have any display to make, or any thing very entertaining to present, but such views as I have to give, I wish *all*, not only in this city, but in this State, and throughout our Confederate Republic, could hear, who have a desire to hear them.

I was remarking, that we are passing through one of the greatest revolutions in the annals of the world. Seven States have within the last three months thrown off an old government and formed a new. This revolution has been signally marked, up to this time, by the fact of its having been accomplished without the loss of a single drop of blood. [Applause.]

This new constitution, or form of government, constitutes the subject to which your attention will be partly invited. In reference to it, I make this first general remark. It amply secures all our ancient rights, franchises, and liberties. All the great principles of Magna Charta are retained in it. No citizen is deprived of life, liberty, or property, but by the judgment of his peers under the laws of the land. The great principle of religious liberty, which was the honor and pride of the old constitution, is still maintained and secured. All the essentials of the old constitution, which have endeared it to the hearts of the American people, have been preserved and perpetuated. [Applause.] Some changes have been made. Of these I shall speak presently. Some of these I should have preferred not to have seen made; but these, perhaps, meet the cordial approbation of a majority of this audience, if not an overwhelming majority of the people of the Confederacy. Of them, therefore, I will not speak. But other important changes do meet my cordial approbation. They form great improvements upon the old constitution. So, taking the whole new constitution, I have no hesitancy in giving it as my judgment that it is decidedly better than the old. [Applause.]

Allow me briefly to allude to some of these improvements. The question of building up class interests, or fostering one branch of industry to the prejudice of another under the exercise of the revenue power, which gave us so much trouble under the old constitution, is put at rest forever under the new. We allow the imposition of no duty with a view of giving advantage to one class of persons, in any trade or business, over those of another. All, under our system, stand upon the same broad principles of perfect equality. Honest labor and enterprise are left free and unrestricted in whatever pursuit they may be engaged. This subject came well nigh causing a rupture of the old Union, under the lead of the gallant Palmetto State, which lies on our border, in 1833. This old thorn of the tariff, which was the cause of so much irritation in the old body politic, is removed forever from the new. [Applause.]

Again, the subject of internal improvements, under the power of Congress to regulate commerce, is put at rest under our system. The power claimed by construction under the old constitution, was at least a doubtful one—it rested solely upon construction. We of the South, generally apart from considerations of constitutional principles, opposed its exercise upon grounds of its inexpediency and injustice. Notwithstanding this opposition, millions of money, from the common treasury had been drawn for such purposes. Our opposition sprang from no hostility to commerce, or all necessary aids for facilitating it. With us it was simply a question, upon *whom* the burden should fall. In Georgia, for instance, we have done as much for the cause of internal improvements as any other portion of the country according to population and means. We have stretched out lines of railroads from the seaboard to the mountains; dug down the hills, and filled up the valleys at a cost of not less than twenty-five millions of dollars. All this was done to open an outlet for our products of the interior, and those to the west of us, to reach the marts of the world. No State was in greater need of such facilities than Georgia, but we did not ask that these works should be made by appropriations out of the common treasury. The cost of the grad-

697

ing, the superstructure, and equipments of our roads, was borne by those who entered on the enterprise. Nay, more—not only the cost of the iron, no small item in the aggregate cost, was borne in the same way—but we were compelled to pay into the common treasury several millions of dollars for the privilege of importing the iron, after the price was paid for it abroad. What justice was there in taking this money, which our people paid into the common treasury on the importation of our iron, and applying it to the improvement of rivers and harbors elsewhere?

The true principle is to subject the commerce of every locality, to whatever burdens may be necessary to facilitate it. If Charleston harbor needs improvement, let the commerce of Charleston bear the burden. If the mouth of the Savannah river has to be cleared out, let the sea-going navigation which is benefitted by it, bear the burden. So with the mouths of the Alabama and Mississippi river. Just as the products of the interior, our cotton, wheat, corn, and other articles, have to bear the necessary rates of freight over our railroads to reach the seas. This is again the broad principle of perfect equality and justice. [Applause.] And it is especially set forth and established in our new constitution.

Another feature to which I will allude, is that the new constitution provides that cabinet ministers and heads of departments may have the privilege of seats upon the floor of the Senate and House of Representatives—may have the right to participate in the debates and discussions upon the various subjects of administration. I should have preferred that this provision should have gone further, and required the President to select his constitutional advisers from the Senate and House of Representatives. That would have conformed entirely to the practice in the British Parliament, which, in my judgment, is one of the wisest provisions in the British constitution. It is the only feature that saves that government. It is that which gives it stability in its facility to change its administration. Ours, as it is, is a great approximation to the right principle.

Under the old constitution, a secretary of the treasury for instance, had no opportunity, save by his annual reports, of presenting any scheme or plan of finance or other matter. He had no opportunity of explaining, expounding, inforcing, or defending his views of policy; his only resort was through the medium of an organ. In the British parliament, the premier brings in his budget and stands before the nation responsible for its every item. If it is indefensible, he falls before the attacks upon it, as he ought to. This will now be the case to a limited extent under our system. In the new constitution, provision has been made by which our heads of departments can speak for themselves and the administration, in behalf of its entire policy, without resorting to the indirect and highly objectionable medium of a newspaper. It is to be greatly hoped that under our system we shall never have what is known as a government organ. [Rapturous applause.]

[A noise again arose from the clamor of the crowd outside, who wished to hear Mr. Stephens, and for some moments interrupted him. The mayor rose and called on the police to preserve order. Quiet being restored, Mr. S. proceeded.]

Another change in the constitution relates to the length of the tenure of the presidential office. In the new constitution it is six years instead of four, and the President rendered ineligible for a re-election. This is certainly a decidedly conservative change. It will remove from the incumbent all temptation to use his office or exert the powers confided to him for any objects of personal ambition. The only incentive to that higher ambition which should move and actuate one holding such high trusts in his hands, will be the good of the people, the advancement, prosperity, happiness, safety, honor, and true glory of the confederacy. [Applause.]

But not to be tedious in enumerating the numerous changes for the better, allow me to allude to one other—though last, not least. The new constitution has put at rest, *forever*, all the agitating questions relating to our peculiar institution—African slavery as it exists amongst us—the proper *status* of the negro in our form of civilization. This was the immediate cause of the late rupture and present revolution. Jefferson in his forecast, had anticipated this, as the "rock upon which the old Union would split." He was right. What was conjecture with him, is now a realized fact. But whether he fully comprehended the great truth upon which that rock *stood* and *stands*, may be doubted. The prevailing ideas entertained by him and most of the leading statesmen at the time of the formation of the old constitution, were that the enslavement of the African was in violation of the laws of nature; that it was wrong in *principle*, socially, morally, and politically. It was an evil they knew not well how to deal with, but the general opinion of the men of that day was that, somehow or other in the order of Providence, the institution would be evanescent and pass away. This idea, though not incorporated in the constitution, was the prevailing idea at that time. The constitution, it is true, secured every essential guarantee to the institution while it should last, and hence no argument can be justly urged against the constitutional guarantees thus secured, because of the common sentiment of the day. Those ideas, however, were fundamentally wrong. They rested upon the assumption of the equality of races. This was an error. It was a sandy foundation, and the government built upon it fell when the "storm came and the wind blew."

Our new government is founded upon exactly the opposite idea; its foundations are laid, its corner-stone rests upon the great truth, that the negro is not equal to the white man; that slavery—subordination to the superior race—is his natural and normal condition. [Applause.]

This, our new government, is the first, in the history of the world, based upon this great physical, philosophical, and moral truth. This truth has been slow in the process of its development, like all other truths in the various departments of science. It has been so even amongst us. Many who hear me, perhaps, can recollect well, that this truth was not generally admitted, even within their day. The errors of the past generation still clung to many as late as twenty years ago. Those at the North, who still cling to these errors, with a zeal above knowledge, we justly denominate fanatics. All fanaticism springs from an aberration of the mind—from a defect in reasoning. It is a species of insanity. One of the most striking characteristics of insanity, in many instances, is forming correct conclusions from fancied or erroneous premises; so with the anti-slavery fanatics; their conclusions are right if their premises were. They assume that the negro is equal, and hence conclude that he is entitled to equal privileges and rights with the white man. If their premises were correct, their conclusions would be logical and just—but their premise being wrong, their whole argument fails. I recollect once of having heard a gentleman from one of the northern States, of great power and ability, announce in the House of Representatives, with imposing effect, that we of the South would be compelled, ultimately, to yield upon this subject of slavery, that it was as impossible to war successfully against a principle in politics, as it was in physics or mechanics. That the principle would ultimately prevail. That we, in maintaining slavery as it exists with us, were warring against a principle, a principle founded in nature, the principle of the equality of men. The reply I made to him was, that upon his own grounds, we should, ultimately, succeed, and that he and his associates, in this crusade against our institutions, would ultimately fail. The truth announced, that it was as impossible to war successfully against a principle in politics as it was in physics and mechanics, I admitted; but told him that it was he, and those acting with him, who were warring against a principle. They were attempting to make things equal which the Creator had made unequal.

In the conflict thus far, success has been on our side, complete throughout the length and breadth of the Confederate States. It is upon this, as I have stated, our social fabric is firmly planted; and I cannot permit myself to doubt the ultimate success of a full recognition of this principle throughout the civilized and enlightened world.

As I have stated, the truth of this principle may be slow in development, as an truths are and ever have been, in the various branches of science. It was so with the principles announced by Galileo—it was so with Adam Smith and his principles of political economy. It was so with Harvey, and his theory of the circulation of the blood. It is stated that not a single one of the medical profession, living at the time of the announcement of the truths made by him, admitted them. Now, they are universally acknowledged. May we not, therefore, look with confidence to the ultimate universal acknowledgment of the truths upon which our system rests? It is the first government ever instituted upon the principles in strict conformity to nature, and the ordination of Providence, in furnishing the materials of human society. Many governments have been founded upon the principle of the subordination and serfdom of certain classes of the same race; such were and are in violation of the laws of nature. Our system commits no such violation of nature's laws. With us, all of the white race, however high or low, rich or poor, are equal in the eye of the law. Not so with the negro. Subordination is his place. He, by nature, or by the curse against Canaan, is fitted for that condition which he occupies in our system. The architect, in the construction of buildings, lays the foundation with the proper material—the granite; then comes the brick or the marble. The substratum of our society is made of the material fitted by nature for it, and by experience we know that it is best, not only for the superior, but for the inferior race, that it should be so. It is, indeed, in conformity with the ordinance of the Creator. It is not for us to inquire into the wisdom of his ordinances, or to question them. For his own purposes, he has made one race to differ from another, as he has made "one star to differ from another star in glory."

The great objects of humanity are best attained when there is conformity to his laws and decrees, in the formation of governments as well as in all things else. Our confederacy is founded upon principles in strict conformity with these laws. This stone which was rejected by the first builders "is become the chief of the corner"—the real "corner-stone"—in our new edifice. [Applause.]

I have been asked, what of the future? It has been apprehended by some that we would have arrayed against us the civilized world. I care not who or how many they may be against us, when we stand upon the eternal principles of truth, *if we are true to ourselves and the principles for which we contend*, we are obliged to, and must triumph. [Immense applause.]

Thousands of people who begin to understand these truths are not yet completely out of the shell; they do not see them in their length and breadth. We hear much of the civilization and christianization of the barbarous tribes of Africa. In my judgment, those ends will never be attained, but by first teaching them the lesson taught to Adam, that "in the sweat of his brow he should eat his bread," [applause,] and teaching them to work, and feed, and clothe themselves.

But to pass on: Some have propounded the inquiry whether it is practicable for us to go on with the confederacy without further accessions? Have we the means and ability to maintain nationality among the powers of the earth? On this point I would barely say, that as anxiously as we all have been, and are, for the border States, with institutions similar to ours, to join us, still we are abundantly able to maintain our position, even if they should ultimately make up their minds not to cast their destiny with us. That they ultimately will join us—be compelled to do it—is my confident belief; but we can get on very well without them, even if they should not.

We have all the essential elements of a high national career. The idea has been given out at the North, and even in the border States, that we are too small and too weak to maintain a separate nationality. This is a great mistake. In extent of territory we embrace five hundred and sixty-four thousand square miles and upward. This is upward of two hundred thousand square miles more than was included within the limits of the original thirteen States. It is an area of country more than double the territory of France or the Austrian empire. France, in round numbers, has but two hundred and twelve thousand square miles. Austria, in round numbers, has two hundred and forty-eight thousand square miles. Ours is greater than both combined. It is greater than all France, Spain, Portugal, and Great Britain, including England, Ireland, and Scotland, together. In population we have upward of five millions, according to the census of 1860; this includes white and black. The entire population, including white and black, of the original thirteen States, was less than four millions in 1790, and still less in '76, when the independence of our fathers was achieved. If they, with a less population, dared maintain their independence against the greatest power on earth, shall we have any apprehension of maintaining ours now?

In point of material wealth and resources, we are greatly in advance of them. The taxable property of the Confederate States cannot be less than twenty-two hundred millions of dollars! This, I think I venture but little in saying, may be considered as five times more than the colonies possessed at the time they achieved their independence. Georgia, alone, possessed last year, according to the report of our comptroller-general, six hundred and seventy-two millions of taxable property. The debts of the seven confederate States sum up in the aggregate less than eighteen millions, while the existing debts of the other of the late United States sum up in the aggregate the enormous amount of one hundred and seventy-four millions of dollars. This is without taking into account the heavy city debts, corporation debts, and railroad debts, which press, and will continue to press, as a heavy incubus upon the resources of those States. These debts, added to others, make a sum total not much under five hundred millions of dollars. With such an area of territory as we have—with such an amount of population—with a climate and soil unsurpassed by any on the face of the earth—with such resources already at our command—with productions which control the commerce of the world—who can entertain any apprehensions as to our ability to succeed, whether others join us or not?

It is true, I believe I state but the common sentiment, when I declare my earnest desire that the border States should join us. The differences of opinion that existed among us anterior to secession, related more to the policy in securing that result by co-operation than from any difference upon the ultimate security we all looked to in common.

These differences of opinion were more in reference to policy than principle, and as Mr. Jefferson said in his inaugural, in 1801, after the heated contest preceding his election, there might be differences of opinion without differences on principle, and that all, to some extent, had been federalists and all republicans; so it may now be said of us, that whatever differences of opinion as to the best policy in having a co-operation with our border sister slave States, if the worst came to the worst, that as we were all co-operationists, we are now all for independence, whether they come or not. [Continued applause.]

In this connection I take this occasion to state, that I was not without grave and serious apprehensions, that if the worst came to the worst, and cutting loose from the old government should be the only remedy for our safety and security, it would be attended with much more serious ills than it has been as yet. Thus far we have seen none of those incidents which usually attend revolutions. No such material as such convulsions usually throw up has been seen. Wisdom, prudence, and patriotism, have marked every step of our progress thus far. This augurs well for the future, and it is a matter of sincere gratification to me, that I am enabled to make the declaration. Of the men I met in the Congress at Montgomery, I may be pardoned for saying this, an abler, wiser, a more conservative, deliberate, determined, resolute, and patriotic body of men, I never met in my life. [Great applause.] Their works speak for them; the provisional government speaks for them; the constitution of the permanent government will be a lasting monument of their worth, merit, and statesmanship. [Applause.]

But to return to the question of the future. What is to be the result of this revolution?

Will every thing, commenced so well, continue as it has begun? In reply to this anxious inquiry, I can only say it all depends upon ourselves. A young man starting out in life on his majority, with health, talent, and ability, under a favoring Providence, may be said to be the architect of his own fortunes. His destinies are in his own hands. He may make for himself a name, of honor or dishonor, according to his own acts. If he plants himself upon truth, integrity, honor and uprightness, with industry, patience and energy, he cannot fail of success. So it is with us. We are a young republic, just entering upon the arena of nations; we will be the architects of our own fortunes. Our destiny, under Providence, is in our own hands. With wisdom, prudence, and statesmanship on the part of our public men, and intelligence, virtue and patriotism on the part of the people, success, to the full measures of our most sanguine hopes, may be looked for. But if unwise counsels prevail—if we become divided—if schisms arise—if dissensions spring up—if factions are engendered—if party spirit, nourished by unholy personal ambition shall rear its hydra head, I have no good to prophesy for you. Without intelligence, virtue, integrity, and patriotism on the part of the people, no republic or representative government can be durable or stable.

We have intelligence, and virtue, and patriotism. All that is required is to cultivate and perpetuate these. Intelligence will not do without virtue. France was a nation of philosophers. These philosophers become Jacobins. They lacked that virtue, that devotion to moral principle, and that patriotism which is essential to good government. Organized upon principles of perfect justice and right—seeking amity and friendship with all other powers—I see no obstacle in the way of our upward and onward progress. Our growth, by accessions from other States, will depend greatly upon whether we present to the world, as I trust we shall, a better government than that to which neighboring States belong. If we do this, North Carolina, Tennessee, and Arkansas cannot hesitate long; neither can Virginia, Kentucky, and Missouri. They will necessarily gravitate to us by an imperious law. We made ample provision in our constitution for the admission of other States; it is more guarded, and wisely so, I think, than the old constitution on the same subject, but not too guarded to receive them as fast as it may be proper. Looking to the distant future, and, perhaps, not very far distant either, it is not beyond the range of possibility, and even probability, that all the great States of the north-west will gravitate this way, as well as Tennessee, Kentucky, Missouri, Arkansas, etc. Should they do so, our doors are wide enough to receive them, but not until they are ready to assimilate with us in principle.

The process of disintegration in the old Union may be expected to go on with almost absolute certainty if we pursue the right course. We are now the nucleus of a growing power which, if we are true to ourselves, our destiny, and high mission, will become the controlling power on this continent. To what extent accessions will go on in the process of time, or where it will end, the future will determine. So far as it concerns States of the old Union, this process will be upon no such principles of *reconstruction* as now spoken of, but upon *reorganization* and new assimilation. [Loud applause.] Such are some of the glimpses of the future as I catch them.

But at first we must necessarily meet with the inconveniences and difficulties and embarrassments incident to all changes of government. These will be felt in our postal affairs and changes in the channel of trade. These inconveniences, it is to be hoped, will be but temporary, and must be borne with patience and forbearance.

As to whether we shall have war with our late confederates, or whether all matters of differences between us shall be amicably settled, I can only say that the prospect for a peaceful adjustment is better, so far as I am informed, than it has been.

The prospect of war is, at least, not so threatening as it has been. The idea of coercion, shadowed forth in President Lincoln's inaugural, seems not to be followed up thus far so vigorously as was expected. Fort Sumter, it is believed, will soon be evacuated. What course will be pursued toward Fort Pickens, and the other forts on the gulf, is not so well understood. It is to be greatly desired that all of them should be surrendered. Our object is *peace*, not only with the North, but with the world. All matters relating to the public property, public liabilities of the Union when we were members of it, we are ready and willing to adjust and settle upon the principles of right, equity, and good faith. War can be of no more benefit to the North than to us. Whether the intention of evacuating Fort Sumter is to be received as an evidence of a desire for a peaceful solution of our difficulties with the United States, or the result of necessity, I will not undertake to say. I would fain hope the former. Rumors are afloat, however, that it is the result of necessity. All I can say to you, therefore, on that point is, keep your armor bright and your powder dry. [Enthusiastic cheering.]

The surest way to secure peace, is to show your ability to maintain your rights. The principles and position of the present administration of the United States—the republican party—present some puzzling questions. While it is a fixed principle with them never to allow the increase of a foot of slave territory, they seem to be equally determined not to part with an inch "of the accursed soil." Notwithstanding their clamor against the institution, they seemed to be equally opposed to getting more, or letting go what they have got. They were ready to fight on the accession of Texas, and are equally ready to fight now on her secession. Why is this? How can this strange paradox be accounted for? There seems to be but one rational solution—and that is, notwithstanding their professions of humanity, they are disinclined to give up the benefits they derive from slave labor. Their philanthropy yields to their interest. The idea of enforcing the laws, has but one object, and that is a collection of the taxes, raised by slave labor to swell the fund, necessary to meet their heavy appropriations. The spoils is what they are after—though they come from the labor of the slave. [Continued applause.]

Mr. Stephens reviewed at some length, the extravagance and profligacy of appropriations by the Congress of the United States for several years past, and in this connection took occasion to allude to another one of the great improvements in our new constitution, which is a clause prohibiting Congress from appropriating any money from the treasury, except by a two-third vote, unless it be for some object which the executive may say is necessary to carry on the government.

When it is thus asked for, and estimated for, he continued, the majority may appropriate. This was a new feature.

Our fathers had guarded the assessment of taxes by insisting that representation and taxation should go together. This was inherited from the mother country, England. It was one of the principles upon which the revolution had been fought. Our fathers also provided in the old constitution, that all appropriation bills should originate in the representative branch of Congress, but our new constitution went a step further, and guarded not only the pockets of the people, but also the public money, after it was taken from their pockets.

He alluded to the difficulties and embarrassments which seemed to surround the question of a peaceful solution of the controversy with the old government. How can it be done? is perplexing many minds. The President seems to think that he cannot recognize our independence, nor can he, with and by the advice of the Senate, do so. The constitution makes no such provision. A general convention of all the States has been suggested by some.

Without proposing to solve the difficulty, he barely made the following suggestion:

"That as the admission of States by Congress under the constitution was an act of legislation, and in the nature of a contract or compact between the States admitted and the others admitting, why should not this contract or compact be regarded as of like character with all other civil contracts—liable to be rescinded by mutual agreement of both parties? The seceding States have rescinded it on their part, they have resumed their sovereignty. Why cannot the whole question be settled, if the north desire peace, simply by the Congress, in both branches, with the concurrence of the President, giving their consent to the separation, and a recognition of our independence?" This he merely offered as a suggestion, as one of the ways in which it might be done with much less violence by constructions to the constitution than many other acts of that government. [Applause.] The difficulty has to be solved in some way or other—this may be regarded as a fixed fact.

Several other points were alluded to by Mr. Stephens, particularly as to the policy of the new government toward foreign nations, and our commercial relations with them. Free trade, as far as practicable, would be the policy of this government. No higher duties would be imposed on foreign importations than would be necessary to support the government upon the strictest economy.

In olden times the olive branch was considered the emblem of peace; we will send to the nations of the earth another and far more potential emblem of the same, the cotton plant. The present duties were levied with a view of meeting the present necessities and exigencies, in preparation for war, if need be; but if we have peace, and he hoped we might, and trade should resume its proper course, a duty of ten per cent. upon foreign importations it was thought might be sufficient to meet the expenditures of the government. If some articles should be left on the free list, as they now are, such as breadstuffs, etc., then, of course, duties upon others would have to be higher—but in no event to an extent to embarrass trade and commerce. He concluded in an earnest appeal for union and harmony, on part of all the people in support of the common cause, in which we were all enlisted, and upon the issues of which such great consequences depend.

If, said he, we are true to ourselves, true to our cause, true to our destiny, true to our high mission, in presenting to the world the highest type of civilization ever exhibited by man—there will be found in our lexicon no such word as fail.

Mr. Stephens took his seat, amid a burst of enthusiasm and applause, such as the Athenæum has never had displayed within its walls, within "the recollection of the oldest inhabitant."

[REPORTER'S NOTE.—Your reporter begs to state that the above is not a perfect report, but only such a sketch of the address of Mr. Stephens as embraces, in his judgment, the most important points presented by the orator.—G.J]

PAROLE OF ROBERT E. LEE AND STAFF

Appomattox, Virginia, April 9, 1865

Reprinted from U.S. War Department, *War of the Rebellion: A Compilation of the Official Records of the Union and Confederate Armies*, Washington, D.C., 1880–1901, ser. 1, vol. 46, pt. 2, p. 667.

We, the undersigned prisoners of war belonging to the Army of Northern Virginia, having been this day surrendered by General Robert E. Lee, C. S. Army, commanding said army, to Lieut. Gen. U. S. Grant, commanding Armies of the United States, do hereby give our solemn parole of honor that we will not hereafter serve in the armies of the Confederate States, or in any military capacity whatever, against the United States of America, or render aid to the enemies of the latter, until properly exchanged, in such manner as shall be mutually approved by the respective authorities.

Done at Appomattox Court-House, Va., this 9th day of April, 1865.
R. E. LEE,
General.
W. H. TAYLOR,
Lieutenant-Colonel and Assistant Adjutant-General.
CHARLES S. VENABLE,
Lieutenant-Colonel and Assistant Adjutant-General.
CHARLES MARSHALL,
Lieutenant-Colonel and Assistant Adjutant-General.
H. E. PEYTON,
Lieutenant-Colonel, Adjutant and Inspector General.
GILES B. COOKE,
Major and Assistant Adjutant and Inspector General.
H. E. YOUNG,
Major, Assistant Adjutant-General, and Judge-Advocate-General.
[Indorsement.]

The within named officers will not be disturbed by the United States authorities so long as they observe their parole and the laws in force where they may reside.
GEORGE H. SHARPE,
Assistant Provost-Marshal-General.

PAROLE OF JOSEPH E. JOHNSTON AND TROOPS

Durham Station, North Carolina, April 26, 1865

Reprinted from U.S. War Department, *War of the Rebellion: A Compilation of the Official Records of the Union and Confederate Armies*, Washington, D.C., 1880–1901, ser. 1, vol. 47, pt. 2, p. 313.

Terms of a military convention entered into this 26th day of April,

1865, at Bennett's house, near Durham's Station, N. C., between General Joseph E. Johnston, commanding the Confederate Army, and Maj. Gen. W. T. Sherman, commanding the United States Army in North Carolina.

1. All acts of war on the part of the troops under General Johnston's command to cease from this date.

2. All arms and public property to be deposited at Greensborough, and delivered to an ordnance officer of the United States Army.

3. Rolls of all the officers and men to be made in duplicate, one copy to be retained by the commander of the troops, and the other to be given to an officer to be designated by General Sherman, each officer and man to give his individual obligation in writing not to take up arms against the Government of the United States until properly released from this obligation.

4. The side-arms of officers and their private horses and baggage to be retained by them.

5. This being done, all the officers and men will be permitted to return to their homes, not to be disturbed by the United States authorities so long as they observe their obligation and the laws in force where they may reside.
W. T. SHERMAN,
Major-General, Commanding U. S. Forces in North Carolina.
J. E. JOHNSTON,
General, Commanding C. S. Forces in North Carolina.
RALEIGH, N. C., APRIL 26, 1865.
Approved:
U. S. GRANT,
Lieutenant-General.

PAROLE OF RICHARD TAYLOR AND TROOPS

Citronelle, Alabama, May 4, 1865 (accepted May 8, 1865)

Reprinted from U.S. War Department, *War of the Rebellion: A Compilation of the Official Records of the Union and Confederate Armies*, Washington, D.C., 1880–1901, ser. 1, vol. 47, pt. 2, p. 609.

Memorandum of the conditions of the surrender of the forces, munitions of war, &c., in the Department of Alabama, Mississippi, and East Louisiana, commanded by Lieut. Gen. Richard Taylor, C. S. Army, to Maj. Gen. Edward R. S. Canby, U. S. Army, entered into on this 4th day of May, 1865, at Citronelle, Ala.

I. The officers and men to be paroled until duly exchanged, or otherwise released from the obligations of their parole by the authority of the Government of the United States. Duplicate rolls of all officers and men surrendered to be made, one copy of which will be delivered to the officer appointed by Major-General Canby and the other retained by the officer appointed by Lieutenant-General Taylor; officers giving their individual paroles and commanders of regiments, batteries, companies, or detachments signing a like parole for the men of their respective commands.

II. Artillery, small-arms, ammunition, and all other property of the Confederate Government to be turned over to the officers appointed for that purpose on the part of the Government of the United States. Duplicate inventories of the property surrendered to be prepared, one copy to be retained by the officer delivering and the other by the officer receiving it, for the information of their respective commanders.

III. The officers and men paroled under this agreement will be allowed to return to their homes, with the assurance that they will not be disturbed by the authorities of the United States so long as they continue to observe the conditions of their paroles and the laws in force where they reside, except that persons residents of Northern States will not be allowed to return without permission.

IV. The surrender of property will not include the side arms or private horses or baggage of officers.

V. All horses which are, in good faith, the private property of enlisted men will not be taken from them; the men will be permitted to take such with them to their homes, to be used for private purposes only.

VI. The time and place of surrender will be fixed by the respective commanders, and will be carried out by the commissioners appointed by them.

VII. The terms and conditions of the surrender to apply to officers and men belonging to the armies lately commanded by Generals Lee and Johnston, now in this department.

VIII. Transportation and subsistence to be furnished at public cost for the officers and men after surrender to the nearest practicable point to their homes.

R. TAYLOR,
Lieutenant-General.
ED. R. S. CANBY,
Major-General.

PAROLE OF E. KIRBY SMITH AND TROOPS

New Orleans, Louisiana, May 26, 1865

Reprinted from U.S. War Department, *War of the Rebellion: A Compilation of the Official Records of the Union and Confederate Armies*, Washington, D.C., 1880–1901, ser. 1, vol. 48, pt. 2, pp. 600–602.

Terms of a military convention entered into this 26th day of May, 1865, at New Orleans, La., between General E. Kirby Smith, C. S. Army, commanding the Department of Trans-Mississippi, and Maj. Gen. E. R. S. Canby, U. S. Army, commanding the Army and Division of West Mississippi, for the surrender of the troops and public property under the control of the military and naval authorities of the Trans-Mississippi Department.

I. All acts of war and resistance against the United States on the part of the troops under General Smith shall cease from this date.

II. The officers and men to be paroled until duly exchanged or otherwise released from the obligation of their parole by the authority of the Government of the United States. Duplicate rolls of all officers and men paroled to be retained by such officers as may be designated by the parties hereto, officers giving their individual paroles and commanders of regiments, battalions, companies, or detachments signing a like parole for the men of their respective commands.

III. Artillery, small-arms, ammunition, and other property of the Confederate States Government, including gun-boats and transports, to be turned over to the officers appointed to receive the same on the part of the Government of the United States. Duplicate inventories of the property to be surrendered to be prepared, one copy to be retained by the officer delivering and the other by the officer receiving it, for the information of their respective commanders.

IV. The officers and men paroled under this agreement will be allowed to return to their homes, with the assurance that they will not be disturbed by the authorities of the United States as long as they continue to observe the conditions of their parole and the laws in force where they reside, except that persons resident in the Northern States, and not excepted in the amnesty proclamation of the President, may return to their homes on taking the oath of allegiance to the United States.

V. The surrender of property will not include the side-arms or private horses or baggage of officers.

VI. All horses which are in good faith the private property of enlisted men will not be taken from them. The men will be permitted to take such with them to their homes, to be used for private purposes only.

VII. The time, mode, and place of paroling and surrender of property will be fixed by the respective commanders, and it will be carried out by commissioners appointed by them.

VIII. The terms and conditions of this convention to extend to all officers and men of the Army and Navy of the Confederate States, or any of them being in or belonging to the Trans-Mississippi Department.

IX. Transportation and subsistence to be furnished at public cost for the officers and men (after being paroled) to the nearest practicable point to their homes.

S. B. BUCKNER,
Lieutenant-General and Chief of Staff.
(For General E. Kirby Smith.)
P. JOS. OSTERHAUS,
Major-General of Volunteers and Chief of Staff.
(For Maj. Gen. E. R. S. Canby, commanding Military Division of West Mississippi.)
Approved:
ED. R. S. CANBY
Major-General, Comdg. Army and Division of West Mississippi.
[First indorsement.]
GALVESTON HARBOR, JUNE *2, 1865.*

Approved, understanding that by the provisions of this convention C. S. officers observing their paroles are permitted to make their homes either in or out of the United States.

E. KIRBY SMITH,
General.

[Second indorsement.]

This question was raised by General Smith's commissioners, but I declined to make any stipulation with regard to it, because I had no authority to determine the policy of the Government in any question of this kind.

ED. R. S. CANBY,
Major-General of Volunteers.
SUPPLEMENTAL ARTICLES.

I. The troops and property to be surrendered within the limits of the Division of the Missouri will be turned over to commissioners appointed by the commander of that division.

II. The men and material of the C. S. Navy will be surrendered to commissioners appointed by the commanders of the Mississippi and West Gulf Squadrons, respectively, according to the limits in which the said men and materials may be found.

III. If the U. S. troops designated for the garrisons of interior points should not reach their destination before the work of paroling is completed, suitable guards will be detailed for the protection of the public property. These guards, when relieved by U. S. troops, will surrender their arms and be paroled in accordance with the terms of this convention.

S. B. BUCKNER,
Lieutenant-General and Chief of Staff.
(FOR GENERAL E. K. SMITH.)
P. JOS. OSTERHAUS,
Major-General of Volunteers and Chief of Staff.
(For Maj. Gen. E. R. S. Canby, commanding Military Division of West Mississippi.)
Approved:
ED. R. S. CANBY,
Major-General, Comdg. Army and Division of West Mississippi.
Approved:
E. KIRBY SMITH,
General.

Glossary

abatis A defensive barrier constructed of felled trees placed lengthwise one over the other.

abolitionism Political and social advocacy of the abolition of slavery, usually on moral grounds.

absenteeism Habitual failure to appear for military duty.

accoutrements Military equipment, excluding uniforms and weapons.

ad valorem tax A tax that is proportional to the value of a commodity or service.

advance guard A **detachment** of **troops** sent ahead of a main force to **reconnoiter** or provide protection.

aide-de-camp A military officer acting as secretary and confidential assistant to a superior officer.

adjutant A **staff** officer who helps a commanding officer with administrative affairs.

agronomy Application of soil and plant sciences to soil management and crop production; scientific agriculture.

ambrotype An early type of photograph made by imaging a negative on glass backed by a dark surface.

American party *See* **Know-Nothing party.**

Andersonville Notorious Confederate prison in southwestern Georgia where horrendous conditions led to the deaths of many Union soldiers.

antebellum Of the period preceding the Civil War.

Appomattox The town in south-central Virginia where General Robert E. Lee surrendered to General Ulysses S. Grant on April 9, 1865, effectively ending the Civil War.

armistice A temporary cessation of fighting by mutual consent; a truce.

armor plate Specially formulated hard steel **plate** used to cover warships. *See* **ironclad.**

armory A building for storing arms and military equipment, which can also serve as headquarters for military **reserve** personnel. *Compare* **arsenal.**

arsenal Establishment for storing, developing, manufacturing, maintaining, or repairing arms, ammunition, and other war **matériel.** *Compare* **armory.**

artificer A skilled worker or craftsperson.

artillery (1) Large-**caliber** weapons, such as cannons, **howitzers,** and missile launchers, that are operated by crews. (2) A combat unit that specializes in the use of such weapons.

assay Qualitative or quantitative analysis of a substance, especially an ore or metal, to determine its components or purity.

attrition The wearing down of an enemy's strength and morale, and the gradual elimination of its **troops,** by unremitting harassment.

AWOL Absent without leave.

axis An alliance of powers, such as nations or states, to promote mutual interests and policies.

bale A large package of raw or finished material, such as cotton, wrapped and tightly bound with twine or wire.

ball A solid spherical or pointed projectile, usually shot from a cannon.

ballast (1) Heavy material used to enhance the stability of a ship or control the depth of a submarine. (2) A water tank on a submarine that is flooded or emptied to control depth.

baptism of fire A soldier's or an army's first experience of actual combat conditions.

barge A large, usually flat-bottomed boat equipped with a passenger cabin, oars, and sails, used to transport freight.

bark A sailing ship with three to five masts.

barracks A building or group of buildings used to house military personnel.

battalion A large body of organized **troops;** in the Confederate Army, a formation consisting of three to eight **companies.**

bateau A small, light, flat-bottomed rowboat.

battery A set of guns or other heavy **artillery,** often located on a warship or riverbank.

bayonet A blade adapted to fit the **muzzle** end of a **rifle** and used as a weapon in close combat.

beachhead A position on an enemy shoreline captured by **troops** in advance of an invading force; more generally, a first achievement that opens the way for further developments.

beam A transverse structural member of a ship's frame, used to support a deck and to brace the sides against stress.

beggar To exceed the limits of.

Belle Isle Confederate prison in North Carolina known for its extremely harsh conditions.

belligerent In wartime, a nation or government that is hostile or aggressive toward another. *Compare* **neutral.**

billet A written order directing that lodging for military **troops** be provided.

bivouac A temporary camp, especially in an unsheltered area.

black belt In the Civil War, an area with many **plantations** and a correspondingly large population of black slaves.

Black Hawk War Conflict between the United States and two Native American tribes, the Sac and Fox, in 1832.

blast furnace A furnace in which combustion is intensified by a blast of air, used in the commercial refinement and production of iron.

blockade The isolation of a nation, area, or harbor by hostile ships or forces to obstruct maritime traffic and commerce.

blockade runner Any of several ships used in the Civil War to penetrate or evade the Union's naval **blockade** of Confederate ports.

bludgeon A short, heavy club, usually of wood, that is thicker or loaded at one end.

bluecoat Member of the Union army.

bluff A steep headland, promontory, riverbank, or cliff.

boatswain An officer in charge of a sailing ship's **rigging,** anchors, cables, and deck crew.

bond (1) A certificate of debt issued by a government guaranteeing payment of the original investment plus interest by a specified date. (2) To secure payment of duties and taxes on goods transported by a ship.

bondman A person obligated to service without wages; also called bondsman or *bondservant.*

booby trap A concealed explosive device triggered by an unsuspecting soldier when a harmless-looking object is touched.

bore The hollow, cylindrical chamber or barrel of a firearm or cannon.

bottom A ship or boat.

breastwork A temporary, quickly constructed **fortification,** usually breast-high; a type of **bulwark.**

bread riots A series of violent political protests in Confederate cities, precipitated by a lack of adequate food supplies at fair prices. A significant bread riot occurred at Richmond, Virginia in April 1863.

breech The part of a firearm behind the barrel. Breech-loading guns developed in the late nineteenth century were technologically superior to their **muzzle**-loading predecessors.

brevet A commission promoting a military officer in rank without a corresponding increase in pay.

bridgehead A fortified position from which **troops** defend the end of a bridge nearest the enemy.

brig A two-masted sailing ship used for military or commercial purposes.

brigade A large Confederate combat unit consisting of a variable number of **regiments.**

brigadier general A high-ranking position in the Confederate Army; at the beginning of the Civil War, the highest grade in that army.

broadhorn A **flatboat** similar to a **scow.**

broadside (1) The simultaneous discharge of all the guns on one side of a warship. (2) A prominent advertisement or public notice printed on a large sheet of paper; also called *broadsheet.*

Bull Run *See* **Manassas.**

bulwark A wall or embankment raised as a defensive **fortification.**

bummer A **forager.**

caisson (1) A large box designed to hold ammunition. (2) A device used to raise ships or sunken objects, consisting of a hollow structure that is submerged, attached tightly to the object, then pumped free of water.

caliber The diameter of the barrel of a firearm, or of a large projectile such as an **artillery shell,** used as a relative measure of destructive potential.

call certificate A short-term **bond** whose value is subject to payment upon notification from the lender.

call up To summon to active military service.

canister A metallic cylinder packed with **shot** that are scattered when the cylinder is fired.

cannonade An extended discharge of **artillery.**

canteen A flask used by soldiers to carry drinking water.

carbine A lightweight **rifle** with a short barrel.

card A wire-toothed brush or a machine fitted with rows of wire teeth, used to disentangle fibers of cotton or wool prior to spinning.

cartel An official agreement between governments at war, especially one concerning the exchange of prisoners.

cartridge A cylindrical, usually metal casing containing the primer and charge of ammunition for firearms.

casemate A fortified enclosure for **artillery** on a warship.

cash crop A crop, such as tobacco or cotton, grown for direct sale.

cavalry Mounted **troops** trained to fight from horseback. Cavalry were important in warfare until the end of the nineteenth century, in spite of technological advances in firearms.

chattel An article of personal, movable property. Under the law before **emancipation,** slaves were considered chattels.

chevron A badge or **insignia** consisting of stripes meeting at an angle, worn on the sleeve of a military uniform to indicate rank, merit, or length of service.

China clipper A large **clipper** built in the mid-nineteenth century, originally designed to transport goods to and from China.

chivalry The qualities idealized by medieval knighthood, such as bravery, courtesy, honor, and gallantry toward women; an important influence in the culture of the Southern United States.

cipher A cryptographic system in which letters or units of text are arbitrarily transposed or substituted according to a predetermined code.

clipper A sharp-bowed sailing vessel of the mid-nineteenth century, having tall masts and sharp lines and built for great speed.

cockleshell A small, light boat.

cohort A group of soldiers.

column A formation of **troops** in which all elements follow one behind the other.

commerce raider In wartime, a ship used to damage, destroy, or seize an enemy's merchant ships or their cargo.

commissary (1) A market or shop for military personnel, usually located within a military installation. (2) A person to whom a specific duty is given by a higher authority; a deputy.

commission An official document issued by a government, conferring on its recipient certain powers or authority, or a high rank in a military force.

compact An agreement or covenant.

company A low-level military subdivision of a Confederate **regiment, battalion,** or **legion.**

Compromise of 1850 Legislation that admitted California as a free state, made New Mexico and Utah territories with no decision on slavery, strengthened the **Fugitive Slave Law** of 1793, and ended slave trading in the District of Columbia. *See also* **Kansas-Nebraska Act, popular sovereignty,** and **Wilmot Proviso.**

Confederate States of America The government established in 1861 by the Southern states after they seceded, consisting initially of South Carolina, Georgia, Louisiana, Mississippi, Florida, Alabama, and Texas. Arkansas, North Carolina, Virginia, and Tennessee joined later in the year.

conscription Compulsory enrollment in the armed forces; also called *draft.*

Conscription Law Confederate legislation enacted in 1862 and 1864 authorizing the government to enforce compulsory enrollment in the armed forces.

Constitution *See* **Provisional Constitution** and **Permanent Constitution.**

Constitutional Union party Political party formed in 1860, as the conflict between North and South broke down older parties. The party platform focused on union of the states, the principles of the United States Constitution, and law enforcement.

consul An official appointed by a government to reside in a foreign country and represent his government's commercial and legal interests there.

contraband (1) In wartime, goods or property that are subject to confiscation if shipped to a **belligerent.** (2) An escaped slave who fled to or was taken behind Union **lines;** in this context, also called *contraband of war.* (3) Smuggled goods.

contract labor Labor undertaken on the basis of a contract as opposed to, e.g., wages or salaries.

cooperationism Opposition to immediate **secession** in favor of cooperation to persuade the federal government to address Southern grievances.

copperhead A Northerner who sympathized with the South during the Civil War; also *Copperhead.*

corduroy To build a road of logs laid down crosswise.

cordwood Wood cut and sold in measured quantities for use as fuel.

corps A **tactical** unit of Confederate combat forces consisting of three or four **divisions** and sometimes other personnel.

corvette An sailing warship usually armed with a single tier of guns.

cotton diplomacy Mainly unsuccessful Confederate policy of regulating cotton exports and offering cotton in exchange for arms, supplies, and diplomatic support; in this context, often called *King Cotton.*

cotton gin A machine that separates seeds, hulls, and other small objects from the fibers of cotton, invented in 1793. Widespread use of the device facilitated development and expansion of the Southern cotton industry.

countermand To cancel or reverse a previously issued command or order.

court-martial A military court of officers appointed by a commander to conduct trials for offenses under military law.

cowcatcher A metal grille or frame projecting from the front of a railroad locomotive that serves to clear the track of obstructions.

Crittenden Compromise Constitutional amendment proposed by Senator John Crittenden of Kentucky in 1860 as a last-minute effort to avert the Civil War. This unsuccessful legislation would have used the **Missouri Compromise** line, extended to California, to divide free and slave states.

cut A passage made by digging or probing.

cutter A single-masted sailing ship with **rigging** similar to that of a **sloop.**

daguerreotype An early photographic process in which the image is made on a light-sensitive silver-coated metallic plate.

Daughters of the Confederacy Patriotic society founded in 1894 for women with ancestors who served in the Civil War; also called *United Daughters of the Confederacy.*

day laborer A laborer hired and paid by the day.

Democratic party Major political party established in the early 1820s, emphasizing personal liberty and the limitation of federal government. The party divided in the 1850s and 1860s, but most Democrats favored the maintenance and expansion of slavery.

dead letter A law or directive still formally in effect but no longer valid or enforced.

depository A place where money is deposited for storage or safekeeping.

depot (1) A storage installation for military equipment and supplies. (2) A station for assembling military recruits and forwarding them to active units.

detachment A small military unit whose members are chosen from a larger body for a special duty or mission.

dispatch (1) An organization or conveyance for delivering messages or goods. (2) In military or diplomatic affairs, an urgent, authoritative message sent by an officer.

disunionism Advocacy of splitting up the Union; **secessionism.**

division An administrative and **tactical** military unit in the Confederate Army that usually consisted of several **infantry brigades, artillery companies,** and sometimes other units. Divisions were typically self-contained and equipped for prolonged combat activity.

doughface A Northerner who sided with the South in the Civil War, especially a member of Congress who supported slavery.

draft (1) Mandatory enrollment in the armed forces; **conscription.** (2) The depth of a vessel's **keel** below the water line, especially when it is loaded.

dragoon A heavily armed **trooper.**

Dred Scott v. Sanford Landmark legal case in which a fugitive slave, Dred Scott, brought suit in 1848 to claim freedom on the ground that he resided in free territory. The U.S. Supreme Court ruled that (1) his residence in Minnesota Territory did not make him free, (2) a black may not bring suit in a federal court, and (3) Congress lacked the authority to ban slavery in the territories.

drill The training of soldiers in marching and the use of arms.

dry dock A large dock in the form of a basin from which the water can be emptied, used for building or repairing a ship below its water line.

due bill A written acknowledgment of indebtedness neither payable to order nor transferable by endorsement; similar to a *promissory note.*

Dunker Member of a group of German-American Baptists opposed to military service and the taking of legal oaths; also called *Dunkard.*

earthwork An earthen embankment, especially one used as a **fortification;** a type of **bulwark.**

echelon A formation of **troops** in which successive combat units are placed in parallel, but with no two on the same alignment, so that each unit has its front clear of the unit in front of it.

emancipation Freedom from bondage, oppression, or restraint; specifically, liberation of the Confederate slaves.

Emancipation Proclamation Executive order issued by President Abraham Lincoln in 1863 abolishing slavery in the Confederacy. It freed only those slaves residing in territory in rebellion "as a fit and necessary war measure."

encamp To set up a military camp; *see also* **bivouac.**

Enfield rifle Any of several **rifles** used in America during the late nineteenth century. The gun takes its name from a borough of London.

enfilade Gunfire directed along the length of a target, such as a **column** of **troops.**

enlisted man Usually, a male member of the armed forces whose rank is below that of officer.

entrenchment A trench dug for the purpose of **fortification** or defense.

entrepôt A place where goods are stored or deposited, and from which they are distributed.

equity A system of jurisprudence supplementing the Confederate law courts in the application of general principles of justice, ethics, and fairness in circumstances not covered by the law.

Erlanger loan A large loan negotiated in 1863 between the Confederacy and Emile Erlanger & Co. of Paris, which was secured by Confederate-owned cotton.

ersatz Being an imitation or a substitute, usually an inferior one; artificial.

factor A merchant or firm that acted as a sales agent or commercial intermediary for Southern planters. Factors also performed concomitant services such as providing loans and vouching for credit.

fagot A twig, stick, or branch, or a bundle of twigs bound together.

fait accompli An accomplished, presumably irreversible deed or fact.

fall line A line connecting the waterfalls of nearly parallel rivers that marks a drop in land level.

ferrotype An early photographic process in which the positive image is made directly on an iron plate varnished with a thin sensitized film; also called *tintype, melanotype,* or *melainotype.*

fiat money Legal tender, especially paper currency, authorized by a government but not based on or convertible into gold or silver.

feint A feigned attack designed to draw defensive action away from an intended target.

fifth column A clandestine subversive organization working within a country or region to further an enemy's military and political aims.

filibuster To take part in a private military action in a foreign country.

fill An embankment.

firebrand A person who stirs up trouble or kindles a rebellion; see also **fire-eater**.

fire-eater A Southern radical or extremist who popularized the right of **secession** among the Southern population.

First Manassas *See* **Manassas**.

Five Civilized Tribes Name used since the mid-nineteenth century for the Cherokee, Chickasaw, Choctaw, Creek, and Seminole tribes, each of which lived on communally held land and had written constitutions, tripartite governments, and public school systems.

flamethrower A weapon that projects ignited incendiary fuel in a steady stream.

flank The right or left side of a military formation.

flatboat A boat with a flat bottom and square ends used for transporting freight on inland waterways.

flint A hard, fine-grained quartz that sparks when struck with steel; used in firearms to produce an ignition spark.

flintlock A gunlock in which a **flint** embedded in the hammer produces a spark that ignites the charge.

flotilla A small fleet of ships.

forager One of a party sent out to gather **forage** for an army; also called *bummer*.

forage (1) Food or provisions. (2) To obtain food or supplies by making a raid.

ford A shallow place in a body of water, such as a river, where one can cross by walking or riding on an animal.

fortification A system of defense structures for protection from enemy attacks, often including walls, fences, or barriers.

Fort Sumter Harbor **fortification** at Charleston, South Carolina, site of the first clash of the Civil War in April 1861.

fraise A defensive barrier of pointed, inclined stakes or barbed wire.

freebooter A person who pillages, plunders, or pirates.

freeboard The distance between the water line and the uppermost full deck of a ship.

Free-Soil party Political party founded in 1848 to oppose the extension of slavery into U.S. territories and the admission of slave states into the Union. The Free-Soilers were absorbed by the **Republican party** in 1854.

frigate A high-speed, medium-sized warship used in the nineteenth century.

frock coat A man's dress coat or suit coat with knee-length skirts; part of the Confederate military uniform.

front The most forward **line** of a combat force.

frontal assault A military attack launched against the front of a fortified area.

Fugitive Slave Law Landmark legislation passed by Congress in 1793 and strengthened by the **Compromise of 1850**. This legislation made it illegal to help a slave escape to freedom, or to give refuge to a runaway slave.

furlough A leave of absence or vacation granted to a member of the armed forces.

gangplank A board or ramp used as a removable footway between a ship and a pier; also called *gangway*.

gauge (1) The distance between the two rails of a railroad. (2) The interior diameter of a shotgun barrel.

garnishment A legal proceeding whereby money or property due a debtor but in the possession of another is applied to the payment of the debt.

garrison A military post, especially a permanent one.

grapnel A small anchor with three or more triangular blades one used for anchoring a small vessel or mine.

Gettysburg Site of a decisive Union victory in southeastern Pennsylvania, marking the turning point of the Civil War in 1863. Abraham Lincoln delivered the Gettysburg Address at the dedication of a cemetery in this town.

gilt A thin layer of gold or something simulating gold.

Great Awakening A series of religious revivals that swept over the American colonies in the middle eighteenth century.

greenback A **note** of United States currency.

guard Often, a unit of soldiers or police charged with defending a region or enforcing its laws.

guerrilla Member of an irregular, unofficial military or paramilitary unit operating in small bands; sometimes called *bushwhacker*.

guidon bearer A soldier bearing a small flag or pennant carried as a **standard** by a military unit.

gunboat A small armed vessel.

habeas corpus In law, a **writ** issued by a court commanding that a person held in custody be brought before the court to determine whether the detention is lawful. Habeas corpus is guaranteed by the U.S. Constitution as a safeguard against illegal imprisonment, but it can be suspended in time of rebellion.

haversack A bag carried over one shoulder to transport supplies.

hegemony The predominant influence of one political group over others.

hinterland The land directly adjacent to and inland from a coast.

hogshead Any of various units of volume or capacity, or a large barrel capable of holding such a quantity.

holding action In military combat, a plan that focuses on defense and maintaining the organization and authority of **troops**.

home guard Member of a Confederate **regiment** whose function was to protect against Northern invaders.

howitzer A relatively short cannon that delivers **shells** at a medium **muzzle** velocity, usually by a high trajectory.

hussar Member of a unit of light **cavalry**.

hydrography The scientific description and analysis of the physical conditions, boundaries, flow, and related characteristics of bodies of water.

impress To seize people or property for public service or use. Southern slaves were sometimes impressed to serve in the Confederate military forces.

Impressment Act Legislation passed by the Confederate Congress in 1863 permitting the seizure of agricultural products and military supplies at a fair price.

infantry A body of soldiers who fight on foot; *compare* **cavalry**.

insignia A badge or emblem of rank or length of service, often worn on the sleeve of a military uniform.

inspector general An officer with general investigative powers within a military organization.

ironclad A nineteenth-century warship having sides armored with metal **plates;** sometimes called *armorclad*.

jayhawkers A group of notorious pro-Union **guerrillas** who operated in Kansas and Missouri.

Johnnie Reb A Confederate soldier.

juggernaut An overwhelming, advancing force that crushes everything in its path.

Juneteenth Commemoration of the official **emancipation** of slaves in Texas on June 19, 1865.

Kansas-Nebraska Act Landmark bill passed in 1854 by the U.S. Congress establishing the Kansas and Nebraska territories, and repealing the ban on slavery in those territories provided by the **Missouri Compromise**. After the Act passed, **sectional** differences gave rise to the formation of the **Republican party** and the candidacy of Abraham Lincoln.

keel The principal structural member of a ship, running lengthwise along the center line from bow to stern, to which supporting structures are attached.

keel boat A riverboat with a heavy timber **keel** down its center.

kepi A military cap with a flat, circular top and a visor; part of the Confederate army uniform.

Know-Nothing party A political party formed in the 1850s that was antagonistic toward recent immigrants and Roman Catholics. They became the *American party,* then disintegrated over the issue of slavery.

knuckle Protruding structure on a ship to protect against **ramming;** also called a *raft.*

laissez faire An economic and political doctrine holding that an economic system functions best without government interference.

lame duck An elected officeholder continuing in office after a successor is elected but before the actual succession.

lanyard A short rope or strap used for fastening something or triggering a naval mine.

legal tender Legally valid currency that may be offered in payment of a debt, which must be accepted by any creditor.

legion In the Confederate Army, a large combat unit consisting of several **companies.**

letters of marque A document issued by a government allowing a private citizen to seize citizens or goods of another government.

limber A two-wheeled, horse-drawn vehicle used to tow a field gun or **caisson.**

line (1) A formation in which elements, such as **troops,** weapons, or ships, are arranged abreast of one another. (2) The regular forces of an army or a navy, in contrast to **staff** and support personnel.

logistics The branch of military operations that deals with the procurement, distribution, maintenance, and replacement of **matériel** and personnel.

Lost Cause The Civil War in the context of Southern defeat, or the region's collective memory of the war.

Louisiana Purchase A large territory of the western United States purchased from France in 1803 that became central in the slavery debate of the late nineteenth century; *see also* **Missouri Compromise.**

lozenge A four-sided planar figure with a diamond-like shape that might appear as part of **insignia** on a military uniform.

magazine (1) A compartment in some firearms from which **cartridges** are fed into a firing chamber. (2) A building within a yard or fort where ammunition and other goods are kept.

malinger To feign illness or other incapacity in order to avoid work or military duty.

Manassas City in northeast Virginia near which the *Battles of Bull Run (First Manassas* and *Second Manassas)* were fought in 1861 and 1862, respectively. First Manassas was the first major land battle of the Civil War.

Manifest Destiny The nineteenth-century doctrine that the United States had the right and duty to expand throughout the North American continent. The question of whether slavery should be permitted in newly acquired territories became the subject of bitter political debates.

manumission The act of freeing from slavery or bondage; **emancipation.**

marksman A man skilled in shooting at a target.

marshal Officer who carries out court orders and discharges duties similar to those of a sheriff.

marine corps A branch of the armed forces composed chiefly of amphibious **troops** under naval authority. The Confederate States Marine Corps was patterned after that of the Union.

martial law Temporary rule by military authorities, imposed on a civilian population in time of war or when civil authority has broken down.

manufactory A factory or manufacturing plant.

martinet One who demands absolute adherence to forms and rules; a rigid disciplinarian.

Mason-Dixon Line The border between Pennsylvania and Maryland, popularly designated as the boundary between the slave states and the free states before the Civil War. It was named for Charles Mason and Jeremiah Dixon, surveyors of the region in the 1760s.

matériel The equipment, apparatus, and supplies of a military force or other organization.

melainotype *See* **ferrotype.**

melee Confused, hand-to-hand fighting in a battle where the opposing **troops** are in close contact.

merchant marine A body of government-licensed commercial cargo ships, or the personnel thereof.

mess hall A building or room used for serving and eating meals at a military installation.

Mexican Cession Provision of the treaty ending the **Mexican War,** under which Mexico ceded two fifths of its territory to the United States and received an indemnity of $15 million.

Mexican War Armed conflict between the United States and Mexico over territorial claims and other issues, occurring from 1846 to 1848.

midshipman A cadet or student in training to be a commissioned naval officer.

militia An army composed of ordinary citizens rather than professional soldiers.

minié ball A conical **rifle** bullet used in the nineteenth century, designed with a hollow base that expands when fired.

miscegenation Genetic mixing of two or more races, common in both Northern and Southern regions of the United States.

Missouri Compromise Measures passed by the U.S. Congress in 1820-1821 to end the crisis concerning the extension of slavery. Maine was admitted as a free state and Missouri as a slave state; slavery was prohibited within the **Louisiana Purchase** north of 36 degrees 30 minutes. *See also* **Compromise of 1850, Kansas-Nebraska Act.**

monitor A heavy **ironclad** warship of the nineteenth century with a low, flat deck and one or more gun **turrets.**

mortar A portable, **muzzle**-loaded cannon used to fire **shells** at low velocities, short ranges, and high trajectories.

mount A horse used as a means of conveyance for a rider.

mulatto A person of mixed white and black ancestry.

musket A shoulder gun that was widely used by both sides in the Civil War. Early muskets were **smoothbore** in design; more accurate weapons with **rifled** barrels were developed in the 1850s.

muster To call **troops** together, as for inspection.

muzzle The forward, discharging end of the barrel of a firearm or cannon.

naval stores Products, such as turpentine or pitch, used in the nineteenth century to caulk the seams of wooden ships.

neutral A nation that does not align itself with either side in a war. *Compare* **belligerent.**

niter Potassium nitrate; *see* **saltpeter.**

note (1) A piece of paper currency. (2) One of a variety of certificates issued by a government or bank, sometimes negotiable as money.

nullification An extremist doctrine of **state rights** holding that a state can declare null and void any federal law it deems unconstitutional.

Nullification was a forerunner of the doctrine of **secession** that brought about the Civil War.

offensive-defensive Confederate military strategy in which forces would conserve resources by standing on the defensive until circumstances allowed concentration against smaller or isolated Union forces.

Old Dominion Informal name for the state of Virginia.

ordinance (1) A statute or regulation, especially one enacted by a small government unit. (2) An authoritative command, order, or agreement.

ordnance Military **matériel,** such as weapons, ammunition, combat vehicles, and equipment.

overseer The manager of a Southern **plantation,** who typically supervised a number of slaves.

packet A boat, usually a coastal or river **steamer,** that covered a regular route and carried passengers, freight, and mail.

parole Word of honor given by a prisoner of war who is granted freedom after promising to lay down arms.

pavilion A temporary building that is easy to erect, disassemble, or move.

paymaster A person in charge of paying wages and salaries to military personnel.

percussion A detonation process in which gunpowder or another explosive material explodes on being struck, usually firing a projectile through the barrel of a weapon.

percussion cap A thin metal cap containing explosive material used to fire a **percussion** firearm.

Permanent Constitution The Constitution of the Confederate States of America as adopted and ratified in late 1861. This document was nearly identical in structure to the United States Constitution. *See also* **Provisional Constitution.**

picket A **detachment** of one or more **troops** held in readiness or advanced to warn of an enemy's approach.

pig iron Crude iron cast in blocks, which are later melted and refined for commercial use.

pincer A military maneuver in which the enemy is attacked simultaneously from two **flanks** and the front.

pirogue A large, flat-bottom riverboat propelled by oars and poles.

pivot Military maneuver in which **troops** swing around a central point.

pivot gun A gun attached to a rotating mechanism, often on a ship.

plantation A large antebellum farm on which crops were raised, usually with the labor of resident slaves. Typical plantations had vast fields, stables, barns, sheds, workshops, and other facilities, as well as a spacious main house occupied by the owner's family.

plate A sheet of hammered, rolled, or cast metal. Iron plates were used in the manufacture of **ironclads.**

platoon A subdivision of a **company** of **troops.**

plebiscite A direct vote in which an electorate decides on a significant proposal, especially the right of national self-determination.

plug-ugly A gangster or ruffian. The original *Plug Uglies* were a gang that operated in several East Coast cities in the 1850s.

ply To traverse a route or course regularly.

point-blank In ballistics, close enough to a target so that missing the target is unlikely or impossible.

pontoon A floating structure, such as a flat-bottomed boat, that is used to support a bridge.

poorhouse An establishment maintained at public expense as housing for the homeless.

popular sovereignty In U.S. history, the doctrine under which slavery was initially permitted in territories, the final question of its legal status being left to territorial settlers when they applied for statehood. It was incorporated into the **Fugitive Slave Law** (*see* **Compromise of 1850**) and the **Kansas-Nebraska Act.** Also called *squatter sovereignty.*

portfolio The office or post of a cabinet member or minister of state.

postbellum Of the period after the Civil War.

powder Any of a variety of explosive mixtures, such as gunpowder.

private A noncommissioned rank in a military or paramilitary organization.

privateer A ship privately owned and manned but authorized by a government to attack and capture enemy vessels during wartime.

prize Property seized during wartime, especially an enemy ship and/or cargo captured at sea.

produce loan A Confederate financing concept in which commodities, or sometimes proceeds from the sale thereof, were exchanged for government bonds.

progressive tax A tax that increases in rate as the taxable amount increases.

proviso A clause in a document making a qualification, condition, or restriction.

provost marshal The head of a military police unit.

Provisional Constitution A temporary Confederate constitution adopted in February 1861 at Montgomery, Alabama, based on the United States Constitution and the earlier Articles of Confederation. *See also* **Permanent Constitution.**

puppet government A government whose behavior is determined by the will of others.

Pyrrhic victory A victory that is offset by staggering losses (after Pyrrhus, king of Epirus).

psychological warfare Propaganda techniques designed to weaken the enemy's morale and to discredit the government of the opposition.

quartermaster An officer responsible for the clothing, equipment (except **ordnance**), and transportation of Confederate **troops.**

railhead A place on a railroad where military supplies are unloaded.

ram A projection on the bow of a warship used to batter or cut into enemy vessels; also, a ship having such a projection.

ranger Member of an armed **troop** charged with patrolling a specific region.

rear guard A **detachment** of **troops** that protects the rear of a military force.

reconnoiter To make a preliminary inspection of an area in order to gather military information; to scout or make a reconnaissance.

Reconstruction The period from 1865 to 1877 during which the states of the Confederacy were controlled by the federal government before being readmitted to the Union.

redoubt A small, often temporary defensive **fortification.**

regiment A large body of organized **troops;** the basic Confederate **infantry** organization.

Republican party Major political party organized to oppose slavery in 1854, whose first major candidate was Abraham Lincoln. Through the 1850s and 1860s, other smaller parties were absorbed into the Republicans.

reserve A fighting force not on active duty but subject to mobilization if needed.

retainer A loyal servant or slave who worked in the household of a person of high rank.

retrocede To cede, give back, or return a territory to its previous owner.

revisionism An academic movement during the 1940s proposing that the legal and social conflicts between North and South were exaggerated by partisan, self-interested extremists on both sides, and that the Civil War was tragic and unnecessary.

rifle (1) To cut spiral grooves inside the **bore** of a weapon. *Compare* **smoothbore**. (2) A firearm with a rifled barrel, designed to be fired from the shoulder, often equipped with a **bayonet**.

rifle-musket A **musket** with a long, **rifled** barrel that usually fired **minié balls**. Rifle-muskets were loaded through the **muzzle** and ignited by **percussion**.

rigging The arrangement of masts, **spars**, and sails on a sailing vessel.

Riot Act An English law enacted in 1715, providing that if twelve or more people unlawfully assemble and disturb the public peace, they must disperse upon proclamation or be considered guilty of felony.

rolling stock Equipment available for use as locomotives or railroad cars owned by a rail carrier.

ropewalk A long alley or pathway used in the manufacture of rope; part of a rope factory.

rout To defeat overwhelmingly in military combat.

saber A heavy cavalry sword with a one-edged, slightly curved blade.

salient The area of a military defense, such as a battle **line**, that projects closest to the enemy.

saltpeter Potassium nitrate, used as a key ingredient in the manufacture of gunpowder and other explosive substances; also called *niter*.

sapper A specialist in field **fortifications**.

schooner A fore-and-aft-rigged sailing vessel with at least two masts.

scorched-earth policy Military strategy of devastating land and buildings in the course of advancing or retreating **troops**, leaving nothing salvageable to the enemy.

scow A large **flatboat**; also called an *ark*.

screw A propeller attached to the engine of a ship.

scrip Paper money issued for temporary emergency use.

scuttle To cut or open holes in a ship's hull, usually with the intention of sinking it.

scurvy A disease caused by deficiency of vitamin C, often prevalent in circumstances where fresh fruits and vegetables are unavailable.

scythe An implement consisting of a long, curved single-edged blade with a long, bent handle, used for mowing or reaping.

search and seizure The search of a person or property and subsequent confiscation of such property by a government authority, as regulated by the United States Bill of Rights.

secessionism In the 1860s, advocacy for the withdrawal of Southern states from the Union, precipitating the U.S. Civil War.

Second Manassas *See* **Manassas**.

secret service A government or military agency engaged in the gathering of intelligence.

section (1) A subdivision of a company of **troops**. (2) An small area or region with distinct political and commercial interests.

sedition Conduct or language inciting rebellion against the authority of a state.

sentinel A person who keeps guard; a sentry.

sentry box A small shelter for a posted sentry.

sequestration Seizure of property authorized by a government or government agency.

set piece A carefully planned and executed military operation.

Seven Days' Battles Confederate counteroffensive in 1862 that ended the Union's drive to capture Richmond, Virginia.

shaft A tall, tapered, monolithic, four-sided shaft of stone that rises to a point, erected as a monument to an important figure; an *obelisk*.

sharecropper A tenant farmer who gives a share of his crops to the landlord in lieu of rent.

sharpshooter In the military, a grade of proficiency in the use of **rifles** and other small arms.

shell A projectile or piece of ammunition, especially the hollow tube containing explosives used to propel such a projectile.

Shenandoah Valley A geographic corridor through Northern Virginia linking important Northern and Southern cities. The area figured prominently in the Civil War, especially the Valley campaign of General Thomas (Stonewall) Jackson in 1862.

shirker In the Civil War, one who avoided work, civic duty, or military obligations.

shot (plural) Solid projectiles designed to be discharged from a firearm or cannon.

shotgun A **smoothbore** gun that fires **shot** (in the form of tiny pellets) over short ranges.

sidewheeler A steamboat with a paddle wheel on each side. *Compare* **sternwheeler**.

siege The surrounding and **blockading** of a city, town, or fortress by an army attempting to capture it.

Signal Corps A branch of the Confederate army responsible for transmitting and receiving coded messages between army units by means of flags, torches, fires, and the like. Signal Corps personnel also observed and reported enemy activities.

skiff A small flat-bottom boat used for local traffic and sometimes carried in tow by larger boats.

skirmish A relatively minor or preliminary battle in war, usually between small forces.

slave driver A slave who was responsible for field production and labor discipline on a **plantation**.

sloop A small, single-masted, fore-and-aft-rigged sailing boat.

smoothbore Characteristic of a firearm having no **rifling**—i.e., spiral grooves—cut inside its barrel. Smoothbore guns fell out of use with the development of more accurate **rifle** technology.

sniper A skilled military gunner detailed to spot and shoot enemy soldiers from a concealed location.

Sons of Confederate Veterans Patriotic society founded in 1896 for male descendants of Confederate veterans.

Sons of Liberty Secret organizations dedicated to the promotion of conservative measures, who defended the Confederacy and its principles during the Civil War.

sortie An armed attack made from a place surrounded by enemy forces.

soubriquet An affectionate or humorous nickname.

Southern Manifesto A political declaration drafted in 1860, stating that North-South differences could not be reconciled within the established order and that the honor, safety, and independence of the South could only be preserved by **secession**.

spar (1) A wooden or metal pole, such as a mast or boom, used to support sails and **rigging**. (2) A pole to which a naval mine or other explosive device is attached.

speak To hail and communicate with a vessel at sea.

specie Coined money.

speculation The practice of buying a commodity in bulk to corner the market, exploiting (or generating) rumors of shortages, and selling at a significant profit.

spearhead To lead forces in a military action, endeavor, or movement.

Spotsylvania Town near Fredericksburg, Virginia which became the focus of a series of battles in May 1864 as part of the **Wilderness campaign**.

spur A short-distance railroad track that connects with a primary rail system.

squadron (1) An armored **cavalry** unit subordinate to a **regiment** and consisting of two or more **troops**. (2) A naval unit consisting of several warships.

staff A group of military officers assigned to assist a commanding officer in an executive or advisory capacity.

standard An emblem or flag of an army, raised on a pole to indicate the rallying point in battle.

Stars and Bars Name for the first Confederate flag.

state guard *See* **guard.**

state rights Political doctrine advocating strict interpretation of the Constitution with regard to the limitation of federal powers and the autonomy of individual states. The Confederate states used this doctrine to justify **secession.**

steamer A large, steam-powered ship propelled by one or more **screws** or paddles; also called *steamship.*

sterling British money, especially the pound as the basic monetary unit of the United Kingdom.

sternpost The principal upright post at the stern of a vessel, usually serving to support the rudder.

sternwheeler A steamboat with a paddle wheel at the stern. *Compare* **sidewheeler.**

stock The rear handle or support of a **rifle** or pistol to which the barrel and mechanism are attached.

stockade A barrier made of strong posts or timbers driven upright side by side into the ground; also, the area protected by such a barrier.

Stonewall brigade A famously brave and disciplined Confederate battle unit initially commanded by General Thomas (Stonewall) Jackson, composed of soldiers from the Shenandoah Valley region of Virginia.

strategic operations The conduct of large-scale combat operations as part of an overall, long-term plan. *Compare* **tactical operations.**

straw boss A worker who acts as a supervisor or crew leader in addition to performing regular duties.

summary justice Legal or disciplinary proceedings carried out speedily and without ceremony, especially during a military operation.

sutler An army camp follower who peddled provisions to the soldiers.

tactical operations Military operations that are relatively small, close to base, and of immediate significance. *Compare* **strategic operations.**

tanner A craftsperson who converts animal skin into leather.

task system Labor method that evolved after the mid-eighteenth century in which a slave was responsible for specified daily tasks or chores; upon completion of his daily work, the slave's time was free.

tax-in-kind Confederate tax paid in the form of agricultural products rather than currency.

temperance movements Organized efforts in the nineteenth and early twentieth centuries to induce people to abstain from alcoholic beverages.

tender (1) A railroad car attached to the rear of a locomotive and designed to carry fuel and water. (2) **Legal tender.**

theater A large geographic area in which military operations are coordinated.

36 degrees 30 minutes *See* **Missouri Compromise.**

three-fifths clause A clause in the United States and Confederate Constitutions stating that each slave counted as three-fifths of a free man for purposes of representation and taxation. The Fourteenth Amendment superseded this rule in 1868.

tidewater Water affected by the ordinary ebb and flow of the tide; also, designating or pertaining to a region, such as eastern Virginia, that is situated on tidewater.

tintype *See* **ferrotype.**

tithe A tax or assessment of one tenth.

torpedo In the Civil War, one of a variety of naval or land mines used primarily by the Confederacy.

total war A war to which all resources and the whole population are committed; also, a war conducted without scruples or limitations.

trace A strap or chain used to transfer movement, usually from a harnessed draft animal to a vehicle.

traverse An earthen wall cutting across an **entrenchment** for the purpose of protecting the **flanks** of the **troops** within.

treasury security A document or certificate indicating ownership or creditorship of a government obligation.

trestle A framework consisting of vertical, slanted supports and horizontal crosspieces supporting a bridge. Railroad trestles were frequent military targets in the Civil War.

troop A group of soldiers, or a member of such a group.

truck A swiveling frame of wheels under each end of a railroad car.

turncoat A soldier who traitorously switches allegiance and joins the enemy.

turret A low, heavily armored structure on a warship, usually rotating horizontally, containing mounted guns and personnel.

Twenty-Slave Law Confederate legislation providing that one white man was exempted from military service for every twenty slaves on a plantation or in a county.

Union The United States of America regarded as a national unit, especially during the Civil War.

Vicksburg campaign Military campaign commanded by Major General Ulysses S. Grant in the region around Vicksburg, Mississippi from October 1862 to July 1863, resulting in the surrender of that city.

vigilance committee A volunteer group of citizens that without authority assumes powers such as pursuing and punishing those suspected of criminal behavior.

unlimber To detach a gun or **caisson** from its **limber.**

vanguard The foremost position in an army or a fleet advancing into battle.

Whig party One of the two dominant American political parties in the second quarter of the nineteenth century (the other being the **Democrats**), advocating high tariffs and loose interpretation of the Constitution. The party disintegrated in the early 1850s, chiefly over the slavery issue.

Wilderness campaign A series of indecisive engagements fought in the Wilderness region near Fredericksburg, Virginia in the spring of 1864, pitting Robert E. Lee against Ulysses S. Grant.

Wilmot Proviso Failed amendment put before Congress during the Mexican War (1846) proposing that slavery be prohibited in any territory acquired in that war.

wing The left or right **flank** of an army.

writ A written order issued by a court, commanding the addressee to perform or cease performing a specified act.

writ of habeas corpus *See* **habeas corpus.**

yeoman (1) A subsistence farmer who cultivated his own land, without slave labor. Confederate yeoman farmers fought against the Union, but some questioned whether their interests were parallel to those of the slave-owners. (2) A low-ranking member of a military unit.

Zouave In the Civil War, member of a group patterned after the French Zouaves, who were known for elaborate, colorful uniforms and precision **drilling.**

Index

proclamation of neutrality, 142

weakness of Confederate purchasing in, 15

Greeley, Horace, 129, 178, 270

Green, George, 534

Green, Philip, 579

Green, Tom, 493

Greene, Israel, 266

Greenhow, Rose O'Neal, 144, 191, 194, 196, 551

profile of, 252–253

Gregg, David, 89

at Brandy Station, 72

Gregg, John, 648

Gregg, Maxcy

and Declaration of Immediate Causes, 167

and Fredericksburg campaign, 230

and Second Manassas, 352

Greyhound (ship), 197

Grierson, Benjamin H., 648

Griffe, 370

Griffin, Charles, 349

Griffith, Richard, 42

Grimke, Angelina, 18

Grimke, Sarah, 18

Grover, Cuvier, 352

Guadalupe (frigate), 317

Guerrilla warfare, 111, 121, 253–259, 347, 379

early activity in border states, 253–254

early activity in Deep South, 254–255

late in war, 258–259

Guilt, 122

Guirot, Anthony J., 622

Gunboats, 298–299

wooden, 389, 390

Guthrie, James, 481, 507, 630

H ———

H. L. Hunley, CSS, 57, 97, 98, 276–277, 345, 395, 597–598

Habeas corpus, writ of, 65, 102, 151

as political issue, 437

slaves securing, 231

suspending, 235

Hague, Parthenia, 430

Hahn, Michael, 496

Hale, John P., and Compromise of 1850, 139

Half-breed, 370

Halleck, Henry, 46

and Henry and Donelson campaign, 271

and prevention of slave insurrection, 561

and Red River campaigns, 493

and Shiloh campaign, 546

and Vicksburg campaign, 646

Hamilton, Alexander

and state rights, 581–583

and state socialism, 473

Hamilton, James, 404

Hammond, James Henry, 156, 208, 463, 509

Hampton, Wade, 30, 80, 287

at Brandy Station, 72

and Carolinas campaign, 85

and cavalry, 86

death of, 262

and Kilpatrick-Dahlgren raid, 314

and Petersburg campaign, 422

and plot against Lincoln, 161

profile of, 261–262

Hampton (gunboat), 298

Hampton Roads conference, 145, 262–263, 280, 283, 528

failure of, 263

Hampton's Legion, 80, 261, 263, 287, 574

Hanckel, Charles F., 621

Hancock, Winfield S.

and Gettysburg campaign, 241

and Petersburg campaign, 419

and Spotsylvania campaign, 576–577

Hanson, Roger W., 408

Harbin, Thomas, 201

Hardcastle, Aaron, 546

profile of, 274–276

and Second Manassas, 352

and Seven Days' Battles, 275, 533

and Sharpsburg campaign, 534, 537

and Spotsylvania campaign, 576

and Wilderness campaign, 677–679

Hill, Benjamin H., 129, 307, 687

and supreme court issue, 306–307

Hill, D. H., 245, 268, 612

and Army of Tennessee, 35

at Bloody Lane, 11

and Confederate Secret Service, 192

and Fredericksburg campaign, 229

and Peninsular campaign, 419

and prisoner exchanges, 451

and Seven Days' Battles, 533

and Sharpsburg campaign, 534

Hillsman farm, 20

Hilton, John, 273

Hindman, Thomas C., 235

and Trans-Mississippi Department, 615

Hines, Thomas H., 129

History of Morgan's Cavalry, A (Duke), 179

Hoarding, 74, 144, 210, 444

shortages and, 377

Hobart-Hampden, August Charles, 62

Hobson, Edward H., 380

Hoffbauer, Charles, 385

Hoffman, William, 435, 459

as commissary general of prisoners, 451

Hoke, Robert, 11

at Drewry's Bluff, 179

Holcombe, James P., 129

Hold, Joseph, 458

Holden, William W., 145, 274, 413, 644

peace policy, 437

Hollins, George N., 345

Holmes, Barbara Galphin, 371

Holmes, Oliver Wendell, Jr., 125

Holmes, Theophilus H., 235, 359, 426

Holt, Joseph, 155

Home for Indigent and Aged Negroes, 17

Home guards, free blacks as, 1

Hood, John Bell, 47, 116, 221, 303

attacking army of Sherman, 279

brigade formation, 291

death of, 280

final offensive under, 36–37

and Franklin and Nashville campaign, 225–228

and Gettysburg campaign, 243

profile of, 277–280

promotion to lieutenant general, 278

resignation of commission in U.S. Army, 278

and Second Manassas, 353

and Sherman's March to the Sea, 354

and Texas Brigade, 279, 288

Hooker, Joseph

at Brandy Station, 72

and Chancellorsville campaign, 27, 91, 93, 94, 182, 323

and Federal Secret Service, 195

and Gettysburg campaign, 237, 241

and Sharpsburg campaign, 534

Horse artillery, 9

Hospitals, 362, 503

Hotchkiss, Jedediah, 543

Hotze, Henry, 172

Housatonic, USS, 277, 345, 395

House divided speech (Lincoln), 178

Houston, Sam, 488, 674

Howard, O. O.

and Chancellorsville campaign, 94

Eleventh Corps and, 182

and First Manassas, 350

and Gettysburg campaign, 241

and Sherman's March to the Sea, 354

Howard-Tilton Memorial Library, Tulane University, 384

Howell, Augustus, 201

Howell, R. H., 442

Hudson, Robert S., 378